Japan

Sapporo & Hokkaidō
p540

Northern Honshū
p474

The Japan Alps & Central Honshū
p199

Tokyo
p66

Hiroshima & Western Honshū
p411

Kyoto
p276

Mt Fuji & Around Tokyo
p146

Shikoku
p606

Kansai
p336

Kyūshū
p647

Okinawa & the Southwest Islands
p721

THIS EDITION WRITTEN AND RESEARCHED BY

Chris Rowthorn,

Andrew Bender, Laura Crawford, Trent Holden, Craig McLachlan,
Rebecca Milner, Kate Morgan, Benedict Walker, Wendy Yanagihara

Contents

MT FUJI P147

PONTO-CHŌ, KYOTO P284

NACHI TAISHA P402

Contents

ON THE ROAD

FRANK CARTER / GETTY IMAGES ©

DAIGO-JI, KYOTO P304

FRANK DEIM / GETTY IMAGES ©

IMPERIAL PALACE, TOKYO P69

Contents

Welcome to Japan

Japan is a world apart – a cultural Galápagos where a unique civilisation blossomed, and today thrives in delicious contrasts of traditional and modern. Its spirit is strong, warm and welcoming.

Culture

Standing at the far-eastern end of the Silk Road and drawing influences from the entire continent, the Japanese have spent millennia taking in and refining the cultural bounties of Asia to produce something distinctly Japanese. From the splendour of a Kyoto geisha dance to the spare beauty of a Zen rock garden, Japan has the power to enthrall even the most jaded traveller. And traditional culture is only half the story: emerging from Tokyo's Shibuya Station and soaking up the energy, lights and sounds of the city is like stepping out of a time capsule into a future world.

Accessible Exoticism

Since the Jesuits first visited Japan in the 17th century, travellers to Japan have found themselves entranced by a culture that is by turns beautiful, unfathomable and downright odd. Staying in a ryokan (traditional Japanese inn) is utterly different from staying in a hotel. Sitting in a robe on tatami (woven floor matting) eating raw fish and mountain vegetables is probably not how you dine back home. And getting naked with a bunch of strangers to soak in an onsen (hot spring) might seem strange at first, but try it and you'll find it's relaxing.

Food

Savouring the delights of Japanese cuisine on its home turf is half the reason to come to Japan, and you can easily build an itinerary around regional specialities and sublime restaurants. Eat just one meal in a top-flight Tokyo sushi restaurant and you'll see what all the fuss is about. The Japanese attention to detail, genius for presentation and insistence on the finest ingredients results in food that can literally change your idea of what is possible in the culinary arena.

Outdoors

The wonders of Japan's natural world are a well-kept secret. The hiking in the Japan Alps and Hokkaidō is world class, and with an extensive hut system you can do multi-day hikes with nothing more than a knapsack on your back. Down south, the coral reefs of Okinawa will have you wondering if you've somehow been transported to Thailand. And you never have to travel far in Japan to get out into nature: from cities such as Kyoto, just a few minutes of travel will get you into forested mountains.

Why I Love Japan

By Chris Rowthorn, Author

I've spent most of my adult life in Japan and now it feels like home to me. I love the food: it's incredibly varied and nourishing and there seems to be no end to the culinary discoveries one can make. I love the combination of a hike in the mountains followed by a long soak in an onsen. But, most of all, I love the meticulous and careful nature of the Japanese people, reflected in every aspect of Japanese life, from trains that run right on time to sublime works of art. Put it all together and you come away with a country that still intrigues me even after almost 20 years of living there.

For more about our authors, see page 880

Above: Matsumoto-jō (p250)

Japan

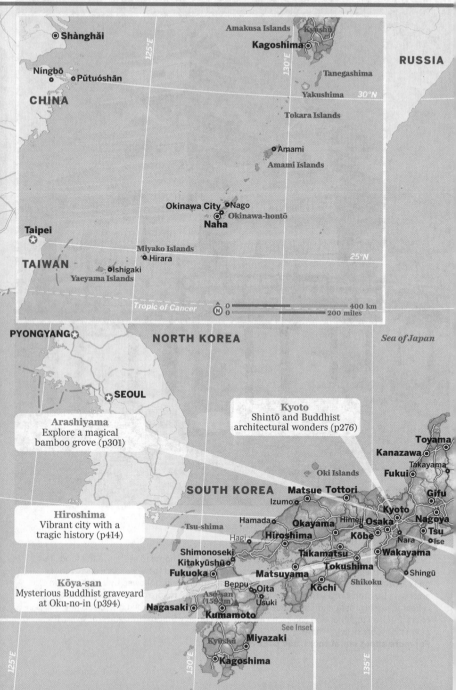

RUSSIA

Shànghǎi
Níngbō
Pǔtuóshān
CHINA
TAIWAN
Taipei

Amakusa Islands
Kyūshū
Kagoshima
Tanegashima
Yakushima · 30°N
Tokara Islands

Amami
Amami Islands

Okinawa City · Nago
Okinawa-hontō
Naha

Miyako Islands
Hirara
Ishigaki
Yaeyama Islands · 25°N

Tropic of Cancer

0 — 400 km
0 — 200 miles

PYONGYANG
NORTH KOREA
Sea of Japan

SEOUL

Arashiyama
Explore a magical
bamboo grove (p301)

Kyoto
Shintō and Buddhist
architectural wonders (p276)

Toyama
Kanazawa
Takayama
Fukui

Oki Islands
SOUTH KOREA
Matsue Tottori
Izumo
Gifu
Kyoto
Nagoya
Hamada Okayama Himeji Osaka
Hiroshima Kōbe Tsu
Hagi Nara Ise
Tsu-shima Takamatsu Wakayama
Shimonoseki Tokushima
Kitakyūshū **Shikoku** Shingū
Fukuoka Matsuyama Kōchi
Beppu Ōita
Aso-san Usuki
(1592m)
Nagasaki Kumamoto
See Inset
Kyūshū **Miyazaki**
Kagoshima

Hiroshima
Vibrant city with a
tragic history (p414)

Kōya-san
Mysterious Buddhist graveyard
at Oku-no-in (p394)

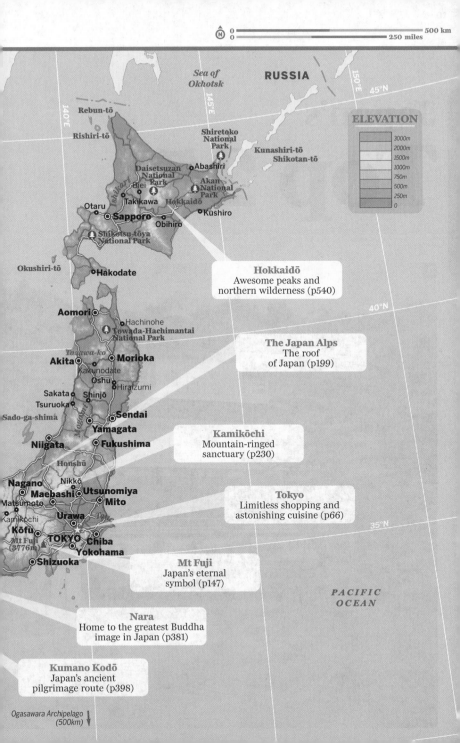

0   0
250 miles
500 km

Sea of Okhotsk

RUSSIA

45°N
150°E
140°E

Rebun-tō

Rishiri-tō

Shiretoko National Park

Kunashiri-tō
Shikotan-tō

ELEVATION

3000m
2000m
1500m
1000m
750m
500m
250m
0

Daisetsuzan National Park
Abashiri
Biei
Akan National Park
Takikawa
Hokkaidō
Otaru
Sapporo
Kushiro
Obihiro
145°E

Shikotsu-tōya National Park

Okushiri-tō

Hakodate

Hokkaidō
Awesome peaks and
northern wilderness (p540)

40°N

Aomori

Hachinohe
Towada-Hachimantai National Park

Tazawa-ko
Akita
Morioka
Kakunodate
Ōshū
Hiraizumi
Sakata
Shinjō
Tsuruoka
Sado-ga-shima
Sendai
Yamagata
Niigata
Fukushima

Honshū

Mogami

The Japan Alps
The roof
of Japan (p199)

Kamikōchi
Mountain-ringed
sanctuary (p230)

Nagano
Nikkō
Maebashi
Utsunomiya
Matsumoto
Mito
Kamikōchi
Urawa
Tōne
Kōfu
TOKYO
Chiba
Mt Fuji
(3776m)
Yokohama
Shizuoka

Tokyo
Limitless shopping and
astonishing cuisine (p66)

35°N

Mt Fuji
Japan's eternal
symbol (p147)

PACIFIC OCEAN

Nara
Home to the greatest Buddha
image in Japan (p381)

Kumano Kodō
Japan's ancient
pilgrimage route (p398)

Ogasawara Archipelago
(500km)

Japan's
Top 25

Kyoto Temples & Gardens

1 With more than 1000 temples to choose from, you're spoiled for choice in Kyoto (p276). Spend your time finding one that suits your taste. If you like things gaudy and grand, you'll love the retina-burning splendour of Kinkaku-ji. If you prefer *wabi-sabi* to rococo, you'll find the tranquillity of Hōnen-in or Shōren-in more to your liking. And don't forget that temples are where you'll find the best gardens: some of them are at Ginkaku-ji, Ryōan-ji and Tōfuku-ji. Kinkaku-ji (p299)

Onsen

2 There's nothing like lowering yourself into the tub at a classic Japanese onsen (natural hot spring bath; p815). You can feel the muscles in your back relax and the 'ahhh' that you emit is just a simple way of saying 'Damn, I'm glad I came to Japan!' If you're lucky, the tub is outside and there's a nice stream running nearby. The Japanese have turned the simple act of bathing into a folk religion and the country is dotted with temples and shrines to this most relaxing of faiths. Bathing in one of the onsen at Yunessun (p172)

FRANK DEIM / GETTY IMAGES ©

BLAINE HARRINGTON III / CORBIS ©

Japanese Cuisine

3 Japan is a food lover's paradise and the cuisine (p786) is incredibly varied, running the gamut from simple *soba* (buckwheat noodles) to multicourse *kaiseki* (haute cuisine) banquets. In a city such as Tokyo or Kyoto, you could eat a different Japanese speciality cuisine every night for a month without repeating your meal. There's no doubt that a food tour of Japan will be memorable, but there's just one problem: once you try the real thing in Japan, the restaurants back home will pale in comparison. The only solution is another trip to Japan! Sushi

Cherry-Blossom Viewing

4 If you think of the Japanese as sober, staid and serious people, join them under a cherry tree laden with blossoms in the springtime. It's as if the cherries release a kind of narcotic that reduces inhibitions. They'll drench you in sake and beer, stuff you with snacks, pull out portable karaoke and perhaps even get up and dance. Japan is a happy place when the cherry blossoms are out, and you're more than welcome to join the party. Two of the best places to join in the fun are Tokyo's Ueno-kōen (p96) and Kyoto's Maruyama-kōen (p293). Cherry blossoms, Kyoto Imperial Palace Park (p286)

Staying in a Ryokan

5 Eat in your bedroom. Spend the day lounging about in a robe. Soak in a bath while looking at a garden. Don't lift a finger except to bring food to your mouth. Sounds relaxing? Then we highly recommend a night in a good ryokan (traditional Japanese inn; p812). The Japanese had the whole spa thing figured out long before they ever heard the word 'spa'. From first class to the most humble, every ryokan will give you a taste of how the Japanese used to live. Tawaraya (p312), Kyoto

Castles

6 Japan's castles have about as much in common with their European counterparts as kimonos have with Western dinner dresses. Their graceful contours belie the grim military realities behind their construction. Towering above the plains, they seem designed more to please the eye than to protect their lords. If you have an interest in the world of samurai, shōguns and military history, you'll love Japan's castles. Now that the castle at Himeji (p370) is under wraps, try the one at Matsuyama (p634) or Hikone (p375). Osaka-jō (p339)

Oku-no-in at Kōya-san

7 Riding the funicular up to the sacred Buddhist monastic complex of Kōya-san (p394), you almost feel like you're ascending to another world. The place is permeated with a kind of august spiritual grandeur, and nowhere is this feeling stronger than in the vast Oku-no-in cemetery. Trails weave their way among towering cryptomeria trees and by the time you arrive at the main hall, the sudden appearance of a Buddha would seem like the most natural thing in the world. Torii, Oku-no-in cemetery

Arashiyama's Bamboo Grove

8 Western Kyoto is home to one of the most magical places in all of Japan: the famed bamboo grove in Arashiyama (p301). The visual effect of the seemingly infinite stalks of bamboo is quite different from any forest we've ever encountered – there's a palpable presence to the place that is utterly impossible to capture in pictures, but don't let that stop you from trying. If you've seen *Crouching Tiger, Hidden Dragon*, you'll have some idea of what this place is about.

Kyoto's Geisha Dances

9 It can't be stressed enough: if you find yourself in Kyoto when the geisha dances (p328) are on – usually in the spring – do everything in your power to see one. It's hard to think of a more colourful, charming and diverting stage spectacle. You might find that the whole thing takes on the appearance of a particularly vivid dream. When the curtain falls after the final burst of colour and song, the geisha might continue to dance in your mind for hours afterwards.

Ogasawara Archipelago

10 This Pacific island chain (p196), located some 1000km south of Tokyo, is one of Japan's best-kept secrets. Inhabited only within the last 180 years, these subtropical islands boast white-sand beaches, warm blue waters and dozens of rare plant and animal species. Divers and snorkellers can swim with dolphins, mantas and sea turtles. Hiking, kayaking, whale-watching and stargazing are also on the bill. The catch? The most accessible main island of Chichi-jima is a 25½-hour ferry ride from Tokyo.

Hiroshima

11 Seeing the city's leafy boulevards, it's hard to picture Hiroshima (p414) as the devastated victim of an atomic bomb. It's not until you walk through the Peace Memorial Museum that the terrible reality becomes clear – the displays of battered personal effects say it all. But outside the quiet of the Peace Memorial Park, energetic Hiroshima rolls on. A visit here is a heartbreaking, important history lesson, but the modern city and its people ensure that's not the only memory you leave with.

Paper cranes, Peace Memorial Park (p414)

Festivals

12 You might imagine the people of Japan as a nation of buttoned-down conformists. If so, you owe it to yourself to check out a really rollicking *matsuri* (festival). The fact is: these people know how to really let loose. From giant festivals like Kyoto's Gion Matsuri (p309) to local ones held in tiny hamlets, a festival may well by the highpoint of your trip. And don't be surprised if you're asked to participate.
Awa-odori Matsuri (p610)

Wild Hokkaidō

13 The last region of Japan to be 'pacified' by the central government, Hokkaidō (p540) remains the wildest part of the country. The scale here is totally different from any other part of Japan: the sky is bigger, the distances are greater and the nature is much wilder (this is the last redoubt of the brown bear in Japan). If you like your nature wild and woolly, make a trip up to Japan's wild northern island. Shiretoko National Park (p593)

Skiing

14 Travellers the world over are finally savvy about one of Japan's greatest secrets: skiing and snowboarding (p48). From the Japan Alps in Central Honshū to the Siberian-blasted Hokkaidō highlands, this is one country where it pays to pack a few extra layers. Well-priced equipment rental shops will have you up on the slopes in no time at all, while onsen are waiting to receive you for a unique après-ski experience. Indeed, there is nothing quite like a hot bath and a cold sake after an adrenaline-fuelled day of black diamonds. Niseko (p564), Hokkaidō

Kabuki

15 For sheer otherworldly bizarreness, few theatrical spectacles come close to kabuki (stylised Japanese theatre). It doesn't really matter if you don't understand the words, as this amps up the 'alien beings who've come down to earth to flummox the earthlings' factor that makes kabuki one of the most entertaining spectacles in Japan. We're pretty sure that you'll find kabuki to be one of those things that resonate long after leaving these islands. The two best places to see kabuki are Kyoto's Minami-za Theatre (p328) and Tokyo's Kabuki-za (p131).

Hiking in the Japan Alps

16 Close your eyes and picture Japan. If all you see are geisha, Zen gardens, bullet trains and hypermodern cities, you might be in for a real surprise when you get into the Japan Alps (p199). Hike right into the heart of the high peaks here and you'll be in awe of so much mountain splendour. You can go hut-to-hut among the peaks for a week with nothing on your back but a solid day pack.

15

Shopping in Tokyo

17 If you want to see some incredible shops, you've got to come to a country that's been running a multibillion-dollar trade surplus for the last several decades. If it's available to humanity, you can buy it in Japan. Whether it's ¥10,000 (US$100) melons or curios from ¥100 shops (where everything goes for about US$1), you'll be amazed at the sheer variety of the goods on offer in Tokyo. Head to the boutiques of Ginza to see the glitterati do their shopping, or join the mere mortals in Shibuya and Shinjuku (p133). And no trip to Tokyo would be complete without a visit to Tsukiji Fish Market (p73), the largest of its kind in the world. Shoppers outside Shibuya 109 (p135)

Tokyo's Modern Architecture

18 Japan may be known for its traditional temples, but Tokyo's cityscape is a veritable open-air museum of contemporary structures (p135). The capital has come a long way from copying the Eiffel Tower – these days you'll find dozens of inspired and original works by a pantheon of the world's greatest designers. Fill up on such architectural eye-candy as the chic boutiques in Omote-sandō, the quirky postmodern projects on Odaiba, or even the new army of office towers in Marunouchi. Interior of the Tokyo International Forum (p69; architect Rafael Viñoly)

Mt Fuji

19 Even from a distance Mt Fuji (p147) will take your breath away. Close up, the perfectly symmetrical cone of Japan's highest peak is nothing short of awesome. Dawn from the summit? Pure magic. Fuji-san is Japan's most revered and timeless attraction. Hundreds of thousands of people climb it every year, continuing a centuries-old tradition of pilgrimages up this sacred volcano. Those who'd rather search for picture-perfect views from the less daunting peaks nearby can follow in the steps of Japan's most famous painters and poets.

Naoshima

20 This island-turned-art museum (p443) in the Inland Sea is one of Japan's more interesting attractions. It's studded with art museums, sculptures and 'art houses' (each of which contains a unique installation). There's even a funky 'art sento' (public bath) which is the most unusual public bath in all of Japan. Hop on a bicycle and work your way around museums, galleries and open-air installations. And if the weather is warm, cool off with a swim at the beach. All the while, soak up the brilliant scenery of the island-studded Inland Sea. 'Red Pumpkin' by Yayoi Kusama

Kumano Kodō

21 On southern Kansai's ancient pilgrimage route, the Kumano Kodō (p398), you can just about imagine the old days when most goods were transported along winding mountain trails on someone's back. If you like the idea of a few days spent wandering through cedar forests, visiting shrines, staying at comfortable lodges and finishing up with a good soak in some of the area's best onsen, this old pilgrims' path might be for you.

Nachi Taisha (p402)

Sumō

22 Sitting ringside when two *yokozuna* (grand champions) clash is like watching two mountains get into a shoving match – you can just about feel the earth shake. Even if you're up in the nosebleed seats, catching a sumō match is a highlight of any Japan trip. It's just so different from any other sport: the salt-throwing ritual, the otherworldly calls of the referee, the drawn-out staring matches before the bout, the whole thing just screams 'only in Japan!' Sumō tournament, Ryōgoku Kokugikan (p132)

Daibutsu (Great Buddha) of Nara

23 Here's the drill: go to the temple of Tōdai-ji (p381) in Nara and stop for a moment outside the main hall. Then, without looking up, step into the hall. Calm your thoughts. Now raise your eyes to behold the Great Buddha. This is probably the closest one can come to enlightenment without years of meditation. Perhaps no other sight in Japan has as much impact as this cosmic Buddha – you can almost feel the energy radiating from its bulk.

Kamikōchi

24 One of the most stunning natural vistas in Japan, Kamikōchi (p230) is a highland valley surrounded by the eye-popping summits of the Northern Japan Alps. Trails start from the photogenic bridge, Kappa-bashi, and follow the pristine Azusa-gawa through tranquil forests of willow, larch and elm trees. The birthplace of Japanese alpinism, Kamikōchi can be the gateway for ascending Yariga-take (3180m) or for a simple one-hour stroll along the river to the local hot springs. In winter, you can trek in through the access tunnel and have the entire valley to yourself for a snowshoe jaunt.

Tsumago– Magome Hike

25 A beautifully preserved post town, Tsumago (p255) has traditional wooden inns which hosted travelling samurai lords. From Tsumago, follow the old Nakasendō post road (p254) through alpine hamlets and old-growth cedar forests to the mountain pass Magome-tōge. Rest here at a teahouse before continuing to Magome (p254), where fantastic mountain views are a backdrop to old inns and shops. The 7.8km hike winds through a world of farmhouses, waterwheels and rice paddies that time seems to have passed by.
Tsumago

Need to Know

For more information, see Survival Guide (p826)

Currency
Yen (¥)

Language
Japanese

Visas
Visas are issued on arrival for most nationalities for stays of up to 90 days.

Money
ATMs in post offices and some convenience stores accept foreign cards. Most hotels and department stores, but only some restaurants and ryokan, accept credit cards.

Mobile Phones
Only 3G phones work in Japan. Voice SIM cards are not presently available. Mobile phone rental is common and easy.

Time
Japan is GMT/UTC +9 hours. Japan's time zone is referred to as Japan Standard Time. There is no daylight savings time in Japan.

When to Go

Hot summers, mild winters
Warm summers, cold winters

Sapporo
GO Apr–Oct

Takayama
GO Apr–Oct

Tokyo
GO any time

Kyoto
GO Mar–Jun or Sep–Nov

Naha
GO Mar–Nov

High Season
(Apr & May, Aug)

➡ Flights are pricey around the Golden Week (early May), O-Bon (mid-August) and New Year.

➡ Honshū cities are busy in the cherry blossom (late March to early April) and autumn foliage (November) seasons.

Shoulder
(Jun & Jul, Sep–Dec)

➡ June and July is rainy season in most of Japan (except Hokkaidō) – it doesn't rain every day but it can be pretty humid.

➡ Autumn (September to mid-December) is usually cool and clear.

Low Season
(Jan–Mar)

➡ Winter is cool or cold in most of Honshū, but it's fine for travel.

➡ Be ready for snow in the mountains.

Websites

Lonely Planet (www.lonely-planet.com/japan) Destination information, hotel bookings, traveller forum and more.

Japan Ministry of Foreign Affairs (www.mofa.go.jp) Links to embassies and consulates.

Japan National Tourism Organization (www.jnto.go.jp) Official tourist site.

Japan Meteorological Agency Tropical Cyclone Page (www.jma.go.jp/en/typh) Up-to-date weather satellite images (good for checking on typhoons).

Tokyo Sights (www.tokyotojp.com) Hours, costs, phone numbers etc for major sights.

Rikai (www.rikai.com/perl/Home.pl) Japanese to English translations.

Important Numbers

Drop the 0 in the area code when dialling from abroad.

Ambulance & fire	☎119
Police	☎110
Country code	☎81
International access code	☎001
International operator	☎0051
Local directory	☎104

Exchange Rates

Australia	A$1	¥99
Canada	C$1	¥98
Europe	€1	¥131
New Zealand	NZ$1	¥82
UK	£1	¥154
US	US$1	¥101

For current exchange rates, see www.xe.com.

Daily Costs

**Budget:
Less than ¥15,000**

➡ Guesthouse room: ¥2800
➡ Two meals: ¥2000
➡ Train/bus tickets: ¥1500
➡ Temple/museum entry: ¥500

**Midrange:
¥15,000–¥20,000**

➡ Business hotel room: ¥9000
➡ Two meals: ¥4000
➡ Train/bus tickets: ¥1500
➡ Two temple/museum entries: ¥1000

**Top end:
Over ¥20,000**

➡ Top-end hotel room: ¥20,000
➡ Two meals: ¥6000
➡ Train/bus/taxi: ¥4500
➡ Two temple/museum entries: ¥1000

Opening Hours

Banks Open 9am to 3pm Monday to Friday.

Bars Open 6pm to midnight or later, closed one day per week.

Department stores Open 10am to 7pm, closed one or two days per month.

Museums Open 9am or 10am to 5pm, closed Monday.

Offices Open 9am to 5pm or 6pm Monday to Friday.

Post offices Local open 9am to 5pm Monday to Friday; central open 9am to 7pm Monday to Friday and 9am to 3pm Saturday.

Restaurants Open 11am to 2pm and 6pm to 11pm, closed one day per week.

Smaller shops Open 9am to 5pm, may be closed Sunday

Arriving in Japan

Narita International Airport

Narita Express – ¥2940; 53 minutes to Tokyo

Limousine bus – ¥3000; two hours to the city

Taxi – around ¥30,000 to the city

Haneda Airport

Monorail – ¥470; 25 minutes to Tokyo

Limousine bus – ¥1000; 45 minutes to the city

Taxi – around ¥6000 to the city

Kansai International Airport

Express trains – ¥2980; 78 minutes to Kyoto

Limousine bus – ¥2500; 90 minutes to the city

Shared taxi – ¥3500; about 90 minutes to the city

Getting Around

Japan has a brilliant public transport system: trains, buses, ferries and planes are all abundant and efficient.

Safe Travel

The Great East Japan Earthquake of March 2011 and the resulting tsunami wrought incredible devastation on parts of northeast Honshū (the main island of Japan).

While most of the tsunami damage has been cleaned up and the local infrastructure largely restored, an exclusion zone with a radius of 20km was in effect around the Fukushima Dai-Ichi nuclear power plant, which was damaged by the tsunami. The plant is in Fukushima Prefecture in northeast Honshū.

For much more on **transport**, see p840

First Time Japan

For more information, see Survival Guide (p825)

Checklist

➡ Purchase your Japan Rail Pass (p848)

➡ Make sure your passport is valid for at least six months past your arrival date

➡ Inform your debit- or credit-card company that you will be travelling abroad

➡ Arrange for travel insurance

➡ Get an international licence if you plan to rent a car in Japan

What to Pack

➡ Slip-on shoes, as you'll be taking off your shoes a lot

➡ Prescription medicines, which can be time-consuming to purchase

➡ As little as possible – you can buy most things you'll need

Top Tips for Your Trip

➡ Get a Japan Rail Pass. This is one of the best travel bargains on earth and it allows you to make unlimited use of the extensive, fast and efficient Japan Rail system. For more information, see the Transport chapter (p848).

➡ Stay at least one night in a ryokan (traditional Japanese inn) and visit at least one onsen (hot spring bath).

What to Wear

Japan can be tough to dress for as it experiences four distinct seasons, each of which has changeable weather. For the hot, humid months (late May to early September) go with light, breathable clothes. For the cold months (early December to March), a fleece and shell/windbreaker is a good idea. For everything in between (ie spring and fall), be flexible: bring a light fleece or jacket that you can put on or take off as needed.

As for dress code, most adult males don't wear shorts in Japan (unless they're exercising or hiking), but foreign males can do so without problems. For upscale restaurants and bars, you don't need anything nicer than 'smart casual' clothing (newish jeans or decent trousers and collared shirts for men and skirts, casual dresses and blouses or similar tops for women).

Sleeping

Booking in advance is an absolute necessity in high seasons, particularly in places like Kyoto and Nara (from late March to mid-May, in mid-August and during the New Year period). It's also a good idea in other seasons as the Japanese are not used to 'walk in' guests. See p826 for more information.

➡ **Hotels** Choose from international luxury brands, efficient business hotels, cramped capsule hotels and slightly scandalous 'love hotels'.

➡ **Ryokan** A night or two in a ryokan (traditional Japanese inn) is highly recommended.

➡ **Guesthouses** Inexpensive lodgings, many of them catering specifically to foreign travellers, are plentiful in tourist destinations.

Money

It's not quite as easy to get cash in Japan as it is in other developed nations. Many Japanese ATMs don't accept foreign-issued cards. However, ATMs in Japanese post offices and 7-Eleven convenience stores *do* accept foreign-issued cards. Likewise, credit cards are not universally accepted in Japan. However, most hotels, department stores, upscale restaurants, JR ticket offices and even some taxis *do* accept credit cards. Still, you should never assume that you can use your credit card – always carry sufficient cash as a backup. For more information see the Directory (p832).

Bargaining

Bargaining is not really done in Japan. The only place where bargaining is widely practised is at flea markets, such as the ones held twice a month in Kyoto. That said, you can always give it a go at big electronics shops – just keep in mind that being pushy won't work in Japan.

Tipping

Tipping is not done in Japan and the Japanese never do it. However, if you feel like you've received excellent service from a guide or your personal maid at a ryokan, then place some money in an envelope and hand it to the person (handing cash over without an envelope is considered crass in these situations).

Language

Most Japanese study English at school, and those who deal with foreign tourists usually speak English. Country folk and the elderly may speak little, if any. But don't worry – people will go to great lengths to understand you. For more on language see p852.

 Is there a Western-/Japanese-style room?
洋室/和室はありますか?
yō·shi·tsu/wa·shi·tsu wa a·ri·mas ka

Some lodgings have only Japanese-style rooms, or a mix of Western and Japanese – ask if you have a preference.

 Please bring a (spoon/knife/fork).
(スプーン/ナイフ/フォーク)をください。
(spūn/nai·fu/fō·ku) o ku·da·sai

If you haven't quite mastered the art of eating with chopsticks, don't be afraid to ask for cutlery at a restaurant.

 How do I get to ...?
…へはどう行けばいいですか?
... e wa dō i·ke·ba ī des ka

Finding a place from its address can be difficult in Japan. Addresses usually give an area (not a street) and numbers aren't always consecutive. Practise asking for directions.

 I'd like a nonsmoking seat, please.
禁煙席をお願いします。
kin·en·se·ki o o·ne·gai shi·mas

There are smoking seats in many restaurants and on bullet trains so be sure to specify if you want to be smoke-free.

5 **What's the local speciality?**
地元料理は何がありますか?
ji·mo·to·ryō·ri wa na·ni ga a·ri·mas ka

Throughout Japan most areas have a speciality dish and locals usually love to talk food.

Etiquette

Although Japan is a formal society with a complex system of manners, no one expects you to know all the rules. Doing what is polite in your own country is a good start, and keep the following in mind (see p786 for eating etiquette):

➡ Use two hands when giving or receiving presents, important documents, or your name/business card (business cards are very important in Japan). When giving money, try to put it in an envelope.

➡ Take off your shoes when stepping up onto tatami mats, into a private home or into the hall of a temple. Step straight out of the shoes onto the mats – the whole point is to keep the inside floor free from the dirt of the street.

➡ Temples are religious places. Speak quietly in the main halls, and don't enter dressed like you're off to the beach.

➡ Don't expect too much flexibility. Not all restaurants are willing to alter dishes to suit dietary preferences or requirements, and not every ryokan has slippers or futons big enough for a foreigner.

What's New

Extended Shinkansen Lines

Shinkansen (bullet train) lines have been extended northeast to the city of Aomori, at the northern tip of Honshū, and south to the city of Kagoshima, in Kyūshū, so that you can now cross almost all of Kyūshū and Honshū by bullet train. The Hokuriku *shinkansen* is also slated to start an extended service in the spring of 2015 to the city of Toyama (great for access to the Japan Alps and the Tateyama–Kurobe Alpine Route). The line will eventually be extended as far as the culturally important city of Kanazawa.

A New Home For Kabuki in Tokyo

Tokyo's new kabuki venue, Kabuki-za, reopened in Ginza (Tokyo) in spring 2013. (p131)

Cheap Airfares to Hokkaidō

Budget airlines are proliferating in Japan and several offer incredibly reasonable fares to Hokkaidō, bringing this once distant destination within easy and inexpensive reach of budget travellers.

Craft Beer & Brewpub Boom

Microbrews are all the rage across the archipelago. Beer lovers will find the widest pickings in Hokkaidō and Kyūshū.

D.T. Suzuki Museum

The new D.T. Suzuki Museum in Kanazawa honours Japan's best known proponent of Zen Buddhism, and the garden here is an eloquent lesson in Zen aesthetics. (p263)

Hip Capsule Hotels

Capsule hotels used to be the refuge of sozzled salarymen who missed the last train home. Not anymore. A wave of cool designer capsule hotels has swept the country; a good example of this is the Capsule Ryokan Kyoto.

Sky Tree Blooms in Tokyo

Opened in 2012, the Tokyo Sky Tree soars to 634m and features two observation decks. (p101)

Gunkanjima Tours

Not exactly new, but these tours have been booming in popularity since the island served as the set for the villain's lair in the Bond film *Skyfall* (2012). (p673)

JR SCMAGLEV & Railway Park

This fantastic new museum on the outskirts of Nagoya features a real Maglev train, *shinkansen* and classic trains. It's a must-see for train lovers. (p211)

Ogasawara Archipelago

The far-flung islands of Ogasawara are Japan's latest site to be awarded World Heritage status by Unesco, listed in 2011 for their unique and varied ecosystem. They're located approximately 1000km from the mainland (yet remarkably still part of Tokyo Prefecture), a 25½-hour ferry journey – but those who make it are rewarded with fantastic opportunities for whale- and dolphin-watching, rugged landscapes and pristine beaches. (p196)

For up-to-date tips and suggestions from travellers, see **lonelyplanet.com/thorntree**

If You Like...

Temples, Shrines & Gardens

You'll find the Japan of your imagination – immaculately raked gardens, quiet Buddhist temples and mysterious Shintō shrines – all across the archipelago, even in the ultramodern capital of Tokyo.

Kyoto If you're after traditional Japan, you could spend your whole trip here and not get bored. (p276)

Nara A short hop, skip and jump from Kyoto, Nara is a compact wonder of a city that some consider the birthplace of Japanese culture. (p377)

Kanazawa Some call this small city a 'mini-Kyoto', but Kanazawa isn't a 'mini' anything – it's big on temples and has one of the best gardens in Japan: Kenroku-en. (p260)

Tokyo That's right: amid all that concrete and neon there are some wonderful hints of traditional culture. (p68)

Culinary Adventure

Who doesn't come to Japan to eat? And we don't just mean 'extreme eating'; we mean some of the Japanese food you might have tried back home, only much better versions. Then there's all the new stuff to try – and did we mention really good sake?

Tokyo With more Michelin stars than any city on earth, this is the place for the best Japanese food in the country, as well as some of the best French and Italian food you'll find anywhere. (p111)

Tsukiji Simply pointing out that the Tsukiji Fish Market is the biggest in the world doesn't begin to convey the size, variety and excitement of the place. (p73)

Kyoto If you want to sample *kaiseki* (haute cuisine) in traditional surroundings, dine with a geisha, or sample the offerings in Japanese sweet shops, this is the place. (p315)

Depachika Department-store food halls in Tokyo and Kyoto are the best food shops on the planet – be prepared to get overwhelmed and lost. (p324)

Hiking

Japan has some *brilliant* hiking and a reasonably priced hut system that rivals anything you'll find elsewhere. Whether you fancy a week-long hike across the peaks with nothing but a daypack or just a few good strolls in the hills between bouts of temple-hopping, Japan will definitely satisfy.

Japan Alps The Japan Alps in Central Honshū form the roof of Japan. If you like big peaks, grand scenery and long walks, this is the place. (p199)

Hokkaidō From incredible coastal treks to the famed Daisetsuzan Grand Traverse, Hokkaidō is a destination for nature lovers. (p540)

Kyūshū If the whiff of volcanic gases and the threat of eruption adds a certain frisson to your hiking, you'll love the southern island of Kyūshū. (p647)

Kumano Kodō Head down to the wooded wilds of southern Kansai to follow the ancient pilgrimage path to the shrines and hot springs of Hongū. (p398)

IF YOU LIKE... CASTLES

The queen of Japanese castles, Himeji-jō (p370) is presently undergoing a multiyear renovation and the main keep will be under wraps until 2015, but it's still an interesting stop for castle fans.

Onsen

Spend some time soaking in a few of Japan's great onsen or, better yet, in an onsen ryokan (a traditional inn built around a private hot spring) and you'll arrive home recharged.

Kinosaki Japan's classic onsen town is all an onsen town ought to be: quaint, friendly and packed with homey ryokan. (p408)

Kayōtei If your finances run to a night or two here, you will surely be glad you made the trip to this sublime onsen. (p274)

Hongū Trek for a few days along Japan's ancient pilgrimage route, the Kumano Kodō, then soak your sore muscles in the three great onsen near the village of Hongū. (p402)

Takaragawa Onsen This is the place to try the classic onsen experience: sitting in a hot bath looking at the snowy banks of a rushing river. (p166)

Urami-ga-taki Onsen They don't make onsen with more scenic, soothing locations than this one on Hachijō-jima. (p183)

Shopping

Forget sumō and judo – Japan's national sport is shopping. And the Japanese go at it with a real passion. Whether your taste runs to expensive boutiques or ¥100 shops, if you're a shopper you have to come to Japan.

Tokyo Japan's capital has the widest selection of stores on the planet, selling everything from gadgets to Gucci bags. (p133)

Kyoto The old capital has a brilliant selection of traditional goods (think ceramics, antiques, scrolls, tea-ceremony articles and kimonos), as well as plenty of

(Above) Cherry blossom, Sensō-ji (p99), Tokyo
(Below) Sand garden, Ginkaku-ji (p295), Kyoto

trendy boutiques, department stores, and the two best flea markets in the country. (p329)

Osaka The Osakans come in for quite a ribbing from their fellow Japanese: they're famed for driving a hard bargain and shopping with abandon. (p354)

Modern Architecture

Japan is where the world's architects come to play. During the heady years of the Bubble Era, wild and wonderful buildings sprouted up and down the archipelago.

Tokyo If Japan is an architect's playground, Tokyo is an architect's Disneyland. Take a stroll and enjoy the nuggets of genius scattered among the concrete afterthoughts. (p68)

Naoshima This island-cum-art-museum is graced with several Andō Tadao creations and other fantastic buildings. (p443)

Kanazawa While it's more famous for its temples and gardens, Kanazawa gets a lot of visits from architecture buffs who come to see the 21st Century Museum of Contemporary Art. (p260)

Skiing

It started as a secret among expats living in Hong Kong and Singapore, and now the word is out: Japan has the best skiing in Asia and some of the most reliable powder snow on earth. If you want to combine culture with snow time, Japan is the perfect place.

Niseko You could be forgiven for thinking that the Japanese word for 'powder snow' is 'Niseko':

this Hokkaidō ski area is just about synonymous with the stuff. (p564)

Hakuba With some excellent advanced runs and a stunning alpine backdrop, Hakuba is a consistent favourite among Japan's expat skiers. (p247)

Nozawa Onsen No place in Japan does the ski-onsen combination better than Nozawa Onsen. With 14 free onsen in which to soak after your day on the slopes, it's a must for hot spring fans who also happen to enjoy skiing. (p245)

Festivals

Perhaps you imagine the Japanese to be a serious and staid people. If so, check out one of the country's wilder *matsuri* (festivals) to see these people bust loose, and join the fun!

Gion Matsuri The main event here (a parade of floats) is pretty tame, but the evenings leading up to this great Kyoto summer festival get pretty wild. Put on a *yukata* (robe) and stroll through town, stopping for beer and snacks as you go. (p309)

Hanami Strictly speaking, the Japanese cherry-blossom-viewing parties *(hanami)* that take place up and down the archipelago in March and April aren't *matsuri,* but they sure feel like festivals.

Hatsumōde Again, the first shrine visit of the year *(hatsu-mōde)* is not a *matsuri* in the strict sense, but if you find yourself at a popular Shintō shrine on New Year's Eve or New Year's Day, you'll see why we've included it here.

Kishiwada Danjiri Matsuri In one of the wilder events in Japan, the locals haul floats through the streets, sometimes

at surprising speeds. Join the fun, but stand well back when those things go by. (p347)

Pop Culture

The folks who brought you Godzilla, Pokémon and Shonen Knife are still hard at work. Tokyo is all about pop culture, so it really deserves its own entry here!

Akihabara Better known as 'Akiba', Tokyo's main electronics district is alive with the pulse of *otaku* (geek) trends. (p92)

Shibuya Shibuya is the shopping hub at the centre of Tokyo's youth universe. Keep your eyes peeled and you'll see several trends coming into being as you walk down the street. (p82)

Ghibli Museum If you know the name Hayao Miyazaki (the king of Japanese anime), or if your kids do, you'll want to make a half-day trip out of Tokyo to see his museum. (p87)

Beaches

Beaches may not be the first thing you associate with Japan, but the archipelago has some real stunners, many of them on the islands of Okinawa.

Sakibaru Kaigan This lovely stretch of white sand and clear water on Amami-Ōshima is a winner by any definition. (p731)

Kerama Islands It's impossible to pick a favourite beach on these three charming islands – the fun is in exploring each one and finding your own white-sand paradise. (p744)

Hoshizuna-no-hama While the beach here is nothing to sneeze at, it's the drop-off at the edge of the coral reef that really gets our motor running. (p756)

Month by Month

January

Japan comes to life after the lull of the New Year holiday. Winter grips the country in the mountains and in the north, but travel is still possible in most places.

✿ Shōgatsu (New Year)

New Year (31 December to 3 January) is one of the most important celebrations in Japan and includes plenty of eating and drinking. The central ritual, *hatsu-mōde,* involves the first visit to the local shrine to pray for health, happiness and prosperity during the coming year. Keep in mind that a lot of businesses and attractions shut down during this period

and transport can be busy as people head back to their hometowns.

🏃 Skiing

While many ski areas open in December, the ski season really gets rolling in January.

✿ Seijin-no-hi (Coming-of-Age Day)

On the second Monday in January, ceremonies are held for boys and girls who have reached the age of 20. A good place to see the action is at large shrines, where you'll find crowds of girls in kimonos and boys in suits or kimonos.

February

It's still cold in February in most of Japan (with the exception of Okinawa). Skiing is in full swing and this is a good time to soak in onsen (hot springs).

✿ Setsubun Matsuri

On 2, 3 or 4 February, to celebrate the end of winter and drive out evil spirits, the Japanese engage in throwing roasted beans while chanting '*oni wa soto, fuku wa uchi*' (meaning 'out with the demons, in with good luck'). Check local shrines for events.

✿ Yuki Matsuri

Drawing over two million annual visitors, Sapporo's famous snow festival (p550) really warms up winter in Hokkaidō in early February. Teams from around the world compete to create the most impressive ice and snow sculptures. After touring the sculptures, head to one of the city's friendly pubs and eateries to warm up with sake and great local food.

March

By March it's starting to warm up on the main islands of Japan. Plums start the annual procession of blossoms across the archipelago. This is a pleasant time to travel in Honshū, Kyūshū and Shikoku.

◉ Plum-Blossom Viewing

Not as famous as the cherries, but quite lovely in their own right, Japan's plum trees bloom from late February into early March. Strolling among the plum orchards at places like Kyoto's Kitano Tenman-gū is a fine way to spend an early spring day in Japan.

April

Spring is in full swing by April. The cherry blossoms usually peak early in April in most of Honshū. Japan is beautiful at this time, but places like Kyoto can be crowded.

⊙ Cherry-Blossom Viewing

When the cherry blossoms burst into bloom, the Japanese hold rollicking *hanami* (cherry-blossom viewing) parties. It's hard to time viewing the blossoms: to hit them at their peak in Tokyo or Kyoto, you have to be in the country from around 25 March to 5 April.

🎎 Takayama Matsuri

The first part of this festival, the Sannō Matsuri (p222), is held on 14 and 15 April. The festival floats here are truly spectacular. Book well in advance if you want to spend the night or come back in October for the second part, the Hachiman Matsuri.

May

May is one of the best months to visit Japan. It's warm and sunny in most of the country. Book accommodation well in advance during the April/May Golden Week holidays.

🎎 Sanja Matsuri

The grandest of all Tokyo festivals is held on the third weekend in May. It features hundreds of *mikoshi* (portable shrines) paraded through Asakusa, starting from Asakusa-jinja.

🎎 Golden Week

Most Japanese are on holiday from 29 April to 5 May, when a series of national holidays coincide. This is one of the busiest times for domestic travel, so be prepared for crowded transport and accommodation.

June

June is generally a lovely time to travel in Japan – it's warm but not sweltering. Keep in mind that the rainy season generally starts in Kyūshū and Honshū sometime in June. It doesn't rain every day but it can be humid.

🏃 Japan Alps Hiking Season

Most of the snow has melted off the high peaks of the Japan Alps by June and hikers flock to the trails. You should check conditions before going, however, as big snow years can mean difficult conditions for skiers.

July

The rainy season ends in Honshū sometime in July and, once it does, the heat cranks up and it can be very hot and humid. Head to Hokkaidō or the Japan Alps to escape the heat.

🏃 Mt Fuji Climbing Season

Mt Fuji officially opens to climbing on 1 July, and the months of July and August are ideal for climbing the peak.

🎎 Gion Matsuri

Held on 17 July, this is the mother of all Japanese festivals. Dozens of huge floats are pulled through the streets of Kyoto by teams of chanting citizens. On the three evenings preceding the parade, people stroll through Shijō-dōri's street stalls dressed in beautiful *yukata* (light cotton kimonos).

🎎 Tenjin Matsuri

Held on 24 and 25 July, this is your chance to see the city of Osaka let its hair down. Try to make the second day of the festival, when huge crowds carry *mikoshi* (portable shrines) through the city.

August

August is hot and humid across most of Japan. Once again, Hokkaidō and the Japan Alps can provide some relief. Several of the year's best festivals and events happen in August.

🎎 Aomori Nebuta Matsuri

Held for several days in early August, this is one of Japan's more colourful festivals (p503). On the final day of the festival enormous parade floats are pulled through Aomori by teams of chanting dancers.

🎎 Matsumoto Bonbon

Matsumoto's biggest event takes place on the first Saturday in August, when hoards people perform the 'bonbon' dance through the city streets.

🎇 Awa-odori Matsuri

The city of Tokushima, on the southern island of Shikoku, comes alive from 12 to 15 August for the nation's largest and most famous *bon* dance (p610). Teams of dancers take to the streets to perform sake-inspired *bon* dances, and the best troupes are awarded prizes. *Bon* dances are performed to welcome the souls of the departed back to this world (and this is usually considered a good excuse to consume vast quantities of sake).

🎇 O-Bon

This Buddhist observance, which honours the spirits of the dead, occurs in mid-August (it is one of the high-season travel periods). This is a time when ancestors return to earth to visit their descendents. Lanterns are lit and floated on rivers, lakes or the sea to help guide them on their journey. See also Daimon-ji Gozan Okuribi.

🎇 Daimon-ji Gozan Okuribi

Huge fires in the shape of Chinese characters and other symbols are set alight in Kyoto during this festival (p310), which forms part of O-Bon (festival of the dead). It's one of Japan's most impressive spectacles.

🎇 Summer Fireworks Festivals

Cities and towns across Japan hold spectacular summer fireworks festivals in August. You'll be amazed at the quality and duration of some of these incredible displays.

(Above) Float in Kyoto's Gion Matsuri parade (p309)
(Below) Shintō festival at Yasaka-jinja (p293), Kyoto

☆ Earth Celebration

The island of Sado-ga-shima, off the coast of Northern Honshū, is the scene of this internationally famous festival of dance, art and music. The festival (p532) is held in the third week of August.

September

Sometime in early to mid-September, the heat breaks and temperatures become very pleasant in the main islands. Skies are generally clear at this time, making it a great time to travel.

🎎 Kishiwada Danjiri Matsuri

Huge *danjiri* (festival floats) are pulled through narrow streets in the south of Osaka during this lively festival on 14 and 15 September. Much alcohol is consumed and occasionally the *danjiri* go off course and crash into houses.

October

October is one of the best months to visit Japan: the weather can be warm or cool and usually sunny. The autumn foliage peaks in the Japan Alps at this time.

🎎 Asama Onsen Taimatsu Matsuri

In early October, Asama Onsen holds this spectacular fire festival (p252). Men, women and children parade burning bales of hay through narrow streets to an enormous bonfire at Misha *jinja* (shrine).

🎎 Kurama-no-hi Matsuri

On 22 October, huge flaming torches are carried through the streets of the tiny hamlet of Kurama in the mountains north of Kyoto. This is one of Japan's more primeval festivals (p252).

November

November is also beautiful for travel in most of Japan. Skies are reliably clear and temperatures are pleasantly cool. Snow starts to fall in the mountains and foliage peaks in places like Kyoto and Nara. Expect crowds.

🎎 Shichi-Go-San (7-5-3 Festival)

This is a festival in honour of girls aged three and seven and boys aged five. On 15 November, children are dressed in their finest clothes and taken to shrines or temples, where prayers are offered for good fortune.

December

December is cool to cold across most of Japan. The Japanese are busy preparing for the New Year. Most things shut down from 29 or 30 December, making travel difficult (but transport runs and accommodation is open).

Plan Your Trip
Itineraries

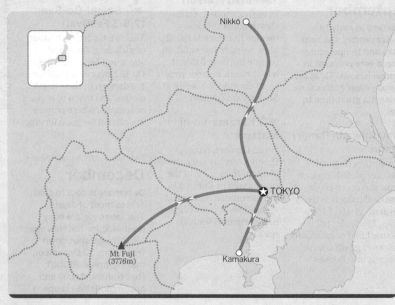

Nikkō

TOKYO

Mt Fuji
(3776m)

Kamakura

1 WEEK Tokyo, Mt Fuji & Around

With air connections to most of the world, as well as some of the world's best restaurants, shops and nightlife, Tokyo makes a great introduction to Japan. And you don't have to travel far outside the city to see some of Japan's great natural and traditional wonders.

To make the most of your stay in **Tokyo**, try to base yourself in an area that's interesting and also well served by transport connections, such as Shinjuku, Shibuya, Ginza, Roppongi or Marunouchi (Tokyo Station area). In any of these places, you can walk to a huge variety of restaurants and shops, and train/subway stations are always nearby. Of course, it's also perfectly possible to stay in slightly less convenient but cheaper areas like Asakusa or Ueno.

On your first morning in town, visit Tsukiji Fish Market – if you're jetlagged and up early anyway, make the best of it with a market tour. After the obligatory sushi breakfast, head up to Asakusa to visit the temple of Sensō-ji, then over to nearby Ueno for the Tokyo National Museum. The next day, take the loop line to Harajuku and walk to Meiji-jingū, the city's finest Shintō shrine, then take a stroll down chic

View over Tokyo from the Sky Deck (p77)

Omote-sandō. From there, head to Shibuya to soak up some of modern Tokyo. Make sure you spend an evening wandering east Shinjuku, where you'll get the full experience of Tokyo's neon madness. Other urban areas to check out include Ginza, for high-end shopping; Akihabara, for electronics and geek culture; and Roppongi, for international nightlife.

Break up your time in Tokyo with day trips to nearby attractions. The temples and shrines at **Nikkō** are among the most spectacular in Japan. For a taste of old Japan, a day poking among the Zen temples at **Kamakura** is a brilliant way to escape the crowds of the capital. Finally, it would be a shame to come all the way to Japan and not see **Mt Fuji**. You can get to the base of the mountain and back in a day from Tokyo, but climbing it will involve spending the night on the mountain. Either way, we recommend checking the weather first – the mountain is socked in by clouds much of the year, so try to wait for a break in the weather to make the trip.

MIKA / GETTY IMAGES ©

10 DAYS Tokyo, the Japan Alps & Kyoto

The Tokyo–Japan Alps–Kyoto route is the classic Japan itinerary and the best way to get a quick taste of the country. You'll experience three faces of Japan: the modern wonders of Tokyo, the traditional culture of Kyoto and the natural beauty of the Japan Alps.

While you can do this itinerary in any season, keep in mind that the Japan Alps can be snow covered any time from early November to late March – this rules out hiking unless you're an experienced winter mountaineer – but you can visit the attractive cities of Takayama and Kanazawa any time of year.

Let's assume that you'll fly into **Tokyo**, where you can spend a few days experiencing the best that the capital has to offer. Don't worry about skipping some of the traditional sights in that itinerary, because you'll be heading to Kyoto, and you'll get your fill of shrines and temples there.

From Tokyo, take the *shinkansen* (bullet train) to **Nagoya**, then an express to **Takayama**. Spend a day here checking out the restored Sanmachi-suji, then head into the Japan Alps via **Kamikōchi** or nearby **Shin-Hotaka Onsen**. Return to Takayama and rent a car so you can visit the thatched-roof villages of **Shirakawa-gō** and **Gokayama**. From there, if you feel like some more alpine scenery, drive northeast and head back into the Japan Alps via the **Tateyama-Kurobe Alpine Route** (the route is open from late spring to early autumn). Next, travel to **Kanazawa** (some rental agencies will allow you to drop the car in Kanazawa). Otherwise, you can also go from Takayama to Kanazawa by bus with a stop in Shirakawa-gō en route. In Kanazawa, check out the famous garden of Kenroku-en, the 21st Century Museum of Contemporary Art and the Nagamachi district.

From Kanazawa, there are several daily express trains that will get you to **Kyoto** in a little over two hours. In Kyoto, take some time to visit the sights, then jump on the *shinkansen* and get yourself back to **Tokyo** in time for your flight home.

FRANK CARTER / GETTY IMAGES ©

Top: *Gasshō-zukuri* style houses, Shirakawa-gō (p227)
Bottom: Carp streamers at a festival, Kanazawa (p260)

Kansai & Points West

While many people fly into Tokyo and base themselves there, Kansai, which is home to the ancient capital of Kyoto, is an equally appealing place to stay, especially if you're a fan of traditional culture. And with a Japan Rail Pass, you can easily head west to see Hiroshima, Miyajima and Naoshima.

Served by Kansai International Airport, which has connections to many parts of the world, **Kyoto** is the obvious place to stay: it's roughly in the middle of Kansai and it's got a wide range of excellent accommodation, not to mention the nation's finest temples, gardens and shrines. Spend a day exploring the Higashiyama area (both southern and northern), followed by another day strolling through the bamboo groves of Arashiyama. Then, hop on a train for a day trip to **Nara** to see the sights of **Nara-kōen**, including **Tōdai-ji**, with its enormous Buddha figure.

If you want to see a modern Japanese metropolis in high gear, then **Osaka** is only about 30 minutes by train from Kyoto. You can easily explore the city, grab some dinner and a drink and make it back to Kyoto before the trains stop running.

For those with a spiritual bent, a trip to the mountaintop Buddhist retreat of **Kōya-san** is highly recommended. Spend the night on one of the many temple lodgings there before returning to Kyoto. More adventurous travellers will also want to check out Japan's ancient pilgrimage route, the **Kumano Kodō**, in southern Kansai.

Kyoto also makes a good base for exploring some of the important sights in Western Honshū and the Inland Sea, especially if you've got a Japan Rail Pass. **Hiroshima** can be visited as a day trip from Kyoto if you use the *shinkansen* (bullet train) and get an early start. However, it's more relaxing to spend the night in nearby **Miyajima**, home of the iconic 'floating torii' (Shintō shrine gate) of Itsukushima-jinja. Art lovers might also consider stopping for a night or two at **Naoshima**, the island-turned-art museum in the Inland Sea.

Finally, if all this bouncing around makes you tired, finish off your adventure with an overnight trip up to **Kinosaki**, where you can soak away your cares in some of Japan's best hot springs.

Top: Itsukushima-jinja (p422), Miyajima
Bottom: Geisha, Kyoto (p328)

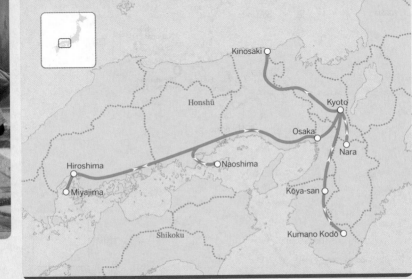

RUSSIA

Rebun-tō
Rishiri-tō

Sōya-misaki
Wakkanai

SEA OF OKHOTSK

Shiretoko
National Park

RUSSIA

Hokkaidō
Shari

Asahikawa

Asahidake Onsen

Biei

Otaru

Furano

Daisetsuzan
National Park

Sapporo

Noboribetsu
Onsen

Hakodate

*SEA OF
JAPAN*

Towada-ko

*PACIFIC
OCEAN*

Tazawa-ko

Honshū

Dewa Sanzan

Sado-ga-shima

The Wilds of Hokkaidō & Tōhoku

3 WEEKS

If you want to step off the main Tokyo–Kyoto tourist trail, head to Hokkaidō, Japan's northernmost major island, and Northern Honshū, the northern tip of Japan's main island. In summer these areas are usually relatively cool, while in winter you can expect cold and snowy weather.

Whether you're on a Japan Rail Pass or flying directly, **Sapporo** makes a good hub for Hokkaidō excursions. If you're here in February, your prize for enduring the arctic cold is a front-row seat at the Sapporo Snow Festival, highlighted by life-size carvings of everything from European cityscapes to elaborate ice mazes.

On a day trip from Sapporo, see romantic **Otaru**, with its Victorian brick warehouses and fresh sushi spreads. If you have more time, a couple of nights in **Hakodate** will recall the era of European colonisation. On the way back to Sapporo, hot-springs fans can take a dip in the waters of **Noboribetsu Onsen**.

Head out again, making a brief stop in **Asahikawa** for a few rounds of Otokoyama sake, before pressing on to **Wakkanai**. From here, take the ferry to **Rishiri-tō** and **Rebun-tō** in search of annual wildflower blooms. On the return, see **Sōya-misaki**, Hokkaidō's northernmost point, from which you might catch a glance of Russia's Sakhalin Island on a clear day.

Travel back to Asahikawa to plan your next move. Make your way to **Asahidake Onsen**, and hike **Daisetsuzan National Park**. Get behind the wheel of a rental car and explore the lavender fields and gourmet attractions around **Furano** and **Biei**. If you really want to leave it all behind, head east to **Shari**, the jumping-off point for **Shiretoko National Park**. Don't forget your bear bells; humans aren't the only creatures that call this remote peninsula home.

If you haven't yet had your fill of natural wonders, take the train south through the Seikan Tunnel (the world's longest underwater tunnel) to Northern Honshū. Visit **Towada-ko**, a crater lake that's home to the Nyūtō Onsen. Then continue south to lovely **Tazawa-ko**, Japan's deepest lake. If you're a hiker, you'll want to make the famed pilgrimage across the three sacred peaks of **Dewa Sanzan**. Finally, if you really want to get off the beaten track, take the ferry to **Sado-ga-shima** and rent a car to explore this beguiling island (home of the Kodo Drummers).

Top: Otaru (p562)
Bottom: View of Rishiri-zan from Rebun-tō (p588)

Kyūshū & Shikoku

2 WEEKS

Relatively few tourists make the journey southwest to the islands of Shikoku and Kyūshū, which is a shame, since these two islands are home to some of the country's most beautiful scenery, welcoming people and great food. They're also good options for escaping the bitter cold of winter, particularly southern Kyūshū.

While there are some international flights to Fukuoka in Kyūshū, it's likely that you'll approach this area from Kansai or Tokyo. Take a *shinkansen* to the city of Okayama in Western Honshū. Here, catch a special *Nampū* express train across the Inland Sea right down into the mountainous heart of Shikoku and spend a night or two in one of the Chiiori Trust's thatched-roof cottages in **Iya Valley** (note that it's also possible to drive here and this gives you more freedom to explore the area). From here, you can head south to do some surfing at **Ohkihama**, or head west to climb **Ishizuchi-san**. Finally, take a dip in the wonderful **Dōgo Onsen** in the castle town of **Matsuyama**.

From Matsuyama you can recross the Inland Sea and join the Sanyō Shinkansen line that will take you southwest to the island of **Kyūshū** (consider a stop at Hiroshima en route). Your first stop in Kyūshū should be **Fukuoka**, Kyūshū's largest city, which is crammed with spirited dining and nightlife in the lanes of Tenjin and Daimyō. From here, you can head southeast to the hot spring resort of **Beppu**, or southwest to **Nagasaki**. While Nagasaki is best known to Westerners for its tragic history, most visitors are surprised to find a vibrant city with great food and lots of opportunities to learn about Japan's early contacts with the West.

From either Beppu or Nagasaki, head south, possibly stopping en route at the semiactive volcano of **Aso-san**, which offers superb hiking, then make your way to **Kagoshima**, a city with a laid-back almost tropical vibe which contrasts sharply with the rest of Japan. Sengan-en garden and Sakurajima volcano are must-sees before going south for a sand bath in the seaside town of **Ibusuki**.

Finally, if you have time and enjoy hiking, take a ferry south from Kagoshima to the island of **Yakushima** for some hiking and onsens before making your way north and homeward.

Top: *Rotemburo* (outdoor bath), Iya Valley (p616)
Bottom: Takachiho-kyō (p711)

Off the Beaten Track: Japan

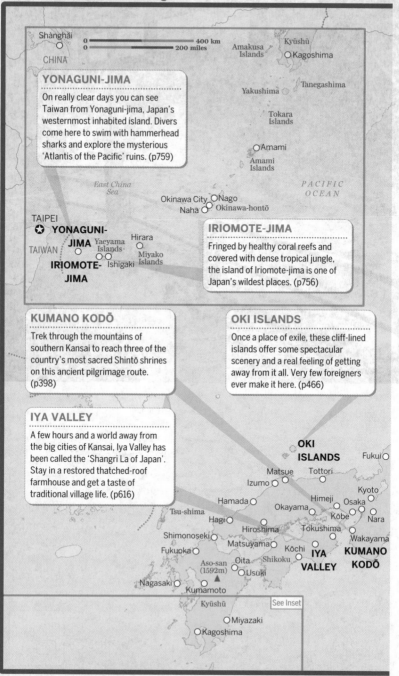

YONAGUNI-JIMA

On really clear days you can see Taiwan from Yonaguni-jima, Japan's westernmost inhabited island. Divers come here to swim with hammerhead sharks and explore the mysterious 'Atlantis of the Pacific' ruins. (p759)

IRIOMOTE-JIMA

Fringed by healthy coral reefs and covered with dense tropical jungle, the island of Iriomote-jima is one of Japan's wildest places. (p756)

KUMANO KODŌ

Trek through the mountains of southern Kansai to reach three of the country's most sacred Shintō shrines on this ancient pilgrimage route. (p398)

OKI ISLANDS

Once a place of exile, these cliff-lined islands offer some spectacular scenery and a real feeling of getting away from it all. Very few foreigners ever make it here. (p466)

IYA VALLEY

A few hours and a world away from the big cities of Kansai, Iya Valley has been called the 'Shangri La of Japan'. Stay in a restored thatched-roof farmhouse and get a taste of traditional village life. (p616)

N
0 — 500 km
0 — 250 miles

RUSSIA

Sea of Okhotsk RUSSIA

RISHIRI-TŌ & REBUN-TŌ

SHIRETOKO NATIONAL PARK

Abashiri

Daisetsuzan National Park

Akan National Park

Takikawa
Biei
Hokkaidō

Otaru
Sapporo
Obihiro
Kushiro

Shikotsu-tōya National Park

Okushiri-tō
Hakodate

Aomori

Towada-Hachimantai National Park
Hachinohe

Akita
Morioka

Kakunodate

Oshu

Sakata
Shinjō

Tsuruoka

Sendai

Yamagata

SADO-GA-SHIMA
Niigata
Fukushima

Noto Peninsula

Toyama
Nagano
Nikkō
Utsunomiya

Sea of Japan

Kanazawa
Maebashi
Mito

Honshū
Urawa
TOKYO

Gifu
Kōfu
Chiba

Nagoya
Yokohama

Tsu
Mt Fuji (3776m)

Ise
Shizuoka

PACIFIC OCEAN

Ogasawara Archipelago (500km) ↓

SHIRETOKO NATIONAL PARK

With no sealed roads and a healthy population of brown bears, Shiretoko earns the title of Japan's last true wilderness. The reward for tackling the tough trails here are long soaks in plentiful hot springs. (p593)

RISHIRI-TŌ & REBUN-TŌ

Almost as far north as you can go in Japan, these two islands burst into riotous blooms of wildflowers each year from May to August. They're a true delight for hikers and photographers. (p585)

SADO-GA-SHIMA

A wild outpost of rugged mountains and coastline, each August this island rocks to the sound of the famous Kodo Drummers during the fabulous Earth Celebration. (p530)

OGASAWARA ARCHIPELAGO

This is as far off the beaten track as you can get in Japan. A full 25½-hour ferry ride from Tokyo, these semitropical islands – complete with whales, sharks and dolphins – feel like a different world. (p196)

Snowboarding, Niseko (p564)

Plan Your Trip
Skiing in Japan

Japan, home to more than 500 ski resorts, may be one of the skiing and snowboarding world's best-kept secrets. Regular snowfall, stunning mountain vistas, well-groomed runs, friendly locals, tasty food and an incredible variety of onsen (hot springs) for that all-important après-ski soak. What's more, cultural experiences are all around! If you plan your itinerary accordingly, it's possible to head from powdery slope to Zen garden with relative ease, allowing for one of the most exotic ski holidays imaginable.

What to Bring

Almost everything you will need is available in Japan. However it's best to bring some things from abroad:

Goggles

They're very expensive in Japan.

Essential toiletries

Sunblock, aspirin and other pharmacy items may be hard to track down.

Large-sized ski boots

Rental places at most resorts have boots of up to 30cm (which is equivalent to men's size 12 in the USA, UK or Australia). Resorts such as Niseko, which attract strong international followings, typically stock larger sizes. But if you have very large feet, play it safe and bring your own boots.

Large-sized clothing and gloves

If you're a bit on the big side, bring your own gear. While larger sizes are becoming more readily available, you might waste time searching for what you need.

Season

The ski season usually kicks off in mid-December, though conditions are highly variable. Early on, resorts will intermittently open runs depending on the quality and quantity of snowfall. January and February are peak months across the country. Things begin to warm up in March, heralding the close of the ski season in early April.

Where to Ski

Japan's best-known ski resorts are found in the Japan Alps region of Central Honshū, and on the northern island of Hokkaidō. The former lays claim to the highest mountains, while the latter boasts the deepest and most regular snowfall in the country.

While the ski resorts of Northern Honshū have seen tough times due to the effects of the Great East Japan Earthquake, they offer some wonderful options. And don't forget Niigata, easily accessed by *shinkansen* (bullet train) from Tokyo.

An excellent website for checking out the Japan ski scene is www.snowjapan. com (in English).

What follows is our overview of 10 top ski areas. This is just to whet your appetite, of course, as there are about 500 more that we don't mention here!

➡ **Niseko** (p564) As far as most foreign skiers are concerned, Niseko is how you say 'powder' in Japanese. This is understandable, as Niseko receives an average snowfall of 15m annually. Located on Hokkaidō, Niseko is actually four interconnected ski areas: Niseko Annupuri, Niseko Village (also known as Higashiyama), Grand Hirafu and Hanazono.

➡ **Furano** (p575) More or less in the centre of Hokkaidō (the town also hosts a belly-button festival, Heso Matsuri, to celebrate being in the middle!), Furano shot to world fame after hosting FIS World Ski and Snowboarding Cup events. Relatively undiscovered in comparison to Niseko, Furano rewards savvy powder fiends with polished runs through pristine birch forests.

➡ **Sapporo Teine** (p549) So close to Sapporo, Hokkaidō's capital, that buses run from downtown hotels. You can swish down slopes used in the 1972 Sapporo Winter Olympics by day and enjoy the raucous restaurants, bars and clubs of Susukino by night.

➡ **Hakuba** (p247) The quintessential Japan Alps ski resort, Hakuba offers eye-popping views in addition to excellent and varied skiing in seven resorts. Hakuba hosted Winter Olympic events in 1998 and is led by the legendary Happō-One Ski Resort (pronounced 'hah-poh-oh-nay').

➡ **Shiga Kōgen** (p244) In the Japan Alps, Shiga Kōgen is one of the largest ski resorts in the world, with an incredible 21 different areas, all interconnected by trails and lifts and accessible with one lift ticket. With such a variety of terrain on offer, there is something for everyone here.

Skiing in Japan

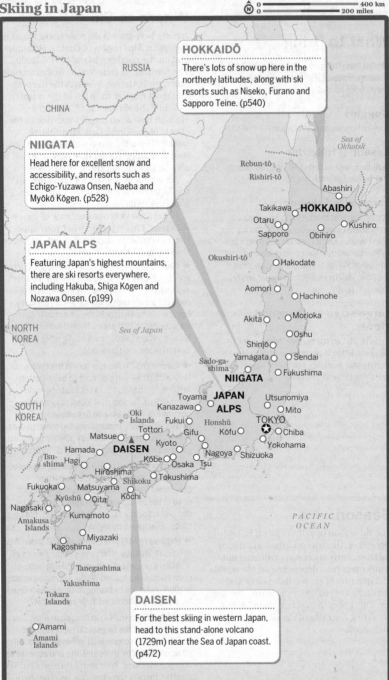

0   400 km
0   200 miles

HOKKAIDŌ

There's lots of snow up here in the northerly latitudes, along with ski resorts such as Niseko, Furano and Sapporo Teine. (p540)

NIIGATA

Head here for excellent snow and accessibility, and resorts such as Echigo-Yuzawa Onsen, Naeba and Myōkō Kōgen. (p528)

JAPAN ALPS

Featuring Japan's highest mountains, there are ski resorts everywhere, including Hakuba, Shiga Kōgen and Nozawa Onsen. (p199)

DAISEN

For the best skiing in western Japan, head to this stand-alone volcano (1729m) near the Sea of Japan coast. (p472)

RUSSIA

CHINA

Sea of Okhotsk

Rebun-tō
Rishiri-tō
Abashiri
Takikawa **HOKKAIDŌ**
Otaru Kushiro
Sapporo Obihiro

Okushiri-tō Hakodate

NORTH KOREA

Sea of Japan

Aomori Hachinohe

Akita Morioka
Oshu
Shinjō
Yamágata Sendai
Sado-ga-shima
NIIGATA Fukushima

Toyama **JAPAN** Utsunomiya
Kanazawa **ALPS** Mito
SOUTH KOREA Oki Fukui Honshū Kōfu TOKYO
Islands Tottori Gifu Chiba
Matsue Kyoto Yokohama
Tsu- Hamada **DAISEN** Nagoya Shizuoka
shima Hagi Kōbe Tsu
Hiroshima Osaka
Fukuoka Matsuyama Shikoku Tokushima
Kyūshū Kōchi
Nagasaki Oita
Amakusa Kumamoto
Islands Miyazaki
Kagoshima

Tanegashima
Yakushima
Tokara Islands

Amami
Amami Islands

PACIFIC OCEAN

Hakuba (p247)

➡ **Nozawa Onsen** (p245) This quaint Swiss-style village is tucked high up in the Japan Alps. It offers a good variety of runs, including some challenging mogul courses. Snowboarders will enjoy the terrain park and half-pipe, and there's even a cross-country skiing course that traverses the peaks.

➡ **Echigo-Yuzawa Onsen** (p536) Talk about easy to get to! Echigo-Yuzawa Onsen has its own *shinkansen* station on the Jōetsu line to Niigata and you can go skiing as a day trip from Tokyo (77 minutes one-way by the fastest service). GALA Yuzawa is the resort to head to here.

➡ **Naeba** (p537) Home to Dragondola, reportedly the longest gondola in the world (5.5km), Naeba has two massive ski areas, centred around the Prince Hotel Naeba, that cater to your every whim and fancy.

➡ **Myōkō Kōgen** (p538) Much less developed than the other resorts listed here, Myōkō Kōgen is directly north of Nagano city and close to the Sea of Japan. Head here for an off-the-beaten-path ski holiday in the powder-rich Myōkō mountain range.

➡ **Daisen** (p472) This is our 'wildcard'! With the best skiing in western Japan, this exposed volcano (1729m) is only 10km from the Sea of Japan in Tottori Prefecture and catches heavy snowfall in winter. Daisen White Resort is where it's at!

Costs

Many people unfamiliar with skiing in Japan often assume that it will cost an arm and a leg to ski here. But, even after factoring in the international air ticket, it might actually be cheaper to ski for a week in Japan than in your home country. Are we mad? Well, let's check the numbers.

➡ **Lift tickets and equipment rental** A full-day lift ticket at most ski areas in Japan costs between ¥4000 and ¥5500. This is significantly less than a full day at large resorts in North America or Europe. Full equipment rental is typically no more than ¥5000 per day (both ski and snowboard sets are available). The Japanese tend to be connoisseurs of quality, which means that you need not worry about getting stuck with shabby and/or outdated gear.

➡ **Accommodation** You can find plenty of upmarket accommodation in the ¥6500 to ¥10,000 range at major ski areas in Japan, and this price will often include one or two meals. This is often less than half of what you'd expect to pay for similar accommodation in North

THE JAPANESE WAY OF SKIING

Snow is snow, skis are skis – right? How different can it be to ski in Japan? Not very much, but keep the following in mind:

➡ Lift-line management is surprisingly poor in Japan. Skiers are often left to jostle and fend for themselves, and even when it's crowded, singles are allowed to ride triple and quad lifts alone.

➡ Not all resorts use the green/blue/black coding system for difficulty. Some have red, purple, orange, dotted lines or black-numbered runs on the map.

➡ The majority of Japanese skiers start skiing at 9am, have lunch exactly at noon, and get off the hill by 3pm. If you work on a slightly different schedule, you will avoid a lot of the crowds.

➡ Off-piste and out-of-bounds skiing is often high quality but also highly illegal and potentially dangerous, resulting in the confiscation of your lift pass if you're caught by the ski patrol. Cut the ropes at your own risk.

America or Europe. The budget traveller will find a variety of backpacker-type hostels near most resorts, and families will be glad to know that young children (under six years of age) can usually stay for free or at a significant discount.

➡ **Food** On-slope meals top out at around ¥1000, which is slightly less than what you'd pay in North America or Europe. The restaurant selection anywhere you go is also varied, including the likes of *rāmen* (egg noodles), *udon* (wheat noodles), *kareraisu* (curry rice) and *gyūdon* (sliced beef on rice), as well as more familiar fast-food options including sandwiches, pizza, burgers and kebabs. Beer and snacks, however, can be quite expensive – better to bring your own rather than buy from one of the ubiquitous convenience stores.

➡ **Transport** Airport-to-resort transport in Japan costs no more than in other countries, and is usually faster and more efficient (and, unlike in North America, you don't need to rent a car).

Can You Say 'Ski' in Japanese?

That's right: it's 'ski' (all right, it's pronounced more like 'sukee'). But the point is that communication won't be much of a problem on your Japan ski trip.

Tackling the language barrier has never been easier: most of the better-known resorts employ a number of English-speaking foreigners on working-holiday visas. They work the lifts and in the cafeterias, and often find employment in the hotels or guesthouses that are most popular with foreign guests.

All major signs and maps are translated into English, and provided you have some experience at large resorts back home, you'll find the layout and organisation of Japanese resorts to be pretty intuitive.

The information counter at the base of the mountain always has helpful and polite staff available to answer questions.

Travel with Children

Japan is a great place to travel with kids. The usual concerns that parents have about safety and hygiene are simply not concerns in ultrasafe and spotless Japan. Instead, your biggest challenge will probably be keeping your kids entertained. In this chapter, we'll show you how.

Japan for Children

You'll find that the Japanese love kids and will fawn over the young ones, declaring them to be *kawaii* (cute).

Entertainment

As far as activities and keeping kids entertained, you'll find Japan is a very easy place to travel.

➡ Most towns and cities have small playgrounds and parks that will keep toddlers and small children entertained.

➡ Older children will likely enjoy the same things that their Japanese peers enjoy: game centres, amusement parks, downtown shopping areas and movies (which are usually screened in English). Some children might even get a kick out of the same sights as their parents: shrines, temples and museums.

➡ And then there are outdoor sports like hiking, skiing/snowboarding and marine sports.

Food

Food can be an issue if your child is a picky or unadventurous eater – even adults can find some Japanese cuisine challenging.

➡ If you're going to a *kaiseki* (haute cuisine) place, have your lodgings call ahead to ask for some kid-friendly dishes. Ditto if you'll be dining at your ryokan.

Best Regions for Children

Tokyo

Tokyo Disneyland and the youth meccas of Shibuya and Harajuku are only the beginning of Tokyo's child-friendly attractions.

Kansai

Nara offers a giant park filled with friendly deer and eye-popping sights like the Great Buddha; there's even a restaurant where they can eat lunch while operating a giant train set.

Okinawa & the Southwest Islands

The sand is white, the water warm and the coral good. If the weather's bad for snorkelling, take the kids to one of the world's best aquariums.

Kyoto

Cycling the backstreets, wandering the shopping arcades, picnicking by the river and hiking in the hills will please the kids. And Kiyomizu-dera is as close to child-friendly as temples come.

Sapporo & Hokkaidō

If your kids ski or snowboard, they'll love the powder snow up in Hokkaidō.

➡ If necessary, have your lodgings write your child's dietary restrictions or allergies for you in Japanese.

➡ You'll find a lot of so-called 'family restaurants' in Japan, which usually serve Western food (pizza, fried chicken, French fries), or offer special kids' meals (sometimes called *o-ko-sama ranchii*). *Shokudō* (all-round eateries) also tend to serve something that children will eat.

➡ Most supermarkets stock a good selection of baby food, but you may need to ask a clerk to help you read the contents.

➡ If your child simply will not eat Japanese food, don't worry: the big cities are chock-a-block with international restaurants, and fast-food joints can be found even in smaller towns. In rural areas, where only Japanese food may be available, you can stock up beforehand on food your child likes at a supermarket.

Facilities

➡ There are nappy-changing facilities in some public places, such as department stores and larger train stations.

➡ Cots are available in most hotels (but not usually in ryokan) and can be booked in advance.

➡ High chairs are available in lots of restaurants (though in many restaurants everyone simply sits on the floor).

➡ There are child-care agencies in larger cities, although outside Tokyo few have English-speaking staff.

Infants

➡ Nappies (diapers) are readily available. A picture on the package usually indicates if they are for boys or girls. Bottles, wipes and medications are available at large pharmacies.

➡ Breastfeeding is generally not done in public, although it's not frowned upon. That said, in a quiet part of a park or a playground, with something like a shawl to cover the child, it is usually fine. Some department stores, hospitals and public attractions have rooms where mothers can breastfeed.

Getting Around

➡ Most trains and buses do have *yūsen zaseki* (priority seating for those who are elderly, handicapped, pregnant or with young children).

➡ Child seats in taxis are generally not available, but most car-rental agencies will provide one if you ask in advance.

➡ Most cities are fairly accessible to those with strollers, and train stations and many large buildings have elevators (lifts). However, many attractions such as temples and shrines do not have ramps. An issue, particularly in Kyoto, is the relative lack of pavements away from the main streets (luckily, the Japanese tend to be safe drivers!).

Children's Highlights

Let's face it: even the most precocious kid will eventually get tired of temples, gardens and shrines. Here are a few hints to keep the little ones entertained in Japan.

Amusement parks Japan is famous for amusement parks, including the famous Tokyo Disneyland and Universal Studios Japan.

Trains Children will love Japan's trains, whether they're riding the *shinkansen* (bullet train) or just watching from the platform.

Game centres On a rainy day when the kids are getting bored, a good game centre might just be a lifesaver. You'll find them in shopping malls across the land.

Movies Hollywood films (and occasionally others) are usually screened in English in Japan.

Shōtengai At the downtown *shōtengai* (market streets) – with ¥100 shops and game centres – there's plenty to keep kids occupied.

Skiing & snowboarding If you're in Japan in the winter, the kids will love spending a day on the slopes.

Beaches While Okinawa has the best beaches in Japan, you'll find decent beaches along the shores of most of Japan's major islands.

Sushi and sashimi

Eat & Drink Like a Local

Japanese food is one of the world's most diverse, refined and delicious cuisines. If you're like most visitors to Japan, enjoying the genuine article on its home turf is a big reason for visiting the country. In this chapter, we'll arm you with the knowledge you need to make a thorough exploration of this sublime cuisine.

The Year in Food

Few cultures are as seasonally aware as the Japanese. Indeed, the ancient Japanese calendar divided the year into 24 separate seasons, and even today most Japanese will start a letter with a reference to the present season. This appreciation of the seasons finds its greatest expression in the country's food culture.

Spring (Mar–Jun)

The new growth of spring finds its way onto tables in the form of *takenoko* (bamboo shoots), *sansai* (mountain vegetables), and *wagashi* (Japanese sweets) with plum and cherry blossom motifs.

Summer (Jul–Sep)

The Japanese fight the heat of summer by eating cooling dishes like *reimen* (cold ramen) and cold *zaru soba* (noodles served on a plate). *Unagi* (eel) is also eaten because it's thought to strengthen the body against the summer heat. After meals, juicy peaches, pears and watermelons are eaten as dessert.

Autumn (Sep–Nov)

Chestnut dishes and persimmons are popular, as are *wagashi* with maple leaf motifs.

Winter (Dec–Feb)

The Japanese warm up in winter by eating *nabe* (hot pot) dishes and drinking warm *amazake* (warm, fermented rice milk). This is also the season for *fugu* (pufferfish) and oysters.

Food Experiences

Eating should be a big part of your Japan journey, and it's perfectly possible to plan an entire trip to include dining experiences such as those below.

➡ **Tsukiji Fish Market, Tokyo** Wake early and visit the famous Tsukiji Fish Market (p73). If it swims in the sea, you can be pretty sure you'll find it for sale here in the world's biggest fish market.

➡ **Kaiseki, Kyoto** Dine at Kyoto's excellent traditional *kaiseki* (Japanese haute cuisine) restaurants. You can get *kaiseki* in other parts of Japan, but it just seems to taste better when served in the classic wooden buildings of the old capital.

➡ **Kuidaore, Osaka** Roll up your sleeves and join the locals in their favourite pastime: *kuidaore* (eating until you drop). Cheap, hearty and tasty are the watchwords for Osaka cuisine.

Street Food

Japan doesn't have a street food culture like Thailand or China. Indeed, until recently, it was considered uncouth for a woman to eat or drink while walking. But, *yatai* (food stalls, usually open only in the evening) have always been a part of the culture, especially at festivals. It's now becoming more common to see street snacks on offer, especially in cities like Osaka and Tokyo. Look out for dishes such as *taco-yaki* (grilled octopus dumplings), *tai-yaki* (fish-shaped bean cakes) and *yaki-imo* (baked sweet potatoes).

Dare to Try

Japan is rivaled only by China as the place to put your taste buds to the test. It's a paradise for the 'been there, eaten that' crowd. Here are a few dishes that will give even the most ardent culinary daredevils pause for thought. Having tried them all, we're happy to report that none of them taste anything like chicken.

➡ **Fugu** This is the 'deadly' pufferfish that gave Homer Simpson so such much trouble. It's a speciality of Western Honshū, best consumed in winter.

➡ **Nattō** These partially fermented soybeans with the scent of ammonia are the litmus test by which Japanese judge a foreigner's sense of culinary adventure (don't be surprised if someone asks you: 'Can you eat *nattō*?').

➡ **Uni** With the flavour of a distilled tidal pool and the appearance of a small orange brain, *uni* (sea urchin) is usually described on English-language sushi menus as 'challenging'.

➡ **Namako** Even most Japanese are put off by sea cucumber. If you can eat this and actually like it, our hats are off to you.

➡ **Shirako** This is the sperm-filled reproductive gland of a male fish. No further comment.

Local Specialities

You'll find that every island and region of Japan has its own *meibutsu* (speciality).

Tokyo

➡ **Sushi** Get it fresh from Tsukiji Fish Market at the sushi counters found around the market or at one of the high-end sushi restaurants across the city.

➡ **Nouveau rāmen** Of course you can get every type of regional Japanese *rāmen* in Tokyo, but you can also sample some new twists on these familiar noodles.

Mt Fuji & Around Tokyo

➡ **Hōtō noodles** A specialty of the Fuji area is *hōtō* (hand-cut noodles), served as part of hearty mountain stews containing thick miso, pumpkin, sweet potato and other vegetables – often served in a cast-iron pot.

➡ **Yuba** A popular traditional dish in the Nikkō area is *yuba* (the skin that forms when making tofu), which is cut into strips and used in everything from *udon* (thick white wheat noodle) dishes, to sashimi to *age yuba manju* (fried bean buns).

The Japan Alps & Central Honshu

➡ **Kishimen** A hearty, flat type of *udon* noodle that is wildly popular in Nagoya.

➡ **Miso-katsu** A type of *tonkatsu* (deep-fried pork cutlet) served with a miso-flavoured sauce.

➡ **Soba** Nagoya prides itself on producing some of Japan's finest *soba* (buckwheat noodles).

➡ **Sashimi & sushi** Kanazawa and the Noto Peninsula are famous for impossibly fresh seafood.

Kyoto

➡ **Kaiseki** Kyoto is the best place to sample Japan's traditional haute cuisine.

➡ **Sweets** You can find *wagashi* (traditional Japanese sweets) from Okinawa to Hokkaidō, but Kyoto has the largest selection and an incredible variety of long-established sweet shops.

➡ **Tofu** Known for its pure underground water and high-quality beans, Kyoto tofu is revered as some of the best in the country.

Diners at an *izakaya* (pub-eatery; p788), Tokyo

Kansai

➡ **Okonomiyaki** For hearty *okonomiyaki* (savoury pancakes), Osaka's Dōtombori is the place to go.

➡ **Rāmen** It's hardly surprising that down-to-earth Osaka is the best place in Japan to get acquainted with *rāmen*.

➡ **Street food** No city in Japan has a better selection of street food, including several *taco-yaki* stands that attract huge crowds from dawn to dusk.

Hiroshima & Western Honshū

➡ **Hiroshima-yaki** You can't visit Hiroshima without sampling the city's distinctive style of *okonomiyaki*, which is topped with a pile of green onions.

➡ **Oysters** In winter, oyster lovers from across Japan seek out the oysters harvested from the Inland Sea near Hiroshima.

Okonomiyaki (savoury pancake)

Northern Honshū (Tōhoku)

➡ **Gyūtan** Beef tongue grilled over charcoal might not sound that appealing, but served with a squeeze of lemon, it's fantastic.

➡ **Kiritanpo** Kneaded rice grilled on bamboo spits may sound a bit odd, but it's pretty tasty, especially when served with a soy-based broth and vegetable hotpot.

➡ **Jaja-men** These flat noodles are Morioka's most famous noodle dish – usually served all-you-can eat.

➡ **Tanrei karakuchi sake** A distinctive style of crisp,dry sake produced in Niigata Prefecture, an area famous for its pure water and rice.

Sapporo & Hokkaidō

➡ **Craft beer** Sapporo is in the middle of a huge craft beer boom and local brews are attracting worldwide attention.

➡ **Crab cuisine** Hokkaidō is famous for its king crab and nothing tastes better than freshly caught crab boiled and served with a bit of melted butter and lemon.

➡ **Jingisukan** The Japanese pronunciation of Ghenghis Khan, this all-you-can-eat lamb dish

is usually washed down with endless mugs of draft beer.

➡ **Sapporo rāmen** A hearty *rāmen* dish based on a miso-flavoured soup.

Shikoku

➡ **Sanuki udon** A speciality of Shikoku's Kagawa Prefecture, Sanuki *udon* is famous for its smooth texture and distinctive taste. It comes in very small bowls and customers often compete to see how many bowls they can eat.

Kyushu

➡ **Hakata rāmen** *Rāmen* served in a soup with an intensely flavourful pork broth; currently enjoying nationwide popularity.

➡ **Yaki-curry** Curry rice topped with cheese and grilled – sort of like curry au gratin.

➡ **Chikin nanban** Sweet fried chicken served with tartar sauce.

➡ **Chirin-chirin** A Nagasaki speciality of sweet citrus-flavoured shaved ice.

➡ **Shippoku-ryori** A type of *kaiseki* cuisine with Portuguese and Chinese influences – a speciality of Nagasaki.

Rāmen (egg noodles)

➡ **Castella** A Portuguese pound cake (pronounced 'kasuterra' in Japanese).

Okinawa & the Southwest Islands

➡ **Goya champuru** A stir-fry containing the bitter melon *goya* (an Okinawan vegetable).

➡ **Soki soba** Bowls of hot noodles served with thick slices of tender marinated pork.

➡ **Mimiga** Sliced pig ears marinated in vinegar.

➡ **Awamori** Okinawan firewater brewed from rice, occasionally 'flavoured' by the addition of a poisonous snake in the bottle.

How to Eat & Drink

When to Eat

➡ **Breakfast** Eaten upon waking, the traditional Japanese breakfast consists of rice, miso soup, and a few side dishes like a small cooked fish and *nattō*. These days, unless they're staying at a ryokan, modern Japanese tend to eat thick slices of supermarket bread and perhaps a boiled egg for breakfast, washed down with tea or coffee.

➡ **Lunch** Eaten at midday and is usually a rice-based meal with side dishes like meat or fish. Noodles (*soba, udon* or *rāmen*) are very popular.

➡ **Dinner** Eaten after work (usually 6pm to 8pm). This is usually a rice-based meal supplemented with meat or fish, although noodles are sometimes consumed in the evening. If a person eats out, especially in cities, they're as likely to eat foreign fare as Japanese.

Of course, it's common for office workers, particularly men, to go out with their colleagues or clients for drinking and dining in the evening, often until around midnight.

Where to Eat

It's said that Japan has the highest number of restaurants per capita of any country. One reason for this is that few Japanese entertain guests at home.

Most Japanese restaurants are speciality restaurants: while Japanese restaurants back home might serve everything from sushi to *gyōza* (dumplings) under one roof, this would be considered very strange in Japan. Because Japanese restaurants tend to specialise in one dish or type of cuisine, they become very good at it.

In addition to Japanese restaurants of every stripe, you'll also find a wide range of foreign restaurants in Japanese cities, with French, Italian, Chinese and Thai being the most popular.

Menu Decoder

Here's a brief list of important Japanese eating words. For a full explanation of the restaurants and dishes you'll encounter, see the Japanese Cuisine chapter, p786. For key phrases and words see p852.

➡ **Setto** (セット) A set menu/course

➡ **Morning setto** (モーニングセット) A breakfast set (usually egg, toast and coffee)

➡ **Teishoku** (定食) Also set menu/course

➡ **Tabehodai** (食べ放題) All-you-can eat

➡ **Viking** (バイキング) Also all-you-can eat

➡ **Choshoku/asa gohan** (朝食 or 朝ご飯) Breakfast

➡ **Chushoku/hiru gohan** (昼食 or 昼ご飯) Lunch

➡ **Yushoku/ban gohan** (夕食 or 晩ご飯) Dinner

➡ **Resutoran** (レストラン) Restaurant

Japan on a Budget

Japan has a reputation as one of the world's most expensive countries. In reality, Japan is one of the least expensive countries in the developed world. Of course, you can still burn through a lot of cash if you're not careful. In this chapter, we'll show you how to really stretch those yen.

Essential Money-Saving Tips

Japan Rail Pass

This is the best way to see a lot of Japan without going broke. See the Transport section of this chapter for details.

Business hotels

Cheap business hotels are proliferating across Japan. In many cases, they are cheaper than youth hostels, especially if you're travelling as a couple. See the Accommodation section of this chapter for details.

Cheap eats

Even in Tokyo, you can fill up on noodles, rice dishes or set meals for as little as ¥500 (US$6). See the Eating section of this chapter for details.

Free attractions

A surprising number of sights in Japan are completely free. See the Attractions section of this chapter for details.

It's Cheaper Than You Think

Everyone has heard the tale of the guy who blundered into a bar in Japan, had two drinks and got stuck with a bill for US$1000. Urban legends like this date back to the heady days of the Bubble Era in the 1980s. Sure, you can still drop money like that on a few drinks in exclusive establishments in Tokyo (if you can get by the guy at the door), but you're more likely to be spending ¥600 (about US$6) per beer in Japan.

The fact is, Japan's image as one of the world's most expensive countries is just that: image. Anyone who has been to Japan recently knows that it can be cheaper to travel in Japan than in parts of Western Europe, the US, Australia or even the big coastal cities of China. Still, there's no denying that Japan is not Thailand. In order to help you stretch those yen, we've put together the following list of money-saving tips.

Accommodation

➡ **Cheap business hotels** There are several good budget business hotel chains in Japan that offer double or twin rooms for about ¥6500 (around US$65). One of the best value is the Toyoko Inn chain that offers free internet, breakfast (sometimes dinner), free phone calls in Japan and a host of other perks.

➡ **Capsule hotels** A night in a capsule hotel will set you back around ¥3000 (around US$34). Best of all, hip new capsule hotels have opened recently that cater to travellers (including women) rather than drunk salarymen.

➡ **Guesthouses** You'll find good, cheap guesthouses in many of Japan's cities, where a night's accommodation costs about ¥3500 (US$39).

➡ **Manga kissa** For real penny pinching (or when stuck with nowhere to stay), there are 24-hour *manga kissa* (comic book internet cafes) that have shower rooms, private booths you can sleep in and good rates (about ¥2000) for overnight hours. They're not the most salubrious or quiet places, but you can't beat the prices.

Transport

➡ **Japan Rail Pass** Like the famous Eurail Pass, this is one of the world's great travel bargains. It allows unlimited travel on Japan's brilliant nationwide rail system, including the lightning-fast *shinkansen* (bullet train). See the Transport chapter (p848) for more information.

➡ **Seishun Jūhachi Kippu** For ¥11,500, you get five one-day tickets good for travel on any regular Japan Railways train. You can literally travel from one end of the country to the other for around US$130. However, these can only be purchased and used during certain periods. See p850 for more information.

➡ **Local travel passes** Always check for special transport passes in the areas you explore. Where possible, we list these in the relevant destination chapters, but it never hurts to enquire at the tourist information office when you arrive, since these deals are being introduced all the time.

➡ **Car hire** Consider renting a car to explore places not well served by public transport, or in places where public transport is expensive. Highway tolls can really add up, but you always have the option of staying on local roads. See the Transport chapter (p844) for more information on car hire.

Shopping

➡ **Hyaku-en shops** *Hyaku-en* means ¥100, and, like the name implies, everything in these shops costs only ¥100, or just a bit more than US$1. You'll be amazed at what you can find in these places – some even sell food.

➡ **Flea markets** A good, new kimono costs an average of ¥200,000 (US$2270), but you can pick up a fine, used kimono at a flea market for ¥1000 (US$11). Whether you're shopping for yourself or for presents for the folks back home, you'll find some incredible bargains at Japan's flea markets.

Attractions

➡ **Shrines and temples** The vast majority of Shintō shrines in Japan cost nothing to enter. Likewise, the grounds of many temples can be toured for free (often, you only have to pay to enter the halls or a walled garden).

➡ **Museums and galleries** A surprising number of museums and galleries in Japan are free, while others are free a few days each month. The local tourist information office can usually supply a list of free places.

➡ **Parks and gardens** Most parks and many gardens in Japan are free to enter.

Eating

➡ **Shokudō** You can get a good filling meal in these all-around Japanese eateries for about ¥700 (US$7), and the tea is free and there's no tipping. Try that in New York.

➡ **Bentō** The ubiquitous Japanese box lunch, or bentō, costs around ¥500 and is both filling and nutritious.

➡ **Use your noodle** You can get a steaming bowl of tasty *rāmen* (egg noodles) in Japan for as little as ¥500, and ordering is a breeze – you just have to say *'rāmen'* and you're away. *Soba* (buckwheat noodles) and *udon* (thick white wheat noodles) are even cheaper – as low as ¥350 per bowl.

Regions at a Glance

Tokyo

Food
Culture
Shopping

Sushi & More

Not only does Tokyo have more restaurants than any other city in the world, it has more great ones. Whether it's sushi right from the source at Tsukiji Fish Market or a late-night bowl of *rāmen* (egg noodles), you will eat well – very well – here.

Past, Present & Future

Tokyo is famous for its pop culture – its eccentric street fashion, lurid anime (Japanese animation) and *kawaii* (cute) characters. But there is so much more: dig deeper in the city's excellent museums, and look to the future on those giant video screens.

Shop, Shop, Shop

Didn't think you were getting out of here empty handed, did you? Tokyo is a shoppers' paradise, offering everything from traditional crafts to the latest lifestyle gadgets.

p66

Mt Fuji & Around Tokyo

Ryokan
Outdoors
Culture

Ryokan & Onsen

Some of Japan's most loved ryokan and onsen are just a few hours from Tokyo. Each area offers its own regional flavour – rugged onsen towns to the north, lakeside resorts to the west, and laid-back villages to the south.

Outdoor Activities

Options include hiking cedar groves, scrambling up volcanoes, white-water rafting, skiing, lazing on beaches, surfing and swimming with dolphins.

Shrines & Temples

The cultural legacies of different historical eras come to life in the vibrant Unesco World Heritage–listed shrines and temples of Nikkō and the more austere ones of medieval Kamakura.

p146

The Japan Alps & Central Honshū

Onsen
Villages
Skiing

Ultimate Onsen

The mountainous heart of Japan bubbles over with exquisite hot springs and fantastic inns to enjoy them. Gaze up at snowy peaks while steam rises from your body.

Thatched Roofs

Travel to the remote village of Shirakawa-gō (or, even remoter, Ainokura) and fall asleep to the sound of chirping frogs in a centuries-old thatched-roof farmhouse.

Powder Peaks

Ski some of Asia's best slopes, commanding breathtaking views of the northern Japan Alps. Après-ski soaking in hot springs is mandatory.

p199

Kyoto

Temples
Culture
Food

Shintō & Buddhist Masterpieces

With over 1000 Buddhist temples and more than 400 Shintō shrines, Kyoto is *the* place to savour Japanese religious architecture and garden design. Find a quiet temple to call your own for the morning or join the throngs at a popular shrine.

Japan's Cultural Storehouse

Whether it's geisha, tea ceremonies, paintings, theatre performances or textiles, Kyoto is Japan's cultural capital.

Cuisine: Refined & Otherwise

If you're after *kaiseki* (haute cuisine) in sublime surroundings, go to Kyoto. But if a steaming bowl of *rāmen* is more your speed, you'll find endless choices here

p276

Kansai

Culture
Nature
Onsen

The Roots of the Nation

Southern Kansai is where Japanese culture came into being. Trace the history of the Yamato people (modern Japanese) from their roots in Asuka, through Nara and up to Kyoto.

Deep Mountains & Pilgrimage Routes

Southern Kansai (Wakayama and southern Nara) is a world of mountains, winding rivers and Shintō shrines. Pilgrims have been communing with the gods here for thousands of years.

Seaside & Riverside Onsen

From the quaint town of Kinosaki in the north to the riverside Hongū in the south, Kansai has plenty of hot springs to soak in after a day of soaking up the culture.

p336

Hiroshima & Western Honshū

Islands
Food
Onsen

Island Adventures

An art-filled weekend, a mountain hike, a beachside frolic or an escape to slow-paced solitude – you can take your pick on one of Western Honshū's countless islands.

Seafood Heaven

Seafood is king along the salty coasts of Western Honshū, and every seaside town has its speciality. Don't miss the chance to risk your life for a plate of pufferfish in *fugu*-mad Shimonoseki.

Onsen Side Trips

Sure, they're not all superstars, and you have to seek them out, but that's what makes the quiet onsen towns here so inviting.

p411

Northern Honshū (Tōhoku)

Outdoors
Onsen
Tradition

Parks & Peaks

Northern Honshū is blessed with some spectacular mountains. Temperate summers lure hikers, while snowy winters attract powder fiends and snow bunnies.

Rustic Escapes

That image you have of milky-white waters and stars over head or the steamy wooden bathhouse all by its lonesome in the mountains – that's Tōhoku.

Festivals & Ancient Rites

Nobody in Japan does festivals like they do up here. Ancient customs and beliefs live on in Tōhoku, preserved by centuries of isolation. Sample food prepared the way it has been for generations, or follow in the footsteps of mountain ascetics.

p474

Sapporo & Hokkaidō

Outdoors
Food
Onsen

Pristine Wilderness

Hokkaidō is where all your preconceived notions of Japan will be shattered. Walks in the park span days on end. Ocean voyages navigate precarious ice floes. Skiers carve snow drifts reaching several metres in depth.

Unique Cuisine

Flash-frozen salmon sashimi, soup curries, massive crabs and Sapporo lager are just some of Hokkaidō's much-revered culinary specialities.

Hidden Onsen

Soak in hidden steaming hot pools surrounded by thick forest and towering mountains.

p540

Shikoku

Nature
Temples
Surfing

Japan's Shangri La Valley

A short drive from the mainland madness, Iya Valley has dramatic gorges, ancient vine bridges and a hint of sustainable living. Raft or hike along the pristine Yoshino-gawa.

Good Buddha

The 88-temple pilgrimage is a rite of passage for many Japanese who, dressed in white and armed with a walking stick, lower the pulse, raise the gaze and seek to honour the great Buddhist saint, Kōbō Daishi.

Surfing Shikoku!

There's good surfing from the fishing villages of Tokushima Prefecture to the wild bluffs at Ashizuri-misaki. And the consistent crowd-free swells at Ohkinohama Beach should be legendary.

p606

Kyūshū

History
Nature
Onsen

Saints & Samurai

Christian rebellions led to over two centuries of seclusion during which Nagasaki's Dejima Island was Japan's window to the world. Visit the city to learn about this fascinating chapter of Japanese history.

Mountains of Fire

The active volcanoes Aso-san and Sakurajima are only the most famous of Kyūshū's mountains, with fantastic hiking in between. The ever-present chance of eruption gives residents a unique *joie de vivre*.

In Hot Water – And Hot Sand

Soak away riverside in intimate Kurokawa Onsen or in one of Beppu's onsen, or get buried in a sand bath in Ibusuki. Even Kyūshū's biggest city, Fukuoka, has natural onsen.

p647

Okinawa & the Southwest Islands

Beaches
Hiking
Food

Sun-Soaked

Splash out on the gorgeous golden beaches of the Kerama Islands, where you can whale-watch in winter and have the sand all to yourself.

Super Cedars

Climb into the green, pulsing heart of Yakushima, where ancient cedar trees grow really, really big. Looking more like a *Star Wars* set than Earth, this is the closest we've come to an otherworldly experience.

Island Cuisine

Tuck into a plateful of *gōya champurū*, Okinawa's signature stir-fry with bitter melon. Add some *awamori*, the local firewater, and you'll be ready to grab the *sanshin* (banjo) and party.

p721

On the
Road

Sapporo & Hokkaidō
p540

**Northern
Honshū**
p474

**The Japan Alps &
Central Honshū**
p199

Tokyo
p66

**Hiroshima &
Western Honshū**
p411

Kyoto
p276

**Mt Fuji &
Around Tokyo**
p146

Shikoku
p606

Kansai
p336

Kyūshū
p647

**Okinawa & the
Southwest Islands**
p721

Tokyo

🔖 03 / POP 13.24 MILLION

Best Places to Eat

➡ Daiwa Sushi (p112)

➡ Nagi (p116)

➡ Hantei (p118)

➡ Tofuya-Ukai (p113)

➡ Tonki (p114)

Best Places to Stay

➡ Sawanoya Ryokan (p110)

➡ Shibuya Granbell (p109)

➡ Nui (p111)

➡ Claska (p108)

➡ Park Hyatt (p109)

Why Go?

Tokyo (東京) offers a tapestry of sensory madness unlike anywhere else. It is a city forever reaching into the future, resulting in sci-fi streetscapes of crackling neon and soaring towers. Yet it is also a city seeped in history, and you can find traces of the shōgun's capital on the kabuki stage or under the cherry blossoms at Ueno Park.

There are excellent museums here, along with everything else you can ask of Japan – grand temples, atmospheric shrines, elegant gardens and, yes, even hot springs. However, Tokyo is also a place where sightseeing can take a backseat. To get to know the city is to enjoy it as the locals do: by splurging on divine sushi, singing karaoke until dawn or shopping for the latest must-have.

Tokyo has a neighbourhood for everyone – be they suit-clad salarymen (white-collar workers), manga-thumbing *otaku* (geek) or *hime gyaru* (princess girl). No doubt it has one for you, too.

When to Go
Tokyo

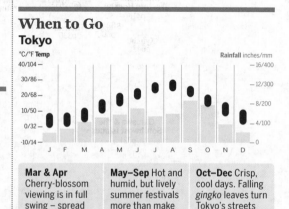

Mar & Apr Cherry-blossom viewing is in full swing – spread the picnic blanket and bring a *bentō*.	**May–Sep** Hot and humid, but lively summer festivals more than make up for it.	**Oct–Dec** Crisp, cool days. Falling *gingko* leaves turn Tokyo's streets to gold.

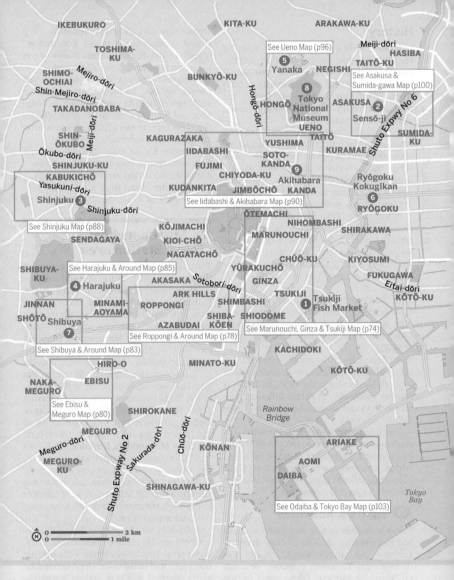

Tokyo Highlights

1 Tucking into some of the freshest sushi on the planet at **Tsukiji Fish Market** (p73)

2 Soaking up the atmosphere (and the incense) at Asakusa's centuries-old temple, **Sensō-ji** (p99)

3 Raising a glass in the nightlife neighbourhood of **Shinjuku** (p128)

4 Joining the eccentric fashion tribes as they shop their way through **Harajuku** (p135)

5 Losing yourself in the vestiges of Shitamachi (low-city) culture in **Yanaka** (p98)

6 Catching the salt-slinging, belly-slapping ritual of sumō at **Ryōgoku Kokugikan** (p132)

7 Getting swept up in the crowds and neon lights of **Shibuya** (p82)

8 Gawking at the gilded screens and glistening swords of the **Tokyo National Museum** (p93)

9 Venturing into the belly of the pop culture beast that is **Akihabara** (p92)

History

Originally called Edo (literally 'Gate of the River') due to its location at the mouth of the Sumida-gawa, this small farming village rose from obscurity in 1603 when Tokugawa Ieyasu established his shōgunate (military government) among Edo's swampy lands.

Edo quickly transformed into a bustling city and, by the late 18th century, it had become the most populous city in the world. When the authority of the emperor was reinstated in 1868, the capital was officially moved from Kyoto to Edo, which was then renamed Tokyo, meaning Eastern Capital.

After more than 250 years of self-prescribed isolation, Tokyo suddenly welcomed foreign influence with open arms. Western fashion and ideas were adopted as the city eagerly sought to take its place among the pantheon of the world's great cities.

In 1923 the Great Kantō Earthquake and ensuing fires levelled much of the city. It was once again torn to shreds during the devastating Allied air raids during the final years of WWII.

Emerging from the rubble after the US occupation, Tokyo quickly propelled itself towards modernity in the 1950s and '60s. A soaring economic crescendo followed, culminating in the giddy heights of the 1980s Bubble Economy.

The humbling 'burst' in the '90s led to a recession that still continues today. Yet Tokyo remains the beating heart of its island nation, never ceasing to reinvent itself while holding significant global influence over pop culture, design and technology.

Sights & Activities

Tokyo is endless in size and scope and can feel more like a collection of cities than one cohesive one. In Edo times, the city was divided into Yamanote ('uptown' or 'high city') and Shitamachi ('downtown' or the 'low city'). On the elevated plain west of the castle (now the Imperial Palace), Yamanote was where the feudal elite built their estates. In the east, along the banks of the Sumida-gawa, Shitamachi was home to the working classes, merchants and artisans.

Even today, remnants of this distinction exist: the east side of the city is still a tangle of alleys and tightly packed quarters. Neighbourhoods such as Asakusa and Ueno retain a down-to-earth vibe, more traditional architecture and an artisan tradition – the closest approximation to old Edo that remains. This is one of the best places to put the guide book away and just explore.

Yamanote developed into the moneyed commercial and business districts. Further west, newer neighbourhoods such as Shinjuku and Shibuya came to life after WWII – this is the hypermodern Tokyo of riotous neon and giant video screens.

Of course it's not really that simple. You'll find incongruous pockets of old and new – a tiny shrine lodged among sky scrapers, a glowing spire rising from a jumble of low-slung buildings – that are oh-so-Tokyo.

Marunouchi 丸の内 (Tokyo Station area 東京駅)

The Imperial Palace marks the centre of the city and just to the east you'll find the bustling business district of Marunouchi. In the past decade, several glossy towers have replaced the tired, almost Soviet-style structures that once characterised Marunouchi. There's the **Marunouchi Building** (丸の内ビル; Maru Biru; Map p74; www.marunouchi.com/marubiru; 2-4-1 Marunouchi, Chiyoda-ku; ⊙11am-9pm Mon-Sat, to 8pm Sun, restaurants 11am-11pm Mon-Sat, to 10pm Sun; ℝ JR Yamanote Line to Tokyo, Marunouchi north exit), towering above the city and offering up restaurants, elegant shopping and privileged views of the imperial grounds. Its sister structure, the **Shin-Marunouchi Building** (新丸の内ビル; Shin-Maru Biru; Map p74; www.marunouchi.com/shinmaru; 1-5-1 Marunouchi, Chiyoda-ku; ⊙11am-9pm Mon-Sat, to 8pm Sun, restaurants 11am-11pm Mon-Sat, to 10pm Sun; ℝ JR Yamanote Line to Tokyo, Marunouchi north exit), soars over the skyline next door.

Naka-dōri, which runs parallel to the palace between Hibiya and Ōtemachi stations, is a pretty, tree-lined avenue with upscale boutiques and patio cafes. Once famous for being deserted at nights and on weekends, Marunouchi is now an increasingly popular place to hang out.

At the heart of the neighbourhood is **Tokyo Station**, which turns 100 in 2014. The elegant red-brick building was heavily damaged during WWII and hastily rebuilt shortly after. A lengthy renovation project, completed in 2012, saw it returned to its former height and glory and its ornate domes restored.

TOKYO IN...

Two Days

Start the day with a pilgrimage to **Meiji-jingū** (p84) in Harajuku, followed by a stroll through the pop-culture bazaar along **Takeshita-dōri** (p136). Take a lunch break at local fave **Harajuku Gyōza Rō** (p115), then check out the stunning contemporary architecture along **Omote-sandō** (p135). Head to **Shinjuku** (p128) in the evening for a dose of neon and a drink in one of the ambient watering holes of Golden Gai.

The following day, visit the old side of town for some sightseeing in **Asakusa** (p99) and **Ueno** (p93), finishing with an afternoon amble through the atmospheric **Yanaka neighbourhood** (p98) and dinner at Hantei (p118).

Four Days

On day three, take a taxi at dawn to the **Tsukiji Fish Market** (p73) to see the legendary **tuna auction** (p73), followed by sushi breakfast at **Daiwa Sushi** (p112). Walk to nearby **Hama-rikyū Onshi-teien** (p75) and take a breather in the garden's teahouse, then scoot over to **Ginza** and its delectable **depachika** (department store basement; p113). Catch an exhibition at the **Mori Art Museum** (p76) in Roppongi, followed by a nightcap at **Mado Lounge** (p121) on the 52nd floor.

Sleep in on day four, then spend your last afternoon exploring one of Tokyo's more off-beat neighbourhoods, such as bohemian **Shimo-Kitazawa** or anime-mad **Akihabara** (p92). Then head to **Shibuya** (p122) to dance and sing the night away.

★**Imperial Palace** PALACE
(皇居; Kōkyo; Map p70; ☏3213-1111; http://sankan. kunaicho.go.jp/english/index.html; 1 Chiyoda, Chiyoda-ku; ⊕Marunouchi Line to Ōtemachi, exits C13b or C8b) FREE The residence of Japan's emperor occupies the site of Edo-jō, the Tokugawa shōgunate's castle. In its heyday the castle was the largest in the world, though little remains of it apart from the moat and walls. The present palace, structurally modern, but traditional in style, was completed in 1968, replacing the one built in 1888 and destroyed during WWII.

The palace itself is closed to the public for all but two days of the year, 2 January and 23 December (the Emperor's birthday). It is possible, however, to take a tour of the imperial grounds, but you must book ahead through the Imperial Household Agency's website. Reserve well in advance – slots become available on the 1st day of the month preceding the month you intend to visit. Tours, leaving from **Kikyō-mon** (桔梗門; Map p74), run twice daily from Monday to Friday (10am and 1.30pm), but only in the mornings from late July through the end of August. There is a thorough list of instructions (in English) on the website.

Imperial Palace East Garden GARDEN
(東御苑; Kōkyo Higashi-gyoen; Map p74; ⊗9am-4pm Nov-Feb, to 4.30pm Mar-Apr, Sep & Oct, to 5pm May-Aug, closed Mon & Fri year-round; ⊕Maru-nouchi Line to Ōtemachi, exit C10) FREE This landscaped garden, entered via **Ōte-mon** (大手門; Map p74), is the only corner of the Imperial Palace grounds open to the public without reservation. Here you can see the massive stones used to build the castle walls, and even climb on the ruins of one of the keeps. Take a token upon arrival and return it at the end of your visit.

Tokyo International Forum ARCHITECTURE
(東京国際フォーラム; Map p74; 3-5-1 Marunouchi, Chiyoda-ku; ⊕JR Yamanote Line to Yūrakuchō, central exit) FREE Looking like a glass ship plying the urban waters, this is one of Tokyo's architectural marvels. Architect Rafael Viñoly won Japan's first international architecture competition with his design; the building was completed in 1996. Although it's used mainly for its meeting halls, casual visitors are free to wander its courtyard-cum-sculpture garden and the glass eastern wing.

National Film Centre ARTS CENTRE
(東京国立近代美術館フィルムセンター; Map p74; www.momat.go.jp/english/nfc/index. html; 3-7-6 Kyōbashi, Chūō-ku; screenings adult/student ¥500/300, gallery only ¥200/70; ⊗gallery 11am-6.30pm Tue-Sat, check website for screening times; ⊕Ginza Line to Kyōbashi, exit 1) The National Film Centre is an archive of Japanese and foreign films affiliated with the National

Greater Tokyo

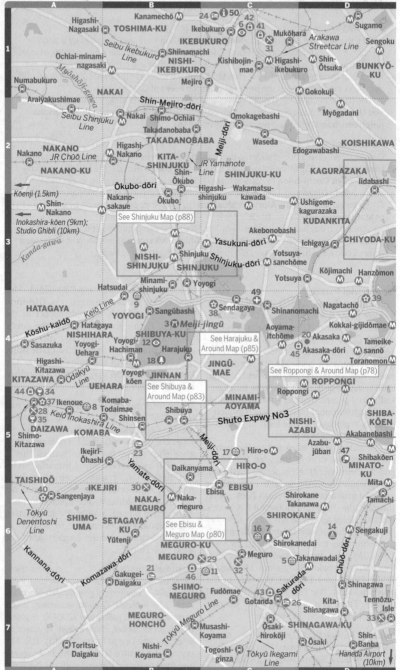

Greater Tokyo

Museum of Modern Art. The 7th-floor gallery offers a concise history (in English) of Japanese cinema, including rare footage of some of the earliest films – when the actors were straight off the kabuki stage – and vintage film memorabilia.

Nihombashi BRIDGE
(日本橋; Map p74; 🚇Ginza Line to Mitsukoshi-mae, exits B5 or B6) The Imperial Palace is the symbolic centre of the city, but this bridge, where Chūō-dōri crosses Nihombashi-gawa, is its geographic centre. All distances were measured from this point during the Edo period. The granite bridge is guarded with bronze lions, though you could still walk past it without noticing, as it's now under the shadow of the city expressway.

Kite Museum MUSEUM
(凧の博物館; Map p74; www.tako.gr.jp/eng/museums_e/tokyo_e.html; 5th fl, 1-12-10 Nihombashi, Chūō-ku; adult/child ¥200/100; ⊙11am-5pm Mon-Sat; 🚇Ginza Line to Nihombashi, exit C5) This tiny museum pays homage to the *Edo-dako* (Edo-style kite), brilliantly coloured and decorated with imagery of folk heroes and warriors. None are particularly old (they're made of paper, after all), but they're amazing to look at nonetheless. The museum is located above the restaurant Taimeiken (たいめいけん).

Mitsubishi Ichigōkan Museum ART GALLERY
(三菱一号館美術館; Map p74; http://mimt.jp/english; 2-6-2 Marunouchi, Chūō-ku; admission ¥1500; ⊙10am-6pm Tue, Wed & Sun, to 8pm Thu-Sat; 🚇Chiyoda Line to Nijūbashimae, exit 1) The

Mitsubishi Ichigōkan was the area's first office building, designed in 1894 by English architect Josiah Conder. The original is long gone but this faithful replica, which houses an art gallery, opened in 2010. Exhibitions cover Western and Japanese art from the time of the original structure's heyday.

◉ Ginza & Tsukiji
銀座 ● 築地

Ginza is Tokyo's answer to New York's Fifth Ave or London's Oxford St. In the 1870s the area was the first neighbourhood in Tokyo to modernise, welcoming Western-style brick buildings, the city's first department stores, gas lamps and other harbingers of globalisation.

Today, other shopping districts rival it in opulence, vitality and popularity, but Ginza retains a distinct snob value. It's therefore a superb place to window-shop and people-watch. Ginza is also Tokyo's original gallery district, and there are still many in the neighbourhood.

The heart of Ginza is the 4-chōme crossing, where Chūō-dōri and Harumi-dōri intersect. Narrow Namiki-dōri is Tokyo's most exclusive nightlife strip, where elegant women in kimono wait on company execs and politicians in members-only bars and clubs. Stroll down here in the evening and you might catch a glimpse of this secretive world.

A short walk to the southeast is a luxury commercial centre of a different sort: Tsukiji Fish Market.

★ **Tsukiji Fish Market** MARKET
(築地市場; Tsukiji Shijō; Map p74; ☑3542-1111; www.tsukiji-market.or.jp; 5-2 Tsukiji, Chūō-ku; ⊙closed Sun & most Wed; ℝŌedo Line to Tsukijishijō, exits A1 & A2) Tsukiji Fish Market is the world's biggest seafood market, moving an astounding 2400 tonnes of seafood a day. All manner of creatures pass through here, but it's the *maguro* (Bluefin tuna) that has emerged as the star. The tuna auction, where middlemen bid for these prized beauties – which can sell for over US$10,000 each – starts at 5am.

Even if you don't arrive at dawn, you can still get a flavour of the frenetic atmosphere of the other parts of the market. Tsukiji is very much a working market, where handcarts and forklifts perform a perfect high-speed choreography not accounting for the odd tourist, and you'll have to exercise caution to avoid getting in the way. Don't come in large groups, with small children or in nice shoes and, by all means, don't touch anything you don't plan to buy.

It almost seems impossible that something as organic, messy and chaotic as the Tsukiji Fish Market, which has stood on its current spot since 1935, can exist in orderly, contemporary Tokyo. Indeed, the market is slated for a controversial move to reclaimed land in Toyosu in the spring of 2015. What will become of the old market is still up in the air.

There's a **Tourist Information Center** (Map p74; 5-2 Tsukiji, Chūō-ku; ⊙8am-2pm) in the Outer Market with maps and English-speaking staff.

➡ **Seafood Intermediate Wholesalers Area**

(水産仲卸業者売場; Map p74; ⊙9-11am) Tsukiji isn't just the tuna auction and this area of the market, which opens to the public from 9am, is arguably more interesting – it is certainly more colourful. Here you can see a truly global haul of sea creatures, from gloriously magenta octopi to gnarled turban shells.

ℹ VISITING THE TUNA AUCTION

Tsukiji's famous tuna auction is without a doubt one of Tokyo's highlights, but it's only for the hardy. Up to 120 visitors a day are allowed to watch from a gallery between 5.25am and 6.15am. You must be at the **Fish Information Center** (おさかな普及センター; Map p74; 6-20-5 Tsukiji, Chūō-ku), by the market's **Kachidoki-mon** (勝どき門; Map p74), at 5am to register as a visitor, though the queue begins to form up to an hour earlier.

It's first come, first served, so to ensure you make the cut, it's a good idea to arrive even earlier (especially on a Saturday morning). Public transportation doesn't start up early enough to get you here on time, so you'll have to take a taxi or hangout nearby all night.

The market is closed on Sundays, most Wednesdays and public holidays; it also closes to visitors during busy periods (like December and January). Check the calendar here: www.tsukiji-market.or.jp/tukiji_e.htm.

The market has banned visitors to the tuna auction in the past, so please be on your best behavior so as not to give the authorities any reason to do so again.

Marunouchi, Ginza & Tsukiji

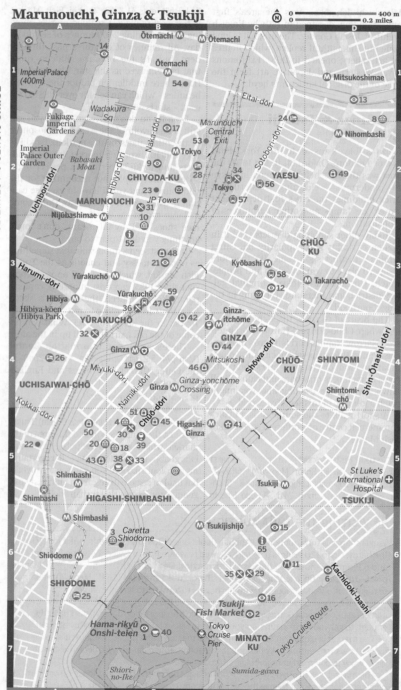

0 — 400 m
0 — 0.2 miles

Ōtemachi Ⓜ Ōtemachi
5
14
Imperial Palace
(400m)
54
Mitsukoshimae
13
7
Eitai-dōri
Fukiage
Imperial
Gardens
Wadakura
Sq
24
8
17
Marunouchi
Central
Exit
Nihombashi
Imperial
Palace Outer
Garden
Babasaki
Moat
53
Tokyo
34
YAESU
49
9
28
Tokyo
56
CHIYODA-KU
23
JP Tower
57
MARUNOUCHI
31
CHŪŌ-
KU
Nijūbashimae
10
52
48
21
Kyōbashi
58
Takarachō
Harumi-dōri
Yūrakuchō
12
Hibiya
Yūrakuchō
59
Hibiya-kōen
(Hibiya Park)
36
47
42
37
Ginza-
itchōme
27
YŪRAKUCHŌ
GINZA
44
32
Mitsukoshi
SHINTOMI
26
19
46
Ginza-yonchōme
Crossing
CHŪŌ-
KU
Miyuki-dōri
Ginza
Shintomi-
chō
UCHISAIWAI-CHŌ
Ginza
51
45
Higashi-
Ginza
41
Kokkai-dōri
50
4
30
39
22
20
18
43
38
33
Shimbashi
@
Tsukiji
St Luke's
International
Hospital
Shimbashi
HIGASHI-SHIMBASHI
TSUKIJI
Shimbashi
Tsukijishijō
15
Caretta
Shiodome
3
55
Shiodome
11
SHIODOME
35
29
25
6
16
Hama-rikyū
Onshi-teien
1
40
Tsukiji
Fish Market
2
Tokyo
Cruise
Pier
MINATO-
KU
Shiori-
no-Ike
Sumida-gawa

Marunouchi, Ginza & Tsukiji

All are laid out for buyers in styrofoam crates – it's a photographer's paradise, though again you'll need to be careful. It's also advisable to get here as early as possible; by 11am the crowds have dwindled and the sprinkler trucks plough through to prep the empty market for tomorrow's sale.

➔ **Outer Market**
(場外市場; Jōgai Shijō; Map p74; ⊘5am-2pm) The outer market is where rows of vendors hawk fish related goods, such as dried fish and seaweed, rubber boots and crockery – it's far more pedestrian friendly. Of particular note is **Uogashi-yokochō** (魚がし横町; Map p74;

sushi set ¥3150; ⊘5am-2pm), a cluster of tiny sushi restaurants inside the market, where you can sink your teeth into some ultrafresh fish.

There's also the market's Shintō shrine, **Namiyoke-jinja** (波除神社; Map p74), whose deity protects seafarers.

★ **Hama-rikyū Onshi-teien**   GARDEN
(浜離宮恩賜庭園; Detached Palace Garden; Map p74; www.tokyo-park.or.jp/park/format/index028. html; 1-1 Hama-rikyū-teien, Chūō-ku; adult/child ¥300/free; ⊘9am-5pm; ℝ Ōedo Line to Shiodome, exit A1) Once the horse stables and hunting

ground of the Tokugawas, this gorgeous garden features perfectly manicured hills set below the imposing towers of Shiodome next door. The complimentary audio guide uses satellite technology to detect your location within the garden and automatically narrates interesting facts and stories about your surroundings.

The park is accessible via Tokyo Cruise (p142) water buses from Asakusa.

Advertising Museum Tokyo　MUSEUM
(アド・ミュージアム東京; Map p74; www. admt.jp; Basement fl, Caretta Bldg, 1-8-2 Higashi-Shimbashi, Minato-ku; ⊙11am-6.30pm Tue-Fri, to 4.30pm Sat; 🚃Ōedo Line to Shiodome, Shimbashi Station exit) FREE Dentsu, Japan's largest advertising agency, curates this museum that includes wood-block printed handbills from the Edo period, art-deco Meiji- and Taisho-era works and the best contemporary campaigns.

Sony Building　SHOWROOM
(ソニービル; Map p74; www.sonybuilding.jp; 5-3-1 Ginza, Chūō-ku; ⊙11am-7pm; 🚃Ginza Line to Ginza, exit B9) FREE Come here to play around with yet-to-be-released Sony gadgets and gizmos, including the latest cameras. There's a duty-free shop on the 4th floor that sells international models of popular products, too.

Tokyo Gallery　ART GALLERY
(東京画廊; Map p74; www.tokyo-gallery.com; 7th fl, 8-10-5 Ginza, Chūō-ku; ⊙11am-7pm Tue-Fri, to 5pm Sat; 🚃JR Yamanote Line to Shimbashi, Ginza exit) FREE Tokyo Gallery collaborates with the Beijing-Tokyo Art Project, and shows challenging, often politically pointed works by Japanese and Chinese artists.

DON'T MISS

NAKAJIMA NO OCHAYA

Nakajima no Ochaya (中島の御茶屋; 1-1 Hama-rikyū-teien, Chūō-ku; tea & sweet ¥500; ⊙9am-4.30pm; 🚃Ōedo Line to Shiodome, exit A1), a beautiful teahouse from 1704, stands elegantly along a cedar bridge in the middle of Hama-rikyū Onshi-teien. It's the ideal spot for a cup of *matcha* (powdered green tea) while contemplating the very faraway 21st century beyond the garden walls.

Ginza Graphic Gallery　ART GALLERY
(ギンザ・グラフィック・ギャラリー; Map p74; www.dnp.co.jp/gallery/ggg; 7-7-2 Ginza, Chūō-ku; ⊙11am-7pm Tue-Fri, to 6pm Sat; 🚃Ginza Line to Ginza, exit A2) FREE This graphic-design showcase celebrates the best in print, from retrospectives of influential designers to suggestions of what's to come.

Shiseido Gallery　ART GALLERY
(資生堂ギャラリー; Map p74; www.shiseido. co.jp/e/gallery/html; Basement fl, 8-8-3 Ginza, Chūō-ku; ⊙11am-7pm Tue-Sat, to 6pm Sun; 🚃JR Yamanote Line to Shimbashi, Ginza exit) FREE An ever-changing selection of up-and-coming artists from around the globe fill this high-ceilinged space.

⊙ Roppongi & Around
六本木

Once primarily known for its debauched nightlife, Roppongi has reinvented itself over the last decade and now has an air of sophistication (at least during the day).

The transformation started with the opening in 2003 of **Roppongi Hills** (六本木ヒルズ; Map p78; www.roppongihills.com/en; Roppongi 6-chōme, Minato-ku; ⊙11am-11pm; 🚃Hibiya Line to Roppongi, exit 1), an enormous complex which includes shops, offices, restaurants and an art museum. It took developer Mori Minoru no fewer than 17 years to acquire the land and construct his labyrinthine kingdom, which he envisioned would improve the quality of urban life by centralising home, work and leisure into a utopian microcity.

A grand vision realised? It's a matter of opinion, but similar structures, such as **Tokyo Midtown** (東京ミッドタウン; Map p78; www.tokyo-midtown.com/en; 9-7 Akasaka, Minato-ku; ⊙11am-11pm; 🚃Ōedo Line to Roppongi, exit 8), which now anchors the other side of Roppongi, followed.

★ Mori Art Museum　MUSEUM
(森美術館; Map p78; www.mori.art.museum; Roppongi Hills, Minato-ku; adult/student ¥1500/1000, Sky Deck additional ¥300; ⊙10am-10pm Wed-Mon, to 5pm Tue, Sky Deck 10am-10pm; 🚃Hibiya Line to Roppongi, exit 1) When this museum, perched on the 52nd and 53rd floors of Mori Tower in the Roppongi Hills complex, opened in 2003 it was a watershed moment for the Tokyo art scene. Previously scattered, contemporary art now had a central, highly visible home with the space to stage large-scale exhibitions.

Shows here cover both global and local movements. Every three years, an exhibition called Roppongi Crossing (next up in autumn 2013) focuses on up-and-coming Japanese artists and has emerged as a barometer of current trends.

Admission to the museum includes entry to **Tokyo City View**, the observatory on the 52nd floor, which has some of the best views in central Tokyo. Weather permitting, the rooftop **Sky Deck** has open-air views.

National Art Center Tokyo   MUSEUM
(国立新美術館; Map p78; www.nact.jp; 7-22-1 Roppongi, Minato-ku; admission varies by exhibition, building admission free; ◎10am-6pm Wed, Thu & Sat-Mon, to 8pm Fri; ℝChiyoda Line to Nogizaka, exit 6) Designed by Kurokawa Kishō, this architectural marvel, which opened in 2007, has no permanent collection. However, it boasts the country's largest exhibition space for visiting shows, which include international blockbusters and the annual **Japan Media Arts Festival**. It's also worth visiting for the undulating glass facade, cafes atop giant inverted cones and the excellent gift shop.

Suntory Museum of Art   MUSEUM
(サントリー美術館; Map p78; www.suntory.co.jp/sma; 4th fl, Tokyo Midtown, Minato-ku; admission varies, children free; ◎10am-6pm Sun-Thu, to 8pm Fri & Sat; ℝŌedo Line to Roppongi, exit 8) From the time of its original opening in 1961, the Suntory has been a champion of lifestyle art. Rotating exhibitions focus on the beauty of useful things: Japanese ceramics, lacquerware, dyeing, weaving and such. Its new Midtown digs by architect Kuma Kengō are at turns understated and breathtaking.

21_21 Design Sight   MUSEUM
(21_21デザインサイト; Map p78; www.2121designsight.jp; Tokyo Midtown, Minato-ku; adult/child ¥1000/free; ◎11am-8pm Wed-Mon; ℝChiyoda Line to Nogizaka, exit 3) Contemporary, and often genre-bending, exhibitions on art, architecture and design are held in this graceful bunker designed by Andō Tadao. Check the website for workshops and talk events and visit the iTunes store to download 21_21's curious iPhone app.

Nogi-jinja   SHINTŌ SHRINE
(乃木神社; Map p78; 8-11-27 Akasaka, Minato-ku; ◎9am-5pm; ℝChiyoda Line to Nogizaka, exit 1) This shrine honours General Nogi, hero of the Russo-Japanese War. Hours after Emperor Meiji's funerary processional, Nogi

and his faithful wife committed ritual suicide (Nogi disembowelled himself; his wife slit her throat), following their leader into death. Nogi's black, wooden residence is on the same grounds.

Musée Tomo   MUSEUM
(智美術館; Map p78; www.musee-tomo.or.jp; 4-1-35 Toranomon, Minato-ku; admission varies; ◎11am-6pm Tue-Sun; ℝHibiya Line to Kamiyachō, exit 4B) Perhaps Tokyo's most elegant museum, Musée Tomo is named for Kikuchi Tomo, whose collection of contemporary Japanese ceramics wowed them in Washington and London before finally being exhibited in Tokyo. Exhibitions change every few months; the displays are always beautifully laid out, with informative exhibition notes. The museum is behind the Hotel Ōkura.

Tokyo Tower   TOWER
(東京タワー; Map p78; www.tokyotower.co.jp/english; 4-2-8 Shiba-kōen, Minato-ku; adult/child main observation deck ¥820/460, special observation deck ¥600/400; ◎observation 9am-10pm; 🖝; ℝŌedo Line to Akabanebashi, Akabanebashi exit) It might look like a garish Eiffel Tower rip-off, but to Tokyoites, Tokyo Tower remains a powerful symbol of the city's post-WWII rebirth. At 333m, Tokyo Tower, finished in 1958, is 13m taller than the French tower that inspired its design. Lifts whisk visitors up to the main **observation deck** at 150m; there's another 'special' deck at 250m.

MUSEUM DISCOUNTS

Tokyo Handy Guide (www.gotokyo.org/book/tokyo_handy_guide) Offers small discounts (around ¥100) to many museums; you can pick one up for free at most tourist information centres and many accommodations.

Grutt Pass (www.rekibun.or.jp/grutto; pass ¥2000) Valid for two months, this booklet has coupons for discounted – and sometimes free – admission to over 70 museums in greater Tokyo, including the biggies (Tokyo National Museum, Edo-Tokyo Museum, Mori Art Museum etc). Purchase the pass at any of the affiliated museums.

Mupon (www.tokyoartbeat.com/apps/mupon.en) This iPhone app offers a year's worth of discounts to art museums in greater Tokyo.

Roppongi & Around

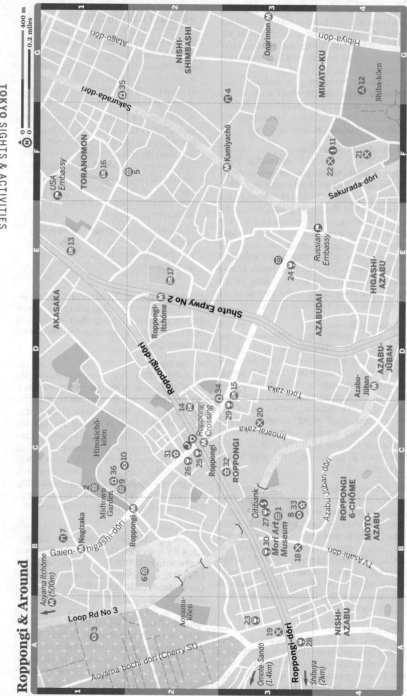

0 400 m
0 0.2 miles

Roppongi & Around

Roughly a third of the steel used to build the tower came from scrap metal salvaged at the end of the war.

While the view from the top can't compete with Tokyo Sky Tree (p101), it's still not too shabby. However, Tokyo Tower is best appreciated when you catch a glimpse of it peeking out from between skyscrapers – like Mt Fuji appearing through the clouds – especially when it's lit up at night.

Zōjō-ji   BUDDHIST TEMPLE
(増上寺; Map p78; www.zojoji.or.jp/en/index.html; Shiba-kōen, Minato-ku; ⊙ dawn-dusk; ⓡ Ōedo Line to Akabanebashi, Akabanebashi exit) **FREE** One of the most important temples of the Jōdō (Pure Land) sect of Buddhism, this is also the former funerary temple of the Tokugawa regime, and the tombs of six shōgun stand out back. Zōjō-ji is most dramatic at dusk when Tokyo Tower lights the grounds from behind.

The temple dates from 1393, yet like many sights in Tokyo its original structures have been relocated and were subject to war, fire and natural disasters. It has been rebuilt several times in recent history, the last time in 1974. The main gate, Sangedatsu-mon, was constructed in 1622 and is the oldest structure on the grounds. The giant bell (1673; 15 tonnes) is considered one of the great three bells of the Edo period.

Atago-jinja   SHINTŌ SHRINE
(愛宕神社; Map p78; www.atago-jinja.com; 1-5-3 Atago, Minato-ku; ⊙ 24hr; ⓡ Hibiya Line to Kamiyachō, exit 3) Originally constructed at the behest of Tokugawa Ieyasu, Atago-jinja's main feature is its giant stone stairway at the entrance, leading up to the highest natural spot in central Tokyo. In Edo times it doubled as a fire watchtower, and thus Homusubi no Mikoto, the Shintō fire god, is worshipped here. Atago-jinja is prettiest at dusk when lit by lanterns.

◎ Ebisu & Meguro
恵比寿・目黒

Named for the prominent beer manufacturer that once provided a lifeline for most of the neighbourhood's residents, Ebisu is now a hip area with a generous smattering of excellent restaurants and bars.

A short zip along the 'Skywalk' from Ebisu Station takes you to **Yebisu Garden Place** (恵比寿ガーデンプレイス; Map p80; www.gardenplace.jp; 4-20 Ebisu, Shibuya-ku; ⓡ JR Yamanote Line to Ebisu, east exit), another one of Tokyo's 'microcities' with a string of shops and restaurants, office buildings and two museums.

Meguro, just one stop south of Ebisu on the JR Yamanote Line, is synonymous with its main drag, Meguro-dōri, which is lined

Ebisu & Meguro

with fantastic interior and antique shops (otherwise known as MISC – Meguro Interior Shops Community).

Beyond Ebisu and Meguro are some of Tokyo's more attractive residential neighbourhoods, including Daikanyama and Naka-Meguro.

★ Tokyo Metropolitan Museum of Photography   MUSEUM

(東京都写真美術館; Map p80; www.syabi.com; 1-13-3 Mita, Meguro-ku; admission ¥500-1650; ⊙10am-6pm Tue, Wed, Sat & Sun, to 8pm Thu & Fri; 圓JR Yamanote Line to Ebisu, east exit) This is the city's top photography museum, with excellent changing exhibitions of both international and Japanese photographers. There are usually several exhibitions going on at once and ticket prices are based on how many you see. Take the Skywalk from Ebisu station to Yebisu Garden Place; the five-storey museum is on the right towards the back.

Beer Museum Yebisu   MUSEUM

(エビスビール記念館; Map p80; www.sapporoholdings.jp/english/guide/yebisu; 4-20-1 Ebisu, Shibuya-ku; ⊙11am-7pm Tue-Sun; 圓JR Yamanote Line to Ebisu, east exit) FREE Yes, this is the site of the original Yebisu brewery (1889). Inside you'll find a gallery of photographs and antique signage that document the rise of Yebisu, and beer in general, in Japan. It's inside Yebisu Garden Place, behind the Mitsukoshi department store.

Skip the tour (¥500), unless your Japanese-language skills can handle a guided tasting. Instead, head for the 'tasting salon' where you can sample four kinds of beer (¥400 each) at your own pace.

Yamatane Museum of Art   MUSEUM

(山種美術館; Map p70; www.yamatane-museum. or.jp; 3-12-36 Hiroo, Shibuya-ku; adult/student/child ¥1000/800/free, special exhibits extra; ⊙10am-5pm Tue-Sun; 圓JR Yamanote Line to Ebisu, west exit) This exceptional collection of *nihonga*

Ebisu & Meguro

(Japanese-style paintings) includes some 1800 works from the Meiji Restoration and onwards, of which a small selection is displayed at any one time. Two names to look for: Hayami Gyoshū (1894–1935), whose *Dancing Flames* is an important cultural property; and Okumura Togyū (1889–1990), whose *Cherry Blossoms at Daigo-ji Temple* is a masterpiece in pastel colours.

Daikanyama   NEIGHBOURHOOD
(代官山; Map p80; 🚉 Tōkyū Tōyoko Line to Daikanyama) Daikanyama is a shopping district that favours small boutiques, quiet streets and a wealthy, impeccably dressed clientele (occasionally walking impeccably dressed dogs). Not everything here is outrageously priced, and the neighbourhood can be an excellent place to discover still-under-the-radar Japanese designers, as many have shops here. Daikanyama is also known for its cafes – perfect for people-watching.

Naka-Meguro   NEIGHBOURHOOD
(中目黒; Map p80; 🚉 Hibiya Line to Naka-Meguro) Known to locals as 'Nakame', Naka-Meguro

doesn't look like much when you exit the station. Cross the street with the tracks overhead, however, and in one block you'll hit the Meguro-gawa, a tree-lined canal flanked by stylish cafes, restaurants and boutiques. Nakame is a favourite haunt (and home) of fashion, art and media types, whose tastes are reflected here.

Meguro Parasitological Museum   MUSEUM
(目黒寄生虫館; Map p70; http://kiseichu.org; 4-1-1 Shimo-Meguro, Meguro-ku; ⏰ 10am-5pm Tue-Sun; 🚌 2 or 7 from Meguro Station to Ōtori-jinja-mae, 🚉 JR Yamanote Line to Meguro, west exit) **FREE** Here's one for fans of the grotesque: this small museum was established in 1953 by a local doctor concerned by the increasing number of parasites he was encountering due to unsanitary postwar conditions. The grisly centrepiece is an 8.8m-long tapeworm found in the body of a 40-year-old Yokohama man.

The museum is about a 1km walk from Meguro Station; the entrance is on the ground floor of a small apartment building, just uphill from the Ōtori-jinja-mae bus stop.

Institute for Nature Study   PARK
(自然教育園; Shizen Kyōiku-en; Map p70; www.ins.kahaku.go.jp; 5-21-5 Shirokanedai, Meguro-ku; adult/child ¥300/free; ⏰ 9am-4.30pm Tue-Sun Sep-Apr, to 5pm Tue-Sun May-Aug, last entry 4pm year-round; 🚉 Namboku Line to Shirokanedai, exit 1) What would Tokyo look like left to its own natural devices? Since 1949 this park, affiliated with the Tokyo National Museum, has let the local flora go wild. There are wonderful walks through its forests, marshes and ponds, making this one of Tokyo's most appealing – yet least known – getaways.

Although the 200,000 sq metres of this land was the estate of a *daimyō* (domain lord) some six centuries ago and was the site of gunpowder warehouses in the early Meiji period, you'd scarcely know it now.

**Tokyo Metropolitan
Teien Art Museum**   MUSEUM
(東京都庭園美術館; Map p70; www.teien-art-museum.ne.jp; 5-21-9 Shirokanedai, Minato-ku; admission varies; ⏰ 10am-6pm, closed 2nd & 4th Wed each month; 🚉 Namboku Line to Shirokanedai, exit 1) Inside a beautiful art-deco structure that was once a princely estate, the Teien museum hosts mostly exhibitions of decorative arts. It began a comprehensive renovation project in 2011 and plans to re-open sometime in 2014; check the website for updates.

TOKYO SIGHTS & ACTIVITIES

CHERRY-BLOSSOM VIEWING

When it comes to cherry-blossom viewing, parks such as Ueno-kōen (p96), Yoyogi-kōen (p84), Inokashira-kōen (p87) and Shinjuku-gyoen (p87) are obvious choices. Here are two spots known only by locals that blissfully fly under the radar in spring:

Meguro-gawa (目黒川; Map p80; Hibiya Line to Naka-Meguro) Naka-Meguro's canal is lined with *sakura* (cherry trees) that form an awesome pale pink canopy. Local restaurants set up food stalls and, rather than staking out a seat, visitors stroll under the blossoms, hot wine in hand.

Aoyama-reien (青山霊園; 2-32-2 Minami-Aoyama, Minato-ku; Ginza Line to Gaienmae, exit 1B) This sprawling cemetery, with many famous inhabitants, comes alive with cherry blossoms blanketing the tombs and statues. It's a pretty, if unusual, *hanami* spot. Why should the living have all the fun?

Hatakeyama Collection   MUSEUM
(畠山記念館; Map p70; www.ebara.co.jp/csr/hatakeyama; 2-20-12 Shirokanedai, Minato-ku; adult/student/child ¥500/300/free; ⊙10am-5pm Tue-Sun Apr-Sep, to 4.30pm Tue-Sun Oct-Mar; Asakusa Line to Takanawadai, exit A2) Glide through the exhibition space in borrowed slippers while perusing earthenware dedicated to the elaborate yet austere tea ceremony. Ponder the elusive *wabi-sabi* (an aesthetic that embraces the notion of ephemerality and imperfection) in the grounds, which cloaks the museum with its army of gnarled trees. Note that the museum can be closed for weeks at a time in between exhibitions so check the schedule on the website.

Sengaku-ji   BUDDHIST TEMPLE
(泉岳寺; Map p70; 2-11-1 Takanawa, Minato-ku; ⊙7am-6pm Apr-Sep, to 5pm Oct-Mar; Asakusa Line to Sengaku-ji, exit A2) Follow the steps up to the tombs of the famous 47 *rōnin* – soldiers without a samurai – who avenged their master Lord Asano's death, then followed him to the grave by committing seppuku (ritual disembowlment) in 1703.

◉ Shibuya & Around 渋谷

Shibuya is the centre of the city's teen culture, and its brightly-dressed, bleached-hair denizens aren't shy about living loud.

If a local friend asks to meet you at Shibuya, you'll probably gather at **Hachikō** (ハチ公) plaza in front of the station. The always-buzzing Shibuya Crossing leads from the station to the pedestrian street **Centre-gai** (センター街; Sentā-gai; Map p83; JR Yamanote Line to Shibuya, Hachikō exit), Shibuya's main artery, with plenty of shops, restaurants and bars. Beyond is Dōgenzaka, also known as **Love Hotel Hill** (ラヴホテルヒル; Map p83; JR Yamanote Line to Shibuya, Hachikō exit), home to nightclubs and by-the-hour hotels.

The newest landmark, opened in 2012, is the 34-floor Shibuya Hikarie (p84) building. Its upmarket shops and restaurants threaten to attract grown-up sophisticates to Shibuya.

Just one express stop from Shibuya is Shimo-Kitazawa, a neighbourhood with a decidedly different vibe – one that's laidback and earthy.

★ Shibuya Crossing   STREET
(渋谷交差点; Map p83; JR Yamanote Line to Shibuya, Hachikō exit) Rumoured to be the world's busiest, this intersection in front of Shibuya Station is famously known as 'The Scramble'. It's an awesome spectacle of giant video screens and neon. People come from all directions at once – sometimes over a thousand with every light change – yet still manage to dodge each other with a practiced, nonchalant agility.

It's worth pausing for a moment to take in a bird's eye view of the crowds from the **Starbucks** (Map p83; 1st & 2nd fl, QFront Bldg, 21-6 Udagawa-chō, Shibuya-ku; ⊙6.30am-4am; ; JR Yamanote Line to Harajuku, Hachikō exit) perched above the easily spotted Tsutaya bookshop, adjacent to the station.

Hachikō Statue   MONUMENT
(ハチ公像; Map p83; Hachikō Plaza; JR Yamanote Line to Shibuya, Hachikō exit) Hachikō, an Akita dog, belonged to a professor who lived near Shibuya Station. The professor died in 1925, but the dog continued to show up and wait at the station for his master until his own death 10 years later. The story became legend and a small statue was erected at the station plaza in the dog's memory.

Shibuya & Around

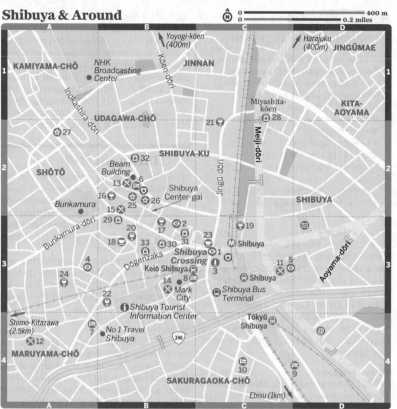

Shibuya & Around

TOKYO SIGHTS & ACTIVITIES

KIKUCHI RINKO: ACTRESS

If a movie were being made about Tokyo, and each neighbourhood was a character, which neighbourhood would you want to play?
I'd want to be Shibuya. There's an amazing overflow of spirit and vigour that the neighbourhood cannot digest! It's seedy, sloppy and reckless – it's filled with tonnes of energy to waste. Seems like it could be a very colourful role.

Academy Award–nominated actress Kikuchi Rinko is a Tokyo native.

Shibuya Hikarie CULTURAL BUILDING
(渋谷ヒカリエ; Map p83; www.hikarie.jp; 2-21-1 Shibuya, Shibuya-ku; ⊙11am-8pm; 🚃JR Yamanote Line to Shibuya, east exit) The 8th floor of this gleaming new tower houses a collection of gallery spaces, including one curated by the influential **Tomio Koyama Gallery** and another, the **d47 Museum**, which showcases crafts from around Japan's 47 prefectures. Head to the 11th floor Sky Lobby for views over Shibuya.

Shimo-Kitazawa NEIGHBOURHOOD
(下北沢; 🚃Keiō Inokashira Line to Shimo-Kitazawa) The narrow streets of 'Shimokita' are barely passable by cars, meaning a streetscape like a dollhouse version of Tokyo. It's been a favourite haunt for generations of students and there's a lively street scene all afternoon and evening, especially on weekends.

Shimokita is one of Tokyo's best neighbourhoods to *bura-bura suru* (to kick around). During the day, head to the north side which is packed with second-hand clothing stores and cafes. Come evening, the south side, with its bars, restaurants, theatres and live-music houses, is the place to be.

There have long been plans to build a road through the centre of this neighbourhood, much to the dismay of local residents and business owners. In a city awash with skyscrapers and new developments, cosy, organic communities such as Shimokita are a rare breed.

Japan Folk Crafts Museum MUSEUM
(日本民芸館; Nihon Mingei-kan; Map p70; www.mingeikan.or.jp/english; 4-3-33 Komaba, Meguro-ku; adult ¥1000, student ¥200-500; ⊙10am-5pm Tue-Sun; 🚃Keiō Inokashira Line to Komaba-Tōdaimae, west exit) The *mingei* (folk crafts) movement was launched in the early 20th century to promote handmade objects over mass-produced ones. The leaders of the movement founded this museum to house some 17,000 examples of exquisite Japanese craftwork; note that the museum closes for stretches a year; note that the museum closes for stretches in between, so check the schedule first.

◉ Harajuku 原宿

Harajuku is Tokyo's catwalk, where the city's fashionistas come to shop and show-off. **Takeshita-dōri** is the neighbourhood's famous subculture bazaar, a pilgrimmage site for teens from all over Japan and particularly famous for its *goth-loli* girls (think zombie Little Bo Peep).

Fans of contemporary architecture will want to check out **Omote-sandō** (p135) – the regal boulevard that connects Harajuku and Aoyama – where the designer boutiques come in designer buildings.

★ Meiji-jingū SHINTŌ SHRINE
(明治神宮; Map p70; www.meijijingu.or.jp; 1-1 Yoyogi Kamizono-chō, Shibuya-ku; ⊙dawn-dusk; 🚃JR Yamanote Line to Harajuku, Omote-sandō exit) **FREE** Tokyo's grandest Shintō shrine is dedicated to the Emperor Meiji and Empress Shōken. Constructed in 1920, the shrine was destroyed in WWII air raids and rebuilt in 1958; however, unlike so many of Japan's postwar reconstructions, Meiji-jingū has an authentic feel. The towering 12m wooden torii gate that marks the entrance was created from a 1500-year-old Taiwanese cyprus.

The shrine itself oocupies only a small fraction of the sprawling forested grounds. **Meiji-jingū-gyoen** (明治神宮御苑; Inner Garden; Map p70; admission ¥500; ⊙9am-4.30pm) was once imperial land; the Meiji emperor himself designed the iris garden here to please the empress. The garden is most impressive when the irises bloom in June.

Yoyogi-kōen PARK
(代々木公園; Map p70; 🚃JR Yamanote Line to Harajuku, Omote-sandō exit) If it's a sunny and warm weekend afternoon you can count on there being a crowd lazing around the large grassy expanse that is Yoyogi-kōen. You can also usually find revellers and noisemakers of all stripes, from hula-hoopers to African drum circles to a group of retro greasers dancing around a boom box.

Harajuku & Around

Harajuku & Around

It's an excellent place for a picnic and probably the only place in the city where you can reasonably toss a frisbee without fear of hitting someone. While you're there, check out the nearby **Yoyogi National Stadium**, an early masterpiece by architect Tange Kenzō, built for the 1964 Olympics.

Ukiyo-e Ōta Memorial Art Museum MUSEUM
(浮世絵太田記念美術館; Map p85; www.ukiyoe-ota-muse.jp; 1-10-10 Jingūmae, Shibuya-ku; adult ¥700-1000, child free; ⏰10.30am-5.30pm Tue-Sun, closed 27th to end of month; ☒JR Yamanote Line to Harajuku, Omote-sandō exit) Pad quietly in slippers through this museum to view the first-rate collection of *ukiyo-e* (woodblock prints) amassed by Ōta Seizo, the former head of the Toho Life Insurance Company. A small selection of the collection, which numbers more than 10,000 prints and includes works by masters such as Hokusai and Hiroshige, is arranged in changing, thematic exhibitions.

Downstairs from the museum is a branch of the shop Kamawanu (p134), which specialises in beautifully printed *tenugui* (traditional hand-dyed thin cotton towels).

Design Festa ART GALLERY
(デザインフェスタ; Map p85; www.designfesta-gallery.com; 3-20-2 Jingūmae, Shibuya-ku; ⏰11am-7pm; ☒JR Yamanote Line to Harajuku, Takeshita exit) **FREE** Design Festa has been a leader in Tokyo's fringe art scene for over a decade. The madhouse building itself is worth a visit; it's always evolving. Inside are a dozen small galleries rented out by artists, who are usually hanging out nearby. Design Festa also sponsors a twice-yearly large-scale exhibition (p106) in Odaiba.

Watari Museum of Contemporary Art (Watari-Um)
MUSEUM
(ワタリウム美術館; Map p85; www.watarium.co.jp; 3-7-6 Jingūmae, Shibuya-ku; adult/student ¥1000/800; ⏰11am-7pm Tue & Thu-Sun, to 9pm Wed; ☒Ginza Line to Gaienmae, exit 3) Progressive and often provocative, this museum was built in 1990 to a design by Swiss architect Mario Botta. Exhibits range from retrospec-

tives of established art-world figures (like Yayoi Kusama and Nam June Paik) to graffiti and landscape artists – with some exhibitions spilling onto the surrounding streets.

The excellent art bookshop in the basement called **On Sundays** has an enormous collection of obscure postcards.

Nezu Museum MUSEUM
(根津美術館; Map p85; www.nezu-muse.or.jp; 6-5-1 Minami-Aoyama, Minato-ku; adult/student/child ¥1000/800/free, special exhibitions extra ¥200; ⏰10am-5pm Tue-Sun; ☒Ginza Line to Omote-sandō, exit A5) This recently renovated museum offers a striking blend of old and new: a renowned collection of Japanese, Chinese and Korean antiquities in a gallery space designed by contemporary architect Kuma Kengō. Select items from the extensive collection are displayed in manageable monthly exhibitions. Behind the galleries there's a woodsy strolling garden studded with teahouses and sculptures.

Shinjuku & West Tokyo
新宿

Here in Shinjuku, much of what makes Tokyo tick is crammed into one busy district: upscale department stores, anachronistic shanty bars, buttoned-up government offices, swarming crowds, streetside video screens, hostess clubs, hidden shrines and soaring skyscrapers.

At the heart of Shinjuku is the sprawling train station, which acts as a nexus for over three million commuters each day, making it one of the busiest in the world. The west side of the station (Nishi-Shinjuku) is a perfectly planned expanse of gridded streets and soaring corporate towers. Tokyo's municipal government moved here in 1991 from Yūrakuchō. Also worth a look is the photogenic **Mode Gakuen Cocoon Tower** (Map p88; 1-7-3 Nishi-shinjuku, Shinjuku-ku; ☒JR Yamanote Line to Shinjuku, west exit).

The east side of Shinjuku is one of Tokyo's largest and liveliest entertainment districts.

The JR Chūō line heads west of Shinjuku to some of Tokyo's original commuter towns, characterised by classic 1960s shopping arcades and an ambivalent, if not dismissive, attitude towards the development seen elsewhere in the city. Here you'll find the charming suburb of **Kichijōji** (吉祥寺; ☒JR Chūō Line to Kichijōji), with its wonderful park, and the Ghibli Museum just beyond.

Tokyo Metropolitan Government Offices
BUILDING

(東京都庁; Tokyo Tochō; Map p88; www.metro. tokyo.jp/ENGLISH/TMG/observat.htm; 2-8-1 Nishi-Shinjuku, Shinjuku-ku; ☺observatories 9.30am-11pm; ⊠Ōedo Line to Tochōmae, exit A4) FREE To-kyo's seat of power is a grey granite complex designed by Tange Kenzō. It has stunning, distinctive architecture and great views from the 202m-high **observatories** on the 45th floors of the twin towers of Building 1 (the views are virtually the same from either tower). On a clear day, look west for a glimpse of Mt Fuji.

Shinjuku-gyoen
PARK

(新宿御苑; Map p88; www.env.go.jp/garden/shin-jukugyoen; 11 Naito-chō, Shinjuku-ku; adult/6-15yr/under 6yr ¥200/50/free; ☺9am-4.30pm Tue-Sun; ⊠Marunouchi Line to Shinjuku-gyoenmae, exit 1) Though Shinjuku-gyoen was designed as an imperial retreat (completed 1906), it's now definitively a park for everyone. The wide lawns make it a favourite for urbanites in need of an escape from the hurly-burly of city life. Pick up a *bentō* (boxed lunch) from a *depachika* (department store food floor) or convenience store on the way for a picnic.

Don't miss the recently renovated greenhouse, with its giant lilypads and perfectly-formed orchids, and the cherry blossoms in spring.

Hanazono-jinja
SHINTŌ SHRINE

(花園神社; Map p88; 5-17 Shinjuku, Shinjuku-ku; ☺24hr; ⊠Marunouchi Line to Shinjuku-sanchōme, exits B10 & E2) During the day merchants from nearby Kabukichō come to this Shintō shrine to pray for the solvency of their business ventures. At night, despite signs asking revellers to refrain, drinking and merrymaking carries over from the nearby bars onto the stairs here.

Japanese Sword Museum
MUSEUM

(刀剣博物館; Map p70; www.touken.or.jp; 4-25-10 Yoyogi, Shibuya-ku; adult/student/child ¥600/300/free; ☺9am-4.30pm Tue-Sun; ⊠Keiō New Line to Hatsudai, east exit) In 1948, after American forces returned the *katana* (Japanese swords) they'd confiscated during the post-war occupation, the national Ministry of Education established a society to preserve the feudal art of Japanese sword-making. There are about 120 swords with their fittings in the collection, of which about one-third are on exhibition at any one time, with English explanations throughout.

The museum's location, in a residential neighbourhood, is not obvious. Head down Kōshū-kaidō to the Park Hyatt and make a left, then the second right under the highway, followed by another quick right and left in succession. There's a map on the website.

Ghibli Museum
MUSEUM

(ジブリ美術館; www.ghibli-museum.jp; 1-1-83 Shimo-Renjaku, Mitaka-shi; adult ¥1000, child ¥100-700; ☺10am-6pm Wed-Mon; ⊠JR Chūō Line to Mitaka, south exit) Master animator Hayao Miyazaki, whose Studio Ghibli (pronounced 'jiburi') produced *Princess Mononoke* and *Spirited Away*, designed this museum himself. Fans will enjoy the original sketches; kids, even if they're not familiar with the movies, will fall in love with the fairy-tale atmosphere and the climbable Cat Bus. Don't miss the original 20-minute animated short playing on the 1st floor.

Getting to Ghibli is all part of the adventure. Tickets must be purchased in advance, and you must also choose the exact time and date of your visit. You can do this online through a travel agent before you arrive in Japan (the easy option) or from a kiosk at any Lawson convenience store in Tokyo (the difficult option, as it will require some Japanese-language ability to navigate the ticket machine). Both options are explained in detail on the website, where you will also find a useful map.

A minibus (return trip/one-way ¥300/200) leaves for the museum approximately every 20 minutes from the south exit of Mitaka Station (bus stop 9). Alternatively, you can walk there in about 15 minutes by following the canal and turning right when you reach a park. The museum is actually on the western edge of Inokashira-kōen and you can walk there through the park from Kichijōji Station in about 30 minutes.

Inokashira-kōen
PARK

(井の頭公園; www.kensetsu.metro.tokyo.jp/seibuk/inokashira/index.html; 1-18-31 Gotenyama, Musashino-shi; ⊠Keiō Inokashira Line to Kichijōji, Kōen exit) At the centre of this gorgeous greenbelt is a pond where you can rent row boats and swan-shaped pedal boats. There's also an ancient shrine to the sea goddess Benzaiten. Be warned: Benzaiten is known to be a jealous goddess and urban legend has it that couples who flaunt their romance and row across the water break up soon afterwards.

Shinjuku

Shinjuku

On weekends, craft vendors and performance artists set up on the eastern end of the park. In cherry blossom season, this is one of the best spots for *yozakura* (night blossoms).

From Kichijōji Station, walk straight from the Kōen exit, crossing at the light and veering to the right of the Marui ('0101') department store; you're on the right path if you see food trucks on your left.

◎ Iidabashi & Northwest Tokyo 飯田橋

Iidabashi and its surrounds formed part of the Edo-era Yamanote district of villas belonging to the governing elite. Kitanomaru-kōen, the leafy expanse north of the Imperial Palace grounds, is home to several museums. The stretch along the moat explodes with cherry blossoms (and flower photographers) in spring.

Yasukuni-jinja   SHINTŌ SHRINE
(靖国神社; Map p90; ☎ 3261-8326; www.yasukuni.or.jp; 3-1-1 Kudan-kita, Chiyoda-ku; 🚇 Hanzōmon Line to Kudanshita, exit 1) Literally 'For the Peace of the Country Shrine', Yasukuni is the memorial shrine to Japan's war dead, around 2.5 million souls. It's a beautiful shrine, completed in 1869 and with torii gates made, un-

usually, out of steel and bronze. It is also incredibly controversial: in 1979 14 class-A war criminals, including WWII general Hideki Tōjō, were enshrined here.

The annual decision by leading politicians whether or not to visit the shrine on 15 August, the anniversary of Japan's defeat in WWII, is closely watched by neighbouring Asian countries and can result in sharp rebukes from their political leaders.

Yūshū-kan   MUSEUM
(遊就館; Map p90; www.yasukuni.or.jp; adult/student ¥800/500; ⊙ 9am-4pm; 🚇 Hanzōmon Line to Kudanshita, exit 1) This contentious war museum, on the ground of Yasukuni-jinja, begins with Japan's samurai tradition and ends with its imperialist aggressions in the first half of the 20th century. While the text has been purportedly toned down over the years, it is still known to boil the blood of some visitors with its particular view of history.

There are also some emotionally harrowing exhibits, such as the messages (translated into English) of kamikaze pilots written to their families before their final missions.

National Shōwa Memorial Museum MUSEUM
(昭和館; Shōwa-kan; Map p90; ☎ 3222-2577; 1-6-1 Kudan-minami, Chiyoda-ku; adult/student/child ¥300/150/80; ⊙ 10am-5.30pm; 🚇 Hanzōmon Line

Iidabashi & Akihabara

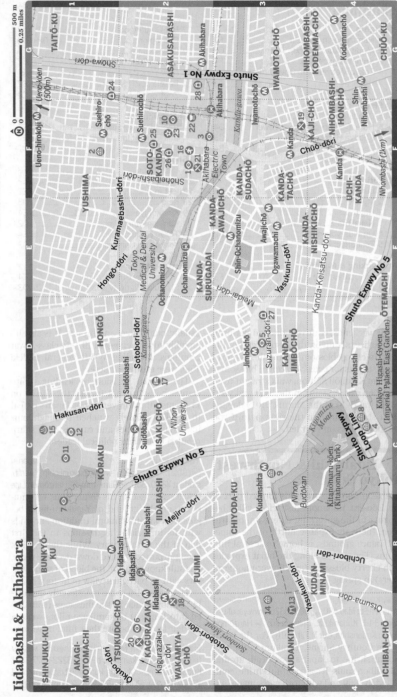

0   500 m
0   0.25 miles

Iidabashi & Akihabara

to Kudanshita, exit 4) This museum of WWII-era Tokyo gives a sense of everyday life for the common people: how they ate, slept, dressed, studied, prepared for war and endured martial law, famine and loss of loved ones. An English audio guide (free) fills in a lot. On the 5th floor, media consoles show film footage shot during the war.

Kagurazaka   NEIGHBOURHOOD
(神楽坂; Map p90; ® JR Sōbu Line to Iidabashi, west exit) Kagurazaka is an old geisha quarter with winding cobblestone streets and some of Tokyo's most exclusive restaurants. Though short on sights, this neighbourhood is heavy on atmosphere, at times feeling like a Tokyo of a hundred years ago. To reach the more ambient area, cross Sotobori-dōri, head up Kagurazaka Hill and turn right at the Royal Host restaurant.

Koishikawa Kōrakuen   GARDEN
(小石川後楽園; Map p90; 1-6-6 Kōraku, Bunkyō-ku; adult/child ¥300/free; ◎9am-5pm; ® JR Sōbu Line to Iidabashi, exit C3) Established in the mid-17th century as the property of the Tokugawa clan, this 7-hectare formal garden incorporates elements of Chinese and Japanese landscaping, although nowadays the *shakkei* (borrowed scenery) includes Tokyo Dome stadium. The garden is famed for plum trees in February, irises in June and autumn colours. Don't miss the Engetsu-kyō (Full-Moon Bridge), which dates from the early Edo period.

Tokyo Dome City   STADIUM
(東京ドームシティ; Map p90; www.tokyo-dome.co.jp/e/; 1-3 Kōraku, Bunkyō-ku; ; ® JR Chūō Line to Suidōbashi, west exit) Tokyo Dome is home to Japan's top baseball team, the Yomiuri Giants, but the 'city' surrounding it contains lots of other attractions, including an upscale bathhouse with real onsen water, **Spa LaQua** (スパラクーア; Map p90; www.laqua.jp; 5th-9th fl; admission from ¥2565; ◎11am-9am), and the amusement park **Tokyo Dome City Attractions** (東京ドームシティアトラクションズ; Map p90; ☎5800-9999; www.tokyo-dome.co.jp/e; day pass adult/child ¥3800/2000, individual rides ¥400-800; ◎10am-9pm; ; ® JR Chūō Line to Suidōbashi, west exit).

Adjacent to Gate 21 of Tokyo Dome, the **Japanese Baseball Hall of Fame & Museum** (野球体育博物館; Map p90; www.baseball-museum.or.jp; 1-3-61 Kōraku, Bunkyō-ku; adult/child ¥500/200; ◎10am-6pm Tue-Sun Mar-Sep, 10am-5pm Tue-Sun Oct-Feb) chronicles baseball's rise from a hobby imported by a US teacher in 1872 to the national obsession it's become.

National Museum of Modern Art (MOMAT)   MUSEUM
(国立近代美術館; Kokuritsu Kindai Bijutsukan; Map p90; www.momat.go.jp/english; 3-1 Kitanomaru-kōen, Chiyoda-ku; adult/student ¥420/130, extra for special exhibitions; ◎10am-5pm Tue-Thu, Sat & Sun, to 8pm Fri; ® Tozai Line to Takebashi, exit 1b) Picking up from the

Meiji period, this excellent museum traces the evolution of Japanese art following the introduction of Western-style techniques in the late 19th century through to the mid-20th century.

Crafts Gallery
MUSEUM

(東京国立近代美術館工芸館; Bijutsukan Kōgeikan; Map p90; www.momat.go.jp/english/craft/index.html; 1-1 Kitanomaru-kōen, Chiyoda-ku; adult/student ¥500/300; ◎10am-5pm Tue-Sun; 圓Tozai Line to Takebashi, exit 1b) This showcase for the works of contemporary artisans features ceramics, lacquer work, wood carving, textiles etc from Japan's so-called 'living treasures'.

Ikebukuro
NEIGHBOURHOOD

(池袋; Map p70; 圓JR Yamanote Line to Ikebukuro) Though Ikebukuro once boasted the world's largest department store, tallest building and longest escalator, these former glories have since been outshone elsewhere. For manga and girl-geek culture, however, **Otome Road** (乙女ロード), the female version of the overwhelmingly male-centric *otaku* zone in Akihabara, is tops.

◎ Akihabara & Around
秋葉原

Akihabara began its evolution into **Electric Town** (秋葉原電気街; Denki-Gai; 圓JR Yamanote to Akihabara, Denki-gai exit) post-WWII, when the area around the station became a black market for radio parts. In more recent decades, Akihabara has been widely known as *the* place to hunt for bargains on new and used electronics. Nowadays, Akiba, as the neighbourhood is called, is also the centre of the *otaku* (geek) universe, catching manga and anime fans in its gravitational pull.

Pick up a map at **Tokyo Anime Center Akiba Info** (東京アニメセンターAkiba Info; Map p90; www.animecenter.jp; 2nd fl, Akihabara UDX Bldg, 4-14-1 Soto-Kanda, Chiyoda-ku; ◎11am-7pm Tue-Sun; 圓JR Yamanote Line to Akihabara, Electric Town exit); the helpful staff here speak English.

@Home Café
POP CULTURE

(@ほぉ〜むカフェ; Map p90; www.cafe-athome.com; 4th-7th fl, 1-11-4 Soto-kanda, Chiyoda-ku; drinks from ¥500; ◎11.30am-10pm Mon-Fri, from 10.30am Sat & Sun; 圓JR Sōbu Line to Akihabara, Electric Town exit) This is Akihabara's most popular maid cafe, where the waitresses dress as french maids and treat customers as *go-shujinsama* (master) with shy, giggling deference. It's more or less innocent fun, and most of the customers here are Japanese tourists (and, surprisingly, often female), rather than hardcore *otaku*.

There's a one drink minimum order. To really get into it though, sign up for some of the extra perks – like having a smiley face drawn in ketchup on your omelet or getting to play a game of *moe moe jankan* (rock, paper, scissors maid-style) with your maid of choice.

Akihabara Radio Center
BUILDING

(秋葉原ラジオセンター; Map p90; 1-14-2 Soto-Kanda, Chiyoda-ku; ◎hours vary; 圓JR Yamanote Line to Akihabara, Electric Town exit) Strictly for old-school electronics *otaku*, this two-storey warren of several dozen electronics stalls under the elevated railway is the original, still-beating heart of Akihabara. By old-school, we mean connectors, jacks, LEDs, switches, semiconductors and other components. The easiest access is the narrow entrance under the tracks on Chūō-dōri.

Super Potato Retro-kan
ARCADE

(スーパーポテトレトロ館; Map p90; 1-11-2 Soto-Kanda, Chiyoda-ku; ◎11am-8pm Mon-Fri, 10am-8pm Sat & Sun; 圓JR Yamanote Line to Akihabara, Electric Town exit) Remember Street Fighter, or PacMan? Used-game shop Super Potato specialises in games of the vintage variety, and on the 5th floor of its Akihabara shop it has even got a retro video arcade where you can get your hands on some old-school consoles.

3331 Arts Chiyoda
ART GALLERY

(Map p90; www.3331.jp/en; 6-11-14 Soto-Kanda, Chiyoda-ku; ◎noon-7pm Mon, Wed, Thu & Sun, to 8pm Fri & Sat; 圓Ginza Line to Suehirochō, exit 4) **FREE** When this junior high school closed for lack of students, a handful of galleries moved in. All are free to enter, though special exhibitions sometimes charge admission. Given its proximity to Akiba, 3331 Chiyoda often has installations with a pop-culture bent. There's a cafe here, too.

Jimbōchō
NEIGHBOURHOOD

(神保町; Map p90; 圓Hanzōmon Line to Jimbōchō) Bibliophiles take note: there are literally over a hundred second-hand booksellers here, concentrated along a stretch of Yasukuni-dōri. While naturally most books are in Japanese, this a good place to trawl for art tomes, vintage manga and other collectibles. Suzuran-dōri, one block behind Yasukuni-dōri, has a retro vibe to go with the books on sale here.

POP PHENOMENON: AKB48

Love them or hate them, these days there's no escaping AKB48, a super girl group with no fewer than 60 rotating members. Formed in 2005, AKB48 was meant to be an accessible idol group for Akiba's *otaku* (geeks). The group performs daily at its own theatre in Akihabara, **AKB48 Theatre** (Map p90; www.akb48.co.jp; 8th fl, Don Quijote, 4-3-3 Soto-kanda, Chiyoda-ku; R JR Yamanote Line to Akihabara, Electric Town exit), and fans can vote for which girls will appear.

Fast-forward a few years and AKB48 is now a full-on mainstream pop phenomenon with its own TV show, countless endorsements and record sales. The group's success is a compelling example of Akiba's growing influence over the culture at large.

While AKB48 has attracted a lot of male fans (and simultaneously picked up criticism for sexualising teens as young as 13), the group has also got a lot of female fans their own age. Sister groups now exist in Jakarta and Singapore.

Getting tickets, which are awarded by lottery, to one of the shows is near impossible. However, if you're curious to see what the big deal is, you can pop into the **AKB48 Cafe** (Map p90; http://akb48cafeshops.com; 1-1 Kanda Hanagaoka-chō, Chiyoda-ku; ⊙ 11am-11pm; R JR Yamanote Line to Akihabara, Electric Town exit) in Akihabara. Here videos of the group play on loop and look-a-like waitresses serve cutesy concoctions to slack-jawed fans.

◉ Ueno 上野

Ueno, revolving around its sprawling park, has been one of Tokyo's top draws since the Edo period. Ueno Hill, where **Kanei-ji** (寛永寺; Map p96; 1-14-11 Ueno-sakuragi, Taitō-ku; R JR Yamanote Line to Uguisudani, north exit) stands, was the site of a last-ditch defence of the Tokugawa shōgunate by 2000 loyalists in 1868. They were duly dispatched by the imperial army, and the new Meiji government set about turning the newly christened Ueno-kōen into a shining example of its 'civilisation and enlightenment' campaign. Grand museums based on European models were built, starting with the Tokyo National Museum.

To the north is **Yanaka** (谷中; Yanaka, Taitō-ku ; R JR Yamanote Line to Nippori, west exit), where not just the spirit, but also the actual structures, that define the old Shitamachi still exist. The neighbourhood miraculously survived the Great Kantō Earthquake of 1923, the allied firebombing of WWII and the slash-and-burn modernisation of the postwar years. But that's not all that makes Yanaka unique: it has more than a hundred temples, relocated from around Tokyo during an Edo-period episode of urban restructuring. It's a magical area, the kind of scene that visitors come hoping to see in Japan but often miss.

★ Tokyo National Museum   MUSEUM
(東京国立博物館; Tokyo Kokuritsu Hakubutsu-kan; Map p96; www.tnm.jp; 13-9 Ueno-kōen, Taitō-ku; adult/student/child ¥600/400/free; ⊙ 9:30am-5pm Tue-Sun, open later some weekends in summer; R JR

Yamanote Line to Ueno, Ueno-kōen exit) If you visit only one museum in Tokyo, make it this one. The world's largest collection of Japanese art covers ancient pottery, religious sculpture, samurai swords, *ukiyo-e* (woodblock prints), exquisite kimono, and much, much more. There are several buildings, the most important of which is the **Honkan** (Main Gallery), built in the imperial style, fusing Western and Japanese architectural motifs.

Another must-see is the **Gallery of Hōryū-ji Treasures**, which displays masks, scrolls and gilt Buddhas from Hōryū-ji – located in Nara Prefecture, and said to be the first Buddhist temple in Japan (founded in 607) – in a spare, elegant box of a contemporary building (1999) by Taniguchi Yoshio, who also designed New York's Museum of Modern Art (MoMA).

The **Heiseikan** (Heisei Hall), which opened in 1993 to commemorate the marriage of Crown Prince Naruhito, houses the Japanese Archaeology Gallery as well as special exhibits.

The **Tōyōkan** (Gallery of Eastern Antiquities), reopened in 2013, showcases pieces from across East and South Asia and the Middle East. The **Hyōkeikan** (Hyōkei Hall) was built in 1909, with Western-style architecture that is reminiscent of a museum you might find in Paris, but is closed for earthquake retrofitting.

The grand **Kuro-mon** (Black Gate) to the west of the main gate was transported from the Edo-era mansion of a feudal lord. For a few weeks in spring and autumn the **garden** behind the Honkan, which has five vintage teahouses, opens to the public.

Tokyo National Museum

HISTORIC HIGHLIGHTS

It would be a challenge to take in everything the sprawling Tokyo National Museum has to offer in a day. Fortunately, the Honkan (Main Gallery) is designed to give visitors a crash course in Japanese art history from the Jōmon era (13,000–300 BC) to the Edo era (AD 1603–1868). The works on display here are rotated regularly, to protect fragile ones and to create seasonal exhibitions – you're always guaranteed to see something new.

Buy your ticket from outside the main gate then head straight to the Honkan with its sloping tile roof. Stow your coat in a locker and take the central staircase up to the 2nd floor, where the exhibitions are arranged chronologically. Allow two hours for this tour of the highlights.

The first room on your right starts from the beginning with **ancient Japanese art** 1. Be sure to pick up a copy of the brochure *Highlights of Japanese Art* at the entrance.

Continue to the **National Treasure Gallery** 2. 'National Treasure' is the highest distinction awarded to a work of art in Japan. Keep an eye out for more National Treasures, labelled in red, on display in other rooms throughout the museum.

Moving on, stop to admire the **art of the Imperial court** 3, the **samurai armour and swords** 4 and the **ukiyo-e and kimono** 5.

Next, take the stairs down to the 1st floor, where each room is dedicated to a different craft, such as lacquerware or ceramics. Don't miss the excellent examples of **religious sculpture** 6 and **folk art** 7.

Finish your visit with a look inside the enchanting **Gallery of Hōryū-ji Treasures** 8.

REBECCA MILNER ©

Ukiyo-e & Kimono (Room 10)
Chic silken kimono and lushly coloured *ukiyo-e* (woodblock prints) are two icons of the Edo era (AD 1603–1868) *ukiyo* – the 'floating world', or world of fleeting beauty and pleasure.

Museum Garden
Don't miss the garden if you visit during the few weeks it's open to the public in spring and autumn.

Japanese Sculpture (Room 11)
Many of Japan's most famous sculptures, religious in nature, are locked away in temple reliquaries. This is a rare chance to see them up close.

Heiseikan & Japanese Archaeology Gallery

Research & Information Centre

8

Hyōkeikan

Kuro-mon

Main Gate

Gallery of Hōryū-ji Treasures
Surround yourself with miniature gilt Buddhas from Hōryū-ji, said to be one of Japan's oldest Buddhist temples, founded in 607. Don't miss the graceful Pitcher with Dragon Head, a National Treasure.

REBECCA MILNER ©

Samurai Armour & Swords (Rooms 5 & 6)
Glistening swords, finely stitched armour and imposing helmets bring to life the samurai, those iconic warriors of Japan's medieval age.

Art of the Imperial Court (Room 3-2)
Literature works, calligraphy and narrative picture scrolls are displayed alongside decorative art objects, which allude to the life of elegance led by courtesans a thousand years ago.

Honkan (Main Gallery) 2nd Floor

National Treasure Gallery (Room 2)
A single, superlative work from the museum's collection of 87 National Treasures (perhaps a painted screen, or a gilded, hand-drawn sutra) is displayed in a serene, contemplative setting.

Museum Garden & Teahouses

Honkan (Main Gallery) 1st Floor

Honkan (Main Gallery)

Tōyōkan (Gallery of Eastern Antiquities)

Gift Shop
The museum gift shop, on the 1st floor of the Honkan, has an excellent collection of Japanese art books in English.

Dawn of Japanese Art (Room 1)
The rise of the Imperial court and the introduction of Buddhism changed the Japanese aesthetic forever. These clay works from previous eras show what came before.

Folk Culture (Room 15)
See artefacts from Japan's historical minorities – the indigenous Ainu of Hokkaidō, the Kirishitan (persecuted Christians of the middle ages) and the former Ryūkyū Empire, now Okinawa.

Ueno

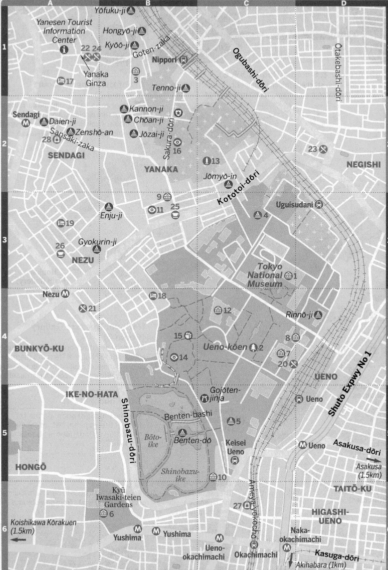

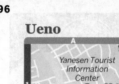

★ **Ueno-kōen**   PARK
(上野公園; Map p96; ◷5am-11pm; ℝJR Yamanote Line to Ueno, Ueno-kōen & Shinobazu exits)
Established in 1873, Ueno-kōen is known
as Japan's first public park (in the Western
sense), but it's much older than that. Struc-

tures here date as far back as the 17th century. There's a **Kiyōmizu Kannon-dō** (清水
観音堂; Map p96; ◷9am-4pm; ℝJR Yamanote
line to Ueno, Shinobazu exit) modelled after the
landmark temple in Kyoto and a **Tōshōgū**
(東照宮; Map p96; admission ¥200; ◷9.30am-

Ueno

TOKYO SIGHTS & ACTIVITIES

4.30pm; Ⓡ JR Yamanote Line to Ueno, Shinobazu exit) like the shrine in Nikkō (under reconstruction until January 2014).

Shinobazu Pond (不忍池), where couples now paddle swan-shaped boats, was likened to the country's central Lake Biwa and Ueno-kōen was billed as a mini-Japan – a sort of prototypical Disney World. During the Edo period, when travel was heavily restricted, Tokyoites could 'see' the country without having to leave home. The park's reputation as the most famous *hanami* (cherry-blossom viewing) spot in the city dates to this era.

Ueno-kōen remains a beloved public space. On weekends look for buskers, acrobats and food vendors. Navigating the park is easy, thanks to large maps (in Japanese and English) around the area.

Shitamachi Museum MUSEUM
(下町風俗資料館; Map p96; www.taitocity.net/taito/shitamachi; 2-1 Ueno-kōen, Taitō-ku; adult/child ¥300/100; ⊙9.30am-4.30pm Tue-Sun; ⊡; Ⓡ JR Yamanote to Ueno, Shinobazu exit) This museum re-creates life in the plebeian quarters of Tokyo during the Meiji and Taishō periods (1868–1926) through an exhibition of typical wooden buildings from that era. Take off your shoes and look inside an old tenement house or around an old sweet shop while soaking up the atmosphere of Shitamachi. Ask for an English-language leaflet; English-speaking guides are available, too.

National Science Museum MUSEUM
(国立科学博物館; Kokuritsu Kagaku Hakubutsu-kan; Map p96; www.kahaku.go.jp; 7-20 Ueno-kōen,

Taitō-ku; adult/child ¥600/free; ⊙9am-5pm Tue-Thu, Sat & Sun, to 8pm Fri; ⊡; Ⓡ JR Yamanote Line to Ueno, Ueno-kōen exit) Of particular interest here is the Japan Gallery, which showcases the rich and varied wildlife of the Japanese archipelago, from the bears of Hokkaido to the giant beetles of Okinawa. Also: a rocket launcher, a giant squid, an Edo-era mummy, and a digital seismograph that charts earthquakes in real time. There's English signage throughout, plus an English-language audio guide (¥300).

Kyū Iwasaki-teien HISTORIC BUILDING
(旧岩崎邸庭園; Map p96; http://teien.tokyo-park.or.jp/en/kyu-iwasaki/index.html; 1-3-45 Ike-no-hata, Taitō-ku; adult/child ¥400/free; ⊙9am-5pm; Ⓡ Chiyoda Line to Yushima, exit 1) This grand residence was once the villa of the founder of the Mitsubishi conglomerate, and is now a fascinating example of how the cultural elite of the early Meiji period tried to straddle east and west. Built in 1896, it was restored and opened to the public in 2001.

National Museum of Western Art MUSEUM
(国立西洋美術館; Kokuritsu Seiyō Bijutsukan; Map p96; www.nmwa.go.jp; 7-7 Ueno-kōen, Taitō-ku; adult/student ¥420/130, permanent collection 2nd & 4th Sat free; ⊙9.30am-5.30pm Tue-Thu, Sat & Sun, to 8pm Fri; Ⓡ JR Yamanote Line to Ueno, Ueno-kōen exit) The permanent collection here runs from medieval Madonna and Child images to 20th-century abstract expressionism, but is strongest in French Impressionism, including a whole gallery of Monet. The main building was designed by Le Corbusier in the late 1950s and is now on Unesco's World Heritage List.

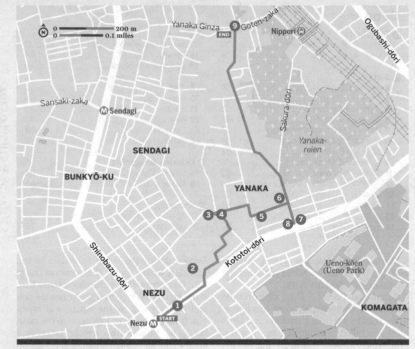

🚶 City Walk
Strolling Yanaka

START NEZU STATION
FINISH YANAKA GINZA
LENGTH 2KM; TWO HOURS

Wander through the vintage Shitamachi neighbourhood of Yanaka. Don't start out too late as many temples close their doors by 5pm.

From exit 1 of Nezu Station head up **①Kototoi-dōri**. Here, a handful of traditional, wooden two-storey merchant's houses – with a shop on the ground floor and the living quarters above – remain alongside the mid-20th-century concrete buildings with colourful awnings. Don't miss the shops selling *sembei* (rice crackers) and *wagashi* (Japanese sweets).

Pay a visit to the temple **②Gyokurin-ji**. Just inside the grounds, on your right, a stone wall guards a narrow alley: follow it. This twisting path, hemmed in by temple walls, takes you deep into Yanaka's most atmospheric quarters.

When you emerge from the back alleys, head left and you'll soon spot a pretty cluster of temples, including **③Enju-ji**, which has some fantastic gnarled trees. Double back towards the fork in the road marked by an

ancient, thick-trunked **④Himalayan cedar tree**. On the left side of the tree is a classic, old-school corner shop. Continue past it to the **⑤studio of painter Allan West** (p99).

The next landmark is **⑥SCAI the Bathhouse** (p99), a centuries-old public bathhouse that became a contemporary art gallery in 1993. One block over, the **⑦Shitamachi Museum Annex** preserves an old liquor shop built in 1910; it's free to enter.

If you're in need of a break, you can soak up more local atmosphere over coffee at **⑧Kayaba Coffee** (p158).

From here, double back, taking a left at the fork and then heading down the narrow road to the left of the Yamazaki shop. Continue on, and enjoy the stroll past temples, tiny galleries and craft shops.

When you reach an intersection with lively vendors – that's **⑨Yanaka Ginza** (p153). Join locals shopping and snacking their way up and down the lane. Walk west and you can pick up the subway at Sendagi Station; to the east is Nippori Station, where you can hop on the JR Yamanote Line.

Tokyo Metropolitan
Museum of Art
MUSEUM

(東京都美術館; Map p96; www.tobikan.jp; 8-36 Ueno-kōen, Taitō-ku; admission varies; ⊙9am-5pm Tue-Sun; ℝJR Yamanote Line to Ueno, Ueno-kōen exit) Newly re-opened after a long renovation, this museum, established in 1926, is back to staging wildly popular temporary exhibits from leading international museums (such as New York's Metropolitan Museum of Art).

Ueno Zoo
ZOO

(上野動物園; Ueno Dōbutsu-en; Map p96; www.tokyo-zoo.net; 9-83 Ueno-kōen, Taitō-ku; adult/child ¥600/free; ⊙9.30am-5pm Tue-Sun; 🚻; ℝJR Yamanote Line to Ueno, Ueno-kōen exit) Japan's oldest zoo was established in 1882, and is home to animals from around the globe, but the biggest attractions are two giant pandas that arrived from China in 2011 – Rī Rī and Shin Shin. Ueno Zoo is larger than you'd think, given the obvious space constraints of Tokyo.

Yanaka-reien
CEMETERY

(谷中霊園; Map p96; 7-5-24 Yanaka, Taitō-ku; ℝJR Yamanote Line to Nippori, west exit) One of Tokyo's largest graveyards, Yanaka-reien is the final resting place of more than 7000 souls, many of whom were quite well known in their day, such as Japan's most famous female novelist of the modern era, Higuchi Ichiyō (you'll find her portrait on ¥5000 bills). It's also where you'll find the **tomb of Yoshinobu Tokugawa** (徳川慶喜の墓; Map p96), the last shōgun.

Asakura Chōso Museum
MUSEUM

(朝倉彫塑館; Map p96; www.taitocity.net/taito/asakura; 7-16-10 Yanaka, Taitō-ku; adult/student ¥400/150; ⊙9.30am-4.30pm Tue-Thu, Sat & Sun; ℝJR Yamanote Line to Nippori, north exit) Sculptor Asakura Fumio (artist name Chōso; 1883–1964) designed this fanciful house and studio himself; it's now a museum with a number of the artist's signature realist works, mostly of people and cats, on display. At the time of research this museum was still closed for renovation, but was set to reopen in autumn 2013.

Studio Allan West
ART STUDIO

(えどころアランウエスト; Map p96; www.allanwest.jp; 1-6-17 Yanaka, Taitō-ku; ⊙1-5pm daily, from 3pm Sun, closed irregularly; ℝChiyoda Line to Nezu, exit 1) A long-time Yanaka resident, Allan West paints gorgeous screens in the traditional Japanese style, making his paints from scratch just as local artists have done for centuries. Visitors are welcome to peek inside his studio when he's there.

SCAI the Bathhouse
ART GALLERY

(Map p96; www.scaithebathhouse.com; 6-1-23 Yanaka, Taitō-ku; ⊙noon-6pm Tue-Sat; ℝChiyoda Line to Nezu, exit 1) Once a 200-year-old bathhouse, now a cutting-edge gallery space, SCAI showcases Japanese and international artists in its austere vaulted space.

⊙ Asakusa &
Sumida-gawa 浅草・隅田川

Asakusa, with its ancient temple, retains a lot of that old Shitamachi spirit. At the turn of the last century, the neighbourhood was a pleasure district likened to Montmartre in Paris, though hardly any of that old bawdiness remains today.

The neighbourhoods across the Sumida-gawa, too, look much like they have for decades, having experienced little of the development seen elsewhere in the city – save for Tokyo Sky Tree. Given its location, among low-lying residential buildings and unburied electrical wires, Tokyo's newest landmark looks as though it were dropped here by aliens.

Ryōgoku, also east of the Sumida-gawa, is home to the national sumō stadium Kokugikan – you'll often see chubby wrestlers waddling around Ryōguku Station.

★ Sensō-ji
BUDDHIST TEMPLE

(浅草寺; Map p100; 2-3-1 Asakusa, Taitō-ku; ⊙24hr; ℝGinza Line to Asakusa, exit 1) FREE Tokyo's most visited temple enshrines a golden image of Kannon (the Buddhist goddess of mercy), which, according to legend, was miraculously pulled out of the nearby Sumida-gawa by two fishermen in AD 628. The image has remained on the spot ever since; the present structure dates from 1950. Entrance to the temple complex is via the fantastic, red **Kaminari-mon** (雷門; Thunder Gate; Map p100).

Through the gate, protected by Fūjin (the god of wind) and Raijin (the god of thunder) is **Nakamise-dōri**, the temple precinct's shopping street. Here everything from tourist trinkets to genuine Edo-style crafts is sold.

At the end of Nakamise-dōri is the temple itself, and to your left you'll spot the 55m **Five-storey Pagoda** (五重塔; Map p100). It's a 1973 reconstruction of a pagoda built by Tokugawa Iemitsu and is even more picturesque at night, all lit up.

Asakusa & Sumida-gawa

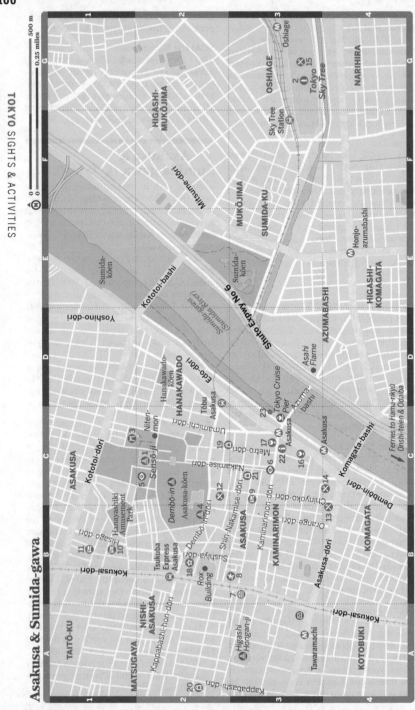

500 m
0.25 miles

G1

TAITŌ-KU

MATSUGAYA

NISHI-ASAKUSA

Kappabashi-hon-dōri

Kappabashi-dōri

Kokusai-dōri

Hisago-dōri

ASAKUSA

Kototoi-dōri

Hanayashiki Amusement Park

Niten-mon

Sensō-ji

Dembo-in

Asakusa-kōen

Dembo-in-dōri

HANAKAWADO

Hanakawado-kōen

Edo-dōri

Umamichi-dōri

Nakamise-dōri

Shin-Nakamise-dōri

Sushiya-dōri

Tsukuba Express Asakusa

Rox Building

Higashi Hongan-ji

ASAKUSA

KAMINARIMON

Kaminarimon-dōri

Metro-dōri

Chinyoko-dōri

Orange-dōri

Asakusa-dōri

Kokusai-dōri

Tawaramachi

KOTOBUKI

KOMAGATA

Demboin-dōri

Komagata-bashi

Asakusa

Asakusa

Azuma-bashi

Tokyo Cruise Pier

Asahi Flame

Ferries to Hama-rikyū
Onshi-teien & Odaiba

Shuto Expwy No 6

Sumida-gawa (Sumida River)

Sumida-kōen

Sumida-kōen

Kototoi-bashi

Yoshino-dōri

Mitsume-dōri

HIGASHI-MUKŌJIMA

MUKŌJIMA

SUMIDA-KU

AZUMABASHI

HIGASHI-KOMAGATA

Honjo-azumabashi

Sky Tree Station

OSHIAGE

Oshiage

Tokyo Sky Tree

NARIHIRA

1 • 2 • 3 • 5 • 10 • 11 • 20 — 4 • 7 • 8 • 12 • 13 • 14 • 23 • 6 • 9 • 16 • 17 • 18 • 19 • 21 • 22 — 15 • 1 • 2

Asakusa & Sumida-gawa

It's a mystery as to whether or not the ancient image of Kannon actually exists, as it's not on public display. This doesn't stop a steady stream of worshippers from visiting. In front of the temple is a large incense cauldron: the smoke is said to bestow health and you'll see people rubbing it into their bodies through their clothes.

★ Tokyo Sky Tree TOWER
(東京スカイツリー; Map p100; www.tokyo-skytree.jp; 1 Oshiage, Sumida-ku; admission to 350m/450m observation decks ¥2000/3000; ◷8am-10pm; ◻Hanzōmon Line to Oshiage, Sky Tree exit) Even if you don't go in for heights, Tokyo Sky Tree is an engineering marvel. It opened in May 2012 as the world's tallest 'free-standing communication tower' at 634m. Its silvery exterior of steel mesh morphs from a triangle at the base to a circle at 300m. There are two observation decks, one at 350m and another at 450m.

The panorama from the lower deck, the Tembō Deck, is plenty spectacular; at peak visibility you can see up to 70km away. To increase your chances of spotting Mt Fuji, go in the early morning or during the winter months. Don't miss the small section of glass floor panels, where you can see – dizzyingly – all the way to the ground.

The upper deck, the Tembō Galleria, beneath the digital broadcasting antennas, features a circular glass corridor for more vertiginous thrills.

The ticket counter is on the 4th floor. Try to avoid visiting on the weekend, when you might have to wait in line.

Asakusa-jinja SHINTŌ SHRINE
(浅草神社; Map p100; 2-3-1 Asakusa, Taitō-ku; ◷9am-4.30pm; ◻Ginza Line to Asakusa, exit 1) Asakusa-jinja was built in honour of the brothers who discovered the Kannon statue that inspired the construction of Sensō-ji. The current building, painted a deep shade of red, dates to 1649 and is an impressive example of an early-Edo architectural style called *gongen-zukuri*. It's also the epicentre of one of Tokyo's most important festivals, May's Sanja Matsuri (p106).

Taiko Drum Museum MUSEUM
(太鼓館; Taiko-kan; Map p100; 2-1-1 Nishi-Asakusa, Taitō-ku; adult/child ¥500/150; ◷10am-5pm Wed-Sun; ◷; ◻Ginza Line to Tawaramachi, exit 3) There are hundreds of drums from around the world here, including several traditional Japanese *taiko*. The best part is that you can actually play most of them (those marked with a music note).

Chingo-dō BUDDHIST TEMPLE
(鎮護堂; Map p100; 2-3-1 Asakusa, Taitō-ku; ◷6am-5pm; ◻Ginza Line to Asakusa, exit 1) This peaceful, overlooked little temple pays tribute to the *tanuki*, 'raccoon dogs' who figure in Japanese myth as mystical shape-shifters and merry pranksters, but are also said to protect against fire and theft.

★ **Edo-Tokyo Museum**   MUSEUM
(江戸東京博物館; Map p70; ☑ 3626-9974; www.
edo-tokyo-museum.or.jp; 1-4-1 Yokoami, Sumida-ku;
adult/child ¥600/free; ◷ 9.30am-5.30pm Tue-Sun,
to 7.30pm Sat; ☒ JR Sōbu Line to Ryōgoku, west
exit) In addition to looking like a retro-future
space station, this city history museum is
among the best we've seen. Exhibitions
document Tokyo's epic transition from Edo
to its modern avatar with heaps of interesting facts. Highlights include a replica of the
original Nihonbashi bridge, real examples
of Edo-era infrastructure and impeccably
detailed scale models of markets and shops.

You could easily spend half a day here if
you want to take a thorough look at things.
There are often special exhibits, but the permanent collection is enough to overwhelm
most visitors. English signage goes a long
way, but the museum really comes to life
with the help of a volunteer guide (free).
There is usually an English-speaking guide
on hand, but if you want to be extra sure
there's one when you visit, contact the museum two weeks in advance.

Arashio Stable   SUMO
(荒汐部屋; Arashio-beya; Map p70; ☑ 3666-7646;
www.arashio.net; 2-47-2 Hama-chō, Nihombashi,
Chūō-ku; ◷ 7.30-10am; ☒ Toei Shinjuku Line to
Hamachō, exit A2) **FREE** Arashio is one of the
more welcoming sumo stables, where you
can catch the big boys in action during their
morning practice. The viewing area is really
just a bench, so only a handful of people can
watch at a time. Complete silence is mandatory. Visit the website (in English) for
additional information about visiting and
etiquette.

Sumō Museum   MUSEUM
(相撲博物館; Map p70; www.sumo.or.jp/museum;
1-3-28 Yokoami, Sumida-ku; ◷ 10am-4.30pm Mon-
Fri; ☒ JR Sōbu Line to Ryōgoku, west exit) **FREE** On
the ground floor of the national sumo stadium, Ryōgoku Kokugikan (p132), this small
museum displays the photos of all the past
yokozuna (top-ranking sumō wrestlers), or
for those who lived before the era of photography, *ukiyo-e* (woodblock prints). During
tournaments, the museum is only open to
ticket holders.

**Museum of Contemporary Art,
Tokyo (MOT)**   MUSEUM
(東京都現代美術館; Map p70; www.mot-art-
museum.jp; 4-1-1 Miyoshi, Kōtō-ku; adult/child
¥500/free; ◷ 10am-6pm Tue-Sun; ☒ Ōedo Line to
Kiyosumi-Shirakawa, exit B2) For a primer in the
major movements of post-WWII Japanese
art, a visit to the permanent collection gallery here should do the trick. The building's
stone, steel and wood architecture by Yana-
gisawa Takahiko is a work of art in its own
right. The museum is on the edge of Kiba-
kōen, a well-signposted 10-minute walk
from the subway station.

Kiyosumi-teien   GARDEN
(清澄庭園; Map p70; 3-3-9 Kiyosumi, Kōtō-ku;
adult/child ¥150/free; ◷ 9am-5pm; ☒ Ōedo Line
to Kiyosumi-Shirakawa, exit A3) Kiyosumi-teien
started out in 1721 as the villa of a *daimyō*.
After the villa was destroyed in the 1923
earthquake, Iwasaki Yatarō, founder of the
Mitsubishi Corporation, purchased the
property. He used company ships to transport prize stones here from all over Japan,
which are set around a pond ringed with
Japanese black pine, hydrangeas and Taiwanese cherry trees.

⊙ Odaiba & Tokyo Bay
お台場・東京湾

Developed mostly in the '90s on reclaimed
land, Odaiba is a bubble-era vision of urban
planning, where the buildings are large, the
streets are wide and the waterfront is the
main attraction. Love it or hate it, you'll definitely feel like you're in an alternate Tokyo.

Viewed from the promenades and elevated walkways of **Odaiba Kaihin-kōen** (お台
場海浜公園; Odaiba Seaside Park; Map p103; 1-4-1

FORTUNE TELLING

Getting an *omikuji* (paper fortune), is part of the fun of visiting a shrine or temple,
and Sensō-ji has them in English (on the reverse). They're sold from what can best be
described as a very analogue vending machine. Put a ¥100 coin in the slot, then grab a
silver canister and shake it. Extract a stick and note its number (in kanji), then find the
matching drawer and withdraw a paper fortune, returning the stick to the canister. If you
get a bad one – and some are harsh! – never fear. Just tie the paper on the nearby rack,
ask the gods for better luck and try again.

Odaiba & Tokyo Bay

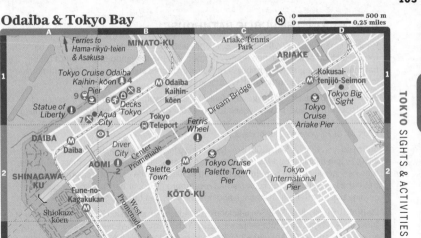

Daiba, Minato-ku; ⊙24hr; ℝYurikamome Line to Odaiba Kaihin-kōen), the city looks less sinister than it does downtown, pretty even – especially at night.

There's some interesting architecture here too, notably the **Fuji TV Building** (フジテレビ; Map p103; ♫info 5500-8888; 2-4-8 Daiba, Minato-ku; observation deck adult/child ¥500/¥300; ⊙10am-6pm Tue-Sun; ℝYurikamome line to Daiba), with its giant suspended orb (which holds an observatory).

At the time of research, an 18m-tall 1:1 scale model of **Gundam** (ガンダム; Map p103), the robotic 'mobile suit' from the immensely popular anime series of the same name, was stationed in front of the Diver City mall – though it was planned as a limited-time only installation.

Travelling to Odaiba is most fun on the driverless Yurikamome monorail, which departs from Shimbashi Station and snakes through skyscrapers before crossing the Rainbow Bridge.

★**Ōedo Onsen Monogatari** ONSEN
(大江戸温泉物語; Map p103; www.ooedoonsen.jp/higaeri/english/index.html; 2-6-3 Aomi, Kōtō-ku; adult/child from ¥1980/900, after 6pm from ¥1480/900; ⊙11am-8am; ♿; ℝYurikamome Line to Telecom Centre, Rinkai Line to Tokyo Teleport

Odaiba & Tokyo Bay

with free shuttle bus) This honest-to-goodness onsen actually pipes in hot-spring water from 1400m below Tokyo Bay. Billed as an 'onsen theme park' – a fantastically Japanese concept – the interior is done up like a Disneyland-style version of an Edo-era town, with games and food stalls. Upon entering, visitors change their clothes for colourful *yukata* (light cotton summer kimono).

URBAN ICON: THE PUBLIC BATHHOUSE

Prior to Japan's post-WWII economic revolution, most private homes didn't have bathrooms. Instead people washed – and gossiped – at their neighbourhood *sentō* (public bathhouse). Though their numbers are dwindling, there are still about 1000 bathhouses in Tokyo; most neighbourhoods have at least one.

Below are two classics of the genre. Unlike fancier onsen, *sentō* don't have soap and towels set out for you, so you'll need to bring your own (or buy some from the counter). **Super Sentos** (www.sunnypages.jp/search/tokyo_sightseeing/super_sentos) also has a good list of Tokyo-area bathhouses.

Jakotsu-yu (蛇骨湯; Map p100; www.jakotsuyu.co.jp; 1-11-11 Asakusa, Taitō-ku; admission ¥450; ⊙ 1pm-midnight Wed-Mon; 🚇 Ginza Line to Tawaramachi, exit 3) Unlike most *sentō*, the tubs here are filled with pure hot-spring water, naturally the color of weak tea. Another treat: the lovely, lantern-lit, rock-framed *rotemburo* (outdoor bath). Jakotsu-yu is a welcoming place, with English signage and no policy against tattoos.

Daikoku-yu (大黒湯; 32-6 Senju-kotobukichō, Adachi-ku; admission ¥450; ⊙ 3pm-midnight Tue-Sun; 🚇 Hibiya Line to Kita-senju, west exit) With an impressive winglike roof befitting an elegant temple, Daikokuyu – constructed in 1929 – is known as the 'king of public bathhouses'. Inside, classic *sentō* murals of idyllic nature scenes adorn the walls.

There are a variety of baths, including *rotemburo* (outdoor baths). Some, like the *iwashioyoku* (hot stone bath) and *tsunaburo* (hot sand bath), cost extra and require reservations. Only the baths themselves are divided by gender, so couples and families can enjoy the rest of the complex, including the outdoor foot-bath, together.

There's an overnight surcharge of ¥1700 per person between 2am and 5am. Note that visitors with tattoos will be denied admission.

National Museum of Emerging Science & Innovation (Mirai-kan) MUSEUM
(未来館; Map p103; www.miraikan.jst.go.jp; 2-3-6 Aomi, Kōtō-ku; adult/child ¥600/200; ⊙10am-5pm Wed-Mon; 🔃; 🚇 Yurikamome Line to Telecom Centre) *Miraikan* means 'hall of the future', and exhibits here present the science and technology that will likely shape the years to come. Lots of hands-on displays make this a great place for kids. Don't miss the demonstration of the humanoid robot ASIMO. The popular Gaia dome theatre/planetarium has an English audio option; reserve your seats as soon as you arrive.

Tokyo Joypolis AMUSEMENT PARK
(東京ジョイポリス; Map p103; http://tokyo-joypolis.com; 3rd-5th fl, Decks Tokyo, 1-6-1 Daiba, Minato-ku; passport adult/child ¥3900/2900, after 5pm ¥2900/1900; ⊙10am-11pm; 🔃; 🚇 Yurikamome Line to Odaiba Kaihin-kōen) Unleash your inner child at this three-storey indoor amusement park, operated by game-maker Sega. You'll find a mix of virtual reality and action rides, including a roller coaster where you can simultaneously shoot zombies (Veil of Dark) and a driving game using real cars (Initial D Arcade Stage 4). Lines are shortest on weekdays when kids are in school.

Separate admission and individual ride tickets (from ¥500) are available, but if you plan to go on more than six attractions the unlimited 'passport' makes sense.

Tokyo Disney Resort AMUSEMENT PARK
(東京ディズニーリゾート; www.tokyodisney resort.co.jp; 1-1 Maihama, Urayasu-shi; 1-day ticket adult/child ¥6200/4100, after 6pm ¥3300; ⊙hours vary by season; 🔃; 🚇JR Keiyō line to Maihama) Pop quiz: what's the most visited sight in Japan? Kyoto's temples? Nope, it's Tokyo Disney Resort. There are actually two parks here: Tokyo Disney, modelled after the California original, and Tokyo Disney-Sea, which has shows and international pavilions that are popular with adults. Invest in a Fast Pass to cut down on time lost waiting in lines.

🍴 Courses

A Taste of Culture COOKING
(www.tasteofculture.com) Noted Japanese culinary expert Elizabeth Andoh leads cooking courses and market tours in English that draw on her deep understanding of Japanese culture. The program is, naturally, seasonal; check the website for current offerings and sign up well in advance.

Sōgetsu Kaikan FLOWERS

(草月会館; Map p70; ☎ 3408-1209; www.sogetsu. or.jp/english/index.html; 7-2-21 Akasaka, Minato-ku; trial lesson ¥3150; 🚇 Ginza line to Aoyama-itchōme, exit 3) This avant-garde school offers classes in ikebana (flower arranging), in English. Trial lessons take place several times a month; see the website for details.

👉 Tours

Walking Tours

Many a seemingly ordinary Tokyo street conceals a fascinating story. A guide can help you uncover them, while cutting down on getting-lost time. All of the following offer tours in English.

Tokyo SGG Club GUIDED TOUR

(www2.ocn.ne.jp/~sgg) **FREE** Volunteer 'Systemized Goodwill Guides' (SGG) lead one-hour tours around Asakusa on Saturdays and Sundays at 11am and 1.15pm, leaving from the Asakusa Tourist Information Center (p140). Ninety-minute tours of Ueno leave from **Green Salon** (グリーンサロン; Map p96; 7-47 Ueno-kōen, Taitō-ku; 🚇 JR Yamanote Line to Ueno, Ueno-kōen exit) in Ueno-kōen on Wednesdays, Fridays and Sundays at 10.30am and 1.30pm. Arrive at least 10 minutes early; tours are on a first-come-first-served basis.

Mr Oka GUIDED TOUR

(www.homestead.com/mroka) Wonderful, English-speaking Mr Oka conducts tours for small, private groups and is particularly knowledgeable about the history of some of the city's older districts.

Haunted Tokyo Tours GUIDED TOUR

(www.hauntedtokyotours.com) Fun and friendly English-speaking guides take amblers to the scenes of some of the city's most notorious ghost haunts and urban legends. You'll never look at Tokyo the same way again!

Tokyo Metropolitan
Government Tours GUIDED TOUR

(www.gotokyo.org/en/tourists/guideservice/guide-service/index.html) The Tokyo government tourism bureau can arrange free or fairly cheap walking tours with volunteer guides in one of seven different languages. There are several routes to choose from, each lasting about three hours.

Institute for Japanese Cultural
Exchange & Experience CULTURAL TOUR

(www.ijcee.com/e.html) This organisation arranges tours with licensed, bilingual guides.

Many have an added cultural experience (ie visiting Tsukiji and learning how to make sushi, or strolling Asakusa in a kimono).

Bus Tours

All of the following companies offer a variety of reliable bus tours with English-speaking guides.

Hato Bus Tours BUS TOUR

(Map p70; ☎ 3435-6081; www.hatobus.com; per person ¥1500-12,000; 🚇 JR Yamanote Line to Hamamatsuchō, south exit) Tokyo's most well-known bus-tour company offers hour-long, half-day, full-day and night-time tours of the city. Shorter tours cruise by the sights in an open-air double-decker bus; longer ones make stops at major sights. Tours leave from the Hato Bus Terminal in Hamamatsuchō.

Japan Gray Line BUS TOUR

(Map p74; ☎ 5275-6511; www.jgl.co.jp/inbound/traveler/traveler.htm; half-day/full day per person from ¥4000/7900) Half-day and full-day tours with stops, covering key downtown sights. Pick-up service from major hotels is available, otherwise most tours leave from in front of the Dai-Ichi Hotel in Shimbashi.

SkyBus BUS TOUR

(Map p74; ☎ 3215-0008; www.skybus.jp; 2-5-2 Marunouchi, Chiyoda-ku; tours adult/child from ¥1500/700, Sky Hop Bus adult/child ¥1800/900; ⏰ ticket office 9am-6pm; 🚇 JR Yamanote Line to Tokyo, Marunouchi south exit) Double-decker buses cruise through different neighbourhoods of the city (for roughly 50 to 80 minutes). The Sky Hop Bus plan allows you to hop on and off buses on any of the three routes.

🎎 Festivals & Events

Tokyo has hundreds of annual festivals, with the biggest ones happening during the warmer months. Here are some of the major ones; see Go Tokyo (p141) for month by month listings.

New Year's Day CULTURAL FESTIVAL

(お正月; O-shōgatsu) Just after midnight on 31 December, Tokyoites start flocking to the city's myriad shrines and temples, and the subway runs until morning.

Hanami CHERRY BLOSSOM FESTIVAL

(花見) In late March to early April, cherry-blossom-viewing obsession takes over as locals gather in the city's parks for rare public displays of euphoria.

TOKYO FOR CHILDREN

In many ways, Tokyo is a parent's dream: hyperclean, safe and with every mod-con. The downside is that most of the top attractions aren't that appealing to little ones.

Older kids and teens, however, should get a kick out of Tokyo's pop culture and neon streetscapes. **Shibuya** and **Harajuku** in particular are packed with the shops, restaurants and arcades that local teens love.

A popular destination for local families is **Odaiba**. Here, kids can meet ASIMO the humanoid robot at the National Museum of Emerging Science & Innovation (p104) and run loose at virtual-reality arcade Tokyo Joypolis (p104).

Tokyo Disney Resort (p104) has all the classic rides and is another top draw. There's also the Ghibli Museum (p87), which honours Japan's own animation genius, Miyazaki Hayao (*Princess Mononoke, Spirited Away*). If your kids have caught the Japanese character bug, reward good behaviour with a trip to toy emporium KiddyLand (p136).

Japanese kids are wild about **trains** – chances are yours will be, too. The southern terrace at Shinjuku Station overlooks the multiple tracks that feed the world's busiest train station. Another treat is a ride on the driverless Yurikamome Line that weaves in between skyscrapers.

Need to Know

➡ Children under 12 get in for free at most city museums and gardens. Under six, they ride for free on public transportation; under-12s are charged half the adult fare.

➡ Most hotels can supply a cot, but it is near impossible to find a room that can sleep four. Ryokan with 'family rooms' can sleep four or five lined up on futons, otherwise a short-term apartment or vacation rental is the way to go.

➡ While not exactly gourmet, large chains (such as Jonathan's, Royal Host and Gusto) cater well to families with small children.

➡ Convenience stores, literally on every block, stock snacks such as ready-made sandwiches and usually have clean restrooms.

➡ Major train stations have elevators, though they might not always be immediately obvious. You do not want to try to get on a rush hour train with a pram.

➡ Department stores, shopping centres and some train station restrooms have nappy-changing facilities. See **Tokyo Urban Baby** (www.tokyourbanbaby.com) for a map of public nursing stations and other baby-friendly places.

Design Festa   ARTS FESTIVAL
(www.designfesta.com) Asia's largest art fair draws budding designers and artists to Tokyo Big Sight in Odaiba in March and November.

Sanja Matsuri   PARADE
(三社祭) The grandest of all Tokyo festivals features hundreds of *mikoshi* (portable shrines) paraded through Asakusa, starting from Asakusa-jinja (p101). On the third weekend in May.

Mitama Matsuri   LANTERN FESTIVAL
(みたままつり) Yasukuni-jinja (p89) celebrates the summer festival of the dead with 30,000 paper lanterns from the 13 to 16 July.

Sumida-gawa Fireworks   FIREWORKS
(隅田川花火大会 | Sumida-gawa Hanabi Taikai) The largest of the summer firework shows sees 20,000 pyrotechnic wonders explode over Asakusa on the last Saturday of July.

Gishi-sai   HISTORICAL FESTIVAL
(義士祭) On 14 December, a memorial service is held at Sengaku-ji (p82) to honour 47 samurai who famously avenged their master, and locals don their best medieval garb.

Emperor's Birthday   IMPERIAL FESTIVAL
(www.kunaicho.go.jp/e-event/sanga01.html) The 23 December is one of the only two days a year that the Imperial Palace (p69) is open to the public and the Imperial family makes a rare appearance; the other is 2nd January.

🛏 Sleeping

Tokyo accomodation ranges from over-the-top luxury hotels to cheap dorm rooms in converted warehouses. While boutique hotels haven't really taken off here, ryokan (traditional inns) fill the need for small-scale sleeping spaces with a personal touch. Prices are higher than elsewhere in Japan, but even backpackers can find a comfortable place to nest, especially on the east side of the city.

Wherever you decide to stay, advanced booking is highly recommended. Not only will you get a better price at most hotels, but even at hostels walk-ins can fluster staff.

Hotel rates can fluctuate wildly; compare prices for your travel dates at hotels around the city with **Japanican** (www.japanican.com), which also does online bookings.

It should be noted that some midrange and budget options do not accept credit cards – come prepared with cash.

🛏 **Marunouchi** 丸の内 (**Tokyo Station area** 東京駅)

Central and convenient for travel in and out of Tokyo, Marunouchi makes sense as a base, though rates here are among the highest in the city.

Hotel Ryumeikan Tokyo　　　　HOTEL ¥¥¥
(ホテル龍名館東京; Map p74; ☑ 3271-0971; www.ryumeikan-tokyo.jp; 1-3-22 Yaesu, Chūō-ku; s/d ¥17,000/30,000; ✆ @ 🛜; 🚈 JR Yamanote to Tokyo, Yaesu north exit) Three minutes on foot from Tokyo Station, Ryumeikan strikes the right balance between comfortable amenities, polite service and winning location. The decor is stylish and modern, with subtle Japanese touches. Bicycle and mobile phone rentals are available, too.

Tokyo Station Hotel　　　LUXURY HOTEL ¥¥¥
(東京ステーションホテル; Map p74; ☑ 5220-1112; www.tokyostationhotel.jp; 1-9-1 Marunouchi, Chiyoda-ku; d from ¥30,030; ✆ @ 🛜; 🚈 JR Yamanote Line to Tokyo, Marunouchi south exit) Part of the newly renovated Tokyo Station, this is the city's newest luxury hotel. Rooms are spacious and decorated in an opulent European fashion, with tall ceilings, marble counters and dripping chandeliers; some have views of the Imperial Palace. It's supremely located for those catching an early *shinkansen* (bullet train).

🛏 **Ginza & Tsukiji** 銀座・築地

In Ginza, you'll have excellent shopping, cafes and restaurants at your doorstep – not to mention the Imperial Palace and Tsukiji Fish Market. This, of course, comes with a price.

Hotel Villa Fontaine Shiodome　　　BUSINESS HOTEL ¥¥
(ホテルヴィラフォンテーヌ汐留; Map p74; ☑ 3569-2220; www.hvf.jp/eng; 1-9-2 Higashi-Shimbashi, Minato-ku; s/d incl breakfast from ¥14,000/16,000; ✆ @ 🛜; 🚈 Ōedo Line to Shiodome, exit 10) Stylish, if not compact, rooms, and a location that puts you within easy striking distance of Tsukiji Fish Market make this a solid choice.

Mercure Hotel Ginza Tokyo BUSINESS HOTEL ¥¥¥
(メルキュールホテル銀座; Map p74; ☑ 4335-1111; www.mercure.com; 2-9-4 Ginza, Chūō-ku; s/d from ¥17,000/21,000; ✆ @ 🛜; 🚈 Yūrakuchō Line to Ginza-itchōme, exit 11) With chinoiserie prints and sprays of orchids, this hotel has more style than other cookie-cutter options in the same price range. It's a short walk from here to Ginza's department-store-lined boulevards.

TOKYO SLEEPING

ℹ LONG-TERM RENTALS

If you're planning to stick around for a week or more, a furnished apartment or a room in a share house (aka gaijin house) might be a better deal.

Sakura House (Map p88; www.sakura-house.com; 2nd fl, 7-2-6 Nishi-Shinjuku, Shinjuku-ku; 🚈 JR Yamanote Line to Shinjuku, west exit) Manages dozens of share houses around the city. It has been around for ages and many, many expats have logged time in one of their lodgings.

Kimi Information Center (Map p70; ☑ 3986 1604; www.kimiwillbe.com; 8th fl, 2-42-3 Ikebukuro, Toshima-ku; 🚈 JR Yamanote Line to Ikebukuro, west exit) Short- and long-stay, furnished and unfurnished apartments for those on a budget, mostly on the west side of the city.

Tokyo Apartments (www.tokyoapartments.jp) Upscale furnished and serviced apartments in central locations, by the week and by the month.

🛏 Roppongi & Around
六本木

If nightlife features prominently on your agenda, Roppongi is a good place to hang your hat. Akasaka, with its embassies and multinational headquarters, is known for its luxury hotels.

B Roppongi   BUSINESS HOTEL ¥¥
(ザ・ビー六本木; Map p78; ☎5412-0451; www.theb-hotels.com/the-b-roppongi/en/index.html; 3-9-8 Roppongi, Minato-ku; s/d incl breakfast from ¥10,000/12,000; ⊜@🛜; ⊠Hibiya Line to Roppongi, exit 5) The B Roppongi has slick, white-brown rooms ranging in size from 10 to 31 sq metres. Atmosphere is business-casual and the location is perfect for Roppongi's nocturnal attractions, though light sleepers should request a quiet room. A light breakfast is included.

Villa Fontaine Roppongi   HOTEL ¥¥
(ヴィラフォンテーヌ六本木; Map p78; ☎3560-1110; www.hvf.jp; 1-6-2 Roppongi, Minato-ku; s/d ¥15,000/17,000; ⊜@🛜; ⊠Namboku Line to Roppongi-itchōme, exit 2) Stylish, modern and reasonably priced, Villa Fontaine offers 160cm-wide beds and a complimentary buffet breakfast. It's close enough to Roppongi's centre to experience its madness, but far enough away for a quiet sleep.

ANA Intercontinental Tokyo   LUXURY HOTEL ¥¥¥
(ANAインターコンチネンタルホテル東京; Map p78; ☎3505-1111; www.anaintercontinental-tokyo.jp/e; 1-12-33 Akasaka, Minato-ku; s/d from ¥26,200/36,750; ⊜@🛜⛵; ⊠Ginza Line to Tameike-sannō, exit 13) The spacious rooms here have fantastic nighttime views and a sophisticated contemporary design. There's a gym, too. Considering the location – within walking distance of Roppongi – and the prices at neighbouring establishments, it's a pretty good deal.

Hotel Ōkura   LUXURY HOTEL ¥¥¥
(ホテルオークラ東京; Map p78; ☎3582-0111; www.okura.com; 2-10-4 Toranomon, Minato-ku; s/d from ¥36,750/42,000; ⊜@🛜⛵; ⊠Ginza Line to Toranomon, exit 3) The Ōkura is equally famed for its vintage Japanese modern design (it was built in 1962) and for its long list of celebrated guests (this is where the Lennon family holed up in the 1970s). It's a sprawling property that includes a museum, a tea-house and a Japanese garden, in addition to expansive rooms.

🛏 Ebisu & Meguro
恵比寿・目黒

Not a conventional area stay but Ebisu and Meguro are both fairly central and close to scores of excellent bars and restaurants.

★Claska   BOUTIQUE HOTEL ¥¥
(クラスカ; Map p70; ☎3719-8121; www.claska.com/en/hotel; 1-3-18 Chūō-chō, Meguro-ku; s/d from ¥12,600/19,950, weekly per night s ¥7875; @; ⊠JR Yamanote Line to Meguro, west exit) The Claska is hands-down Tokyo's most stylish hotel; its handful of rooms have been done up by local designers. Some have tatami and floor cushions; others have terraces and glass-walled bathrooms. The hotel is smack in the middle of the city's interior design district, along Meguro-dōri. It's a 10-minute (about ¥1000) taxi ride from Meguro Station, 2km away. Book early.

Hotel Excellent Ebisu   BUSINESS HOTEL ¥¥
(ホテルエクセレント恵比寿; Map p80; ☎5458-0087; www.soeikikaku.co.jp/english/index.html; 1-9-5 Ebisu-nishi, Shibuya-ku; s/d from ¥9150/11,550; ⊜@; ⊠JR Yamanote Line to Ebisu, west exit) Though the rooms here are utterly ordinary, and rather small, this is a solid choice if you want to take advantage of the excellent bars and restaurants in and around Ebisu. The hotel is right in front of the train station.

Ryokan Sansuisō   RYOKAN ¥¥
(旅館山水荘; Map p70; ☎3441-7475; www.sansuiso.net; 2-9-5 Higashi-Gotanda, Shinagawa-ku; s/d from ¥5000/8600; ⊜@🛜; ⊠JR Yamanote Line to Gotanda, east exit) This small, Japanese-style inn is a little shabby, but the older couple who run it are incredibly friendly. 'Splurge' on a room with an attached bath (an extra ¥400). It's a 500m walk from here to Gotanda Station, one stop past Meguro on the Yamanote Line.

🛏 Shibuya & Around 渋谷

Staying in Shibuya puts you right in the thick of things, and the rail access is excellent. Though if you're not planning on taking advantage of the local nightlife, you might want to pick somewhere a little more peaceful.

Capsule & Sauna Century   CAPSULE HOTEL ¥
(カプセル＆サウナセンチュリー; Map p83; ☎3464-1777; 1-19-14 Dōgenzaka, Shibuya-ku; capsules from ¥3700; ⊠JR Yamanote Line to Shibuya,

Hachikō exit) This men-only capsule hotel perched atop Dōgenzaka hill was recently redone, and extras include large shared bathrooms and massage chairs. It's a clean, well-run place. Note that it fills up fast on weekends, so come claim your capsule before heading out for the night.

Hotel Fukudaya
RYOKAN ¥¥

(ホテル福田屋; Map p70; ☎ 3467-5833; www2. gol.com/users/ryokan-fukudaya/index.html; 4-5-9 Aobadai, Meguro-ku; s/d from ¥6300/10,500; ⊜@⊗; ℝ JR Yamanote Line to Shibuya, south exit) Hotel Fukudaya is pretty classy for its price, with well-tended tatami rooms both with and without private bathrooms. It's located near the upscale residential neighbourhoods of Daikanyama and Ikejiri-Ōhashi. While Shibuya is technically the closest station, it's still a 20-minute walk (or about a ¥1000 taxi ride) away.

★ Shibuya Granbell Hotel
BOUTIQUE HOTEL ¥¥¥

(渋谷グランベルホテル; Map p83; ☎ 5457-2681; www.granbellhotel.jp; 15-17 Sakuragaoka-chō, Shibuya-ku; s/d from ¥13,000/22,000; ⊜@⊗; ℝ JR Yamanote Line to Shibuya, south exit) One of the city's few boutique hotels, the Granbell is a step up from a business hotel, but priced about the same. Stylish rooms have glass-enclosed bathrooms, Simmons beds and pop-art curtains. Only a few minutes' walk from Shibuya Station, on a narrow lane, the Granbell is the best place to hole up in Shibuya. Try to book early.

Hotel Mets Shibuya
BUSINESS HOTEL ¥¥¥

(ホテルメッツ渋谷; Map p83; ☎ 3409-0011; www.hotelmets.jp/shibuya; 3-29-17 Shibuya, Shibuya-ku; s/d incl breakfast from ¥13,500/22,000, wheelchair-accessible r ¥22,000; ⊜@; ℝ JR Yamanote Line to Shibuya, new south exit) Comfortable and super convenient, the Hotel Mets is attached to Shibuya Station's quiet south exit. The premium rooms have beds with Simmons mattresses and better decor, but the regular rooms aren't shabby.

Excel Hotel Tōkyū
HOTEL ¥¥¥

(エクセルホテル東急; Map p83; ☎ 5457-0109; www.tokyuhotelsjapan.com/en/; 1-12-2 Dōgenzaka, Shibuya-ku; s/d from ¥22,500/30,000; ⊜@; ℝ JR Yamanote Line to Shibuya, Shibuya Mark City exit) This tower, connected to Shibuya Station, boasts excellent night views from the upper floors. Rooms are spacious though ordinary, but at least you're right on top of the action.

LOVE HOTELS

These hotels for amorous encounters aren't just for the sleazy: sky-high residential rents mean many young people live at home in cramped quarters until marriage. If you're travelling as a couple, a night in a *rabuho* (love hotel) can be a cheap alternative to a business hotel: an all-night 'stay' starts around ¥6000 (a three-hour daytime 'rest' goes for about ¥4000).

Dōgenzaka, aka **Love Hotel Hill**, is a stone's throw from the nightclubs of Shibuya. While patrons these days seem to favour a 'classy' look, you can still find hotels with kitschy themes evoking tropical islands and Arabian palaces.

Shinjuku & West Tokyo
新宿

As a major transportation hub on the west side of the city, Shinjuku makes for a convenient base, though it's mostly big-name hotels here.

Citadines
APARTMENT HOTEL ¥¥

(シタディーン; Map p88; ☎ 5379-7208; www.citadines.com; 1-28-13 Shinjuku, Shinjuku-ku; r from ¥13,800; ⊜@⊗; ℝ Marunouchi Line to Shinjuku-gyoenmae, exit 2) Rooms at the recently opened Citadines are bright and modern, if not compact, and include a small kitchenette. The hotel is a bit far from the Shinjuku action, though travellers staying for more than a few days will likely come to appreciate the relative quiet. Weekly rates available, too.

Kadoya Hotel
BUSINESS HOTEL ¥¥

(かどやホテル; Map p88; ☎ 3346-2561; www.kadoya-hotel.co.jp; 1-23-1 Nishi-Shinjuku, Shinjuku-ku; s/d from ¥7560/13,650; ⊜@; ℝ JR Yamanote Line to Shinjuku, west exit) A steal for its Nishi-Shinjuku address, this family-run hotel has simple, clean rooms and friendly service. The newer 'comfort' rooms have Simmons beds and better decor. Check online for packages that include breakfast, early check-in, or mobile phone rental.

★ Park Hyatt Tokyo
LUXURY HOTEL ¥¥¥

(パークハイアット東京; Map p88; ☎ 5322-1234; http://tokyo.park.hyatt.com; 3-7-1-2 Nishi-Shinjuku, Shinjuku-ku; r from ¥52,175; ⊜@⊗✉; ℝ Ōedo Line to Tochōmae, exit A4) Tokyo's most famous hotel has 177 rooms spread out over a dozen floors of a Tange Kenzō–designed skyscraper in Nishi-Shinjuku. The hotel starts from the 41st floor, meaning even the entry-level rooms have otherworldly views. The service here is gracious and above all accommodating; perks for guests include complimentary mobile phone rentals.

Hotel Century Southern Tower   HOTEL ¥¥¥

(ホテルセンチュリーサザンタワー; Map p88; ☑ 5354-0111; www.southerntower.co.jp/english; 2-2-1 Yoyogi, Shibuya-ku; s/d ¥18,480/27,720; ❷ @ 🛜; 🚇 JR Yamanote Line to Shinjuku, south exit) The location – just outside Shinjuku Station's south exit – is the big draw here. Rooms are comfortable but not splashy, with winter views of Mt Fuji possible from one side and the green space of Shinjuku-gyoen on the other. Rates may decrease for longer stays.

🏨 Iidabashi & Northwest Tokyo 飯田橋

Less touristy, the city's northwest neighbourhoods offer reasonable prices.

Kimi Ryokan   RYOKAN ¥

(貴美旅館; Map p70; ☑ 3971-3766; www.kimi-ryokan.jp; 2-36-8 Ikebukuro, Toshima-ku; s/d ¥4200/6100; ❷ 🛜; 🚇 JR Yamanote Line to Ikebukuro, west exit) Easily one of the best budget ryokan in Tokyo, this convivial inn has small, but not cramped, tatami rooms and a comfortable wood-floored lounge area where you can meet fellow travellers over green tea. The shared showers and toilets are clean and there's also a lovely Japanese cypress bath. Book in advance.

Hotel Niwa Tokyo   HOTEL ¥¥¥

(庭のホテル東京; Map p90; ☑ 3293-0028; www.hotelniwa.jp; 1-1-16 Misaki-chō, Chiyoda-ku; s/d from ¥20,790/25,410; ❷ @ 🛜; 🚇 JR Sōbu Line to Suidōbashi, east exit) This modern hotel takes its design cues from Japan's traditional aesthetic, with simple lines and natural hues. It also has a convenient central location and is easily accessible from Narita via the Tokyo Dome Hotel limousine bus stop.

🏨 Ueno 上野

If you'd like to immerse yourself in historic Tokyo, then Ueno, with its welcoming, inexpensive ryokan, is an excellent choice. A direct train connects Ueno with Narita Airport.

★ Sawanoya Ryokan   RYOKAN ¥¥

(旅館澤の屋; Map p96; ☑ 3822-2251; www.sawanoya.com; 2-3-11 Yanaka, Taitō-ku; s/d from ¥5040/10,080; ❷ 🛜 🚻; 🚇 Chiyoda Line to Nezu, exit 1) Sawanoya is a gem in quiet Yanaka, with very friendly staff and all the traditional hospitality you would expect of a ryokan – even origami cranes perched on your pillow. The shared cypress and earthenware baths are the perfect balm after a long day. The lobby overflows with information about travel options in Japan and bicycles are available for rent.

★ Hōmeikan   RYOKAN ¥¥

(鳳明館; Map p70; ☑ 3811-1181; www.homeikan.com; 5-10-5 Hongō, Bunkyō-ku; s/d from ¥6825/11,550; 🛜; 🚇 Ōedo Line to Kasuga, exit A6) Atop a slope in a quiet residential neighbourhood, this beautifully crafted wooden ryokan is an old-world oasis in the middle of Tokyo. The main Honkan wing dates from the Meiji era and is registered as an important cultural property. Rooms are tatami, with shared bathrooms. The only drawback is that it's a little out of the way.

Annex Katsutarō Ryokan   RYOKAN ¥¥

(アネックス勝太郎旅館; Map p96; ☑ 3828-2500; www.katsutaro.com; 3-8-4 Yanaka, Taitō-ku; s/d ¥6300/10,500; ❷ @ 🛜; 🚇 Chiyoda Line to Sendagi, exit 2) More like a modern hotel than a traditional ryokan, the family-run Annex Katsutarō has spotless, thoughtfully arranged tatami rooms with attached bathrooms. Though a bit of a walk from the sights in Ueno, it's ideal for exploring the old Yanaka district.

Ryokan Katsutarō   RYOKAN ¥¥

(旅館勝太郎; Map p96; ☑ 3821-9808; www.katsutaro.com; 4-16-8 Ike-no-hata, Taitō-ku; s/d ¥5200/8400; ❷ @ 🛜; 🚇 Chiyoda Line to Nezu, exit 2) The original Ryokan Katsutarō has a quiet and family-like atmosphere, with very affable managers. Though the building may be aged, the eight tatami rooms here have been renovated without ruining the inn's character. Bicycle rental available.

TokHouse   APARTMENT ¥¥

(Map p70; www.tokhouse.com; 3-52-9 Sendagi, Bunkyō-ku; s/d/q from ¥8000/10,000/12,000; ❷ 🛜; 🚇 JR Yamanote Line to Nishi-Nippori, west exit) For the price of a room in a crammed business hotel you'll get your very own apartment in the heart of Shitamachi. Amenities are basic, but the apartments are clean and include a kitchen. Richard, the

American owner, has been living in Tokyo for nearly two decades and has lots of tips for exploring the area.

Asakusa & Sumida-gawa 浅草·隅田川

While not central, Asakusa has an attractive, unpretentious, traditional atmosphere and the city's best hostels.

★Nui HOSTEL ¥
(ヌイ; Map p70; ☑ 6240-9854; http://backpackersjapan.co.jp/nui_en; 2-14-13 Kuramae, Taitō-ku; dm/d from ¥2700/6500; ☻@☎; ⓡ Ōedo Line to Kuramae, exit A7) In a former warehouse, this brand-new hostel raises the bar for stylish budget digs in Tokyo. High ceilings means bunks you can comfortably sit up in and there's an enormous kitchen and workspace. Best of all is the ground floor bar and lounge, with its glass front, grand piano and furniture handmade from salvaged timber.

Khaosan Tokyo Kabuki HOSTEL ¥
(Map p100; ☑ 5830-3673; www.khaosan-tokyo.com/en/kabuki; 1-17-2 Asakusa, Taitō-ku; dm/d from ¥3000/7800; ☻@☎; ⓡ Ginza Line to Asakusa, exit 3) This is the nicest of Khaosan's mini-empire of quirky hostels. It's a short walk from the sights in Asakusa. All rooms have en suite bathrooms and there's a cozy lounge done up like a traditional Japanese living room. Staff speak English.

K's House Tokyo Oasis HOSTEL ¥¥
(ケイズハウス東京オアシス; Map p100; ☑ 3844-4447; http://kshouse.jp/tokyo-oasis-e/index.html; 2-14-10 Asakusa, Taitō-ku; dm/d/tr from ¥2900/8800/11,700; ☻@☎; ⓡ Tsukuba Express to Asakusa, exit A1) Just a few minutes from Sensō-ji, this is a clean, modern hostel with heaps of resources for travellers and friendly, English-speaking staff. The nicer dorm rooms and all the private rooms have en suite bathrooms.

Sukeroku No Yado Sadachiyo RYOKAN ¥¥¥
(助六の宿貞千代; Map p100; ☑ 3842-6431; www.sadachiyo.co.jp; 2-20-1 Asakusa, Taitō-ku; s/d from ¥14,000/19,000; @☎; ⓡ Ginza Line to Asakusa, exit 1) This traditional ryokan virtually transports its guests to old Edo. The well-maintained tatami rooms are spacious for two people, and all come with modern, Western-style bathrooms. Splurge on an exquisite meal here, and make time for the *o-furo* (tradi-tional Japanese baths), one made of fragrant Japanese cypress and the other of black granite. Look for the rickshaw parked outside.

✕ Eating

When it comes to Tokyo superlatives, the city's eating scene takes the cake. There are more restaurants in this pulsing megalopolis than in any other city in the world. Tokyo's victual vocabulary extends far beyond fish and noodles: the cosmopolitan city boasts some of the best international cuisine on the planet. And the quality is unparalleled, too – you're rarely more than 500m from a good, if not great, restaurant.

Best of all, you can eat well on any budget in pretty much every neighbourhood. Lunch is usually excellent value, with many pricier restaurants offering cheaper courses during the noontime hours. Reservations are neces-sary only at upmarket restaurants, though they're a good idea at midrange places (es-pecially on Friday and Saturday evenings) if you have a party larger than two.

If you want to dig deeper, **Tabelog** (http://tabelog.com) is Japan's most popular word-of-mouth dining website, with thousands of entries arranged by cuisine and location. And remember – the local critics are harsh.

LOCAL KNOWLEDGE

THE WAY OF RĀMEN

Chef Ivan Orkin of **Ivan's Rāmen** (www.ivanramen.com; 3-24-7 Minami-Karasuyama, Setagaya-ku; ⏱ 11.30am-2pm & 6pm-11pm Mon-Fri, 11.30am-9.30pm Sat & Sun, closed Wed & 4th Tue; ⊡; ⓡ Keio Line to Rokakōen) filled us in on the art of noodle slurping and his favourite shops.

How to Eat It
Rāmen is like a brick-oven pizza – if you let it sit for a few minutes it becomes something different. So you need to start slurping right away, even if it burns a little. Keep slurping, make noise and don't chew.

Where to Eat It
Nagi (p116) is one of my favourites. The one in Golden Gai is a great place to go after drinking. I also like Kikanbō (p117) in Kanda. It's sort of new wave. It serves very serious, delicious spicy miso *rāmen*.

✖ **Marunouchi** 丸の内
(**Tokyo Station area** 東京駅)

Marunouchi is experiencing a dining renaissance along with its redevelopment. The 5th floor of the Shin-Marunouchi Building (p68) has dozens of restaurants and is popular with the young, after-work crowd. Nearby **Marunouchi Brick Square** (丸の内ブリックスクエア; Map p74; www.marunouchi.com/brick; 2-6-1 Marunouchi, Chiyoda-ku; ⏰11am-11pm; 🚇Chiyoda Line to Nijūbashimae, exit 1) has several upscale alfresco options.

There are also plenty of places to eat within Tokyo Station.

Tokyo Rāmen Street　　　　　RĀMEN ¥

(東京ラーメンストリート; Map p74; www.tokyoeki-1bangai.co.jp/ramenstreet; basement fl, Tokyo Station; rāmen from ¥750; ⏰7.30am-10.30pm; 🚇JR Yamanote Line to Tokyo Station, Yaesu south exit) Eight of Japan's famous *rāmen-ya* (*rāmen* shops) operate minibranches out of a corner of Tokyo Station (in the basement on the Yaesu side). All of the major styles are covered, from *shōyu* (soy sauce base) to *tsukemen* (noodles served on the side). Good luck picking just one!

Ishii　　　　　　　　　　KUSHIYAKI ¥

(い志井; Map p74; 5th fl, Shin-Marunouchi Bldg, 1-5-1 Marunouchi, Chiyoda-ku; skewers from ¥140; ⏰11am-2pm & 4pm-2am Mon-Sat, 11am-10pm Sun; 🈺; 🚇JR Yamanote Line to Tokyo, Marunouchi north exit) *Yakiton* (grilled pork skewers) – rather than the more common *yakitori* (grilled chicken skewers) – is the specialty here. Trendy Ishii is done up like a retro, post-WWII food stand and is notorious for using all of the pig (and we mean *all* of it). Look for the lanterns.

Meal MUJI　　　　　　　　　DELI ¥

(Map p74; www.muji.net/cafemeal/; 3-8-3 Marunouchi, Chiyoda-ku; meals from ¥780; ⏰10am-9pm; 🈺🍴; 🚇JR Yamanote Line to Yūrakuchō, Kyōbashi exit) On the 2nd floor of the Yūrakuchō MUJI shop, this deli follows the brand's 'simpler is better' mantra with fresh, natural fare. First claim your seat than head to the counter and point to your picks from the variety of hot and cold dishes.

✖ **Ginza & Tsukiji** 銀座

Sushi breakfast at Tsukiji is a classic Tokyo experience. In the evening, the day's catch is sliced up by expert hands in Ginza's sushi restaurants, which are among the most highly regarded in the world. But budget diners needn't fear Ginza; look instead to the inexpensive **yakitori stands** (Map p74; skewers from ¥120; ⏰5pm-11pm) crammed under the JR tracks around Yūrakuchō Station.

Ginza Bairin　　　　　　　TONKATSU ¥

(銀座梅林; Map p74; www.ginzabairin.com; 7-8-1 Ginza, Chūō-ku; meals from ¥980; ⏰11.30am-8.45pm; 🈺🍴; 🚇Ginza Line to Ginza, exit A2) Cheap and cheerful *tonkatsu* (deep-fried pork cutlet) is the name of the game at this salaryman favourite in the heart of Ginza, in business since 1927. Look for the plastic food models in the window.

Robata Honten　　　　　　　IZAKAYA ¥

(爐端本店; Map p74; ☎3591-1905; 1-3-8 Yūrakuchō, Chiyoda-ku; dishes ¥1000-1500; ⏰5-11pm Mon-Sat; 🚇Ginza Line to Hibiya, exit A4) Alongside the train tracks and inside an old wooden building blackened by the years, this *izakaya* (pub-eatery) has enough ambience that it needn't worry about the food. Fortunately, it does: filling, home-style dishes, a mix of Japanese and Western, are served family-style, piled high in bowls along the counter – just point to what you want.

★ **Daiwa Sushi**　　　　　　SUSHI ¥¥

(大和寿司; Map p74; ☎3547-6807; Bldg 6, 5-2-1 Tsukiji, Chūō-ku; sushi set ¥3500; ⏰5am-1.30pm Mon-Sat, closed occasional Wed; 🈺; 🚇Ōedo Line to Tsukijishijō, exit A2) This is one of Tsukiji's most famous sushi counters and waits of over an hour are commonplace. Trust us, it's worth it. The standard set is a solid bet and includes *chū-toro* (medium-grade tuna) and *uni* (sea urchin roe); there's a picture menu, too. Though the staff may be too polite to say so, you're expected to eat and run.

★ **Sushi Kanesaka**　　　　SUSHI ¥¥¥

(鮨かねさか; Map p74; ☎5568-4411; www.sushi-kanesaka.com; basement fl, 8-10-3 Ginza, Chūō-ku; lunch/dinner course from ¥5000/20,000; ⏰11.30am-1pm & 5-10pm Mon-Fri, to 9pm Sat & Sun; 🈺; 🚇JR Yamanote Line to Shimbashi, Ginza exit) Tucked away below street level, this sushi superstar is the workshop of the eponymous master chef who slices through premium pieces of fresh fish with a surgeon's precision. If you're contemplating a sushi splurge during your time in Tokyo, this is the place to do it. But book ahead – there are only 20 seats. A small square lantern marks the entrance.

> **DEPARTMENT-STORE FOODHALLS**
>
> *Depachika* (デパ地下; department-store basements) house food halls with a staggering array of tempting edibles, both sweet and savoury. Everything is of the highest quality and gorgeously packaged for presentation as gifts.
>
> Treat yourself to museum-quality cakes, flower-shaped *wagashi* (Japanese-style sweets) or a *bentō* (boxed meal) that almost looks too good to eat. After 5pm the prices of some items, such as sushi sets, are slashed – a boon for those looking for a cheap, tasty dinner to go. This is also the place to pick-up souvenirs such as green tea and rice crackers.
>
> Two *depachika* to try are Isetan (p137) in Shinjuku and Mitsukoshi (p133) in Ginza.

✖ Roppongi & Around
六本木

It's only logical that there's an abundance of international options in Tokyo's capital of *gaijin*-dom, and you can find everything from a classic eggs benedict brunch to late-night kebab stands here.

Roppongi, a playground for those with expense accounts, is also known for high-end dining and ambitious concept restaurants.

The basement of Tokyo Midtown (p76) has dozens of reasonably-priced options as well as takeaway counters – perfect for a picnic lunch in the garden out back.

Chinese Cafe 8   CHINESE ¥
(中国茶房8; Map p78; www.chinesecafe8.com; 2nd fl, 3-2-13 Nishi-Azabu, Minato-ku; dishes from ¥780; ⊙24hr; ✆⊚; ℝHibiya Line to Roppongi, exit 3) This all-night eatery is a Roppongi landmark, famous for its cheeky decor, Peking duck, and abrupt service (in that order). There's a neon English sign out front.

Tokyo Curry Lab   CURRY ¥
(東京カレーラボ; Map p78; 2nd fl, Tokyo Tower, 4-2-8 Shiba-kōen, Minato-ku; meals ¥1000-1350; ⊙11am-10pm; ⊚; ℝHibiya Line to Kamiyachō, exit 1) Under Tokyo Tower, this space-station-like restaurant specialises in the curiously addicting Japanese dish *kare-raisu* (curry-rice). There are personal TVs at each bar stool and hilariously illustrated placemats (you'll see).

Gonpachi   IZAKAYA ¥
(権八; Map p78; ☎5771-0170; www.gonpachi.jp/nishiazabu; 1-13-11 Nishi-Azabu, Minato-ku; skewers ¥180-1500, lunch sets weekday/weekend from ¥800/2050; ⊙11.30am-3.30am; ⊜⊚; ℝHibiya Line to Roppongi, exit 1) Gonpachi is a Tokyo institution, serving charcoal-grilled skewers plus tempura, noodles etc. Cavernous by local standards, it looks like an Edo-era night market on the inside and a feudal villa on the outside. If it looks vaguely familiar, that's because the restaurant inspired the set for one of the epic fight scenes in the movie *Kill Bill*.

Jōmon   IZAKAYA ¥¥
(ジョウモン; Map p78; ☎3405-2585; www.teyan-dei.com; 5-9-17 Roppongi, Minato-ku; skewers ¥150-1600; ⊙6pm-5am; ⊚; ℝHibiya Line to Roppongi, exit 3) Slide open the wooden door to enter a cosy kitchen with bar seating and rows of ornate *shochū* (liquor) jugs lining the wall. Skewers of grilled meat and vegetables are the specialty here, from straight up divine (top grade beef) to ingeniously delicious (bacon-wrapped quail eggs). The restaurant is almost directly across from the Family Mart; book ahead on weekends.

★Tofuya-Ukai   KAISEKI ¥¥¥
(とうふ屋うかい; Map p78; ☎3436-1028; www.ukai.co.jp; 4-4-13 Shiba-kōen, Minato-ku; lunch/dinner courses from ¥5500/8400; ⊙11am-10pm; ✆⊚; ℝToei Ōedo Line to Akabanebashi, exit 8) One of the city's most impressive restaurants, Tofuya-Ukai has only private rooms, all of which overlook a beautiful, manicured garden. The *kaiseki* (Japanese haute cuisine) courses feature delicate, handmade tofu served a variety of ways, but may also include sashimi and grilled fish; considering the spread, it's excellent value. Inquire when booking about vegetarian meals; reserve well in advance.

✖ Ebisu & Meguro
恵比寿・目黒

Ebisu is one of the best places in the city for eating out: there are scores of unpretentious restaurants that serve just plain good food. There are some creative, stylish places too, especially as you move further out to Daikanyama and Naka-meguro.

★ **Tonki**   TONKATSU ¥

(とんき; Map p70; 1-2-1 Shimo-Meguro, Meguro-ku; meals ¥1800; ☺ 4-11pm Wed-Mon, closed 3rd Mon of month; ☺ ⓘ; ⓡ JR Yamanote Line to Meguro, west exit) There are only two things on the menu here – *rosu-katsu* (fatty loin cutlet) and *hire-katsu* (lean fillet cutlet) – but Tonki's loyal customers never tire of it. Sit at the counter to watch the perfectly choreographed chefs breading, frying and garnishing the tender cutlets. Look for a white sign and *noren* (doorway curtains) across the sliding doors.

From Meguro Station, walk down Meguro-dōri and take the first left in front of the Pachinko parlour.

Afuri   RĀMEN ¥

(あふり; Map p80; 1-1-7 Ebisu, Shibuya-ku; noodles from ¥750; ☺ 11am-5am; ☺ ⓘ; ⓡ JR Yamanote Line to Ebisu, east exit) Hardly your typical, surly *rāmen-ya*, Afuri has upbeat young cooks and a hip industrial interior. The unorthodox menu might draw eye-rolls from purists, but house specialties such as *yuzu-shio* (a light, salty broth flavoured with *yuzu* – a type of citrus – peel) draw lines at lunchtime.

Chano-ma   JAPANESE ¥

(チャノマ; Map p80; 1-22-4 Kami-Meguro, Meguro-ku; lunch set & mains from ¥880; ☺ noon-2am Sun-Thu, to 4am Fri & Sat; ☒ ⓘ; ⓡ Hibiya Line to Naka-Meguro) By day, Chano-ma is a laid-back cafe with a popular 'deli lunch' special of healthy Japanese food. By night, it's a chilled-out lounge where you can sip cocktails by candlelight on a row of raised mattresses. It's in an impossibly narrow building across the street from Naka-Meguro Station.

Ganko Dako   STREET FOOD ¥

(頑固蛸; Map p70; 3-11-6 Meguro, Meguro-ku; takoyaki ¥500; ☺ 11am-1am; ⓡ JR Yamanote Line to Meguro, west exit) This street stall dishes out steaming hot *tako-yaki* (grilled octopus dumplings), topped with everything from kimchi to Worcestershire sauce. It's located, unfortunately, across from the Meguro Parasitological Museum (p81); nonetheless, Ganko Dako draws them in – check out the celebrity signings on the wall.

Ippo   IZAKAYA ¥

(一歩; Map p80; ☏ 3445-8418; 2nd fl, 1-22-10 Ebisu, Shibuya-ku; mains ¥800-1500; ☺ 6pm-3am; ⓡ JR Yamanote Line to Ebisu, east exit) This mellow joint specialises in simple pleasures: fish and sake (there's an English sign out front

that says just that). There's only a counter and a few small tables, so groups should call ahead; staff speak English. Follow the wooden stairs under the sage ball.

Ebisu-Yokochō   STREET FOOD ¥

(恵比寿横町; Map p80; www.ebisu-yokocho.com; 1-7-4 Ebisu, Shibuya-ku; dishes ¥500-1500; ☺ 5pm-late; ⓡ JR Yamanote Line to Ebisu, east exit) This retro arcade, marked by colourful signs, is lined with counters dishing up everything from grilled scallops to *yaki soba* (fried buckwheat noodles). Even if you don't stop to eat it's worth strolling through. If you do eat here, be warned that, this being Ebisu, the food is not as cheap as the decor might suggest.

★ **Higashi-Yama**   JAPANESE ¥¥

(ヒガシヤマ; Map p70; ☏ 5720-1300; www.higashiyama-tokyo.jp; 1-21-25 Higashiyama, Meguro-ku; lunch/dinner course from ¥2100/4000; ☺ 11.30am-2pm & 6pm-1am Mon-Sat; ☺; ⓡ Hibiya Line to Naka-Meguro) Chic, starkly minamalist, and all but completely hidden, Higashi-Yama serves set courses of seasonal, all-natural, modern Japanese cuisine on gorgeous crockery. The basement lounge – an even better-kept secret – is perfect for an after-dinner drink. From Naka-Meguro Station, walk 10 minutes down Yamate-dōri towards Shibuya, turning left in front of the Family Mart; Hagashi-Yama will be on your left. Reservations recommended.

✕ Shibuya & Around 渋谷

Shibuya is choc-a-block with fast-food joints and cheap *izakaya* catering to the youthful crowd who hang out here. Shibuya Hikarie (p84) has some more sophisticated, yet still reasonably priced, restaurants on the 6th and 7th floors that stay open until 4am Friday and Saturday nights, and a basement (level 3) foodcourt with good takeaway options.

For more eccentric eateries hop on the train and head to Shimo-Kitazawa.

d47 Shokudō   SHOKUDŌ ¥

(d47食堂; Map p83; www.hikarie8.com/d47shoku-do/about.shtml; 6th fl, Shibuya Hikarie, 2-21-1 Shibuya, Shibuya-ku; meals ¥950-1680; ☺ 11am-11pm; ☺; ⓡ JR Line to Shibuya, east exit) There are 47 prefectures in Japan and d47 serves a changing line-up of *teishoku* (set meals) with the specialties of each. Only the prefecture names are on the menu in English, so you'll have to take a chance on wherever strikes your fancy. Counter seats offer a bird's eye view of the trains coming and going at Shibuya Station.

Nabezō
SHABU-SHABU ¥

(鍋ぞう; Map p83; www.nabe-zo.com; 6th fl, Beam Bldg, 31-2 Udagawa-chō, Shibuya-ku; meals from ¥1980; ☺ 11.30am-3pm & 5-11pm Mon-Fri, 11.30am-11pm Sat & Sun; ⊠; ⓡ Yamanote Line to Shibuya, Hachikō exit) Here's one for when you're really hungry: diners get a bubbling tabletop pot of broth and 90 minutes to dunk as much beef or pork as they like into it. Though it's a chain, Nabezō gets points for including a veggie bar with plenty of greens and mushrooms. The restaurant is inside the silver and concrete Beam Building.

Angelica
BAKERY ¥

(アンゼリカ; Map p70; 2-19-15 Kitazawa, Setagaya-ku; miso-pan ¥140; ☺ 10am until sold out; ⓡ Keiō Inokashira Line to Shimo-Kitazawa) This tiny Shimo-Kitazawa bakery is famous for its *miso-pan*, a fluffy bun spiked with just a hint of miso. Look for the green awning on the main road leading down from the south exit of the train station.

Viron
BAKERY ¥

(Map p83; ☎ 5458-1770; 33-8 Udagawachō, Shibuya-ku; sandwiches ¥525-1050; ☺ 9am-10pm; ⓡ JR Yamanote Line to Shibuya, Hachikō exit) A fantastic French bakery (it apparently imports the flour from the motherland), Viron serves up sandwiches and quiches to take away.

Shirube
IZAKAYA ¥

(汁べゑ; Map p70; ☎ 3413-3785; 2-18-2 Kitazawa, Setagaya-ku; dishes ¥580-880; ☺ 5.30pm-midnight Mon-Thu & Sun, to 2am Fri & Sat; ☎⊠; ⓡ Keiō Inokashira Line to Shimo-Kitazawa, south exit) This lively *izakaya* serves a mix of classic dishes and inventive fusion ones around an open kitchen. Don't miss the *aburi saba* (blow torch grilled mackerel). Heading down the hill from the train station, make a right in front of Mr Donuts and look for the white *noren* (doorway curtains) on your right. Reservations recommended on weekends.

Kaikaya
SEAFOOD ¥¥

(開花屋; Map p83; ☎ 3770-0878; www.kaikaya.com; 23-7 Maruyama-chō, Shibuya-ku; lunch from ¥780, dishes ¥680-2500; ☺ 11.30am-3pm, 5.30-11.30pm Mon-Fri, 5.30-11.30pm Sat & Sun; ☎⊠; ⓡ Yamanote Line to Shibuya, Hachikō exit) 🖉 The chef here is a self-professed ocean lover and Kaikaiya is his attempt to bring the beach to Shibuya. Everything on the menu is caught in nearby Sagami

Bay. It's a boisterous, popular place; reservations are recommended. From Dōgenzaka, turn right after the police box and the restaurant, with a red awning, will be on your right.

Sushi-no-Midori
SUSHI ¥¥

(寿司の美登利; Map p83; 4th fl, Mark City, 1-12-3 Dōgenzaka, Shibuya-ku; sets from ¥2100; ☺ 11am-10pm Mon-Fri, to 9pm Sat & Sun; ☎⊠; ⓡ JR Yamanote Line to Shibuya, Hachikō exit) Sushi-no-midori, famed for being excellent value, almost always has a line. Don't let the wait put you off; service is quick and the generous sushi sets are worth it. Look for the signs to the Mark City complex inside Shibuya Station, near the Inokashira Line.

✖ **Harajuku** 原宿

Sticky sweet crepes are the official food of Takeshita-dōri. Elsewhere you'll find plenty of fashionable restaurants and cafes.

★ Harajuku Gyōza Rō
GYŌZA ¥

(原宿餃子楼; Map p85; 6-4-2 Jingūmae, Shibuya-ku; 6 gyōza ¥290; ☺ 11.30am-4.30am; ⊠; ⓡ JR Yamanote Line to Harajuku, Omote-sandō exit) *Gyōza* (dumplings) are the only thing on the menu here, but you won't hear any complaints from the regulars who queue up to get their fix. Have them *sui* (boiled) or *yaki* (pan-fried), with or without *niniku* (garlic) or *nira* (chives) – they're all delicious. Expect to wait on weekends.

Maisen
TONKATSU ¥

(まい泉; Map p85; http://mai-sen.com; 4-8-5 Jingūmae, Shibuya-ku; lunch/dinner from ¥995/1680; ☺ 11am-10pm; ☎⊠; ⓡ Ginza Line to Omote-sandō, exit A2) You could order something else, but pretty much everyone is here for the famous *tonkatsu* (breaded, deep-fried pork cutlets). Price is determined by grade of meat: you can splurge on the prized *kurobuta* (black pig), but even the cheapest is melt-in-your-mouth divine. The restaurant is housed in an old public bathhouse. A takeaway window serves delicious *tonkatsu sando* (sandwich).

A to Z Cafe
CAFE ¥

(Map p85; http://atozcafe.exblog.jp; 5th fl, 5-8-3 Minami-Aoyama, Minato-ku; mains ¥500-1500; ☺ noon-11.30pm; ⊠; ⓡ Ginza Line to Omote-sandō, exit B3) Artist Yoshitomo Nara teamed up with design firm Graf to create this spacious and only slightly off-kilter cafe. Along with wooden schoolhouse chairs, whitewashed walls and a small cottage, you can find a few scattered examples of Nara's work. The Japanese-style diner food – think fried chicken with *yuzu* (citrus) sauce – is delicious, too.

Marukaku ⠀⠀⠀⠀⠀⠀⠀⠀⠀⠀JAPANESE ¥

(丸角; Map p85; 4th fl, Gyre Bldg, 5-10-1 Jingūmae, Shibuya-ku; lunch set ¥900, small dishes ¥380-700; ⏱11.30am-11pm; 😊🍴; 🚇JR Yamanote Line to Harajuku, Omote-sandō exit) The lunchtime *sakana teishoku* (fish set meal) here has a loyal following; it's fresh, filling and a steal – especially considering the location on top of Chanel. Options change daily, depending on what's in season. The dinner menu expands to include sashimi, small dishes and skewers of grilled meat and vegetables. Look for the white *noren* (curtains).

⭐Agaru Sagaru Nishi Iru Higashi Iru ⠀⠀⠀⠀⠀⠀⠀⠀KAISEKI ¥¥

(上ル下ル西入ル東入ル; Map p85; 📞3403-6968; www.agarusagaru.com; Basement fl, 3-25-8 Jingūmae, Shibuya-ku; course ¥3990; ⏱5.30-10pm Mon-Sat; 🚇JR Yamanote Line to Harajuku, Takeshita exit) The young, unpretentious chefs here serve up artful dishes that are Kyoto-inspired but tweaked for Tokyoites' been-there-done-that tastes. Also, the restaurant looks like a cave – even from the street. There's only a counter and a few tables, so call ahead on weekends. Sitting at the counter is more fun.

Mominoki House ⠀⠀⠀⠀⠀⠀⠀⠀⠀⠀ORGANIC ¥¥

(もみの木ハウス; Map p85; http://omotesando.mominokihouse.net; 2-18-5 Jingūmae, Shibuya-ku; lunch/dinner set from ¥800/3200; ⏱11.30am-10pm; 😊🖋🍴; 🚇JR Yamanote Line to Harajuku, Takeshita exit) 🍃 Boho Tokyoites have been coming here for tasty and nourishing macrobiotic fare since 1976. The casual, cosy dining room has seen some famous visitors too, like Paul McCartney. Chef Yamada's menu is heavily vegetarian, but also includes free-range chicken and *Ezo shika* (Hokkaidō venison; ¥4800).

🍴 Shinjuku & West Tokyo
新宿

Shinjuku has an overwhelming number of restaurants in all styles and budgets. If you want to narrow down your choices – or grab a quick bite without having to brave the crowds – head to one of the *resutoran-gai* (restaurant 'towns') found on the top floor of most department stores; both **Lumine** (ルミネ; Map p88; ⏱11am-11pm) and **Mylord** (ミロード; Map p88; ⏱11am-11pm), inside Shinjuku Station near the south exit, have reasonably-priced options.

One stop north of Shinjuku on the Yamanote Line, **Shin-Ōkubo** is Tokyo's Little Seoul, home to many authentic Korean restaurants.

⭐Nagi ⠀⠀⠀⠀⠀⠀⠀⠀⠀⠀⠀⠀⠀⠀RĀMEN ¥

(凪; Map p88; www.n-nagi.com; 2nd fl, Golden Gai G2, 1-1-10 Kabukichō, Shinjuku-ku; rāmen from ¥750; ⏱11:30am-3pm & 6pm-5am Mon-Sat, to 2am Sun; 🚇JR Yamanote Line to Shinjuku, east exit) The excellent noodles at this tiny Golden Gai joint, up a treacherous flight of stairs, are served in a dark broth deeply flavoured with *niboshi* (dried sardines). There is almost always a wait; first purchase your order from the vending machine inside, then claim your spot at the end of the line. Look for the sign with a red circle.

Nakajima ⠀⠀⠀⠀⠀⠀⠀⠀⠀⠀⠀⠀⠀KAISEKI ¥

(中嶋; Map p88; 📞3356-7962; www.shinjyuku-nakajima.com; Basement fl, 3-32-5 Shinjuku, Shinjuku-ku; lunch/dinner from ¥800/8400; ⏱11.30am-2pm & 5.30-10pm Mon-Sat; 😊; 🚇Marunouchi Line to Shinjuku-sanchōme, exit A1) In the evening, this Michelin-starred restaurant serves exquisite *kaiseki* dinners. On weekdays it does a set lunch of humble *iwashi* (sardines) for one-tenth the price. In the hands of Nakajima's chefs they're divine; get yours sashimi or *yanagawa nabe* (stewed with egg). The line for lunch starts to form shortly before the restaurant opens. Reservations are necessary for dinner.

A tiny sign marks the stairs leading down to the restaurant, which has white door curtains out front.

Omoide-yokochō   YAKITORI ¥
(思い出横丁; Map p88; Nishi-Shinjuku 1-chōme, Shinjuku-ku; skewers from ¥100; ⏱ noon-midnight, hours vary by shop; 🚇 JR Yamanote Line to Shinjuku, west exit) Since the postwar days, smoke has been billowing night and day from the *yakitori* stalls that line this alley by the train tracks, literally translated as 'Memory Lane' (and less politely known as Shonben-yokochō, or 'Piss Alley'). A few stalls have English menus.

Pepa Cafe Forest   THAI ¥
(ペパカフェフォレスト; www.peppermintcafe. com/forest/index.html; 4-1-5 Inokashira, Mitaka-shi; mains from ¥1000; ⏱ noon-10pm; ⏱ 📶; 🚇 JR Chūō Line to Kichijōji, Kōen exit) This funky terrace cafe sits inside Inokashira-kōen and serves authentic Thai food, plus coffee and sweets. It's across the pond, if you're coming through the park from Kichijōji Station.

Tsunahachi   TEMPURA ¥¥
(つな八; Map p88; www.tunahachi.co.jp; 3-31-8 Shinjuku, Shinjuku-ku; sets ¥1995-3990; ⏱ 11am-10pm; ⏱ 📶; 🚇 JR Yamanote Line to Shinjuku, east exit) Tsunahachi has been expertly frying prawns and seasonal vegetables for nearly 90 years. The sets are served in courses so each dish comes piping hot. Sit at the counter for the added pleasure of watching the chefs at work. Indigo *noren* (curtains) mark the entrance.

🍴 Iidabashi & Northwest Tokyo 飯田橋

Kagurazaka is famous for having the highest concentration of French restaurants of anywhere outside of France. Tokyo Dome City has dozens of restaurants, mostly of the fast-food variety. The eastern side of Ikebukuro Station is crammed with cheap options, including *rāmen* shops and *kaiten-sushi* (conveyer belt sushi) restaurants.

Le Bretagne   FRENCH ¥
(ル ブルターニュ; Map p90; www.le-bretagne. com/e/top.html; 4-2 Kagurazaka, Shinjuku-ku; crêpes ¥950-1680; ⏱ 11.30am-11.30pm Tue-Sat, 11.30am-9pm Sun; 📶 📶; 🚇 JR Sōbu Line to Iida-bashi, west exit) This French-owned cafe, hidden on a cobblestone lane in Kagurazaka, is credited with starting the Japanese rage for crêpes. Savoury buckwheat *galettes* are made with ham and cheese imported from France and farm fresh vegetables; the sweet ones – with the likes of caramelised butter, apple compote and ice cream – are divine.

Namco Namjatown   ECCLECTIC ¥
(ナムコ・ナンジャタウン; Map p70; 2nd fl, Sunshine City, 3-1-3 Higashi-Ikebukuro, Toshima-ku; adult/child ¥300/200; ⏱ 10am-10pm; 🚸; 🚇 JR Yamanote Line to Ikebukuro, exit 35) Tokyo's original 'food themepark' has attractions such as 'Ice Cream City' and 'Gyōza Stadium' – each with dozens of vendors in a setting that looks lifted from a cartoon. Admission only gets you in; you'll have to pay extra for the treats you want to sample.

Canal Café   ITALIAN ¥¥
(カナルカフェ; Map p90; 📞 3260-8068; 1-9 Kagurazaka, Shinjuku-ku; lunch set from ¥1600; dinner mains ¥1500-2800; ⏱ 11.30am-11pm Tue-Sat, to 9.30pm Sun; 📶 📶; 🚇 JR Sōbu Line to Iidabashi, west exit) Along the languid moat that forms the edge of Kitanomaru-kōen, this is one of Tokyo's best alfresco dining spots. The restaurant serves tasty wood-fired pizzas, seafood pastas and grilled meats, while over on the 'deck side' you can settle in with a sandwich, muffin or just a cup of coffee.

🍴 Akihabara & Around 秋葉原

Akihabara and nearby Jimbōchō are good places to sample *b-kyū gurume* (b-grade gourmet), a term used to describe comfort food done well. Think *tonkatsu*, *rāmen* and all those other stick-to-your-ribs dishes that defy Japanese food's generally healthy image.

Kikanbō   RĀMEN ¥
(鬼金棒; Map p90; http://karashibi.com; 2-10-8 Kaji-chō, Chiyoda-ku; rāmen from ¥780; ⏱ 11am-9.30pm Mon-Sat, to 4pm Sun; 🚇 JR Yamanote Line to Kanda, north exit) The '*karashibi*' (カ ラシビ) spicy miso *rāmen* here has a cult following. You can choose the level of *kara* (spice) and *shibi* (strange mouth-numbing sensation created by Japanese *sanshō* pepper). We recommend *futsū-futsū* (regular for both) for first-timers; *oni* (devil) level costs an extra ¥100. Look for the red door curtains and purchase your order from the vending machine.

Marugo

TONKATSU ¥

(丸五; Map p90; ☎ 3255-6595; 1-8-14 Soto-Kanda, Chiyoda-ku; meals from ¥1400; ⏰ 11.30am-3pm & 5-8.20pm; 🚻; ⓡ JR Yamanote Line to Akihabara, Electric Town exit) Dine among a cast of regulars who tuck into their meals of slow-cooked pork and chicken cutlets side-by-side at the bar on the ground level, or amid old clocks upstairs. Look for the brown door curtains.

✖ Ueno 上野

Ueno has some wonderful traditional restaurants. In and around the Ameya-yokochō shopping street there are dozens of places for a quick bite.

Yanaka Ginza

STREET FOOD ¥

(谷中銀座; Map p96; snacks from ¥60; ⓡ JR Yamanote Line to Nippori, north exit) Yanaka Ginza's cluttered cluster of street stalls feels more like a bustling village thoroughfare than a Tokyo street. Amblers will be treated to a variety of cheap eats from *yakitori* skewers to crunchy croquettes. Hunker down on a milk carton with the locals and wash it all down with a beer.

★ Hantei

JAPANESE ¥¥

(はん亭; Map p96; ☎ 3828-1440; www.hantei. co.jp/nedu.html; 2-12-15 Nezu, Bunkyō-ku; lunch/dinner course from ¥3150/2835; ⏰ noon-3pm & 5-10pm Tue-Sun; ⓡ Chiyoda Line to Nezu, exit 2) Housed in a beautifully maintained, nearly 100-year-old traditional wooden building, Hantei is a local landmark. Delectable skewers of seasonal *kushiage* (fried meat, fish and vegetables) are served with small, refreshing side dishes. Lunch courses include eight sticks and dinner courses start with six, after which you'll continue to receive additional rounds (¥210 per skewer) until you say stop

Sasa-no-Yuki

TOFU ¥¥

(笹乃雪; Map p96; ☎ 3873-1145; 2-15-10 Negishi, Taitō-ku; dishes ¥350-1000, set meals ¥2600-4500; ⏰ 11.30am-8pm Tue-Sun; 🖋🚻; ⓡ JR Yamanote Line to Uguisudani, north exit) 🌿 Sasa-no-Yuki opened its doors in the Edo period, and continues to serve its signature dishes, with tofu made fresh every morning with water from the shop's own well. The best seats overlook a tiny garden with a koi pond. Vegetarians should not assume every thing is purely veggie – ask before ordering. There is bamboo and a bench out front.

Nagomi

YAKITORI ¥¥

(和味; Map p96; ☎ 3821-5972; 3-11-11 Yanaka, Taitō-ku; skewers from ¥180; ⏰ 5pm-midnight; 🚻; ⓡ JR Yamanote Line to Nippori, north exit) On Yanaka Ginza, Nagomi deals in juicy skewers of *jidori* (free range chicken). There are plenty of grilled veggie options, too. Wash it all down with a bowl of chicken soup *rāmen*. Look for the sake bottles in the window.

✖ Asakusa & Sumida-gawa 浅草・隅田川

Down-home, unpretentious fare is an Asakusa speciality. Don't miss the snack vendors on Nakamise-dōri, dishing out traditional treats such as *mochi* (sticky-rice cakes) stuffed with sweet bean paste.

Daikokuya

TEMPURA ¥

(大黒家; Map p100; 1-38-10 Asakusa, Taitō-ku; meals ¥1500-2050; ⏰ 11am-8.30pm Mon-Fri, to 9pm Sat; 🚻; ⓡ Ginza Line to Asakusa, exit 6) Near Nakamise-dōri, this is the place to get old-fashioned tempura fried in pure sesame oil, an Asakusa specialty. It's in a white building with a tile roof. If there's a queue (and there often is), you can try your luck at the annexe one block over.

Rokurinsha

RĀMEN ¥

(六厘舎; Map p100; www.rokurinsha.com; 6th fl, Solamachi, 1-1-2 Oshiage, Sumida-ku; rāmen from ¥850; ⏰ 11am-11pm; ⓡ Hanzōmon Line to Oshiage, Sky Tree exit) Rokurinsha's speciailty is *tsukemen – rāmen* noodles served on the side with a bowl of concentrated soup for dipping. The noodles here are thick and perfectly al dente, the soup is a rich *tonkotsu* (pork bone) base topped with pork, hard-boiled egg and bamboo shoots. It's an addicting combination.

Hana no Mai

JAPANESE ¥

(花の舞; Map p70; 1-3-20 Yokoami, Sumida-ku; chanko-nabe ¥980-2980; ⏰ 11.30am-2pm & 4pm-midnight; 🚻; ⓡ JR Sōbu Line to Ryōgoku, west exit) If you're curious about a sumō wrestler's diet, you can sample *chanko-nabe*, a protein-rich hotpot that is a key part of wrestlers' weight-gain strategy, along with sushi and other typical Japanese dishes. Hana no Mai is just to the right outside the west exit of JR Ryōgoku Station, in the old station building.

Namiki Yabu Soba

SOBA ¥

(並木藪蕎麦; Map p100; ☎ 3841-1340; 2-11-9 Kaminarimon, Taitō-ku; noodles ¥700-1800; ⏰ 11am-

7.30pm Fri-Wed; 😊 📷 ; 🚇 Ginza Line to Asakusa, exit 2) Delicate, hand-made noodles draw locals and tourists alike to this timeless, classy *soba* shop, in business since 1913. Seating is on tatami mats or at communal tables. There's a raised white vertical sign out front.

Irokawa UNAGI ¥¥

(色川; Map p100; 📞 3844-1187; 2-6-11 Kaminari-mon, Taitō-ku; sets from ¥2500; 🕙 11.30am-1.30pm & 5-8.30pm Mon-Sat; 😊 📷 ; 🚇 Ginza Line to Asakusa, exit 2) This tiny restaurant has a real old Edo flavour and is one of the best, unpretentious *unagi* (eel) restaurants in town. The menu is simple: a 'small' gets you two slices of charcoal-grilled eel over rice, a 'large' gets you three. The chef grills everything right behind the counter. Look for the light green building.

🍴 Odaiba & Tokyo Bay
お台場・東京湾

All of Odaiba's giant malls have restaurant floors. The **Odaiba Takoyaki Museum** (お台場たこ焼きミュージアム; Map p103; 4th fl, Decks Tokyo, 1-6-1 Daiba, Minato-ku; six takoyaki ¥350 ; 🕙 11am-9pm; 🚇 Yurikamome Line to Odaiba Kaihin-kōen) has a half-dozen different venders serving up different styles of *tako-yaki* (grilled octopus dumplings).

Gonpachi IZAKAYA ¥

(権八; Map p103; 📞 3599-4807; 4th fl, Aqua City, 1-7-1 Daiba, Minato-ku; dishes ¥250-1350, lunch set ¥800-1050; 🕙 11am-3am; 📷 ; 🚇 Yurikamome Line to Daiba, south exit) This branch of the famous Nishi-Azabu restaurant serves tasty *soba* sets at lunch and charcoal-grilled skewers, tempura and salads in the evening. The traditional interior is a nice break from concrete Odaiba.

Bills INTERNATIONAL ¥

(ビルズ; Map p103; 3rd fl, Decks Tokyo, 1-6-1 Daiba, Minato-ku; mains from ¥1300; 🕙 9am-11pm; 😊 📷 👶 ; 🚇 Yurikamome Line to Odaiba Kaihin-kōen) This Odaiba outpost from Australian chef Bill Granger is an inviting, spacious place with bay views from the terrace. The menu includes breakfast classics such as ricotta hotcakes and lunch and dinner mains such as *wagyū* burgers.

TY Harbor Brewery AMERICAN ¥¥

(Map p70; 📞 5479-4555; www.tyharborbrewing.co.jp; 2-1-3 Higashi-Shinagawa, Shinagawa-ku; lunch set ¥1200-1700, dinner mains from ¥1700; 🕙 11.30am-2pm & 5.30-10pm; 📷 ; 🚇 Rinkai Line to Tennōzu Isle, exit B) In a former warehouse on the waterfront, TY Harbor serves up excellent burgers, steaks and crab cakes with views of the canals around Tennōzu Isle. It also brews its own beer on the premises – a rare feat in central Tokyo. Weekend brunch here is an expat institution; call ahead to book a seat on the terrace.

🍷 Drinking & Nightlife

Tokyo's nightlife is undoubtably one of the city's highlights. Whatever stereotypes you may have held about Japanese people being quiet and reserved will fall to pieces after dark. Tokyo is a 'work hard, play hard' kind of place and you'll find people out any night of the week.

There is truly something for everyone here, from sky-high lounges to grungy holes-in-the-wall. In the last few years, the craft beer scene has exploded. Another trend is *tachinomi-ya* ('standing bars') – small, lively joints where patrons crowd around the bar.

Tokyo has a healthy club scene, centred mostly on Shibuya and Roppongi. Check out **Clubberia** (www.clubberia.com) and **iFlyer** (www.iflyer.tv) to find out what's going on when you're in town. Most of the big clubs have discount flyers that can be printed or downloaded from their websites. Be prepared to show photo ID at the door.

🍺 Marunouchi 丸の内 (Tokyo Station area 東京駅)

The 7th floor of the Shin-Marunouchi Building (p68) is filled with late-night bars and restaurants; it's the liveliest place in Marunouchi after dark.

Bar Oak BAR

(バーオーク; Map p74; 2nd fl, Tokyo Station Hotel, 1-9-1 Marunouchi, Chiyoda-ku; 🕙 5pm-midnight; 🚇 JR Yamanote Line to Tokyo, Marunouchi south exit) The Tokyo Station Hotel's bar is the perfect place to linger over a martini (¥1100) before or after catching the *shinkansen*. Though with its dark wood panelling, jazz piano soundtrack and black-tie bartenders it's easy to forget that something as modern as the *shinkansen* exists.

So Tired BAR

(Map p74; www.heads-west.com/shop/so-tired.html; 7th fl, Shin-Marunouchi Bldg, 1-5-1 Marunouchi, Chiyoda-ku; 🕙 11am-4am Mon-Sat, 11am-11pm Sun; 🚇 JR Yamanote Line to Tokyo, Marunouchi north

KARAOKE: WAY MORE FUN THAN IT SOUNDS

Of course no discussion of Tokyo nightlife would be complete without mentioning the national past-time that is karaoke (カラオケ). You'll find branches of major chains such as **Big Echo** (ビッグエコー; Map p83; http://big-echo.jp; 24-10 Udagawa-chō, Shibuya-ku; per 30min before/after 7pm ¥225/380, ¥480 after 7pm Fri & Sat; ⏰ 1pm-5am Mon-Thu, to 6am Fri & Sat; ⓡ JR Yamanote Line to Shibuya, Hachikō exit) and **Karaoke-kan** (カラオケ館; Map p83; www.karaokekan.jp; 25-6 Udagawa-chō, Shibuya-ku; per 30min before/after 6pm Mon-Thu ¥53/520, Fri-Sun ¥160/640; ⏰ 11am-6am; ⓡ JR Yamanote Line to Shibuya, Hachikō exit) in Shibuya, and also around major train stations. Most offer a sizeable selection of songs in English. It's often cheaper to go for a meal plan – though we make no promises about the food. Tack on a *nomihōdai* (飲み放題; all-you-can-drink) option and let your inner diva shine.

These favourites are a cut above the typical yodelling parlour:

Festa Iikura (フェスタ飯倉; Map p78; ☎ 5570-1500; www.festa-iikura.com; 3-5-7 Azabudai, Minato-ku; 3hr room & meal plan from ¥3000; ⏰ 5pm-5am Mon-Sat; ⓡ Hibiya Line to Kamiyachō, exit 2) Serves the best karaoke food in town. Classy sushi dinner courses include three hours of karaoke, and there's a rack of costumes to play with free of charge.

Lovenet (ラブネット; Map p78; www.lovenet-jp.com; 7-14-4 Roppongi, 3rd fl, Hotel Ibis, Minato-ku; suites per hr ¥2400-25,000; ⏰ 6pm-5am; ⓡ Hibiya Line to Roppongi, exit 4A) Looks like what you'd get if a karaoke parlour mated with a love hotel. The most outrageous of its themed rooms is the Aqua Suite, complete with a large Jacuzzi.

Pasela (パセラ; Map p88; www.pasela.co.jp/shop/shinjuku; 1-3-16 Kabuki-chō, Shinjuku-ku; per 30min before/after 6pm ¥200/400, Fri & Sat after 6pm ¥480; ⏰ 3pm-8am Mon-Fri, noon-8.30am Sat & Sun; ⓡ JR Yamanote Line to Shinjuku, east exit) Boasts more songs than anywhere else and this Shinjuku outpost has a curious facade meant to evoke a Southeast Asian resort.

Shidax Village (シダックスビレッジ; ☎ 3461-9356; http://yoyaku.sdx.co.jp/pc/shopinfo_64030.html; 1-12-13 Jinnan, Shibuya-ku; per 30min Mon-Thu ¥540, Fri-Sun ¥590, 3hr room & meal plan from ¥2500; ⏰ 11am-5am; ⓡ JR Yamanote Line to Shibuya, Hachikō exit) Outshines all the other karaoke joints in Shibuya with comparatively spacious rooms.

exit) The best thing about this bar, popular with 20- and 30-somethings is that you can buy a drink at the counter and take it out to the terrace. The views aren't sky-high, instead you feel curiously suspended among the office towers.

🍷 Ginza & Tsukiji
銀座・築地

Ginza is where people dress to the nines to go out and splurge, though not every bar here charges a premium. Towards Shimbashi, there are many salaryman joints, where workday warriors go to let off steam.

Aux Amis Des Vins WINE BAR
(オザミデヴァン; Map p74; 2-5-6 Ginza, Chūō-ku; ⏰ 5.30pm-2am Mon-Fri, noon-midnight Sat; ⓡ Yūrakuchō Line to Ginza-itchōme, exits 5 & 8) Even when it rains, the plastic tarp comes down over the small terrace and good wine is drunk alleyside. The enclosed upstairs seating area is warm and informal, and you can order snacks or full *prix-fixe* dinners. A solid selection of wine, mostly French, comes by the glass (from ¥800) or by the bottle.

Ginza Lion BEER HALL
(銀座ライオン; Map p74; www.ginzalion.jp; 7-9-20 Ginza, Chūō-ku; ⏰ 11.30am-11pm; ⓡ Ginza Line to Ginza, exit A4) An institution, the Lion was one of Japan's first beer halls when Yebisu rose to popularity during the early Meiji period. This fantastically kitsch incarnation dates to 1934. Come for the atmosphere – skip the food.

🍺 Roppongi & Around
六本木

Exiting the subway station at Roppongi Crossing at night can feel like entering the world of *Bladerunner* or *Star Wars,* where throngs of the galaxy's most unscrupulous citizens gather to engage in a host of unsavoury activities under the sizzling neon lights. Club music thumps, and the streets are filled with catcalls and other shady offers.

Here, *gaijin* (foreigners) and locals mix it up and boozily schmooze until the first trains at dawn. There are loads of shot bars and cheap dives for getting wasted, but also plenty of spots that offer style as well as stiff drinks.

★**SuperDeluxe** LOUNGE

(スーパー・デラックス; Map p78; www.super-deluxe.com; Basement fl, 3-1-25 Nishi-Azabu, Minato-ku; admission varies; ☒Hibiya Line to Roppongi, exit 1B) This basement bunker morphs from lounge to gallery to club to performance space from night to night; check the website for event details. Whatever is happening, you're guaranteed to run into an interesting mix of creative types from Tokyo and beyond. It's in an otherwise unremarkable building; look for the tiny sign and the staircase leading down.

★**Pink Cow** BAR

(ピンクカウ; Map p78; www.thepinkcow.com; Basement fl, Roi Bldg, 5-5-1 Roppongi, Minato-ku; ☉5pm-late Tue-Sun; ☒Hibiya Line to Roppongi, exit 3) The Pink Cow is a funky, friendly place to hang out, with excellent California-style food and yummy, reasonably-priced wines by the glass. It's a hub for the artsy expat community – with events such as indie film screenings, writers' salons and Burlesque nights – and a good bet if you're in the mood to mix with a creative crowd.

Muse CLUB

(ミューズ; Map p78; www.muse-web.com; B1 fl, 4-1-1 Nishi-Azabu, Minato-ku; admission women/ men incl 2 drinks free/¥3000; ☒Hibiya Line to Roppongi, exit 3) Muse is a catacomb-like underground space that looks like something out of a Tim Burton film. There's something for everyone here: two dance floors playing house and hip-hop, plenty of sofas and a billiard table. Muse draws a mix of locals and foreigners and really picks up after midnight. The cover charge is usually less on weekday nights; ID required.

Mado Lounge LOUNGE

(マドラウンジ; Map p78; www.ma-do.jp; 52nd fl, Mori Tower, Roppongi Hills, 6-10-1 Roppongi, Minato-ku; ☒Hibiya Line to Roppongi, exit 1c) On the 52nd floor of Mori Tower, the views are stunning from the floor-to-ceiling windows of this swank, dimly-lit lounge. You have to pay admission to the Mori Art Museum and/ or Tokyo City View to take the elevator this high, so it makes sense to visit after hitting the museum.

Eleven CLUB

(イレブン; Map p78; www.go-to-eleven.com; Basement fl, 1-10-11 Nishi-Azabu, Minato-ku; admission ¥3000-4000; ☒Hibiya Line to Roppongi, exit 2) The reincarnation of notorious party box 'Yellow', Eleven is as hot, and as stylish, as ever. Dive down to the lower basement and dance the night away to electro, dub and house music.

Geronimo BAR

(ジェロニモ; Map p78; ☎3478-7449; www.geronimoshotbar.com; 2nd fl, 7-14-10 Roppongi, Minato-ku; ☉6pm-6am Mon-Fri, from 7pm Sat & Sun; ☒Hibiya Line to Roppongi, exit 4) Love it or hate it, this shot bar at Roppongi Crossing is a neighbourhood institution. If someone bangs the drum (and it happens more often than you'd think) they buy a round of shots for the whole bar – which means if you get lucky you can drink here all night for very little.

🍺 Ebisu & Meguro
恵比寿・目黒

Ebisu is known for its lively *tachinomi-ya* (standing bars), Naka-Meguro for its riverside cafes and hard-to-find lounges.

★**Buri** BAR

(ぶり; Map p80; www.buri-group.com; 1-14-1 Ebisu-nishi, Shibuya-ku; ☉5pm-3am; ☒JR Yamanote Line to Ebisu, west exit) The name means 'super' in Hiroshima dialect and the lively crowd that packs in on weekends certainly seems to agree. Generous quantities of sake (over 50 varieties; ¥750) are served semifrozen in colourful jars. Although there are some stools around the horseshoe-shaped counter, Buri is a *tachinomi-ya* (standing bar) at heart.

DON'T MISS

SUMMER BEER GARDENS

From June through mid-September, Tokyo department stores transform their rooftops into beer gardens, and knocking back frosty mugs under the stars is a time-honoured Tokyo tradition. **Keiō** (京王; Map p88; http://info.keionet.com/shinjuku/index.html; 1-1-4 Nishi-Shinjuku, Shinjuku-ku; ☒JR Yamanote Line to Shinjuku, west exit) in Shinjuku and **Matsuzakaya** (松坂屋; Map p74; www.matsuzakaya.co.jp; 6-10-1 Ginza, Chūō-ku; ☒Ginza Line to Ginza, exit A3) in Ginza are two long-time favourites.

Kinfolk Lounge
LOUNGE

(キンフォーク; Map p80; http://wegotways. com/kinfolk; 2nd fl, 1-11-1 Kami-Meguro, Meguro-ku; ◎6pm-midnight; 🚇Hibiya Line to Naka-Meguro) Sip mojitos under wooden rafters in this dim, moody lounge run by custom bicycle makers Kinfolk. From Naka-Meguro Station, cross Yamate-dōri and the river, then take the first left. It's a few minutes' walk on the left, up a rickety metal staircase above a cafe.

What the Dickens!
PUB

(ワット・ザ・ディッキンズ; Map p80; whatthedickens.jp; 4th fl, 1-13-3 Ebisu-nishi, Shibuya-ku; ◎5pm-late Tue-Sat, to midnight Sun; 🚇JR Yamanote Line to Ebisu, west exit) This British pub is a long-time favourite of both Japanese locals and down-to-earth expats. The beer and pub grub are well up to scratch and local bands play nightly. It has an unlikely location inside a building that looks like adobe decorated with a mosaic of a hummingbird.

🍷 Shibuya & Around 渋谷

Shibuya is Tokyo's most musically inclined neighbourhood: some of the best clubs are here, along with live-music houses and bars where the soundtrack *is* the atmosphere. There are lots of bars here in general; most, but not all, are cheap joints catering to 20-somethings. **Nonbei-yokochō** (のんべえ横丁; Map p83), northeast of Shibuya Station near the JR tracks, is a gaggle of cramped bars each seating but a handful of people.

Bohemian Shimo-Kitazawa has some fun, funky places, too.

★ Womb
CLUB

(ウーム; Map p83; www.womb.co.jp; 2-16 Maruyama-chō, Shibuya-ku; admission varies; ◎11pm-late; 🚇JR Yamanote Line to Shibuya, Hachikō exit) Womb's state-of-the art sound system, enormous mirror ball and frenetic

---

laser lighting go perfectly with the house and techno music played here. Though it draws more diehard music fans than scene chasers, Womb's four floors still get jammed at weekends. Photo ID is required.

Beat Cafe
BAR

(Map p83; 3rd fl, 33-13 Udagawa-chō, Shibuya-ku; ◎7pm-5am; 🚇JR Yamanote line to Shibuya, Hachikō exit) It's all about the music at this shabby bar on Center Gai, run by an indie music promoter. Join an eclectic mix of local and international regulars who swig beers (¥650) and chat beats under the watchful eyes of taxidermic elk. Sister club **Echo** downstairs has a small dancefloor and a groovy yardsale decor.

Sound Museum Vision
CLUB

(Map p83; www.vision-tokyo.com; Basement fl, 2-10-7 Dōgenzaka, Shibuya-ku; ◎admission ¥3000-4000; 🚇JR Yamanote line to Shibuya, Hachikō exit) One of Tokyo's newer clubs, Sound Museum Vision is a cavernous space with four dance floors. With a sleek modern interior and not so much of a cruisy vibe, Vision is downright classy for this side of Shibuya. A solid line-up of international DJs plays mostly house and techno. Bring ID.

Mother
BAR

(マザー; Map p70; www.rock-mother.com/index. html; 5-36-14 Kitazawa, Setagaya-ku; ◎6pm-2am; 🚇Keiō Inokashira Line to Shimo-Kitazawa) Mother is classic Shimo-Kitazawa, with a funky decor (it looks like a tiled cave) and a soundtrack straight out of the '60s and '70s. But this is no dive: the food and drink here are plenty tasty. With McDonalds on your left, head down the hill until the road widens, hang a right and look for the wooden door.

Ruby Room
CLUB

(ルビールーム; Map p83; www.rubyroomtokyo. com; 2nd fl, 2-25-17 Dōgenzaka, Shibuya-ku; admission incl 1 drink ¥1500; ◎8pm-late; 🚇JR Yamanote Line to Shibuya, Hachikō exit) This tiny, sparkly gem of a club hosts both DJ and live-music events. It's an appealing spot for older kids hanging out in Shibuya. Tuesday is open mic night (free entry with two-drink minimum); if you're musically-inclined, you're welcome to join the stage.

Flower Bar Gardena
BAR

(Map p70; 📞6638-8714; flkawashima@yahoo.co.jp; 2-34-6 Kitazawa, Setagaya-ku; ◎5pm-midnight Wed, Fri & Sat; 🚇Keiō Inokashira Line to Shimo-Kitazawa, north exit) A flower shop by day, Gar-

---

TEA CEREMONIES

A few of Tokyo's most prestigious hotels have tea rooms where ceremonies are performed in English. These include the Hotel Ōkura (p108) and the **Imperial Hotel** (帝国ホテル; Map p74; 📞3504-1111; www.imperialhotel.co.jp; 1-1-1 Uchisaiwaichō, Chiyoda-ku; 🚇Hibiya Line to Hibiya, exit A13). Call ahead to reserve; fees are usually ¥1000 to ¥1500 per person.

TOKYO'S COFFEE SHOP CULTURE

Japan may, historically, be a land of tea, but since coffee shops were introduced at the turn of the last century Tokyo has never looked back. Sample the city's vast and varied cafe scene at these favourites.

Cafe de l'Ambre (カフェ・ド・ランブル; Map p74; www.h6.dion.ne.jp/~lambre; 8-10-15 Ginza, Chūō-ku; coffee from ¥650; ⊙noon-10pm Mon-Sat, to 7pm Sun; 🚇Ginza Line to Ginza, exit A4) The sign over the door here reads 'Coffee Only' but, oh, what a selection! In business since 1948, l'Ambre specialises in aged beans from all over the world, which the owner still roasts himself.

Omotesando Koffee (Map p85; http://ooo-koffee.com; 4-15-3 Jingūmae, Shibuya-ku; espresso ¥250; ⊙10am-7pm; 🚇Ginza Line to Omotesandō, exit A2) Tokyo's most *oshare* (stylish) coffee stand is a minimalist cube set up inside a half-century-old traditional house. Be prepared to circle the block trying to find it, but know that an immaculate macchiato and a seat in the garden await you.

Coffee Maldive (コーヒーモルティブ; Map p70; 2-14-7 Kitazawa, Setagaya-ku; ⊙10am-9pm; 🚇Keiō Inokashira Line to Shimo-Kitazawa, south exit) Stop by this Shimo-Kitazawa landmark, featured in Yoshimoto Banana's novel *Moshi Moshi Shimo-Kitazawa*, for an iced cafe au lait laced with cubes of coffee-flavoured jelly.

Kayaba Coffee (カヤバ珈琲; Map p96; http://kayaba-coffee.com; 6-1-29 Yanaka, Taitō-ku; drinks from ¥400; ⊙8am-11pm Mon-Sat, to 6pm Sun; 🚇Chiyoda Line to Nezu, exit 1) This vintage 1930s coffee shop in Yanaka is a hangout for local students and artists, morphing into a bar in the evenings.

Meikyoku Kissa Lion (名曲喫茶ライオン; Map p83; http://lion.main.jp; 2-19-13 Dōgenzaka, Shibuya-ku; coffee ¥500; ⊙11am-10.30pm; 🚇JR Yamanote Line to Shibuya, Hachikō exit) Think theme cafes are a recent thing? Lion, which opened in 1926, is a classical music cafe where patrons come to listen to what was then the latest recordings. Whispering only, here.

Nekomachi Cafe 29 (猫町カフェ２９; Map p96; http://nyancafe29.blog.fc2.com; 2-1-22 Yanaka, Taitō-ku; coffee ¥500; ⊙noon-7pm Wed-Sun; 🚇Chiyoda Line to Nezu, exit 1) Cat cafes are the newest trend, but while some feel like petting zoos, this is more like a cosy cafe that just happens to be inhabited by five silky-furred beauties.

dena invites customers to linger after hours at a small counter literally awash with cut flowers. Smells heavenly and the house wine is delish, too. Happy hour from 5pm to 7pm. It's a green building.

🍸 Harajuku 原宿

Harajuku has a handful of hidden gems, but feels pretty quiet after the shops close. Scoot down to Aoyama to hang out with the fashion crowd.

Two Rooms   BAR
(トゥールームス; Map p85; ☎3498-0002; www.tworooms.jp; 5th fl, AO Bldg, 3-11-7 Kita-Aoyama, Minato-ku; ⊙11.30am-2am Mon-Sat, to 10pm Sun; 🚇Ginza Line to Omote-sandō, exit B2) With its sleek contemporary design, this restaurant and bar, popular with expats, could be anywhere – save for the sweeping view towards the Shinjuku skyline from the terrace. Expect a crowd dressed like they don't care that wine by the glass starts at ¥1400. You can eat here too, but the real scene is at night by the bar.

Harajuku Taproom   PUB
(原宿タップルーム; Map p85; http://baird-beer.com/en/taproom; 2nd fl, 1-20-13 Jingūmae, Shibuya-ku; ⊙5pm-midnight Mon-Fri, noon-midnight Sat & Sun; 🚇JR Yamanote Line to Harajuku, Takeshita exit) Come here to sample more than a dozen different beers on tap from respected local craft brewer Baird's Brewery. Heading down Takeshita-dōri, take a left after Cafe Solare and the bar will be at the end of the lane on the right.

Le Baron   CLUB
(Map p85; www.lebaron.jp; 3-8-40 Minami-Aoyama, Minato-ku; admission ¥3000-4000; ⊙Wed-Sun; 🚇Ginza Line to Omotesandō, exit A4) A swank import from Paris, Le Baron is Tokyo's new *it* venue for the partying jet set. It's at the end of an alley, right before the Poplar convenience store.

歌舞伎町一番街

FRANK DEIM / GETTY IMAGES ©

1. Shinjuku nightlife (p128)
Shinjuku's Kabukichō area is full of cabarets, love hotels, bars and clubs.

2. Tokyo Sky Tree (p101)
Rising 643m, Tokyo Sky Tree is the world's tallest free-standing communication tower and offers spectacular views over Tokyo.

3. Sensō-ji (p99)
Enshrined in this Buddhist temple is a golden image of Kannon, goddess of mercy, which is said to have been kept on this spot since AD 628..

1. Imperial Palace (p69)

The Imperial Palace was built on the site of the Tokugawa shōgunate's castle. All that remains of the original castle are the moat and walls.

2. Prada building (p135)

This shop, shaped like a convex glass fishbowl, is the work of Herzog & de Meuron.

3. Mt Fuji (p147)

An iconic Japanese image, Mt Fuji is currently under consideration for listing as a World Heritage Site.

🍷 Shinjuku & West Tokyo
新宿

The main drag on the east side of Shinjuku Station, Yasukuni-dōri, is wall-to-wall *izakaya*. The most ambient watering holes can be found further down in **Golden Gai** (ゴールデン街; Map p88; 🚇 JR Yamanote Line to Shinjuku, east exit), a cluster of eccentric, closet-sized bars in what was originally a post-WWII black market. It's known to be a haunt for writers and artists. Though most establishments are likely to give tourists a cool reception, there are a few friendly places. Cover charges (of ¥500 and up) are standard at bars in Golden Gai.

Kabukichō is Tokyo's most notorious red-light district, full of cabarets, hostess (and host) clubs, love hotels and fetish bars. It's generally safe to stroll through, though not wise not to go alone. Note that if you follow a tout to a bar or club here you will likely end up with a hefty bill.

★ **Zoetrope** BAR
(ゾートロープ; Map p88; http://homepage2.nifty.com/zoetrope; 3rd fl, 7-10-14 Nishi-Shinjuku, Shinjuku-ku; ⏰ 7pm-4am Mon-Sat; 🚇 JR Yamanote Line to Shinjuku, west exit) Behind the small counter here are more than 300 varieties of Japanese whisky – more than you'll find anywhere else in the world. If you tell the barman what you like, he'll help you narrow down some choices from the daunting menu. Meanwhile silent films are screened on the wall.

Araku BAR
(亜楽; Map p88; www.arakubar.com; 2nd fl, G2-dōri, 1-1-9 Kabukichō, Shinjuku-ku; cover charge ¥500; ⏰ 8pm-5am Mon-Sat; 🚇 JR Yamanote Line to Shinjuku, east exit) If you're looking for a welcoming place to hole up in Golden Gai, this bar is a good option. It has a sofa, Australian wines by the glass and a groovy atmosphere. Look for the steps carpeted with red shag.

GAY & LESBIAN TOKYO

Tokyo's gay and lesbian enclave is **Shinjuku-nichōme** ('Ni-chōme'). There are hundreds of establishments crammed into a few blocks, including bars, dance clubs, saunas and love hotels. Unfortunately, not all welcome foreigners, so it's best to ask around before getting the cold shoulder at the door. **Utopia Asia** (www.utopia-asia.com) has a good list of friendly places (including a small map of Ni-chōme), though some listings are out of date.

Outside of the neighbourhood, parties take place at larger venues. Don't miss the carnivalesque **Shangri-La** (www.ageha.com/gn/ja/events/index.html), held roughly every other month at Odaiba super club Ageha (p130), if you're in town. The **Tokyo Rainbow Pride** (http://tokyorainbowpride.com/en/parade) parade is held in April and the **Tokyo International Lesbian & Gay Film Festival** (www.tokyo-lgff.org) usually hits screens in mid-July.

Other venues to check out include the following:

Advocates Cafe (アドボケイツカフェ; Map p88; http://advocates-cafe.com; 2-18-1 Shinjuku, Shinjuku-ku; ⏰ 6pm-4am, to 1am Sun; 🚇 Marunouchi Line to Shinjuku-sanchōme, exit C8) Many a night out in Ni-chōme starts 'on the corner' at this tiny bar that spills out onto the street. Anyone and everyone is welcome.

Arty Farty (アーティファーティ; Map p88; www.arty-farty.net; 2nd fl, 2-11-7 Shinjuku, Shinjuku-ku; ⏰ 7pm-3am Mon-Thu, to 5am Fri & Sat, 5pm-3am Sun; 🚇 Marunouchi Line to Shinjuku-sanchōme, exit C8) A welcoming spot open to men and women, Arty Farty has been a gateway to the community for many a moon. There's a small dance floor here that gets packed on weekends.

Bar Goldfinger (Map p88; http://goldfingerparty.com/bar/top; 2-12-11 Shinjuku, Shinjuku-ku; ⏰ 6pm-2am Sun, Mon, Wed & Thu, to 4am Fri & Sat; 🚇 Marunouchi Line to Shinjuku-sanchōme, exit C8) The most popular of the few ladies-only joints in Ni-chōme also hosts Tokyo's hottest lesbian party, **Goldfinger** (www.goldfingerparty.com). Men are welcome here on Fridays.

Cocolo Cafe (ココロカフェ; Map p88; 2-14-6 Shinjuku, Shinjuku-ku; ⏰ 11am-5am Mon-Thu, to 7am Fri, 3pm-7am Sat, 3pm-4am Sun; 🚇 Marunouchi Line to Shinjuku-sanchōme, exit C8) This neighbourhood hub is a good place to browse flyers for upcoming events.

MISSING THE MIDNIGHT TRAIN

Cinderellas who've stayed out partying past midnight and found that their last train has turned into a *kabocha* (pumpkin) needn't fret. If dancing the night away doesn't appeal, and an astronomically priced taxi ride doesn't compute, try a **manga kissa** instead. These 'comic book coffee shops' have private cubicles for reading, watching DVDs, catching up on email and, more often than not, sleeping.

Overnight packages – as low as ¥1500 for up to eight hours – are a bargain. Check in at the reception desk, prepay for your stay and while away the wee hours; some even have shower stalls and will rent you a blanket and a hair dryer.

Aprecio (アプレシオ; Map p83; www.aprecio.co.jp; 5th fl Beam Bldg, 31-2 Udagawa-chō, Shibuya-ku; ⌚24hr; @; ⓡJR Yamanote Line to Shibuya, Hachikō exit) and **Gran Cyber Cafe Bagus** (グランサイバーカフェバグース; Map p78; ☎5786-2280; www.gcc-bagus.jp; 12th fl, Roi Bldg, 5-5-1 Roppongi, Minato-ku; ⌚24hr; ⊖@; ⓡHibiya Line to Roppongi, exit 3) are two of the nicer chains with convenient branches in Shibuya and Roppongi, respectively.

New York Bar
BAR

(ニューヨークバー; Map p88; ☎5323-3458; http://tokyo.park.hyatt.com; 52nd fl, Park Hyatt, 3-7-1-2 Nishi-Shinjuku, Shinjuku-ku; ⌚5pm-midnight Sun-Wed, to 1am Thu-Sat; ⓡŌedo Line to Tochōmae, exit A4) You may not be lodging at the Park Hyatt, but you can still ascend to the 52nd floor to swoon over the sweeping nightscape. Live music plays nightly at this bar famed for its appearance in the movie *Lost in Translation*. There's a cover charge of ¥2200 after 8pm (7pm Sunday) and a dress code (no shorts or sandals).

Champion
BAR

(チャンピオン; Map p88; G2-dōri, 1-1-10 Kabukichō, Shinjuku-ku; ⌚6pm-5am; ⓡJR Yamanote Line to Shinjuku, east exit) At the entrance to Golden Gai, Champion isn't exactly representative of the district, but it's fun just the same. There's no cover charge, drinks are just ¥500 a pop and the karaoke is loud.

Asakusa & Sumida-gawa 浅草・隅田川

A century ago, this was one of the most debauched corners of the city, though it's a lot more sedate now. Still, it's possible to find pockets of nostalgia.

★ Popeye
PUB

(ポパイ; Map p70; www.40beersontap.com; 2-18-7 Ryōgoku, Sumida-ku; ⌚5-11pm Mon-Sat; ⓡJR Sōbu Line to Ryōgoku, west exit) Popeye boasts the largest selection of Japanese beer in the world. The excellent happy-hour deal (5pm to 8pm) includes free half-plates of pizza, sausages and other munchables. From Ryōgoku Station's west exit, take a left on the main road and pass under the tracks; take the second left and look for Popeye on the right.

Kamiya Bar
BAR

(神谷バー; Map p100; www.kamiya-bar.com; 1-1-1 Asakusa, Taitō-ku; ⌚11.30am-10pm Wed-Mon; ⓡGinza Line to Asakusa, exit 3) One of Tokyo's oldest Western-style bars, Kamiya opened in 1880 and is still hugely popular – though probably more so today for its enormous, cheap draft beer (¥1020 for a litre). It's real speciality, however, is Denki Bran, a herbal liquor that's been produced in-house for over a century. Order at the counter, then give your tickets to the server.

Ef
BAR

(エフ; Map p100; www.gallery-ef.com; 2-19-18 Kaminarimon, Taitō-ku; ⌚11am-midnight Mon, Wed & Thu, to 2am Fri & Sat, to 10pm Sun; ⓡGinza Line to Asakusa, exit 2) Set in a wobbly wooden house that beat the 1923 earthquake and WWII, this wonderfully cosy space serves coffee, tea and, after 6pm, cocktails and beer. You can eat here too, and be sure to check out the gallery in the back.

Odaiba & Tokyo Bay お台場・東京湾

★ Jicoo the Floating Bar
COCKTAIL BAR

(ジークザフローティングバー; Map p103; ☎0120-049-490; www.jicoofloatingbar.com; admission ¥2500; ⌚8-10.30pm Thu-Sat; ⓡYurikamome Line to Hinode or Odaiba Kaihin-kōen) Manga (Japanese comics) artist Leiji Matsumoto designed this spaceshiplike ship that cruises around Tokyo Bay. The evening-long 'floating pass' usually includes some sort of live-music entertainment and a clubby vibe makes it popular with 20- and 30-somethings. Board on the hour at Hinode or on the half-hour at Odaiba Kaihin-kōen. Naturally, space is limited; reservations recommended.

Ageha
CLUB

(アゲハ; www.ageha.com; 2-2-10 Shin-Kiba, Kōtō-ku; admission ¥2500-4000; ⏰11pm-5am Fri & Sat; 🚉Yūrakuchō Line to Shin-Kiba, main exit) This enormous waterside club, the largest in Tokyo, rivals any you'd find in LA or Ibiza. It's essentially a giant warehouse, so events set the atmosphere; check the schedule before trekking out here. Free shuttle buses run all night between the club and the east side of Shibuya Station on Roppongi-dōri; bring photo ID.

☆ Entertainment

Cinemas

Going to the cinema in Tokyo can be surprisingly expensive: tickets go for around ¥1800. Many cinemas offer a 'ladies' day' discount (about ¥1000) on Wednesdays and the same discount – to everyone – on the first of the month. Imported films are usually subtitled in Japanese, so the sound tends to be in the original language.

The **Tokyo International Film Festival** (TIFF; www.tiff-jp.net/en/) takes place in October and screens a number of Japanese and Asian films among others. The less-commercial **Tokyo Filmex** (http://filmex.net), held in November, focuses on the works of local and Asian directors. Both screen (most) films with English subtitles.

National Film Center
CINEMA

(Map p74; www.momat.go.jp/fc.html; 3-7-6 Kyōbashi, Chūō-ku; screenings ¥500; 🚉Kyōbashi, exit 1) Japanese classics are screened here daily, though unfortunately without English subtitles.

Uplink
CINEMA

(アップリンク; Map p83; www.uplink.co.jp; 2nd fl, 37-18 Udagawa-chō, Shibuya-ku; 🚉JR Yamanote Line to Shibuya, Hachikō exit) Day and night Uplink screens quirky independent films (domestic and foreign) in a tiny art-house cinema with comfy armchairs.

Toho Cinemas Roppongi Hills
CINEMA

(TOHOシネマズ六本木ヒルズ; Map p78; https://hlo.tohotheater.jp/net/schedule/009/TNPI2000J01.do; 6-10-2 Roppongi, Minato-ku; adult ¥1800-3000, child ¥1000, 1st day of month & women on Wed ¥1000; ⏰10am-midnight Sun-Wed, to 5am Thu-Sat; 🚉Hibiya Line to Roppongi, exit 1C) Toho's nine-screen multiplex has luxurious reclining seats and internet booking up to two days in advance for reserved seats. Look for all-night screenings on nights before holidays.

Live Music

Tokyo's home-grown live-music scene has turned out some good acts, often found playing around Shibuya and Ebisu. If you wander a bit further, the tiny underground bars and clubs in Shimo-Kitazawa, Kōenji and Kichijōji are where the local talent cuts their teeth.

Check out **Tokyo Gig Guide** (www.tokyo-gigguide.com) for a directory of venues and recommended shows.

★Unit
LIVE MUSIC

(ユニット; Map p80; ☎5459-8630; www.unit-tokyo.com; 1-34-17 Ebisu-nishi, Shibuya-ku; admission ¥2500-5000; 🚉Tōkyū Tōyoko Line to Daikanyama) This subterranean club often has two shows: live music in the evening and a DJ-hosted event after hours. It's an excellent place to catch Japanese indie bands or overseas artists making their Japan debut. In stylish Daikanyama, Unit isn't as grungy as other Tokyo live-music houses, but the bookings are solid.

Shinjuku Pit Inn
JAZZ

(新宿ピットイン; Map p88; ☎3354-2024; www.pit-inn.com; Basement fl, 2-12-4 Shinjuku, Shinjuku-ku; admission from ¥3000; ⏰matinee 2.30pm, evening show 7.30pm; 🚉Marunouchi Line to Shinjuku-sanchōme, exit C5) This is not the kind of place where you come to talk over the music. Aficionados have been coming here for over 40 years to listen to Japan's best jazz performers. Ocassional all-night shows carry the aura of another era. Weekday matinees feature young artists and cost only ¥1300.

Club Quattro
LIVE MUSIC

(クラブクアトロ; Map p83; www.club-quattro.com; 32-13-4 Udagawa-chō, Shibuya-ku; admission ¥3000-4000; 🚉JR Yamanote Line to Shibuya, Hachikō exit) This venue feels like a concert hall, but it's actually more along the lines of a slick club. Though there's no explicit musical focus, emphasis is on rock and roll and world music, and the quality is generally high. Expect a more varied, artsy crowd than the club's location – near Sentā-gai in Shibuya – might lead you to expect.

Abbey Road
LIVE MUSIC

(アビーロード; Map p78; ☑3402-0017; www.ab-beyroad.ne.jp; Basement fl, 4-11-5 Roppongi, Minato-ku; admission ¥1900-2300; ☺6-11:30pm Mon-Sat; ⓇHibiya Line to Roppongi, exit 4a) Abbey Road is, appropriately, the home of the Parrots, who reproduce a variety of Beatles hits with uncanny accuracy. They perform several nights a week; check the website for their schedule and set list. Advance bookings are recommended.

Shelter
LIVE MUSIC

(シェルター; Map p70; www.loft-prj.co.jp/SHEL-TER; 2-6-10 Kitazawa, Setagaya-ku; admission ¥2000-3500; ⓇKeiō Inokashira Line to Shimo-Kitazawa, south exit) Of all the venues on the Shimo-Kitazawa circuit, this small basement club has the most consistently solid line-up. It can be an excellent place to catch (and even meet) up-and-coming musicians, usu-ally of the rock persuasion.

Alfie
JAZZ

(アルフィー; Map p78; http://homepage1.nifty.com/live/alfie; 5th fl, 6-2-35 Roppongi, Minato-ku; admission ¥3000-4000; ☺shows 8pm Mon-Sat, 7pm Sun; ⓇHibiya Line to Roppongi, exit 1) This is Roppongi's classiest jazz venue, where a soft amber lighting melts over the lounge singers while the patrons nurse their cocktails.

Theatre & Dance

Intensely visual kabuki developed in Edo during the 18th and 19th centuries and an afternoon at the theatre has been a favourite local pastime ever since.

A full kabuki performance lasts several hours and comprises several acts (usually from different plays), with long intervals in between. Get tickets for Tokyo performances via www.kabuki-bito.jp/eng.

You can also catch other forms of tradi-tional theatre, such as nō (stylised dance-drama) and *bunraku* (classic puppet thea-tre), throughout the year, though perform-ances are irregular.

Contemporary theatre in Tokyo doesn't hold the same cultural sway that kabuki did in its heyday. Still, in pockets of the city, public and underground theatres play to full houses. **Festival/Tokyo** (http://festival-tokyo.jp/en/), the city's annual international thea-tre festival, takes place in November.

Fans of dance should seek out perform-ances of *butoh*, a fascinating contemporary form that originated in Japan.

★Kabuki-za
TRADITIONAL THEATRE

(歌舞伎座; Map p74; ☑3545-6800; www.ka-bukibito.jp/eng; 4-12-15 Ginza, Chūō-ku; tickets ¥4000-20,000; ⓇHibiya Line to Higashi-Ginza, exit 3) Established in 1889, Tokyo's designated kabuki theatre reopened in 2013 after a lengthy reconstruction. The new building, designed by architect Kuma Kengo, has a traditional facade but its scarlet and gold interior is thoroughly modern. A full kabuki performance comprises several acts (usually from different plays) and lasts several hours. Tickets can be purchased on the website, in English. Be sure to rent a headset for blow-by-blow explanations in English (¥700, plus ¥1000 deposit), and pick up a *bentō* for the long intermission.

It may be possible to buy same-day, single act 'makumi' tickets (availability-pending), though only for seats in the upper tiers.

Setagaya Public Theatre
PERFORMING ARTS

(世田谷パブリックシアター; Map p70; ☑5432-1526; www.setagaya-pt.jp; 4-1-1 Taishidō, Setagaya-ku; tickets ¥3500-7500; ⓇTōkyū Den-en-toshi Line to Sangenjaya, Carrot Tower exit) This Tokyo theatre is both commercially success-ful and consistently interesting, producing contemporary dramas along with modern nō and sometimes butoh. The smaller Theatre Tram shows more experimental works.

National Nō Theatre
TRADITIONAL THEATRE

(国立能楽堂; Kokuritsu Nō-gakudō; Map p70; ☑3423-1331; www.ntj.jac.go.jp/english; 4-18-1 Sendagaya, Shibuya-ku; tickets from ¥2600; ⓇJR Sōbu Line to Sendagaya) This theatre stages the traditional music, poetry and dances that nō is famous for, as well as the interludes of *kyōgen* (short, lively comic farces). Each seat has a small screen that can display an English translation of the dialogue. It's a five-minute walk west of the station; tickets go fast.

ⓘ GETTING TICKETS

Found a show or event that strikes your fancy? **Ticket Pia** (チケットぴあ; ☑0570-02-9111; http://t.pia.jp/; ☺10am-8pm) handles just about everything, including concerts and theatre perform-ances major and minor. Tickets (unless sold-out) can be purchased up to three days before the show. There are conven-ient branches on the 4th floor of Shibuya Hikarie (p84) and inside the Asakusa Tourist Information Center (p140).

Robot Restaurant
CABARET

(ロボットレストラン; Map p88; ☑3200-
5500; www.robot-restaurant.com/top.html; 1-7-1
Kabukichō, Shinjuku-ku; tickets ¥4000; ☺shows
at 7pm, 8.30pm & 10pm; ℝJR Yamanote Line to
Shinjuku, east exit) This Kabukichō spectacle is
part girly show (though with no nudity) and
part hilarity, the highlight being giant robots manned by bikini-clad women. There's
enough neon and lights in the small theatre to light all of Shinjuku. Trust us, you'll
know it when you see it. Reservations recommended, but not necessary. Dinner is a
small *bentō*.

National Theatre
TRADITIONAL THEATRE

(国立劇場; Kokuritsu Gekijō; Map p70; ☑3230-
3000; www.ntj.jac.go.jp/english; 4-1 Hayabusa-
chō, Chiyoda-ku; tickets from ¥1500; ℝHanzōmon
Line to Hanzōmon, exit 1) Performances at the
prestigious National Theatre include kabuki, *gagaku* (music of the imperial court)
and *bunraku* (classic puppet theatre).
Earphones with English translation are
available for hire (¥650 plus ¥1000 deposit). Check the website for performance
schedules.

Asakusa Engei Hall
COMEDY

(浅草演芸ホール; Map p100; www.asakusaen
gei.com; 1-43-12 Asakusa, Taitō-ku; adult/child
¥2500/1100; ☺shows 11.40am-4.30pm & 4.40-
9pm; ℝGinza Line to Tawaramachi, exit 3) Asakusa
was once full of theatres like this one, where
traditional *rakugo* (comedic monologue)
and other forms of comedy are performed
along with jugglers, magicians and the like.
It's all in Japanese, but the lively acts are fun
all the same – and form the basis for a lot of
what appears on Japanese TV.

Honda Theatre
THEATRE

(本多劇場; Map p70; www.honda-geki.com; 2-10-
15 Kitazawa, Shibuya-ku; ℝKeiō Inokashira Line
to Shimo-Kitazawa, south exit) This is the original – and the biggest – of a collection of
shōgekijō (small theatres) that set up in Shimo-Kitazawa in the early '80s and turned
the neighbourhood into a contemporary
theatre hub. Naturally, you'll need a fair
amount of Japanese ability to get through
the performances.

Sport

Sumō is fascinating, highly ritualised and
steeped in Shintō tradition. It's also the
only traditional Japanese sport that still has
enough clout to draw big crowds and dominate primetime TV.

Tournaments take place in Tokyo at
Ryōgoku Kokugikan in January, May and
September. Other times of year you can drop
in on an early morning practice session at
one of the stables, like Arashio Stable (p102).

Baseball is more of an obsession than a
sport in Japan, and it's worth getting tickets
to a game if only to see the fans go wild at
each play and to witness the perfectly choreographed 7th-inning stretch. Within Tokyo,
the Yomiuri Giants and Yakult Swallows are
crosstown rivals.

Baseball season runs from April through
October. Check the schedules on the stadium websites.

★ Ryōgoku Kokugikan
SUMŌ

(両国国技館; Ryōgoku Sumō Stadium; Map p70;
☑3623-5111; www.sumo.or.jp/eng/ticket/index.
html; 1-3-28 Yokoami, Sumida-ku; ☺tournaments
Jan, May & Sep; ℝJR Sōbu Line to Ryōgoku, west
exit) If you're in town when a tournament is
on, don't miss the chance to catch a match
at Japan's largest sumō stadium. Doors open
at 8am, but the action doesn't really heat up
until the senior wrestlers hit the ring around
2pm. You can rent a radio (¥100 fee, plus
¥2000 deposit) to listen to commentary in
English.

Ringside tickets cost ¥14,300, boxes cost
between ¥9200 and ¥11,300 per person,
and arena tickets will set you back between
¥2100 and ¥8200. Tickets can be purchased
online in English (for a ¥1000 handling fee)
up to a month prior to the tournament. You
can also usually turn up on the day and get
an arena ticket (but you'll have to arrive very
early, say 6am, to snag seats during the last
days of a tournament).

Tokyo Dome
BASEBALL

(東京ドーム; Map p90; ☑5800-9999; www.to
kyo-dome.co.jp/e/dome; 1-3-61 Kōraku, Bunkyō-ku;
ℝJR Chūō Line to Suidōbashi, west exit) The 'Big
Egg' is home to Japan's favourite baseball
team, the Yomiuri Giants. Tickets often sell
out in advance; get them online at www.e-
tix.jp/ticket_giants/en/ticket_pc_en.php.

Jingū Baseball Stadium
BASEBALL

(神宮球場; Jingū Kyūjō; Map p85; ☑3404-8999;
www.jingu-stadium.com; 3-1 Kasumigaoka-machi,
Shinjuku-ku; ℝGinza Line to Gaienmae, exit 3) Jingū
Baseball Stadium was originally built to host
the 1964 Olympics, and today it's the Yakult
Swallows' home field. Games start at 6pm,
and nonreserved outfield seats go for just
¥1500. The ticket box is located near Gate 9.

Shopping

Tokyo is the trendsetter for the rest of Japan, and its residents shop (economy be damned) with an infectious enthusiasm. Merchandise is generally of excellent quality, and not as wildly expensive as you might think.

ŌEDO ANTIQUE MARKET

Vintage kimono, delicate sake cups, Buddhist statuary... These are just a few examples of the treasures to be found at the **Ōedo Antique Market** (大江戸骨董市; Map p74; www.antique-market.jp; ⊘9am-4pm 1st & 3rd Sun of month), held in the courtyard at the Tokyo International Forum (p69). With around 250 vendors, it's the largest in the country.

Marunouchi 丸の内 (Tokyo Station area 東京駅)

Takashimaya　　　　　　　DEPARTMENT STORE
(高島屋; Map p74; 2-4-1 Nihombashi, Chūō-ku; ⊘10am-8pm; ℞Ginza Line to Nihombashi, Takashimaya exit) Takashimaya's branch on New York's Fifth Ave is renowned for its cutting-edge Japanese-inspired interior, but the design of the Tokyo flagship store (1933) tips its pillbox hat to New York's Gilded Age. Uniformed female elevator operators still announce each floor in high-pitched sing-song voices.

★**Muji**　　　　　　　CLOTHING, HOMEWARES
(無印良品; Map p74; www.mujiyurakucho.com; 3-8-3 Marunouchi, Chiyoda-ku; ⊘10am-9pm; ℞JR Yamanote to Yūrakuchō, Kyōbashi exit) Muji (short for Mujirushi) means 'no brand', though by now the label's simple, functional aesthetic is just as iconic as any brand. This Yūrakuchō outpost is one of the largest in Tokyo and carries clothes for men and women, housewares and Muji's unbeatable line of travel accessories.

There's another sizeable branch in **Tokyo Midtown** (無印良品; Map p78; Basement fl, Tokyo Midtown, 9-7 Akasaka, Minato-ku; ⊘11am-9pm; ℞Ōedo Line to Roppongi, exit 8).

Ginza 銀座

Ginza is Tokyo's original shopping neighbourhood, and although other areas have risen in power, it is still the benchmark to which all of the other boutique-filled districts are compared. Don't miss the grandiose department stores, vestiges of the 1950s and '60s when ceremony and much ado were wrapped up in the shopping experience.

★**Mitsukoshi**　　　　　　　DEPARTMENT STORE
(三越; Map p74; www.mitsukoshi.co.jp; 4-6-16 Ginza, Chūō-ku; ⊘10am-8pm; ℞Ginza Line to Ginza, exits A7 & A11) One of Ginza's grande dames, Mitsukoshi is the quintessential Tokyo department store, and it gleams after a recent renovation. The housewares department on the 8th floor has beautiful made-in-Japan crockery and chopsticks and the basement food court is peerless. The tax refund counter is on the 2nd-floor mezzanine.

Uniqlo　　　　　　　CLOTHING
(ユニクロ; Map p74; www.uniqlo.com; 5-7-7 Ginza, Chūō-ku; ⊘11am-9pm; ℞Ginza Line to Ginza, exit A2) Uniqlo made its name with inexpensive, well-made basics that are tweaked with style – designers such as Jil Sander and Takahashi Jun have participated in recent capsule collections. This enormous, 12-storey outpost offers everything in the Uniqlo cannon, from socks to coats. Check out the T-shirts on the 11th floor and the limited-edition items on the 12th floor.

There are Uniqlo all over the city, including another fairly big – though not nearly 12-storey – branch in **Shibuya** (Map p83; 2-29-5 Dōgenzaka, Shibuya-ku; ⊘11am-9pm Mon-Fri, from 10am Sat & Sun; ℞JR Yamanote Line to Shibuya, Hachikō exit).

Dover Street Market Ginza　　　　　　　FASHION
(DSM; Map p74; http://ginza.doverstreetmarket.com; 6-9-5 Ginza, Chūō-ku; ⊘11am-8pm Sun-Thu, to 9pm Fri & Sat; ℞Ginza Line to Ginza, exit A2) A department store as envisioned by Kawakubo Rei (of Comme des Garçons), DSM has seven floors of avant-garde brands, including several Japanese labels and everything in the Comme des Garçons line-up. The quirky installations alone make it worth the visit.

Itōya　　　　　　　ARTS & CRAFTS
(伊東屋; Map p74; 2-7-15 Ginza, Chūō-ku; ⊘10.30am-8pm Mon-Sat, to 7pm Sun; ℞Ginza Line to Ginza, exit A13) Nine floors of stationery-shop love await visitors to this century-old purveyor of fountain pens and paper-bound luxuries. The 6th floor offers more traditional Japanese wares including *washi* (fine Japanese handmade paper) and *furoshiki* (wrapping cloths).

Takumi
CRAFT

(たくみ; Map p74; www.ginza-takumi.co.jp; 8-4-2 Ginza, Chūō-ku; ⏰11am-7pm Mon-Sat; 🚇Ginza Line to Shimbashi, exit 5) Takumi has been around for more than 60 years and has acquired an elegant selection of toys, textiles, ceramics and other traditional folk crafts from around Japan.

Hakuhinkan
CHILDREN

(博品館; Map p74; www.hakuhinkan.co.jp; 8-8-11 Ginza, Chūō-ku; ⏰11am-8pm; 🚇JR Yamanote Line to Shimbashi, Ginza exit) This layer cake of a toy store is crammed with plush toys, character goods and novelty items. There's another branch at Narita Airport (Terminal 1) that opens at 7.30am for last-chance purchases.

🔒 Roppongi 六本木

A worthwhile place to check out is the 3rd floor of Tokyo Midtown (p76), which has a cluster of homewares shops.

Japan Sword
ANTIQUES

(日本刀剣; Map p78; www.japansword.co.jp; 3-8-1 Toranomon, Minato-ku; ⏰9.30am-6pm Mon-Fri, to 5pm Sat; 🚇Ginza Line to Toranomon, exit 2) Japan Sword sells the genuine article: antique swords and samurai helmets dating from the Edo period and modern creations from 'living treasure' artisans. The 2nd-floor gallery is one of the few places you can see real swords that aren't behind glass. The staff speak English and can arrange the necessary export paperwork. It also sells convincing replicas.

Japan Traditional Craft Center
CRAFT

(全国伝統的工芸品センター; Map p70; http://kougeihin.jp/en/top; 8-1-22 Akasaka, Minato-ku; ⏰11am-7pm Mon-Sat; 🚇Ginza Line to Aoyama-itchōme, exit 4) Supported by the Japanese Ministry of Economy, Trade and Industry, this shop showcases crafts from around Japan, from potter to lacquerwork boxes. The emphasis is on high-end goods, but you can find beautiful things in all price ranges here.

🔒 Ebisu & Meguro
恵比寿・目黒

Daikanyama and Naka-Meguro are two good places to hunt for one-of-a-kind fashion finds. In Daikanyama, look for boutiques wedged in the space between main drags Kyū-Yamate-dōri and Hachiman-dōri. In Naka-Meguro check the riverside and the narrow streets behind it.

⭐Okura
FASHION, ACCESSORIES

(オクラ; Map p80; 20-11 Sarugaku-chō, Shibuya-ku; ⏰11.30am-8pm, 11am-8.30pm Sat & Sun; 🚇Tōkyū Tōyoko Line to Daikanyama) Almost everything in this enchanting shop is dyed a deep indigo blue – from sweatshirts to scarves. There are some beautiful, original items, though unfortunately most aren't cheap. The shop itself looks like a rural house, with worn wooden floorboards and whitewashed walls. Note: there's no sign out the front, but look for the traditional building.

Meguro Interior Shops Community (MISC)
HOMEWARES, ANTIQUES

(ミスク; Map p70; http://misc.co.jp/; Meguro-dōri; 🚇JR Yamanote Line to Meguro, west exit) This is Tokyo's interior design district and there are dozens of shops here, spread out on both sides of a 3km stretch of Meguro-dōri. Even if you're not planning to buy, it's interesting to poke around and imagine what Tokyo's concrete-box apartments might look like on the inside. Note that many stores close on Wednesdays.

Kamawanu
CRAFT

(かまわぬ; Map p80; www.kamawanu.co.jp; 23-1 Sarugaku-chō, Shibuya-ku; ⏰11am-7pm; 🚇Tōkyū Tōyoko Line to Daikanyama) Kamawanu specialises in *tenugui*: dyed rectangular cloths of thin cotton, which can be used as tea towels, kerchiefs or gift wrap (the list goes on; they're surprisingly versatile). There are more than 200 different patterns available here, with motifs from traditional to modern. Turn down the little street to the right of the post office, and look for a traditional building.

Good Day Books
BOOKS

(グッド デイ ブックス; Map p70; www.gooddaybooks.com; 2-4-2 Nishi-Gotanda, Shinagawa-ku; ⏰11am-8pm Mon-Sat, to 6pm Sun; 🚇JR Yamanote Line to Gotanda, west exit) Tokyo's best shop for secondhand English-language books has a good selection on Japanese culture and language, and also hosts discussion events. It's above the Big-B shop; check the website for step-by-step directions.

🔒 Shibuya & Around 渋谷

Shibuya is the stomping ground of fashion-conscious *joshikōsei* (high school girls), though you'll find more grown-up clothes in the new Shibuya Hikarie building. It's also an excellent place to hunt for *zakka* (miscellaneous goods), such as cute stationery, lifestyle gadgets and bizarre beauty products.

There are some great shopping spots in Shimo-Kitazawa (p84), too, where you'll find everything from used clothes and costumes to quirky and questionable trinkets.

★ Tōkyū Hands
VARIETY

(東急ハンズ; Map p83; http://shibuya.tokyu-hands.co.jp; 12-18 Udagawa-chō, Shibuya-ku; ⊙10am-8.30pm; 🚇JR Yamanote Line to Shibuya, Hachikō exit) This DIY and *zakka* store has eight fascinating floors of everything you didn't know you needed. It's perfect for souvenir hunting – surely someone you know needs reflexology slippers, right?

There's another branch in Shinjuku (新宿ハンズ; Map p88; Takashimaya Times Square, 5-24-2 Sendagaya, Shibuya-ku; ⊙10am-8.30pm; 🚇JR Yamanote Line to Shinjuku, new south exit) and an upscale version in Ginza, **Ginza Hands** (銀座ハンズ; Map p74; http://ginza.tokyu-hands.co.jp/; 5th-9th fl, Marronnier Gate, 2-2-14 Ginza, Chūō-ku; ⊙11am-9pm; 🚇JR Yamanote to Yūrakuchō, Kyōbashi exit).

Shibuya 109
FASHION

(渋谷109; Ichimarukyū; Map p83; 2-29-1 Dōgenzaka, Shibuya-ku; ⊙10am-9pm; 🚇JR Yamanote Line to Shibuya, Hachikō exit) See all those dolled-up teens walking around Shibuya? This is where they shop. Even if you don't intend to buy anything, you can't understand Shibuya without making a stop here.

Sister
FASHION

(シスター; Map p83; www.faketokyo.com; 2nd fl, 18-4 Udagawa-cho, Shibuya-ku; ⊙noon-10pm; 🚇JR Yamanote Line to Shibuya, Hachikō exit) One of the best places in Tokyo to find hot new Japanese designers. Look for the 'Fake Tokyo' banners.

Aquvii
ACCESSORIES

(アクビ; Map p83; 6-19-16 Jingūmae, Shibuya-ku; ⊙noon-8pm; 🚇JR Yamanote Line to Shibuya, Hachikō exit) Come see what the cool kids are wearing (and making) at this showcase for quirky, made-in-Tokyo accessories and other oddities from local designers.

Haight & Ashbury
VINTAGE

(Map p70; 2nd fl, 2-37-2 Kitazawa, Setagaya-ku; ⊙noon-10pm; 🚇Odakyu Line to Shimo-Kitazawa, north exit) Shimo-Kitazawa's best thrift shop, H&A – not H&M – provides all the props and costumes you'd need to re-enact almost any theatrical number, from the goatherd scene in *The Sound of Music* to the opening act of *Cabaret*.

Village Vanguard
VARIETY

(ヴィレッジ・ヴァンガード; Map p70; 2-10-15 Kitazawa, Setagaya-ku; ⊙10am-midnight; 🚇Odakyu Line to Shimo-Kitazawa, south exit) This pop-culture emporium is crammed with all the magazines, music, gadgets, toys and character goods that everyone's talking about.

🔒 Harajuku 原宿

Omote-sandō is lined with upscale boutiques. Narrow, meandering Cat St, which intersects it, offers a more chilled-out shopping experience. The web of alleys surrounding the two, known as Ura-Hara (literally 'behind Harajuku'), is where you'll find the small boutiques and vintage shops that keep the neighbourhood's indie spirit alive.

RETAIL ARCHITECTURE IN OMOTE-SANDŌ

The magnificent parade of sculpturelike stores along Omote-sandō also functions as a walk-through showroom for the who's who of contemporary (mostly) Japanese architects.

Omotesandō Hills (表参道ヒルズ; Map p85; 4-12-10 Jingūmae, Shibuya-ku; 🚇Omote-sando, exit A2) This concrete mall, designed by Andō Tadao, spirals round a sunken atrium.

Dior (Map p85; 5-9-11 Jingūmae, Shibuya-ku; 🚇Omote-sando, exit A1) The filmy exterior, which seems to hang like a dress, is the work of Pritzker Prize–winner SANAA (Sejima Kazuyo and Nishizawa Ryūe).

Louis Vuitton (Map p85; 5-7-5 Jingūmae, Shibuya-ku; 🚇Omote-sando, exit A1) Aoki Jun's design is meant to evoke a stack of trunks.

Tod's (Map p85; 5-1-15 Jingūmae, Shibuya-ku; 🚇Omote-sando, exit A1) Itō Toyo designed the criss-crossing ribbons of concrete that take their inspiration from the zelkova trees below; what's more impressive is that they're also structural.

Prada (Map p85; 5-2-6 Minami-aoyama, Minato-ku; 🚇Omote-sando, exit A4) This convex glass fishbowl is the work of Herzog & de Meuron, also Pritzker Prize winners.

★ Takeshita-dōri VARIETY

(竹下通り; Map p85; ℝ JR Yamanote Line to Harajuku, Takeshita exit) This teaming alley is where aspiring goths, Lolitas and punks come to shop, and you'll spot some pretty wild stuff. Even if you're not in the market for a dress inspired by the Victorian-era, there is still plenty to pull out your wallet for here, like funky tights and mobile-phone charms.

★ KiddyLand CHILDREN

(キデイランド; Map p85; www.kiddyland.co.jp/en/index.html; 6-1-9 Jingūmae, Shibuya-ku; ⊘ 10am-9pm; ℝ JR Yamanote Line to Harajuku, Omote-sandō exit) This multistorey toy emporium is packed to the rafters with character goods, from Hello Kitty to Studio Ghibli. It's not just for kids either; you'll spot plenty of teens and even adults indulging their love of *kawaii* (cute).

Laforet FASHION

(ラフォーレ; Map p85; www.laforet.ne.jp; 1-11-6 Jingūmae, Shibuya-ku; ⊘ 11am-8pm; ℝ JR Yamanote Line to Harajuku, Omote-sandō exit) Laforet has been a beacon of cutting-edge Harajuku style for decades. It's been looking a little mainstream lately (see the Topshop on the ground floor) but you can still find plenty inside here to turn your head. And guys: don't let the gaggles of girls put you off, there's stuff for you in here, too.

There's also a gallery, **Laforet Museum Harajuku** (ラフォーレミュジアム原宿; Map p85; ✆ info 3475 3127; www.lapnet.jp/index.html; 6th fl, Laforet Bldg, 1-11-6 Jingūmae, Shibuya-ku; ⊘ 11am-8pm; ℝ JR Yamanote line to Harajuku, Omote-sandō exit) **FREE**, on the 6th floor that hosts exhibitions with a pop-culture slant.

Pass the Baton VINTAGE

(パスザバトン; Map p85; www.pass-the-baton.com; 4-12-10 Jingūmae, Shibuya-ku; ⊘ 11am-9pm Mon-Sat, to 8pm Sun; ℝ Ginza Line to Omote-sandō, exit A3) This concept store bills itself as a 'curated' consignment shop. From personal castaways to dead stock from long defunct retailers, everything here comes tagged with a profile of its previous owner. It's in the basement of the Omotesandō Hills West Wing, but you'll need to enter from a separate street entrance on Omote-sandō.

Oriental Bazaar SOUVENIRS

(オリエンタルバザー; Map p85; www.orientalbazaar.co.jp; 5-9-13 Jingūmae, Shibuya-ku; ⊘ 10am-6pm Mon-Wed & Fri, to 7pm Sat & Sun; ℝ JR Yamanote Line to Harajuku, Omote-sandō exit) Stocking a wide selection of souvenirs at very reasonable prices, Oriental Bazaar is an easy one-stop destination. Items to be found here include fans, pottery, *yukata* (light summer kimono) and T-shirts, some made in Japan, some not (check the labels).

Hysteric Glamour FASHION

(Map p85; www.hystericglamour.jp; 6-23-2 Jingūmae, Shibuya-ku; ⊘ 11am-8pm; ℝ Chiyoda Line to Meiji-jingū-mae, exit 4) It's more tongue-in-cheek than hysterical or glamorous, but whatever you want to call it, it's fun stuff spiked generously with that trademark Tokyo flavour. It even has a toddler line, the ultimate designer punk for your diapered rocker.

Chicago Thrift Store VINTAGE

(シカゴ; Map p85; 6-31-21 Jingūmae, Shibuya-ku; ⊘ 10am-8pm; ℝ JR Yamanote Line to Harajuku, Omote-sandō exit) This treasure trove of vintage clothing is stuffed to the rafters with funky hats, ties and coats Don't miss the used kimono and *yukata* in the back corner.

Condomania SPECIALITY SHOP

(コンドマニア; Map p85; 6-30-1 Jingūmae, Shibuya-ku; ⊘ 11am-9.30pm; ℝ JR Yamanote Line to Harajuku, Omote-sandō exit) This may be Tokyo's cheekiest rendezvous point. Popular items include *omamori* (traditional good-luck charms) with condoms tucked inside.

RECYCLE SHOPS

Take Tokyoites' love of fashion, pair it with impossibly small closets and what do you get? Possibly the world's best consignment shops, called *risaikuru shoppu* (recycle shops). Check out the huge **RagTag** (ラグタグ; Map p85; 6-14-2 Jingūmae, Shibuya-ku; ⊘ 11am-8pm; ℝ JR Yamanote Line to Harajuku, Omote-Sandō exit) on Cat St, stocked with the brands locals love, like Comme des Garçons and Vivienne Westwood.

⌂ Shinjuku & West Tokyo
新宿

Shinjuku is a major shopping hub. You'll find branches of most major fashion retailers in the department stores attached to the train station. Nearby are several electronics outlets, such as **Yodobashi Camera** (ヨドバシカメラ; Map p88; 1-11-1 Nishi-Shinjuku, Shinjuku-ku; ⊘ 9.30am-10pm; ℝ JR Yamanote Line to Shinjuku, west exit).

★**Don Quijote** VARIETY

(ドン・キホーテ; Map p88; ☎5291-9211; www.donki.com; 1-16-5 Kabukichō, Shinjuku-ku; ⏰24hr; 🚇JR Yamanote line to Shinjuku, east exit) In Kabukichō, this fluorescent-lit bargain castle is filled to the brink with weird loot. Chaotic piles of knockoff electronics and designer goods sit alongside sex toys, fetish costumes and packaged foods.

Look for other branches in **Roppongi** (Map p78; 3-14-10 Roppongi, Minato-ku; ⏰24hr; 🚇Hibiya Line to Roppongi, exit 3) and **Shibuya** (Map p83; 2-25-8 Dōgenzaka, Shibuya-ku; ⏰10am-4.30am; 🚇JR Yamanote Line to Shibuya, Hachikō exit).

Disk Union MUSIC

(ディスクユニオン; Map p88; 3-31-4 Shinjuku, Shinjuku-ku; ⏰11am-9pm; 🚇JR Yamanote Line to Shinjuku, east exit) Scruffy Disk Union is known by local audiophiles as Tokyo's best used CD and vinyl store. Eight storeys carry a variety of musical styles; if you still can't find what you're looking for there are several other branches in Shinjuku that stock more obscure genres (pick up a map here).

Isetan DEPARTMENT STORE

(伊勢丹; Map p88; www.isetan.co.jp; 3-14-1 Shinjuku, Shinjuku-ku; ⏰10am-8pm; 🚇Marunouchi Line to Shinjuku-sanchōme, exits B3, B4 & B5) Most department stores play to conservative tastes, but this one is an exception. The recently redone 3rd floor has some edgy womenswear, including collections from famous and not-yet-famous Japanese designers. Men get a whole building of their own (connected by a passageway). The basement food hall here is tops, too.

Kinokuniya BOOKS

(紀伊國屋書店; Map p88; www.kinokuniya.co.jp; Takashimaya Times Sq, 5-24-2 Sendagaya, Shibuya-ku; ⏰10am-8pm; 🚇JR Yamanote Line to Shinjuku, south exit) The 6th floor here has a broad selection of foreign-language books and magazines, including English-teaching texts.

RankingRanqueen VARIETY

(ランキンランキン; Map p88; Basement fl, Shinjuku Station, Shinjuku-ku; ⏰10am-11pm; 🚇JR Yamanote Line to Shinjuku, east exit) If it's trendy, it's here. This clever shop stocks only the top-selling products in any given category, from eyeliner and soft drinks to leg-slimming massage rollers. Look for it just outside the east exit ticket gates of JR Shinjuku Station. It's a popular meeting spot and usually has a crowd out front.

🔒 Iidabashi & Northwest Tokyo 飯田橋

Otome Rd in Ikebukuro is the locus of the girl geek movement, where you'll find a row of shops selling manga, costumes and drawing supplies. It runs alongside the western street-level entrance to the Sunshine City shopping complex, at the end of Sunshine 60-dōri and past the elevated highway.

Animate MANGA, ANIME

(アニメイト; Map p70; www.animate.co.jp; 3-2-1 Higashi-Ikebukuro, Toshima-ku; ⏰10am-9pm; 🚇JR Yamanote Line to Ikebukuro, exit 35) This landmark comic (and more) shop is credited with putting Otome Rd on the map. It's since moved to a new location just off Sunshine 60-dori (look for the big blue sign to the left). Animate turned its old location, on Otome Rd, into **ACOS** (Map p70; 3-2-1 Higashi-Ikebukuro, Toshima-ku; ⏰11am-8pm; 🚇JR Yamanote Line to Ikebukuro, exit 35), a *cos-play* (costume play) speciality store.

🔒 Akihabara & Around 秋葉原

Akihabara's Electric Town is crowded with stores hawking gadgets and *otaku* paraphernalia (anime, manga, figures etc). Many of the big electronics retailers have tax-exemption counters, so make sure to have your passport on you. Nearby Jimbōchō (p92) is famous for its second-hand bookshops.

★**Mandarake Complex** MANGA, ANIME

(まんだらけコンプレックス; Map p90; www.mandarake.co.jp; 3-11-2 Soto-Kanda, Chiyoda-ku; ⏰noon-8pm; 🚇JR Yamanote Line to Akihabara, Electric Town exit) When *otaku* dream of heaven, it probably looks a lot like this giant store. Mandarake has long been Tokyo's go-to store for manga and anime, and its Akihabara branch is the largest. Eight storeys are piled high with comic books and DVDs, action figures and cel art just for starters.

It also has a trippy basement branch in **Shibuya** (Map p83; Basement fl, Beam Bldg, 31-2 Udagawa-chō, Shibuya-ku; ⏰noon-8pm; 🚇JR Yamanote Line to Shibuya, Hachikō exit).

★**2k540 Aki-Oka Artisan** CRAFT

(アキオカアルチザン; Map p90; www.jrtk.jp/2k540; 5-9 Ueno, Taitō-ku; ⏰hours vary; 🚇Ginza Line to Suehirochō, exit 2) *Monozukuri* (the art of making things) is the focus of the few dozen shops gathered in this minimalist arcade under the JR tracks. This is the place to find fans in cool geometric patterns and mobile phone cases carved from wood.

Ohya Shobō
BOOKS

(大屋書房; Map p90; www.ohya-shobo.com; 1-1 Kanda-Jimbōchō, Chiyoda-ku; ⏰10am-6pm Mon-Sat; 🚇Hanzōmon Line to Jimbōchō, exit A7) You really could lose yourself for hours in this splendid, musty old bookshop that carries *ukiyo-e* (woodblock prints), Edo-era manga and vintage maps. The staff are friendly and helpful.

Yodobashi Akiba
ELECTRONICS

(ヨドバシカメラAkiba; Map p90; www.yodobashi-akiba.com; 1-1 Kanda Hanaoka-chō, Chiyoda-ku; ⏰9.30am-10pm; 🚇JR Yamanote Line to Akihabara, Shōwa-tōriguchi exit) Inside this complex are six monster floors of electronics, cameras, toys and appliances – if you can plug it in, it's probably here. For all the modern convenience that it hawks, Yodobashi Camera feels like an old-time bazaar with all the sights and sounds clamouring for your attention.

Gachapon Kaikan
CHILDREN

(ガチャポン会館; Map p90; www.akibagacha.com; 3-15-5 Soto-Kanda, Chiyoda-ku; ⏰11am-8pm Mon-Fri, to 10pm Sat, to 7pm Sun; 🚇Ginza Line to Suehiro-chō, exit 3) Come with pockets full of ¥100 coins, because this shop houses hundreds of *gachapon* (capsule-vending machines) dispensing manga character toys, keychain trinkets and assembly-required figurines – perfect prepackaged Tokyo souvenirs.

🏯 Ueno 上野

Ameya-yokochō
MARKET

(アメヤ横町; Map p96; ⏰10am-7pm; 🚇JR Yamanote Line to Ueno, Ueno-kōen exit) The gravelly *irasshai* ('welcome') of the fishmongers and clothing vendors at this old-fashioned open-air market couldn't be further from Ginza or Shibuya. Ameya Yokochō got its start as a black market after WWII when American goods were sold here, and you can still find the blue jeans and Hawaiian shirts that were in vogue at the time.

Isetatsu
CRAFT

(いせ辰; Map p96; ☎3823-1453; 2-18-9 Yanaka, Taitō-ku; ⏰10am-6pm; 🚇Chiyoda Line to Sendagi, exit 1) Dating back to 1864, this venerable stationery shop specialises in *chiyogami*: gorgeous, colourful paper made using woodblocks.

🏯 Asakusa & Sumida-gawa 浅草・隅田川

In Asakusa you'll find many traditional craft shops that have been making things – knives, combs, make-up brushes for kabuki actors, for example – much as they did a hundred years ago.

Nakamise-dōri
STREET

(仲見世通り; Map p100; www.asakusa-nakamise.jp; 🚇Ginza Line to Asakusa, exit 1) This lively pedestrian street leading up to Sensō-ji is chock-a-block with shops selling tourist wares like *geta* (wooden sandals worn with kimonos) and Edo-style toys and trinkets.

Solamachi
SOUVENIRS

(ソラマチ; Map p100; 1-1-2 Oshiage, Sumida-ku; ⏰10am-9pm; 🚇Hanzōmon Line to Oshiage, Sky Tree exit) It's not all cheesy Sky Tree swag at this mall under the tower (though you can get 634m long rolls of Sky Tree toilet paper). Shops on the 4th floor offer a better-than-usual selection of Japanese-y souvenirs, including pretty accessories made from kimono fabric.

Kappabashi-dōri
STREET

(合羽橋通り; Map p100; 🚇Ginza Line to Tawaramachi, exit 3) Kappabashi-dōri supplies many a Tokyo restaurant with all the necessities (matching sets of chopsticks, crockery, uniforms and neon signs, for example) but is most famous for its shops selling plastic food models. You can pick up key chains and the like here shaped like sushi, which look almost good enough to eat.

Bengara
CRAFT

(べんがら; Map p100; www.bengara.com; 1-35-6 Asakusa, Taitō-ku; ⏰10am-6pm, to 7pm Sat & Sun, closed 3rd Thu; 🚇Ginza Line to Asakusa, exit 1) This little shop specialises in *noren*, the curtains that hang in front of shop doors, as well as other useful indigo-dyed goods.

ℹ️ Orientation

Officially, central Tokyo is made up of 23 *ku* (wards). Unofficially, central Tokyo is whatever falls within the JR Yamanote Line, the elevated rail loop that circles the city. Many of the stations on the Yamanote Line are transit hubs and, as a result, are the most developed. A good many of the city's sights, accommodations, bars and restaurants lie in neighbourhoods on the loop, which include Marunouchi (Tokyo Station), Ebisu, Shibuya, Harajuku, Shinjuku, Akihabara and Ueno.

The Imperial Palace grounds form the city's incongruously verdant core. No roads pass through here, and no subways pass under, meaning that navigating the very centre of the city is necessarily a circuitous affair. The Sumida-gawa runs down the eastern half of Tokyo, draining into Tokyo Bay along the city's southeast border.

Tokyo is the antithesis of the neat grid, which can make it difficult to connect the dots without a map (smart phones are a lifesaver). Only major boulevards have names, though even these sometimes change when the road bends or joins with another. One useful boulevard on the west side of the city is Meiji-dōri, which runs between Ebisu, Shibuya, Harajuku and Shinjuku, roughly parallel to the JR Yamanote Line.

Central neighbourhoods with significant tourist spots usually have maps and street signs posted in English.

ℹ️ Information

DANGERS & ANNOYANCES

For a megalopolis with over 35-million people, Tokyo is a surprisingly safe place. That said, you should exercise the same caution you would in your home country.

Touts for bars and clubs in Roppongi and Shinjuku's Kabukichō can be aggressive. Be wary of following them; while not common, spiked drinks followed by theft or, worse, beatings, have occurred. Overcharging is the more likely outcome.

Women should note that *chikan* (gropers) do haunt crowded trains, though they usually prey on local women (who are presumed less likely to make a scene). During rush hour, many express trains heading to the suburbs have women-only cars (marked in pink).

Tokyo has a different take on smoking than most Western cities: it is OK to smoke in most restaurants, bars and clubs, but not on city streets. Look for official smoking areas (easily spotted by oversized ashtray bins and clouds of smoke) around train stations.

EMERGENCY

Ambulance (☑119)

Emergency Interpretation (☑5285-8181; www.himawari.metro.tokyo.jp/qq/qq13enmnlt.asp; ⏰9am-8pm) In English, Chinese, Korean, Thai and Spanish.

Police (警視庁; Keishichō; ☑emergency 110, general 3501-0110; www.keishicho.metro.tokyo.jp) *Kōban* (police boxes), staffed 24 hours, are located near most major train stations.

Tokyo English Life Line (TELL; ☑5774-0992; www.telljp.com; ⏰9am-11pm) Free, anonymous telephone counselling.

INTERNET ACCESS

Most accommodations in Tokyo have, at the very least, complimentary wi-fi in the lobby. You can also now log on to a free wireless network at any one of the 200+ **Starbucks** (http://starbucks.wi2.co.jp/pc/index_en.html) in Tokyo (yes, there are over 200!), though you'll need to register an email address first.

Visit **Freespot** (www.freespot.com/users/map_e.html) for a list of other free hotspots around the city. Both Narita and Haneda airports have free wi-fi, too.

If you need to get on a computer, here are some options:

FedEx Kinko's (フェデックスキンコーズ; http://english-fedexkinkos-cojp.presencehost.net/companyinfo/locations.html; per 10 min ¥250; @) Outposts all over central Tokyo have a few computer terminals each, as well as printing and photocopying services.

Terminal (http://theterminal.jp/index.html; 3rd fl, 3-22-12 Jingūmae, Shibuya-ku; per hr ¥380; ⏰24hr; @📶; 🚉JR Yamanote Line to Harajuku, Takeshita exit) Tokyo's nicest internet cafe has big-screen Macs kitted out with Adobe software, and good coffee.

Wired Café 360 (ワイアードカフェ360; www.cafecompany.co.jp/brands/wired/360/index.html; 5th fl, KDDI Design Studio, 4-32-16 Jingūmae, Shibuya-ku; coffee ¥450; ⏰10am-8pm; @📶; 🚉JR Yamanote Line to Harajuku, Takeshita exit) Has five computers that you can use if you buy a drink or a meal.

LEFT LUGGAGE

Most train stations have coin lockers (priced ¥300 to ¥600 per day, depending on size), where you can store stuff for up to three days.

Both Narita and Haneda airports have luggage-keep facilities, which average about ¥500 per day. Porter services can ship your bags ahead to your hotel for about ¥2000.

JR East Travel Service Center (p141) keeps bags for ¥500 per day and can transport your luggage anywhere within the city for ¥1500.

LOST & FOUND

Lost items are recovered at an astonishing rate – it is always worth trying. If you lose something on the street, check in with the nearest *kōban* (police box) or contact the **Tokyo Metropolitan Police Lost and Found Center** (☑3814-4151; http://www.keishicho.metro.tokyo.jp/kouhoushi/no4/welcome/kensaku.htm).

If you leave something in a taxi, contact the **Tokyo Taxi Center** (☑3648-0300; www.tokyo-tc.or.jp/user/u_frame.html).

Major train stations have 'Lost & Found' windows (marked in English); at smaller ones inquire at the station window. If that fails, have your accomodation call the hotline number for the appropriate train operator:

JR East Infoline (☑ in English 050-2016-1603; www.jreast.co.jp/e/customer_support/infoline. html; ☺ 10am-6pm)

Toei Transportation Lost & Found (☑ 3812-2011; ☺ 9am-7pm Mon-Fri, 9am-5pm Sat & Sun)

Tokyo Metro Lost & Found (☑ 3834-5577; www.tokyometro.jp/en/support/lost/index.html; ☺ 9.30am-7pm Mon-Fri, 9.30am-4pm Sat & Sun)

MEDIA

Japan's longest-running English-language newspaper, the *Japan Times* (www.japantimes.co.jp), can be found in convenience stores and train station kiosks, as well as online. You can also read English versions of Japanese newspapers *Daily Yomiuri* (www.yomiuri.co.jp/dy) and *Asahi Shimbun* (http://ajw.asahi.com) online.

Metropolis (http://metropolis.co.jp) is a free English-language magazine for the expat community, with reviews and event listings. It comes out twice a month and can be found at places popular with foreigners; the online version is updated more frequently.

MEDICAL SERVICES

For a comprehensive list of medical services with English-speaking staff, check out http://japan.usembassy.gov/e/acs/tacs-tokyodoctors. html.

Keiō University Hospital (慶應義塾大学病院; Map p70; ☑ 3353-1211; www.hosp.med. keio.ac.jp; 35 Shinanomachi, Shinjuku-ku; ☺ 24hr emergency care; ᰮ JR Sōbu line to Shinanomachi)

St Luke's International Hospital (聖路加国際病院; Seiroka Kokusai Byōin; ☑ 3541-5151; www.luke.or.jp; 9-1 Akashi-chō, Chūō-ku; ☺ 24hr emergency care, outpatient service 8am-11am Mon-Fri; ᰮ Hibiya Line to Tsukiji, exits 3 & 4)

MONEY

Getting cash is easier in Tokyo than elsewhere in Japan, and even though most places take credit cards, it's still a good idea to have some cash as back-up.

7-Eleven (セブン・イレブン; www.sevenbank. co.jp/english) Have 24-hour cash dispensers that routinely work with overseas ATM cards; you'll find one in most neighbourhoods.

Citibank (シティバンク; www.citibank.co.jp/en) The only bank with ATMs that accept cards from every country; its ATMs are 24-hour, though locations are few and far between.

Post offices (ゆうちょ銀行; www.jp-bank. japanpost.jp/en/ias/en_ias_index.html) Have English-language ATMs, though they often close early in the evenings and on weekends.

POST

You're never more than a couple hundred metres from a post office in central Tokyo. The **Tokyo Central Post Office** (東京中央郵便局; ☑ 3217-5231; 2-7-2 Marunouchi, Chiyoda-ku; ☺ post 24hr, ATM 12.05am-11.55pm Mon-Sat, to 9pm Sun; ᰮ JR Yamanote Line to Tokyo Station, Marunouchi south exit) is on the ground floor of the JP Tower in Marunouchi and keeps later hours than most. The **Azabu Post Office** (☑ 3582-7431; 1-6-19 Azabudai, Minato-ku; ☺ post 9am-7pm Mon-Fri, ATM 8am-9pm Mon-Fri, 9am-5pm Sat & Sun; ᰮ Kamiyachō, exit 2) near Roppongi is accustomed to foreigners. Post offices can hold post restante mail for 10 days.

TELEPHONE

There are several mobile phone rental companies operating out of Narita airport: www.narita-airport.jp/en/guide/service/list/svc_19.html.

Some have cheaper base fees, while others have cheaper call rates; it's a good idea to shop around for a package that best suits your needs. Some even offer smart phones, which are invaluable for navigating Tokyo's confusing address system.

There are a few rental shops at Haneda, too: http://www.haneda-airport.jp/inter/en/premises/service/internet.html#mobilePhone.

Depending on how long you're staying, it may be a better deal to buy a prepaid mobile. Mobile carrier **Softbank** (http://mb.softbank. jp/en/prepaid_service) has them, and the shops in **Roppongi** (☑ 5775-5011; 4-9-7 Roppongi, Minato-ku; ☺ 10am-9pm; ᰮ Hibiya Line to Roppongi, exit 4) and **Omote-sandō** (☑ 03-6406-0711; 1-13-9 Jingūmae, Shibuya-ku; ☺ 10am-9pm; ᰮ JR Yamanote Line to Harajuku, Omote-sandō exit) have English-speaking staff who can help you get sorted. They don't keep many in stock though, so it's a good idea to visit early, or call ahead. You'll need your passport and a photo ID with your home address printed on it.

TOURIST INFORMATION

There are tourist information centres at both terminals at Narita Airport with English-speaking staff who can help you get oriented.

Asakusa Tourist Information Center (浅草文化観光センター; Map p100; http://taitonavi. jp; 2-18-9 Kaminarimon, Taitō-ku; ☺ 9am-8pm; @ ☏; ᰮ Ginza Line to Asakusa, exit 2) Maps and pamphlets in English, and excellent views of Tokyo Sky Tree from the 8th floor. Tokyo SGG Club (p105) guided tours leave from here.

JNTO Tourist Information Center (TIC; Map p74; ☑ 3201-3331; www.jnto.go.jp; 1st fl, Shin-Tokyo Bldg, 3-3-1 Marunouchi, Chiyoda-ku; ☺ 9am-5pm; ᰮ JR Yamanote line to Yūrakuchō, Tokyo International Forum exit) This main TIC operated by the Japan National Tourism Organisation (JNTO) has the most comprehensive information on travel in Tokyo and Japan, and knowledgeable, English-speaking staff.

Marunouchi Cafe Seek (Map p74; www.marunouchicafe.com; 2nd fl, Shin-Tokyo Bldg, 3-3-1 Marunouchi, Chiyoda-ku; ⊙9am-8pm Mon-Fri, 11am-6pm Sat & Sun; @ ⊙) Upstairs from the JNTO TIC, this comfy lounge has an impressive library of books on Tokyo and Japan, free internet and friendly, English-speaking staff.

Shibuya Tourist Information Center (渋谷観光案内所; http://shibuyakukanko.jp.e.ea. hp.transer.com; 4th fl, Mark City, Shibuya Station; ⊙11am-9pm; ⊠JR Yamanote Line to Shibuya, Hachikō exit) Maps and brochures that cover some of Shibuya's more off-the-beaten-path locales.

Tokyo Tourist Information Center (東京観光情報センター; ☑5321-3077; www.gotokyo. org/en/index.html; 1st fl, Tokyo Metropolitan Government Bldg 1, 2-8-1 Nishi-Shinjuku, Shinjuku-ku; ⊙9.30am-6.30pm; ⊠Ōedo line to Tochōmae, exit A4) Run by the municipal government, this TIC has local info (including tons of English maps and brochures), but can't make bookings.

There's also a branch at Keisei Ueno Station (☑3836-3471; ⊙9.30am-6.30pm) and at the international terminal in Haneda Airport.

Yanesen Tourist Information Center (☑3828-7878; www.ti-yanesen.jp/en; 3-16-6 Yanaka, Taitō-ku; ⊙9am-5pm; ⊠Chiyoda Line to Sendagi, exit 2) Local information about the Yanaka area; check the website for information on cultural experiences and guided tours.

TRAVEL AGENCIES

JR East Travel Service Center (JR東日本訪日旅行センター; Map p74; www.jreast.co.jp/e/ customer_support/information_center.html; Tokyo Station Marunouchi North; ⊙7.30am-8.30pm; ⊠JR Yamanote Line to Tokyo, Marunouchi north exit) Cash in your Japan Rail Pass voucher, or purchase a Japan Rail Pass here. English-speaking staff can also book *shinkansen* tickets, discount onsen and ski packages, and budget accommodations in Tokyo. Check the website for other JR travel service centre locations

JTB (Map p74; ☑3213-9181; www.jtb.co.jp; 1-4-1 Marunouchi, Chiyoda-ku; ⊙11am-7pm; ⊠JR Yamanote Line to Tokyo, Marunouchi north exit) Japan's most ubiquitous travel agency specialises in domestic travel packages and can book some highway bus and ferry tickets. There are dozens of branches around the city.

No 1 Travel (☑3200-8871; www.no1-travel. com; 7th fl, Don Quijote Bldg, 1-16-5 Kabukichō, Shinjuku-ku; ⊙10am-6.30pm Mon-Fri, 11am-6pm Sat; ⊠JR Yamanote Line to Shinjuku, east exit) Discount air tickets and packages for overseas travel from Japan. Staff are fluent in English and other languages. There's another branch in Shibuya (6th fl, Osawa Bldg, 1-20-1 Dōgenzaka, Shibuya-ku; ⊙10am-6.30pm Mon-Fri, 11am-4.30pm Sat; ⊠JR Yamanote Line to Shibuya, Hachikō exit).

USEFUL WEBSITES

Go Tokyo (www.gotokyo.org/en/index.html) Tokyo metropolitan goverment tourism website, with attraction and festival information.

Metropolis (http://metropolis.co.jp) Comprehensive events listings, plus articles on what's going on in Tokyo.

Time Out Tokyo (www.timeout.jp/en/tokyo) Lots of reviews, plus a reliable weekend guide (published on Thursdays).

Tokyo Art Beat (www.tokyoartbeat.com) Bilingual art and design guide with regularly updated list of exhibitions.

Tokyo Fashion (http://tokyofashion.com) The lowdown on the latest trends and brands, as well as fashion-related events.

Tokyo Food Page (www.bento.com) Restaurant directory compiled by a *Japan Times* dining columnist; note that some information is outdated.

Tokyo Parks (www.tokyo-park.or.jp/english/ index.html) Resource of picturesque places to unwind in the capital.

Tokyo Pocket Guide (www.tokyopocketguide. com/tokyo) A web library of English pdf maps detailing major neighbourhoods in the city centre.

VISA EXTENSION

Tokyo Regional Immigration Bureau (東京入国管理局; Tokyo Nyūkoku Kanrikyoku; Map p70; ☑5796-7111; www.immi-moj.go.jp/english/ index.html; 5-5-30 Kōnan, Minato-ku; ⊙9am-noon & 1-4pm Mon-Fri; ⊠99 from Shinagawa Station east exit to Tokyo Nyūkoku Kanrikyoku-mae, ⊠Rinkai Line to Tennōzu Isle) Handles all things visa-related for greater Tokyo.

ⓘ Getting There & Away

AIR

Tokyo has two major airports: **Narita Airport** (成田空港; ☑0476-34-8000; www.narita-airport.jp/en; Narita-shi, Chiba-ken) and **Haneda Airport** (羽田空港; ☑5757-8111; international terminal 6428-0888; www.tokyo-airport-bldg. co.jp/en; Ōta-ku). Most international flights operate through the former while domestic travel is usually funnelled through the latter. However, Haneda opened an international wing in October 2010. In general, flights to Narita are cheaper, but on the other hand Narita is considerably further from the city centre than Haneda.

Immigration and customs procedures are usually straightforward, but they can be time-consuming. Note that Japanese customs officials can be very scrupulous; backpackers arriving from anywhere even remotely exotic (the Philippines, Thailand etc) can expect some questions and perhaps a thorough search.

It is important to note that there are two distinct terminals at Narita, separated by a five-minute train ride. Be sure to check which terminal your flight departs from, and give yourself plenty of time to get out to Narita. Airport officials recommend leaving at least four hours before your flight.

BOAT

Ferries and high-speed jet foils depart for the Izu and Ogasawara Islands from **Takeshiba Pier** (竹芝桟橋; Takeshiba Sanbashi; www.tptc.co.jp/tabid/329/Default.aspx; 1-16-3 Kaigan, Minato-ku; ℝ JR Yamanote Line to Hamamatsuchō, north exit).

BUS

Long-distance buses, managed by most rail companies, including Japan Rail, are usually cheaper than trains and every once in a while actually more convenient. The most popular bus route is the one that travels to Mt Fuji from the **Shinjuku Highway Bus Terminal** (新宿高速バスターミナル; Map p88; ☑ 5376-2222; www.highwaybus.com/html/gp/foreign/en/access/index.html; 1-10-1 Nishi-Shinjuku, Shinjuku-ku; ◷ 6am-11.30pm; ℝ JR Yamanote Line to Shinjuku, west exit). Same-day tickets can be purchased on the ground floor of the terminal, where there is a timetable in English; advanced ticket sales are sold on the 2nd floor.

JR Highway Buses (JR 高速バス; www.jrbuskanto.co.jp/bus_route_e/) depart for major cities throughout Honshu from bus terminals in **Shinjuku** (Map p88; ◷ 6.20am-12.05am; ℝ JR Yamanote Line to Shinjuku, south exit) and at **Tokyo Station** (Map p74; ◷ 6am-12.30am; ℝ JR Yamanote Line to Tokyo, Yaesu south exit).

TRAIN

The following information pertains to cross-country travel from Tokyo.

JR Lines

There are several *shinkansen* (bullet train) lines that connect Tokyo with the rest of Japan – they are the most convenient way to move around the country. Note that some make more stops than others; Japan Rail Pass holders can't ride the fastest trains, Nozomi and Mizuho, on the Tōkaidō line.

Akita Line Branches off from the Tōhoku line at Morioka, heading to Akita.

Jōetsu Line Northbound for Niigata.

Nagano Line Splinters off from the Jōetsu line, bound for Nagano.

Tōhoku Line Runs northeast through Sendai all the way to Shin-Aomori, from where you can continue on to Hokkaidō.

Tōkaidō Line Zips through Central Honshū, stopping in Kyoto and Osaka, then changes its name to the Sanyō line before terminating in Kyūshū.

Yamagata Line Splinters off from the Tōhoku line at Fukushima, bound for Yamagata. All lines pass through Tokyo Station, though you can ride the Tōkaidō line to Shinagawa Station and the Jōetsu or Tōhoku lines to Ueno Station. Shinagawa and Ueno are both on the JR Yamanote line, like Tokyo Station.

There is also a local Tōkaidō Line service that shadows the bullet train, making regular stops throughout Central Honshū as it trundles towards Nagoya, Kyoto and Osaka. The Tōhoku main line crawls alongside the Tōhoku *shinkansen*, from Ueno to Morioka. Both require multiple transfers to go the length of the route.

Private Lines

Tokyo's private train lines service the city's sprawling suburbia, but also connect the capital to several worthwhile day-trip destinations. All private lines depart from a major station along the JR Yamanote line, with the exception of the Tobu Nikkō line.

RIVERBOAT CRUISE

Riverboats were once a primary means of transportation in Tokyo, and the Sumida-gawa was the main 'highway'. You can experience this centuries-old tradition (and happily combine sightseeing and transport) by hopping on one of the water buses run by **Tokyo Cruise** (水上バス; Suijō Bus; http://suijobus.co.jp).

Of the four routes, the Sumida-gawa line is the most popular, which runs from Asakusa to Hama-rikyū-teien (¥720, 35 minutes) and terminates at **Hinode Pier** (日の出桟橋; ℝ Yurikamome Line to Hinode, east exit) on Tokyo Bay.

The Asakusa-Odaiba Direct Line connects Asakusa with Odaiba Kaihin-kōen (¥1520, 50 minutes), also via the Sumida-gawa. If you're planning to take this route, try to catch one of the two spaceshiplike boats, *Himiko* and *Hotaluna*, designed by famous manga artist Leiji Matsumoto.

ⓘ SUICA CARDS & DISCOUNT PACKAGES

Transferring between multiple lines and calculating fares becomes a no-brainer with this prepaid train pass kitted out with an electromagnetic chip. Simply swipe the card over the reader on the ticket gates. Suica is good on all subway, rail and bus lines in greater Tokyo and can be charged at most electronic ticket machines. The cards require a ¥500 deposit, refundable when you return it to a JR window.

Pick up a Suica charged with ¥2000 and get a deal on airport transport with the **Suica & N'EX** (from Narita) or **Suica & Monorail** (from Haneda) packages, available from JR East Travel Service Centers at either airport. A round-trip package from Narita to Tokyo Station costs ¥5880 (saving you ¥2000).

Keiō Line Connects Shinjuku with the popular hiking spot, Takao-san.

Odakyū Line Heads southwest from Shinjuku to Odawara, where you can transfer to trains for Hakone.

Tobu Nikkō Line Connects Asakusa with Nikkō to the north.

Tōkyū Tōyoko Line Runs south from Shibuya to Yokohama.

ⓘ Getting Around

TO/FROM NARITA AIRPORT

Narita Airport is 66km from central Tokyo. With the exception of very early morning flights, public transportation can usually meet all arrival and departure times.

Depending on where you're headed, it's generally cheaper and faster to travel into Tokyo by train than by limousine bus. However, rail users will probably need to change trains somewhere, and this can be frustrating on a jetlagged first visit.

Bus services provide a hassle-free direct route to many major hotels, and you don't have to be a hotel guest to use them; a short taxi ride (and there are always taxis waiting in front of big hotels) can take you the rest of the way.

We don't recommend taking a taxi from Narita – it'll set you back around ¥30,000. Figure one to two hours into your itinerary to get to/from Narita.

Bus

Limousine Bus (リムジンバス; www.limousinebus.co.jp/en) Convenient, hourly shuttle buses connect Narita to major hotels and train stations, such as Shinjuku (¥3000, 1½ hours to two hours). Buses also run between Narita and Haneda airport (¥3000, one to 1½ hours).

Heiwa Kōtsū (平和交通; Map p74; http://heiwakotsu.com/na_top_english.htm#3) Discount buses run between Ginza, Tokyo Station and Narita Airport (¥1000, one to 1¼ hours); however you'll have to reserve online (in Japanese) or take your chances on there being a spare seat.

Train

The local JR 'Airport Narita' train costs ¥1280 and takes 1½ hours to or from Tokyo Station.

Keisei Skyliner (京成スカイライナー; www.keisei.co.jp) Zips between the airport and Ueno Station (¥2400, 45 minutes), also stopping at Nippori Station. The economical Keisei Limited Express (¥1000, 1½ hours) is its main line (read: turtle speed) counterpart. If you're transferring to/from the JR Yamanote line, access the train from Nippori Station; subway passengers should use Ueno Station.

Narita Express (N'EX; www.jreast.co.jp/e/nex/index.html) Runs approximately every half-hour, linking the airport to Tokyo Station (¥2940, 53 minutes) before branching off to either Shinjuku, Shibuya or Shinagawa stations (all ¥3110, 1½ hours). Seats are reserved, but tickets can be bought immediately before departure if they are available from the ticket counters in either airport terminal. Japan Rail Pass holders can ride for free.

TO/FROM HANEDA AIRPORT

From downtown Tokyo, it takes far less time to reach Haneda Airport than Narita. Taxis to the city centre cost around ¥6000; this will be your only option if your flight gets in before dawn.

Keikyu Line (www.haneda-tokyo-access.com/en) 'Airport Express' trains run between Shinagawa Station and Keikyu Haneda Station (¥400, 16 minutes).

Limousine Bus (p143) Coach buses connect Haneda with major centres such as Shibuya (¥1000), Shinjuku (¥1200) and Tokyo Station (¥900), as well as Narita Airport (¥3000, one to 1½ hours). Travel time depends on traffic, but averages about 45 minutes to most points in the city centre. The last bus of the evening from Haneda leaves for Shibuya Station at 12.30am; buses start up again around 5am.

Tokyo Monorail (www.tokyo-monorail.co.jp/english) A direct link to Haneda from Hamamatsuchō Station on the JR Yamanote line (¥470, 25 minutes).

BICYCLE

Tokyo may not have many bike lanes, but that doesn't stop a lot of locals from taking to the city on two wheels. Cycling is an excellent way to get around, and to see how the city fits together. Some guesthouses (especially around Ueno and Asakusa) have bikes to lend. Otherwise, check out these rental shops, and make sure to have photo ID on you.

Muji Yūrakuchō Rent a Cycle (無印有楽町 レンタサイクル; Map p74; ☑ 5208-8241; www. mujiyurakucho.com/renta/index.asp; 3-8-3 Marunouchi, Chiyoda-ku; weekday/weekend ¥525/1050; ⊙10am-8pm; ℝ JR Yamanote Line to Yūrakuchō, Kyōbashi exit) These bicyles go quickly on weekends, but you can usually score one early on a weekday; a ¥3000 deposit is required. The rental counter is inside the Muji shop.

Sumida-kōen Bicycle Parking Lot (隅田公園 駐輪場; Map p100; 1-1 Hanakawado, Taitō-ku; ¥200; ⊙6am-8pm; ℝ Ginza Line to Asakusa, exit 5) City bikes for rent, just next to the Tokyo Cruise Pier in Asakusa.

Tokyo Rent a Bike (☑ mobile 090-6516-9992; www.tokyorentabike.com; 8th fl, 3-5-11 Naka-Meguro, Meguro-ku; per day ¥1000; ⊙pick up 10am-1pm Sat & Sun, by reservation on weekdays; ℝ Hibiya Line to Naka-Meguro) Six-gear city bikes, mountain bikes, cycling maps and tours.

BUS

Municipal buses criss-cross the city and cost ¥200 a ride; there are no transfer tickets. That said, few tourists find the bus system, with its limited English, convenient, save for the the superhandy Shiubya-to-Roppongi service, which departs outside the east exit of Shibuya Station.

The **Megurin** (めぐりん; www.city.taito.lg.jp/index/kurashi/kotsu/megurin/index.html; one ride/day pass ¥100/300; ⊙ every 15 minutes, 7am-7pm) bus runs around Taitō-ku, stopping near many sights and accommodations in Ueno and Asakusa; look for a route map at any of the TICs in those neighbourhoods.

Free Shuttles

Several neighbourhoods have free local shuttles.

Marunouchi Shuttle (www.hinomaru.co.jp/metrolink/marunouchi/index.html; ⊙every 15min 10am-8pm) Transports passengers up Daimyōkoji and down Hibiya-dōri.

Metro Link Nihonbashi (Map p74; www. hinomaru.co.jp/metrolink/nihonbashi/index. html; ⊙every 10min 10am-8pm) Connects Kyōbashi and Mitsukoshimae subway stations with Tokyo Station.

Tokyo Bay Shuttle (www.hinomaru.co.jp/metrolink/odaiba/index.html; ⊙every 15-20min 11am-8pm) Loops around Odaiba; there's a stop just outside exit B of Tokyo Teleport Station.

Panda Bus (http://www.pandabus.net/Route. html; ⊙hourly 10am-5pm) Has two routes that connect Ueno, Asakusa and Tokyo Sky Tree. The bus really does look like a panda, though unfortunately it runs infrequently.

CAR & MOTORCYCLE

Riding a bike through Tokyo can actually be faster than driving a car. With the city's chaotic traffic, exorbitant parking rates and network of one-way streets, we do not recommend renting a vehicle to get around – especially since the public transport network is so efficient.

If you're keen on renting a car to get out of the metropolis, consider taking a train away from central Tokyo (or at least to the edge) and renting a car from there.

Major Japanese car rental chains (Toyota, Nissan, Mazda etc) have numerous branches in and around Tokyo (including the airports) and take online reservations in English.

TAXI

It rarely makes economic sense to take a taxi, unless you've got a group of four. The meter starts at a steep ¥710, which gives you 2km of travel. After that, the meter starts to clock an additional ¥100 for every 350m (and up to ¥100 for every two minutes you sit idly in traffic). Figure around ¥2500 for a ride from Roppongi to Ginza. It's best to have cash on you, as not all taxis take credit cards.

While it's possible to hail a cab from the street, you're best bet is a taxi stand in front of a train station. Taxis with their indicator in red are free; green means taken.

Even in Tokyo, most cabbies don't speak English and have trouble finding all but the most well-known spots. Fortunately many have GPS systems, so have an address or a business card for your destination handy.

TRAIN

Tokyo's train network includes JR lines, a subway system, and private commuter lines. It's so thorough, especially in the city centre, that you rarely have to walk more than 10 minutes from a station to your destination. Stations have English signage.

Tickets are sold from vending machines near the automated ticket gates. Look for the newer touch screen ones that have an English option. Fares are determined by how far you ride; there should be a fare chart above the ticket machines. You'll need a valid train ticket to exit the station.

ℹ TRAIN TIPS

As far as public transport networks go, no city can touch Tokyo's awesome network of trains and subway lines. It's clean, quick, efficient and convenient, but it does have it's quirks. Some tips:

➡ Avoid rush hour (around 8am to 9.30am and 5pm to 8pm), when 'packed in like sardines' is an understatement.

➡ Note your last train. The whole system shuts down from approximately midnight to 5am. The last train of the night can also be especially crowded (often with swaying drunks).

➡ If you can't work out how much to pay, one easy trick is to buy a ticket at the cheapest fare (¥130 for JR; ¥160 for Tokyo Metro; ¥170 for Toei) and use one of the 'fare adjustment' machines, near the exit gates, to settle the difference at the end of your journey.

➡ Tokyo's competing rail lines can make getting from point A to point B – in the cheapest, most economical way – a little confusing. **Jorudan** (www.jorudan.co.jp/english/norikae), also available as an iPhone app, is a lifesaver: it calculates routes by speed and fare.

➡ Most train stations have multiple exits – make sure you get the right one (which can save you a lot of time and confusion above ground). There are usually maps in the station that show which exits are closest to major area landmarks.

Day Passes

Day passes can save you money, though only if you plan to cover a lot of ground in one day. You'll need to get one that covers the rail lines you'll be using, and purchase it from one of the station windows on those lines.

Tokyo Metro 1-Day Open Ticket Costs ¥710 (child ¥360) and covers Tokyo Metro subway lines.

Common 1-Day Ticket Costs ¥1000 (child ¥500) and covers both Tokyo Metro and Toei subway lines.

Tokyo Combination Ticket Costs ¥1580 (child ¥790) and covers JR trains in Tokyo, all subway lines and Toei buses.

JR Lines

Carving out the city's centre, the elevated **Yamanote Line** does a 35km-long loop around the metropolis, taking in most of the important areas. Another useful JR route is the **Chūō**

Line, also above ground, which cuts across the city centre from Tokyo Station to Shinjuku and points further west. Tickets are transferable on all JR lines.

Private Lines

Private lines connect downtown Tokyo with the suburbs, but a few service popular destinations.

Keiō Inokashira Line Travels from Shibuya to Kichijōji, stopping at Shimo-Kitazawa and Inokashira-kōen.

Tōkyū Tōyoko Line Connects Shibuya with Daikanyama and Naka-Meguro.

Subway Lines

There are a total of 13 colour-coded subway lines zigzagging through Tokyo. Four are operated by TOEI; nine belong to Tokyo Metro. Transfers between lines within the same group are seamless; if you plan to switch between TOEI trains and Tokyo Metro trains, you'll need to purchase a transfer ticket at the start of your journey.

Mt Fuji & Around Tokyo

Includes ➡

Best Onsen

➡ Jinata Onsen (p183)

➡ Urami-ga-taki Onsen (p184)

➡ Takaragawa Onsen (p166)

➡ Sai-no-kawara (p164)

Best Culture

➡ Hakone Open-Air Museum (p172)

➡ Tōshō-gū (p159)

➡ Kairaku-en (p167)

➡ Kenchō-ji (p190)

Why Go?

With ancient sanctuaries, hot springs, mountains and beaches, the region surrounding Tokyo is a natural foil for the dizzying capital. Really, you couldn't design it any better if you tried.

Authentic country ryokan, regional cuisines and cedar-lined trails are all within two hours of central Tokyo, as well as the symbol of Japan itself, alluring Mt Fuji. There's history here too, including an old medieval capital and ports that were among the first to open to the West. These are, for better or for worse, well-visited places and you'll find transport and communication to be a comparative breeze.

The Izu Islands and World Heritage–listed Ogasawara, island chains that trickle some 1000km south from Tokyo, are the exception. Though they're technically still part of the capital, you'll find many Tokyoites are only vaguely familiar with them – so much the better for those looking for total escape.

When to Go
Kawaguchi-ko

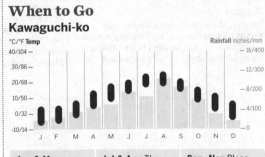

Apr & May Experience the flush of spring in the mountains north and west of Tokyo.

Jul & Aug The official season for Mt Fuji climbing and beach-hopping around the Izu Peninsula.

Sep–Nov Pleasant temperatures and fewer crowds, save when the autumn leaves blaze red.

MT FUJI AREA

Mt Fuji (富士山周辺; Fuji-san; 3776m), Japan's highest and most famous peak, is obviously this region's natural draw. In addition to climbing Fuji-san, visitors can hunt for precious views of the sacred volcano, and get outdoorsy around the Fuji Five Lakes (Fuji go-ko) with plenty of camping, hiking and lake activities.

👉 Tours

Discover Japan Tours   GUIDED TOUR
(www.discover-japan-tours.com/en) Reputable tour company running guided group tours of Mt Fuji from Tokyo (¥10,000 per person for groups of two or more), specialising in less frequented routes. Private tours also available.

Fujiyama Guides   GUIDED TOUR
(☏0555-23-7554; www.fujiyamaguides.com) Delve into the rich history of the mountain with a three-day pilgrim tour; price depends on group size (private tour/per person for two ¥116,000/¥61,000). It also offers two-day off-season guided climbs of Mt Fuji (June to October, weather permitting; private tour/per person for two ¥65,000/36,000).

ℹ Information

All of the following have English-speaking staff and brochures on climbing and sights.
Fuji-Yoshida Tourist Information Center
(☏0555-22-7000; ⊙9am-5pm) Inside Fujisan (Mt Fuji) Station. Has all the info on climbing, and brochures and maps of the area.
Kawaguchi-ko Tourist Information Center
(☏0555-72-6700; ⊙8.30am-5.30pm Sun-Fri, until 7pm Sat) At Kawaguchi-ko Station, with maps and brochures.
Shin-Fuji Station Tourist Information Center
(☏0545-64-2430; ⊙8.45am-5.30pm) On the 1st floor of the *shinkansen* (bullet train) station in Tokyo.

ℹ Getting There & Away

The Mt Fuji area is most easily reached from Tokyo by bus or train. The two main towns on the north side of the mountain, Fuji-Yoshida and Kawaguchi-ko, are the principal gateways. It's also possible to bus in straight from Tokyo to the Kawaguchi-ko Fifth Station on the mountain during the official climbing season.

Coming from Western Japan (Kyoto, Osaka), you can take an overnight bus to Kawaguchi-ko.

BUS

Frequent Keiō Dentetsu (p152) and Fujikyū Express (p153) buses (¥1700, one hours and 50 minutes) operate directly to Kawaguchi-ko Station, and Fujisan Station in Fuji-Yoshida, from the **Shinjuku Highway Bus Terminal** (☏03-5376-2222).

Coming from Western Japan, the overnight bus departs from Osaka's Higashi-Umeda Subway Station (¥8500, 10.15pm) via Kyoto Station (¥8000, 11.18pm) to Kawaguchi-ko Station (arrives 8.32am).

TRAIN

JR Chūō line trains go from Shinjuku to Ōtsuki (*tokkyū* ¥2980, one hour; *futsū* ¥1280, 1½ hours), where you transfer to the Fuji Kyūkō line for Fujisan Station (¥990, 45 minutes) and Kawaguchi-ko (¥1110, 50 minutes).

Mt Fuji   富士山

Of all the iconic images of Japan, Mt Fuji is the real deal. Admiration for the mountain appears in Japan's earliest recorded literature, dating from the 8th century. Back then the now dormant volcano was prone to spewing smoke, making it all the more revered. Mt Fuji continues to captivate both Japanese and international visitors; in 2012, some 318,000 people climbed it. It's currently under consideration to become a World Heritage Listed Site.

The Japanese proverb 'He who climbs Mount Fuji once is a wise man, he who climbs it twice is a fool' remains as valid as ever. While reaching the top brings a great sense of achievement (particularly at sunrise), be aware it's a grueling climb and one that's not known for its beautiful scenery or being at one with nature. It's often packed with trekkers, and its barren apocalyptic-looking landscape is worlds away from Fuji's beauty that's viewed from afar.

At the summit, the crater has circumference of 4km. As expected, views are spectacular, but be prepared for it to be clouded over. The highest point (3776m) is on the opposite side of the crater, and there's a post office if you want to send a postcard back home.

Mt Fuji Climbing Guide (www.mountfujiguide.com) and **Climbing Mt Fuji** (www17.plala.or.jp/climb_fujiyama/index.html) are both excellent online resources with all the info climbers need. The *Climbing Mt Fuji* brochure, available at the Fuji-Yoshida Tourist Information Center, is also worth picking up.

Mt Fuji & Around Tokyo Highlights

1 Watching the sunrise from the summit of majestic **Mt Fuji** (p147), Japan's highest mountain and national symbol

2 Taking in old Edo's grandeur at the shrines and temples of **Nikkō** (p157)

3 Flip-flopping between sandy beaches and seaside hot springs on the **Izu Peninsula** (p174)

4 Dipping into onsen culture in the mountains of **Gunma Prefecture** (p164)

5 Resetting your senses in the Zen temples of the medieval capital of **Kamakura** (p190)

6 Getting the Japanese resort experience in timeless **Hakone** (p169)

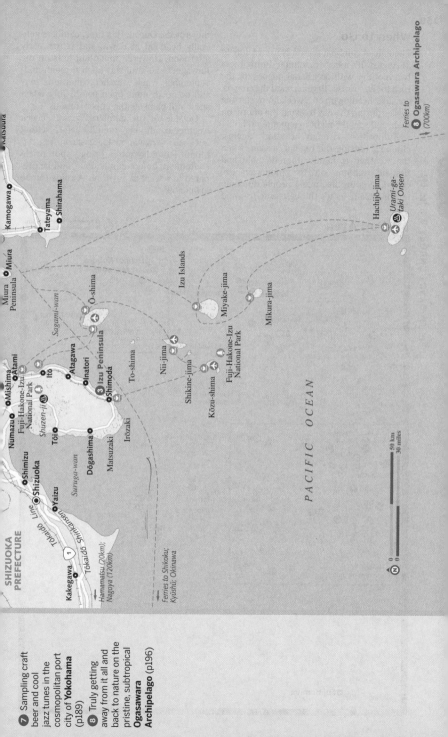

7 Sampling craft beer and cool jazz tunes in the cosmopolitan port city of **Yokohama** (p189)

8 Truly getting away from it all and back to nature on the pristine, subtropical **Ogasawara Archipelago** (p196)

SHIZUOKA PREFECTURE

Kakegawa

Tōkaidō Line

Tōkaidō Shinkansen

Yaizu

Shimizu

Shizuoka

Hamamatsu (20km); Nagoya (120km)

Ferries to Shikoku; Kyūshū; Okinawa

Numazu

Mishima

Atami

Fuji-Hakone-Izu National Park

Shuzen-ji

Tōi

Dōgashima

Matsuzaki

Irōzaki

Suruga-wan

Itō

Atagawa

Inatori

Shimoda

Izu Peninsula

Tō-shima

Nii-jima

Shikine-jima

Kōzu-shima

3

Numazu

Miura Peninsula

Miura

Sagami-wan

Ō-shima

Izu Islands

Kamogawa

Tateyama

Shirahama

Katsuura

Miyake-jima

Mikura-jima

Fuji-Hakone-Izu National Park

Hachijō-jima

Urami-ga-taki Onsen

Ferries to **8** Ogasawara Archipelago (700km)

PACIFIC OCEAN

0   50 km
0   30 miles

When to Go

The official climbing season is from 1 July to 31 August. It's a busy mountain during these two months, with occasional queues for the rush to see sunrise. To get around the crowds, consider heading up on a weekday or starting earlier during the day to avoid the afternoon rush, and spend a night in a mountain hut.

Authorities strongly caution against climbing outside the regular season, when the weather is highly unpredictable and first-aid stations on the mountain are closed. Despite this, many people do climb out of season, as it's the best time to avoid

the crowds. During this time, climbers generally head off at dawn, and return early afternoon. However, mountain huts on the Kawaguchi-ko Trail stay open through mid-September when weather conditions may still be good; none open before July, when snow still blankets the upper stations.

Outside of the climbing season, check weather conditions carefully before setting out (see www.snow-forecast.com/resorts/Mount-Fuji/6day/top), bring appropriate equipment, do not climb alone, and be prepared to retreat at any time. A guide can be invaluable.

Mt Fuji Area

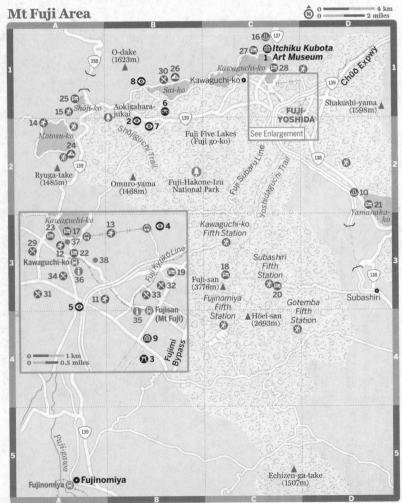

Once snow or ice is on the mountain, Fuji becomes a very serious and dangerous undertaking and should only be attempted by those with winter mountaineering equipment and plenty of experience. It's highly advised that off-season climbers register with the local police department for safety reasons; fill out the form at the Kawaguchi-ko or Fuji-Yoshida Tourist Information Centers.

Trails

The mountain is divided into 10 'stations' from base (First Station) to summit (Tenth). From the base station is the original pilgrim trail, but these days most climbers start from the halfway point at one of the four Fifth Stations, which are accessed via bus. All the routes converge at the Eighth Station, so be sure you take the right path on the way down.

To time your arrival for dawn you can either start up in the afternoon, stay overnight in a mountain hut and continue early in the morning, or climb the whole way at night. You do not want to arrive at the top too long before dawn, as it's likely to be very cold and windy.

Traditional Route

The completion of the road to Kawaguchi-ko Fifth Station in 1964 dramatically changed the culture of climbing Mt Fuji, allowing busy Tokyoites to bus in after work and bus out the next morning. Historically, Fuji pilgrims began at Sengen-jinja near present-day Fuji-Yoshida, paying their homage to the shrine gods before beginning their 19km ascent up Japan's most sacred mountain. Today, the **Yoshidaguchi Trail**, the oldest up the mountain, offers climbers a chance to participate in this centuries-old tradition. Purists will tell you this is the only way to climb, saying that the lower reaches are the most beautiful, through lush forests along an isolated path.

It takes about five hours to reach the old Yoshidaguchi Fifth Station; the trail meets up with the one leaving from the new Kawaguchi-ko Fifth Station at the Sixth Station. Count on it taking around 12 hours climb from Fuji's base to summit.

Fifth Station Routes

Around 90% of climbers opt for this more convenient route, which halves the trekking time. There are four Fifth Station trails for

Mt Fuji Area

ⓘ CLIMBING MT FUJI: KNOW BEFORE YOU GO

Although children and grandparents regularly reach the summit of Mt Fuji, this is a serious mountain. It's high enough for altitude sickness, and on the summit it can go from sunny and warm to wet, windy and cold remarkably quickly. Even if conditions are fine, you can count on it being close to freezing in the morning, even in summer. Also be aware that visibility can rapidly disappear with a blanket of mist rolling in suddenly. At a minimum, bring clothing appropriate for cold and wet weather, including a hat and gloves. You should also bring water, a map and light snacks. If you're climbing at night, bring a torch (flashlight) or headlamp, and spare batteries.

Descending the mountain is much harder on the knees than ascending; hiking poles can help. To avoid altitude sickness, be sure to take it slowly and take regular breaks. If you're suffering severe symptoms, you'll need to make an immediate descent.

The *Shobunsha Yama-to-kōgen Mt Fuji Map* (山と高原地図・富士山; in Japanese), available at major book stores, is the most comprehensive map of the area.

For summit weather conditions, see www.snow-forecast.com/resorts/Mount-Fuji/6day/top.

climbing Mt Fuji: Kawaguchi-ko, also known as Yoshida (2305m); Subashiri (1980m); Fujinomiya (2380m); and Gotemba (1440m). Allow five to six hours to reach the top (though some climb it in half the time) and about three hours to descend, plus 1½ hours for circling the crater at the top.

The **Kawaguchi-ko Trail** is by far and away the most popular route. It's accessed from Kawaguchi-ko Fifth Station (aka Mt Fuji Fifth Station), and it has the most modern facilities and is easiest to reach from Kawaguchi-ko town.

The less trodden, but more scenic forested **Subashiri Trail**, is a good alternative. As it merges with the Kawaguchi-ko Trail at the Eighth Station, it's possible to combine the two by heading up via the Kawaguchi-ko path and descending via Subashiri by running, schussing and sliding down its loose sand. Though be aware you'll end up at Subarashi Fifth Station, so it might not be an option if you've parked your car at Kawaguchi-ko Fifth Station.

Other Fifth Stations are **Fujinomiya**, which is best for climbers coming from the west (Nagoya, Kyoto and beyond) and the seldom-used and neglected **Gotemba Trail**, a 7½ hour climb to the summit.

Mountain Accommodation

From the Fifth Stations and up, dozens of mountain huts offer hikers simple hot meals and a place to sleep (with/without meals from ¥7350/5250). Though much maligned for their spartan conditions (a blanket on the floor sandwiched between other climbers), they can fill up fast – reservations are recommended and are essential on weekends. **Taishikan** (太子館; ☑ 22-1947) and **Fujisan Hotel** (富士山ホテル; ☑ 22-0237; www.fujisanhotel.com) at the Eighth Station (Kawaguchi-ko Trail) usually have an English speaker on hand. Most huts allow you to rest inside as long as you order something. Camping on the mountain is not permitted, other than at the designated campsite near the Kawaguchi-ko Fifth Station.

The Subashiri Fifth Station has the atmospheric **Higashi Fuji Lodge** (☑ 75-2113; r ¥5000), which is very convenient for off-season trekkers, and cooks up steaming *soba* (buckwheat noodles) with mushrooms and Fuji herbs.

ⓘ Getting There & Around

For those wanting to start trekking as soon as they arrive from Tokyo, **Keiō Dentetsu Bus** (☑ 03-5376-2222; www.highwaybus.com) runs direct buses (¥2600, 2½ hours; reservations necessary) from the Shinjuku Highway Bus Terminal to Kawaguchi-ko Fifth Station (does not operate in winter).

Buses run from both Kawaguchi-ko Station and Fujisan Station to the starting point at Kawaguchi-ko Fifth Station (one-way/return ¥1500/2000, 50 minutes) roughly mid-April to early December. In the trekking season, buses depart hourly from around 7am until 8pm (ideal for climbers intending to make an overnight ascent). Returning from Fifth Station, buses head back to town from 8am to 9pm.

In the off-season, the first bus inconveniently leaves Kawaguchi-ko and Fujisan Stations at 9.30am, and the last bus returns at 3.30pm, meaning most trekkers will need to get a taxi (around ¥12,000, plus tolls) in the morning to have enough time before getting the bus back. The bus schedule is highly seasonal; call **Fujikyū Yamanashi bus** (📞 0555-72-2922; http://transportation.fujikyu.co.jp) or your hotel for details.

In the low season you should be able to find other trekkers to share a taxi at K's House (p155). Car hire is another option (particularly if there's a group), costing around ¥6800 per day, plus ¥2000 in tolls.

To get to the Subashiri Fifth Station trail, you can catch a train from Kawaguchi-ko to Gotemba (¥1470), from where regular buses head to the Subashiri access point. Check timetables carefully before heading off.

Fuji Five Lakes 富士五湖

📞 555

The Fuji Five Lakes (Fuji go-ko) region is a postcard-like area around Fuji's northern foothills; its lakes act as natural reflecting pools for the mountain's perfect cone. Yamanaka-ko is the easternmost lake, followed by Kawaguchi-ko, Sai-ko, Shōji-ko and Motosu-ko. Particularly during the autumn *kōyō* (foliage) season, the lakes make a good overnight trip out of Tokyo, for leisurely strolling, lake activities and for hiking in the nearby mountains.

Fuji-Yoshida and Kawaguchi-ko are the most accessible and developed areas. Kawaguchi-ko is the most popular place to stay, with the best range of accommodation, but

both make good bases if you plan on climbing Mt Fuji and don't intend on overnighting in a mountain hut.

Fuji-Yoshida 富士吉田

Not actually a lake, Fuji-Yoshida is one of the main gateway towns for the Fuji Five Lakes area. The central district, **Gekkō-ji**, feels like the little town that time forgot, with original mid-20th-century facades. The Fujisan Station is in the centre of Fuji-Yoshida.

⊙ Sights & Activities

Fuji Sengen-jinja   SHINTŌ SHRINE
(5558 Kami-Yoshida) A necessary preliminary to the Mt Fuji ascent is a visit to this deeply wooded, atmospheric temple, built in 1615 but thought to have been the site of a shrine as early as 788. It's worth a visit for its 1000-year-old cedar; its main gate, which is rebuilt every 60 years (slightly larger each time); and its two 1-tonne *mikoshi* (portable shrines) used in the annual Yoshida no Hi-matsuri (Yoshida Fire Festival). From Fujisan Station it's a 15-minute walk, or take a bus to Sengen-jinja-mae (¥150, five minutes).

Togawa-ke Oshi-no-ie
Restored Pilgrim's Inn   HISTORIC BUILDING
(御師旧外川家住宅; 3-14-8 Kami-Yoshida; adult/child ¥100/50; ⊙ 9.30am-4.30pm, Wed-Mon) Fuji-Yoshida's *oshi-no-ie* (pilgrims' inns) have served visitors to the mountain since the

TOP VIEWS OF MT FUJI

Mt Fuji has many different personalities depending on the season. Winter and spring months are your best bet for seeing it in all its clichéd glory; however, even during these times the snow-capped peak may be visible only in the morning before it retreats behind its cloud curtain. Its elusiveness, however, is part of the appeal, making sightings all the more special. Here are some of our top spots for viewing, both in the immediate and greater area:

Kawaguchi-ko On the north side of the lake, where Fuji looms large over its shimmering reflection.

Motosu-ko The famous view depicted on the ¥1000 bill can be seen from the northwest side of the lake.

Hakone The mountain soars in the background of Ashino-ko and the red torii (shrine gate) rising from the water.

Izu Peninsula Journey along the west coast to catch glimpses of Fuji and the ocean, bathed in glorious sunsets.

Panorama-dai The end of this hiking trail (p156) rewards you with a magnificent front-on view of the mountain.

Kōyō-dai Mt Fuji can be seen from this lookout (p156), particularly stunning in the autumn colours.

ⓘ FUJISAN TRAIN STATION

In 2011, Fuji-Yoshida Station changed its name to Fujisan Station. It's also commonly referred to as Mt Fuji Station in English. This is not to be confused with the Kawaguchi-ko Fifth Station which is also commonly referred to as Mt Fuji Fifth Station. It's not a train station but a climbing access point (and bus stop) on the mountain, the starting point for the Kawaguchi-ko Trail to the summit. Confused yet?

days when climbing Mt Fuji was a pilgrimage rather than a tourist event. Very few still function as inns but Togawa-ke Oshi-no-ie offers some insight into the fascinating Edoera practice of Mt Fuji worship.

Fuji-Q Highland   AMUSEMENT PARK

(www.fuji-q.com; 5-6-1 Shin-Nishihara; admission only adult/child ¥1300/700, day pass ¥5000/3700; ⊙9am-5pm Mon-Fri, to 8pm Sat & Sun) A high-octane amusement park with spectacular roller coasters providing a memorable way to bag Fuji views. It's one stop west of Fujisan Station.

🛏 Sleeping & Eating

Fuji-Yoshida Youth Hostel   HOSTEL ¥

(☑22-0533; www.jyh.or.jp; 2-339 Honchō; r per person from ¥2900; ☻) This popular old lodging in Gekkō-ji has small, slightly dingy, tatami rooms, but some have mountain views. There are basic self-catering facilities and limited English is spoken. It's a 15-minute walk on the main road away from Fujisan Station; look for the sign on the left-hand side and turn down the small alley on the left just before it.

Mt Fuji Hostel Michael's   HOSTEL ¥

(☑72-9139; www.mfi.or.jp/mtfujihostel; 3-21-37 Shimo-Yoshida; dm from ¥2900; ☻@🛜) No-frills Western-style hostel above Michael's American Pub in Gekkō-ji.

Matsuya Cafe   CAFE ¥

(まつや茶房; 294-3 Shimo-Yoshida; sandwiches from ¥500; ⊙10am-7pm Tue-Sun; @🛜🖉🍴) Stop by for well-brewed coffee, grilled-cheese sandwiches and a chat with the savvy, English-speaking owner. It's in a wooden merchant's house from the 1930s on the main drag in Gekkō-ji; look for an old hanging wooden sign.

Michael's American Pub   PUB ¥¥

(マイケルズアメリカンパブ; 795-1 Shimo-Yoshida; meals ¥600-1200; ⊙11.30am-3.30pm Sun-Fri, 7pm-2am Fri-Wed; 🍴) For traditional Americana (burgers, pizzas and brew), drop by this expat and local favourite in Gekkō-ji.

Kawaguchi-ko 河口湖

Easily the most popular place to stay in the Fuji Five Lakes region, Kawaguchi-ko is the closest town to four of the five lakes and departure points for climbing Mt Fuji. Set around the lake, even if you have no intention of climbing, this is a great spot to hang out and enjoy what the Fuji Five Lakes region has to offer, along with great Mt Fuji views.

⊙ Sights & Activities

Kachi Kachi Yama Ropeway   ROPEWAY

(カチカチ山ロープウェイ; 1163-1 Azagawa; one-way/return adult ¥400/700, child ¥200/350; ⊙9am-5pm) Around 600m north of Kawaguchi-ko Station, on the lower eastern edge of the lake, this ropeway runs to the Fuji Viewing Platform (1104m). If you have time, there is a 3½-hour hike from here to Mitsutōge-yama (三つ峠山; 1785m); it's an old trail with excellent Fuji views. Ask at the Kawaguchi-ko Tourist Information Center for a map.

★ Itchiku Kubota Art Museum   MUSEUM

(久保田一竹美術館; http://itchiku-museum.com; 2255 Kawaguchi; adult/child ¥1300/400; ⊙9.30am-5.30pm) In an attractive Gaudí-influenced building, this excellent museum exhibits the kimono art of Itchiku Kubota. A small number of lavishly dyed kimonos from his life's work of continuous landscapes are displayed at any one time, in a grand hall of cypress. You might see Mt Fuji in the wintertime or the cherry blossoms of spring spread across oversized kimonos. Take the Retro-bus to Kubota Itchiku Bijyutukan Mae stop.

Fuji Visitor Center   VISITORS CENTRE

(富士ビジターセンター; ☑72-0259; 6663-1 Funatsu; ⊙8.30am-5pm) 𝗙𝗥𝗘𝗘 It's worth dropping in before your climb to get up to speed on Mt Fuji at this well-presented visitors centre. An English video (12 minutes) with a blockbuster movie soundtrack is a little cheesy but gives a good summary of the mountain and its geological history. There's also an observation deck.

Tensui Onsen ONSEN

(天水; http://tensui-kawaguchiko.com; admission ¥1000; ⏱10am-10pm) A 10-minute walk up-hill behind the Itchiku Kubota Art Museum, this onsen has a large indoor bath and rocky *rotemburo* (outdoor baths) with mountain views, although none of Fuji unfortunately. Towel rental is ¥200.

Ide Sake Brewery BREWERY

(☑72-0006; www.kainokaiun.jp; 8 Funatsu; ¥500; ⏱tours 9am & 3pm) Using the spring waters from Mt Fuji, this small-scale sake brewery has been producing Japan's favourite tipple for over 150 years, and its tours provide a fascinating insight to the production process. Tours are around 40 minutes, and include tasting of various sakes and a souvenir glass. The brewing season is November to March, but it's a fascinating visit any time of the year; reservations are essential. Also has a lovely Japanese garden.

Onsen-ji ONSEN

(☑72-6111; www.onsenji.net; ⏱11am-10pm Mon-Fri, 10am-10pm Sat & Sun) Just the place to soothe those aching legs, the waters of this popular *rotemburo* will feel like heaven for those returning from a day's trekking.

🛏 Sleeping

K's House Mt Fuji HOSTEL ¥

(☑83-5556; http://kshouse.jp/fuji-e/index.html; 6713-108 Funatsu; dm from ¥2500, d with/without bathroom ¥7800/6800; ⊝@🛜) The best budget choice in the Fuji area, this clean modern hostel has a welcoming atmosphere, spacious Japanese-style rooms and helpful English-speaking staff. There's a fully loaded kitchen, mountain bikes for hire and comfy common areas to meet fellow travellers/climbers. There's a bar around the corner and staff offer free pick-up from Kawaguchi-ko Station. Rooms fill up fast during the climbing season.

Kawaguchi-ko Station Inn HOSTEL ¥

(☑72-0015; www.st-inn.com; 3639-2 Funatsu; dm/s/d ¥2700/4500/8000) Across from the station, this spotless hostel offers mixed dorms (some with Fuji views), laundry facilities, English-speaking staff and a top-floor onsen looking out to Mt Fuji in the distance. There's an 11.30pm curfew.

Tominoko Hotel HOTEL ¥¥

(☑72-5080; www.tominoko.net; 55 Asakawa; r per person with 2 meals ¥12,000) Most lodgings on the lake with these views come with hefty price tags, but this place is a steal. Rooms are modern, smart Western-style twins. Ask for one on an upper level to score a balcony and take in the spectacular view of Mt Fuji across the lake. Also has a *rotemburo*.

Fuji Lake Hotel HOTEL ¥¥

(☑72-2209; www.fujilake.co.jp; 1 Funatsu; r per person with 2 meals from ¥15,750; @🛜) Near the Kawaguchi-ko town centre, and right on the shores of the lake, this historic 1935 hotel offers either Mt Fuji or lake views from its Japanese-Western combo rooms. Some rooms have private *rotemburo,* otherwise there's a common onsen.

Sunnide Resort HOTEL ¥¥¥

(サニーデリゾート; ☑76-6004; www.sunnide. com; 2549-1 Ōishi; d from ¥21,000, cottages from ¥16,000; @🛜) Offering views of Mt Fuji from the far side of Kawaguchi-ko, friendly Sunnide has hotel rooms and cottages with a delicious outdoor bath. You can splash out in the stylish suites or the discounted 'backpacker' rates (¥4200, no views), if same-day rooms are available. Breakfast/dinner costs ¥1500/1575.

Kozantei Ubuya RYOKAN ¥¥¥

(湖山亭うぶや; ☑72-1145; www.ubuya.co.jp; Asakawa; r per person with 2 meals from ¥20,100) Elegant and ultra stylish, Ubuya offers some of the best views we've seen from any hotel room. The unobstructed panoramic view of Mt Fuji reflected in Kawaguchi-ko is simply unbeatable, especially when soaking in an outdoor tub on your balcony decking. One for the honeymooners.

🍴 Eating

Kawaguchi-ko's local noodles are *hōtō*, hand-cut and served in a thick miso stew with pumpkin, sweet potato and other vegetables.

Akai IZAKAYA ¥

(mains from ¥525; ⏱6-11pm Fri-Wed; 🍴) Great little *izakaya* (pub-eatery), popular with the locals, serving sensational whole grilled fish and *ika yakisoba* (fried noodles with squid). It's off Rte 137, down an alleyway next to the petrol station near the Ogino supermarket.

Hōtō Fudō NOODLES ¥¥

(ほうとう不動; 707 Kawaguchi; hōtō ¥1050; ⏱11am-7pm) Four branches around town serve this massive hearty stew, bubbling in its own cast-iron pot, but certainly the most interesting is this one. South of the lake, this architecturally designed igloo-like concrete building sits against the Mt Fuji backdrop.

Sanrokuen TEPPANYAKI ¥¥
(3370-1 Funatsu; set meals ¥2100-4200; ⊘10am-7.30pm Fri-Wed; 🅟) Here diners sit on the floor around traditional *irori* (charcoal pits) grilling their own meals – skewers of fish, meat, tofu and vegies. From Kawaguchi-ko Station, turn left, left again after the 7-Eleven and after 600m you'll see the thatched roof on the right.

Sai-ko 紅葉台

Sai-ko is a quiet lake area good for hiking, fishing and boating. Mt Fuji is mostly obstructed but there are great views from the **Kōyō-dai** lookout, near the main road, and from the western end of the lake.

⊙ Sights

Narusawa Ice Cave CAVE
(adult/child ¥280/130; ⊘9am-5pm) Narusawa Ice Cave was formed by lava flows from a prehistoric eruption of Mt Fuji. Walk through the chilly cave to the end to see the lava display.

Fugaku Wind Cave CAVE
(adult/child ¥280/130; ⊘8am-5pm) Accessed via a 1.4km path from the Narusawa Ice Cave, Fugaku was also formed by prehistoric lava flows from Mt Fuji, you'll need to crawl through some tight ice-walled spaces here to see what was once used as cold storage.

Sai-ko Iyashi-no-Sato Nenba CULTURAL CENTRE
(西湖いやしの里根場; 2710 Nenba; adult/child ¥350/150; ⊘9am-5pm) Built in 2006 on the site of historic thatched-roof houses washed away in a typhoon 40 years earlier, these reconstructed frames offer an insight into a forgotten time. There are demonstrations of silk and paper crafts as well as restaurants specialising in *soba* and *hōtō*. The Retro bus stops right out front.

🛏 Sleeping & Eating

There are a few campgrounds around the lake; however, none of these are particularly appealing.

Sai-ko Otto Camp Jo CAMPGROUND ¥
(☑82-2921; camping for two incl tent rental ¥6000) Opposite the Hamayou Resort; has BBQ and water facilities, tent hire and canoe rental (¥3000, two hours).

Cafe M CAFE ¥¥
(mains from ¥1160; ⊘noon-5pm, Fri-Wed) By far the best feed on the lake, this cutesy country-style cafe has partial Fuji views from its outdoor decking and excellent cafe fare such as crab linguine. Also has a boutique gift store.

Shōji-ko 精進湖

Further west from Sai-ko, low-key and tiny Shōji-ko is said to be the prettiest of the Fuji Lakes and offers Mt Fuji views, fishing and boating.

Murahamasō (村浜荘; ☑83-2375, 87-2436; www.murahamasou.com; 807 Shōji; r per person with 2 meals ¥7000; 🛜) is a traditional lodging where some rooms have lake and mountain (not Mt Fuji) views and all have shared bathrooms. Some English is spoken.

Motosu-ko 本栖湖

Famous as the site of the image on the ¥1000 bill, where Mt Fuji rises majestically from the north shore of Motosu-ko.

It's a popular spot for outdoor activities. The **Panorama-dai** (パノラマ台) hiking trail ends here in a spectacular, spot-on view of Mt Fuji. It's a one-hour hike from the trailhead, a 20-minute walk beyond the Motosu-Iriguchi bus stop (¥1240, 45 minutes from Kawaguchi-ko).

Koan Motosu (☑38-0117) offers paddleboarding (¥1500/4000 per hour/day), kayaking (¥2000 per person, one hour) and even scuba diving in the lake!

🛏 Sleeping

Koan Motosu Inn INN ¥
(☑38-0117; www.motosuko.com/shop/shop/koan/koancamp.html; camping ¥2000, r per person from ¥5500) A lovely inn and campground on the lake, with Fuji views, private Jacuzzi, helpful English-speaking owner and attached restaurant and shop. It's a short walk downhill from the Tourist Information Centre.

Lake Motosu Campground CAMPGROUND ¥
(☑87-2345; camping with/without car ¥2500/1500, bungalow 2/4/6 person ¥4730/5250/6300) Another camping option with its simple tatami mat bungalows set in a wooded area on the lake, with campfires, shared bathroom blocks and a store selling basic snacks, beer and camping items. Futon rental is an extra ¥620 per set and no English is spoken. It's on the main road, about 300m on the left from the lake entrance.

Yamanaka-ko 山中湖村

The largest lake in the region, Yamanaka-ko is more popular with locals than overseas tourists. The southern side of the lake is overdeveloped and has a Japanese tourist-trap feel but the northern side is more appealing with a sleepier vibe.

One of the reasons to visit is for the **Benifuji-no-yu** (山中湖温泉紅富士の湯; www.benifuji.co.jp; adult/child ¥700/200, towel rental ¥210; ☺10am-9pm) onsen. Ignore the faded hotel facade, inside the views improve dramatically when Mt Fuji is clear in sight as you soak in the outdoor stone and *hinoki* (cypress) baths.

If you're staying overnight, **Hotorinite** (ホトリニテ; ☑62-0548; r per person ¥3000; @☎) has tasteful, well-equipped rooms in a generations-old worker's lodge set in leafy surrounds. The young English-speaking owner is a great source of information on the area.

The bus from Fuji-yoshida (¥480, 25 minutes) stops at the entrance of Yamanaka-ko. Turn left at the traffic lights and 7-Eleven and it's about 500m on the left on the main road just past the old bowling alley.

🎎 Festivals & Events

Yoshida no Himatsuri   FIRE
This annual festival (26–27 August) is held to mark the end of the climbing season and to offer thanks for the safety of the year's climbers. The first day involves a *mikoshi* procession and the lighting of bonfires on the town's main street. On the second day, festivals are held at Sengen-jinja (p153).

ℹ Getting Around

City buses run from Kawaguchi-ko to Fujinomiya Fifth Station (¥2040, 75 minutes), via the three smaller lakes.

From Fujisan Station it's an eight-minute bus ride (¥230) or five-minute train (¥210) to Kawaguchi-ko Station.

The **Retro-bus** has hop-on-hop-off service from Kawaguchi-ko Station to all of the sightseeing spots around the western lakes. One route (two-day passes adult/child ¥1000/500) follows Kawaguchi-ko's northern shore, and the other (¥1300/650) heads south and around Sai-ko and Aokigahara.

There is a **Toyota Rent-a-Car** (☑72-1100, in English 0800-7000-815) a few minutes' walk from Kawaguchi-ko Station; head right from the station, turning right at the next intersection. **Sazanami** (☺7am-5pm summer, 9am-5pm win-

ter), on Kawaguchi-ko's southeast shore, rents regular bicycles (per hour/day ¥400/1500), electric pedal-assisting bicycle (per hour/day ¥600/2600) and rowboats (per hour ¥1000).

NORTH OF TOKYO

North of Tokyo, the Kantō plain gives way to mountain country. This rugged landscape makes a fine backdrop for the spectacular shrines of Nikkō and the bubbling hot springs of Gunma Prefecture.

Nikkō   日光

☑0288 / POP 90,000

Ancient moss clinging to a stone wall; rows of perfectly aligned stone lanterns; vermilion gates; and towering cedars: this is only a pathway in Nikkō, a sanctuary that enshrines the glories of the Edo period (1600–1868). Scattered among hilly woodlands, Nikkō is one of Japan's major attractions. The drawback is that plenty of other people have discovered it too; high season (summer and autumn) and weekends can be extremely crowded where the spirituality of the area can feel a little lost.

Nikkō is certainly possible as a day trip from Tokyo, though spending at least one night allows for an early start before the crowds arrive. And a couple of nights gives you time to explore the gorgeous natural scenery in the surrounding area.

History

Nikkō's religious history dates back to the middle of the 8th century, when the Buddhist priest Shōdō Shōnin (735–817) established a hermitage here. For centuries the mountains served as a training ground for Buddhist monks, though the area fell gradually into obscurity. Nikkō became famous when chosen as the site for the mausoleum of Tokugawa Ieyasu, the warlord who took control of Japan and established the shōgunate that ruled for more than 250 years, until the Meiji Restoration ended the feudal era.

Ieyasu was laid to rest among Nikkō's towering cedars in 1617, and in 1634 his grandson, Tokugawa Iemitsu, commenced work on the shrine that can be seen today. The original shrine, Tōshō-gū, was completely rebuilt using an army of some 15,000 artisans from across Japan, who took two

Nikkō

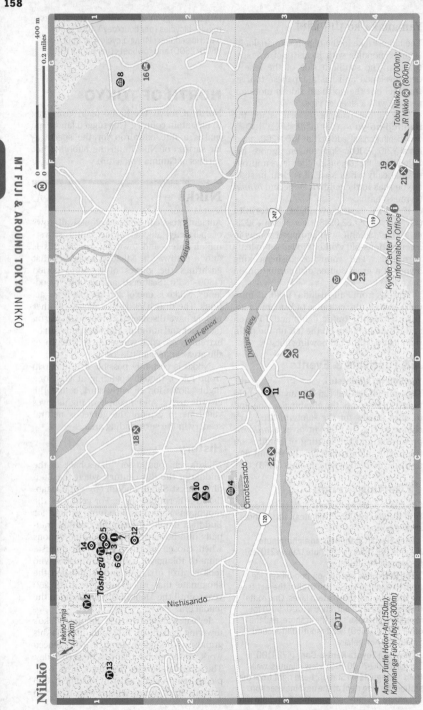

400 m
0.2 miles

8
16

Daiya-gawa

247

Tobu Nikkō (700m);
JR Nikkō (800m)

19
21

119

Kyodo Center Tourist
Information Office

Inari-gawa

23

20

Daiya-gawa

11

15

18

22

10
9

4

Omotesandō

120

5
3
12
7
14
1
6

Tōshō-gū

2

Nishisandō

17

Takino-Jinja
(1.2km)

13

Annex Turtle Hotori-An (150m);
Kanman-ga-Fuchi Abyss (300m)

Nikkō

MT FUJI & AROUND TOKYO NIKKŌ

years to complete the shrine and mausoleum. Whatever one's opinion of Ieyasu, the grandeur at Nikkō is awesome, a display of wealth and power by a family that for two and a half centuries was Japan's supreme arbiter of power.

⊙ Sights

The World Heritage Sites around Tōshō-gū are Nikkō's centrepiece. A **combination ticket** (¥1000), valid for two days and available at booths in the area, covers entry to Rinnō-ji, Tōshō-gū and Futarasan-jinja. The Nemuri-Neko (Sleeping Cat) and Ieyasu's tomb in Tōshō-gū require a separate admission ticket (¥520).

Most sites are open from 8am to 4.30pm (until 3.30pm from November to March). To avoid the hordes, visit early on a weekday. Be sure to pick up a map from the tourist information office, as finding the English signposts to the shrines and temples can be tricky.

★ **Tōshō-gū**   SHINTŌ SHRINE
(東照宮) The entrance to the main shrine is through the torii (shrine gate) at **Omote-mon** (表門), a gate protected on either side by Deva kings.

Just inside are the **Sanjinko** (三神庫; Three Sacred Storehouses). On the upper storey of the last storehouse are imaginative relief carvings of elephants by an artist who famously had never seen the real thing. To the left of the entrance is **Shinkyūsha** (神厩舎; Sacred Stable), adorned with allegorical relief carvings of monkeys. The famous 'hear no evil, see no evil, speak no evil' monkeys demonstrate three principles of Tendai Buddhism.

Pass through another torii, climb another flight of stairs, and on the left and right are a drum tower and a belfry. To the left of the drum tower is **Honji-dō** (本地堂). This hall is best known for the painting on its ceiling of the Nakiryū (Crying Dragon). Monks demonstrate the acoustical properties of this hall by clapping two sticks together. The dragon 'roars' (a bit of a stretch) when the sticks are clapped beneath the dragon's mouth, but not elsewhere.

Next comes **Yōmei-mon** (陽明門; Sunset Gate), dazzlingly decorated with glimmering gold leaf and intricate, coloured carvings and paintings of flowers, dancing girls, mythical beasts and Chinese sages. Worrying that its perfection might arouse envy in the gods, those responsible for its construction had the final supporting pillar placed upside down as a deliberate error. Although the style is more Chinese than Japanese and some critics deride it as gaudy, it's a grand spectacle.

To the left of Yōmei-mon is **Jin-yōsha** (神輿舎), the storage for the *mikoshi* used during festivals.

Tōshō-gū's **Honden** (本殿; Main Hall) and **Haiden** (拝殿; Hall of Worship) are across the enclosure. Inside – open only to *daimyō* (domain lords) during the Edo period – are paintings of the 36 immortal poets of Kyoto, and a ceiling-painting pattern from the Momoyama period; note the 100 dragons, each different. *Fusuma* (sliding door) paintings depict a *kirin* (a mythical beast that's part giraffe and part dragon). It's said that the creature will appear only when the world is at peace.

ℹ️ UNDER RESTORATION

A few of Nikkō's temples have been undergoing restoration work for the past few years and this is set to continue. The Sanbutsudo Hall at Rinnō-ji, the temple's main hall, is undergoing major renovation works and is due for completion in 2020. At Tōshō-gū, the Yomeimon Gate is scheduled for renovation in 2013 where scaffolding will shroud the gate so visitors will be unable to fully view the shrine. Haiden Hall and Taiyūin-byō's Nitennmon Gate (second gate) were also being restored at the time of research.

While this does mean you might only get partial exterior views of some temples, it shouldn't put people off visiting. The interiors are completely on display and the temples remain impressive sights. You can check in with the Tourist Information Office for an update before you visit.

Through Yōmei-mon and to the right is **Nemuri-Neko** (眠り猫), a small wooden sculpture of a sleeping cat that's famous throughout Japan for its lifelike appearance (though admittedly the attraction is lost on some visitors). From here, **Sakashita-mon** (坂下門) opens onto an uphill path through towering cedars to the appropriately solemn **Tomb of Ieyasu** (奥社 (徳川家康の墓)).

Rinnō-ji   BUDDHIST TEMPLE

(輪王寺) This Tendai-sect temple was founded 1200 years ago by Shōdō Shōnin. The **Sambutsu-dō** (三仏堂; Three-Buddha Hall) is constructed from some 360m of zelkova trees and is the main attraction. Inside are three 8m gilded wooden Buddha statues. The central image is Amida Nyorai (one of the primal deities in the Mahayana Buddhist canon), flanked by Senjū (1000-armed Kannon, deity of mercy and compassion) and Batō (a horse-headed Kannon), whose special domain is the animal kingdom.

Rinnō-ji's **Hōmotsu-den** (宝物殿; Treasure Hall; admission ¥300) houses some 6000 treasures associated with the temple; the separate admission ticket includes entrance to the **Shōyō-en** strolling garden.

Taiyūin-byō   SHINTŌ SHRINE

(大猷院廟) Enshrining Ieyasu's grandson Iemitsu (1604–51) is Taiyūin-byō. Though it houses many of the same elements as Tōshō-gū (storehouses, drum tower, Chinese-style gates etc), its smaller, more intimate scale and setting in a cryptomeria forest make it very appealing.

Among Taiyūin-byō's many structures, look for dozens of lanterns donated by *daimyō*, and the gate Niō-mon, whose guardian deities have a hand up (to welcome those with pure hearts) and a hand down (to suppress those with impure hearts). Inside the main hall, 140 dragons painted on the ceiling are said to carry prayers to the heavens; those holding pearls are on their way up, and those without are returning to gather more prayers.

Futarasan-jinja   SHINTŌ SHRINE

(二荒山神社) Shōdō Shōnin founded this shrine; the current building dates from 1619, making it Nikkō's oldest. Set among cypress trees, it's very atmospheric. It's the protector shrine of Nikkō itself, dedicated to the nearby mountain, Nantai-san (2484m), the mountain's consort, Nyotai-san, and their mountainous progeny, Tarō. There are other shrine branches on Nantai-san and by Chūzenji-ko.

Takinō-jinja   SHINTŌ SHRINE

(滝尾神社) In between Futarasan-jinja and Taiyūin-byō, a 25-minute walk along a stone-paved path leads to Takinō-jinja, less grand than the main attractions and thus delightfully less crowded. The stone torii, called **Unmeshi-no-torii**, dates back to Iemitsu's time (1696). Before entering, it's customary to try your luck tossing three stones through the small hole near the top. Head back down to the fork in the path and take the trail to the left to pass a handful of small temples and the tomb of Shōdō Shōnin before coming out behind Rinnō-ji.

Shin-kyō   HISTORIC SITE

(神橋; crossing fee ¥300) This much-photographed red bridge over the Daiya-gawa is located at the sacred spot where Shōdō Shōnin was said to have been carried across the river on the backs of two giant serpents. It's a reconstruction of the 17th-century original.

Kanman-ga-Fuchi Abyss   PARK

(憾満ガ淵) Another quiet alternative is the 20-minute walk to Kanman-ga-Fuchi Abyss, a collection of *jizō* statues (the small stone statues of the Buddhist protector of travellers and children) set along a wooded path. It's said that if you try to count them there and back you'll end up with a different number, hence the nickname 'Bake-jizō' (ghost *jizō*). Take a left after passing the Shin-kyō bridge and follow the river for about 800m, crossing another bridge en route.

Nikkō Woodcarving Center   MUSEUM
(日光木彫りの里 工芸センター; ☑53-0070; 2848 Tokorono; ☉9am-5pm, closed Tue Nov-Apr) **FREE** You've seen Nikkō-bori, the traditional local woodcraft, all over temples and gift shops. Here you can try your hand at making your own hand mirrors, plates and other crafts, daily from 9am to 11am and 1pm to 3pm (from ¥900 depending on your choice of craft). There's also a shop and on the 2nd floor a collection of museum-grade showpieces.

✵✵ Festivals & Events

Yayoi Matsuri   MIKOSHI
Procession of *mikoshi* held at Futarasan-jinja on 16 and 17 April.

Tōshō-gū Grand Festival   HISTORICAL
Nikkō's most important annual festival is held on 17 and 18 May and features horseback archery on the first day and a 1000-strong costumed re-enactment of the delivery of Ieyasu's remains to Nikkō on the second.

Tōshō-gū Autumn Festival   HISTORICAL
Autumnal repeat on 16 and 17 October of the May festival.

🛏 Sleeping

Rindō-no-Ie   MINSHUKU ¥
(りんどうの家; ☑53-0131; www3.ocn.ne.jp/~garrr/Rindou.html; 1462 Tokorono; r per person without bathroom from ¥3500; ☺@☎) Small but thoughtfully arranged tatami rooms; tasty meals and pick-up service. Breakfast/dinner is ¥700/1800. It's across the river, a 15-minute walk northwest of the train station; see the website for a map.

Nikkō Guesthouse   GUESTHOUSE ¥
(日光ゲストハウス; ☑090-1838-7873; www.nikko-guesthouse.com; 5-12 Aioi-chō; dm/d without bathroom from ¥2600/6500) Run by a lovely couple, this tiny guesthouse is set in a renovated old house near Tōbu Station. Female and male dorms are a bit cramped, but they're tidy, as are the private doubles; all with fan only and shared bathrooms. There's an 11pm curfew.

Nikkō Park Lodge   GUESTHOUSE ¥
(日光パークロッヂ; ☑53-1201; www.nikkoparklodge.com; 2828-5 Tokorono; dm/d from ¥2990/7980; ☺@☎) In the wooded hills north of town, this cute, well-kept guesthouse has Western-style rooms, a spacious dorm, homely lounge with log fire and English-speaking staff who are a great source of info. Take advantage of the afternoon pick-up service, otherwise it's around ¥700 by taxi from the station. There is also a newer **guesthouse** across from Tōbu Station.

Nikkō Station Classic Hotel   HOTEL ¥¥
(☑53-1000; www.nikko-stationhotel.jp; s/d from ¥11,000/20,000; ☺@☎) Centrally located, this smart midrange hotel has modern stylish decor, comfortable Western-style rooms and buffet breakfast.

Annex Turtle Hotori-An   INN ¥¥
(☑53-3663; www.turtle-nikko.com; 8-28 Takumi-chō; s/tw ¥6650/12,700; ☺@☎) The Turtle Inn's newer annexe is more modern, with Japanese- and Western-style rooms plus river views from the onsen.

Turtle Inn Nikkō   INN ¥¥
(タートル・イン・日光; ☑53-3168; www.turtle-nikko.com; 2-16 Takumi-chō; s/tw without bathroom ¥4950/9300, with bathroom ¥5750/10,900; ☺@☎) This long-time favourite is still in the running with recently touched-up spacious rooms, both Japanese- and Western-style. Take a bus to Sōgō-kaikan-mae, backtrack

---

WORTH A TRIP

NIKKŌ INN

Located just 30 minutes from Nikkō in positively pastoral Shimogoshiro, **Nikko Inn** (☑0288-27-0008; www.nikko-inn.jp; 333 Koshiro; r per person ¥5000; ☎) offers an antidote to the concrete boxes of modern Japan. Creative unit Nikko Design reworked six old-style Japanese homes into guest cottages that sleep four to seven people. Each vintage wooden structure features tatami rooms and traditional verandahs, plus modern kitchen and bathroom facilities. Beyond is little more than rice fields, a village of 1000 people and the mountains of Nikkō. Shimogoshiro is on the Tōbu line from Asakusa Station (2¼ hours; ¥1160), four stops before Nikkō.

about 50m, turn right along the river and walk for about five minutes; you'll see the turtle sign on the left.

Nikkō Kanaya Hotel   HOTEL ¥¥¥
(日光金谷ホテル; ☑54-0001; www.kanayahotel. co.jp; 1300 Kamihatsu-ishimachi; tw from ¥17,325; ＠) This grand lady from 1893 wears her history like a well-loved, if not slightly worn, dress. The newer wing has Japanese-style rooms with excellent vistas, spacious quarters and private bathrooms; the cheaper rooms in the main building by contrast are rather ordinary. The lobby bar is deliciously dark and amenable to drinking whisky. Rates rise steeply in high seasons.

✖ Eating & Drinking

A local speciality is *yuba* (the skin that forms when making tofu) cut into strips; better than it sounds, it's a staple of *shōjin ryōri* (Buddhist vegetarian cuisine). You'll see it all over town, in everything from noodles *(yuba soba)* to fried bean buns *(age yuba manju)*.

Hippari Dako   YAKITORI ¥
(ひっぱり凧; 1011 Kamihatsu-ishimachi; meals ¥500-850; ☉11am-8pm; ☑🍴) An institution among foreign travellers, as years of business cards tacked to the walls testify, this tiny restaurant serves filling meals, including curry *udon, yuba* sashimi and *yaki udon* (fried noodles). It has an English sign.

Hi no Kuruma   OKONOMIYAKI ¥
(ひの車; 597-2 Gokō-machi; mains ¥500-1500; ☉noon-3pm & 6-9pm Thu-Tue; 🍴) A popular choice for cheap and easy grill-your-own meals. Look for the small parking lot and red-black-green-and-white Japanese sign.

Yuzawaya   CAFE ¥
(湯沢屋; 946 Kamihatsu-ishimachi; tea sets from ¥450; ☉11am-5pm) A 200-year-old teahouse specialising in *manju* (bean-jam buns) and other traditional sweets; look for the green-and-white banners.

Yuba Yūzen   KAISEKI ¥¥
(日光ゆば遊膳; 1-22 Yasukawachō; sets ¥2700-3200; ☉11am-2pm Thu-Tue) A *yuba*-speciality restaurant that serves it sashimi-style, with tofu and soy milk, and with the addition of a variety of seasonal side dishes. There's no English menu, but there are only two choices for sets: ¥2700 if you're hungry and ¥3200 if you're really hungry. Look for the two-storey tan building across from the first left turn after Shin-kyō.

Shokudō Suzuki   SHOKUDŌ ¥¥
(食堂すゞき; 581-2 Gokō-machi; mains from ¥1100; ☉11.30am-2.30pm & 5.30-8.30pm) A tiny joint that's strewn with wine bottles, comic books and autographs from celebrity diners. Equally eclectic is the menu of pasta (get the *tarioriini;* it's fresh tagliolini) and inventive *yuba* dishes. Look for the beige building on the corner with the giant pasta picture.

★ Gyōshintei   KAISEKI ¥¥¥
(尭心亭; ☑53-3751; www.meiji-yakata.com/gy-oushin; 2339-1 Sannai; set courses ¥3465-8400; ☉11am-7pm; ☑🍴) Splurge here on deluxe spreads of *shōjin ryōri,* featuring local bean curd and vegetables served half a dozen delectable ways. The elegant tatami dining room overlooks a carefully tended garden. It's directly north of the Shin-kyō bridge (about 250m) and there's a three-peaked emblem on the door curtain.

Nikko Park Lodge Cafe   CAFE
(11-6 Matsubaracho; ☉10am-7pm; ＠🛜) Across the street from the Tōbu Station, this guesthouse cafe serves a good brew, cheap beer and has free wi-fi and internet. A good place to meet fellow travellers.

❶ Information

Kyōdo Center Tourist Information Office
(☑54-2496; www.nikko-jp.org; 591 Gokomachi; internet per 15min ¥50, wi-fi for 20min free; ☉9am-5pm) The main tourist information office with English speakers (guaranteed between 10am and 2pm) and maps for sightseeing and hiking. Has internet access.

Post Office (日光郵便局; ☑54-0101; 896-1 Nakahatsuishi-chō) There's one on the main road, three blocks past the Kyōdo Center, and another across the street from Tōbu Nikkō Station on Rte 119; both have international ATMs.

Tōbu Nikkō Station Tourist Information Desk (☑53-4511; ☉8.30am-5pm) At the Nikkō Station, there's a small information desk where you can pick up a town map and get help in English to find buses, restaurants and hotels.

Tochigi Volunteer Interpreters & Guides Association (NikkoTVIGA@hotmail.co.jp) Offers free guided tours. Contact in advance.

❶ Getting There & Away

Nikkō is best reached from Tokyo via the Tōbu Nikkō line from Asakusa Station. You can usually get last-minute seats on the hourly reserved *tokkyū* (limited-express) trains (¥2620, 1¾ hours). *Kaisoku* (rapid) trains (¥1320, 2½ hours, hourly from 6.20am to 4.50pm) require no reservation. For the *tokkyū*, you may have to change at Shimo-imaichi. Be sure to ride in the last two cars to reach Nikkō (some cars may separate at an intermediate stop).

JR Pass holders can take the Tohoku *shinkansen* from Tokyo to Utsunomiya (¥4800, 54 minutes) and change there for an ordinary train to Nikkō (¥740, 45 minutes).

Both JR Nikkō Station (designed by Frank Lloyd Wright) and the nearby Tōbu Nikkō Station lie southeast of the shrine area within a block of Nikkō's main road (Rte 119, the old Nikkō-kaidō). From the station, follow this road uphill for 20 minutes to reach the shrine area, past restaurants, souvenir shops and the main tourist information centre, or take a bus to the Shin-kyō bus stop (¥190). Bus stops are announced in English. Buses leave from both JR and Tōbu Nikkō Station; buses bound for both Chūzen-ji Onsen and Yumoto Onsen stop at Shin-kyō and other stops around the World Heritage Sites.

TRAIN/BUS PASSES

Tōbu Railway (www.tobu.co.jp/foreign; ⊙Sightseeing Service Center 7.45am-5pm) Offers two passes covering rail transport from Asakusa to Nikkō (though not the *tokkyū* surcharge, from ¥1040) and unlimited hop-on-hop-off bus services around Nikkō. Purchase these passes at the **Tōbu Sightseeing Service Center** in Asakusa Station.

All Nikko Pass (adult/child ¥4400/2210) Valid for four days and includes buses to Chūzen-ji Onsen and Yumoto Onsen.

World Heritage Pass (adult/child ¥3600/1700) Valid for two days and includes buses to the World Heritage Sites, plus admission to Tōshō-gū, Rinnō-ji and Futarasan-jinja.

TŌBU NIKKŌ BUS FREE PASS

If you've already got your rail ticket, two-day bus-only passes allow unlimited rides between Nikkō and Chūzen-ji Onsen (adult/child ¥2000/1000) or Yumoto Onsen (adult/child ¥3000/1500), including the World Heritage Site area. The **Sekai-isan-meguri** (World Heritage Bus Pass; adult/child ¥500/250) covers the area between the stations and the shrine precincts. Buy these at Tōbu Nikkō Station.

Around Nikkō 日光周辺

Nikkō is part of Nikkō National Park, 1400 sq km sprawling over Fukushima, Tochigi, Gunma and Niigata Prefectures. This mountainous region features extinct volcanoes, lakes, waterfalls and marshlands. There are good hiking opportunities and some remote hot-spring resorts.

Chūzen-ji Onsen 中禅寺温泉

📷 0288

This highland area 11.5km west of Nikkō offers some natural seclusion and striking views of Nantai-san from Chūzen-ji's lake, Chuzenji-ko. The lake itself is 161m deep and a fabulous shade of deep blue in good weather, with the usual flotilla of sightseeing boats.

⊙ Sights

Kegon-no-taki WATERFALL
(華厳ノ滝 | Kegon Falls; 2479-2 Chūgushi; adult/child ¥530/320; ⊙8am-5pm) The big-ticket attraction of the area is this billowing, 97m-high waterfall. Take the elevator down to a platform to observe the full force of the plunging water or view up high on the viewing platform.

Futarasan-jinja SHRINE
(二荒山神社; 2484 Chūgushi; ⊙8am-4.30pm) This shrine complements the shrines at Tōshō-gū and is the starting point for pilgrimages up Nantai-san. The shrine is about 1km west of the falls, along the lake's north shore.

Chūzen-ji Tachiki-kannon TEMPLE
(中禅寺立木観音; 2578 Chūgūshi; adult/child ¥500/200; ⊙8am-4.30pm) This eponymous temple, located on the lake's eastern shore, was founded in the 8th century and houses a 6m-tall Kannon statue from that time.

OFF THE BEATEN TRACK

KANIYU ONSEN

In the midst of mountains and rivers in the scenic Oku Nikkō region you'll find **Kaniyu Onsen** (加仁湯; 📷96-0311; 871 Kawamata; admission ¥1000; ⊙day visitors 9am-3pm), a rustic atmospheric ryokan-onsen with milky sulphuric waters in its multiple outdoor baths. To get here, take the Tōbu line to Shimoimachi, change to a Kinugawa Onsen–bound train then board the bus to Kaniyu Onsen. From here, it's a two-hour hike exploring the absolute beauty of the area. For more information, ask at the Kyodo Center Tourist Information Office in Nikkō before setting out. From Nikkō, allow around four hours all up to reach the onsen.

Italian Embassy Villa Memorial Park

PARK

(イタリアン大使館別荘記念公園; 2482 Chū-gūshi; admission ¥100; ⊙9am-4.30pm Tue-Sun) Beyond Chūzen-ji Tachiki-kannon, the former summer residence of Italy's ambassadors (from 1928 to 1997) has a pleasant sun terrace with excellent lake views.

🛏 Sleeping

Chūzenji Pension

INN ¥

(中禅寺ペンション; ☎55-0888; www.chuzenji-pension.com; 2482 Chūgūshi; r per person from ¥5250; ⊜@) A pink hostelry set back from the lake's eastern shore has nine mostly Western-style rooms that feel a bit like grandma's house. There's a cosy fireplace and two onsen baths.

Nikkō Lakeside Hotel

HOTEL ¥¥¥

(日光レークサイドホテル; ☎55-0321; www.tobuhotel.co.jp/nikkolake; 2482 Chūgūshi; s/tw from ¥13,000/26,000; 🚱) The rooms at this Meiji-era hotel (1894) are a little worn, but the classy dining room still carries an old-time resort feel and there's a smart cafe with outdoor decking overlooking manicured lawns. The wooden bathhouse with milky sulphuric water is also open to day trippers (admission ¥1000).

Hotel Shikisai

HOTEL ¥¥¥

(奥日光ホテル四季彩; ☎55-1010; www.hotel-shikisai.co.jp; 2485 Chugushi Nikko; tw incl 2 meals from ¥15,000; 🚱) High on a hill on the lake's eastern shore is this peaceful hideaway hotel offering mostly Japanese-style rooms and a couple of stylish suites, one with its own private garden and *rotemburo*. It has a lovely onsen looking out to the leafy garden; also open to day trippers (¥1000). Free afternoon pick-up service from Nikkō.

ℹ Getting There & Away

Buses run from Tōbu Nikkō Station to Chūzen-ji Onsen (¥1100, 45 minutes) or use the economical Tōbu Nikkō Bus Free Pass, available at Tōbu Nikkō Station.

Yumoto Onsen 湯元温泉

From Chūzen-ji Onsen, you might continue on to the quieter hot-springs resort of Yumoto Onsen by bus (¥840, 30 minutes) or reach it by a rewarding three-hour hike on the **Senjōgahara Shizen-kenkyu-rō** (戦場ヶ原自然研究路; Senjōgahara Plain Nature Trail).

For the latter option, take a Yumoto-bound bus and get off at Ryūzu-no-taki (竜頭ノ滝; ¥410, 20 minutes), a waterfall that marks the start of the trail. The hike follows the Yu-gawa across the picturesque marshland of Senjōgahara (partly on wooden plank paths), alongside the 75m-high falls of Yu-daki (湯滝) to the lake Yu-no-ko (湯の湖), then around the lake to Yumoto Onsen.

Towards the back of the town, the hot-spring temple **Onsen-ji** (温泉時; adult/child ¥500/300; ⊙9am-4pm) has a humble bathhouse (with extremely hot water) and a tatami lounge for resting weary muscles.

From Yumoto Onsen you can return to Nikkō by bus (¥1650, 1½ hours).

Gunma Prefecture 群馬県

The star in the Kantō-area hot-spring firmament is Gunma Prefecture (Gunma-ken). Mineral baths seem to bubble out of the ground at every turn in this mountainous landscape, and some small towns feel delightfully traditional. Here's just a small selection.

Kusatsu Onsen 草津温泉

☎0279 / POP 7400

Kusatsu has been voted Japan's favourite onsen town year after year since the Edo period. Apparently shōgun Tokugawa Ieyasu himself was a fan. The pungent, emerald-coloured waters are relatively heavy in sulphuric acid, which has an antibacterial effect, and the smell permeates the town.

In winter, the Kusatsu area is known for it's great skiing with several slopes, the most popular being **Furikozawa** at an elevation of 3000m and **Tenguyama** where the main run is suitable for all levels.

◉ Sights & Activities

Yubatake

SPRING

(湯畑, hot-water field) The main attraction in the town centre and the source of hot-spring water in the area. Its milky blue sulphuric water flows like a waterfall at 4000L per minute and is topped with wooden tanks from which Kusatsu's ryokan fill their baths. The area is atmospherically lit up at night.

★ Sai-no-kawara

ONSEN

(西の河原露天風呂; 521-3 Ōaza Kusatsu; adult/child ¥500/300; ⊙7am-8pm) West of town in Sai-no-kawara kōen is this incredibly tran-

quil 500-sq-metre *rotemburo*, separated by a
bamboo wall into men's and women's baths,
that can fit 100 people. It's a 15-minute walk
from the town centre or a 20-minute ride
(¥100) on the 'A course' bus from Kusatsu
bus terminal. There's no towel rental so
bring your own.

Mt Shirane   MOUNTAIN
Head up into the hills to the volcanic peak
of Mt Shirane, famous for its striking milky-
green sulphur **Yugama crater lake**. A bus
runs from Kusatsu Station (¥2000 return,
30 minutes) up the steep, winding road to
the Shirane Resthouse, from where it's a
15-minute stair climb to the lake.

Ōtakinoyu   ONSEN
(大瀧乃湯; 596-13 Ōaza Kusatsu; adult/child
¥800/400; ⊙9am-9pm) Known for its tubs at
a variety of temperatures; try different ones
for an experience known as *awase-yu* (mix-
and-match waters).

🛏 Sleeping & Eating

Hotel Ichii   HOTEL ¥¥
(ホテル一井; ☑88-0011; www.hotel-ichii.co.jp;
411 Kusatsu-machi; r per person incl 2 meals from
¥12,000; 🐾) Though you might not know
it from looking at this concrete tower next
to Yubatake, this hotel has been a Kusatsu
institution for over 300 years. It's rambling,
retrodecor features Japanese-style rooms,
plus indoor and outdoor onsen and is centrally located.

Ijimaken Ryokan   RYOKAN ¥¥
(☑88-3457; r per person with shared bathroom
from ¥6500) Run by friendly owners, this
slightly run-down ryokan-meets-hotel remains a good deal despite the mish-mash of
odd decor; stuffed animals and fake flowers.
Go for the upstairs rooms with balcony area
and loads of natural light. A little tricky to
find, it's a 10-minute walk downhill from the
bus terminal with no English sign.

Kusatsu Onsen Boun   RYOKAN ¥¥¥
(草津温泉望雲; ☑88-3251; www.hotelboun.com;
433-1 Kusatsu-machi; r per person from ¥18,000) A
stunning ryokan that fuses traditional decor with elegant touches, featuring tatami
rooms and common areas brightened with
ikebana artwork, mossy gardens, waterfalls
and a bamboo decking atrium. There's a
large onsen in a big wooden bathhouse and
rotemburo with garden outlook. It's conveniently located, a three-minute walk from
Yubatake.

> **DON'T MISS**
>
> ### YUMOMI
> From 1 April to 30 November, Kusatsu
> offers a touristy but unique opportunity
> to see **yumomi** (adult/child ¥500/250;
> 4 to 5 shows daily), in which local women
> stir the waters to cool them while sing-
> ing folk songs. Otherwise you can opt
> to do-it-yourself between 11.30am and
> 2pm (¥200). It's next to Yubatake at the
> bathhouse **Netsu-no-Yu** (熱の湯; 414
> Kusatsu-machi).

Mikuniya   NOODLES ¥
(三国家; 386 Ōaza Kusatsu; dishes from ¥650;
⊙11am-2pm) Fill up on tasty bowls of *sansai soba* (buckwheat noodles with mountain
vegetables; ¥800) at this popular place on
the shopping street that runs behind Yubatake towards Sai-no-kawara. Look for the
renovated wooden building with the black
door curtains, or the line out the front.

Yumehana   JAPANESE ¥
(夢花; http://kusatsu-yumehana.com; sets from
¥980; ⊙10am-10pm) This popular lunch spot
diagonally opposite the bus station serves filling *teishoku* (set meals); the jumbo tempura
set (¥1200) easily feeds two. Yumehana has a
picture menu, but no English menu. It closes
on certain days depending on the season.

ℹ Information
Stop in at the **City Hall Tourist Section** (☑88-
0001; ⊙8.30am-5.30pm Mon-Fri), next to the
bus station. Occasionally there's an English
speaker on hand and there is a touch screen
information terminal in English. Otherwise, the
Kusatsu Onsen Ryokan Information Centre
(☑88-3722; ⊙9am-5pm), the white building
opposite the bus station, can help with accommodation bookings and has a recommended
walking map. For more town info, see www.
kusatsu-onsen.ne.jp/foreign/index.html.

ℹ Getting There & Away
Buses 2,3 and 4 connect Kusatsu Onsen to
Naganohara-Kusatsuguchi Station (¥670, 25
minutes). *Tokkyū* Kusatsu trains run from Ueno to
Naganohara-Kusatsuguchi Station (¥4620, 2½
hours) three times a day. Alternatively, take the
Joetsu *shinkansen* to Takasaki (¥4600, one hour)
and transfer to the JR Agatsuma line (¥1110, 1½
hours). **JR Bus Kantō** (☑03-3844-1950; www.
jrbuskanto.co.jp) offers direct service to Kusatsu
Onsen (¥3200, four hours) from Shinjuku Station's New South exit; reservations required.

Minakami & Takaragawa Onsen
水上温泉・宝川温泉

📞 0278 / POP 21,000

In the northern region of the Gunma Prefecture is the sprawling onsen town of Minakami, an all-year-round destination and mecca for outdoor-adventure sports, hiking and skiing. When the spring snow melts between April and June, the Tone Gawa (利根川) is the source of some of the best **white-water rafting** and **kayaking** in Japan. It's also home to Takaragawa Onsen (about 30 minutes away by road), a riverside spa ranked among the nation's best.

The train station is in the village of Minakami.

🏃 Activities

★ Takaragawa Onsen
ONSEN

(www.takaragawa.com; admission ¥1500; ⊘ 9am-5pm) This stunning outdoor onsen is idyllic. All of the bathing pools – save one just for women – are mixed out there and will appeal more to the exhibitionists out there. Women can take modesty towels (rental is ¥100) into the mixed baths. The curious junk and gems you'll pass on your way to the baths are decades' worth of gifts from local villagers. The bears in cages are the only downside here. Buses run hourly between Minakami Station and Takaragawa Onsen (¥1100, 40 minutes) or Takaragawa Iriguchi (¥1000, 30 minutes), from where it's a short walk to the onsen.

Hōshi Onsen Chōjūkan
ONSEN

(法師温泉長寿館; www.houshi-onsen.jp; 650 Nagai; admission for day trippers ¥1000; ⊘ 10.30am-1.30pm) The main bathhouse at this ryokan is a stunning wooden structure from 1896, with rows of individual bathing pools and a unique style of water bubbling up from below. It's mixed bathing, with an additional modern bathhouse just for women and *rotemburo*.

Tanigawadake Ropeway
ROPEWAY

(谷川岳ロープウェイ; www.tanigawadake-rw.com; return ¥2000; ⊘ 8am-5pm) Tanigawadake ropeway takes you via gondola to the peak of Tenjin-daira, from where hiking trips, ranging from a couple of hours to all day, are available from May to November. There's skiing and snowboarding in winter. From Minakami Station, take a 20-minute bus to Ropeway-Eki-mae bus stop (¥650, about hourly).

Adventure Sports

Summer is the high season for outdoor adventure when you can get your adrenalin fix through canyoning, hiking, mountain biking and white-water rafting. Winter meanwhile is all about snow sports, with many ski resorts in the region, plus snowshoeing and climbing opportunities around **Mt Tanigawa** (Tanigawadake; 1977m), **Mt Tenjin** and **Ichinokura**. All are more suited for experienced hikers, Tanigawadake particularly, which has claimed quadruple the number of deaths on Mt Everest. There are also bears in the area, so take caution.

Canyons Minakami
TOUR OPERATOR

(キャニオンズみなかみ; 📞 72-2811; www.canyons.jp;) Professional English-speaking team, which has long been the leader in Minakami's outdoor scene and sustainable development. Offers four-season packages.

I Love Outdoors
TOUR OPERATOR

(📞 72-1337; www.iloveoutdoors.jp/en; 169-1 Shikanosawa) A relative new-comer to the scene, which was set up by one of the Aussie founders of Canyons with his Japanese wife.

Bungy Japan
ADVENTURE SPORTS

(www.bungeejapan.com; 143 Obinata; first jump ¥7500; ⊘ hours vary) Japan's only bridge bungy jump, with over 15 years of experience from Aussie and Kiwi operators. Check website for details.

🛏 Sleeping

Alpine Lodge
LODGE ¥

(アルパイン・ロッジ; 📞 72-2811; www.lodge.canyons.jp; 45 Yubiso; dm/d from ¥4000/5000; ⊘ closed Nov; 🐾) Run by the Canyons team, this is the place to meet fellow adventure travellers over drinks and live music (on weekends) in the popular bar or tucking into riverside BBQs. While the dorms are simple (with pine bunk beds) and private tatami rooms are on the small side, there are free pool tables and station pick-up, a half-pipe ramp out front and self-catering facilities. Staff can take care of all your adventure needs here.

Tenjin Lodge
LODGE ¥

(天神・ロッジ; 📞 25-3540; www.tenjinlodge.com; 220-4 Yubiso; r per person from ¥5000; 🐾) Across from a waterfall and nearby swimming holes, this Australian-/Korean-run lodge offers comfy, spacious Japanese and Western rooms; ask for a riverside one. Kieran and Bo are welcoming hosts and offer home-cooked meals (¥1000), and BBQs in the warmer months; they also lead guided hiking and snowshoeing tours. There are plans for backpacker dorms. Located at the foot of Taniga-wadake. Take the Jōetsu *shinkansen* from Tokyo Station to Jōmō Kōgen Station (70 minutes, ¥5750), from where it's free pick-up.

★ Hōshi Onsen Chōjūkan
RYOKAN ¥¥

(法師温泉長寿館; ☑ 66-0005; www.houshi-onsen.jp; 650 Nagai; r per person incl 2 meals from ¥13,800) Perfectly rustic and supremely photogenic, this lodging is one of Japan's finest onsen ryokan on the southwestern fringes of Minakami. Its onsen (p166) is a stunner. To get here, take a bus from Gokan Station (two stops before Minakami on the Jōetsu line) or from the Jōmō Kōgen *shinkansen* station to Sarugakyō (40 minutes); at the last stop, take another bus for Hōshi Onsen (15 minutes).

Ōsenkaku
RYOKAN ¥¥

(汪泉閣; ☑ 75-2121; www.takaragawa.com; 1899 Fujiwara; r per person ¥10,000) Adjacent to Takaragawa Onsen, this inn has gorgeous riverfront rooms over several buildings and an old-style feel. It also has 24-hour use of the Takaragawa baths. Prices rise steeply for nicer rooms with better views and private baths, but aim for the 1930s-vintage No 1 annexe. Note that dinner includes bear-meat soup; if you'd prefer not to eat this, ask for *no kuma-jiru* (熊汁) when reserving.

✕ Eating

I Love Nature Cafe
CAFE ¥

(☑ 72-1337; www.iloveoutdoors.jp/cafe; 169-1 Shikanosawa; mains from ¥500; ⊙ 9am-9pm; ☎) Part of I Love Outdoors, this bright funky cafe has a bohemian vibe thanks to its Mexican throw rugs and colourful wallpaper. A five-minute walk from Minakami Station, it serves burgers and pizza, as well as cold beer.

Kadoya
SOBA ¥¥

(そば処角弥; www.kadoya-soba.com; soba for two from ¥2700; ⊙ 11am-2.30pm) Expect to queue at this popular 'local' specialising in *hegi soba* (soba flavoured with seaweed and served on a special plate, a *hegi*). The noodles are hand-rolled fresh every day and they close up shop once they sell out. A five-minute walk from Alpine Lodge on the main street, look for the back-and-white building.

La Biere
PIZZERIA ¥¥

(pizzas from ¥800; ⊙ 11am-2.30pm & 5-8.30pm, Wed-Mon; ▣) Simple and tasty wood-fired pizzas in this cute pizzeria with pot plants

and umbrella-covered decking out the front. Takeway is also available. In Minakami Village, a short walk from the station.

❶ Information

Minakami Tourist Information Center (水上観光協会; ☑ 62-0401; www.enjoy-minakami.jp/eng; ⊙ 8.30am-5.30pm) Across from the station, this office has very helpful English-speaking staff, brochures and bus schedules.

❶ Getting There & Away

From Ueno, take the Joetsu *shinkansen* (¥4600, 50 minutes) or JR Takasaki line (¥1890, two hours) to Takasaki and transfer to the Jōetsu line (¥950, one hour). You can also catch the Jōetsu *shinkansen* to Jōmō Kōgen from Tokyo/Ueno (¥5750/5550, 1¼ hours), from where buses run to Minakami (¥600, 25 minutes).

Mito
水戸

☑ 029

Capital of Ibaraki Prefecture and a one-time castle town, Mito is best known for **Kairaku-en** (偕楽園; 1-3-3 Tokwachō; ⊙ 6am-7pm) FREE, one of the three most celebrated landscape gardens in Japan.

Kairaku-en dates back to 1842 when it was built by the *daimyō* of the Mito *han* (domain), a member of the clan of the Tokugawa shōgun. 'Kairaku-en' means 'the garden to enjoy with people', and it was one of the first gardens in the nation to open to the public. Sadly, it closed after it was damaged in the Great Eastern Japan Earthquake in 2011 but was fully reopened in early 2012 after undergoing repairs.

The 32-acre gardens are popular for their 3000 *ume* (plum-blossom) trees; some 100 varieties bloom in late February or early March. A **plum-blossom festival** happens around this time; check at the **Kairaku-en Park Center** (☑ 244-5454; www.koen.pref.iba-raki.jp/park/kairakuen01.html; ⊙ 6am-7pm) for dates. The three-storey pavilion **Kobun-tei** (好文亭; admission ¥190; ⊙ 9am-5pm) is a 1950s reproduction of the *daimyō's* villa (the original was destroyed in WWII).

From Tokyo, JR Jōban line trains depart from Ueno Station for Mito (*tokkyū;* ¥3510, 75 minutes). During the plum-blossom festival, connect by local train to Kairaku-en Station (¥180, five minutes); otherwise take a bus to Kairaku-en bus stop (¥230, 15 minutes) or walk (about 30 minutes) from the station's south exit along the lake Senba-ko.

WEST OF TOKYO

Nature reasserts herself at the western edge of Tokyo, spreading green through the scenic Fuji Five Lakes region towards Mt Fuji. To the southwest are the classic hot-spring resorts of Hakone and the seaside onsen and beach towns of the Izu Peninsula.

Takao-san 高尾山

📍 042

Gentle Takao-san is one of Tokyo's most popular day trips. Although it's often busy on weekends and holidays and rather built up compared with other regional hikes, it can make for a perfect family outing.

One of the chief attractions on this 599m mountain is the temple **Yaku-ō-in** (薬王院; 📞 661-1115; ⏰ 24hr), best known for the **Hi-watari Matsuri** (Fire-crossing Ceremony), which takes place on the second Sunday in March, near Takaosanguchi Station. Priests walk across hot coals with bare feet amid the ceremonial blowing of conch shells. The public is also welcome to participate.

Year-round, Takao-san offers **nature hikes**. Keio-line offices have free trail maps in English, or check www.takaotozan.co.jp.

The most popular trail (No 1) leads you past the temple; allow about 3¼ hours return for the 400m ascent. Alternatively, a cable car and a chair lift can take you part of the way up (adult/child one-way ¥470/230, return ¥900/450).

From Shinjuku Station, take the Keio line (*jun-tokkyū*; ¥370, 47 minutes) to Takaosanguchi. The tourist village, trail entrances, cable car and chairlift are a few minutes away to the right. JR Pass holders can travel to Takao Station on the JR Chūō line (48 minutes) and transfer to the Keio line to Takaosanguchi (¥120, two minutes).

Oku-Tama Region 奥多摩周辺

📍 042

Oku-Tama is Tokyo's best spot for hiking getaways. Here, the Tama-gawa runs through magnificent mountains with waterfalls, woodlands and hiking trails, ideal for day trips or overnight stays.

Mitake-san (御岳山; elevation 939m) is a charming old-world mountain hamlet that seems light years from Tokyo's bustle. Access is easiest by cable car, and about 30 minutes

on foot from the terminus, up dozens of steps, is **Musashi Mitake-jinja** (武蔵御嶽神社; 176 Mitake-san; ⏰ 24hr), a Shintō shrine and pilgrimage site said to date back some 1200 years. The site commands stunning views of the surrounding mountains. Pick up maps at the **Mitake Visitors Centre** (御岳ビジターセンター; 📞 878-9363; fax 878-9445; 38-5 Mitake-san; ⏰ 9am-4.30pm Tue-Sun), 250m beyond the cable car, near the start of the village.

If you've got time, the five-hour round-trip **hike** from Musashi Mitake-jinja to the summit of **Ōtake-san** (大岳山; 1266m) is highly recommended. Although there's some climbing involved, it's a fairly easy hike and the views from the summit are excellent – Mt Fuji is visible on clear days.

If you're not spending the night on Mitake-san, note that the cable car operates 7.30am to 6.30pm only.

🛏 Sleeping & Eating

The following places are all near Musashi Mitake-jinja.

Komadori San-sō　　　　MINSHUKU ¥
(駒鳥山荘; 📞 878-8472; www.hkr.ne.jp/~komadori; 155 Mitake-san; r per person with shared bathroom from ¥4500; @) Below the shrine near the back end of the village, this former pilgrims' inn brims with bric-a-brac and history – it's been in the same family for 17 generations. Rooms and the verandah have excellent views.

Mitake Youth Hostel　　　　HOSTEL ¥
(御嶽ユースホステル; 📞 878-8501; www.jyh. or.jp; 57 Mitake-san; dm member/nonmember ¥2880/3440; 🖙) This comfortable hostel has fine tatami rooms inside a handsome old building that used to be a pilgrims' lodge. It's midway between the top of the cable car and Musashi Mitake-jinja, about a minute beyond the visitors centre.

Momiji-ya　　　　NOODLES ¥
(紅葉屋; 📞 878-8475; 151 Mitake-san; mains ¥735-1155; ⏰ 10am-5pm; 🖘) Near the shrine gate, this cosy shop has mountain views out the back windows and *kamonanban soba* (noodles in hearty duck broth). Look for the brown-and-white curtain outside.

❶ Getting There & Away

Take the JR Chūō line from Shinjuku Station, changing to the JR Ōme line at Tachikawa Station or Ōme Station depending on the service, and get off at Mitake (¥890, 90 minutes). Buses (¥270, 10 minutes) run from Mitake Station to Takimoto, where a cable car takes you near Mitake village (one-way/return ¥570/1090, six minutes, 7.30am to 6.30pm); on foot, the climb takes about one hour.

Hakone 箱根

☎ 0460 / POP 13,500

If you only have a day or two outside Tokyo, Hakone can give you almost everything you could desire from the Japanese countryside: spectacular mountain scenery crowned by Mt Fuji, onsen and traditional inns. It's also home to world-class art museums. Ashino-ko is in the centre of it all and provides the foreground for the iconic image of Mt Fuji with the torii of the Hakone-jinja rising from the lake.

During holidays, Hakone can be quite busy and feel highly packaged. To beat the crowds, plan your trip during the week. For more information, try www.hakone.or.jp/english.

ℹ Getting There & Away

The private **Odakyū line** (www.odakyu.jp) from Shinjuku Station goes directly into Hakone-Yumoto, the region's transit hub. Use either the convenient Romance Car (¥2020, 90 minutes) or *kyūkō* (regular-express) service (¥1150, two hours); the latter may require a transfer at Odawara. The last trains from Hakone-Yumoto to Shinjuku run at 7.45pm weekdays and 8.50pm Saturday and Sunday for the Romance Car, and 10.30pm weekdays and 11pm Saturday and Sunday for the Odakyū line.

JR Pass holders can take the Kodama *shinkansen* (¥3840, 50 minutes) or the JR Tōkaidō line (*futsū* ¥1750, one hour; *tokkyū* ¥2350, one hour) from Tokyo Station or the Shōnan-Shinjuku line from Shinjuku (¥1450, 80 minutes) to Odawara and change there for trains or buses for Hakone-Yumoto.

The narrow-gauge, switchback Hakone-Tōzan line runs from Odawara via Hakone-Yumoto to Gōra (¥650, one hour).

Odakyū's **Hakone Freepass** (箱根フリーパス), available at Odakyū stations and Odakyū Travel branches, is an excellent deal, covering the return fare to Hakone and unlimited use of most modes of transport within the region, plus other discounts. It's available as a two-day pass (adult/child from Shinjuku ¥5000/1500, from Odawara if you're not planning on returning to Shinjuku, ¥3900/1000) or a three-day pass (adult/child from Shinjuku ¥5500/1750, from Odawara ¥4400/1250). Freepass-holders need to pay an additional limited-express surcharge (¥870 each way) to ride the Romance Car.

For those wanting to combine Hakone with Mt Fuji on their itinerary, there is the **Fuji Hakone Pass** (¥7200), a three-day pass offering discount round-trip travel from Shinjuku as well as unlimited use of most transportation in the Hakone and Fuji areas.

ℹ Getting Around

Part of Hakone's popularity comes from the chance to ride assorted *norimono* (modes of transport): switchback train (from Hakone-Yumoto to Gōra), cable car (funicular), ropeway (gondola), ship and bus. Check out www.odakyu.jp, which describes this circuit.

BOAT

From Tōgendai, sightseeing boats criss-cross Ashino-ko to Hakone-machi and Moto-Hakone (¥970, 30 minutes).

BUS

The Hakone-Tōzan and Izu Hakone bus companies service the Hakone area, linking most of the sights. Hakone-Tōzan buses, included in the Hakone Freepass, run between Hakone-machi and Odawara (¥1150, 55 minutes) and between Moto-Hakone and Hakone-Yumoto (¥930, 35 minutes).

CABLE CAR & ROPEWAY

Gōra is the terminus of the Hakone-Tōzan railway and the beginning of the cable car to Sōun-zan, from where you can catch the Hakone Ropeway line to Ōwakudani and Tōgendai.

LUGGAGE FORWARDING

At Hakone-Yumoto Station, deposit your luggage with **Hakone Baggage Service** (箱根キャリーサービス; ☎ 86-4140; per piece from ¥700; ⊙ 8.30am-7pm) by noon, and it will be delivered to your inn within Hakone from 3pm. Hakone Freepass holders get a discount of ¥100 per bag.

Hakone-Yumoto Onsen 箱根湯元温泉

Hakone-Yumoto is the starting point for most visits to Hakone. Though heavily visited, it's an ambient riverside resort town with a high concentration of onsen, the main attraction here.

◉ Sights & Activities

Key Hiraga Museum   MUSEUM
(平賀敬美術館; 613 Yumoto; admission ¥600; ⊙ 11am-5pm Fri-Tue) Dedicated to the bold, Pigalle-inspired paintings of Key Hiraga (1936–2000), this museum is run by the late artist's wife in their old-style villa. You can combine admiring the art with a soak in the villa's onsen for an extra fee of ¥500.

Hakone Region

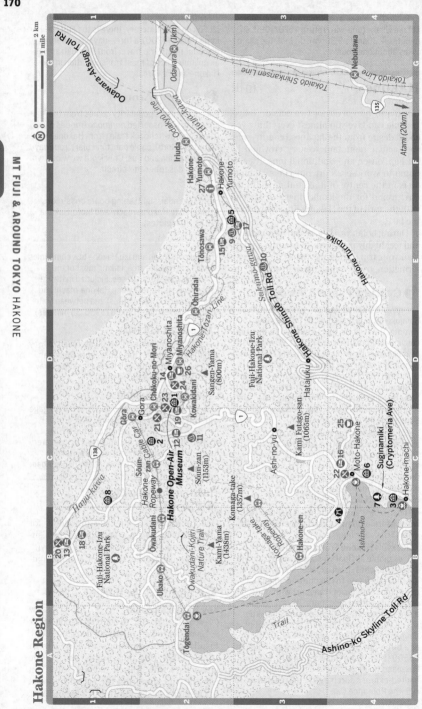

Hakone Region

Cross the Haya-kawa at Yumoto-bashi and take the first right; the museum is down a small lane.

Tenzan Tōji-kyo ONSEN
(天山湯治郷; www.tenzan.jp; 208 Yumoto-chaya; admission ¥1200; ⊙9am-10pm) Soak in *rotemburo* of varying temperatures and designs (one is constructed to resemble a natural cave) at this popular bath 2km southwest of town; weekends and holidays can be busy. Take the 'B' course shuttle bus from the bridge outside the Hakone-Yumoto Station (¥100).

Furasato ONSEN
(ふるさと; ☑85-5559; www.hakone-furasato.com; admission ¥850; ⊙9am-6pm Mon-Fri, to 8pm Sat & Sun) This ryokan has atmospheric *rotemburo* and indoor onsen; open to day trippers.

Yu-no-Sato ONSEN
(湯の里; www.yunosato-y.jp; 191 Yumotochaya; admission ¥1400; ⊙11am-11pm) A spa complex with several baths, including a *rotemburo* amid the fresh mountain air, jet bubble bath, plasma bath and private onsen for two, available by reservation. Towel rental is ¥200.

🛏 Sleeping

Hakone-no-Mori Okada HOTEL ¥
(箱根の森おかだ; ☑85-6711; www.hakonenomori-okada.jp; 191 Yumoto-chaya; r per person from ¥5930) Adjacent to the Hotel Okada, it includes access to the onsen at Yu-no-Sato.

Omiya Ryokan RYOKAN ¥¥
(☑85-7345; www.o-miya.com; 116 Yumotochaya; r from ¥6150, weekends with meals ¥13,000; ☏) This ryokan has well-priced midweek tatami rooms, some with mountain views. There's a small indoor onsen, but it offers 50% discount to a more attractive *rotemburo*, a short walk away. To get here, take the 'B' course bus from Hakone-Yumoto Station.

★Fukuzumirō RYOKAN ¥¥¥
(福住楼; ☑85-5301; www.fukuzumi-ro.com; 74 Tōnozawa; r per person incl 2 meals from ¥18,000) No two rooms are alike at this 100-year-old inn, though all have exquisite original woodwork. Most have sun terraces that rub up against the Haya-kawa; the small, quiet room overlooking the garden was a favourite of author Kawabata Yasunori. There are onsen baths but no private facilities. The inn is just below Tōnozawa Station on the Hakone-Tōzan railway, on the river side of the road, or a short taxi ride from Hakone-Yumoto Station.

Hotel Okada HOTEL ¥¥¥
(ホテルおかだ; ☑85-6000; www.hotel-okada.co.jp; 191 Yumoto-chaya; r per person from ¥15,000; ⊜☏⊠) This rambling hotel on the edge of the Sukumo-gawa has excellent Japanese- and Western-style rooms and baths including direct entry to the large Yu-no-Sato complex nearby. Take bus A from the train station (¥100, 10 minutes).

ⓘ Information

Tourist Information Center (☎85-8911; www.hakone.or.jp; ⊙9am-5.45pm) Pick up maps and info at the excellent Tourist Information Center with English speakers. By the bus stop across the main road from the train station. There are large coin lockers for luggage storage at the station (¥500).

Miyanoshita 宮ノ下

The first worthwhile stop on the Hakone-Tōzan railway towards Gōra, this village has antique shops along the main road, some splendid ryokan and a pleasant **hiking trail** skirting up 800m Sengen-yama (浅間山). The trailhead is just below Fujiya Hotel, marked by a shrine.

🛏 Sleeping & Eating

Fujiya Hotel　　　　　　　　　　　HOTEL ¥¥¥
(富士屋ホテル; ☎82-2211; www.fujiyahotel.jp; 359 Miyanoshita; d from ¥19,830; ⊙@☎✈) One of Japan's finest Western-heritage hotels. It opened in 1878 and played host to Charlie Chaplin back in the day (Room 45). Now sprawled across several wings, it remains dreamily elegant due to its old-world lounge areas and hillside garden. It's worth a visit to soak up the atmosphere and have tea in the lounge.

Miyafuji　　　　　　　　　　　　　SUSHI ¥¥
(鮨みやふじ; 310 Miyanoshita; meals from ¥1500; ⊙11.30am-3pm & 5.30-8pm; 🎫) A short walk up the street from Fujiya Hotel this friendly sushi shop is known for its *aji-don* (brook trout over rice). Look for the English sign.

🍷 Drinking

Naraya Cafe　　　　　　　　　　　　CAFE
(ナラヤカフェ; 404-13 Miyanoshita; coffee from ¥350; ⊙10.30am-6pm, closed Wed; 🎫) On the slope from the station, this cafe is in a renovated derelict structure that was once part of the grand, 300-year-old Naraya Hotel. You can take your espresso while soaking in the free footbath on the terrace looking out over the mountains.

Chōkoku-no-Mori & Gōra 彫刻の森・強羅

Gōra, one stop after Chōkoku-no-Mori, is the terminus of the Hakone-Tōzan line and the starting point for the funicular and cable-car trip to Tōgendai on Ashino-ko.

⊙ Sights & Activities

★**Hakone Open-Air Museum**　　　　MUSEUM
(彫刻の森美術館; www.hakone-oam.or.jp; 1121 Ninotaira; adult/child ¥1600/500; ⊙9am-4.30pm; 🎫) On a rolling hillside setting, this museum is a safari for art lovers, as you tick off an impressive selection of 19th- and 20th-century Japanese and Western sculptures (including works by Henry Moore, Rodin and Miró) found among the foliage. It also has an excellent Picasso Pavilion with more than 300 works including paintings, glass art and tapestry. Kids will love the giant crochet artwork/playground with its Jenga-like exterior walls. End the day by soaking your feet in the outdoor footbath. Located two stops beyond Miyanoshita, uphill from the Chōkoku-no-Mori Station. Hakone Freepass holders get ¥200 off the admission price.

POLA Museum of Art　　　　　　　MUSEUM
(www.polamuseum.or.jp; 1285 Kozukayama; adult/child ¥1800/700; ⊙9am-5pm) Showcasing the impressive private collection of the late Suzuki Tsuneshi, son of the founder of the Pola Orbis Group (cosmetics company), this quality museum is located in an equally impressive architecturally designed building. Artworks in the collection include those from such famous names as Van Gogh, Cézanne, Renoir, Matisse, Picasso and Rodin.

Hakone Museum of Art　　　　　　MUSEUM
(箱根美術館; www.moaart.or.jp; 1300 Gōra; adult/child ¥900/free; ⊙9.30am-4.30pm closed Thu) Sharing grounds with a lovey velvety moss garden and teahouse (¥700 *matcha* green tea and sweet), this museum has a collection of Japanese pottery dating from as far back as the Jōmon period (ie some 5000 years ago).

Yunessun　　　　　　　　　　　　ONSEN
(箱根小涌園ユネッサン; www.yunessun.com; 1297 Ninotaira; adult/child ¥2600/1300; ⊙9am-7pm; 🎫) Best described as an onsen amusement park, here you can soak in everything from green tea and sake to red wine and coffee. It's mixed bathing here so you'll need to bring a swimsuit. Buses running to Hakone-machi from Gōra or Hakone-Yumoto (via Chōkoku-no-Mori or Miyanoshita, respectively) stop at Yunessun.

🛏 Sleeping & Eating

Yudokoro Chōraku　　　　　　　　RYOKAN ¥
(湯処長楽; ☎82-2192; 525 Kowakudani; r per person from ¥5150) This simple, homely

ryokan has lovely owners, surprisingly spacious tatami rooms with kitchenettes and onsen bath and outdoor barrel tubs (available for day use, ¥550). It's a 10-minute walk uphill from the Hakone Open-Air Museum, on the left.

B&B Pension
PENSION ¥¥

(☎87-7800; http://en.pensionhakone.com; 1297 Ninotaira; s/d incl breakfast from ¥5000/10,000) This sprawling hotel is a little dated but offers clean, simple Western-style rooms with shared bathrooms and a public onsen. A good cheaper option. It's up the hill from Yunessun, signposted along the way.

Gyōza Center
JAPANESE ¥

(餃子センター; www.gyozacenter.com; 1300 Gōra; mains from ¥735; ⏱11.30am-3pm & 5-8pm, closed Sat; ▣) The humble *gyōza* (dumpling) stars at this cosy restaurant in a dozen different roles, from plain pan-fried *(nōmaru)* and filled with crabmeat or shrimp, to boiled in soup with kimchi *(kimchi sui-gyōza)*. No vegetarian options here, sorry. The restaurant is between Gōra and Chōkoku-no-Mori Stations on a corner, with an English sign.

Kappeizushi
SUSHI ¥

(かっ平寿し; 1143-49 Ni-no-taira; meals from ¥980; ⏱9am-8pm Wed-Mon; ▨▣) A few doors downhill from the Hakone Open-Air Museum, Kappeizushi does tasty *chirashi-zushi* (rice topped with assorted sashimi). Look for the small sign in the window.

Sōun-zan & Ōwakudani 早雲山・大桶谷

From Gōra, continue to near the 1153m-high summit of Sōun-zan by cable car (¥410, 10 minutes).

From Sōun-zan, there are several **hiking trails** including one to Kami-yama (1¾ hours) and another up to Ōwakudani (1¼ hours). The latter is sometimes closed due to the mountain's toxic gases. Check at the tourist information office.

Sōun-zan is the starting point for the **Hakone Ropeway**, a 30-minute, 4km gondola ride to Tōgendai (one-way/return ¥1330/2340), stopping at Ōwakudani en route. In fine weather Mt Fuji looks fabulous from here.

Ōwakudani is a volcanic cauldron of steam, bubbling mud and mysterious smells where you can buy onsen *tamago* (eggs boiled and blackened in the sulphurous waters). Don't linger, as the gases are poisonous. From here you can take the **Ōwakudani-Togendai Nature Trail**, a one-hour hike.

🛏 Sleeping & Eating

Hakone Sengokuhara Youth Hostel
HOSTEL ¥

(箱根仙石原ユースホステル; ☎84-8966; www.theyh.com; dm members/nonmembers ¥3510/4140, r per person ¥5400; ➡@@🛜) Part of the Fuji Hakone Guest House, located behind the main guesthouse, this hostel has Japanese-style shared and private rooms. Rates rise by ¥1000 to ¥2000 in high seasons. Use of the outdoor bath is ¥500 per person for 30 minutes.

Ryokan Masuya
RYOKAN ¥

(☎84-8057; www.onsen-masuya.com; 1-6-0 Sengokuhara; r per person from ¥4000; @) Simple onsen ryokan with spacious balcony rooms in a quiet leafy setting in Sengokuhara. Bicycles are for hire (¥3500 per day) and breakfast is available (¥1000). Take the bus to Sengoku annaijo-mae (Sengoku tourist information) stop from where it's a three-minute walk.

Fuji Hakone Guest House
GUESTHOUSE ¥¥

(富士箱根ゲストハウス; ☎84-6577; www.fujihakone.com; 912 Sengokuhara; s/d from ¥5925/11,850; ➡@@🛜) Run by a welcoming English-speaking family, this guesthouse has handsome tatami rooms, cosy indoor and outdoor onsen with divine volcanic waters, and a wealth of information on sights and hiking in the area. Take the 'T' course bus to Senkyōrō-mae from Odawara Station (stop 4; ¥1020, 50 minutes) or Tōgendai (¥370, 10 minutes). There's an English sign close by.

Daichi
IZAKAYA ¥

(75 Sengokuhara; meals from ¥400; ⏱11.30am-2pm & 5.30-8pm, closed Thu; ▣) Rub shoulders with the locals at this farmhouse-style restaurant that cooks up simple, tasty homestyle meals. The *tako-yaki* (grilled octopus dumplings) comes cripsy and set meals are under ¥1000. A short walk from the Fuji Hakone Guest House.

Ashi-no-ko 芦ノ湖

Between Tōgendai, Hakone-machi and Moto-Hakone, this lake is touted as the primary attraction of the Hakone region; but it's Mt Fuji, with its snow-clad slopes glimmering in the reflection on the water, that lends the lake its poetry.

Hakone-machi & Moto-Hakone 箱根町・元箱根

The sightseeing boats across Ashino-ko deposit you at either of these two towns, both well touristed and with sights of historical interest.

⊙ Sights

Hakone Sekisho MUSEUM
(箱根関所, Hakone Checkpoint Museum; 1 Hakone-machi; adult/child ¥500/250; ⊙9am-4pm Dec-Feb, to 4.30pm Mar-Nov) A recent reconstruction of the feudal-era checkpoint on the Old Tōkaidō Hwy, this museum has Darth Vader–like armour and grisly implements used on lawbreakers. Unfortunately it only has basic English explanations on some displays.

Narukawa Art Museum MUSEUM
(www.narukawamuseum.co.jp; 570 Moto Hakone; adult/child ¥1200/800; ⊙9am-5pm) Art comes in two forms here – in the exquisite *nihon-ga* (Japanese-style paintings) on display, and in the stunning Mt Fuji views from the panarama lounge looking out across the lake. Don't miss the cool kaleidoscope displays.

Hakone-jinja SHINTŌ SHRINE
(箱根神社; ⊙9am-4pm) A pleasant stroll around the lake follows a cedar line path to this shrine set in a wooded grove in Moto-Hakone. Its signature red torii rises from the lake; get your camera ready for that picture-postcard shot.

Onshi Hakone Kōen PARK
(恩賜箱根公園; 171 Moto-Hakone; ⊙9am-4.30pm) FREE On a small peninsula near the

---

DON'T MISS

AMAZAKE-JAYA

Up the hill from the Moto-Hakone bus stop is the entrance to the stone-paved Old Hakone Hwy (箱根旧街道), part of the Edo-era Tokkaidō Hwy, which leads back to Hakone-Yumoto (about 3½ hours). Along the way you'll pass this 350-year-old **Amazake-jaya** (甘酒茶屋; ⊙7am-5.30pm), an isolated, traditional-looking teahouse where you can enjoy a cup of *amazake* (a thick sweet drink made from rice used to make sake; ¥400) with a traditional sweet, *mochi* (sticky rice cake; from ¥400).

Hakone Sekisho is this scenic park. Its elegant Western-style building was once used by the imperial family, and has Fuji views across the lake.

🛏 Sleeping & Eating

Moto-Hakone Guesthouse MINSHUKU ¥
(元箱根ゲストハウス; ☑83-7880; www.fujiha-kone.com; 103 Moto-Hakone; r per person without bathroom ¥5250; ⊕@🛜) Offering simple but pleasant Japanese-style rooms and common areas with laundry and kitchen facilities. From Odawara Station, take the stop 3 bus to Hakone-machi or Moto-Hakone and get off at Ōshiba (¥1100, one hour); the guesthouse is a one-minute walk away.

Honjin Ieyasu YAKITORI ¥
(本陣家康; 107-1 Moto-Hakone; meals from ¥700; ⊙11.30am-3pm summer & 6pm-midnight; 🅿) You won't pay tourist prices at this casual, counter restaurant. The lunch set – try the *shōga yaki* (grilled pork and ginger) – is a steal and in the evening *yakitori* (skewers from ¥130) is served until midnight. It's on a side street opposite La Terrazza, one block past the Moto-Hakone bus stop; look for the white lanterns.

Izu Peninsula 伊豆半島

The Izu Peninsula (Izu-hantō), about 100km southwest of Tokyo in Shizuoka Prefecture, has a cool surfer vibe backed by plenty of history, particularly the famed *Kurofune* (Black Ships) of US Commodore Perry. It also packs lush greenery, rugged coastlines and abundant onsen. Weekends and holidays can be crowded on the east coast, particularly in summer. It's always quieter on the rugged west coast, which has Mt Fuji views over Suruga-wan.

Atami 熱海

☑0557 / POP 40,000
Atami is both the gateway to Izu, and its largest town. While this overdeveloped hot-springs resort lacks charm, there are a few sights and onsen that make it a worthwhile visit.

Overlooking the coastline, the sleek **MOA Museum of Art** (MOA美術館; ☑84-2511; www.moaart.or.jp; 26-2 Momoyama-chō; adult/student ¥1600/800; ⊙9.30am-4.30pm, closed Thu) has an excellent collection of Japanese and Chinese pottery and paintings, spanning more than 1000 years and including national treasures. It also has a serene tea garden set among Japanese maple and bubbling brooks. Stealing the show, however, is MOA's grandiose entrance, with escalators leading up 200m past ceilings that glow in changing neon colours that make you feel like you're about to board a spaceship.

Take bus 6 outside Atami Station to the last stop (¥160, eight minutes). Otherwise you can get here via the **Yu-Yu** (¥800) bus if you plan to spend the day sightseeing.

Sun Beach is an attractive sight in the evening, with its sands illuminated by coloured floodlights. If you plan to hang around, **Toyoko-Inn** (☑86-1045; www.toyoko-inn.com; 12-4 Kasuga-cho; s/d incl breakfast ¥5840/6980; @⊟) has well-priced, comfortable rooms.

Discount tickets to the museum (¥1400) and good English brochures and transport info are available at the tourist office, at the station building.

ℹ **Getting There & Away**

JR trains run from Tokyo Station to Atami on the Tōkaidō line (Kodama *shinkansen* ¥4080, 50 minutes; Odoriko ¥3700, 1¼ hours; Acty *kaisoku* ¥1890, 1½ hours).

Tokai Kisen (☑5472-9999; www.tokaikisen. co.jp; ⊘9.30am-8pm) runs jet ferries from Atami port to Ō-Shima in the Izu Islands (¥4660, 45 minutes). Prices are seasonal and dependent on fuel surcharges. To reach Atami port, take bus 7 from the station.

Itō & Around 伊東

☑0557

Itō is a commendably laid-back seaside town with some wonderful ryokan and onsen that provide a lovely antidote to the hectic city pace.

◉ **Sights & Activities**

Tōkaikan   HISTORIC BUILDING
(東海館; 12-10 Higashi Matsubara-chō; adult/child ¥200/100; ⊘9am-9pm) Next to K's House hostel, this 1920s inn is now a national monument for its elegant woodwork, each of its three storeys designed by a different architect. Its large bath is still open to bathers (¥500).

Ryokufuen   ONSEN
(緑風園; ☑37-1885; www.ryokufuen.com; 3-1 Otonashi-Cho; admission ¥1000; ⊘1.30pm-10pm) Soak away in this tranquil *rotemburo* with

its rocky waterfall under a canopy of trees. K's House guests receive a 50% discount with voucher. It's about a 15-minute walk on the main road leading from the station. Turn right at Saiseiji-jinja off the main road and it's a two-minute walk on your right.

Yokikan   ONSEN
(☑36-6488; www.yokikan.co.jp/english_top.html; 2-24 Suehiro-chō, Yokikan; admission ¥1000; ⊘11am-3pm) Part of a hotel, this outdoor rooftop *rotemburo* has the novelty of only being accessible via a rickety in-house cable car. It's mixed bathing, with distant views over the town and the water.

Sunhatoya Onsen   ONSEN
(Main Rd, Sunhatoya Hotel; admission ¥2000; ⊘8.30am-7pm) In a region famous for onsen, it's not surprising people are starting to get creative, with this plush bathhouse boasting not only ocean views, but fish-tank–lined walls full of colourful fish, turtles and sharks.

Ikeda Museum of 20th Century Art   MUSEUM
(☑45-2211; www.nichireki.co.jp/ikeda; 614 Totari; adult/child ¥900/500; ⊘9am-5pm, closed Wed) Art lovers will not want to miss out on this treasure trove of big names, such as Dalí, Warhol, Picasso, Lichtenstein and Miró, all on show in an abstract silver cube-shaped building. Take bus 6 from Itō Station.

Mt Omuro   MOUNTAIN
(return chairlift ¥500; ⊘9am-4pm) Ride the four-minute chairlift to the summit of Mt Omuro, a grassy dormant rice-bowl volcano crater, where you can take in coastal views of Mt Fuji. There's a 1km walk around the summit, bizarrely enough with an archery centre in the middle. Take the bus bound for Shaboten Koen and Omuroyama from Itō Station (¥690, 40 minutes).

Jōgasaki   HIKING
South of Itō is the striking Jōgasaki coast, with its windswept cliffs formed by lava. A moderately strenuous cliffside hike, with volcanic rock and pine forests, winds south of the sci-fi–looking lighthouse to Izu Kōgen Station (about 6.5km). It's a 1.5km walk from Jōgasaki-kaigan Station to the coast. There is also a 48m-long suspension bridge with waves crashing 23m below. From Itō Station, take the Jogasakiguchi-bound bus (¥700, 35 minutes).

Izu Peninsula

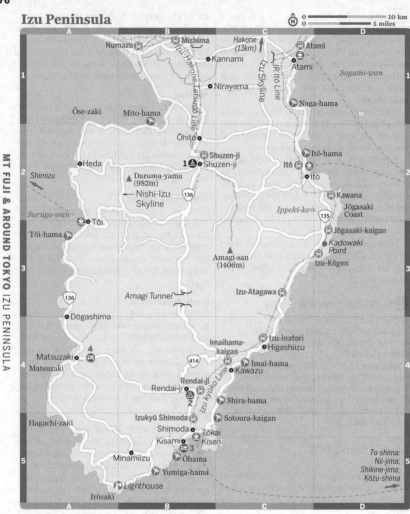

Sculpture Park PARK

On the far end of Orange Beach, a short walk from K's House, this photogenic sculpture park has a wonderful coastal backdrop.

🛏 Sleeping

★ K's House Itō Onsen HOSTEL ¥

(ケイズハウス伊東温泉; ☑ 35-9444; http://kshouse.jp/ito-e/index.html; 12-13 Higashi Matsubara-chō; dm from ¥2950, s/d per person from ¥3900/3400; ➡ @ 🛜) A 100-year-old ryokan with a charming riverside setting full of carp and heron, K's House is the real reason to come to Itō. The Japanese-style dorms, private rooms and common areas are beautifully maintained and classically stylish. With a fully equipped kitchen, helpful staff, and public and private onsen, this may be the best deal in the country.

Yamaki Ryokan RYOKAN ¥¥

(山喜旅館; ☑ 37-4123; www.ito-yamaki.co.jp; 4-7 Higashi Matsubara-chō; r per person from ¥6000; 🛜) A block east of the Tōkaikan is this charming wooden inn from the 1940s with an onsen bath and pleasant rooms; some with ocean views. Limited English. Ask for reservations at the Tourist Information Center.

Izu Peninsula

✖ Eating & Drinking

For a small seaside town, Itō is jam-packed with eateries and small bars.

Kunihachi   IZAKAYA ¥

(国八; 12-13 Higashimatsubara-chō; dishes ¥370-800; ⊙5.30pm-midnight; 🖉📶) A cute *izakaya* cluttered with eclectic decor, the menu caters to all with cheap and tasy dishes such as jumbo *okonomiyaki* (pancake; ¥730). It has a great vegetarian selection as well as exotic game such as horse sashimi.

Hamazushi   SUSHI ¥

(はま寿司; sushi from ¥100; ⊙11am-11pm) In a town famous for fish, it says something about this *kaiten* sushi (sushi train) place that people are prepared to queue for cheap and tasty morsels of seafood. Opposite the beach near Marine Town.

Sweet House Wakaba   ICE CREAM ¥

(6-4 Chuo-chō; ice cream from ¥450; ⊙9am-10pm) Serving old-school sundaes with generous dollops of soft handmade ice cream, with your choice of topping. Go the creamy red *adzuki* bean. It's in the *shotengai* (shopping arcade).

Fuji Ichi   SUSHI ¥¥

(ふじいち; www.fujiichi.com/eng.html; 7-6 Shizumi-chō; sets from ¥1500; ⊙10am-3pm Mon-Fri, to 3.30pm Sat) The coastal road is lined with restaurants and fishmongers – this is both. Run by a laid-back Japanese-Kiwi, this casual upstairs eatery is noted for its grilled fish and squid (cooked DIY on hot plates), but you can't miss with the sashimi set (*sashimi teishoku*, ¥1100). Heading south, it's a block past the Aoki supermarket; look for the vertical blue signs on the right.

Izu Kogen Brewery   PUB ¥¥

(Marine Town; pizzas from ¥1000; ⊙10am-9pm) Enjoy delicious thin-crust pizzas while sipping microbrewed beer and looking out to the sea. Then soak your toes in the foot onsen outside afterwards. Can life get any better?

Freaks   BAR

(⊙8pm-1am) Intimate bar spinning soul and funk vinyl, on the main road towards the station from K's House.

ℹ Information

Tourist Information Center (📞37-6105; ⊙9am-5pm) Across from Itō Station with helpful, English-speaking staff, loads of info on the Izu Peninsula and a detailed Itō map. For more info, check out www.itospa.com.

ℹ Getting There & Away

The JR limited-express Odoriko service runs from Tokyo Station to Itō (¥4020, one hour and 40 minutes). Itō is connected to Atami by the JR Itō line (¥320, 22 minutes).

From Itō, the Izukyūkō (aka Izukyū) line goes to Shimoda, stopping at Jōgasaki-kaigan (¥560, 25 minutes). There are six buses daily to Shuzen-ji (¥1100, one hour).

Shimoda 下田

📞0558 / POP 25,000

Shimoda's laid-back vibe is perfectly suited to an exploration of its surrounding beaches. It also holds a pivotal place in Japan's history as the spot where the nation officially opened to the outside world after centuries of isolation.

◉ Sights

★ Perry Road   STREET

This quaint cobbled street leads along a canal to Ryōsen-ji temple and is a pleasant place to stroll around on a lazy afternoon. The old traditional houses under willow trees are now full of cafes, jazz bars, boutique shops and restaurants.

Ryōsen-ji & Chōraku-ji   BUDDHIST TEMPLE

(了仙寺・長楽寺) A 25-minute walk south of Shimoda Station is **Ryōsen-ji**, site of the treaty that opened Shimoda, signed by Commodore Perry and representatives of the Tokugawa shōgunate. The temple's **Black Ship Art Gallery** (了仙寺宝物館, Hōmotsukan; 3-12-12 Shichiken-chō; adult/child ¥500/150; ⊙8.30am-5pm) displays artefacts relating to Perry, the Black Ships, and Japan as seen through foreign eyes and vice versa.

Shimoda

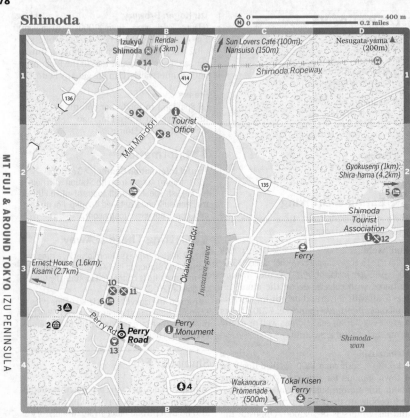

Behind and up the steps from Ryōsen-ji is **Chōraku-ji**, where a Russo-Japanese treaty was signed in 1854; look for the cemetery and *namako-kabe* (black-and-white lattice-patterned) walls.

Gyokusenji
TEMPLE

(玉泉寺; 31-6 Kakizaki; museum adult/child ¥400/200; ⏰8am-5pm) Founded in 1590 this Zen temple is famous as the first Western consulate in Japan, established in 1856. A small **museum** has artefacts of Townsend Harris, the first consul general. It's a 25-minute walk from Shimoda Station, or take bus 9 to Kakizaki-jinja-mae (¥160, five minutes).

Shimoda Kōen & Wakanoura Promenade Park
PARK

(下田公園・和歌の浦遊歩道) If you keep walking east from Perry Rd, you'll reach the pleasant hillside park of Shimoda Kōen, which overlooks the bay. It's loveliest in June, when the hydrangeas are in bloom.

🛏 Sleeping

Ōizu Ryokan
RYOKAN ¥

(大伊豆旅館; ☑22-0123; 3-3-25 Shimoda; r per person ¥3500) Popular with international travellers for its excellent prices, Ōizu has plain but comfy Japanese-style rooms with TV, and a two-seater onsen. It's at the southern end of town, two blocks north of Perry Rd. Check-in is from 3pm. It's often closed on weekdays, so phone ahead.

Nansuisō
RYOKAN ¥

(南水荘; ☑22-2039; 1-21-17 Higashi Hongo; r per person ¥4000) A quiet old inn along the river with simple rooms and a shared onsen bath; it's pretty in the spring when the cherry trees bloom.

Yamane Ryokan
RYOKAN ¥¥

(やまね旅館; ☑22-0482; 1-19-15 Shimoda; r per person ¥4500) You wouldn't guess this place has been running for 60 years from its tidy,

Shimoda

well-maintained Japanese-style rooms. The owner speaks little English but is very friendly and the central location is excellent. Facilities are shared; breakfast is available for ¥1000.

Kurofune Hotel   HOTEL ¥¥¥
(黒船ホテル; ☏22-1234; www.kurofune-hotel. com; 3-8 Kakizaki; r per person ¥5900; @⊠) This glitzy old-line hotel has bay views, seafood dinners, palm trees by the *rotemburo* and a heated swimming pool. Rooms are Japanese-style except for the suites, some of which have their own *rotemburo* (from ¥37,000 per person).

✕ Eating & Drinking

Musashi   NOODLES ¥
(むさし; 1-13-1 Shimoda; mains ¥650-1000; ⊘11am-2pm Wed-Mon) In business since 1916, serving hearty comfort food such as *kamo nabeyaki udon* (duck hotpot; ¥1000); there's a big badger out the front.

Ra-Maru   CAFE ¥
(burgers from ¥900; ⊘10am-4.30pm; 🍴) Retro diner serving tasty Shimoda fish burgers with camembert, and shrimp burgers with a big dollop of fresh avocado, with a side of onion rings and cold beer. Just behind the harbour museum at the port.

★**Gorosaya**   JAPANESE ¥¥
(ごろさや; 1-5-25 Shimoda; lunch ¥1575, dinner ¥3150; ⊘11.30am-2pm & 5-9pm closed Thu; 🍴) Elegant, understated ambience and fantastic seafood. The *Isōjiru* soup is made from over a dozen varieties of shellfish and looks like a tide pool in a bowl. It's two streets on the left past the tourist information office off the main road; look for the wooden fish decorating the entrance.

Porto Caro   ITALIAN ¥¥
(ポルトカーロ; 3-3-7 Shimoda; mains from ¥950; ⊘11am-2.30pm & 6.30-10pm, closed Wed; 🍴🍴) Upstairs Italian trattoria run by a friendly writer who's great for a chat about all things Shimoda. The Shimoda seafood pasta with wasabi sauce is sensational, as are the tasty simple pizzas. Look for the English sign two blocks down from the post office.

Nami Nami   IZAKAYA ¥¥
(開国厨房なみなみ; 3-3-26 Shimoda; skewers/ small plates from ¥120/550; ⊘5pm-midnight) This friendly counter bar has a retro vibe and an inventive menu. Local fish *(honjitsu no sakana)* and assorted delicacies served *yakitori*-style or breaded and fried. It's two doors up from Ōizu Ryokan, with a yellow sign.

Soul Bar Tosaya   BAR
(土佐屋; http://tosaya.net; 3-14-30 Shimoda; snacks from ¥600; ⊘6pm-midnight) In the heart of Perry Rd, this is one of the oddest mashups we've seen: a traditional residence from the era of the Black Ships that's now a soul-music bar complete with disco ball. It also serves meals.

ℹ Information

Shimoda information can be found online at www.shimoda-city.info.

Shimoda International Club (sicshimoda@ yahoo.co.jp) Offers guided tours (¥200 per person) on weekends and holidays.

Shimoda Tourist Association (☏22-11531; 1-1 Sotogaoka; ⊘9am-5pm) In the port area near the harbour museum with English-speaking staff, useful Shimoda Guidebook (¥840)and free walking map. Can book accommodation.

Sun Lovers Cafe (⊘11am-5.30pm Tue-Sat) Free internet, book swapping and light meals.

Tourist Office (観光案内所; ☏22-1531; http://shimoda-city.info; 1-1 Sotogaoka; ⊘10am-5pm) In the city centre, with no English spoken, but staff can call the Shimoda Tourist Association at the port.

SURFIN' SHIMODA

At the southern tip of Izu Peninsula, the beaches around Shimoda are some of Japan's best surf spots. While it's an all-year-round surfing destination, waves are best between May and August. **Shira-hama** (白浜海岸) is the most popular and its small but constant break gets packed in summer. There's also a **reef break** at the front of the Shimoda Prince Hotel, a short walk uphill from Papa's Restaurant) **Shirahama Mariner** (☑ 0558-22-6002; www.mariner.co.jp; ☺ 9am-9pm) and **Irie Surf & Cafe** (☺ 9.30am-7pm, closed Tue) both rent boards (¥3000) and lessons (per two hours ¥5000).

The beaches in **Kisami** (きさみ), just south of Shimoda, are among some of the best. **Ōhama beach** (大浜) has the largest stretch of sand and consistent waves; **Irita** (いりたはま) is especially good when a southerly rolls in; and **Tatado** (多々戸) has arguably the most consistent waves on the peninsula. **Baguse Surf School** (☑ 0558-22-2558; http://baguse.jp; 58-8 Tatado; 10am-4pm Apr-Nov) offers lessons (from ¥5500, 1½ hours) and board rentals (from ¥3300) in Tatado.

ⓘ Getting There & Away

Shimoda is as far as you can go by train on the Izu Peninsula. Limited-express *tokkyū* trains run to Shimoda from Tokyo Station (¥6090, 2¾ hours) or Atami (¥3400, 80 minutes); regular Izukyūkō trains run from Atami (¥1890, 1½ hours) and Itō (¥1570, one hour). Try to catch Izukyū's Resort 21 train, with sideways-facing seats for full-on sea views.

Tōkai buses run to Dōgashima (¥1360, one hour) via Matsuzaki.

Tōkai Kisen (東海汽船; ☑ 5472-9999; ☺ 9.30am-8pm) ferries serve the Izu Islands Kōzu-shima, Shikine-jima and Nii-jima (all ¥4070).

Car rental is available at **Toyota Rent-a-Car** (トヨタレンタカー; ☑ reservations in English 0800 7000 815; car rental per day from ¥6500; ☺ 8am-8pm) by the train station.

Shira-hama 白浜海岸

☑ 0558

North of Shimoda, Shira-hama (meaning white-sand beach) is an attractive beach town full of young beachgoers and a popular spot with Kantō-area surfers on their summer break.

Off the main road is the pleasant 2400-year-old **Shirahama-jinja** shrine, a nice spot to wander with striking torii on the rocky edge of the beach.

🛏 Sleeping & Eating

Pension Sakuraya　　　　　　　PENSION ¥¥

(☑ 23-4470; www.izu-sakuraya.jp; 2584-20 Shirahama; r from ¥10,600; ☎) A 10-minute walk up a steep hill from the beach, this homely guesthouse has been welcoming visitors for over 25 years. All rooms have fridges, as well as sea or mountain views. The English-speaking owner is a good source of info.

Pension Shirahama Mariner　　　PENSION ¥¥

(☑ 22-6002; www.mariner.co.jp; 2752-16 Shirahama; r per person ¥8000) Upstairs from Hana Cafe and run by the guys from the Shirahama Mariner surf shop, rooms here are comfy with homely touches such as colourful bedspreads and rugs. There's a bit of traffic noise but with these spectacular ocean views, who cares?

Hana Cafe　　　　　　　　　　　CAFE ¥

(2752-16 Shirahama; pizzas from ¥980; ☺ 9am-9pm; ☎) Just across from the ocean, this sun-drenched beach cafe offers cheap and cheerful meals, beer, cocktails and Hawaiian coffee.

Papa's Restaurant　　　　　　　CAFE ¥¥

(☑ 22-0225; pizzas from ¥1050; ☺ 11am-3pm & 5-10pm, closed Tue) Cosy diner with vintage toy cars, gingham tablecloths and surfboards on the walls, serves light fare such as shrimp tacos and pizza. It's a five-minute walk uphill from the beach on the right.

ⓘ Getting There & Away

Bus 9 runs from Shimoda to Shira-hama (¥320, 10 minutes).

Kisami きさみ

Most famous for **Ōhama beach** (大浜), laidback Kisami is another surf town with good vibrations. There are other surf beaches in the area including **Irita** and **Tatado** (多々戸).

A two-minute walk from Ō-hama beach, **Ernest House** (アーネストハウス; ☑ 22-5880; www.ernest-house.com; 1893-1 Kisami; r ¥10,500-13,650; ☺ @ ☎) is a quaint clapboard pension with beach-house vibe and an outdoor Jacuzzi. Attached is **Cafe Mellow** (meals ¥300-950; ⊙11am-11pm closed Tue), with long counter bar, outdoor decking, comfy chairs, and beach fare such as burgers, green curry and seafood BBQs.

Tabí Tabí (☑22-4188; www.tabitabiizu.com; r from ¥4500; 🖲) up the road is another cosy lodge, and a great source of info.

To get here From Izukyū Shimoda Station, take an Irōzaki-bound bus (stop 3 or 4; ¥360) to Kisami, from where it's a 15-minute walk.

Rendai-ji & Kanaya Onsen 蓮台寺・金谷温泉

The town of Rendai-ji is home to one of the best onsen on the peninsula, **Kanaya Onsen** (金谷温泉; 114-2 Kouchi; admission ¥1000; ⊙9am-10pm). Its rambling building houses the biggest all-wood (*hinoki*) bath in the nation (mixed), called the *sennin-furo* (1000-person bath, a vast exaggeration). Women can cover up with a towel (BYO or buy one for ¥200). The women-only bath is nothing to sneeze at, and both sides have private outdoor baths as well.

The same building also houses the fabulously traditional **Kanaya Ryokan** (☑22-0325; 114-2 Kouchi; r per person from ¥7500), which was built in 1929 and feels like it. Some of the tatami rooms are simple, while others are vast suites with private toilet. There are no restaurants nearby, so go for the inn's meals or pack your own.

Rendaijiso (☑22-3501; www.rendaijiso.jp; admission ¥1000; ⊙noon-7pm) has several separate men's and women's baths on offer with a beautiful rockpool *rotemburo* and *hinoki* outdoor bath under a wooden hut where you can soak to the sounds of whistling birds.

From Izukyū Shimoda Station take the Izukyū line to Rendai-ji Station (¥160, five minutes) but note that the express doesn't stop here. For Kanaya, go straight across the river and main road to the T-junction and turn left; the onsen is 50m ahead on the right.

Matsuzaki 松崎

☑0558

Things are much quieter on the west coast. The sleepy port of Matsuzaki is known for its streetscapes and attractive river setting: some 200 traditional houses with *namako-kabe* walls are concentrated in the south of town, on the far side of the river.

Izu Chōhachi Art Museum (伊豆の長八美術館; 23 Matsuzaki; adult/child ¥500/ free; ⊙9am-5pm) showcases the work of native son Irie Chōhachi (1815–99) including Shungyo-no-zu (Dawn in Spring 1875) and unimaginably detailed frescos and plaster works; staff supply magnifying glasses so you can get a better look. You can find more of his pieces at **Chōhachi Memorial Hall** (長八記念館; 234-1 Matsuzaki; adult/ child ¥500/300; ⊙9am-5pm) and **Iwashina Elementary School** (岩科学校; 442 Iwashina-hokusoku; adult/child ¥300/free; ⊙9am-5pm).

Sanyo-sō Youth Hostel (三余荘ユースホステル; ☑42-0408; www.jyh.or.jp; 73-1 Naka; dm member/nonmember ¥3360/3960) is a good sleeping option, 3km east of Matsuzaki with shared tatami rooms close to the water. For a good feed, **Mingei Sabō** (民芸茶房; 495-7 Matsuzaki; sets ¥1050-3150; ⊙7.30am-8.30pm), near the port, has filling sets of fresh local seafood.

The **Tourist Information Center** (☑42-1190; ⊙8.30am-5pm) at the bus stop will hold your luggage for the day (¥100).

From Shimoda Station take a Dōgashima-bound bus and get off at the Yūsu-hosteru-mae bus stop (¥1160, 50 minutes); it's another ¥240 to Matsuzaki. Buses run to Shuzen-ji (¥2090, 1½ hours) via Dōgashima, complete with fantastic views over Suruga-wan to Mt Fuji.

Dōgashima 堂ヶ島

Dōgashima, a short bus ride from Matsuzaki, is famous for its dramatic rock formations, which line the seashore.

Cruises (¥920/1880 for 20/50 minutes) from the nearby jetty take in the town's famous shoreline cave. The park just across the street from the bus stop has excellent views too; don't miss the **Tensōdō** (天窓洞), a natural window in the cave's roof.

Sawada-kōen Rotemburo (沢田公園; 2817-1 Sawada Nishina; adult/child ¥500/150; ⊙7am-8pm in summer, closed Tue) has an amazing spot on a cliff overlooking the ocean, but gets very busy at sunset. To get here, take a Dōgsahima bus from Matsuzaki and get off at the sixth stop, Sawada. It's a little tricky to find but it's about a 10-minute walk from here heading towards the fisherman's harbour.

Seaside Dogashima (2121-3 Nishina; d from ¥10,500) has simple clean rooms with ocean views and shared bathrooms. A step up is **Umibe No Kakureyu Seiryu** (☑52-1118;

www.n-komatu.co.jp; 2941 Nishina; r per person incl 2 meals from ¥50,000; 🛜), where traditional design meets modern standards at this popular ryokan on the beach. A variety of baths are on offer; it has a sensational men's *rotemburo* right on the beach with crashing waves. It's a five-minute walk from the Dōgashima bus stop.

The **Tourist Information Center** (📞52-1268; ⏰8.30am-5pm Mon-Sat), in front of the bus stop, can help with onward bookings and transport info.

Buses to Dōgashima (¥1360, one hour), via Matsuzaki (¥260, eight minutes), leave from in front of Shimoda Station.

Shuzen-ji Onsen 修善寺温泉

📞 0558

Inland Shuzen-ji Onsen is a quaint hot-spring village in a lush valley bisected by the rushing Katsura-gawa. The narrow lanes and criss-crossing bridges are perfect for strolling. Some of Japan's finest onsen ryokan are here as well.

There's a **Tourist Information Office** (📞72-2501; ⏰9am-5pm) at Shuzen-ji Station; no English is spoken but you can pick up a sightseeing map in English and there is a free internet terminal. Shuzen-ji Onsen is a 10-minute bus ride from the station.

In the middle of Shuzen-ji Onsen is its namesake temple, **Shuzen-ji** (964 Shuzen-ji; adult/child ¥300/200; ⏰8.30am-4.30pm). It's said to have been founded over 1200 years ago by Kōbō Daishi, the Heian-period priest credited with spreading Buddhism throughout much of Japan. You can wander the pleasant temple grounds free of admission.

History aside, the real reason to visit Shuzen-ji is to take a dip in one of its famous onsen. Inns around town offer day-use bathing. Try **Hako-yu** (筥湯; 925 Shuzen-ji; admission ¥350; ⏰noon-8.30pm), an elegant, contemporary facility identified by its 12m-high wooden tower.

Right on the river is a foot bath called **Tokko-no-yu** (独鈷の湯, Iron-Club Waters; ⏰24hr) `FREE`, rumoured to be Izu's oldest hot spring.

🛏 Sleeping & Eating

Goyōkan
MINSHUKU ¥¥

(五葉館; 📞72-2066; www.goyokan.co.jp; 765-2 Shuzen-ji; r per person without bathroom from ¥10,650) Simple tatami rooms in the centre of everything, with river views. There are

no private facilities, but the shared (indoor) baths are made of stone and *hinoki*. Some English is spoken.

⭐ Arai Ryokan
RYOKAN ¥¥¥

(新井旅館; 📞72-2007; www.arairyokan.net; 970 Shuzen-ji; r per person incl 2 meals from ¥25,000; 🛜♨) Long beloved by Japanese artists and writers, this gem of an inn was founded in 1872 and has kept its traditional, wood-crafted heritage. The bath hall, designed by artist Yasuda Yukihiko, is grand and the riverside rooms are magnificent in autumn, when the maples are ablaze. Take your pick between rooms looking onto the river or peaceful garden.

Zendera Soba
NOODLES ¥¥

(禅寺そば; 761-1-3 Shuzen-ji; meals ¥630-1890; ⏰11am-2pm Fri-Wed; 🔲) This local institution serves its speciality namesake Zendera *soba* (¥1260) with a stalk of fresh wasabi root to grate yourself. It's steps from the bus station on the river side of the street, and has white and black banners.

ℹ Getting There & Away

From Tokyo, take the Tōkaidō line to Mishima (Kodama *shinkansen* ¥4400, one hour) then transfer to the Izu-Hakone Tetsudō for Shuzen-ji (¥500, 35 minutes). Buses connect Shuzen-ji Station to Shuzen-ji Onsen (¥210, 10 minutes), Itō (¥1100, one hour), Shimoda (¥2140, 1½ hours) and Dōgashima (¥1970, 1½ hours).

Izu Islands

The Izu Islands (伊豆諸島; Izu-shotō) comprise peaks of a submerged volcanic chain extending 300km into the Pacific. Although easily reached by ferry from Tokyo, the islands feel worlds away and not many tourists make it here. Soaking in an onsen while gazing at the Pacific is the classic Izu Islands activity, as is hiking up the mostly dormant volcanoes and along the pristine beaches.

Note the islands can get very crowded during summer and most onsen are mixed bathing requiring swimsuits. For more information on the whole chain, see www.tokyo-islands.com.

ℹ Getting There & Away

Ferries sail to/from Tokyo's Takeshiba Pier, a 10-minute walk from the north exit of Hamamatsu-chō Station. High-speed hydrofoils service the inner islands – Ō-shima (from ¥7410, 1¾ hours), Nii-jima (¥9560, 2½ hours) and Shikine-jima (¥9560, 2½ hours).

The outer islands are serviced by the large passenger ferry *Salvia-maru*: Miyake-jima (¥8230, seven hours), Mikura-jima (¥9250, eight hours) and Hachijō-jima (¥8580, 11 hours).

The islands are also serviced by ferries from the Izu Peninsula from Atami and Shimoda ports; see relevant sections for details.

Island hopping is also easy on the daily ferries that run up and down the island chains. Note that prices may change seasonally or to reflect fuel prices.

For up to date ferry schedules, visit www.tokyo-islands.com.

Ō-SHIMA 大島'

🎵 04992

The largest of the islands and closest to Tokyo, here you can peer into the maw of a recently erupted volcano, on a trip to the 754m summit of **Mihara-san**. Ō-shima's southernmost point, **Toushiki-no-hana** (トウシキの鼻), is rocky and wave beaten, with good swimming in sheltered pools below Tōshiki Camp-jō.

Round out your trip with a dip in one of Ō-shima's onsen. **Motomachi Hama-no-yu** (元町浜の湯; adult/child ¥400/240; ⏰1-7pm Sep-Jun, 11am-7pm Jul & Aug) is a fine outdoor onsen with great views of the ocean and Mt Fuji too if the weather is clear. It's a three-minute walk from the Motomachi Port.

Tōshiki Camp-jō (トウシキキャンプ場) FREE, close to the Minami-kōkō-mae bus stop, is a well-maintained campsite right near the sea, with showers and communal cooking area. Or try **Akamon** (ホテル赤門; 🎵2-1213; www.ooshima-akamon.com; 1-16-7 Motomachi; r per person from ¥12,000) hotel, with tatami rooms and onsen.

The **Ō-shima Tourist Association** (大島観光協会; 🎵2-2177; ⏰8.30am-5.15pm) is located near the pier in Motomachi. Find more information at www.town.oshima.tokyo.jp.

NII-JIMA 新島

Nii-jima has a ripping white-sand beach, two fine onsen and an easy laid-back vibe. **Habushi-ura** (羽伏浦) is a blazing 6.5km stretch of white sand that runs over half the length of the island. It attracts surfers from all over Kantō; the waves and tide are very strong so take care.

The island's other main attraction is one of Japan's most whimsical onsen, **Yunohama Onsen** (湯の浜温泉; ⏰24hr) FREE, a *rotemburo* which has several tubs built into the rocks overlooking the Pacific.

You can camp at **Habushi-ura Camp-jo** (羽伏浦キャンプ場) FREE with a stunning mountain backdrop and only 10 minutes' walk to the Habushi-ura beach. There are showers and plenty of barbecue pits. Otherwise **Saro** (サロー; 🎵5-2703; www.saro-niijima.jp; 3-3-4 Honmura; r per person from ¥5500; ⊜☎) guesthouse offers simple but stylish rooms and a hip cafe; some English is spoken. The **Nii-jima Tourist Association** (新島観光協会; 🎵5-0001; ⏰8am-4pm) is about 200m south of the pier.

SHIKINE-JIMA 式根島

About 6km south of Nii-jima, tiny Shikine-jima is a natural marvel: excellent seaside onsen and several sandy beaches all in just 3.8 sq km. **Jinata Onsen** (地鉈温泉; ⏰24hr) FREE, at the end of a narrow cleft in the rocky coastline, is one of the most dramatically located onsen we've seen. The waters, stained a rich orange from iron sulphide, are naturally 80°C; mixed with the cool ocean, they're just right. The tide affects the temperature, so bathing times change daily; check before making the steep descent.

Kamanoshita Camp-jo (釜の下キャンプ場; ⏰Sep-Nov & Mar-Jun) FREE is right near a fine beach and two free onsen. No showers here. The **Shikine-jima Tourist Association** (式根島観光協会; 🎵7-0170; ⏰8am-5pm) is at the pier.

MIYAKE-JIMA & MIKURA-JIMA

Lava flows in 1983 left some spectacular apocalyptic scenery on **Miyake-jima** (三宅島), 180km south of Tokyo. Check with the **Miyake-jima Tourism Association** (🎵0499-45-1144; ⏰8.30am-5.30pm) for volcanic-gas warnings. Underwater arches and coral beds make this island particularly attractive to divers.

Tiny **Mikura-jima** (御蔵島), just 20km further south, offers the rare chance to swim up close with dolphins from April to October contact **Snorkel Tours** (per 2hr about ¥6500) or the **Mikura-jima Tourism Association** (🎵0499-48-2022; fax 0499-48-7070; ⏰9am-5pm). Camping is not permitted on either island.

HACHIJŌ-JIMA 八丈島

About 290km south of Tokyo, Hachijō-jima has a culture all its own, with two dormant volcanos, 854m **Hachijō-Fuji** (八丈富士) and **Mihara-yama** (三原山), and plenty of palms attracting visitors for its hiking, diving and onsen.

★**Urami-ga-taki Onsen** (裏見ケ滝温泉; ⊘10am-9pm) **FREE** is not to be missed. At the southern end of the island, a 30-minute drive from Sokodo Port, just below the road, it overlooks a waterfall – pure magic in the early evening.

Project WAVE (⌂2-5407; www3.ocn.ne.jp/~p-wave/english.html) offers a variety of ecotourism options, including hiking, bird-watching, sea-kayaking and scuba diving. **Sokodo Camp-jō** (底土キャンプ場; 4188 Mitsune) **FREE** is an excellent camping ground with toilets, cold showers and cooking facilities. **Hachijōjima Tourism Association** (八丈島観光協会; ⌂2-1377; ⊘8.15am-5.15pm) is next to the town hall on the main road.

SOUTH OF TOKYO

Tokyo's cultural presence looms large in the Kantō area, but the area just to the south stands on its own. Yokohama, Japan's second-largest city, has an entirely different urban spirit. Further south, the fascinating old capital and coastal town of Kamakura brims with temples, shrines and surprisingly hip restaurants.

Yokohama   横浜

⌂045 / POP 3.7 MILLION

While there are no big drawcards in the way of sights, scratch the surface a little and you'll find out why Yokohama prides itself on its cosmopolitan roots. Though just 20 minutes south of central Tokyo, the city has a flavour and history all its own. Locals are likely to cite the uncrowded streets or neighbourhood atmosphere as the main draw, but for visitors it's the breezy bay front, microbreweries, jazz clubs and great international dining.

History

For most of its history, Yokohama was an unnoticed fishing village. Its fate changed abruptly in 1853–54 when the American fleet under Commodore Matthew Perry arrived off the coast to persuade Japan to open to foreign trade; in 1858 this little village was designated an international port.

Throughout the late 19th and early 20th centuries, Yokohama served as a gateway for foreign influence and ideas. Among the city's firsts-in-Japan: a daily newspaper, gas lamps and a train terminus (connected to Shimbashi in Tokyo).

The Great Kantō Earthquake of 1923 destroyed much of the city, but the rubble was used to reclaim more land, including Yamashita-kōen. The city was devastated yet again in WWII air raids; occupation forces were initially based here but later moved down the coast to Yokosuka.

⊙ Sights & Activities

⊙ Minato Mirai 21
みなとみらい 21

This district of artificial islands used to be shipping docks, but the last three decades have transformed them into a planned city of tomorrow ('Minato Mirai' means 'port future'). Certain areas, namely the concrete sprawl and commercial complexes created in the early-'90s boom years, appear dated in retrospect. Recent additions, however, are of a more pedestrian sort, including the waterfront **Zō-no-hana Park** and a series of **promenades** connecting the area's main attractions.

Landmark Tower   NOTABLE BUILDING
(ランドマークタワー; 2-2-1 Minato Mirai; adult/child ¥1000/500; ⊘10am-10pm; 🚇Minato Mirai) It may not be Japan's tallest building any more, thanks to the Tokyo Skytree, but it's still impressive standing at 296m high (70 storeys) and has one of the world's fastest lifts (45km/h). The Landmark Tower Sky Garden observatory is on the 69th floor; on clear days there are views to Tokyo and Mt Fuji, and you can get a glimpse into games taking place at Yokohama Stadium.

Yokohama Museum of Art   ART GALLERY
(横浜美術館; www.yaf.or.jp/yma; 3-4-1 Minato Mirai; adult/child ¥500/free; ⊘10am-6pm, closed Thu; 🚇Minato Mirai) Behind Landmark Tower, this modern-art museum hosts exhibitions that swing between safe-bet shows with European headliners to more daring contemporary Japanese artists. There's also permanent works including Picasso, Miró and Dalí in the catalogue.

Yokohama Port Museum   MUSEUM
(横浜みなと博物館; 2-1-1 Minato Mirai; museum & ship adult/child ¥600/300; ⊘10am-5pm, closed Mon; 🚇Minato Mirai) On the harbour in front of Landmark Tower, sits the docked **Nippon Maru sailing ship** (日本丸). Take a tour through the ship; the four-masted barque (built in 1930) retains many original fittings.

Yokohama

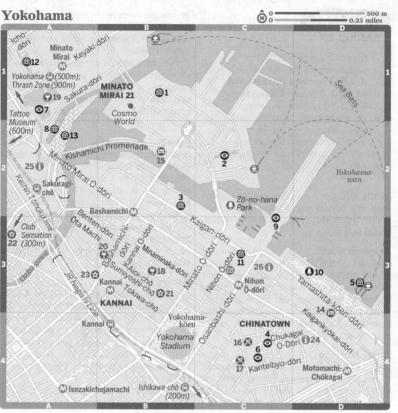

Yokohama

◉ Sights

1	!!! Cup Noodles Museum B1
2	Akarenga Sōkō C2
3	BankART Studio NYK B2
4	Chinatown C4
5	Hikawa Maru D3
6	Kantei-byō C4
7	Landmark Tower A1
8	Nippon Maru Sailing Ship A2
9	Ōsanbashi International
	Passenger Terminal C3
10	Yamashita-kōen D3
11	Yokohama Archives of History C3
12	Yokohama Museum of Art A1
13	Yokohama Port Museum A2

⬤ Sleeping

14	Hotel New Grand D3
15	Navios Yokohama B2

⊗ Eating

	Bills .... (see 2)
16	Manchinrō Honten C4

17	Ryūsen C4

⊖ Drinking & Nightlife

18	Craft Beer Bar B3
19	Sirius A1
20	Taproom B3

✪ Entertainment

	Airegin .... (see 20)
21	Bar Bar Bar B3
22	Downbeat Bar A3
23	Kamome A3

⬡ Shopping

	Akarenga Sōkō .... (see 2)

ⓘ Information

24	Chinatown 80 Information
	Center D4
25	Sakuragi-chō Station Tourist
	Information A2
26	Yokohama Convention &
	Visitors Bureau C3

WORTH A TRIP

SANKEI-EN 三渓園

Opened to the public in 1906, the landscaped gardens of **Sankei-en** (三渓園; 58-1 Honmoku-sannotani; adult/child ¥500/200; ⏱9am-4.30pm) feature walking paths and bridges among ponds and medieval structures, and provide a peaceful escape. From Yokohama or Sakuragi-chō Station, take bus 8 to Honmoku Sankei-en-mae (30 minutes).

As you exit, the comprehensive, and somewhat dry, port museum takes you through the city's port history; kids will love the simulated ship ride.

Akarenga Sōkō   HISTORIC BUILDING

(横浜赤レンガ倉庫; www.yokohama-akarenga.jp; 1-1-2 Shinkō; ⏱11am-8pm, some restaurants later; ®Bashamichi) Akarenga Sōkō means 'red-brick warehouse', and these attractive century-old structures have been refurbished into boutiques, restaurants, cafes and event spaces.

Tattoo Museum   MUSEUM

(☎323-1073; www.ne.jp/asahi/tattoo/horiyoshi3; 1F Imai Bldg, 1-11-7 Hiranuma Nishi-ku; admission ¥1000; ⏱noon-6pm; ®Tobe) Famous tattoo artist Horiyoshi III set up this museum with his wife, and it's a must not only for tattoo lovers but anyone interested in Japan's subculture. It's so packed you can hardly move with its display of tattoo needles and other tattoo paraphernalia set over two floors. It's a quick train ride from Minato Mirai to Tobe.

👁 Yamashita-kōen Area 山下公園周辺

This seaside, landscaped **park** (山下公園周辺; ®Motomachi-Chukagai) is perfect for strolling and ship watching.

Ōsanbashi International Passenger Terminal   NOTABLE BUILDING

(大さん橋国際客船ターミナル; 1-1-4 Kaigan-dōri; ⏱24hr; ®Nihon-ō-dōri) FREE Just to the west of Yamashita-kōen, this sleek, award-winning pier, completed in 2002, has an attractive roof deck where you can sit on the lawn or benches to take in the harbour views.

Yokohama Archives of History   MUSEUM

(横浜開港資料館; 3 Nihon ō-dōri; adult/child ¥200/100; ⏱9.30am-5pm, closed Mon; ®Nihon-ō-dōri) Displays in English chronicle the city's history with paintings, sketches, model ships and photographs, from the opening of Japan at the Yokohama port through to the mid-20th century. It's inside the former British consulate, on the main road across from Ōsanbashi pier.

BankART Studio NYK   GALLERY

(www.bankart1929.com; 3-9 Kaigan-dōri; admission varies; ⏱cafe 11.30am-11pm, gallery hours vary; ®Bashamichi) In a former warehouse, this gallery and theatre is a fixture on the local arts scene. It hosts changing exhibitions from local and international artists, and you can sift through flyers for local events over drinks in the 1st-floor cafe before stocking up on art and design books in the excellent attached shop.

Hikawa Maru   MUSEUM

(氷川丸; adult/child ¥200/100; ⏱10am-4.30pm Tue-Sun; ®Motomachi-Chūkagai) Moored at the eastern end of Yamashita-kōen, this restored 1930s passenger ship has art-deco fixings and stories to tell. Inside, you can wander from the 1st-class cabins (one of the staterooms was used by Charlie Chaplin) to the engine room.

👁 Chinatown 中華街

Yokohama's sprawling **Chinatown** (中華街; Chūkagai; ®Moto machi-Chūkagai, Ishikawa-chō) packs speciality shops and some 300 restaurants within a space of several blocks, marked by 10 elaborately painted gates. It's very touristy, but still worth popping in for a meal. At its heart is the Chinese temple **Kantei-byō** (関帝廟; 140 Yamashita-chō; ⏱9am-7pm) FREE, dedicated to Kanwu, the god of business.

🛏 Sleeping

Yokohama has plenty of midrange business hotel chains such as **Toyoko Inn** (www.toyoko-inn.com/eng) and the **Washington Hotel** (www.wh-rsv.com/english). Backpackers on a budget should head to Kotobukichō and Matsukage-chō – near the Ishikawachō and Kannai Stations – an area with a high concentration of hostels. It's a neighbourhood known for the down and out, but it's perfectly safe, cheap and a five-minute walk to Chinatown.

Hostel Zen
HOSTEL ¥

(☎342-9553; http://zen.ilee.jp; 3-10-5 Matsukage-chō; r incl breakfast from ¥3000; 🔊; 🚇Ishikawa-chō) An impeccably clean and bright hostel with Japanese–style rooms, some are decent sized, others are squashy, so ask the helpful staff to let you check out a few first. There's a good breakfast spread, clean shared bathrooms, and rooftop-decking area with funky furniture and umbrellas.

Hostel A Silk Tree
HOSTEL ¥

(www.hostel-nemunoki.com; 3-9-4 Matsukage-chō; s/d ¥3000/4500; @; 🚇Ishikawa-chō) Tiny rooms at this hostel, even for Japanese standards, but they come spotlessly clean and there's a well-equipped communal kitchen, rooftop garden and friendly English-speaking staff. Showers cost ¥200.

Navios Yokohama
HOTEL ¥¥

(ナビオス横浜; ☎633-6000; www.navios-yokohama.com; 2-1-1 Shinkō; s/d from ¥8400/14,700; ➡@🔊; 🚇Bashamichi) Well located in convenient Minato Mirai, despite the ugly '70s brick exterior, this is Yokohama's best mid-range deal. Rooms are spotless and central, with city or sea views. Rates increase on weekends.

Hotel New Grand
HOTEL ¥¥¥

(ホテルニューグランド; ☎681-1841; www.hotel-newgrand.co.jp; 10 Yamashita-kōen-dōri; s/tw from ¥13,860/32,340; ➡@; 🚇Motomachi-Chūkagai) This old-line hotel (1927) has a prime waterfront location and elegant old-world charm (check out the timeless original lobby), despite the addition of a tower in 1992. It was once a favourite of visiting foreign dignitaries such as General McArthur and Charlie Chaplin.

✖ Eating

Colombus Okonomiyaki
OKONOMIYAKI ¥

(お好み焼き ころんぶす 石川町店; mains ¥690-1120; ⊙ Mon-Thur 11.30am-10pm, Fri & Sat 11.30am-11pm, Sun 3-10pm; 🚇Ishikawa-chō) Friendly staff grill up tasty *okonomiyaki* at your table from a choice of prawn, squid or veg at this smart eatery. It's a two-minute walk from the Ishikawa-chō Station. Turn right from the north exit, then take a left at the first traffic lights and Colombus is 50m on your right.

Kin no Kura Jr
IZAKAYA ¥

(金の蔵Jr.; dishes ¥270; ⊙4pm-4am; 🎴; 🚇Yokohama) Popular for cheap drinks and typical *izakaya* snacks, such as the delicious salmon-belly sashimi, ordered on-screen at your table (English available). All dishes and drinks are ¥270, making it sensational value. From Yokohama Station's main exit, turn right and walk over the bridge and along the main strip. It's 80m on your right.

Bills
INTERNATIONAL ¥¥

(ビルズ; Akarenga Sōko Bldg 2; mains ¥1000-2000; ⊙9am-11pm; 🎴; 🚇Bashamichi) The latest outpost from Australian celebrity chef Bill Granger proves Yokohama still has an appetite for foreign flavours. There's a glass terrace and a long line for Sunday brunch. Try his famous ricotta hotcakes or berry berry pancakes.

OODLES OF NOODLES

Noodle lovers, take note: two Yokohama museums pay homage to the humble noodle and both are highly entertaining kitsch sights. **Shin-Yokohama Rāmen Museum** (新横浜ラーメン博物館; www.raumen.co.jp/ramen; 2-14-21 Shin-Yokohama; adult/child ¥300/100, dishes around ¥900; ⊙11am-10pm Mon-Sat, 10.30am-10pm Sun; 🚇Shin-Yokohama) is devoted solely to *rāmen*, the Chinese-style noodles that (it's fair to say) Japan is bonkers about. Nine *rāmen* restaurants from around the country were handpicked to sell their wares in this replica of a 1958 *shitamachi* (downtown district). When this clever 'food theme park' opened in 1994, it set off a wave of copycat establishments around the country. It's a short walk from the Shin-Yokohama station – ask for directions at the information centre at the station.

The !!! **Cup Noodles Museum** (www.cupnoodles-museum.jp; 2-3-4 Shinko; adult/child 500/free; ⊙10am-6pm, last entry 5pm, closed Tue; 🚇Bashamichi) is dedicated to Momofuku Ando's instant *rāmen* invention. This slick new museum has an 'instant noodles history cube' showcasing instant rāmen cups from the first one developed in 1958; a cutesy animation theatre on the history of the invention; and fun interactive activities making it a hit with kids and adults alike. At the end, you can make your own noodles; design and colour your cup, select your ingredients and air seal it to take home to enjoy.

Grassroots
INTERNATIONAL ¥¥

(レストラン　グラスルーツ; www.stovesy-okohama.com/grassroots; 2-13-3 Watanabe Bldg, Tsuruya-chō; mains ¥950-1400; ◎5pm-midnight; 🄬; 🄬Yokohama) There's a psychedelic vibe here with its paint-splattered floors, lava lamps and old car-seat chairs. Grassroots serves a good selection of international beers and tasty pub meals such as fish burgers and grilled tuna steaks with avocado mash. Happy hour (half-price beer) is 5pm to 8pm. From Yokohama Station's main exit, turn right and walk over the bridge, then right at Mosburger, walk one minute and it's on your left.

Charcoal Grill Green
GASTROPUB ¥¥

(http://ishikawacho.greenyokohama.com; 1-8-1F Ishikawa-chō; mains ¥1100-1400; ◎5pm-2am Mon-Fri & 4pm-2am Sat & Sun; 🄬; 🄬Ishikawa-chō) A charcoal grill and bar with three craft beers on tap to go with smoky steaks, BBQ pork and delicious prawn pizzas.

Ryūsen
CHINESE ¥¥

(馬さんの店龍仙; www.ma-fam.com; 218-5 Yamashita-chō; mains from ¥1050; ◎7am-3am; 🄬; 🄬Ishikawa-chō) You can't miss friendly old Mr Ma sitting outside his small Shanghai-style eatery, as he has done for years. The walls are literally wallpapered with photos of tasty-looking dishes. It has two other branches in Chinatown.

Manchinrō Honten
CHINESE ¥¥¥

(萬珍樓本店; ☎681-4004; www.english.manchinro.com; 153 Yamashita-chō; lunch/dinner courses from ¥2500/6000; ◎11am-10pm; 🄬🄬; 🄬Motomachi-Chūkagai) With chefs from Hong Kong, this elegant Cantonese restuarant is one of Chinatown's oldest (1892) and most respected. It serves a great selection of dim sum from 11am to 5pm.

🍷 Drinking & Nightlife

Yokohama is a live-music city, particularly noted for its love of jazz. The Kannai-Bashamichi area is considered a jazz hub.

★ Kamome
LIVE MUSIC

(カモメ; www.yokohama-kamome.com; 6-76 Sumiyoshi-chō; cover ¥2000-3500; ◎7-10.30pm Mon-Fri, 6-10.30pm Sat & Sun; 🄬Bashamichi, exit 3) The best place for serious live music, with a line-up that includes veteran and up-and-coming talents playing jazz, funk, fusion and bossa nova. The interior is stark and sophisticated, the crowd stylish and multi-generational.

Taproom
PUB

(馬車道　タップルーム; www.bairdbeer.com; 5-63-1, Sumiyoshi-chō; meals from ¥700; ◎5pm-midnight Mon-Fri, noon-midnight Sat & Sun; 🄬Bashamichi) Part of the Baird Brewing Company, this pub is set over three floors with a rooftop beer garden. Fourteen beers are served from wooden taps, 10 of which are from the brewery itself, ranging from pale ales to chocolate flavours. Try a sampler set for ¥1000 if you're struggling to decide. It also dishes up authentic American-style BBQ dishes. Has other branches around town.

Thrash Zone
BAR

(1F Tamura Bldg, 2-10-7 Tsuruyachō; ◎6-11.30pm; 🄬Yokohama) Stacked Marshall amps and walls covered with punk posters set the scene at this small bar popular with local beer-and-music fans. Knock back frothies from a choice of 13 craft 'extreme' beers (full body and high alcohol) from Japan and American breweries to a soundtrack of heavy metal and punk tunes on the screen. It also does great Belgian fries with basil mayo (¥500).

Club Sensation
LIVE MUSIC

(http://sensation-jp.com; 3-80 Miyagawa-chō; ◎6pm-1am, closed Mon; 🄬Hinodecho) Intimate British-themed rock cafe-bar, run by Japanese rockers, hosting local and international bands.

Airegin
JAZZ

(www.yokohama-airegin.com; 5-60 Sumiyoshi-chō; cover incl 1 drink ¥2500; ◎7.30-11pm; 🄬Bashamichi) Up a flight of stairs is where you'll find this intimate, smoky and genuine jazz bar that's been swinging since '72. It's run by a passionate jazz-loving couple and top-notch performances bring in an appreciative and knowledgeable audience.

Bar Bar Bar
JAZZ

(www.barbarbar.jp; 1-25 Aioi-chō, 2fl; cover ¥2000-3000; ◎6pm-3am; 🄬Kannai) A classy jazz bar with live performances every night by local and international artists.

Craft Beer Bar
BAR

(クラフトビアバー; 2-31-3 Ōta-chō; drinks from ¥700; ◎4-11.30pm, closed Mon; 🄬Bashamichi) One for the purists, this intimate counter bar has a revolving selection of 11 domestic craft brews, poured from brass taps. There's no English menu, but you can just tell the barman what you want (ale, stout etc) and how you want it (pint or glass). Look for

BEER LOVERS REJOICE

Yokohama locals sure love a cold beer and recent years has seen a growing trend of microbreweries and quality craft-beer bars popping up all over town. Perhaps the passion arises from the fact that it's home to **Yokohama Brewery** (www.yokohamabeer.com; 1-6-68 Sumiyoshi-chō), the oldest craft brewery in Japan, and one of the most famous Japanese beer producers, **Kirin Brewery** (☑045-503-8250; ⊙closed Mon) FREE. Kirin Brewery tours take you through the entire process of brewing, malting and fermentation and finish up with tasting of three beers, including one with a 'soft serve'–style head. Tours are in Japanese but you get an English pamphlet as a guide. Call ahead to book.

Another way to experience the city's passon is at one of its many beer festivals. **Yokohama Oktoberfest** is held over two weeks at Akarenga Sōkō in late September/early October annually and features around 80 beers in the spirit of the German festival with sausages, pretzels and music. Of the several smaller craft-beer festivals, the **Great Japan Beer Festival Yokohama** is one of the most popular, taking place in mid-September and featuring around 200 craft beers from across Japan.

The city even has a publication dedicated to beer, the free *Yokohama Beer Magazine* (in English), available from the tourist offices.

a plain wooden door in the alleyway, with English on the awning. Also has an impressive selection of 400 single malts.

Downbeat Bar　　　　　　BAR
(ダウンビート; www.yokohama-downbeat.com; 1-43 Hanasaki-chō Bldg 2; ⊙4-11.30pm Mon-Sat; ⛫Sakuragi-chō) *Jazz kissa,* which fall somewhere between cafes and bars, boast extensive jazz-record collections. This is one of the oldest (1956) in Yokohama, with more than 3000 albums and some serious speakers. Occasional live music means an occasional cover charge. Look for the 2nd-floor red awning.

Sirius　　　　　　BAR
(シリウス; ☑221-1111; 2-2-1-3 Minato Mirai; cover charge for jazz after 10pm ¥1050, cocktails from ¥1260; ⊙7am-1am; ⛫Sakuragi-chō) Cocktails with a view from the 70th floor of the Yokohama Royal Park Hotel.

🛍 Shopping

Akarenga Sōkō　　　　SHOPPING CENTRE
(横浜赤レンガ倉庫; www.yokohama-akarenga.jp; 1-1-2 Shinkō; ⊙11am-8pm) The red-brick warehouses are home to boutique clothing and accessories, unique gifts, design and watches and homewares. Made up of two buildings: warehouse 1 is better for shopping.

ⓘ Information

POST

The **Yokohama Port Post Office** (9am-7pm Mon-Fri, to 5pm Sat, to 12.30pm Sun) has an international ATM and parcel/post facilities.

TOURIST INFORMATION

Information about Yokohama is available at www.welcome.city.yokohama.jp/eng/tourism, as well as the following tourist offices, all of which have an English speaker.

Chinatown 80 Information Center (横浜中華街インフォメーションセンター; ☑662-1252; ⊙10am-9pm) A few blocks from Motomachi-Chūgakai Station.

Sakuragi-chō Station Tourist Information (☑211-0111; ⊙9am-6pm) Maps, brochures and hotel bookings. Outside the northern exit of Sakuragi-chō Station.

Yokohama Convention & Visitors Bureau (☑221-2111; www.welcome.city.yokohama.jp; 2 Yamashita-cho, Naka-ku, 1st fl, Sangyo-Boeki Center; ⊙9am-5pm Mon-Fri) A 10-minute walk from Nihon-odori Station with helpful staff, maps and brochures. Also has a great website.

Yokohama Station Tourist Information Center (☑441-7300; ⊙9am-7pm) Staff are helpful and can book accommodation. In the east–west corridor at the station.

ⓘ Getting There & Away

JR Tōkaidō, Yokosuka and Keihin Tōhoku lines run from Tokyo Station (¥450, 40 minutes) via Shinagawa (¥280, 18 minutes) to Yokohama Station. Some Keihin Tōhoku line trains continue along the Negishi line to Sakuragi-chō, Kannai and Ishikawa-chō. From Shinjuku, take the Shōnan-Shinjuku line (¥540, 35 minutes).

The private Tōkyū Tōyoko line runs from Shibuya to Yokohama (¥260, 30 minutes), after which it becomes the Minato Mirai subway line to Minato Mirai (¥440, 34 minutes) and Motomachi-Chūkagai (¥460, 40 minutes).

The Tōkaidō *shinkansen* stops at Shin-Yokohama Station, northwest of town, connected to the city centre by the Yokohama line.

ℹ Getting Around

BOAT

Sea Bass ferries connect Yokohama Station with Minato Mirai 21 (¥400, 10 minutes) and Yamashita-kōen (¥700, express/local 20/30 minutes) from approximately 10am to 7pm. From Yokohama Station, take the east exit and pass through Sogō department store to reach the dock.

BUS

Although trains are more convenient, Yokohama has an extensive bus network (adult/child ¥210/110 per ride). A special Akai-kutsu ('red shoe') bus loops every 20 minutes from 10am to around 7pm through the major tourist spots for ¥100 per ride.

SUBWAY

The Yokohama City blue line (*shiei chikatetsu*) connects Yokohama with Shin-Yokohama (¥230, 11 minutes), Sakuragi-chō (¥200, six minutes) and Kannai (¥200, five minutes). The cheaper JR line connects Yokohama with Shin-Yokohama (¥160, 15 minutes), Sakuragi-chō (¥130, three minutes) and Kannai (¥130, five minutes).

The **Minato Burari** day pass covers municipal subway and bus rides (including the Akai-kutsu bus, but not the Minato Mirai line) around Minato Mirai and Yamashita-kōen (adult/child ¥500/250); purchase at any subway station.

Kamakura 鎌倉

♩ 0467 / POP 174,000

An hour from Tokyo, Kamakura was Japan's first feudal capital, between 1185 and 1333, and its glory days coincided with the spread of populist Buddhism in Japan. This legacy is reflected in the area's high concentration of stunning temples. The town has a laid-back, earthy vibe complete with organic restaurants and summer beach shacks – which can be added to sunrise meditation and hillside hikes as reasons to visit. Kamakura does tend to get packed on weekends and in holiday periods, so plan accordingly.

History

The end of the Heian period was marked by a legendary feud between two great warrior families, the Minamoto (Genji) and the Taira (Heike). After the Taira routed the Minamoto, the third son of the Minamoto clan,

called Yoritomo, was sent to live at a temple on the Izu Peninsula. When the boy grew old enough, he began to gather support for a counterattack on his clan's old rivals. In 1180 Yoritomo set up his base at Kamakura, far away from the debilitating influences of Kyoto court life, close to other clans loyal to the Minamoto and, having the sea on one side and densely wooded hills on the others, easy to defend.

After victories over the Taira, Minamoto Yoritomo was appointed shōgun in 1192 and governed Japan from Kamakura. When he died without an heir, power passed to the Hōjō, the family of Yoritomo's wife.

The Hōjō clan ruled Japan from Kamakura for more than a century until, in 1333, weakened by the cost of maintaining defences against threats of attack from Kublai Khan in China, the Hōjō clan was defeated by Emperor Go-Daigo. Kyoto once again became the capital.

By the Edo period, Kamakura was practically a village again. With the opening of a rail line at the turn of the last century, the seaside town was reborn as a summer resort. Summer homes of wealthy Tokyoites still line the Shōnan coast.

◎ Sights & Activities

★ Kenchō-ji BUDDHIST TEMPLE

(建長寺; 8 Yamanouchi; adult/child ¥300/100; ⏲ 8.30am-4.30pm) Established in 1253, Kenchō-ji is Japan's oldest Zen monastery and is still active today. It once comprised seven buildings and 49 subtemples, most of which were destroyed in the fires of the 14th and 15th centuries. However, the 17th and 18th centuries saw its restoration, and you can still get a sense of its splendour. The central Butsuden (Buddha Hall) was brought piece by piece from Tokyo in 1647. Its Jizō Bosatsu statue, unusual for a Zen temple, reflects the valley's ancient function as an execution ground – Jizō consoles lost souls. Other highlights include a bell cast in 1253 and the juniper grove, believed to have sprouted from seeds brought from China by Kenchō-ji's founder some seven centuries ago.

Engaku-ji BUDDHIST TEMPLE

(円覚寺; 409 Yamanouchi; adult/child ¥300/100; ⏲ 8am-5pm Apr-Oct, to 4pm Nov-Mar) Engaku-ji, one of the five major Rinzai Zen temples in Kamakura, is on the left as you exit Kita-Kamakura Station. It was founded in 1282, allegedly as a place where Zen monks might pray for soldiers who lost their lives defending Japan against Kublai Khan. Engaku-ji remains an important temple, and a number of notable priests have trained here. All of the temple structures have been rebuilt over the centuries; the Shariden, a Song-style reliquary, is the oldest structure, last rebuilt in the 16th century. At the top of the long flight of stairs is the Engaku-ji bell, the largest bell in Kamakura, cast in 1301.

Tsurugaoka Hachiman-gū SHINTŌ SHRINE
(鶴岡八幡宮; 2-1-31 Yukinoshita; treasure hall adult/child ¥200/100; ☺9am-4pm) Kamakura's most important shrine is, naturally, dedicated to Hachiman, the god of war. Minamoto Yoritomo himself ordered its construction in 1191 and designed the pine-flanked central promenade that leads to the coast. The sprawling grounds are ripe with historical symbolism: the Gempei Pond, bisected by bridges, is said to depict the rift between the Minamoto (Genji) and Taira (Heike) clans. Behind the pond is the **Kamakura National Treasure Museum** (鎌倉国宝館; ☏22-0753; 2-1-1 Yukinoshita, Kamakura Kokuhōkan; admission ¥300; ☺9am-4.30pm Tue-Sun), housing remarkable Buddhist sculptures from the 12th to 16th centuries.

Daibutsu MONUMENT
(大仏; 4-2-28 Hase, Great Buddha; adult/child ¥200/150; ☺8am-5.30pm Apr-Sep, to 5pm Oct & Nov) Kamakura's most iconic sight, an 11.4m bronze statue of Amida Buddha (*amitābha* in Sanskrit), is in Kōtoku-in, a Jōdo sect temple. Completed in 1252, it's said to have been inspired by Yoritomo's visit to Nara (where Japan's biggest Daibutsu holds court) after the Minamoto clan's victory over the Taira clan. Once housed in a huge hall, today the statue sits in the open, the hall having been washed away by a tsunami in 1495. For an extra ¥20, you can duck inside to see how the sculptors pieced the 850-tonne statue together.

Buses from stops 1 and 6 in front of Kamakura Station run to the Daibutsu-mae stop. Alternatively, take the Enoden Enoshima line to Hase Station and walk north for about five minutes. Better yet, take the Daibutsu Hiking Course (p192).

Hase-dera BUDDHIST TEMPLE
(長谷寺, Hase Kannon; 3-11-2 Hase; adult/child ¥300/100; ☺8am-4.30pm) About 10 minutes' walk from the Daibutsu, Hase-dera (Jōdo sect) is one of the most popular temples in the Kantō region. The focal point of the

temple's main hall is a 9m-high carved wooden *jūichimen* (11-faced) Kannon statue. Kannon (*avalokiteshvara* in Sanskrit) is the bodhisattva of infinite compassion and, along with Jizō, is one of Japan's most popular Buddhist deities. According to legend, the temple dates back to AD 736, when the statue is said to have washed up on the shore near Kamakura.

Ennō-ji BUDDHIST TEMPLE
(円応寺; 1543 Yamanouchi; admission ¥200; ☺9am-3.30pm) Ennō-ji is distinguished by its statues depicting the judges of hell. According to the Juo concept of Taoism, which was introduced to Japan from China during the Heian period (794–1185), these 10 judges decide the fate of souls, who, being neither truly good nor truly evil, must be assigned to spend eternity in either heaven or hell. Presiding over them is Emma (Yama), a Hindu deity known as the gruesome king of the infernal regions.

Jomyo-ji BUDDHIST TEMPLE
(3-8-31 Jomyoji; admission adult/child ¥100/50; ☺9.30am-4.30pm) This Tokasan temple of the Rinzaishu Kenchō-ji sect was originally a tantric Buddhist temple and converted to a Zen temple. Behind the main temple is the Tomb of Ashikaga Sadauji, the father of Takauji, the founder of the Muromachi era. But the real reason to visit is for the atmospheric rock garden and teahouse where you can sip on *matcha* tea in a traditional tea ceremony (¥600). To get here, take the Keikyu bus 4 from Kamakura Station and get off at the Jumyōji stop from where it's a two-minute walk.

GET ZEN

Too many temples and before you know it you're feeling anything but 'Zen'. *Zazen* (seated meditation) can help you discover what you're missing – after all, temples were originally designed for this purpose (and not sightseeing). Both **Engaku-ji** (☺5.30-6.30am Apr-Oct, 6-7am Nov-Mar) FREE and **Kenchō-ji** (temple admission ¥300; ☺5-6pm Fri & Sat, enter before 4.30pm) hold beginner-friendly, public *zazen* sessions. Instruction is in Japanese, but you can easily manage by watching everyone else; arrive at least 15 minutes early.

Kamakura

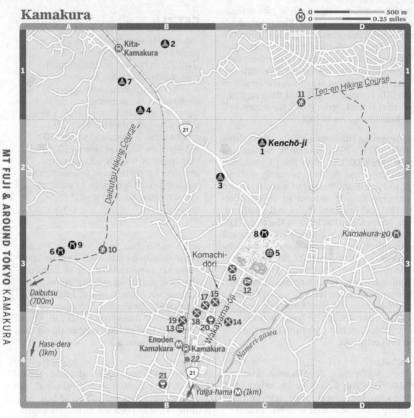

Tōkei-ji BUDDHIST TEMPLE
(東慶寺; 1367 Yamanouchi; admission adult/child ¥200/100; ◷8.30am-4.30pm) Across the railway tracks from Engaku-ji, Tōkei-ji is famed as having served as a women's refuge. A woman could be officially recognised as divorced after three years as a nun in the temple precincts. Today, there are no nuns; the grave of the last abbess can be found in the cemetery, shrouded by cypress trees.

Daibutsu Hiking Course HIKING
This 3km wooded trail connects Kita-Kamakura with the Daibutsu in Hase (allow about 1½ hours). The path begins at the steps just up the lane from pretty **Jōchi-ji** (浄智寺; 1402 Yamanouchi; adult/child ¥200/100; ◷9am-4.30pm), a few minutes from Tōkei-ji. Along the course you'll pass **Zeniarai-benten** (銭洗弁天; ◷8am-4pm) **FREE**, one of Kamakura's most alluring Shintō shrines. A cavelike entrance leads to a clearing where visitors come to bathe their money in natural springs, with the hope of bringing financial success. From here, continue down the paved road, turning right at the first intersection, walking along a path lined with cryptomeria and ascending through a succession of torii to **Sasuke-inari-jinja** (佐助稲荷神社; ◷24hr) **FREE** before meeting up with the Daibutsu path once again. To hike in the opposite direction, follow the road beyond Daibutsu and the trail entrance is on the right, just before a tunnel.

Sugimoto-dera TEMPLE
(杉本寺; 903 Nikaidō; adult/child ¥200/100; ◷8am-4.30pm) This small temple, founded in AD 734, is reputed to be the oldest in Kamakura. The ferocious-looking guardian deities and statues of Kannon are its main draw. Take a bus from stop 5 at Kamakura Station to the Sugimoto Kannon bus stop (¥190, 10 minutes).

Kamakura

Hōkoku-ji   TEMPLE
(報国寺; 2-7-4 Jōmyōji; bamboo garden ¥200; ⊙9am-4pm) Down the road from Sugimoto-dera, on the right-hand side, is this Rinzai Zen temple with quiet, landscaped gardens where you can relax under a red parasol with a cup of Japanese tea.

Zuisen-ji   TEMPLE
(瑞泉寺; 710 Nikaidō; adult/child ¥200/100; ⊙9am-4.30pm) The grounds of this secluded pictur-esque Zen temple make for a pleasant stroll and include gardens laid out by Musō Soseki, the temple's esteemed founder. To get here, take the bus from stop 4 at Kamakura Station and get off at Ōtōnomiya (¥190, 10 minutes); turn right where the bus turns left in front of Kamakura-gū, take the next left and keep fol-lowing the road for 10 or 15 minutes.

Ten-en Hiking Course   HIKING
(天園ハイキングコース) From Zuisen-ji you can access this trail, which winds through the hills for two hours before coming out at Kenchō-ji. From Kenchō-ji, walk around the Hojo (Main Hall) and up the steps to the trail.

☆ Festivals & Events

Kamakura Matsuri   HISTORICAL
A week of celebrations held from the sec-ond Sunday to the third Sunday in April. It includes a wide range of activities, most of which are centred on Tsurugaoka Hachiman-gū.

Bonbori Matsuri   LANTERNS
From 7 to 9 August, hundreds of lanterns are strung up around Tsurugaoka Hachiman-gū.

Reitai Matsuri   MIKOSHI
Festivities between 14 and 16 September in-clude a procession of *mikoshi* as well as, on the last day, a display of horseback archery.

🛏 Sleeping

Kamakura Guesthouse   GUESTHOUSE ¥
(鎌倉ゲストハウス; ☑67-6078; www.kamaku-ra-guesthouse.com; 273-3 Tokiwa; dm ¥3000; ⊖⊛) While it's away from the action, the cheap Japanese dorms and common area with *irori* set in a traditional cypress home make this a nice place to hang out. There's bicycles for rent (¥500 per day), communal kitchen and *zazen* (seated meditation) tours to Engakūji temple are offered during the week. Take the Enoden bus from the station to the Kajiwaraguchi stop; it's a one-minute walk from here.

Kamejikan Guesthouse   GUESTHOUSE ¥¥
(☑25-166; www.kamejikan.com; 3-17-21 Za-imokuza; dm/d from ¥3200/9000; ⊖@⊛) A three-minute walk to the beach, this lovely guesthouse has nice touches such as paper lampshades, a small cafe and bar. Choose from six-bed dorms or private doubles, all with common tiled bathrooms. The English-speaking owner is a good source of info and rents bodyboards and bicycles (¥500 per day). Catch bus 12, 40 or 41 to Kuhonji from Kamakura Station.

Hotel New Kamakura   HOTEL ¥¥
(ホテルニューカマクラ; ☑22-2230; www. newkamakura.com; 13-2 Onarimachi; s/d from ¥4200/11,000; @) Charming, slightly shabby, ultraconvenient and a steal, this hotel built

in 1924 has both Western- and Japanese-style rooms. There's red carpet and a vintage vibe, though the economy rooms are rather plain. Exit west from Kamakura Station, and take a sharp right down the alley.

Classical Hotel Ajisai
HOTEL ¥¥

(クラシカルホテルあじさい; ☑22-3492; www.hotel-ajisai.com; 1-12-4 Yukinoshita; s/tw from ¥5780/11,560; @) Across from Tsurugaoka Hachiman-gū, the 10-room Ajisai is a businesslike, affordable option with small, basic Western-style rooms. The 4th-floor rooms have shrine views.

Kamakura Park Hotel
HOTEL ¥¥¥

(鎌倉パークホテル; ☑25-5121; www.kamakura-parkhotel.co.jp; 33-6 Sakanoshita; s/tw from ¥17,850/31,500; ☺☎) A bit 1980s plush, the Japanese- and Western-style rooms come with ocean views and marble baths. It's a 12-minute walk along the coast from Hase Station.

🍴 Eating

Vegetarians can eat well in Kamakura; pick up the free, bilingual *Vegetarian Culture Map* at the Tourist Information Center.

Bowls Donburi Café
JAPANESE ¥

(鎌倉どんぶりカフェbowls; 2-14-7 Komachi; meals ¥880-1680; ☺11am-3pm & 5-10pm; ☺@ ☎🍴) The humble *donburi* (rice bowl) gets a hip, healthy remake here at this modern bright cafe, with toppings such as roasted tuna, soy sauce and sesame oil. You get a discount if you discover the word *atari* at the bottom of the bowl. Also serves excellent coffee and has free wi-fi and computer terminals with internet.

Sông Bé Cafe
ASIAN FUSION ¥

(ソンベカフェ; www.song-be-cafe.com; 13-32 Onarimachi; dishes from ¥780; ☺11.30am-8.30pm, closed Wed; 🍴🍴) This mellow day-to-evening joint across from the train tracks just near the Hotel New Kamakura serves up dishes such as pad thai and green curry, with vegies sourced from the local farmers market, and Southeast Asian beers to match. The friendly owner also serves a good selection of teas and tasty *zenzai* desserts.

Milk Hall
CAFE ¥

(ミルクホール; www.milkhall.co.jp; 2-3-8 Komachi; mains from ¥600-1050; ☺11am-8pm Mon-Fri, to 9pm Sat & Sun; 🍴) This local cafe-scene landmark is also an antiques shop and, by evening, a moody bar with a good whiskey menu and live jazz some nights. Head two blocks down Komachi-dōri, take a left and then another left down the first alley; the door has an English sign.

Kamakura Ichibanya
JAPANESE ¥

(鎌倉壱番屋; 22-6156 Komachi-dōri; packages from ¥80; ☺9am-6.30pm) Specialises in *senbei* (rice crackers); watch staff grilling them in the window or buy some 50 packaged varieties, including curry, wasabi, garlic, *mentaiko* (spicy cod roe) or *uni* (sea urchin); look for the baskets on the corner.

Imo-no-kichikan
ICE CREAM ¥

(いも吉館; Komachi-dōri; ☺10am-6pm) Famous for soft-serve sweet-potato ice cream (¥295). Look for the giant plastic cone with lavender-hued ice cream.

⭐Matsubara-an
NOODLES ¥¥

(松原庵; 4-10-3 Yuiga-hama; mains from ¥550-1800; ☺11am-9pm; 🍴) In a former residence tucked in a quiet backstreet is this upscale *soba* restaurant capturing the feel of early-20th-century Kamakura. You can't go wrong with the tempura *goma seiro soba* (al dente noodles served cold with sesame dipping sauce). Dine alfresco or indoors where you can watch noodles being handmade. From Yuiga-hama Station (on the Enoden line) head towards the beach and then take the first right. Look for the blue sign; the entrance is just to the left.

Bonzo
SOBA ¥¥

(☑73-7315; http://bonzokamakura.com; 3-17-33 Zaimokuza; dishes from ¥300-1700; ☺11.30am-3pm & 6-9pm, closed Thu; 🍴) Intimate and suave Michelin-star restaurant that specialises in handmade *ju-wari* (100% soba), including *kamo seiro* (cold soba in hot broth) with wild duck imported from France. The homemade sesame tofu is incredibly creamy and not to be missed. Catch bus 12, 40 or 41 to Kuhonj.

Issan-an
SOBA ¥¥

(meals from ¥950-2000; ☺11am-8pm) Opposite Tsurugaoka Hachiman-gū, this popular *soba* restaurant with tatami-mat seating overlooking a pleasant garden is a good place to refuel when temple hopping.

Magokoro
FUSION ¥¥

(麻心; 2nd fl, 2-8-11 Hase; meals from ¥1000; ☺11am-3pm & 5-9pm Tue-Sun; ☎🍴🍴) ✏ Mixing ocean views with an organic hemp-based menu, including vegetarian hemp taco rice, macrobiotic cakes and hemp beer on tap. From Hase Station, walk to the beach and turn left onto the coastal road; you'll see the 2nd-floor picture windows on your left.

Good Mellows CAFE ¥¥
(www.goodmellows.com; burgers from ¥850; ⊘9am-8.30pm) A small dose of Americana meets Japanese kitsch opposite the beach, with neatly stacked charcoal-grilled burgers of bacon, mozarella and avocado washed down with a Dr Pepper or a cold beer.

🍷 Drinking

Univibe BAR
(☑67-8458; www.univibe.jp; 7-13-2F Onaricho; ⊘11am-5pm & 6pm-late) Spacious upstairs bar with retro vintage decor, friendly bartenders, fooseball and a relaxed vibe. A five-minute walk from the Kamakura JR station.

Bar Ram BAR
(バー・ラム; 2-11-11 Komachi; drinks from ¥500; ⊘5pm-late) Kamakura has pockets of nightlife, including this hole in the wall in the lanes off Komachi-dōri. It's a *tachinomi-ya* (drink-while-standing bar) with plenty of old Rolling Stones vinyls and friendly banter. Look for the English sign.

ℹ️ Information

For information about Kamakura, see www.city.kamakura.kanagawa.jp/english.

Kamakura Post Office (郵便局; ☑22-1200; 1-10-3 Komachi; ⊘9am-7pm Mon-Fri, to 3pm Sat) Has ATMs inside.

Kamakura Welcome Guides (www1.kamakura net.ne.jp/kwga) Offers half-day tours on Fridays with English-speaking volunteer guides for a nominal fee; five days' notice is required.

Tourist Information Center (鎌倉市観光協会 観光総合案内所; ☑22-3350; ⊘9am-5.30pm Apr-Sep, to 5pm Oct-Mar) Just outside the east exit of Kamakura Station, the English-speaking staff are helpful and can book accommodation. Pick up a guide to Kamakura's temples (¥1575), as well as free brochures and maps for the area.

ℹ️ Getting There & Away

JR Yokosuka-line trains run to Kamakura from Tokyo (¥890, 56 minutes) and Shinagawa (¥690, 46 minutes), via Yokohama (¥330, 27 minutes). Alternatively, the Shōnan Shinjuku line runs from the west side of Tokyo (Shibuya, Shinjuku and Ikebukuro, all ¥890) in about one hour, though some trains require a transfer at Ōfuna, one stop before Kita-Kamakura. The last train from Kamakura back to Tokyo Station is 11.28pm and Shinjuku 9.15pm.

JR Kamakura-Enoshima Free Pass (from Tokyo/Yokohama ¥1970/1130) Valid for two days; covers the trip to and from Tokyo/Yokohama and unlimited use of JR trains around Kamakura, the Shōnan monorail between Ōfuna and Enoshima, and the Enoden Enoshima line.

Odakyū Enoshima/Kamakura Free Pass (from Shinjuku/Machida ¥1430/990) Valid for one day; includes transport to Fujisawa Station (where it meets the Enoden Enoshima line), plus use of the Enoden.

ℹ️ Getting Around

You can walk to most temples and shrines from Kamakura or Kita-Kamakura Stations. Sites in the west, like the Daibutsu, can be reached via the Enoden line from Kamakura Station to Hase (¥190) or by bus from Kamakura Station stops 1 and 6.

Kamakura Rent-a-Cycle (レンタサイクル; per hr/day ¥600/1600; ⊘8.30am-5pm) is outside the east exit of Kamakura Station, and right up the incline.

EAST OF TOKYO

Chiba Prefecture, east and southeast of Tokyo, has few attractions for travellers, save the city of Narita. There are also decent surf beaches along the Kujūkuri-hama coastline, on the Pacific side of the Bōsō Peninsula.

Narita 成田

☑0476 / POP 127,000
Narita is chiefly known as the home of Japan's main international airport, but the older part of the city is a surprisingly pleasant stop.

⊙ Sights

Narita-san Shinshōji TEMPLE
(成田山新勝寺; 1 Narita; ⊘24hr) **FREE** Impressive temple surrounded by a pretty park, Narita-san Kōen (成田山公園), laced with walking paths, trees and ponds.

Omote-sandō STREET
Omote-sandō, Narita's main drag, winds like an eel towards the Narita-san Shinshōji, past souvenir shops and restaurants and makes for a pleasant stroll. Most of the traditional shops shut around 5pm.

Tourist Pavilion MUSEUM
(Omote-sandō; ⊘9am-5pm, closed Mon) **FREE** Halfway down Omote-sandō, this museum has local-history exhibits, as well as floats used in the Narita Gion Matsuri on display.

NARITA LAYOVER

If you have a long layover – including at least three hours to get out, away and back into the airport – consider making a quick detour into Narita city. There are international ATMs and luggage-storage facilities in both terminals; enquire at the English-speaking information counters.

🛏 Sleeping

Numerous chains operate hotels near the airport for those facing early flights.

Kirinoya Ryokan   RYOKAN ¥¥
(桐之屋旅館; ☎ 22-0724; www.naritakanko.jp/kirinoya; 58 Tamachi; s/d without bathroom ¥5250/9450; @) None of the chain hotels here can compete with Kirinoya Ryokan when it comes to history. The owner can trace his lineage back 50 generations, and his rambling inn is full of samurai armour and swords. Rooms are Japanese-style; call for pick-up (til 7pm) from either of Narita's train stations.

Narita Excel Hotel Tokyu   HOTEL ¥¥¥
(☎ 33-0109; www.tokyuhotelsjapan.com; 31 Oyama; s/d from ¥13,800/23,100; ☎) A good airport hotel with several restaurants, comfy modern rooms and a free shuttle bus to the airport and into town. Heavily discounted rates are available online.

🍴 Eating & Drinking

Kawatoyo Honten   JAPANESE ¥¥
(川豊本店; 386 Naka-machi; meals ¥1260-1890; ⊙10am-5pm, closed Mon) Opposite the Tourist Pavillion is the landmark eel house Kawatoyo Honten. The speciality here is *unajū* (¥1500; eel grilled, sauced and served over rice in a lacquer box). You can watch the chefs carving up the whiplike creatures right at the front table (perhaps not for the squeamish).

5.2.4 Garage Cafe   CAFE
(www.5-2-4.net; Omote-sandō; coffee from ¥350; ⊙10am-10pm; ☎) Cool little cafe with free wi-fi serving good coffee, homemade ginger ale, beer and hot dogs from its chalkboard menu. Occasionally has live music.

ℹ Information

Narita Tourist Information Center (☎ 24-3198; ⊙8.30am-5.15pm) Pick up a map at the Narita Tourist Information Center, just outside the eastern exit of JR Narita Station.

ℹ Getting There & Away

From Narita International Airport you can take the private Keisei line (¥250, 10 minutes) or JR (¥190/230 from Terminal 2/1, 10 minutes); Keisei-line trains are more frequent. From Tokyo, the easiest way to get to Narita is via the Keisei line from Keisei Ueno Station, taking the Cityliner (¥1730, 57minutes), or the express (*tokkyu*; ¥810, 70 minutes). Note that most JR Narita Express trains do not stop at Narita.

OGASAWARA ARCHIPELAGO

You won't believe you're still in Japan, much less Tokyo! About 1000km south of downtown in the middle of the Pacific Ocean, this far-flung outpost of Tokyo Prefecture has pristine beaches and star-studded night skies. The Ogasawara Archipelago (小笠原諸島; Ogasawara-shotō) was recently designated a World Heritage Site. This is a nature-lover's paradise, surrounded by tropical waters and coral reefs. Snorkelling, whale-watching, swimming with dolphins, and hiking are all on the bill.

The islands' earliest inhabitants were Westerners who set up provisioning stations for whaling ships working the Japan whaling grounds. You still see the occasional Western family name and face. You'll also see disused gun emplacements at the ends of most of the islands' beaches, built by the Japanese in hopes of repelling an anticipated Allied invasion in WWII (the big battles were fought further south on Iwo-jima).

The only way to get here is a 25½-hour ferry ride from Tokyo. The ferry docks at Chichijima (父島; Father Island), the main island of the group. A smaller ferry connects it to Haha-jima (母島), the other inhabited island.

Given the islands' nature, history and location, a trip here is one of Japan's great little adventures.

ℹ Getting There & Away

The *Ogasawara-maru* sails once a week between Tokyo's Takeshiba Pier (10 minutes from Hamamatsu-chō Station) and Chichi-jima (2nd class Jul–Aug/Sep–Jun from ¥25,100/¥22,570, 25½ hours). The *Hahajima-maru* sails five times a week between Chichi-jima and Haha-jima (¥3780, two hours). Contact **Ogasawara Kaiun** (小笠原海運; ☎ 03-3451-5171; www.ogasawarakaiun.co.jp/english); prices may change as per fuel charges. Other operators run day cruises from Chichi-jima to Haha-jima.

Chichi-jima   父島

📞 04998 / POP 2100

Beautifully preserved Chichi-jima has plenty of accommodation, restaurants and even a bit of tame nightlife. But the real attractions are excellent beaches and outdoor activities.

👁 Sights & Activities

The two best beaches for snorkelling are on the north side of the island, a short walk over the hill from the village. **Miya-no-hama** (宮之浜) has decent coral and is sheltered, making it suitable for beginners. About 500m along the coast (more easily accessed from town) is **Tsuri-hama** (釣浜), a rocky beach that has better coral but is more exposed.

Good swimming beaches line the west side of the island, getting better the further south you go. The neighbouring coves of **Copepe** (コペペ海岸) and **Kominato-kaigan** (小港海岸) are particularly attractive. From Kominato-kaigan, you can walk along a trail over the hill and along the coast to the beguiling white sand of **John Beach** (ジョンビーチ), but note that it's a two-hour walk in each direction and there is no drinking water – bring at least 3L per person. The path to nearby Jinny beach is currently off-limits; the strong current makes it unsafe to swim to there, though sea kayaking is possible.

Many operators offer whale-watching and dolphin swimming, as well as trips to Minami-jima, an uninhabited island with a magical beach called **Ōgi-ike** (扇池). Stanley Minami, the English-speaking skipper of the **Pink Dolphin** (📞 2-2096; www15.ocn.ne.jp/~pdolphin) runs half-/full-day tours (¥5000/8000) to Minami-jima and Haha-jima that include snorkelling and dolphin-watching.

Pelan Sea Kayak Club (📞 2-3386; www.pelan. jp) offers tours to some of the island's more enchanting spots (half-/full day ¥5000/10,000). Fees include equipment rental and meals cooked Pelan-style, on a wood-burning camp stove. Catching and grilling your own fish is optional.

At Ōgiura Beach, **Rao Adventure Tours** (📞 2-2081; http://web.me.com/boninrao/RAO/English_Page.html) runs jungle tours (¥5000 per half-day) and a surf school (¥15,000 per day).

🛌 Sleeping & Eating

Rockwells   GUESTHOUSE ¥
(ロックウェルズ; 📞 2-3838; http://rockwells. co.jp/ogasawara; dm ¥3000, r per person with 2 meals from ¥6900; 🛜) The closest thing you'll

find to a beach shack on the island – simple accommodation and a bar three seconds from Ōgiura beach.

Ogasawara Youth Hostel   HOSTEL ¥
(小笠原ユースホステル; 📞 2-2682; www.oyh. jp; dm members/nonmembers ¥3750/4350; P @) Clean, well-run hostel about 400m southwest of the pier; book early during summer.

⭐ **Pelan Village**   ECO RESORT ¥¥
(📞 2-3386; www.pelan.jp; r per person from ¥4500; 🛜 🍃) A Never-Never Land of cosy wooden cabins, walkways and ladders perched on a leafy mountainside, Pelan Village offers a sustainable eco retreat. On an island that sources most of its food from Tokyo, Pelan stands out for growing a fair amount of its own. It is not, however, for dilettantes – conventional soaps and detergents are banned because water run-off goes directly to the crops.

Tetsuya Healing Guest House   GUESTHOUSE ¥¥
(てつ家; 📞 2-7725; www.tetuyabonin.com; r per person from ¥7800; ⊖ @ 🛜) The talk of the island for its multicourse meals that make innovative use of local ingredients. The thoughtfully designed rooms and open-air baths are even better. It's a five-minute walk from the beach of Kominato-kaigan.

Banana Inn   GUESTHOUSE ¥¥
(バナナ荘; 📞 2-2051; http://pinkdolphin.p1.bindsite .jp/banana.html; r from ¥5250) Steps from the ferry pier, this humble inn has very basic Japanese- and Western-style rooms but lots of hospitality from owner John Washington, an Ernest Hemingway type who enjoys discussing local history. Note that the guesthouse may be closed September to December.

ℹ️ KNOW BEFORE YOU GO

There is no foreign currency-exchange service in the Ogasawara and while a few places accept credit card, you can't rely on it. Make sure you have plenty of yen on you before you set out for the islands.

If you plan on visiting Ogasawara in summer (July to August) make sure you book accommodation well in advance as everywhere gets booked up very quickly. Note there's no camping on the islands. For more information, check out the excellent Ogasawara Village Tourist Information website (www. ogasawaramura.com).

ONLY IN OGASAWARA

When scientists photographed the fabled giant squid *Architeuthis* for the first time ever in 2004, there is no wonder it was just off the Ogasawaras. The chain is home to dozens of rare and endangered species, such as the Bonin flying fox. From January to April humpback whales come within 500m of shore. On a clear night, from the top deck of the *Ogasawara-maru* ferry, you'll see the Milky Way stretching from horizon to horizon through a breathtaking field of stars.

Bonina   INTERNATIONAL ¥

(☎ 2-3027; mains from ¥500; ⏰ 6pm-midnight) A delightful popular beach shack with ocean views serving simple fare of pizza and tacos. Closes the day after the ship arrives and occasionally open for lunch. It's in front of Futami Bay, not far from the port.

🍷 Drinking

Yankee Town   BAR

(ヤンキータウン; ⏰ 8pm-2am Thu-Tue) A 15-minute walk east of the main pier, this driftwood bar is the perfect spot to chill with a cocktail. Occasionally has live music. Follow the main coastal road towards Okumura and you'll see its coloured lights on the left.

ℹ Information

Chichi-jima Tourism Association (父島観光協会; ☎ 2-2587; ⏰ 8am-noon & 1.30-5pm) In the B-Ship building, about 250m west of the pier, near the post office. Ask for the helpful *Guide Map of Chichi-jima;* English spoken.

Ogasawara Visitor Center (小笠原ビジターセンター; ⏰ 8.30am-5pm) Right on the beach past the village office, it has displays in English about the local ecosystem and history.

ℹ Getting Around

Rental scooter is the best way to get around the island as buses are infrequent and you'll be able to explore more of the island (available from ¥3000 per day). You can rent them from Ogasawara Kanko if you have an international drivers licence.

Haha-jima   母島

☎ 04998 / POP 500

Haha-jima is less developed than Chichi-jima and, with limited lodgings, sees far fewer visitors. Outside the summer season,

you may even find yourself staring out over cerulean waters or spotting rare birds all by your lonesome.

👁 Sights & Activities

A road runs south from the village to the start of the **Minami-zaki Yūhodō** (南崎遊歩道), a hiking course that continues all the way to the **Minami-zaki** (南崎; literally 'southern point'). Along the way you'll find **Hōraine-kaigan** (蓬莱根海岸), a narrow beach with a decent offshore coral garden, and **Wai Beach** (ワイビーチ), with a drop-off that sometimes attracts eagle rays. Minami-zaki itself has a rocky, coral-strewn beach with ripping views of smaller islands to the south. Though tempting, the waters beyond the cove can whisk swimmers away.

Above Minami-zaki you'll find **Kofuji** (小富士), an 86m-high peak with fantastic views in all directions. Back in town, a four-hour hike loops through rare indigenous flora to **Mt Chibusa** (乳房山; 463m), the highest peak on the island.

Dive shop **Club Noah** (クラブノア母島; ☎ 3-2442; http://noah88.web.fc2.com; ⏰ cafe 1-6pm) runs jungle-hiking and marine-life ecotours. It's in a white building on the far side of the fishing port; inside there's a **cafe** serving light meals (from ¥500).

🛏 Sleeping & Eating

Anna Beach Haha-jima Youth Hostel   HOSTEL ¥

(アンナビーチ母島ユースホステル; ☎ 3-2468; www.k4.dion.ne.jp/~annayh; dm members/nonmembers from ¥3960/3360; ⊜ 🛜) A young family runs this tidy, cheery youth hostel in a bright yellow Western-style house overlooking the fishing port.

Island Resort Nanpū   HOTEL ¥¥

(民宿 ナンプー; ☎ 3-2462; www.hahajima-nanpu.com/english; d with breakfast from ¥10,500; ⊜ @ 🛜) Cosy lodge with glossy wood-panelled rooms, friendly owners and good food.

ℹ Information

Haha-jima Tourist Association (母島観光協会; ☎ 3-2300; ⏰ 8am-noon & 1-5pm) Located in the passenger waiting room at the pier.

ℹ Getting Around

Scooter (from ¥3000 per day) is the best way to get around the island. They can be rented from most lodgings.

The Japan Alps & Central Honshū

Includes ➡

Why Go?

Japan's heartland in both geography and outlook, Central Honshū (本州中部; 'Honshū Chūbu') stretches out between the sprawling leviathans of Greater Tokyo and Kansai. The awesome Japan Alps (日本アルプス) rise sharply near the border of Gifu and Nagano Prefectures before rolling north to the dramatic Sea of Japan coast.

World-class skiing, hiking and onsen can be found in the region's photogenic alpine uplands. All but one of Japan's 30 highest peaks (Fuji-san) are here. Kanazawa oozes culture: temples and tearooms that served lords and housed geisha are beautifully preserved. Takayama's riverside streetscapes satisfy admirers from Japan and abroad. Matsumoto's magnificent castle and alpine backdrop ensure its popularity.

Nagoya, famed for technical know-how, is Japan's fourth largest city. Combining urban delights with excellent transport connections to just about everywhere, Nagoya secures the region's worthy place as a high priority on any itinerary.

Best Vistas

➡ Kamikōchi (p230)

➡ Shin-hotaka Ropeway (p234)

➡ Tateyama-Kurobe Alpine Route (p259)

➡ Utsukushi-ga-hara-kōgen (p251)

Best Rotemburo

➡ Nakabusa Onsen (p257)

➡ Yarimikan (p235)

➡ Takayama Ouan Hotel (p222)

➡ Ōshirakawa Rotemburo (p228)

When to Go
Nagoya

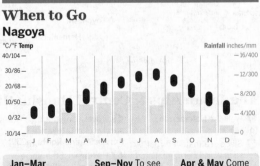

Jan–Mar Nagano's myriad slopes won't disappoint snowbunnies.

Sep–Nov To see autumn's brilliant show, head for Kamikōchi or the Hida region's mountain onsen.

Apr & May Come for cherry blossoms and one of Japan's best festivals, Takayama Matsuri.

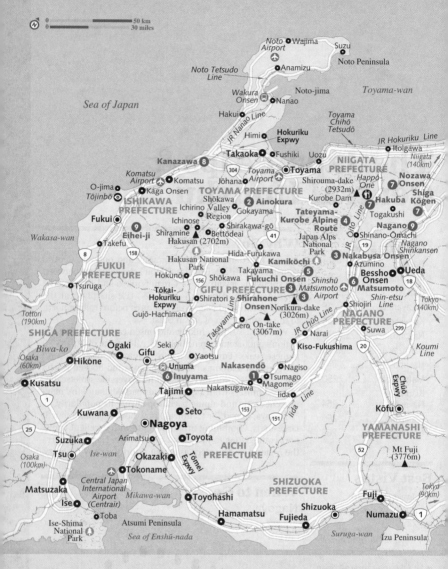

The Japan Alps & Central Honshū Highlights

1 Walk the **Nakasendō** (p254)

2 Sleep in a thatched-roof house at World Heritage–listed **Ainokura** (p229)

3 Dissolve your troubles in the mountain-ringed *rotemburo* of **Fukuchi Onsen** (p234), **Shirahone Onsen** (p233) or **Nakabusa Onsen** (p257)

4 Travel along the spectacular **Tateyama-Kurobe Alpine Route** (p259)

5 Hike against the alpine backdrop of **Kamikōchi** (p230)

6 Recall a shōgun's reign at **Inuyama-jō** (p213) and **Matsumoto-jō** (p250)

7 Ski at the Olympic resorts of **Hakuba** (p247), **Nozawa**

Onsen (p245) and **Shiga Kōgen** (p244)

8 Visit Kanazawa's **D.T. Suzuki Museum** (p263) or the ancient garden, **Kenroku-en** (p263)

9 Contemplate Zen at **Eihei-ji** (p274) or seek the key to salvation in Nagano's **Zenkō-ji** (p237)

Climate

Central Honshū's climate varies with its landscape. The best times to visit are generally April through May and late September to early November; temperatures are mild and clear skies prevail. Expect heavy rains in the *tsuyu* (monsoon) season, typically a few weeks in June, then sticky summers capped with typhoons, as late as October. Road closures are commonplace in the Japan Alps when the snow sets in, from November to March, although higher peaks might remain snowcapped as late as June. Hiking season runs from July to September until autumn ushers in a brilliant display of *kōyō* (turning leaves), at its peak in mid-October.

ℹ Getting There & Away

Chūbu Centrair International Airport (NGO), outside Nagoya, is one of the best airports we've seen, providing easy access from abroad. Some intra-Asia routes serve Komatsu (near Kanazawa) and Toyama. Nagoya is a major rail hub on the Tōkaidō *shinkansen* (bullet train) line between Tokyo and Osaka. The Nagano *shinkansen* connects Tokyo and Nagano. The Hokuriku extension of this line into Kanazawa is set to open in spring 2015.

ℹ Getting Around

Nagoya is Chūbu's transport terminus. Rail access is by the north–south JR Takayama and Chūō lines, with hubs in Takayama, Matsumoto and Nagano. The JR Hokuriku line follows the Sea of Japan coast, linking Fukui, Kanazawa and Toyama, with connections to Kyoto and Osaka.

Bus companies JR, Meitetsu, Nōhi and Alpico operate seasonal services from Nagoya, Takayama and Matsumoto to numerous destinations in Chūbu's mountainous middle.

Renting a car is well suited for trips to the Noto Peninsula, or for those wanting to get up high and off the beaten track. Be prepared for slow, steep and windy roads, which can be treacherous at times and not for the fainthearted; plan your explorations carefully. An excellent resource is www.navitime.co.jp/en.

NAGOYA

♪ 052 / POP 2.26 MILLION

Home proud Nagoya, birthplace of Toyota and pachinko, is a manufacturing powerhouse. Although Nagoya's GDP tops that of many small countries, this middle child has grown accustomed to life in the shadow of its bigger brothers, Tokyo and Kansai.

> ℹ **HIKING THE JAPAN ALPS**
>
> Central Honshū, a hiker's delight, is blessed with half of the nation's 100 famous mountains, amid many national parks – this chapter presents the most popular locations. Enthusiastic hikers should pick up Lonely Planet's *Hiking in Japan*.

Despite the shackles of industry, Nagoya has cosmopolitan aspects, including some fantastic museums, significant temples and great shopping. Parks and green spaces in the inner wards are prevalent and well maintained. In general, locals take pride in the homely character of this friendly city.

Nagoya is located in the centre of the largest fertile plain in the region, between Tokyo and Kyoto/Osaka, on the Tōkaidō *shinkansen* line. It's the gateway for journeys north into Chūbu's big mountain heart and a great base for day trips: factory visits, ceramic villages and cormorant fishing are on the radar.

All lines lead to 'Meiekī', a hybrid terminus of the JR and private Meitetsu and Kintetsu lines, as well as subway and bus stations. Here you'll find a labyrinthine world of passageways, restaurants and retailers, and above, the soaring JR Central Towers and Midland Square complexes. Be sure to leave enough time if making a transfer.

East of the station, Sakura-dōri, Nishiki-dōri and Hirokōji-dōri (from north to south) are the three main drags, intersected first by Fushimi-dōri then Otsu-dōri. The majority of the mainstream action is found within this grid. Just east of Otsu-dōri is the long and narrow Hisaya-ōdōri-kōen (aka Central Park), Nagoya's much loved Eiffel-esque TV Tower and the wacky Oasis 21 complex. Following Otsu-dōri north will get you to the castle, while the vibrant Ōsu district, Atsuta Jingū shrine and bustling Kanayama Station area are to the south.

Nagoya's excellent English signposted subway services all the hotspots – Fushimi and Sakae Stations are your mainstays for shopping, accommodation and nightlife.

History

Although Nagoya did not become a unified city until 1889, it had a strong influence for centuries before. It is the ancestral home of Japan's 'three heroes': Oda Nobunaga (unifier of Japan), shōgun Toyotomi Hideyoshi and

202

Central Nagoya

0   500 m
0   0.25 miles

THE JAPAN ALPS & CENTRAL HONSHŪ NAGOYA

Tokugawa Ieyasu, the latter whose dictatorial reign from Edo also heralded an era of peace, prosperity and the Arts. Tokugawa ordered the construction of Nagoya-jō, which became an important outpost for 16 generations of the Tokugawa family, also called the Owari clan.

Nagoya grew into a centre for commerce, industry and transport; during WWII some 10,000 Mitsubishi Zero fighter planes were produced here. Manufacturing prominence led to massive Allied bombing – citizens were evacuated and roughly one quarter

Central Nagoya

of the city was destroyed. From these ashes rose the Nagoya of today, with its wide avenues, subways, skyscrapers and parks.

Nagoya's manufacturing sector continues to thrive. The city's countless department stores reflect a flourishing commercial sector, although it's an indicator of Japan's economic downturn that even Nagoyans are tightening their belts.

◉ Sights

◎ Nagoya Station Area

Midland Square   LANDMARK
(ミッドランドスクエア; ☑527-8877; www.midland-square.com/english; 4-7-1 Meieki; ⊙ shops 11am-8pm, restaurants 11am-11pm; ℝ Nagoya) Nagoya's tallest building (247m) houses Toy-

ota's corporate HQ and showroom, boutique shopping on the lower floors and a beehive of offices in the middle. At the top, **Sky Promenade** (スカイプロメナード; ☑527-8877; www.midland-square.com/sky-promenade; 4-7-1 Meieki; adult/child/senior ¥700/300/500; ⊙11am-9.30pm; ℝ Nagoya), with Japan's tallest open-air observation deck and some restaurants with killer views, is reached via adventurously lit passageways. 'Scraper fans should also check out the exterior of the **Mode Gakuen Spiral Towers** educational facility, unmissable a few blocks south.

Noritake Garden   GARDEN
(ノリタケの森; ☑561-7290; www.noritake.co.jp/eng/mori; 3-1-36 Noritake-shinmachi; ⊙10am-6pm Tue-Sun; ℝ Kamejima) Pottery fans will enjoy a stroll around Noritake Garden,

the 1904 factory grounds of one of Japan's best-known porcelain makers. The grounds feature old chimneys and remnants of early kilns as well as the **Noritake Gallery** (☎562-9811; ◷10am-6pm Tue-Sun), exhibiting paintings, sculptures and ceramic works. The **Craft Centre** (☎561-7114; adult/child ¥500/free; ◷10am-5pm Tue-Sun) houses a museum and demonstrates the production process. You can also glaze your own dish (from ¥1800). Signage is in English throughout. The on-site 'Box Outlet Shop' has (ironically unboxed) wares at discounted prices.

Toyota Commemorative Museum of Industry & Technology   MUSEUM
(トヨタテクノミュージアム産業技術記念館; ☎551-6115; www.tcmit.org/english; 4-1-35 Noritake-shinmachi; ◷9.30am-5pm Tue-Sat; ☐Sako, Meitetsu Nagoya line) The world's largest car manufacturer had humble beginnings in the weaving industry. This interesting museum occupies the site of Toyota's original weaving plant. Rev-heads will find things textile heavy before warming to the 7900 sq m automotive and robotics pavilion. Science-minded folk will enjoy countless hands-on exhibits. Displays are bilingual and there's an English-language audio tour available. Don't confuse this museum with the Toyota Kaikan Exhibition Hall and plant tours – see p211.

◉ Nagoya Castle Area

Nagoya-jō   CASTLE
(名古屋城; www.nagoyajo.city.nagoya.jp; 1-1 Honmaru; adult/child ¥500/free; ◷9am-4.30pm; ☐Shiyakusho, exit 7) The original structure, built between 1610 to 1614 by Tokugawa Ieyasu for his ninth son, was levelled in WWII. Today's castle is a concrete replica (with elevator), completed in 1959. At each end of the roof you can see the 3m-long gilded *shachi-hoko* – legendary creatures possessing a tiger's head and carp's body. The museum houses treasures, an armour collection and the histories of the Oda, Toyotomi and Tokugawa families. Within the castle grounds, the beautiful year-round garden, Ninomaru-en (二の丸園) has a number of pretty teahouses.

Nagoya Nō Theatre   THEATRE
(名古屋能楽堂; ☎231-0088; 1-1-1 San-no-maru; museum entry free, performance prices vary; ◷9am-5pm) Outside the main gate of Nagoya-jō, this theatre has a small museum

of costumes and antiquities related to nō, one of the world's oldest continuously performed theatre forms.

Tokugawa Art Museum   MUSEUM
(徳川美術館; www.tokugawa-art-museum.jp/english; 1017 Tokugawa-chō; adult/child ¥1200/500; ◷10am-5pm Tue-Sun; ☐Me-guru stop 11) A must for anyone interested in Japanese culture and history, this museum has a 10,000-plus piece collection that includes National Treasures and Important Cultural Properties once belonging to the shōgunal family. A priceless 12th-century scroll depicting *The Tale of Genji* is locked away except for a short stint in late November; the rest of the year, visitors must remain content with a video.

Tokugawa-en   GARDEN
(徳川園; ☎935-8988; www.tokugawaen.city.nagoya.jp/english; 1001 Tokugawa-chō; admission ¥300; ◷9.30am-5.30pm Tue-Sun; ☐Me-guru stop 10) This delightful Japanese garden adjacent the Tokugawa Art Museum was donated by the Tokugawa family to Nagoya city in 1931, but destroyed by bombing in 1945. From that time, until a three year restoration project was completed in 2004, the site was used as a park. Water is its key element – there's a lake, river, bridges and waterfall. Each spring 2000 peonies and irises burst into bloom, and maples ignite in the autumn.

◉ Fushimi & Sakae

The area between Fushimi and Sakae subway stations is ground zero for shopping and people-watching. Hisaya-ōdōri-kōen (Central Park) is usually bustling and Sakae's side streets fill with revellers well into the night.

Nagoya TV Tower   LANDMARK
(名古屋テレビ塔; ☎971-8546; www.nagoya-tv-tower.co.jp; 3-6-15 Nishiki; adult/child/senior ¥600/300/500; ◷10am-9pm; ☐Sakae, exit 4b, 5a) Nagoya's much-loved TV tower, completed in 1954, was the first of its kind in Japan. The tower's central location makes its 100m-high Sky Balcony a great place to get the lie of the land. Better still, the sprawling beer garden and Korean barbecue at its base is unrivalled in town.

Oasis 21   LANDMARK
(オアシス２１) Oasis 21 is a bus terminal and transit hub featuring a Tourist Information Center and some decent shops and eateries. Its iconic 'galaxy platform' – an elliptical

glass and steel structure filled with water for visual effect and cooling purposes – caused quite a stir when it was first built. Feel free to climb the stairs and walk around it while you're waiting for your next ride; it's most fun at night when it's adventurously lit.

Nagoya City Science Museum
MUSEUM
(名古屋市科学館; ☑ 201-4486; www.ncsm.city. nagoya.jp/en; 2-17-1 Sakae; adult/child ¥800/500; ⏱ 9.30am-5pm Tue-Sun; 🚇 Fushimi, exit 5) This spanking new hands-on museum claims the world's largest dome-screen planetarium with some seriously out of this world projection technology. There's also a tornado lab and a deep-freeze lab complete with indoor aurora. Despite scheduled shows being kid-centric and in Japanese, the cutting edge technology of this impressive, centrally located facility is worth experiencing.

International Design Centre Nagoya
GALLERY
(国際デザインセンター; ☑ 265-2105; www. idcn.jp/e; 4th fl, 3-18-1 Sakae; ⏱ 11am-8pm, closed Tue; 🚇 Yaba-chō, exit 5 or 6) **FREE** Housed in the swooping Nadya Park complex is this secular shrine to the deities of conceptualisation, form and function. From art deco to post modernism, Electrolux to Isamu Noguchi and Arne Jacobsen to the Mini Cooper, all are represented in this significant collection. Once sated, design-heads should gravitate to the **Loft department store**, also in Nadya Park, to burn some cash.

◉ Southside

The area between Ōsu-Kannon and Kami-maezu Stations, crammed with retailers, eateries and street vendors, has a delightfully young and alternative vibe. Patient shoppers will be rewarded with funky vintage threads and offbeat souvenirs.

From Kamimaezu Station, take exit 9 and walk north two blocks. Turn left onto Bansho-ji street (万松寺通), a covered shopping arcade which becomes Osu-Kannon street and continues on to the temple. The streets either side are alive with activity. Further south, the busy yet compact Kanayama Station area is an alternative base to Meieki and Sakae.

Ōsu Kannon
BUDDHIST TEMPLE
(大須観音; ☑ 231-6525; ⏱ 5.30am-7pm; 🚇 Ōsu Kannon, exit 2) The much-visited Ōsu Kannon temple traces its roots back to 1333. The temple, devoted to the Buddha of Compassion was moved to its present location by Toku-

gawa Ieyasu in 1610, although the present buildings date from 1970. The library inside holds the oldest known handwritten copy of the *kojiki* – the ancient mythological history of Japan.

Atsuta-jingū
SHINTŌ SHRINE
(熱田神宮; www.atsutajingu.or.jp; 1-1-1 Jingū; 🚇 Jingū-mae or Jingū-nishi, exit 2) Although the current buildings were completed in 1966, Atsuta-jingū has been a shrine for over 1900 years and is one of the most sacred Shintō shrines in Japan. Nestled among ancient cypress trees, it houses the sacred *kusanagi-no-tsurugi* (grass-cutting sword), one of the three regalia that, according to legend, were presented to the imperial family by the sun goddess Amaterasu-Ōmikami. There's also a changing collection of over 4000 Tokugawa-era swords, masks and paintings on display in the **Treasure Hall** (宝物館; adult/child ¥300/150; ⏱ 9am-4.30pm, closed last Wed & Thu of each month).

Nagoya/Boston Museum of Fine Arts
MUSEUM
(名古屋ボストン美術館; ☑ 684-0101; www. nagoya-boston.or.jp/english; 1-1-1 Kanayama-chō; adult/senior/child ¥1200/900/free; ⏱ 10am-7pm Tue-Fri, to 5pm weekends; 🚇 Kanayama, south exit) This collaborative effort between Japanese backers and the Museum of Fine Arts Boston showcases an impressive collection of Japanese and international masterpieces.

Nagoya Urban Institute
MUSEUM
(名古屋都市センター; ☑ 678-2200; www.nui. or.jp; 1-1-1 Kanayama-cho; ⏱ 9am-5pm Tue-Sun) **FREE** Atop the Nagoya/Boston Museum of Fine Arts, visitors can learn about the history of Nagoya's postwar redevelopment and enjoy a great view over the city.

✯✯ Festivals & Events

Atsuta Matsuri
FESTIVAL
The largest and most auspicious celebration held at Atsuta-jingū, with parades, martial arts displays and fireworks. On 5 June.

Dekimachi Tennō-sai
PARADE
On the first Saturday and Sunday of June there's a parade of floats with large *karakuri ningyō* (marionettes) around the Susano-o-jinja shrine, near the Tokugawa Art Museum.

Nagoya Bashō
SUMŌ
(愛知県体育館 Aichi-ken Taiiku-kan; ☑ 971-2516; www.sumo.or.jp/eng; 1-1 Ninomaru; tickets from

¥3000) One of six annual sumō champion-ship tournaments, held over two weeks in July at Aichi Prefectural Gymnasium. Arrive early in the afternoon to watch the lower-ranked wrestlers up close.

Minato Matsuri   PARADE
Held around 'Ocean Day' (third Monday in July) is this street festival in Nagoya Port, with parade, dancing, fireworks and a water-logging contest dating back to the Edo period.

Nagoya Matsuri   PARADE
Nagoya's big sha-bang takes place mid-October in Hisaya-ōdōri-kōen. Celebrating Nagoya's 'three heroes', the lively procession includes costumes, *karakuri ningyō* floats, folk dancing and decorated cars.

🛏 Sleeping

If you're passing through, stay near Nagoya or Kanayama Stations for convenience. The area between Fushimi and Sakae will suit better if you want to hit the town or drop 'til you drop. Ryokan listed here do not have en suite facilities. Be sure to take note of the station exits for each listing.

Hostel Ann   HOSTEL ¥
(Hostel Ann案; ☏253-7710; www.hostelann.com; 2-4-2 Kanayama; dm/s/d ¥2500/3500/6000; @; ® Kanayama, north exit) A short walk north of Kanayama Station in a pleasant residential block, this former ryokan has been nicely remodelled to offer cheap digs for backpack-ers. From the station, walk north on Otsu-dōri, pass NTK hall (on your left) and turn right. Walk two short blocks and then turn left – the hostel is to the right.

Ryokan Marutame   RYOKAN ¥¥
(旅館丸為; ☏321-7130; www.jin.ne.jp/marutame; 2-6-17 Tachibana; s/tw ¥5040/8820; ® Higashi Betsuin, exit 4) Opposite Higashi Betsuin tem-ple, this ryokan is beyond the shadows of skyscrapers. Rooms have a traditional feel, and there's a lovely *hanare* (separate) room by the back garden. Staff speak some Eng-lish and simple Japanese meals are avail-able. From the station, walk past the Nagoya Terebi building, then the temple and turn right. It's on the left.

★ the b Nagoya   HOTEL ¥¥
(ザ・ビー 名古屋; ☏241-1500; www.theb-hotels. com/en; 4-15-23 Sakae; s/d from ¥5500/7000; ⊝@; ® Sakae, exit 13) A smart, well-managed hotel with a brilliant location opposite Hisaya-ōdōri-kōen, between Sakae and Yaba-cho subway stations. Well-designed rooms are tiny but tasteful. Online special rates including breakfast can make for excellent value.

★ Richmond Hotel Nagoya Nayabashi   HOTEL ¥¥
(リッチモンドホテル名古屋納屋橋; ☏212-1055; www.richmondhotel.jp/en/nagoya; 1-2-7 Sakae; s/tw/tr from ¥6500/12,000/15,000; P⊝@; ® Fushimi, exit 7) Occupying a prime riverside Nayabashi location, this modern business hotel with crisp, clean lines and dark-wood furniture is an excellent choice of accommodation. Rooms are larger than most in this class, with big twin rooms (31 sq m) for the price.

Best Western Nagoya   HOTEL ¥¥
(ベストウエスタンホテル名古屋; ☏263-3411; www.nagoya.bwhotels.jp; 4-6-1 Sakae; ⊙s/d from ¥5500/7800; @; ® Sakae, exit 12) Formerly the 'Precede', this hotel boasts a convenient Sakae location, pleasant staff and discount-ed online rates. Although showing signs of age, neutral rooms are larger than most and serviced well. There's a Starbucks down-stairs.

Petit Ryokan Ichifuji   RYOKAN ¥¥
(☏914-2867; www.ichifuji-nagoya.com; 1-7 Saikō-bashi-dōri; s/d from ¥6600/9800; @; ® Heian-dōri, exit 2 via elevator) Some will find its location and lack of a restaurant inconvenient, while others will love the ambience of this small inn with traditional rooms and a communal cypress bath. From Heian-dōri subway, turn right and walk about 300m. There's a sign in English.

Hamilton Hotel -Black-   HOTEL ¥¥
(ハミルトンホテルブラック; ☏231-8310; www.hamilton-hotel.jp/black; 1-11-17 Sakae; s/d from ¥7000/9000; P@; ® Fushimi, exit 6) This slick-looking hotel has ubercompact rooms and a youthful, stylish vibe in an enviable Fushimi location, near the Hilton. Cheaper rates may be available online.

Meitetsu Inn Nagoya Nishiki   HOTEL ¥¥
(名鉄イン名古屋錦; ☏951-3434; www.m-inn.com/en/hotel; 3-3-22 Nishiki; s/d from ¥7200/11,300; P@; ® Hisaya Ōdōri, exit 4) Smack in the middle of party central, you'll find this hospital-crisp and -clean, modern buisness hotel with 264 rooms and free breakfast. It's so central that you can crawl home if need be.

Hilton Nagoya
HOTEL ¥¥¥

(ヒルトン名古屋; ☑212-1111; www.hilton.com; 1-3-3 Sakae; s/d from ¥19,500/26,500; ℙ❸@✉; ☒Fushimi, exit 7) This characteristic Hilton benefits from an excellent location and features spacious, stylish rooms with Japanese accents, a selection of suites and an Executive floor. There's also complimentary bicycle rental, a courtesy station shuttle service, two restaurants, three bars and a gym. Most rooms have good views.

ANA Crowne Plaza Grand Court
HOTEL ¥¥¥

(ANAクラウンプラザホテルグランコート名古屋; ☑683-4111; www.anacrowneplaza-nagoya.jp/english; Kanayama 1-1-1; s/d ¥20,000/28,000; ℙ@; ☒Kanayama, south exit) Conveniently located adjacent Kanayama Station, this solid international hotel offers decent-sized, well-appointed rooms with a view. Significantly lower rates can usually be found through Crowne Plaza in your home country.

Nagoya Marriott Associa Hotel
HOTEL ¥¥¥

(名古屋マリオットアソシアホテル; ☑584-1111; www.associa.com/english/nma; 1-1-4 Meieki; s/d from ¥24,000/32,000; ❸@; ☒Nagoya) Perched above JR Nagoya Station, the mammoth Marriott Associa literally tops everything in town, including in price. The 774 spacious rooms located between the 20th and 49th floors have an incredible outlook and luxurious appointments – many even have views from the tub.

✖ Eating

Nagoya is famous for bold local specialities that translate well to non-Japanese palates. *Kishimen* are soft, flat, handmade wheat noodles; *miso-nikomi udon* are noodles in hearty miso broth; and *miso-katsu* is a fried breaded pork cutlet topped with miso sauce. *Kōchin* (free-range chicken) is another local speciality, as are *tebasaki* (chicken wings). *Hitsumabushi* (charcoal-grilled eel) is also popular.

For cheap, international eats, head to the Ōsu storefronts. **Osso Brasil** (オッソ・ブラジル; ☑238-5151; 3-41-13 Ōsu; mains ¥700-1500; ◷10.30am-9pm Tue-Sun; ☒Kamimaezu, exit 8) serves lunchtime grills (all-you-can-eat on weekends, ¥1600), **Lee's Taiwan Kitchen** (李さんの台湾名物屋台; ☑251-8992; 3-35-10 Ōsu; mains around ¥450; ◷noon-8pm, closed Wed; ☒Kamimaezu, exit 8) does take-out bubble tea and crackly *kara-age* (deep-fried chicken), while other stands range from kebabs to crêpes to pizza.

Misen
CHINESE ¥

(味仙; ☑238-7357; 3-6-3 Ōsu; dishes ¥580-1680; ◷lunch & dinner, until 2am Fri & Sat; ☑; ☒Yaba-chō, exit 4) Folks line up for opening at this big Chinese joint where the *Taiwan rāmen* (台湾ラーメン) induces rapture – it's a spicy concoction of ground meat, chilli, garlic and green onion, served over noodles in a hearty clear broth. Other faves include *gomoku yakisoba* (五目焼きそば; stir-fried noodles) and *kinoko-itame* (stir-fried mushrooms). There's a limited picture menu.

Indus
INDIAN ¥

(インダス; ☑261-8819; 3-13-31 Sakae, Princess Garden Hotel 1F; lunch from ¥580, buffet ¥980; ◷11am-10pm; ☑◨; ☒Yaba-chō exit 6 or Sakae, exit 7) A cheery Indian institution where vegetarians can get serious with curry. The all-you-can-eat buffet is great value (¥980) and includes your choice of three curries (including meat), an enormous naan, rice, salad, pappadums and a drink. There's also a full à la carte menu.

Ōsho
DUMPLINGS ¥

(王将; ☑231-6887; Ōsu 2-2601; sets ¥577-1029, small plates from ¥200; ◷11am-10.30pm) This spotless new branch of a popular *gyōza* (dumpling) chain is in a great location opposite Ōsu Kannon. Set meals are excellent value including *rāmen*, *gyōza* and fried rice. There's an extensive picture menu.

Tiger Café
CAFE ¥

(タイガーカフェ; ☑220-0031; 1-8-26 Nishiki; mains ¥600-2000, specials ¥650-850; ◷11am-11pm; ◨; ☒Fushimi, exit 10) Fashionistas grace the windows of this replica Parisian bistro, with tiled floors, white-shirted staff, sidewalk seating and art-deco details. The smoked-salmon sandwich and *croque monsieur* are favourites, as are the good-value lunch specials.

Ebisuya
NOODLES ¥

(えびすや; ☑961-3412; 3-20-7 Sakae; dishes from ¥700; ◷lunch & dinner Mon-Sat; ☒Sakae, exit 3) One of Nagoya's best-known *kishimen* chains, the huge noodle bowls are tasty and cheap. You can often see noodles being made by the chefs, and the menu has pictures.

Chomoranmen
NOODLES ¥

(ちょもらん麺; ☑963-5121; 3-15-10 Nishiki; bowls ¥590-790; ◷11.30am-midnight; ☒Sakae, exit 3) Opposite the Nagoya TV tower, these cheap, chunky handmade *rāmen* bowls will fill you up. The walls are enshrined with photos of the owner's share of famous patrons. Someone should be happy to help you with the vending machine used to take orders if you get stuck.

★ Yabaton Honten
TONKATSU ¥¥

(矢場とん本店; ☑ 252-8810; www.english.yabaton.com; 3-6-18 Ōsu; dishes ¥1050-2520; ☺ lunch & dinner Tue-Sun; ⧉; ⟐ Yaba-chō, exit 4) Since 1947, this has been the place to try Nagoya's famed *miso-katsu*. Signature dishes are *Waraji-tonkatsu* (breaded pork flattened schnitzel-style) and *teppan-tonkatsu* (breaded pork cutlet with miso on a sizzling plate of cabbage). Walk under the expressway and look for the four-storey pig, across the street to your right. It's on the corner, next to McDonalds. Check the website for other locations.

Tarafuku
IZAKAYA ¥¥

(たら福; ☑ 566-5600; 3-17-26 Meieki; dishes ¥400-980; ☺ dinner; ⧉; ⟐ Nagoya) Atmosphere seeps from this ambitious *izakaya* (pub eatery), which transformed a decrepit building into an airy urban oasis. French and seasonally influenced dishes may include potato croquettes in a fried tofu crust; tomato and eggplant au gratin; house-cured beef in wine sauce; plus wine and cocktail lists. Located diagonally across from two Tōyoko Inns.

Tori Tori Tei
IZAKAYA ¥¥

(とりとり亭; ☑ 263-3360; Ōsu 3-18-29; small plates ¥420-1000; ☺ 5.30pm-1am; ⟐ Kamimaezu, exit 9) This Ōsu branch of *izakaya*, specialising in Nagoya chicken, has atmosphere and beer aplenty. Try the *tebasaki* (fried chicken wings; ¥150 each), *chikin namban furai* (Namban-style fried chicken; ¥620), and daikon salad (¥470). The building, on a corner off Akamon-dōri, has paper lanterns and red signage with black lettering.

Yamamotoya Sōhonke
NOODLES ¥¥

(山本屋総本家; ☑ 241-5617; 3-12-19 Sakae; dishes ¥976-1890; ☺ lunch & dinner; ⧉; ⟐ Yaba-chō, exit 6) This is the place to go for soupy *miso-nikomi udon* – the chain has been doing it since 1925. The basic dish costs ¥976 and goes up from there. From Yaba-chō Station, take exit 6, turn left, cross Otsu-dōri and walk two blocks down Shirakawa-dōri. It's on your right and has a large white sign with black Japanese writing.

★ Torigin Honten
JAPANESE ¥¥¥

(鳥銀本店; ☑ 973-3000; 3-14-22 Nishiki; kaiseki courses ¥4500-7800; ☺ dinner; ⧉; ⟐ Sakae, exit 2) Come here for a unique *kōchin kaiseki* experience with immaculately presented servers and a wonderfully traditional atmosphere. Courses consist of *kōchin* chicken served in many forms, including *kushiyaki* (skewered), *kara-age* (deep-fried), *zōsui* (mild rice hotpot) and sashimi (what you think it is).

★ Atsuta Hōraiken Honten
EEL ¥¥¥

(あつた蓬莱軒本店; ☑ 671-8686; 503 Kōbe-chō; sets from ¥2500; ☺ lunch & dinner Thu-Tue) This *hitsumabushi* chain near Atsuta-jingū, in business since 1873, is revered with good reason. Patrons queue during the summer peak season for *hitsumabushi,* eel basted in a secret *tare* (sauce) served atop rice in a covered lacquered bowl (¥3100); add green onion, wasabi and *dashi* (fish broth) to your taste. Other *teishoku* (set menus) include tempura and steak.

🍷 Drinking

★ GROK
CAFE, BAR

(☑ 332-2331; 1-6-13 Tachibana; ☺ 5pm-late Fri-Wed; ⟐ Kamimaezu, exit 7) FREE We love this friendly, colourful and a little bit hippy two-storey cafe/bar. Whether you're with friends or flying solo, you're bound to feel comfortable. It's a little off the beaten track, but that's part of its charm. You can't miss it from the street.

Shooters
BAR

(シューターズ; ☑ 202-7077; www.shooters-nagoya.com; 2-9-26 Sakae; ☺ 5pm-1am Mon-Thu, 11.30am-3am Fri-Sun; ⟐ Fushimi, exit 5) Things can get raucous at Nagoya's largest US-style sports bar with over a dozen screens attracts lots of *gaijin* (foreigners) and their admirers. The bar menu includes mouth-watering burgers, hearty pasta and spicy Tex-Mex – some come just for the food.

Red Rock Bar & Grill
PUB

(レッドロックバーアンドグリル; ☑ 262-7893; www.theredrock.jp; 4-14-6 Sakae; ☺ 5.30pm-late Tue-Sun; ⟐ Sakae, exit 13) On a Sakae side street, Aussie-owned Red Rock attracts locals and expats alike. A fun menu includes such imports from Terra Australis as crocodile nuggets (that's right), lamb wrap, and (we're told) the best meat pies north of Down Under.

The 59's Cafe & Diner
CAFE, BAR

(☑ 971-0566; 3-15-10 Nishiki; ☺ 5pm-late; @; ⟐ Sakae, exit 3) Cowboys and cowgirls greet you in this cruisy, colourful, fun and friendly basement bar. Staff will make you feel welcome and may try to matchmake;

all-you-can-drink nights are Mondays, Wednesdays and Fridays for the ladies (¥1500), and for the gents, Sundays and Thursdays (¥1800).

Smash Head
PUB

(スマッシュヘッド; ☑201-2790; 2-21-90 Ōsu; ⊙noon-midnight Wed-Mon; 圓Ōsu Kannon, exit 2) Through the passageway to the left of the main Ōsu Kannon temple building, you'll find this motorcycle repair shop/pub. Guinness is the beverage of choice, patrons are cool and fish and chips cost ¥850.

Eric Life
CAFE

(エリックライフ; ☑222-1555; 2-11-18 Ōsu; ⊙noon-midnight Thu-Tue; 圓Ōsu Kannon, exit 2) This trendy cafe is a sweet spot to chill over a coffee, cake or cocktail. Artsy folk come to people-watch.

☆ Entertainment

Nagoya's nightlife might not match Tokyo's or Osaka's in scale but it makes up for this in enthusiasm. Check venue websites for listings.

Club JB's
NIGHTCLUB

(クラブジェービーズ; ☑241-2234; www.club-jbs.jp; B1F Marumikonkō Bldg, 4-3-15 Sakae; 圓Sakae, exit 13) Beats, hip-hop, house and techno all feature at different times at this popular club with a central location and killer sound system.

Club Mago
NIGHTCLUB

(☑243-1818; www.club-mago.co.jp; 2-1-9 Shinsakae; cover charge varies; 圓Shinsakae, exit 2) You'll love it or you'll hate it. This 'sexy' mega-club complex sometimes pulls international acts. Its throng of *gaijin* and Japanese punters often pulses with excitement.

Electric Lady Land
LIVE MUSIC

(エレクトリックレディランド; ☑201-5004; www.ell.co.jp; 2-10-43 Ōsu; 圓Ōsu Kannon, exit 2) An intimate live venue showcasing the underground music scene in a cool, post-industrial setting. Nationally known bands play the 1st-floor hall, while up-and-coming acts have the smaller 3rd.

Nagoya Blue Note
LIVE MUSIC

(名古屋ブルーノート; ☑961-6311; www.nagoya-bluenote.com; B2F 3-22-20 Nishiki; 圓Sakae, exit 8) If you're into jazz, big band or blues, you're likely to find your fancy at this long-standing Nagoyan institution.

Misono-za
THEATRE

(御園座; ☑222-1481; www.misonoza.co.jp; 1-6-14 Sakae; 圓Fushimi, exit 6) This is the city's venue for kabuki theatre in February and October, although it does not have the translation facilities of theatres in other cities.

Nagoya Dome
SPORTS

(☑719-2121; 圓Nagoya Dome-mae Yada) This 45,000-seat stadium is home to the Chunichi Dragons baseball team and a venue for large concerts.

🔒 Shopping

Komehyō
DEPARTMENT STORE

(コメ兵; ☑242-0088; 2-20-25 Ōsu; 圓Ōsu Kannon, exit 2) Enjoy the genius of Komehyō, Japan's largest discounter of secondhand, well... everything. Housed over seven floors in the main building, clothes, jewellery and accessories are of excellent quality and at reasonable prices. With patience, you can find some real bargains, especially at 'yen=g' on the 7th floor, where clothing is sold by weight.

SHOPPING IN NAGOYA

Nagoya's manufacturing roots make it a great place to shop. Both Meieki and Sakae boast gargantuan malls and department stores, good for clothing, crafts and foods. Big players are **Maruei** (丸栄; ☑264-1211; 3-3-1 Sakae), **Mitsukoshi** (三越; ☑252-1111; 3-5-1 Sakae) and **Matsuzakaya** (松坂屋; ☑251-1111; 3-16-1 Sakae) in Sakae; and **Takashimaya** (高島屋; ☑566-1101; 1-1-4 Meieki), **Meitetsu** (名鉄・近鉄; ☑585-1111; 1-2-1 Meieki) and **Kintetsu** (☑582-3411; 1-2-2 Meieki) near Nagoya Station. Regional crafts include *Arimatsunarumi shibori* (elegant tie-dying), cloisonné ceramics and *seki* blades (swords, knives, scissors etc).

In Ōsu, along Akamon-dōri, Banshō-ji-dōri and Niomon-dōri, there are hundreds of funky vintage boutiques and discount clothing retailers. Ōsu Kannon temple hosts a colourful antique market on the 18th and 28th of each month, while Higashi Betsuin temple has a flea market on the 12th of each month.

East of Ōsu, Otsu-dōri has a proliferation of manga shops.

Momijiya FASHION
(もみじや; ☑251-1313; 3-37-46 Ōsu; ☒Ōsu Kannon, exit 2) For something different, Momijiya creates clothing and accessories patterned with antique kimono fabric. Look for cute, contemporary twists.

Maruzen BOOKS
(丸善; ☑261-2251; 3-3-1 Sakae; ☉10am-7pm; ☒Sakae, exit 15) English-language titles can be purchased here, on the 6th and 7th floors of the Maruei department store.

Junkudo Books Loft Nagoya BOOKS
(ジュンク堂書店ロフト名古屋店; ☑249-5592; B1F & 7F Nadya Park, 3-18-1 Sakae; ☉10.30am-8pm; @) Split between the basement and 7th floor of Loft department store in Nadya Park, there are over half a million books here, including English and foreign language titles.

ⓘ Information

EMERGENCY
Ambulance & Fire (☑119)
Police (☑110)

INTERNET ACCESS
Nagoya International Centre (名古屋国際センター; ☑581-0100; www.nic-nagoya.or.jp/en; 1-47-1 Nagono; ☉9am-7pm Tue-Sun; ☒Kokusai Centre) This not-for-profit organisation provides information, consultation and referral services in English. There's also an internet corner on the 3rd floor (per 15 minutes ¥100) and a library with over 30,000 items in various languages.
FedEx Kinko's Fushimi (フェデックスキンコーズ伏見店; 1F Kirin Hirokoji Bldg, 2-3-31 Sakae; first 10min ¥262.50 then ¥210 per 10min block thereafter; ☉24hr; ☒Fushimi, exit 4) Rental PCs available for internet access.

INTERNET RESOURCES
There are a number of useful websites for up-to-date information on what's happening in Nagoya. The Nagoya Convention and Visitors Bureau (www.ncvb.or.jp/en) and Nagoya International Centre (www.nic-nagoya.or.jp/en) homepages are brimming with information. Also try www.nagoya-info.com for English-language listings.

MEDICAL SERVICES
Aichi Prefectural Emergency Medical Guide (愛知県救急医療ガイド; ☑263-1133, automated service 050-5810-5884; www.qq.pref.aichi.jp) Phone or follow the English link on this prefectural homepage for a list of medical institutions with English-speaking staff, including specialities and hours of operation.

Tachino Clinic (たちのクリニック; ☑541-9130; 3F Dai-Nagoya Bldg, 3-26-8 Meieki; ☉9.30am-1pm & 2.30-6pm Mon-Wed & Fri; 9.30am-1pm Thu & Sat) Opposite the east exit of Nagoya Station; with English-speaking staff.

MONEY & POST
Citibank has 24-hour Cirrus ATMs on the 1st floor of the Sugi building (☒Sakae, exit 7) and in the arrival lobby at Central Japan International Airport.
JR Towers Post Office (タワーズ内郵便局; ☒Nagoya) Within the JR station complex, on the Sakura-dōri side.
Nagoya Station Post Office (名古屋中央郵便局名古屋駅前分室) Just east of the station on Hirokōji-dōri, before the elevated expressway.

TOURIST INFORMATION
English-language street and subway maps are widely available at tourist information centres and hotels. The free *Live Map Nagoya* has the city covered and the *Nagoya Pocket Guide* and *Nagoya InfoGuide* maps are particularly handy. English-language listings publications include *Nagmag, RAN* and *Nagoya Calendar*. For rail-related queries, the staff at JR Nagoya Station's ticket windows speak some English.

Nagoya has three helpful Tourist Information Centre branches, stacked with resources in English and Japanese and at least one English speaker on hand.
Tourist Information Centre (Nagoya Station) (観光案内所; ☑541-4301; 1-1-14 Meieki; ☉9am-7pm; ☒Nagoya, in the central concourse)
Tourist Information Centre (Kanayama) (観光案内所; ☑323-0161; LOOP Kanayama 1F, 1-17-18 Kanayama; ☉9am-8pm; ☒Kanayama)
Tourist Information Centre (Sakae) (観光案内所; ☑963-5252; Oasis 21 B1F, 1-11-1 Higashi-sakura; ☉10am-8pm; ☒Sakae)

ⓘ Getting There & Away

AIR
Central Japan International Airport (p840), opened in 2005 on a manmade island in Ise Bay, 35km south of the city, has become a tourist attraction for locals. They come for the dozens of well-priced shopping and dining options, plane-spotting from the enormous observation deck, or to soak in the **Fū-no-yu** (風の湯; adult/child with towel ¥1000/600; ☉8am-10pm), hot-spring baths. For travellers, the airport is far friendlier and less frantic than its big brothers in Tokyo and Osaka. With excellent transport connections, it's a great arrival port into Japan from around 30 international destinations in Europe, North America and Asia. Domestic routes serve around 20 Japanese cities, though you'll find some are reached faster by train.

BOAT

Taiheiyo Ferry (www.taiheiyo-ferry.co.jp/
english) sails snazzy ships between Nagoya and
Tomakomai (Hokkaidō, from ¥9500, 40 hours)
via Sendai (from ¥6500, 21 hours 40 minutes)
every other evening at 7pm, with daily services to Sendai. Take the Meikō subway line to
Nagoya-kō Station and go to Nagoya Port.

BUS

JR and **Meitetsu Highway buses** operate
services between Nagoya and Kyoto (¥2500,
2½ hours, hourly), Osaka (¥3000, three hours,
hourly), Kobe (¥3300, 3½ hours), Kanazawa
(¥4060, four hours, 10 daily), Nagano (¥4500,
4½ hours) and Tokyo (¥6500, six hours, 14
daily). Overnight buses run to Hiroshima
(¥8500, nine hours).

New kid on the block, **Willer Express** (www.
willerexpress.com) offers airline style seating
and online reservations in English at *heavily* discounted rates. Key routes from Nagoya include
Tokyo (from ¥3200, six hours) and Fukuoka
(from ¥6500, 11½ hours overnight).

Departure points vary by carrier and destination, although almost all highway buses depart
from the Nagoya Station Bus Terminal. Some
routes also depart from Oasis 21. Confirm your
departure location at time of booking.

TRAIN

Nagoya is a major *shinkansen* hub, connecting
with Tokyo (¥10,070, 1¾ hours), Shin-Osaka
(¥5670, 50 minutes), Kyoto (¥4930, 35 minutes), Hiroshima (¥12,920, 2½ hours) and
Hakata/Fukuoka (¥17,020, 3½ hours).

To get into the Japan Alps, take the JR Chūō
line to Matsumoto (*Shinano tokkyū* – limited
express – ¥5360, two hours) or onwards to Nagano (¥6620, 2¾ hours). A separate line serves
Takayama (Hida *tokkyū*, ¥5360, 2¼ hours).

The private Meitetsu line has routes in and
around Nagoya (Tokonome, Inuyama, Gifu)
covered.

ⓘ Getting Around

TO/FROM THE AIRPORT

Central Japan International Airport is easily accessed from Nagoya and Kanayama Stations via
the Meitetsu *Kūkō* (Airport) line (*tokkyū*, ¥850,
28 minutes). A taxi from central Nagoya costs
upwards of ¥13,000.

BUS

The gold **Me~guru bus** (名古屋観光ルートバスメ
ーグル; www.ncvb.or.jp/routebus; day pass adult/
child ¥500/250) follows a one-way loop near
attractions in the Meieki, Sakae and castle areas.
Ticket holders recieve discounted admissions. It
runs 9.30am to 5pm, hourly Tuesday to Friday and
twice hourly on weekends. No bus on Mondays.

SUBWAY

Nagoya has an excellent subway system with
six lines, clearly signposted in English and Japanese. Fares cost ¥200 to ¥320 depending on
distance. One-day passes (¥740, ¥850 including
city buses), available at ticket machines, include
subway transport and discounted admission to
many attractions. On Saturday and Sunday the
donichi eco-kippu (Saturday-Sunday eco-ticket)
gives the same benefits for ¥600 per day.

AROUND NAGOYA

In the suburbs of Nagoya, outlying Aichi-ken
and the southern part of Gifu-ken, there are
some interesting destination museums and
towns reached easily by train. Gifu city, ben-
efitting from recent redevelopment and a
pretty position at the foothills of the mountains, is worth considering as an alternative
base to Nagoya. Neighbouring Inuyama
boasts National Treasures – its castle and
teahouse. Both Inuyama and Gifu city are
famed for the spectacle of *ukai* (fishing with
trained cormorants).

⦿ Sights & Activities

★ **JR SCMAGLEV & Railway Park** MUSEUM
(JR リニア・鉄道館; ☑050-3772-3910; www.
museum.jr-central.co.jp/en; Kinjofuto 3-2-2; adult/
child ¥1000/500; ⊙10am-5.30pm Wed-Mon; ⊠JR
Aonami line, Kinjofuto station) Trainspotters will
be in heaven at this fantastic hands-on museum. Featuring actual *Maglev* (world's fastest train – 581km/h), *shinkansen* and historical rolling stock and rail simulators, this
massive museum offers a fascinating insight
into Japanese postwar history, through the
development of a railroad like no other. The
'hangar' is 20 minutes from Nagoya on the
Aonami line, found on the Taiko-dōri side of
JR Nagoya Station.

**Toyota Kaikan Exhibition Hall
& Factory Tour** FACTORY, MUSEUM
(トヨタ会館; ☑0565-29-3345 (museum),
0565-29-3355 (tour); www.toyota.co.jp/en/
about_toyota/facility/toyota_kaikan; 1 Toyota-chō;
⊙9.30-5pm Mon-Sat) **FREE** Here, in Toyota
city, is a changing exhibit of up to 20 shiny
examples of the latest automotive technology, hot off the production line, and
you have the rare opportunity to see how
they're made, for free. Two-hour tours of
Toyota Motor Corporation's main factory
begin here, every Monday through Saturday, at 11am, but, you need to book between

two weeks and three months ahead and allow two hours to get to Toyota city from central Nagoya. See the website for directions and reservations.

Arimatsu Tie-Dyeing Museum
MUSEUM

(有松鳴海絞会館 Arimatsu Narumi-shibori Kaikan; ☑621-0111; www.shibori-kaikan.com; 3008 Arimatsu; adult/child 300/100; ⊙9.30am-5pm Thu-Tue; ⍟Meitetsu Arimatsu) This museum upholds the 400-year-old tradition of *shibori* (tie-dyeing). Downstairs, you'll find historical artefacts, a gift shop and a video introducing this painstaking and beautiful craft. Upstairs, a number of women patiently demonstrate the art. If you fancy and have the time (up to three hours) you can try it yourself. It's ¥1050 to ¥3150 depending on the item (all materials provided), plus postage for the finished product to be sent to you – reservations are required. Arimatsu is about 20 minutes from Nagoya on the Meitetsu main line, towards Toyohashi.

Tokoname
常滑

☑0569 / POP 56,570

Clay beneath the ground of this bayside community has made Tokoname a hub for ceramic-making for centuries – during peak produiction some 400 chimneys rose above its centre. The area still produces some ¥60 trillion in ceramics annually and makes an interesting excursion from Nagoya, or nearby Centrair Airport.

Yakimono Sanpo Michi (やきもの散歩道; Pottery Footpath) is a hilly 1.8km trail around the town's historic centre. Pick up a walking map in English from Tokoname Tourist Information inside Tokoname Station. Lining the well-signposted path are kilns, cafes and galleries. Numbered plaques corresponding to the walking map indicate stops along the way. A series of *maneki-neko* (ceramic 'lucky' cats) greet you as you head toward the beginning of the path. If you look up, you'll see Toko-nyan, the mother of all *maneki-neko*, looming above.

The restored **Takita Residence** (滝田家 Takita-ke; Takita Residence, stop 8; admission ¥300; ⊙9am-4.30pm Tue-Sun), c. 1850, was the home of a shipping magnate. Inside are replicas of the *bishu-kaisen* (local trading ships) and displays of ceramics, lacquer and furniture. Look for the *suikinkutsu*, a ceramic jar buried in the ground so that it rings like a *koto* (Japanese musical instrument) when water drips into it.

The pipe-and-jug-lined lane at **Dokanzaka** (土管坂; Dokan-zaka hill, stop 9) is particularly photogenic. Around the back of **Noborigama-hiroba** (登窯広場; Climbing Kiln Sq, stop 13) are 10 square chimneys that served the gigantic 1887 kiln. It's a five-minute detour from here to **Inax Live Museum** (イナックスライブミュージアム; www1.lixil.co.jp/ilm/english; 1-130 Okueichō; adult/child ¥600/200; ⊙10am-5pm, closed 3rd Wed of each month), the showpiece of one of Japan's largest plumbing-equipment manufacturers, housing some 150 elaborately decorated Meiji- and Taisho-era toilets and Japan's only tile museum, with over 1000 tiles from around the world.

When you need a rest, atmospheric **Koyōan** (古窯庵; ☑35-8350; mains ¥880-2100; ⊙11.30am-5pm Tue-Sun, dinner by reservation) serves homemade *soba* (buckwheat noodles) on beautiful local ceramics. Eel fans should try **Nakamura-ya** (うなぎの中村屋; ☑35-0120; 2-53 Sakaemachi; ⊙lunch Thu-Tue), for Unagi-don (eel on rice) or *hitsumabushi*. It's in a great spot, near Toko-nyan, the giant cat.

❶ Getting There & Around

The private Meitetsu line connects Tokoname with Nagoya (*kyūkō*, ¥650, 40 minutes; *tokkyū*, ¥1000, 30 minutes) and Central Japan International Airport (¥300, five minutes). The Pottery Footpath begins a few hundred metres from the train station.

Inuyama
犬山

☑0568 / POP 75,130

Inuyama's Kiso-gawa (river), aka the 'Japanese Rhine', paints a pretty picture beneath its castle, a National Treasure. By day, the castle, quaint streets, manicured Uraku-en and 17th-century Jo-an Teahouse make for pleasant strolling, while at night the scene turns cinematic as fishermen practise *ukai* by firelight (1 June to 15 October).

Just south of the temple are the shrines **Haritsuna Jinja** (針綱神社) and **Sankō-Inari Jinja** (三光稲荷神社), the latter with interesting statues of *komainu* (protective dogs).

Since 1635, townsfolk have celebrated the Inuyama *Matsuri* (Festival) on the on first Saturday and Sunday in April. A scaled-down version is held on the fourth Saturday in October. A government designated Intangible Cultural Asset, the festival features a parade of 13 three-tiered floats strewn with 365 lanterns. Atop each float elaborate *kara-kuri ningyō* perform to music.

◉ Sights & Activities

★ Inuyama-jō CASTLE
(犬山城; ☎ 61-1711; 65-2 Kitakoken; adult/child ¥500/100; ⏰ 9am-4.30pm; ⓡ Meitetsu Inuyama-yuen) A National Treasure, Japan's oldest standing castle is said to have originated as a fort in 1440. The current *donjon* (main keep) built atop a 40m rise beside the Kiso-gawa dates from 1537 and has resisted war, earthquake and restoration, remaining the penultimate example of Momoyama-era architecture. Inside are steep, narrow staircases and military displays – the view from the top is worth the climb. The castle is 15 minutes' walk from Meitetsu Inuyama-yuen Station.

Inuyama Artifacts Museum (Main) / Castle & Town Museum MUSEUM
(犬山市文化史料館（本館）・城とまちミュージアム; ☎ 62-4802; 8 Kitakoken; ¥100, included in admission to Inuyama-jō; ⏰ 9am-4.30pm; ⓡ Meitetsu Inuyama-yuen station) This museum, located one block south of Haritsuna Jinja and Sankō-Inari Jinja, was reopened in October 2012 after extensive renovations. It houses two of the Inuyama festival floats and various artefacts related to cormorant fishing, Inuyama-jō and the town's history.

Karakuri Exhibition Room (Annex) MUSEUM
(からくり展示館（別館）; ☎ 61-3932; 69-2/69-3 Kitakoken; ¥100, included in admission to Inuyama-jō; ⏰ 9am-4.30pm; ⓡ Meitetsu Inuyama-yuen station) This small annex exhibits Edo- and Meiji-era *karakuri ningyō*. On Saturday and Sunday at 10.30am and 2pm, you can see the wooden characters in action. On Friday and Saturday between 10am and 4pm, there are demonstrations of how the puppets are made by artisan Tamaya Shobei the 9th, who, at time of writing, is the only living *karakuri ningyō* Master from an unbroken lineage.

Dondenkan MUSEUM
(どんでん館; ☎ 65-1728; Higashi-koken 62; adult/child ¥200/100; ⏰ 9am-4.30pm; ⓡ Meitetsu Inuyama) Four of the 13 impressive Inuyama Matsuri floats are on year-round display in this custom-made building.

Uraku-en & Jo-an Teahouse GARDEN
(有楽園・茶室如安; 1 Gomonsaki; admission adult/child ¥1000/600; ⏰ 9am-5pm Mar-Nov, to 4pm Dec-Feb; ⓡ Meitetsu Inuyama-yuen station) Within this pretty garden in the grounds of the Meitetsu Inuyama Hotel, you'll find

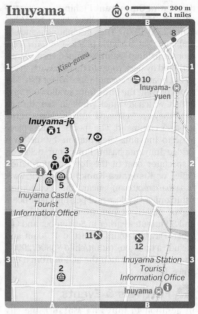

Inuyama

Jo-an, one of the finest teahouses in Japan. Another of Inuyama's National Treasures, Jo-an was built in 1618 in Kyoto by Oda Urakusai, younger brother of Oda Nobunaga, and relocated here in 1972. You can enjoy tea on the grounds for an additional ¥500.

Kiso-gawa Cormorant Fishing   BOAT TRIP

(木曽川鵜飼い; evening boat tours, adult/child from ¥2500/1250) The fascinating, ancient and some say barbaric practise of *ukai* (cormorant fishing) features trained cormorants. Tethered by neck ropes to their masters in adjacent boats, the cormorants dive for fish. The ropes prevent the birds from swallowing larger fish, which get stuck whole in their throats until they are 'retrieved' into the boats at the master's command. The spectacle takes place close to Inuyama-yūen Station, by the Twin Bridge Inuyama-bashi. Book your ticket on a spectator boat at the Tourist Information Office or **Kisogawa Kankō** (☎61-0057; www.kisogawa-kankou.com), near the cormorant-fishing pier. Up close and personal tour boats depart nightly at 7pm from June to August and 30 minutes earlier in September and October. Daylight tours depart at 11.30am and include a lunchbox (adult/child ¥3800/2900). You can always watch the action from a distance, for free.

✿ Festivals & Events

In addition to **Inuyama Matsuri**, the city also hosts the summer **Nihon Rhine Matsuri**, every 10 August on the banks of the river, culminating in fireworks.

🛏 Sleeping & Eating

Inuyama International
Youth Hostel   HOSTEL ¥

(犬山国際ユースホステル; ☎61-1111; www.inuyama-hostel.com/en; 161 Himuro; s/d/tr from ¥3300/6200/8700; @; ☒ Meitetsu Inuyama-yuen) Some will enjoy the isolation of this large hostel with a variety of room types and communal bathing – others won't. Meals must be reserved (breakfast/dinner ¥840/1580) and there are no facilities nearby. It's a 30 minute walk from Inuyama-yuen Station, or about ¥1350 in a taxi.

Geihanrō   RYOKAN ¥¥

(迎帆楼; ☎61-2205; www.geihanro.com; 41-6 Kitakoken; P @; ☒ Meitetsu Inuyama-yuen) Recently renovated to a high standard, you'll be hard-pressed to find nicer accommodation in town. This large ryokan/hotel accepts single travellers and has a prime riverside location beneath the castle. The view from the communal bath is wonderful.

Rinkō-kan   RYOKAN ¥¥

(臨江館; ☎61-0977; www.rinkokan.jp; 8-1 Nishidaimon; r per person with/without 2 meals from ¥10,500/5250; @; ☒ Meitetsu Inuyama-yuen,

west exit) Overlooking the river, this cheery, 20-room ryokan has stone common baths including *rotemburo*. Some rooms have in-room bathrooms and a variety of packages are available, including good deals for single travellers.

Kōhii Fū   CAFE ¥

(珈琲ふう; ☎61-6515; 558 Higashikoken; lunch ¥600; ◷8am-6pm Thu-Tue; ☒ Meitetsu Inuyama, west exit) This family-run cafe serves a hearty lunch 'of the day'. Otherwise, there's coffee, cake and the usual suspects. From the station, turn right at the lights, walk two blocks to the next set of lights, then turn left. Walk another block and a half and it's on your left.

Narita   FRENCH ¥¥

(フレンチ創作料理なり多; ☎65-2447; 395 Higashikoken; 5-course meal from ¥3000; ◷lunch & dinner; ☒ Meitetsu Inuyama, west exit) Fancy five-course French cuisine in an Edo period building with an attractive garden. From the station, turn right at the lights, walk two blocks to the next set of lights, then turn right. It's on your right.

ℹ Information

Inuyama has two Tourist Information Offices to dispense English-language materials and assist with accommodation and activities reservations. On the web, visit www.ml.inuyama.gr.jp/en.

Inuyama Station Tourist Information Office

(犬山市観光案内所（犬山駅）; ☎61-6000; ◷9am-5pm)

Inuyama Castle Tourist Information Office

(犬山市観光案内所（犬山城）; ☎61-2825; 12 Kitakoken; ◷9am-5pm)

ℹ Getting There & Around

Inuyama is connected with Nagoya (*tokkyū*, ¥540, 25 minutes) and Gifu (¥440, 35 minutes) via the Meitetsu Inuyama line. JR travellers can connect via Gifu to Unuma (¥320, 20 minutes) and walk across the Kiso-gawa to Inuyama. The castle and ukai area are slightly closer to Inuyama-yūen Station than Inuyama Station.

Around Inuyama   犬山近辺

The region surrounding Inuyama has a few unusual and worthwhile attractions, as well as some decent farmland scenery. Be sure to check transport connections before you set out.

Sights

Museum Meiji-mura MUSEUM
(明治村; ☎0568-67-0314; www.meijimura.com/english; 1 Uchiyama; adult/senior/child ¥1600/1200/600; ⏲9.30am-5pm Mar-Oct, to 4pm Nov-Feb, closed Mon Dec-Feb; 🚌departs Meitetsu Inuyama Station, east exit) Few Meiji-era buildings (known for unifying Western and Japanese architectural elements) have survived war, earthquake or rabid development. In 1965, this open-air museum was created to preserve the unique style. Over 60 buildings from around Japan were painstakingly dismantled, transported and reassembled in this leafy lakeside location. Favourites include the entry facade of Frank Lloyd Wright's Tokyo Imperial Hotel, Kyoto's St Francis Xavier's Cathedral, and Sapporo's telephone exchange. Buses to Meiji-mura (¥410, 20 minutes) depart every 20 to 30 minutes from Inuyama Station's east exit. If you're driving, parking is ¥800.

Ōagata-jinja SHINTŌ SHRINE
(大縣神社; ☎67-1017; 3 Aza Miyayama; 🚊Meitetsu Komaki line, Gakuden station) This ancient shrine, set on a lovely hillside with a plum orchard at the back, is dedicated to the female Shintō deity Izanami and attracts women seeking marriage or fertility. See if you can find the large *hime-ishi* (姫石; princess stone) and other items resembling giant female genitals.

The popular **Hime-no-miya Matsuri** takes place here on the Sunday before 15 March (or on 15 March if it's a Sunday). Locals pray for good harvests and prosperity by parading through the streets bearing a *mikoshi* (portable shrine) with replica vaginas.

Ōagata-jinja is a 25-minute walk from Gakuden Station (¥220 from Inuyama, seven minutes). To reach the shrine, turn right at the exit and follow Rte177 east, all the way, across the river and up the hill. Sadly, recent expansion of a nearby industrial landfill threatens the tranquility of the shrine. Beware the many noisy, smelly dumptrucks sharing the narrow road to your destination.

Tagata-jinja SHINTŌ SHRINE
(田県神社; 152 Tagata-chō; 🚊Meitetsu Komaki Line, Tagata-jinjamae station) Izanagi, the male counterpart of female deity Izanami, is commemorated at this shrine, with countless wooden and stone phalluses to celebrate. You can buy souvenirs from ¥500.

The **Tagata Hōnen-sai Matsuri** takes place on 15 March at Tagata-jinja, when the highly photogenic, 2m-long, 60kg 'sacred object' is paraded excitedly around the neighbourhood. Arrive well before the procession starts at 2pm.

Tagata-jinja is about a five minute walk west of Tagata-jinja-mae Station on the Meitetsu Komaki line (¥290 from Inuyama, nine minutes).

Gifu 岐阜

☎058 / POP 413,150

Historically, Gifu has a strong association with Oda Nobunaga, *daimyō* (domain lord) of the castle and bestower of the city's name in 1567. It was later visited by famed haiku poet Matsuō Bashō, who witnessed *ukai* here in 1688; Charlie Chaplin did the same in his day.

Although contemporary Gifu shows little evidence of those historic times (due to a colossal earthquake in 1891 and the decimation of WWII), recent redevelopment has created a vibrant and accessible downtown core. Noteworthy attractions include the lovely Gifu Park and one of the three Great Buddhas of Japan. Add some pretty mountains, a wide river and excellent transport links, and a stopover here becomes a viable alternative to big city Nagoya.

Sights & Activities

Visitors generally arrive at JR Gifu or Meitetsu Gifu stations, but sightseeing is centred about 15 minutes north of this area, by bus, around Gifu-koen, the Nagara River and the picturesque 'old-town' of Kawara-machi.

Cormorant Fishing SPECTACLE
(鵜飼い) *Ukai* is an ancient tradition where *ukai* masters in boats use trained birds, tethered at the neck, to dive for fish. *Ukai* takes place at night, by firelight. Although some will find the ancient practise cruel, the glow of the lanterns along the riverbanks east of the *Nagara-bashi* bridge is a sight to behold, and masters claim the birds are not harmed by their training. For a closer view, sightseeing boats depart nightly in season (11 May to 15 October) from the **Cormorant Fishing Viewing Boat Office** (鵜飼観覧船事務所; Ukai kanran fune jimusho; ☎262-0104; www.gifucvb.or.jp/en; 1-2 Minato-machi; adult/child ¥3300/2900; ⏲departures 6.15pm, 6.45pm & 7.15pm; 🚌N80, N32-N86, direction Takatomi, stop Nagara-bashi) below the bridge, which also takes

reservations by phone; strongly advised. Food and drinks are not available on the boats.

Nagara River Ukai Museum
MUSEUM

(長良川うかいミュージアム; ☎ 210-1555; http://ukaimuseum.jp; 51-2 Choryo; adult/child ¥500/250; ⏰ 9am-6.30pm Wed-Mon, 1 May-15 Oct, 9am-4.30pm Wed-Mon, 16 Oct-30 Apr; 🚌 City loop or N-line bus, stop Ukai-ya) This shiny new museum, opened in 2012, is the only one of its kind and features exhibits on everything you could possibly want to know about cormorant fishing in Japan.

Gifu-kōen
PARK

(岐阜公園; 🅿; 🚌 N80, N32-N86, stop Gifu-kōen) At the foot of Mt Kinka-zan, this is one of the loveliest city parks in Japan, with plenty of water and trees set into the hillside.

Gifu City History Museum
MUSEUM

(岐阜市歴史博物館; 2-18-1 Ōmiya-chō; adult/child ¥300/150; ⏰ 9am-4.30pm Tue-Sun; 🚌 N80, N32-N86, stop Gifu-kōen) Located within the grounds of Gifu-kōen, this museum focuses on the Sengoku period, when daimyo Oda Nobunaga was at the height of his power.

Kinka-zan Ropeway
ROPEWAY

(金華山ロープウエー; 257 Senjōjiki-shita; return adult/child ¥1050/520; ⏰ 9am-5pm year-round, extended hours during holiday periods) Gifu's castle is most easily reached by this cable car within Gifu-kōen. It will whisk you the 329m to the summit of Mt Kinka-zan in under five minutes.

Gifu-jō
CASTLE

(岐阜城; 18 Tenshukaku; adult/child ¥200/100; ⏰ 9.30am-30min before ropeway closure; 🚌 N80, N32-N86, stop Gifu-kōen) Perched atop Mt Kinka-zan with sweeping views over the cities of Gifu and Nagoya, the castle is a 1956 concrete replica of Oda Nobunaga's stronghold, destroyed in 1600, the ruins of which were finished off in WWII. There's an hour-long hiking trail from the park below.

Shōhō-ji
(Gifu Great Buddha)
BUDDHIST TEMPLE

(正法寺; ☎ 264-2760; 8 Daibutsu-chō; adult/child ¥200/100; ⏰ 9am-5pm; 🚌 N80, N32-N86, stop Gifu-kōen) The main attraction of this orange-and-white temple is the papier-mâché *daibutsu* (Great Buddha; c 1832), one of the three Great Buddha statues of Japan. It's 13.7m tall and is said to have been fashioned over 38 years using a tonne of paper sutras.

🛏 Sleeping & Eating

The narrow streets a few blocks north of JR Gifu and west of Meitetsu Gifu stations, between Kinkabashi-dōri and Nagarabashi-dōri, are dotted with open eateries, *izakaya* and a welcoming night vibe. Hotels listed are in this general vicinity.

★ Dormy Inn Gifu Ekimae
HOTEL ¥¥

(ドーミーイン岐阜; ☎ 267-5489; www.hotespa.net/hotels/gifu; 6-31 Yoshino-machi; s/d from ¥6500/9000; 🚌 JR Gifu, north exit) Opened in September 2012, this new kid on the block is five minutes' stroll along the elevated walkway from JR Gifu station. Light-filled rooms are functionally compact with fresh, inviting decor. There's an on-site onsen and the guest laundry has gas-powered dryers. Breakfast is available.

Comfort Hotel Gifu
HOTEL ¥¥

(コンフォートホテル岐阜; ☎ 267-1311; www.comfortinn.com/hotel-gifu-japan-JP030; 6-6 Yoshino-machi; s/tw with breakfast ¥6500/11,550; ⊜@🛜; 🚌 JR Gifu, north exit) Across from JR Gifu Station, this unpretentious, 219-room business hotel includes a breakfast buffet in the rate.

Daiwa Roynet Hotel Gifu
HOTEL ¥¥

(ダイワロイネットホテル岐阜; ☎ 212-0055; www.daiwaroynet.jp/gifu; 8-5 Kanda-machi; s/d ¥11,000/20,000; ⊜@; 🚌 Meitetsu Gifu) Closest to Meitetsu-Gifu station, there's a splash of colour in the rooms of this pleasant business hotel, where everything is at your doorstep.

★ Gyōza Gishuu
DUMPLINGS ¥

(餃子専門店 岐州; ☎ 266-6227; 1-31 Sumida-machi; items from ¥200; ⏰ 5.30pm until sold out, Wed-Mon) This humming hole-in-the-wall does soupy fried *gyōza* and *ebi chahan* (shrimp fried rice). Go straight from JR station along the street between Kinkabashi-dōri and Nagarabashi-dōri. It's on the corner of the second block, to your right.

Shanthy
INDIAN ¥

(☎ 262-7328; 2-13-2 Sumida-machi; lunch from ¥500, dinner set ¥1280; ⏰ lunch & dinner; 🍽) This spacious Indian restaurant offers great value – the dinner sets include salad, curry, naan or rice and a drink (options include wine).

Utsuboya
CAFE ¥

(空穂屋; ☎ 215-7077; www.utsuboya.info; 38 Utsuboya-chō; doughnuts from ¥200; ⏰ 10am-

6pm Fri-Wed; N80, N32-N86, stop Hon-machi 3-chōme) In Kawara-machi, this charming cafe and antiques gallery makes home-made doughnuts. From the bus stop, walk east along Nagarabashi-dōri and then turn right on the second street; it's on the right in an old, tile-roofed shophouse.

Bier Hall
BAR

(ビアホール; 266-8868; 2-8 Tamamiya-chō; 5.30pm-1am Mon-Sat) The friendly staff of this popular and spacious pub will make you feel welcome. Guinness is the beer of choice and simple meals are cheap and tasty. It's easily likable.

🔒 Shopping

Gifu's craft tradition includes *wagasa* (oiled paper parasols/umbrellas) and elegantly painted *chōchin* (paper lanterns), though the number of real artisans is dwindling – souvenir shops generally sell mass-produced versions. The Tourist Information Office has a map of high-quality makers and retailers. Expect to pay ¥10,000 and over for the good stuff.

Sakaida Eikichi Honten
HANDICRAFTS

(坂井田永吉本店; 271-6958; 27 Kanōnakahiroe-chō; 9.30am-5.30pm Mon-Sat) This high-end *wagasa* maker is a 10-minute walk from JR Gifu Station. Turn left from the south exit, and turn right at the second stoplight. It's at the next corner.

Ozeki Chōchin
HANDICRAFTS

(オゼキ; 263-0111; www.ozeki-lantern.co.jp; 1-18 Oguma-chō; 9am-5pm Mon-Fri; stop Ken-Sōgōchōsha-mae) Find beautiful paper lanterns here, near the Higashi Betsuin temple.

ℹ️ Information

Tourist Information Office (262-4415; 9am-7pm Mar-Dec, to 6pm Jan & Feb) Friendly staff can assist with English maps and accommodation recommendations. On the 2nd floor of JR Gifu Station.

ℹ️ Getting There & Around

Gifu is a blink from Nagoya on the JR Tōkaidō line (*tokkyū*, ¥450, 18 minutes). Meitetsu trains take longer and are more expensive (¥540, 35 minutes) but also serve Inuyama (¥440, 35 minutes) and Central Japan International Airport (*tokkyū*, ¥1310, 64 minutes).

JR Gifu and Meitetsu-Gifu Stations are a few minutes' walk apart, joined by a covered elevated walkway.

Buses to sights (¥200) depart from stops 11 and 12 of the bus terminal by JR Gifu Station's Nagara exit, stopping at Meitetsu-Gifu en route. There's also a city-loop bus from stop 10. Check before boarding as not all buses make all stops.

Gujō-Hachiman   郡上八幡
0575 / POP 44,490

Nestled in the mountains at the confluence of several rivers, Gujō-Hachiman is a picturesque town famed for its **Gujō Odori** folk dance festival. It's also where plastic food models were invented.

Following a tradition dating to the 1590s, townsfolk engage in frenzied dancing on 32 nights between mid-July and early September. Visitor participation is encouraged, especially during *tetsuya odori,* the four main days of the festival (13 to 16 August), when the dancing goes all night.

Otherwise, the town's sparkling rivers, narrow lanes and stone bridges maintain appeal. A famous spring, **Sōgi-sui,** near the centre of town, is something of a pilgrimage site, named for a Momoyama-era poet. People who rank such things place Sōgi-sui at the top of the list for clarity.

👁 Sights & Activities

Gujō Hachiman-jō
CASTLE

(郡上八幡城; adult/child ¥300/150; 9am-5pm) Twenty minutes' hike from Jōka-machi Plaza bus terminal you'll find the pride of Gujō, a hilltop castle dating from 1933. Prior to its construction, the site had been a humble fortress since around 1600. The castle contains various weaponry and has wonderful views across the valley.

Shokuhin Sample Kōbō
WORKSHOP

(食品サンプル工房創作館; 67-1870; www.samplekobo.com; samples vary; 9am-5pm, Fri-Wed) **FREE** Realistic food models have been one of life's great mysteries, until now. In an old merchant house, this hands-on workshop lets you see how it's done and try creating them yourself (reservation required). Tempura (three pieces; ¥1000) and lettuce (free) make memorable souvenirs. It's about five minutes' walk from Jōka-machi Plaza, across the river.

🛏 Sleeping & Eating

Bizenya Ryokan
RYOKAN ¥¥

(備前屋旅館; 65-2068; www.gujyo-bizenya.jp; 264 Yanagi-machi; r per person without meals from ¥5,250; P) This quietly upscale ryokan near

Shin-bashi bridge faces a lovely garden. Some rooms have private facilities and plans with or without meals are available.

Nakashimaya Ryokan RYOKAN ¥¥
(中嶋屋旅館; ☏65-2191; www.nakashimaya.net; 940 Shinmachi; s/d without meals ¥5800/11600; ℗) Nakashimaya Ryokan is a delightfully well kept, compact and comfortable inn, with shared facilities. It's between the station and the Tourist Association. There's an organic cafe next door.

Yoshida-ya Ryokan & City Hotel RYOKAN ¥¥
(旅館吉田屋; www.yoshidayaryokan.com; 160 Tonomachi; Japanese r per person with 2 meals from ¥15,750; Western r without meals s/d ¥6825/12,600) By the bus terminal, this pleasant ryokan has both traditional Japanese (shared bathroom and toilet) and spacious Western-style rooms. It has an on-site restaurant.

ℹ Information

Tourist Association (観光協会; ☏67-0002; pupi@zd.wakwak.com; bike rental per hr/day ¥300/1500; ⏰8.30am-5pm) By the Shin-bashi bridge, pick up a walking map in English, or rent a bicycle. For guided tours in English, email Gujoinus in advance.

ℹ Getting There & Away

The most convenient access to Gujō-Hachiman is via bus from Gifu (¥1480, one hour). Be sure to get off at the Jōka-machi Plaza stop, which is not the end of the line. Nohi bus also operates services from Nagoya (¥2900, 2½ hours) and Takayama (¥1600, 1¼ hours).

The private Nagaragawa Tetsudō line serves Gujō-Hachiman from Mino-Ōta (¥1320, 80 minutes, hourly), with connections via the JR Takayama line to Nagoya (¥1110, one hour) and Takayama (tokkyū, ¥4180, 1¾ hours; futsū, ¥1890, three hours), but the station is located inconveniently away from sights.

HIDA DISTRICT 飛騨地域

Visitors flock to this ancient mountainous region for its onsen ryokan (traditional hotspring inn), the World Heritage villages of Ogimachi and Ainokura, and its centrepiece, Takayama, one of Japan's most likeable cities. Hida's signature architectural style is the thatch-roofed gasshō-zukuri, while its culinary fame rests in Hida-gyū (Hida beef), hoba-miso (sweet miso paste grilled at the table on a magnolia leaf) and soba.

Takayama 高山

☏0577 / POP 92,750

A working city that has retained its traditional charm, Takayama boasts one of Japan's most atmospheric townscapes and best-loved festivals. Its present layout dates from the late 17th century and includes a wealth of museums, galleries and temples for a city of this size.

Takayama should be considered a high priority on any visit to Central Honshū. Meiji-era inns, hillside shrines and temples, and a pretty riverside setting beckon you. Excellent infrastructure and friendly, welcoming locals seal the deal. Give yourself two or three days to enjoy it all, if you can. Takayama is easily explored on foot or by bicycle and is the perfect start or end point for trips into Hida and the Northern Japan Alps.

Almost all the main sights are clearly signposted in English and in walking distance of the station, which sits between the main streets of Kokubunji-dōri and Hirokōji-dōri. Both run east and cross the Miya-gawa where they become Yasugawa-dōri and Sanmachi-dōri, respectively. Once across the river (about 10 minutes' walk), you're in the middle of the infinitely photogenic Sanmachi-suji (district) of sake breweries, cafes, retailers and immaculately preserved old private houses (古い町並み; furui machinami).

◉ Sights & Activities

Morning Markets MARKET
(朝市; Asa-ichi; ⏰7am-noon Nov-Mar, 6am-noon Apr-Oct) Daily Asa-ichi (morning markets) are a wonderful way to start the day and meet the people. The **Jinya-mae Morning Market** (1-5 Hachiken-machi) is in front of Takayama-jinya; the larger **Miya-gawa Morning Market** (宮川朝市) runs along the east bank of the Miya-gawa, between Kaji-bashi and Yayoi-bashi. Stalls range from farm-fresh produce to local arts and crafts. Autumnal apples are out of this world.

Sanmachi-suji NEIGHBOURHOOD
(三町筋) This original district of three main streets (Ichino-machi, Nino-machi and San-no-machi) of merchants has been immaculately preserved. Sake breweries are designated by spheres of cedar fronds hanging above their doors; some open to the public in January and early February, but year-round, most just sell their brews. Day or night, photographic opportunities abound.

Fujii Folk Museum MUSEUM
(藤井美術民芸館; Fujii Bijutsu Mingeikan; 69 Kamisanno-machi; adult/child ¥700/350; ☉9am-5pm, often closed Tue-Fri early Dec-early Mar) A private collection in an old merchant's house, with folk craft and ceramics from the Muromachi and Edo periods.

Hida Folk
Archaeological Museum MUSEUM
(飛騨民族考古館; Hida Minzoku Kōkō-kan; 82 Kamisanno-machi; adult/child ¥500/200; ☉7am-5pm Mar-Nov, 9.30am-4pm Nov-Feb) A former samurai house boasting interesting secret passageways and an old well in the courtyard.

Yoshijima Heritage House HISTORIC BUILDING
(吉島家; Yoshijima-ke; 1-51 Ōjin-machi; adult/child ¥500/300; ☉9am-5pm Mar-Nov, to 4.30pm Wed-Sun Dec-Feb) Design buffs shouldn't miss Yoshijima-*ke*, which is well covered in architectural publications. Its lack of ornamentation allows you to focus on the spare lines, soaring roof and skylight. Admission includes a cup of delicious shiitake tea, which you can also purchase for ¥600 per can.

Takayama-jinya HISTORIC BUILDING
(高山陣屋; ☑32-0643; 1-5 Hachiken-machi; adult/child ¥420/free; ☉8.45am-4.30pm, to 6pm Aug) These sprawling grounds south of Sanmachi-suji house the only remaining prefectural office building of the Tokugawa shōgunate, originally the administrative centre for the Kanamori clan. The present main building dates back to 1816 and was used as local government offices until 1969. There's also a rice granary, garden and a tor-ture chamber with explanatory detail. Free guided tours in English are available (reservations advised).

Kusakabe Folk Crafts Museum MUSEUM
(日下部民藝館; Kusakabe Mingeikan; 1-52 Ōjin-machi; adult/child ¥500/300; ☉9am-4.30pm Mar-Nov, to 4pm Wed-Mon Dec-Feb) This building dating from the 1890s showcases the striking craftsmanship of traditional Takayama carpenters. Inside is a collection of folk art.

Takayama Festival
Floats Exhibition Hall MUSEUM
(高山屋台会館; Takayama Yatai-kaikan; 178 Sakura-machi; adult/child ¥820/410; ☉8.30am-5pm Mar-Nov, 9am-4.30pm Dec-Feb) A rotating selection of four of the 23 multi-tiered *yatai* (floats) used in the Takayama Matsuri can be seen here. These spectacular creations, some from the 17th century, are prized for their flamboyant carvings, metalwork and lacquerwork. Some feature *karakuri ningyō* that perform courtesy of eight accomplished puppeteers manipulating 36 strings. The museum is on the grounds of the stately **Sakurayama Hachiman-gū** shrine, which presides over the festival and is dedicated to the protection of Takayama.

Karakuri Museum MUSEUM
((飛騨高山獅子会館)からくりミュージアム; ☑32-0881; 53-1 Sakura-machi; adult/child ¥600/400; ☉9am-4.30pm) On display are over 800 *shishi* (lion) masks, instruments and drums related to festival dances. The main draw are the twice-hourly puppet shows where you can see the mechanical *karakuri ningyō* in action.

GASSHŌ-ZUKURI ARCHITECTURE

Hida winters are unforgiving. Inhabitants braved the elements long before the advent of propane heaters and 4WD vehicles. The most visible symbol of their adaptability is *gasshō-zukuri* architecture; steeply slanted straw-roofed homes that dot the regional landscape.

Sharply angled roofs prevent snow accumulation, a serious concern in an area where most mountain roads close from December to April. The name *gasshō* comes from the Japanese word for prayer, because the shape of the roofs was thought to resemble hands clasped together. *Gasshō* buildings often featured pillars crafted from stout cedars to lend extra support. The attic areas were ideal for silk cultivation. Larger *gasshō-zukuri* buildings were inhabited by wealthy families, with up to 30 people under one roof. Peasant families lived in huts so small that today they'd only be considered fit for toolsheds.

The art of *gasshō-zukuri* construction is dying out. Most remaining examples have been relocated to folk villages, including Hida-no-Sato, Ogimachi, Suganuma and Ainokura. Homes that are now neighbours may once have been separated by several days of travel on foot or sled. These cultural preservation efforts have made it possible to imagine a bygone life in the Hida hills.

Takayama

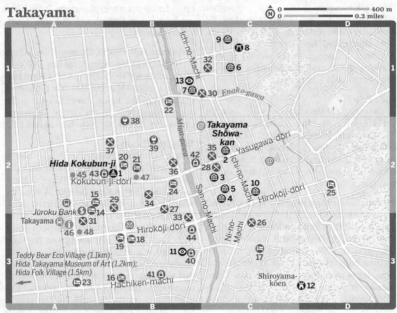

⭐ **Hida Kokubun-ji** BUDDHIST TEMPLE
(飛騨国分寺; 1-83 Sōwa-chō; treasure hall adult/
child ¥300/250; ⊙9am-4pm) The original
buildings of this, Takayama's oldest temple, were constructed in the 8th century,
but later destroyed by fire. The oldest of
the present buildings dates from the 16th
century. The temple's treasure hall houses
some Important Cultural Properties, and the
courtyard boasts a three-storey pagoda and
an impressively gnarled gingko tree believed
to be 1200 years old.

⭐ **Takayama Shōwa-kan** MUSEUM
(高山昭和館; 6 Shimoichino-machi; adult/child
¥500/300; ⊙9am-5pm) We love this nostalgia
bonanza from the Shōwa era (1926–1989),
concentrating on the period between 1955
and 1965, a time of great optimism between
Japan's postwar malaise and pre-Titan
boom. Lose yourself among the delightful
mishmash of endless objects, from movie
posters to cars and everything between,
haphazardly arranged in a series of themed
rooms.

Teramachi & Shiroyama-kōen NEIGHBOURHOOD
(寺町・城山公園) These lovely, hilly districts
to the east are linked by a well-signposted
walking path. Teramachi has over a dozen

temples and shrines you can wander around
before taking in the greenery of Shiroyama-
kōen. Various trails lead through the park
and up the mountainside to the ruins of the
castle, **Takayama-jō** (高山城跡).

Takayama Museum of History & Art MUSEUM
(飛騨高山まちの博物館; Hida-Takayama Machi
no Hakubutsukan; ☑32-1205; 75 Kamiichino-
machi; ⊙museum 9am-7pm, garden 7am-9pm)
FREE Not to be confused with the Hida
Takayama Museum of Art, this free museum
is situated around pretty gardens and features 14 themed exhibition rooms relating
to local history, culture, literature and the
arts.

Hirata Folk Art Museum MUSEUM
(平田記念館; Hirata Kinenkan; ☑33-1354; 39
Kaminino-machi; ⊙9am-5pm) Hirata Folk Art
Museum dates from the turn of the 20th
century and displays items from everyday
rural Japanese life.

Hida Takayama Museum of Art MUSEUM
(飛騨高山美術館; Hida Takayama Bijutsukan;
☑35-3535; 1-124-1 Kamiokamoto-cho; adult/child
¥1300/800; ⊙9am-5pm) Set back from town,
lovers of art nouveau and art deco glassware
and furniture will appreciate this large pri-

Takayama

vate gallery with a ritzy cafe, its own London Bus shuttle (ask at the Tourist Information Office) and a spectacular glass fountain by Ren Lalique.

Teddy Bear Eco Village　　　　GALLERY
(飛騨高山テディベアエコビレッジ; ☎37-3525; 3-829-4 Nishinoishiki-machi; adult/child ¥600/400; ◷10am-4pm) You'll know if you're one of *those* people who *have* to see this collection of over 1000 little fluffy guys from around the world, some over 140 years old, housed in a building just a little bit older. The annexed cafe is a lovely spot to enjoy a healthy something in the outdoors. Ask for directions at the Tourist Information Office.

Hida Folk Village　　　　HISTORIC BUILDING
(飛騨の里　Hida-no-sato; www.hidanosato-tpo. jp/english12.htm; 1-590 Kamiokamoto-chō; adult/child ¥700/200; ◷8.30am-5pm) The sprawling, open-air Hida-no-Sato is a highly recommended half-day trip. It features dozens of traditional houses and buildings, which were dismantled at their original sites throughout the region and rebuilt here. Well-presented displays offer the opportunity to envision rural life in previous centuries. During clear weather, there are good views of the Japan Alps. To get here, hire a bicycle, or catch a bus from Takayama bus station (¥200, 10 minutes). The *Hida-no-Sato setto ken* ticket combines return fare and admission to the park for ¥900. Be sure to check return times for the bus.

🛏 Sleeping

One of Takayama's pleasures is its variety of high-quality accommodation, both Japanese and Western, for all budgets. If visiting during festival times, book accommodation months in advance and expect to pay a 20% premium. The **Ryokan Hotel Association** (www.takayamaryokan.jp/english) can further assist with lodging enquiries.

TAKAYAMA MATSURI

One of Japan's great festivals, the **Takayama Matsuri** is in two parts. On 14 and 15 April is the Sannō Matsuri; a dozen *yatai* (floats), decorated with carvings, dolls, colourful curtains and blinds, are paraded through the town. In the evening the floats are decked out with lanterns and the procession is accompanied by sacred music. Hachiman Matsuri, on 9 and 10 October, is a slightly smaller version. Book accommodation months in advance.

Guesthouse Tomaru   GUESTHOUSE ¥

(飛騨高山ゲストハウスとまる; www.hidatakayama-guesthouse.com; 6-5 Hanasato-machi; dm/s/d & tr per person ¥2500/6000/3000; @ 🛜) Visitors love the friendly homestay vibe of this small, centrally located guesthouse. Pleasant rooms with homely touches are kept spotlessly clean. There's free wi-fi and a shared kitchen.

**Hida Takayama
Temple Inn Zenkō-ji**   HOSTEL ¥

(飛騨高山善光寺宿坊; ☎ 32-8470; www.takayamahostelzenkoji.com; 4-3 Tenman-chō; dm/s per person ¥2500/3000; P 🚌 🛜) Good karma washes over this branch of Nagano's famous Zenkō-ji temple, where donations are accepted in return for accommodation. Private rooms are generously proportioned around a courtyard garden. Even the dorms have temple-charm. There's a shared kitchen and no curfew for respectful guests.

K's House Takayama   HOSTEL ¥

(☎ 34-4410; www.kshouse.jp/takayama-e; 4-45-1 Tenman-cho; dm/s/d/tr per person from ¥2800/4500/3900/3600; 🛜) Opened in October 2012, this sparkly hostel is likely to cause a stir on the Takayama hostel scene. All rooms, including dorms, have private bathroom, TV and wi-fi. It has a kitchen and common area, and bicycle rentals are available.

J-Hoppers   HOSTEL ¥

(ジェイホッパーズ飛騨高山ゲストハウス; ☎ 32-3278; www.takayama.j-hoppers.com; 5-52 Nada-machi; dm/s/d-tw-tr per person from ¥2500/3500/3000; 🛜) A convenient location, large dorm beds, Japanese-style private rooms and outgoing, active staff (who can assist with local tours and activities) make this social hostel a good budget option. For families, there are also quad private rooms with bunkbeds.

★ Rickshaw Inn   HOTEL ¥

(力車イン; ☎ 32-2890; www.rickshawinn.com; 54 Suehiro-chō; s without bathroom from ¥4900, tw with/without bathroom from ¥11,900/10,200; 🚌 @) Well positioned on the fringe of Takayama's entertainment district, this travellers' favourite is great value. There's a range of room types, a small kitchen, laundry facilities and a cosy lounge. Friendly English-speaking owners are founts of information about Takayama.

Minshuku Kuwataniya   MINSHUKU ¥

(民宿桑谷屋; ☎ 32-5021; www.kuwataniya.com; 1-50-30 Sowa-machi; r per person with/without bathroom ¥6450/4350; P @) Takayama's longest-running *minshuku* (Japanese guesthouse) has both Japanese- and Western-style rooms, onsen baths and free bicycles. It offers meals featuring Hida's famed beef, as well as vegetarian options. The location is a little dull.

★ Yamakyū   RYOKAN ¥¥

(山久; ☎ 32-3756; www.takayama-yamakyu.com; 58 Tenshōji-machi; r with/without meals ¥7980/5880; P @ 🛜) Occupying a lovely hillside spot opposite Hokke-ji temple, Yamakyū is a 20-minute walk from the station. Inside, antique-filled curio cabinets, clocks and lamps line the red-carpeted corridors. All 20 tatami rooms have a sink and toilet and the common bathrooms are of a high standard. Some English is spoken. This is an excellent choice for a ryokan experience without the expense.

★ Takayama Ouan   HOTEL ¥¥

(高山桜庵; ☎ 37-2230; www.hotespa.net/hotels/takayama; 4-126 Hanasato; s/d from ¥9000/20,000; P @) Although the popularity of this hulking recent addition to the Takayama hotel scene is evident in wear and tear, we love how east meets west and new meets old here. Reasonable rates are appropriate for well-proportioned, Western-style rooms with big comfortable beds and traditional design elements; dark woods, tatami and moody lighting set the scene. The rooftop *rotemburo*, including free private *kazoku-buro* (family baths), will make your friends jealous. The hotel has a lot of tatami, so you'll be leaving your shoes in a locked box in the lobby. As you leave the station, look to your right – it's the tallest building in sight.

★**Tanabe Ryokan**   RYOKAN ¥¥

(旅館田邊; ☑ 32-0529; www.tanabe-ryokan.jp; 58 Aioi-chō; r per person with 2 meals from ¥12,600; ❀@) This elegant, atmospheric inn has a premium, central location and friendly, welcoming staff who speak some English. Tatami rooms are stylish and spacious – each has an en-suite bath, although the lovely common baths with their beamed ceilings are worth enjoying. A sumptuous dinner of *kaiseki* (Japanese haute cuisine)-style Hida cuisine completes the experience.

Sumiyoshi Ryokan   RYOKAN ¥¥

(寿美吉旅館; ☑ 32-0228; www.sumiyoshi-ryokan. com; 4-21 Hon-machi; r per person with/without meals from ¥10,500/6300; Ⓟ @) The kind owners of this delightfully antique-y inn, set in a Meiji-era merchant's house, have been welcoming guests from abroad for years. Some rooms have river views through panes of antique glass, and the common baths are made of wood and slate tiles. One room has a private bath.

Spa Hotel Alpina   HOTEL ¥¥

(スパホテルアルピナ; ☑ 33-0033; www. spa-hotel-alpina.com; 5-41 Nada-chō; s/tw from ¥7200/13,000; Ⓟ❀@) This glorified business hotel has a slightly clinical feel for a 'spa hotel', but offers comfortable beds, bright rooms and a fantastic rooftop onsen with views across the city. Discounted rates can be secured online.

Best Western Hotel   HOTEL ¥¥

(ベストウェスタンホテル高山; ☑ 37-2000; www.bestwestern.co.jp; 6-6 Hanasato-machi; s/d/ tw from ¥7000/11,000/13,000; ❀⊗) Popular with overseas guests, this tourist hotel's refurbished rooms have a splash of colour. Good-value rates can be found online and usually include the decent breakfast buffet.

Hōshōkaku   RYOKAN ¥¥¥

(宝生閣; ☑ 34-0700; www.hoshokaku.co.jp; 1-88 Baba-machi; r per person with 2 meals from ¥15,750; Ⓟ) Surrounded by the greenery of Shiroyama-kōen, this upscale hillside ryokan on the edge of town has outdoor hot springs with city views and sumptuous *kaiseki* cuisine. It's easiest to grab a taxi when you arrive.

✕ **Eating**

Takayama's specialities include *soba, hoba-miso, sansai* (mountain vegetables) and *Hida-gyū*. Street foods include *mitarashi-dango* (skewers of grilled riceballs seasoned

with soy sauce) and *shio-sembei* (salty rice crackers). *Hida-gyū* turns up on *kushi-yaki* (skewers), in *korokke* (croquettes) and *niku-man* (steamed buns). If you're on a budget, keep an eye out for the numerous bakeries around town where you can stock up on delicious, inexpensive fresh breads and sandwiches.

★**Chapala**   MEXICAN ¥

(チャパラ; ☑ 34-9800; 1 Hanakawa-chō; mains ¥600-980; ⊗dinner Mon-Sat, closed 1st Mon of each month; Ⓘ) The enthusiastic, local owner of this friendly restaurant does a great job bringing the flavours of Mexico to a quiet Japanese street. The taste and dainty portions of tacos, quesadillas and guac' and chips won't match California or Guadalajara, but the place is adorable and patrons love it. Where else can you eat tacos with chopsticks while swilling Coronas and sake?

★**Center4 Hamburgers**   BURGERS ¥

(☑ 36-4527; www.tiger-center4.com; 94 Kamiichi-no-machi; ⊗11.00am-9.30pm; Ⓘ) This young Japanese couple are livin' their dream, welcoming visitors from around the world. Delicious comfort food is prepared with love – juicy homestyle burgers, including veggie, club sandwiches, chilli and clam chowder – served in a retro dining room that feels like the extension of someone's home. If you can, top it off with a world beer, a decent red or a milkshake and you'll be too full and floaty to waste time feeling guilty about taking a break from *soba*. It's tucked away behind Agariya Antiques.

Rakuda   CAFE ¥

(らくだ; ☑ 34-5574; 1-94 Ōjin-machi; lunch from ¥850; ⊗10am-6pm Wed-Mon; Ⓘ) As laid-back as its namesake ('camel'), comfy and sunny Rakuda has curry lunches, open sandwiches topped with omelette and veggies, and daily homemade cakes. It's in a small square beside a mini parking lot.

Ebisu-Honten   NOODLES ¥

(恵比寿本店; ☑ 32-0209; 46 Kami-Ni-no-machi; soba dishes ¥830-1530; ⊗10am-5pm Thu-Tue; ☑) This Sanmachi shop has been making *teuchi* (handmade) *soba* since 1898. The menu explains the *soba*-making process. Try cold *zaru soba* (¥830) for the real flavour of the buckwheat, or delicious tempura *soba* (¥1350). It has an interesting red-glass sign with white characters and a little roof on it.

★**Kotarō** TONKATSU ¥¥

(小太郎; ☑32-7353; 6-1 Tenmanmachi; meals ¥1050-2100; ⏰11.30am-2pm & 5-9pm Thu-Tue; 📖) Expect satisfaction from this compact workmanlike eatery whose chef has spent over 25 years mastering the art of *tonkatsu* and other fried goodies. Generous *teishoku* (from ¥1050) feature crispy, crunchy katsu, cooked to perfection, accompanied by perfectly balanced sides; fluffy rice, rich miso soup, fruit, salad and pickles. Try the cheese katsu (¥1350) for something different.

Kyōya SHOKUDŌ ¥¥

(京や; ☑34-7660; 1-77 Ōjin-machi; mains ¥600-5000; ⏰11am-10pm Wed-Mon; 📖) This traditional eatery specialises in regional dishes such as *hoba-miso* and *Hida-gyū soba*. Seating is on tatami mats around long charcoal grills, under a cathedral ceiling supported by dark timbers. It's on a corner, by a bridge over the canal. Look for the sacks of rice over the door.

Suzuya SHOKUDŌ ¥¥

(寿々や; ☑32-2484; 24 Hanakawa-chō; sets ¥1155-4200; ⏰11am-3pm & 5-9pm Wed-Mon; 🌱📖) In the centre of town, Suzuya is one of Takayama's longstanding favourites, serving local specialities such as *Hida-gyū*, *hoba-miso* and various stews. There's plenty of signage to direct you.

Takumi-ya BEEF ¥¥

(匠家; ☑36-2989; 2 Shimo-Ni-no-Machi; mains downstairs ¥680-980, upstairs from ¥1500; ⏰11am-3pm & 5-9pm Thu-Tue; 📖) Hida beef on a burger budget. Adjacent to Takumi-ya's butcher shop is a casual restaurant specialising in *rāmen* in Hida-beef broth and Hida *gyū-don* (beef and onion over rice). The pricier upstairs restaurant serves *yakiniku* (Korean-style barbecue).

Myōgaya VEGAN ¥¥

(茗荷舎; ☑32-0426; 5-15 Hanasato-chō; mains around ¥1000; ⏰lunch Wed-Sun; 🌱📖) Healthy and delicious go hand in hand at this cosy vegan eatery, a block east of the train station. Look for tasty veggie curry with brown rice, samosas, juices and dandelion tea. Reservations requested on Saturdays.

Yamatake-Shōten SHOKUDŌ ¥¥

(山武商店; ☑32-0571; www.hida-yamatake.jp; 1-70 Sōwa-chō; meals per person from around ¥3500; ⏰lunch & dinner Thu-Tue) This butchery

with upstairs restaurant is a unique, though not uncomplicated place to sample Hida-*gyū* at retail prices. You choose your own cut of meat, sold by weight (per 100g) which is plated and brought to the table for you to cook on an inset charcoal grill. Vegetables and simple desserts are included. Check the website for the lowdown. There's a ¥420 seating charge.

Tenaga Ashinaga SHOKUDŌ ¥¥

(てながあしなが; ☑34-5855; 3-58-11 Hon-machi; small plates from ¥180, meals ¥650-3450; ⏰lunch & dinner; 📖) If you're looking for a tasty, uncomplicated meal, this large, well-positioned eatery, near Kaji-bashi, is a good choice. A diverse English and Japanese photo menu has most of your favourites, such as *udon*, *rāmen* and *donburi*, as well as gristlier, meatier choices. The location attracts many foreign clientele whose smiling faces line the photo wall outside.

★**Restaurant Le Midi** FRENCH ¥¥¥

(☑36-6386; www.le-midi.jp/english; 2-85 Hon-machi; appetisers ¥650-3400; Hida beef dishes ¥2400-7500; ⏰11.30am-2pm & 6-9pm Fri-Wed; 📖) One street back from the river, this upscale restaurant serves traditional French cuisine with a Japanese twist. Mouthwatering appetisers include Hida beef carpaccio and onion gratin soup. Lunch sets range from ¥1800 to ¥4800 and course dinners including hors d'oeuvres, mains, soup, salad and coffee start at ¥4800. For dessert, the local *sukune kabocha* (pumpkin) pudding is a must. If you're feeling French and fancy, you're unlikely to be disappointed.

🍷 Drinking

Once you've had a wonderful day in the sun, you might feel like carrying on into the night. Unfortunately, Takayama disappoints a little in this regard. Asahi-machi, north of Kokubun-ji-dōri and west of the Miya-gawa, is Takayama's sprawly bar district, but don't expect too much.

★**Red Hill Pub** PUB

(レッド・ヒル; ☑33-8139; 2-4 Sowa-chō; ⏰7pm-midnight; 🎤) You'll feel like you're walking into a friend's living room in this cosy, dimly lit basement bar. The hip and happy owner, Hisayo, deftly adjusts the vibe to suit the patrons who present. It's sometimes soulful and smooth, sometimes rocking and raucous. If it's quiet and you're alone, you'll still have someone fascinating to talk to – Hisayo speaks excellent English. She also prepares tasty snacks and offers an excellent selection of brews and killer cocktails.

Desolation Row
BAR

(☎ (090) 8077-5966; 30 Asahi-machi; ⏰ 8pm-late) If you're a fan of Bob Dylan, you'll likely connect with the owner of this mellow bar with a real rustic charm. He doesn't speak much English, but music transcends language, after all. As does whisky... and beer. Look for the galvanised iron front and the big blue door.

Rum Dance Hall
BAR

(☎ 36-1682; 29 Asahi-machi; cover charge ¥300; ⏰ 7pm-late Mon-Sat) This stylish bar appeals to a cool, older crowd. There's a plethora of cocktails on the menu and the English-speaking owner spins jazz, blues and soul in crystal stereo. It's a concrete building with a staircase and glass wall in the middle.

🛍 Shopping

Takayama is renowned for arts and crafts. Look for *ichii ittobori* (woodcarvings), *shunkei* lacquerware, and the rustic *yama-da-yaki* and decorative *shibukusa-yaki* styles of pottery. Between Sanmachi-dōri and Yasugawa-dōri, near the Takayama Museum of History & Art, are plenty of wonderful antique (古物; *kobutsu*) shops. With patience and smarts you can find some excellent deals. Seking them out is half the fun.

Takayama's most ubiquitous souvenirs are *saru-bobo* (monkey babies); little red dolls with pointy limbs and featureless faces, recalling the days when grandmothers fashioned dolls for children out of whatever materials were available.

Suzuki Chōkoku
ARTS & CRAFTS

(鈴木彫刻; ☎ 32-1367; 1-2 Hatsuda-machi; ⏰ 9am-7pm Wed-Mon) Helmed by the one-time head of the local *ittobori* association, here you'll find figurines from ¥750 to *how much?*

Washi no Yamazaki
ARTS & CRAFTS

(和紙の山崎; ☎ 32-4132; 1-22 Honmachi; ⏰ 9am-5pm) We can't keep this wonderful family-run *washi* (handmade Japanese paper) store a secret any longer.

LOTUS BLUE
ARTS & CRAFTS

(☎ 62-9611; 2-70 Hachiken-machi; ⏰ 10am-4pm) This chic boutique has design smarts and style, featuring some fantastic plastic from the '50s and '60s. Sometimes exhibitions are held upstairs.

ℹ Information

Jūroku Bank (十六銀行) Can change cash or travellers cheques.

Takayama Post Office (高山郵便局; ☎ 32-0540; 5-95-1 Nada-machi) Has an ATM; a few blocks east of the station.

Tourist Information Office (飛騨高山観光案内所; ☎ 32-5328; www.hida.jp/english; ⏰ 8.30am-5pm Nov-Mar, to 6.30pm Apr-Oct) Directly in front of JR Takayama Station, knowledgeable English-speaking staff dispense English-language maps and a wealth of pamphlets on sights, accommodation, special events and regional transit. Staff are unable to assist with accommodation reservations.

Hida-chi Cafe (ひだっちカフェ; ☎ 57-8831; 79-2 Kamisanno-machi; ⏰ 11am-5pm) This cafe has wi-fi and internet facilities, inexpensive meals and dispenses English-language maps and information.

City Library (高山市図書館; ⏰ 9.30am-9.30pm) Internet access, east of Sanmachi-suji.

Kinki Nippon Tourist (☎ 32-6901; 1-17 Hanaoka-machi; ⏰ 9.15am-6pm Mon-Fri) This travel agency can make limited bus, train, hotel and tour reservations within Japan.

ℹ Getting There & Away

From Tokyo or Kansai, the most efficient way to reach Takayama is via Nagoya on the JR Takayama line (Hida *tokkyū*, ¥5360, 2¼ hours); the mountainous train ride along the Hida-gawa is *gorge*-ous. Some trains continue on to Toyama (¥2770, 90 minutes), where you can connect to Kanazawa (¥2100, 40 minutes).

Nōhi Bus (濃飛バス; ☎ 32-1688; www.nouhibus.co.jp/english) Operates highway bus services between Takayama and Tokyo's Shinjuku Station (¥6500, 5½ hours, several daily, reservations required) and Matsumoto (¥3100, 2½ hours). Takayama's bus station is adjacent to the train station. Schedules vary seasonally and some routes don't run at all during winter, when many roads are closed.

Toyota Rent-a-Car (トヨタレンタカー; ☎ 36-6110) Opposite the station, to the right.

ℹ Getting Around

Most sights in Takayama can be covered easily on foot. You can amble from the train station to Teramachi in about 20 minutes. Takayama is bicycle-friendly. Some lodgings lend bikes, or you can hire one from **Hara Cycle** (ハラサイクル; ☎ 32-1657; 61 Suehiro-cho; the first hour ¥300, each additional hour ¥200; per day ¥1300; ⏰ 9am-8pm Wed-Mon).

Hida-Furukawa 飛騨古川

📞 0577 / POP 26,000

Just 15 minutes by train from Takayama, Hida-Furukawa is a relaxing riverside town with an ageing population. Photogenic streetscapes, peaceful temples and interesting museums are framed by the Hida mountains. Each April, the town comes to life for the Hida Furukawa Matsuri.

👁 Sights & Activities

Seto-kawa and
Shirakabe-dōzō   HISTORIC DISTRICT

(瀬戸川と白壁土蔵街) You'll find this lovely historic canal district five minutes' walk from JR Hida-Furukawa station, boasting whitewalled shops, storehouses, private homes and carp-filled waterways. Across the canal, Ichino-machi street is sprinkled with woodworking shops, sake breweries (marked by spheres of cedar fronds above the entrance) and traditional storehouses. At its western extent, riverside **Honkō-ji** (本光寺) is Hida's largest wooden temple, showcasing the fine craftsmanship of Furukawa's carpenters. Originally established in 1532, current buildings date from 1913 following a fire that destroyed 90% of the town.

Hida Furukawa Matsuri Kaikan   MUSEUM

(飛騨古川まつり会館; 14-15 Ichinomachi; adult/child ¥800/400; ⊙9am-5pm Mar-Nov, to 4.30pm Dec-Feb) Observe Furukawa's famous festival year-round in this canal-district museum. There's a 3D video of the festivities (with English narration), three of the massive *yatai* that are paraded through the streets, and a *karakuri ningyō* show. You can also try your hand at manipulating the puppets and watch craftsmen demonstrating *kirie* (paper cut-outs) or *ittobori*. Festival drums can be seen to the left as you exit the exhibition hall.

Carpentry Museum   MUSEUM

(匠文化館 Takumi Bunkakan; 10-1 Ichinomachi; adult/child ¥300/100; ⊙9am-5pm, to 4.30pm winter Fri-Wed) Across from Hida Furukawa Matsuri Kaikan, this museum, dedicated to the history of Japanese carpentry and its unique methods, is a must for woodworkers and design fans. In a hands-on room, you can try assembling blocks of wood cut into different joint patterns – not as easy as it sounds.

★ Hida Satoyama Cycling   CYCLING

(飛騨里山サイクリング; 📞73-5715; www.satoyama-cycling.com; 8-8 Furukawa-chō Nino-machi; half-day tour ¥4500, standard tour ¥7000; ⊙9am-6pm Fri-Wed) The fantastic crew at Satoyama Cycling love what they do and do it with excellence. Small group tours are a fun way to meet the locals and experience the sights. They include a friendly, professional, English speaking guide, mountain-bike rental and insurance. Various tours cater to different levels of fitness. All capture the spirit and scenery of this working rural town. A one-stop-shop for all things Hida, the team can also connect you with some unique, traditional accommodation (for longer stays) in town and around – just ask. Highly recommended.

🎊 Festivals & Events

Furukawa Matsuri   PARADE

(古川祭り) Furukawa Matsuri – informally known as Hadaka Matsuri (Naked Festival) – takes place every 19 and 20 April with parades of *yatai*. The highlight is an event known as Okoshi Daiko in which, on the night of the 19th, squads of boisterous young men dressed in *fundoshi* (loincloths) and fuelled by sake, parade through town, competing to place small drums atop a stage bearing a giant drum. OK, it's not *naked*-naked, but we didn't make up the name.

Kitsune Himatsuri   PARADE

(きつね火祭り) During the 'Fox Fire Festival' on the fourth Saturday in September, locals dress up as foxes, parade through the town by lantern light and enact a wedding at Okura Inari-jinja. The ceremony, deemed to bring good fortune, climaxes with a bonfire.

🛏 Sleeping & Eating

Hida Tomoe Hotel   HOTEL ¥¥

(飛騨ともえホテル; 📞73-2056; www.tomoe-jp.com; 10-27 Kanamori-cho; r per person with/without meals from ¥10,290/5250; @) This attractive business hotel by the station with Western- and Japanese-style rooms, most with bath and toilet, also has a pretty common bath. Including meals means farm-fresh local *kaiseki* cuisine by the *irori* (open hearth).

Ichino-machi Cafe   CAFE ¥

(壱之町珈琲店; 📞73-7099; 1-12 Ichino-machi; ⊙11am-5pm Wed-Mon; 🛜) Chiffon cake, melon bread and local Hida-beef curry are all items you might find on the menu at this handsome cafe within a restored traditional *machi-ya* (merchant house). Free wi-fi is a bonus.

ℹ️ Information

Hida-Furukawa train and bus stations adjoin each other east of the town centre. Sights are within 10 minutes' walk. There's a **Tourist Information Office** (観光案内所; ☑73-3180; ⊘8.30am-5pm) at the bus station, with some English maps and leaflets, though little English is spoken.

ℹ️ Getting There & Around

Trains run frequently between Takayama and Hida-Furukawa, three stops north of Takayama (*futsū*, ¥230, 15 minutes). Central Furukawa is an easy stroll, or hire a bike at the taxi office **Miyagawa** (☑73-2321; per hr ¥200), near the station. Staff here can also store your luggage for ¥200 per day.

Shirakawa-gō & Gokayama 白川郷・五箇山

These remote, mountainous districts between Takayama and Kanazawa are best known for farmhouses in the thatched *gasshō-zukuri* style. They're rustic and lovely; against the vibrant colours of spring, draped with the gentle mists of autumn, or peeking through a carpet of snow, they hold a special place in the Japanese heart. For more information, see the boxed text p219.

In the 12th century, the region's isolation is said to have attracted survivors from the Taira (Heike) clan which was virtually wiped out by the Minamoto (Genji) clan in a brutal battle in 1185. During feudal times, Shirakawa-gō, like the rest of Hida, was under direct control of the Kanamori clan, connected to the Tokugawa shōgun, while Gokayama was a centre for the production of gunpowder for the Kaga region, under the ruling Maeda clan.

Fast-forward to the 1960s, when construction of the gigantic Miboro Dam over the Shōkawa river was to submerge entire villages. Many *gasshō* houses were relocated to their current sites. Although primarily preserved for tourism, these working villages still present a view of rural life found in few other parts of Japan.

Most of Shirakawa-gō's sights are in the heavily visited village of Ogimachi, linked by expressway to Takayama. The less-crowded, more isolated villages of Suganuma and Ainokura, in the Gokayama district of Toyama Prefecture, have the most ambience; other sights are spread over many kilometres along Rte 156. All three villages are Unesco World Heritage Sites.

Passionate debate continues around the impact tour buses have upon these unique communities, and how best to mitigate disruption to daily life. It's a case of not biting the hand which feeds you.

To avoid the crowds, steer clear of weekends, holidays, and cherry-blossom and autumn-foliage seasons. To best appreciate life here, stay overnight in a *gasshō-zukuri* inn. Accomodation is basic and advance reservations are recommended.

Ogimachi 荻町

☑05769

The Shirakawa-gō region's central settlement has some 600 residents and the largest concentration of *gasshō-zukuri* buildings – over 110. It's also the most accessible. Pick up a free English-language map at the **Tourist Information Office** (観光案内所; ☑6-1013; 2495-3 Ogimachi; ⊘9am-5pm), by the main bus stop outside the Folk Village. Be sure to bring enough cash – there are no ATMs and credit cards are not accepted.

👁 Sights & Activities

On the site of the former castle, **Shiroyama Tenbōdai** (Observation Point) provides a lovely overview of the valley. It's a 15-minute walk via the road behind the east side of town. You can climb the path (five minutes) from near the intersection of Rtes 156 and 360, or there's a shuttle bus (¥200 one-way) from the Shirakawa-gō bus stop.

Shirakawa-gō's big festival is held on 14 and 15 October at **Shirakawa Hachimanjinja** (other festivals continue until the 19th), and features groups of dancing locals, taking part in the lion dance and *niwaka* (improvised buffoonery). The star is *doburoku*, a very potent unrefined sake.

Gasshō-zukuri Folk Village   MUSEUM
(合掌造り民家園; Gasshō-zukuri Minka-en; ☑6-1231; 2499 Ogimachi; adult/child ¥500/300; ⊘8.40am-5pm Apr-Nov, 9am-6pm Fri-Wed Dec-Mar) Over two dozen *gasshō-zukuri* buildings have been relocated here, although the arrangement feels contrived. Several houses are used for demonstrating regional crafts such as woodwork, straw handicrafts and ceramics (in Japanese only, reservations required); many items are for sale. You're free to wander the grounds for a picnic, but be sure to carry your rubbish out of town.

Wada-ke
HISTORIC BUILDING

(和田家; adult/child ¥300/150; ⊙9am-5pm)
Shirakawa-gō's largest *gasshō* house is a designated National Treasure. It once belonged to a wealthy silk-trading family and dates back to the mid–Edo period. Upstairs are silk-harvesting equipment and a valuable lacquerware collection.

Kanda-ke
HISTORIC BUILDING

(神田家; adult/child ¥300/150; ⊙9am-5pm) Of the other open *gasshō* houses, Kanda-ke is the least cluttered with exhibits, leaving you to appreciate the architectural details – enjoy a cup of tea in the massive 36-tatami room on the ground floor.

Nagase-ke
HISTORIC BUILDING

(長瀬家; adult/child ¥300/150; ⊙9am-5pm)
This former home of the doctors to the Maeda clan has exhibits of herbal medicine. The *butsudan* (Buddhist altar) dates from the Muromachi period. In the attic, you can get an up-close look at the construction of the roof, which took 530 people to re-thatch.

Myōzen-ji Folk Museum
MUSEUM

(明善寺郷土館; adult/child ¥300/150; ⊙8.30am-5pm Apr-Nov, 9am-4pm Dec-Mar) Adjacent to Myōzen-ji, Ogimachi's small temple, Myōzen-ji Folk Museum displays the traditional paraphernalia of daily rural life.

Shirakawa-gō-no-Yu
ONSEN

(白川郷の湯; adult/child ¥700/300; ⊙10am-9.30pm) In central Ogimachi, Shirakawa-gō-no-Yu boasts a sauna, small *rotemburo* and large bath. Visitors staying at lodgings in town get a ¥200 discount.

Shiramizu-no-Yu
ONSEN

(しらみずの湯; ☑5-4126; 247-7 Hirase; adult/child ¥600/400; ⊙10am-9pm Thu-Tue) About 12km south of Ogimachi, off Rte 156 in Hirase Onsen, Shiramizu-no-Yu is a new onsen facility with views across the river valley, a treat during autumn. Its waters are said to be beneficial for fertility.

Ōshirakawa Rotemburo
ONSEN

(大白川露天風呂; ☑6-1311; admission ¥300; ⊙8.30am-5pm mid-Jun–Oct, to 6pm Jul & Aug) This tiny middle-of-nowhere onsen is 40km from Ogimachi, along a mountainous windy road with blind curves, impassible much of the year. There's no public transport, which is part of the charm, as are the views of Lake Shiramizu. Getting there from Ogimachi takes at least 90 minutes and requires determination and a car, or a taxi and lots of cash.

🍴 Sleeping & Eating

For online reservations at one of Ogimachi's many *gasshō* inns, try www.japaneseguesthouses.com/db/shirakawago. Rates include two meals. Expect a nightly heating surcharge (¥400 and up) during cold weather.

★ Magoemon
INN ¥¥

(孫右エ門; ☑6-1167; 360 Ogimachi; r per person Apr-Sep ¥9800, Oct-Mar ¥10,500; ℗) For an authentic and atmospheric retreat, this building is 300 years old and oozes history and charm. The friendly family owners speak no English and appreciate your efforts to communicate in Japanese. Meals are served around the handsome *irori*. Three of the six large rooms (shared facilities) face the river.

Kōemon
INN ¥¥

(幸エ門; ☑6-1446; 546 Ogimachi; r per person ¥8400; ℗) In the centre of Ogimachi, Kōemon has five rooms with heated floors, dark-wood panelling and shared bathrooms. The fifth-generation owner speaks English well and his love of Shirakawa-gō is infectious.

Shimizu
INN ¥¥

(民宿志みづ; ☑6-1914; www.shimizuinn.com; 2613 Ogimachi; r per person ¥8400; ℗) This homestyle inn at the southern end of town enjoys a picturesque outlook. There are three small guestrooms and a common bath. The building is over 200 years old.

Toyota Shirakawa-gō Eco-Institute
HOTEL ¥¥

(トヨタ白川郷自然学校; ☑6-1187; www.toyota.eco-inst.jp; 223 Magari; d per person from ¥12,200; ℗) 🖉 Ten minutes' drive from Ogimachi, this eco-lodge caters heavily to groups, but welcomes individual travellers. Countless activities and tours are available and sumptuous French cuisine is served. Varying rates reflect the variety of room types.

Ochūdo
CAFE ¥

(落人; ☑090-5458-0418; 792 Ogimachi; lunch ¥1000; ⊙10.30am-5pm; 🖬) Set around a large *irori* in a 350-year-old *gasshō* house, this delightful cafe serves curry rice, tea and coffee.

Irori
SHOKUDŌ ¥

(いろり; ☑6-1737; 374-1 Ogimachi; dishes ¥315-1100; lunch sets ¥1050-1575; ⊙lunch; 🖉🖬) At the entrance to Ogimachi, this bustling eatery serves regional specialities such as *hoba-miso*, *yakidofu* (fried tofu) and *soba* or *udon teishoku*. You can eat at tables or around the *irori*.

Gokayama District 五箇山

☎0763

North along the Shōkawa river, in Toyama Prefecture, the Gokayama district has always been sparsely populated and quite isolated. Although there are a number of *gasshō-zukuri* buildings scattered along Rte 156, the villages of Suganuma and Ainokura have the best examples. To get here, drive north on Rte 156 from Shirakawa-gō. You'll reach Suganuma first, then Ainokura. The **Gokayama Tourist Information Office** (五箇山観光総合案内所; ☎66-2468; 754 Kaminashi; ◷9am-5pm) is in the village of Kaminashi.

◉ Sights & Activities

★**Suganuma**   HISTORIC BUILDING
(菅沼; www.gokayama.jp/english) Down a steep hill off Rte 156, 15km north of Ogimachi, this pretty riverside collection of nine *gasshō-zukuri* houses is a World Heritage Site. It feels more like a residential museum than a working village. There is no accommodation in the village.

Gokayama Minzoku-kan   MUSEUM
(五箇山民族間; ☎67-3652; 436 Suganuma; adult/child ¥300/150; ◷9am-4.30pm) Folklore museum in Suganuma. You can see items from traditional life and displays illustrating traditional gunpowder production, for which the area was famed.

Murakami-ke   HISTORIC BUILDING
(村上家; ☎66-2711; www.murakamike.jp; 742 Kaminashi; adult/child ¥300/150; ◷8.30am-5pm Apr-Nov, 9am-4pm Dec-Mar) Between Suganuma and Ainokura, in the hamlet of Kaminashi (上梨), you'll find one of the oldest *gasshō* houses in the region (dating from 1578). Now a small museum, the proud owner delights in showing visitors around and might sing you some local folk songs. Close by, the main hall of Hakusan-gū shrine dates from 1502. It's an Important Cultural Property. On 25 and 26 September, the Kokiriko Matsuri features costumed dancers performing with rattles that move like snakes. On day two, everyone joins in.

★**Ainokura**   HISTORIC VILLAGE
(相倉) Enchanting Ainokura, a World Heritage Site, is the most impressive of Gokayama's villages. The valley boasts over 20 *gasshō* buildings amid splendid mountain views. The village's remote location attracts less tour buses than Ogimachi, so it's much quieter. If you want to really step back in time and hear the sound of your thoughts, spend a night here – it's magical after the buses leave.

Ainokura Folklore Museum   MUSEUM
(相倉民族館 Ainokura Minzoku-kan; admission ¥200; ◷8.30am-5pm) Stroll through the village to this interesting museum, with displays of local crafts and paper. It's divided into two buildings, the former Ozaki and Nakaya residences.

Gokayama Washi-no-Sato   GALLERY
(五箇山和紙の里; adult/child ¥200/150; ◷8.30am-5pm) Further north on Rte 156 you'll find this roadside attraction which explains the art of making *washi* (handmade paper) and gives you the chance to try it out (from ¥500, reservations required, limited English). There's also a gift shop.

Kuroba Onsen   ONSEN
(くろば温泉; 1098 Kamitaira-hosojima; adult/child ¥600/300; ◷10am-9pm Wed-Mon) About 1km north of Suganuma along Rte 156, Kuroba Onsen is a complex of indoor-outdoor baths with a lovely view. Its low-alkaline waters are good for fatigue and sore muscles.

🛏 Sleeping

Remote Ainokura is a great place for a *gasshō-zukuri* stay. Some Japanese ability will help you with reservations and getting by. Rates may be higher in winter due to a heating charge.

Camping Ground   CAMPGROUND ¥
(相倉キャンプ場; ☎66-2123; 611 Ainokura; per person ¥500; ◷mid-Apr–late Oct) This lovely, basic campground is about 1km from the village of Ainokura.

Yomoshiro   INN ¥¥
(民宿与茂四郎; ☎66-2377; 395 Ainokura; per person with 2 meals ¥8400) Try this welcoming four-room inn, whose owner will demonstrate the *sasara*, a kind of noisemaker, upon request.

Goyomon   INN ¥¥
(民宿五ヨ門; ☎66-2154; 438 Ainokura; per person with 2 meals ¥8000) This is a small family-oriented homestay.

Chōyomon   INN ¥¥
(民宿長ヨ門; ☎66-2755; 418 Ainokura; per person with 2 meals ¥8000) You can't get much more rustic than this 350-year-old place, in the centre of the village.

ℹ Getting There & Away

Nōhi Bus Company (www.nouhibus.co.jp/english) operates seven buses daily linking Shirakawa-gō with Takayama (one-way/return ¥2400/4300, 50 minutes) and Kanazawa (¥1800/3200, 1¼ hours). Some buses require a reservation. Weather delays and cancellations are possible between December and March.

Just before Ainokura, buses divert from Rte 156 for Rte 304 towards Kanazawa. From the Ainokura-guchi bus stop it's about 400m uphill to Ainokura before the descent into the village.

Kaetsuno Bus operates at least four buses a day between Takaoka station on the JR Hokuriku line, Ainokura (¥1450, 90 minutes) and Ogimachi (¥2350, 2½ hours), stopping at all major sights. If you want to get off at unofficial stops (eg Kuroba Onsen), tell the driver.

For self-drivers, there are exits for Shirakawa-gō (Ogimachi) and Gokayama (Ainokura) on the Tokai-Hokuriku expressway from Takayama. Alternatively, take the expressway to Shirakawa-gō (Ogimachi) then follow windy Rte 156 to the villages of Gokayama. From Hakusan, the scenic toll road Hakusan Super-Rindō ends near Ogimachi (cars ¥3150). In colder months, check conditions in advance with regional tourist offices before setting out on any National roads.

NORTHERN JAPAN ALPS
北日本アルプス

Boasting some of Japan's most dramatic scenery, the Northern Japan Alps of Gifu, Toyama and Nagano Prefectures contain stunning peaks above 3000m, accessible even to amateur hikers. Also called the Hida Ranges, the most spectacular scenery is protected within the 174,323 hectare Chūbu-Sangaku National Park (中部山岳国立公園). Highlights include hiking the valleys and peaks of Kamikōchi, doing it easy on the Shin-Hotaka Ropeway and soaking up the splendour of Hida's many mountain *rotemburo*. The northern part of the park extends to the Tateyama-Kurobe Alpine Route.

ℹ Information

Numerous English-language maps and pamphlets are published by the Japan National Tourism Organization (JNTO) and local authorities. Most detailed hiking maps are in Japanese.

There are few banks in the area, and the only ATM in the communities listed in this section is at Hirayu Onsen's post office, which keeps shorter hours than most. Be sure you have enough cash before setting out.

ℹ Getting There & Around

Matsumoto and Takayama are the gateway cities into the peaks, while the main transit hubs where you're up there are Hirayu Onsen and Kamikōchi. Buses make the journey from Takayama. From Matsumoto, it's a ride on the private Matsumoto Dentetsu train to Shin-Shimashima, then a bus. Either way, the journey is breathtaking.

Hiring a car is a good option if windy roads don't bother you, and you're not overnighting in Kamikōchi – the road between Naka-no-yu and Kamikōchi is open only to buses and taxis.

Kamikōchi 上高地
☑ 0260

Some of Japan's most spectacular scenery is found here – majestic snowcapped peaks, bubbling crystal brooks, wild monkeys, wildflowers and ancient forests. That said, it wouldn't be Japan without the crowds. Timing is everything.

In the late 19th century, foreigners 'discovered' this mountainous region and coined the term 'Japan Alps'. A British missionary, Reverend Walter Weston, toiled from peak to peak and sparked Japanese interest in mountaineering as a sport. He is now honoured with a festival on the first Sunday in June, the official opening of the hiking season. Kamikōchi has become a base for daytrippers, hikers and climbers.

Kamikōchi is closed from 15 November to 22 April, and in peak times (late July to late August, and during the foliage season in October) can seem busier than Shinjuku Station – plan to arrive early in the day. June to July is rainy season. It's perfectly feasible to visit as a day trip but you'll miss out on the pleasures of staying in the mountains and taking uncrowded early-morning or late-afternoon walks.

Visitors arrive at Kamikōchi's sprawling bus station, surrounded by visitor facilities. A 10-minute walk along the Azusa-gawa takes you to *Kappa-bashi*, a bridge named after a legendary water sprite. Hiking trails begin here.

◉ Sights & Activities

Kamikōchi Onsen Hotel ONSEN
(www.kamikouchi-onsen-spa.com; admission ¥800; ⊙7-9am & 12.30-3pm) Open to non-hotel guests during limited off-hours, the baths here are a refreshing respite, especially on drizzly days.

Bokuden-no-yu   ONSEN

(admission ¥700; ⊙ noon-5pm) Not for the claustrophobic, the area's most unusual on-sen is a tiny cave bath dripping with miner-als. Find it near the Naka-no-yu bus stop, right before the bus-only tunnel towards Kamikōchi proper. Pay at the small shop for the key to the little mountain hut hous-ing the onsen. It's yours privately for up to 30 minutes.

🛏 Sleeping & Eating

Accommodation in Kamikōchi is expensive and advance reservations are essential. Ex-cept for camping, rates quoted here include two meals. Some lodgings shut down power in the middle of the night (emergency light-ing stays on).

Dotted along the trails and around the mountains are dozens of spartan *yama-goya* (mountain huts), which provide two meals and a futon from around ¥8000 per person; some also serve simple lunches. En-quire before setting out to make sure there's one on your intended route.

The bus station has a very limited range of eateries and retailers. Depending on your length of stay, bring essential munchies and take your rubbish with you.

Kamikōchi Gosenjaku Hotel & Lodge   HOTEL ¥¥

(上高地五千尺ホテル・ロッヂ; ☎ hotel 95-2111, lodge 95-2221; www.gosenjaku.co.jp/eng-lish; 4468 Kamikōchi; lodge skier's bed per person ¥10,500, s/tw ¥23,805/17,850; hotel r per person from ¥28,000) By Kappa-bashi, this com-pact lodge recently expanded to include a small hotel. The lodge has 34 Japanese-style rooms and some 'skier's beds'; basically curtained-off bunks. Rooms all have sink and toilet, but baths are shared. The hotel is more upscale with a combination of com-fortable Western and Japanese rooms, some with balconies.

Kamikōchi Nishiitoya San-sō   INN ¥¥

(上高地西糸屋山荘; ☎ 95-2206; www.nishiitoya.com; 4469-1 Kamikōchi; dm from ¥8000, d per per-son from ¥10,500; ⊙ @ 🛜) This friendly lodge, west of Kappa-bashi, has a cosy lounge and

---

SAMPLE BUS ROUTES & DISCOUNTS: NORTHERN JAPAN ALPS

Within the Alps, schedules change seasonally. A number of discount passes are available.

Alpico's '3-day Free Kippu' (¥6400) offers unlimited rides between Matsumoto, Takaya-ma and within the Chūbu-Sangaku National Park. The 'Alps-wide Free Passport' (¥10,000) gives you an extra day and also includes Shirakawa-gō.

Meitetsu's 'Marugoto value kippu' (¥5000) includes two days' travel anywhere between Takayama and Shin-Hotaka, a ride on the Shin-Hotaka Ropeway and a soak in the *rotem-buro* at Hirayu Onsen bus station.

Tourist Information Offices should direct you to the latest schedules and fares.

FROM	TO	FARE (¥; ONE-WAY, OR ONE-WAY/RETURN)	DURATION (MIN; ONE-WAY)
Takayama	Hirayu Onsen	1530	55
	Kamikōchi	2660/4900	80
	Shin-Hotaka	2100	90
Matsumoto	Shin-Shimashima	680 (train)	30
	Kamikōchi	2400/4400	95
Shin-Shimashima	Naka-no-yu	1550	50
	Kamikōchi	1900/3300	70
	Shirahone Onsen	1400/2300	75
Kamikōchi	Naka-no-yu	600	15
	Hirayu Onsen	1130/2000	25
	Shirahone Onsen	1350	35
Hirayu Onsen	Naka-no-yu	540	10
	Shin-Hotaka	870	30

HIKING & CLIMBING IN KAMIKŌCHI

The river valley offers mostly level, short-distance, signposted walks.

A four-hour round trip starts east of Kappa-bashi past Myōjin-bashi (one hour) to Tokusawa (another hour) before returning. By Myōjin-bashi, the idyllic Myōjin-ike (pond) marks the innermost shrine of Hotaka-jinja (admission ¥300). West of Kappa-bashi, you can amble alongside the river to Weston Relief (monument to Walter Weston; 15 minutes) or to Taishō-ike (40 minutes).

Other popular hikes include the mountain hut at Dakesawa (2½ hours up) and fiery Yakedake (four hours up, starting about 20 minutes west of the Weston Relief, at Hotaka-bashi). From the peaks, it's possible to see all the way to Mt Fuji in clear weather – it's a breathtaking view.

Numerous long-distance hikes vary in duration from a few days to a week. Japanese-language maps of the area show routes and average hiking times between huts, major peaks and landmarks. Favourite hikes and climbs (which can mean human traffic jams during peak seasons) include Yariga-take (3180m) and Hotaka-dake (3190m).

A steep but worthwhile hike connects Kamikōchi and Shin-Hotaka. From Kappa-bashi, the trail crosses the ridge below Nishi-Hotaka-dake (2909m) at Nishi-Hotaka San-sō (cottage; three hours) and continues to Nishi-Hotaka-guchi, the top station of the Shin-Hotaka Ropeway. The hike takes nearly four hours in this direction but is far easier in reverse. To reach the ropeway, take a bus from Takayama or Hirayu Onsen.

Serious hikers should consider treks to pristine Nakabusa Onsen (three days) or Murodō (five days); the latter, on the Tateyama-Kurobe Alpine Route, includes a soak en route in idyllic Takama-ga-hara Onsen.

Long-distance hikes have access to mountain huts; enquire at the Information Centre for details. Hikers and climbers should be well prepared. Even during summer, temperatures can plummet or the whole area can be covered in sleeting rain or blinding fog. There is no refuge on the peaks during thunderstorms.

In winter, Kamikōchi is empty, but makes a beautiful spot for snowshoeing or cross-country skiing. You'll have to hike in from the entrance to the Kama Tunnel on Rte 158.

dates from the early 20th century. Rooms are a mix of Japanese and Western styles, all with toilet. The shared bath is a large onsen facing the Hotaka mountains.

Tokusawa-en CAMPGROUND ¥¥
(徳澤園; ☎95-2508; www.tokusawaen.com/english; campsite/dm/s-tw per person ¥500/9500/13,900-15,900) A marvellously secluded place, in a wooded dell about 7km northeast of Kappa-bashi. It's both a camping ground and a lodge, and has Japanese-style rooms (shared facilities) and hearty meals served in a busy dining hall. Access is by walking only, and takes about two hours.

★ **Kamikochi Imperial Hotel** HOTEL ¥¥¥
(上高地帝国ホテル; ☎95-2001; www.imperial hotel.co.jp/j/kamikochi; Azumino Kamikochi; r without meals from ¥29,400; @) Expect exceptional service and rustic, European Alps–styled rooms in this historic red-gabled lodge, completed in 1933. Prices are elevated, but a wide range of stay plans are available and the hotel occasionally offers excellent packages including French haute cuisine.

Forest Resort Konashi CAMPGROUND ¥
(森のリゾート小梨 Mori no rizōto Konashi; ☎95-2321; www.nihonalpskankou.co.jp; campsite per person from ¥700, cabins per person tw from ¥10,000; ⊙office 7am-7pm) About 200m past the Kamikōchi Visitor Centre, this camping ground can get crowded. Rental tents are available from ¥7000 (July and August) and and there's a small shop and restaurant.

Kamonji-goya SHOKUDŌ ¥
(☎95-2418; dishes ¥600-2000; ⊙8.30am-4pm; 📖) Kamikōchi's signature dish is *iwana* (river trout) grilled whole over an *irori*. This is *the* place to try it. The *iwana* set is ¥1500, or there's *oden* (fish-cake stew), *soba* and *kotsu-sake* (dried *iwana* in sake) served in a lovely ceramic bowl. It's just outside the entrance to Myōjin-ike.

ℹ Information

Kamikōchi is entirely closed from 16 November to 22 April. Serious hikers should consider insurance (保険; *hoken*; from ¥1000 per day) available at Kamikōchi bus station.

Kamikōchi Information Centre (上高地インフォメーションセンター; ☑95-2433; ☺8am-5pm) This invaluable resource at the bus station complex provides information on hiking and weather conditions and distributes the English-language *Kamikōchi Pocket Guide* with a map of the main walking tracks.

Kamikōchi Visitor Centre (上高地ビジターセンター; ☑95-2606; ☺8am-5pm) Ten minutes' walk from Kamikōchi bus station along the main trail; this is the place for information on Kamikōchi's flora, fauna, geology and history. You can also book guided walks to destinations including Taishō-ike and Myōjin-ike (per person from ¥500). Nature guides (from ¥2000/hour) and climbing guides (approx ¥30,000/day) may be available. English speakers may be offered but cannot be guaranteed.

Ryokan Association (地観光旅館組合 Kankō Ryokan Kumiai; ☑95-2405; 4468 Kamikōchi; ☺7am-5pm) If you're after a last-minute room and speak some Japanese, this excellent service at the bus station books accommodation.

ⓘ Getting Around

Private vehicles are prohibited between Naka-no-yu and Kamikōchi; access is only by bus or taxi as far as the Kamikōchi bus station. Those with private cars can use car parks en route to Naka-no-yu in the hamlet of Sawando for ¥500 per day; shuttle buses (¥1800 return) run a few times per hour.

Buses run via Naka-no-yu and Taishō-ike to the bus station. Hiking trails commence at Kappa-bashi, which is a short walk from the bus station.

Shirahone Onsen 白骨温泉

☑0263
Intimate, dramatic and straddling a deep gorge, this onsen resort town is one Japan's most beautiful – heavenly during autumn and a white wonderland in winter. Onsen ryokan with open-air baths surround the gorge. Meaning 'white bone', it is said that bathing in the milky-blue hydrogen-sulphide waters of 'Shirahone' for three days ensures three years without a cold. The waters have a wonderful silky feel. The riverside **Kōshū Rotemburo** (公衆露天風呂; admission ¥500; ☺8.30am-5pm Apr-Oct), deep within the gorge, is separated by gender; the entrance is by the bus stop. Budget travellers may wish to sample the waters (from ¥600) and move on; nightly rates here begin at ¥9000 (per person, twin share,

including two meals) and advance reservations are strongly recommended.

🛏 Sleeping & Eating

★ **Awanoyu Ryokan**   RYOKAN ¥¥¥
(泡の湯旅館; ☑93-2101; www.awanoyu-ryokan.com; 4181 Shirahone Onsen; r per person incl 2 meals from ¥25,150; P) Awanoyu Ryokan typifies mountain onsen ryokan. Uphill from Shirahone, it has been an inn since 1912 (the current building dates from 1940). Light-filled guestrooms have private facilities. There are also single-sex common baths and *konyoku* (mixed bathing): the waters are so milky that you can't see below the surface, so don't be shy.

Tsuruya Ryokan   RYOKAN ¥¥
(つるや旅館; ☑93-2331; www.tsuruya-ryokan.jp; 4202-6 Shirahone Onsen; r per person with 2 meals from ¥10,650; P) Tsuruya Ryokan has both contemporary and traditional touches and great indoor and outdoor baths. Each of its 28 rooms has lovely views of the gorge; rooms with private toilet and sink are available for an extra charge.

ⓘ Information

The **Tourist Information Office** (観光案内所; ☑93-3251; www.shirahone.org; 4197-4 Azumino; ☺9am-5pm) maintains a list of inns that have opened their baths (admission from ¥600) to the public each day.

Hirayu Onsen 平湯温泉

☑0578
This onsen village is a hub for bus transport and the best base for day trips to Kamikōchi, neighbouring Shirahone and Fukuchi Onsens, and the Shin-Hotaka Ropeway. There is a pleasant, low-to-the-ground cluster of onsen lodgings, about half of which open for day-bathers; even the bus station has a rooftop *rotemburo* (¥600).

🛏 Sleeping & Eating

Ryosō Tsuyukusa   MINSHUKU ¥
(旅荘つゆくさ; ☑89-2620; http://tuyukusa.okuhida-onsengo.com; 621 Hirayu; r per person with 2 meals ¥7500; P) Ryosō Tsuyukusa is an eight-room mum 'n' dad *minshuku* with decent tatami rooms and a cosy mountain-view *rotemburo* of *hinoki* (cypress). Go downhill from the bus station and left at the first narrow street, it's on the left. No English is spoken.

Okada Ryokan
RYOKAN ¥¥

(岡田旅館; ☑89-2336; www.okadaryokan.com; 505 Hirayu; s/tw without meals from ¥8400/10,500) Although not much English is spoken, the kind staff at this hulking ryokan downhill from the bus station provide a warm welcome. Large rooms have private facilities and the common baths and *rotemburo* are excellent. Unlike many ryokan in the area, single travellers on a budget can get rates here without meals – but beware the slim pickings for nearby restaurants. Meal plans are available.

Hirayu-kan
RYOKAN ¥¥

(平湯館; ☑89-3111; www.hirayukan.com; 726 Hirayu; r per person with 2 meals from ¥13,800; P) Dignified Hirayu-kan has 79 rooms with private facilities in both Japanese and Western style and beautiful *rotemburo* amid a wonderful garden. It's a short walk downhill from the bus terminal.

Hirayu-no-mori
RESORT ¥¥

(ひらゆの森; ☑89-3338; www.hirayunomori. co.jp/contents/english; 763-1 Hirayu; r per person with 2 meals from ¥8000, bath day use ¥500; P) Practically in its own forest uphill from the bus station, this sprawling onsen ryokan boasts 16 different *rotemburo* pools, plus indoor and private baths. After 9pm, they're exclusively for overnight guests. Rooms are Japanese-style, and meals are hearty and local.

★ Miyama Ouan
RYOKAN ¥¥¥

(深山桜庵; ☑89-2799; www.hotespa.net/hotels/ miyamaouan; 229 Hirayu; r per person with meals from ¥19,000) We adore this sparkling new ryokan with traditional service, modern technology and personal touches. Seventy-two rooms of a variety of sizes and styles are beautifully finished with cypress woods and chic design – all have private facilities. The private *kazoku-buro rotemburo* is a little piece of heaven. They'll even collect you from the bus station.

Hirayu Camping Ground
CAMPGROUND

(平湯キャンプ場; ☑89-2610; www.hirayu-camp.com; 768-36 Hirayu; campsite per adult/child ¥600/400, bungalow from ¥5800, parking ¥1500; ⊙end Apr–end Oct) To reach the small Hirayu Camping Ground, turn right from the bus station – it's about 700m ahead, on the left.

ⓘ Information

The **Tourist Information Office** (観光案内所; ☑89-3030; 763-1 Hirayu; ⊙9.30am-5.30pm) opposite the bus station has leaflets, maps and can book accommodation. No English is spoken.

Fukuchi Onsen 福地温泉
☑0578

This tiny onsen town a short ride north of Hirayu Onsen follows a steep hill and has beautiful views and a handful of outstanding baths. Otherwise, there's not much else here. By bus from Hirayu Onsen, you can get off at Fukuchi-Onsen-Kami stop and walk downhill to check out the ryokan, then pick up the bus to return to Hirayu or travel onward to Shirahone Onsen.

◉ Sights & Activities

Mukashibanashi-no-sato
ONSEN

(昔ばなしの里; ☑89-2793; bath ¥500; ⊙8am-5pm, closed irregularly) This restaurant-cum-onsen is set back from the street in a traditional farmhouse with fine indoor and outdoor baths, free on the 26th of each month. Out front is an unmissable vintage knick-knack shop adorned with Shōwa-era movie posters and advertisements. By bus, get off at Fukuchi-Onsen-kami bus stop.

⊨ Sleeping & Eating

★ Yumoto Chōza
RYOKAN ¥¥¥

(湯元長座; ☑89-2146; www.cyouza.com; r per person with 2 meals from ¥23,000; P) In terms of guestrooms, baths and cuisine, this is close to onsen ryokan prefection; reservations are essential. Opposite Fukuchi-Onsen-shimo bus stop, the entrance to Yumoto Chōza is reached by a rustic, covered walkway, as if to take you back in time. Bold, dark woods denote handsome traditional architecture. Half of the 32 rooms have en-suite *irori* and there are five indoor baths and two stunning *rotemburo* – day visitors can bathe between 2pm and 6pm for ¥750.

Shin-Hotaka Onsen 新穂高温泉
☑0578

The main reason people visit Shin-Hotaka Onsen, an otherwise sleepy hollow north of Fukuchi Onsen, is the Shin-Hotaka Ropeway, Japan's longest.

◉ Sights & Activities

Shin-Hotaka Ropeway
ROPEWAY

(新穂高ロープウェイ; www.okuhi.jp/rop/frtop; Shin-Hotaka; oneway/return ¥1500/2800; ⊙8.30am-4.30pm) A few minutes' walk uphill from the Shin-Hotaka Onsen bus terminus, the ropeway celebrated its 40th anniversary in 2010. From a starting elevation of 1308m, two cable cars whisk you to 2156m towards the peak of Nishi Hotaka-dake (2909m). Views from the top are spectacular, from observation decks and walking trails – in winter, snows can be shoulder deep. In season, properly equipped hikers with ample time can choose longer options from the top cable-car station, Nishi Hotaka-guchi, including hiking over to Kamikōchi (three hours), which is much easier than going the other way.

Nakazaki Sansou Okuhida-no-yu　　ONSEN
(中崎山荘奥飛騨の湯; adult/child ¥800/400; ☉8am-8pm) Over 50 years old but completely rebuilt in 2010, the facility still commands a spectacular vista of the mountains. The milky waters of its large indoor baths and *rotemburo* do wonders for dry skin. There's a small dining room. It's next to Hotel Hotaka.

Shin-Hotaka-no-yu　　ONSEN
(新穂高の湯; ☎89-2458; Okuhida Onsengo Kansaka; ☉8am-9pm May-Oct, closed Nov-Apr) **FREE** Exhibitionists will love this barebones *konyoku rotemburo*, by the Kamata-gawa, visible from the bridge which passes over it. Entry is free (or by donation). Enter through segregated change rooms, and emerge into a single large pool.

🍴 Sleeping & Eating

⭐Yarimikan　　RYOKAN ¥¥
(槍見舘; ☎89-2808; www.yarimikan.com; Okuhida Onsen-gun Kansaka; r per person with meals from ¥15,900; 🅿) Yarimikan is a wonderfully traditional onsen ryokan on the Kamata-gawa (river), with two indoor baths, eight riverside *rotemburo* (some available for private use) and only 15 rooms. Guests can bathe 24 hours a day (it's stunning by moonlight) and day visitors are accepted between 10am and 2pm for ¥500. Cuisine features local Hida beef and grilled freshwater fish. It's just off Rte 475, a few kilometres before the Shin-Hotaka Ropeway.

Nonohana Sansō　　INN ¥¥
(野の花山荘; ☎89-0030; www.nono87.jp; r per person with 2 meals from ¥13,800; day guests adult/child ¥800/500; ☉day guests 10am-5pm; 🅿) Along a road that ascends from Rte 475, Nonohana Sansō opened its doors in 2010. All tatami guestrooms are traditionally styled and have private facilities, although the lobby and lounge are refreshingly contemporary. There's an open kitchen preparing local specialties and the large *rotemburo* have a fantastic outlook – they're open to visitors.

ⓘ Information

Oku-Hida Spa Tourist Information Centre (奥飛騨温泉郷観光案内所; ☎89-2458; ☉10am-5pm) By the bus terminus.

NAGANO PREFECTURE 長野県

Formerly known as Shinshū and often referred to as the 'Roof of Japan', Nagano Prefecture is a wonderful place to visit for its regal mountains, rich cultural history, fine architecture and cuisine.

In addition to a hefty chunk of the Japan Alps National Park, Nagano boasts several quasi-national parks that attract skiers, mountaineers and onsen aficionados.

Of its two main cities, Nagano, the prefectural capital and past host of the Olympic Games is home to Zenkō-ji, a spectacular temple of national significance. Ever-lovable Matsumoto makes the most of its wonderful geography, vibrant city centre and photogenic original castle.

Nagano 長野
☑026 / POP 381,500
Mountain-ringed prefectural capital Nagano has been a place of pilgrimage since the Kamakura period, when it was a temple town centred on the magnificent Zenkō-ji, which still draws more than four million visitors per year.

Following Nagano's flirtation with international fame, hosting the Winter Olympic Games in 1998, the city has reverted to its friendly small-town self. While Zenkō-ji is the only real attraction in the city centre, Nagano is a pleasant regional base with plenty of accommodation and some excellent restaurants.

Zenkō-ji occupies a prominent place to the north of this grid city. Chūō-dōri leads south from the temple, doing a quick dogleg before hitting JR Nagano Station, 1.8km away; it is said that street-planners considered Zenkō-ji so auspicious that it should not be approached directly from the train. The bus terminus and private Nagano Dentetsu ('Nagaden') line are also at JR Nagano Station.

Nagano Prefecture

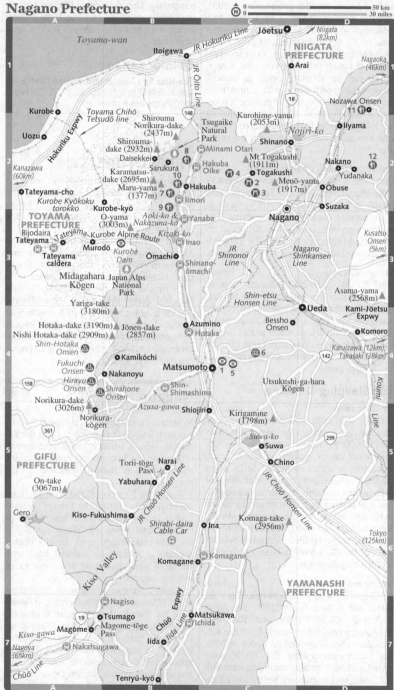

Nagano Prefecture

◉ Sights

Zenkō-ji   BUDDHIST TEMPLE
(善光寺; ☎ 234-3591; www.zenkoji.jp; 491 Motoyoshi-chō; ⏰ 4.30am-4.30pm summer, 6am-4pm winter, hours vary rest of year) FREE Founded in the 7th century, Zenkō-ji is home to the revered statue Ikkō-Sanzon, claimed as the first Buddhist image to arrive in Japan (in AD 552). It is said that not even 37 generations of emperors have seen the image, though millions of visitors flock here to view a copy every seven years during the Gokaichō Matsuri. Zenkō-ji's immense popularity stems partly from its liberal welcoming of pilgrims, regardless of gender, creed or religious belief. Its chief officiants are both a priest and a priestess. The current building dates from 1707 and is a National Treasure.

Visitors enter the temple via Nakamise-dōri and the impressive gates **Niō-mon** (仁王門) and **San-mon** (山門 (三門)). In the *hondō* (main hall), the Ikkō-Sanzon image is in an ark left of the central altar, behind a dragon-embroidered curtain. To the right, visitors may descend **Okaidan** (admission ¥500), a staircase to a twisting pitch-black tunnel beneath the altar. Not for the claustrophobic, the idea is that in the darkness, all are equal, seeking the same thing – a heavy metallic object said to be the key to salvation. The method is basically to grope the right-hand wall while avoiding your fellow aspirants. The admission is a small price to pay if you find the key.

Any bus from bus stop 1 in front of JR Nagano Station's Zenkō-ji exit will get you to the temple (¥100, about 10 minutes; alight at the Daimon bus stop).

✸ Festivals & Events

Gokaichō Matsuri   RELIGIOUS
Five million pilgrims come to Zenkō-ji every seven years from early April to mid-May to view a copy of Zenkō-ji's sacred Buddha image – the only time it can be seen. The next festival is in 2015.

Enka Taikai   FIREWORKS
A fireworks festival with street food on 23 November.

⏺ Sleeping

Visitors have the unique opportunity to experience *shukubō* (temple lodging) at one of Zenkō-ji's subtemples. Contact Zenkō-ji to book, at least one day in advance. Expect to pay ¥7000 to ¥10,000 per person with two meals.

Shimizuya Ryokan   RYOKAN ¥
(清水屋旅館; ☎ 232-2580, (fax) 234-5911; www.chuoukan-shimizuya.com; 49 Daimon-chō; r per person from ¥4725; @ 🛜) On Chūō-dōri, a few blocks south of Zenkō-ji, this ryokan has been in the family for 130 years. The rustic dark-wood interior has plenty of interesting ups, downs, nooks and crannies. There are shared bathrooms and a laundry. Meal plans are available.

1166 Backpackers   HOSTEL ¥
(1166 バックパッカーズ; ☎ 217-2816; www.1166bp.com; 1048 Nishi-machi; dm/r ¥2600/5600; @ 🛜) Opened in 2010, this intimate, woody hostel is set amid older buildings in the back streets near Zenkō-ji. Look for the beige building with a chalk signboard outside. No meals are served, but there's a kitchen and dining area for guests.

Moritomizu Backpackers   BACKPACKERS ¥
(森と水バックパッカーズ; ☎ 217-5188; www.moritomizu.net/backpackers/backpackers-e; 1-6-2 Nakagosho; dm/s/tw per person from ¥2500/3000/2500; ➖@🛜) This friendly budget backpackers has clean, simple rooms with shared facilities five minutes' walk from JR Nagano Station. Cheapest rooms have no heating and face the railway. There's a heating surcharge for other rooms in the colder months.

Matsuya Ryokan   RYOKAN ¥¥
(松屋旅館; ☎ 232-2811; www14.ocn.ne.jp/~matuya; Zenkō-ji Kannai; r per person from ¥5250, with 2 meals from ¥9450) Six generations of the Suzuki family have maintained this traditional inn just inside Zenkō-ji's Niō-mon, next to the statue of

ZENKŌ-JI LEGENDS

Few Japanese temples have the fascination of Zenkō-ji, thanks in part to the legends related to it. The following are just a few:

Ikkō-Sanzon This image, containing three statues of the Amida Buddha, was brought to Japan from Korea in the 6th century and remains the temple's raison d'être, wrapped like a mummy and kept in an ark behind the main altar. It's said that nobody has seen it for 1000 years, but in 1702, to quell rumours that the ark was empty, the shōgunate ordered a priest to confirm its existence and take measurements. That priest remains the last confirmed person to have viewed it.

Following an Ox to Zenkō-ji Long ago, an impious old woman was washing her kimono when an ox appeared, caught a piece of the cloth on his horn and ran away, the angry woman in hot pursuit. The ox led her to Zenkō-ji, where, exhausted, she fell asleep under its eaves. While she slept, the ox appeared in her dream and revealed himself to be the image of the Amida Buddha, then disappeared. The woman saw this as a miracle and became a pious believer. Today, locals say 'I followed an ox to Zenkō-ji', to mean that something good happened unexpectedly.

The Doves of San-mon Legend claims there are five white doves hidden in the plaque of the San-mon gate; the five short strokes in the characters for Zenkō-ji do look remarkably dove-like. See if you can spot them too. In the upper character (善, zen) they're the two uppermost strokes; in the middle character (光, kō) they're the strokes on either side of the top; and in the 'ji' (寺) it's the short stroke on the bottom left.

Binzuru It is said that Binzuru, a healer and one of Buddha's disciples had attained enlightenment, but was was instructed to remain on earth to do good works. At most temples, images of Binzuru are outside the main hall. At Zenkō-ji you'll find his statue just inside, worn down where visitors have touched it to help heal ailments of the corresponding parts of their own bodies; you can see the lines where the face was once replaced.

Enmei Jizō. It's the closest lodging to the temple. Meals are seasonal *kaiseki*. Add ¥1000 per person for rooms with private facilities.

Island Hotel
HOTEL ¥¥
(アイランドホテル; ☎226-3388; www.island-hotel.co.jp; 2-15-8 Minamichitose; s/d/tw ¥6000/9000/11,500; @) This simple tourist hotel a few blocks from the station has bright, compact rooms and welcomes overseas guests. There's a free light breakfast and a nice bar downstairs.

Hotel Metropolitan Nagano
HOTEL ¥¥
(ホテルメトロポリタン長野; ☎291-7000; www.metro-n.co.jp; 1346 Minami-Ishido-chō; s from ¥8800, d & tw from ¥12,000; P@) Situated opposite the station, the Metropolitan has elegant and spacious rooms by Japanese standards. There's a cafe, restaurant and top-floor lounge with sweeping views. Japan Rail Pass holders get a 20% discount.

Chisun Grand Nagano
HOTEL ¥¥
(チサングランド長野; ☎264-6000; www.solarehotels.com; 2-17-1 Minami-Chitose; s/d/tw from ¥6300/8900/10,600; @) Formerly the

Holiday Inn, this hotel was built for Olympic guests of overseas proportions and features large Western-style rooms, including impressive Junior Suites. Excellent rates can be found online.

Eating

India the Spice
CAFE ¥
(インディア・ザ・すぱいす; ☎226-6136; 1418 Minami-ishido-chō; mains from ¥800; ☺11.30am-11pm Mon-Thu & Sun, to midnight Fri & Sat) This eccentric cafe is festooned with every kind of wall clock imaginable, and specialises in variations on the theme of curry; lunch sets include *omu-karē* (rice wrapped in an omelette in keema curry sauce; ¥900). Going up Chūō-dōri, turn right at the 'Joy Style' London Bus, then take another right. There are vine leaves around the entrance.

Chō Bali Bali
ASIAN ¥
(チョーバリバリ; ☎229-5226; 1366-1 Ishido-chō; mains from ¥600; ☺lunch & dinner Tue-Sun;) This stylish space gathers lively crowds and serves eclectic dishes from Indonesia, Thai-

land and Vietnam, with a touch of Italian for good measure; *yam-un-sen* is a spicy Thai salad with vermicelli. Highly recommended.

Bakery's Street&Cafe
CAFE ¥

(☑ 232-0269; 1583 Nishi-go-chō; items ¥200-890; ☺ 10am-6pm) This delightful cafe near the Olympic torch monument, serves freshly baked bread and delicious sandwiches to eat in or take out, as well as pizza, pasta, salad and desserts. There's a picture menu and serve-yourself items.

Asian Night Market
CAFE ¥

(アジアンナイトマーケット; http://asian-night-market.net; 2-1 Higashi-go-chō; most dishes under ¥1000; ☺ noon-11pm; 📶 📷) This hippy joint is part boutique selling clothes and nick-nacks from Southeast Asia, and part bar-restaurant with English speaking staff serving sumptuous Thai food. There's also free wi-fi. You can view the menu online. The Chinese broccoli and obligatory pad thai are wonderful.

Marusei
SHOKUDŌ ¥

(丸清食堂; ☑ 232-5776; 486 Motoyoshi-chō; dishes ¥600-1800; ☺ 11am-6pm Thu-Tue) A stone's throw from Zenkō-ji on Nakamise-dōri, unassuming Marusei serves *soba* and *tonkatsu* among others; the generous Marusei *bentō* (¥1350) lets you try both.

★Yayoi-za
SHUKUDŌ ¥¥

(弥生座; ☑ 232-2311; 503 Daimon-chō; dishes ¥525-4200; ☺ lunch & dinner, closed Tue & 2nd Wed of each month; 📷) This establishment has been serving *seiro-mushi* (ingredients steamed in a wood and bamboo box) for over 150 years. The standard is *monzen seiro-mushi* (local beef and vegetables). For dessert, try *kuri-an cream* (chestnut-paste mousse).

★Gohonjin Fujiya
FUSION ¥¥

(藤屋御本陣; ☑ 232-1241; 80 Daimon-chō; mains ¥600-1400, courses ¥2400-7500; ☺ lunch Mon-Fri, dinner nightly; 📷) Until recently, this imposing 1923 building was Nagano's most venerable Hotel Fujiya, and had been since 1648. It's since transformed itself into the city's most elegant Western restaurant and function centre. The spectacular dining

Nagano

0 — 400 m
0 — 0.2 miles

SHINSHŪ CUISINE: A ROGUE'S GALLERY

Nagano Prefecture is renowned for foods ranging from familiar to… challenging. Local foods are usually preceded by the region's ancient name, *Shinshu* (信州).

Ringo (りんご) Apples, often as big as grapefruits and we think the best in the world. Ubiquitous in autumn.

Kuri (栗) Chestnuts, especially in Obuse.

Soba (そば) Buckwheat noodles, handmade from 100% buckwheat in speciality shops (ordinary *soba* contains as little as 50% buckwheat). These can be eaten either cold (*zaru-soba;* with wasabi and soy-based dipping sauce) or hot (*kake-soba;* in broth).

Oyaki (おやき) Little wheat buns filled with vegetables, baked or steamed.

Wasabi (わさび) Japanese horseradish, grown in bogs particularly in Hotaka. You know grated wasabi from sushi and *soba*, and locals parboil the greens as drinking snacks. Some shops sell wasabi in cakes and ice cream.

Basashi (馬刺し) Raw horse meat.

Hachinoko (蜂の子) Bee larvae.

Inago (稲子) Crickets.

room is called Wisteria and mixes Japanese and art deco motifs. Everchanging chef's menus (lunch ¥2400, dinner ¥5000) are usually a good bet. For dessert, the *Shinshū ringo-pai* (apple pie) is a little slice of heaven.

Fujiki-an　　　　　　　　　NOODLES ¥¥
(藤木庵; ☑232-2531; 67 Daimon-chō; mains ¥800-1500; ☉lunch Wed-Mon, dinner Thu-Sat in Mar-Nov only; ☑) Fujiki-an have been making fresh *soba* in the north of Nagano-ken since 1827, but you wouldn't know it by the clean contemporary lines of this outlet. There's a picture menu. *Seiro-mori soba* (cold *soba* on a bamboo mat) lets the flavour shine; other favourites are tempura, *kinoko* (mushroom) and *nishin* (herring).

🍷 Drinking

⭐ **Izakaya Hanbey**　　　　　　IZAKAYA
(居酒屋半兵ヱ; ☑269-8000; Takahashi Dai 2 Bldg 1F, 1418 Minami-ishido-chō; items from ¥50; ☉5pm-late) The Nagano branch of this national *izakaya* chain, plastered with Shōwa-era movie posters and advertisements, is particularly cool, as are the occasional two-hour all-you-can-drink deals for ¥980. The extensive and amusing English menu features such delights as 'raw guts' and 'raw uterus' – both for ¥70, bargain. Otherwise, there's *gyōza*, *yakitori* (skewers of grilled chicken), *okonomiyaki* (pancake) and *kushiage* (grilled skewers).

Groovy　　　　　　　　　　LIVE MUSIC
(グルービー; ☑227-0480; www.naganogroovy. web.fc2.com; 1398 Kitaishido-chō; cover ¥1000-3500) A music spot popular with jazz lovers for its live shows; check the website for schedule info.

ℹ Information

The Nagano Visitor's Guide can be found online at www.nagano-cvb.or.jp. There's a **post office** with international ATM in the West Plaza Nagano building opposite the station's Zenkō-ji exit, as well as the **Central Post Office** (長野中央郵便局; Chūō-dōri).

Internet Cafe Chari Chari (インターネットカフェ茶里茶里; 2F Daitō Bldg, Minami-ishido-chō; per hr ¥390; ☉24hr)

Nagano Tourist Information Centre (長野市観光情報センター; ☑226-5626; ☉9am-6pm) Inside JR Nagano Station, this friendly outfit has good English-language colour maps and guides to Nagano and the surrounding areas.

ℹ Getting There & Away

Nagano *shinkansen* run twice hourly from Tokyo Station (Asama, ¥7460, 1¾ hours). The JR Shinonoi line connects Nagano with Matsumoto (Shinano *tokkyū*, ¥2260, 50 minutes; Chūō *futsū*, ¥1110, 1¼ hours) and Nagoya (Shinano *tokkyū*, ¥6620, three hours).

　If you're travelling on *futsū* (local) trains on the JR Chūō line between Nagano, Matsumoto and beyond, don't schedule too tight an onward connection, as trains are occasionally delayed (unusual in Japan).

Togakushi 戸隠

 026

Popular with hikers in spring, summer and autumn and with skiers in the winter, this pretty forested region in the mountains northwest of Nagano city makes a lovely day trip or a peaceful overnight stay. Togakushi has been famed for *soba* for centuries. Pick up English-language maps from the Nagano Tourist Information Centre or download one at www.togakushi-21.jp.

◉ Sights

Togakushi Jinja SHINTŌ SHRINE

(戸隠神社) Comprising three sub-shrines: Togakushi-Hōkōsha (宝光社), Togakushi-Chūsha (中社) and Togakushi-Okusha (奥社). A few kilometres apart, Togakushi Jinja honours the 1911m-high Mt Togakushi. Intimate Chūsha is the most easily accessible; one tree here is said to be 700 years old. There's a little village with some shops, ryokan and restaurants here.

Okusha, the innermost shrine, can be reached via bus or hiking trail. The direct path from Chūsha to Okusha bus stop takes about 25 minutes, or there's a longer route via **Kagami-ike** (鏡池; Mirror Pond) and the **Togakushi Botanic Garden** (森林植物園). From Okusha bus stop it's another 2km (40 minutes) to the shrine buildings, via a magnificent 500m-long cedar-lined path (杉並木; *suginamiki*), planted in 1612.

From Okusha, avid alpinists can make the strenuous climb to the top of Mt Togakushi. In winter, Okusha is inaccessible except for hearty snowshoers, and businesses are closed.

Togakushi Folk Museum & Ninja House MUSEUM

(戸隠民俗館・忍者からくり屋敷; Togakushi Minzoku-kan & Ninja Karakuri Yashiki; ☑254-2395; 3688-12 Togakushi; adult/child ¥500/350; ⊙9am-5pm mid-Apr–mid-Nov; ☐Okusha) Above the Okusha bus stop you'll find this museum housing artefacts from a time when local *yamabushi* (mountain monks) practised what became known as *ninpo* (the art of stealth). The 'Ninja House' is the most fun, cleverly concocted with trick doors, hidden staircases and a room that slopes upwards.

🛌 Sleeping & Eating

★ Togakushi Campground CAMPGROUND ¥

(戸隠キャンプ場; ☑254-3581; www.togakushi.com/camp; 3694 Togakushi; sites from ¥3000, bungalows from ¥5000, cabins from ¥9000, cottages from ¥18,000; ⊙end Apr-end Oct; ☐Togakushi Kyanpu-jo) This beautiful, sprawling campground a few kilometres from Okusha has its own babbling brook, 350 campsites, 30 bungalows, 33 cabins and six self-contained cottages – avoid summer holidays. It's best in October when the leaves are turning and it's just about ready to close for the winter. Rental tents are available (¥4000). From Nagano, take the bus to 'Togakushi Kyanpu-jo' stop.

Yokokura Ryokan RYOKAN ¥

(横倉旅館; ☑254-2030; 3347 Chūsha; dm/with 2 meals ¥3045/5065, r per person with meals from ¥7800; ℙ) In Chūsha, Yokokura Ryokan is in a thatch-roofed building from the early Meiji-era, about 150m from the steps up to Chūsha. It's both a hostel and a ryokan, with tatami-room dorms (gender-separate) and private rooms. Room-only plans are available.

Okusha no Chaya CAFE ¥

(奥社の茶屋; ☑254-2222; 3506 Togakushi; mains ¥800-1680; ⊙10am-4.30pm late Apr-late Nov) By Okusha bus stop, Okusha no Chaya serves fresh *soba* and other staples behind a glass wall overlooking the forest; delicious soft-serve ice cream comes in seasonal flavours such as tomato, chestnut and wasabi.

Uzuraya Soba NOODLES ¥

(うずら家そば; ☑0120-833-090; 3229 Togakushi; dishes ¥400-1800; ⊙10.30am-4pm Thu-Tue; ⊛) This wonderful noodle shop claims that Togakushi is the home of *soba* and they may be right. It's directly across from the steps to Chūsha shrine. Tempura *soba* is king.

❶ Getting There & Away

Buses depart Nagano hourly (7am to 7pm) and arrive at Chūsha-Miyamae bus stop by Chūsha shrine in about an hour (one-way/return ¥1300/2400). To Okusha the one-way/return fare is ¥1280/2300. The Togakushi Kōgen Free Kippu pass (¥2500) gives unlimited rides on buses to and around Togakushi for three days. Buy tickets inside the Alpico Bus office in front of Nagano Station's Zenkō-ji exit.

Karuizawa 軽井沢

☑0267 / POP 19,020

Karuizawa is a picturesque resort town situated in a small fertile valley beneath the shadow of Mt Asama, one of the most active volcanoes on Honshū. Its last significant eruption was in 2009, from which ashfall was reported as far as Tokyo. Despite the distant potential for volcanic cataclysm, Karuizawa has long been a popular retreat from Tokyo's summer heat. In 1957, a young Emperor Akihito met his future bride, Empress Micihiko, on a tennis court here. Since then, the town has had a reputation as a place for romance, and it's a popular spot for weddings.

With easy access from both Tokyo and Nagano by *shinkansen*, Karuizawa makes an excellent day trip or overnight stop, with a wide range of high-end accommodation, cafes, restaurants and a shopping outlet that even antishoppers will find hard to resist.

Accommodation can be a little spread out, although many hotels have their own shuttles. Hiring a car here will help you enjoy all the area has to offer.

◎ Sights & Activities

Karuizawa Prince Shopping Outlet   MALL
(☎42-5211; www.karuizawa-psp.jp/en; ⏰10am-7pm) Outside the south exit of Karuizawa station, this gargantuan outlet shopping mall has most of the big names. There's a high likelihood of finding bargains and hard to find or only-in-Japan merchandise. Set among acres of grassland, with its own lake, plenty of dining options and great views to Mt Asama, it's easy to lose time here, even if you're not a big shopper. Shopaholics should allocate *plenty* of time.

Old Karuizawa   NEIGHBOURHOOD
(旧軽井沢) Also known as 'Old Karuizawa Ginza', this attractive main street is lined with classy boutiques, galleries and cafes. Follow Karuizawa-hondōri north from the station for about 1km, then turn right onto Kyū-karuizawa Main Street – you can't miss it.

Former Mikasa Hotel   MUSEUM
(旧三笠ホテル; ☎42-7072; 1339-342 Karuizawa; admission ¥400; ⏰9am-5pm) This property, one of the first Western hotels in Japan, welcomed guests from 1906 to 1970. An exceptional example of elaborate Meiji-era architecture, it's now a museum for you to explore.

Mt Asama Magma Stone Park   MUSEUM
(鬼押出し園; Onioshidashi-en; ☎86-4141; www.princehotels.co.jp/amuse/onioshidashi; 1053 Kanbara, Tsumagoi-mura, Gunma-ken; adult/child ¥600/400, varies seasonally; ⏰8am-4.30pm) In nearby Gunma-ken, here's your chance to get up close and personal with Mt Asama – so close, you could almost touch it. Formed in 1783 by Asama's last violent eruption, this *'Hurled by Demons'* Park has a surreal landscape of jagged hardened magma juxtaposed with verdant green fields; volcanic soil is extremely fertile. Enquire at the Tourist Information Office for bus fares and times.

'Umi' Museum of Contemporary Art   GALLERY
(軽井沢現代美術館; Karuizawa Gendai-bijutsukan; ☎31-5141; 2052-2 Nagakura; adult/senior/child ¥1000/800/500; ⏰10am-5pm Fri-Mon Apr-Jun & Oct-Nov; Mon-Sun, Jul-Sep) This light-filled gallery showcases an impressive collection of contemporary works by Japanese artists who have found fame abroad. It's in a lovely forested spot.

🛏 Sleeping & Eating

APA Hotel Karuizawa Ekimae   HOTEL ¥¥
(APAホテル軽井沢駅前; ☎42-0665; www.apahotel.com; 1178-1135 Karuizawa; s/d from ¥8000/14,000; ℗@) Only two minutes' walk from the north exit of JR Karuizawa Station, this neat business hotel is a great choice if you're here to shop and are looking for value and convenience.

Cottage Inn Log Cabin   CABIN ¥¥
(☎45-6007; www.log-cabin.co.jp/en; 3148-1 Naka-Karuizawa; s/tw/tr per person from ¥12,000/6000/5700) As the name suggests, these fully self-contained cabins have a rustic appeal in a forested setting, five minutes' walk from Naka-Karuizawa Station. It's a great option for travelling families.

Dormy Club Karuizawa   HOTEL ¥¥
(ドーミー倶楽部軽井沢; ☎44-3411; www.hotespa.net/hotels/karuizawa; 482 Senrigataki-naka; s/d from ¥15,800/25,600; ℗@) This secluded 24-room tourist hotel between Karuizawa and Hoshino Onsen has friendly staff and stylish, well-designed rooms. *Shinkan* (new-wing) rooms have balconies and gorgeous light-filled bathrooms.

★ Hoshino-ya   RESORT ¥¥¥
(星のや; ☎050-3786-0066; www.global.hoshinoresort.com/hoshinoya_karuizawa; Hoshino Karuizawa; r per person from ¥16,000; 🐕) ✿ This stunning eco resort in the onsen village of Hoshino, just outside Karuizawa, is anything but basic. Modern rooms and villas incorporate traditional design elements and are positioned around a pond in a beautiful forest setting.

All have cypress tubs and are exquisitely furnished around the premise that less is more. Enjoy 24-hour room service from the resort's three restaurants. You may have to share the decadent onsen pools with day visitors (¥1200).

Tokyu Harvest Club HOTEL ¥¥¥
(☑41-3000; www.resorthotels109.com/en/kyuka-ruizawa; 1178-493 Karuizawa; r from 26,000; ☐ @ ☎) Expect a high level of service from this elegant resort hotel with spacious, comfortable rooms, filled with natural light. It's in a quiet spot a few minutes' drive from JR Karuizawa Station and has wonderful indoor/outdoor baths.

Torimaru Prince-ten CHICKEN ¥
(とりまるプリンス店; ☑42-0525; Karuizawa Prince Shopping Plaza, 1178-161 Karuizawa; sets from ¥850; ☺lunch & dinner Thu-Tue) In Karuizawa Prince Shopping Plaza you'll find this traditional chicken-joint serving juicy, crispy *kara-age*. There's a picture menu.

ℹ Information

Karuizawa Tourist Association (軽井沢観光協会 Karuizawa Kankō Kyōkai; ☑45-6050; www.karuizawa-kankokyokai.jp) In the JR Karuizawa Station building, grab your English-language pamphets, magazines and maps, here. Some English is spoken.

ℹ Getting There & Away

Karuizawa is a stop on the Nagano *shinkansen* line, from Nagano (Asama, ¥3070, 33 minutes) or Tokyo (Asama, ¥5240, 70 minutes). There are twice-hourly services in both directions at most times.

Alternatively, the private *Shinano Tetsudō* line from Nagano operates local trains (¥1590, 1¼ hours) and there are five buses per day from Tokyo's Ikebukuro Station (¥2500, three hours).

Obuse 小布施

☑ 026 / POP 11,070
This lovely little town northeast of Nagano occupies a big place in Japanese art history and has a handful of interesting museums. The famed *ukiyo-e* (woodblock print) artist Hokusai (1760–1849) worked here during his final years. Obuse is also famed for *kuri* (chestnuts), which you can sample steamed with rice or in ice cream and sweets.

The town is increasingly popular with local day trippers – avoid weekends and holidays if you can.

◉ Sights

Hokusai Museum GALLERY
(北斎館; Hokusai-kan; ☑247-5206; 485 Ōaza Obuse; adult/child ¥500/free; ☺9am-5.30pm Apr-Sep, to 4.30pm Oct-Mar) Japan's most famous *ukiyo-e* (woodblock) artist, Hokusai, spent his final years in Obuse. Over 30 of his works are exhibited in this gallery, including several colourful floats decorated with his imaginative ceiling panels. It's a 10-minute well-signposted walk from the station.

Takai Kōzan Kinenkan MUSEUM
(高井鴻山記念館; ☑247-4049; 805-1 Ōaza Obuse; admission ¥300; ☺9am-6pm Apr-Sep, to 5pm Oct-Mar) Takai Kōzan, Hokusai's friend and patron, was a businessman and an accomplished classical artist specialising in elegant Chinese-style landscapes. His life and work is commemorated in this small museum.

**Japanese Lamp &
Lighting Museum** MUSEUM
(日本のあかり博物館; Nihon no Akari Hakubutsukan; ☑247-5669; 973 Obuse-machi; adult/child ¥500/free; ☺9am-4.30pm, closed Wed except May, Aug, Oct, Nov) Showcasing lighting through Japanese history, including oil lamps and lanterns, this neat museum will flip the switches of design aficionados.

Taikan Bonsai Gallery GALLERY
(盆栽美術館大観; Bonsai Bijutsukan Taikan; ☑247-3000; 10-20 Obuse-machi; adult/child Apr-Nov ¥500/300, Dec-Mar ¥300/free; ☺9am-5pm) Come here to appreciate the delicate art of bonsai including some rare species. Admission includes entry to a small gallery of landscapes.

✕ Eating

Chikufūdō DESSERT ¥
(竹風堂; 973 Obuse-machi; ☺8am-6pm) Sample chestnut confections at Chikufūdō, established in 1893. *Dorayakisan* (chestnut paste in pancake dumplings) are the standard.

ℹ Information

The **A la Obuse Guide Centre** (ア・ラ・小布施ガイドセンター; ☑247-5050; 789-1 Ōaza Obuse; ☺9am-5pm) has maps and bicycles for hire (¥400/half-day). It is en route to the museums from the station.

It also has a cafe, gift store and quaint little guesthouse (s/tw from ¥8400/12,600) if you decide to stick around.

ⓘ Getting There & Away

Obuse is reached via the Nagano Dentetsu (Nagaden) line from Nagano (*tokkyū*, ¥750, 26 minutes; *futsū*, ¥650, 34 minutes).

Yudanaka 湯田中

♪ 0269

One of Japan's most infamous tourist traps, Yudanaka is best known for its over-photographed snow monkeys. Otherwise, it's a rather sprawling and unappealing onsen village.

◉ Sights & Activities

Jigokudani Monkey Park ZOO

(地獄谷野猿公苑; Jigokudani Yaen-kōen; www.jigokudani-yaenkoen.co.jp; 6845 Ōaza-heian; adult/child ¥500/250; ⊙ 8.30am-5pm Apr-Oct, 9am-4pm Nov-Mar) In operation since 1964 and clearly in a state of disrepair, thousands flock here each year to see the troupe of Japanese macaques who may once have bathed naturally in the waters, but for decades have been lured into them by the promise of food. They're at times a little savage and run wildly around you as you observe them on the paths and in the man-made onsen. The monkeys are a few hundred steps climb from the car park, which is itself at the end of a 1.6km winding uphill road with no public transport. The ruse is most convincing in winter when the snow hides the industrial debris by the river; although the only way in is via a limited operation shuttle bus on that slippery, windy road.

Kaede no Yu ONSEN

(楓の湯; 3227-1 Heian; admission ¥300; ⊙ 10am-9pm, closed first Tue of every month) This onsen at Yudanaka Station has footbaths, indoor baths and *rotemburo*.

🛏 Sleeping

Uotoshi Ryokan RYOKAN ¥

(魚蔵旅館; ☎ 33-1215; www.avis.ne.jp/~miyasaka; 2563 Sano; s/d/tr/q from ¥4300/7980/11,970/15,960; @) In sleepy Yudanaka, Uotoshi Ryokan is basic but hospitable. The English-speaking owner will demonstrate and let you try *kyūdō* (Japanese archery), pick you up at Yudanaka Station, or drop you off at the start of the Monkey Park trail on request. Dinner and breakfast are available. It's a 10-minute walk from the station: exit left and follow the road over the river; when the road ends, turn right. It's a two-storey white building.

ⓘ Getting There & Around

From Nagano, take the Nagano Dentetsu (Nagaden) line to Yudanaka terminus (*tokkyū*, ¥1230, 45 minutes; futsū, ¥1130, 1¼ hours). Not all trains go as far as Yudanaka.

For Jigokudani Monkey Park, take the bus for Kanbayashi Onsen Guchi and get off at Kanbayashi Onsen (¥220, 15 minutes, eight daily), walk uphill along the road about 400m, and you'll see a sign reading 'Monkey Park' at the start of a rather gruelling 1.6km walk, further uphill.

Shiga Kōgen 志賀高原

♪ 0269

The site of several events in the 1998 Nagano Olympics and the 2005 Special Olympics World Winter Games, Shiga Kōgen is Japan's largest ski resort and one of the largest in the world: there are 21 linked areas covering 80 runs. One lift ticket gives access to all areas as well as the shuttle bus between the various base lodges. There is a huge variety of terrain for all skill levels, as well as ski-only areas.

Outside winter, the mountains' lakes, ponds and overlooks make an excellent destination for hikers. Otherwise, there's no compelling reason to visit. If you're a skier, read on...

If time is limited, base yourself somewhere central like the Ichinose Family Ski Area, which has a central location and wide variety of accommodation and restaurants. The Nishitateyama area has good wide runs and generally ungroomed terrain. The Terakoya area is a little hard to get to but it is generally uncrowded and has good short runs and a pleasant atmosphere.

🛏 Sleeping & Eating

Hotel Shirakabasō HOTEL ¥¥

(ホテル白樺荘; ☎ 34-3311; www.shirakaba.co.jp/english; 7148 Hirao; r per person with 2 meals from ¥11,700; P 🛜) Close to the cable-car base station and the Sun Valley ski area is this pleasant little hotel with a variety of rooms and its own indoor and outdoor onsen baths.

Hotel Heights Shiga Kōgen HOTEL ¥¥

(ホテルハイツ志賀高原; ☎ 34-3030; www.shigakogen.jp/heights; r per person with 2 meals from ¥8300; P) Near the base of the Kumanoyu ski area, the large Hotel Heights boasts clean Japanese- and Western-style rooms and its own onsen.

Hotel Sunroute Shiga Kōgen
HOTEL ¥¥

(ホテルサンルート志賀高原; ☎34-2020; r per person with 2 meals from ¥10,500; P) Popular with a Western crowd, this hotel is a three-minute walk from the Ichinose Diamond ski lift, with great access to other ski areas. The rooms are Western style with en suite baths; some have mountain views.

Villa Ichinose
INN ¥¥

(ヴィラ・一の瀬; ☎34-2704; www.villa101.biz/english; 7149 Hirao; r per person from ¥6000; P🌐) With a great location in front of the Ichinose bus stop, English-speaking staff and a friendly atmosphere, this inn is popular with overseas guests. Japanese-style rooms have toilet only and Western-style rooms have their own bathroom. There's wi-fi in the lobby and a 24-hour public bath on the 2nd floor.

Chalet Shiga
INN ¥¥

(シャレー志賀; ☎34-2235; www.shigakogen.jp/chalet; r per person with 2 meals from ¥10,500; P) Chalet Shiga is both convenient to the slopes and has a popular sports bar on-site. Both Western- and Japanese-style rooms are available.

❶ Information

Shiga Kōgen Ropeway Association (志賀高原索道協会; ☎34-2404; www.shigakogen.gr.jp; 1-day lift ticket ¥4800; ⊙8.30am-4.30pm Dec-Apr) The conglomeration of hills are managed by this central body – limited information in English can be found on their website. Lift passes are available in a variety of durations and a wide range of equipment can be rented from numerous outlets. In the Hasuike area, in front of the Shiga Kōgen ropeway station, their office has English speakers who can help you navigate the slopes and book accommodation.

❶ Getting There & Away

Direct buses run between Nagano Station and Shiga Kōgen, with frequent departures in ski season (¥1600, 70 minutes). You can also take a train from Nagano to Yudanaka and continue to Shiga Kōgen by bus – take a Hase-ike–bound bus and get off at the last stop (¥760, approximately 40 minutes).

Nozawa Onsen 野沢温泉

☎0269 / POP 3800

This wonderful working village tucked in a picturesque corner of the eastern Japan Alps is both a humming ski resort winter-long and a year-round onsen town – worth visiting any time of year.

Settled as early as the 8th century, its compact and quaint, though the maze of narrow streets will challenge even the best of drivers. Dotted throughout are 13 free public onsen and a range of excellent accommodation. Outside the busy ski-season, it's possible to briefly escape modernity and get a sense of life in an ancient mountain village.

⊙ Sights & Activities

Nozawa Onsen Snow Resort
SKI AREA

(野沢温泉スキー場; www.nozawaski.com/winter/en/; 1-day lift ticket ¥4600; ⊙8.30am-4.30pm Dec-Apr;) Nozawa Onsen Snow Resort, one of Honshū's best, dominates the 'upper' village. The relatively compact ski face is easy to navigate and enjoy with a variety of terrain at all levels. The main base is around the Higake gondola station, where there are beginner and kid-friendly runs. Snowboarders should try the Karasawa terrain park or the half-pipe at Uenotaira and advanced skiers will enjoy the steep and often mogulled Schneider Course.

Onsen
ONSEN

(⊙6am-11pm) Onsen-water is still wisely used by many villagers for laundry, cooking and heating, and there are 13 free onsen (for bathing) dotted about the town, each with a history. Our favourite is **Ō-yu**, with its fine wooden building, followed by the scalding-hot **Shin-yu**, and the atmospheric old **Kuma-no-tearai** (Bear's Bathroom). The waters here are *hot* and full of minerals - if you have silver jewellery, leave it in your room unless you don't mind it temporarily turning black. Some baths are cordoned off because they are so hot that only hardened locals are permitted to enter them!

✹ Festivals & Events

Dōsojin Matsuri
FESTIVAL

(道祖神祭り) Each year on the 15th January crowds gather to witness the spectacle of the famous Dōsojin Matsuri (Fire Festival). Crudely, it's a kind of cleansing ritual for men aged 25 and 42, the so-called 'unlucky ages' in Japan. The real unlucky ones are the 42 year olds, whose task is to sit atop and defend a purpose-built two-storey shrine which is beseiged by fire at the hands of the 25-year-olds and random onlookers. Copious amounts of sake is imbibed by all, and after a few hours, the defenders climb down (if they can) and the shrine is set ablaze to much joy and excitement. Really!

🛏 Sleeping & Eating

Pension Schnee INN ¥
(ペンションシュネー; ☎85-2012; www.pension-schnee.com; 8276 Hikage-suki-jō; r per person with meals from ¥8400; @) Near the Higake gondola base, you can ski in and out of this super friendly, family-run chalet, popular with Western clientele, who appreciate its premium location. European pension-style rooms are spacious and there's a woody dining room/bar.

Lodge Nagano INN ¥
(ロッジながの; ☎090-8670-9597; www.lodgenagano.com; 6846-1 Toyosato; r per person with breakfast from ¥4000, r in summer from ¥2500; 🛜) This popular foreign-run guesthouse attracts lots of Aussie skiers – there's Vegemite in the dining room. It's a friendly, fun place with bunk dorm and tatami rooms, some with private bath.

★ Address Nozawa APARTMENT ¥¥
(アドレス野沢; ☎67-0360; www.addressnozawa.com; 9535 Nozawa Onsen; studio s/d from ¥12,750/17,000; @🛜🎿) We love this innovative, boutique property, opened in 2011. Formerly a traditional inn, new owners sought to recreate a space which combined Japanese and European design elements and have done just that. Large Western-style rooms with tatami floors feature fresh colours, soft downy beds, bright bathrooms and a full kitchen stocked with breakfast provisions. There's an on-site onsen bath, kids' room, ski storage and plenty of high technology.

Kiriya Ryokan RYOKAN ¥¥
(桐屋旅館; ☎85-2020; www.kiriya.jp; 8714-2 Nozawa Onsen; r per person with meals from ¥12,000; P🛜🎿) This friendly ryokan has been in the family for generations. The owner's attentive service and excellent English ensure its abiding popularity with overseas guests. All rooms have private toilets. Some have their own baths in addition to the large communal onsen baths. There's a guest laundry and a wonderful garden.

Mura-no-hoteru Sumiyoshi-ya RYOKAN ¥¥
(村のホテル住吉屋; ☎85-2005; www.sumiyoshiya.co.jp; 8713 Toyosato; r per person with meals from ¥18,900; @) This wonderful ryokan, the oldest in town, has a wide range of traditional room types, many with private bathrooms and great views. The communal onsen baths with stained glass windows are dreamy. Limited English is spoken but the friendly staff are committed to excellence in service.

Haus St Anton INN ¥¥
(サンアントンの家; ☎85-3597; www.nozawa.com/stanton; 9515 Nozawa Onsen; r per person with meals with/without bathroom from ¥14,000/11,550; P@) Owned by a two-time former Olympian, this comfortable Austrian-themed inn has helpful staff and is close to the village's main street. There are six handsome Western-style bedrooms and a dining area/bar with a woody, warm atmosphere.

Lodge Matsuya INN ¥¥
(ロッヂまつや; ☎85-2082; www2u.biglobe.ne.jp/~onotaka; 9553 Nozawa Onsen; r per person with breakfast from ¥6500, with 2 meals from ¥8500; @) In the centre of town this large, family-run ski lodge has both Western- and Japanese-style rooms.

Pasta di Pasta ITALIAN ¥
(パスタディパスタ; ☎85-5055; www.pastadipasta.net; 8376-145 Toyosato; dishes ¥500-1200; ⏱lunch and dinner, hours vary seasonally) Freshly cooked pasta, pizza and appetisers are order of the day in this cosy upstairs eatery. The not too creamy *wafū sanshū no kinoko* pasta (three kinds of mushroom) is delicious.

Tōyō Rāmen NOODLES ¥
(東洋ラーメン; ☎85-3363; 9347 Toyosato; ⏱lunch & dinner) Chunky *rāmen* bowls and mouthwatering *tezukuri* (handmade) *gyōza* are dished out year-round in this 30-seat Chinese eatery.

🍷 Drinking

Main Street Bar Foot BAR
(マインストリトバーフット; @) A casual place on the main street, with free internet (with drink purchase) and fussball.

Stay BAR
(ステイ; www.seisenso.com) Stay is a cosy basement bar that's open late and run by a music-loving Japanese man who has lived abroad.

Minato Bar IZAKAYA
(みなと) On the slopes near the base of the gondola, Minato appeals to an older crowd. It's a Japanese-style place that seats 50 and offers karaoke next door.

ℹ Information

In the centre of the village, **Nozawa Onsen Visitor Centre** (野沢温泉ビジターセンター; ☎85-3155; www.nozawakanko.jp/english; 9780-4 Toyosato; ⏱8.30am-6pm) has English-speaking staff who can assist with accommodation and tour bookings.

❶ Getting There & Away

There are direct buses between Nagano Station's east exit and Nozawa Onsen (¥1400, 90 minutes, seven buses per day in winter, three buses per day in summer). Alternatively, take a JR Iiyama-line train between Nagano and Togari Nozawa Onsen Station (¥740, 55 minutes). Regular buses connect Togari Nozawa Onsen Station and Nozawa Onsen (¥300, 20 minutes, nine per day). The bus station/ticket office is about 200m from the main bus stop, which is directly in the middle of town. This can be a little confusing, but there are staff around to help get people where they need to be.

Hakuba 白馬

☎ 0261

At the base of one of the highest sections of the Northern Japan Alps, Hakuba is one of Japan's main skiing and hiking centres. In winter, skiers from across Japan and increasingly overseas flock to Hakuba's seven ski resorts. In summer, the region draws hikers attracted by easy access to the high peaks. There are many onsen in and around Hakuba-mura, the main village, and a long soak after a day of action is the perfect way to ease your muscles.

◉ Sights & Activities

Mimizuku-no-yu　ONSEN
(みみずくの湯; 5480 Ō-aza Hokujō; adult/child ¥500/250; ◎10am-9.30pm, enter by 9pm) One of Hakuba's many onsen, many contend this has the best mountain views from the tub.

Skiing

Happō-One Ski Resort　SKIING
(八方尾根スキー所; www.happo-one.jp/english; 1-day lift ticket ¥4600; ◎Dec-Apr) Host of the downhill races at the 1998 Winter Olympics, Happō-One is one of Japan's best ski areas, with superb mountain views and beginner, intermediate and advanced runs catering to skiers and snowboarders. For the lowdown, check the excellent website (in English).

Most runs go right down the face of the mountain, with several good burners descending from Usagidaira 109, the mountain's centre point. Above this, two chairlifts run to the top. On busy days, avoid lift bottlenecks by heading to areas like the Skyline 2.

The rest house at Usagidaira 109 is the largest eating establishment with a selection of vendors. There are plenty of hire places in the streets around the base of the mountain,

some with boots up to 31cm. All have roughly the same selection and prices (¥2500 to ¥3000 per day for skis/board and boots).

From Hakuba Station, a five-minute bus ride (¥260) takes you into the middle of Hakuba-mura; from there it's a 10-minute walk to the base of Happō-One and the main 'Adam' gondola base station. In winter, a shuttle bus makes the rounds of the village, lodges and ski base.

Hakuba 47 Winter Sports Park & Hakuba Goryū Ski Resort　SKIING
(www.hakuba47.co.jp; one-day lift ticket ¥4800; ◎Dec-Apr) The interlinked areas of Hakuba 47 Winter Sports Park and Hakuba Goryū Ski Resort form the second major ski resort in the Hakuba area. There's a good variety of terrain at both areas, but you'll have to be at least an intermediate skier to ski the runs linking the two. Like Happō-One, this area boasts fantastic mountain views. The Genki Go shuttle bus from Hakuba-mura and Hakuba-eki provides the easiest access.

Hakuba Cortina Kokusai　SKIING
(白馬コルチナ国際; www.hakubacortina.jp/ski; 1-day lift ticket ¥3500; ◎Dec-Apr) This smaller ski area at the north end of the valley is popular with an upwardly mobile Japanese crowd who dig the resort – a massive European gothic structure with hotel, restaurants, ski rental and deluxe onsen – and those who want quieter slopes. It also caters to more advanced skiers, but can be icy when there isn't new snow.

Hiking

In summer, you can take the gondola and the two upper chairlifts, then hike along a trail for an hour or so to Happō-*ike* (pond) on a ridge below Karamatsu-dake (唐松岳; 2695m). From here, follow a trail another hour up to Maru-yama, continue for 1½ hours to the Karamatsu-dake San-sō (mountain hut) and then climb to the peak of Karamatsu-dake in about 30 minutes. The return fare is ¥2340 if purchased at the Hakuba tourist office, ¥2600 otherwise.

Evergreen Outdoor　ADVENTURE SPORTS
(www.evergreen-hakuba.com) This gang of friendly, healthy, outdoorsy folk offer an array of adventures with English-speaking guides from about ¥5000 year-round, including canyoning and mountain biking, as well as snowshoeing and backcountry treks in the winter.

🛏 Sleeping & Eating

Snowbeds Backpackers
HOSTEL ¥

(スノーベッズバックパッカーズ; ☏72-5242; www.snowbedsjapan.com; dm per person from ¥3510; [P][@][🛜]) This foreign-run backpackers has cheap but cramped bunk rooms and a nice communal area with a wood stove. It's close to the nightlife. Private rooms are also available.

Hakuba Panorama Hotel
INN ¥¥

(白馬パノラマホテル; ☏85-4031; www.hakuba-panorama.com; 3322-1 Hokujō; s/d with breakfast from ¥10,900/16,900; [P][🛜]) About 300m from one of the lifts at Happō-One, this Australian-run outfit has bilingual Japanese staff, an on-site travel agency and a variety of room types with en suite bathrooms. There's a guest laundry and a wonderful onsen.

Hakuba Highland Hotel
HOTEL ¥¥

(白馬ハイランドホテル; ☏72-3450; www.hakuba-highland.net; 1582 Hokujō; r per person with meals from ¥9680; [P]) This older hotel has sensational views over the Hakuba range and a great indoor-outdoor onsen, but it's away from the action. In winter, there's a free shuttle bus to the main resorts, each about 20 minutes' drive.

★ Ridge Hotel & Apartments
HOTEL ¥¥¥

(☏85-4301; www.theridge.jp; 4608 Hakuba; s/d from ¥16,350/10,900, apartment r from ¥36,000; [P][@][🛜]) Sophisticated, sexy and stylish, this stunning property has it all, year-round: location, amenities, views. A variety of room types range from the sublime – Western rooms with Japanese elements, to the ridiculous – a gorgeous loft balcony suite in the shadow of the slopes. Obliging, attentive staff speak English well. Splurge if you can.

Hakuba Tokyu Hotel
HOTEL ¥¥¥

(白馬東急ホテル; ☏72-3001; www.tokyuhotelsjapan.com/en; Happō-wadanomori; s/d with breakfast from ¥18,400/25,400; [P][🛜]) This elegant year-round hotel has large rooms with great views and a wonderful garden, popular for weddings. The Grand Spa boasts the highest alkaline content in the area, and there's both French and Japanese restaurants.

Bamboo Coffee Bar
CAFE ¥

(☏090-7017-5331; ⊙8am-6pm; [🛜][📶]) On the left as you exit Hakuba Staion, this wonderful modern cafe serves delicious speciality coffees, sweet treats and panini sandwiches. The mellow tunes, friendly staff and free wi-fi (with purchases) make this a great place to log on and get your bearings.

🍷 Drinking & Entertainment

Tanuki's
SPORTS BAR

(タヌキ; ☏090-7202-9809; 6350-3 Hokujo; ⊙noon-late, Thu-Tue) This neat little bar to your right as you exit the station serves juicy original burgers as well as your favourite fast foods in a welcoming environment which includes free pool, darts and foosball on the 2nd floor.

Tracks Bar
BAR

(☏75-4366) Located between Kamishiro Station and Goryū, this is one of the favourite night spots for the younger, foreign crowd, with live music, pool tables, wood-burner stoves and sports on a huge screen.

The Pub
PUB

(☏72-4453; www.thepubhakuba.com; ⊙4.30pm-late; [@][🛜]) The only English pub in the village is found in a Swiss-style chalet on the grounds of the Momonoki hotel. By Japanese standards, it's huge and happening. There's a daily happy hour and free internet and wi-fi.

Hakuba Bike Bar
BAR

(www.bikebar-hakuba.com) This fun, disco-lit basement bar in Hakuba Goryū has a refreshingly hippie vibe – these guys think they're pretty cool, and by many standards, they are. It's about 10 minutes' walk from the Sky 4 Gondola and has billiards, early-evening film nights for families (Ninja juice is served) and karaoke.

ℹ Information

Hakuba Accomodation Information Centre (白馬宿泊情報センター; Hakuba Shukuhaku Jōhō Sentā; ☏72-6900; www.hakuba1.com; ⊙7am-6pm) For information, maps and lodging assistance. Located to the right of Hakuba Station.

Hakuba Tourist Information Office (白馬村観光案内所; ☏72-3232; www.vill.hakuba.nagano.jp/english; ⊙8.30am-5.30pm) Provides maps and leaflets relating to tourism in the area. In addition to all things winter, the website has detailed information on summer gondola operating schedules and fares. It's just outside Hakuba Station.

ℹ Getting There & Away

Hakuba is connected with Matsumoto by the JR Ōito line (tokkyū, ¥2260, one hour; futsū, ¥1110, 1½ hours). Continuing north, change trains at

Minami Otari to meet the JR Hokuriku line at Itoigawa, with connections to Niigata, Toyama and Kanazawa.

Alpico group operates buses from Nagano Station (¥1500, approximately 70 minutes) and Shinjuku Nishi-guchi, in Tokyo (¥4700, 4½ hours).

Bessho Onsen 別所温泉

☑ 0268

With some interesting temples and reputedly excellent waters, this mountain-ringed onsen town is worth passing through if you're nearby, but overall lacks something cohesive as a destination.

Historically, it's been referred to as 'Little Kamakura' for the fact that it served as an administrative centre during the Kamakura period (1185–1333). It was also mentioned in *The Pillow Book* by the Heian-era poetess Sei Shōnagon – no doubt it was infinitely more appealing then. That said, it does have some lovely elements, a National Treasure temple and a stunning example of traditional onsen ryokan.

◉ Sights & Activities

Anraku-ji TEMPLE
(安楽寺; ☑ 38-2062; adult/child ¥300/100; ⊙8am-5pm Mar-Oct, to 4pm Nov-Feb) Of the Sōtō zen sect, Anraku-ji is the oldest Zen temple in Nagano. Dating from AD 824–34, it's a National Treasure, renowned for its octagonal pagoda. The temple is a 10-minute walk from the station.

Kitamuki Kannon TEMPLE
(北向観音; ☑ 38-2023; ⊙24hr) **FREE** The grounds of this Tendai temple have some impressive ancient trees and sweeping valley views, although there's no longer anything particularly contemplative about the valley development below, once an awe-inspiring vista. The temple's name comes from the fact that this Kannon image faces north, a counterpart to the south-facing image at Zenkō-ji in Nagano. A further 5km hike from here are the temples Chūzen-ji and Zenzan-ji, which do feel like a real escape.

Onsen ONSEN
(admission ¥150; ⊙6am-10pm) There are three central public baths: Ō-yu (大湯) has a small *rotemburo*; Ishi-yu (石湯) is famed for its stone bath; and Daishi-yu (大師湯), most frequented by the locals, is relatively cool.

🛏 Sleeping & Eating

★ **Ryokan Hanaya** RYOKAN ¥¥
(旅館花屋; ☑ 38-3131; www.hanaya.naganoken.jp; 169 Bessho Onsen; r per person for groups of 2 or more, with meals from ¥13,650) Ryokan Hanaya is a warp back in time to the Taisho era (1912–1925) – a traditional gem set among wonderful manicured Japanese gardens. Spacious tatami rooms open onto the scenery; 14 beautiful though ageing rooms each have unique motifs and history. All have their own toilets, some have onsen baths. Expect the most attentive level of service and cuisine (served in your room), though little English is spoken. The *rotemburo* in the garden are blissful.

Uematsu-ya INN ¥¥
(上松屋; ☑ 38-2300; www.uematsuya.com/english; 1628 Bessho Onsen; r per person with 2 meals from ¥11,550) Uematsu-ya is a well-kept, good-value inn occupying a nine-storey building atop a hill. Its rooms (Japanese and Western style) all have their own bathrooms. Deluxe rooms are larger, on higher floors and have a private terrace. There are also indoor onsen and lovely *rotemburo*. Some English is spoken.

ℹ Information

Bessho Onsen Ryokan Association (別所温泉旅館組合; ☑ 38-3510; www.bessho-spa.jp; ⊙9am-5pm) Located at the train station, this small office provides tourist information and can assist with lodging reservations, though some Japanese ability will be handy.

ℹ Getting There & Away

Access is by train, via Ueda. From Nagano, take the JR *shinkansen* (Asama, ¥1410, 12 minutes) or the private Shinano Tetsudō line (¥750, 42 minutes). From Tokyo, take the JR *shinkansen* (Asama, ¥5980, 1½ hours). Once at Ueda, change to the private Ueda Dentetsu line to Bessho Onsen (¥570, 28 minutes).

Matsumoto 松本

☑ 0263 / POP 243,000

Embraced by seven great peaks to the west (including Yariga-take, Hotaka-dake and Norikura-dake, each above 3000m) and three smaller sentinels to the east (including beautiful Utsukushi-ga-hara-kōgen), Matsumoto occupies a protected position in a fertile valley no more than 20km across at its widest. Views of the regal Alps are never far away and sunsets are breathtaking.

Formerly known as Fukashi, Nagano Prefecture's second-largest city has been here since the 8th century. In the 14th and 15th centuries, it was the castle town of the Ogasawara clan and continued to prosper through the Edo period, to the present.

Today, Matsumoto is one of Japan's finest cities – an attractive, cosmopolitan place loved by its residents. Admirers from around the world come to enjoy its superb castle, pretty streets, galleries, cafes and endearing vistas. With plenty of well-priced, quality accommodation and excellent access to/from and around the town, Matsumoto is the perfect base for exploring the Japan Alps and the Kiso and Azumino Valleys.

⊙ Sights & Activities

Matsumoto-jō
CASTLE

(松本城; 4-1 Marunōchi; adult/child ¥600/300; ⊙8.30am-5pm early-Sep–mid-Jul, to 6pm mid-Jul–Aug) Magnificent, must-see Matsumoto-jō is Japan's oldest wooden castle and one of four castles designated National Treasures – the others are Hikone, Himeji and Inuyama. The magnificent three-turreted *donjon* was completed around 1595, in contrasting black and white, leading to the nickname Karasu-jō (Crow Castle). Steep steps lead up six storeys, with impressive views from each level. Lower floors display guns, bombs and gadgets with which to storm castles, and a delightful *tsukimi yagura* (moon-viewing pavilion). It has a tranquil moat full of carp, with the occasional swan gliding beneath the red bridges. The basics are explained over loudspeakers in English and Japanese. You can also ask at the entrance about a free tour in English (subject to availability), or call the Goodwill Guide Group (☑32-7140), which gives free one-hour tours by reservation.

Matsumoto City Museum
MUSEUM

(松本市立博物館; Matsumoto Shiritsu Hakubutsukan; 4-1 Marunōchi; ⊙8.30am-4.30pm) The castle grounds (and your admission ticket) also include the Matsumoto City Museum, with its small displays relating to the region's history and folklore.

Former Kaichi School
MUSEUM

(旧開智学校; Kyū Kaichi Gakkō; ☑32-5275; 2-4-12 Kaichi; adult/child ¥300; ⊙8.30am-4.30pm, closed Mon Dec-Feb) A few blocks north of the castle, the former Kaichi School is both an Important Cultural Property and the oldest elementary school in Japan, founded in 1873. It opened its doors as a museum in 1965, and has been

a fascinating homage to turn-of-the-century education ever since. The building itself is an excellent example of Meiji-era architecture.

Nawate-dōri
STREET

(縄手道り) Nawate-dōri is a popular place for a stroll, a few blocks from the castle. Vendors of this riverside walk sell antiques, souvenirs and delicious *taiyaki* (filled waffle in the shape of a carp) of varying flavours. Look for the big frog statue, by the bridge.

Nakamachi
NEIGHBOURHOOD

(中町) This charming former merchant district by the Metoba-*gawa* (river), with its *namako-kabe kura* (lattice walled storehouses) and Edo-period streetscapes, makes for a wonderful stroll. Many buildings have been preserved and transformed into cafes, galleries and craft shops specialising in wood, glass, fabric, ceramics and antiques.

Matsumoto Timepiece Museum
MUSEUM

(松本市時計博物館; Matsumoto-shi Tokei Hakubutsukan; 4-21-15 Chūō; adult/student ¥300/150; ⊙9am-5pm Tue-Sun) Home to Japan's largest pendulum clock (on the building's exterior) and over 300 other timepieces, incuding fascinating medieval Japanese creations, this museum shows Japan's love of *monozukuri* (the art of creating things).

Matsumoto

Matsumoto City Museum of Art MUSEUM
(松本市美術館; Matsumoto-shi Bijutsukan; 4-2-22 Chūō; adult/child ¥400/free; ⊙9am-5pm Tue-Sun) This sleek museum has a good collection of Japanese artists, many of whom hail from Matsumoto or depict scenes of the surrounding countryside. Highlights include the striking avant-garde works of Kusama Yayoi (look for the 'Infinity Mirrored Room').

Japan Ukiyo-e Museum MUSEUM
(日本浮世絵美術館; 2206-1 Koshiba; adult/child ¥1050/530; ⊙10am-5pm Tue-Sun) Housing more than 100,000 woodblock prints, paintings, screens and old books, this renowned museum exhibits a minuscule fraction of its collection. The museum is approximately 3km from Matsumoto Station, 15 minutes' walk from Ōniwa Station on the Matsumoto Dentetsu line (¥170, six minutes), or about ¥2000 by taxi.

Matsumoto Open-Air Architectural Museum MUSEUM
(松本市歴史の里 Matsumoto-shi Rekishi-no-sato; ☑47-4515; 2196-1 Shimadachi; ¥400; ⊙9am-4.30pm Tue-Sun) Adjacent to the better known Japan Ukiyo-e Museum, amid fields and rice paddies, beneath the gaze of the Alps stand these five examples of striking late Edo- and early Showa-era architecture for you to explore.

Utsukushi-ga-hara Onsen & Asama Onsen ONSEN
(美ヶ原温泉・浅間温泉) Northeast of downtown, Utsukushi-ga-hara Onsen (not to be confused with Utsukushi-ga-hara-kōgen) is the prettier of these spa villages, with a quaint main street and views across the valley. Asama Onsen's history is said to date back to the 10th century and includes writers

and poets, though it looks quite generic now. Both areas are easily reached by bus from Matsumoto's bus terminal (Utsukushi-ga-hara Onsen: ¥330, 18 minutes, twice hourly; Asama Onsen: ¥350, 23 minutes, hourly).

Hot Plaza Asama ONSEN
(ホットプラザ浅間; ☑46-6278; 3-16 Asama-onsen; adult/child ¥630/350; ⊙10am-11pm Wed-Mon) Among dozens of baths and inns at Asama Onsen, Hot Plaza Asama has numerous indoor and outdoor baths in a traditional building. Rental towels are available (¥200). Buses from Matsumoto Station take about 20 minutes.

Utsukushi-ga-hara-kōgen PLATEAU
(美ヶ原高原) This stunning alpine plateau (2000m) boasts over 200 varieties of flora, which come alive in summer. It's a great day trip from Matsumoto (612m), reached via an ooh-and-ahh drive on twisty mountain roads called Azalea Line and Venus Line (open late April to early November). A car gives you freedom to explore the beauty, but there's also a bus, in season (¥1500 one-way, 1½ hours).

Utsukushi-ga-hara Open Air Museum MUSEUM
(美ヶ原美術館; Utsukushi-ga-hara Bijutsukan; adult/child/student ¥1000/700/800; ⊙9am-5pm late Apr-early Nov) Atop Utsukushi-ga-hara-kōgen you'll find this seemingly random sculpture garden with some 350 pieces, mostly by Japanese sculptors. The surrounding countryside provides an inspiring backdrop. Nearby are pleasant walks and the opportunity to see cows in pasture (a constant source of fascination in Japan). **Furusato-kan** (ふる里館), the shop at the hilltop farm, sells ice cream made from local *kokemomo* (lingonberries). Buses (¥1500, 1½ hours)

run several times daily during the warmer months, athough a rental car is good option if windy roads don't phase you.

✸ Festivals & Events

Locals love to celebrate – you're never far from a festival here.

Matsumoto-jō
Sakura Matsuri
CHERRY BLOSSOM

Three days after the cherry blossoms are declared in full bloom (early April), the castle and its *sakura* trees are illuminated spectacularly, and entry to the inner compound is free.

Matsumoto-jō Taiko Matsuri
DRUMMING

The castle grounds and beyond ring out with the sound and energy of Taiko drumming during this awesome festival, held the balmy last weekend of July.

Tenjin Matsuri
PARADE

The festival at Fukashi-jinja on 23 and 24 July features elaborately decorated *yatai*.

Matsumoto Bonbon
PARADE

Matsumoto's biggest event takes place on the first Saturday in August, when over 25,000 people of all ages perform the 'bonbon' dance through the streets, well into the hot summer's night. Be prepared to be drawn into the action.

Takigi Nō Matsuri
THEATRE

This atmospheric festival during August features nō performances by torchlight, outdoors on a stage in the park below the castle.

Saitō Kinen Matsuri
MUSIC

About a dozen classical music concerts in memory of revered Japanese conductor and music educator Saitō Hideo (1902–72) held from mid-August to mid-September. Ozawa Seiji, conductor emeritus of the Boston Symphony Orchestra, is festival director.

Dōsojin Matsuri
CULTURAL

On the fourth Saturday in September, much merriment is to be had at the festival held in honour of *dōsojin* (roadside guardians) at Utsukushi-ga-hara Onsen.

Asama Onsen Taimatsu Matsuri
PARADE

Around the start of October, Asama Onsen celebrates the spectacular and slightly manic fire festival, wherein groups of men, women and children, shouting 'wa-sshoi!', like a mantra, parade burning bales of hay through narrow streets to an enormous bonfire at Misha-jinja.

Oshiro Matsuri
CULTURAL

The Castle Festival, from mid-October to 3 November, is a cultural jamboree that includes costume parades, puppet displays and flower shows.

🛏 Sleeping

Matsumoto is compact enough that you can stay anywhere downtown and get around easily. Most business hotels are by the station, but there are some great traditional options in picturesque Nakamachi.

★ Nunoya
INN ¥

(ぬのや旅館; ☎32-0545; www.mcci.or.jp/www/nunoya/en; 3-5-7 Chūō; r per person from ¥4500) Few inns have more heart than this simple, traditional charmer, meticulously kept by its friendly owner. The spotless inn has shiny dark-wood floors and atmospheric tatami rooms. No meals are served, but you're right in the heart of the best part of town. If you don't mind sharing a bathroom, the rate is wonderful for this much character.

Richmond Hotel
HOTEL ¥

(リッチモンドホテル松本; ☎37-5000; www.richmondhotel.jp/en/matsumoto; 1-10-7 Chūō; s/d from ¥5200/8500; ☺@) A few minutes' walk from JR Matsumoto Station, this 204-room business hotel is in great shape and a great location. The deluxe double rooms are large by Japanese standards, and reasonably priced. There's a Gusto family restaurant (with picture menu) downstairs.

Marumo
RYOKAN ¥

(まるも; ☎32-0115; 3-3-10 Chūō; r per person ¥5250, with breakfast ¥6300) Between Nakamachi and the river, this creaky wooden ryokan dates from 1868 and has lots of traditional charm, including a bamboo garden and coffee shop. Although the rooms aren't huge and don't have private facilities, it's quite popular, so book ahead.

Seifūsō
RYOKAN ¥

(静風荘; ☎46-0639; www.ryokanseifuso.jp/english; 634-5 Minami-asama; r per person from ¥4700; P@) Free pick-up (arrange in advance) and free bicycles make up for the fact that this inn is closer to Asama-onsen than Matsumoto. Otherwise, it's run by a friendly family who love to welcome overseas guests. Japanese-style rooms are clean and bright, have a nice outlook and shared baths. Once you're there, take bus 2 to get back into town.

★ **Hotel Buena Vista** HOTEL ¥¥
(ホテルブエナビスタ; ☏37-0111; www.
buena-vista.co.jp/english; 1-2-1 Honjo; s/tw from
¥9240/17,640; ◉@） An oldie but a goodie –
Matsumoto's sharpest Western hotel recently received a makeover in its public spaces
and rooms, leaving it looking quite the part.
The executive rooms and the suites are the
way to go, if you're going to do it. Many
rooms have exceptional views.

Dormy Inn Matsumoto HOTEL ¥¥
(ドーミーイン松本; ☏33-5489; www.hotespa.
net/hotels/matsumoto; 2-2-1 Fukashi; s/d from
¥8000/10,500; P@） This newer property has
compact, well-designed rooms with pleasant, neutral decor. There's an onsen featuring a sunny *rotemburo* and the breakfast
buffet is decent. Otherwise, there's all the
things travellers need, including a laundry.
Deals can be found online (in Japanese).

Sugimoto RYOKAN ¥¥¥
(旅館すぎもと; ☏32-3379; 451-7 Satoyamabe; r
per person from ¥15,000; ☒ Utsukushigahara Onsen
Line/Town Sneaker North Course) The lack of English spoken at this upscale ryokan in Utsukushi-ga-hara Onsen may be its only downfall
for non-Japanese speakers. With some fascinating elements, such as the art collection,
underground passageway and bar full of single malts, this is a unique property. Rooms
range in size and decor (Japanese, Western
and mixed), but all are ineffably stylish.

✖ Eating & Drinking

For a quick coffee and cake, cafes line the
banks of the Metoba-gawa and Nawate-dōri.

Kura SHOKUDŌ ¥
(蔵; ☏33-6444; 1-10-22 Chūō; dishes from ¥300,
teishoku ¥945-2100; ◷lunch & dinner Thu-Tue)
Near Nakamachi, Kura serves meticulously
prepared sushi and tempura for lunch and
dinner in a stylish former warehouse. For
the daring: *basashi* (raw horse meat).

Delhi CURRY ¥
(デリー; ☏35-2408; 2-4-13 Chūō; curries with rice
¥650-850; ◉） One of our favourites, this little
'ma and pa' outfit has been serving delicious
curry rice (Japanese style) in an adorable
former storehouse by the river, since 1970.
If you like *tonkatsu*, you must try the *katsu
karē* (¥850). Cheap and cheerful.

Kane TAIWANESE ¥
(香根; ☏36-1303; 2-8-5 Ōte; ◷5.30pm-late; ◹)
This simple Taiwanese eatery near the castle serves amazing spicy soups, noodles and
veggies as well as the standard array of Chinese fare at very reasonable prices. There's a
picture menu.

Nomugi NOODLES ¥
(野麦; ☏36-3753; 2-9-11 Chūō; soba ¥1100;
◷lunch Thu-Mon; ◹) In Nakamachi, this is
one of central Japan's finest *soba* shops. Its
owner used to run a French restaurant in
Tokyo before returning to his home town.
Keeping things Zen, there are two dishes:
zaru-soba and *kake-soba*. Oh, and beer.

Robata Shōya GRILL ¥
(炉ばた庄屋; ☏37-1000; 11-1 Chūō; dishes
¥300-900; ◷lunch & dinner) Close to the station you'll find this lively *robatayaki* (grill)
house, doing it before your eyes to a wide
range of seafood, chicken, meats and mountain delights. Order lots of small plates.

Shizuka IZAKAYA ¥¥
(しづか; ☏32-0547; 4-10-8 Ōte; dishes ¥480-
4410; ◷lunch & dinner Mon-Sat; ◉） This wonderfully traditional *izakaya* serving favourites like *oden* and *yakitori* (skewers of
grilled chicken) as well as some more challenging specialities.

Old Rock PUB
(オールドロック; ☏38-0069; 2-30-20 Chūō;
mains from ¥750; ◷lunch & dinner) In the perfect spot, a block south of the river, across
from Nakamachi, you'll find this popular
pub with good lunch specials and, appropriately, a wide range of beers.

Coat BAR
(メインバーコート; ☏34-7133; 2-3-24 Chūō;
◷6pm-12.30am Tue-Sun) This sophisticated
little whisky bar is run by a colourful character who'd love to pour you a single malt or
one of his original cocktails.

Sorpresa BAR
(ソルプレーサ; ☏37-0510; Buena Vista Hotel,
14F; ◷5.30pm-midnight) You can't beat the
views from this swanky top-floor bar at the
Buena Vista Hotel. It's also a French restaurant, if you fancy it, but it's possible to come
here just to imbibe.

🔒 Shopping

Matsumoto is synonymous with *temari* (embroidered balls) and doll-making. Takasago
street, one block south of Nakamachi, has
several doll shops. **Parco department store**
(パルコ) has pride of place in the city centre.

Belle Amie HANDICRAFTS
(ベラミ; ☑33-1314; ⊙9am-7pm Mon, Tue, Thu,
Fri & Sat, 10am-6pm Sun) *Temari* and dolls are
found here. Doll styles include *tanabata*
and *oshie-bina* (dressed in fine cloth).

Nakamachi Kura-chic-kan ARTS & CRAFTS
(中町・蔵シック館; ☑36-3053; 2-9-15 Chūō;
⊙9am-5pm) A pun on 'classic' in English,
'kura' in Japanese and 'chic' in French, Nakamachi Kura-chic-kan showcases locally
produced arts and crafts.

Chikiri-ya GLASS
(ちきりや; ☑33-2522; 3-4-18 Chūō ⊙9am-5pm)
Glass and pottery aficionados will find this
wonderful boutique a must.

ⓘ Information

Although small streets radiate somewhat confusingly from the train station, soon you're on a
grid. Any place on our Matsumoto map is within
20 minutes' walk of the train station.

On the web, visit: www.city.matsumoto.
nagano.jp.

Main Post Office (Honmachi-dōri)

JTB (☑35-3311; 1-2-11 Fukashi) For train and
bus reservations.

Tourist Information Office (松本市観光案内
所; ☑32-2814; 1-1-1 Fukashi; ⊙9.30am-5.45pm)
This excellent Tourist Information Office
inside Matsumoto Station has friendly English-
speaking staff and a wide range of well-produced
English language materials on the area.

ⓘ Getting There & Away

AIR
Shinshū Matsumoto airport has flights to Fukuoka, Osaka and Sapporo.

BUS
Alpico runs buses between Matsumoto and
Shinjuku in Tokyo (¥3400, 3¼ hours, 18 daily),
Osaka (¥5700, 5¾ hours, two daily, and one
longer overnight service), and Nagoya (¥3460,
3½ hours, eight daily). **Nohi Bus** services
Takayama (¥3100, 2½ hours, six daily). Reservations are advised. The **Matsumoto bus
station** is in the basement of the Espa building
across from the train station.

CAR
Renting a car is a great way to explore the beau-
ty outside town, but expect narrow, windy roads.
There are several agencies around the station.
Rates generally around ¥6500 per day.

TRAIN
'Matsumotooo... Matsumotooo...' is connected
with Tokyo's Shinjuku Station (*tokkyū*, ¥6200,

2¾ hours, hourly), Nagoya (*tokkyū*, ¥5360, two
hours) and Nagano (Shinano *tokkyū*, ¥2260, 50
minutes; Chūō *futsū*, ¥1110, 1¼ hours).

ⓘ Getting Around

Matsumoto-jō and the city centre are easily covered on foot and free bicycles are available for
loan – enquire at the Tourist Information Office.
Three 'town sneaker' loop bus routes operate
between 9am and 5.30pm for ¥190/500 per
ride/day; the blue and orange routes cover the
castle and Nakamachi.

An airport shuttle bus connects Shinshū
Matsumoto airport with downtown (¥540, 25
minutes). A taxi costs around ¥4500.

Kiso Valley Nakasendō 木曽谷中仙道
☑0264

The Nakasendō was one of the five highways
of the Edo period connecting Edo (now Tokyo) with Kyoto. Much of the route is now
followed by National Roads, however, in this
thickly forested section of the Kiso Valley,
there exists several sections of the twisty,
craggy post road which have been carefully
restored, the most impressive being the
7.8km stretch between Magome and Tsumago, two of the most attractive Nakasendō
towns. Walking this route is one of Japan's
most rewarding tourist experiences.

It's worth a stay in any or all of these special towns to have them to yourself once the
day trippers clear out. For street foods, look
for *gohei-mochi* (skewered rice dumplings
coated with sesame-walnut sauce) and in
autumn you can't miss *kuri-kinton* (chestnut dumplings).

MAGOME 馬篭
In Gifu-ken, pretty Magome is the furthest
south of the Kiso Valley post towns. Its
buildings line a steep, cobblestone pedestrian road which is unfriendly to heavy wheelie
suitcases, but whose rustic shopfronts and
mountain views will keep your finger on the
shutter.

From Magome, the 7.8km hike to Tsumago follows a steep, largely paved road until
it reaches its peak at the top of Magome-
tōge (pass) – elevation 801m. After the pass,
the trail meanders by waterfalls, forest and
farmland. The route is easiest in this direction, from Magome (elevation 600m)
to Tsumago (elevation 420m). The route is
clearly signposted in English; allow three to
six hours to enjoy it.

If fitness or a disability might prevent you from appreciating this amazing walk, there is an easier way. The Magome-Tsumago bus (¥600, 30 minutes, two to three daily in each direction) also stops at Magome-*tōge*. If you alight and begin the walk here, it's a picturesque 5.2km downhill run through to Tsumago.

If you do the hike, both towns offer a handy baggage forwarding service from either Tourist Information Office to the other. Deposit your bags between 8.30am and 11.30am, for delivery by 1pm.

Tōson Kinenkan　　　　　　　MUSEUM
(藤村記念館; ☎69-2047; admission ¥500; ☺9am-4pm) Magome was the birthplace of author Shimazaki Tōson (1872–1943). His work records the decline of two provincial Kiso families – this heavily Japanese museum is devoted to his life and times.

🛏 Sleeping & Eating

Minshuku Tajimaya　　　　　　INN ¥
(民宿但馬屋; ☎69-2048; www.kiso-taji-maya.com; 4266 Magome; s/d inc two meals ¥8925/16,800; ☺🛜) This pleasant historical inn has compact rooms and friendly staff, although the location of the bathrooms can be inconvenient. The array of local specialties served in the common dining area is impressive, as are the *hinoki* baths.

Magome-Chaya　　　　　　　INN ¥¥
(馬籠茶屋; ☎59-2038; www.magomechaya.com; r per person inc 2 meals from ¥9450) This popular *minshuku* is almost halfway up the hill, near the water wheel. Room-only plans are available.

ℹ Information

Tourist Information Office (観光案内館; ☎59-2336; fax 59-2653; ☺9am-5pm) Inconveniently halfway up the hill to the right, you can pick up maps here and staff can book accommodation.

TSUMAGO 妻籠

Tsumago feels like an open-air museum, about 15 minutes' walk from end to end. It was designated by the government as a protected area for the preservation of traditional buildings, where modern developments such as telephone poles aren't allowed to mar the scene. The dark-wood glory of its lattice-fronted buildings is particularly beautiful at dawn and dusk. Film and TV crews are often spotted here.

On 23 November, the **Fūzoku Emaki** parade is held along the Nakasendō in Tsumago, featuring townsfolk in Edo-period costume.

◉ Sights & Activities

Waki-honjin (Okuya) &
Local History Museum　　　　MUSEUM
(脇本陣（奥谷） ・歴史資料館　Rekishi Shiryōkan; adult/child ¥600/300; ☺9am-5pm) The former rest stop for the *daimyō's* retainers, this Waki-honjin was reconstructed in 1877 by a former castle builder under special dispensation from Emperor Meiji. It contains a lovely moss garden and a special toilet built in case Meiji happened to show up. He never did. The adjacent Local History Museum houses elegant exhibitions about Kiso and the Nakasendō, with some English signage.

Tsumago-honjin　　　HISTORIC BUILDING
(妻籠本陣; adult/child ¥300/150; ☺9am-5pm) Here is where *daimyō* themselves would spend the night, although the building's architecture is more noteworthy than its exhibits. A combined ticket (adult/child ¥700/350) also gives you admission to Waki-honjin and the Local History Museum, opposite.

Kisoji Resort　　　　　　　ONSEN
(木曽路館　Kisoji-kan; ☎58-2046; 2278 Azuma; baths ¥700; ☺9am-7pm) A few kilometres above Tsumago, you'll find this *rotemburo* with panoramic mountain vistas, a sprawling dining room and a souvenir shop.

🛏 Sleeping & Eating

Oyado Daikichi　　　　　　　INN ¥
(御宿大吉; ☎57-2595; www17.plala.or.jp/daikiti/english; r per person with 2 meals from ¥9000; ☺@) Popular with foreign visitors, this traditional looking inn benefits from modern construction and has a prime top of the hill location – all rooms have a lovely outlook. It's at the very edge of town.

★ Fujioto　　　　　　　　RYOKAN ¥¥
(藤乙; ☎57-3009; www.takenet.or.jp/~fujioto; r per person from ¥10,500; ☺🛜) The owner of this unpretentious, welcoming inn has ability in English, French, Italian and Spanish. It's a great place to have your first ryokan experience as most staff are able to communicate well, especially over the wonderful *kaiseki* dinner, served in the dining room. Corner upstairs rooms have lovely views. You can also stop by for lunch – try the Kiso Valley trout (*teishoku* ¥1350).

Matsushiro-ya RYOKAN ¥¥
(松代屋旅館; ☑ 57-3022; fax 57-3386; r per person ¥10,500; ☺ Thu-Tue) Showing signs of age, this is one of Tsumago's most historic lodgings (parts date from 1804). It has large tatami rooms and plenty of authentic charm.

Yoshimura-ya NOODLES ¥
(吉村屋; ☑ 57-3265; dishes ¥700-1500; ☺ lunch, closed Thu; ☑ 🖳) If you're hungry after a long walk, this handmade *soba* will fill you up.

ⓘ Information

Tourist Information Office (観光案内館; ☑ 57-3123; fax 57-4036; ☺ 8.30am-5pm) Tsumago's Tourist Information Office is in the centre of town, by the antique phone booth. Some English is spoken and there's English-language literature. Ask here for any directions.

ⓘ Getting There & Away

Nakatsugawa and Nagiso Stations on the JR Chūō line serve Magome and Tsumago respectively, though both are still at some distance. Nakatsugawa is connected with Nagoya (*tokkyū*, ¥2430, 57 minutes) and Matsumoto (*tokkyū*, ¥3670, 1¼ hours). A few *tokkyū* daily stop in Nagiso (from Nagoya ¥2770, one hour); otherwise change at Nakatsugawa (*futsū* ¥320, 20 minutes).

Buses leave hourly from Nakatsugawa Station for Magome (¥540, 30 minutes). There's also an infrequent bus service between Magome and Tsumago (¥600, 25 minutes), via Magome-tōge.

Buses run between Tsumago and Nagiso Station (¥270, 10 minutes, eight per day), or it's an hour's walk.

Meitetsu operate highway buses that connect Tokyo's Shinjuku Station with Magome (¥4500, 4½ hours). Note that the stop is at the highway interchange, from where it's a 1.3km uphill walk, unless timed with the bus from Nakatsugawa.

KISO-FUKUSHIMA 木曽福島

North of Tsumago and Magome, Kiso-Fukushima is larger and considerably more developed, but its historical significance as an important checkpoint on the Nakasendō and its riverside position make it a pleasant lunch stop en route to (or from) Matsumoto.

From Kiso-Fukushima station, turn right and head downhill towards the town centre and the Kiso-gawa. Sights are well signposted. Look for **Ue-no-dan** (上の段), the historic district of atmospheric houses, many of which are now retailers.

⊙ Sights

Fukushima Checkpoint Site MUSEUM
(福島関所跡 Fukushima Sekisho-ato; adult/child ¥300/150; ☺ 8am-5pm Apr-Oct, 8.30am-4pm Nov-Mar) This is a reconstruction of one of the most significant checkpoints on the Edo-period trunk roads. From its perch above the river valley, it's easy to see the barrier's strategic importance. Displays inside show the implements used to maintain order, including weaponry and tegata (wooden travel passes), as well as the special treatment women travellers received.

✕ Eating

★ Kurumaya Honten NOODLES ¥
(くるまや本店; ☑ 22-2200; 5367-2 Kiso-machi Fukushima; mains ¥630-1575; ☺ 10am-5pm Thu-Tue; ☑ 🖳) One of Japan's most renowned *soba* shops. The classic presentation is cold *mori* (plain) or *zaru* (with strips of nori seaweed) with a sweetish dipping sauce. It's near the first bridge at the bottom of the hill. Look for the gears above the doorway.

Bistro Matsushima-tei ITALIAN ¥
(ビストロ松島体; ☑ 23-3625; 5250-1 Ue-no-dan; mains ¥1155-1900, lunch sets ¥1200-1800; ☺ lunch & dinner daily Jul-Oct, closed Wed Nov-Jun) In Ue-no-dan, Bistro Matsushima-tei serves a changing selection of handmade pizzas and pastas in a chichi-atmospheric setting befitting the building's history.

ⓘ Information

Tourist Office (木曽町観光協会 Kiso-machi Kankō Kyōkai; ☑ 22-4000; 2012-10 Kiso-machi Fukushima; ☺ 9am-4.45pm) Across from the station, these friendly ladies have some English maps, but appreciate some Japanese ability.

ⓘ Getting There & Away

Kiso-Fukushima is on the JR Chūō line (*Shinano tokkyū*), easily reached from Matsumoto (¥2100, 38 minutes), Nakatsugawa (¥2100, 34 minutes) and Nagoya (¥4500, 1½ hours).

NARAI 奈良井

A less known but equally important example of a Nakasendō post town, Narai is one of our favourites, tucked away in the folds of a narrow valley. Once called 'Narai of a thousand houses', it flourished in the Edo period when its proximity to the highest pass on the Nakasendō made it a popular resting place for travellers. Today, it's a conservation area with a preserved main street showcasing some wonderful examples of Edo period architecture.

Narai is famed for *shikki* (lacquerware). Plenty of quality souvenir shops line the street, many at reasonable prices.

◉ Sights

Nakamura House   HISTORIC BUILDING

(中村邸; ☑34-2655; adult/child ¥300/free; ◷9am-4pm) This wonderfully preserved former merchant's house and garden looks as if it has stood still while time passed by.

⊨ Sleeping & Eating

★Echigo-ya   RYOKAN ¥¥

(ゑちごや旅館; ☑34-3011; www.naraijyuku-echigoya.jp; 493 Narai; r per person inc 2 meals from ¥13,650) In business for over 220 years, this charming family-run ryokan is one of a kind. With only two guestrooms, this is a unique opportunity to experience the Japanese art of hospitality in its most undiluted form. Expect to feel like you've stepped back in time. Some Japanese ability will help make the most of the experience. Book well in advance. Cash only.

Oyado Iseya   INN ¥¥

(御宿伊勢屋; ☑34-3051; www.oyado-iseya.jp; 388 Narai; r per person inc 2 meals from ¥9000) The streetfront of this former merchant house built in 1818 has been beautifully preserved. Now a pleasant 10-room inn, guestrooms are in the main house and a newer building out back.

Matsunami   SHOKUDŌ ¥

(松波; ☑34-3750; 397-1 Narai; meals ¥850; ◷11.30am-8pm Wed-Mon) This delightful little eatery on a corner serves simple favourites such as special-sauce *tonkatsu-don*.

❶ Information

Tourist Information Office (奈良井宿観光協会; ☑54-2001; www.naraijuku.com) Inside Narai station, it has some English language leaflets and a map. Little English is spoken.

❶ Getting There & Away

Only *futsū* trains stop at Narai, which is on the JR Chūō line. It takes no more than an hour or three to see the sights, making a neat day trip from Matsumoto (¥560, 50 minutes), but you could easily pass a peaceful evening here. From Nagoya, change trains at Nakatsugawa (¥1280, 1½ hours) or Kiso-Fukushima (¥400, 20 minutes).

Azumino   安曇野

☑0263

The city of Azumino was formed in 2005, when the towns of Akashina, Hotaka, Toyoshina and three smaller villages amalgamated. It's also the traditional name of the picturesque valley in which they're located. An easy day trip from Matsumoto, the area is home to Japan's largest wasabi farm and is a popular starting point for mountain hikes.

◉ Sights & Activities

Dai-ō Wasabi-Nōjo   FARM

(大王わさび農場; ☑82-2118; 1692 Hotaka; ◷9am-5pm) **FREE** Fancy some wasabi beer? This farm, a 15-minute bike ride from Hotaka Station, is de rigueur for wasabi lovers. An English map guides you among wasabi plants (130 tons of wasabi are grown in flooded fields here annually) amid rolling hills, restaurants, shops and workspaces.

Rokuzan Bijutsukan   MUSEUM

(碌山美術館; ☑82-2094; 5095-1 Hotaka; adult/child ¥700/150; ◷9am-4pm, closed Mon Nov-Apr) Ten minutes' walk from JR Hotaka Station, Rokuzan Bijutsukan showcases the work of Meiji-era sculptor Rokuzan Ogiwara (aka 'Rodin of the Orient') and his Japanese contemporaries, in a pleasant garden setting.

Jōnen-dake   HIKING

(常念岳) From Hotaka Station, it's 30 minutes by taxi (around ¥5000) to reach the Ichinosawa trailhead, from where experienced hikers can climb Jōnen-dake (2857m); the ascent takes about 5½ hours. There are many options for hikes extending over several days, but you must be properly prepared. Hiking maps are available at the Tourist Information Centre, although the detailed ones are in Japanese.

⊨ Sleeping & Eating

★Nakabusa Onsen   RYOKAN ¥¥

(中房温泉; ☑77-1488; www.nakabusa.com; 7226 Nakabusa; r per person with 2 meals from ¥9390; ◷Apr-Nov) With over a dozen indoor, outdoor and sand baths, this rambling old resort at the end of a twisty mountain road to the middle of nowhere, will delight onsen-fans and those seeking a peaceful retreat. The older *honkan* wing has basic rooms wheras the newer *bekkan* wing is more comfortable. In late fall, the outlook is breathtaking, when stunningly colourful foliage is topped by the snowcapped peaks. Enquire at the

Tourist Information Centre for the limited bus schedule (¥1700; one hour) or rent a car (and some nerves of steel).

Ariake-so INN ¥¥
(有明荘; ☑ 090-2321-9991; www.enzanso.co.jp/ariake/english; r per person with meals from ¥9500; ☺ Apr-late Nov) En route to Nakabusa Onsen, this seasonal forest lodge has basic dorm-style rooms and a nourishing onsen (day use ¥600).

ℹ Information

Tourist Information Office (観光案内所; ☑ 82-9363; ☺ 9am-5pm Apr-Nov, 10am-4pm Dec-Mar) This friendly, home-proud tourist office opposite JR Hotaka station has helpful English speaking staff and rents out bicycles – a great way to explore.

ℹ Getting There & Away

Hotaka is the gateway city to the Azumino valley. JR Hotaka Station is 28 minutes (*futsū*, ¥320) from Matsumoto on the JR Ōito line.

TOYAMA PREFECTURE
富山県

Toyama Prefecture is big in pharmaceuticals, zipper manufacturing and mountains. Visitors come for the latter, the Tateyama range, to the city's east and south, as well as the traditional thatched-roof houses of the Gokayama district.

Toyama 富山
☑ 076 / POP 421,950

The most likely reason you'll find yourself here is a journey on the Tateyama-Kurobe Alpine Route. A transit hub on the Hokuriku coast, the city lacks charm and isn't hugely geared for tourism – that may change when the Hokuriku *shinkansen* flies into town in 2014. If you do pass through, be sure to sample the local seafood, including *hotaruika* (firefly squid) and *shiroebi* (white shrimp). There are plenty of seafood restaurants outside the station's south exit, which is also where the hotels are. Sights can be reached by tram or bus.

◉ Sights

Iwase NEIGHBOURHOOD
(岩瀬) North of the city centre is the bayside Iwase neighbourhood, the well-preserved main street of the former shipping business district. Now it's filled with shops and private homes; even the banks look interesting. Take the Portram light rail line from Toyama Station's north exit to the terminus, Iwasehama (¥200, 25 minutes), make a sharp left to cross the canal via Iwase-bashi (岩瀬橋) and you'll see signs in English. Rather than backtrack, you can return via Higashi-Iwase Station on the Portram.

Chōkei-ji TEMPLE
(長慶寺; ☺ 24hr) This hilltop temple has a wonderful outlook, but you'll come to see the 500 plus stone statues of *rakan* (Buddha's disciples) lined up in the forest.

Toyama Municipal Folkcraft Village MUSEUM
(富山市民俗民芸村; 1118-1 Anyōbō; adult/child ¥500/250; ☺ 9am-5pm) Here you'll find folk art, ceramics, *sumi-e* (ink brush) paintings and more, in a cluster of hillside buildings. Toyama's free Museum Bus can get you here (10 minutes, hourly from 10.30am to 4.30pm), from in front of the Toyama Excel Hotel Tōkyū.

🛏 Sleeping & Eating

Comfort Hotel Toyama Eki-mae HOTEL ¥
(コンフォートホテル富山駅前; ☑ 433-6811; www.choice-hotels.jp; 1-3-2 Takara-machi; s/d with breakfast from ¥5800/8500; @ ☎) Across the street and to the right as you exit the station, this business hotel has pleasant, well-maintained, modern rooms and professional staff.

Toyama Excel Hotel Tōkyū HOTEL ¥¥
(富山エクセルホテル東急; ☑ 441-0109; www.tokyuhotelsjapan.com/en; 1-2-3 Shintomi-chō; s/d from ¥10,900/18,400; ℗ @) Toyama's fanciest digs has 210 rooms in a variety of configurations and two restaurants. Rooms on higher floors have fantastic views.

Shiroebi-tei SEAFOOD ¥
(白えび亭; ☑ 432-7575; mains ¥730-2200; ☺ 10am-8pm) Locals swear by this workmanlike institution on the 3rd floor of Toyama Station. The staple is *shiroebi ten-don* (white shrimp tempura over rice; ¥730). There's a picture menu.

🍷 Drinking

Pot Still PUB
(☑ 433-3347; www.pot-still.net/english; 2-3-27 Sakura-chō; ☺ 7pm-late) This Irish pub has a weird name and a weirder sign, but more importantly, Guinness on tap, killer fish and chips (¥900), pool, darts and a foreigner-friendly environment.

TATEYAMA-KUROBE ALPINE ROUTE　　立山黒部アルペンルート

Open from mid-April to mid-November, this popular seasonal 90km route connects Shinano-ōmachi in Nagano-ken with Tateyama (Toyama-ken) via a sacred mountain, a deep gorge, a boiling-hot spring and glory-hallelujah mountain scenery. It's divided into nine sections with different modes of transport including your own two feet. During peak season (August to October), transport and accommodation reservations are strongly advised.

Travel is possible in either direction; instructions here are from Shinano-ōmachi. As it's usually only travelled one-way, we'd suggest an itinerary that uses the route to get between Matsumoto and Toyama/Kanazawa, or the reverse.

Full details are online at: www.alpen-route.com/english. There are hundreds of steps en route and plenty of walking. Be sure to forward your baggage to your destination hotel before you set off (details on the website).

The fare for the entire route is ¥10,560/17,730 one-way/return; tickets for individual sections are available. It takes *at least* six hours, one-way. If you're starting in Toyama, you may find a return trip to Murodō (¥6530), the route's highest point, sufficient.

Setting off in the morning from Matsumoto, take a local train to Shinano-ōmachi station (elevation 712m). Buses depart in front of the station for **Ogizawa** (¥1330, 40 minutes), where you'll board the trolley-buses that take you through a 5.8km tunnel to the colossal **Kurobe-dam** (¥1500, 16 minutes). After soaking in the views from the impressive observation deck, it's a 15-minute walk across the dam to **Kurobeko**, then an underground cable car to **Kurobe-daira** (¥840, five minutes). From here, the Tateyama Ropeway whisks you 488m up to **Daikanbō** (¥1260, seven minutes) for breathtaking views of the valley below. When you're ready, board another trolley bus – this one tunnelling through Mt Tateyama for 3.7km to **Murodō** (¥2100, 10 minutes).

At 2450m, Murodō is the route's highest point. Its beauty is somewhat marred by the monstrous bus station, but a short hike takes you back to nature. Ten minutes' walk north is the pond **Mikuri-ga-ike** (みくりが池), home to an inn of the same name that houses a small restaurant and Japan's highest onsen. Twenty minutes further on is **Jigokudani Onsen** (Hell Valley Hot Springs): no bathing here, the waters are boiling! To the east, you can hike for about two hours – including a very steep final section – to the peak of **O-yama** (雄山; 3003m) for an astounding panorama. Keen long-distance hikers with several days or a week to spare can continue south to Kamikōchi.

The trek down continues with a bus to **Bijodaira** (美女平; ¥1660, 50 minutes) via the spectacular alpine plateau of **Midagahara Kōgen**. You can break the trip at Midagahara and do the 15-minute walk to see Tateyama caldera (立山カルデラ), the largest nonactive crater in Japan. The upper part of the plateau is often covered with deep snow well into spring; snowploughs keep the road clear by pushing vast walls of snow to each side of the road, forming a virtual tunnel of ice.

The last stage of the route is the cable car down to **Tateyama** (立山; ¥700, seven minutes). There's plenty of accommodation in Tateyama if you make an early start or late finish, or, continue on through rural scenery on the chug-a-lug regional Chitetsu line (not part of the route) to Toyama (¥1170, one hour).

ℹ Information

Information Office (観光案内所; ☏ 432-9751; ⊙ 8.30am-8pm) The helpful information office, inside Toyama Station, stocks maps and pamphlets on the city and Tateyama-Kurobe Alpine Route. Some English is spoken.

ℹ Getting There & Away

Daily flights operate between Toyama and major Japanese cities, with less-frequent flights to Seoul (South Korea) and Shanghai (China).

The JR Takayama line runs south to Takayama (*tokkyū*, ¥2770, 90 minutes) and Nagoya (*tokkyū*, ¥6930, four hours). JR's Hokuriku line runs west to Kanazawa (*tokkyū*, ¥2100, 39 minutes; *futsū*, ¥950, one hour) and Osaka (tokkyū, ¥7980, 3¼ hours); and northeast to Niigata (¥6620, three hours).

The Hokuriku *shinkansen*, set to open in 2014, will create a high-speed link with Nagano, onwards to Tokyo.

ISHIKAWA PREFECTURE

Ishikawa Prefecture (石川県; Ishikawa-ken), made up of the former Kaga and Noto fiefs, offers a blend of cultural and historical sights and natural beauty. Kanazawa, the Kaga capital and power base of the feudal Maeda clan, boasts traditional architecture and one of Japan's most famous gardens. To the north, the peninsula, Noto-hantō, has sweeping seascapes and quiet fishing villages. Hakusan National Park, near the southern tip of the prefecture, offers great hiking. You can find good overviews at www.hot-ishikawa.jp.

Kanazawa 金沢

♪ 076 / POP 462.360

Kanazawa's array of cultural attractions makes it the drawcard of the Hokuriku region. Best known for Kenroku-en, a castle garden dating from the 17th century, it also boasts beautifully preserved samurai and geisha districts, attractive temples and a wealth of museums. We recommend a two- or three-day stay to take it all in.

History

During the 15th century, Kanazawa was under the control of an autonomous Buddhist government, ousted in 1583 by Maeda Toshiie, head of the powerful Maeda clan. Kanazawa means 'golden marsh' – in its heyday, the region was Japan's richest, producing about five million bushels of rice, annually. This wealth allowed the Maeda to patronise culture and the arts. Kanazawa remains a national cultural hotspot.

An absence of military targets spared the city from destruction during WWII. Its myriad of historical and cultural sites are wonderfully preserved and integrate neatly with the city's share of contemporary architecture.

◉ Sights & Activities

Kanazawa is a sprawling city, but unfortunately public transport isn't the best. You'll orient yourself soon enough; a plethora of city maps are available from the Tourist Information Office in JR Kanazawa Station.

The station area has its own vibe but is set back from most of the action. Heading south of the station along Hyakumangoku-dōri, you'll first reach Kōrinbō, the shopping and business district, before arriving in Katamachi, by the banks of the Sai-gawa; this is where to eat, drink and be merry. If you're staying near the station, note that buses stop early evening. Taxis back from the area's countless bars and restaurants will set you back at least ¥1300.

Tera-machi and Nishi-chaya-gai are just over the bridge from Kata-machi, but the big name sights are to its east: Kenroku-en, Castle Park and many museums are here. To their north, across the Asano-gawa, lies pretty Higashi-chaya-gai in the shadow of hilly Utatsuyama's many temples. Heading west will loop you back to the station, passing Ōmichō Market.

Nagamachi District   NEIGHBOURHOOD

(長町) Once inhabited by samurai, this attractive, well-preserved district (Nagamachi Buke Yashiki) framed by two canals features winding streets lined with tile-roofed mud walls.

Nagamachi Yūzen-kan   MUSEUM

(長町友禅館; 2-6-16 Nagamachi; admission ¥350; ⊙9am-noon & 1-4.30pm Fri-Wed) In a non-traditional building at the edge of the district, the Nagamachi Yūzen-kan displays some splendid examples of Kaga yūzen kimono-dyeing and demonstrates the process. Enquire ahead about trying the silk-dyeing process yourself (¥4000).

Nomura Samurai House   HISTORIC BUILDING

(武家屋敷跡 野村家; 1-3-32 Nagamachi; adult/child/student ¥500/250/400; ⊙8.30am-5.30pm Apr-Sep, to 4.30pm Oct-Mar) Nomura Samurai House, though partly transplanted from outside Kanazawa, is worth a visit for its decorative garden.

21st Century Museum of
Contemporary Art   MUSEUM

(金沢21世紀美術館; www.kanazawa21.jp; 1-2-1 Hirosaka; adult/child ¥350/free; ⊙10am-6pm Tue-Thu & Sun, to 8pm Fri & Sat) A low-slung glass cylinder, 113m in diameter, forms the perimeter of this 2004 'it' building. Inside, galleries are arranged like boxes on a tray, showcasing works by leading contemporary artists from Japan and abroad, with occasional music and dance performances. Check the website for events; admission fees may vary for special exhibitions.

Kanazawa Noh Museum   MUSEUM

(金沢能楽美術館; 1-2-25 Hirosaka; adult/child ¥300/free; ⊙10am-6pm Tue-Sun) Come here for a basic introduction to the ancient art of nō

TRADITIONAL CRAFTS

During the Edo period, Kanazawa's ruling Maeda family fuelled the growth of important crafts. Many are still practised today.

Kanazawa & Wajima Lacquerware

This luminous black lacquerware starts with hard, durable wood finely carved with any imperfections removed. Many layers of undercoating are applied, each rubbed down with *washi* (Japanese paper) before the next application. Before the final topcoat, decoration is applied through *maki-e* (painting) or gilding. With the last coat of lacquer, artists must take great care that dust does not settle on the final product.

Ōhi Pottery

An aesthetic central to the tea ceremony, *wabi-sabi* means introspective, humble and understated, yet profound and prepared with great thought. The deliberately simple, almost primitive designs, rough surfaces, irregular shapes and monochromatic glazes of Ōhi pottery have long been favoured by tea practitioners. The same family, with the professional name Chōzaemon, has been keeper of the Ōhi tradition since the early Edo period.

Kutani Porcelain

Known for elegant shapes, graceful designs and bold hues of red, blue, yellow, purple and green, this underglaze ware could hardly be more different from Ōhi pottery. It is said to date back to the early Edo period, and shares design characteristics with Chinese porcelain and Japanese Imari ware. Typical motifs include birds, flowers, trees and landscapes.

Kaga Yūzen Silk Dyeing

This laborious, specialised method of silk-dyeing is characterised by strong colours and realistic depictions of nature, such as flower petals that have begun to brown around the edges. A pattern is drawn on the fabric with the grey-blue ink of spiderwort flowers. The lines are traced over with rice paste to keep the dyes from running. Colours are filled in and coated with more rice paste before the entire silk is dyed with the kimono's background colour. Only then is the fabric rinsed and steamed to fix the colours. White lines between the elements, where the initial spiderwort ink has washed away, are a characteristic of *Kaga yūzen*.

Gold Leaf

It starts with a lump of pure gold the size of a ¥10 coin, which is rolled to the size of a tatami mat, as little as 0.0001mm thick. The gold leaf is cut into squares of 10.9cm – the size used for mounting on walls, murals or paintings – or then cut again for gilding on lacquerware or pottery. Tiny particles find their way into tea, sweets and hand lotion. Kanazawa makes over 98% of Japan's gold leaf.

THE JAPAN ALPS & CENTRAL HONSHŪ KANAZAWA

(noh), one of the world's oldest continuously performed theatre forms. With special emphasis on Kaga-style performance, changing exhibits complement permanent displays. The ground floor is marked with the outline of a nō stage.

Kanazawa Castle Park HISTORIC BUILDING
(金沢城公園 Kanazawa-jō Kōen; 1-1 Marunouchi; grounds/bldg free/¥300; ⊙grounds 5am-6pm Mar-15 Oct, 6am-4.30pm 16 Oct-Feb, castle 9am-4.30pm) Originally built in 1580, this massive structure was called the 'castle of 1000 tatami' and housed the Maeda clan for 14 generations until it was ultimately destroyed by fire in 1881. What remains is the elegant gate Ishikawa-mon (石川門), rebuilt in 1788, providing a dramatic entry from Kenroku-en; holes in its turret were designed for *ishi-otoshi* (hurling rocks at invaders). Two additional buildings, the Hishi-yagura (菱櫓; diamond-shaped turret) and Gojikken-Nagaya (五十間長屋; armoury), were reconstructed in 2001, offering a glimpse of the castle's unique wood-frame construction. Restoration and archaeological work continues.

Kanazawa

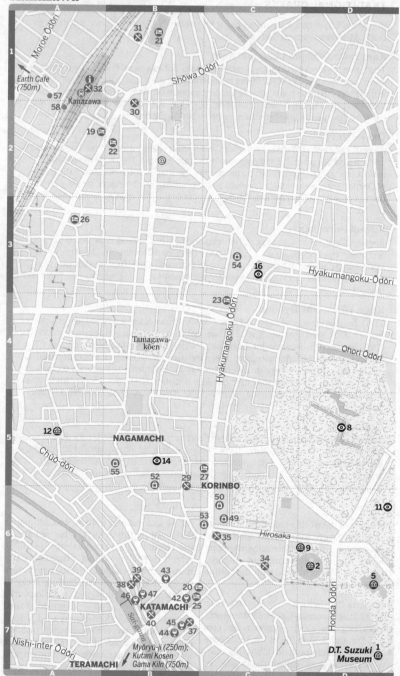

Moroe-Ōdōri

Earth Cafe
(750m)

57

58

32

Kanazawa

31

21

Shōwa-Ōdōri

30

19

22

@

26

54

16

Hyakumangoku-Ōdōri

23

Ohori-Ōdōri

Tamagawa-
kōen

Hyakumangoku-Ōdōri

12

NAGAMACHI

Chūō-dōri

55

14

52

29

27

KORINBO

50

53

49

8

11

35

Hirosaka

9

34

2

5

39

43

38

46

47

20

42

45

25

KATAMACHI

40

44

37

Nishi-inter-Ōdōri

Sai-gawa

Honda-Ōdōri

TERAMACHI

Myōryū-ji (250m);
Kutani Kosen
Gama Kiln (750m)

D.T. Suzuki
Museum

1

Seison-kaku
HISTORIC BUILDING

(☎221-0580; 2-1 Dewa-machi; adult/student ¥700/300; ⏰9am-5pm Thu-Tue) Inside the Castle Park, Seison-kaku is a retirement villa built by a Maeda lord for his mother in 1863. Elegant chambers named for trees and animals are filled with furniture, clothing and furnishings. A detailed English-language pamphlet is available.

Kenroku-en
GARDEN

(兼六園; 1-1 Marunouchi; adult/child ¥300/100; ⏰7am-6pm Mar-15 Oct, 8am-4.30pm 16 Oct-Feb) Ranked as one of the top three gardens in Japan (the other two are Kairaku-en in Mito, and Kōraku-en in Okayama), this Edo period garden draws its name (*kenroku*; 'combined six') from a renowned Sung-dynasty garden in China that dictated six attributes for perfection: seclusion, spaciousness, artificiality, antiquity, abundant water and broad views. Kenroku-en has them all. The garden, originally belonging to an outer villa of Kanazawa-jō, began in 1876 but was later enlarged to serve the castle itself. It was 'completed' in the early 19th century and opened to the public in 1871.

In winter the branches of Kenroku-en's trees are famously suspended with ropes via a post at each tree's centre, forming elegant conical shapes that protect the trees from breaking under Kanazawa's heavy snows. In spring, irises turn Kenroku-en's waterways into rivers of purple. Arrive before the crowds to increase potential for silent contemplation.

★ D.T. Suzuki Museum
MUSEUM

(鈴木大拙館; ☎221-8011; www.kanazawa-museum.jp/daisetz/english; 3-4-20 Honda-machi; adult/senior/child 300/200/free; ⏰9.30am-4.30pm, Tue-Sun) Opened in 2012, this wonderful new museum is a tribute to Daisetsu Teitaro Suzuki, one of the foremost Buddhist philosophers and writers (in both Japanese and English) of our time, largely credited for introducing Zen to the west. This stunning concrete complex embodies the heart of Zen. Come to learn about the man and contemplate by the immaculate water mirror garden.

Ishikawa Prefectural Museum of Traditional Products & Crafts
MUSEUM

(石川県立伝統産業工芸館; 2-1 Kenroku-machi; adult/child ¥250/100; ⏰9am-5pm, closed 3rd Thu of month Apr-Nov, closed Thu Dec-Mar) This small museum offers fine displays of over 20 regional crafts. Pick up the free English-language headphone guide.

Kanazawa

Top Sights
1 D.T. Suzuki Museum D7

Sights
2 21st Century Museum of Contemporary Art D6
3 Gyokusen-en E5
4 Honda Museum E7
5 Ishikawa Prefectural Art Museum D6
6 Ishikawa Prefectural Museum of Traditional Products & Crafts E6
7 Kaikarō F3
8 Kanazawa Castle Park D5
9 Kanazawa Noh Museum D6
10 Kanazawa Phonograph Museum E3
11 Kenroku-en D6
12 Nagamachi Yūzen-kan A5
13 Nakamura Memorial Museum E7
14 Nomura Samurai House B5
15 Ōhi Pottery Museum E3
16 Ōmichō Market C3
17 Seison-kaku E6
18 Shima F3

Sleeping
19 ANA Crowne Plaza Kanazawa A2
20 APA Hotel Kanazawa Chūō B7
21 Hotel Dormy Inn Kanazawa B1
22 Hotel Nikkō Kanazawa B2
23 Hotel Resol Trinity C4
24 Kanazawa Hakuchōrō Hotel E4
25 Murataya Ryokan B7
26 Pongyi A3
27 Tōyoko Inn Kanazawa Kenroku-en Kōrinbō C5
28 Yōgetsu F3

Eating
29 Cottage B5
30 Daiba Kanazawa Ekimae B2
31 Forus Department Store B1
32 Fureai-kan A1
33 Hotaruya F3
34 Itaru Honten C6
35 Janome-sushi Honten C6
36 Kanazawa Todoroki-tei E3
37 Oden Miyuki Honten B7
38 Osteria del Campagne B7
39 Spice Box B6
40 Tamazushi B7
41 Tamura E4

Drinking & Nightlife
42 Baby Rick B7
43 Event House Apres B6
44 I no Ichiban B7
45 Pilsen B7
46 Polé Polé B7
47 RMX B7

Entertainment
48 Ishikawa Prefectural Nō Theatre E7

Shopping
49 Atrio Shopping Plaza C6
50 Daiwa Department Store C6
51 Ishikawa Craft Store E5
52 Kanazawa Kutani Museum B5
53 Kōrinbō 109 .... C6
54 Meitetsu M'Za Department Store C3
55 Murakami B5
56 Sakuda Gold Leaf Company F3

Transport
57 Hokutetsu Bicycle Rental A1
58 JR Kanazawa Station Rent-a-Cycle A2

Kanazawa Phonograph Museum MUSEUM
(金沢蓄音器館; 2-11-21 Owari-chō; admission ¥300; ⏲10am-5pm) Audio buffs will dig this museum of old-time phonographs and SP records, with daily demonstrations at 11am, 2pm and 4pm.

Ishikawa Prefectural Art Museum MUSEUM
(石川県立美術館; 2-1 Dewa-machi; adult/child ¥350/free; ⏲9.30am-5pm) All the local specialties are covered here with an emphasis on Kutani porcelain, Japanese painting and *Kaga yūzen* (silk-dyed) fabrics and costumes. Admission prices vary during special exhibitions.

Nakamura Memorial Museum MUSEUM
(中村記念美術館; 3-2-29 Honda-machi; adult/child ¥300/free; ⏲9.30am-5pm) Rotating exhibitions from the 600-piece private collection of wealthy sake brewer Nakamura Eishun are displayed here, beneath the Ishikawa Prefectural Art Museum. They include *chanoyu* (tea ceremony) utensils, calligraphy and traditional crafts.

Honda Museum MUSEUM
(本多蔵品館; 3-1 Dewa-machi; admission ¥500; ⏲9am-5pm daily Mar-Oct, Fri-Wed Nov-Feb) This museum exhibits the Honda family (chief retainers to the Maeda clan) collection of armour, household utensils and art. There's a detailed catalogue in English.

Gyokusen-en GARDEN
(玉泉園; 1-1 Marunouchi; adult/child ¥500/350; ⏲9am-4pm Mar–mid-Nov) For more intimacy and fewer crowds than Kenroku-en, this

Edo-period garden rises up a steep slope. Enjoy a cup of tea here for an additional ¥700, while contemplating the tranquil setting.

Ōhi Pottery Museum — MUSEUM
(大樋美術館; Hashiba-chō; adult/child ¥700/500; ⊙9am-5pm) This museum was established by the Chōzaemon family, now in its 10th generation. The first Chōzaemon developed this style in nearby Ōhi village, using a special slow-fired amber glaze, specifically for use in *chanoyu*.

Higashi-chaya-gai — NEIGHBOURHOOD
(東茶屋街) Across Asano-gawa, Higashi-chaya-gai (Higashi Geisha District) is an enclave of narrow streets established early in the 19th century for geisha to entertain wealthy patrons. The slatted wooden facades of the geisha houses are romantically preserved.

Shima — MUSEUM
(志摩; 1-13-21 Higashiyama; adult/child ¥400/300; ⊙9am-6pm) This well-known former geisha house in traditional style dates from 1820 and has an impressive collection of elaborate combs and *shamisen* (a three-stringed instrument) picks

Kaikarō — MUSEUM
(懐華樓; 1-14-8 Higashiyama; admission ¥700; ⊙9am-5pm) In Higashi-chaya-gai, Kaikarō is an early-19th-century geisha house refinished with contemporary fittings and art including a red lacquered staircase.

Teramachi District — NEIGHBOURHOOD
(寺町) This hilly neighbourhood across Saigawa, southwest of the centre, was established as a first line of defence and contains dozens of temples.

Myōryū-ji — TEMPLE
(妙立寺; ☑241-0888; 1-2-12 Nomachi; admission ¥800; ⊙9am-4.30pm Mar-Nov, to 4pm Dec-Feb, reservations required) In Teramachi, fascinating Myōryū-ji (aka Ninja-dera), completed in 1643, was designed to protect its Lord in case of attack. It contains hidden stairways, escape routes, secret chambers, concealed tunnels and trick doors. Contrary to popular belief, this ancient temple has nothing to do with ninja. Admission is by tour only (in Japanese with an English guidebook). Phone for reservations (in English).

Kutani Kosen Gama Kiln — GALLERY
(九谷光仙窯; 5-3-3 Nomachi; ⊙9am-5pm) `FREE` The Kutani Kosen Gama Kiln is a must for pottery lovers. Short tours give visitors a glimpse of the process and history of this fine craft. You can decorate porcelain yourself.

Ōmichō Market — MARKET
(近江町市場; 35 Ōmichō; ⊙9am-5pm) Between Kanazawa Station and Katamachi, this market, reminiscent of Tokyo's Tsukiji, is a bustling warren of fishmongers, buyers and restaurants. It's a great place to watch everyday people in action or indulge in the freshest of sashimi. The nearest bus stop is Musashi-ga-tsuji.

🎉 Festivals & Events

Kagatobi Dezomeshiki — CULTURAL
In early January, scantily clad firemen brave the cold, imbibe sake and demonstrate ancient fire-fighting skills on ladders.

Asano-gawa Enyūkai — MUSIC
Performances of traditional Japanese dance and music are held on the banks of the Asano-gawa during the second weekend of April.

Hyakumangoku Matsuri — PARADE
In early June, Kanazawa's main annual festival commemorates the first time the region's rice production hit one million *koku* (around 150,000 tonnes). There's a parade of townsfolk in 16th-century costumes, *takigi nō* (torch-lit performances of nō drama), *tōrō nagashi* (lanterns floated down the river at dusk) and a special *chanoyu*. It's at Kenroku-en.

🛏 Sleeping

★ Pongyi — GUESTHOUSE ¥
(ポンギー; ☑225-7369; www.pongyi.com; 2-22 Rokumai-machi; dm per person from ¥2600; @) Run by a friendly Japanese man who did a stint in Southeast Asia as a monk, Pongyi is a charmingly renovated old shop alongside a canal. Cosy dorms are located in the attached vintage *kura* warehouse. Private rooms are available from ¥6000.

Tōyoko Inn Kanazawa Kenroku-en Kōrinbō — HOTEL ¥
(東横イン金沢兼六園香林坊; ☑232-1045; www.toyoko-inn.com; 2-4-28 Korinbo; s/d from ¥3980/5980) In Kōrinbō, this business hotel has clean, cheap and cheerful little rooms and a free shuttle to the train station. It's about 15 minutes' walk from both Katamachi and JR Kanazawa Station, in either direction.

Yōgetsu
MINSHUKU ¥

(陽月; ☎252-0497; 1-13-22 Higashiyama; r per person with/without breakfast from ¥5000/4500) This beautifully renovated 200-year-old geisha teahouse has only three rooms and features a circular *goemonburo* bath. It's located right in the picturesque Higashi-chaya district. No English is spoken.

Murataya Ryokan
RYOKAN ¥

(村田屋; ☎263-0455; www.murataya-ryokan.com; 1-5-2 Katamachi; s/tw ¥4700/9000; ⊜@) Eleven well-kept rooms around a lovely courtyard and friendly hosts await at this travellers' favourite in Katamachi. It's central to nightlife and restaurants, but that can also make things noisy.

★ Hotel Resol Trinity
HOTEL ¥¥

(ホテルレソルトリニティ; ☎221-9629; www. trinity-kanazawa.com; 1-18 Musashi-machi; r from s/d ¥5000/7000; @) This lovely niche hotel is a breath of fresh air. Rooms have a splash of colour and have been designed to make you feel comfortable in a compact space. Its location is central to everything; you can walk to the station, Katamachi and Kenroku-en in about 15 minutes.

APA Hotel Kanazawa Chūō
HOTEL ¥¥

(アパホテル金沢中央; ☎235-2111; www. apahotel.com; 1-5-24 Katamachi; s/d/tw from ¥8000/11,000/15,000; ⊜@) This mammoth business hotel has compact, inoffensive rooms and an unbeatable Katamachi location. The indoor and outdoor onsen baths on the 14th floor are a major bonus.

Hotel Dormy Inn Kanazawa
HOTEL ¥¥

(ドーミーイン金沢; ☎263-9888; www.hotespa. net/hotels/kanazawa; 2-25 Horikawa-shinmachi; s/d/tw ¥8500/12,000/15,000; ⊜@) Around the corner from the station, this popular, modern tourist hotel has well-designed, functional rooms, a terrarium and a calcium-rich onsen *rotemburo* on the top floor, and a coin laundry.

ANA Crowne Plaza Kanazawa
HOTEL ¥¥

(☎224-6111; www.anacrowneplaza-kanazawa.jp; 16-3 Showa-machi; s/d/tw from ¥9945/10,115/12,415; P@) By the station, most of the Crowne Plaza's almost 250 rooms could be considered small for an international hotel, but they are well furnished and many have great views. Recommended if you want to be by the station and can get a deal online in your home country.

Kanazawa Hakuchōro Hotel
HOTEL ¥¥

(金沢白鳥路ホテル; ☎222-1212; www.hakuchoro .com; 6-3 Marunouchi; s/tw from ¥12,000/18,000; P⊜@) This interesting hotel between the Castle Park and Higashi-chaya-gai is removed from the action. Formal, Western-style rooms are showing their age, but their dimensions make up for it. There's a lovely lobby, a restaurant and common onsen baths. Parking is free.

★ Hotel Nikkō Kanazawa
HOTEL ¥¥¥

(ホテル日航金沢; ☎234-1111; www.hnkanazawa. jp; 2-15-1 Hon-machi; s/d from ¥26,250) Kanazawa's most luxurious hotel, near the station, has a wide range of room types from singles to lavish suites and an impressive selection of on-site restaurants and bars. Most rooms have exceptional views. The 'Luxe Style' and 'Stylish' rooms are the most recently refurbished and worthy of the extra coin.

✗ Eating

Seafood is the staple of Kanazawa's *Kaga ryōri* (Kaga cuisine); even the most humble train-station *bentō* usually features some type of fish. *Oshi-zushi* (a thin layer of fish pressed atop vinegared rice) is said to be the precursor to modern sushi. Another favourite is *jibuni* (which is flour-coated duck or chicken stewed with shiitake and green vegetables).

The JR Kanazawa Station building has plenty of food outlets in its **Fureai-kan** (ふれあい館); otherwise, the neighbouring **Forus department store** has the 'Kuugo Dining Resort' on its 6th floor, with over 15 restaurants. Otherwise, head to Katamachi. Closer by, Ōmichō market (p265) has fresh-from-the-boat eateries; both are great for browsing.

★ Itaru Honten
SEAFOOD, IZAKAYA ¥¥

(いたる本店; ☎252-5755; 3-8 Kakinokibatake; ⊙dinner Mon-Sat; ⒟) Here you'll find some of the best sushi and sashimi in Japan, including regional specialties *hotaru-ika* and *shiro-ebi*. The Kanazawa *Omakase* (leave it to the chef) course is ¥3000. Otherwise, you can try *jibuni*.

Oden Miyuki Honten
IZAKAYA ¥

(三幸本店; ☎222-6117; 1-10-3 Katamachi; oden ¥100-400, most other dishes ¥400-600; ⊙dinner Mon-Sat) For fish in another form (ground and pressed into cakes and served in broth), *oden* is very satisfying, especially on chilly nights. Some of the staff are English-speaking.

Spice Box
INDIAN ¥¥

(スパイスボックス; ☑234-3313; 2-30-8 Katamachi; tapas ¥300-800, lunch sets from ¥780; ♨) Authentic and delicious, this little Indian and Sri Lankan gem is in the heart of Katamachi. The chef's recommendation tandoori plate feeds two for ¥1,800. Lunch sets start at ¥780. Vegetarians welcomed!

Daiba Kanazawa Ekimae
IZAKAYA ¥¥

(台場金沢駅前店; ☑263-9191; 6-10 Konohanamachi, Kanazawa Miyako Hotel 1F; items from ¥420; ♨lunch & dinner; 📖) This trendy spot in the Kanazawa Miyako hotel building has a comprehensive Japanese menu and a limited English one with all the Western favourites and some local specialties. It's a great place for your first *izakaya* experience.

Osteria del Campagne
ITALIAN ¥¥

(オステリアデルカンパーニュ; ☑261-2156; 2-31-33 Katamachi; mains ¥650-1950, set menu from ¥2500; ♨dinner Mon-Sat; 📖) This cosy, quietly fashionable Italian bistro serves lovely set menus, including house-made focaccia, salads, pastas and desserts, plus hors d'oeuvres you can eat with chopsticks. It has an English menu and friendly, professional staff.

Earth Cafe
VEGAN ¥¥

(☑233-0722; www.earth-p.net/cafe; 2-12-30 Ekinishi-honmachi; items ¥550-1480; ♨11am-6pm Mon-Sat; 📖) Vegans (and those feeling the need for healthy food) will rejoice at this wholesome, airy cafe. It's a little pricey for what you get, but there's no comparison in town. Keeping it simple, we rate both the veggie burgers and the curries. It's about 1km northwest of the station, on Rte 60.

Tamazushi
SUSHI ¥¥

(玉寿司; ☑221-2644; 2-21-18 Katamachi; mains ¥1300-3300; ♨dinner Mon-Sat) Near the river in Katamachi, this classic sushi counter is one of Kanazawa's best. There's no English, but there is a picture menu. It's a brown-white building on your right as you enter from the main street.

Janome-sushi Honten
SUSHI ¥¥

(蛇之目寿司本店; ☑231-0093; 1-1-12 Kōrinbō; mains ¥1000-3400, Kaga ryōri sets from ¥4000; ♨lunch & dinner Thu-Tue; 📖) Regarded for sashimi and Kaga cuisine since 1931, one of our Japanese friends says that when he eats here, he knows he's really in Kanazawa. You can't go wrong with the lunch of the day (¥1000).

Kanazawa Todoroki-tei
BISTRO ¥¥

(金沢とどろき亭; ☑252-5755; 1-2-1 Higashiyama; plates from ¥1200; ♨lunch & dinner) In a wonderful Taisho-era (1912–26) building with vaulted ceilings, near Higashi-chaya-gai, you'll find this atmospheric Western restaurant. Think art deco, wooden tables and candlelight. It's looking a little rough around the edges, but that's part of its charm – not too snooty. Romantic eight-course dinners for two are good value at ¥3675 per person.

Cottage
WESTERN ¥¥

(コテージ; ☑262-3277; 2-12-10 Kōrinbō; ♨lunch & dinner Mon-Fri, closed Wed; dinner only Sat & Sun) Expect tasty home-style cooking at this cosy Kōrinbō restaurant, run by a friendly Irish and Japanese husband-and-wife team. Italian and Irish fare is on the English menu.

★Hotaruya
KAISEKI ¥¥¥

(蛍屋; ☑251-8585; 1-13-24 Higashiyama; lunch/dinner courses from ¥3675/6300) To splurge on *Kaga ryōri* and step back in time, visit this shop in Higashi Chaya-gai; it's on the corner in a little square. You'll be rewarded with wood-beam and tatami room surroundings, and understated, standard-setting course meals. For lunch, try the *hanamachi kaiseki* set, ¥6300.

Tamura
SEAFOOD, IZAKAYA ¥¥¥

(田村; ☑222-0517; 2-18 Namiki-machi; courses from ¥2000; ♨5-11.30pm Tue-Sun; 📖) Favoured by Japanese celebrities, this riverside jaunt is as affable as its owner who speaks some English. If you're going to do it, you're best to let him run the show. Courses start at ¥2000, with the deluxe *omakase* at ¥8800.

🍷 Drinking

Most of Kanazawa's bars are jam-packed into high-rises in Katamachi – many are barely disguised hostess bars. There's plenty of wholesome action too – weekends are busy. For a mellower evening, soak in the ambient *izakaya* and cafes of Higashi-chaya-gai.

Polé Polé
BAR

(ポレポレ; ☑260-1138; 2-31-30 Katamachi) This reggae bar's reputation as a *gaijin* institution precedes it. In reality, it's a dark and grungy hole in the wall, littered with years of sawdust and peanut shells. What makes it worthwhile, is the friendly, chilled staff who are happy to oblige if you're looking to chat, chill, or tune out of da rat race, mon.

Pilsen
PUB

(ぴるぜん; ☎221-0688; 1-9-20 Katamachi; ◷Mon-Sat) This decent-sized German bierhall has been pulling pints and serving wurst, cheese and pasta since 1968 to a usually interesting mix of locals and foreigners.

Baby Rick
BAR

(ベイビーリック; 1-5-20 Katamachi) Class and character in the heart of Katamachi; this bar has an extensive picture menu, a billiard table and attracts a lively crowd. It's in the basement level beneath Shidax karaoke. There's a ¥500 cover after 10pm.

I no Ichiban
IZAKAYA

(いの一番; ☎261-0001; 1-9-20 Katamachi) This above-average izakaya exudes ambience and is strong with cuisine and mixology alike. Look for the wood-panel screen and tiny stand of bamboo.

Event House Apres
NIGHTCLUB

(イベントハウスアプレ; ☎222-0004; Space 237 Bldg 7F, 2-3-7 Katamachi; ◷7pm-late Tue-Sun) Apres is the most happening joint for a younger crowd; cheap drinks, thumping tunes and lots of locals and expat party people on the floor. Say no more.

RMX
GAY

(☎262-0881; 2-30-2 Katamachi) There's a ¥1500 cover charge at this friendly little bar for gay men.

☆ Entertainment

Ishikawa Prefectural Nō Theatre
THEATRE

(石川県立能楽堂; ☎264-2598; www.nohgaku.or.jp; 3-1 Dewa-machi; performance tickets vary; ◷9am-4.30pm Tue-Sun) Nō theatre is alive and well in Kanazawa. Weekly performances take place here, during summer.

🛍 Shopping

The Hirosaka shopping street, between **Kōrinbō 109** department store and Kenroku-en, has some upmarket craft shops on its south side. Other major department stores are near JR Kanazawa Station (Forus, **Meitetsu M'za**) and on Hyakumangoku-dōri between Kōrinbō and Katamachi (**Daiwa**, **Atrio Shopping Plaza**), where you'll also find the fresh and funky Tatemachi Shopping Promenade.

Ishikawa Craft Store
ARTS & CRAFTS

(石川県観光物産館 Ishikawa-ken Kankō-bussankan; ☎222-7788; 2-20 Kenroku-machi; ◷10am-6pm) An overview of Kanazawa crafts, under one roof.

Kanazawa Kutani Museum
CERAMICS

(金沢九谷ミュウジアム) In a wonderful old storehouse in the Nagamachi samurai district, this lovely museum is actually more of an outlet for high-end ceramic ware. There's also a small museum of historic Kutani-yaki pottery and a cafe.

Murakami
FOOD

(村上; ☎264-4223; 2-3-32 Nagamachi; ◷8.30am-5pm) If a flowering tree made of candy excites you, slake it at Murakami, this handsome wagashi (Japanese candy) shop, where you'll also find fukusamochi (red-bean paste and pounded rice in a crêpe) and kakiho (soybean flour rolled in black sesame seeds).

Sakuda Gold Leaf Company
ARTS & CRAFTS

(金銀箔工芸さくだ; ☎251-6777; www.goldleaf-sakuda.jp; 1-3-27 Higashiyama; ◷9am-6pm) Here you can observe the kinpaku (gold leaf) process and pick up all sorts of gilded souvenirs including pottery, lacquerware and, er, golf balls. They also serve tea containing flecks of gold leaf, reputedly good for rheumatism. Even the toilet walls are lined with gold and platinum.

ℹ Information

There are post offices in Katamachi and in Kanazawa Station. Coin-operated laundries can be found in Higashi Chaya-gai and Katamachi. Online, check out www4.city.kanazawa.lg.jp for general city information.

Kanazawa Tourist Information Centre (石川県金沢観光情報センター; ☎232-3933 KGGN, 232-6200; http://kggn.sakura.ne.jp; 1 Hirooka-machi; ◷9am-7pm) This excellent office inside Kanazawa Station has incredibly helpful staff and a plethora of well-made English language maps, pamphlets and magazines, including, Eye on Kanazawa. The friendly folk from the Goodwill Guide Network (KGGN) are also here to assist with hotel recommendations and free guiding in English – two weeks' notice is requested.

Ishikawa Foundation for International Exchange (☎262-5931; www.ifie.or.jp; 1-5-3 Honmachi; ◷9am-8pm Mon-Fri, to 5pm Sat & Sun) Offers information, a library, satellite TV news and free internet access. It's on the 3rd floor of the Rifare building, a few minutes' walk southeast of JR Kanazawa Station.

ℹ️ Getting There & Away

AIR

Nearby **Komatsu airport** (KMQ; www.komatsuairport.jp) has air connections with major Japanese cities, as well as Seoul, Shanghai and Taipei.

BUS

JR Highway Bus operates express buses from in front of Kanazawa Station's east exit to Tokyo's Shinjuku Station (¥7840, 7½ hours) and Kyoto (¥4060, 4¼ hours). Hokutetsu Buses serve Nagoya (¥4060, four hours). Nōhi Bus Company services Takayama, via Shirakawa-go (¥3300, 2½ hours).

TRAIN

The JR Hokuriku line links Kanazawa with Fukui (*tokkyū*, ¥2430, 50 minutes; *futsū*, ¥1280, 80 minutes), Kyoto (*tokkyū*, ¥6200, 2¼ hours), Osaka (*tokkyū*, ¥6930, 2¾ hours) and Toyama (*tokkyū*, ¥2100, 35 minutes), with connections to Takayama (total ¥4870, additional 90 minutes).

From Tokyo take the Jōetsu *shinkansen* and change at Echigo-Yuzawa in Northern Honshū (¥11,840, four hours), until Spring 2015, when the Hokuriku *shinkansen* makes its bold entry into Kanazawa, slashing travel times and increasing visitor numbers dramatically.

ℹ️ Getting Around

JR Kanazawa Station is the hub for transit to/ from and around Kanazawa.

Full-size bikes can be rented from **JR Kanazawa Station Rent-a-Cycle** (駅レンタサイクル; 📞 261-1721; per hr/day ¥200/1200; ⏰ 8am-8.30pm) and **Hokutetsu Bicycle Rental** (北鉄レンタルサイクル; 📞 263-0919; per 4hr/ day ¥630/1050; ⏰ 8am-5.30pm) in the offices of Nippon Rentacar. Both are by the west exit.

The city recently introduced a pay-as-you-go bicycle rental system called 'Machi-nori'. The bikes are a bit dinky, but with a bit of planning, the system functions well. For the lowdown on how it works, in English, go to: www.machi-nori.jp.

Buses depart from the circular terminus in front of the station's east exit. Any bus from station stop 7, 8 or 9 will take you to the city centre (¥200, day pass ¥900). The Kanazawa Loop Bus (single ride/day pass ¥200/500, every 15 minutes from 8.30am to 6pm) circles the major tourist attractions in 45 minutes. On Saturday, Sunday and holidays, the Machi-bus goes to Kōrinbō for ¥100.

Airport buses (¥1100, 40 minutes) depart from station stop 6. Some services are via Katamachi and Kōrinbō 109, but take one hour to reach the airport.

Numerous car-rental agencies are dotted around the station's west exit.

Noto Peninsula   能登半島

With rugged seascapes, traditional rural life, fresh seafood and a light diet of cultural sights, Noto Peninsula (Noto-hantō) atop Ishikawa-ken is a picturesque escape from the Hokuriku region's urban sprawl. The lacquer-making town of Wajima is the hub of the rugged north, known as Oku-Noto, and the best place to stay overnight. Famous products include *Wajima-nuri* lacquerware, renowned for its durability and rich colours, Suzu-style pottery and locally harvested sea salt and *iwanori* seaweed.

ℹ️ Getting There & Around

In the centre of Oku-Noto, **Noto airport** connects the peninsula with Tokyo. **Furusato Taxi** (📞 0768-22-7411) is a van service to locations around the peninsula. Fares start at ¥700 to nearby communities including Wajima (about 30 minutes).

Although there are trains, most sights can be reached by road only. For the west Noto coast, take the JR Nanao line from Kanazawa to Hakui (*tokkyū*, ¥1370; *futsū*, ¥740) and connect to buses. For Oku-Noto, trains continue to Wakura Onsen, connecting to less frequent buses. **Hokutetsu** (📞 076-234-0123) runs buses between Kanazawa and Wajima (¥2200, two hours, 10 daily).

Self driving is easily the best way to see the peninsula. The 83km Noto Yūryo (能登有料; Noto Toll Rd) speeds you as far as Anamizu (toll ¥1180). Noto's mostly flat west coast also appeals to cyclists. However, cycling is not recommended on the Noto-kongō coast and east because of steep, blind curves.

Lower Noto Peninsula 能登半島下

📞 0767

The small town of **Hakui** (羽咋) is Noto's western transit hub, with frequent train connections to Kanazawa and less frequent bus connections along Noto's west coast. With about twice the population, the town of **Himi** (氷見) in neighbouring Toyama-ken, about 40 minutes drive east, is also a pleasant starting point to tackle the peninsula.

👁️ Sights & Activities

Kita-ke   HISTORIC BUILDING
(喜多家; 📞 28-2546; adult/child ¥500/200; ⏰ 8.30am-5pm Apr-Oct, to 4pm Nov-Mar) During the Edo period, the Kita family administered over 200 villages from Kita-ke, at the pivotal crossroads of the Kaga, Etchū and Noto

Noto Peninsula

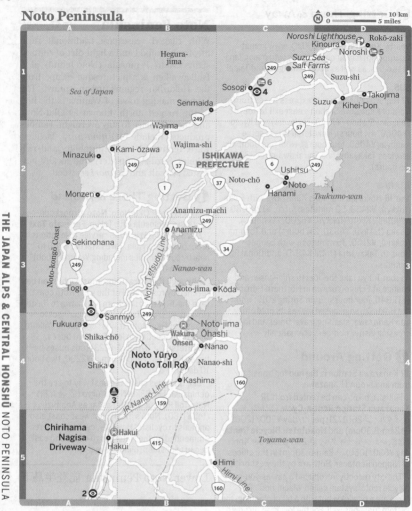

fiefs. Inside this splendid, sprawling family home and museum are displays of weapons, ceramics, farming tools, fine and folk art, and documents. The garden has been called the Moss Temple of Noto. It's about 1km from the Komedashi exit on the Noto Toll Rd. By train, take the JR Nanao line to Menden Station and walk for 20 minutes.

Myōjō-ji
BUDDHIST TEMPLE

(妙成寺; ☎ 27-1226; admission ¥500; ⊙ 8am-5pm Apr-Oct, to 4.30pm Nov-Mar) Founded in 1294 by Nichizō, a disciple of Nichiren, the imposing Myōjō-ji remains an important temple for the sect. The grounds comprise 10 Important Cultural Properties, most notably the strikingly elegant five-storeyed pagoda. The Togi-bound bus from Hakui Station can drop you at Myōjō-ji-guchi bus stop (¥420, 18 minutes); from here, it's under 10 minutes' walk.

Chirihama Nagisa Driveway
DRIVING

(千里浜なぎさドライブウエイ) At times the 8km Chirihama Nagisa Driveway, in the Chirihama district of Hakui, resembles an early Daytona as buses, motorcycles and cars roar past the breakers and revellers barbecue in the sun on this compacted strip of hard sand.

Noto Peninsula

🛏 Sleeping

Hotel Grantia Himi   HOTEL ¥¥
(ホテルグランティア氷見; ☑ 0766-73-1771;
443-5 Kanō; s/d from ¥5500/9500) This smart,
comfortable business hotel is a good resting
point if you're driving to the Noto Peninsula
from Toyama or Gokayama. It's in the car-
park of a shopping mall and there are plenty
of shops and amenities nearby to keep you
occupied.

Noto-kongō Coast 能登金剛
☑ 0768

This rocky, cliff-lined shoreline extends for
about 16km between Fukūra and Sekino-
hana, and is adorned with dramatic rock
formations.

The manicured little town of **Monzen** is
the area's transport hub, with buses servicing
Kanazawa (¥2200, 2½ hours), Hakui (¥1510,
1½ hours) and Wajima (¥740, 35 minutes).

◉ Sights

Sōji-ji   BUDDHIST TEMPLE
(総持寺; ☑ 42-0005; fax 42-1002; adult/child
¥400/150; ⊙8am-5pm) In Monzen, this beautiful temple was established in 1321 as the head
of the Sōtō school of Zen, but now functions as
a branch temple. Temple buildings were damaged by the 2007 Noto earthquake and are under fastidious reconstruction which may take
many years. Still, Sōji-ji welcomes visitors to
experience one hour of *zazen* (seated meditation; ¥300, 9am to 3pm), serves *shōjin-ryōri*
(Buddhist vegetarian cuisine; ¥2500 to ¥3500)
and can accommodate visitors (with two
meals ¥6500; single women are prohibited).
Reserve at least two days in advance.

Ganmon   CAVE
(厳門) There's a lot of hype about this interesting, though not entirely attractive, sea
cave carved into the cliff by the force of the
waves. There are souvenir shops and restaurants galore.

Wajima 輪島
☑ 0768 / POP 31,500

About 20km north of Monzen, this fishing
port is the largest town in Oku-Noto and is
historically famed for Wajima-nuri (lacquerware). Although significantly damaged in the
2007 Noto earthquake (magnitude 6.9), the
town centre has been lovingly rebuilt, making it a pleasant place to spend a night and
wake to enjoy the lively morning market.

◉ Sights & Activities

Asa-ichi   MARKET
(Morning Market; ⊙8am-noon, closed 10th & 25th of
each month) This entertaining morning market features a few hundred ageing fishwives
hawking fresh off-the-trawler seafood, lacquerware, pottery and souvenirs – all with
saleslady sass and humour that knows no
language barriers. Haggle politely if you dare.

Ishikawa Wajima Urushi
Art Museum   MUSEUM
(石川輪島漆芸美術館; ☑ 22-9788; adult/stu-
dent ¥600/300; ⊙9am-4.30pm) This modern
museum, about a 15-minute walk west of
the former train station, has a large, rotating
collection of lacquerware in galleries on two
floors. Phone ahead, as this museum closes
between exhibitions.

Kiriko Kaikan   MUSEUM
(キリコ会館; ☑ 22-7100; adult/child ¥600/350;
⊙8am-5pm) A selection of the impressive illuminated lacquered floats used in the Wajima Taisai festival, some up to 15m tall, is
on display in this hall. It's 20 minutes' walk
from JR Kanazawa Station, or take the bus
to Tsukada bus stop (¥150, six minutes).

✹ Festivals & Events

Gojinjō Daikō Nabune Matsuri   DRUMMING
This festival culminating on 31 July features
wild drumming by performers wearing demon masks and seaweed headgear.

Wajima Taisai   PARADE
Wajima's famous, towering, illuminated
kiriko (woodcarved) festival floats parade
through the streets to much excitement, in
late August.

🛏 Sleeping & Eating

Wajima has dozens of *minshuku* known for
seafood meals worth staying in for. There
are also some lovely restaurants by the harbour, though some close by early evening.

★ **Tanaka** RYOKAN ¥¥
(お宿たなか; ☑22-5155; www.oyado-tanaka.jp; 22-38 Kawai-machi; r per person with meals from ¥9450; P) This immaculate 10-room inn has beds on tatami, hot-spring baths (including a private-use *rotemburo,* extra charge), dark woodwork, paper lanterns and ambience aplenty. The *kaiseki* meals here feature local seafood and laquerware.

Route Inn Wajima HOTEL ¥¥
(ホテルルートイン輪島; ☑22-7700; 1-2 Marine Town; s/d ¥6500/10,500) With decent-sized rooms and great views from the upper floors, this modern harbourside tourist hotel has all you need if you're passing through, including free breakfast.

Wafū-no-yado Mangetsu MINSHUKU ¥¥
(和風の宿満月; ☑22-4487; 20-1-44 Kawaimachi; r per person with 2 meals from ¥8400; P) The delightfully senior lifetime owners of this inn near the station speak no English, but would love to welcome you as best they can. Recently renovated rooms are charming and traditional, although bathrooms are shared.

Sodegahama Camping Ground CAMPGROUND ¥
(袖ヶ浜キャンプ場; ☑23-1146; fax 23-1855; campsites per person ¥1000) Take the local *no-ranke* bus (umi course, ¥100) or Nishiho bus (direction Zōza 雑座) to Sodegahama, or hike for 20 minutes to reach this beachfront campground.

Madara-yakata SEAFOOD ¥
(まだら館; ☑22-3453; mains ¥800-2100; ☺lunch & dinner) This restaurant near the Asa-ichi serves local specialities, including *zosui* (rice hotpot), *yaki-zakana* (grilled fish) and seasonal seafood, surrounded by folk crafts.

Umi-tei Notokichi SEAFOOD ¥¥
(海亭のと吉; ☑22-6636; 4-153 Kawaimachi; dishes ¥600-2500; ☺dinner Thu-Tue) A popular local haunt for generations, you'll be hard pressed to better experience seafood elsewhere in Japan. Purists should keep it simple and go for the *sashimi moriawase* (¥1500). They also do a mean version of *katsudon* (¥1000).

Shinpuku SEAFOOD ¥¥
(伸幅; ☑22-8133; sushi per piece from ¥150, sets ¥1000-2500; ☺lunch & dinner, closed irregularly, mostly Wed) This tiny, assiduously local sushi shop serves fabulously fresh fish and seafood, and *iwanori* seaweed in the miso soup. Meals such as the *nigiri* set (¥1200) are a sure bet, while *asa-ichi-don* (¥2500) is a selection from the morning market over rice. It's on the main street, one block east of the Cosmo petrol station. There's a picture menu.

❶ Information

Tourist Information Office (輪島観光協会; ☑22-1503; ☺8am-7pm) Limited English is spoken by the friendly staff of this office at the former Wajima train station, now the bus station. They do have English-language maps and can help with accommodation.

❶ Getting There & Away

Hokutetsu runs buses between Kanazawa and Wajima (¥2200, two hours, 10 daily) and, less frequently, Monzen (¥740, 35 minutes).

Suzu & Noto-chō 珠洲・能登町

☑0768

From Wajima, towards the tip of the peninsula, you'll pass the famous slivered *dandan-batake* (rice terraces) at **Senmaida** (千枚田) before arriving in the coastal village of **Sosogi** (曽々木). From Wajima, Ushitsu-bound buses stop in Sosogi (¥740, 40 minutes).

Closeby you'll find the **mado-iwa** (窓岩; window rock) rock formation, just offshore, and a number of hiking trails. In winter, look for *nami-no-hana* (flowers of the waves), masses of foam that form when waves gnash Sosogi's rocky shore.

The road northeast from Sosogi village passes sea-salt farms (珠洲製塩) onward to the tiny village of Suzu and remote cape Rokkō, the peninsula's furthest point. Nearby, you can amble up to the lighthouse in the village of **Noroshi** (狼煙) and west along the cape.

The road circles around the tip of the peninsula, heading south past less dramatic scenery, back to civilisation.

◎ Sights

Senmaida Rice Terraces LANDMARK
(白米千枚田段々畑) Once a common sight in Japan, this ancient method of farming has all but died out – these 'thousand' terraced rice paddies snaking up the hillside are both fascinating and beautiful in all seasons.

Tokikuni Residences HISTORIC BUILDINGS
(時国家・上時国家 Tokikuni-ke & Kami-tokikuni-ke; Tokikuni-ke: adult/child ¥600/300; Kami-tokikuni-ke adult/child ¥500/400; ☺8.30am-5pm)

One of the few survivors of the Taira clan, Taira Tokitada was exiled to this region in 1185. His ancestors eventually divided and established separate family residences here, both now Important Cultural Properties. The first, Tokikuni-ke, was built in 1590 in the style of the Kamakura period and has a *meishō tei-en* (famous garden). A few minutes' walk away, Kami-tokikuni-ke has an impressive thatched roof and elegant interior. It was completed in the early 19th century.

🛏 Sleeping & Eating

Yokoiwaya   MINSHUKU ¥¥
(横岩屋; ☎ 32-0603; Ku-2 Machino-machi Sosogi; r per person with meals from ¥8350; [P]) In Sosogi, waterfront *minshuku* Yokoiwaya has welcomed guests for over 150 years and is known for its outstanding seafood dinners. Look for the paper lantern, or request pick-up from Sosogi-guchi bus stop (曽々木口バス停).

★ Lamp no Yado   RYOKAN ¥¥¥
(ランプの宿; ☎ 86-8000; www.lampnoyado. co.jp; 10-11 Jike; r per person incl 2 meals from ¥20,100; [P] ⊠) Remote Lamp no Yado is a place of its own: a 13-room wooden waterside village beneath a cliff. The building goes back four centuries, to when people would escape to its curative waters for weeks at a time. It's been an inn since the 1970s. Decadent rooms have private bathrooms, and some have their own *rotemburo*. The pool is almost superfluous. This is a romantic destination ryokan, but not for those on a budget or with a fear of tsunami.

Kaga Onsen   加賀温泉
☎ 0761
This broad area consisting of three hot-spring villages, **Katayamazu Onsen**, **Yamashiro Onsen** and **Yamanaka Onsen**, is centred on Kaga Onsen and Daishōji Stations along the JR Hokuriku line and is famed for its *onsen ryokan*, lacquerware and porcelain. Of the three villages, Yamanaka Onsen is the most scenic.

◉ Sights & Activities

Kutaniyaki Art Museum   MUSEUM
(石川県九谷焼美術館; 1-10-13 Jikata-machi; admission ¥500; ⊙ 9am-5pm, closed Mon) Stunning examples of bright and colourful local porcelain are on display here, an eight-minute walk from Daishōji Station.

Zenshō-ji   BUDDHIST TEMPLE
(全昌寺; 1 Daishōji Shinmei-chō; admission ¥500; ⊙ 9am-5pm) The Daishōji Station area is crammed with temples including Zenshō-ji, which houses over 500 amusingly carved Buddhist arhat sculptures.

Yamanaka Onsen   ONSEN
In lovely Yamanaka Onsen, the 17th-century haiku poet Basho rhapsodised on the chrysanthemum fragrance of the local mineral springs. It's still an ideal spot for chilling at the bathhouse **Kiku no Yu** (菊の湯; admission ¥420; ⊙ 6.45am-10.30pm), and for river walks by the Kokusenkei gorge, spanned by the elegant **Korogi-bashi** (Cricket bridge) and the whimsical, modern-art **Ayatori-hashi** (Cat's Cradle bridge). Yamanaka Onsen is accessible by bus (¥410, 30 minutes) from Kaga Onsen station.

Yamashiro Onsen   ONSEN
(総湯) A few kilometres closer to Kaga Onsen Station, Yamashiro Onsen is a sleepy town centred on a magnificent wooden bathhouse that was recently rebuilt. **Kosōyu** (古総湯; admission ¥500, Sōyu combined ticket ¥700; ⊙ 6am-10pm) has beautiful stained-glass windows and a rest area on the top floor; neighbouring **Sōyu** is a larger, more modern bathhouse.

🛏 Sleeping

The friendly folk at the **Yamanaka Onsen Tourism Association** (山中温泉観光協会; ☎ 78-0330; www.yamanaka-spa.or.jp/english; Yamanaka Onsen Bunka Kaikan, 5-1 Yamanaka Onsen) can help with the difficult task of picking the right ryokan for your budget and tastes – there are many in this region. Our two favourites are the following.

★ Beniya Mukayū   RYOKAN ¥¥¥
(べにや無何有; ☎ 77-1340; www.mukayu.com; 55-1-3 Yamashiro Onsen; per person with meals from ¥47,400; [P] @) The friendly staff at this award-winning ryokan are committed to upholding the Japanese art of hospitality. Gorgeously minimalist, with an interior designed by renowned architect Kiyoshi Sey Takayama, there's a quiet, Zen-like philosophy that pervades every aspect of the guest experience, from a welcoming private tea ceremony to the gentle morning yoga classes. Rooms are a beautiful coming together of traditional and contemporary – all feature private outdoor cypress baths and elements of understated luxury. Spa treatments are

out of this world. Mukayu's cuisine features only the best and freshest local seasonal ingredients, exquisitely prepared. This is truly a special place.

Kayōtei RYOKAN ¥¥¥
(かよう亭; ☑ 78-1410; www.kayotei.jp; 1-20 Higashi-machi; per person with meals from ¥39,000; P @) This delightful, opulent ryokan along the scenic Kokusenkei gorge has only 10 rooms, giving it an intimate feel. Some rooms have private outdoor baths facing the inn's own mountain.

ⓘ Getting There & Away

The JR Hokuriku line links Kaga Onsen with Kanazawa (*tokkyū*, ¥1470, 25 minutes; *futsū*, ¥740, 44 minutes) and Fukui (*tokkyū*, ¥1300, 20 minutes; *futsū*, ¥570, 48 minutes). A bus (¥700, 45 minutes, one daily April to November) links Yamanaka Onsen with Fukui-ken's famous Eihei-ji temple.

Hakusan National Park 白山国立公園

This national park, geared for serious hikers and naturalists, straddles four prefectures – Ishikawa, Fukui, Toyama and Gifu – and has several peaks above 2500m; the tallest is Hakusan (2702m), a sacred mountain that, along with Mt Fuji, has been worshipped since ancient times. In summer, hiking and scrambling uphill to catch mountain sunrises are the main activities, while in winter skiing and onsen bathing take over. The alpine section of the park is crisscrossed with trails, offering treks of up to 25km. For hikers who are well equipped and in no hurry, there is a 26km trek to Ogimachi in Shōkawa Valley.

Those looking to hike on and around the peaks are required to stay overnight, mostly in giant dorms at either **Murodō Centre** (Tateyama Murodō Sansō; ☑ 076-463-1228; www.murodou.co.jp; dm with 2 meals ¥7700; ⊙ 1 May-15 Oct) or **Nanryū Sansō** (南竜 ☑ 076-259-2022; http://city-hakusan.com/stay/nanryu.html; dm with 2 meals ¥7600, campsites ¥300, tent rental ¥2200, 5-person cabins ¥12,000; ⊙ Jul-Sep). Getting to either of these requires a hike of 3½ to five hours, and when the lodges are full, each person gets about one tatami mat's worth of sleeping space. Camping is prohibited in the park except at Nanryū Sansō camping ground; there are several camping grounds outside the park. That doesn't stop the park

from swarming with visitors, however. Reservations are recommended at least one week in advance.

The closest access point is Bettōdeai. From here it's 6km to Murodō (about 4½ hours' walk) and 5km to Nanryū (3½ hours). Ichirino, Chūgū Onsen, Shiramine and Ichinose have *minshuku*, ryokan and camping. Rates per person start from around ¥300 for campsites, or around ¥7500 for rooms in inns with two meals.

ⓘ Getting There & Away

This is not easily done, even during the peak summer period. The main mode of transport is the **Hokutetsu Kankō** (☑ 076-237-5115) bus from Kanazawa Station to Bettōdeai. From late June to mid-October, up to three buses operate daily (¥2000, two hours). Return fares include a coupon for a stay at Murodō Centre (¥10,600).

If you're driving from the Shōkawa Valley, you can take the spectacular Hakusan Super-Rindō toll road (cars ¥3150).

FUKUI PREFECTURE

Fukui-ken (福井県) is off the beaten path for most travellers in Japan and doesn't hold much interest for overseas visitors, with the exception of a very special temple and some coastal rocks.

Fukui 福井

☑ 0776 / POP 268,000
Unfortunate Fukui was decimated in the 1940s, first by war then by earthquake. For most tourists, it's now just a working-class city en-route to Eihei-ji or Tojinbō. Enquire at the **Fukui Tourist Information Centre** (☑ 20-5348; ⊙ 8.30am-7pm) about a Free Pass (¥2000), offering unlimited bus transport to these destinations for two days.

JR trains connect Fukui with Kanazawa (*tokkyū*, ¥2940, 50 minutes; *futsū*, ¥1280, 1½ hours), Tsuruga (*tokkyū*, ¥2610, 35 minutes; *futsū*, ¥950, 55 minutes), Kyoto (¥4810, 1½ hours) and Osaka (¥5870, 1¾ hours).

Eihei-ji 永平寺

☑ 0776
In 1244 the great Zen master Dōgen (1200–53), founder of the Sōtō sect of Zen Buddhism, established Eihei-ji in a forest near Fukui. Today it's one of Sōtō's two head tem-

ples, one of the world's most influential Zen centres and a palpably spiritual place amid mountains, mosses and ancient cedars. Serious students of Zen should consider a retreat here – there are commonly some 150 priests and disciples in residence – but all are welcome to visit.

Comprising over 70 buildings, the **temple** (☑ 63-3102; adult/child ¥500/200; ⊘ 9am-5pm) receives huge numbers of visitors for tourism and training, each year, and is often closed for periods varying from a week to 10 days for religious observance. Check with http://global.sotozen-net.or.jp/eng, before you start planning.

Aspirants can attend the temple's four-day, three-night **sanrō experience program** (Religious Trainee Program; ☑ 63-3640; www.sotozen-net.or.jp/kokusai/list/eiheiji.htm; fee ¥11,000), which follows the monks' training schedule, complete with 3.50am prayers, cleaning, *zazen* and ritual meals in which not a grain of rice may be left behind. Knowledge of Japanese isn't necessary, but it helps to be able to sit in the half-lotus position. Everyone we've spoken to who has completed this course agrees it is a remarkable experience. Book at least two weeks in advance.

To get to Eihei-ji from Fukui, take the Keifuku bus (¥720, 35 minutes, at least three daily); buses depart from the east exit of Fukui Station.

Tōjinbō 東尋坊

On the coast about 25km northwest of Fukui these towering **rock formations** are the stuff of legend: one says that Tōjinbō, an evil priest, was cast off the cliff by angry villagers in 1182; the sea surged for 49 days thereafter, a demonstration of the priest's fury from beyond his watery grave.

Visitors can take a boat trip (¥1010, 30 minutes) to view the rock formations or travel further up the coast to **O-jima**, a small island with a shrine that is joined to the mainland by a bridge.

From Fukui, catch a train to Awara Onsen Station (*futsū*, ¥320, 16 minutes) and then a bus (¥730, 40 minutes).

Tsuruga 敦賀

Tsuruga, south of Fukui and north of Biwako, is a thriving port and train junction. **Shin Nihonkai ferry company** (☑ 0770-23-2222; www.snf.jp) has nine sailings a week to Tomakomai, Hokkaidō (2nd class from ¥9300, 19½ hours nonstop, 30½ hours with stops). Several of these stop en route at Niigata (¥5200, 12½ hours) and Akita (¥6500, 20 hours). Buses timed to ferry departures serve Tsuruga-kō port from Tsuruga Station (¥340, 20 minutes).

Kyoto

075 / POP 1.47 MILLION

Best Temples & Shrines

➡ Fushimi-Inari Taisha (p304)

➡ Nanzen-ji (p299)

➡ Kinkaku-ji (p299)

➡ Ginkaku-ji (p295)

Best Places to Stay

➡ Tawaraya (p312)

➡ Hyatt Regency Kyoto (p313)

➡ Westin Miyako, Kyoto (p314)

➡ Kyoto Hotel Ōkura (p312)

➡ Chion-in (p293)

Why Go?

For much of its history, Kyoto (京都) *was* Japan. Even today, Kyoto is *the* place to go to see what Japan is all about. Here is where you'll find all those things you associate with the Land of the Rising Sun: ancient temples, colourful shrines and sublime gardens. Indeed, Kyoto is the storehouse of Japan's traditional culture, and it's even the place where the Japanese go to learn about their own culture.

With 17 Unesco World Heritage Sites, more than 1600 Buddhist temples and over 400 Shintō shrines, Kyoto is one of the world's most culturally rich cities. And traditional architecture is only half the story: there are also dazzling geisha dances, otherworldly kabuki performances, and an incredible range of shops and restaurants. All told, it's fair to say that Kyoto ranks with Paris, London and Rome as one of those cities that everyone should see at least once in their lives. Thus, Kyoto should rank at the top of any Japan itinerary.

When to Go
Kyoto

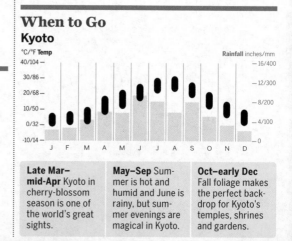

Late Mar–mid-Apr Kyoto in cherry-blossom season is one of the world's great sights.

May–Sep Summer is hot and humid and June is rainy, but summer evenings are magical in Kyoto.

Oct–early Dec Fall foliage makes the perfect backdrop for Kyoto's temples, shrines and gardens.

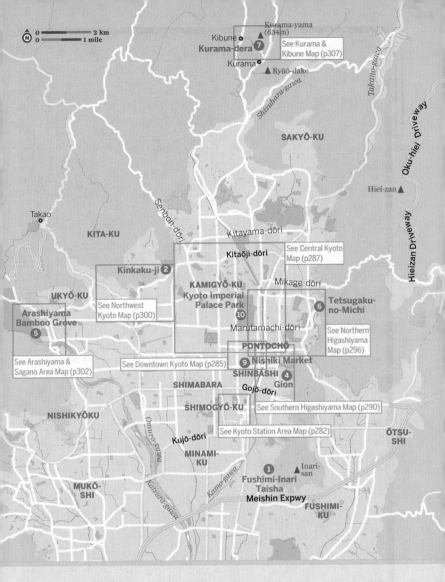

Kyoto Highlights

1 Pass through vermilion shrine gates at **Fushimi-Inari Taisha** (p304)

2 Marvel at the golden hall of **Kinkaku-ji** (p299) floating over its tranquil pond

3 Spend a night in a traditional **ryokan** (p310)

4 Take an evening stroll through **Gion** (p293) and keep your eyes peeled for geisha

5 Immerse yourself in a green fantasy world at **Arashiyama's Bamboo Grove** (p301)

6 Wander along the **Tetsugaku-no-Michi** (p295)

7 Visit **Kurama-dera** (p307), and the hot spring below

8 Be dazzled by the spring or autumn **geisha dances**

9 Explore **Nishiki Market** (p284), known to locals as 'Kyoto's pantry'

10 Relax in the **Kyoto Imperial Palace Park** (p286)

Greater Kyoto

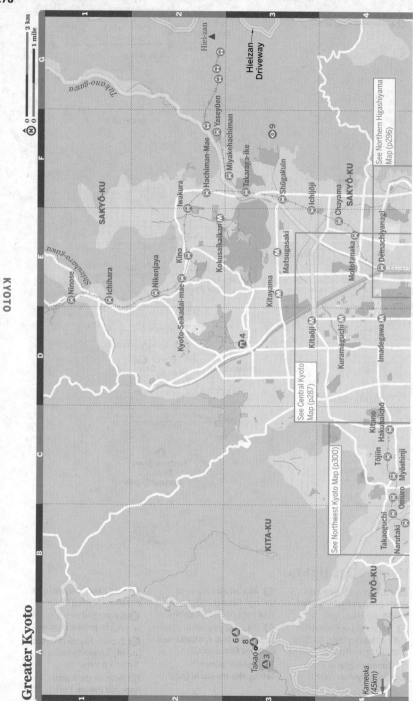

Hiei-zan

Hieizan Driveway

Yaseyūen

Hachiman-Mae

Miyakehachiman

Takaraga-Ike

9

Shūgakuin

Ichijōji

Chayama

SAKYŌ-KU

See Northern Higashiyama Map (p296)

Iwakura

Kokusaikaikan

Kino

Matsugasaki

Mototanaka

Demachiyanagi

SAKYŌ-KU

Ninose

Ichihara

Nikenjaya

Kitayama

Kyoto-Seikadai-mae

4

Kitaōji

Kuramaguchi

Imadegawa

See Central Kyoto Map (p287)

Kitano

Hakubaichō

See Northwest Kyoto Map (p300)

Tōjin

Myōshinji

KITA-KU

Takaoguchi

Narutaki

Omuro

UKYŌ-KU

6

8

Takao

3

Kameoka (45km)

Kurama-gawa

Takano-gawa

2 km

1 mile

N

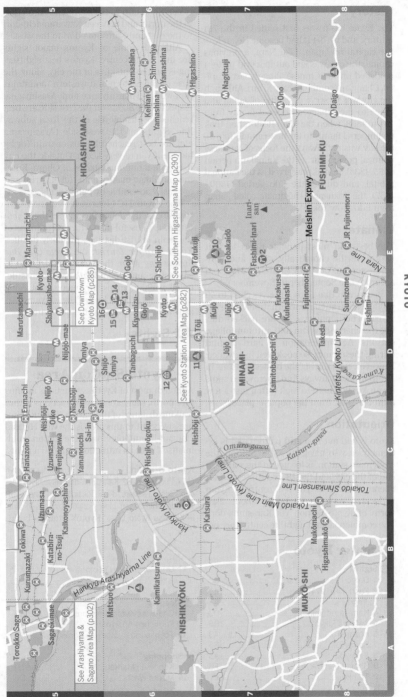

KYOTO

HIGASHIYAMA-KU

FUSHIMI-KU

MINAMI-KU

NISHIKYŌKU

MUKO-SHI

Meishin Expwy

Nara Line

Kintetsu Kyoto Line

Tokaido Main Line (Kyoto Line)

Tokaido Shinkansen Line

Hankyu Kyoto Line

Hankyu Arashiyama Line

Kamo-gawa

Omuro-gawa

Katsura-gawa

See Southern Higashiyama Map (p290)

See Downtown Kyoto Map (p285)

See Kyoto Station Area Map (p282)

See Arashiyama & Sagano Area Map (p302)

Inari-san

Stations / places (left to right, top area):
Yamashina, Shinomiya, Keihan Yamashina, Yamashina, Higashino, Nagitsuji, Ono, Daigo

Marutamachi, Marutamachi, Kyoto-Shiyakusho-mae, Gojō, Shichijō, Tōfukuji, Tobakaidō, Fushimi-Inari, Fujinomori, JR Fujinomori

Shijaikusho-mae, Nijōjō-mae, Kiyomizu-Gojō, Kyoto, Kujō, Jūjō, Fukakusa Kuinabashi, Fujinomori, Sumizome, Fushimi

Enmachi, Nijō, Nishiōji-Oike, Sanjō, Shijō-Ōmiya, Tōji, Kamitobaguchi, Takeda

Hanazono, Uzumasa, Tenjingawa, Yamanouchi, Sai-in, Sai, Nishiōji, Nishikyōgoku

Uzumasa, Katabira-no-Tsuji, Kaikonoyashiro, Nishijō-Sanjō

Tokiwa, Kurumazaki, Arisugawa, Kamikatsura, Katsura, Mukōmachi, Higashimukō

Torokko Saga, Sagaekimae, Matsuo, Kamikatsura

Nijō, Ōmiya, Tanbaguchi, Nishiōji

History

The Kyoto basin was first settled in the 7th century, and by 794 it had become Heian-kyō, the capital of Japan. Like Nara, a previous capital, the city was laid out in a grid pattern modelled on the Chinese Tang-dynasty capital, Chang'an (contemporary Xi'an). Although the city was to serve as capital of Japan and home to the Japanese imperial family from 794 to 1868 (when the Meiji Restoration took the imperial family to the new capital, Tokyo), the city was not always the focus of Japanese political power. During the Kamakura period (1185–1333), Kamakura served as the national capital, and during the Edo period (1600–1867), the Tokugawa shōgunate ruled Japan from Edo (now Tokyo).

Climate

The best and most popular times to visit Kyoto are the climatically stable and temperate seasons of spring (March to May) and autumn (late September to November).

Be warned that Kyoto receives close to 50 million domestic and international tourists a year. The popular sights are packed during the cherry-blossom and autumn-foliage seasons. Accommodation is hard to find during these times, so book well in advance. However, even during the busiest seasons in Kyoto, you can always find uncrowded spots if you know where to look (often just a few minutes' walk from the popular places).

Orientation

Kyoto is laid out in a grid pattern and is extremely easy to navigate. Kyoto Station, the city's main station, is located at the southern end of the city, and the JR and Kintetsu lines operate from here. The real centre of Kyoto is located around Shijō-dōri, about 2km north of Kyoto Station via Karasuma-dōri. The commercial and nightlife centres are between Shijō-dōri to the south and Sanjō-dōri to the north, and between Kawaramachi-dōri to the east and Karasuma-dōri to the west.

Although some of Kyoto's major sights are in the city centre, Kyoto's best sightseeing is on the outskirts of the city, along the base of the eastern and western mountains (known as Higashiyama and Arashiyama, respectively). Sights on the east side are best reached by bus, bicycle or the Tōzai subway line. Sights on the west side (Arashiyama etc) are best reached by bus or train (or by bicycle if you're very keen). Outside the city itself, the mountain villages of Ōhara, Kurama and Takao make wonderful day trips and are easily accessible by public transport.

The Kyoto TIC (Tourist Information Centre) stocks the following maps: the *Kyoto City Map*, a useful map with decent insets of the main tourist districts; the fairly detailed *Kyoto Map for Tourist*; the *Kyoto City Bus Sightseeing Map*, the most useful guide to city buses; and *Kyoto Walks*, which has detailed walking maps for major sightseeing areas in and around Kyoto (Higashiyama, Arashiyama, northwest Kyoto and Ōhara).

◉ Sights

◉ Kyoto Station Area

Although most of Kyoto's attractions are further north, there are a few attractions within walking distance of the station. The most impressive sight in this area is the vast Higashi Hongan-ji, but don't forget the station building itself – it's an attraction in its own right.

Kyoto Station　　　　　　　　　　NOTABLE BUILDING
(京都駅; Map p282; Karasuma-dōri, Higashishiokōji-chō, Shiokōji sagaru; ℝ JR Tōkaidō Main Line, ℝ JR Tōkaidō Shinkansen Line, Sanyō Shinkansen Line, ℝ Kintetsu Kyoto Line) Kyoto's station build-

KYOTO IN...

Two Days

Even two days are enough to get a taste for the magic of Kyoto. On the morning of the first day, head to **Southern Higashiyama** and – if the energy level permits – spend the afternoon exploring **Northern Higashiyama**. You could just about make it from Kiyomizu-dera to Ginkaku-ji in one long day. The following day, head west to the Arashiyama and Sagano Area to visit the famed **Bamboo Grove** and **Ōkōchi Sansō**.

Four Days

Four days is about the perfect amount of time to allot Kyoto on a typical 10-day Japan trip. It gives you enough time to see quite a few of the big-name spots and add in a few *anaba* (secret spots). On the first two days, basically do the above two-day itinerary, but consider visiting **Southern Higashiyama** and **Northern Higashiyama** on separate days. After hitting these areas and the **Arashiyama and Sagano** area, you've probably got one more day to play with. Maybe take a break from temple-hopping and hit some museums, or wander downtown and head up into the mountains to check out **Kibune** and **Kurama**.

One Week

If you're blessed with a full week in the old capital, our first advice is this: *slow down*. You'll want to do everything we mention in the above four-day itinerary, but at a slower pace, and you should consider 'stepping off the map' – ie just wandering into some temples or shrines and shops that aren't mentioned in this guide or hiking in the hills. Find your own perfect little garden and spend some time in meditation, thinking or napping. You'll also want to make a day trip to **Nara** and maybe even another one down to **Ise**.

ing is a striking steel-and-glass structure – a futuristic cathedral for the transport age. In the station building you'll find several food courts, the Kyoto Prefectural International Centre (京都府国際センター), a performance space and an Isetan department store.

While train stations don't usually qualify as stand-alone attractions, the Kyoto Station building is a great exception to this rule. In addition to serving as the city's transport hub, it's chock-a-bloc with shops, performance spaces and things to see and do. Take some time to explore the many levels of the station, all the way up to the 15th-floor observation level. If you don't suffer from fear of heights, try riding the escalator from the 7th floor on the eastern side of the building up to the 11th-floor aerial skywalk, high over the main concourse.

Kyoto Tower   NOTABLE BUILDING

(京都タワー; Map p282; Karasuma-dōri, Shichijō sagaru; admission ¥770; ⏰9am-9pm, last entry 8.40pm; 🚆JR Main Line, 🚆JR Tōkaidō Shinkansen Line, Sanyō Shinkansen Line, 🚆Kintetsu Kyoto Line) If you want to orient yourself and get an idea of the layout of Kyoto as soon as you arrive in town, Kyoto Tower is the place to do it. Located right outside the Karasuma (north)

gate of the station, this retro tower looks like a rocket perched atop the Kyoto Tower Hotel.

The tower provides excellent views in all directions and you can really see why Kyotoites describe their city as a *bonchi* (a flat tray with raised edges). There are free mounted binoculars to use, and these allow ripping views over to Kiyomizu-dera and as far south as Osaka.

Higashi Hongan-ji   TEMPLE

(東本願寺; Map p282; Karasuma-dōri, Shichijō agaru; ⏰5.50am-5.30pm Mar-Oct, 6.20am-4.30pm Nov-Feb; 🚆JR Tōkaidō Main Line, 🚆JR Tōkaidō Shinkansen Line, Sanyō Shinkansen Line, 🚆Kintetsu Kyoto Line) **FREE** A short walk north of Kyoto Station, this temple is the last word in all things grand and gaudy. Considering the proximity to the station, the free admission, the awesome structures and the dazzling interiors, this temple is an obvious spot to visit if you find yourself near the station.

In 1602, when Tokugawa Ieyasu engineered the rift in the Jōdo Shin-shū school, he founded this temple as a competitor to Nishi Hongan-ji. Rebuilt in 1895 after a series of fires destroyed all of the original structures, the temple is now the headquarters of the Ōtani branch of Jōdo Shin-shū.

Kyoto Station Area

Kyoto Station Area

In the corridor between the two main buildings you'll find a curious item encased in glass: a tremendous coil of rope made from human hair. Following the destruction of the temple in the 1880s, an eager group of female temple devotees donated their locks to make the ropes that hauled the massive timbers used for reconstruction.

The enormous **Goei-dō** (main hall) is one of the world's largest wooden structures, standing 38m high, 76m long and 58m wide.

Nishi Hongan-ji   TEMPLE
(西本願寺; Map p282; Horikawa-dōri, Hanaya-chō sagaru; ⊙ 6am-5pm Nov-Feb, 5.30am-5.30pm Mar, Apr, Sep & Oct, to 6pm May-Aug; 🚉 JR Tōkaidō

Main Line, 🚉JR Tōkaidō Shinkansen Line, Sanyō Shinkansen Line, 🚉Kintetsu Kyoto Line) `FREE` This temple contains five buildings, featuring some of the finest examples of architecture and artistic achievement from the Azuchi-Momoyama period (1568–1600). The **Goei-dō** is a marvellous sight and the **Daisho-in Hall** has sumptuous paintings, carvings and metal ornamentation. A small garden and two nō (stylised Japanese dance-drama) stages are connected with the hall. The dazzling **Kara-mon** has intricate ornamental carvings.

In 1591 Toyotomi Hideyoshi built this temple, known as Hongan-ji, as the new headquarters for the Jōdo Shin-shū (True Pure Land) school of Buddhism, which had accumulated immense power. Later, Tokugawa Ieyasu saw this power as a threat and sought to weaken it by encouraging a breakaway faction of this school to found Higashi Hongan-ji (*higashi* means 'east') in 1602. The original Hongan-ji then became known as Nishi Hongan-ji (*nishi* means 'west'). It now functions as the headquarters of the Hongan-ji branch of the Jōdo Shin-shū school, with over 10,000 temples and 12 million followers worldwide.

Tō-ji BUDDHIST TEMPLE
(東寺; Map p278; 1 Kujō-chō; admission to grounds free, Kondō, Kōdō & Treasure Hall ¥500 each, pagoda, Kondō & Kōdō ¥800; ⊙ 8.30am-5.30pm Apr-Aug, to 4.30pm Sep-Mar; 🚉JR Tōkaidō Main Line, 🚉JR Tōkaidō Shinkansen Line, Sanyō Shinkansen Line, 🚉Kintetsu Kyoto Line) This temple was established in 794 by imperial decree to protect the city. In 818 the emperor handed the temple over to Kūkai, the founder of the

Shingon school of Buddhism. Many of the buildings were destroyed by fire or fighting during the 15th century; most of those that remain date from the 17th century.

The Kōdō (Lecture Hall) contains 21 images representing a Mikkyō (Esoteric Buddhism) mandala. The Kondō (Main Hall) contains statues depicting the Yakushi (Healing Buddha) trinity. In the southern part of the garden stands the five-storey pagoda, which burnt down five times. It was rebuilt in 1643 and is now the highest pagoda in Japan, standing 57m tall.

The Kōbō-san market-fair is held here on the 21st of each month. The fairs held in December and January are particularly lively.

Tō-ji is a 15-minute walk southwest of Kyoto Station or a five-minute walk from Tōji Station on the Kintetsu line.

**Umekōji Steam Locomotive
Museum** MUSEUM
(梅小路蒸気機関車館; Map p278; Kankiji-chō, Shimogyō-ku; adult/child ¥400/100, train ride ¥200/100; ⊙10am-5pm, closed Mon, except during spring break (25 Mar-7 Apr) and summer break (21 Jul-7 Aug); 🚌Kyoto City Bus from Kyoto Station, take bus 33, 205 or 208 to the Umekō-ji Kōen-mae stop) A hit with steam-train buffs and kids, this museum features 18 vintage steam locomotives (dating from 1914 to 1948) and related displays. It's in the former Nijō Station building, which was recently relocated here and carefully reconstructed. For an extra few yen, you can take a 10-minute ride on one of the fabulous old trains (departures at 11am, 1.30pm and 3.30pm).

If catching the bus to the museum, make sure you get on a westbound service.

ℹ **KYOTO TIPS**

Common sense varies from place to place. In Kyoto, even if you dispense with common sense, you don't run the risk of serious trouble, but there are a few things to keep in mind to make everything easier and perhaps a little safer:

➡ Look both ways when exiting a shop or hotel onto a sidewalk, especially if you have young ones in tow: Kyoto is a city of cyclists and there is almost always someone on a bicycle tearing in your direction.

➡ Bring a pair of slip-on shoes to save you from tying and untying your shoes each time you visit a temple.

➡ Don't take a taxi in the main Higashiyama sightseeing district during cherry-blossom season – the streets will be so crowded that it will be faster to walk or cycle.

➡ Head for the hills to find the most beautiful sights. Yes, the middle of the city has some great sights, but as a general rule, the closer you get to the mountains, the more attractive the city gets.

Downtown Kyoto

Downtown Kyoto looks much like any other Japanese city, but there are some excellent attractions to be found here, including Nishiki Market, the Museum of Kyoto, the Kyoto International Manga Museum and Ponto-chō. If you'd like a break from temples and shrines, then downtown Kyoto can be a welcome change. It's also good on a rainy day, because of the number of covered arcades and indoor attractions.

Nishiki Market   MARKET
(錦市場; Map p285; Nishikikōji-dōri, btwn Teramachi & Takakura; ⊙9am-5pm; Ⓢ Karasuma Line to Shijō Station, Ⓡ Hankyū Line to Karasuma or Kawaramachi Stations) If you are interested in seeing all the weird and wonderful foods that go into Kyoto cuisine, wander through Nishiki Market. It's in the centre of town, one block north of (and parallel to) Shijō-dōri, running west off Teramachi Shopping arcade and ending shortly before Daimaru department store.

This market is a great place to visit on a rainy day or if you need a break from temple-hopping (note that some stalls are closed on Wednesdays). The variety of foods on display is staggering, and the frequent cries of *irasshaimase!* (welcome!) are heartwarming.

Museum of Kyoto   MUSEUM
(京都文化博物館; Map p285; Takakura-dōri, Sanjō aguru; admission ¥500, extra for special exhibitions; ⊙10am-7.30pm, closed Mon; Ⓢ Karasuma or Tōzai lines to Karasuma-Oike Station) This museum is worth visiting if a special exhibition is on. The regular exhibits, which include models of ancient Kyoto, audiovisual presentations and a small gallery dedicated to Kyoto's film industry, are not worth a special visit.

On the 1st floor, the Roji Tempō is a reconstructed Edo-period merchant area showing 10 types of exterior latticework (this section can be entered free; some of the shops sell souvenirs and serve local dishes). The museum has English-speaking volunteer tour guides. The museum is a three-minute walk southeast of the Karasuma-Oike stop on the Karasuma and Tōzai subway lines.

**Kyoto International
Manga Museum**   MUSEUM
(京都国際マンガミュージアム; Map p285; www.kyotomm.com/english; Karasuma-dōri, Oike aguru; adult/child ¥800/300; ⊙10am-6pm, closed Wed; Ⓢ Karasuma or Tōzai lines to Karasuma-Oike Station) This fine museum has a collection of some 300,000 manga (Japanese comic books). Located in an old elementary school building, the museum is the perfect introduction to the art of manga. While most of the manga and displays are in Japanese, the collection of translated works is growing.

In addition to the galleries that show both the historical development of manga and original artwork done in manga style, there are beginners' workshops and portrait drawings on weekends. Visitors with children will appreciate the children's library and the occasional performances of *kami-shibai* (humorous traditional Japanese sliding-picture shows), not to mention the Astroturf lawn where the kids can run free. The museum hosts six month-long special exhibits yearly: check the website for details.

It's a short walk from the Karasuma-Oike Station on the Karuma line subway or the Tōzai line subway.

Ponto-chō   NEIGHBOURHOOD
(先斗町; Map p285; Ponto-chō, Nakagyō-ku; Ⓡ Keihan Line to Sanjo Station, Ⓢ Tōzai Line to Sanjo-Keihan or Kyoto Shiyakusho-mae stations, Ⓡ Hankyū Line to Kawaramachi Station) A traditional nightlife district and one of Kyoto's five geisha districts, Ponto-chō is a narrow alley running between Sanjō-dōri and Shijō-dōri, just west of Kamo-gawa. It's best visited in the evening, when the traditional wooden buildings and hanging lanterns create a wonderful atmosphere of old Japan, perhaps combined with a walk in nearby Gion.

Central Kyoto

The area we refer to as Central Kyoto includes the Kyoto Imperial Palace Park, Nijō-jō, a couple of important shrines and the Nishijin weaving district, among other things. It's flat and easy to explore by bicycle or on foot.

**Kyoto Imperial Palace
(Gosho)**   HISTORICAL BUILDING
(京都御所; Map p287; Kyoto Gosho; Kyoto-gosho, Nakagyō-ku; Ⓢ Karasuma Line to Marutamachi or Imadegawa stations) The original imperial palace was built in 794 and was replaced numerous times after destruction by fire. The present building, on a different site and smaller than the original, was constructed in 1855. Enthronement of a new emperor and other state ceremonies are still held here.

The Gosho does not rate highly in comparison with other attractions in Kyoto and

Downtown Kyoto

Downtown Kyoto

◎ Sights
1 Kyoto International Manga
  Museum A1
2 Museum of Kyoto B2
3 Nishiki Market B3
4 Ponto-chō D2

◎ Sleeping
5 Best Western Hotel Kyoto C2
6 Hiiragiya Ryokan C1
7 Hotel Unizo D2
8 JAM Hostel Kyoto Gion D3
9 Kyoto Hotel Ōkura D1
10 Mitsui Garden Hotel Kyoto Sanjō A2
11 Tawaraya C1
  Yoshikawa .... (see 33)

◎ Eating
12 A-Bar D3
13 Biotei B2
14 Café Independants C2
15 Ganko Zushi D2
16 Hinaka D3
17 Honke Tagoto C2
18 Ippūdō B3
19 Kane-yo C2
20 Karafuneya Coffee Honten D2
21 Kerala C1
22 Kiyamachi Sakuragawa D1
23 Merry Island Café D1
24 Mishima-tei C2
25 Musashi Sushi D2

26 Ootoya D2
27 Park Café C1
28 Rāmen Kairikiya D2
29 Shizenha Restaurant Obanzai A1
30 Tagoto Honten D3
31 Tsukiji Sushisei B3
32 Warai B3
33 Yoshikawa C1

◎ Drinking & Nightlife
34 Ike Tsuru C3
35 Ing Bar D2
36 McLoughlin's Irish Bar &
  Restaurant D1
37 Sama Sama D1
38 Yoramu B1

◎ Entertainment
39 Minami-za Theatre D3
40 Ponto-chō Kaburen-jō Theatre D2
41 World Peace Love D3

◎ Shopping
42 Aritsugu C3
43 Art Factory C2
44 Daimaru Department Store B3
45 Fujii Daimaru Department Store C3
46 Junkudō D2
47 Kyūkyo-dō C1
48 Marui D3
49 Rakushikan B2
50 Takashimaya Department Store D3

you must apply for permission to visit at the Imperial Household Agency (see below). However, you shouldn't miss the park surrounding the Gosho.

To get there, take the Karasuma line subway to Imadegawa or a bus to the Karasuma-Imadegawa stop and walk 600m southeast.

Imperial Household Agency　BOOKING OFFICE
(宮内庁京都事務所; ☎ 211-1215; ⓧ 8.45am-noon & 1-5pm Mon-Fri; ⓢ Karasuma Line to Imadegawa Station) Permission to visit the Gosho is granted by the Kunaichō, the Imperial Household Agency, which is inside the walled park surrounding the palace, a short walk from Imadegawa Station on the Karasuma line. The Imperial Household Agency is also the place to make reservations to see the Sentō Gosho, Katsura Rikyū and Shūgaku-in Rikyū. You have to fill out an application form and show your passport.

Children can visit the Imperial Palace if accompanied by adults over 20 years of age (but are forbidden entry to the other three imperial properties of Katsura Rikyū, Sentō Gosho and Shūgaku-in Rikyū). Permission to tour the palace is usually granted the same day (try to arrive at the office at least 30 minutes before the start of the tour you'd like to join). Guided tours, sometimes in English, are given at 10am and 2pm from Monday to Friday. The tour lasts about 50 minutes.

The Gosho can be visited without reservation on two occasions each year, once in spring and once in autumn. The dates vary each year, but as a general guide, the spring opening is around the last week of April and the autumn opening is in the middle of November. Check with the TIC for exact dates.

Sentō Gosho Palace　HISTORICAL BUILDING
(仙洞御所; Map p287; ☎ 211-1215; Kyoto gyōen, Nakagyō-ku; ⓢ Karasuma Line to Marutamachi or Imadegawa stations) This palace is a few hundred metres southeast of the main Kyoto Gosho. It was originally built in 1630 during the reign of Emperor Go-Mizunō as a residence for retired emperors. The palace was repeatedly destroyed by fire and reconstructed but served its purpose until a final blaze in 1854 (it was never rebuilt).

The gardens, which were laid out in 1630 by Kobori Enshū, are superb. The route takes you past lovely ponds and pathways, and in many ways, a visit here is more enjoyable than a visit to the Gosho, especially if you are a fan of Japanese gardens. Visitors must obtain advance permission from the Imperial Household Agency and be over 20 years old. Tours (in Japanese) start at 11am and 1.30pm.

Kyoto Imperial Palace Park　PARK
(京都御苑; Map p287; Kyoto gyōen, Nakagyō-ku; ⓧ dawn to dusk; ⓢ Karasuma Line to Marutamachi or Imadegawa stations) FREE The Kyoto Gosho and Sentō Gosho are surrounded by the spacious Kyoto Imperial Palace Park, which is planted with a huge variety of flowering trees and open fields. It's perfect for picnics, strolls and just about any sport you can think of. Take some time to visit the pond at the park's southern end, which contains gorgeous carp.

The park is most beautiful in the plum- and cherry-blossom seasons (late February and late March, respectively). The plum arbour is located about midway along the park on the west side. There are several large *shidareze-zakura* ('weeping' cherry trees) at the north end of the park, making it a great cherry-blossom destination. The park is between Teramachi-dōri and Karasuma-dōri (to the east and west) and Imadegawa-dōri and Marutamachi-dōri (to the north and south).

★ **Daitoku-ji**　TEMPLE
(大徳寺; Map p287; 53 Daitokuji-chō, Murasakino; ⓧ dawn-dusk; ⓢ Karasuma Line to Kitaōji Station) FREE Daitoku-ji, a collection of Zen temples, raked gravel gardens and wandering lanes, is a separate world within Kyoto. It is also one of the most rewarding destinations in this part of the city, particularly for those with an interest in Japanese gardens.

The name Daitoku-ji confusingly refers to both the main temple here and the entire complex, which contains a total of 24 temples and subtemples. We discuss three of them here, but another five are open to the public.

The eponymous **Daitoku-ji** is on the eastern side of the grounds. It was founded in 1319, burnt down in the next century and rebuilt in the 16th century. The San-mon contains an image of the famous tea master, Sen-no-Rikyū, on the 2nd storey. If you enter via the main gate on the east side of the complex, Daitoku-ji will be on your right, a short walk north.

Just north of Daitoku-ji, **Daisen-in** is famous for its two small gardens. At the west-

Central Kyoto

Central Kyoto

ern edge of the complex, **Kōtō-in** is famous for its stunning bamboo-lined approach and the maple trees in its main garden (try to visit in the foliage season).

The temple bus stop is Daitoku-ji-mae and buses 205 and 206 are convenient from Kyoto Station. Daitoku-ji is also a short walk west of Kitaō-ji subway station on the Karasuma line.

Nijō-jō
CASTLE

(二条城; Map p287; 541 Nijōjō-chō, Nijō-dōri, Horikawa Nishi iru; admission ¥600; ⊙8.45am-5pm, closed Tue in Dec, Jan, Jul & Aug; Ⓢ Tōzai Line to Nijō-jō-mae) This castle was built in 1603 as the official Kyoto residence of the first Tokugawa shōgun, Ieyasu. The ostentatious style of its construction was intended as a demonstration of Ieyasu's prestige and also to signal the demise of the emperor's power. As a safeguard against treachery, Ieyasu had the interior fitted with 'nightingale' floors, as well as concealed chambers where bodyguards could keep watch.

After passing through the grand Karamon gate, you enter Ninomaru Palace, which is divided into five buildings with numerous chambers. The Ohiroma Yon-no-Ma (Fourth Chamber) has spectacular screen paintings. Don't miss the excellent Ninomaru Palace Garden, which was designed by the tea master and landscape architect Kobori Enshū.

Nishijin
NEIGHBOURHOOD

(西陣; Nishijin; ⊒ Kyoto City Bus 9 to the Horikawa-Imadegawa stop) The Nishijin district is the home of Kyoto's textile industry, the source of the fantastically ornate kimonos and *obi* (ornamental kimono belts) for which the city is famous. It's one of Kyoto's more traditional districts, and there are still lots of good old *machiya* (traditional town houses) scattered about.

Nishijin Textile Center
MUSEUM

(西陣織会館; Map p287; Horikawa-dōri, Imadegawa Minami iru; ⊙9am-5pm; ⊒ Kyoto City Bus 9 to the Horikawa-Imadegawa stop) FREE In the heart of the Nishijin textile district, this is worth a peek before starting a walk around the area. There are also displays of completed fabrics and kimonos, as well as weaving demonstrations and occasional kimono fashion shows. Unfortunately, these days, it's often overrun with large bus tours. It's on the southwest corner of the Horikawa-dōri and Imadegawa-dōri intersection.

Orinasu-kan
MUSEUM

(織成館; Map p287; 693 Daikoku-chō; adult/child ¥500/350; ⊙10am-4pm, closed Mon; ⊒ Kyoto City Bus 9 to the Horikawa-Imadegawa stop) This museum, housed in a Nishijin weaving factory, has impressive exhibits of Nishijin textiles. It's more atmospheric and usually quieter than the Nishijin Textile Center. The Susameisha building across the street is also open to the public and worth a look. It's a short walk north of the Nishijin Textile Center.

Shimogamo-jinja
SHINTŌ SHRINE

(下鴨神社; Map p287; 59 Izumigawa-chō, Shimogamo; ⊙6.30am-5pm; Ⓢ Keihan Line to Demachiyanagi Station, ⊒ Kyoto City Bus 205 to the Shimogamo-jinja-mae stop) FREE Dating from the 8th century, this shrine is a Unesco World Heritage Site. It is nestled in the fork of the Kamo-gawa and Takano-gawa rivers, and is approached along a shady path through the lovely Tadasu-no-mori. This wooded area is said to be a place where lies cannot be concealed and is considered a prime location to sort out disputes. The trees here are mostly broadleaf (a rarity in Kyoto) and they are gorgeous in the springtime.

The shrine is dedicated to the god of harvest. Traditionally, pure water was drawn from the nearby rivers for purification and agricultural ceremonies. The *hondō* (main hall) dates from 1863 and, like the Haiden hall at its sister shrine, Kamigamo-jinja, is an excellent example of *nagare*-style shrine architecture. The annual *yabusame* (horseback archery) event here is spectacular. It happens on 3 May from 1pm to 3.30pm in Tadasu-no-mori.

Kyoto Botanical Gardens
PARK

(京都府立植物園; Map p287; Shimogamohangichō, Sakyō-ku; gardens adult ¥200, child ¥80-150; greenhouse adult ¥200, child ¥80-150; ⊙9am-5pm, greenhouse 9am-4pm; Ⓢ Karasuma Line to Kitayama Station) The Kyoto Botanical Gardens, opened in 1914, occupy 240,000 sq metres and feature 12,000 plants, flowers and trees. It is pleasant to stroll through the rose, cherry and herb gardens or see the rows of camphor trees and the large tropical greenhouse.

This is a good spot for a picnic or a bit of frisbee throwing. It's also a great spot for a *hanami* (cherry-blossom viewing) party and the blossoms here tend to hold on a little longer than those elsewhere in the city. The gardens are a five-minute walk west of Kitayama subway station (Karasuma line).

Kamigamo-jinja
SHINTŌ SHRINE

(上賀茂神社; Map p278; 339 Motoyama, Kamigamo; ⊙6am-5pm; ⊒ Kyoto City Bus 9 to the Kamigamo-misonobashi stop) FREE This shrine is one of Japan's oldest and predates the founding of Kyoto. Established in 679, it is dedicated to Raijin, the god of thunder, and is one of Kyoto's 17 Unesco World Heritage Sites.

The present buildings (over 40 in all), including the impressive Haiden hall, are exact reproductions of the originals, dating from the 17th to 19th centuries. The shrine is entered from a long approach through two torii (shrine gates). The two large conical white-sand mounds in front of Hosodono hall are said to represent mountains sculpted for gods to descend upon.

The shrine is a five-minute walk from Kamigamo-misonobashi bus stop.

⊙ Southern Higashiyama

The Higashiyama district, which runs along the base of the Higashiyama mountains (Eastern Mountains), is the main sightseeing district in Kyoto and it should be at the top of your Kyoto itinerary. It is thick with impressive sights: fine temples, shrines, gardens, museums, traditional neighbourhoods and parks.

★ Shōren-in   BUDDHIST TEMPLE
(青蓮院; Map p290; 69-1 Sanjōbō-chō, Awataguchi, Higashiyama-ku; admission ¥500; ⊙9am-5pm; Ⓢ Tōzai Line to Higashiyama Station) This temple is hard to miss, with the giant camphor trees growing just outside its walls. Shōren-in was originally the residence of the chief abbot of the Tendai school of Buddhism. The present building dates from 1895, but the main hall has sliding screens with paintings from the 16th and 17th centuries.

Often overlooked by the crowds that descend on other Higashiyama temples, this is a pleasant place to sit and think while gazing out over the beautiful gardens. The temple is a five-minute walk north of Chion-in.

Sanjūsangen-dō Temple   BUDDHIST TEMPLE
(三十三間堂; Map p290; 657 Sanjūsangendōmawari-chō, Higashiyama-ku; admission ¥600; ⊙8am-4.30pm, 9am-3.30pm Nov-Mar; Ⓢ Keihan Line to Shichijō Station, Ⓤ Kyoto City Bus No 206 or 208 to the Sanjūsangen-dō-mae stop) The original Sanjūsangen-dō was built in 1164 at the request of the retired emperor Go-shirakawa. The temple's name refers to the 33 *(sanjūsan)* bays between the pillars of this long, narrow building, which houses 1001 statues of the 1000-armed Kannon (the Buddhist goddess of mercy). The largest Kannon is flanked on either side by 500 smaller Kannon images, neatly lined up in rows.

Kyoto National Museum   MUSEUM
(京都国立博物館; Map p290; www.kyohaku.go.jp; 527 Chaya-machi, Higashiyama-ku; adult/student ¥500/250; ⊙9.30am-6pm, to 8pm Fri, closed Mon; Ⓡ Keihan Line to Shichijō Station, Ⓤ Kyoto City Bus 206 or 208 to the Sanjūsangen-dō-mae stop) The Kyoto National Museum is housed in two buildings opposite Sanjūsangen-dō temple. It was founded in 1895 as an imperial repository for art and treasures from local temples and shrines. There are 17 rooms with displays of over 1000 artworks, historical artefacts and handicrafts.

The permanent collection is excellent but somewhat poorly displayed; unless you have a particular interest in Japanese traditional arts, we recommend visiting this museum only when a special exhibition is on. Note that the museum is presently undergoing a partial reconstruction; you can still enter the museum but construction will be going on until late 2013.

Kawai Kanjirō Memorial Hall   MUSEUM
(河井寛次郎記念館; Map p290; 569 Kaneichō, Gojō-zaka, Higashiyama-ku; admission ¥900; ⊙10am-5pm, closed Mon; Ⓤ Kyoto City Bus 206 or 207 from Kyoto Station to the Umamachi stop.) This museum is one of Kyoto's overlooked little gems, especially for those with an interest in Japanese crafts such as pottery and furniture. The hall was the home and workshop of one of Japan's most famous potters, Kawai Kanjirō (1890–1966).

The 1937 house is built in rural style and contains examples of Kanjirō's work, his collection of folk art and ceramics, and his workshop and a fascinating *nobori-gama* (a stepped kiln).

The hall is a 10-minute walk north of the Kyoto National Museum. Or, take a Kyoto City bus. Note that it closes from around the 10th to the 20th of August and the 24th of December to the 7th of January; dates vary each year.

Kiyomizu-dera   BUDDHIST TEMPLE
(清水寺; Map p290; 1-294 Kiyomizu, Higashiyama-ku; admission ¥300; ⊙6am-6pm; Ⓤ Kyoto City Bus 206 to the Kiyōmizu-michi or Gojō-zaka stops, Ⓡ Keihan Line to Kiyomizu-Gojō Station) This ancient temple was first built in 798, but the present buildings are reconstructions dating from 1633. As an affiliate of the Hossō school of Buddhism, which originated in Nara, it has successfully survived the many intrigues of local Kyoto schools of Buddhism through the centuries and is now one of the most famous landmarks of the city (it can get crowded during spring and autumn).

The main hall has a huge verandah that is supported by pillars and juts out over the hillside. Just below this hall is the waterfall **Otowa-no-taki**, where visitors drink sacred waters believed to bestow health and

Southern Higashiyama

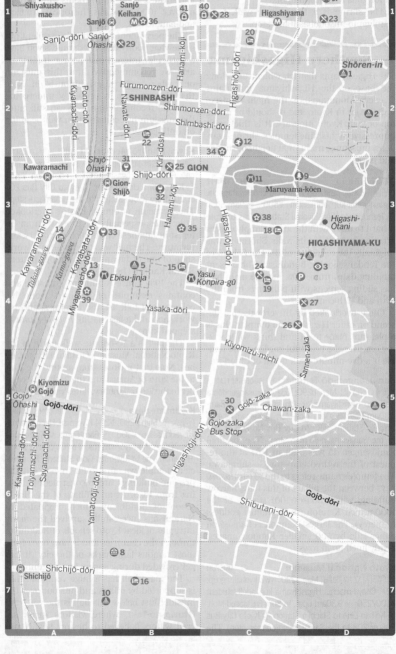

N 0 400 m
0 0.2 miles

Oike-dōri
Kyoto-
Shiyakusho-
mae
Oike-
Ōhashi

Sanjō
Keihan

41
40
28

Higashiyama
37
17

23

Sanjō
Sanjō
36

Sanjō-dōri
Sanjō-
Ōhashi
29

Shōren-in
1

Ponto-chō
Kiyamachi-dōri

Furumonzen-dōri

Hanami-kōji

20

Higashiōji-dōri

2

SHINBASHI
Shinmonzen-dōri

Nawate-dōri
Shimbashi-dōri

22
Kiri-dōshi

34
12

Kawaramachi

Shijō-
Ōhashi
31
25 GION
Shijō-dōri

11
9

Maruyama-kōen

Gion-
Shijō
32

Kawaramachi-dōri
Takase-gawa

Kamo-gawa

14
33

35

Higashiōji-dōri

38
18

Higashi-
Ōtani

HIGASHIYAMA-KU

7

3

Kawabata-dōri
Miyagawacho-dōri
13
5
15

Ebisu-jinja

Yasui
Konpira-gū

24
19

P

39

Yasaka-dōri

27

26

Sannen-zaka

Kiyomizu-michi

Kiyomizu
Gojō

Kiyamachi-dōri

Gojō-
Ōhashi
Gojō-dōri

30
Gojō-zaka

Chawan-zaka

6

Kawabata-dōri
Toiyamachi-dōri
21

Gojō-zaka
Bus Stop

Sayamachi-dōri

Yamatooji-dōri

4
Higashiōji-dōri

Gojō-dōri

Shibutani-dōri

8

Shichijō-dōri

Shichijō
16

10

Southern Higashiyama

KYOTO SIGHTS

longevity. Dotted around the precincts are other halls and shrines. At **Jishu-jinja**, the shrine up the steps above the main hall, visitors try to ensure success in love by closing their eyes and walking about 18m between a pair of stones – if you miss the stone, your desire for love won't be fulfilled! Note that you can ask someone to guide you, but if you do, you'll need someone's assistance to find your true love.

Before you enter the actual temple precincts, check out the **Tainai-meguri**, the entrance to which is just to the left (north) of the pagoda that is located in front of the main entrance to the temple (there is no English sign). We won't tell you too much about it as it will ruin the experience. Suffice to say that by entering the Tainai-meguri, you are symbolically entering the womb of a female bodhisattva. When you get to the rock in the darkness, spin it in either direction to make a wish.

The steep approach to the temple is known as Chawan-zaka (Teapot Lane) and is lined with shops selling Kyoto handicrafts, local snacks and souvenirs.

Check at the TIC for the scheduling of special night-time illuminations of the temple held in the spring and fall.

It's about 10 minutes' walk uphill from the Kiyōmizu-michi or Gojō-zaka bus stops or 20 minutes walk uphill from the Keihan Line's Kiyomizu-Gojō Station.

Ninen-zaka & Sannen-zaka   NEIGHBOURHOOD
(二年坂・三年坂; Higashiyama-ku; ◻ Kyoto City Bus 206 to the Kiyomizu-michi or Gojō-zaka stops, ◻ Keihan Line to Kiyomizu-Gojō Station) Just below and slightly to the north of Kiyomizudera, you will find one of Kyoto's loveliest restored neighbourhoods, the Ninen-zaka and Sannen-zaka area. The name refers to the two main streets of the area: Ninen-zaka and Sannen-zaka, literally 'Two-Year Hill' and 'Three-Year Hill' (the years referring to the ancient imperial years when they were first laid out).

These two charming streets are lined with old wooden houses, traditional shops and restaurants. If you fancy a break, there are many teahouses and cafes along these lanes.

Southern Higashiyama Walking Tour

Hills, Temples & Lanes Of Southern Higashiyama

START GOJŌ-ZAKA BUS STOP ON HIGASHIŌJI-DŌRI (BUS 18, 100, 206 OR 207)
END JINGŪ-MICHI BUS STOP ON SANJŌ-DŌRI (BUS 5 OR 100); HIGASHIYAMA-SANJŌ STATION ON THE TŌZAI SUBWAY LINE
DISTANCE ABOUT 5KM
DURATION FOUR HOURS

Walk up Gojō-zaka slope. Head uphill until you reach the first fork in the road; bear right and continue up Chawan-zaka (Teapot Lane). At the top of the hill, you'll come to Kiyomizu-dera. Before you enter the temple pay ¥100 to descend into the ❶**Tainai-meguri**, the entrance to which is just left of the main temple entrance. Next, enter ❷**Kiyomizu-dera**.

After touring Kiyomizu-dera, exit down Kiyomizu-michi. Continue downhill until you reach a four-way intersection; head right down the stone-paved steps. This is Sannen-zaka, where you will find tiny little ❸**Kasagi-ya**, which has been serving tea and Japanese-style sweets for as long as anyone can remember.

Halfway down Sannen-zaka, the road curves to the left. Follow it a short distance, then go right down a flight of steps into Ninen-zaka. At the end of Ninen-zaka zigzag left (at the vending machines), then right (just past the parking lot), and continue north. Very soon, on your left, will be ❹**Ishibei-kōji**, perhaps Kyoto's most beautiful street. Explore this, then retrace your steps to continue north, passing almost immediately the entrance to ❺**Kōdai-ji** on the right up a long flight of stairs.

After Kōdai-ji continue north to the T-junction; turn right at this junction and then take a quick left. You'll cross the wide pedestrian arcade that leads to Ōtani cemetery and then descend into ❻**Maruyama-kōen**. In the centre of the park you'll see the giant Gion *shidare-zakura*, Kyoto's most famous cherry tree.

From the park, you can head west into the grounds of ❼**Yasaka-jinja**. Return to the park and head north to tour the grounds of the impressive ❽**Chion-in**. From here it's a quick walk to ❾**Shōren-in**. From Shōren-in walk down to Sanjō-dōri.

Kōdai-ji
BUDDHIST TEMPLE

(高台寺; Map p290; 526 Shimokawara-chō, Kōdai-ji, Higashiyama-ku; admission ¥600; ⊙9am-5pm; ⑤Tōzai Line to Higashiyama Station, ☒Kyoto City Bus 206 to the Yasui stop) This temple was founded in 1605 by Kita-no-Mandokoro in memory of her late husband, Toyotomi Hideyoshi. The extensive grounds include gardens that were designed by the famed landscape architect Kobori Enshū, and tea-houses designed by the renowned master of the tea ceremony, Sen-no-Rikyū.

The temple is a 10-minute walk north of Kiyomizu-dera or a 10-minute walk south of Maruyama-kōen. The easiest access is probably from the Tōzai subway line's Higashiyama Station. Check at the TIC for the scheduling of special night-time illuminations of the temple (when the gardens are lit by multicoloured spotlights).

Maruyama-kōen
PARK

(円山公園; Map p290; Maruyama-chō, Higashiyama-ku; ⑤Tōzai Line to Higashiyama Station) This park is a great place to escape the bustle of the city centre and amble around gardens, ponds, souvenir shops and restaurants. Peaceful paths meander through the trees and carp glide through the waters of a small pond in the centre of the park.

For two weeks in late March/early April, when the park's many cherry trees come into bloom, the calm atmosphere of the park is shattered by hordes of revellers enjoying *hanami* (blossom-viewing). For those who don't mind crowds, this is a good place to observe the Japanese at their most uninhibited. It is best to arrive early and claim a good spot high on the eastern side of the park, from which point you can safely peer down on the mayhem below.

The park is a five-minute walk east of the Shijō-Higashiōji intersection. To get there from Kyoto Station, take bus 206 and get off at the Gion stop. Alternatively, take the Tōzai subway line to the Higashiyama stop and walk south for about 10 minutes.

Yasaka-jinja
SHINTŌ SHRINE

(八坂神社; Map p290; 625 Gion-machi Kitagawa, Higashiyama-ku; ⊙24hr; ⑤Tōzai Line to Higashiyama Station) **FREE** This colourful shrine is just down the hill from Maruyama-kōen. It's considered to be the guardian shrine of neighbouring Gion and is sometimes endearingly referred to as 'Gion-san'. This shrine is particularly popular as a spot for *hatsu-mōde* (the first shrine visit of the new year).

If you don't mind a stampede, come here around midnight on New Year's Eve or over the next few days. Surviving the crush is proof that you're blessed by the gods! Yasaka-jinja also sponsors Kyoto's biggest festival, Gion Matsuri (p309).

Chion-in
BUDDHIST TEMPLE

(知恩院; Map p290; 400 Rinka-chō, Higashiyama-ku; admission to inner buildings & garden ¥300, grounds free; ⊙9am-4.30pm; ⑤Tōzai Line to Higashiyama Station) Chion-in was established in 1234 on the site where Hōnen, one of the most famous figures in Japanes Buddhism, taught his brand of Buddhism (Jōdo, or Pure Land, Buddhism) and eventually fasted to death. Today, the temple serves as the headquarters of the Jōdo sect, the most popular sect of Buddhism in Japan. It's the most popular pilgrimage temple in Kyoto and it's always a hive of activity. For visitors with a taste for the grand, this temple is sure to satisfy.

The oldest of the present buildings date back to the 17th century. The two-storey San-mon, a Buddhist temple gate at the main entrance, is the largest temple gate in Japan and prepares you for the massive scale of the temple. The immense main hall contains an image of Hōnen. It's connected to another hall, the Dai Hōjō, by a 'nightingale' floor (that sings and squeaks at every move, making it difficult for intruders to move about quietly).

Up a flight of steps southeast of the main hall is the temple's giant bell, which was cast in 1633 and weighs 70 tonnes. It is the largest bell in Japan. The bell is rung by the temple's monks 108 times on New Year's Eve each year.

The temple is close to the northeastern corner of Maruyama-kōen.

Gion
NEIGHBOURHOOD

(祇園周辺; Higashiyama-ku; ☒Keihan line to Gion-Shijō Station, ⑤Tōzai Line to Sanjō-Keihan Station) Gion is Kyoto's famous entertainment and geisha district on the eastern bank of the Kamo-gawa. Modern architecture, congested traffic and contemporary nightlife establishments rob the area of some of its historical beauty, but there are still some lovely places left for a stroll and the district looks very attractive in the evening.

Gion falls roughly between Sanjō-dōri and Gojō-dōri (north and south, respectively) and Higashiōji-dōri and Kawabata-dōri (east and west, respectively). In case you're wondering, Gion rhymes with 'key on'.

Hanami-kōji is the main north–south avenue of Gion, and the section south of Shijō-dōri is lined with 17th-century restaurants and teahouses, many of which are exclusive establishments for geisha entertainment.

Another must-see spot in Gion is **Shimbashi** (sometimes called Shirakawa Minami-dōri), which is one of Kyoto's most beautiful streets, and, arguably, among the most beautiful streets in all of Asia, especially in the evening and during cherry-blossom season. To get there, start at the intersection of Shijō-dōri and Hanami-kōji and walk north, then take the third left.

Kenin-ji Temple   BUDDHIST TEMPLE
(建仁寺; Map p290; Komatsu-chō, Shijo sagaru, Yamatoōji-dōri, Higashiyama-ku; admission ¥500; ☻10am-5pm Mar-Oct, to 4pm Nov-Feb; 🚉Keihan Line to Gion-Shijō Station) Founded in 1202 by the monk Eisai, Kenin-ji is the oldest Zen temple in Kyoto. It's an island of peace and calm on the border of the boisterous Gion nightlife district and it makes a fine counterpoint to the worldly pleasures of that area. The highlight here is the fine and expansive *kare-sansui* (dry landscape) garden.

The painting of the twin dragons on the roof of the Hōdō hall is also fantastic; access to this hall is via two gates with rather puzzling English operating instructions (you'll see what we mean).

It's at the southern end of Hanami-kōji street.

◉ Northern Higashiyama

The northern Higashiyama area at the base of the Higashiyama mountains is one of the city's richest areas for sightseeing. It includes such first-rate attractions as Nanzen-ji, Ginkaku-ji, Hōnen-in and Shūgaku-in Rikyū. You can spend a wonderful day walking from Keage Station on the Tōzai subway line all the way north to Ginkaku-ji via the Tetsugaku-no-Michi (the Path of Philosophy), stopping in the countless temples and shrines en route.

★ Nanzen-ji   BUDDHIST TEMPLE
(南禅寺; Map p296; Fukuchi-chō, Nanzen-ji, Sakyō-ku; admission Hōjō garden ¥500, San-mon gate ¥300-400, grounds free; ☻8.40am-5pm Mar-Nov, to 4.30pm Dec-Feb; 🚇Tōzai Line to Keage Station, 🚌Kyoto City Bus 5 to the Eikandō-michi stop) This is one of the finest temples in Kyoto, with its expansive grounds and numerous subtemples. It began as a retirement villa for

Emperor Kameyama but was dedicated as a Zen temple on his death in 1291. Civil war in the 15th century destroyed most of the temple; the present buildings date from the 17th century. It operates now as headquarters for the Rinzai school of Zen.

At its entrance stands the massive San-mon. Steps lead up to the 2nd storey, which has a fine view over the city. Beyond the gate is the main hall of the temple, above which you will find the Hōjō, where the Leaping Tiger Garden is a classic Zen garden well worth a look. (Try to ignore the annoying taped explanation of the garden.) While you're in the Hōjō, you can enjoy a cup of tea while gazing at a small waterfall (¥500, ask at the reception desk of the Hōjō).

Dotted around the grounds of Nanzen-ji are several subtemples that are often skipped by the crowds.

To get to Nanzen-ji from JR Kyoto or Keihan Sanjō Station, take bus 5 and get off at the Nanzen-ji Eikan-dō-michi stop. You can also take the Tōzai subway line from the city centre to Keage and walk for five minutes downhill. Turn right (east, towards the mountains) opposite the police box and walk slightly uphill (toward the mountains) and you will arrive at the main gate of the temple.

Nanzen-ji Oku-no-in   BUDDHIST TEMPLE
(南禅寺奥の院; Map p296; Fukuchi-chō, Nanzen-ji, Sakyō-ku; ☻dawn-dusk; 🚇Tōzai Line to Keage Station, 🚌Kyoto City Bus 5 to the Eikandō-michi stop) **FREE** Perhaps the best part of Nanzen-ji is overlooked by most visitors: Oku-no-in, a small shrine-temple hidden in a forested hollow behind the main precinct.

To get there, walk up to the red-brick aqueduct in front of the subtemple of **Nanzen-in** (☎771 0365; Map p296; Fukuchi-chō, Nanzen-ji; adult ¥300, child ¥150-250; ☻8.40am-5pm; underground rail, 10-min walk from Keage Station, Tōzai subway line). Follow the road/path that runs parallel to the aqueduct up into the hills, until you reach a waterfall in a beautiful mountain glen. Keep in mind that this is a sacred spot and worshippers come here to pray in peace. Please try to maintain a respectful silence.

Tenju-an   BUDDHIST TEMPLE
(天授庵; Map p296; 86-8 Fukuchi-chō, Nanzen-ji, Sakyō-ku; admission ¥400; ☻9am-5pm Mar–mid-Nov, to 4.30pm mid-Nov–Feb; 🚇Tōzai Line to Keage Station, 🚌Kyoto City Bus 5 to the Eikandō-michi stop) This temple stands at the side of the

San-mon. Built in 1337, the temple has a splendid garden and a great collection of carp in its pond.

Konchi-in
BUDDHIST TEMPLE

(金地院; Map p296; 86-12 Fukuchi-chō, Nanzen-ji, Sakyō-ku; admission ¥400; ⊙ 8.30am-5pm Mar-Nov, to 4.30pm Dec-Feb; ⑤ Tōzai Line to Keage Station, ⊡ Kyoto City Bus 5 to the Eikandō-michi stop) Just west of the main gate to Nanzen-ji (up some steps and down a side street), you will find Konchi-in, which has a dry garden designed by the master landscape designer Kobori Enshū. This garden is a good example of *shakkei* (borrowed scenery); note how the mountains behind are drawn into the design.

Eikan-dō
BUDDHIST TEMPLE

(永観堂; Map p296; 48 Eikandō-chō, Sakyō-ku; admission ¥600; ⊙ 9am-5pm; ⑤ Tōzai Line to Keage Station, ⊡ Kyoto City Bus 5 to the Eikandō-michi stop) Eikan-dō is a large temple famed for its varied architecture, gardens and works of art. It was founded in 855 by the priest Shinshō, but the name was changed to Eikan-dō in the 11th century to honour the philanthropic priest Eikan.

In the Amida-dō Hall, at the southern end of the complex, is the statue of Mikaeri Amida (Buddha Glancing Backwards). From the Amida-dō Hall, head north to the end of the covered walkway. Change into the sandals provided, then climb the steep steps up the mountainside to the Tahō-tō (Tahō Pagoda), where there's a fine view across the city.

Note that this temple is one of the city's most popular fall foliage spots; while it is stunning in November when the maples turn crimson, it also gets completely packed.

The temple is a 10-minute walk north of Nanzen-ji.

Tetsugaku-no-Michi (Path of Philosophy)
NEIGHBOURHOOD

(哲学の道; Map p296; Sakyō-ku; ⑤ Tōzai Line to Keage Station, ⊡ Kyoto City Bus 5 to the Eikandō-michi or Ginkakuji-michi stops) The Tetsugaku-no-Michi is a pedestrian path that runs along a canal near the base of the Higashiyama. It's lined with cherry trees and a host of other blooming trees and flowers.

The path takes its name from one of its most famous strollers: 20th-century philosopher Nishida Kitarō, who is said to have meandered along the path lost in thought. It only takes 30 minutes to complete the walk, which starts just north of Eikan-dō and ends at Ginkaku-ji.

★ Hōnen-in
BUDDHIST TEMPLE

(法然院; Map p296; 30 Goshonodan-chō, Shishigatani, Sakyō-ku; ⊙ 6am-4pm; ⊡ Kyoto City Bus 5 to the Eikandō-michi or Ginkakuji-michi stops) **FREE** This fine temple was established in 1680 to honour Hōnen, the charismatic founder of the Jōdo school. It's a lovely, secluded temple with carefully raked gardens set back in the woods.

Be sure to visit in November for the maple leaves. Normally, you cannot enter the main hall, but two special openings happen yearly (admission autumn/spring ¥500/800; 1 to 17 April and 1 to 7 November).

The temple is a 10-minute walk from Ginkaku-ji, on a side street that is accessible from the Tetsugaku-no-Michi; heading south on the path, look for the English sign on your left, then cross the bridge over the canal and follow the road uphill.

Ginkaku-ji
BUDDHIST TEMPLE

(銀閣寺; Map p296; 2 Ginkaku-ji-chō, Sakyō-ku; admission ¥500; ⊙ 8.30am-5pm Mar-Nov, 9am-4.30pm Dec-Feb; ⊡ Kyoto City Bus 5 to the Ginkakuji-michi stop) In 1482 Shōgun Ashikaga Yoshimasa constructed a villa here as a genteel retreat from the turmoil of civil war. The villa's name translates as 'Silver Pavilion', but the shōgun's ambition to cover the building with silver was never realised. After Yoshimasa's death, the villa was converted into a temple.

Walkways lead through the gardens, which include meticulously raked cones of white sand (said to be symbolic of a mountain and a lake), tall pines and a pond in front of the temple. A path also leads up the mountainside through the trees.

Note that Ginkaku-ji is one of the city's most popular sites, and it is almost always crowded, especially during the spring and autumn. We strongly recommend visiting right after it opens or just before it closes.

From JR Kyoto or Keihan Sanjō Station, take bus 5 and get off at the Ginkakuji-michi stop. From Demachiyanagi Station or Shijō Station, take bus 203 to the same stop.

Okazaki-kōen Area
NEIGHBOURHOOD

(岡崎公園; Map p296; Okazaki, Sakyo-ku; ⑤ Tōzai Line to Higashiyama Station) Right in the heart of the northern Higashiyama area, you'll find Okazaki-kōen, which is Kyoto's museum district, and the home of one of Kyoto's most popular shrines, Heian-jingū.

Take bus 5 from Kyoto Station or Keihan Sanjō Station and get off at the Kyoto Kaikan Bijutsu-kan-mae stop and walk north,

Northern Higashiyama

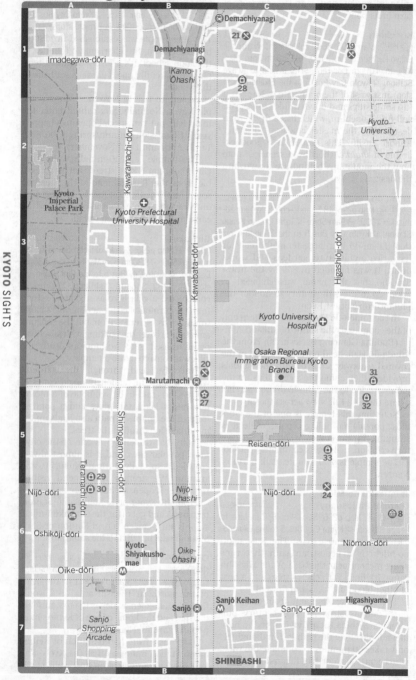

Demachiyanagi

21

19

Imadegawa-dōri

Demachiyanagi

Kamo-Ōhashi

28

Kyoto University

Kawaramachi-dōri

Kyoto Imperial Palace Park

Kyoto Prefectural University Hospital

Kawabata-dōri

Higashiōji-dōri

Kamo-gawa

Kyoto University Hospital

Osaka Regional Immigration Bureau Kyoto Branch

20

Marutamachi

31

27

32

Reisen-dōri

Shimogamohon-dōri

33

Teramachi-dōri

29

30

Nijō-dōri

Nijō-Ōhashi

Nijō-dōri

24

15

8

Oshikōji-dōri

Kyoto-Shiyakusho-mae

Oike-Ōhashi

Niōmon-dōri

Oike-dōri

Sanjō Shopping Arcade

Sanjō

Sanjō Keihan

Sanjō-dōri

Higashiyama

SHINBASHI

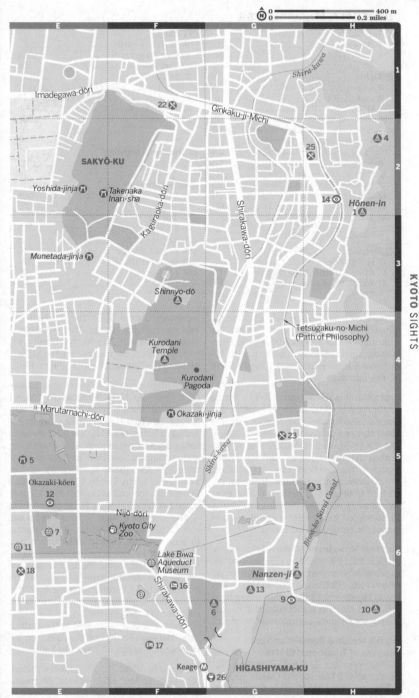

0 400 m
0 0.2 miles

Shira-kawa

22 ✕

Ginkaku-ji-Michi

SAKYŌ-KU

25 ✕

Imadegawa-dōri

4 ▲

Yoshida-jinja 🛉

Takenaka Inari-sha 🛉

14 ◉ Hōnen-in 1 ▲

Kaguraoka-dōri

Shirakawa-dōri

Munetada-jinja 🛉

Shinnyo-dō ▲

Tetsugaku-no-Michi (Path of Philosophy)

Kurodani Temple ▲

Kurodani Pagoda

Marutamachi-dōri

Okazaki-jinja 🛉

23 ✕

5 🏛

Shira-kawa

Okazaki-kōen

12 ◉

3 ▲

Nijō-dōri

Kyoto City Zoo 🛉

Biwa-ko Sosui Canal

7 🏛

Lake Biwa Aqueduct Museum 🏛

11 🏛

16 ▲

2 ▲ Nanzen-ji ▲

18 ✕

13 ▲

9 ◉

10 ▲

Shirakawa-dōri

@

6 ▲

17 🏛

Keage Ⓜ

26 🏛 HIGASHIYAMA-KU

Northern Higashiyama

or walk up from Keihan Sanjō Station (15 minutes). Most of the area's sights are within five minutes' walk of this stop. Alternatively, take the Tōzai subway line to Higashiyama Station and walk roughly north for five minutes.

Kyoto Municipal Museum of Art MUSEUM
(京都市美術館; Map p296; 124 Enshōji-chō, Okazaki, Sakyō-ku; admission varies; ⊙9am-5pm, closed Mon; ⓢTōzai Line to Higashiyama Station) The Kyoto Municipal Museum of Art organises several major exhibitions a year, including the excellent Kyoten exhibition, which showcases Japan's best living artists. It's held from late May until early June most years (check with the TIC for exact dates). Kyoto-related works form a significant portion of the permanent collection.

National Museum of Modern Art MUSEUM
(京都国立近代美術館; Map p296; www.momak. go.jp/english; Enshōji-chō, Okazaki, Sakyō-ku; admission ¥420; ⊙9.30am-5pm, closed Mon; ⓢTōzai Line to Higashiyama Station) This museum is renowned for its compact collection of contemporary Japanese ceramics and paintings.

Miyako Messe & Fureai-Kan Kyoto Museum of Traditional Crafts MUSEUM
(みやこめっせ・京都伝統産業ふれあい館; Map p296; 9-1 Seishōji-chō, Okazaki, Sakyō-ku; ⊙9am-5pm, closed Dec 29-Jan 3; ⓢTōzai Line to Higashiyama Station) FREE The museum has exhibits covering things like wood-block prints, lacquerware, bamboo goods and gold-leaf work. It's in the basement of the Miyako Messe (Kyoto International Exhibition Hall).

Heian-jingū SHINTŌ SHRINE
(平安神宮; Map p296; Nishitennō-chō, Okazaki, Sakyō-ku; admission to garden ¥600; ⊙6am-5pm Nov-Feb, 6am-6pm Mar-Oct; ⓢTōzai Line to Higashiyama Station, 🚍Kyoto City Bus 5 to the Kyoto Kaikan/Bijyutsukan-mae stop) This impressive shrine complex was built in 1895 to commemorate the 1100th anniversary of the founding of Kyoto. The buildings are colourful replicas, reduced to two-thirds of the size of the Kyoto Gosho of the Heian period.

The spacious garden, with its large pond and Chinese-inspired bridge, is also meant to represent the kind of garden that was popular in the Heian period. About 500m in front of the shrine there is a massive orange torii (Shintō shrine gate). Although it appears to be entirely separate from the shrine, this is actually considered the main entrance to the shrine itself.

Two major events are held at the shrine: Jidai Matsuri (Festival of the Ages), on 22 October, and *takigi nō*, from 1 to 2 June.

Shūgaku-in Rikyū HISTORICAL BUILDING
(修学院離宮; Map p278; Yabusoe, Shūgakuin, Sakyō-ku; 🚍Kyoto City Bus 5 to the Shūgaku-in

Rikyū-michi stop) FREE This imperial villa was begun in the 1650s by the abdicated emperor Go-Mizunoo, and work was continued after his death in 1680 by his daughter Akenomiya. Designed as an imperial retreat, the villa grounds are divided into three large garden areas on a hillside: lower, middle and upper.

The gardens' reputation rests on their ponds, pathways and impressive use of 'borrowed scenery' in the form of the surrounding hills; the view from the Rinun-tei Teahouse in the upper garden is particularly impressive.

Tours, in Japanese, start at 9am, 10am, 11am, 1.30pm and 3pm (50 minutes). You must make advance reservations through the Imperial Household Agency (p286). An audio guide is available for non-Japanese speakers.

From Kyoto Station, take bus 5 and get off at the Shūgaku-in Rikyū-michi stop. The trip takes about 45 minutes. From the bus stop it's a 15-minute walk (about 1km) to the villa. You can also take the Eiden Eizan line from Demachiyanagi Station to the Shūgaku-in stop and walk east about 25 minutes (about 1.5km) towards the mountains. Needless to say, a taxi is also a good option here.

Hiei-zan & Enryaku-ji
TEMPLE
(延暦寺; 4220 Honmachi, Sakamoto, Sakyō-ku; admission ¥550; ⊙8.30am-4.30pm, 9am-4pm in winter; 🚍Kyoto Bus (not Kyoto City Bus) to Enryakuji Bus Center, 🚍Keihan Bus to Enryakuji Bus Center) A visit to 848m-high Hiei-zan and the vast Enryaku-ji complex is a good way to spend half a day hiking, poking around temples and enjoying the atmosphere of a key site in Japanese history.

Enryaku-ji was founded in 788 by Saichō, also known as Dengyō-daishi, the priest who established the Tendai school. The complex is divided into three sections – Tōtō, Saitō and Yokawa. The Tōtō (eastern pagoda section) contains the Kompon Chū-dō (primary central hall), which is the most important building in the complex. The flames on the three Dharma (the law, in Sanskrit) lamps in front of the altar have been kept lit for over 1200 years. The Daikō-dō (great lecture hall) displays life-sized wooden statues of the founders of various Buddhist schools.

The Saitō (western pagoda section) contains the Shaka-dō, which dates from 1595 and houses a rare Buddha sculpture of the Shaka Nyorai (Historical Buddha). The Saitō, with its stone paths winding through forests of tall trees, temples shrouded in mist and the sound of distant gongs, is the most atmospheric part of the temple. Hold onto your ticket from the Tōtō section, as you may need to show it here.

The Yokawa is of minimal interest and a 4km bus ride away from the Saitō area.

You can reach Hiei-zan and Enryaku-ji by either train or bus. The most interesting way is the train-cable car-ropeway route.

By train, take the Keihan line north to the last stop, Demachiyanagi, and change to the Yase-Hieizanguchi-bound Eizan Dentetsu Eizan-line train (be careful not to board the Kurama-bound train that sometimes leaves from the same platform). At the last stop, Yase-Hieizanguchi (¥260), board the cable car (¥530, nine minutes) and then the ropeway (¥310, three minutes) to the peak, then walk down to the temples.

Alternatively, if you want to save money (by avoiding the cable car and ropeway), there are direct Kyoto and Keihan buses from Kyoto and Demachiyanagi stations to the Enryaku-ji Bus Center, which take about 65 and 45 minutes, respectively (both cost ¥750).

⊙ Northwest Kyoto

Northwest Kyoto has many excellent sights spread over a large area. Highlights include Kinkaku-ji (the famed Golden Pavilion) and Ryōan-ji, with its mysterious stone garden. Note that three of the area's main sights – Kinkaku-ji, Ryōan-ji and Ninna-ji – can easily be linked together to form a great half-day tour out of the city centre.

Kitano Tenman-gū
SHINTŌ SHRINE
(北野天満宮; Map p287; Bakuro-chō, Kamigyō-ku; ⊙5am-6pm Apr-Oct, 5.30am-5.30pm Nov-Mar; 🚍Kyoto City Bus 50 from Kyoto Station or Bus 10 from Sanjo-Keihan to the Kitano-Tenmangū-mae stop) FREE This is a fine, spacious shrine on Imadegawa-dōri. If you're in town on the 25th of any month, be sure to catch the Tenjin-san Market (p330) here. It's one of Kyoto's two biggest markets and is a great place to pick up some interesting souvenirs.

Kinkaku-ji
BUDDHIST TEMPLE
(金閣寺; Map p300; 1 Kinkaku-ji-chō, Kita-ku; admission ¥400; ⊙9am-5pm; 🚍Kyoto City Bus 205 from Kyoto Station to the Kinkakuji-michi stop, 🚍Kyoto City Bus 59 from Sanjo-Keihan to the Kinkakuji-mae stop) Kyoto's famed 'Golden Pavilion', Kinkaku-ji is one of Japan's best-known

Northwest Kyoto

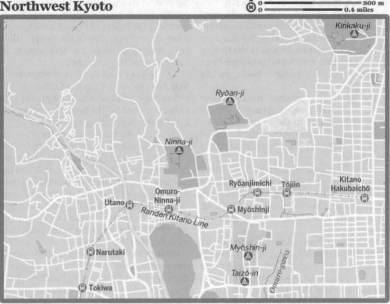

sights. The original building was built in 1397 as a retirement villa for Shōgun Ashikaga Yoshimitsu. His son converted it into a temple.

In 1950 a young monk consummated his obsession with the temple by burning it to the ground. The monk's story was fictionalised in Mishima Yukio's *Golden Pavilion*. In 1955 a full reconstruction was completed that exactly followed the original design, but the gold-foil covering was extended to the lower floors.

Note that this temple can be packed almost any day of the year. We recommend going early in the day or just before closing.

Ryōan-ji
BUDDHIST TEMPLE

(龍安寺; Map p300; 13 Goryōnoshitamachi, Ryōan-ji, Ukyō-ku; admission ¥500; ⊙ 8am-5pm Mar-Nov, 8.30am-4.30pm Dec-Feb; 🚌 Kyoto City Bus 59 from Sanjō-Keihan to the Ryoanji-mae stop) This temple belongs to the Rinzai school of Zen and was founded in 1450. The main attraction is the garden arranged in the *kare-sansui* style. An austere collection of 15 rocks, apparently adrift in a sea of sand, is enclosed by an earthen wall. The designer, who remains unknown, provided no explanation.

The viewing platform for the garden can be packed solid but the other parts of the temple grounds are also interesting and less crowded. Among these, Kyoyo-chi pond is

perhaps the most beautiful, particularly in autumn. If you want to enjoy the *kare-sansui* garden without the crowds, try to come right at opening time.

Note that you can walk to Ryōan-ji from Kinkaku-ji in about half an hour.

Ninna-ji
BUDDHIST TEMPLE

(仁和寺; Map p300; 33 Omuroōuchi, Ukyō-ku; admission to Kondō Hall & Treasure Hall ¥500, grounds free; ⊙ 9am-5pm Mar-Nov, 9am-4.30pm Dec-Feb; 🚌 Kyoto City Bus 59 from Sanjo-Keihan to the Omuro Ninna-ji stop, 🚌 Kyoto City Bus 26 from Kyoto Station to the Omuro Ninna-ji stop) This temple was built in 842 and is the head temple of the Omura branch of the Shingon school of Buddhism. The present temple buildings, including a five-storey pagoda, are from the 17th century. The extensive grounds are full of cherry trees that bloom in early April.

Admission to most of the grounds is free, but separate admission fees are charged for some of the temple's buildings, many of which are closed most of the year.

Myōshin-ji
BUDDHIST TEMPLE

(妙心寺; Map p300; 64 Myoshin-ji-chō, Hanazono, Ukyō-ku; admission to main temple free, other areas of the complex ¥500; ⊙ 9.10-11.40am & 1pm-3.40pm; 🚌 Kyoto City Bus No 10 from Sanjo-Keihan to the Myōshin-ji Kita-mon-mae stop) The vast temple complex Myōshin-ji is a separate world within Kyoto, a walled-off complex of temples and subtemples that invites lazy strolling. Myōshin-ji dates back to 1342, and belongs to the Rinzai school. There are 47 subtemples, but only a few are open to the public.

From the north gate, follow the broad stone avenue flanked by rows of temples to the southern part of the complex. The eponymous Myōshin-ji is roughly in the middle of the complex. Your entry fee here entitles you to a tour of several of the buildings of the temple. The ceiling of the *hattō* (lecture hall) features Tanyū Kanō's unnerving painting Unryūzu (meaning 'dragon glaring in eight directions'). Your guide will invite you to stand directly beneath the dragon; doing so makes it appear that it's spiralling up or down.

Another highlight of the complex is the wonderful garden of **Taizō-in** (退蔵院; admission ¥500; ⊙9am-5pm), a subtemple in the southwestern corner of the grounds.

Note that the northern gate of Myōshin-ji is an easy 10-minute walk south of Ninna-ji.

◎ Arashiyama & Sagano Area

Arashiyama and Sagano, at the base of Kyoto's western mountains (known as the Arashiyama), is Kyoto's second-most important sightseeing district after Higashiyama. On first sight, you may wonder what all the fuss is about: the main street and the area around the famous Tōgetsu-kyō bridge have all the makings of a classic Japanese tourist trap. But once you head up the hills to the temples hidden among the greenery, you will understand the appeal.

Bus 28 links Kyoto Station with Arashiyama. Bus 11 connects Keihan Sanjō Station with Arashiyama. The most convenient rail connection is the ride from Shijō-Ōmiya Station on the Keifuku-Arashiyama line to Arashiyama Station (take the Hankyū train from downtown to get to Shijō-Ōmiya). You can also take the JR San-in line from Kyoto Station or Nijō Station and get off at Saga Arashiyama Station (be careful to take only the local train, as the express does not stop in Arashiyama). Finally, a fast way to get there from the middle of Kyoto (downtown and central Kyoto) is to take the Tōzai subway line to the western-most stop (Uzumasa-Tenjin-gawa) and take a taxi from there to Arashiyama (the taxi ride will take about 15 minutes and cost around ¥1600).

The sites in this section are all within walking distance of Arashiyama Station. We suggest walking from this station to Tenryū-ji, exiting the north gate, checking out the bamboo grove, visiting Ōkōchi Sansō, then walking north to Giō-ji or Adashino Nembutsu-ji. If you have time for only one temple in the area, we recommend Tenryū-ji. If you have time for two, we suggest adding Giō-ji.

Kameyama-kōen
PARK

(亀山公園; Map p302; ⊜Kyoto City Bus 28 from Kyoto Station to the Arashiyama-Tenryuji-mae stop) Southwest of Tenryū-ji, this park is a nice place to escape the crowds of Arashiyama. It's laced with trails, the best of which leads to a lookout over Katsura-gawa and up into the Arashiyama mountains.

Keep an eye out for the monkeys, and keep children well away from the occasionally nasty critters. If you turn left when you reach the top of the bamboo grove, you'll find yourself in the park.

Tenryū-ji
BUDDHIST TEMPLE

(天龍寺; Map p302; 68 Susukinobaba-chō, Saga Tenryū-ji, Ukyō-ku; admission ¥600; ⊙8.30am-5.30pm, to 5pm 21 Oct-20 Mar; ⊜Kyoto City Bus 28 from Kyoto Station to the Arashiyama-Tenryuji-mae stop) One of the major temples of the Rinzai school of Zen, Tenryū-ji was built in 1339 on the former site of Emperor Go-Daigo's villa after a priest had dreamt of a dragon rising from the nearby river. The dream was interpreted as a sign that the emperor's spirit was uneasy and the temple was constructed as appeasement – hence the name *tenryū* (heavenly dragon).

The present buildings date from 1900, but the main attraction is the 14th-century Zen garden.

Arashiyama's famous bamboo grove lies just outside the north gate of the temple.

Arashiyama Bamboo Grove
PARK

(嵐山竹林; Map p302; Ogurayama, Saga, Ukyō-ku; ⊙dawn-dusk; ⊜Hankyū Line to Arashiyama Station) FREE Arashiyama's famed Bamboo Grove is a magical place. The atmosphere is otherworldly and it's quite unlike any other forest we've ever experienced. The effect is quite hypnotic as the bamboo stalks seem to continue forever in all directions.

It's best accessed from the north gate of Tenryū-ji Temple, which brings you right into the thick of it. From here, you can make a leisurely stroll up to the lovely Ōkōchi Sansō Villa.

KYOTO SIGHTS

Arashiyama & Sagano Area

Arashiyama & Sagano Area

You can try to take pictures if you want, but in our experience, cameras simply cannot capture the mystical atmosphere of the place.

★ **Ōkōchi Sansō**　　HISTORICAL BUILDING
(大河内山荘; Map p302; 8 Tabuchiyama-chō, Sagaogurayama, Ukyō-ku; admission ¥1000; ☺9am–5pm; ⬚ Kyoto City Bus 28 from Kyoto Station to the

Arashiyama-Tenryuji-mae stop) This villa is the home of Ōkōchi Denjiro, an actor in samurai films. The superb gardens allow fine views over the city and are open to visitors. The gardens are particularly lovely during the autumn foliage season. The admission fee is hefty but includes tea and a cake (save the tea/cake ticket that comes with your admission). The villa is a 10-minute walk through the bamboo grove north of Tenryū-ji. When you get to the top of the bamboo grove, the entrance will be diagonally in front of you to the right.

The following sights are all located north of Ōkōchi Sansō. Strolling from Ōkōchi-Sansō all the way to Adashino Nembutsu-ji is a nice way to spend a few hours in Arashiyama/Sagano.

Jōjakkō-ji
BUDDHIST TEMPLE
(常寂光寺; Map p302; 3 Ogura-chō, Sagaogurayama, Ukyō-ku; admission ¥400; ⊙9am-5pm; 🚌Kyoto City Bus 28 from Kyoto Station to the Arashiyama-Tenryuji-mae stop) If you continue north of Ōkōchi Sansō, the narrow road soon passes stone steps on your left that lead up to the pleasant grounds of Jōjakkō-ji. The temple is famous for its maple leaves and the Tahōtō pagoda. The upper area of the temple precinct affords good views east over Kyoto. The temple is a 10-minute walk north of Ōkōchi Sansō.

Rakushisha
HISTORICAL BUILDING
(落柿舎; Map p302; 20 Himyōjin-chō, Sagaogurayama, Ukyō-ku; admission ¥200; ⊙9am-5pm Mar-Dec, 10am-4pm Jan & Feb; 🚌Kyoto City Bus 28 from Kyoto Station to the Arashiyama-Tenryuji-mae stop) This hut belonged to Mukai Kyorai, the best-known disciple of illustrious haiku poet Bashō. Literally meaning 'House of the Fallen Persimmons', legend holds that Kyorai dubbed the house Rakushisha after waking one morning after a storm to find the persimmons he had planned to sell from the garden's trees scattered on the ground.

The hut is a short walk downhill and to the north of Jōjakkō-ji.

Nison-in
BUDDHIST TEMPLE
(二尊院; Map p302; 27 Monzenchōjin-chō, Saganison-in, Ukyō-ku; admission ¥500; ⊙9am-4.30pm; 🚌Kyoto City Bus 28 from Kyoto Station to the Arashiyama-Tenryuji-mae stop) Nison-in is in an attractive setting on a wooded hillside. The long approach to the temple, which is lined with lovely maple trees, is the biggest drawcard. The temple is located a short walk north of Jōjakkō-ji.

Giō-ji
BUDDHIST TEMPLE
(祇王寺; Map p302; 32 Kozaka, Sagatoriimoto, Ukyō-ku; admission ¥300; ⊙9am-5pm, with seasonal variations; 🚌Kyoto City Bus 28 from Kyoto Station to the Arashiyama-Tenryuji-mae stop) This quiet temple was named for a Heian-era *shirabyōshi* (traditional dancer) named Giō. Aged 21, Giō committed herself here as a nun after her romance with Taira-no-Kiyomori, the commander of the Heike clan. The temple is famous for its lovely expanse of moss, which lies in front of the thatch-roof main hall. It's about 10 minutes' walk north of Nison-in.

Adashino Nembutsu-ji
BUDDHIST TEMPLE
(化野念仏寺; Map p302; 17 Adashino-chō, Sagatoriimoto, Ukyō-ku; admission ¥500; ⊙9am-4.30pm, to 3.30pm Dec-Feb; 🚌Kyoto City Bus 28 from Kyoto Station to the Arashiyama-Tenryuji-mae stop) This rather unusual temple is where the abandoned bones of paupers and destitutes without next of kin were gathered. Thousands of stone images are crammed into the temple grounds, and these abandoned souls are remembered each year with candles here in the **Sentō Kuyō ceremony** held on the evenings of 23 and 24 August.

The temple is about 15 minutes' walk north of Giō-ji.

Arashiyama Monkey Park Iwatayama
PARK
(嵐山モンキーパークいわたやま; Map p302; 8 Genro-kuzan-chō, Arashiyama, Ukyō-ku; adult/child ¥550/250; ⊙9am-5pm 15 Mar-Oct, to 4pm Nov-14 Mar; 🚌Kyoto City Bus 28 from Kyoto Station to the Arashiyama-Tenryuji-mae stop) Home to some 200 Japanese monkeys of all sizes and ages, this park is fun for kids and animal lovers of all ages. Though it is common to spot wild monkeys in the nearby mountains, here you can see them close up. It makes for an excellent photo opportunity, not only for the monkeys but for the panoramic view over Kyoto.

Refreshingly, it is the animals who are free to roam while the humans who feed them are caged in a box! Just be warned: it's a steep climb up the hill to get to the monkeys. If it's a hot day, you're going to be drenched by the time you get to the spot where they gather.

The entrance to the park is up a flight of steps just upstream of the Tōgetsu-kyō bridge (near the orange torii of Ichitanijinja). Buy your tickets from the machine to the left of the shrine at the top of the steps.

⊙ Southeast Kyoto

Southeast Kyoto contains some of Kyoto's most impressive sights, including Tōfuku-ji, with its lovely garden, and Fushi-Inari-Taisha, with its hypnotically beautiful arcades of Shintō shrine gates.

Tōfuku-ji
BUDDHIST TEMPLE

(東福寺; Map p278; 15-778 Honmahi, Higashi-yama-ku; admission to garden ¥400, Tsūtenkyō bridge ¥400, grounds free; ⊘9am-4pm Apr-Oct, 8.30am-4pm Nov-early Dec, 9am-3.30pm early Dec-Mar; ◉JR Nara Line to Tōfukuji Station) Founded in 1236 by the priest Enni, Tōfuku-ji belongs to the Rinzai sect of Zen Buddhism. The present temple complex includes 24 subtemples. The huge San-mon is the oldest Zen main gate in Japan. The Hōjō (abbot's hall) was reconstructed in 1890. The **gardens**, laid out in 1938, are well worth a visit.

Tōfuku-ji is a 20-minute walk (2km) southeast of Kyoto Station. You can also take a local train on the JR Nara line and get off at JR Tōfukuji Station, from which it's a 10-minute walk southeast. Alternatively, you can take the Keihan line to Keihan Tōfukuji Station, from which it's also a 10-minute walk.

Fushimi-Inari Taisha
SHINTŌ SHRINE

(伏見稲荷大社; Map p278; 68 Yabunouchi-chō, Fukakusa, Fushimi-ku; ⊘dawn to dusk; ◉JR Nara Line to Inari Station) FREE This stunning shrine complex was dedicated to the gods of rice and sake by the Hata family in the 8th century. As the role of agriculture diminished, deities were enrolled to ensure prosperity in business.

Nowadays, the shrine is one of Japan's most popular, and is the head shrine for some 30,000 Inari shrines scattered the length and breadth of Japan.

The entire complex sprawls across the wooded slopes of Inari-yama. A pathway wanders 4km up the mountain and is lined with thousands of red torii. There are also dozens of stone foxes. The fox is considered the messenger of Inari, the god of the rice harvest (and, more recently, business). The Japanese traditionally see the fox as a sacred, somewhat mysterious figure capable of 'possessing' humans. The key often seen in the fox's mouth is for the rice granary.

The walk around the upper precincts of the shrine is a pleasant day hike. It also makes for a very eerie stroll in the late afternoon and early evening, when the various graveyards and miniature shrines along the path take on a mysterious air.

To get to the shrine from Kyoto Station, take a JR Nara line train to Inari Station. From Keihan Sanjō Station take the Keihan line to Fushimi-Inari Station. The shrine is just east of both of these stations.

Daigo-ji
BUDDHIST TEMPLE

(醍醐寺; Map p278; 22 Higashiōji-chō, Daigo, Fushimi-ku; admission ¥600, grounds free; ⊘9am-5pm Mar-Nov, to 4pm Dec-Feb; ⑤Tōzai Line to Daigo Station) Daigo-ji was founded in 874 by the priest Shobo, who gave it the name of Daigo. This refers to the five periods of Buddha's teaching, which were often compared to the five forms of milk prepared in India, the highest form of which is called *daigo* (ultimate essence of milk). The temple was expanded into a vast complex of buildings on two levels: Shimo Daigo (Lower Daigo) and Kami Daigo (Upper Daigo).

During the 15th century, the lower-level buildings were destroyed, with the sole exception of the five-storey **pagoda**. Built in 951, this pagoda still stands and is lovingly noted as the oldest of its kind in Japan and the oldest existing building in Kyoto.

To get to Daigo-ji, take the Tōzai subway line from central Kyoto to the Daigo stop, and walk east (towards the mountains) for about 10 minutes. Make sure that the train you board is bound for Daigo (board a train heading to Rokujizo NOT one heading to Hama-Ōtsu).

Admission to the temple grounds is free for most of the year; during the cherry-blossom and autumn-foliage seasons it will cost you ¥600 to enter.

◉ Uji

Uji is a small city to the south of Kyoto. Its main claims to fame are Byōdō-in and tea cultivation. Uji's stone bridge – the oldest of its kind in Japan – has been the scene of many bitter clashes in previous centuries.

Uji is also home to **Ujigami-jinja** (宇治上神社; ☑0774 21 4634; Uji Yamada 59; admission free; ⊘9am-4.30pm; ⑤5min walk from Uji Station, Keihan Uji line), a Unesco World Heritage Site. Despite this status, it's not one of the Kyoto area's more interesting sights. Those who wish to see it can find it by crossing the river (using the bridge near Byōdō-in) and walking about 10 minutes uphill (there are signs).

Uji can be reached by rail in about 40 minutes from Kyoto on the Keihan Uji line or JR Nara line.

When arriving in Uji by Keihan train, leave the station, cross the river via the first bridge on the right, and then turn left to find Byōdō-in. When coming by JR, the temple is about 10 minutes' walk east (towards the river) of Uji Station.

Byōdō-in TEMPLE
(平等院; 116 Uji renge, Uji-shi; admission ¥600 (¥300 while the Phoenix Hall is being renovated); ⏰8.30am-5.30pm; ☒JR Nara Line to Uji Station) This Buddhist temple was converted from a Fujiwara villa in 1052. The Hōō-dō (Phoenix Hall), more properly known as the Amida-dō, was built in 1053 and is the only original remaining building. The phoenix was a popular mythical bird in China and was revered by the Japanese as a protector of Buddha. The architecture of the building resembles the shape of the bird, and there are two bronze phoenixes perched opposite each other on the roof.

The building was originally intended to represent Amida's heavenly palace in the Pure Land. This building is one of the few extant examples of Heian-period architecture, and its graceful lines make one wish that far more of its type had survived to the present day. For a preview, take a look at the ¥10 coin.

Inside the hall is the famous statue of Amida and 52 Bosatsu (bodhisattvas) dating from the 11th century and attributed to the priest-sculptor Jōchō.

⊙ Southwest Kyoto

Southwest Kyoto is home to two notable sights, including the famous 'Moss Temple' (Saihō-ji) and Katsura-Rikyū.

Saihō-ji BUDDHIST TEMPLE
(西芳寺; Map p278; 56 Jingatani-chō, Matsuo, Nishikyō-ku; admission ¥3000; ☒Kyoto City Bus 28 from Kyoto Station to the Matsuo-taisha-mae stop) The main attraction at this temple is the heart-shaped garden designed in 1339 by Musō Kokushi. The garden is famous for its luxuriant moss, hence the temple's other name, Koke-dera (Moss Temple). While the reservation procedure is troublesome and the entry fee rather steep, a visit to the temple is highly recommended – the lush, shady garden is among the best in Kyoto.

Before you visit the garden, you will be asked to copy a Sutra using a Japanese ink brush. It's not as hard as it sounds, as you can trace the faint letters on the page – and don't worry about finishing. Once in the garden, you're free to move about as you wish.

Take bus 28 from Kyoto Station to the Matsuo-taisha-mae stop and walk 15 minutes southwest. From Keihan Sanjō Station, take Kyoto bus 63 to Koke-dera, the last stop, and walk for two minutes.

Entry to Saihō-ji is part of a tour only, and advance reservation is required. To visit, send a postcard at least one week before the date you wish to come and include your name, number of visitors, address in Japan, occupation, age (you must be over 18) and desired date (choice of alternative dates preferred). Enclose a stamped, self-addressed postcard for a reply to your Japanese address – eg buy an ōfuku-hagaki (send-and-return postcard set) at a Japanese post office. The address:

Saihō-ji
56 Jingatani-chō
Matsuo, Nishikyō-ku
Kyoto-shi 615-8286

Katsura Rikyū HISTORICAL BUILDING
(桂離宮; Map p278; Katsura Detached Palace; Katsura Misono, Nishikyō-ku; ☒Kyoto City Bus 33 to the Katsura Rikyū-mae stop) **FREE** This palace is considered to be one of the finest examples of Japanese traditional architecture. It was built in 1624 for the emperor's brother, Prince Toshihito. Every conceivable detail of the villa, the teahouses, the large pond with islets and the surrounding garden has been given meticulous attention.

Tours (around 40 minutes), in Japanese, commence at 10am, 11am, 2pm and 3pm. You should be there 20 minutes beforehand. An explanatory video is shown in the waiting room and a leaflet is provided in English. You must make advance reservations with the Imperial Household Agency (p286). Visitors must be over 20 years of age.

To get to the villa from Kyoto Station, take bus 33 and get off at the Katsura Rikyū-mae stop, which is a five-minute walk from the villa. The easiest access from the city centre is to take a Hankyū line train from Hankyū Kawaramachi Station to Hankyū Katsura Station, which is a 15-minute walk from the villa. A taxi from Hankyū Katsura Station to the villa will cost about ¥700. Note that some tokkyū (express) trains don't stop in Katsura.

⊙ Kitayama Area

Starting on the north side of Kyoto city and stretching almost all the way to the Sea of Japan, the Kitayama (Northern Mountains) are a natural escape prized by Kyoto city dwellers. Attractions here include the village of Ōhara, with its pastoral beauty, the fine mountain temple at Kurama, the river dining platforms at Kibune, and the trio of mountain temples in Takao.

Ōhara
NEIGHBOURHOOD

(大原; Ōhara; 🚌 Kyoto Bus 17 or 18 from Kyoto Station to the Ōhara stop) Since ancient times Ōhara, a quiet farming town about 10km north of Kyoto, has been regarded as a holy site by followers of the Jōdo school of Buddhism. The region provides a charming glimpse of rural Japan, along with the picturesque Sanzen-in, Jakkō-in and several other fine temples.

It's most popular in autumn, when the maple leaves change colour and the mountain views are spectacular. During the peak foliage season of November, this area can get very crowded, especially on weekends.

It's most easily accessed by a Kyoto bus from Kyoto Station. Note, these are tan coloured, unlike Kyoto City buses, which are usually light green.

Sanzen-in
TEMPLE

(三千院; 540 Raigōin-chō, Ōhara, Sakyō-ku; admission ¥700; ⊘ 8.30am-5pm Mar-Nov, to 4.30pm Dec-Feb; 🚌 Kyoto Bus 17 or 18 from Kyoto Station to the Ōhara stop) Founded in 784 by the priest Saichō, Sanzen-in belongs to the Tendai sect of Buddhism. The temple's **Yusei-en** is one of the most photographed gardens in Japan, and rightly so. Take some time to sit and enjoy the garden.

After seeing Yusei-en, head off to the **Ojogokuraku Hall** (Temple of Rebirth in Paradise) to see the impressive Amitabha trinity, a large Amida image flanked by attendants Kannon, goddess of mercy, and Seishi, god of wisdom. After this, walk up to the hydrangea garden at the back of the temple, where in late spring and summer you can walk among hectares of blooming hydrangeas.

To get to Sanzen-in, follow the signs from Ōhara's main bus stop up the hill past a long arcade of souvenir stalls. The entrance is on your left as you crest the hill.

Jakkō-in
TEMPLE

(寂光院; 676 Kusao-chō, Ōhara; admission ¥600; ⊘ 9am-5pm Mar-Nov, to 4.30pm Dec-Feb; 🚌 Kyoto Bus 17 or 18 from Kyoto Station to the Ōhara stop) This fine little temple lies on the other side of the village from the more famous Sanzen-in. It's worth a visit both for its intimate atmosphere and the pleasant walk that takes you there.

The history of Jakkō-in is exceedingly tragic. The actual founding date of the temple is subject to some debate (somewhere between the 6th and 11th centuries), but it gained fame as the temple that harboured Kenrei Mon-in, a lady of the Taira clan. In 1185 the Taira were soundly defeated in a sea battle with the Minamoto clan at Dan-no-ura. With the entire Taira clan slaughtered or drowned, Kenrei Mon-in threw herself into the waves with her grandson Antoku, the infant emperor; she was fished out – the only member of the clan to survive.

Unfortunately the main building of the temple burned down in 2000 and the newly reconstructed main hall is lacking some of the charm of the original. Nonetheless, it's a nice spot and the walk there is pleasant.

Jakkō-in lies to the west of Ōhara. Walk out of the bus station up the road to the traffic lights, then follow the small road to the left. It's easy to get lost on the way, but any villager will be happy to point you in the right direction.

Kurama & Kibune
NEIGHBOURHOOD

(鞍馬・貴船; Map p307; Kurama, Sakyō-ku; 🚃 Eiden Eizan line from Demachiyanagi Station to Kibune-guchi Station for Kibune, or Kurama Station for Kurama) Only 30 minutes north of Kyoto on the Eiden Eizan main line, Kurama and Kibune are a pair of tranquil valleys long favoured by Kyotoites as places to escape the crowds and stresses of the city below. Kurama's main attractions are its mountain temple and its onsen (hot springs). Kibune, over the ridge, is a cluster of ryokan overlooking a mountain stream. It is best enjoyed in the summer, when the ryokan serve dinner on platforms built over the rushing waters of the Kibune-gawa, providing welcome relief from the summer heat.

The two valleys lend themselves to being explored together. In the winter one can start from Kibune, walk for an hour or so over the ridge, visit Kurama-dera and then soak in the onsen before heading back to Kyoto. In the summer the reverse is best; start from Kurama, walk up to the temple, then down the other side to Kibune to enjoy a meal suspended above the cool river (unfortunately, restaurants in Kibune are known to refuse solo diners).

If you happen to be in Kyoto on the night of 22 October, be sure not to miss the Kurama-no-hi Matsuri (Kurama Fire Festival), one of the most exciting festivals in the Kyoto area.

To get to Kurama and Kibune, take the Eiden Eizan line from Kyoto's Demachiyanagi Station. For Kibune, get off at the second-to-last stop, Kibune Guchi, take a right out of the station and walk about 20 minutes up the hill. For Kurama, go to the last stop,

Kurama & Kibune

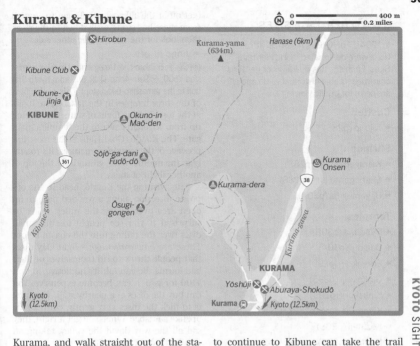

Kurama-yama
(634 m)
Hanase (6km)

Hirobun

Kibune Club

Kibune-jinja

KIBUNE

Okuno-in
Maō-den

Sōjō-ga-dani
Fudō-dō

361

Kurama
Onsen

Kurama-dera

Ōsugi-
gongen

38

KURAMA

Kyoto
(12.5km)

Yōshūji   Aburaya-Shokudō

Kurama   Kyoto (12.5km)

Kurama, and walk straight out of the station. Both destinations are ¥410 and take about 30 minutes to reach.

Kurama-dera   BUDDHIST TEMPLE
(鞍馬寺; Map p307; 1074 Kurama Honmachi, Sakyō-ku; admission ¥200; ⊙9am-4.30pm; ℝ Eiden Eizan line from Demachiyanagi Station to Kurama Station) This temple was established in 770 by the monk Gantei from Nara's Tōshōdai-ji. After seeing a vision of the deity Bishamon-ten, guardian of the northern quarter of the Buddhist heaven, Gantei established Kurama-dera just below the peak of Kurama-yama. Originally under the Tendai sect, Kurama has been independent since 1949, describing its own brand of Buddhism as Kurama Kyō.

The entrance to the temple is just up the hill from the Eiden Eizan main line's Kurama Station. A tram goes to the top for ¥100; alternatively, hike up by following the main path past the tram station. The trail is worth taking if it's not too hot, as it winds through a forest of towering old-growth *sugi* (cryptomeria) trees. At the top there is a courtyard dominated by the *honden* (main hall). Behind the *honden*, a trail leads off to the mountain's peak.

At the top, you can take a brief detour across the ridge to **Ōsugi-gongen**, a quiet shrine in a grove of trees. Those who want

to continue to Kibune can take the trail down the other side. It's a 1.2km, 30-minute hike from the *honden* to the valley floor of Kibune. On the way down are two pleasant mountain shrines, **Sōjō-ga-dani Fudō-dō** and **Okuno-in Maō-den**.

Kurama Onsen   ONSEN
(鞍馬温泉; Map p307; 520 Kurama Honmachi, Sakyō-ku; admission to outdoor/indoor bath ¥1000/2500; ⊙10am-9pm; ℝ Eiden Eizan line from Demachiyanagi Station to Kurama Station) One of few onsen within easy reach of Kyoto, Kurama Onsen is a great place to relax after a hike. The outdoor bath has a fine view of Kurama-yama; the indoor bath includes use of sauna and relaxation areas. Buy tickets from the machine outside the door of the main building (instructions are in Japanese and English).

To get to Kurama Onsen, walk straight out of Kurama Station, turn left up the main road and follow it for about 10 minutes. You'll see the baths down on your right. There's also a free shuttle bus that runs between the station and the onsen, leaving approximately every 30 minutes.

Kibune-jinja   SHINTŌ SHRINE
(貴船神社; Map p307; 180 Kibune-chō, Kurama, Sakyō-ku; ⊙6am-6pm Jan-Apr & Dec, 6am-8pm May-Nov; ℝ Eiden Eizan line from Demachiyanagi

KYOTO HERITAGE SITES

In 1994, 17 of Kyoto's historical attractions were designated World Heritage Sites. Each site has buildings or gardens of immeasurable historical value and all are open for public viewing.

Castles
➡ Nijō-jō (p288)

Shrines
➡ Kamigamo-jinja (p288)
➡ Shimogamo-jinja (p288)
➡ Ujigami-jinja (p304)

Temples
➡ Byōdō-in (p305)
➡ Daigo-ji (p304)
➡ Enryaku-ji (p299)
➡ Ginkaku-ji (p295)
➡ Kinkaku-ji (p299)
➡ Kiyomizu-dera (p289)
➡ Kōzan-ji (p308)
➡ Ninna-ji (p300)
➡ Nishi Hongan-ji (p282)
➡ Ryōan-ji (p300)
➡ Saihō-ji (p305)
➡ Tenryū-ji (p301)
➡ Tō-ji (p283)

Station to Kibune-guchi Station) **FREE** This shrine, halfway up the valley-town of Kibune, is worth a quick look, particularly if you can ignore the unfortunate plastic horse statue at its entrance. From Kibune you can hike over the mountain to Kurama-dera, along a trail that starts halfway up the village on the eastern side (or vice versa).

Takao   NEIGHBOURHOOD
(高雄; Map p278; Takao; 🚌 JR Bus from Kyoto Station to the Yamashiro-Takao stop) Takao is a secluded mountain village tucked far away in the northwestern part of Kyoto. It is famed for autumn foliage and the temples of Jingo-ji, Saimyō-ji and Kōzan-ji.

There are two options for buses to Takao: an hourly JR bus leaves from Kyoto Station, which takes about an hour to reach the Takao stop (get off at the Yamashiro-Takao stop); and Kyoto city bus 8 from Shijō-Karasuma

(get off at the Takao stop). To get to Jingo-ji from these bus stops, walk down to the river, then look for the steps on the other side.

➡ **Jingo-ji**
(神護寺; 5 Takao-chō, Umegahata, Ukyō-ku; admission ¥500; ⊘9am-4pm; 🚌 JR Bus from Kyoto Station to the Yamashiro-Takao stop) This is the best of the three temples in the Takao area. It sits at the top of a long flight of stairs that stretch up from Kiyotaki-gawa to the temple's main gate. The Kondō (Gold Hall) is the most impressive of the temple's structures; it's roughly in the middle of the grounds, at the top of another flight of stairs.

After visiting the Kondō, head in the opposite direction along a wooded path to an open area overlooking the valley. Don't be surprised if you see people tossing small discs over the railing into the chasm below. These are *kawarakenage* – light clay discs that people throw to rid themselves of their bad karma. Be careful: it's addictive, and at ¥100 for two, it can become expensive. You can buy the discs at a nearby stall. The trick is to flick the discs very gently, convex side up, like a Frisbee. When you get it right, they sail all the way down the valley, taking all that bad karma away with them.

The other two temples are within easy walking distance of Jingo-ji.

➡ **Saimyō-ji**
(西明寺; 2 Makino-chō, Umegahata, Ukyō-ku; admission ¥500; ⊘9am-5pm; 🚌 JR Bus from Kyoto Station to the Yamashiro-Takao stop) This is the better of the two other temples. It's about five minutes' walk north of the base of the steps that lead up to Jingo-ji (follow the river upstream).

➡ **Kōzan-ji**
(高山寺; 8 Toganoo-chō, Umegahata, Ukyō-ku; admission ¥600; ⊘8.30am-5pm; 🚌 JR Bus from Kyoto Station to the Yamashiro-Takao stop) This temple is of slightly less interest than Saimyō-ji, but the approach is stunning – it's lined with towering cryptomeria trees. To get to Kōzan-ji you must walk back up to the main road and follow it north for about 10 minutes.

🏃 Activities

Funaoka Onsen   ONSEN
(船岡温泉; Map p287; 82-1 Minami-Funaoka-chō-Murasakino, Kita-ku; admission ¥410; ⊘3pm-1am Mon-Sat, 8am-1am Sun & holidays; 🚌 Kyoto City Bus 9 from Kyoto Station to the Horikawa-Kuramaguchi stop) This old bath on Kuramaguchi-dōri is Kyoto's best. It boasts an outdoor bath, a sauna, a cypress-wood tub, an electric bath,

a herbal bath and a few more for good measure. Be sure to check out the *ranma* (carved wooden panels) in the changing room. Carved during Japan's invasion of Manchuria, the panels offer insight into the prevailing mindset of that era. (Note the panels do contain some violent imagery, which may disturb some visitors.)

To find the bath, head west about 400m on Kuramaguchi-dōri from the Kuramaguchi-Horiikawa intersection. It's on the left, not far past Lawson convenience store. Look for the large rocks out the front.

Maika   GEISHA COSTUME
(舞香; Map p290; ☎ 551-1661; www.maica.tv/e; Miyagawa suji 4-chōme 297, Higashiyama-ku; maiko/geisha from ¥6500/8000; ☒ Keihan Line to Gion-Shijo or Kiyomizu-Gojo stations) If you ever wondered how you might look as a geisha, Kyoto has several shops that offer *maiko-henshin* (geisha transformation). Maika is a popular *maiko-henshin* shop in Gion. If you don't mind spending a bit extra, it's possible to head out in costume for a stroll through Gion (and be stared at like never before!).

The process takes about an hour. Call to reserve at least one day in advance.

Club Ōkitsu Kyoto   JAPANESE CULTURE
(京都桜橘倶楽部「桜橘庵; Map p287; ☎ 411-8585; www.okitsu-kyoto.com; 524-1 Mototsuchi-mikado-chō, Shinmachi-Higashi-iru, Kamichōjamachi-dōri, in the Kōdōkan; ☒ Karasuma Line to Imadegawa Station) Kyoto is a fine place to get a taste of traditional Japanese culture. Club Ōkitsu Kyoto offers an upscale introduction to various aspects of Japanese culture including tea ceremony and the incense ceremony. It also offers kimono dressing upon request (note that kimono dressing is not offered alone: it must be part of a package).

The introduction is performed in an exquisite Japanese villa near the Kyoto Gosho and participants get a sense of the elegance and refinement of traditional Japanese culture.

En   TEA CEREMONY
(えん; Map p290; ☎ 080-3782-2706; 272 Matsubara-chō, Higashiyama-ku; tea ceremony per person ¥2000; ⊙ 3-6pm, closed Wed; ☒ Kyoto City Bus 206 to the Gion or Chionin-mae stops) A small teahouse near Gion where you can experience the Japanese tea ceremony with a minimum of fuss or expense. English explanations are provided and tea ceremonies are held at 3pm, 4pm, 5pm or 6pm (check the website for the latest times, as these may change). Reservations are recommended in high season.

It's a little tricky to find: it's located down a little alley off Higashiōji-dōri – look for the sign just south of Tenkaippin Rāmen.

🍴 Courses

Uzuki   COOKING
(www.kyotouzuki.com; 3hr class per person ¥4500) If you want to learn how to cook some of the delightful foods you've tried in Kyoto, we highly recommend Uzuki, a small cooking class conducted in a Japanese home for groups of two to four people. You will learn how to cook a variety of dishes and then sit down and enjoy the fruits of your labour.

You can consult beforehand if you have particular dishes you'd like to cook. The fee includes all ingredients. Reserve via website.

✹ Festivals & Events

There are hundreds of festivals happening in Kyoto throughout the year. Listings of these can be found in the *Kyoto Visitor's Guide* or *Kansai Scene*. The following are some of the major and most spectacular festivals. These attract hordes of spectators from out of town, so you will need to book accommodation well in advance.

Setsubun Matsuri at Yoshida-jinja FESTIVAL
This festival is held on the day of *setsubun* (2, 3 or 4 February; check with the TIC), which marks the last day of winter in the Japanese lunar calendar. In this festival, people climb up to Yoshida-jinja in the northern Higashiyama area to watch a huge bonfire (in which old good-luck charms are burned). It's one of Kyoto's more dramatic festivals. The action starts at dusk.

Aoi Matsuri   PARADE
The Hollyhock Festival dates back to the 6th century and commemorates the successful prayers of the people for the gods to stop calamitous weather. These days the procession involves imperial messengers carried in ox carts and a retinue of 600 people dressed in traditional costume. The procession leaves at around 10am on 15 May from the Kyoto Gosho and heads for Shimogamo-jinja.

Gion Matsuri   PARADE
Perhaps the most renowned of all Japanese festivals, Gion Matsuri reaches a climax on 17 July with a parade of over 30 floats depicting ancient themes and decked out in incredible finery. On the three evenings preceding the main festival day, people gather on Shijō-dōri, many of them dressed in beautiful

yukata (light summer kimonos), to look at the floats and carouse from one street stall to the next.

Daimon-ji Gozan Okuribi FESTIVAL
This festival, commonly known as Daimon-ji Yaki, is performed on 16 August as a means of bidding farewell to the souls of ancestors. Enormous fires are lit on five mountains in the form of Chinese characters or other shapes. The largest fire is always burned on Daimon-ji-yama, just above Ginkaku-ji, in northern Higashiyama. The fires start at 8pm and the best position to watch from is the banks of the Kamo-gawa or, alternatively, pay for a rooftop view from a hotel.

Jidai Matsuri PARADE
The Festival of the Ages is of comparatively recent origin, only dating back to 1895. More than 2000 people, dressed in costumes ranging from the 8th century to the 19th century, parade from Kyoto Gosho to Heian-jingū on 22 October.

Kurama-no-hi Matsuri FESTIVAL
In perhaps Kyoto's most dramatic festival, the Kurama Fire Festival, huge flaming torches are carried through the streets of Kurama by men in loincloths on 22 October (the same day as the Jidai Matsuri). Note that trains to and from Kurama will be completely packed with passengers on the evening of the festival (we suggest going early and returning late).

🛏 Sleeping

The most convenient areas in which to be based, in terms of easy access to shopping, dining and sightseeing attractions, are downtown Kyoto and the Higashiyama area. The Kyoto Station area is also a good location, with excellent access to transport and plenty of shops and restaurants about. Transport information in the following listings is from Kyoto Station unless otherwise noted.

🛏 Kyoto Station Area

★ Capsule Ryokan Kyoto CAPSULE HOTEL ¥
(カプセル旅館京都; Map p282; ☑344-1510; www.capsule-ryokan-kyoto.com; capsule ¥3500, tw per person ¥3990; @ 🛜; ᴿ JR Tōkaidō Main Line to Kyoto Station, 🆂 Karasuma Line to Kyoto Station) This unique accommodation offers ryokan-style capsules (meaning tatami mats inside the capsules), as well as comfortable, cleverly designed private rooms. Each capsule also has its own TV and cable internet access point, while the private rooms have en suite bathrooms and all the amenities you might need. Free internet, wi-fi and other amenities are available in the comfortable lounge.

It's located a seven-minute walk from Kyoto Station, near the southeast corner of the Horikawa-Shichijo intersection.

★ Tour Club GUESTHOUSE ¥
(ツアークラブ; Map p282; ☑075 353 6968; www.kyotojp.com; 362 Momiji-chō, Higashinakasuji, Shōmen-sagaru, Shimogyō-ku; dm ¥2450, d per person ¥3490, tw per person ¥3490-3885, tr per person ¥2960-3240; ⊕@🛜; ᴿ JR Tōkaidō Main Line, JR Tōkaidō Shinkansen Line, 🆂 Karasuma Line, Kyoto Station, ᴿ Kintetsu Kyoto Line) Run by a charming and friendly family, this clean, well-maintained guesthouse is a favourite of many foreign visitors. Facilities include wi-fi, a small Zen garden, laundry and free tea and coffee. The private rooms, which were recently refurbished, have en suite bathrooms.

It's a 10-minute walk from Kyoto Station; turn north off Shichijō-dōri at the Nagomi-kan coffee shop (looks like a bank) and keep an eye out for the English sign.

Budget Inn GUESTHOUSE ¥
(バジェットイン; Map p282; ☑075 344 1510; www.budgetinnjp.com; 295 Aburanokōji-chō, Aburanokōji, Shichijō sagaru, Shimogyō-ku; per person tr/q/5-person ¥3660/3245/2996; ⊕@🛜; ᴿ JR Tōkaidō Main Line, JR Tōkaidō Shinkansen Line, 🆂 Karasuma Line, Kyoto Station, ᴿ Kintetsu Kyoto Line) This well-run guesthouse is an excellent choice. It's got eight Japanese-style private rooms, all of which are clean and well maintained. All rooms have their own bathroom and can accommodate up to five people, making this a good spot for families. The staff here is very helpful and friendly, and laundry and bicycle rental are available. All in all, this is a great choice in this price range. It's a seven-minute walk from Kyoto Station; from the station, walk west on Shiokōji-dōri, turn north one street before Horikawa and look for the English-language sign out front.

Matsubaya Ryokan RYOKAN ¥
(松葉家; Map p282; ☑075 351 3727; www.matsubayainn.com; Higashinotōin Nishi-iru, Kamijuzū-yachō-dōri, Shimogyō-ku; r per person from ¥4200; @🛜; ᴿ JR Tōkaidō Main Line, JR Tōkaidō Shinkansen Line, 🆂 Karasuma Line, Kyoto Station, ᴿ Kintetsu Kyoto Line) A short walk from Kyoto Station, this newly renovated ryokan has clean, well-kept rooms and a management that is used

to foreign guests. Some rooms on the 1st floor look out on small gardens. Average room rates here run about ¥6510 per person.

Matsubaya also has several serviced apartments in its adjoining Bamboo House section – these would be great for anyone planning a longer stay in the city. Breakfast is available from ¥500 to ¥800 (Western) or ¥1000 (Japanese). Note that wi-fi is available in all rooms except those on the 5th floor (on this floor, each room has LAN cable internet access).

Ryokan Shimizu RYOKAN ¥

(☑ 371-5538; Map p282; www.kyoto-shimizu.net; 644 Kagiya-chō, Shichijō-dōri, Wakamiya agaru, Shimogyō-ku; r per person from ¥5250; ❷ @; ꤯ JR Tōkaidō Main Line, JR Tōkaidō Shinkansen Line, Ⓢ Karasuma Line, Kyoto Station, ꤯ Kintetsu Line) A short walk north of Kyoto Station, this travellers' ryokan is quickly building a loyal following of foreign guests, and for good reason: it's clean, well run and friendly. Rooms are standard ryokan style with one difference: all have bathrooms. Bicycle rental is available. Prices rise on Saturdays and nights before holidays.

K's House Kyoto GUESTHOUSE ¥

(ケイズハウス京都; Map p282; ☑ 342-2444; http://kshouse.jp; 418 Naya-chō, Shichijō agaru, Dotemachi-dōri, Shimogyō-ku; dm from ¥2300, s/d/ tw per person from ¥3500/2900/2900; ❷ @ 🛜; ꤯ JR Tōkaidō Main Line, JR Tōkaidō Shinkansen Line, Ⓢ Karasuma Line, Kyoto Station, ꤯ Kintetsu Kyoto Line) K's House is a large Western-style backpackers' guesthouse with both private and dorm rooms. The rooms are simple but adequate and there are spacious common areas. There's also an on-site restaurant that serves cheap cafe drinks, alcohol and snacks, making this a great place to meet and hang out with other travellers. The staff can help arrange inexpensive onward travel around Japan. It's about a 10-minute walk from Kyoto Station.

APA Hotel Kyoto Ekimae BUSINESS HOTEL ¥¥

(アパホテル京都駅前; Map p282; ☑ 365-4111; www.apahotel.com; Shiokōji sagaru, Nishinotōin-dōri, Shimogyō-ku; s/tw per person from ¥9500/9000; ❷ @ 🛜; ꤯ JR Tōkaidō Main Line, JR Tōkaidō Shinkansen Line, Ⓢ Karasuma Line, Kyoto Station, ꤯ Kintetsu Kyoto Line) Only five minutes on foot from Kyoto Station, this efficient business hotel is a good choice for those who want the convenience of a nearly stationside location. Rooms are adequate, with firm, clean beds and unit bathrooms. The staff is professional and is used to dealing with foreign guests.

★ Hotel Granvia Kyoto HOTEL ¥¥¥

(ホテルグランヴィア京都; Map p282; ☑ 344-8888; www.granvia-kyoto.co.jp; Shiokōji sagaru, Karasuma-dōri, Shimogyō-ku; tw/d from ¥32,340/28,875; ❷ @ 🛁; ꤯ JR Tōkaidō Main Line, JR Tōkaidō Shinkansen Line, Ⓢ Karasuma Line, Kyoto Station, ꤯ Kintetsu Kyoto Line) Imagine stepping straight out of bed and into the *shinkansen* (bullet train). This is almost possible when you stay at the Granvia, an excellent hotel located directly above Kyoto Station. Rooms are clean, spacious and well appointed, with deep bathtubs. This is a very professional operation with some good on-site restaurants, some of which have views over the city.

The hotel also has family rooms.

★ Dormy Inn Premium Kyoto Ekimae HOTEL ¥¥¥

(ドーミーインPREMIUM京都駅; Map p282; ☑ 371-5489; www.hotespa.net/hotels/kyoto; Higashishiokōji-chō 558-8, Shimogyō-ku; tw/d from ¥26,000/22,000; @; ꤯ JR Tōkaidō Main Line to Kyoto Station, Ⓢ Karasuma Subway Line to Kyoto Station) Located almost directly across the street from Kyoto Station, this clean, efficient new hotel is a great choice for those who want to be near the station. Rooms are clean and well maintained and the on-site spa bath is a nice plus. Note that you can often get better rates online.

🛏 Downtown Kyoto

Hotel Unizo BUSINESS HOTEL ¥¥

(ホテルユニゾ京都; Map p285; ☑ 241-3351; www. hotelunizo.com/eng/kyoto; Kawaramachi-dōri-Sanjō sagaru, Nakagyō-ku; s/d/tw from ¥10,000/17,000/ 19,000; ❷ @ 🛜; 🚌 Kyoto City Bus 5 to the Kawaramachi-Sanjō stop, Ⓢ Tōzai Line to Kyoto Shiyakusho-mae Station) They don't get more central than this downtown business hotel: it's right in the middle of Kyoto's nightlife, shopping and dining district, and you can walk to hundreds of restaurants and shops within five minutes. It's a standard-issue business hotel, with small but adequate rooms and unit bathrooms. Considering the location and the condition of the rooms, it's great value.

Best Western Hotel Kyoto HOTEL ¥¥

(ベストウェスタンホテル京都; Map p285; ☑ 254-4055; http://kyoto.bwhotels.jp; Matsugae-chō 457, Kawaramachi-Rokkaku, Nakagyō-ku; s/tw from ¥18,000/33,000; @; Ⓢ Tōzai Line to Kyoto Shiyakusho-mae Station) Plonked down right in the middle of downtown Kyoto's main shopping district, the Best Western claims one of the most convenient locations in Kyoto. It's brand new and off to a good start. Rooms are small but spotless, with everything you might need, including a helpful staff. You can get cheaper rates online.

Mitsui Garden Hotel Kyoto Sanjō   HOTEL ¥¥

(三井ガーデンホテル　京都三条; Map p285; ☑ 256-3331; www.gardenhotels.co.jp/eng/sanjo; 80 Mikura-chō, Nishiiru, Karasuma, Sanjō-dōri, Nakagyō-ku; s/d/tw from ¥10,500/17,600/18,800; @; ⓢ Tōzai & Karasuma lines to Karasuma-Oike Station, exit 6) Just west of the downtown dining and shopping district, this is a clean and efficient hotel that offers good value for the price and reasonably comfortable rooms. It's just a minute or two to the nearest subway station.

★ Tawaraya   RYOKAN ¥¥¥

(俵屋; Map p285; ☑ 211-5566; Fuyachō-Oike sagaru, Nakagyō-ku; r per person incl 2 meals ¥42,263-84,525; ⊜ @; ⓢ Tōzai Line to Kyoto Shiyakusho-mae Station, exit 8) Tawaraya has been operating for over three centuries and is one of the finest places to stay in Japan. Entering this ryokan is like entering another world, and you just might not want to leave. The ryokan has an intimate, private feeling and all rooms have bathrooms.

The gardens are sublime and the cosy study is the perfect place to linger with a book. A night here is sure to be memorable and is *highly* recommended.

Kyoto Hotel Ōkura   HOTEL ¥¥¥

(京都ホテルオークラ; Map p285; ☑ 211-5111; http://okura.kyotohotel.co.jp; Kawaramachi-dōri, Oike, Nakagyō-ku; s/d/tw from ¥21,945/31,185/31,185; ⊜ @; ⓢ Tōzai Line to Kyoto Shiyakusho-mae Station, exit 3) Located right in the midst of downtown, this is a well-run, comfortable hotel that claims the most convenient location of any luxury hotel in Kyoto. Rooms here are clean, spacious and comfortable; and those on the upper floors have great views.

There are several excellent on-site restaurants and bars, along with hundreds within easy walking distance of the hotel. If you exhaust the possibilities in and around the hotel, you can walk downstairs and hop right onto the subway.

Aoi Kyoto Stay   RENTAL HOUSE ¥¥¥

(葵KYOTO STAY; Map p290; ☑ 354-7770; http://en.kyoto-stay.jp; Tenno-chō 145-1-4F, Kiyamachi Bukkōji Agaru, Shimogyō-ku; from ¥15,000 per person, varying by season and house; ⓡ; Ⓡ Hankyū Line to Kawaramachi Station) Aoi Kyoto Stay has

a collection of beautifully refurbished Kyoto *machiya* (traditional townhouses) located in the middle of downtown Kyoto. This is your chance to stay in a *machiya* without forsaking comforts such as air conditioning, floor heating, Western-style beds and wi-fi. You can peruse the collection on the website. The office is shown on our map.

Some of the larger houses are suitable for families, but those with small children might be worried about their children damaging some of the decorations. The smaller houses would make perfect romantic getaways. Houses have laundry facilities and simple cooking facilities. The company can arrange to have meals sent to your house or you can self-cater at the food floors of the nearby department stores. All in all, these are highly recommended.

★ Hiiragiya Ryokan   RYOKAN ¥¥¥

(柊屋; Map p285; ☑ 221-1136; www.hiiragiya.co.jp/en; Anekōji-agaru, Fuya-chō, Nakagyō-ku; r per person incl 2 meals ¥36,750-86,900; ⊜ @; ⓢ Tōzai Line to Kyoto Shiyakushomae Station, exit 8) This classic ryokan has hosted celebrities and dignitaries from around the world. From the decorations to the service to the food, everything at the Hiiragiya is first class. Rooms in the old wing have great old Japan style, while those in the new wing are pristine and comfortable.

It's centrally located downtown within easy walking distance of two subway stations and lots of good restaurants.

Hiiragiya Bekkan   RYOKAN ¥¥¥

(柊屋別館; Map p290; ☑ 231-0151, 231-0153; www.hiiragiya.com; Gokōmachi-dōri, Nijō sagaru; r per person incl 2 meals from ¥16,800; ⊜ @ ⓡ; ⓢ Tōzai Line to Shiyakusho-mae Station, exit North-10) An annex of the Hiiragiya ryokan and not far from the main building, Hiiragiya Bekkan offers the traditional ryokan experience at slightly more affordable rates. The *kaiseki* (Japanese haute cuisine) served here is delicious, and the gardens are lovely. Rooms have en-suite bathrooms, but bathtubs are shared (there are four lovely bathtubs). As with many ryokan, some rooms can be a bit noisy.

Yoshikawa   RYOKAN ¥¥¥

(吉川; Map p285; ☑ 221-5544; www.kyoto-yoshikawa.co.jp; Tominokōji, Oike-sagaru, Nakagyō-ku; r per person incl 2 meals low season/high season from ¥36,225/48,300; @; ⓢ Tōzai & Karasuma lines to Karasuma-Oike Station or Kyoto Shiyakusho-mae Station) Located downtown, within easy walking distance of two subway stations

and the entire dining and nightlife district, this superb traditional ryokan has beautiful rooms and a stunning garden. The ryokan is famous for its tempura and meals are of a high standard.

Central Kyoto

Palace Side Hotel   HOTEL ¥
(ザ・パレスサイドホテル; Map p287; ☎415-8887; www.palacesidehotel.co.jp; Karasuma-dōri, Shimotachiuri agaru, Kamigyō-ku; s/tw/d from ¥6000/9000/9800; ⊕@; ⑤Karasuma Line to Marutamachi Station) Overlooking the Kyoto Imperial Palace Park, this excellent value budget hotel has a lot going for it, starting with a friendly English-speaking staff, great service, washing machines, an on-site restaurant, well-maintained rooms and free internet terminals. The rooms are small but serviceable. It's a three-minute walk from the subway.

Ryokan Rakuchō   RYOKAN ¥
(洛頂旅館; Map p287; ☎721-2174; 67 Higashi-hangi chō, Shimogamo, Sakyō-ku; s/tw/tr ¥5300/9240/12,600; ⊕@♜; ⑤Karasuma Line to Kitaōji Station, ▥Kyoto City Bus 205 to Furitsudaigaku-mae stop) There is a lot to like about this fine little foreigner-friendly ryokan in the northern part of town: it's entirely non-smoking, there is a nice little garden and the rooms are clean and simple. Meals aren't served, but the owners can supply a good map of local eateries.

Tōyoko Inn Kyoto Gojō Karasuma   HOTEL ¥¥
(東横INN京都五条烏丸; Map p278; ☎344-1045; www.toyoko-inn.com; Karasuma-dōri, Matsubara sagaru, Gojō Karasuma-chō 393, Shimogyō-ku; s/tw from ¥6480/9480; @; ⑤Karasuama Line to Gojō Station) Those familiar with the Tōyoko Inn chain know that this hotel brand specialises in simple, clean, fully equipped but small rooms at the lowest price possible. There are all kinds of interesting extras: free breakfast, free telephone calls inside Japan, and reduced rates on rental cars. They'll even lend you a laptop if you need to do some emailing.

It's a little south of the city centre, but easily accessed by the Karasuma subway line.

Citadines Kyoto Karasuma Gojō   HOTEL ¥¥¥
(シタディーン京都 烏丸五条; Map p278; ☎352-8900; www.citadines.jp/kyoto; Gojō-dōri, Karasuma Higashi iru, Matsuya-chō 432, Shimogyō-ku; tw/d from ¥23,100/23,100; @; ⑤Karasuma Line to Gojō Station) On Gojō-dōri, a bit south of the main downtown district, but within

easy walking distance of the Karasuma subway line (as well as the Keihan line), this serviced apartment/hotel is a welcome addition to the Kyoto accommodation scene. The kitchens allow you to do your own cooking and other touches make you feel right at home.

Furnished Apartment   APARTMENT
(ザ・ファーニッシュドアパートメント; Map p278; ☎090-6660-7645; www.kyotojp.com/furnished-apartment.html; 34 Hinoshitachō, Takakura-dōri, Matsubara-sagaru, Shimogyō-ku; apt per month 1/2 person from ¥98,000/140,000; ♜; ⑤Karasuma Subway Line to Gojō Station) Located in the middle of Kyoto, these apartments have everything you need for a longer stay in Kyoto, including simple kitchens, bathrooms and basic furniture. They're within walking distance of the shops and restaurants of downtown, as well as Gojō Station on the Karasuma subway line.

Southern Higashiyama

JAM Hostel Kyoto Gion   GUESTHOUSE ¥
(ジャムホステル京都祇園; Map p285; ☎201-3374; www.jamhostel.com; 170 Tokiwa-chō, Higashiyama-ku; per person ¥2000-4000; ♜; ▥Keihan Line to Gion Shijō Station) This new guesthouse boasts a convenient location on the edge of Gion and a sake bar downstairs that is a convivial place for guests to mix with local regulars. There are a variety of simple but clean dorm rooms here and common bathing facilities.

Ryokan Uemura   RYOKAN ¥¥
(旅館うえむら; Map p290; ☎fax 561-0377; Ishibe-kōji, Shimogawara, Higashiyama-ku; r with breakfast per person ¥9000, r without meals per person ¥7500; ⊕; ▥Kyoto City Bus 206 to the Higashiyama-Yasui stop) This beautiful little ryokan is at ease with foreign guests. It's on a quaint cobblestone alley, just down the hill from Kōdai-ji. Rates include breakfast, and there is a 10pm curfew. Book well in advance, as there are only three rooms.

Note that the manager prefers bookings by fax and asks that cancellations also be made by fax (with so few rooms, it can be costly when bookings are broken without notice).

★Hyatt Regency Kyoto   HOTEL ¥¥¥
(ハイアットリージェンシー京都; Map p290; ☎541-1234; www.kyoto.regency.hyatt.com; 644-2 Sanjūsangendō-mawari, Higashiyama-ku; r ¥19,000-49,000; ⊕@♜; ▥Keihan Shichijō Station) The

Hyatt Regency is an excellent, stylish, foreigner-friendly hotel at the southern end of Kyoto's southern Higashiyama sightseeing district. Many travellers consider this the best hotel in Kyoto. The staff here is extremely efficient and helpful (there are even foreign staff members – something of a rarity in Japan).

The on-site restaurants and bar are excellent. The stylish rooms and bathrooms have lots of neat touches. The concierges are knowledgeable about the city and they'll even lend you a laptop to check your email if you don't have your own. It's a five-minute walk from the station.

Shiraume   RYOKAN ¥¥¥

(白梅; Map p290; ☎ 561-1459; Gion Shinbashi Shirakawa hotori, Shijōnawate agaru, Higashi iru, Higashiyama-ku; per person incl meals ¥22,000-35,000, per person incl breakfast ¥15,000-25,000; @; ⓡ Keihan Line to Sanjō Station, Ⓢ Tōzai Line to Sanjō-Keihan Station) Looking out over the Shirakawa Canal in Shimbashi, a lovely street in Gion, this ryokan offers an excellent location, atmosphere and service. The decor is traditional with a small inner garden and nice wooden bathtubs. This would be a great spot to sample the Japanese ryokan experience.

Gion Hatanaka   RYOKAN ¥¥¥

(祇園畑中; Map p290; ☎ 541-5315; www.thehatanaka.co.jp; Yasaka-jinja Minami-mon mae, Higashiyama-ku; r per person incl 2 meals from ¥30,000; ⊜ ⓢ; ⓡ Kyoto City Bus 206 to the Higashiyama-Yasui stop) Climb a flight of beautiful stone stairs to reach the entrance to Gion Hatanaka, a fine ryokan right in the heart of the Southern Higashiyama sightseeing district (less than a minute's walk from Yasaka-jinja). Despite being fairly large, this ryokan manages to retain an intimate and private feeling. In addition to bathtubs in each room, there is a huge wooden communal bath.

The rooms are clean, well designed and relaxing. This ryokan offers regularly scheduled geisha entertainment that non-guests are welcome to join. Wi-fi is in the lobby only.

Seikōrō Ryokan   RYOKAN ¥¥¥

(晴鴨楼; Map p290; ☎ 561-0771; http://ryokan. asia/seikoro; 467 Nishi Tachibana-chō, 3 chō-me, Gojō sagaru, Toiyamachi-dori, Higashiyama-ku; r per person incl 2 meals from ¥26,250; ⊜ @ ⓢ; ⓡ Kyoto City Bus 17 or 205 to the Kawaramachi-Gojō stop) The Seikōrō is a classic ryokan with fine rooms and a grandly decorated lobby. It's fairly spacious, with excellent, comfortable rooms, attentive service and a fairly convenient midtown location. Several rooms look over gardens and all have private baths.

Ryokan Motonago   RYOKAN ¥¥¥

(旅館元奈古; Map p290; ☎ 561-2087; www. motonago.com; 511 Washio-chō, Kōdaiji-michi, Higashiyama-ku; r per person incl 2 meals from ¥17,850; ⊜ @ ⓢ; ⓡ Kyoto City Bus 206 to the Gion stop) This ryokan may have the best location of any ryokan in the city: right on Nene-no-Michi in the heart of the Higashiyama sightseeing district. It's got traditional decor, friendly service, nice bathtubs and a few small Japanese gardens.

Sakara Kyoto   INN ¥¥¥

(桜香楽; Map p290; http://sakarakyoto.com; 541-2 Furukawa-chō, Higashiyama-ku; r ¥10,000-¥24,000; @ ⓢ; Ⓢ Tōzai Line to Higashiyama Station) This modern Japanese-style inn is conveniently located in a covered pedestrian shopping arcade just south of Sanjō-dōri, about 50m from Higashiyama Subway Station. It's great for couples and families, and rooms can accommodate up to five people. Each room has bath/shower, kitchenette and laundry facilities. Reservation is by email only.

Gion House   RENTAL HOUSE ¥¥¥

(ザ・祇園ハウス; Map p290; ☎ 353-8282; www. thegionhouse.com; 563-12 Komatsu-chō, Higashiyama-ku; per night from ¥23,000; ⓢ; ⓡ Kyoto City Bus 206 to the Higashiyama Yasui stop, ⓡ Keihan Line to Gion-Shijō Station) This beautifually decorated traditional Japanese house right on the edge of Gion makes the perfect getaway for those seeking something other than a run-of-the-mill hotel. It's spacious and comfortable and has everything you need to take care of yourselves for a few days in the old capital. Step outside the door and a few minutes' walk will bring you to Gion's most atmospheric lanes. And if you can force yourself off the comfortable futons in the morning, you can take your morning tea on a rooftop verandah.

🏯 Northern Higashiyama

★ Westin Miyako, Kyoto   HOTEL ¥¥¥

(ウェスティン都ホテル京都; Map p296; ☎ 771-7111; www.miyakohotels.ne.jp/westinkyoto; Keage, Sanjō-dōri, Higashiyama-ku; d & tw from ¥33,500, Japanese-style r from ¥41,500; ⊜ @ ⓢ ⓢ; Ⓢ Tōzai Line to Keage Station, exit 2) The grande dame of Kyoto hotels occupies a commanding position overlooking the Higashiyama sightseeing district (making it one of the best locations for sightseeing in Kyoto). Rooms are clean and well maintained, and the staff is at home with foreign guests.

Rooms on the north side have great views over the city to the Kitayama mountains. There is a fitness centre, as well as a private garden and walking trail. The hotel even has its own ryokan section for those who want to try staying in a ryokan without giving up the convenience of a hotel.

Koto Inn RENTAL HOUSE ¥¥¥
(古都イン; Map p290; ☑751–2753; koto.inn@gmail.com; 373 Horiike-chō, Higashiyama-ku; per night from ¥15,000; ☻@☎; ⑤Tōzai Line to Higashiyama station) Conveniently located near the Higashiyama sightseeing district and two-minutes' walk from the Tōzai subway line, this vacation rental is good for families, couples and groups who want a bit of privacy. It's got everything you need and is decorated with lovely Japanese antiques. While the building is traditionally Japanese, all the facilities are fully modernised.

The house can hold up to four or five people. Due to the antiques and sliding doors, it's probably not suitable for families with young children.

Kyoto Garden Ryokan Yachiyo RYOKAN ¥¥¥
(旅館八千代; Map p296; ☑771-4148; www.ryokan-yachiyo.com; 34 Fukuchi-chō, Nanzen-ji, Sakyō-ku; r per person incl 2 meals ¥18,900-42,000; ☻☎; ⑤Tōzai Line to Keage Station, exit 2) Located just down the street from Nanzen-ji temple, this large ryokan is at home with foreign guests. Rooms are spacious and clean, and some look out over private gardens. There is an excellent on-site restaurant with a choice of tatami and table seating. For convenient evening strolling, this is a good bet. The price varies depending on dates and meals.

🛏 Arashiyama & Sagano

Hoshinoya HOTEL ¥¥¥
(星のや; Map p302; ☑871-0001; http://global.hoshinoresort.com/hoshinoya_kyoto; Genrokuzan-chō, Arashiyama 11-2, Nishikyō-ku; r per person from ¥51,660; ☎; ⑯Hankyū Line to Arashiyama Station) Sitting in a secluded area on the south bank of the Oi-gawa in Arashiyama (upstream from the main sightseeing district), this modern take on the classic Japanese inn is quickly becoming a favourite of well-heeled visitors to Kyoto in search of privacy and a unique experience. Rooms feature incredible views of the river and the surrounding mountains.

The best part is the approach: you'll be chauffeured by a private boat from a dock near Togetsu-kyō bridge to the inn (note that on days following heavy rains, you'll have to go by car instead). This is easily one of the most unique places to stay in Kyoto.

🛏 Kansai Airport

Hotel Nikkō Kansai Airport HOTEL ¥¥¥
(ホテル日航関西空港; ☑072-455-1111; www.nikkokix.com; Senshū Kūkō Kita 1, Izumisano-shi, Osaka-fu; s/tw/d from ¥21,945/32,340/30,030; ☻☎♿; ℝJR Line Haruka Airport Express to Kansai Airport) The only hotel at the airport is the excellent Hotel Nikkō Kansai Airport, just a five-minute walk from the international arrivals hall. The rooms here are spacious and comfortable. It's the perfect place to stay if you arrive late or have an early departure. There are several places to eat nearby. You can often get better rates by booking online.

🍴 Eating

Kyoto is a great place to explore Japanese cuisine and you'll find good restaurants regardless of your budget. If you tire of Japanese food, there are plenty of excellent international restaurants to choose from. You'll find the thickest concentration of eateries in downtown Kyoto, but also great choices in Southern Higashiyama/Gion and in and around Kyoto Station.

Because Kyoto gets a lot of foreign travellers, you'll find a surprising number of English menus and most places are quite comfortable with foreign guests.

🍴 Kyoto Station Area

The new Kyoto Station building is chock-a-block with restaurants, and if you find yourself anywhere near the station around mealtime, this is probably your best bet in terms of variety and price.

There are several food courts scattered about the station building. The best of these can be found on the 11th floor on the west side of the building: the **Cube** (Map p282; ☺11am-10pm) food court and Isetan department store's **Eat Paradise** (Map p282; ☺11am-10pm) food court. In Eat Paradise, we like Tonkatsu Wako for *tonkatsu* (deep-fried breaded pork cutlet), Tenichi for sublime tempura, and Wakuden for approachable *kaiseki* fare.

KYOTO EATING

FRANK DEIM / GETTY IMAGES ©

MORTEN LEGARTH / GETTY IMAGES ©

Dōtombori (p341), Osaka
With its glittering nightscapes and plenty of restaurants, shops and theatres, this is Osaka's liveliest night spot.

Himeji-jō (p370)
Japan's most magnificent castle, Himeji-jo was built in 1580 and is one of only a handful of original castles remaining.

Cherry-blossom viewing (p33), Kyoto
Hanami (cherry-blossom viewing parties) take place throughout Japan in March and April.

1. Daigo-ji (p304)

This Buddhist temple was founded in AD 874. Its pagoda is the oldest of its kind in Japan.

2. Geisha in Ponto-chō, Kyoto (p284)

One of Kyoto's five geisha districts, Ponto-chō is a narrow alley lined with traditional wooden buildings and hanging lanterns.

3. Daibutsu, Tōdai-ji (p381)

The Daibutsu (Great Buddha) at Tōdai-ji, standing around 15m tall and weighing over 500 tonnes, is c of the largest bronze figures in the world.

To get to these food courts, take the west escalators from the main concourse all the way up to the 11th floor and look for the Cube on your left and Eat Paradise straight in front of you.

Other options in the station include **Kyoto Rāmen Koji** (Map p282; ⏱11am-10pm), a collection of seven *rāmen* restaurants on the 10th floor (underneath the Cube). Buy tickets from the machines, which don't have English but have pictures on the buttons. In addition to *rāmen,* you can get green-tea ice cream and other Japanese desserts at Chasen, and *tako-yaki* (battered octopus pieces) at Miyako.

About five minutes' walk north of the station, Yodobashi Camera (p330) has a wide selection of restaurants on the 6th floor, and an international supermarket with lots of take-away items on the B2 floor.

✕ Central Kyoto

Chez Luc EUROPEAN ¥¥
(シェ・ルーク; Map p287; ☑708-2610; Ebisugawa-dōri Taka-kura Nishi iru, Yamanaka-chō 552, Nakagyō-ku; lunch sets around ¥1850, dinner sets around ¥3900; ⏱11.30am-2.30pm, last order 1.30pm & 6-10pm, last order 9pm, closed Sunday dinner and national holidays; 🅼; ⓢKarasuma Line to Marutamachi Station) This comfortable little bistro serves hearty and very authentic Alsatian cuisine. It also serves a variety of excellent Alsatian and French wines at reasonable prices. The owner speaks French, English and German. Reservations are recommended on weekends.

✕ Downtown Kyoto

Downtown Kyoto has the best variety of approachable Japanese and international restaurants.

★ Ippūdō RĀMEN ¥
(一風堂; Map p285; ☑213-8800; 653-1 Bantōya-chō, Nishikikōji higashiiru, Higashinotō-in, Nakagyō-ku; rāmen ¥750-950; ⏱11am-2am; 🅼; ⓢKarasuma Line to Shijō Station) There's a reason that there's usually a line outside this *rāmen* joint at lunchtime: the *rāmen* is awesome and the bite-sized *gyōza* (dumplings) are to die for. We recommend the *gyōza* set meal, which costs ¥750 or ¥850, depending on your choice of *rāmen*. It's on Nishiki-dōri, next to a post office and diagonally across from a Starbucks.

Kerala INDIAN ¥
(ケララ; Map p285; ☑251-0141; 2F KUS Bldg, Kawaramachi, Sanjō agaru, Nakagyō-ku; lunch/dinner from ¥850/2600; ⏱11.30am-2pm & 5-9pm; 🅿🅼; ⓢTōzai Line to Kyoto Shiyakusho-mae Station) This is where we go for reliable Indian lunch sets – great *thalis* that include two curries, good naan bread, some rice, a small salad etc. Dinners are à la carte. It's on the 2nd floor; look for the display of food in the glass case at street level.

Warai OKONOMIYAKI ¥
(わらい; Map p285; ☑257-5966; 1F Mizukōto Bldg, 597 Nishiuoya-chō, Nishikikōji-dōri, Takakura Nishiiru, Nakagyō-ku; okonomiyaki from ¥600; ⏱11.30am-1am; 🅼; ⓢKarasuma Line to Shijō Station, 🅡Hankyū Line to Karasuma Station) A great place to try *okonomiyaki* (savoury pancakes) in casual surroundings. It can get a little smoky, but it's a fun spot to eat. It's got sets from as little as ¥650 at lunch. It's about 20m west of the west end of Nishiki Market; look for the English sign in the window.

Karafuneya Coffee Honten CAFE ¥
(からふねや珈琲本店; Map p285; ☑254-8774; Kawaramachi Sanjō sagaru, Nakagyō-ku; simple meals ¥800-900; ⏱9am-1am; 🅼; ⓢTōzai Line to Kyoto Shiyakusho-mae Station, 🅡Keihan Line to Sanjō Station) Japan is famous for its plastic food models, but this place takes them to a whole new level – it's like some sort of futuristic dessert museum. We like the centrepiece of the display: the mother of all sundaes that goes for ¥10,000 to 18,000 and requires advance reservation to order. Lesser mortals can try the tasty matcha parfait for ¥780 or any of the cafe drinks and light meals.

Biotei VEGETARIAN ¥
(びお亭; Map p285; ☑255-0086; 2F M&I Bldg, 28 Umetada-chō, Sanjō-dōri, Higashinotōin Nishi iru, Nakagyō-ku; lunch from ¥840; ⏱lunch & dinner, closed Sun & Mon, dinner Thu & lunch Sat; 🅿🅼; ⓢTōzai & Karasuma Lines to Karasuma-Oike Station) Located diagonally across from the Nakagyō post office, this is a favourite of Kyoto vegetarians. Best for lunch, it serves a daily set meal of Japanese vegetarian food (the occasional bit of meat is offered as an option, but you'll be asked your preference). It's up the metal spiral steps. Closed on national holidays.

Café Bibliotec HELLO! CAFE ¥
(カフェビブリオティックハロー！; Map p287; ☑231-8625; 650 Seimei-chō, Yanaginobanba higashi iru, Nijō, Nakagyō-ku; meals from ¥850, coffee

¥450; 11.30am-midnight; ; S Tōzai Line to Kyoto Shiyakusho-mae Station) Like its name suggests, books line the walls of this cool cafe located in a converted *machiya*. You can get the usual range of coffee and tea here, as well as light cafe lunches. Overall, this may be our favourite cafe in Kyoto, and it's worth the walk from the centre of town. Look for the plants out front.

Honke Tagoto
NOODLES ¥

(本家田每; Map p285; 221-3030; 12 Ishibashi-chō, Sanjō-dōri, Kawaramachi Nishi iru, Nakagyō-ku; noodle dishes from ¥840; 11am-9pm; ; S Tōzai Line to Kyoto Shiyakusho-mae Station) One of Kyoto's oldest *soba* restaurants makes a good break for those who have overdosed on *rāmen*. It's in the Sanjō covered arcade and you can see inside to the tables.

Rāmen Kairikiya
RĀMEN ¥

(ラーメン魁力屋; Map p285; 251-0303; 1F Hijikata Bldg, 435-2 Ebisu-chō, Kawaramachi-dōri, Sanjō agaru, Nakagyō-ku; rāmen from ¥600; 11am-3am; ; S Tōzai Line to Kyoto Shiyakusho-mae Station) Not far from the Sanjō-Kawaramachi intersection, this popular *rāmen* specialist welcomes foreigners with friendly staff. It's got several types of *rāmen* to choose from and tasty sets that include things such as fried rice, fried chicken or *gyōza*, all for about ¥900. It's pretty easy to spot: look for the red and white sign.

Park Café
CAFE ¥

(パークカフェ; Map p285; 211-8954; 1F Gion Bldg, 340-1 Aneyakō-ji kado, Gokomachi-dōri, Nakagyō-ku; drinks from ¥450; noon-11pm; S Tōzai Line to Kyoto Shiyakusho-mae Station) This hip little cafe always reminds us of a Melbourne coffeeshop. It's on the edge of the downtown shopping district and a convenient place to take a break.

Café Independants
CAFE ¥

(カフェ　アンデパンダン; Map p285; 255-4312; B1F 1928 Bldg, Sanjō Gokomachi kado, Nakagyō-ku; salads from ¥400, sandwiches from ¥800; 11.30am-midnight; S Tōzai Line to Kyoto Shiyakusho-mae Station) Located beneath a gallery, this cool subterranean cafe offers a range of light meals in a bohemian atmosphere. A lot of the food offerings are laid out on display for you to choose from – with the emphasis on healthy sandwiches and salads. Take the stairs on your left before the gallery.

Ootoya
SHOKUDŌ ¥

(大戸屋; Map p285; 255-4811; 2F Goshoame Bldg, Sanjō-dōri, Kawaramachi higashi iru, Nakagyō-ku; meals from ¥600; 11am-11pm; S Tōzai Line to Kyoto Shiyakusho-mae Station, Keihan Line to Sanjō Station) Ootoya is a clean, modern Japanese restaurant that serves a range of standard Japanese dishes at bargain-basement prices. It's popular with Kyoto students and young office workers. The large picture menu makes ordering a breeze. Look for the English sign just west of Ganko Sushi.

Shizenha Restaurant Obanzai
VEGETARIAN ¥

(自然派レストランおばんざい; Map p285; 223-6623; 199 Shimomyōkaku-ji-chō, Koromonotana-dōri, Oike agaru, Nakagyō-ku; lunch/dinner ¥840/2100; 11am-2pm & 5-9pm, closed dinner Wed; ; S Tōzai & Karasuma Lines to Karasuma-Oike Station) A little out of the way but good value, Obanzai serves a buffet-style lunch/dinner of mostly organic vegetarian food. It's northwest of the Karasuma-Oike crossing, set back from the street a bit. Lunch on weekends is ¥1050.

Musashi Sushi
SUSHI ¥

(寿しのむさし; Map p285; 222-0634; Kawaramachi-dōri, Sanjō agaru, Nakagyō-ku; all plates ¥137; 11am-10pm; ; S Tōzai Line to Kyoto Shiyakusho-mae Station, Keihan Line to Sanjō Station) This is the place to go to try *kaiten-zushi* (conveyor-belt sushi). Sure, it's not the best sushi in the world, but it's cheap, easy and fun. Look for the mini sushi conveyor belt in the window. It's just outside the entrance to the Sanjō covered arcade.

A-Bar
IZAKAYA ¥

(居酒屋A（あ）; Map p285; 213-2129; 2F Reiho Bldg, Nishikiyamachi-dōri, Shijō agaru, Nakagyō-ku; dishes ¥160-680; 6pm-1am; ; Keihan Line to Shijō Station, Hankyū Line to Kawaramachi Station) This student *izakaya* (pub-eatery) with a log-cabin interior is popular with expats and Japanese students for a raucous night out. The food is fairly typical *izakaya* fare, with plenty of fried items and some decent salads. It's a little tough to find – look for the small black-and-white sign at the top of a flight of steps.

Hinaka
KAISEKI ¥¥

(旬肴ひなか; Map p285; 231-5525; Asahi Pontochō Bldg. 1F, Nabeya-chō 214-1, Nakagyō-ku; dinner from around ¥3000; 5-11pm, closed Mon; ; Hankyū Line to Kawaramachi Station) Hinaka is a small locals' favourite on Ponto-chō, one of Kyoto's most atmospheric walkways. The menu includes Kyoto specialities such as tofu and *yuba* (tofu skim), as well as seasonal vegetables and fish. The chef hails from one of Kyoto's best-known restaurants. Diners sit at the counter or at tables with sunken floors (no knee strain here).

Kane-yo EEL (UNAGI) ¥¥
(かねよ; Map p285; 221-0669; 456 Matsugaechō, Rokkaku, Shinkyōgoku, Nakagyō-ku; unagi over rice from ¥1200; 11.30am-8.30pm; ; Tōzai Line to Kyoto Shiyakusho-mae Station) This is a good place to try *unagi* (eel). You can sit downstairs with a nice view of the waterfall or upstairs on the tatami. The *kane-yo donburi* set (¥1200) is good value; it's served until 2pm. Look for the barrels of live eels outside and the wooden facade.

Ganko Zushi SUSHI ¥¥
(がんこ寿司; Map p285; 255-1128; 101 Nakajima-chō, Sanjō-dōri, Kawaramachi Higashi iru, Nakagyō-ku; lunch ¥1000-2000, dinner 3000; 11am-11pm; ; Tōzai Line to Kyoto Shiyakusho-mae Station or Sanjō Keihan Station, Keihan Line to Sanjō Station) Near Sanjō-ōhashi bridge, this is a good place for sushi or just about anything else. There are plenty of sets to choose from, but we recommend ordering sushi à la carte. There's a full English menu, the kitchen is fast and they are used to foreigners. Look for the large display of plastic food models in the window.

Merry Island Café INTERNATIONAL ¥¥
(メリーアイランド カフェ; Map p285; 213-0214; Kiyamachi-dōri, Oike agaru, Nakagyō-ku; lunch from ¥1050; 11.30am-11pm; ; Tōzai Line to Kyoto Shiyakusho-mae Station) This popular lunch/dinner restaurant strives to create the atmosphere of a tropical resort. The menu is *mukokuseki* (without nationality) and most of what is on offer is tasty. It does a good risotto and occasionally has a nice piece of Japanese steak. In warm weather the front doors are opened and the place becomes a sidewalk cafe.

Tsukiji Sushisei SUSHI ¥¥
(築地寿司清; Map p285; 252-1537; Takakura-dōri, Nishikikōji sagaru, Obiya-chō 581, Nakagyō; sushi sets ¥1260-3150; 11:30am-3pm & 5-10pm Mon-Fri; 11:30am-10pm Sat, Sun & holidays; ; Karasuma Line to Shijō Station) On the basement floor, opposite Daimaru, this simple sushi restaurant serves excellent sushi at the counter or tables. You can order a set or just point at what looks good. You can see inside the restaurant from street level, so it should be easy to spot.

Mishima-tei JAPANESE ¥¥
(三嶋亭; Map p285; 221-0003; 405 Sakurano-chō, Teramachi-dōri, Sanjō sagaru, Nakagyō-ku; sukiyaki lunch/dinner from ¥8700/12,700; 11.30am-10pm, closed Wed; ; Tōzai Line to Kyoto Shiyakusho-mae Station) In the Sanjō covered arcade, this is a good place to sample sukiyaki. There's even a discount for foreign travellers! Special lunch ¥4505 until 3pm.

Tagoto Honten KAISEKI ¥¥
(田ごと本店; Map p285; 221-1811; 34 Otabi-chō, Shijō dōri, Kawaramachi Nishiiru, Nakagyō-ku; lunch/dinner from ¥1600/3700; 11am-3pm & 4.30-9pm; ; Keihan Line to Shijō Station, Hankyū Line to Kawaramachi Station) Across the street from Takashimaya department store, this long-standing Kyoto restaurant serves approachable *kaiseki* fare in a variety of rooms, both private and common. The *kiku* set includes some sashimi, a bit of tempura and a variety of other nibblies. *Kaiseki* dinner courses start at ¥6300 and you must reserve in advance.

This is a good spot for those who want a civilised meal downtown in relaxing surroundings. At present, there's no English sign. Look for pictures of the food and the stone and wooden front; the entrance is down the narrow alley.

Kiyamachi Sakuragawa KAISEKI ¥¥¥
(木屋町 櫻川; Map p285; 255-4477; Kiyamachi-dōri, Nijō sagaru, Kamikoriki-chō 491 1F, Nakagyō-ku; lunch/dinner sets from ¥5000/10,000; 11.30am-2pm & 5-9pm, closed Sun; Tōzai Line to Kyoto Shiyakusho-mae Station) This elegant restaurant, just north of downtown on Kiyamachi-dōri, is an excellent place to try *kaiseki* (Japanese haute cuisine). The modest but fully satisfying food is beautifully presented and it's a joy to watch the chefs in action. Reservations are strongly recommended and smart casual clothes are the way to go.

★**Yoshikawa** TEMPURA ¥¥¥
(吉川; Map p285; 221-5544; Oike sagaru, Tominokōji, Nakagyō-ku; lunch ¥3000-25,000, dinner ¥6000-25,000; 11am-2pm & 5-8.30pm; ; Tōzai & Karasuma Lines to Karasuma-Oike Station or Kyoto Shiyakusho-mae Station) This is the place to go for delectable tempura. It offers table seating, but it's much more interesting to sit and eat around the small counter and observe the chefs at work. It's near Oike-dōri in a fine traditional Japanese-style building. Reservation required for tatami room; counter and table seating unavailable on Sunday.

✕ Southern Higashiyama

Kasagi-ya TEAHOUSE ¥
(かさぎ屋; Map p290; ☎ 561-9562; 349 Masuya chō, Kōdai-ji, Higashiyama-ku; ⏰ 11am-6pm, closed Tue; 📷; 🚌 Kyoto City Bus 206 to Higashiyama-Yasui stop) At Kasagi-ya, on the Ninen-zaka slope near Kiyomizu-dera, this funky old wooden shop has atmosphere to boot and friendly staff. It's a great place for a cup of green tea and a Japanese sweet to power you through a day of sightseeing in Higashiyama. *Matcha* tea with a sweet costs ¥700.

It's hard to spot; you may have to ask someone in the area to point it out.

Kagizen Yoshifusa TEAHOUSE ¥
(鍵善良房; Map p290; ☎ 561-1818; 264 Gion machi Kita gawa, Higashiyama-ku; kuzukiri ¥900; ⏰ 9.30am-6pm, closed Mon; 📷; 🚇 Hankyū Line to Kawaramachi Station, 🚇 Keihan Line to Gion-Shijō Station) One of Kyoto's oldest and best-known *okashi-ya* (sweet shops) sells a variety of traditional sweets and has a peaceful tearoom in back where you can sample cold *kuzukiri* (transparent arrowroot noodles), served with a *kuro-mitsu* (sweet black sugar) dipping sauce. It's in a traditional *machiya* up a flight of stone steps.

Santōka RĀMEN ¥
(山頭火; Map p290; ☎ 532-1335; Sanjō kudaru Higashi gawa, Higashiyama-ku; rāmen from ¥790; ⏰ 11am-2am Mon-Sat, 11am-midnight Sun & national holidays; 📷; 🚇 Keihan Line to Sanjō Station, 🚇 Tōzai Line to Sanjō-Keihan Station) The young chefs at this sleek restaurant dish out some seriously good Hokkaidō-style *rāmen*. You will be given a choice of three kinds of soup when you order: *shio* (salt), *shōyu* or miso – we highly recommend you go for the miso soup.

For something decadent, try the *tokusen toroniku rāmen*, which is made from pork cheeks, of which only 200g can be obtained from one animal. The pork will come on a separate plate from the *rāmen* – just shovel it all into your bowl. The restaurant is located on the east side and ground floor of the new Kyōen restaurant and shopping complex.

Asuka SHOKUDŌ ¥
(明日香; Map p290; ☎ 751-9809; 144 Nishi-machi, Sanjō-dōri, Jingū-michi Nishi iru, Higashiyama-ku; meals from ¥850; ⏰ 11am-10pm, closed Mon; 📷; 🚇 Tōzai Line to Higashiyama Station) With an English menu, and a staff of old Kyoto *mama-sans* at home with foreign customers, this is a great place for a cheap lunch or dinner while sightseeing in the Higashiyama area. The tempura *moriawase* (assorted tempura set) is a big pile of tempura for only ¥1000. Look for the red lantern and the pictures of the set meals.

Hisago NOODLES ¥
(ひさご; Map p290; ☎ 561-2109; 484 Shimokawara-chō, Higashiyama-ku; meals from ¥900; ⏰ 11.30am-7.30pm, closed Mon; 📷; 🚌 Kyoto City Bus 206 to Higashiyama-Yasui stop) If you need a quick meal while in the main southern Higashiyama sightseeing district, this simple noodle and rice restaurant is a good bet. It's within easy walking distance of Kiyomizu-dera and Maruyama-kōen. *Oyako-donburi* (chicken and egg over rice; ¥980) is the speciality of the house.

There is no English sign; look for the traditional front and the small collection of food models on display. In the busy seasons, there's almost always a queue outside.

Omen Kodai-ji NOODLES ¥¥
(おめん　高台寺店; Map p290; ☎ 541-5007; Kodaiji-dōri, Shimokawara Higashi iru, Masuya-chō 358, Higashiyama-ku; noodles from ¥1100, set menu ¥2980; ⏰ 11:30am-8:30pm; 🚌 5-min walk from Higashiyama-Yasui bus stop) This branch of Kyoto's famed Omen noodle chain is the best place to stop while exploring the Southern Higashiyama district. It's in a remodelled Japanese building with a light, airy feeling. The signature udon noodles are delicious and there are many other à la carte offerings.

Shibazaki NOODLES ¥¥
(柴崎; Map p290; ☎ 525-3600; 4-190-3 Kiyomizu, Higashiyama-ku; soba from ¥1000; ⏰ 11am-6pm, closed Tue except national holidays; 📷; 🚌 Kyoto City Bus 206 to the Kiyomizu-michi stop, 🚇 Keihan Line to Kiyomizu-Gojō Station) For excellent *soba* noodles and well-presented tempura sets (among other things) in the vicinity of Kiyomizu-dera, try this comfortable and spacious restaurant. After your meal, head upstairs to check out the sublime collection of Japanese lacquerware – it's the best we've seen anywhere. Look for the low stone wall and the *noren* curtains hanging in the entryway.

Ryūmon CHINESE ¥¥
(龍門; Map p290; ☎ 752-8181; Kita gawa, Sanjō-dōri, Higashiōji Nishi iru, Higashiyama-ku; dinner set from ¥3000; ⏰ 5pm-5am; 🚇 Tōzai Line to Higashiyama Station or Sanjō-Keihan Station, 🚇 Keihan Line to Sanjō Station) The place looks like a total dive, but the food is reliable and authentic, as the

DEPARTMENT-STORE DINING

Yes, we know: the idea of dining in a department store sounds as appetising as dining in a gas station. However, Japanese department stores, especially those in large cities such as Tokyo and Kyoto, are loaded with good dining options. And, unlike many street-level shops, they're usually fairly comfortable with foreign diners (if there's any communication trouble, they can always call down to the bilingual ladies at the information counter).

On their basement floors, you'll find *depachika* (from the English word 'department' and the Japanese word *chika,* which means 'underground'). A good *depachika* is like an Aladdin's cave of gustatory delights that rivals the best gourmet shops in any Western city. Meanwhile, on their upper floors, you'll usually find a *resutoran-gai* ('restaurant city') that includes restaurants serving all the Japanese standards – sushi, noodles, *tonkatsu,* tempura – along with a few international restaurants, usually French, Italian and Chinese.

If you find yourself feeling peckish in downtown Kyoto, here are some good department dining options:

Takashimaya (Map p285; ☑ 221 8811; Shijō Tominokōji kado; ☉ 10am-8pm, restaurants 10am-10pm; ⑤ Kawaramachi Station, Hankyū Kyoto line) At the corner of Shijō and Kawaramachi streets, this elegant department store has an incredible food floor (on the B1 level) and the best department store *resutoran-gai* in the city (on the 7th floor).

Daimaru (Map p285; ☑ 211 8111; Tachiuri Nishi-machi 79, Shijō-dōri Takakura Nishi iru; ☉ 10am-8pm, restaurants 11am-9pm, closed Jan 1; ⑤ Shijō Station, Karasuma Line or Karasuma Station, Hankyū Kyoto Line) On the north side of Shijō, between Kawaramachi and Karasuma streets, Daimaru has a food floor that rivals the one at Takashimaya (note the awesome Japanese sweet section) and a solid *resutoran-gai* on the 8th floor.

Fujii Daimaru (Map p285; ☑ 221 8181; Shijō-dōri Teramachi; ☉ 10:30am to 8pm; ⑤ Kawaramachi Station, Hankyū Line) On the south side of the Shijō-Teramachi intersection, the Tavelt food floor on the B1 level of this department store is the cheapest of the three. It usually has a great selection of take-away sushi/sashimi and fruit.

crowds of Chinese diners will attest. There's no English menu, but there is a picture menu and some of the waiters can speak English.

Decor is strictly Chinese kitsch, with the exception of the deer head over the cash register – we're still trying to figure that one out.

✖ **Northern Higashiyama**

Goya
OKINAWAN ¥

(ゴーヤ; Map p296; ☑ 752-1158; 114-6 Nishida-chō, Jōdo-ji, Sakyō-ku; ☉ 11.30am-4pm & 5.30-11pm, closed Wed; ⌨ Kyoto City Bus 5 to Ginkakuji-michi stop) We love this Okinawan-themed restaurant for its tasty food, stylish interior and comfortable upstairs seating. It's the perfect place for lunch while exploring northern Higashiyama and it's just a short walk from Ginkaku-ji. At lunch it serves simple things like taco rice (¥880) and *gōya champurū* (bitter melon stir-fry; ¥680).

Dinners are more à la carte affairs with a wide range of *izakaya* fare, much of it with an Okinawan twist.

Au Temps Perdu
FRENCH ¥

(オ・タン・ペルデュ; Map p296; ☑ 762-1299; 64 Okazaki Enshōji-chō, Higashiyama-ku; food from ¥500; ☉ closed Mon; ⓓ; ⑤ Tōzai Subway Line to Higashiyama Station) Overlooking the Shirakawa Canal, this tiny indoor/outdoor French-style cafe offers some of the best people-watching in Northern Higashiyama, along with great bread, quiche and pastries. It's easy to pull a baby stroller up to these outdoor tables.

Karako
RĀMEN ¥

(唐子; Map p296; ☑ 752-8234; 12-3 Tokusei-chō, Okazaki, Sakyō-ku; rāmen from ¥630; ☉ 11.30am-2pm & 5pm-midnight, closed Tue; ⓓ; ⌨ Kyoto City Bus 206 to Higashiyama-Nijō stop) This is our favourite *rāmen* restaurant in Kyoto. While it's not much on atmosphere, Karako has excellent *rāmen* – the soup is thick and rich and the *chāshū* (pork slices) melt in your mouth. We recommend the *kotteri* (thick soup) *rāmen*. Look for the red lantern outside.

Falafel Garden
ISRAELI ¥

(ファラフェルガーデン; Map p296; ☑712 1856; 3-16 Tanaka Shimoyanagi-chō, Sakyō-ku; falafel from ¥380; ⊙11am-9.30pm, closed Wed; ⬛; ◨Keihan Line to exit 7, Demachiyanagi Station) Close to the Keihan and Eizan lines' Demachiyanagi Station, this funky Israeli-run place has excellent falafel and a range of other dishes, as well as offering a set menu (¥1150). We like the style of the open-plan converted Japanese house and the minigarden out the back, but the main draw is those tasty falafels!

Hinode Udon
NOODLES ¥

(日の出うどん; Map p296; ☑751-9251; 36 Kitanobō-chō, Nanzenji, Sakyō-ku; noodle dishes from ¥450; ⊙11am-5pm, closed Sun except for Apr & Nov; ⬛; ◨Kyoto City Bus 5 to the Eikandō-michi stop) Filling noodle and rice dishes are served at this pleasant little shop. Plain *udon* (thick white noodles) here is only ¥450, but we recommend you spring for the *nabeyaki udon* (pot-baked *udon* in broth) for between ¥850 and ¥1000. This is a good spot for lunch when temple-hopping near Ginkaku-ji or Nanzen-ji.

Cafe Proverbs 15:17
VEGETARIAN ¥

(カフェプロバーブズ15:17; Map p296; ☑707-6856; Domus Hyakumanben 3F, 28-20 Tanakamonzen-chō, Sakyō-ku; drinks/food from ¥300/450; ⊙11.45am-10pm, to 6pm Wed, closed Mon; ⬛⬛⬛; ◨Kyoto Bus 206 to the Hyakumamben stop) ⬛ This is a pleasant spot for a cuppa or a light vegetarian meal. Lunch sets include green curry, sandwiches and Japanese fare. It's on the 3rd floor but there's a small sign on street level.

Earth Kitchen Company
BENTŌ ¥

(アースキッチンカンパニー; Map p296; ☑771-1897; 9-7 Higashi Maruta-chō, Kawabata, Marutamachi, Sakyō-ku; lunch ¥735; ⊙10.30am-6.30pm Mon-Fri; ⬛; ◨Keihan Line to Marutamachi Station) ⬛ Located on Marutamachi-dōri near the Kamo-gawa, this is a tiny spot that seats just two people but does a bustling business serving tasty takeaway lunch. If you fancy a picnic lunch for your temple-hopping, this is the place.

★Omen
NOODLES ¥¥

(おめん; Map p296; ☑771-8994; 74 Jōdo-ji Ishibashi-chō, Sakyō-ku; noodles from ¥1100; ⊙11am-9pm; ⬛; ◨Kyoto City Bus 5 to Ginkakuji-michi stop) This noodle shop is named after the thick, white noodles served in a hot broth with a selection of seven fresh vegetables. Just say '*omen*' and you'll be given your choice of hot or cold

noodles, a bowl of soup to dip them in and a plate of vegetables (you put these into the soup along with some sesame seeds).

It's a great bowl of noodles but don't stop there: the à la carte menu is also fantastic – ranging from excellent tempura to healthy vegetable dishes. It's about five minutes' walk from Ginkaku-ji in a traditional Japanese house with a lantern outside. Note that there's often a line during tourist high season.

Grotto
KAISEKI ¥¥

(ぐろっと; Map p296; ☑771-0606; 114 Jōdo-ji Nishida-chō, Sakyō-ku; dinner course ¥4750; ⊙6pm-midnight, closed Sun; ⬛; ◨Kyoto City Bus 5 to Ginkakuji-michi stop) This stylish little place along Imadegawa-dōri serves a tasty dinner set menu that will take you through the major tastes in Japanese gastronomy. The fare is simple counter *kaiseki* or *kappō* (a series of little dishes). It's a great way to spend two or three hours with someone special. Reservations are recommended. The master speaks English.

✕ Arashiyama & Sagano Area, Northwest Kyoto

Komichi
CAFE ¥

(こみち; Map p302; ☑872-5313; 23 Ōjōin-chō, Nison-in Monzen, Saga, Ukyō-ku; matcha ¥650; ⊙10am-5pm, closed Wed; ◨Kyoto City Bus 28 from Kyoto Station to Arashiyama-Tenryuji-mae stop) This friendly little teahouse is perfectly located along the Arashiyama tourist trail. In addition to hot and cold tea/coffee drinks, it serves *uji kintoki* (sweet *matcha* over shaved ice, sweetened milk and sweet beans – sort of a Japanese Italian ice) in summer and a variety of light noodle dishes year-round. The picture menu helps with ordering.

The sign is green and black on a white background.

Yoshida-ya
SHOKUDŌ ¥

(よしだや; Map p302; ☑861-0213; 20-24 Tsukurimichi-chō, Saga Tenryū-ji, Ukyō-ku; lunch from ¥750; ⊙10.30am-4pm, closed Wed; ◨Kyoto City Bus 28 from Kyoto Station to Arashiyama-Tenryuji-mae stop) This quaint and friendly little *teishoku-ya* (set-meal restaurant) is the perfect place to grab a simple lunch while in Arashiyama. All the standard *teishoku* favourites are on offer, including things like *oyako-donburi* for ¥850. You can also cool off here with a refreshing *uji kintoki* (¥650). It's the first place south of the station and it's got a rustic front.

Arashiyama Yoshimura　　NOODLES ¥¥
(嵐山よしむら; Map p302; ☑ 863-5700; Togetsu-
kyō kita, Ukyō-ku; soba dishes from ¥1050, set meals
from ¥1575; ⏱ 11am-5pm; 🅿; 🚌 Kyoto City Bus
28 from Kyoto Station to Arashiyama-Tenryuji-mae
stop) For a tasty bowl of *soba* noodles and
a million-dollar view over the Arashiyama
mountains and the Togetsu-kyō bridge, head
to this extremely popular eatery just north of
the famous bridge, overlooking the Katsura-
gawa. There's an English menu but no English sign; look for the big glass windows and
the stone wall.

Shigetsu　　VEGETARIAN, JAPANESE ¥¥
(篩月; Map p302; ☑ 882-9725; 68 Susukinobaba-
machi, Saga Tenryū-ji, Ukyō-ku; lunch sets incl
temple entry ¥3500, ¥5500 & ¥7500; ⏱ 11am-
2pm; 🚌 Kyoto City Bus 59 from Sanjō-Keihan to
the Ryoanji-mae stop) To sample *shōjin-ryōri*
(Buddhist vegetarian cuisine) try Shigetsu
in the precinct of Tenryū-ji. It has beautiful
garden views.

🍴 **Ōhara**

Seryō-Jaya　　SHOKUDŌ ¥¥
(芹生茶屋; ☑ 744-2301; Ōhara Sanzenin hotori,
Sakyō-ku; lunch sets from ¥2000; ⏱ 11am-5pm;
🚌 Kyoto Bus 17 or 18 from Kyoto Station to Ōhara
stop) Just by the entry gate to Sanzen-in,
Seryō-jaya serves tasty *soba* noodles and
other fare. There is outdoor seating in the
warmer months. Look for the food models
(which will also help with ordering).

🍴 **Kurama**

Aburaya-Shokudō　　SHOKUDŌ ¥
(鞍馬　油屋食堂; Map p307; ☑ 741-2009; 252
Honmachi, Kurama, Sakyō-ku; udon & soba from
¥600; ⏱ 9.30am-4.30pm; 🚃 Eiden Eizan Line from
Demachiyanagi Station to Kurama Station) Just
down the steps from Kurama-dera's main
gate, this classic old-style *shokudō* (all-round
restaurant) reminds us of what Japan was
like before it got rich. The *sansai teishoku*
(¥1750) is a delightful selection of vegetables,
rice and *soba* topped with grated yam.

★ **Yōshūji**　　VEGETARIAN ¥¥
(雍州路; Map p307; ☑ 741-2848; 1074 Honmachi,
Kurama, Sakyō-ku; meals from ¥1050; ⏱ 10am-
6pm, closed Tue; 🅿; 🚃 Eiden Eizan Line from
Demachiyanagi Station to Kurama Station) Yōshūji
serves superb *shōjin-ryōri* in a delightful
old Japanese farmhouse with an *irori* (open

hearth). The house special, a sumptuous
selection of vegetarian dishes served in red
lacquered bowls, is called *kurama-yama
shōjin zen* (¥2600). Or if you just feel like
a quick bite, try the *uzu-soba* (*soba* topped
with mountain vegetables).

You'll find it halfway up the steps leading
to the main gate of Kurama-dera; look for
the orange lanterns out the front.

🍴 **Kibune**

Visitors to Kibune from June to September
should not miss the chance to cool down by
dining at one of the picturesque restaurants
beside the Kibune-gawa. Meals are served
here on platforms (known as *kawa-doko*)
suspended over the river, as cool water flows
just underneath. Most of the restaurants offer some kind of lunch special for around
¥3000. For a full *kaiseki* dinner spread
(¥5000 to ¥10,000) have a Japanese speaker
call to reserve in advance. Be warned that
restaurants in Kibune have been known to
turn away solo diners.

Kibune Club　　CAFE ¥
(貴船倶楽部; Map p307; ☑ 741-3039; 76
Kibune-chō, Kurama, Sakyō-ku; coffee from ¥500;
⏱ 11.30am-6pm summer, 11.30am-5pm winter,
11.30am-7pm during foliage light-up in Nov; 🅿;
🚃 Eiden Eizan Line from Demachiyanagi Station
to Kibune-guchi Station) The exposed wooden
beams and open, airy feel of this rustic cafe
make it a great spot to stop for a cuppa
while exploring Kibune. In the winter, staff
sometimes crank up the wood stove, which
makes the place rather cosy. It's easy to spot.

Hirobun　　JAPANESE ¥¥
(ひろ文; Map p307; ☑ 741-2147; 87 Kibune-chō,
Kurama, Sakyō-ku; noodles served until 4pm from
¥600, kaiseki courses from ¥8400; ⏱ 11am-9pm;
🚃 Eiden Eizan line from Demachiyanagi Station
to Kibune-guchi Station) This is a good place
to sample riverside or 'above-river' dining
in Kibune. There's a friendly crew of ladies
here who run the show and the food is quite
good. Note that it does not accept solo diners for *kaiseki* courses (but you can have
noodles). Look for the black-and-white sign
and the lantern. Reserve for dinner.

🍷 **Drinking**

Kyoto has a great variety of bars, clubs and
izakayas, all of which are good places to
meet Japanese folks. And if you happen to
be in Kyoto in the summer, many hotels and

department stores operate rooftop beer gardens with all-you-can-eat-and-drink deals and good views of the city.

In addition to the places listed here, all the top-end hotels listed in the Sleeping section have at least one good bar on their premises. We particularly like the **Tōzan** (Map p290; Sanjūsangendō-mawari, Hyatt Regency Kyoto; 🚇 Keihan Line to Shichijō Station) at the Hyatt.

McLoughlin's Irish Bar & Restaurant BAR
(マクラクランズ・アイリッシュバー＆レストラン; Map p285; 🖉 212-6339; 8F The Empire Bldg, Kiyamachi, Sanjō-agaru, Nakagyō-ku; ⏰ 6pm-midnight, later on Fri & Sat, closed Tue; 🕿; 🚇 Tōzai Line to Kyoto Shiyakusho-mae Station) With a fine view over the city, free wi-fi and good food, this bar is a nice place to spend an evening in Kyoto. There's a great selection of local and international craft beers. It's also a good place to meet local expats and Japanese. It hosts music events as well.

Gael Irish Pub BAR
(ザガエルアイリッシュパップ; Map p290; 🖉 525-0680; 2F Ôtô Bldg, Nijûikken-chō, Yamatoōji-dōri agaru, Shijō, Higashiyama-ku; drinks from ¥500; ⏰ 5pm-1am, later Thu-Sun; 🚇 Keihan Line to Gion-Shijō Station) A cosy little Irish bar on the doorstep of Gion. It offers good food, excellent beer and friendly staff, as well as occasional live music. It's up a flight of steps.

Sama Sama BAR
(サマサマ; Map p285; 🖉 241-4100; 532 Kamiōsaka-chō, Kiyamachi, Sanjō agaru, , Nakagyō-ku; drinks ¥600-700; ⏰ 8pm-3am, closed Thu; 🚇 Tōzai Line to Kyoto Shiyakusho-mae Station) This place seems like a very comfortable cave somewhere near the Mediterranean. Scoot up to the counter or make yourself at home on the cushions on the floor and enjoy a wide variety of drinks, some of them Indonesian (where the owner hails from). It's down an alley just north of Sanjō; the alley has a sign for Sukiyaki Komai Tei.

Kisui IZAKAYA
(器粹; Map p290; 🖉 585-6639; 1F 2-239 Miyagawa-suji, Higashiyama-ku; drinks from ¥600; ⏰ 6pm-midnight, closed Sun; 🚇 Keihan Line to Gion-Shijō Station) This little one-counter *izakaya* at the north end of the Miyagawa geisha district is a good place to knock a few back. The cheerful owner is sure to make you welcome and you can order food from the upstairs restaurant to eat. It's on the 1st floor, opposite a park, on the corner. There is no English sign.

Gion Finlandia Bar BAR
(ぎをん　フィンランディアバー; Map p290; 🖉 541-3482; Gion-machi minamigawa (Hanamikōji Shijō sagaru hitosujime Nishi iru minamigawa), Higashiyama-ku; drinks around ¥900; ⏰ 6pm-3am; 🚇 Keihan Line to Gion-Shijō Station) This stylish Gion bar in an old geisha house is a great place for a civilised drink in Southern Higashiyama. The 1st floor is decorated with Finnish touches, while the upstairs retains a Japanese feeling, with sunken floors and tatami mats. There's a wide selection of vodka on offer here. The cover charge is ¥500.

Yoramu BAR
(ヨラム; Map p285; 🖉 213-1512; 35-1 Matsuya-chō, Nijō-dōri, Higashinotoin, higashi-iru, Nakagyō-ku; sake tasting sets from ¥1200; ⏰ 6pm-midnight Wed-Sat; 🚇 Karasuma or Tōzai Lines to Karasuma-Oike Station) Named for Yoramu, the Israeli sake expert who runs the place, this is highly recommended for anyone who wants an education in sake. It's very small and can only accommodate a handful of people. By day, it's a *soba* restaurant.

Ing Bar BAR
(イング; Map p285; 🖉 255-5087; 2F Royal Building, 288 Minamikurayama-chō, Nishikiyamachi-dōri, Takoyakushi-agaru, Nakagyō-ku; drinks from ¥500; ⏰ 6pm-2am Mon-Thu, to 5am Fri-Sun; 🚇 Hankyū Line to Kawaramachi Station) This little joint is the place for cheap bar snacks, drinks and good music. It's on the 2nd floor of the Royal building.

Kick Up BAR
(キックアップ; Map p296; 🖉 761-5604; Higashikomonoza-chō 331, Higashiyama-ku; drinks from ¥600, food from ¥500; ⏰ 7pm-midnight, closed Wed; 🚇 Tōzai Line to Keage Station) Located just across the street from Keage Station on the Tōzai subway line (take exit No 1), this wonderful bar attracts a regular crowd of Kyoto expats, local Japanese and guests from nearby hotels. It's relaxing and friendly.

Ike Tsuru JUICE BAR
(池鶴; Map p285; 🖉 221-3368; Nishikikōji-dōri, Yanaginobanba-Higashi-iru, Nakagyō-ku; juice ¥450; ⏰ 9am-6.30pm, closed Wed; 🕿; 🚇 Karasuma Line to Shijō Station, 🚇 Hankyū Line to Karasuma Station) We love this fruit juice specialist in Nishiki Market. In addition to all the usual favourites, it sometimes has durian on hand and can whip up a very unusual durian juice. Look for the fruit on display – it's on the south side of the market, a little east of Yanaginobanba-dōri.

☆ Entertainment

Most of Kyoto's cultural entertainment is of an occasional nature, and you'll need to check with the TIC or *Kansai Scene* to find out whether anything interesting coincides with your visit.

Clubs

World Peace Love　　　　NIGHTCLUB
(ワールドピースラブ; Map p285; ☎213-4119; 97 Shinmachi Shijō-agaru, Shimogyō-ku; admission ¥2500-3000; ⊗8pm-1am Wed & Fri-Sun; ℝHankyū Line to Kawaramachi Station) World is Kyoto's biggest club and it naturally hosts some of the biggest events. It has two floors, a dance floor and lockers where you can leave your stuff while you dance the night away. Events include everything from deep soul to reggae to techno to salsa. Drinks from ¥500.

Metro　　　　NIGHTCLUB
(メトロ; Map p296; ☎752-4765; BF Ebisu Bldg, Marutamachi sagaru, Kawabata, Sakyō-ku; admission ¥500-3000; ⊗9pm-3am; ℝKeihan Line to Marutamachi Station) This is one of the most popular and vibrant clubs in town. It holds a variety of themed events and occasional live bands or international DJ events. It's inside exit 2 of the Keihan Marutamachi Station.

Geisha Dances

In the spring and autumn, Kyoto's geisha (or, properly speaking, *geiko* and *maiko*) perform fantastic dances, usually on seasonal themes. For a small additional fee, you can participate in a brief tea ceremony before the show. We *highly* recommend seeing one of these dances if you are in town when they are being held. Ask at the tourist information centre or at your lodgings for help with ticket purchase. Tour companies can also help with tickets.

★ Gion Odori　　　　DANCE
(祇園をどり; ☎561-0224; Gion, Higashiyama-ku; admission/with tea ¥3500/4000; ⊗shows 1.30pm & 4pm) Held at **Gion Kaikan Theatre** (祇園会館; Map p290; Gion, Higashiyama-ku) near Yasaka-jinja; 1 to 10 November.

★ Miyako Odori　　　　DANCE
(都をどり; ☎561-1115; Gion-chō South, Higashiyama-ku; seat reserved/nonreserved/reserved with tea ¥4000/2000/4500; ⊗shows 12.30pm, 2pm, 3.30pm & 4.50pm) At **Gion Kōbu Kaburen-jō Theatre** (祇園甲部歌舞練場; Map p290; Gion-chō South, Higashiyama-ku), near Gion Corner; throughout April.

Kamogawa Odori　　　　DANCE
(鴨川をどり; ☎221-2025; Ponto-chō, Sanjō sagaru, Nakagyō-ku; normal/special seat/special seat with tea ¥2000/4000/4500; ⊗shows 12.30pm, 2.20pm & 4.10pm) Held at **Ponto-chō Kaburen-jō Theatre** (Map p285; Ponto-chō, Sanjō sagaru, Nakagyō-ku), 1 to 24 May.

Kitano Odori　　　　DANCE
(北野をどり; ☎461-0148; Imadegawa-dōri, Nishi-honmatsu nishi iru, Kamigyō-ku; admission/with tea ¥4000/4500; ⊗shows 1.30pm & 4pm) At **Kamishichiken Kaburen-jō Theatre** (上七軒歌舞練場; Map p287; Imadegawa-dōri, Nishihonmatsu nishi iru, Kamigyō-ku), 25 March to 7 April.

Kyō Odori　　　　DANCE
(京をどり; Map p290; ☎561-1151; Kawabata-dōri, Shijō sagaru; non-reserved/reserved seat ¥2000/4000, plus ¥500 with tea) ⊗shows 12.30pm, 2.30pm & 4.30pm) Held at **Miyagawa-chō Kaburen-jō Theatre** (宮川町歌舞練場), east of the Kamo-gawa between Shijō-dōri and Gojō-dōri; from the first Saturday to the third Sunday in April.

Geisha Entertainment

If you want to see geisha perform and actually speak with them, one of the best ways is at Gion Hatanaka (p314), a Gion ryokan that offers the **Kyoto Cuisine & Maiko Evening** (Map p290; ☎541-5315; www.kyoto-maiko.jp; 505 Minamigawa, Gion-machi, Yasaka Jinja Minamimonmae; per person ¥18,000; ⊗6-8pm, every Mon, Wed, Fri & Sat). Here, you can enjoy elegant Kyoto *kaiseki* food while being entertained by real Kyoto *geiko* and *maiko*.

Kabuki

★ Minami-za Theatre　　　　THEATRE
(南座; Map p285; ☎561-0160; Shijō-Ōhashi, Higashiyama-ku; performances ¥4200-27,000; ℝKeihan Line to Gion-Shijō Station) This grand theatre in Gion is the oldest kabuki venue in Japan and it's a great place to get acquainted with this most beguiling of Japanese theatrical arts. The major event of the year is the Kao-mise Festival (1 to 26 December), which features Japan's finest kabuki actors. Other performances take place on an irregular basis.

Ask at the tourist information centre or at your lodgings for help with ticket purchase. Tour companies can also help with tickets.

Karaoke

**Jumbo Karaoke Hiroba
Kawaramachi Branch**　　　　KARAOKE
(ジャンボカラオケ広場; Map p290; ☎231-6777; 29-1 Ishibashi-chō, Sanjō dōri, Kawaramachi Ni-

shi iru, Nakagyō-ku; per person per 30min before/after 7pm from ¥150/350; ⏱11am-5am; ⑤Tōzai Line to Kyoto Shiyakusho-mae Station) If you feel like giving the vocal chords a workout with the Japanese national pastime (karaoke), then head to this popular 'karaoke box' in the Sanjō shopping arcade. It has enough English songs to keep foreign guests entertained.

Musical Performances

Musical performances featuring the koto, *shamisen* and *shakuhachi* are held in Kyoto on an irregular basis. Traditional performances of *bugaku* (court music and dance) are often held at Kyoto shrines during festival periods. Occasionally contemporary butoh dance is also performed in Kyoto. Check with the tourist information centre to see if any performances are scheduled to be held while you are visiting the city.

Nō

Kanze Kaikan Nō Theatre THEATRE
(観世会館; Map p290; ☎771-6114; 44 Okazaki Enshoji-chō, Sakyō-ku; ⏱9am-5pm Tue-Sun; ⑤Tōzai Line to Higashiyama Station) This is the main theatre for performances of nō. *Takigi nō* is a picturesque form of nō performed in the light of blazing fires. In Kyoto this takes place on the evenings of 2 and 3 June at Heian-jingū – tickets cost ¥3000 if you pay in advance.

Ask at the tourist information office for the location of ticket agencies or you can pay ¥4000 at the entrance gate.

Traditional Dance, Theatre & Music

Gion Corner THEATRE
(ギオンコーナー; Map p290; ☎561-1119; Yasaka Hall, 570-2 Gionmachi Minamigawa, Higashiyama-ku; admission ¥3150; ⏱performances nightly at 6pm & 7pm; ⓡKeihan Line to Gion-Shijō Station) The shows presented here are a sort of crash course in Japanese traditional arts. You get a chance to see snippets of the tea ceremony, koto music, ikebana, *gagaku* (court music), *kyōgen* (ancient comic plays), *Kyōmai* (Kyoto-style dance) and *bunraku* (puppet plays).

From 1 December to the second week of March, performances take place only on Fridays, Saturdays and Sundays.

🔒 Shopping

The heart of Kyoto's shopping district is around the intersection of Shijō-dōri and Kawaramachi-dōri. The blocks to the north and west of here are packed with stores selling both traditional and modern goods. This area is also home to Kyoto's largest department stores: **Marui** (マルイ (OIOI); Map p285; ☎075-257-0101; 68 Shin-chō, Shijō-dōri Kawaramachi Higashi-iru, Shimogyō-ku; ⏱10.30am-8.30pm, restaurants 11am-10pm, supermarket 8am-10pm), Takashimaya (p324), Daimaru (p324) and Fujii Daimaru (p324)).

Some of the best shopping and people-watching can be had along Kyoto's three downtown shopping arcades: **Shinkyōgoku shopping arcade**, **Teramachi shopping arcade** and Nishiki Market (p284). Teramachi and Shinkyōgoku run parallel to each other in the heart of downtown. The former has a mix of tasteful and tacky shops; the latter specialises in tacky stuff for the hordes of schoolkids who visit Kyoto every year. Nishiki branches off Teramachi to the west, about 100m north of Shijō-dōri.

The place to look for antiques in Kyoto is Shinmonzen-dōri, in Gion. The street is lined with great old shops, many of them specialising in one thing or another (furniture, pottery, scrolls, prints etc). You can easily spend an afternoon strolling from shop to shop, but be warned: if something strikes your fancy you're going to have to break out the credit card – prices here are steep!

Teramachi-dōri, between Oike-dōri and Marutamachi-dōri, has a number of classic old Kyoto arts, crafts, antiques and tea shops. This is probably the best place for shopping if you're after 'old Kyoto' items.

⭐**Aritsugu** KNIVES
(有次; Map p285; ☎221-1091; 219 Kajiya-chō, Nishikikōji-dōri, Gokomachi nishi iru, Nakagyō-ku; ⏱9am-5.30pm; ⓡHankyū Line to Kawaramachi Station) Located in Nishiki Market, this is one of the finest knife shops in Japan. There's usually someone on hand who can help you in English. If you purchase a knife, staff put a final edge on it with a giant stone sharpening wheel before packaging it.

⭐**Morita Washi** HANDICRAFTS
(森田和紙; Map p278; ☎341-1419; 1F Kajinoha Bldg, 298 Ōgisakaya-chō, Higashinotōin-dōri, Bukkōji agaru, Shimogyō-ku; ⏱9.30am-5.30pm Mon-Fri, to 4.30pm Sat; ⑤Karasuma Line to Shijō Station) Not far from Shijo-Karasuma, this wonderful shop sells a fabulous variety of handmade *washi* (Japanese paper) for reasonable prices. It could be our favourite shop in Kyoto.

⭐**Zōhiko** HANDICRAFTS
(象彦; Map p296; ☎752-7777; 10 Okazaki Saishōji-chō, Sakyō-ku; ⏱9.30am-6pm, closed Wed; ⓠKyoto City Bus 206 from Kyoto Station to Kumano-jinja-mae

MARKETS

If you're in town when one of the following markets is on, by all means go! Markets are the best places to find antiques and bric-a-brac at reasonable prices and are the only places in Japan where you can actually bargain for a better price.

On the 21st of each month, **Kōbō-san Market** (弘法さん（東寺露天市）; Map p278; ☎ 691 3325; Kujō-chō 1, Tō-ji; ⏱ dawn to dusk, 21st of each month; Ⓢ 10min walk from Kyoto Station) is held at Tō-ji to commemorate the death of Kōbō Daishi (Kūkai), who in 823 was appointed abbot of the temple.

Another major market, **Tenjin-san Market** (天神さん（北野天満宮露天市）; Map p287; ☎ 461 0005; Bakuro-chō, Kitano Tenman-gū; ⏱ dawn to dusk, 25th of each month; 🚌 1min walk from Kitano Tenmangū-mae bus stop, 🚌 50 or 101 from Kyoto Station), is held on the 25th of each month at Kitano Tenman-gū, marking the day of the birth (and, coincidentally, the death) of the Heian-era statesman Sugawara Michizane (845–903).

stop) This is our favourite lacquerware shop in Kyoto. Inside is a treasure trove of beautiful lacquerware and there's a fine gallery upstairs. It's very near Heian-jingū.

Kōjitsu Sansō OUTDOOR GEAR
(好日山荘; Map p282; ☎ 708-5178; 5F Kyoto Yodobashi, 590-2 Higashi shiokōji-chō, Shichijō sagaru, Shimogyō-ku; ⏱ 9.30am-10pm; 🚃 JR Tōkaidō Main Line to Kyoto Station, Ⓢ Karasuma Line to Kyoto Station) If you plan to do some hiking or camping while in Japan, you can stock up on equipment at this excellent little shop. It's down a flight of steps, the entrance to which is to the right of a convenience store.

Art Factory CLOTHING
(アートファクトリー; Map p285; ☎ 213-3131; 498 Higashigawa-chō, Teramachi, Takoyakushi agaru, Nakagyō-ku; ⏱ 11am-8pm; 🚃 Hankyū Line to Kawaramachi Station, Ⓢ Karasuma Line to Shijō Station) A T-shirt with your name written in kanji, katakana or hiragana across the chest is a great souvenir, and this place can make them in just a few minutes. If you don't fancy your own name on the shirt, you can also get the name of your country or choose from a variety of Japanese words and slogans.

Look for the T-shirts displayed outside (strangely, there is no sign in English or Japanese, but they call themselves 'Art Factory').

Bic Camera ELECTRONICS
(ビックカメラ; Map p282; ☎ 353-1111; Kyoto Station Bldg, 927 Higashi Shiokōji-chō, Shimogyō-ku; ⏱ 10am-9pm; 🚃 JR Tōkaidō Main Line to Kyoto Station, Ⓢ Karasuma Line to Kyoto Station) Vast new electronics/camera shop, directly connected to Kyoto Station via the Nishinotōin gate; otherwise, it's accessed by leaving the north (Karasuma) gate and walking west. You will be amazed by the sheer amount of goods it has on display. Just make sure that an English operating manual is available.

For computer parts, note that not all items work with English operating systems.

Yodobashi Camera ELECTRONICS
(ヨドバシカメラ; Map p282; ☎ 351-1010; 590-2 Higashi Shiokōji-chō, Shimogyō-ku; ⏱ 9.30am-10pm; 🚃 JR Tōkaidō Main Line to Kyoto Station, Ⓢ Karasuma Line to Kyoto Station) This mammoth shop sells a range of electronic goods, camera and computer products and also has a restaurant floor, supermarket, bookshop, cafe and, well, the list goes on. It's a few minutes' walk north of Kyoto Station.

Kamiji Kakimoto HANDICRAFTS
(紙司柿本; Map p296; ☎ 211-3481; 54 Tokiwagi-chō, Nijō agaru, Teramachi; ⏱ 9am-6pm) Sells a good selection of *washi* (Japanese paper). It even stocks *washi* computer paper.

Rakushikan HANDICRAFTS
(楽紙館; Map p285; ☎ 221-1070; Takoyakushi-dōri, Takakura nishi iru, Nakagyō-ku; ⏱ 10.30am-6pm, closed Mon, first/last week of the year; Ⓢ Karasuma Line to Shijō Station) This downtown Kyoto paper specialist carries an incredible variety of *washi* and other paper products in its spacious store. You can also try making your own *washi* here (ask at the counter for details).

Kyūkyo-dō HANDICRAFTS
(鳩居堂; Map p285; ☎ 231-0510; 520 Shimohonnōjimae-chō, Teramachi, Aneyakōji agaru,, Nakagyō-ku; ⏱ 10am-6pm Mon-Sat, closed Sun & 1-3 Jan; Ⓢ Tōzai Line to Kyoto Shiyakusho-mae Station) An old shop in the Teramachi covered arcade selling a selection of incense, *shodō* (calligraphy) goods, tea-ceremony supplies and *washi*. Prices are on the high side but the quality is good.

**Kyoto
Handicraft Center**   HANDICRAFTS, SOUVENIRS
(京都ハンディクラフトセンター; Map p296;
☑ 761-5080; 21 Entomi-chō, Shōgoin, Sakyō-ku;
◷ 10am-6pm, closed 1-3 Jan; ☐ Kyoto City Bus 206
from Kyoto Station to Kumano-jinja-mae stop) Just
north of the Heian-jingū, this is a huge co-
operative that sells, demonstrates and exhibits crafts (wood-block prints and *yukata* are
a good buy here). It's the best spot in town
for buying Japanese souvenirs and is highly
recommended.

Kagoshin   HANDICRAFTS
(籠新; Map p290; ☑ 771-0209; 4 chō-me, Sanjō-
dōri, Sanjō-Ōhashi higashi; ◷ 9am-6pm, closed
Mon; ⒮ Tōzai Line to Sanjō-Keihan Station) Small
shop selling a wide variety of inexpensive
bamboo products such as flower holders
and baskets.

Kyoto Sanjō Takematsu   HANDICRAFTS
(京都三条竹松; Map p290; ☑ 751-2444; 3-39
Sanjō-dōri, Higashiyama-ku; ◷ 10am-7pm; ⒮ Tōzai
Line to Sanjō-Keihan Station) A great spot to
pick up bamboo crafts. It's a short walk from
Sanjō-Keihan Station and downtown.

Tōzandō   SWORDS
(東山堂; Map p296; ☑ 762-1341; 24 Shōgoin
Entomi-chō, Sakyō-ku; ◷ 10am-7pm; ☐ Kyoto City
Bus 206 from Kyoto Station to Kumano-jinja-mae
stop) If you're a fan of Japanese swords and
armour, you have to visit this wonderful shop
on Marutamachi (diagonally opposite the
Kyoto Handicraft Center). It's got authentic
swords, newly made Japanese armour, martial arts goods etc and there's usually someone on hand who can speak English.

Ippōdō   TEA
(一保堂; Map p296; ☑ 211-3421; Teramachi-dōri,
Nijō, Nakagyō-ku; ◷ 9am-7pm Mon-Sat, to 6pm
Sun & holidays, cafe 11am-5.30pm; ⒮ Tōzai Line
to Kyoto Shiyakusho-mae Station) This is an
old-fashioned tea shop selling all sorts of
Japanese tea. You can ask to sample the
tea before buying. There's an excellent adjoining cafe that sells a variety of green tea
drinks and Japanese sweets – it's a highly
recommended spot to relax while shopping
on Teramachi.

Junkudō   BOOKSHOP
(ジュンク堂書店; Map p285; ☑ 253-6460; Kyoto
BAL Bldg, 2-251 Yamazaki-chō, Kawaramachi-dōri,
Sanjō sagaru, Nakagyō-ku; ◷ 11am-8pm; ⒮ Tōzai
Line to Sanjō-Keihan Station, ☒ Keihan Line to Sanjō
Station) In the BAL Building, this shop has a

great selection of English-language books on
the 7th floor. This is Kyoto's best bookshop
now that the old Maruzen and Random Walk
bookshops have closed (you may remember
these shops if you visited in the past).

There is an excellent cafe on the top floor,
which has a great view over Kyoto to the
Higashiyama mountains. You can get light
meals here as well as drinks.

ⓘ Information

IMMIGRATION OFFICE

**Osaka Regional Immigration Bureau Kyoto
Branch** (大阪入国管理局京都出張所; Map
p296; ☑ 752-5997; 4F Kyoto Second Local
Joint Government Bldg, 34-12 Higashimaruta-
chō, Marutamachi-dōri, Kawabata Higashi iru,
Sakyō-ku; ◷ 9am-noon & 1-4pm Mon-Fri) To
extend a short-stay visa beyond the standard
90 days or three months, apply here. You
must provide two copies of an Application for
Extension of Stay (available at the bureau), a
letter stating the reasons for the extension
and supporting documentation, as well as your
passport. There is a processing fee of ¥4000;
be prepared to spend well over an hour completing the process. Note that extensions are
not guaranteed and rules vary by nationality.

INTERNET ACCESS

The city of Kyoto has recently launched a free
wi-fi access program for foreign travellers, with
hotspots across the city. You must email to get
the access code. Go to http://kanko.city.kyoto.
lg.jp/wifi/en/ to find a map of hotspots and to
get started. Note that access is limited to three
hours, but you can get another access code for
additional hours.

Kinko's (キンコーズ; ☑ 213-6802; 651-1
Tearaimizu-chō, Karasuma-dōri, Takoyakushi
sagaru, Nakagyō-ku; first 10min ¥262, then
every 10min ¥210; ◷ 24hr) This copy shop has
several terminals where you can log on to the
internet and do tasks like scanning and writing.
It's expensive but conveniently located.

Kyoto International Community House
(KICH; ☑ 752-3010; 2-1 Torii-chō, Awataguchi,
Sakyō-ku; ◷ 9am-9pm, closed Mon) An essential stop for those planning a long-term stay in
Kyoto, but it can also be quite useful for short-
term visitors. Here you can send and receive
faxes, and use the internet (there are terminals
and wi-fi). Note that you must register to use
wi-fi and the internet terminals (ask at the
information counter).

It's closed Monday, except when Monday is a
national holiday, then it's closed Tuesday. Take
the Tōzai line subway from central Kyoto and
get off at Keage Station, from which it's a 350m
(five-minute) walk downhill.

Media Café Popeye (ポパイ; ☎253-5300; B1, 42-6 Ebisu-cho, Kawaramachi, Sanjō agaru, Nakagyō-ku; ¥420 for the first hour, ¥95 per 15min thereafter; ☻24hr) This is convenient when you're downtown. It's underground, in front of the Catholic Church.

Tops Café (トップスカフェ; ☎681-9270; www.topsnet.co.jp; Kyoto-eki, Hachijō-guchi, Shimogyō-ku; per 15min ¥120, plus ¥200 registration fee; ☻24hr) This is an all-night manga/internet cafe where you can actually spend the night in the booths if you want. It's just outside the south (Hachijō) exit of Kyoto Station.

INTERNET RESOURCES

Kyoto Temple Admission Fees (www.temple-fees.com)

Kyoto Visitor's Guide (www.kyotoguide.com)

MEDICAL SERVICES

Kyoto University Hospital (京都大学医学部附属病院; Map p296; ☎751-3111; 54 Shōgoinkawahara-chō, Sakyō-ku; ☻8.30am-11am; ℝKeihan Line to Marutamachi Station) Best hospital in Kyoto. There is an information counter near the entrance that can point you in the right direction. If you can, try to arrive at 8.30am to register. If you arrive later, you'll face a longer wait.

MONEY

Most of the major banks are near the Shijō-Karasuma intersection, two stops north of Kyoto Station on the Karasuma line subway.

International transactions (such as wire transfers) can be made at **Bank of Tokyo-Mitsubishi UFJ** (三菱東京UFJ銀行; Map p285; ☎221-7161; ☻9am-3pm Mon-Fri, 10am-5pm Sat, ATM 24hr), which is at the southeast corner of this intersection. There is another branch one block southwest of the intersection. Other international transactions can be made at **Citibank** (シティバンク; Map p285; ☎212-5387; ☻ office 9am-3pm Mon-Fri, ATM 24hr), just west of this intersection.

Finally, you can change travellers cheques at most post offices around town, including the Kyoto Central Post Office, next to Kyoto Station. Post offices also have ATMs that accept most foreign-issued cards. If your card doesn't work at postal ATMs, try the ATMs in 7-Eleven convenience stores. Failing that, try Citibank, which has a 24-hour ATM that accepts most foreign-issued cards.

POST

Kyoto Central Post Office (京都中央郵便局; ☎365-2471; 843-12 Higashishiokōji-chō, Shimogyō-ku; ☻9am-9pm Mon-Fri, to 7pm Sat & Sun, ATMs 12.05am-11.55pm Mon-Sat, to 9pm Sun & holidays) Conveniently located next to Kyoto Station (take the Karasuma exit; the post office is on the northwestern side of the

station). There's an after-hours service counter on the southern side of the post office, open 24 hours a day, 365 days a year. The ATMs here are open *almost* 24 hours a day.

TOURIST INFORMATION

Kyoto Tourist Information Center (京都総合観光案内所; TIC; Map p282; ☎343-0548; 2F Kyoto Station Bldg, Shimogyō-ku; ☻8.30am-7pm) Located in the main concourse on the 2nd floor of the Kyoto Station building that runs between the *shinkansen* station and the front of the station (near Isetan department store), this is the main tourist information centre in Kyoto.

English speakers are always on hand and occasionally, speakers of other European and Asian languages are available. It stocks useful maps of the city, as well as bus maps, and can answer most of your questions. Note that it's called 'Kyo Navi' in Japanese (in case you have to ask someone).

TRAVEL AGENCIES

IACE TRAVEL (IACE トラベル; Map p285; ☎212-8944; 4F Dai15 Hase Bldg, 688 Takanna-chō, Karasuma dōri, Shijo agaru, Nakagyō-ku; ☻10am-7pm Mon-Fri, to 11am-6pm Sat) A good central travel agency that can arrange discount air tickets, car rental and accommodation, as well as other services.

KNT (近畿日本ツーリスト; Map p285; ☎255-0489; 437 Ebisu-chō, Sanjo agaru, Kawaramachi dōri; ☻10.30am-7pm Mon-Fri, to 6.30pm Sat & Sun) This travel agency, while not geared for foreign travellers, is a useful place to make domestic travel arrangements (train, bus, ferry and plane tickets).

❶ Getting There & Away

Travel between Kyoto and other parts of Japan is a breeze. Kansai is served by the Tōkaidō and San-yō *shinkansen* (bullet train) lines, several JR main lines and a few private rail lines. It is also possible to travel to/from Kyoto and other parts of Honshū, Shikoku and Kyūshū by long-distance highway buses. Finally, Kyoto is served by two airports (Kansai International Airport and Osaka Itami Airport). Kyoto is also relatively close to Nagoya, in case you can only get a flight to Centrair airport.

AIR

Kyoto is served by Osaka Itami Airport (ITM), which principally handles domestic traffic, and the Kansai International Airport (KIX), which principally handles international flights. There are frequent flights between Tokyo and Itami (around ¥24,600, 80 minutes), but unless you're very lucky with airport connections you'll probably find it as quick and more convenient to take the *shinkansen*. There are ample connections to/from both airports, though the trip to/from Kansai International Airport takes longer and costs more.

BUS

Overnight JR buses run between Tokyo Station (Nihonbashi-guchi/arrival, Yaesu-guchi/departure long-distance bus stop) and Kyoto Station Bus Terminal (京都駅前バスターミナル; Map p282).The trip takes about eight hours and there are usually departures nightly in either direction, at 10.10pm, 10.30pm, 11pm (daily from Tokyo to Kyoto) and 11pm (daily from Kyoto to Tokyo). The fare is ¥6700 to ¥8100 one-way. You should be able to grab some sleep in the reclining seats. There is a similar service to/from Shinjuku Station's Shin-minami-guchi in Tokyo.

Other JR bus transport possibilities include Kanazawa (one-way ¥3800 to ¥4060) and Hiroshima (one-way ¥4300 to ¥5500).

TRAIN

Shinkansen (Tokyo, Osaka, Nagoya & Hakata) Kyoto is on the Tōkaidō-San-yō *shinkansen* line, which runs between Tokyo and Kyūshū, with stops at places such as Nagoya, Osaka, Kōbe, Himeji and Hiroshima en route. The *shinkansen* operates to/from Kyoto Station (Kyoto's main train station). On the Tokyo end, it operates from Tokyo, Shinagawa and Shin-Yokohama stations. Fares and times for Hikari (the second-fastest type of *shinkansen*) between Kyoto and the following cities are as follows:

Tokyo (¥13,220; 2¾ hours)

Nagoya (¥5440; 40 minutes)

Shin-Osaka (¥2730; 15 minutes)

Hiroshima (¥10,790; two hours)

Hakata (¥15,210; three hours, 22 minutes)

Nara The private Kintetsu line (sometimes written in English as the Kinki Nippon railway) links Kyoto (Kintetsu Kyoto Station, south side of the main Kyoto Station building) and Nara (Kintetsu Nara Station). There are fast direct *tokkyū* (¥1110, 33 minutes) and ordinary express trains (¥610, 40 minutes), which may require a change at Saidai-ji.

The JR Nara line also connects Kyoto Station with JR Nara Station (express, ¥690, 41 minutes), and this is a great option for Japan Rail Pass holders.

Osaka The fastest train other than the *shinkansen* between Kyoto Station and Osaka is the JR *shinkaisoku* (special rapid train), which takes 29 minutes (¥540). In Osaka, the train stops at both Shin-Osaka and Osaka Stations.

There is also the cheaper private Hankyū line, which runs between Hankyū Kawaramachi, Karasuma and Ōmiya Stations in Kyoto and Hankyū Umeda Station in Osaka (*tokkyū* or limited express Umeda-Kawaramachi, ¥390, 40 minutes). These trains are usually more comfortable than the JR trains, and if you board at Kawaramachi or Umeda, you can usually get a seat.

Alternatively, you can take the Keihan main line between Demachiyanagi, Sanjō, Shijō or Shichijō Stations in Kyoto and Keihan Yodoyabashi Station in Osaka (*tokkyū* to/from Sanjō ¥400, 51 minutes). Yodoyabashi is on the Midō-suji subway line. Again, these are more comfortable than JR trains and you can usually get a seat if you board in Demachiyanagi or Yodoyabashi.

Tokyo The *shinkansen* line has the fastest and most frequent rail links. The journey can also be undertaken by a series of regular JR express trains, but keep in mind that it takes around eight hours and involves at least two (often three or four) changes along the way. The fare is ¥7980. Get the staff at the ticket counter to write down the exact details of each transfer for you when you buy your ticket.

ⓘ Getting Around

TO/FROM THE AIRPORT

Osaka Itami Airport 大阪伊丹空港

There are frequent limousine buses between Osaka Itami airport and Kyoto Station (the Kyoto Station airport bus stop is opposite the south side of the station, in front of Avanti department store). Buses also run between the airport and various hotels around town, but on a less regular basis (check with your hotel). The journey should take around 55 minutes and the cost is ¥1280. Be sure to allow extra time in case of traffic.

At Itami, the stand for these buses is outside the arrivals hall; buy your tickets from the machines and ask one of the attendants which stand is for Kyoto (hint: you've got a better chance of getting a seat if you board at the South Terminal).

MK Taxi (☑ 778-5489) offers limousine van service to/from the airport for ¥2300. Call at least two days in advance to reserve, or ask at the information counter in the arrivals hall on arrival in Osaka.

Kansai International Airport (KIX)
関西国際空港

The fastest, most convenient way to travel between KIX and Kyoto is on the special Haruka airport express, which makes the trip in about 78 minutes. Most seats are reserved (¥3290, ¥3490 or ¥3690 depending on season) but there are usually two cars on each train with unreserved seats (¥2980). Open seats are almost always available, so you don't have to purchase tickets in advance. First and last departures from Kyoto to KIX are 5.46am and 8.15pm; first and last departures from KIX to Kyoto are 6.33am Mon-Fri, 6.42am Sat, Sun and holidays and 10.16pm. Note that the Haruka is one of the few trains in Japan that is frequently late (although not usually by more than a few minutes). We suggest leaving a little extra time when heading from Kyoto to the airport to catch a flight.

If you have time to spare, you can save some money by taking the *kankū kaisoku* (Kansai airport express) between the airport and Osaka Station and taking a regular *shinkaisoku* to/ from Kyoto. The total journey by this method takes about 92 minutes with good connections and costs ¥1830, making it the cheapest option (note that you can save ¥130 by exiting and re-entering at Osaka Station).

It's also possible to travel by limousine bus between Kyoto and KIX (¥2500, about 90 minutes). In Kyoto, the bus departs from the same place as the Itami-bound bus.

A final option is the **MK Taxi Sky Gate Shuttle limousine van service** (☑ 778-5489), which will pick you up anywhere in Kyoto city and deliver you to KIX for ¥3500. Call at least two days in advance to reserve. The advantage of this method is that you are delivered from door to door and you don't have to lug your baggage through the train station. MK has a counter in the arrivals hall of KIX, and if there's room they'll put you on the next van to Kyoto. A similar service is offered by **Yasaka Taxi** (☑ 803-4800).

BICYCLE

Kyoto is a great city to explore on a bicycle; with the exception of outlying areas it's mostly flat and there is a bike path running the length of the Kamo-gawa.

Unfortunately, Kyoto must rank near the top in having the world's worst public facilities for bike parking, and the city regularly impounds bikes parked outside regulation bike-parking areas. If your bike does disappear, check for a poster in the vicinity (in both Japanese and English) indicating the time of seizure and the inconvenient place you'll have to go to pay a ¥2000 fine and retrieve your bike.

There are two bicycle-parking lots in town that are convenient for tourists: one in front of Kyoto Station and another off Kiyamachi-dōri, between Sanjō-dōri and Shijō-dōri. It costs ¥150 per day to park your bicycle here. Be sure to hang onto the ticket you pick up as you enter.

WANT MORE?

For in-depth information, reviews and recommendations at your fingertips, head to the Apple App Store to purchase Lonely Planet's *Kyoto City Guide* iPhone app.

Alternatively, head to **Lonely Planet** (www.lonelyplanet.com/kyoto) for planning advice, author recommendations, traveller reviews and insider tips.

Bicycle Purchase

If you plan on spending more than a week or so exploring Kyoto by bicycle, it might make sense to purchase a used bicycle. A simple *mama chari* (shopping bike) can be had for as little as ¥3000. Try the used-cycle shop **Ei Rin** (栄輪; Map p296; ☑ 752-0292; 28-4 Sekiden-chō, Tanaka, Sakyō-ku; ⏱ 9.30am-8.30pm) on Imadegawa-dōri, near Kyoto University. Otherwise, you'll find a good selection of used bikes advertised for sale on the message board of the Kyoto International Community House (p331).

Bicycle Rental

Kyoto Cycling Tour Project (京都サイクリング ツアープロジェクト; KCTP; Map p296; ☑ 354-3636; www.kctp.net; ⏱ 9am-7pm) A great place to rent a bike. These folk rent bikes (¥1000 per day) that are perfect for getting around the city. KCTP also conducts a variety of excellent bicycle tours of Kyoto with English-speaking guides. These are a great way to see the city (check the website for details).

PUBLIC TRANSPORT
Bus

Kyoto has an extensive network of bus routes providing an efficient way of getting around at moderate cost. Many of the routes used by visitors have announcements in English. The core timetable for buses is between 7am and 9pm, though a few run earlier or later.

The main bus terminals are Kyoto Station on the JR and Kintetsu lines, Sanjō Station on the Keihan line/Tōzai subway line, Karasuma-Shijō Station on the Hankyū line/Karasuma subway line, and Kitaōji Station on the Karasuma subway line. The bus terminal at Kyoto Station is on the north side and has three main departure bays (departure points are indicated by the letter of the bay and number of the stop within that bay).

The TIC stocks the *Bus Navi: Kyoto City Bus Sightseeing Map*, which is a good map of the city's main bus lines. This map is not exhaustive. If you can read a little Japanese, pick up a copy of the regular (and more detailed) Japanese bus map available at major bus terminals throughout the city.

Bus stops usually display a map of destinations from that stop on the top section. On the bottom section there's a timetable for the buses serving that stop. Unfortunately, all of this information is in Japanese, and nonspeakers will simply have to ask locals for help.

Entry to the bus is usually through the back door and exit is via the front door. Inner-city buses charge a flat fare (¥220), which you drop into the clear plastic receptacle on top of the machine next to the driver on your way out. A separate machine gives change for ¥100 and ¥500 coins or ¥1000 notes.

On buses serving the outer areas, you take a numbered ticket *(seiri-ken)* when entering. When you leave, an electronic board above the driver displays the fare corresponding to your ticket number (drop the *seiri-ken* into the ticket box with your fare).

The main **Kyoto Bus Information Centre** (京都バス案内書) is located in front of Kyoto Station. Here you can pick up bus maps, purchase bus tickets and passes (on all lines, including highway buses), and get additional information. Nearby, there's a convenient English/Japanese bus-information computer terminal; just enter your intended destination and it will tell you the correct bus and bus stop.

Three-digit numbers written against a red background denote loop lines: bus 204 runs around the northern part of the city and buses 205 and 206 circle the city via Kyoto Station. Buses with route numbers on a blue background take other routes.

When heading for locations outside the city centre, be careful which bus you board. Kyoto city buses are green, Kyoto buses are tan and Keihan buses are red and white.

Subway

Kyoto has two efficient subway lines, which operate from around 5.30am to around 11.30pm. The minimum fare is ¥210 (children ¥110).

The quickest way to travel between the north and south of the city is the Karasuma subway line. The line has 15 stops and runs from Takeda in the far south, via Kyoto Station, to the Kyoto International Conference Hall (Kokusaikaikan Station) in the north.

The east–west Tōzai subway line crosses Kyoto from Uzumasa-Tenjingawa in the west, meeting the Karasuma line at Karasuma-Oike Station, and continuing east to Sanjō Keihan, Yamashina and Rokujizō, in the east and southeast.

TAXI

Kyoto taxi fares start at ¥640 for the first 2km. The exception is **MK Taxis** (☏ 778-4141), whose fares start at ¥580.

MK Taxis also provides tours of the city with English-speaking drivers. For a group of up to four, prices start at ¥21,800 for a three-hour tour. Another company offering a similar service is **Kyōren Taxi Service** (☏ 672-5111).

Most Kyoto taxis are equipped with satellite navigation systems. If you are going somewhere unusual, it will help the driver if you have the address or phone number of your destination, as both of these can be programmed into the system.

Kansai

Best Places to Eat

➡ Café Absinthe (p349)

➡ Misono (p369)

➡ Imai Honten (p351)

➡ Fukutei (p373)

Best Places to Stay

➡ Nishimuraya Honkan (p409)

➡ Guesthouse Sakuraya (p385)

➡ Arietta Hotel (p348)

➡ Blue Sky Guesthouse (p403)

Why Go?

Kansai (関西) is the heart of Japan. Nowhere else in the country can you find so much of historical and cultural interest in such a compact area. Indeed, if you had to choose only one region of Japan to explore, Kansai would be the easy choice. Kyoto, covered in the preceding chapter, makes the perfect base for exploring Kansai and is home to an extraordinary range of first-rate attractions.

Nara, Japan's first permanent capital, is thick with traditional sights and is home to the awe-inspiring Tōdai-ji Temple. Osaka is a great place to sample Japanese city life in all its mind-boggling intensity, while Kōbe retains some of the international feeling that dates back to its days as a foreign treaty port. In Mie-ken, you'll find Ise-jingū, one of Japan's three most important shrines, and in Wakayama-ken there are great onsen, a rugged coastline and the temple complex of Kōya-san, Japan's mountaintop Buddhist retreat centre.

When to Go
Osaka

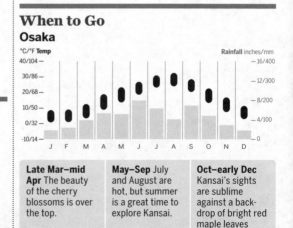

Late Mar–mid Apr The beauty of the cherry blossoms is over the top.

May–Sep July and August are hot, but summer is a great time to explore Kansai.

Oct–early Dec Kansai's sights are sublime against a backdrop of bright red maple leaves

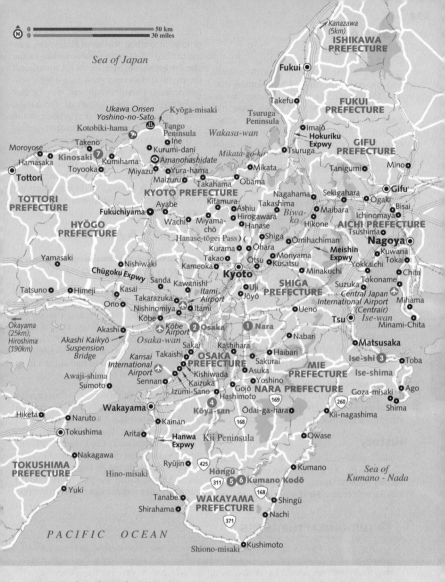

Kansai Highlights

1 Gaze in awe at the **Great Buddha** (p381) at Nara's Tōdai-ji

2 Feast your eyes on the colourful human parade of Osaka's **Dōtombori area** (p341)

3 Feel the power radiating from the main hall of **Ise-jingū** (p404), Japan's most sacred Shintō shrine

4 Wander the mystical forest of Kōya-san's **Oku-no-in** (p395)

5 Soak in the restorative waters of the three onsen of **Hongū** (p402)

6 Walk the ancient pilgrimage trails of Wakayama's **Kumano Kodō** (p398)

7 Put on your *yukata* (light cotton kimono) and stroll from onsen to onsen in the quaint town of **Kinosaki** (p408)

OSAKA

⏹ 06 / POP 2.8 MILLION

Osaka (大阪) is the working heart of Kansai. Famous for its down-to-earth citizens and the colourful *Kansai-ben* (Kansai dialect) they speak, it's a good counterpart to the refined atmosphere of Kyoto. First and foremost, Osaka is famous for good eating: the phrase *kuidaore* (eat 'til you drop) was coined to describe Osakans' love for good food. Osaka is also a good place to experience a modern Japanese city. It's only surpassed by Tokyo as a showcase of the Japanese urban phenomenon.

This isn't to say that Osaka is particularly attractive; it's an endless expanse of concrete boxes, pachinko (pinball) parlours and elevated highways. But the city somehow manages to rise above this and exert a peculiar charm, and a few architectural gems keep it interesting. At night, Osaka really comes into its own – this is when the streets come alive with flashing neon, beckoning residents with promises of tasty food and good times.

Osaka's highlights include Osaka-jō and its surrounding park, Osaka Aquarium, the *Blade Runner* nightscapes of the Dōtombori area, and the wonderful Open-Air Museum of Old Japanese Farmhouses. But Osaka has more to offer than its specific sights, and casual strolls are likely to be as rewarding as structured sightseeing tours.

History

Osaka has been a major port and mercantile centre from the beginning of Japan's recorded history. During its early days, Osaka was Japan's centre for trade with Korea and China. In the late 16th century, Osaka rose to prominence when Toyotomi Hideyoshi, having unified all of Japan, chose Osaka as the site for his castle. Merchants set up around the castle and the city grew into a busy economic hub. This development was further encouraged by the Tokugawa shōgunate, which adopted a hands-off approach to the city, allowing merchants to prosper unhindered by government interference.

In the modern period, Tokyo has usurped Osaka's position as the economic centre of Japan, but it's still an economic powerhouse, and the city is ringed by factories churning out the latest in electronics and hi-tech products.

⊙ Sights & Activities

◉ Kita Area キタ

By day, Osaka's centre of gravity is the Kita area. There are few great attractions, but it does have the eye-catching Umeda Sky building, department stores, lots of eateries, and the activity of the big city. The past couple of years has seen a complete revamping of Osaka Station and there's more to come (see boxed text p364).

★**Umeda Sky Building**   NOTABLE BUILDING
(梅田スカイビル; Map p340; www.kuchu-teien. com; 1-1-88 Ōyodonaka, Kita-ku; admission ¥700; ⊙ observation decks 10am-10.30pm, last entry 10pm; ☒ JR line to Osaka) The Umeda Sky Building is Osaka's most dramatic piece of modern architecture, designed by Hara Hiroshi, who also designed Kyoto Station. Its twin-tower complex is like a space-age Arc de Triomphe,

---

ℹ **THE KANSAI THRU PASS**

The Kansai Thru Pass is an excellent way to get around Kansai on the cheap. This pass – available at the travel counter in the arrivals hall of Kansai International Airport and at the main bus information centre in front of Kyoto station – allows unlimited travel on most bus and train lines in Kansai except the Japan Railways (JR) line. (The pass covers travel on the Nankai line, which serves Kansai International Airport.) It also qualifies you for discounts at several attractions around Kansai. The pass does not cover the Ise-Shima region.

When you buy the pass, be sure to pick up the handy companion English guide-map, which shows all the bus and train lines available.

Two-/three-day passes cost ¥3800/5000. It's possible to purchase multiple passes for longer explorations of Kansai. Like the Japan Rail Pass, however, these passes are only available to travellers on temporary visitor visas (you'll have to show your passport). For more on the pass, visit the Kansai Thru Pass website (www.surutto.com/tickets/kansai_thru_english.html).

and from the top you can marvel at the incredible sprawl of humanity in all directions. Getting to the top is half the fun – for the final five storeys you take a glassed-in escalator across the open space between the two towers (definitely not one for vertigo sufferers). Tickets for the observation decks can be purchased once you get off the escalator.

Below the towers, you'll find **Takimi-kōji Alley** (滝見小路), a re-creation of an early Shōwa-era market street crammed with restaurants and *izakaya* (pub-eateries).

The building is reached via an underground passage that starts just north of both Osaka and Umeda stations.

Osaka Museum of Housing & Living
MUSEUM

(大阪くらしの今昔館, Osaka Kurashi no Konjakukan; Map p340; http://konjyakukan.com; 6-4-20 Tenjinbashi; admission ¥600; ◷10am-5pm, closed Tue, day after national holiday & 3rd Mon; ⑤Tanimachi line to Tenjinbashisuji-rokuchōme, exit 3) Two subway stops from Umeda, this museum contains a life-sized reproduction of an 1830s Edo-period Osaka neighbourhood, including shophouses, drug stores, and even an old-style *sentō* (public bath). The rooms and houses are dimly lit to recreate the ambience of pre-electric Osaka. It makes for an interesting experience in the middle of the city. It's in the building right behind exit 3 of Tenjinbashisuji-rokuchōme station.

◉ Central Osaka

Osaka-jō
CASTLE

(大阪城; Map p340; www.osakacastle.net; 1-1 Osaka-jō; grounds/castle keep free/¥600, combined entry with Osaka Museum of History ¥900; ◷9am-5pm, to 7pm Aug; ⑧JR Osaka Loop line to Osaka-jō-kōen) This castle was built as a display of power by Toyotomi Hideyoshi after he achieved his goal of unifying Japan. One hundred thousand workers toiled for three years to construct an 'impregnable' granite castle, finishing the job in 1583. It was destroyed 32 years later by the armies of Tokugawa Ieyasu, rebuilt within 10 years, then suffered a further calamity when another generation of the Tokugawa clan razed it rather than let it fall to the forces of the Meiji Restoration in 1868.

The present structure is a 1931 concrete reconstruction of the original, which was refurbished in 1997. The interior houses an excellent collection of displays relating to the castle, Toyotomi Hideyoshi and the city of Osaka. On the 8th floor is an observation deck with 360-degree views. The castle and park are at their colourful best in the cherry-blossom and autumn-foliage seasons.

The Ōte-mon gate, the main entrance to the park, is a 10-minute walk northeast of Tanimachi-yonchōme Station (Tanimachi 4-chome) on the Chūō and Tanimachi subway lines. You can also take the JR Osaka Loop line, get off at Osaka-jō-kōen and enter through the back of the castle.

Osaka Museum of History
MUSEUM

(大阪歴史博物館, Osaka Rekishi Hakubutsukan; Map p340; www.mus-his.city.osaka.jp; 4-1-32 Ōtemae; admission ¥600, combined entry with Osaka Castle Museum ¥900; ◷9.30am-5pm, to 8pm Fri, closed Tue; ⑤Tanimachi line to Tanimachi-yonchōme, exit 2) Just southwest of Osaka-jō, the Osaka Museum of History is housed in a sail-shaped building adjoining the NHK Broadcast Center. The museum is built where the Naniwa Palace (c 650) stood, and you can see archaeological remains on the basement floor. There are also great views of Osaka-jō from the upper floors. There aren't full English explanations for everything so grab an audio guide. From the station exit, go right (east) about 300 metres.

Modern Transportation Museum
MUSEUM

(交通科学博物館; www.mtm.or.jp; 3-11-10 Namiyoke; adult/child ¥400/100; ◷10am-5.30pm, closed Mon; ⑧JR Osaka Loop line to Bentenchō, south exit) Transport fanciers and people with kids in tow will want to check out this small museum. There are interactive displays, a life-sized *shinkansen* that you can climb inside, and it also has models of ships and aircraft. Don't miss the great model-train layout at the far end of the building.

◉ Nakano-shima 中之島

Sandwiched between Dōjima-gawa and Tosabori-gawa, this island is an oasis of trees and riverside walkways in the midst of Osaka's unrelenting grey. It's home to **Osaka City Hall** (大阪市役所; Map p340), the neo-Renaissance **Osaka Central Public Hall** (大阪市中央公会堂; Map p340) and **Nakano-shima-kōen** (中之島公園; Map p340) on the eastern end of the island, a good place for an afternoon stroll or picnic lunch. If coming from Kyoto, take the Keihan line to Yodoyabashi Station. If you're coming by JR, walk about 1km south of JR Osaka Station.

Osaka

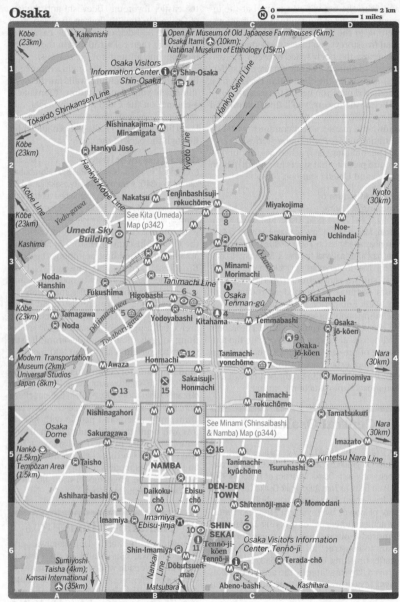

Museum of Oriental Ceramics MUSEUM
(大阪市立東洋陶磁美術館; Map p340; www.
moco.or.jp; 1-1-26 Nakano-shima; admission ¥500;
⏰9.30am-5pm, closed Mon; ⓈMidō-suji line to Yodoyabashi, exit 1) This museum has one of the
finest collections of Chinese and Korean ceramics anywhere in the world, with a smaller
Japanese gallery. At any one time, approximately 400 of the gorgeous pieces from the
permanent collection are on display, and
there are often special exhibits (which cost
extra). There's also an interesting exhibition

Osaka

of Chinese snuff bottles. From Yodoyabashi Station exit 1, cross the river and go right, passing the Central Public Hall.

National Museum of Art, Osaka   MUSEUM
(国立国際美術館; Map p340; www.nmao.go.jp; 4-2-55 Nakano-shima; admission ¥420; ⊙10am–5pm, to 7pm Fri, closed Mon) This impressive underground museum has regularly changing exhibitions of modern local and international art. You'll know it by the large steel plant-like structure on the ground above. It's near the western end of Nakano-shima.

⊙ Dōtombori 道頓堀

Dōtombori, in Osaka's Minami area, is the city's liveliest night spot. It's centred on Dōtombori-gawa and **Dōtombori Arcade** (道頓堀; Map p344), a strip of restaurants and theatres where a peculiar type of Darwinism is the rule for both people and shops: survival of the flashiest. In the evening, head to **Ebisu-bashi** (戎橋; Map p344) to sample the glittering nightscape. Below, the banks of the Dōtombori-gawa have been turned into attractive pedestrian walkways.

South of Dōtombori Arcade is **Hōzen-ji** (法善寺; Map p344), a tiny temple hidden down a narrow paved alley off Senichi-mae arcade. It's built around a moss-covered **Fudō-myōō statue**. In place of standard offerings, people show respects at the temple by splashing water over the statue, hence its bushy appearance. Running parallel to this alley is atmospheric **Hōzen-ji Yokochō** (法善寺横丁; Hōzen-ji Alley; Map p344), dotted with traditional restaurants and bars.

To the south of Dōtombori, in the direction of Nankai Namba Station, is a maze of arcades with more restaurants, pachinko parlours, strip clubs and who knows what else. To the north of Dōtombori, between Midō-suji and Sakai-suji, the streets are crowded with hostess bars, clubs and pubs.

Namba, on the Midō-suji line, or Nipponbashi, on the Sakai-suji and Sennichimae lines, are the nearest stations for Dōtombori.

For more on Dōtombori, see the walking tour on p346.

⊙ Amerika-Mura
アメリカ村

Amerika-Mura (America Village, also known as Ame-Mura) is a compact enclave of hip, youth-focused and offbeat shops, plus cafes, bars, and a few discreet love hotels thrown in for good measure. The peculiar name comes from the presence of several shops that sprang up here after the war and sold various bits of Americana such as Zippo lighters and T-shirts.

The best reason to come is to check out the hordes of Japanese teens sporting the latest fads in clothing and hair. This is also a good area if you're looking for secondhand clothes or record shops. Keep your eyes peeled for signboards at street level advertising 'vintage' and 'used'.

In the middle of it all is **Triangle Park** (三角公園, Sankaku-kōen; Map p344), an all-concrete 'park' with benches where you can sit and watch the parade of fashion victims. As you walk around, you may notice odd human-like **street lamps** in different poses. Artists were recently commissioned to paint a few – look out for these around the park and in front of Big Step. Another landmark

KANSAI OSAKA

Kita (Umeda)

N
0 ——————— 400 m
0 ——————— 0.2 miles

Kita (Umeda)

is the **Peace on Earth mural** (1983), painted by Osaka artist Seitaro Kuroda; and, of course, there's the mini **Statue of Liberty**.

If you're on a budget, the southern end of Ame-Mura is the best place to eat and drink in Osaka in the evening, with its many cheap *izakaya* and restaurants.

Ame-Mura is west of Midō-suji and Shinsaibashi Station, running a few blocks south to Dōtombori-gawa. From the Midō-suji subway station, take exit 7 and walk west past OPA.

◉ Tennō-ji & Around
天王寺公園

Shin-Sekai   NEIGHBOURHOOD
(新世界; Map p340; S Sakai-suji line to Ebisu-chō, exit 3 or Midō-suji line to Dōbutsuen-mae, exit 5) For something different, take a walk through this retro entertainment district. At the heart of it is crusty old **Tsūten-kaku** (通天閣; Map p340), a 103m-high tower that dates back to 1912 (it was rebuilt in 1969). It once symbolised everything new and exciting about this neighbourhood (*shin-sekai* is Japanese for 'new world') but today's Shin-Sekai is home to ancient pachinko parlours, rundown theatres and all manner of suspicious characters. But it is packed with cheap eateries: the must-try dish here is *kushikatsu* (deep-fried meat and vegetables on skewers). While you're in the neighbourhood, pop in for a drink at the friendly and colourful bar **Nocosare-jima** (のこされ島; Map p340; www.nocoto.com; ⊙ 7pm-1am), where you can also get food. It's just near the base of the tower.

Shitennō-ji   BUDDHIST TEMPLE
(四天王寺; Map p340; 1-11-18 Shitennō-ji; admission ¥300; ⊙ 8.30am-4.30pm Apr-Sep, to 4pm Oct-Mar; S Tanimachi line to Shitennōji-mae, south exit) Founded in 593, Shitennō-ji is one of the oldest Buddhist temples in Japan, though only the big stone torii (shrine gate) is original, dating to 1294, making it oldest of its kind in the country. In the temple's central precinct there is a five-storey pagoda, which (unusually) you can climb up. The grounds are a somewhat desolate expanse of raked gravel, but there is a pleasant garden, **Honbō Teien** (本坊庭園; Map p340; admission ¥300; ⊙ 10am-4pm), just to the northeast of the central precinct. There is also a very good **flea market** outside the temple on

the 21st and 22nd of each month, with antiques and secondhand goods, including old kimonos.

Sumiyoshi Taisha   SHINTŌ SHRINE
(住吉大社; 2-9-89 Sumiyoshi; ⊙ dawn-dusk; R Nankai main line to Sumiyoshi-taisha) **FREE**
Dedicated to Shintō deities associated with the sea and sea travel, this shrine was founded in the early 3rd century and is considered the 'headquarters' for all Sumiyoshi shrines in Japan. The buildings today are faithful replicas of the ancient originals, with a couple that date back to 1810. They offer visitors a rare opportunity to see a Shintō shrine that predates the influence of Chinese Buddhist architectural styles.

The shrine is next to both Sumiyoshi-taisha Station on the Nankai main line and Sumiyoshi-tori-mae Station on the Hankai line (the tram line that leaves from Tennō-ji Station).

◉ Tempōzan 天保山

Trudging through the streets of Kita or Minami, you could easily forget that Osaka is actually a port city. A good remedy for this is a trip down to the Tempōzan seaside development, where there are several attractions, especially appealing for those with children. To get here, take the Chūō subway line to Osakakō Station, come down the stairs of exit 1 and walk towards the big wheel.

Giant Ferris Wheel   FERRIS WHEEL
(大観覧車, Daikanransha; 1-1-10 Kaigan-dōri; admission ¥700; ⊙ 10am-10pm, last ticket 9.30pm; S Chūō line to Osakakō) Among the biggest in the world, this 112m-high Ferris wheel offers unbeatable views of Osaka, Osaka Bay and Kōbe. Give it a whirl at night to enjoy the vast carpet of lights formed by the Osaka/Kōbe conurbation.

★Osaka Aquarium   AQUARIUM
(海遊館; www.kaiyukan.com; 1-1-10 Kaigan-dōri; adult/child ¥2000/900; ⊙ 10am-8pm; S Chūō line to Osakakō) Osaka Aquarium is easily one of the best aquariums in the world and it's well worth a visit. A walkway winds its way past displays of life found on different ocean levels around the Pacific's 'ring of fire' region, from Antarctic penguins to coral-reef Butter-flyfish to unearthly jellyfish from the deep. Most impressive is the enormous central

Minami (Shinsaibashi & Namba)

tank, which houses a whale shark and manta, among a huge variety of other fish and rays. There are good English explanations throughout. Not surprisingly, this is a very popular attraction, especially with families and school groups.

Tempōzan Marketplace   MALL
(天保山マーケットプレース; 1-1-10 Kaigan-dōri; ⊙11am-8pm; ⑤Chuō line to Osakakō) FREE
Next to the Ferris wheel and aquarium, Tempōzan Marketplace is a shopping and dining complex that includes the **Naniwa Kuishinbo Yokochō** (なにわ食いしんぼ

横丁; 1-1-10 Kaigan-dōri; ⊙11am-8pm), a faux 1960s–70s food court, where you can sample all of Osaka's culinary specialities. It's a fun spot to stop in for a bite to eat after visiting the aquarium.

◉ Other Areas

The Open-Air Museum of Japanese Farmhouses and the National Museum of Ethnology are both north of Osaka and accessible via the Midō-suji line, so it's feasible to see the two in the same day if you set out early.

Minami (Shinsaibashi & Namba)

★ **Open-Air Museum of**
Old Japanese Farmhouses   MUSEUM, PARK
(日本民家集落博物館, Nihon Minkashuraku Hakubutsukan; ☎ 6862-3137; www.occh.or.jp/minka; 1-2 Hattori Ryokuchi; admission ¥500; ⊙9.30am-5pm, closed Mon; ®Midō-suji line to Ryokuchi-kōen, west exit) In Ryokuchi-kōen, this fine open-air museum features a collection of traditional Japanese country houses, transported here and painstakingly reconstructed within a leafy park. Most striking is the giant *gasshō-zukuri* (steeply slanting thatch-roofed) farmhouse from Gifu-ken, and a thatched-wall farmhouse from Nagano, which looks to be wearing a shaggy coat. The whole place comes alive with fiery red maple leaves during November.

From the west exit of Ryokuchi-kōen Station, go straight out the doors (past the McDonald's), follow this road down to Hattori Ryokuchi park (服部緑地公園), then walk through the park to the museum.

★ **National Museum of**
Ethnology   MUSEUM
(国立民族学博物館; ☎ 6876-2151; www.minpaku.ac.jp; 10-1 Senri Expo Park; adult/child ¥420/110; ⊙10am-5pm, closed Wed; ®Midō-suji line to Senri-chūō, then Osaka Monorail to Banpaku-kinen-

kōen) Located within the expansive Osaka Banpaku-kōen (World Expo Park), this fabulous museum is brimming with interesting and colourful artefacts, providing a whirlwind tour through many of the world's cultures. Exhibits range from Bollywood movie posters to Ainu textiles, Ghanaian barbershop signboards to Bhutanese mandalas and Japanese festival floats; there's even a Filipino jeepney in here. Note there's limited English signage so it's best to get an audio guide.

From the station, cross the bridge to the park and follow the signs to the museum. You can buy tickets at the park entrance. From Kyoto, take the Hankyū line to Minami Ibaraki Station and change there to the Osaka Monorail.

Universal Studios Japan   AMUSEMENT PARK
(ユニバーサルスタジオジャパン, Universal City; www.usj.co.jp; adult/child ¥6400/4300; ⊙10am-6pm Mon-Fri, to 8pm Sat, Sun & holidays, longer hours summer; ®JR Osaka Loop line to Universal City) Universal Studios Japan is closely based on its sister parks in the USA, featuring a variety of movie-related rides, shows and other attractions, plus restaurants. Hours vary seasonally. To get here, take the JR Loop line to Nishi-kujō Station, then

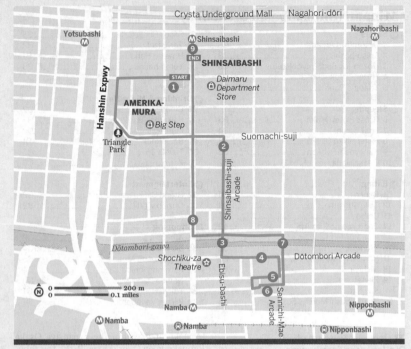

🏃 City Walk
Sights of Minami

START SHINSAIBASHI STATION
END SHINSAIBASHI STATION
LENGTH 2.2KM; 2½ HOURS

Try to time your walk so you're in Dōtombori after dark for the full neon-lit experience. Start with a wander around the colourful neighbourhood of ❶ **Amerika-Mura** (p341). Then cross over Midō-suji, take a deep breath, and step into the throng in ❷ **Shinsaibashi-suji**, Shinsaibashi's famous, and famously long, *shōtengai* (market street).

After inching past shops, game parlours and eateries, with thumping music and the high-pitched call of *irasshaimase!* coming at you from every angle, you'll be released out the end and onto ❸ **Ebisu-bashi**. This bridge is a popular place for photos down Dōtombori-gawa, with the neon garishness of the buildings on both sides. Here also is the perennially joyful Glico running man. Be sure to glance back to see the masses coming down the arcade.

At the end of the bridge, look right to glimpse the neo-Renaissance facade of Shochiku-za Theatre. Go left by Kani Dōroku's giant crab, another local landmark, into ❹ **Dōtombori Arcade**. Walk past countless restaurants, takoyaki stands, spiky-haired touts and more big signs (big pufferfish, big dragon, big hand holding sushi). Look out for Kuidaore Taro, the 60-odd-year-old mechanical clown found drumming here when not on tour.

Before the big cow, take a right down Senichi-mae arcade. Turn again at the cobblestoned alley with the wooden signboard for ❺ **Hōzen-ji Yokochō** (法善寺横丁), and you're suddenly in an older, quieter Osaka, charmingly lantern-lit in the evening. At the end, go left then through the temple gateway to tiny ❻ **Hōzen-ji** (p109).

Continue past the temple back to Senichi-mae arcade and the Dōtombori strip, then cross over ❼ **Tazaemon-bashi**. At the other side of the bridge, head down to the waterside walkway – a good spot to grab a plate of *takoyaki* (octopus balls) and take a seat.

Follow the walkway under Ebisu-bashi and up onto ❽ **Midō-suji-dōri**, where you can stroll the boulevard all the way north to **Shinsaibashi Station**.

switch to a Universal Studios shuttle train (total trip ¥170, 15 minutes). There are also some direct trains from Osaka Station (the price is the same).

✖✖ Festivals & Events

Tōka Ebisu   TRADITIONAL FESTIVAL
From 9 to 11 January, huge crowds of more than a million people flock to the Imamiya Ebisu-jinja (今宮戎神社) to receive bamboo branches hung with auspicious tokens. The shrine is near Imamiya Ebisu Station on the Nankai line.

Sumō Spring Tournament   SUMŌ
(Haru Bashō; www.sumo.or.jp) The big fellas rumble into Osaka in March for this major tournament in the sumō calendar, held in the Prefectural Gymnasium (府立体育会館, Furitsu Taiiku-kan) in Namba. Tickets go from around ¥3500 to ¥10,000.

★ Tenjin Matsuri   TRADITIONAL FESTIVAL
Held on 24 and 25 July, this is one of Japan's three biggest festivals. Try to make the second day, when processions of *mikoshi* (portable shrines) and people in traditional attire start at Osaka Temman-gū and end up in hundreds of boats on the O-kawa. As night falls, there is a huge fireworks display.

Kishiwada Danjiri Matsuri TRADITIONAL FESTIVAL
Osaka's wildest festival, on 14 and 15 September, is a kind of running of the bulls except with *danjiri* (festival floats), many weighing over 3000kg. The *danjiri* are hauled through the streets by hundreds of people using ropes – take care and stand back. Most of the action takes place on the second day and the best place to see it is west of Kishiwada Station on the Nankai *honsen* line (main rail line, from Nankai Station).

🛏 Sleeping

There are plenty of places to stay in and around the two centres of Kita and Minami. You can also explore Osaka from a base in Kyoto, and you'll find more budget accommodation in the old capital, which is only about 40 minutes away by train. But keep in mind that the trains stop running a little before midnight (party-goers take note). Minami, including Shinsaibashi, Dōtombori and Namba, has a bigger selection of restaurants and shops, but the Kita area is convenient if you want fast access to transport, with plenty of hotels around the stations.

🛏 Kita Area

Hearton Hotel Kita Umeda   HOTEL ¥¥
(ハートンホテル北梅田; Map p342; ☎ 6377-0810; www.heartonhotel.com/kit; 3-12-10 Toyosaki; s/tw ¥11,550/18,900; ✿@; ⑤ Midō-suji line to Nakatsu) This is a good midrange option in a pleasant area a short walk north of Hankyū Umeda Station (even shorter from Nakatsu subway station), putting you right near transport and the restaurants and shops of Umeda. The clean, light rooms have a modern design and are slightly bigger than average for Japanese hotels. Staff are friendly and some English is spoken. Don't be put off by the rack-rate prices; you'll pay significantly less booking online.

Hotel Sunroute Umeda   HOTEL ¥¥
(ホテルサンルート梅田; Map p342; ☎ 6373-1111; www.sunroute.jp/english; 3-9-1 Toyosaki; s/d from ¥8820/12,600; ✿@☎; ⑤ Midō-suji line to Nakatsu) The Sunroute is a good business hotel about 15 minutes' walk north of JR Osaka Station, in a convenient spot just north of Hankyū Umeda. The rooms are small but fresh, with neutral colours, and some with good views over Osaka.

Hilton Osaka   HOTEL ¥¥¥
(ヒルトン大阪; Map p342; ☎ 6347-7111; www3.hilton.com; 1-8-8 Umeda; s ¥18,000; tw from ¥22,000-51,000; ✿@☎☎; ℝ JR line to Osaka) Just south of JR Osaka Station, this is an excellent hotel at home with foreign guests. The rooms have a Japanese touch, there's a 15m pool in the fitness centre and the views from the 35th-floor Windows on the World bar are awesome. Handily, there are two floors of great restaurants below the hotel.

🛏 Minami Area

Osaka Hana Hostel   HOSTEL ¥
(大阪花宿; Map p344; ☎ 6281-8786; http://osaka.hanahostel.com; 1-8-4 Nishi-Shinsaibashi; dm/tw/tr ¥2800/7200/9600; ✿@☎️; ⑤ Midō-suji line to Shinsaibashi, exit 7) This is a great new budget option in the heart of Shinsaibashi. Besides the six-bed dorms, there are private, mostly Japanese-style rooms with and without (small) ensuite; plus good options for groups and families, including studios with kitchenette and bigger ensuite. There are two kitchen/lounge areas, clean shared facilities, and a helpful team of well-travelled English-speaking staff.

First Cabin
HOTEL ¥

(ファーストキャビン; Map p344; ☑6631-8090; www.first-cabin.jp; 4th fl, Midōsuji-Namba Bldg, 4-2-1 Namba; per person ¥4800; ⊜@; Ⓢ Midō-suji line to Namba, exit 13) Here you get a tiny private room, sort of like a suite on an Airbus A380 (hence the name), with a big TV, a locker and LAN internet access. Rooms are segregated by gender, as are the large common baths and showers. Service is friendly and it's a top location close to Midō-suji and Nankai Namba Stations, but rooms can be noisy.

★ Arietta Hotel
HOTEL ¥¥

(アリエッタホテル大阪; Map p340; ☑6267-2787; www.thehotel.co.jp/en/arietta_osaka; 3-2-6 Azuchi-machi; s/tw with breakfast from ¥7500/15,000; ⊜@; Ⓢ Midō-suji line to Honmachi, exit 3) In Honmachi, about 10 minutes' walk north of the Minami district (served by the Midō-suji subway line), the Arietta has a warm, boutique-hotel feel. The good-sized rooms are minimalist, with wood floors and tiled bathrooms offering something different to the norm. Staff are welcoming and a breakfast of breads, coffee and juice is included. It's got all you need at a competitive price.

Kaneyoshi Ryokan
RYOKAN ¥¥

(かねよし旅館; Map p344; ☑6211-6337; www.kaneyosi.jp; 3-12 Soemonchō; per person from ¥5250; @⚙; Ⓢ Sennichimae line to Nipponbashi, exit 2 or Midō-suji line to Namba, exit 14) Kaneyoshi is a bit dated, but it's clean, the tatami rooms are comfortable with private bathrooms, and management are eager to please. Try for a room at the back, where you'll have views of the river. Staying here you'll be in the thick of the nightlife district – not unsafe, but expect a few cheerful businessmen in the vicinity after dark. There are no non-smoking rooms (though rooms are well aired) and there's a midnight curfew.

★ Cross Hotel Osaka
HOTEL ¥¥¥

(クロスホテル大阪; Map p344; ☑6213-8281; www.crosshotel.com/osaka; 2-5-15 Shinsaibashi-suji; s/d/tw from ¥16,170/24,255/27,720; ⊜@; Ⓢ Midō-suji line to Namba, exit 14) Cross Hotel is going for a trendy urban look, with black, white and dark red featuring in the stylish rooms and common areas. Rooms are average size, but they had us at the spacious Japanese-style bathrooms – a rare treat. Service is excellent and you'd have to sleep under Ebisu-bashi bridge to achieve a more central location. Online deals bump this into upper-midrange territory.

Hotel Nikkō Osaka
HOTEL ¥¥¥

(ホテル日航大阪; Map p344; ☑6244-1281; www.hno.co.jp; 1-3-3 Nishi-Shinsaibashi; s ¥11,000-24,000, d ¥13,000-30,000; ⊜@; Ⓢ Midō-suji line to Shinsaibashi, exit 6) The Nikkō is a good central base in Minami and has direct access to Shinsaibashi subway station. Service is professional, rooms are modern and comfortable with spacious deluxe options, and there's even a 'ladies' floor, with special bathroom amenities. There are restaurants and bars on-site, and good views from the upper floors.

🛏 Other Areas

★ Hostel 64 Osaka
HOSTEL ¥

(☑6556-6586; Map p340; www.hostel64.com; 3-11-20 Shinmachi; dm/s/d from ¥3300/5900/7800; ⊜@🛜; Ⓢ Chuō line to Awaza, exit 2) This non-traditional hostel in a quiet neighbourhood just west of Shinsaibashi is a little out of the way but worth the effort, especially if you're in town a few days. There are Japanese- and Western-style private rooms, a small dorm of individual beds separated by screens, and a cosy lounge that doubles as a cafe-bar. Besides the welcoming, knowledgeable staff, the main appeal is the thoughtfully designed interiors, all kitted out with retro furnishings sensitive to the 1960s building. Bathrooms are shared and there's no elevator.

Shin-Osaka Youth Hostel
HOSTEL ¥

(新大阪ユースホステル; Map p340; ☑6370-5427; http://osaka-yha.or.jp/shin-osaka-eng; 1-13-13 Higashinakajima; dm/tw ¥3300/9000; ⊜@🛜⚙; 🚃 JR line to Shin-Osaka, east exit) Five minutes from Shin-Osaka Station, this efficiently run hostel is in a large building with great views across the city. There are a few rules, such as a day-time lockout (you can still use the lounge) and midnight curfew, but the rooms and common areas are big, well equipped and spotlessly clean. Private rooms are good value, with one designated room for the physically disabled.

🍴 Eating

🍴 Kita

Umeda Hagakure
NOODLES ¥

(梅田はがくれ; Map p342; ☑6341-1409; B2 fl, Osaka Ekimae Daisan Bldg, 1-1 Umeda; noodles ¥600-1100; ⊙11am-2.45pm & 5-7.45pm Mon-Fri, 11am-2.30pm Sat & Sun; 🚃 JR line to Osaka) Locals line up here for the delicious house-made *udon* noodles, which come hot or cold (cold is the speciality) and sometimes with a side of instructions from the owner on how to eat them. There are pictures to help with ordering; our pick is the *tenzaru* (cold *udon* served with tempura; ¥1100). Avoid weekdays between noon and 1pm, when the office-worker lunch crowd descends.

★ **Robatayaki Isaribi**   IZAKAYA, YAKITORI ¥¥
(炉ばた焼き漁火; Map p342; ☎6373-2969; www.rikimaru-group.com/shop/isaribi.html; 1-5-12 Shibata; dishes ¥315; ⏰5-11.15pm; ☐; ☐JR line to Osaka) Enjoy the lively atmosphere and Osakan friendliness here while you fill up on tasty meat, seafood and vegetable dishes served fresh off the grill. Individual items are all ¥315, or loosen the belt and make a night of it with the all-you-can-eat-and-drink option (from ¥3500). Find Isaribi in the basement, accessed via stairs in front of a liquor store. It's best to book for groups.

Yukari   OKONOMIYAKI ¥¥
(ゆかり; Map p342; ☎6311-0214; www.yukari chan.co.jp; Ohatsutenjin-dōri; okonomiyaki ¥1000-2000; ⏰11am-1am; ☐☐; ☐JR line to Osaka) This popular restaurant in the Ohatsutenjin-dōri arcade serves up that great Osaka favourite, *okonomiyaki* (a mix of batter with shredded cabbage and various fillings, slathered in a Worcestershire-style sauce and mayonnaise), cooked on a griddle right in front of you. There's lots to choose from on the picture menu, including veg options, but you can't really go wrong with the *tokusen mikkusu yaki* (okonomiyaki with fried pork, shrimp and squid; ¥1080). Look for the red and white signage out front.

Ganko Umeda Honten   JAPANESE, SUSHI ¥¥
(がんこ梅田本店; Map p342; ☎6376-2001; www.gankofood.co.jp; 1-5-11 Shibata; meals ¥780-5000; ⏰11.30am-4am, to midnight Sun; ☐; ☐JR line to Osaka) This large dining hall serves a wide variety of set-course meals and sushi (à la carte or in sets), offering traditional, quality ingredients at a reasonable price. It's on the street along the west side of Hankyū Umeda Station. Look for the picture of the guy wearing a headband.

Satoyama Dining   BUFFET ¥¥
(里山ダイニング; Map p342; 17fl Hankyū Terminal Bldg, 1-1-4 Shibata; lunch/dinner ¥1890/2480; ⏰11am-10.30pm; ☐☐☐; ☐JR line to Osaka) Satoyama's all-you-can-eat buffet is perfect for those who want to try a few things without having to commit. Roam around at leisure and take your pick from the range of mostly Japanese home-style dishes, while enjoying great views of the Hep Five Ferris wheel. Tip: come after 8.30pm and you'll pay the lunch price for dinner. It's non-smoking throughout and there are discounts for kids.

Restaurant Org...   CAFE ¥¥
(レストランオルグ; Map p342; ☎6312-0529; www.restaurant-org.com; 7-7 Dōyama-chō; lunch ¥900-1400, dinner ¥1200-3000; ⏰11.00am-10pm Mon-Thu, to 10.30pm Fri-Sun; ☐; ☐JR line to Osaka) At this spacious, wooden-table-filled cafe you can grab a light meal or quick coffee pick-me-up while exploring Kita. The menu features pizzas, pastas, risottos and salads, with some vegetarian-friendly options (let them know what you don't eat). There's no English menu, but there are pictures and 'pasta lunch' or 'pizza lunch' will get your point across.

Tucusi Tapas & Charcoal Grill   SPANISH ¥¥
(ツクシタパスアンドチャコールグリル; Map p342; ☎6362-2948; http://tucusi.com; 2-5-30 Sonezaki; lunch from ¥800, tapas ¥400-1500; ⏰11.30am-3pm & 5pm-3am; ☐; ☐Tanimachi line to Higashi-Umeda) Spanish food is all the rage in Japan and Tucusi has the good stuff. It's a slick, modern spot oddly located in a sort of netherworld east of Kita-Shinchi. Like most tapas spots, this place is as much about drinking as eating.

✕ Shinsaibashi & Around

Green Earth   VEGETARIAN ¥
(Map p340; 4-2-2 Kita-kyūhōji-machi; ¥550-850; ⏰11.30am-5pm Mon-Sat; ☐☐☐; ☐Midō-suji line to Shinsaibashi, exit 3) A haven for vegetarians and vegans, this small cafe serves up hearty sandwiches, curries and pastas, with a generous daily lunch set for ¥700 (with drink ¥850). It's also entirely smoke-free. From Shinsaibashi, walk north up Midō-suji, turn left immediately after Namba Shrine (難波神社), take the second right and look for the English sign on the right.

★ **Café Absinthe**   MEDITERRANEAN ¥¥
(カフェアブサン; Map p344; ☎6534-6635; www.absinthe-jp.com; 1-2-27 Kitahorie; meals ¥1000-3000; ⏰3pm-3am, to 5am Sat & Sun, closed Tue; ☐; ☐Midō-suji line to Shinsaibashi, exit 7) For fantastic cocktails, non-alcoholic drinks and juices and a diverse Mediterranean menu (something of a rarity in Kansai),

RESTAURANT HALLS

A lot of the dining action in Osaka can be found in the numerous food halls found on the upper floors of department stores, in underground shopping arcades and in basement floors of hotels. These typically have a variety of reasonably priced restaurants clustered together in one floor, all with food displays and prices in the windows, making it easy to browse and find something that takes your fancy.

Namba Parks Mall A huge variety of places under one roof just south of Namba Station. Try **Sai-ji-ki** (菜蒔季; Map p344; ☑6636-8123; 6th fl, Namba Parks, 2-10-70 Namba-naka; lunch/dinner from ¥1468/1888; ⏱11am-11pm, enter by 9pm; ⊖☑❖; ⑤Midō-suji, Sennichi-mae, or Yotsubashi line to Namba), an organic all-you-can-eat restaurant.

Gourmet Traveler (グルメトラベラー; Map p342; B2 fl, Herbis Plaza complex) Gourmet Traveler at the Herbis Plaza complex is located west of JR Osaka Station between the Hilton and the Ritz Carlton hotels. It has everything from a Belgian beer restaurant to Indian curry, as well as a smattering of Japanese places.

Hankyū Sanbangai (阪急三番街; Map p342; www.h-sanbangai.com; ⑧Hankyū line to Umeda) Go down to the B2 floor of Hankyū Umeda Station for Japanese and international restaurants, as well as a good collection of shops selling cakes, pastries and chocolates. You'll know you're in the right place when you see the canal.

Osaka Maru Bldg (大阪丸ビル; Map p342; www.marubiru.com/restaurant; ⑧JR line to Osaka) There is a good variety of restaurants on the B2 floor of the distinctive cylindrical Maru Building, including Korean, Indian, *yakitori* and an *omuraisu* (fried rice wrapped in a thin omelette topped with sauce) specialist.

Hilton Plaza (ヒルトンプラザ; Map p342; www.hiltonplaza.com; ⑧JR line to Osaka) On the B2 floor beneath the Hilton Plaza. Among the restaurants worth trying here is the tempura specialist, **Shinkiraku** (新善楽; Map p342; ☑6345-3461; East B2 fl Hilton Plaza, 1-8-16 Umeda; lunch/dinner from ¥780/2000; ⏱11am-2.30pm & 5-11pm Mon-Fri, 11am-2.30pm & 4-10pm Sat & Sun & holidays; ⓐ; ⑧JR line to Osaka).

this friendly restaurant near the western edge of Ame-Mura is a must. The drinks and food here cost a little more, but it's good value when you factor in quality ingredients, stylish surrounds and a friendly, laid-back atmosphere. And, yes, it does serve the eponymous absinthe.

Nishiya　　　　　　　　NOODLES ¥¥
(にし家; Map p344; ☑6241-9221; 1-18-18 Higashi Shinsaibashi; noodle dishes from ¥630, dinner courses ¥3000-5000; ⏱11am-11pm Mon-Sat, to 9.30pm Sun; ⓐ; ⑤Midō-suji line to Shinsaibashi, exit 5 or 6) A peaceful spot on the busy streets of Shinsaibashi, this welcoming Osaka landmark serves *udon* noodles, a variety of hearty *nabe* (cast-iron pot) dishes, and *shabu-shabu* (thin slices of meat and vegetables cooked in a broth and dipped in sauce) courses for reasonable prices. Look for the traditional wooden sliding-door entrance and the food models.

Ume no Hana　　　　TOFU, JAPANESE ¥¥
(梅の花; Map p344; ☑6258-3766; www.umenohana.co.jp; 11th fl, OPA Bldg, 1-4-3 Nishi-Shinsaibashi; lunch/dinner from ¥2000/5000; ⏱11am-3pm & 5-10pm; ⓐ; ⑤Midō-suji line to Shinsaibashi, exit 7) Ume no Hana is part of an upscale chain serving a variety of tofu-based dishes, all beautifully presented with sides of vegetables, pickles and fish, depending on the course you choose. It makes for a pleasant traditional dining experience, high above the hustle and bustle on the 11th floor. Take the OPA building elevator from street level on Midō-suji or from the subway.

Cuorerudino Pizzeria　　　ITALIAN ¥¥
(ピッツェリア・クオーレルディーノ; ☑4390-1383; Map p344; www.cuorerudino.com; 1-14-26 Minamihorie; meals ¥700-1400; ⏱11.30am-11pm; ⊖; ⑤Midō-suji line to Shinsaibashi or Yotsubashi line to Yotsubashi) This new, casual pizzeria has an open kitchen with a large brick oven, so you can see the delicious thin-crust pizzas being prepared. Staff are enthusiastic and there's an interesting menu (in Japanese and Italian) of mostly pizzas but also antipasto and desserts. Smoking only on the outdoor terrace.

Amerika-Mura

Amerika-Mura is home to some good cafes and cheap eateries, including some of Japan's cheapest *izakaya* (which, not surprisingly, tend to come and go).

★Shinsaibashi Madras 5 · CURRY ¥

(マドラス心斎橋店; Map p344; ☑ 6213-0858; 2-7-22 Nishi-Shinsaibashi; meals ¥680-1480; ☺ 11am-1am; ✔️ 🍴; Ⓢ Midō-suji line to Namba) If you've never tried Japanese-style curry rice, this is a good place to get acquainted with its warm, saucy charms. Choose from tomato-, beef- or chicken-based curries and a variety of toppings. You can even get *genmai* (brown rice) if you wish. It's not far from either Namba or Shinsaibashi stations.

Banco · CAFE ¥

(バンコ; Map p344; ☑ 080-6113-2504; http://banco.ciao.jp; 1-9-26 Nishi-Shinsaibashi; lunch ¥850; ☺ noon-2am; 🍴; Ⓢ Midō-suji line to Shinsaibashi, exit 7) A handy Ame-Mura location, an intimate space with art-filled walls and streetside tables, friendly service, and, importantly, good coffee – Banco has all the makings for a relaxed lunchtime or evening pit stop. Alcohol is also served.

Slices Bar & Cafe · CAFE, BAR ¥

(スライセズバーアンドカフェ; Map p344; ☑ 6211-2231; www.slicesjapan.com; 1st fl, Yoshimoto Bldg, 2-3-21 Nishi-Shinsaibashi; pizza slices/whole from ¥400/1600; ☺ noon-midnight, to 2am Sat; 🍴; Ⓢ Midō-suji line to Namba or Shinsaibashi) If you need a break from Japanese food, stop into this casual foreigner-friendly joint. The pizza lunch sets are especially good value, but there are also calzones, wraps, bagels, desserts and bubble teas, plus brunch-time pancakes on the menu. Canadian owners serve a few Canadian specialities (Hosers, get your poutine here), and it has cocktails to suit any mood.

Planet 3rd · CAFE ¥

(Map p344; 1-5-24 Nishi-Shinsaibashi; ☺ 7am-midnight; 🖥️@🍴) A large cafe, with a few iPads for use, good coffee, drinks and light meals.

Tori Kizoku · IZAKAYA, YAKITORI ¥

(鳥貴族; Map p344; ☑ 6251-7114; 2nd fl, 1-8-15 Nishi-Shinsaibashi; dishes/drinks ¥294; ☺ 6pm-5am; 🍴; Ⓢ Midō-suji line to Shinsaibashi) The name means 'chicken nobility', but the prices at this popular *yakitori-ya* chain are decidedly common. Look for the yellow and red sign and the number 280 (indicating that all grilled skewers cost just ¥280).

Yume-hachi · IZAKAYA ¥

(ゆめ八; Map p344; ☑ 6212-7078; www.yume-hachi.jp; 1st fl, 2-16-9 Nishi-Shinsaibashi; dishes ¥380; ☺ 5pm-5am; Ⓢ Midō-suji line to Namba or Shinsaibashi) A good choice for a cheap feed where the food is actually not bad and portions are decent. This funky spot attracts a younger crowd out for late-night drinks. The drinks menu has English, and there are some pictures on the food menu, which has pasta, fried chicken, rice dishes and other light meals.

Dōtombori & Around

Dōtombori Arcade is crammed with eateries. The dining isn't refined, but if you want heaping portions of tasty food in a very casual atmosphere, it can be a lot of fun. And because it sees a lot of tourists, most of the big restaurants here have English menus.

★Imai Honten · NOODLES ¥¥

(今井本店; Map p344; ☑ 6211-0319; http://d-imai.com; 1-7-22 Dōtombori; dishes from ¥630; ☺ 11am-10pm, closed Wed; 🍴; Ⓢ Midō-suji line to Namba) Step into an oasis of calm amid the chaos to be welcomed by kimono-clad staff at one of the area's oldest and most revered *udon* specialists. Try the *kitsune udon* – noodles topped with soup-soaked slices of fried tofu. There's no English sign outside, but look for the traditional front and the tree.

★Chibō · OKONOMIYAKI ¥¥

(千房; Map p344; ☑ 6212-2211; www.chibo.com; 1-5-5 Dōtombori; meals from ¥850; ☺ 11am-1am Mon-Sat, to midnight Sun; 🍴; Ⓢ Midō-suji line to Namba) This popular *okonomiyaki* specialist is a good place to expand your Japanese-pancake repertoire. Try the house special *Dōtombori yaki*, a toothsome treat with pork, beef, squid, shrimp and cheese for ¥1550. For something different, go for a *stamina yaki*, cooked with kimchi and topped with an egg. Some tables look out over the canal.

★Zauo · SEAFOOD ¥¥

(ざうお難波本店; Map p344; ☑ 6212-5882; www.zauo.com; Washington Hotel Plaza B1 fl, Nipponbashi 1-1-13; meals ¥680-6000; ☺ 5pm-midnight Mon-Fri, 11.30am-midnight Sat & Sun; Ⓢ Sakai-suji line to Nipponbashi, exit 6, or Midō-suji line to Namba) In a country where seafood is sometimes eaten so fresh it's still moving, it makes sense to find a restaurant where fish swim around the tables and patrons try to catch them for dinner. If you're lucky enough to hook something, there's celebratory drumming and your fish is whisked away to be prepared how you like (you pay based on the type of fish). It's best to order from the menu in case nothing is biting – try an eight-piece sushi *omakase nigiri*, or a very tasty *shio-yaki* (salt-grilled) fish set. There's a ¥300-per-person table charge. Reserve to get a table on a 'boat'.

Krungtep
THAI ¥¥

(クンテープ; Map p344; 4708-0088; www.krungtep.co.jp; 1-6-14 Dōtombori; lunch buffet ¥1200, dinner dishes from ¥980; 11.30am-11pm, closed 3-5pm weekdays; ; S Midō-suji line to Namba) This long-running Thai place serves fairly authentic versions of the standard favourites like green curry and tom yum kung, and does a great-value lunch buffet. Tables at the back have views of the canal. Look for the small English sign a couple of buildings past the giant crab – it's in the basement.

Drinking & Nightlife

Osaka is a hard-working city, but when quitting time rolls around, Osakans know how to party. Take a stroll through Minami on a Friday night and you'd be excused for thinking there's one bar for every resident of the city. In summer, head up to one of the city's rooftop **beer gardens** for all you can drink and eat in fun, casual surrounds – the one atop Hanshin Department Store is particularly good. For up-to-date info on upcoming bar/club/music events in Osaka, check **iflyer** (http://iflyer.tv).

Kita

Minami might be Osaka's real nightlife district, but there are bars, clubs and *izakaya* in the neighbourhoods to the south and east of Osaka Station, and around Hankyū Umeda Station.

Karma
BAR, RESTAURANT

(カーマ; Map p342; www.club-karma.com; B1 fl Zero Bldg, 1-5-18 Sonezakishinchi; 5pm-3am Mon-Sat, to 11pm Sun; JR line to Osaka) Spacious and white-wall stylish, Karma is a fine bar-restaurant to kick back in if you enjoy a bit of pumping music with your evening drink. It also serves light meals (dishes ¥600 to ¥1200). Some Saturdays have techno events with cover charges averaging ¥2500.

Blarney Stone
PUB

(Map p342; www.the-blarney-stone.com; 6th fl Sonezaki Center Bldg, 2-10-15 Sonezaki; 5pm-1am Mon-Thu, to 5am Fri & Sat, 3.30pm-1am Sun; JR

line to Osaka) In Umeda's Ohatsutenjin-dōri arcade, have a Guinness or two and relax in the friendly atmosphere of this Irish-style pub, well liked among expats and Japanese for after-work drinks and the free live music on weekends. There's a sign at street level.

Captain Kangaroo
BAR

(Map p342; 1-5-20 Sonezakishinchi; 6pm-5am Mon-Sat, to midnight Sun; JR line to Osaka) This popular, dimly lit bar in the Kita-Shinchi district is a short walk from JR Osaka Station and draws a good crowd of expats and Japanese. Among other bar-menu standards, it does a good burger with chunky fries, and you can get a meat pie.

Windows on the World
BAR

(ウィンドーズオンザワールド; Map p342; 1-8-8 Umeda; 5.30pm-12.30am Mon-Thu & Sun, to 1am Fri & Sat; JR line to Osaka) An unbeatable spot for sophisticated drinks with a view – it's on the 35th floor of the Hilton Osaka. There's a ¥1750 per person table charge and drinks average ¥2000.

Minami

This is the place for a big night out in Osaka, with numerous bars, clubs and restaurants packed into the streets and alleys of Shinsaibashi and Namba.

Zerro
BAR

(ゼロ; Map p344; 2-3-2 Shinsaibashi-suji; 7pm-5am; S Midō-suji line to Namba or Shinsaibashi) Zerro has a good range of drinks and food, energetic bilingual bartenders, and a street-level location ideal for a spot of people-watching. Come early for relaxed drinks and conversation; come late on the weekend for DJs, dancing and a lively crowd.

Folk Rock Bar Phoebe
BAR

(Map p344; 108 Dōtombori Heights, 2-7-22 Nishi-Shinsaibashi; 6pm-2am; S Midō-suji line to Namba or Shinsaibashi) Imagine a storeroom crammed with old records, CDs, worn-out knick-knacks and random ornaments. Then imagine a bar in the middle of it. That's kind of what to expect at this tiny, quirky place, where you'll be heartily welcomed by the long-haired owner as he spins folk-rock tunes on the record player and serves drinks. There's an English sign out front.

Murphy's
BAR

(マーフィーズ; Map p344; 6th fl Reed Plaza Bldg, 1-6-3 Higashi-Shinsaibashi; 5pm-1am Sun-Thu, to

LOOK UP, LOOK DOWN

As in all major Japanese cities, space is at a premium in Osaka, and many bars and pubs are hidden away in the upper floors and basements of buildings. When you're wandering around the narrow streets of Shinsaibashi or Namba late at night, convinced that bar you're looking for must have closed or moved, remember to keep looking up to check the signs on the sides of buildings showing what's on each floor, and look down for signboards pointing to what's below ground. Oh, and best learn how to ask 'Where is...' in Japanese.

4am Fri & Sat; S Sakai-suji line to Nagahoribashi) This is one of the oldest Irish-style pubs in Japan, and a good place to rub shoulders with expats and Japanese, enjoy free live music, catch sports matches, and, of course, have a pint. It's on the 6th floor of a futuristic building with what looks like a rocket on the front.

Rock Rock   BAR
(ロックロック; Map p344344; www.rockrock. co.jp; 3rd fl Shinsaibashi Atrium Bldg, 1-8-1 Nishi-Shinsaibashi; ⊙7pm-5am Mon-Sat, to 1am Sun; S Midō-suji line to Shinsaibashi, exit 7) Serving the music-loving community since 1995, Rock Rock has a history of hosting after parties for international acts and attracting a host of celeb visitors. Regular events with a modest cover charge showcase some of Osaka's finest rock DJs. Check the website for what's happening (and for a list of famous guests, if you're curious).

Cinquecento   BAR
(チンクエチェント; Map p344; 2-1-10 Higashi-Shinsaibashi; ⊙7.30pm-5am Mon-Sat, 8pm-3am Sun; S Midō-suji line to Namba or Shinsaibashi) Everything at this cosy, aptly named bar is ¥500, including a hearty selection of food and the impressively extensive martini menu. It's not far from the corner of Sakai-suji; look for the 5 in a red circle.

Tavola 36   BAR
(タボラ36; Map p344; 5-1-60 Namba; ⊙6-11.30pm Mon-Thu, to midnight Fri, Sat & Sun; ℝ Midō-suji line to Namba) If you want drinks, a killer view and classy surroundings, this is where to go in Minami. It's an Italian restaurant-bar on the 36th floor of the Swissotel Nankai Osaka. There's a ¥1260 per person table charge after 6pm and drinks start from around ¥1100.

★ Onzieme (11)   NIGHTCLUB
(オンジェム; Map p344; www.onzi-eme.com; 11th fl Midō-suji Bldg, 1-4-5 Nishi-Shinsaibashi; S Midō-suji line to Shinsaibashi, exit 7) Those eager for a taste of Osaka nightlife at its craziest should head to the city's largest and most lively club. An assortment of local and internationally acclaimed house, hip-hop and techno DJs showcase their talents nightly, with the posh interior reminiscent of some of the more famous London establishments. Cover charges average ¥2500.

Grand Café   NIGHTCLUB
(グランドカフェ; Map p344; http://grandcafe osaka.com; B1 fl Spazio Bldg, 2-10-21 Nishi-Shinsaibashi; S Midō-suji to Shinsaibashi) This hip club hosts a variety of electronica-DJ and hip-hop events. There's a comfy seating area and several dance floors. Look for the English sign at street level.

☆ Entertainment

For information on upcoming shows, events and concerts, chat to the tourist offices or pick up a copy of *Kansai Scene* (you can also check the listings on its website: www.kansaiscene.com). A number of the foreigner-friendly pubs and bars have free live music on weekends, including Murphy's (p352) and the Blarney Stone (p352).

★ National Bunraku Theatre   THEATRE
(国立文楽劇場; Map p340; ☎6212-2531; www. ntj.jac.go.jp; 1-12-10 Nipponbashi; S Sennichimae or Sakai-suji line to Nipponbashi) This is probably the best place in Japan to see the mesmerising puppet-mastery of *bunraku*. Attending a full performance can be an all-day affair, with two parts running about four hours each. You can just buy a ticket to one part, or, a fantastic option for time-poor travellers is the single-act ticket. These are sold on the day (from 9.45am) and can't be reserved, so you need to show up at the box office in the morning and hope seats are available for one of the acts. Tickets for full plays start at around ¥2300 or ¥5800 depending on seats, with single-act tickets proportionally cheaper. English audio guides can be hired (¥650) and the theatre provides English programs explaining the

BUNRAKU

Japanese traditional puppet theatre, known as *bunraku*, did not originate in Osaka but the art form was popularised here. The most famous *bunraku* playwright was Chikamatsu Monzaemon (1653–1724), who wrote plays set in Osaka concerning the classes that traditionally had no place in Japanese art: merchants and the denizens of the pleasure quarters. Not surprisingly, *bunraku* found a wide audience among these people, and a theatre was established to put on the plays of Chikamatsu in Dōtombori. Today's National Bunraku Theatre works to keep the tradition alive.

Learn more about the history, puppeteers and main characters of *bunraku* in the lobby and exhibition room (free entry) of the National Bunraku Theatre (p353), where you can of course also see performances – it's well worth it if you have the opportunity.

stories. Performances are usually held in January, April, July, August and November: check the website or at the tourist offices for current dates. Shows sell out quickly.

Osaka Nōgaku Hall THEATRE
(大阪能楽会館; Map p342; www.pp.iij4u.or.jp/~rohnishi; 2-3-17 Nakasakinishi; 🚉 JR line to Osaka) A five-minute walk east of Osaka Station, this hall holds nō (stylised dance-drama) shows about twice a month, most of which cost ¥5000 to ¥6000. See p803 for more on nō.

🛍 Shopping

Osaka has almost as many shops as it has restaurants, with major department stores, high-end fashion, independent boutiques, electronic goods and secondhand stores. Most major department stores will refund the sales tax on purchases over ¥10,000 – make sure you bring your passport along, and ask at the information counters for details.

🛍 Kita

Kita is the place to come if you like browsing department stores. Many are clustered around the stations, including **Hankyū** (阪急梅田本店; Map p342; www.hankyu-dept.co.jp/honten) and **Hanshin** (阪神梅田; www.hanshin-dept.jp/hshonten), the more youth-oriented **Hep Five** (Map p342; www.hepfive.jp), with the giant Ferris wheel on top; as well as recent additions to the Osaka retail scene **Lucua** (ルクア; Map p342; www.lucua.jp), in JR Osaka Station, and **NU Chayamachi** (NU 茶屋町; Map p342; http://nu-chayamachi.com). Fashion-savvy guys should also check out **Hankyū Men's** (阪急メンズ; Map p342; www.hankyu-dept.co.jp/mens) in the ship-shaped Hep Navio building. The department stores all have similar hours, opening 10am or 11am and closing 8.30pm or 9pm.

Maruzen & Junkudō Umeda BOOKS
(MARUZEN&ジュンク堂書店梅田店; Map p342; www.junkudo.co.jp/MJumeda.html; 7-20 Chayamachi; ⊘10am-10pm; 🚉 JR line to Osaka) This new behemoth bookshop, the largest in Osaka, is the result of two book specialists joining forces. There's a big range of English-language books on the 6th floor, with travel guides on the 3rd floor. It's in the new Andō Tadao–designed Chaska Chayamachi building.

Kōjitsu Sansō OUTDOOR GEAR
(好日山荘; Map p342; www.kojitsusanso.jp; Osaka Ekimae Daisan Bldg, 1-1-3 Umeda; ⊘11am-9pm; 🚉 JR line to Osaka) If you need a new backpack or any other kind of outdoor gear, head to this excellent shop on the ground floor at the northwest corner of the Ekimae Daisan building.

Junkudō BOOKS
(ジュンク堂書店; Map p342; www.junkudo.co.jp; 1-6-20 Dōjima Avanza; ⊘10am-9pm; 🚉 JR line to Osaka) This large bookshop has a great selection of foreign- and Japanese-language books. It's inside the Dōjima Avanza Building, about 10 minutes' walk from Osaka Station. Most English-language books are on the 3rd floor, along with a cafe. English travel guides are on the 2nd floor.

🛍 Minami

Minami has a huge range of shops. International high-end brands have their outlets along Midō-suji, the main boulevard of Minami, between Shinsaibashi and Namba subway stations. Head to the jam-packed Shinsaibashi-suji arcade (which connects to more arcades) for popular local and international chains, and Ame-Mura for out-there and vintage clothes, accessories and music.

★**Dōguya-suji Arcade**   MARKET
(道具屋筋; Map p344; www.doguyasuji.or.jp/map_
eng.html; [S] Midō-suji line to Namba) Come here
for all manner of pots, pans, knives, kitchen
gadgets and just about anything related to the
preparation, consumption and selling of food.
There are even shopfront lanterns, bar signs
and plastic food models (which make for interesting souvenirs). Start thinking about how
to make room in the suitcase for that *rāmen*
strainer you never realised you needed.

★**Village Vanguard**   BOOKS, HOMEWARES
(ヴィレッジヴァンガード; Map p344; www.
village-v.co.jp; 1-10-28 Nishi-Shinsaibashi; ⏰11am-
11pm; [S] Midō-suji line to Shinsaibashi, exit 7) Village Vanguard bills itself as an 'exciting'
bookstore, but books are only half the story:
between the cluttered racks of books and
magazines are various odd items, amusing
kitchen devices, homewares and more –
probably the stuff that Tokyu Hands rejected. It's a good spot to find a non-traditional
memento of your time in Japan.

Tokyu Hands   DEPARTMENT STORE
(東急ハンズ; Map p344; www.tokyu-hands.co.jp;
3-4-12 Minamisenba; ⏰10.30am-8.30pm; [S] Midō-
suji line to Shinsaibashi) If you love gadgets,
don't miss Tokyu Hands. From tools for jobs
you didn't know existed to curios to please
people with everything, this place is stocked
to the rafters with things that you probably
don't need but may very well want. Even if
you don't buy anything, it's fun to browse.
There's a smaller, new branch in **Umeda**
(東急ハンズ; Map p342; www.tokyu-hands.co.jp;
10th-12th fl, Daimaru, 3-1-1 Umeda; ⏰10am-9pm
Mon-Fri, to 8.30pm Sun; [R] JR line to Osaka).

Bic Camera   ELECTRONICS
(ビックカメラ; Map p344; www.biccamera.co.jp/
shoplist/nanba.html; 2-10-1 Sennichimae; ⏰10am-
9pm; [S] Midō-suji or Sennichimae line to Namba)

Bic Camera is a one-stop shop for everything
related to cameras, electronics and computers (but note that many computer-related
items are designed for operation with a Japanese system). You are likely to find some of
the best prices in the city at this vast shop.

Namba Parks Mall   SHOPPING MALL
(なんばパークス; Map p344; www.nambaparks.
com; 2-10-70 Namba-naka; ⏰11am-9pm; [S] Midō-
suji, Sennichimae, Yotsubashi line to Namba) They
call it 'Namba Parks' because of all the trees
in flower pots around the upper levels of this
shopping complex in Namba. It consists of
floor after floor of shops selling fashion, accessories, homewares and more. There are
also numerous restaurants and cafes. It's a
good place to go for a break from the Minami mayhem.

Athens   BOOKS
(アセンス; Map p344; www.athens.co.jp; 1-6-10
Shinsaibashi-suji; ⏰10am-10pm; [S] Midō-suji line
to Shinsaibashi, exit 6) Athens has a good selection of English books and magazines on the
4th floor, with a focus on art and design.

ⓘ Orientation

Osaka is generally divided into two main areas:
Kita and Minami. Kita (Japanese for 'north')
contains the main business and administrative
centre of Umeda, and two of Osaka's biggest
train stations: JR Osaka and Hankyū Umeda.
Minami (Japanese for 'south') contains the
bustling shopping and nightlife zones of Namba,
Shinsaibashi, Amerika-Mura and Dōtombori. It's
also home to major train stations JR Namba and
Nankai Namba.

Between north and south are two rivers, the
Dōjima-gawa and the Tosabori-gawa, and the
island of Nakano-shima. About 1km southeast
of Nakano-shima is Osaka-jō. There are also a
handful of sights in the Tennō-ji area just south
of Minami. The bay area, with the excellent
Osaka Aquarium, is west of the city.

FOODIE SHOPPING

If you're after groceries or something for a picnic, drop by **Kuromon Ichiba** (黒門市場;
Kuromon Market; Map p344; www.kuromon.com; [S] Sennichimae or Sakai-suji line to Nipponbashi, exit 10) to shop with the locals for fresh fish, meat, vegetables, pickles and more.
There are numerous stores in this long covered market, some also selling *bentō*, and a
few with counters where you can sit and have lunch. Most places open 9am or 10am,
closing 5pm or 6pm, and are closed Sundays.

For gourmet gifts, sake and confectionary, as well as fresh food, check out the
Hanshin Food Hall (阪神食品館; Map p342; B1 fl Hanshin Department Store; ⏰10am-8pm;
[R] JR line to Osaka), where the some 100 outlets and counters could keep gourmands
busy browsing for hours.

DEN DEN TOWN

Taking its name from the Japanese word for electricity (*denki*), Den Den Town – Osaka's version of Tokyo's Akihabara – is looking a bit tired these days, no doubt suffering from the competition of flash electronic megastores like Bic Camera. It consists of a long stretch of electronic-goods shops, but there are also manga stores, shops selling secondhand video games and CDs, and a couple of cosplay outlets adding a touch of seediness. If you can ignore the rough edges, you'll find it's a good place to find some bargains, and there are so many shops here you're bound to come across the gadget you need (though make sure it will work in your home country). To avoid sales tax, check if the store has a 'Tax Free' sign outside and bring your passport. Note that most stores are closed on Wednesday.

Den Den Town runs along Sakai-suji, starting southeast of Nankai Namba Station and continuing down to Ebisu-chō Station, which is on the Sakai-suji subway line (exit 1 or 2).

Note that If you're arriving by *shinkansen* (bullet train), you'll arrive at Shin-Osaka Station, which is three stops (about five minutes) north of Umeda and JR Osaka Station on the Midō-suji subway line.

❶ Information

INTERNET ACCESS

Unless you're sleeping on a park bench, you will almost certainly have some form of internet access at your accommodation. An increasing number of cafes also have wi-fi. Otherwise, you can find large internet cafes dotted around the city, most with a range of seat options (from basic chair to cosy booth), refreshments, shower rooms and special deals for night-time hours.

Media Cafe Popeye (メディアカフェポパイ; www.media-cafe.ne.jp; 5th fl, Raise Umeda Bldg, 2-1-21 Umeda; per hr from ¥360; ⊘24hr; ⓇJR line to Osaka) Not far from JR Osaka Station.

MONEY

ATMs at Citibank, large post offices, and 7-Eleven stores take international cards. Major banks and post offices have currency exchange services.

Citibank (シティバンク; http://citibank.co.jp; 2nd fl Dai-ichi Semei Bldg, 1-8-17 Umeda; ⊘9am-8pm Mon-Fri, 10am-5pm Sat & Sun, ATM 24hr; ⓇJR line to Osaka) Other branches at Shinsaibashi (Midō-suji Diamond Bldg, 2-1-2 Nishi Shinsaibashi; ⊘9am-3pm Mon-Fri, ATM 24hr; ⓈMidō-suji line to Shinsaibashi) and Umeda (7th fl ABC-MART Umeda Bldg, 1-27 Chaya-machi, across from Hankyū Station; ⊘9am-3pm & 5-7pm Mon-Fri, 10am-4pm Sat, ATM 8am-10pm; ⓇHankyū line to Umeda or JR line to Osaka); there's also a 24-hour ATM at Kansai International Airport.

POST

Osaka Central Post Office (大阪中央郵便局; Osaka Eki-mae Dai-ichi Bldg, Umeda 1-3-1; postal services 9am-9pm, ATM 24hr, closed 9pm-midnight Sun; ⓇJR line to Osaka) The post office also has a postal-service window operating 7am to midnight daily. Currency exchange available 9am to 6pm weekdays. Near JR Osaka Station.

TOURIST INFORMATION

Tourist offices can help book accommodation if you visit in person. There are offices in the main stations, and information counters at the airports. To get the lowdown on upcoming events, pick up a copy of *Kansai Scene* magazine, available for free at major bookshops.

Osaka Visitors Information Center, Umeda (大阪市ビジターズインフォメーションセンター・梅田; ☎6345-2189; www.osaka-info.jp; ⊘8am-8pm) This is the main tourist office, inside JR Osaka Station at the north end of the central concourse. If you were coming out of the central gates, you'd turn left (towards the North Gate Bldg and Lucua); it's on a corner on the left. There are other offices on the 1st floor of Nankai Namba Station (大阪市ビジターズインフォメーションセンター・なんば; ☎6631-9100; ⊘9am-8pm), the 3rd floor of Shin-Osaka Station (大阪市ビジターズインフォメーションセンター・新大阪; ☎6305-3311; ⊘9am-6pm), and at Tennō-ji Station (大阪市ビジターズインフォメーションセンター・天王寺; ☎6774-3077; ⊘9am-6pm).

TRAVEL AGENCIES

HIS No 1 Travel Osaka (大阪No1トラベル; ☎6133-0273; www.no1.his-west.jp; 1st fl Dai-ichi Semei Bldg, 1-8-17 Umeda; ⊘11am-7pm Mon-Sat, to 6.30pm Sun; ⓇJR line to Osaka) In Umeda, this helpful travel agency has English speakers and competitive prices.

KANSAI OSAKA

ℹ Getting There & Away

AIR

Osaka is served by two airports: **Kansai International Airport** (http://www.kansai-airport.or.jp/en), which handles all international and some domestic flights; and **Osaka Itami Airport** (ITM; http://osaka-airport.co.jp/), also called Osaka International Airport, which handles only domestic traffic. KIX is about 50km southwest of the city, on an artificial island in the bay. Itami is located in Osaka itself.

BOAT
China & Korea

The **Japan China International Ferry Company** (www.shinganjin.com) connects Shanghai and Osaka/Kōbe (one-way 2nd class ¥20,000, around 48 hours), departing Osaka on Tuesdays. A similar service at similar prices is provided by the **Shanghai Ferry Company** (www.shanghai-ferry.co.jp), departing Osaka on Fridays.

Panstar Ferry Company (www.panstar.co.kr) connects Osaka and Busan, South Korea (one-way from around ¥13,000, 19 hours), departing Osaka three times a week. There is scant information online in English – ask at the tourist offices for the latest schedules and costs.

These ferries operate from the Osaka Port International Ferry Terminal, which can be reached by taking the Chuō line or the Nankō Port Town line (aka New Tram) to Cosmo Square Station. It's about a 15-minute walk from the station to the terminal; there are also shuttle buses.

Within Japan

Destinations include Beppu (from ¥10,600, 11½ hours), Miyazaki (from ¥10,000, 12¾ hours), Shibushi (from ¥12,700, 14¾ hours) and Shinmoji (from ¥6500, 12 hours) in Kyūshū; and Toyō (from ¥6500, 9¼ hours) in Shikoku. There are also services to the Amami Islands (p733) and Naha, Okinawa (p742). At the time of writing there were no services running from Osaka to Shōdo-shima.

Domestic ferries operate from piers at Nankō Cosmo Port Ferry Terminal, Kamome Ferry Terminal, and Nankō Ferry Terminal, all accessible from the Nankō Port Town line. See www.osaka-ferry.net for links to ferry companies and route information.

BUS

Long-distance buses run between Osaka and cities all across Honshū (to Tokyo one-way from ¥3600, eight hours), Shikoku and some cities in Kyūshū (to Nagasaki one-way ¥11,000, 10 hours). Most buses depart from **JR Osaka Station Bus Terminal** (大阪駅 JR 高速バスターミナル), at the north end of Osaka Station, and from **OCAT Bus Terminal** (Osaka City Air Terminal; www.ocat.co.jp) at JR Namba Station. Check with the tourist offices for more details.

TRAIN

Osaka is on the Tōkaidō–San-yō *shinkansen* line that runs between Tokyo and Hakata (in Kyūshū). Hikari *shinkansen* run from Shin-Osaka Station to Tokyo (¥13,750, three hours) and Hakata (¥14,590, three hours). Other cities on this line include Hiroshima (¥9950, 1½ hours), Kyoto, Kōbe and Okayama.

Kyoto

While *shinkansen* is the fastest way to travel between Kyoto and Shin-Osaka (from ¥1380, 15 minutes), the JR *shinkaisoku* (special rapid train) between JR Kyoto Station and the central JR Osaka Station (¥540, 28 minutes) is more convenient if you want to avoid a change at Shin-Osaka.

The Hankyū line runs between Hankyū Umeda Station in Osaka and Hankyū Kawaramachi, Karasuma and Ōmiya stations in Kyoto (*tokkyū* limited express train to Kawaramachi ¥390, 44 minutes). The Keihan line runs between Sanjō, Shijō or Shichijō stations in Kyoto and Keihan Yodoyabashi Station in Osaka (*tokkyū* to Sanjō ¥400, 51 minutes). Yodoyabashi is on the Midō-suji subway line.

Kobe

The *shinkansen* runs between Shin-Kōbe Station and Shin-Osaka Station (from ¥1450, 13 minutes). There is also a JR *shinkaisoku* train between JR Osaka Station and Kōbe's Sannomiya and Kōbe stations (¥390, 24 minutes).

The Hankyū line is a little cheaper and usually less crowded. It runs from Osaka's Hankyū Umeda Station to Kōbe's Sannomiya Station (*tokkyū*, ¥310, 29 minutes).

Nara

The JR Kansai line links Osaka's Namba and Tennō-ji stations to JR Nara Station via Hōryū-ji (*yamatoji kaisoku*, ¥540, 50 minutes). The Kintetsu Nara line runs from Namba (Kintetsu Namba Station) to Kintetsu Nara Station (¥540, 40 minutes).

ℹ Getting Around

TO/FROM THE AIRPORT
Kansai International Airport (KIX)

KIX is well connected to the city with a direct train line and regular buses.

The fastest way to travel between KIX and Osaka is the private Nankai Express Rapit, which runs to/from Nankai Namba Station (¥1390, 35 minutes). The JR Haruka limited airport express runs between KIX and Tennō-ji Station (unreserved seat ¥1760, 29 minutes) and Shin-Osaka Station (¥2470, 49 minutes). Regular JR express trains called *kankū kaisoku* also run between KIX and Osaka (¥1160, 70 minutes), Tennō-ji (¥1030, 52 minutes) and JR Namba (¥1030, 62 minutes) Stations, which all connect to the Midō-suji subway.

JOHN ELK / GETTY IMAGES ©

IMRE CIKAJLO / GETTY IMAGES ©

1. Ginkaku-ji (p295)
Once a shogun's retreat from the turmoil of civil war, this temple is now a popular site during the spring-blossom and autumn-foliage seasons.

2. Asahi-dake (p578)
Asahi-dake is Hokkaidō's highest peak and offers plenty of hiking options, as well as onsen to relax in afterwards.

3. Kōbe port (p364)
Cosmopolitan Kōbe has served as a maritime gateway since the earliest days of trade with China.

MARISA VEGA PHOTOGRAPHER / GETTY IMAGES ©

IPPEI NAOI / GETTY IMAGES ©

apporo Snow Festival (p550)
elaborate snow sculptures created for
festival have included full-size theatres,
lides and Hello Kitty statues.

2. Umi Jigoku (p712)
Part of Kannawa's circuit of hells (hot
springs), Umi Jigoku is known as the 'sea
hell' because of its blue water.

3. Tokashiku Beach (p746)
On the west coast of Tokashiki-jima, the
biggest of the Kerama Islands, this beach is
popular with Japanese tourists.

ALEXANDRE SHIMOISHI / GETTY IMAGES ©

1. Arashiyama Bamboo Grove (p301)

The seemingly endless stretches of bamboo give thi grove an otherworldly atmosphere.

2. Nachi Taisha (p402)

Nachi Taisha was built near Japan's highest waterfa Nachi-no-taki, to honour its *kami* (Shintō spirit god).

3. Macaques, Jigokudani Monkey Par (p244)

Japanese macaques (also known as 'snow monkeys are unique to the country and attract plenty of visito

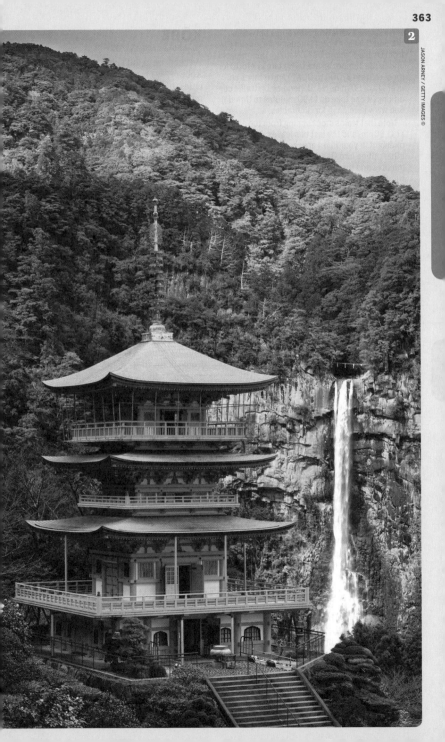

There are a variety of bus routes between KIX and Osaka. Airport limousine buses run to/from Osaka Station, OCAT Namba, Uehonmachi and to the Tempōzan area. The fare is ¥1500 for most routes (¥1000 to OCAT) and it takes an average of 50 minutes, depending on traffic conditions (it can take up to 90 minutes to Umeda). See www.kate.co.jp for timetables.

Note that trains stop running from the airport at 11.30pm, and the last bus leaves just after midnight. If your flight arrives after this, your other option into Osaka is taxi. It takes about 50 minutes and there are standard fares to Osaka Umeda (¥14,000) and Namba (¥13,500). The late-night fare is an additional ¥2500. It's about ¥18,000 to Shin-Osaka.

Osaka Itami Airport

Frequent limousine buses run between the airport and various parts of Osaka. Buses run to/from Shin-Osaka Station every 20 minutes from about 8am to 9pm (¥490, 25 minutes). Buses run at about the same frequency to/from Osaka and Namba stations (¥620, 25 minutes). At Itami, buy your tickets from the machine outside the arrivals hall. See www.okkbus.co.jp for timetables.

BUS

Osaka has an extensive bus system, but it is nowhere near as easy to use as the train and subway network.

TRAIN

Osaka has a good subway network and, like Tokyo, a JR loop line (known as the Kanjō-sen) that circles the city area, intersecting with the subways and other train lines. You're not likely to need any other form of transport unless you stay out late and miss the last train.

Of the eight subway lines, the one that short-term visitors will find most useful is the Midō-suji line (the red line), which runs north to south, stopping at Shin-Osaka, Umeda (next to Osaka Station), Shinsaibashi, Namba and Tennō-ji stations. Most rides cost between ¥200 and ¥300.

There are a couple of good discount passes for train and subway travel (see opposite).

KŌBE

⏺ 078 / POP 1.54 MILLION

Perched on a hillside overlooking the sea, Kōbe (神戸) is one of Japan's most attractive cities. It's also one of the country's most cosmopolitan places, having served as a maritime gateway to Kansai from the earliest days of trade with China. One of Kōbe's best features is its relatively small size – most of the sights can be reached on foot from the main train stations. And this is the main appeal of Kōbe: rather than a collection of sights, Kōbe is a city that is best enjoyed by casual wandering, enjoying the neighbourhoods and stopping in the many good restaurants and cafes as the whim strikes you. The most pleasant neighbourhoods to explore are Kitano, Chinatown and, after dark, the bustling area around Sannomiya Station.

◉ Sights

Kōbe's two main entry points are Sannomiya and Shin-Kōbe stations. Shin-Kōbe Station, in the northeast of town, is where the *shinkansen* stops. A subway (Seishin-Yamate Line, Y¥200, two minutes) runs from here to the downtown Sannomiya Station, which has frequent rail connections with Osaka and Kyoto. It's possible to walk between the two stations in around 20 minutes. Sannomiya Station marks the city centre, although a spate of development in Kōbe Harbor Land is starting to swing the city's centre of gravity towards the southwest. Before starting your exploration of Kōbe, pick up a map of the city at one of the two information offices (one is inside Sannomiya Station and one is inside Shin-Kōbe Station).

Kitano   NEIGHBOURHOOD
(北野; ⒭JR San-yō Shinkansen to Shin-Kōbe or JR, Hankyū or Hanshin lines to Sannomiya Station) Twenty minutes' walk north of Sannomiya

---

JR OSAKA STATION RENEWAL

Osaka Station has recently been transformed into an attractive modern complex, most notably with the addition of an enormous sloping glass roof across the tracks. Take the escalators up to Toki-no-Hiroba Plaza to fully appreciate it (you can also get a coffee here). Among the other open public spaces is the 11th-floor Kaze-no-Hiroba Plaza, where there are great views of Umeda Sky Building. There are also shops aplenty, and, of course, a ridiculous number of restaurants – check out the upper levels of the new North Gate and South Gate buildings. See http://osakastationcity.com for more or pick up a station guide at the tourist information centre.

DISCOUNT PASSES

The **Kansai Thru Pass** (www.surutto.com) allows unlimited travel on most train, subway and bus lines throughout Kansai, except the JR line. That includes travel on the Nankai line, which serves Kansai International Airport. (The pass doesn't cover the Ise-shima region.) It also qualifies you for discounts at several attractions. Two-/three-day passes cost ¥3800/5000. It's possible to purchase multiple passes, and passes can be used on nonconsecutive days. Pick one up at the travel desk in the arrivals hall of Kansai International Airport, at Osaka's main tourist offices, or at the main bus information centre in front of Kyoto Station. Note that the Thru Pass is only available to travellers on temporary visitor visas (you'll have to show your passport).

If you expect to take more than a few subway rides in Osaka, consider buying the good-value **Enjoy Eco Card** one-day pass. For ¥800, or ¥600 on weekends and holidays, you get unlimited travel on all subways, the Nankō Port Town line) and all city buses, but not the JR line. (Note that on the Midō-suji line the pass is good as far north as Esaka, from where you need to pay a fare adjustment.) At the subway ticket machine, push the 'English' button, insert your money, select 'one-day pass' or 'one-day pass weekend' then press the illuminated button showing '¥800' or '¥600'.

is the pleasant hillside neighbourhood of Kitano, where local tourists come to enjoy the feeling of foreign travel without leaving Japanese soil. A European–American atmosphere is created by the winding streets and *ijinkan* (literally 'foreigners' houses'), which housed some of Kōbe's early Western residents. Admission to some houses is free, for others it costs ¥300 to ¥700, and most are open from 9am to 5pm daily. Although these brick and weatherboard dwellings may not hold the same fascination for Western travellers that they hold for local tourists, the area itself is pleasant to stroll around and is dotted with good cafes and restaurants.

Kitano Tenman-jinja   SHINTŌ SHRINE
(北野天満神社; ☎221-2139; 3-12-1 Kitano-cho, Chūō-ku; ⊙dawn to dusk; ®JR San-yō Shinkansen to Shin-Kōbe or JR, Hankyū or Hanshin lines to Sannomiya Station) Dedicated to academic pursuits, the lovely little shrine holds pride of place overlooking the Kitano district, with views all the way down to the Inland Sea. Even if you aren't studying for an upcoming exam, this is a great place to take a breather and do some lazy people-watching.

Nunobiki Falls   WATERFALL
(布引の滝; ®JR San-yō Shinkansen to Shin-Kōbe or JR, Hankyū or Hanshin lines to Sannomiya Station) Accessible by a path that leaves from behind Shin-Kōbe Station (walk out the ground-floor exit, take a left and walk through the underpass that runs under the station building), this waterfall is a refreshing surprise – you'd never have guessed that

this beautiful natural sanctuary lies but a stone's throw from the busy train station. Note that the walk up the stone steps can leave you a sweaty mess in the summer – take it nice and slow and enjoy the river views as you ascend.

Shin-Kōbe Cable Car   CABLE CAR
(新神戸ロープウェイ; Shin-Kōbe Ropeway; one-way/return ¥900/1400, round trip from 5pm-9pm ¥800); ⊙9.30am-9pm; ®JR San-yō Shinkansen to Shin-Kōbe or JR, Hankyū or Hanshin lines to Sannomiya Station) The Shin-Kōbe Cable Car leaves from a building near Shin-Kōbe station and ascends to a mountain ridge 400m above the city. The views from the top over Kōbe and the bay are particularly pretty after sunset.

Nunobiki Hābu-kōen   GARDEN
(布引ハーブ公園; Nunobiki Herb Garden; admission ¥200; ⊙10am-5pm) A garden and park complex on the peaks behind Shin-Kōbe Station, Nunobiki Hābu-kōen is a great place to go to escape the city for a while. The views from the top over Kōbe and the bay are particularly pretty after sunset. The complex of gardens, restaurants and shops below the top station is known as the Nunobiki Hābu-kōen. Note that you can easily walk down to the bottom station from the Herb Garden in about 30 minutes.

Kōbe City Museum   MUSEUM
(神戸市立博物館; Kōbe Shiritsu Hakubutsukan; 24 Kyō-machi; admission ¥200; ⊙10am-5pm, to 7pm Fri, closed Mon & New Year holidays; ®JR, Hankyū or Hanshin lines to Sannomiya Station)

Kōbe

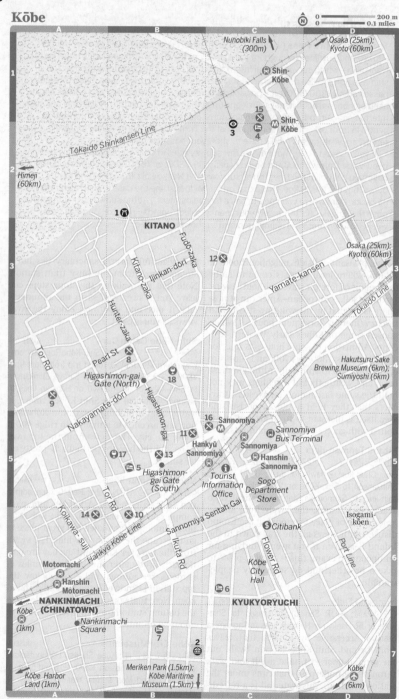

N

0 ——————— 200 m
0 ——————— 0.1 miles

Nunobiki Falls
(300m)

Osaka (25km);
Kyoto (60km)

Shin-
Kōbe

15

Shin-
Kōbe

4

3

Tōkaidō Shinkansen Line

Himeji
(60km)

1

KITANO

Fudō-zaka

12

Osaka (25km);
Kyoto (60km)

Yamate-kansen

Kitano-zaka

Ijinkan-dōri

Tōkaidō Line

Hunter-zaka

Pearl St

8

18

Higashimon-gai
Gate (North)

Tor Rd

9

Higashimon-gai

Hakutsuru Sake
Brewing Museum (6km);
Sumiyoshi (6km)

Nakayamate-dōri

16   Sannomiya
     M

11

Hankyū
Sannomiya

Sannomiya

Sannomiya
Bus Terminal

Sannomiya

17

13

5

Higashimon-
gai Gate
(South)

Hanshin
Sannomiya

Tourist
Information
Office

Sōgō
Department
Store

Isogami-
kōen

Tor Rd

14

10

Koikawa Suji

Hankyū Kōbe Line

Ikuta Rd

Sannomiya Sentah Gai

Flower Rd

Citibank

Kōbe
City
Hall

Port Line

KYUKYORYUCHI

Motomachi

Hanshin
Motomachi

NANKINMACHI
(CHINATOWN)

Kōbe
(1km)

Nankinmachi
Square

6

7

2

Kōbe Harbor
Land (1km)

Meriken Park (1.5km);
Kōbe Maritime
Museum (1.5km)

Kōbe
(6km)

Kōbe

This museum has a collection of so-called *namban* (literally 'southern barbarian') art and occasional special exhibits. *Namban* art is a school of painting that developed under the influence of early Jesuit missionaries in Japan, who taught Western painting techniques to Japanese students. The entrance is on the building's east side.

Nankinmachi (Chinatown) NEIGHBOURHOOD
(南京町; Ⓡ JR line to Motomachi Station) Nankinmachi is a gaudy, bustling, unabashedly touristy collection of Chinese restaurants and stores that should be familiar to anyone who's visited Chinatowns elsewhere in the world. The restaurants here tend to be overpriced and may disappoint sophisticated palates, but the place is fun for a stroll, particularly in the evening when the lights of the area illuminate the gaudily painted facades of the shops.

Kōbe Harbor Land & Meriken Park NEIGHBOURHOOD
(神戸ハーバーランド・メリケンパーク; Ⓢ Kaigan Subway Line to Harbor Land Station, Ⓡ JR Line to Kōbe Station) Five minutes' walk southeast of Kōbe Station, **Kōbe Harbor Land** is awash with megamall shopping and dining developments. This may not appeal to foreign travellers the way it does to the local youth, but it's still a nice place for a stroll in the afternoon.

A five-minute walk to the east of Harbor Land you'll find **Meriken Park**, on a spit of reclaimed land jutting out into the bay. The main attraction here is the Kōbe Maritime Museum.

Kōbe Maritime Museum MUSEUM
(神戸海洋博物館 Kōbe Kaiyō Hakubutsukan; 2-2 Hatoba-chō, Chūō-ku; admission ¥500; ⏰10am-5pm, closed Mon & 29 Dec-3 Jan; Ⓢ Kaigan Subway Line to Minato Motomachi Station, Ⓡ JR Kōbe line to Motomachi) An extensive collection of high-quality model ships and displays with some English explanations. It's about a 10 minute walk from Kōbe Station.

Hakutsuru Sake Brewery Museum MUSEUM
(白鶴造酒資料館; 4-5-5 Sumiyoshi Minami-machi, Higashinada-ku; ⏰9.30am-4.30pm, closed New Year holiday & O-Bon; Ⓡ Hanshin main line to Sumiyoshi) 🆓 The Nada-ku area of Kōbe is one of Japan's major sake-brewing centres and the dominant brewer here is the famous Hakutsuru company. The Hakutsuru Sake Brewery Museum provides a fascinating look into traditional sake-making methods. There is not much in the way of English explanations, but the free English pamphlet should get you started. Free sake tasting is possible after you tour the facilities (ask at the counter).

Take the Hanshin line eight stops east from Sannomiya (¥180, seven minutes if you switch train at Mikage, 15 minutes if you take the Hanshin *honsen* train; express trains do not stop) and get off at Hanshin Sumiyoshi Station. Exit the station, walk south to the elevated highway and cross the pedestrian overpass; take a right at the bottom of the steps; take your first left, then a right and look for it on the right (there is no English sign). You have to sign in at the gate. Use the blue-and-white crane logo atop the modern wing of the factory as your guide.

✪ Festivals & Events

Luminarie FESTIVAL
Kōbe's biggest yearly event is held every evening from around 2 to 13 December to celebrate the city's miraculous recovery from a 1995 earthquake that killed over 6000 people

KANSAI KŌBE

(check with the Kōbe tourist information office as the exact dates change slightly every year). The streets southwest of Kōbe City Hall are decorated with countless illuminated metal archways, which when viewed from within look like the interior of some otherworldly cathedral.

🛏 Sleeping

Hotel Trusty
BOUTIQUE HOTEL ¥¥

(ホテルトラスティ神戸; ☑ 330-9111; www.trusty.jp/kobe; 63 Naniwamachi, Chūō-ku; s/d/tw from ¥6300/11,200/13,200; @; ☒ JR, Hankyū or Hanshin lines to Sannomiya Station) The name of the place screams 'standard-issue business hotel', but this intimate little hotel in Kōbe's Kyūkyoryūchi district is actually a superstylish boutique hotel. The rooms are on the small side, but they are very clean and have all the amenities that you might need. It's within relatively easy walking distance of the stations.

B Kōbe
HOTEL ¥¥

(ザ・ビー神戸; ☑ 333-4880; www.theb-hotels.com/the-b-kobe/en; 2-11-5 Shimoyamate St, Chūō-ku; s/d/tw from ¥5500/8800/7600; @; ⑤ Seishin-Yamate subway line to Sannomiya) The centrally located B Kōbe is a good utilitarian choice if you've got business in Kōbe or just want a clean place to lay your head in the evening. Some of the rooms are quite small, but if you're only there at night this shouldn't matter too much.

ANA Crowne Plaza Hotel Kōbe
HOTEL ¥¥¥

(ANAクラウンプラザ神戸; ☑ 291-1121; www.anacrowneplaza-kobe.jp/en; 1-Chome, Kitano, Chūō-ku; s/d/tw from ¥8800/14,000/14,000; @ 🛜; ⑤ Seishin-Yamate subway line or JR San-yō shinkansen to Shin-Kōbe) You'll feel on top of the world as you survey the bright lights of Kōbe from this perch atop the city. Conveniently located near JR Shin-Kōbe Station, this first-class hotel offers clean and fairly spacious rooms and has an English-speaking staff. Downstairs in the **Oriental Avenue shopping centre** (アベニュー), you'll find several good restaurants to choose from.

Oriental Hotel
HOTEL ¥¥¥

(神戸旧居留地オリエンタルホテル; ☑ 326-1500; www.orientalhotel.jp/en; 25 Kyōmachi, Chūō-ku; d/tw from ¥15,500/17,800; @; ☒ JR Kōbe line, Hanshin or Hankyū to Sannnomiya or Motomachi) Not to be confused with the two other Oriental hotels in Kōbe, this refurbished hotel in the Kyūkyoryūchi district is very well designed, with smart rooms, competent staff and a convenient location next to the Kōbe City Museum.

🍴 Eating

Mikami
SHOKUDŌ ¥

(味加味; ☑ 242-5200; 2-5-9 Kanō-chō; meals from about ¥500; ⊙ lunch & dinner, closed Wed; 🖸; ☒ JR, Hankyū or Hanshin lines to Sannomiya Station) A friendly spot for good-value lunch and dinner sets of standard Japanese fare. Noodle dishes are available from ¥460 and *teishoku* (set meal) from ¥640. There's a small English sign.

Modernark Pharm
INTERNATIONAL ¥

(モダナーク ファーム; ☑ 391-3060; 3-11-15 Kitanagasa-dōri, Chūō-ku; lunch & dinner from ¥850; ⊙ lunch & dinner; 🖋 🖸; ☒ JR Kōbe line to Motomachi) An interesting little restaurant serving tasty sets of Japanese and Western options, including burritos and rice dishes. There are some veggie choices here. Look for the plants.

⭐ R Valentino
ITALIAN ¥¥

(アール ヴァレンティーノ; ☑ 332-1268; 3rd fl, 4-5-13 Kanō-chō, Chūō-ku; pasta from ¥1500, lunch/dinner main from ¥1600/3800; ⊙ lunch & dinner; 🖸; ☒ JR, Hanshin or Hankyū lines to Sannomiya Station) Pizzas cooked in a brick oven are the draw at this Sannomiya Italian restaurant. It's very casual and comfortable and there's an English/Italian menu. The Italian owner can explain the specials and make recommendations.

Wakkoqu
STEAKHOUSE ¥¥

(和黒; ☑ 262-2838; 3rd fl, Shin Kōbe Oriental Avenue shopping mall, 1-1 Kitano-chō; lunch/dinner from ¥2940/7500; ⊙ lunch & dinner; 🖸; ☒ Seishin-Yamate line or JR San-yō Shinkansen to Shin-Kōbe) An elegant spot to try Kōbe beef, you'll find Wakkoqu on the 3rd floor of the Oriental Avenue shopping centre at the base of the Crowne Plaza Kōbe hotel (just outside the elevator bank on the south side). The name 'Wakkoqu' is written in English on the menu displayed outside (and the menu is partially translated into English).

Azzuri
PIZZA ¥¥

(アズーリ; ☑ 241-6036; 3-7-3 Yamamoto-dori, Chūō-ku; pizza from ¥1155; ⊙ lunch & dinner; ☒ JR line to Motomachi Station) Said to be certified by the True Neapolitan Pizza Association (Associazione Verace Pizza Napoletana), this busy pizzeria is worth the walk to get there – just hope that there's a seat when you arrive (it's very popular with locals).

Arti   INDIAN ¥¥
(アールティ　神戸北野ハンター坂本店;
☑222-8665; 2-14-13 Nakayamate-dori, Chu-o-ku;
dinner with one curry from ¥1120; ◷ lunch & dinner;
🖫; 🚊 JR, Hanshin, Hankyū lines to Sannomiya Station) Kōbe is awash with Indian restaurants, but Arti stands head and shoulders above the crowd. There are two branches, but we like this one in Kitano for its pleasant surroundings. With an English menu and English-speaking staff, you'll have no trouble picking your favourite curries and breads to go with them.

Hirai   IZAKAYA ¥¥
(ひら井; ☑327-6040; 1-21-8 Kitanagasa-dori, Chūo-ku; dinner from ¥1500; ◷dinner; 🖫; 🚊JR, Hanshin, Hankyū lines to Sannomiya Station) The area northwest of Sannomiya Station is salaryman central, with myriad *izakaya* and bars to detain workers on their way home. Hirai is a good place to sample the vibe, with an English menu and reasonably tasty and generous portions of all the usual *izakaya* favourites. There's no English sign; look for the sake barrels and the red lantern outside.

Ganko Sushi   SUSHI ¥¥
(がんこ寿司; ☑331-6868; 2-5-1 Kitanagasa-dōri, Chūo-ku; lunch/dinner from ¥700/2000; ◷ lunch & dinner; 🖫; 🚊JR Kōbe line to Sannomiya or Motomachi) For good sushi and just about any other Japanese dish you crave, this casual, easy-to-enter restaurant near Motomachi Station is a good call. We particularly recommend ordering sushi à la carte here. The staff are used to foreigners; look for the small sign that says 'Japanese food restaurant'.

Misono   STEAKHOUSE ¥¥
(みその; ☑331-2890; 7th & 8th fl, Misono Bldg, 1-1-2 Shimoyamate dōri, Chūo-ku; lunch/dinner ¥2500/12,000; ◷ lunch & dinner; 🖫; 🚊JR, Hankyū or Hanshin lines to Sannomiya Station) If you're a carnivore, you probably want to sample some of Kōbe's famous beef. One of the more approachable spots to try these heavenly steaks is at Misono, which occupies two of the upper floors of a building not far from Sannomiya Station. The restaurant isn't particularly luxurious, but the steaks are good and you can enjoy a bit of a view as you dine. There's an English sign at street level.

🍷 Drinking

Kōbe has a large foreign community and a number of bars that see mixed Japanese and foreign crowds. For Japanese-style drink-ing establishments, try the *izakaya* in the neighbourhood between the JR tracks and Ikuta-jinja. Also bear in mind that a lot of Kōbe's nightlife is centred around the city's many cafes, most of which transform into bars come evening.

Bar Ashibe   BAR
(バーアシベ; ☑391-2039; 2-12-21 Shimoyamate-dori, Chu-o-ku; beer from ¥600, cocktails from ¥800; ◷6pm-5am; 🚊JR, Hanshin, Hankyū lines to Sannomiya Station) If you fancy a mellow drink, this genteel bar near Ikuta-jinja is a good choice. The lighting is subdued, the staff are discreet and efficient and the whole vibe just invites soulful meditations. The down tempo R&B soundtrack goes perfectly with the wide selection of spirits.

Sonic   BAR
(ソニック; 1-13-7, Nakayamate-dōri; drink/food from ¥750/850; ◷5-11.30pm Mon-Sat, to 11pm Sun; 🚊JR, Hanshin or Hankyū lines to Sannomiya Station) This friendly international sports bar is a good place to meet local Japanese and expats.

🛈 Information

Citibank (シティバンク; ◷9am-3pm Mon-Fri, ATM 24hr; 🚊JR, Hankyū or Hanshin lines to Sannomiya Station) South of Sogo Department Store; the ATM accepts international cards.

Tourist Information Office (神戸市総合インフォメーションセンター; ☑322-0220; ◷9am-7pm; 🚊JR, Hankyū or Hanshin lines to Sannomiya Station) The city's main tourist information office is on the ground floor on the south side of JR Sannomiya Station's east gate. There's a smaller information counter on the 2nd floor of Shin-Kōbe Station, right outside the main *shinkansen* gate. Both information centres carry reasonably good free maps of the city, as well as a variety of pamphlets.

🛈 Getting There & Away

AIR

Skymark Airlines (www.skymark.jp/en) Operates out of Kōbe Airport, with destinations including Tokyo (Haneda; ¥11,800, 70 minutes), Sapporo (Shin-Chitose; ¥13,800, two hours) and Okinawa (Naha; ¥12,800, 2¼ hours).

BOAT

There are regular ferries between Kōbe and Shinmoji with **Hankyū Ferry** (☑0120-56-3268; www.han9f.co.jp/en, ¥6000), Niihama with **Orange Ferry** (www.orange-ferry.co.jp, ¥5500) and **Ōita** (¥8800).

BUS

Buses run between Kōbe's **Sannomiya Bus Terminal** and Tokyo (Shinjuku highway bus terminal and JR highway bus terminal – JR 高速バスターミナル) at Tokyo Station. The journey costs from ¥6000 and takes around 9½ hours. Buses depart in the evening and arrive early the following day.

TRAIN

Kōbe's JR Sannomiya Station is on the JR Tōkaidō line. A JR *shinkaisoku* train on this line is the fastest way between Kōbe and Osaka Station (¥390, 22 minutes) or Kyoto (¥1050, 54 minutes).

Two private lines, the Hankyū and Hanshin lines, also connect Kōbe and Osaka. The Hankyū line is the more convenient of the two, running between Kōbe's Hankyū Sannomiya Station and Osaka's Hankyū Umeda Station (*tokkyū*, ¥310, 27 minutes). The Hankyū line also has connections between Kyoto and Osaka, so you can travel between Kyoto and Kōbe (*tokkyū*, ¥600, 65 minutes, change at Jūsō or Umeda).

Shin-Kōbe Station is on the Tōkaidō/San-yō *Shinkansen* line. The Hikari *Shinkansen* goes to/from Fukuoka (¥14,270, two hours and 52 minutes) and to/from Tokyo (¥14,270, three hours and 10 minutes). Nozomi *Shinkansen* are slightly faster. Other stations on this line include Osaka, Kyoto, Nagoya and Hiroshima.

ⓘ Getting Around

TO/FROM THE AIRPORT
Itami Osaka Airport

There are direct limousine buses to/from Osaka's Itami airport (¥1020, 40 minutes). In Kōbe, the buses stop on the southwestern side of Sannomiya Station.

Kōbe Airport

The easiest way to get to/from Kōbe's spanking-new airport is with the Portliner, which makes the trip between Sannomiya (downtown Kōbe) and the airport in 18 minutes and costs ¥320. A taxi costs between ¥2500 and ¥3000, and takes 15 to 20 minutes.

Kansai International Airport (KIX)

There are a number of routes between Kōbe and KIX. By train, the fastest way is the JR *shinkaisoku* to/from Osaka Station, and the JR *kanku kaisoku* between Osaka Station and the airport (total cost ¥1660, total time 1¾ hours with good connections). There is also a direct limousine bus to/from the airport (¥2000, 1¼ hours), which is more convenient if you have a lot of luggage. The Kōbe airport bus stop is on the southwestern side of Sannomiya Station.

PUBLIC TRANSPORT

Kōbe is small enough to travel around on foot. The JR, Hankyū and Hanshin railway lines run east to west across Kōbe, providing access to most of Kōbe's more distant sights. A subway line (the Seishin-Yamate Line) also connects Shin-Kōbe Station with Sannomiya Station (¥200, two minutes). Another subway line (the Kaigan Line) runs from just south of Sannomiya Station south toward the Harbor Land area. There is also a city-loop bus service that makes a grand-circle tour of most of the city's sightseeing spots (per ride/all-day pass ¥200/600). The bus stops at both Sannomiya and Shin-Kōbe stations; look for the retro-style green buses.

HIMEJI

♪ 079 / POP 536,300

Himeji-jō, the finest castle in all of Japan, towers over the small city of Himeji (姫路), a quiet city on the San-yō Shinkansen route between Osaka and Okayama/Hiroshima. In addition to the castle, the city is home to the Hyōgo Prefectural Museum of History and Kōko-en, a small garden alongside the castle. If you're a fan of castles, a visit to Himeji is a must. You can visit it as a day trip from Kyoto, Nara or Osaka, or as a stopover en route to Hiroshima.

◉ Sights

Himeji-jō CASTLE
(姫路城; 68 Honmachi; adult/child ¥400/100; ⊙9am-5pm Sep-May, to 6pm Jun-Aug) The most magnificent castle in Japan, Himeji-jō is also one of only a handful of original castles in the country (most others are modern concrete reconstructions). In Japanese it is sometimes called *shirasagi*, or 'white heron', a title that derives from the castle's stately white form.

Although there have been fortifications in Himeji since 1333, today's castle was built in 1580 by Toyotomi Hideyoshi and enlarged some 30 years later by Ikeda Terumasa. Ikeda was awarded the castle by Tokugawa Ieyasu when the latter's forces defeated the Toyotomi armies. In the following centuries it was home to 48 successive lords.

The castle has a five-storey main keep (*tenshū*) and three smaller keeps, and the entire structure is surrounded by moats and defensive walls punctuated with rectangular, circular and triangular openings for firing guns and shooting arrows. The walls of the main keep also feature *ishiotoshi* – openings that allowed defenders to pour boiling water or oil onto anyone who made it past the defensive slits and was thinking of scaling the walls. All things considered, visitors are recommended to pay the admission charge and enter the castle by legitimate means.

It takes around 1½ hours to follow the arrow-marked route around the castle. Last entry is an hour before closing.

Kōko-en GARDEN

(好古園; 68 Honmachi; admission ¥300; ⊗ 9am-6pm 29 Apr-31 Aug, to 5pm 1 Sep-28 Apr, closed 29 & 30 Dec) Just across the moat on the western side of Himeji-jō is Kōko-en, a reconstruction of the former samurai quarters of the castle. There are nine separate Edo-style gardens, two ponds, a stream, a tea arbour (¥500 for *matcha* powdered green tea and a Japanese sweet) and the restaurant Kassuiken (活水軒), where you can enjoy a *bentō* (boxed meal) of *anago* (conger eel, a local speciality) while gazing over the gardens. While the garden doesn't have the subtle beauty of some of Japan's older gardens, it is well done and especially lovely in the autumn-foliage season.

Note that a joint ticket to both the Kōkoen and Himeji-jō costs only ¥560, a saving of ¥140. These can be purchased at both the entrance to Kōko-en and Himeji-jō. Last entry 30 minutes before closing.

Hyōgo Prefectural Museum of History MUSEUM

(兵庫県立歴史博物館; Hyōgo Kenritsu Rekishi Hakubutsukan; 68 Honmachi; admission ¥200; ⊗10am-5pm, closed Mon; ❒ JR San-yo line to Himeji Station) This museum has good displays on Himeji-jō and other castles around Japan. In addition, the museum covers the main periods of Japanese history, with some English explanations. At 10.30am, 1.30pm and 3.30pm, one lucky person can even try on a suit of samurai armour or a kimono (ask at the front desk to be included in the lottery).

The museum is a five-minute walk north of the castle. Last entry 30 minutes before closing.

✿✿ Festivals & Events

Nada-no-Kenka Matsuri FESTIVAL

(灘のけんか祭り) Held on 14 and 15 October, Nada-no-Kenka involves a battle between three *mikoshi* (portable shrines), which are battered against each other until one smashes. Try to go on the second day, when

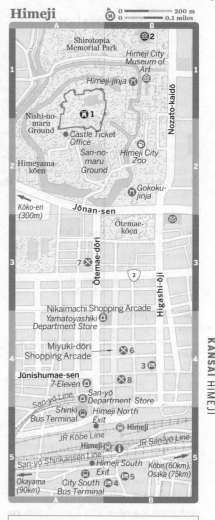

KANSAI HIMEJI

HIMEJI-JŌ RENOVATION

Himeji-jō is undergoing a massive renovation that is slated to finish in early 2015. Until it's completed, the main keep *(tenshū)* of the castle will be covered by a scaffoldlike structure that will obscure it from view. The rest of the castle will not be covered by any structure. It will be possible to enter the castle during the reconstruction period, although some areas (most notably, the castle keep) may be closed to the public from time to time. Call Himeji tourist information office if you have any questions.

An Alternative Castle

While Himeji-jō is undergoing renovations, those who wish to see an original (rather than rebuilt) castle in Kansai should consider a trip out to Hikone to see Hikone-jō. While it's nowhere near as big or impressive as Himeji-jō, it's quite lovely in its own right and is a good example of Japanese castle architecture. If you've got a Japan Rail Pass and can take the *shinkansen* as far as Maibara, you can do this as a half-day trip from Kyoto.

the festival reaches its peak (around noon). It is held five minutes' walk from Shirahamanomiya Station (10 minutes from Himeji Station on the San-yō-Dentetsu line); follow the crowds. The train company lays on extra trains on the day of the *matsuri*.

🛌 Sleeping

Himeji is best visited as a day trip from other parts of Kansai. If you'd like to stay, however, there are plenty of choices.

Tōyoko Inn   HOTEL ¥
(東横イン; ☑284-1045; 97 Minamiekimae-chō; s/d/tw incl breakfast ¥5480/7980/8480; @ 🛜) This efficient business hotel is a good choice if you want to be close to the station. The rooms are serviceable, well maintained and, as usual in a business hotel, fairly small. As with other Tōyoko Inns, just about everything you need is supplied, including free breakfast. Both wi-fi and LAN cable internet are available in each room for free.

APA Hotel Himejieki-kita   HOTEL ¥¥¥
(APAホテル姫路駅北; ☑284-4111; 98 Higashiekimae-chō; s/d/tw from ¥7500/13,000/14,000; @ 🛜) This centrally located business hotel is pretty much everything a good hotel should be: well run and clean with reasonable-sized rooms (for a business hotel, that is). It's within easy walking distance of the castle and lots of restaurants. There's free wi-fi in the lobby and free LAN cable internet in each room.

Hotel Nikkō Himeji   HOTEL ¥¥¥
(ホテル日航姫路; ☑222-2231; 100 Minamiekimae-chō; s/d/tw ¥6800/13,000/12,000; @ 🛜) A stone's throw from the south side of the

station, this hotel offers stylish and fairly spacious rooms and is the best choice for those who are looking for something nicer than a business hotel. The rooms here are larger and the bathtubs have almost enough room to stretch out in. Some of the upper rooms on the north side have views of the top of the castle. Free wi-fi is available in the lobby and restaurant; free LAN cable internet is available in guest rooms.

🍴 Eating

Most of the restaurants in Himeji are located in the shopping arcades north of the station (on the way to the castle).

Me-n-Me   NOODLES ¥
(めんめ; ☑225-0118; 68 Honmachi; noodles from ¥550; ⏰11.30am-7pm, closed Wed; 🈳) They make their own noodles at this homey little noodle joint a few minutes' walk from the castle. It's not fancy, but if you want an honest, tasty bowl of *udon* to power you through the day, this is the spot. There's no English sign: look for the white *noren* (curtains) in the doorway that show noodles being rolled out.

Rāmen Tsurukameya   RĀMEN ¥
(ラーメン鶴亀家; ☑288-1230; 316 Eki-mae-chō; rāmen from about ¥600; ⏰11.30am-midnight Mon-Sat, to 11pm Sun) For good *gyōza* and hearty bowls of thick pork-bone soy-flavoured soup *rāmen* we recommend this friendly *rāmen* joint near the station. Buy your tickets from the machine (staff usually rush around to help you do this, since the buttons are labelled in Japanese). It's roughly opposite Starbucks – look for the faux wooden facade painted with large white swirls.

★ Fukutei
KAISEKI ¥¥

(福亭; ☑222-8150; 75 Kamei-chō; lunch/dinner from ¥1500/3500; ☺11.30am-2.30pm & 5-10pm Mon-Fri, 11.30am-2.30pm & 5-9pm Sat & Sun; ⏍) This stylish, approachable restaurant is a great lunch choice if you want something a little civilised. The fare here is casual *kaiseki*: a little sashimi, some tempura and the usual nibbles on the side. At lunch try the excellent *omakese-zen* (tasting set; ¥1500). There's a small English sign. There's an English menu available at lunch, but not at dinner.

ℹ Information

In Himeji Station, you'll find the **Himeji Tourist Information Office** (姫路市観光案内所[姫路観光なびポート]; ☑287-0003; ☺9am-7pm, closed 29 & 30 Dec) on the ground floor of Himeji Station, not far from the central gate (clearly marked with signs as you exit the turnstiles). While you're there, pick up a copy of the useful *Places of Interest Downtown Himeji* map or *Himeji Tourist Guide & Map*. The castle is a 15-minute walk (1200m) straight up the main road from the north exit of the station. If you don't feel like walking, free rental cycles are available from an underground parking area halfway between the station and the castle; enquire at the information office.

ℹ Getting There & Away

If you've got a Japan Rail Pass or are in a hurry, a *shinkansen* is the best way to reach Himeji to/from Kyoto (Hikari, ¥4930, 55 minutes), Hiroshima (Hikari, ¥7870, 61 minutes), and Shin-Osaka (Hikari, ¥3440, 28 minutes). Note that you cannot use the Nozomi *Shinkansen* if you have a Japan Rail Pass, but you can use the Sakura *Shinkansen*, which run fairly frequently between Himeji and Shin-Osaka stations. If you don't have a pass, a *shinkaisoku* on the JR Tōkaidō line is the best way to reach Himeji from Kyoto (¥2210, 94 minutes), Osaka (¥1450, 63 minutes) and Kōbe's Sannomiya Station (¥950, 37 minutes). From Okayama, to the west, a *tokkyū* JR train on the San-yō line takes approximately two hours including transit time and costs ¥1450.

SHIGA PREFECTURE

Just across the Higashiyama mountains from Kyoto is Shiga Prefecture (滋賀県; Shiga-ken), dominated by Biwa-ko, Japan's largest lake. The small prefecture has a variety of attractions that are easily visited as day trips from Kyoto. The major attractions here are the towns of Nagahama, with its Kurokabe Square neighbourhood of glass artisans, and Hikone, with its fine original castle. Other worthwhile destinations include temples like Mii-dera and Ishiyama-dera, and the Miho Museum, which is worth a trip just to see the building and the compound in which it is located.

Ōtsu
大津

☑077 / POP 341,457

Ōtsu has developed from a 7th-century imperial residence (the city was capital of Japan for just five years) into a lake port and major post station on the Tōkaidō highway between eastern and western Japan. It is now the capital of Shiga-ken.

The **information office** (☑522-3830; ☺8.40am-5.25pm) is at JR Ōtsu Station.

◉ Sights

Mii-dera Temple
BUDDHIST TEMPLE

(三井寺; 246 Onjōji-chō; admission ¥500; ☺8am-5pm) Mii-dera is a short walk northwest from Keihan Hama-Ōtsu Station. The temple, founded in the late 7th century, is the head branch of the Jimon branch of Tendai Buddhism. It started its days as a branch of Enryaku-ji (延暦寺) on Hiei-zan, but later the two fell into conflict, and Mii-dera was repeatedly razed by Enryaku-ji's warrior monks. The Niō-mon gate here is unusual for its roof, made of layers of tree bark rather than tiles. It looks particularly fine when framed by the cherry trees in early April.

★ Festivals & Events

Ōtsu Dai Hanabi Taikai
FIREWORKS

If you're in town on 8 August, be sure to catch the Ōtsu Grand Fireworks Festival. Starting at dusk, the best spots to watch are along the waterfront near Keihan Hama-Ōtsu Station. Be warned that trains to and from Kyoto are packed for hours before and after the event.

Ōtsu Matsuri
FESTIVAL

Takes place in early to mid-October at Tenson-jinja, close to JR Ōtsu Station. Ornate floats are displayed on the first day and paraded around the town on the second day.

ℹ Getting There & Away

From Kyoto, take the JR Tōkaidō line from JR Kyoto Station to JR Ōtsu Station (¥190, nine minutes), or travel on the Kyoto Tōzai subway line to Hama-Ōtsu Station (¥410, 21 minutes from Sanjō Keihan Station).

Shiga Prefecture

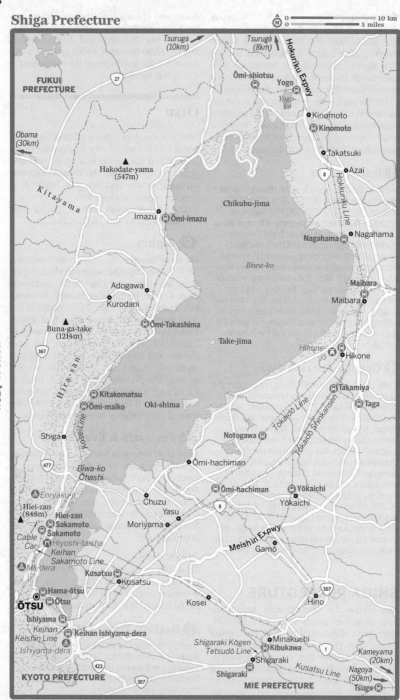

Ishiyama-dera

This Shingon-sect **temple** (石山寺; 1-1-1
Ishiyama-dera; admission ¥500; ⏰8am-4.30pm)
was founded in the 8th century. The room
beside the *hondō* (main hall) is famed as the
place where Lady Murasaki wrote *The Tale
of Genji*. The temple precincts are in a lovely
forest with lots of good trails to explore, including the one that leads up to Tsukimitei
hall, from which there are great views over
Biwa-ko.

The temple is a 10-minute walk from
Keihan Ishiyama-dera Station (continue
along the road in the direction that the
train was travelling). Take the Kyoto Tōzai-
line subway from Sanjō Keihan Station in
Kyoto to Keihan Hama-Ōtsu and change
there to a Keihan-line Ishiyama-dera-
bound *futsū* (¥540, 42 minutes including
transit time).

Alternatively, take the JR Tōkaidō line
from JR Kyoto Station to JR Ishiyama Station (*kaisoku* or *futsū* trains only, ¥230, 13
minutes) and switch to the Keihan line for
the short journey to Keihan Ishiyama-dera
Station (¥160).

Miho Museum

Located in the countryside of Shiga-ken
near the village of Shigaraki, the visually
stunning **Miho Museum** (ミホミュージア
ム; ☎0748-82-3411; www.miho.or.jp; 300, Tashiro
Momodani; adult/child ¥1000/300; ⏰10am-5pm,
Mon, January, February, mid Jun-mid July, mid-end
Aug, mid-end Dec , mid-end Dec) houses the Shu-
mei Family art collection, which includes
examples of Japanese, Middle Eastern, Chinese and south Asian art.

A trip to the IM Pei–designed building
is something like a visit to the secret hide-
out of an archvillain in a James Bond film,
and there is no doubt that the facility is
at least as impressive as the collection it
houses. Since a trip to the museum from
Kyoto or Osaka can take the better part of
a day, we highly recommend checking the
website first, to see what's on before making the trip.

To get here, take the JR Tōkaidō line
from Kyoto or Osaka to Ishiyama Station.
From here, change to a **Teisan Bus** (Teisan
Konan Kōtsu; www.teisan-konan-kotsu.co.jp)
bound for the museum (¥800, approximately 50 minutes).

Hikone 彦根

☎0749 / POP 112,632

Hikone is the second-largest city in the prefecture and of special interest to visitors for
its lovely castle, which dominates the town.
The adjoining garden is also a classic and is
a must-see after your visit to the castle.

⊙ Sights

Hikone-jō CASTLE
(彦根城; 1-1 Konki-chō; admission ¥600;
⏰8.30am-5pm) This castle was completed in
1622 by the Ii family, who ruled as *daimyō*
(domain lords) over Hikone. It is rightly
considered one of the finest castles in the
country. Much of the building is original,
and you can get a great view across the lake
from its upper storeys. Surrounded by more
than 1000 cherry trees, the castle is a very
popular spot for springtime *hanami* (blossom-viewing).

Genkyū-en GARDEN
(玄宮園; admission incl in castle ticket; ⏰8.30am-
5pm) After visiting Hikone-jō, don't miss
nearby Genkyū-en, a lovely Chinese-influ-
enced garden that was completed in 1677.
Ask someone at the castle to point you in
the right direction. There's a teahouse in
the garden where ¥500 gets you a cup of
matcha and a sweet to enjoy as you relax
and gaze over the scenery.

**Yumekyō-bashi
Castle Road** NEIGHBOURHOOD
(夢京橋キャッスルロード) About 400m
southwest of the castle (marked on the
Street Map & Guide to Hikone map and accessible via the Omote-mon or Ōte-mon gate
of the castle), this street of traditional shops
and restaurants is the ideal spot for lunch
after exploring the castle, and a browse in
the shops is a nice way to round out your
visit to Hikone.

✗ Eating

Monzen-ya NOODLES ¥
(もんぜんや; ☎24-2297; soba ¥780; ⏰11am-
7pm, closed Tue) Our favourite spot for a bite
in Yumekyō-bashi Castle Rd is Monzen-ya, a
great little *soba* place that serves such things
as *nishin-soba* (*soba* with herring; ¥880).
Starting from the castle end of the street, it's
about 100m on the left – look for the white
noren curtain with black lettering in the
doorway.

ℹ Information

The good **tourist information office** (☎ 22-2954; ⊙ 9am-5.30pm) is on your left at the bottom of the steps as you take the west exit of Hikone Station. It stocks the excellent *Street Map & Guide to Hikone*, which is good for navigating the town, and *A Journey to Hikone*, which has good detail on the castle itself.

The castle is a 10-minute walk straight up the street from the station (take a left before the shrine, then a quick right, or walk through the shrine grounds).

ℹ Getting There & Away

Hikone is about an hour (*shinkaisoku*, ¥1110) from Kyoto on the JR Tōkaidō line. If you have a Japan Rail Pass or are in a hurry, you can take the *shinkansen* to Maibara (¥3300, 20 minutes from Kyoto) and then backtrack from there on the JR Tōkaidō line to Hikone (¥180, five minutes).

Nagahama　　　　　長浜

☎ 0749 / POP 124,054

Nagahama is a surprisingly appealing little town on the northeast shore of Biwa-ko, which can easily be paired with a trip to Hikone. The main attraction here is the Kurokabe Square neighbourhood northeast of the station.

If you're in the area from 14 to 16 April, check out the **Nagahama Hikiyama Matsuri**, in which costumed children perform Hikiyama *kyōgen* (comic drama) on top of a dozen festival floats decked out with elaborate ornamentation.

⊙ Sights

Kurokabe Square　　　NEIGHBOURHOOD
(黒壁スクエア) Many of the old *machiya* (townhouses) and *kura* (storehouses) in this attractive old neighbourhood (it's not really a square) have been converted into shops and galleries highlighting the town's traditional (and modern) glass industry. Exit the east side of Nagahama Station, cross the bus boarding area towards Heiwado supermarket, walk around the supermarket to the left, then go right on the main street and take the first left after Shiga Bank; after about 100m you will find yourself in the heart of the Kurokabe Square district.

Kurokabe Museum of Glass Art　　　MUSEUM
(黒壁美術館; admission ¥600; ⊙ 10am-5pm) We like the small collection of glass *objets* at this museum. While you're here, ask them

to demonstrate the *suikinkutsu*, a strange 'musical instrument' formed from an over-turned urn into which water is dripped. It's on the main street of Kurokabe Square. There's a small English sign.

Giant Kaleidoscope　　　LANDMARK
(巨大万華鏡; kyodaimangekyō; ⊙ dawn-dusk) Our hands-down favourite attraction in Kurokabe Square is the Giant Kaleidoscope, which is located off a shopping arcade north of the Kurokabe Museum of Glass Art. From the museum, walk north to the next street and take a right. About 30m after entering the arcade, you will see a sign reading 'Antique Gallery London'. It's in an open area behind this shop.

Daisū-ji　　　BUDDHIST TEMPLE
(大通寺; admission to garden ¥500, grounds free; ⊙ 9am-4.30pm, closed year-end/new-year holidays) Daitsū-ji, a Jodo-Shin-sect temple on the outskirts of the Kurokabe Square area (ask someone to point you in the right direction), is worth a quick look. We don't recommend paying to enter the garden, though.

✖ Eating

Yokarō　　　NOODLES ¥
(翼果楼; ☎ 63-3663; dishes from ¥840; ⊙ from 11am until noodles are sold out, closed Mon) For a tasty lunch while exploring Nagahama, drop into this atmospheric restaurant, which positively oozes 'old Japan' charm. The signature dish here is *yakisaba-sōmen* (thin noodles with cooked mackerel) – it's a toothsome dish indeed. There is no English menu, but there are pictures on the Japanese menu. It's roughly in the middle of the Kurokabe Square district – ask a passerby if you can't find it. The name is written in English on the sign.

ℹ Getting There & Away

Nagahama is on the JR Tōkaidō line (*shinkaisoku*, ¥1280, 66 minutes from Kyoto). Be aware that not all *shinkaisoku* from Kyoto go all the way to Nagahama; you may have to change in Maibara, which is a 10-minute ride south of Nagahama by *shinkaisoku* (¥190). If you've got a Japan Rail Pass, you can take the *shinkansen* to Maibara (¥3300, 20 minutes from Kyoto) and then switch to a local JR train for the short trip to Nagahama. There are good street maps of the area, with some English, on street level soon after you exit the east side of Nagahama Station.

NARA

☎ 0742 / POP 366,165

The first permanent capital of Japan, Nara (奈良) is one of the most rewarding destinations in the country. Indeed, with eight Unesco World Heritage Sites, Nara is second only to Kyoto as a repository of Japan's cultural legacy. The centrepiece is, of course, the Daibutsu, or Great Buddha, which rivals Mt Fuji and Kyoto's Golden Pavilion (Kinkaku-ji) as Japan's single most impressive sight. The Great Buddha is housed in Tōdai-ji, a soaring temple that presides over Nara-kōen, a park filled with other fascinating sights that lends itself to relaxed strolling amid the greenery and tame deer.

Nara's best feature is its small size: it's quite possible to pack the most worthwhile sights into one full day. Many people visit Nara as a side trip from Kyoto, and comfortable express trains link the cities in about half an hour. Of course, it's preferable to spend two days here if you can. If your schedule allows for two days in Nara, you might spend one in Nara-kōen and the other seeing the sights to the west and southwest of Nara city (areas known as Nishinokyō and Ikaruga, respectively).

History

Nara is at the northern end of the Yamato Plain, where members of the Yamato clan rose to power as the original emperors of Japan. Until the 7th century, however, Japan had no permanent capital, as Shintō taboos concerning death stipulated that the capital be moved with the passing of each emperor. This practice died out under the influence of Buddhism and with the Taika reforms of 646, when the entire country came under imperial control.

At this time it was decreed that a permanent capital be built. Two locations were tried before a permanent capital was finally established at Nara (which was then known as Heijōkyō) in 710. Permanent status, however, lasted a mere 75 years. When a priest by the name of Dōkyō managed to seduce an empress and nearly usurp the throne, it was decided to move the court to a new location, out of reach of Nara's increasingly powerful clergy. This led to the new capital being established at Kyoto, about 35km to the north.

Although brief, the Nara period was extraordinarily vigorous in its absorption of influences from China, a process that laid the foundations of Japanese culture and civilisation. And with the exception of an assault on the area by the Taira clan in the 12th century, Nara was subsequently spared the periodic bouts of destruction wreaked upon Kyoto, and a number of magnificent buildings have survived.

◉ Sights

Nara retains the grid pattern of streets laid out in Chinese style during the 8th century. There are two main train stations: JR Nara and Kintetsu Nara. JR Nara Station is a little west of the city centre (but still within walking distance of the sights), while Kintetsu Nara is right in the centre of town. Nara-kōen, which contains most of the important sights, is on the eastern side, against the bare flank of Wakakusa-yama. Most of the other sights are west or southwest of the city and are best reached by bus or train. It's easy to cover the city centre and the major attractions in nearby Nara-kōen on foot, although buses and taxis do ply the city.

Nara tourist information offices stock the useful *Nara Sightseeing Map*. If you want something more detailed, ask if they have any copies of the excellent *Nara City Sightseeing Map*. If you read a bit of Japanese and want to explore Nara Prefecture, ask for a copy of *Nara-Yamatoji Kankō Mappu*.

◉ Nara-kōen Area
奈良公園

Many of Nara's most important sites are located in Nara-kōen, a fine park that occupies much of the east side of the city. The park is home to about 1200 deer, which in pre-Buddhist times were considered messengers of the gods and today enjoy the status of National Treasures. They roam the park and surrounding areas in search of handouts from tourists, often descending on petrified children who have the misfortune to be carrying food. You can buy *shika-sembei* (deer biscuits) from vendors for ¥150 to feed to the deer.

Our Nara-kōen walking tour is the best way to take in all the major sights in a day.

Nara National Museum   MUSEUM
(奈良国立博物館; Nara Kokuritsu Hakubutsukan; ☎ 050-5542-8600; 50 Noboriōji-chō; admission ¥500; ◷ 9.30am-5pm) The Nara National Museum is devoted to Buddhist art and is divided into two sections, housed in different

Nara

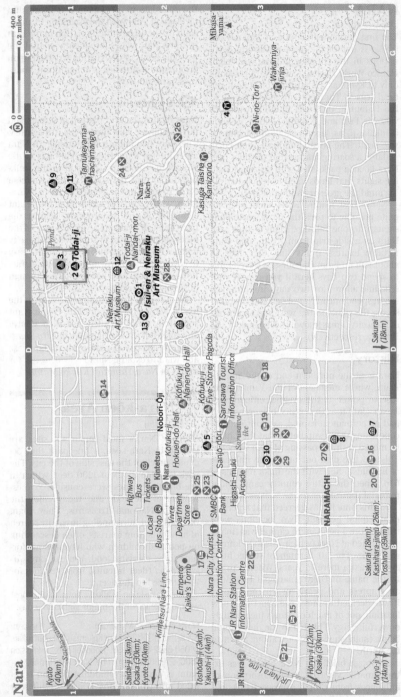

0 400 m
0 0.2 miles

Mikasa-yama

Wakamiya-jinja

Ni-no-Torii

4

26

24

Tamukeyama-hachimangū

9

11

Kasuga Taisha Kamizono

Nara-kōen

Pond

3

2 Tōdai-ji

Tōdai-ji Nandai-mon

12

Todai-ji

Isui-en & Neiraku Art Museum

1

28

Neiraku Art Museum

13

6

Kōfuku-ji Nanen-do Hall

Kōfuku-ji Five-Storey Pagoda

14

18

Kōfuku-ji Hokuen-do Hall

Sanjō-dōri

Sarusawa Tourist Information Office

Sarusawa-ike

Noburi-Ōji

Kintetsu Nara

Highway Bus Tickets

Local Bus Stop

Vivre Department Store

Nara City Tourist Information Centre

19

5

SMBC Bank

25

23

Higashi-muki Arcade

30

10

29

27

8

7

16

20

NARAMACHI

17

Emperor Kaika's Tomb

Nara City Tourist Information Centre

22

JR Nara Station Information Centre

15

JR Nara

JR Nara Line

Kintetsu Nara Line

Kyoto (40km)

Saidai-ji (3km); Osaka (30km); Kyoto (40km)

Tōshōdai-ji (3km); Yakushi-ji (4km)

Hōryū-ji (12km); Osaka (30km)

Hōryū-ji (14km)

Sakurai (18km); Kashihara-jingū (26km); Yoshino (39km)

Sakurai (18km)

Sakurai (18km)

Nara

buildings. Built in 1894, the **Nara Buddhist Sculpture Hall & Ritual Bronzes Gallery** contains a fine collection of *butsu-zō* (statues of Buddhas and Bodhisattvas). The Buddhist images here are divided into categories, each with an excellent English explanation, making this an excellent introduction to Mahayana Buddhist iconography. The newer East and West wings, a short walk away, contain the permanent collections (sculptures, paintings and calligraphy) and are used for special exhibitions.

A special exhibition featuring the treasures of the **Shōsō-in Hall**, which holds the treasures of Tōdai-ji, is held in the newer wings from late October to early November (call the Nara City Tourist Information Centre to check, as these dates vary slightly each year). The exhibits include priceless items from the cultures along the Silk Road. If you are in Nara during these periods and are a fan of Japanese antiquities, you should make a point of visiting the museum, but be prepared for crowds. Admission is ¥1000. Enter by 4.30pm.

Kōfuku-ji
BUDDHIST TEMPLE

(興福寺) This temple was transferred here from Kyoto in 710 as the main temple for the Fujiwara family. Although the original temple complex had 175 buildings, fires and destruction as a result of power struggles have left only a dozen standing. There are two pagodas – three storeys and five storeys – dating from 1143 and 1426, respectively. The taller of the two is the second-tallest in Ja-

pan, outclassed by the one at Kyoto's Tō-ji by a few centimetres. Note that a new hall is being built in the centre of the temple grounds and construction isn't expected to be completed until 2018.

The **Kōfuku-ji National Treasure Hall** (興福寺国宝館; 48 Noborioji-chō; admission ¥600; ⊙9am-5pm) contains a variety of statues and art objects salvaged from previous structures. Enter by 4.45pm.

★ Isui-en & Neiraku Art Museum
GARDEN

(依水園・寧楽美術館; 74 Suimon-chō; admission museum & garden ¥650; ⊙9.30am-4.30pm, closed Tue (except for Apr, May, Oct & Nov) & New Year holidays) This garden, dating from the Meiji era, is beautifully laid out and features abundant greenery and a pond with ornamental carp. It's without a doubt the best garden in the city and well worth a visit. For ¥500 you can enjoy a cup of tea on tatami mats overlooking the garden. Note that you can also enjoy a cup without paying admission at the adjoining Sanshū restaurant (you sill have to pay for the tea, though).

The adjoining art museum, Neiraku Bijutsukan, displays Chinese and Korean ceramics and bronzes (admission is included in garden entry). Enter by 4pm.

Yoshiki-en
GARDEN

(吉城園; 68 Noborioji-chō; ⊙9.30am-5pm Mar–27 Dec) **FREE** This garden, located next door to Isui-en (to the right when you're facing the

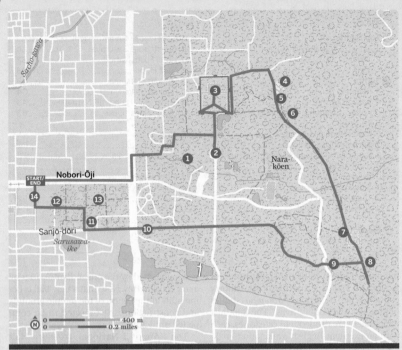

🏃 Walking Tour
Nara-kōen

START KINTETSU NARA STATION
END KINTETSU NARA STATION
DISTANCE 5KM
DURATION HALF A DAY

Walk straight up Nobori-Ōji, passing Kōfuku-ji on your right. Go left and visit **1 Isui-en** (p379), one of Nara's finest gardens. Head north from the garden entrance, take the next major right after about 100m and walk east to come out in front of Tōdai-ji. Go right to see the massive **2 Nandai-mon**. Admire the Niō guardians, then continue to **3 Tōdai-ji** (p141)

Take the southeast exit, then a hard left and walk along the temple enclosure. Just past the pond, take a right up the hill following the stone-paved path, which leads to an atmospheric stretch up to an open plaza in front of **4 Nigatsu-dō** (p141) and **5 Sangatsu-dō** (p141) halls. Climb the steps to Nigatsu-dō to enjoy the view, which takes in Daibutsu-den's graceful curves and most of the Nara plain.

Return to the plaza and head south, passing between a log-cabinlike structure and gaudy **6 Tamukeyama-hachimangū**, a small shrine

overlooking the plaza. Follow the broad path through the woods, descend two staircases and follow the 'Kasuga Shrine' signs. You'll come to a road leading uphill to the left; follow it, passing under the slopes of Wakakusa-yama. At Musashino Ryokan (look for the small English sign), walk straight down the steps, cross a bridge, jog left, and at the T-intersection take a left up to **7 Kasuga Taisha** (p142). Go around the side to find the main entrance.

Leave the shrine via the main entrance and bear left up the path to **8 Wakamiya-jinja** (若宮神社), passing several small shrines on the way. Retrace your steps towards Kasuga Taisha and take a left down the steps which lead back towards the centre of town. Pass through **9 Ni-no-Torii**, a large Shintō shrine gate, and continue down the wooded arcade to **10 Ichi-no-Torii**, another shrine gate. Cross the street and to the **11 Kōfuku-ji pagoda**. Walk through its grounds, passing between the **12 Nanen-dō** and **13 Hokuen-dō** halls, and take the narrow lane that leads down to Higashi-muki Arcade. A quick right here brings you back to **14 Kintetsu Nara Station**.

entrance of Isui-en), is a stunner. Originally a residence of the high priest of Tōdai-ji, it fell into private hands. The present garden was laid out in 1918 and contains a lovely thatch-roof cottage, a pond and several walking paths. It's particularly lovely in November and early December, when the maples turn a blazing crimson. Best of all, at the time of writing, entry was free for foreign tourists! Enter by 4.30pm. Look for the small English sign.

⭐ **Tōdai-ji**   BUDDHIST TEMPLE
(東大寺) Nara's famous Daibutsu (Great Buddha) is housed in the Daibutsu-den Hall of this grand temple. It's Nara's star attraction and is often packed with tour groups and schoolchildren from across the country, but it's big enough to absorb huge crowds and it belongs at the top of any Nara itinerary.

Before you enter the temple be sure to check out the **Nandai-mon** (東大寺南大門), an enormous gate containing two fierce-looking **Niō guardians**. These recently restored wooden images, carved in the 13th century by the sculptor Unkei, are some of the finest wooden statues in all of Japan, if not the world. They are truly dramatic works of art and seem ready to spring to life at any moment. The gate is about 200m south of the temple enclosure.

Note that most of Tōdai-ji's grounds can be visited free of charge, with the exception of the main hall, the Daibutsu-den Hall.

For more information turn to the illustration on the next page.

Daibutsu-den Hall   BUDDHIST TEMPLE
(大仏殿; Hall of the Great Buddha; 406-1 Zōshi-chō; admission ¥500; ⊙8am-4.30pm Nov-Feb, to 5pm Mar, 7.30am-5.30pm Apr-Sep, to 5pm Oct) Tōdai-ji's Daibutsu-den is the largest wooden building in the world. Unbelievably, the present structure, rebuilt twice (most recently in 1709), is a mere two-thirds of the size of the original! The Daibutsu (Great Buddha) contained within is one of the largest bronze figures in the world and was originally cast in 746. The present statue, recast in the Edo period, stands around 15m high and consists of 437 tonnes of bronze and 130kg of gold.

The Daibutsu is an image of Dainichi Buddha (also known as Vairocana Buddha), the cosmic Buddha believed to give rise to all worlds and their respective Buddhas. Historians believe that Emperor Shōmu ordered the building of the Buddha as a charm against smallpox, which ravaged Japan in preceding years. Over the centuries the statue took quite a beating from earthquakes and fires, losing its head a couple of times (note the slight difference in colour between the head and the body).

As you circle the statue towards the back, you'll see a wooden column with a hole through its base. Popular belief maintains that those who can squeeze through the hole, which is exactly the same size as one of the Great Buddha's nostrils, are ensured of enlightenment. There's usually a line of children waiting to give it a try and parents waiting to snap their pictures. Adults sometimes try it, but it's really something for the kids. A hint for big kids: it's a lot easier to go through with both arms held above your head – and someone on either end to push and pull helps, too.

Nigatsu-dō & Sangatsu-dō   BUDDHIST TEMPLE
The Nigatsu-dō and Sangatsu-dō halls are almost sub-temples of Tōdai-ji. They are an easy (uphill from the Daibutsu-den) walk east. You can walk straight east up the hill, but we recommend taking a hard left out of the Daibutsu-den exit, following the enclosure past the pond and turning up the hill. This pathway is among the most scenic walks in all of Nara.

As you reach the plaza at the top of the hill, the **Nigatsu-dō** (二月堂; ⊙8am-4.30pm Nov-Feb, to 5pm Mar, 7.30am-5.30pm Apr-Sep, to 5pm Oct) FREE is the temple hall with the verandah overlooking the plaza. This is where Nara's Omizutori Matsuri is held. The verandah affords a great view over Nara, especially at dusk.

A short walk south of Nigatsu-dō is **Sangatsu-dō** (三月堂; admission ¥500; ⊙8am-4.30pm Nov-Feb, to 5pm Mar, 7.30am-5.30pm Apr-Sep, to 5pm Oct), which is the oldest building in the Tōdai-ji complex. This hall contains a small collection of fine statues from the Nara period.

Tōdai-ji Museum   MUSEUM
(東大寺ミュージアム; ☑20-5511; Nara-shi, Suimon-chō 100; admission ¥500; ⊙9.30am-4.30pm) Not far from the Daibutsu-den and the Nandai-mon, the Tōdai-ji Museum adds another dimension to a visit to the temple, but its appeal is mostly limited to scholars and serious fans of early Nara Buddhism. Several Bodhisattva are on display and the air-conditioning is welcome on a hot summer's day. A joint ticket to the Daibutsu-den and the museum costs ¥800.

Tōdai-ji

The Daibutsu (Great Buddha) at Nara's Tōdai-ji is one of the most arresting sights in Japan. The awe-inspiring physical presence of the vast image is striking. It's one of the largest bronze Buddha images in the world and it's contained in an equally huge building, the Daibutsu-den Hall, which is among the largest wooden buildings on earth.

Tōdai-ji was built by order of Emperor Shōmu during the Nara period (710–784) and the complex was finally completed in 798, after the capital had been moved from Nara to Kyoto. Most historians agree that the temple was built to consolidate the country and serve as its spiritual focus. Legend has it that over two million labourers worked on the temple, but this is probably apocryphal. What's certain is that its construction brought the country to the brink of bankruptcy.

The original Daibutsu was cast in bronze in eight castings over a period of three years. The Daibutsu, or certain parts of it, has been recast several times over the centuries. The original Daibutsu was covered in gold leaf and one can only imagine its impact on Japanese visitors during the eighth century AD.

The temple belongs to the Kegon school of Buddhism, one of the six schools of Buddhism popular in Japan during the Nara period. Kegon Buddhism, which comes from the Chinese Huayan Buddhist sect, is based on the Flower Garland Sutra. This sutra expresses the idea of worlds within worlds, all manifested by the Cosmic Buddha (Vairocana or Dainichi Nyorai). The Great Buddha and the figures that surround him in the Daibutsu-den Hall are the perfect physical symbol of this cosmological map.

Kokuzo Bosatsu
Seated to the left of the Daibutsu is Kokuzo Bosatsu, the bodhisattva of memory and wisdom, to whom students pray for help in their studies and the faithful pray for help on the path to enlightenment.

The Daibutsu (Great Buddha)
Known in Sanskrit as 'Vairocana' and in Japanese as the 'Daibutsu', this is the Cosmic Buddha that gives rise to all other Buddhas, according to Kegon doctrine. The Buddha's hands send the messages 'fear not' and 'welcome'.

FACT FILE

The Daibutsu

- » **Height:** 14.98m
- » **Weight:** 500 tonnes
- » **Nostril width:** 50cm

The Daibutsu-den Hall

- » **Height:** 48.74m
- » **Length:** 57m
- » **Number of roof tiles:** 112,589

Komokuten

Standing to the left of the Daibutsu is Komokuten (Lord of Limitless Vision), who serves as a guardian of the Buddha. He stands upon a demon (*jaki*), which symbolises ignorance, and wields a brush and scroll, which symbolises wisdom.

Buddhas Around Dainichi

Sixteen smaller Buddhas are arranged in a halo around the Daibutsu's head, each of which symbolises one of the Daibutsu's different manifestations. They are graduated in size to appear the same size when viewed from the ground.

Tamonten

To the right of the Daibutsu stands Tamonten (Lord Who Hears All), another of the Buddha's guardians. He holds a pagoda, which is said to represent a divine storehouse of wisdom.

Hole in Pillar

Behind the Daibutsu you will find a pillar with a 50cm hole through its base (the size of one of the Daibutsu's nostrils). It's said that if you can crawl through this, you are assured of enlightenment.

Nyoirin Kannon

Seated to the right of the Daibutsu is Nyoirin Kannon, one of the esoteric forms of Kannon Bodhisattva. This is one of the bodhisattva that preside over the six different realms of karmic rebirth.

Kasuga Taisha
SHINTŌ SHRINE

(春日大社; 160 Kasugano-chō; ☺dawn-dusk) **FREE** This shrine was founded in the 8th century by the Fujiwara family and was completely rebuilt every 20 years, according to Shintō tradition, until the end of the 19th century. It lies at the foot of the hill in a pleasant, wooded setting with herds of sacred deer awaiting handouts. As with similar shrines in Japan, you will find several subshrines around the main hall.

The approaches to the shrine are lined with hundreds of lanterns, and there are many hundreds more in the shrine itself. The lantern festivals held twice a year at the shrine are a major attraction.

While you're in the area, it's worth walking a few minutes south to the nearby shrine of Wakamiya-jinja.

⊙ Naramachi 奈良町

South of Sanjō-dōri and Sarusawa-ike pond you will find Naramachi, a traditional neighbourhood with many well-preserved *machiya* and *kura*. It's a nice place for a stroll before or after hitting the big sights of Nara-kōen, and there are several good restaurants in the area to entice the hungry traveller. There is a lot of creative energy here and residents are eager to share their culture with travellers.

Naramachi Koushi-no-Ie
HISTORIC BUILDING

(ならまち資料館; 44 Gangōji-chō; ☺9am-5pm, closed Mon) **FREE** A traditional Japanese house that you can enter and explore.

Naramachi Monogatari-kan
GALLERY

(奈良町物語館; 2-1 Nakanoshinya-chō; ☺10am-5pm) **FREE** An interesting little gallery that holds some worthwhile exhibitions, ranging from traditional to modern.

Saka-gura Sasaya
SAKE

(酒蔵ささや; ☎27-3383; ☺10am-7pm, closed Thu) **FREE** If all this sightseeing has made you thirsty, drop in for a tasting (prices range from ¥100 to ¥500 per sample) of the various types of sake produced in Nara Prefecture (all sake is also available for purchase). There is a useful English explanation sheet. Look for the sake barrels and a sign in the window reading 'Nara's Local Sake'.

✵ Festivals & Events

The dates for some of these festivals vary, so it's best to check with the Nara or Kyoto tourist information offices.

Yamayaki
TRADITIONAL

(Grass Burning Festival; ☺4th Saturday in January) In early January (on the day before Seijin-no-hi or Coming-of-Age Day), the Grass Burning Festival commemorates a feud many centuries ago between the monks of Tōdai-ji and Kōfuku-ji: Wakakusa-yama is set alight at 6pm, with an accompanying display of fireworks.

Mantōrō
LANTERNS

(☺3 February on Setsubun from 6pm) Held in early February at Kasuga Taisha at 6pm, the Lantern Festival involves the lighting of 3000 stone and bronze lanterns around Kasuga Taisha – it's impossibly atmospheric, as you can imagine. A *bugaku* dance takes place in the Apple Garden on the last day. This festival is also held around 14 August in the O-Bon (Festival of the Dead) holiday period.

Omizutori/Otaimatsu
TRADITIONAL

Every evening from 1 March to 14 March, the monks of Tōdai-ji parade huge flaming torches around the balcony of Nigatsu-dō and rain down embers on the spectators to purify them. On the evening of 12 March, the monks hold a water-drawing ceremony from which the festival takes its name (*mizutori* means "to take water"). The water-drawing ceremony is performed after midnight.

Takigi Onō
NŌ

Open-air performances of nō are held after dark by the light of blazing torches at Kōfuku-ji and Kasuga Taisha, on the third Friday and Saturday of March.

Shika-no-Tsunokiri
DEER-ANTLER CUTTING

Those deer in Nara-kōen are pursued in a type of elegant rodeo into the Roku-en (deer enclosure) close to Kasuga Taisha on the second Saturday, Sunday and the following Monday in October. They are then wrestled to the ground and their antlers sawn off. Tourist brochures hint that this is to avoid personal harm, though it's not clear whether they are referring to the deer fighting each other or the deer mugging the tourists.

🛏 Sleeping

Although Nara can be visited as a day trip from Kyoto, it is pleasant to spend the night here, allowing for a more relaxing pace.

Guesthouse Nara Backpackers
GUESTHOUSE ¥

(ゲストハウス奈良バックパッカーズ; ☎22-4557; www.nara-backpackers.com; 31 Yurugichō; dorm ¥2400, r per person from ¥3800; ☏) In a lovely traditional Japanese building that used to be the home of a tea master, this gorgeous new guesthouse is an utterly charming place to stay for those who want to sample a night or two in a truly Japanese setting. You can choose from dorm rooms or three fine private tatami-mat rooms of varying sizes, some of which have garden views. Due to the presence of *shōji* (sliding paper doors) and traditional glass windows, they cannot accept children below the age of 10 (which is just as well, because parents of young children would spend their time on tenterhooks here), but for anyone else, it's highly recommended. Note that bathing facilities are shared and cooking facilities are available for those who want to self-cater.

Ryokan Seikansō　　　RYOKAN ¥
(旅館静観荘; fax 22-2670; 29 Higashikitsuji-chō; per person without bathroom from ¥4200; 🖀) This traditional ryokan has reasonable rates and a good Naramachi location. The rooms are clean and spacious with shared bathrooms and a large communal bathtub. The management is used to foreign guests and there is a nice Japanese garden. It's a little long in the tooth, but the friendly reception makes up for it.

Ryokan Matsumae　　　RYOKAN ¥
(旅館松前; ☎22-3686; www.matsumae.co.jp/english/index_e.html; 28-1 Higashitera hayashi-chō; per person without bathroom from ¥5250; @🖀) This friendly little ryokan lays claim to an incredibly convenient location in Naramachi, a short walk from all the sights. The rooms are typical of a ryokan: tatami mats, low tables, TVs and futons. Some of the rooms are a little dark, but the feeling here is warm and relaxing. Two computers are available for rent for ¥100 per hour in the lobby.

Guesthouse Nara Komachi　　GUESTHOUSE ¥
(ゲストハウス奈良小町; ☎87-0556; guesthouse@wave.plala.or.jp; 41-2 Surugamachi; dm from ¥2500, r per person from ¥2900; @🖀) One of the best accommodation bargains in Nara is this excellent guesthouse. Choose from dorm rooms or Western- and Japanese-style private rooms with en suite bathrooms/showers. There's a self-catering kitchen and cheap bicycle rentals.

Ugaya Guesthouse　　　GUESTHOUSE ¥
(ウガヤゲストハウス; ☎95-7739; www.ugaya.net; 4-1 Okumomori-chō; dm from ¥2500, r per person without bathroom from ¥3000; @🖀) This casual backpackers' guesthouse offers a tight warren of rooms and dorms and convivial communal areas a short walk from the sights of Naramachi. This is a sociable place and a good place to meet other travellers. Grab a copy of the excellent map when you check in. It has a free computer for guests' use in the lobby.

★**Guesthouse Sakuraya**　　GUESTHOUSE ¥¥
(桜舎; www.guesthouse-sakuraya.com; 1 Narukawa-chō; per person incl breakfast ¥6000; 🖀) This brand-new three-room guesthouse is a charming place to stay. It's described as a guesthouse, but it feels more like a ryokan. The rooms are traditional and the building is an atmospheric stunner. There's a lovely little central garden and a comfortable common room. The owner offers a Discovery of Japanese Culture course for ¥3000. Keep in mind that it's a traditional and relatively small place, so if you're looking for a party, head elsewhere.

Hotel Fujita Nara　　　HOTEL ¥¥
(ホテルフジタ奈良; ☎23-8111; http://en.fujita-nara.com; 47-1 Shimosanjō-chō; s/tw from ¥6500/8400; @🖀) Right smack in downtown Nara and close to both main train stations, this efficient midrange hotel hits all the right notes: clean rooms, reasonable prices and some English-speaking staff. It's a good choice for those who want a conveniently located hotel.

Super Hotel Lohas JR Nara-eki　HOTEL ¥¥
(スーパーホテルLohas・JR奈良駅; ☎27-9000; www.superhoteljapan.com/en/s-hotels/nara-lohas.html; 1-2 Sanjōhonmachi; s/tw ¥6980/12,800; @🖀) Connected to JR Nara Station by an elevated walkway, this new Super Hotel has a lot going for it: clean compact rooms with en suite bathrooms, efficient service and a large communal 'onsen' bath. Room rates include breakfast. Free wi-fi in lobby and free LAN cable internet in guest rooms.

Nara Hotel　　　　　HOTEL ¥¥¥
(奈良ホテル; ☎26-3300; www.narahotel.co.jp/en; 1096 Takabatake-chō; s/tw from ¥18,480/33,495; @🖀) This grande dame of Nara hotels is a classic, with high ceilings and the smell of polished wood all around. All the rooms are spacious and comfortable with big beds. Unfortunately, some of the rooms have cramped unit bathrooms. The rooms in the Shinkan (new wing) are nice, but we recommend the Honkan (main building) for its great retro atmosphere. Free wi-fi in lobby; free LAN cable internet in guest rooms.

KANSAI NARA

✖ Eating

Nara is chock-a-block with good restaurants, most of which are near the train stations and in Naramachi. There aren't many good choices in Nara-kōen, but we list one spot halfway between Tōdai-ji and Kasuga Taisha for those exploring that area.

Mellow Café
CAFE ¥

(メロー カフェ; ☑27-9099; 1-8 Konishi-chō; lunch from ¥980; ◷11am-11.30pm; 📶📱) Located down a narrow alley (look for the palm tree) not far from Kintetsu Nara Station, this open-plan cafe is a pleasant spot to fuel up for a day of sightseeing. The menu centres on pasta and pizza (there's a brick oven). It has an English sign and menu, and offers free wi-fi.

Mizutani-chaya
TEAHOUSE ¥

(水谷茶屋; ☑22-0627; 30 Kasugano-chō; tea from ¥400, noodle dishes from ¥650; ◷10am-4pm, closed Wed; 📱) Located in a small wooded grotto between Nigatsu-dō and Kasuga Taisha, this quaint thatched-roof teahouse is easily the most atmospheric spot for a cuppa in Nara. It's perfectly located for a quick cup of *matcha* (powdered green tea) or some noodles to power your way through a day of sightseeing. In warm seasons, you can sit outside among the greenery. All in all, it's one of the more atmospheric places to eat in all of Nara.

Nonohana Ohka
CAFE ¥

(野の花黄花; ☑22-1139; 13 Nakashinyamachi; coffee & tea ¥500-600; ◷11am-5pm, closed Mon) With indoor and outdoor garden seating, this cafe is one of our favourite places for a pick-me-up when in Naramachi. The cakes are usually very good here and they go down a treat with the excellent tea. Look for the glass front and the sign reading 'cafe'. There's no English menu, but there are photographs on the menu that make ordering pretty simple.

Tachibana
CAFE ¥

(たちばな; ☑31-6439; 18-1 Nishiterabayashi-chō; coffee from ¥400; ◷11am-6pm, closed Wed; 📱) This friendly little cafe/gallery in Naramachi is a great place to sample a cup of green tea. Once you're done enjoying your tea, head upstairs to check out the wonderful collection of ceramics from Kyoto and Nara artists. There's no English sign at present, but the English/Japanese menu is displayed outside.

Kasugano
SHOKUDŌ ¥

(春日野; meals from ¥600; ◷8.30am-5pm; 📶📱) If you're exploring Nara-kōen, lunchtime often finds you somewhere between Tōdai-ji and Kasuga Taisha. A good choice in this area is Kasugano, a restaurant/souvenir shop at the base of Wakakusa-yama. Take a seat in the woodsy annexe cafe section rather than the main tables in the shop area (the menu is the same). Dishes include things like tempura *soba* (¥800). It's the third shophouse from the northern end of this strip. Note that most of the souvenir shops in this same strip also have on-site restaurants that serve similar fare and most have English menus.

Doutor
CAFE ¥

(ドトール) If you need a quick cuppa or a sandwich, there is a branch of the coffee shop chain in the Konishi Arcade (a five-minute walk from Kintetsu Nara).

Silk Road
SHOKUDŌ ¥¥

(シルクロードの終着駅; ☑25-0231; 16 Kasugano-chō; meals ¥1000; ◷10am-7pm; 📱) If you've got kids in tow, head into the Yume-Kaze Plaza (Yumekaze Hiroba in Japanese) dining/shopping complex across from the Nara National Museum to find this wonderful 'train-centric' restaurant. There are two huge model train layouts, which kids can actually control while eating bowls of standard Japanese curry rice and similar favourites.

ℹ Information

The main **JR Nara Station information centre** (☑22-9821; ◷9am-5pm), in the old Nara Station building just outside the east exit of JR Nara Station, is the city's main tourist information centre and English speakers are usually on hand. If you start from Kintetsu Nara Station, try the helpful **Kintetsu Nara Station information office** (☑24-4858; ◷9am-9pm), which is near the top of the stairs above exit 3 from the station.

There are several other information offices in Nara, including the **Nara City Tourist Information Centre** (奈良市観光センター; ☑22-3900; ◷9am-9pm) and the **Sarusawa Tourist Information Office** (猿沢観光案内所; ☑26-1991; ◷9am-5pm).

All of the information offices stock the useful *Nara Sightseeing Map*.

The information centres can put you in touch with volunteer guides who speak English and other foreign languages, but you must book at least one day in advance. Two of these services are the **YMCA Goodwill Guides** (☑45-5920; http://egg-nara.tripod.com/home.htm) and **Nara Student Guides** (☑26-4753; www.narastudentguide.org).

ℹ Getting There & Away

BUS

There is an overnight bus service between To-kyo's Shinjuku (Shinjuku highway bus terminal) and Nara (one-way/return ¥8400/15,120). In Nara, call **Nara Kōtsū Bus** (🖂 22-5110; www.narakotsu.co.jp/kousoku) or check with the Nara City Tourist Information Centre for more details. In Nara, overnight buses leave from stop 8 in front of JR Nara Station and from stop 20 outside Kintetsu Nara Station. In Tokyo, call **Kantō Bus** (🖂 03-3371-1225; www.kanto-bus.co.jp) or visit the Shinjuku highway bus terminal in person.

Airport limousines (¥2000, 90 minutes to Kansai International Airport; ¥1440, 60 minutes to Itami Airport) leave from stop 9 in front of JR Nara Station and stop 20 (Kansai International Airport) and 12 (Itami Airport) outside Kintetsu Nara Station.

Buses to sights west (Yakushi-ji and Tōshōdai-ji) and southwest (Hōryū-ji) leave from stop 10, diagonally across from JR Nara Station, and stop 8 outside Kintetsu Nara Station.

TRAIN
Kyoto

The JR Nara line connects JR Kyoto Station with JR Nara Station (JR *Miyakoji Kaisoku*, ¥690, 45 minutes) and there are several departures an hour during the day. This is the best option for those with Japan Rail Passes.

The Kintetsu line, which runs between Kintetsu Kyoto Station (in Kyoto Station) and Kintetsu Nara Station, is the fastest and most convenient way to travel between Nara and Kyoto. There are *tokkyū* (¥1110, 33 minutes) and *kyūkō* (¥610, 40 minutes). The *tokkyū* trains run directly and are very comfortable; the *kyūkō* usually require a change at Yamato-Saidai-ji.

Osaka

The JR Kansai line links Osaka (Namba and Tennō-ji stations) and Nara (JR Nara Station). A *kaisoku* connects Namba and JR Nara Station (¥540, 45 minutes) and Tennō-ji and JR Nara Station (¥450, 30 minutes).

The Kintetsu Nara line connects Osaka (Kintetsu Osaka Namba Station) with Nara (Kintetsu Nara Station). *Kaisoku* and *futsū* services take about 36 minutes and cost ¥540. *Tokkyū* services do the journey in five minutes less but cost almost double, making them a poor option.

ℹ Getting Around

TO/FROM THE AIRPORT

Nara is served by Kansai International Airport (KIX). There is a **limousine bus service** (Nara Kōtsū; www.narakotsu.co.jp/kousoku/limousine/nara_kanku.html) between Nara and the airport with departures roughly every hour in both directions (¥2000, 90 minutes). At Kansai International Airport, ask at the information counter in the arrivals hall, and in Nara visit the ticket office in the building across from Kintetsu Nara Station. Reservations are a good idea.

For domestic flights, there are **limousine buses** (Nara Kōtsū; www.narakotsu.co.jp/kousoku/limousine/nara_itami.html) to/from Osaka's Itami airport (¥1440, 60 minutes).

BUS

Most of the area around Nara-kōen is covered by two circular bus routes: bus 1 runs anticlockwise and bus 2 runs clockwise. There's a ¥200 flat fare. You can easily see the main sights in the park on foot and use the bus as an option if you are pushed for time or get tired of walking. If you plan to ride a lot, the one-day Free Pass costs ¥500.

Buses to Ikaruga and Nishinokyō (for Yakushi-ji, Tōshōdai-ji and Hōryū-ji) leave from stop 10 diagonally across from JR Nara Station and from stop 8 outside Kintetsu Nara Station.

AROUND NARA

In the area around Nara, southern Nara-ken was the birthplace of imperial rule and is rich in historical sites that are easily accessible as day trips from Osaka, Kyoto or Nara, provided that you make an early start. Of particular historical interest are the *kofun* (burial mounds) that mark the graves of Japan's first emperors; these are concentrated around Asuka. There are also several isolated temples where you can escape the crowds that plague Nara's city centre. Further afield, the mountaintop town of Yoshino is one of Japan's cherry-blossom meccas.

Easily reached by rail, Yamato-Yagi and Sakurai serve as useful transport hubs for the region. Keep in mind that the Kintetsu line is more convenient than JR for most of the destinations in this section.

Temples Southwest of Nara

While Nara city has some impressive ancient temples and Buddhist statues, if you want to go right back to the roots of Japanese Buddhism it's necessary to head to three temples southwest of Nara: Hōryū-ji, Yakushi-ji and Tōshōdai-ji.

Hōryū-ji is one of the most important temples in all of Japan, largely for historical reasons. However, its appeal is more academic than aesthetic, and it's quite a slog through drab suburbs to get there. Thus, for

Around Nara

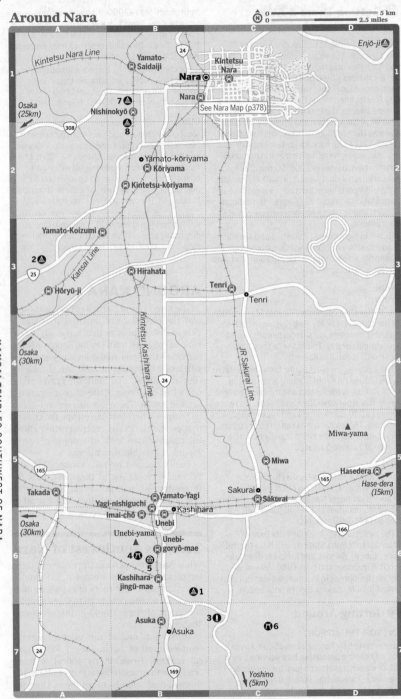

0 — 5 km
0 — 2.5 miles

Kintetsu Nara Line

Osaka (25km)

Yamato-Saidaiji

24

Nara

Kintetsu Nara

Nara

See Nara Map (p378)

Enjō-ji

7

Nishinokyō

8

Yamato-kōriyama

Kōriyama

Kintetsu-kōriyama

Yamato-Koizumi

Kansai Line

2

25

Hōryū-ji

Hirahata

Tenri

Tenri

Osaka (30km)

Kintetsu Kashihara Line

24

JR Sakurai Line

Miwa-yama

Miwa

Hasedera

165

Hase-dera (15km)

Takada

165

Yamato-Yagi

Sakurai

Sakurai

Yagi-nishiguchi

Kashihara

Imai-chō

Unebi

166

Osaka (30km)

Unebi-yama

Unebi-goryō-mae

4

5

Kashihara-jingū-mae

1

Asuka

3

6

Asuka

24

169

Yoshino (5km)

Around Nara

most people we recommend a half-day trip to Yakushi-ji and Tōshōdai-ji, which are easy to get to from Nara and very pleasant for strolling.

If you want to visit all three temples, head to Hōryū-ji first (it's the most distant from the centre of Nara) and then continue by bus 97 or 98 (¥560, 39 minutes) up to Yakushi-ji and Tōshōdai-ji, which are a 10-minute walk apart. Obviously, this can also be done in reverse. Of all the buses that ply the southwest temple route, bus 97 is the most convenient, with English announcements and route maps (it also pulls off the main road and enters the Yakushi-ji parking lot).

Hōryū-ji 法隆寺

Hōryū-ji (法隆寺; admission ¥1000; ⊙8am-5pm 22 Feb-3 Nov, to 4.30pm 4 Nov-21 Feb) was founded in 607 by Prince Shōtoku, who is considered by many to be the patron saint of Japanese Buddhism. Legend has it that moments after his birth, Shōtoku stood up and started praying. Hōryū-ji is renowned not only as the oldest temple in Japan but also as a repository for some of the country's rarest treasures. Several of the temple's wooden buildings have survived earthquakes and fires to become the oldest of their kind in the world.

The temple is divided into two parts, **Sai-in** (West Temple) and **Tō-in** (East Temple). The entrance ticket allows admission to Sai-in, Tō-in and the Great Treasure Hall. A detailed map is provided and a guidebook is available in English and several other languages.

The main approach to the temple proceeds from the south along a tree-lined avenue and continues through the Nandai-mon and Chū-mon gates before entering the Sai-in precinct. As you enter, you'll see the **Kondō** (Main Hall) on your right and a pagoda on your left.

The Kondō houses several treasures, including the triad of the **Buddha Sakyamuni**, with two attendant Bodhisattvas. Though it is one of Japan's great Buddhist treasures, it's dimly lit and barely visible – you will need a torch (flashlight) to see it. Likewise, the pagoda contains clay images depicting scenes from the life of Buddha, which are barely visible without a torch.

On the eastern side of Sai-in are the two concrete buildings of the **Daihōzō-in** (Great Treasure Hall), containing numerous treasures from Hōryū-ji's long history.

Given the cost of admission and the time it takes to get here from central Nara, we recommend that you give careful thought to committing at least half a day to visiting this temple.

ⓘ Getting There & Away

To get to Hōryū-ji, take the JR Kansai line from JR Nara Station to Hōryū-ji Station (¥210, 11 minutes). From there, bus 72 shuttles the short distance between the station and the bus stop Hōryū-ji Monmae (¥180, eight minutes). Alternatively, take bus 52 or 97 from either JR Nara Station or Kintetsu Nara Station and get off at the Hōryū-ji-mae stop (¥760, 60 minutes). Leave the bus stop and walk west for about 50m, cross the road and you will see the tree-lined approach to the temple.

Yakushi-ji 薬師寺

This **temple** (admission ¥500; ⊙8.30am-5pm) houses some of the most beautiful Buddhist statues in all Japan. It was established by Emperor Temmu in 680. With the exception of the **East Pagoda**, which dates to 730, the present buildings either date from the 13th century or are very recent reconstructions.

Entering from the south, turn to the right before going through the gate with guardian figures and walk to the **Tōin-dō** (East Hall). The hall houses a famous Shō-Kannon image, built in the 7th century and showing obvious influences of Indian sculptural styles. Exit the Tōin-dō and walk west to the **Kondō** (Main Hall).

The Kondō was rebuilt in 1976 and houses several images, including the famous **Yakushi Triad** (the Buddha Yakushi flanked by the Bodhisattvas of the sun and moon), dating from the 8th century. They were originally gold, but a fire in the 16th century turned the images an appealingly mellow black.

Behind (north of) the Kondō is the **Kō-dō** (Lecture Hall), which houses yet another fine Buddhist trinity, this time Miroku Buddha with two Bodhisattva attendants. You can exit to the north behind this hall and make your way to Tōshōdai-ji.

ℹ Getting There & Away

To get to Yakushi-ji, take bus 97 from JR Nara Station or Kintetsu Nara Station and get off at the Yakushi-ji Parking Lot stop (Yakushijo Chūshajō in Japanese; ¥340, 22 minutes). The temple is a short walk north of the parking lot. You can also take bus 52, 88 or 97 from these stations and get off at the Yakushi-ji Higashiguchi stop (¥250, 15 minutes). From this stop, walk 100m south (same direction the bus was travelling) to a Mobil station, cross the road to the west, and walk west across a canal. From the main road it's 250m to the temple's south entrance.

You can also take a *futsū* on the Kintetsu Kashihara line (which runs between Kyoto and Kashihara-jingū-mae) and get off at Nishinokyō Station, which is about a 200m walk northwest of Yakushi-ji (and 600m walk south of Tōshōdai-ji). If you're coming from Nara, you will have to change trains at Yamato-Saidaiji (¥200, five minutes; *kyūkō* and *tokkyū* do not stop at Nishinokyō). If you're coming from Kyoto, take a *kyūkō* as far as Yamato Saidaiji and change to the *futsū* (¥610, 40 minutes).

Tōshōdai-ji 唐招提寺

This **temple** (admission ¥600; ◷ 8.30am-5pm, last entry 4.30pm) was established in 759 by the Chinese priest Ganjin (Jian Zhen), who had been recruited by Emperor Shōmu to reform Buddhism in Japan. The temple grounds are pleasantly wooded and make a good contrast to nearby Yakushi-ji, which is largely devoid of greenery.

The **Kondō** (Golden Hall), roughly in the middle of the grounds, contains a stunning Senjū (thousand-armed) Kannon image. Behind this, the **Kōdō** (Lecture Hall), contains a beautiful image of Miroku Buddha.

Tōshōdai-ji is a 500m walk north of Yakushi-ji's northern gate.

Around Yamato-Yagi
大和八木周辺

Easily reached on the Kintetsu line from Osaka, Kyoto or Nara, Yamato-Yagi is the most convenient transport hub for sights in southern Nara-ken. From Kyoto take the Kintetsu

Nara/Kashihara line direct (*kyūkō*, ¥860, 57 minutes). From Nara take the Kintetsu Nara line to Saidaiji and change to the Kintetsu Kashihara line (*kyūkō*, ¥430, 27 minutes). From Osaka's Uehonmachi Station, take the Kintetsu Osaka line direct (*kyūkō*, ¥540, 34 minutes). If you've got a Japan Rail Pass, you can reach the Kashihara area from Nara by taking the JR Nara/Sakurai lines and getting off at Unebi (¥480, 39 minutes).

Kashihara 橿原

Three stops south of Yamato-Yagi, on the Kintetsu Kashihara line, is Kashihara-jingū-mae Station (¥200 from Yamato-Yagi, five minutes; all trains stop). You can also take the JR Nara/Sakurai line from Nara. There are a couple of interesting sights within easy walking distance of this station.

◉ Sights

Kashihara-jingū   SHINTŌ SHRINE
(橿原神宮) **FREE** This shrine, at the foot of Unebi-yama, dates back to 1889, when many of the buildings were moved here from Kyoto Gosho (Kyoto Imperial Palace). The shrine buildings are built in the same style as those of Ise-jingū's Grand Shrine and are a good example of classical Shintō architecture. The shrine is dedicated to Japan's mythical first emperor, Jimmu, and an annual festival is held here on 11 February, the legendary date of Jimmu's enthronement. The vast, parklike grounds are pleasant to stroll around.

The shrine is five minutes' walk from Kashihara-jingū-mae Station; take the central exit out of the station and follow the main street in the direction of the mountain.

**Nara Prefecture Kashihara
Archaeological Museum**   MUSEUM
(奈良県橿原考古学研究所付属博物館; Nara Ken-ritsu Kashihara Kōkogaku Kenkyūjo Fuzoku Hakubutsukan; ☎ 0744-24-1185; admission ¥400, foreign passport holders free; ◷ 9am-5pm, closed Mon) This museum is highly recommended for those with an interest in the history of the Japanese people. The objects on display come from various archaeological sites in the area, including several *kofun*. Although most of the explanations are in Japanese, there's enough English to give you an idea of what's going on. However, if you want to get the most out of the museum, bring a Japanese friend to explain things. Foreigners can enter free, but you'll need your passport to take advantage of this great deal.

To get there from Kashihara-jingū, walk out the northern gate of the shrine (to your left when you stand with your back to the main hall), follow the wooded avenue for five minutes, cross the main road and continue on in the same direction for 100m before turning left at the first intersection. It's on the left soon after this turn. Note that it's not well marked in English (look for a sign reading 'The Museum, Archeological Institute of Kashihara, Nara Prefecture').

Asuka 飛鳥

♪ 0744 / POP 6141

The Yamato Plain in central Nara-ken is where the forerunners of Japan's ruling Yamato dynasty cemented their grip on power. In these pre-Buddhist days, huge earthen burial mounds were used to entomb deceased emperors. Some of the best examples of these burial mounds, or *kofun,* can be found around the town of Asuka, an hour or so south of Nara on the Kintetsu line.

There's a **tourist information office** (☑ 54-3624; ☺ 8.30am-5pm, closed New Year holidays) outside Asuka Station, but it didn't stock any useful maps when we were there. The best way to explore the area is by bicycle. **Manyō Rent-a-Cycle** (レンタサイクル万葉) rents bikes for ¥300 an hour or ¥900 a day (¥1000 a day on weekends). Manyō is across the street from the station, and also stocks a useful English map of the area.

Two tombs worth seeing are **Takamatsuzuka-kofun** (高松塚古墳) and **Ishibutai-kofun** (石舞台古墳; admission ¥250; ☺ 8.30am-5pm). Takamatsuzuka-kofun, which looks like a grassy mound, is located in a pleasant wooded park that you can explore on foot or by bicycle. Ishibutai-kofun, which is composed of vast rocks in an open area, is said to have housed the remains of Soga no Umako but is now completely empty.

If you have time, take a look at **Asuka-dera** (飛鳥寺; admission ¥350; ☺ 9am-5.15pm Apr-Sep, to 4.45pm Oct-Mar), which dates from 596 and is considered the first true temple in all of Japan. Housed within is the oldest remaining image of Buddha in Japan – it looks pretty good considering it's been around for more than 1300 years.

Asuka is five stops south of Yamato-Yagi (change at Kashihara-jingū-mae) and two south of Kashihara-jingū-mae on the Kintetsu Yoshino line (¥220 from Yamato-Yagi, 10 minutes; *tokkyū* trains stop at Asuka).

Around Sakurai 桜井周辺

There are a few interesting places to visit close to the town of Sakurai, which can be reached directly from Nara on the JR Nara/Sakurai line (*futsū,* ¥320, 30 minutes). To reach Sakurai via Yamato-Yagi (when coming from Kyoto or Osaka), take the Kintetsu Osaka line from Yamato-Yagi (*junkyū,* ¥200, seven minutes).

◉ Sights

Tanzan-jinja SHINTŌ SHRINE
(談山神社; admission ¥500; ☺ 8.30am-4.30pm) South of Sakurai, this shrine can be reached by Sakurai City Community Bus from stand 1 outside the southern exit of Sakurai Station (¥480, 25 minutes). Enshrined here is Nakatomi no Kamatari, patriarch of the Fujiwara line, which effectively ruled Japan for nearly 500 years. Legend has it that Nakatomi met here secretly with Prince Naka no Ōe over games of kickball to discuss the overthrow of the ruling Soga clan. This event is commemorated on 29 April and 3 November by by priests playing a game of kickball.

The central structure of the shrine is an attractive 13-storey pagoda, best viewed against a backdrop of maple trees ablaze with autumn colours (November and early December).

Hase-dera BUDDHIST TEMPLE
(長谷寺; admission ¥500; ☺ 8.30am-5pm Apr-Sep, 9am-4.30pm Oct-Mar) Two stops east of Sakurai on the Kintetsu Osaka line is Hasedera Station (¥200, six minutes). From the station, it's a 20-minute walk to lovely Hase-dera. After a long climb up seemingly endless steps, you enter the main hall and are rewarded with a splendid view from the gallery, which juts out on stilts over the mountainside. Inside the top hall, the huge Kannon image is well worth a look. The best times to visit this temple are in the spring, when the way is lined with blooming peonies, and in autumn, when the temple's maple trees turn a vivid red. From the station, walk down through the archway, cross the river and turn right onto the main street that leads to the temple.

Murō-ji BUDDHIST TEMPLE
(室生寺; admission ¥600; ☺ 8.30am-5pm Mar-Nov, to 4pm Dec-Feb) Founded in the 9th century, this temple has strong connections with Esoteric Buddhism (the Shingon sect). Women were never excluded from Murō-ji as they were from other Shingon temples,

and it is for this reason that it came to be known as 'the Woman's Koya'. Unfortunately, the temple's lovely five-storey pagoda, which dates from the 8th or 9th century, was severely damaged in a typhoon in the summer of 1999. The newly rebuilt pagoda lacks some of the rustic charm of the old one. Nonetheless, Murō-ji is a secluded place in thick forest and is well worth a visit.

After visiting the main hall, walk up to the pagoda and then continue on behind the pagoda in the direction of **Oku-no-in**, a temple hall located at the top of a very steep flight of steps. If you don't feel like making the climb, at least go about 100m past the pagoda to see the mammoth cedar tree growing over a huge rock here.

To get there from Sakurai, take the Kintetsu Osaka line from Sakurai to Murōguchi-ōno Station (*kyūkō*, ¥340, 16 minutes). Then switch to a bus to Murō-ji (bus 43, ¥420, 15 minutes). In spring and autumn, there is a direct bus from Hase-dera and Murō-ji (¥830). It runs from the end of April to early May and on weekends from the start of November to the start of December, with one or two buses per hour between 11am and 3pm.

Yoshino 吉野

☑ 0746 / POP 9053

Yoshino is Japan's top cherry-blossom destination. For a few weeks in early to mid-April, the blossoms of thousands of cherry trees form a floral carpet gradually ascending the mountainsides. It's definitely a sight worth seeing, but the narrow streets of the village become jammed tight with thousands of visitors at this time, and you'll have to be content with a day trip unless you've booked accommodation long in advance. Once the cherry-blossom petals fall, the crowds depart and Yoshino reverts to a sleepy village with a handful of shrines and a couple of temples to entertain day trippers.

◉ Sights

Kimpusen-ji   BUDDHIST TEMPLE

(金峯山寺; admission ¥400; ◷8.30am-4.30pm, last entry 4pm) Walk about 400m uphill from the cable-car station and you will come to the stone steps leading to the Niō-mon gate of the temple. Check out the fearsome **Kongō Rikishi** (guardian figure statues) in the gate and then continue on to the massive **Zaō-dō Hall** of the temple. Said to be the second-largest wooden building in Ja-

pan, the hall is most interesting for its unfinished wooden columns. For many centuries Kimpusen-ji has been one of the major centres for Shugendō, and pilgrims have often stopped here to pray for good fortune on the journey to Ōmine-san.

Yoshimizu-jinja   SHINTŌ SHRINE

(吉水神社) Continuing another 300m up the street brings you to a side road to the left (the first turn past the post office) that leads to this small shrine that has a good view back to Kimpusen-ji and the *hito-me-sen-bon* (1000 trees in a glance) viewpoint.

The shrine has played host to several important historical figures. Minamoto Yoshitsune, a legendary swordsman and general, fled here after incurring the wrath of his brother, the first Kamakura shōgun. Emperor Go-Daigo set up a rival southern court in Yoshino after a dispute for succession broke out in Kyoto, and stayed here while his palace was being built. The shrine displays a collection of scrolls, armour and painted murals from the emperor's stay (admission ¥400). It also entertained Toyotomi Hideyoshi and his 5000-person *hanami* party in 1594.

Nyoirin-ji   BUDDHIST TEMPLE

(如意輪時; admission ¥400; ◷9am-4pm, 7am-5pm during cherry blossom season in April) Take the left fork on the road just above Yoshimizu-jinja and the dilapidated Katte-jinja (勝手神社) shrine to reach Nyoirin-ji, a temple that preserves both the relics of Emperor Go-Daigo's unlucky court and his tomb itself.

⌂ Sleeping

Yoshino-yama Kizō-in   SHUKUBŌ ¥

(吉野山喜蔵院; ☑32-3014; per person with two meals ¥10,000; ◷Mar-Dec) Kizō-in temple doubles as the local youth hostel and is the cheapest option in town. It's a pleasant place to stay, and several of the hostel's rooms look out across the valley.

Chikurin-in Gumpōen   RYOKAN ¥¥¥

(竹林院群芳園; ☑32-8081; www.chikurin.co.jp /e/home.htm; r per person with two meals ¥13,650-78,000, without bathroom ¥12,600-21,000, temple r per person ¥10,500-18,000; @) This exquisite temple now operates primarily as a ryokan. Both present and previous emperors have stayed here, and a look at the view afforded by some of the rooms explains why. Reservations are essential for the cherry-blossom season, and a good idea at all other times. Even if you don't plan to stay at the temple, you should at least visit its splendid garden (admission ¥300). Note that the ryokan charges a single-traveller supplement of ¥5250.

🍴 Eating

Hōkon-an
CAFE ¥

(芳魂庵; ☎ 32-8207; ⏰ 9am-5.30pm, open daily during cherry blossom and fall foliage season) An atmospheric little teahouse where you can sip your tea while enjoying a lovely view over the valley. The *matcha* comes with a homemade Japanese sweet. Look for the rustic wooden facade and large ceramic urn on the left, just past the post office. Hours are irregular but it's open daily in April. There's no English menu, but the menu does have pictures.

Nakai Shunpūdō
SHOKUDŌ ¥

(中井春風堂; ☎ 32-3043; ⏰ 9am-5pm, open daily during cherry blossom and fall foliage season) With a limited picture menu, this restaurant serves a *kamameshi teishoku* (rice cooked in an iron pot) and other typical lunch favourites; the view from the windows is great. It's about 5m past the information office, on the opposite side – look for the ceramic *tanuki* (Japanese raccoon dog) figure out front.

Nishizawaya
SHOKUDŌ ¥

(西澤屋; ☎ 32-8600; ⏰ 9am-6pm, open daily during cherry blossom season and fall foliage season; 🍴) Run by a bunch of friendly ladies, this homey restaurant serves a *shizuka gozen* set, which includes a broiled *ayu* (sweetfish) and a small hotpot filled with vegetables and tofu. It's directly across the street from Katte-jinja: look for the plastic food on display.

ℹ️ Information

Yoshinoyama Visitor Centre (☎ 32-3081/8014; ⏰ 9am-5pm Tue-Sun, closed Dec, Jan, Feb; open only weekends; open every day only during cherry-blossom season & national holidays) is about 500m up the main street from the top cable-car station, on your right just after Kimpusen-ji (look for the large tan-and-white building). It can help with *minshuku* (guesthouse) bookings if necessary.

ℹ️ Getting There & Away

Visitors to Yoshino first arrive at Yoshino Station, and then make their way up to the village proper by cable car or on foot. The cable car costs ¥350/600 one-way/return. The walk takes about 15 minutes; follow the path that leaves from beside the cable-car station. Note that the cable car stops running at 5pm (except from 1 April to 22 April, when it runs until 6:40pm) – plan your day accordingly or you'll have to walk down.

To get to Yoshino Station from Kyoto or Nara, take the Kintetsu Nara Kashihara line to Kashihara-jingū-mae (*kyūkō* from Kyoto, ¥860, 66 minutes; *kyūkō* from Nara, ¥480, 36 minutes) and change to the Kintetsu Yoshino line (*kyūkō*, ¥460, 52 minutes; *tokkyū* ¥960, 39 minutes).

You can take a direct train on the Kintetsu Minami Osaka–Yoshino line from Osaka (Abenobashi Station, close to Tennō-ji Station) to Yoshino (*kyūkō* ¥950, 93 minutes; *tokkyū* ¥1450, 75 minutes).

The closest JR station to Yoshino is Yoshino-guchi, which has connections with Nara, Osaka and Wakayama. From there, you'll have to take the private Kintetsu line (*kyūkō* ¥370, 35 minutes; *tokkyū* ¥870, 26 minutes).

KII PENINSULA

The remote and mountainous Kii Peninsula (紀伊半島; Kii-hantō) is a far cry from central Kansai's bustling urban sprawl. Most of the attractions are found in Wakayama-ken, including the mountaintop temple complex of Kōya-san, one of Japan's most important Buddhist centres. To the south, the ancient pilgrimage trails of the Kumano Kodō converge on the town of Hongū, which is also home to several fine onsen.

ℹ️ THE KANSAI WAKAYAMA PASS (W-PASS)

The Kansai Wakayama Pass (W-PASS) is a transport pass for use on buses and trains (excluding JR train lines) in southern Kansai (the Kii Peninsula). It's particularly useful for those who wish to explore Kōya-san, Ryūjin Onsen, the onsens around Hongū and the Kumano Kodō. It was developed for foreign travellers to explore areas that were not covered by other passes at an economical price. Transportation to some of the more remote areas requires planning and bilingual bus timetables are available online to help you organise your journey. Two- and three-day passes cost ¥3500 and ¥5500. See www.kumano-travel.com/index/en/action_ContentsDetail_Detail/id176 for more details.

Kii Peninsula

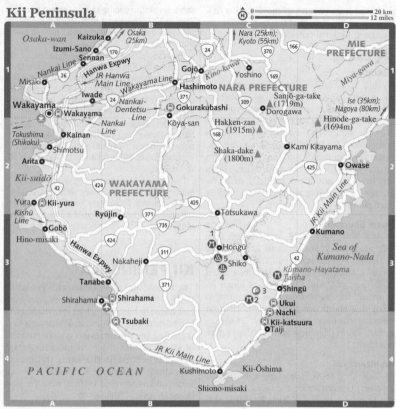

Other Wakayama-ken attractions include the beachside onsen resort of Shirahama, on the west coast of the peninsula, and the rugged coastline of Shiono-misaki and Kii-Ōshima, at the southern tip of the peninsula.

The JR Kii main line (Kinokuni line) runs around the coast of the Kii-hantō, linking Shin-Osaka and Nagoya stations (some trains originate/terminate at Kyoto Station). Special Kuroshio and Nankii *tokkyū* trains can get you around the peninsula fairly quickly, but once you step off these express trains you're at the mercy of slow local trains and buses, so plan accordingly.

Fortunately, area bus and train companies (with the exception of JR, or Japan Railways), have recently launched the Kansai Wakayama Pass (known as the W-PASS; see the boxed text p393). Of course, for most freedom of movement, a rental car is the best way to get around the area, and all of Japan's major car rental companies have branches at Kansai International Airport, which makes a good starting/finishing point for an exploration of the Kii Peninsula.

Kōya-san 高野山

☏ 0736 / POP 3797

Kōya-san is a raised tableland in northern Wakayama-ken covered with thick forests and surrounded by eight peaks. The major attraction here is the Kōya-san monastic complex, which is the headquarters of the Shingon school of Esoteric Buddhism. Though not quite the Shangri-la it's occasionally described as, Kōya-san is one of the most rewarding places to visit in Kansai, not just for the natural setting of the area but also as an opportunity to stay in temples and get a glimpse of long-held traditions of Japanese religious life.

Kii Peninsula

Although it is just possible to visit Kōya-san as a day trip from Nara, Kyoto or Osaka, it's *much* better to reduce the travel stress and stay overnight in one of the town's excellent *shukubō* (temple lodgings). Keep in mind that Kōya-san tends to be around 5°C colder than down on the plains, so bring warm clothes if you're visiting in winter, spring or autumn.

Whenever you go, you'll find that getting there is half the fun – near the end of its journey, the train winds through a series of tight valleys with mountains soaring on all sides, and the final vertiginous cable-car leg is not for the faint of heart.

History

The founder of the Shingon school of Esoteric Buddhism, Kūkai (known after his death as Kōbō Daishi), established a religious community here in 816. Kōbō Daishi travelled as a young priest to China and returned after two years to found the school. He is one of Japan's most famous religious figures and is revered as a Bodhisattva, calligrapher, scholar and inventor of the Japanese *kana* syllabary.

Followers of Shingon believe that Kōbō Daishi is not dead, but rather that he is meditating in his tomb in Kōya-san's Oku-no-in Cemetery, awaiting the arrival of Miroku (Maitreya, the future Buddha). Food is ritually offered in front of the tomb daily to sustain him during this meditation. When Miroku returns, it is thought that only Kōbō Daishi will be able to interpret his heavenly message for humanity. Thus, the vast cemetery here is like an amphitheatre crowded with souls gathered in expectation of this heavenly sermon.

Over the centuries, the temple complex grew in size and attracted many followers of the Jōdo (Pure Land) school of Buddhism. During the 11th century, it became popular with both nobles and commoners to leave hair or ashes from deceased relatives close to Kōbō Daishi's tomb.

Kōya-san is now a thriving centre for Japanese Buddhism, with more than 110 temples remaining and a large population. It is the headquarters of the Shingon school, which numbers 10 million members and presides over nearly 4000 temples all over Japan.

◉ Sights

The precincts of Kōya-san are divided into two main areas: the Garan (Sacred Precinct) in the west, where you will find interesting temples and pagodas, and the Oku-no-in, with its vast cemetery, in the east.

★**Oku-no-in**　　　　　　BUDDHIST TEMPLE
(奥の院) The Oku-no-in is a memorial hall/temple complex surrounded by a vast Buddhist cemetery. Any Buddhist worth their salt in Japan has had their remains, or just a lock or two of hair, interred here just to ensure pole position when the Buddha of the Future (Miroku Buddha) comes to earth.

The best way to approach Oku-no-in is to walk or take the bus east to Ichi-no-hashi-mae bus stop. From here you cross the bridge, **Ichi-no-hashi** (一の橋), and enter the cemetery grounds along a winding, cobbled path lined by tall cedar trees and thousands of tombs. As the trees close in and the mist swirls, the atmosphere can be enchanting, especially as night falls.

At the northern end of the graveyard, you will find the **Tōrō-dō** (燈籠堂; Lantern Hall), which is the main building of the complex. It houses hundreds of lamps, including two believed to have been burning for more than 900 years. Behind the hall you can see the closed doors of the **Kūkai mausoleum** (空海の墓).

On the way to the Lantern Hall is the bridge **Mimyo-no-hashi** (御廟橋). Worshippers ladle water from the river and pour it over the nearby Jizō statues as an offering for the dead. The inscribed wooden plaques in the river are in memory of aborted babies and those who died by drowning.

Between the bridge and the Tōrō-dō is a small wooden building the size of a large phone booth, which contains the **Miroku-ishi** (みろく石). Pilgrims reach through the holes in the wall to try to lift a large, smooth boulder onto a shelf. The weight of the stone is supposed to change according to your weight of sin. We can only report that the thing was damn heavy!

Buses return to the centre of town from the Oku-no-mae bus stop, or you can walk back in about 30 minutes.

KANSAI KŌYA-SAN

Kōya-san

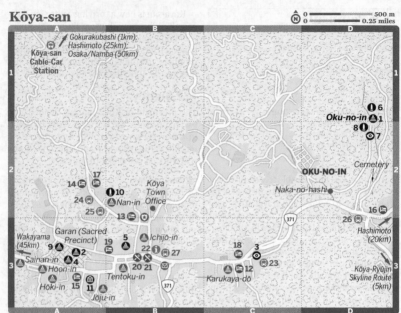

Kōya-san

Kongōbu-ji　　　　　BUDDHIST TEMPLE

(金剛峯寺; admission ¥500; ◷8.30am-5pm)
This is the headquarters of the Shingon
school and the residence of Kōya-san's abbot. The present structure dates from the
19th century and is definitely worth a visit.

The main hall's **Ohiro-ma room** has ornate 16th-century screens painted by Kanō
Tanyu. The **rock garden** is interesting for the

sheer number of rocks used in its composition, giving the effect of a throng of petrified
worshippers listening to a monk's sermon.

Admission includes tea and rice cakes
served beside the stone garden.

Garan　　　　　BUDDHIST TEMPLE

(伽藍; admission to each bldg ¥200; ◷8.30am-
5pm) In this temple complex of several halls

and pagodas, the most important buildings are the **Dai-tō** (大塔; Great Pagoda) and **Kondō** (金堂; Main Hall). The Dai-tō, rebuilt in 1934 after a fire, is said to be the centre of the lotus-flower mandala formed by the eight mountains around Kōya-san. It's well worth entering the Dai-tō to see the **Dainichi-nyōrai** (Cosmic Buddha) and his four attendant Buddhas. It's been repainted and is an awesome sight. The nearby **Sai-tō** (西塔; Western Pagoda) was most recently rebuilt in 1834 and is more subdued.

Treasure Museum
MUSEUM

(霊宝館; Reihōkan; admission ¥600; ⊙ 8.30am-5.30pm May-Oct, to 5pm Nov-Apr) The Treasure Museum has a compact display of Buddhist works of art, all collected in Kōya-san. There are some very fine statues, painted scrolls and mandalas. Enter 30 minutes before closing.

Tokugawa Mausoleum
MONUMENT

(徳川家霊台; Tokugawa-ke Reidai; admission without joint ticket ¥200; ⊙ 8.30am-5pm) Built in 1643, the Tokugawa Mausoleum consists of two adjoining structures that serve as the mausoleums of Tokugawa Ieyasu (on the right) and Tokugawa Hidetada (on the left), the first and second Tokugawa shōguns, respectively. They are ornately decorated, as with most structures associated with the Tokugawa shōguns. The mausoleum is not far from the Namikiri-fudō-mae bus stop (波切不動前バス亭).

✿ Festivals & Events

Aoba Matsuri
TRADITIONAL

Held on 15 June to celebrate the birth of Kōbō Daishi. Various traditional ceremonies are performed at the temples around town.

Rōsoku Matsuri
TRADITIONAL

This more interesting festival is held on 13 August in remembrance of departed souls. Thousands of mourners light candles along the approaches to Oku-no-in.

🛏 Sleeping

More than 50 temples in Kōya-san offer temple lodgings (*shukubō*). A stay at a *shukubō* is a good way to try *shōjin-ryōri* (Buddhist vegetarian cuisine – no meat, fish, onions or garlic). Most *shukubō* also hold morning prayer sessions, which guests are welcome to join.

Most lodgings *start* at ¥9500 per person including two meals. Note that most places add a supplemental charge for solo guests.

There is a lot of variation in prices, not just between temples but also within them, depending upon room, meals and season (needless to say, the more you pay, the better will be the room and the meals). Most places ask that you check in by 5pm.

While we list phone numbers for the *shukubō* in this section, most places prefer that you reserve at least a week in advance by fax through the Kōya-san Tourist Association (p399); the homepage has a form to be used for fax reservations. Even if you contact the temples directly, you will usually be asked to go to the Tourist Association to pick up a reservation slip-voucher. If you prefer to reserve by email, you can call the Tourist Association and request their email address.

Koyasan Guest House Kokuu
GUESTHOUSE ¥

(高野山ゲストハウスKokuu; ☎ 26-7216; http://koyasanguesthouse.com; 49-43 Itogun Kōyachō Kōyasan; capsules from ¥3500, s/d from ¥6000/9000; @ 🛜) A capsule hotel on Kōya-san? Okay, this place is *not* your typical capsule hotel. It's a clean, woodsy, light and airy spot, with a variety of nice private rooms in addition to the capsules. With the closure of the only other budget accommodations on Kōya-san, this is now the only inexpensive place to stay on the mountain.

It's a convivial place and it's now brought the Kōya-san experience within the range of even the most budget conscious backpackers.

Fukuchi-in
SHUKUBŌ ¥¥

(福智院; ☎ 56-2021; fax 56-4736; r per person with meals from ¥12,600, single travellers ¥15,750; @ 🛜) This fine temple has outdoor baths with onsen water and a lovely garden designed by the famous designer Shigemori Mirei. Wi-fi is available for limited durations near the temple office.

Sōji-in
SHUKUBŌ ¥¥

(総持院; ☎ 56-2111; fax 56-4311; r per person with meals from ¥15,750, single travellers ¥18,900) At home with foreign guests, this temple has a lovely garden and some rooms with en suite baths. There is one barrier-free room with Western-style beds. The top rooms here are among the best in Kōya-san.

Rengejō-in
SHUKUBŌ ¥¥

(蓮華定院; ☎ 56-2233; fax 56-4743; r per person with meals from ¥9500, single travellers ¥12,500) This lovely temple has superb rooms, many with garden views, fine painted *fusuma*

KANSAI KŌYA-SAN

KUMANO KODŌ: JAPAN'S ANCIENT PILGRIMAGE ROUTE

From the earliest times, the Japanese believed the wilds of the Kii Peninsula to be inhabited by *kami*, Shintō deities. When Buddhism swept Japan in the 6th century, these *kami* became *gongen* – manifestations of the Buddha or a Bodhisattva – in a syncretic faith known as *ryōbu*, or 'dual Shintō'.

Japan's early emperors made pilgrimages into the area. The route they followed from Kyoto, via Osaka, Tanabe and over the inner mountains of Wakayama, is known today as the Kumano Kodō: the Kumano Old Road. Over time, the popularity of this pilgrimage spread from nobles to common folk and *yamabushi* priests (wandering mountain ascetics).

The Kumano faith is based on prehistoric forms of nature worship and over the centuries has mixed with other religions, such as Buddhism. The focal points of worship are the Hongū Taisha, Hayatama Taisha and Nachi Taisha 'grand shrines', which are connected via the Kumano Kodo pilgrimage routes. Interestingly, the Kumano faith is not defined or standardised, and is open to reinterpretation by those who visit; it's a universal sacred site.

In 2004 Unesco declared the Sacred Sites and Pilgrimage Routes in the Kii Mountain Range to be World Heritage sites. Many sections of the route have been restored and there is good accommodation en route, making it possible to perform your own 'pilgrimage' through the mountains of Wakayama.

The best way to visit Kumano would probably be to follow the general flow of pilgrims from the 9th century – how could over 1000 years of pilgrimage tradition be wrong? Find your way down the west coast of the Kii-hantō peninsula from Kyoto or Osaka to Tanabe (or travel through Kōya-san). Tanabe has some great *izakaya* pubs. From here, head into the mountainous Hongū area. Following the pilgrimage route from Hosshinmon-oji to Kumano Hongū Taisha is a great half-day walk. There are some excellent onsen in Hongū, including Yunomine and Kawa-yu, and many visitors spend a few nights here.

Most of the routes converge on the town of Hongū, which is home to Hongū Taisha, the most important of the three sacred shrines of the pilgrimage; the other two are Hayatama Taisha in Shingū and Nachi Taisha in Nachi Katsuura. Typical routes involve taking a bus from the town of Tanabe, on the west coast of Wakayama, and walking for two days to Hongū, but many variations and longer/shorter trips are possible.

The **Tanabe City Kumano Tourism Bureau** (www.tb-kumano.jp/en/index.html), one of the most progressive tourism outfits in all Japan, has detailed information and maps on the routes. You can access its English-language accommodation booking site via the homepage, making trip planning a snap.

(sliding doors) and interesting art on display. English is spoken here and an explanation of Buddhist practices and meditation is available in the early evening most days. Wi-fi not available but there is LAN cable access available in a common room.

Ekō-in
SHUKUBŌ ¥¥

(恵光院; ☑ 56-2514; ekoin@mbox.co.jp; r per person with meals from ¥10,000; @ 🛜) One of the nicer temples in town, Ekō-in is run by a friendly bunch of young monks and the rooms look onto beautiful gardens. This is also one of the two temples in town (the other is Kongōbu-ji) where you can study *zazen* (seated meditation); call ahead to make arrangements for this. Unlike other *shukubō*, this temple does not charge extra for solo travellers.

Henjōson-in
SHUKUBŌ ¥¥

(遍照尊院; ☑ 56-2434; fax 56-3641; r per person with meals from ¥15,750, without bathroom ¥12,600) Nice rooms and communal baths make this a good choice.

Haryō-in
SHUKUBŌ ¥¥

(巴陵院; ☑ 56-2702; fax 56-2936; r per person with meals from ¥6825, single travellers from ¥7825) This temple is one of the cheaper *shukubō* and functions as a *kokumin-shukusha* (people's lodge).

Shōjōshin-in   SHUKUBŌ ¥¥
(清浄心院; ☑56-2006; fax 56-4770; r per person with meals from ¥9,600 or ¥11,100; 🛜) Friendly spot with free in-room wi-fi and no extra charge for solo travellers.

✖ Eating

The culinary speciality of Kōya-san is *shōjin-ryōri*, which you can sample at your temple lodgings. If you're just in town for the day, you can try *shōjin-ryōri* at any of the temples that offer *shukubō*. Ask at the Kōya-san Tourist Association office and staff will call ahead to make reservations. Prices are fixed at ¥2700, ¥3700 and ¥5300, depending on how many courses you have. In addition, there are a few *shokudō* around town (but note that most close late in the afternoon).

Maruman   SHOKUDŌ ¥
(丸万; ☑56-2049; noodle dishes from ¥370; ⏰9am-5pm, closed irregularly, but usually on Tue or Wed) This simple *shokudō* is a good spot for lunch (opening hours are irregular, though it's usually closed on Wednesday). All the standard lunch items are represented by plastic food models in the window; *katsu-don* (fried pork cutlet over rice) is ¥820. It's just west of the tourist office on the main street – look for the food models in the window. If this is full or doesn't suit, **Nankai Shokudō** next door is similar.

ℹ Information

A joint ticket (*shodōkyōtsu-naihaiken;* ¥1500) that covers entry to Kongōbu-ji, the Kondō, Dai-tō, Treasure Museum and Tokugawa Mausoleum can be purchased at the Tourist Association office.

Kōya-san Tourist Association (高野山観光協会; ☑56-2616; http://eng.shukubo.net/; ⏰8:30am-4:30pm Dec-Feb, 8:30am-5:00pm Mar-Jun, 8:30am-5:45pm Jul & Aug, 8:30am-5pm Sep-Nov) In the centre of town in front of the Senjūin-bashi bus stop (千手院橋バス停), this tourist information centre stocks maps and brochures, and English speakers are usually on hand. While you're there, consider buying a joint ticket, and pick up a copy of the excellent English-language *Koya San* map/pamphlet.

Kōyasan Interpreter Guide Club (☑090-3263-5184, 090-1486-2588; www.geocities.jp/koyasan_i_g_c) This club offers four-hour private tours of Kōya-san for ¥5000 per group with a volunteer guide. Professional guides cost from ¥10,000 per four-hour tour. It also offers regularly scheduled tours on Wednes-

day from April to September for ¥1000 per person. The morning tour meets at Ichi-no-hashi at 8.30am, lasts three hours and covers Oku-no-in, Garan and Kongōbu-ji. The after-noon tour meets at Kongōbu-ji at 1pm, takes three hours, and covers Kongōbu-ji, Garan and Oku-no-in.

ℹ Getting There & Away

Unless you have a rental car, the best way to reach Kōya-san is by train on the Nankai-Dentetsu line from Osaka's Namba Station. The trains terminate at Gokurakubashi, at the base of the mountain, where you board a funicular railway (price included in train tickets) up to Kōya-san itself. From the cable-car station, you take a bus into the centre of town (walking is prohibited on the connecting road).

From Osaka (Namba Station) you can travel directly on a Nankai-Dentetsu line *kyūkō* to Kōya-san (¥1230, one hour and 40 minutes). For the slightly faster *tokkyū* service with reserved seats you need to pay a supplement (¥760). Nankai-Dentetsu offers the Kōya-san World Heritage ticket for ¥3310; this ticket covers entry to the main sites and round trip *tokkyū* fare from Osaka's Nankai Namba Station (check at the Nankai office in Namba since conditions change all the time).

From Kyoto go via Namba in Osaka (taking the Nankai-Dentetsu line from Namba). Or, if you've got a Japan Rail Pass, take the JR line to Hashi-moto, changing at Nara, Sakurai and Takada en route. From Hashimoto, you have no choice but to take the private Nankai-Dentetsu line to Kōya-san (¥810, 50 minutes).

If you plan to continue on from Kōya-san to Hongū in Wakayama, return to Hashimoto and take the JR line to Gōjō (¥200, 15 minutes), then continue by bus to Hongū (¥3200, four hours).

ℹ Getting Around

Buses run on three routes from the top cable-car station via the centre of town to Ichi-no-hashi and Oku-no-in. The fare to the tourist office in the centre of town at Senjūin-bashi is ¥280. The fare to the final stop, Oku-no-in, is ¥400. An all-day bus pass (*ichi-nichi furee kippu;* ¥800) is available from the bus office outside the top cable-car station, but once you get into the centre of town you can reach most destinations quite easily on foot (including Oku-no-in, which takes about 30 minutes). Note that buses run infrequently, so you should make a note of the schedule before setting out to see the sights.

If you don't feel like walking, bicycles can be rented (per hour/day ¥400/1200) at the Kōya-san Tourist Association office.

Tanabe 田辺

☎ 0739 / POP 80,518

Tanabe, a small city on the west coast of Wakayama, serves as the main gateway to the Kumano Kodō. It's a friendly place with a local government that has made huge efforts to welcome foreign tourists.

Just outside the train station, there's a useful **tourist information office** (☎ 25-4919) that stocks useful maps of the area as well as a 'gourmet map' that lists local restaurants with English menus.

Miyoshiya Ryokan (美吉屋旅館; ☎ 22-3448; www.miyoshiya-ryokan.com/english.html; r per person from ¥3200; @) is a simple travellers' ryokan. It is located three minutes' walk from the Kii-Tanabe station. Once you exit the station, turn left at the first traffic signal. Follow this road about 300m and it will be on your right. There is a small English sign near the door.

The JR Kii main line connects Shingū with JR Shin-Osaka Station (*tokkyū*, ¥6810, four hours).

Buses running between Tanabe and Hongū (¥2000, two hours) make a loop of the three surrounding onsen (Watarase, Yunomine and Kawa-yu). These buses also stop at several places, which serve as trailheads for the Kumano Kodō.

Shirahama 白浜

☎ 0739 / POP 23,201

Shirahama, on the southwest coast of the Kii-hantō, is Kansai's leading beach resort and has all the trappings of a major Japanese tourist attraction – huge resort hotels, aquariums, amusement parks etc. However, it also has several good onsen, a great white-sand beach and rugged coastal scenery.

Because the Japanese like to do things according to the rules – and the rules say the only time you can swim in the ocean is from late July to the end of August – the place is almost deserted outside the peak season. Therefore this is a great place to visit in June or September, and we've swum in the sea here as late as mid-October.

There's a **tourist information office** (☎ 42-2900; ⊙ 9.30am-6pm) in the station where you can pick up a map to the main sights and accommodation. Since the station is a fair distance from the main sights, you'll need to take a bus (one-way/all-day pass ¥330/1000, 15 minutes to the beach) if you arrive by rail.

◉ Sights & Activities

Shirara-hama   BEACH

(白良浜) Shirara-hama, the town's main beach, is famous for its white sand. If it reminds you of Australia, don't be surprised; the town had to import sand from Down Under after the original stuff washed away. This place is packed during July and August, but in the low season it can actually be quite pleasant. The beach is hard to miss, as it dominates the western side of town.

Onsen

In addition to its great beach, Shirahama has some of Japan's oldest developed onsen (they're even mentioned in the *Nihon Shoki*, one of Japan's earliest literary texts).

Shirasuna-yu   ONSEN

(しらすな湯; 864 Shirahama-chō; admission May-Sep ¥100, Oct-Apr free; ⊙ 10am-3pm Tue-Sun, to 7pm daily 1 Jul-15 Sep) An open-air onsen off the boardwalk in the middle of Shirara-hama. You can soak here and then dash into the ocean to cool off – not a bad way to spend an afternoon.

Sakino-yu Onsen   ONSEN

(崎の湯温泉; 1668 Shirahama-chō Yusaki, Nishimuro-gun; admission ¥400; ⊙ 8am-6pm Apr-Jun, 7am-7pm Jul-Aug, 8am-5pm Sep-Mar, closed Wed) A fantastic bath built on a rocky point with great views of the Pacific Ocean (and you can climb down the rocks to cool off if the waves aren't too big). Come early in the day to beat the crowds. It's 1km south of the main beach; walk along the seafront road and look for the point below the big Hotel Seamore.

Shirara-yu   ONSEN

(白良湯; 3313-1 Shirahama-chō; admission ¥400; ⊙ 7am-10pm, closed Thu) A pleasant bath right on the north end of Shirara-hama (the main beach).

Murono-yu   ONSEN

(牟婁の湯; 1665 Shirahama-chō, Yusaki; admission ¥400; ⊙ 7am-10pm, closed Tue) A simple onsen in front of Shirahama post office, on the way to the Sakino-yu Onsen.

Coastal Scenery

Just around the point south of the Sakino-yu Onsen are two of Shirahama's natural wonders. **Senjō-jiki** (千畳敷; Thousand Tatami Mat Point) is a wildly eroded point with stratified layers that actually resemble the thousand tatami mats it is named for.

More impressive is the 50m cliff face of **Sandan-heki** (三段壁; Three-Step Cliff), which drops away vertiginously into the sea. While you can pay ¥1200 to take a lift down to a cave at the base of the cliff, it's better simply to clamber along the rocks to the north of the cliff – it's stunning, particularly when the big rollers are pounding in from the Pacific.

If you'd like to enjoy more rugged coastal scenery, walk south along the coast another 1km from Sandan-heki to **Isogi-kōen** (いそぎ公園), a park where the crowds are likely to be thinner and the scenery just as impressive.

These natural attractions can be reached on foot or bicycle from the main beach in around 30 minutes, or you can take a bus from the station (¥430, 20 minutes to Senjō-jiki, bus stop 'Senjō-guchi'), from which you can walk to the others.

🛏 Sleeping

Minshuku Katsuya   MINSHUKU ¥
(民宿かつ屋; ☎ 42-3814; fax 42-3817; 3118-5 Shirahama-chō; r per person ¥4000; @) Katsuya is the best-value *minshuku* in town and it's very central, only two minutes' walk from the main beach. It's built around a small Japanese garden and has its own natural onsen bath. There is red-and-white Japanese writing on the building and faint English on a small sign.

Kokumin-shukusha
Hotel Shirahama   GUESTHOUSE ¥
(国民宿舎ホテルシラハマ; ☎ 42-3039; fax 42-4643; 813 Shirahama-chō; r per person with meals ¥6900, without meals ¥3500) This is a decent place to stay if you are on a budget. It's a little dark and showing its age, but the rooms are spacious and there is an onsen bath. It's just off Miyuki-dōri, 100m past the post office towards the beach (look for a parking lot and the black, blue, red and white sign). The tourist information office at the station has maps.

Hotel Ginsui   HOTEL ¥¥
(ホテル銀翠; ☎ 42-3316; fax 43-1301; Hama dō-ri, Shirahama-chō; s/d/tw from ¥6300/10,290/12,600; 🛜) If you'd prefer a hotel, this is a very reasonable choice within easy walking distance of the beach. It's got everything you need and the staff are efficient. Considering the location, it's a good deal. There's wi-fi in the lobby and LAN cable internet in some rooms (for a fee).

🍴 Eating

There are many restaurants in the streets just in from the beach. If you'd like to self-cater, Sakae Supermarket is five minutes' walk from the main beach.

Kiraku   SHOKUDŌ ¥
(喜楽; ☎ 42-3916; 890-48 Shirahama-chō; ☒ 11am-2pm & 4-9pm, closed Tue; 📷) There is nothing fancy about this friendly little *shokudō* that serves standard *teishoku* for around ¥1200. There is a limited picture menu to help with ordering. It's about 5m in from Miyuki-dōri, on the beach side, close to a coin laundry (look for the plants out the front). There's a limited English menu.

ℹ Getting There & Away

Shirahama is on the JR Kii main line. There are *tokkyū* trains from Shin-Osaka Station (¥5250, two hours and 35 minutes). There also *futsū* trains on the same line (¥3260, 4½ hours). The same line also connects Shirahama to other cities on Kii-hantō such as Kushimoto, Nachi, Shingū and Wakayama city. A cheaper alternative is offered by **Meikō Bus** (www13.ocn.ne.jp/~meikobus; ☒ 9am-6pm), which runs buses between JR Osaka Station and Shirahama (one-way/return ¥2700/5000, about 3½ to four hours).

Kushimoto, Shiono-misaki & Kii-Ōshima
串本・潮岬・紀伊大島
☎ 0735

The southern tip of the Kii Peninsula has some stunning coastal scenery. Shiono-misaki, connected to the mainland by a narrow isthmus, has some fine rocky vistas, but the real action is over on Kii-Ōshima, a rocky island accessible by bridge.

The main attraction on Kii-Ōshima are the coastal cliffs at the eastern end of the island, which can be viewed from the park around **Kashino-zaki Lighthouse** (樫野崎灯台). Just before the park, you'll find the **Toruko-Kinenkan Museum** (トルコ記念館; 1025-25 Kashino, Kushimoto-chō; admission ¥250; ☒ 9am-5pm), which commemorates the sinking of the Turkish ship *Ertugrul* in 1890.

Backtracking about 1km towards the bridge, there are small English signs to the **Japan–US Memorial Museum** (日米修交記念館; 1033 Kashino, Kushimoto-chō; admission ¥250; ☒ 9am-5pm), which commemorates the visit of the US ship *Lady Washington* in 1791, a full 62 years before Commodore Perry's much more famous landing in Yokohama in 1853. There is a lookout just beyond the museum from which you can see the magnificent **Umi-kongō** (海金剛) formations along the eastern end of the island.

If you're without your own transport, the best way to explore Kii-Ōshima is by renting a bicycle at Kushimoto Station. There's a place at the station that rents electric/pedal bicycles for ¥1500 per day. Otherwise, there are buses from the station, but take note of schedules, as departures are few and far between.

Misaki Lodge Youth Hostel (みさき ロッジユースホステル; ☎62-1474; fax 62-0529; 2864-1 Shionomisaki; per person dm without meals/minshuku with two meals from ¥3960/7120) is the best place to stay in the area. It's on the southern side of the cape overlooking the Pacific. Take a Shiono-misaki–bound bus from Kushimoto Station (20 minutes) and get off at Koroshio-mae.

Kushimoto is one hour from Shirahama by JR *tokkyū* (¥2200) and 3½ hours (¥6080) from Shin-Osaka. *Futsū* services are significantly cheaper but take almost twice as long.

Nachi & Kii-Katsuura
那智・紀伊勝浦

The Nachi and Kii-Katsuura area has several sights grouped around the sacred **Nachi-no-taki** (那智の滝), Japan's highest waterfall (133m). **Nachi Taisha** (那智大社), near the waterfall, was built in homage to the waterfall's *kami* (Shintō spirit god). It is one of the three great shrines of Kii-hantō, and worth the climb up the steep steps to get there. Next to the shrine, **Sanseiganto-ji** (山青岸渡寺) is a fine old temple.

The most atmospheric approach to the falls and the shrine is the fantastic tree-lined arcade of **Daimon-zaka** (大門坂). To get to Daimon-zaka, take a bus from Nachi or Kii-Katsuura Station and get off at the Daimon-zaka stop (ask the bus driver to drop you at Daimon-zaka and he'll point you in the right direction from the stop). The way isn't marked in English, but it's roughly straight uphill just in from the road. From the bus stop to the shrine is roughly 800m, most of it uphill. It's fine in winter, but in summer you'll get soaked, so consider doing it in reverse (check bus schedules carefully before setting out).

Daimon-zaka takes you up to the steps at the base of the shrine. After visiting the shrine, walk down to the falls. At the base of the falls is **Nachiyama-oku-no-in** (那智山

奥の院), where you can pay ¥300 to hike up to a lookout with a better view of the falls.

The **Nachi-no-Hi Matsuri** (Fire Festival) takes place at the falls on 14 July. During this lively event, *mikoshi* are brought down from the mountain and met by groups bearing flaming torches.

Buses to the waterfall and shrine leave from Nachi Station (¥470, 17 minutes) and from Kii-Katsuura Station (¥600, 25 minutes). Buses to the Daimon-zaka stop leave from Nachi Station (¥330, 11 minutes) and from Kii-Katsuura Station (¥410, 19 minutes).

ℹ Getting There & Away

Nachi and Kii-Katsuura (the stations are only two stops apart) can be reached by JR Kii main-line trains from Shin-Osaka Station (*tokkyū*, ¥6500, three hours and 45 minutes; *futsū*, ¥4310, six hours excluding transit times) and from Nagoya Station (*tokkyū*, ¥7310, three hours and 40 minutes; *futsū*, ¥4380, 5½ hours excluding transit times). *Futsū* are significantly cheaper but take almost twice as long.

Shingū 新宮

☎0735 / POP 26,998

The small city of Shingū on the east coast of Wakayama functions as a useful transport hub for access to the Kumano Kodō pilgrimage route and the onsen village of Hongū. There's a helpful **information office** (☎22-2840; ◷9am-5.30pm) at the station.

A two-minute walk north of the station, **Hase Ryokan** (長谷旅館; ☎22-2185; fax 21-6677; r per person with meals from ¥6300, no dinner served on Sun; @🐾) is a comfortable and reasonable choice. Call from the station and someone will collect you, or ask at the information office for a map.

The JR Kii main line connects Shingū with Nagoya Station (*tokkyū*, ¥6990, three to 3½ hours) and Shin-Osaka Station (*tokkyū*, ¥6810, four hours).

There are buses between Shingū and Hongū, about half of which make a loop of the three surrounding onsen (Watarase, Yunomine and Kawa-yu).

Hongū 本宮

Hongū is a good starting point for the onsen nearby. The **Kumano Hongū Heritage Centre** (◷9am-5pm) has detailed information in English about the sacred Kumano region. Hongū is also home to **Kumano**

Hongū Taisha (熊野本宮大社), one of the three famous shrines of the Kumano San-zan. The shrine is close to the Hongū Taisha-mae bus stop (the buses listed in this section stop there).

Blue Sky Guesthouse (蒼空げすとはうす; ☑ 42-0800; www.kumano-guesthouse.com/eng.html; 1526 Hongū, Hongū-chō; r per person incl breakfast from ¥6000, single travellers ¥7000; ☎) is an excellent new guesthouse with clean, comfortable rooms a short walk from the Hongū information centre. Follow the main highway 10 minutes to the south end of town and there are signs in English pointing the way.

Buses leave for Hongū from JR Gojō Sta-tion in the north (¥3200, four hours), Kintetsu Yamato-Yagi Station in the south (¥3950, five hours and 10 minutes), Kii-Tanabe in the west (¥2000, two hours) and Shingū in the south-east (¥1500, 60 to 80 minutes), which has the most departures of these three access points. Most Hongū buses also stop at Kawa-yu, Wa-tarase and Yunomine onsen (in that order), but be sure to ask before boarding. Keep in mind that departures are few in any direction.

Needless to say, since bus departures are limited, exploring the area by rental car is a good idea. Renting a car at Tanabe, Shira-hama or Wakayama City and heading inland is the normal route, but you can also start further north and go via Kōya-san.

Yunomine, Watarase & Kawa-yu Onsen

These three onsen are among the best in all of Kansai. Because each has its own distinct character, it's worth doing a circuit of all three. There are several ryokan and min-shuku in the area, but if you are on a tight budget it's possible to camp on the riverbanks above and below Kumano Hongū Taisha.

Note that you can walk between the three onsen in this section relatively easily. The tunnel at the west end of the village at Kawa-yu connects to Watarase Onsen (the total journey is a little less than 1km). From Watarase Onsen, it's about 3km west along Rte 311 to reach Yunomine.

Yunomine Onsen 湯峰温泉

The town of Yunomine is nestled around a narrow river in a wooded valley. Most of the town's onsen are contained inside ryokan or minshuku but charming little **Tsubo-yu**

Onsen (つぼ湯温泉; admission ¥750; ☺ 6am-9.30pm, last entry 9pm) is open to all. It's right in the middle of town, inside a tiny wooden shack built on an island in the river. Buy a ticket at the sentō next to **Tōkō-ji** (東光寺), the temple in the middle of town. The sentō itself is open the same hours as the onsen and entry is ¥250; of the two baths at the sentō, we suggest the kusuri-yu (medicine water; ¥380), which is 100% pure hot-spring water. Note that if you've paid to enter Tsubo-yu Onsen, you can enter the sentō for free.

🛏 Sleeping

Yunomine has plenty of minshuku and ry-okan for you to choose from.

Minshuku Yunotanisō MINSHUKU ¥¥ (民宿湯の谷荘; ☑ 0735-42-1620; r per person with two meals ¥8500) At the upper end of the village, this minshuku is exactly what a minshuku should be: simple, clean and wel-coming. The food is very good and there's an excellent onsen bath on the premises.

Ryokan Yoshino-ya RYOKAN ¥¥ (旅館よしのや; ☑ 0735-42-0101; r per person with two meals from ¥8970, ¥2100 surcharge for solo travellers; ☎) Located very close to Tsubo-yu, this is a slightly more upscale place with a lovely rotemburo (outdoor bath). It's fairly new and the location can't be beat. Like Yunotanisō, it's a friendly and well-run spot. There's free wi-fi in the lobby.

Watarase Onsen わたらせ温泉

This **onsen** (わたらせ温泉; admission ¥700; ☺ 6am-10pm, last entry 9.30pm) is built around a bend in the river directly between Yunom-ine Onsen and Kawa-yu Onsen. It's not as interesting as its neighbours, but does boast a nice collection of rotemburo. Baths get progressively cooler as you work your way out from the inside bath.

Kawa-yu Onsen 川湯温泉

Kawa-yu Onsen is a natural wonder where geothermally heated water percolates up through the gravel banks of the river that runs through the middle of the town. You can make your own private bath here by dig-ging out some of the stones and letting the hole fill with hot water; you can then spend the rest of the day jumping back and forth between the bath and the cool waters of the river. Admission is free and the best spots along the river are in front of Fujiya ryokan. We suggest bringing a bathing suit unless you fancy putting on a 'naked *gaijin*' show for the whole town.

In the winter, from December to 28 February, bulldozers are used to turn the river into a giant *rotemburo*. Known as the **Sennin Buro** (仙人風呂; ⊙ 6.30am-10pm) `FREE`, the name is a play on the word for 'thousand', a reference to the fact that you could just about squeeze 1000 bathers into this open-air tub.

🛏 Sleeping

⭐ Fujiya   RYOKAN ¥¥
(冨士屋; ☑ 0735-42-0007; www.fuziya.co.jp/english; r per person with meals from ¥15,900; 🛜) This is an upmarket ryokan with tasteful rooms: spacious, clean and tastefully decorated. For a very civilised place to stay after a day in the river baths, this is the spot. Needless to say, it's got its own private onsen bath as well. A surcharge of ¥5000 to ¥10,000 applies to solo travellers.

Pension Ashita-no-Mori   HOTEL ¥¥
(ペンションあしたの森; ☑ 0735-42-1525; ashitanomori-kawayu@za.ztv.ne.jp; r per person with meals from ¥10,650) This hotel is in a pleasant wooden building with a good riverside location. Rooms are adequate in size and well maintained. It has its own private onsen bath, and inside baths are onsen as well.

ISE

☑ 0596 / POP 132,711

The Ise (伊勢) region, on Mie Prefecture's Shima Peninsula, is famous for Ise-jingū, Japan's most sacred Shintō shrine. The shrine is in Ise-shi, the main city of the region. Although Ise-shi is rather drab, it's worth making the trip to visit the spectacular shrine, arguably Japan's most impressive. Its only rival is Nikkō's Tōshō-gū, which is as gaudy as Ise-jingū is austere. Ise is also home to a lovely traditional street, Kawasaki Kaiwai.

Ise is easily reached from Nagoya, Kyoto or Osaka and makes a good two-day trip from any of these cities (you can even do it as a day trip from these cities if you take Kintetsu express trains). If you're wondering about how to pronounce Ise, it sounds like 'ee-say'.

◉ Sights & Activities

If you have some time to kill in town before or after visiting the shrines, take a stroll down atmospheric **Kawasaki Kaiwai** (河崎界隈), a street lined with traditional Japanese houses and shops. It's a little tricky to find: start at the Ise Pearl Pier Hotel, cross the street, go down the side street that runs next to and behind Eddy's Supermarket (yes, that's the name), and take a left down the street 50m before the canal; Kawasaki Kaiwai parallels this canal, on its west side (but it's not the street that runs right along its banks – it's the one before that). The atmospheric old buildings begin about 200m north of where you turn left.

Ise-jingū   SHINTŌ SHRINE
(伊勢神宮; ⊙ sunrise-sunset) `FREE` Dating back to the 3rd century, Ise-jingū is the most venerated Shintō shrine in Japan. Shintō tradition has dictated for centuries that the shrine buildings be replaced every 20 years, with exact imitations built on adjacent sites according to ancient techniques using no nails, only wooden dowels and interlocking joints.

Upon completion of the new buildings, the god of the shrine is ritually transferred to its new home in the Sengū No Gi ceremony, first witnessed by Western eyes in 1953. The wood from the old shrine is then used to reconstruct the torii at the shrine's entrance or is sent to shrines around Japan for use in rebuilding their structures. The present buildings were rebuilt in 1993 (for the 61st time) at a cost exceeding ¥5 billion. They'll next be rebuilt in 2013.

You may be surprised to discover that the main shrine buildings are almost completely hidden from view behind wooden fences. Only members of the imperial family and certain shrine priests are allowed to enter the sacred inner sanctum. This is unfortunate, as the buildings are stunning examples of pre-Buddhist Japanese architecture. Don't despair, though, as determined neck craning over fences will be rewarded with glimpses of the upper parts of buildings (at least if you're tall). You can get a good idea of the shrine's architecture by looking at any of the lesser shrines nearby, which are exact replicas that have been built on a smaller scale.

There are two parts to the shrine, Gekū and Naikū. The former is an easy 10-minute walk from Ise-shi Station; the latter is ac-

Ise-Shima

0 — 10 km
0 — 5 miles

MIE PREFECTURE

Ise Okitsu
Matsuzaka
166
Nagoya (105km)
42
Tsu (20km)
Meiwa
23
Kintetsu Yamada Line
Ise-wan
Irago (10km)
Taki
Taki
Tamaki
Sangū Line
Kisei Line
368
Miya-gawa
Shingū (120km)
Kushida-gawa
Ise-shi **Ise**
Ise-Jingū Gekū
Ise-Jingū Naikū
Uji-Yamada
Futami
Futaminoura
Meoto-iwa
Mikimoto Pearl Island
Toba
Ise-shima Skyline Rd
Kintetsu Shima Line
167
Nanahora-dake (778m)
Taka-yama (497m)
Nansei
Owase (50km)
260
Nantō
Kamizaki-wan
Sea of Kumano-Nada
Gokasho-wan
260
Goza
Goza Shira-hama
Anagawa
Ise-Shima Youth Hostel
Matoya-wan
Ugata
Ago
Kashikojima
Ago-wan
Shima
260
Daiō

KANSAI ISE

cessible by bus from the station or from the stop outside Gekū. If you only have time to visit one of the shrines, Naikū is the more impressive of the two.

Smoking is prohibited throughout the grounds of both shrines, and photography is forbidden around their main halls. Also, you might notice that many Japanese tend to dress fairly neatly to visit the shrines. You might feel distinctly out of place in tatty jeans, flip flops and sleeveless T-shirts. You don't have to dress formally and you can even wear shorts, but opt on the side of neatness.

➡ Gekū

(外宮; Outer Shrine) The Outer Shrine dates from the 5th century and enshrines the god of food, clothing and housing, Toyouke-no-Ōkami. Daily offerings of rice are made by shrine priests to the goddess, who is charged with providing food to Amaterasu-Ōmikami, the goddess enshrined in the Naikū. A stall at the entrance to the shrine provides a leaflet in English with a map.

The main shrine building here is the **Goshōden**, which is about 10 minutes' walk from the entrance to the shrine. Across the river from the Goshōden, you'll find three smaller shrines that are worth a look (and are usually less crowded).

From Ise-shi Station or Uji-Yamada Station it's a 10-minute walk down the main street to the shrine entrance; the shrine is southwest of both stations. Note that it's slightly easier to find if you start from Ise-shi Station (be sure to exit the south side of the station).

➡ Naikū

(内宮; Inner Shrine) The Inner Shrine is thought to date from the 3rd century and enshrines the sun goddess, Amaterasu-Ōmikami, who is considered the ancestral goddess of the imperial family and the guardian deity of the Japanese nation.

Naikū is held in even higher reverence than Gekū because it houses the sacred mirror of the emperor, one of the three imperial regalia (the other two are the sacred beads and the sacred sword).

A stall just before the entrance to the shrine provides the same English leaflet given out at Gekū. Next to this stall is the **Uji-bashi**, which leads over the crystal-clear Isuzu-gawa into the shrine. Just off the main gravel path is a **Mitarashi**, the place for pilgrims to purify themselves in the river before entering the shrine.

The path continues along an avenue lined with towering cryptomeria trees to the **Goshōden**, the main shrine building. As at Gekū, you can only catch a glimpse of the top of the structure from here, as four rows of wooden fences obstruct the view. If you feel the temptation to jump over the fence when nobody's around, think again – they're watching you on closed-circuit TV cameras not so cleverly disguised as trees!

To get to Naikū, take bus 51 or 55 from bus stop 11 outside Ise-shi Station or the stop on the main road in front of Gekū (¥410, 15 to 20 minutes). Note that bus stop 11 is located about 100m past the main bus stop outside the south exit of Ise-shi Station (walk south on the main street). Get off at the Naikūmae stop. From Naikū there are buses back to Ise-shi Station via Gekū (¥410, 15 to 20 minutes from bus stop 2). Alternatively, a taxi between Ise-shi Station and Naikū costs about ¥2000.

✦ Festivals & Events

Ise-jingū is Japan's most sacred shrine and it's not surprising that it's a favourite destination for *hatsu-mōde* (first shrine visit of the new year). Most of the action takes place in the first three days of the year, when millions of worshippers pack the area and accommodation is booked out for months in advance.

The **Kagura-sai**, celebrated in late April and mid-September, is a good chance to see performances of *kagura* (sacred dance), *bugaku* dance, nō and Shintō music.

🛏 Sleeping

Hoshide-kan   RYOKAN ¥
(星出館; ☎28-2377; fax 27-2830; 2-15-2 Kawasaki; r per person with/without meals ¥7900/5200; @ 🛜) In Ise-shi, this is a quaint wooden ryokan with some nice traditional touches. Go straight past Ise City Hotel, and it's on

the right (there is a small English sign). It's at the second light (400m) past the train tracks. Look for the large traditional building with cedars poking out of tiny gardens. There's free in-room wi-fi.

Ise-Shima Youth Hostel   HOSTEL ¥
(伊勢志摩ユースホステル; ☎0599-55-0226; ise@jyh.gr.jp; 1219-82 Anagawa, Isobe-chō; r per person with breakfast from ¥4620; 🛜) Built on a hill overlooking an attractive bay, this is a great place to stay for budget travellers. There's free wi-fi available in the lobby. It's close to Anagawa Station on the Kintetsu line south of Ise-shi (only *futsū* trains stop). Walk east out of the station along the waterfront road; it's uphill on the right.

Asakichi Ryokan   RYOKAN ¥¥
(麻吉旅館; ☎22-4101; fax 22-4102; 109 Nakano chō; r per person with meals ¥12,600) Located a short bus or taxi ride outside the city centre, this charming ryokan is a nice place to stay if you want a real Japanese experience. The ryokan is built on a hillside, with rooms at various levels. There's a nice common bath and three rooms have en suite baths. A taxi from the station will cost about ¥1000, or take bus 1 or 2 from stop 2 outside Uji-Yamada Station to the Nakano-chō bus stop.

Ise Pearl Pier Hotel   HOTEL ¥¥
(パールピアホテル; ☎26-1111; www.pearlpier.com; 2-26-22 Miyajiri; s ¥7875-8400, d ¥15,750, tw ¥16,800-18,900; @ 🛜) The Pearl Pier is a good business hotel a short walk from Ise-shi Station. The 'deluxe' rooms may be worth the cash if you've been feeling cramped in business hotels. Wi-fi is available in rooms for ¥210 per night. To get there from Ise-shi Station, take a left (east) outside the station, walk past a JTB travel agency, take a left at the first traffic light, and cross the tracks. You'll see it on the left.

🍴 Eating & Drinking

Nikōdōshiten   JAPANESE ¥
(二光堂支店; ☎24-4409; 19 Ujiimazaike-chō; ⏱11am-4pm, closed Wed & Thu; 📷) At Naikū there are plenty of good restaurants in the Okage-yokochō Arcade, just outside the shrine (to find this place, look to your left as you cross Uji-bashi bridge to enter the shrine). In the arcade, Nikōdōshiten is a good place to try some of the local dishes in a rough, roadhouse atmosphere. *Ise-udon* (thick noodles in a dark broth; small/large bowl ¥450/600) is the speciality. For a

bigger meal, try the *ume-chiri gohan setto* (*ise-udon* with rice and side dishes; ¥800). Carnivores might also like their *ise-udon* with beef (¥800). The restaurant is 100m up from the southern (shrine) end of the arcade, on the right. There is no English sign; Ichishina, the shop just before it, has an English sign.

Daiki SHOKUDŌ ¥¥

(大善; ☎ 28-0281; meals from ¥1000; ☻ 11am-9pm; ▣) Our favourite place to eat in Ise-shi bills itself as 'Japan's most famous restaurant'. It's a great place to sample seafood, including *ise-ebi* (Japanese lobsters), served as set meals for ¥5000; ask for the *ise-ebi teishoku* and specify *yaki* (grilled), *niita* (boiled) or *sashimi* (raw). Simpler meals include tempura *teishoku* (¥1500). It's outside and to the right of Uji-Yamada Station (walk past the Toyota Rentacar lot); there's a small English sign reading 'Kappo Daiki' and 'Royal Family Endorsed'. At the time of writing, the main building was under construction, but it should be done by the time you read this.

❶ Information

Across the street from Naiku (about 10 minutes' walk from Ise-shi Station), **Ise Tourist Information Centre** (伊勢市観光協会; ☎ 28-3705; ☻ 8.30am-5pm) has the useful *Map of Ise* and can answer your questions and help you find accommodation. There are smaller information offices in both Ise-shi Station and Uji-Yamada Station.

❶ Getting There & Away

There are rail connections between Ise-shi and Nagoya, Osaka and Kyoto on both the JR and the Kintetsu lines. If you've got a Japan Rail Pass, the easiest way to get there (even if coming from Kyoto/Osaka) is to take a *shinkansen* to JR Nagoya Station, then switch to a JR *kaisoku* Mie train to Ise-shi Station (¥1940, 90 minutes).

For those travelling without a Japan Rail Pass, the Kintetsu line is by far the most convenient way to go and the *tokkyū* are comfortable and fast. Kintetsu fares and travel times to/from Ise-shi include Nagoya (*tokkyū*, ¥2690, one hour and 20 minutes), Osaka (Uehonmachi or Namba stations, *tokkyū*, ¥3030, one hour and 46 minutes) and Kyoto (*tokkyū*, ¥3520, two hours).

Note that there are two stations in Ise: Ise-shi Station and Uji-Yamada Station, which are only a few hundred metres apart (most trains stop at both). Get off at Ise-shi Station for destinations and accommodation described in this section.

NORTHERN KANSAI

The spectacular coastline of northern Kansai (関西北部) is known for its sandy beaches, rugged headlands, rocky islets and laid-back atmosphere. The JR San-in line runs the length of the area, but it spends a fair bit of time inland and in tunnels. The best way to see the coastline is on wheels, whether it be a rental car, a motorbike, a bicycle or by thumb.

Without a doubt, the best place to base yourself for an exploration of this area is the onsen town of Kinosaki, which is just over two hours from Kyoto by comfortable JR express trains.

Moroyose 諸寄

Moroyose, in Hyōgo-ken, near the border with Tottori-ken, is a pleasant little seaside town with a decent sand beach. **Youth Hostel Moroyose-sō** (諸寄荘ユースホステル; ☎ 0796-82-1279; 461 Moroyose; r per person ¥3435, in winter ¥3645) is a good spot to stay for backpackers, with fairly large rooms for a YH and breakfast/dinner for ¥630/1050. It's a 10-minute climb uphill from the eastern end of the beach. Moroyose is on the JR San-in line; the station is in the centre of town, very close to the beach.

Takeno 竹野

Takeno is a pleasant little fishing village and summer resort with two good sandy beaches: **Benten-hama** (弁天浜) to the west and **Takeno-hama** (竹野浜) to the east. To get to Benten-hama, exit Takeno Station and turn left at the first light and walk straight for about 15 minutes (you will cross one big street en route). To get to Takeno-hama, go straight out of the station and walk for around 20 minutes. There is an **information office** (☎ 0796-47-1080; ☻ 8.30am-5pm) on the beachfront at Takeno-hama in an orange brick building. This office can help with accommodation in local *minshuku* and ryokan.

Bentenhama camping area (弁天浜キャンプ場; ☎ 0796-47-0888; campsites per adult/child ¥1000/500; ☻ Jul & Aug) is on the seafront at Benten-hama. It's a decent, if crowded, spot to pitch a tent. **Kitamaekan** (北前館; ☎ 0796-47-2020; onsen adult/child ¥500/300; ☻ 10am-10pm Mon-Sat, from 7am Sun, closed Thu Sep-Jun) is an onsen complex where the baths are on the 2nd floor with a great view of the beach and sea. It's at Takeno-hama, in a large grey building about 150m west of the information office.

Takeno Station is on the JR San-in line, an easy trip from Kinosaki (¥190, nine minutes). The train trip is a good chance to enjoy some of the coastal scenery.

Kinosaki 城崎

☏ 0796 / POP 4134

Kinosaki is one of the best places in Japan to sample the classic Japanese onsen experience. A willow-lined canal runs through the town centre, and many of the houses, shops and restaurants retain something of their traditional charm. Add the delights of crab fresh from the Sea of Japan in winter, and you'll understand why this is one of our favourite overnight trips from the cities of Kansai.

◎ Sights & Activities

Kinosaki's biggest attraction is its seven onsen. Guests staying in town stroll the canal from bath to bath wearing a *yukata* (light cotton kimono) and *geta* (wooden sandals). Most of the ryokan and hotels in town have their own *uchi-yu* (private baths), but also provide their guests with free tickets to the ones outside (*soto-yu*).

In addition to the town's great onsen, visitors might want to have a peek at the **Kinosaki Mugiwarazaikudenshokan** (城崎麦わら細工伝承館; admission ¥300; ⊙9am-5pm, last entry 4.30pm, closed last Wed of every month), which has displays on one of the local handicrafts known as *mugiwarazaiku*, a decorative technique that employs barley straw cut into tiny pieces and applied to wood to form incredibly beautiful patterns. It's located off the canal, a short walk from Ichi-no-yu onsen.

The following is the full list of Kinosaki's onsen, in order of preference (you can get a map from the information office or your lodgings):

★ Gosho-no-yu   ONSEN

(御所の湯; admission ¥800; ⊙7am-11pm, last entry 10.30pm, closed 1st & 3rd Thu) Lovely log construction, a nice two-level *rotemburo* and fine maple colours in autumn. The entry area is decorated like the Kyoto Gosho (Imperial Palace).

Sato-no-yu   ONSEN

(さとの湯; admission ¥800; ⊙1-9pm, last entry 8.40pm, closed Mon) Fantastic variety of baths, including Arab-themed saunas, rooftop *rotem-*

buro and a 'Penguin Sauna' (basically a walk-in freezer – the only one we've seen. Good after a hot bath). Women's and men's baths shift floors daily, so you'll have to go two days in a row to sample everything.

Kou-no-yu   ONSEN

(鴻の湯; admission ¥600; ⊙7am-11pm, last entry 10.30pm, closed Tue) Nothing fancy, but a good *rotemburo* and pleasant inside baths.

Ichi-no-yu   ONSEN

(一の湯; admission ¥600; ⊙7am-11pm, last entry 10.30pm, closed Wed) Wonderful 'cave' bath.

Yanagi-yu   ONSEN

(柳湯; admission ¥600; ⊙3-11pm, last entry 10.40pm, closed Thu) Worth a quick soak as you make your way around town. Nice wooden construction.

Mandara-yu   ONSEN

(まんだら湯; admission ¥600; ⊙3-11pm, last entry 10.40pm, closed Wed) Small wooden *rotemburo*.

Jizo-yu   ONSEN

(地蔵湯; admission ¥600; ⊙7am-11pm, last entry 10.40pm, closed Fri) Spacious main inside tub but no *rotemburo*. Good if others are crowded.

⌂ Sleeping

Ryokan Yamamotoya   RYOKAN ¥¥

(旅館山本屋; ☏32-2114; www.kinosaki.com/en; 835 Yushima, Kinosakichō; r per person with meals from ¥13,650; ☎) This fine ryokan is comfortable with foreign guests, has lovely rooms and excellent food. It's roughly in the middle of town, very close to Ichi-no-yu onsen. There's free wi-fi in the lobby. Note that solo travellers are only accepted in the spring and autumn and must pay a single supplement.

Suishōen   RYOKAN ¥¥

(水翔苑; ☏32-4571; www.suisyou.com/en; r per person with meals from ¥17,850, Japanese/Western room per person without meals Sun-Thu ¥12,495/6,300, Japanese/Western room per person without meals Fri-Sat ¥15,645/9,450; @☎) This excellent modern ryokan is a short drive from the town centre, but they'll whisk you straight to the onsen of your choice in their own London taxi and pick you up when you're done. It's a strangely pleasant feeling to ride in the back wearing nothing but a *yukata*! The rooms are clean and well kept, and the private onsen is great, with indoor and outdoor baths. Solo travellers are charged extra.

Mikuniya
RYOKAN ¥¥

(三国屋; ☎ 32-2414; www.kinosaki3928.com/english/index.htm; r per person with/without meals from ¥17,850/9450; ☎) About 150m on the right on the street heading into town from the station, this ryokan is a good choice. The rooms are clean, with nice Japanese decorations, and the onsen bath is soothing. There is an English sign. Wi-fi in main building only.

Tsuruya
RYOKAN ¥¥

(つるや; ☎ 32-2924; www.kinosaki-tsuruya.com/english.html; r per person with meals from ¥10,330, without meals from ¥5590) A few metres before Kou-no-yu onsen (as you approach from the station), this simple ryokan is comfortable with foreign guests. The rooms are plain but sufficient and the manager is helpful and speaks some English.

★ Nishimuraya Honkan
RYOKAN ¥¥¥

(西村屋本館; ☎ 32-2211; www.nishimuraya.ne.jp/honkan/english; r per person incl 2 meals from ¥29,400, solo travellers from ¥44,100; ☎) This classic is the ultimate inn here, and a good place to try the high-class ryokan experience. The two onsen baths are exquisite and most of the rooms look out over private gardens. The excellent food is the final touch.

🍴 Eating

Crab from the Sea of Japan is a speciality in Kinosaki during the winter months. It's called *kani* and the way to enjoy it is in *kani-suki*, cooked right at your table in a broth with vegetables. Note that most restaurants in Kinosaki shut down very early. This is because most people opt for the two-meal option at their accommodation. You should consider doing the same, at least during *kani* season.

Cafee Sorella
CAFE ¥

(カフェ ソレッラ; ☎ 32-2059; 84 Yushima, Kinosaki-chō; coffee from ¥320; ⏰ 9:30am-5:30pm, closed irregularly; ☎) This simple coffee shop about 75 metres north of the Kinosaki Station on the main street is a good place for a cuppa and an internet fix (there's free wi-fi if you order a drink). There's an English sign and a picture menu.

Daikō Shōten
SHOKUDŌ ¥¥

(大幸商店; ☎ 32-3684; ⏰ 10am-9pm, to 11pm in summer; 🏮) This seafood shop/*izakaya* is a great place to try freshly caught local seafood in a casual atmosphere. From November until mid-April (the busy tourist season for Kinosaki), the restaurant section is upstairs, while the downstairs is given over to selling vast quantities of crabs and other delights. For the rest of the year, the restaurant is on the ground floor. *Teishoku* are available from ¥1480, but you'll never go wrong by just asking for the master's *osusume* (recommendations). It's diagonally across from Mikuniya, about 50m back toward the station.

Orizuru
SUSHI ¥¥

(をり鶴; ☎ 32-2203; meals ¥3000; ⏰ lunch & dinner, closed Tue; 🏮) For decent sushi and crab dishes, try this popular local sushi restaurant on the main street. You can get a *jō-nigiri* (superior sushi set; ¥3700) or try the crab dishes in winter. It's between Ichi-no-yu and Gosho-no-yu, on the opposite side of the street. There is a small English sign.

Koyume
IZAKAYA ¥¥

(こ夢; ☎ 32-2695; ⏰ 11.30am-2.30pm & 5pm-11.30pm) This tiny *izakaya* serves a variety of food and sake, and is a good place to rub shoulders with the locals. There are a few counter seats and some tatami mat seating. It's on the small street behind Jizo-yu and Yanagi-yu. There is no English sign, so find it by looking for the script listed here. There's no English menu, but there are some pictures on the Japanese menu.

ℹ Information

Opposite the station is an **accommodation information office** (お宿案内所; ☎ 32-4141; ⏰ 9am-6pm), where the staff will gladly help you find a place to stay and make bookings, as well as provide maps of the town. The same office has rental bicycles available for ¥400/800 per two hours/day (return by 5pm).

ℹ Getting There & Away

Kinosaki is on the JR San-in line and there are a few daily *tokkyū* from Kyoto (¥4710, two hours and 22 minutes) and Osaka (¥5450, two hours and 42 minutes).

Tango Peninsula 丹後半島

Tango-hantō juts up into the Sea of Japan on the north coast of Kansai. The inside of the peninsula is covered with thick forest, idyllic mountain villages and babbling streams, while the serrated coast alternates between good sandy beaches and rocky points.

The private Kita-kinki Tango Tetsudō rail line runs between Toyooka and Nishi-Maizuru, cutting across the southern base of the peninsula and stopping en route at

Amanohashidate. Thus, if you want to check out the rest of the peninsula you'll have to go by road, and renting a car is highly recommended to explore this area (Kinosaki would be a good place to rent a car and start your journey). Follow the coastal road, Route 178, around the peninsula for truly spectacular scenery. Along the way, stop for a dip at beautiful **Kotobiki-hama Beach** (琴引浜) in the town of Amino. Further along is the wonderful **Ukawa Onsen Yoshino-no-Sato** (宇川温泉 よし野の里), a fine onsen in Kyusō.

Cape Kyōga-misaki (経ヶ岬) is the northernmost point of the Tango Peninsula. A car park marks the start of the 0.4km hike to the **Kyōga-misaki Lighthouse** (経ヶ岬灯台), which sits at the end of this cape. To be honest, it's not the most impressive part of the peninsula.

Ine (伊根), on a perfect little bay on the eastern side of the Tango-hantō, is fairly interesting village. *Funaya* houses are built right out over the water, under which boats are drawn in, as if in a carport. The best way to check it out is by boat, and **Ine-wan Meguri** (伊根湾めぐり; ☑ 0772-42-0321; ¥660, 30 minutes Mar to Dec) tour boats putter around the bay. Buses (¥910) reach Ine in half an hour from Amanohashidate.

Amanohashidate 天橋立

☑ 0772 / POP 19,993

Amanohashidate (the Bridge to Heaven) is rated as one of Japan's 'three great views'. The 'bridge' is really a long, narrow sand spit, 3.5km in length and covered with 8000 pine trees. It has decent swimming, as well as beach showers, toilet facilities and covered rest areas, the length of the spit. It's a good example of a Japanese tourist circus, but it is pleasant enough and there are some decent nearby attractions such as the village of **Ine**.

The town of Amanohashidate consists of two parts, one at each end of the spit. At the southern end there are a number of hotels, ryokan and restaurants, a popular temple and Amanohashidate Station. There's an **information counter** (☑ 22-8030; ⊙ 9am-6pm) at the station. To get to the bridge from the station, turn right and walk 200m along the main road to the first light and go left.

🛏 Sleeping & Eating

Amanohashidate Youth Hostel HOSTEL ¥
(天橋立ユースホステル; ☑ 27-0121; per person with/without meals ¥4500/2950; @ 🛜) This fine

hostel has good views down towards Amanohashidate, friendly owners, well-kept rooms and an excellent hillside location. To get there, take a bus (¥510, 20 minutes) from JR Amanohashidate Station and get off at the Jinja-mae bus stop. From the stop, walk to the main hall of the shrine, take a right and leave the shrine precinct then turn left up the hill and walk 50m, take a right and follow the sign for Manai Shrine. Turn at the stone torii, walk 200m uphill and it's on the right. Internet costs ¥100 per 20 minutes but wi-fi in the lobby is free.

Resutoran Monju NOODLES ¥¥
(れすとらん文殊; ☑ 22-2805; meals from ¥1000; ⊙ 9.30am-4pm, closed Thu) There are several decent but slightly overpriced *shokudō* at the southern end of Amanohashidate, including Resutoran Monju, which has *asari udon* (noodles with clams), a local speciality, for ¥1000. Look for the red-and-white sign as you approach Chion-ji (the temple at the southern end of Amanohashidate).

❶ Getting There & Away

The Kita-kinki Tango Tetsudō line runs between JR stations at Toyooka to the west and Nishi-Maizuru to the east. Amanohashidate Station is on this line, 1¼ hours from Toyooka (*futsū*, ¥1160) and 40 minutes from Nishi-Maizuru (*futsū*, ¥620). There are several direct trains from Kyoto daily, but JR pass holders will have to fork out for the Kita-kinki Tango Tetsudō part of the route (from Kyoto ¥4380, two hours; from Osaka ¥5240, 2¼ hours).

❶ Getting Around

You can cross Amanohashidate on foot, by bicycle or on a motorcycle of less than 125cc capacity. Bicycles can be hired at a number of places for ¥400 for two hours or ¥1600 per day.

Maizuru 舞鶴

There's nothing overly appealing about the two ports of Nishi-Maizuru and Higashi-Maizuru, but they play an important part in the area's transport networks. If you've come from the west on the Kita-kinki Tango Tetsudō trains, Nishi-Maizuru is the end of the line and where the JR Obama line comes out to meet the coast. If you're on your way to Amanohashidate, this is where you'll have to change to the private line.

There are regular ferry services between Higashi-Maizuru and Otaru in Hokkaidō (2nd class ¥9300, 20 hours). Call **Shin-Nihonkai Ferry** (☑ 06-6345-3881; www.snf.jp/pdf/english.pdf) for details.

Hiroshima & Western Honshū

Includes ➡

Best Island Living

➡ Naoshima (p443)

➡ Miyajima (p422)

➡ Oki Islands (p466)

➡ Shiraishi-jima (p447)

Best Historic Sites

➡ Itsukushima-jinja (p422)

➡ Izumo Taisha (p467)

➡ Atomic Bomb Dome (p414)

➡ Iwami Ginzan silver mine (p468)

➡ Matsue-jō (p463)

Why Go?

Travellers to Western Honshū (本州西部) will find two contrasting coastlines. San-yō (literally 'sunny side of the mountains'), looking out over the Inland Sea, boasts the bigger cities, the narrow-laned portside and hillside towns, ceramic history and the bullet train. This is the coast that holds the region's big name – indelibly scarred, thriving, warm-hearted Hiroshima.

On the other side of the dividing Chūgoku mountain range, San-in (literally 'in the shade of the mountains') gazes out across the expanse of the Japan Sea. Up here, it's all about an unhurried pace, onsen villages that see few foreigners, histporic sites, wind-battered coastlines, and great hospitality.

Head inland for hikes along gorges and through caves. Or you can escape the mainland all together – to the Inland Sea and its galaxy of islands, or to the remote and rugged Oki-shotō in the Sea of Japan.

When to Go
Hiroshima

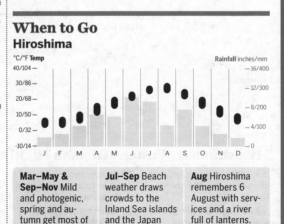

Mar–May & Sep–Nov Mild and photogenic, spring and autumn get most of the attention.

Jul–Sep Beach weather draws crowds to the Inland Sea islands and the Japan Sea coast.

Aug Hiroshima remembers 6 August with services and a river full of lanterns.

Daisen-Oki
National Park
Shimane Peninsula **9**
Kaga

Hirata
Matsue **9**

Hino-misaki **8**
Izumo Taisha **6**

Izumo
Hirose

Sea of Japan

Ōda
Nima
Yunotsu
Iwami
Ginzan **10**
Gōtsu
▲
Sanbe-san
(1126m)

54
314

HONSHŪ

Hamada
9

SHIMANE
PREFECTURE

Shōbara
Miyoshi

Masuda

HIROSHIMA
PREFECTURE

Hibiki-
nada
Sea

Sandan-kyō

54

Expwy

Saijō

Hiroshima
Airport

Mihara

Nagato
Hagi

Tsuwano

Chūgoku

Hiroshima **1**

Hatsukaichi

Higashi-
Hiroshima

2

Takehara
Setod

YAMAGUCHI
PREFECTURE

9

Chōmon-kyō

Miyajima **3**

Ōtake

Kure

Ōmi-shima

Tawarayama Onsen

Mine

◎ *Akiyoshi-dō*

San-yō *Shinkansen Line*

Iwakuni

Eta-jima

Ōshima

Shimanami
Kaidō **4**

Ogōri

Yamaguchi

Tokuyama

Yanai

Sea of
Aki

Imabari

Asa

Hōfu

Kudamatsu

Hōjō

2

Onoda **Ube**

Shimonoseki

Kanmon Straits

Yashiro-shima

Matsuyama

Sea of
Suo

Hime-jima

Sea of
Iyo

Yukuhashi

Hiroshima & Western Honshū Highlights

1 Reflecting on a tragic past in cosmopolitan **Hiroshima** (p414)

2 Gaining a new perspective at the art installations of **Naoshima** (p443)

3 Photographing the floating shrine and staying at a ryokan on **Miyajima** (p422)

4 Island hopping by bicycle via the **Shimanami Kaidō** (p429) to Shikoku

5 Slowing down and listening to the waves on the **Kasaoka Islands** (p446)

6 Seeing where the gods go on holiday at **Izumo Taisha** (p467)

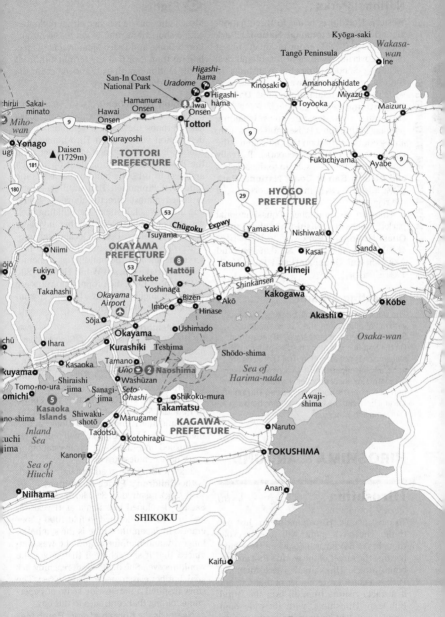

National Parks

Western Honshū is home to three national parks. The **Setonaikai National Park** (瀬戸内海国立公園) is one of Japan's oldest parks, covering swathes of the Inland Sea, including Shōdo-shima and Naoshima in the east, through to Miyajima in the west with its shrine Itsukushima-jinja. **Daisen-Oki National Park** (大山隠岐国立公園) incorporates a few separate areas, including popular hiking spots Daisen and Sanbe-san, and sections of coast on the Oki Islands (the Oki Islands are also a Geopark). To really get off the beaten track, head to the beaches and islets of **San-in Coast National Park** (山陰海岸国立公園), in the far northeast of the region.

There are also a number of quasi-national parks, such as **Nishi-Chūgoku-Sanchi Quasi-National Park** (西中国山地国定公園), with its ravine Sandan-kyō, and **Akiyoshi-dai Quasi-National Park** (秋吉台国定公園).

ⓘ Getting Around

The *shinkansen* (bullet train), linking Okayama with major cities along the San-yō coast to Shimonoseki, is the fastest way to get around. On the San-in coast along the Sea of Japan, the *shinkansen* is not an option. Train services are generally infrequent and it's hard to completely avoid the slow local services. If you're really in a hurry up here, it's worth hiring a car. The major rail link between the two coasts runs between Okayama and Yonago.

HIROSHIMA & AROUND

Hiroshima 広島

☑ 082 / POP 1,174,200

To most people, Hiroshima means just one thing. The city's name will forever evoke thoughts of 6 August 1945, when Hiroshima became the target of the world's first atomic-bomb attack. Hiroshima's Peace Memorial Park is a constant reminder of that day, and it attracts visitors from all over the world. But leafy Hiroshima, with its wide boulevards and laid-back friendliness, is a far from depressing place. Present-day Hiroshima is home to a thriving and internationally minded community, and it's worth spending a couple of nights here to experience the city at its vibrant best.

◉ Sights

Most sights can be reached either on foot or with a short tram ride. To get to the Atomic Bomb Dome and Peace Memorial Park area, hop on tram 2 or 6 at the terminal in front of the station (south exit) and get off at the Genbaku-dōmu-mae stop.

★ Atomic Bomb Dome HISTORIC SITE

(原爆ドーム, Genbaku Dome; 🚊 Genbaku-dōmu-mae) Perhaps the starkest reminder of the destruction visited upon Hiroshima is the Atomic Bomb Dome, across the river from the Peace Memorial Park. Built by a Czech architect in 1915, the building served as the Industrial Promotion Hall until the bomb exploded almost directly above it. Everyone inside was killed, but the building itself was one of very few left standing anywhere near the epicentre. Despite local misgivings, a decision was taken after the war to preserve the shell of the building as a memorial. Declared a Unesco World Heritage Site in December 1996, the propped-up ruins are floodlit at night, and have become a grim symbol of the city's tragic past.

Peace Memorial Park PARK

(平和記念公園; Heiwa-kōen; 🚊 Genbaku-dōmu-mae) The large, leafy Peace Memorial Park is dotted with memorials, including the **cenotaph** (原爆死没者慰霊碑), which contains the names of all the known victims of the bomb. The cenotaph frames the **Flame of Peace** (平和の灯) at the other end of the pond, and the Atomic Bomb Dome across the river. The Flame of Peace will only be extinguished once the last nuclear weapon on earth has been destroyed.

Just north of the road through the park is the **Children's Peace Monument** (原爆の子の像), inspired by Sadako Sasaki. When Sadako developed leukaemia at 11 years of age in 1955, she decided to fold 1000 paper cranes. In Japan, the crane is the symbol of longevity and happiness, and she was convinced that if she achieved that target she would recover. She died before reaching her goal, but her classmates folded the rest. The story inspired a nationwide spate of paper-crane folding that continues to this day.

Nearby is the **Korean Atomic Bomb Memorial** (韓国人原爆犠牲者慰霊碑). Many Koreans were shipped over to work as slave labourers during WWII, and Koreans accounted for more than one in 10 of those killed by the atomic bomb. Just north of this memorial is the **Atomic Bomb Memo-**

NAKA INCINERATION PLANT

Naka Incineration Plant (中工場, Naka Kōjō; 1-5-1 Minami-Yoshijima) Going to a garbage processing plant might not be high up on your list, but if you're an architecture fan or looking for something different, this striking building is worth a visit. The waterfront plant is a large sleek-lined glass-and-metal construction designed by Taniguchi Yoshio, architect of the MoMA redesign in New York; with internal signage by Yagi Tamotsu, known for work for Apple and Esprit. Among the features is a tree-lined central passage, the Ecorium, where you can see the internal workings of the plant. From the upper levels there are views across the water. There is no smell of garbage, but you may get a waft of *furikake* (seasoning) from a nearby factory.

You can look around inside freely between 9am and 4pm. There is an office on level 6 where you can ask for a pamphlet. To get to the plant, take bus 24 for Yoshijima Eigyō-sho and get off at Minami-Yoshijima (¥220, 20 minutes).

rial Mound – the ashes of thousands of unclaimed or unidentified victims are interred in a vault below.

There are other monuments throughout the park, and plenty of benches, including along the riverside looking across to the Atomic Bomb Dome, making this a pleasant area to take a break and reflect.

★ **Peace Memorial Museum**   MUSEUM
(平和記念資料館; www.pcf.city.hiroshima.jp; admission ¥50; ⊙ 8.30am-5pm, to 6pm Mar-Nov, to 7pm Aug; 📵 Genbaku-dōmu-mae or Chūden-mae) The lower floor of Hiroshima's peace museum presents the history of the city and, interestingly, explains the living conditions and sentiment during the war years. Upstairs is a depressing display showing the development of even more destructive weapons in the years since the dropping of the bomb, and rooms filled with items salvaged from the aftermath of the explosion. The displays are confronting and personal – ragged clothes, glasses, a child's melted lunch box – and there are some gruesome photographs of victims. Some will find it upsetting, but it's a must-see in Hiroshima. In the corridor on the way out, it's worth taking time to watch the video testimonials of survivors. There are also English-speaking guides within the museum who can offer interesting insights.

Hiroshima National Peace Memorial Hall for the Atomic Bomb Victims   MEMORIAL
(国立広島原爆死没者追悼平和祈念館; www.hiro-tsuitokinenkan.go.jp; 1-6 Nakajima-chō; ⊙ 8.30am-6pm Mar-Nov, to 5pm Dec-Feb, to 7pm Aug; 📵 Genbaku-dōmu-mae or Hon-dōri) **FREE** A walkway circles down into this peaceful, contemplative underground hall of remem-

brance, where there is a small central fountain. The shape of the fountain represents the time the bomb was dropped (8.15), while the water is an offering of relief to the victims. There is an adjoining room where the names and photographs of atomic-bomb victims are kept, along with evocative testimonies from survivors. The hall was built by architect Tange Kenzō, who also designed the Peace Museum, cenotaph and eternal flame.

Shukkei-en   GARDEN
(縮景園; 2-11 Kami-nobori-chō; admission ¥250, combined ticket with museum ¥600; ⊙ 9am-6pm Apr-Sep, to 5pm Oct-Mar; 📵 Shukkei-en-mae) Modelled after Xi Hu (West Lake) in Hangzhou, China, Shukkei-en was built in 1620 for *daimyō* (domain lord) Asano Nagaakira. The garden's name means 'contracted view', and it attempts to recreate grand vistas in miniature. Pathways lead you through a series of 'landscapes' and views. The garden was destroyed by the bomb, though many of the trees and plants survived to blossom again the following year, and the park and its buildings have long since been restored to their original splendour.

Mazda Museum   MUSEUM
(マツダミュージアム; 📞 252-5050; www.mazda.com/mazdaspirit/museum; ⊙ closed weekends & holidays) **FREE** Popular for the chance to see the impressive 7km assembly line, the longest in the world. English-language tours are available; it's best to check the website or at the tourist office for the latest times. Reservations are required. The museum is a short walk from JR Mukainada (向洋) Station, two stops from Hiroshima on the San-yō line.

Hiroshima

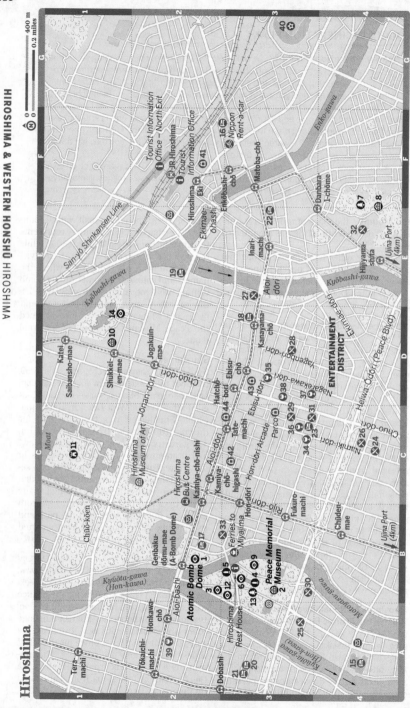

N

0   400 m
0   0.2 miles

Hiroshima

**Hiroshima Prefectural
Art Museum**   MUSEUM
(広島県立美術館; 2-22 Kami-nobori-chō; admission ¥500; ⊘ 9am-5pm, closed Mon; 🚃 Shukkei-en-mae) Next to the Shukkei-en garden is the Hiroshima Prefectural Art Museum, featuring Salvador Dalí's *Dream of Venus* and the artwork of Hirayama Ikuo, who was in the city during the bombing.

Hiroshima-jō   CASTLE
(広島城, Hiroshima Castle; 21-1 Moto-machi; admission ¥360; ⊘ 9am-6pm, to 5pm Dec-Feb; 🚃 Kamiya-chō) Also known as Carp Castle (Rijō; 鯉城), Hiroshima-jō was originally constructed in 1589, but much of it was dismantled following the Meiji Restoration. The remainder was totally destroyed by the bomb and rebuilt in 1958. There's not a lot to see inside, but there's a moat, and the surrounding park is a pleasant place for a stroll.

Hijiyama-kōen   PARK
(比治山公園; 🚃 Hijiyama-shita) Hijiyama-kōen is a hilly tree-filled park, noted for its cherry blossoms in spring and autumn foliage. It's also home to the **Museum of Contemporary Art** (広島市現代美術館; www.hcmca.cf.city.hiro shima.jp; 1-1 Hijiyama-kōen; admission ¥360, additional cost for special exhibits; ⊘ 10am-5pm, closed Mon; 🚃 Hijiyama-shita), and a small manga library. Take the number 5 tram (for Hiroshima Port), or walk about 20 minutes south of JR Hiroshima Station.

🎎 Festivals & Events

Peace Memorial Ceremony MEMORIAL SERVICE
On 6 August, the anniversary of the atomic bombing, a memorial service is held in Peace Memorial Park and thousands of paper lanterns for the souls of the dead are floated down the Kyūōta-gawa from in front of the Atomic Bomb Dome.

🛏 Sleeping

Hiroshima has numerous places to stay in every price bracket. Most accommodation options also have their own bikes for rent (around ¥500 per day).

SANDAN GORGE

Sandan Gorge (三段峡, Sandan-kyō) is an 11km ravine about 50km northwest of Hiroshima within the Nishi-Chūgoku-Sanchi Quasi-National Park. A mostly paved trail follows the Shiki-gawa through the gorge, providing visitors with access to waterfalls, swimming holes, forests and fresh air. The hike is very popular in autumn, when the leaves change colour. The tourist office in Hiroshima has a hiking map in English, or pick up a copy of Lonely Planet's *Hiking in Japan* for more details.

A dozen buses a day run from the Hiroshima bus centre to Sandan-kyō (¥1200, 2 hours; or ¥1400, 75 minutes), dropping you at the southern end of the gorge.

★Hana Hostel HOSTEL ¥
(広島花宿; ☎263-2980; http://hiroshimahostel.jp; 1-15 Kojin-machi; dm/s/tw ¥2500/3900/6400; ⊖@☏) Hana has a choice of Japanese- or Western-style private rooms, some with (small) en suite. Cosy lamp lighting and traditional decoration make the tatami rooms the best pick. The only downside for light sleepers is occasional noise from the street and train line. From the station go immediately left along the train tracks, continue past the railway crossing (not over it) and turn right. It's opposite the temple.

★K's House Hiroshima HOSTEL ¥
(ケイズハウス広島; ☎568-7244; www.kshouse.jp/hiroshima-e; 1-8-9 Matoba-chō; dm/s/tw from ¥2500/4500/7000; ⊖@☏; 🚊Matoba-chō) K's House has a great location not far from the station. There are small dorms and comfortable tatami rooms with shared shower rooms, or pay a little more for a room with bed and en suite. The kitchen-lounge is modern and a good size, there's a rooftop terrace, and staff are helpful. Enter the back of the block – turn left off Aioi-dōri.

J-Hoppers Hiroshima HOSTEL ¥
(ジェイホッパーズ広島ゲストハウス; ☎233-1360; http://hiroshima.j-hoppers.com; 5-16 Dobashi-chō; dm/s/tw per person with shared bathroom ¥2300/3500/2800; ⊖@☏; 🚊Dobashi) This popular old favourite feels more like someone's house than a standard hostel. The rooms are small, but it's a cosy place with a friendly crew. There are both dorm beds and private tatami rooms.

Aster Plaza International Youth House HOTEL ¥
(広島市国際青年会館; ☎247-8700; http://hiyh.pr.arena.ne.jp; 4-17 Kako-machi; s/tw ¥3620/6260; ⊖@; 🚊Funairi-machi or Shiyakusho-mae) With good views from the top floors of a huge municipal building, this city-run hotel represents excellent value for foreign travellers, who get roomy well-equipped modern accommodation at budget prices. There's a 1am curfew.

Ikawa Ryokan RYOKAN ¥
(いかわ旅館; ☎231-5058; www.ikawaryokan.net; 5-11 Dobashi-chō; s/tw from ¥4725/9450; @☏; 🚊Dobashi) On a quiet side street, this is a large family-run hotel-style ryokan with three connected wings. There are Japanese- and Western-style rooms, all very clean, and most have private bathrooms (though there's also a large public bath). Wi-fi in the lobby.

Hotel Active! HOTEL ¥¥
(ホテルアクティブ！広島; ☎212-0001; www.hotel-active.com/hiroshima; 15-3 Nobori-chō; s/d incl breakfast from ¥5980/7875; ⊖@; 🚊Kanayama-chō) This chic hotel has designer couches, satiny coverlets and extra-comfy desk chairs. It's right in the heart of things – within stumbling distance of bars and restaurants – and the bejewelled staff are pleasant. A buffet-style breakfast is included, making this a good-value option.

Sera Bekkan RYOKAN ¥¥
(世羅別館; ☎248-2251; www.yado.to; 4-20 Mikawa-chō; per person with/without meals from ¥12,600/8400; ⊖@; 🚊Ebisu-chō) Off Namiki-dōri is this traditional ryokan with good-sized tatami rooms, large baths, a peaceful garden and great hospitality. Look for the dark-red-brick building on a corner across from a small car park.

Hotel Flex HOTEL ¥¥
(ホテルフレックス; ☎223-1000; www.hotel-flex.co.jp; 7-1 Kaminobori-chō; s/d from ¥6825/11,550; ⊖@) Curves and concrete are the features at this designer hotel in a great spot on the river. Rooms are light with large windows; naturally, the ones on the river side of the building have the views. There's a bright, breezy cafe downstairs and a light breakfast is included.

★ Hiroshima Inn Aioi
RYOKAN ¥¥¥

(広島の宿相生; ☑247-9331; www.galilei.ne.jp/aioi; 1-3-14 Ōtemachi; per person with meals from ¥19,900; ☐Genbaku-dōmu-mae) Kick back in your split-toe socks and *yukata* and enjoy city and park views from your room, or from the large bath on the 7th floor. The meals are an elaborate traditional spread of dishes, and you can opt for breakfast or dinner only. Friendly staff speak just a little English, but they do their best to manage.

✖ Eating

Hiroshima is famous for oysters and *okonomiyaki* (savoury pancakes; batter and cabbage, with vegetables and seafood or meat cooked on a griddle), served Hiroshima-style with individual layers and noodles. You'll come across plenty of places serving both. If you're looking for groceries and cheap eats, check out Aiyū-ichiba market-place (p421).

★ Hassei
OKONOMIYAKI ¥

(八誠; 4-17 Fujimi-chō; dishes ¥450-1200; ⊙11.30am-2pm & 5.30-11pm, dinner only Sun, closed Mon; ☐; ☐Chūden-mae) The walls of this popular *okonomiyaki* specialist are covered with the signatures and messages of famous and not-so-famous visitors. Unless you're a sumō wrestler, you'll probably find a half-order more than enough to be getting on with at lunchtime. It's one block south of Heiwa-Ōdōri.

★ Okonomi-mura
OKONOMIYAKI ¥

(お好み村; 2nd-4th fl, 5-13 Shintenchi; dishes ¥700-1000; ⊙11am-2am; ☐; ☐Ebisu-chō) Twenty-five stalls spread over three floors, all of them serving up hearty variations of tasty *okonomiyaki* – this Hiroshima institution is a great place to get acquainted with the local speciality, and chat with the cooks over a hot griddle. It's in a building off Chūō-dōri, on the opposite side of the square to Parco.

Bakudanya
NOODLES ¥

(ばくだん屋; www.bakudanya.net; 6-13 Fujimi-chō; noodles ¥680-1000; ⊙11.30am-midnight; ☐; ☐Chūden-mae) Come to this simple street-corner eatery to try another famous Hiroshima dish: *tsukemen*, a *rāmen*-like dish in which noodles and soup come separately. This is the original outlet; the chain has now spread across the country. A *nami* (medium-sized) serving of *tsukemen* is ¥780. Look for the green awning on the corner.

Shanti Vegan Cafe
VEGAN ¥

(ヴィーガンカフェ; www.shanti-yoga.net; 2nd fl, Mondano Bldg 2-20 Mikawa-chō; lunch/dinner from ¥850/1500; ⊙11.30am-9.30pm; ☐☐☐; ☐Ebisu-chō) ✿ Eat hearty vegan and vegetarian meals and cakes at this simple cafe beneath a yoga studio. Locally sourced organic vegetables go into tasty, thoughtfully prepared dishes featuring pasta, brown rice, burgers and salads. It's around the corner from Sera Bekkan.

Chari
CAFE ¥

(茶里; 2-5 Nakajima-chō; dishes from ¥750; ⊙11am-10pm; ☐; ☐Chūden-mae) This low-ceilinged narrow cafe-restaurant near the Peace Memorial Museum is a good place for a coffee or lunch stop after walking around the park. There are a few wooden tables and a solo-diner-friendly long bench. Lunch offerings include a *teishoku* (set meal) of *udon*, and there are curries and cakes on the menu.

Nawanai
IZAKAYA ¥

(なわない; Fujimi Bldg, 12-10 Kanayama-chō; ⊙6pm-midnight; ☐Kanayama-chō) In a basement and through a wooden door is this welcoming *izakaya*, where you can mingle with locals over fresh fish and a range of local sakes. Try *ko-iwashi* (baby sardines), available either as sashimi or delicious tempura (¥600). There's a basic English menu. From Aioi-dōri, go down Yagenbori-dōri and take the fourth left; look up and left for the sign in Japanese.

★ Kaki-tei
OYSTERS ¥¥

(牡蠣亭; ☑221-8990; www.kakitei.jp; 11 Hashimoto-chō; lunch/dinner from ¥1000/3800; ⊙11.30am-2.30pm & 5-10pm, closed Tue & 1st & 3rd Wed of month; ☐; ☐Kanayama-chō) Come to this intimate bistro on the riverbank for oysters prepared in a variety of mouth-watering ways. There are also oyster sets at lunch and dinner. Look for the green *noren* (cloth curtain hung in the entrance) and the words 'Oyster Conclave'.

Tōshō
TOFU ¥¥

(豆匠; ☑506-1028; www.toufu-tosho.jp; 6-24 Hijiyama-chō; lunch/dinner courses from ¥1890/3150; ⊙11am-3pm & 5-10pm, to 9pm Sun; ☐Danbara-1-chōme) Housed in a traditional wooden building in a beautiful garden setting by Hijiyama-kōen, Tōshō specialises in home-made tofu, served in a surprising variety of tasty forms by kimono-clad staff. Choose from a range of set courses; there are some pictures on the menu. From the tram stop, continue walking in the direction of the tram and turn left uphill after Hijiyama shrine.

Zucchini
TAPAS ¥¥

(ズッキーニ; ☎546-0777; http://in-smart.co.jp/zucchini; 1-5-18 Ōtemachi; dishes ¥450-2500; ⏰11.30pm-1am; 🚭🈂; 🚋Hon-dōri) Zucchini is a lively Spanish-style tapas restaurant with wooden floors and warm, chandelier lighting. All the usual ham, cheese and fish goodies are served, as well as paellas from ¥1400. It's a two-storey glass-fronted affair near the end of Hon-dōri arcade.

Ristorante Mario
ITALIAN ¥¥

(リストランテマリオ; ☎248-4956; www.san-mario.com; 4-11 Nakajima-chō; lunch/dinner courses ¥1480/5800; ⏰11.30am-2.30pm & 5-10pm; 🈂) A cosy ivy-covered place across from the Peace Park serving honest Italian food with good service, and a romantic atmosphere in the evenings. It's also open afternoons on Saturday and Sunday. Reservations are recommended for weekends.

🍷 Drinking & Nightlife

Hiroshima is a great city for a night out, with bars and pubs to suit whatever mood you're in. The city's main entertainment district is made up of hundreds of bars, restaurants and karaoke joints crowding the lanes between Aioi-dōri and Heiwa-Ōdōri in the city centre. Most places also serve light meals or snacks, and some have live music.

★ Organza
BAR, CAFE

(ヲルガン座; ☎295-1553; www.organ-za.com; 2nd fl Morimoto Bldg, Tōkaichi-machi; ⏰5.30pm-2am Tue-Fri, 11.30am-2am Sat, 11.30am-midnight Sun, closed Mon; 🚋Honkawa-chō) Bookshelves, old-fashioned furniture, a piano, and a stuffed deer head all add to the busy surrounds at this smoky lounge-bar. Organza hosts an eclectic schedule of live events (from acoustic guitar to cabaret), some with a cover charge, and it can get busy. Lunch is served on weekends.

★ Koba
BAR

(コバ; 3rd fl Rego Bldg, 1-4 Naka-machi; ⏰6pm-2am, closed Wed) It's bound to be a good night if you drop into this laid-back place, where the friendly metal-loving musician owner serves drinks and cooks up small tasty meals. There is occasional live music. It's up the stairs in a concrete building, just behind Stussy.

Kuro-sawa
BAR

(黒澤; 5th fl Tenmaya Ebisu Bldg, 3-20 Horikawa-chō; ⏰5.30pm-1am, to 2am Sat & Sun; 🚋Ebisu-chō) This is a trendy, dimly lit joint, with seating at the sleek bar or on low-to-the-ground velvet chairs. Food is also served: try the avocado tempura, or the ko-iwashi tempura (with lemon and green-tea powder for dipping). Make sure you check out the bizarre toilet before you leave. Kuro-sawa is in Ebisu-dōri arcade, in a building opposite the Italian Tomato Café.

Molly Malone's
PUB

(www.mollymalones.jp; 4th fl Teigeki Bldg, 1-20 Shintenchi; ⏰5pm-1am Mon-Thu, 5pm-2am Fri, 11.30am-2.30am Sat, 11.30am-midnight Sun; 🚋Ebisu-chō) A reliable Irish-style pub with Irish management, good beer, good food and occasional live music. It draws a mixed crowd of local expats and Japanese.

Mac
BAR

(マック; 6-18 Nagarekawa-chō; ⏰8pm-late; 🚋Ebisu-chō) Chat, drink and be merry into the wee hours while listening to music from the wall of CDs. The owners take requests; choose wisely. Look for the small sign pointing up a stairway at the side of a building.

Lotus
BAR

(ロータス; 5th fl Namiki Curl Bldg, 3-12 Mikawa-chō; ⏰6pm-3am; 🚋Ebisu-chō) Take off your shoes and unwind here while reclining among the cushions, or sip cocktails at the bar. It's on a side street just off Namiki-dōri.

☆ Entertainment

Hiroshima is a good place to catch a baseball game and see the beloved local team, the Carp. A love of baseball is not a prerequisite for having a great time – it's fun just watching the rowdy yet organised enthusiasm of the crowd, especially when the despised Tokyo Giants come to town. Games are played in the **Mazda Zoom Zoom Stadium** (Hiroshima Municipal Stadium; 2-3-1 Minami-Kaniya), a short walk southeast of the station. For schedule information in English, see www.japanball.com, or ask at the tourist office.

🛍 Shopping

Hiroshima has branches of the big-name department stores, such as **Tokyu Hands** (東急ハンズ広島店; http://hiroshima.tokyu-hands.co.jp; 16-10 Hatchō-bori; ⏰10am-8pm, to 8.30pm Fri & Sat; 🚋Tate-machi), packed with homewares, must-have gadgets, and gifts; and

421

HIROSHIMA & WESTERN HONSHŪ HIROSHIMA

HIROSHIMA READING

➡ *Hiroshima* (1946; by John Hersey) Book of the article by the Pulitzer-winning writer.

➡ *Hiroshima: Three Witnesses* (1990; ed Richard H Minear) Translation of first-hand accounts of three authors.

➡ *Black Rain* (1965; by Masuji Ibuse) A novel depicting the lives of those who survived.

➡ *Sadako & the Thousand Paper Cranes* (1977; by Eleanor Coerr) Aimed at younger readers, based on the true story of Sadako Sasaki.

classy **Mitsukoshi** (広島三越; 5-1 Ebisu-chō; ⊘10.30am-7.30pm; 🚇Ebisu-chō), with its designer labels and great basement-floor food hall. Take a walk down Namiki-dōri for a range of fashionable boutiques, or browse the busy shop-filled Hon-dōri arcade.

Aiyū-ichiba   MARKET
(愛友市場; I You Mart; www.iu-mart.jp) There has been a market in some form here in front of the station since black markets sprang up after the war. Aiyū-ichiba today is an old-school narrow-laned covered marketplace with stores selling fresh fish, meat, vegetables and other goods. Hours vary by store but most open from early morning to evening and some close Sunday.

Global Lounge   BOOKS
(グローバル・ラウンジ; www.hiroshima-no1.com/lounge.html; 2nd fl Kensei Bldg, 1-5-17 Kamiya-chō; ⊘noon-9pm Mon-Thu, to 11pm Fri & Sat, closed Sun; 🚇Kamiya-chō) Global Lounge (aka Outsider) has a big selection of secondhand English-language books (mostly paperbacks). You can grab a coffee and use the internet (¥200 per 15 minutes) while you're here.

ⓘ Information

INTERNET ACCESS

There is free wi-fi in the Peace Park. To get a password, visit the Hiroshima Rest House (p421) tourist office, or the information counter in the Peace Museum. There's also free internet access (30-minute limit) at the **International Exchange Lounge** (国際交流ラウンジ; Peace Memorial Park; ⊘9am-7pm, to 6pm Oct-Mar; 🚇Chūden-mae) by the museum, and internet access at Global Lounge (p421).

MONEY

Higashi Post Office has ATMs that accept international cards and has currency exchange services. ATMs in 7-Elevens also take international cards. Hiroshima Rest House tourist information centre has a list of banks and post offices that change money and travellers cheques.

POST

Higashi Post Office (広島東郵便局; 2-62 Matsubara-chō; ⊘9am-7pm Mon-Fri, to 5pm Sat, to 12.30pm Sun) The post office most convenient to the station.

TOURIST INFORMATION

Tourist Information Office (観光案内所; 🕿261-1877; ⊘9am-5.30pm) Inside the station near the south exit. There is another branch at the north exit (🕿263-6822; ⊘9am-5.30pm).

Hiroshima Rest House (広島市平和記念公園レストハウス; 🕿247-6738; www.mk-kousan.co.jp/rest-house; 1-1 Nakajima-machi; ⊘9.30am-6pm, to 5pm Oct-Mar, to 7pm Aug; 🚇Genbaku-dōmu-mae) In Peace Memorial Park, next to Motoyasubashi. Offers comprehensive information about the city and the island of Miyajima.

USEFUL WEBSITES

Hiroshima Navigator (www.hcvb.city.hiroshima.jp) Tourist and practical information, multiple downloadable audio guides to the sights and more.

Get Hiroshima (www.gethiroshima.com) Events calendar, restaurant and bar reviews, and feature articles.

ⓘ Getting There & Away

AIR

Hiroshima Airport (www.hij.airport.jp) Hiroshima's airport is 40km east of the city, with limousine bus connections to/from Hiroshima Station (¥1300, 48 minutes), operating from 8.20am to 9.40pm.

BUS

Long-distance buses connect Hiroshima with all the major cities. Buses depart from the **Hiroshima Bus Centre** (広島バスセンター; www.h-buscenter.com; 🚇Kamiya-chō), located on the 3rd floor between the Sogo and AQ'A shopping centres.

FERRY

There are connections to Matsuyama in Shikoku, with **Setonaikai Kisen Ferry** (瀬戸内海汽船フェリー; 🕿253-1212; www.setonaikaikisen.co.jp), via standard car ferry (¥3500, 2½ hours, 10 daily) or high-speed service (¥6900, one hour and 15 minutes, 13 daily). The port (広島港) is the last stop on trams 1, 3 and 5 bound for Ujina (宇品). Tram 5 runs from Hiroshima Station. There are frequent ferry services to Miyajima (p426).

ⓘ **TRAM PASSES**

If you'll be taking at least four tram trips in a day, get a **One-day Trip Card**, which gets unlimited travel for ¥600. A one-day card that covers trams plus return ferry to Miyajima is ¥840. The **Two-days Trip Card** is a good deal at ¥2000, covering tram rides, ferry, and ticket for the ropeway on Miyajima (which normally costs ¥1800 return or ¥1000 one-way). Buy passes from the tram terminal at the station, from the conductors on board (one-day cards only), or at various hotels and hostels.

TRAIN

Hiroshima Station is on the JR San-yō line, which passes through and westwards to Shimonoseki. It's also a major stop on the Tokyo–Osaka–Hakata *shinkansen* line. Example *shinkansen* fares from Hiroshima:

Hakata ¥8190, 1¼ hours

Osaka ¥9440, 1½ hours

Tokyo ¥17,540, four hours

ⓘ Getting Around

TRAM

Hiroshima has an extensive tram service that will get you almost anywhere you want to go for a flat fare of ¥150. You pay by dropping the fare into the machine by the driver as you get off the tram. If you have to change trams to get to your destination, you should ask for a *norikae-ken* (transfer ticket). Daily tram passes are also available and convenient if you're taking a few tram rides.

BICYCLE

Hiroshima is fairly compact and easy for cycling. Many hostels and hotels have bikes for hire from around ¥500 per day. **Nippon Rent-a-car** (ニッポンレンタカー; ☑264-0919; 3-14 Kojin-machi; ☺24hr), a few blocks southeast of the station, has a limited number of bikes.

Miyajima   宮島

☑0829 / POP 1970

The small island of Miyajima is a Unesco World Heritage Site and one of Japan's most-visited tourist spots. Its star attraction is the oft-photographed vermilion torii (shrine gate) of Itsukushima-jinja, which seems to float on the waves at high tide – a scene that has traditionally been ranked as one of the three best views in Japan. Besides this feted view, Miyajima has some good hikes, temples, and cheeky deer that rove the streets and will snatch anything out of the hands of unsuspecting tourists.

Turn right as you emerge from the ferry terminal and follow the waterfront for 10 minutes to get to the shrine. The shopping street, packed with souvenir outlets and restaurants, as well as the world's largest *shakushi* (rice scoop), is a block back from the waterfront.

⊙ Sights

Allow a few hours to wander around the sights; more if you plan on hiking Misen (p424). Ideally, try to stay overnight on the island to experience it in the quiet of the evening, and for photos of the 'floating torii' at sunset.

★**Itsukushima-jinja**   SHINTŌ SHRINE

(厳島神社; 1-1 Miyajima-chō; admission ¥300; ☺6.30am-6pm Mar–mid-Oct, to 5.30pm mid-Oct–Nov, Jan & Feb, to 5pm Dec) Going back as far as the late 6th century, Itsukushima-jinja gives the island its real name. The shrine's present form dates from 1168, when it was rebuilt under the patronage of Taira no Kiyomori, head of the doomed Heike clan. Its pier-like construction is a result of the island's holy status: commoners were not allowed to set foot on the island and had to approach the shrine by boat through the **floating torii** (大鳥居) out in the bay. Much of the time, however, the shrine and torii are surrounded by mud: to get the classic view of the torii that adorns the brochures, you'll need to come at high tide.

On one side of the floating shrine is a **floating nō stage** (能舞台), built by local lord Asano Tsunanaga in 1680 and still used for nō (stylised dance-drama) performances every year from 16 to 18 April.

Senjō-kaku   PAVILION

(1-1 Miyajima-chō; admission ¥100; ☺8.30am-4.30pm) Dominating the hill immediately to the north of Itsukushima-jinja is this huge pavilion built in 1587 by Toyotomi Hideyoshi. The atmospheric hall is constructed with massive pillars and beams, and the ceiling is hung with paintings. It looks out onto a colourful five-storey **pagoda** (五重塔) dating from 1407.

Daigan-ji   BUDDHIST TEMPLE

(大願寺; 3 Miyajima-chō; ☺9am-5pm) Miyajima has several important Buddhist temples, in-

Miyajima

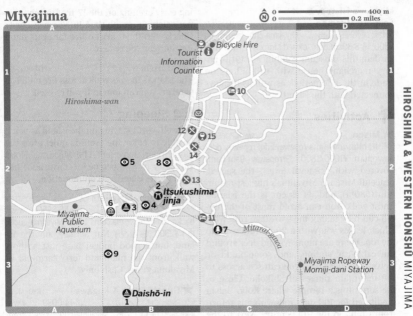

cluding the 1201 Daigan-ji, just south of the shrine, which dates back to the Heian period and is dedicated to Benzaiten, the Japanese name for Saraswati (the Hindu goddess of good fortune). The seated image of Yakushi Nyorai here is said to have been carved by Kōbō Daishi.

★ Daishō-in
BUDDHIST TEMPLE

(大聖院; 210 Miyajima-chō; ⊙ 8am-5pm) Just south of town at the foot of Misen, Daishō-in is a worthwhile stopping point on the way up or down the mountain. This hingon temple is crowded with interesting things to look at: from Buddhist images and prayer wheels to sharp-beaked *tengu* (bird-like demons) and a cave containing images from each of the 88 Shikoku pilgrimage temples.

Momiji-dani-kōen
PARK

(紅葉谷公園; Momiji-dani Park) Momiji means 'maple', and their leaves come alive in autumn here in this pretty park along the river. It's at the foot of Misen, close to the ropeway station.

Tahō-tō
PAGODA

(多宝塔) South of Itsukushima-jinja, stone steps (before the History & Folklore Museum) lead up from the road to this picturesque pagoda. There's a pleasant, short path looping around from here and back down to the road.

Miyajima History & Folklore Museum

MUSEUM

(歴史民俗資料館; 57 Miyajima-chō; admission ¥300; ⏲ 8.30am-5pm, closed Mon) Set in a fine garden, this museum combines a 19th-century merchant house with exhibitions on trade in the Edo period, as well as displays connected with the island.

🏃 Activities

⭐ Misen

WALK, ROPEWAY

(弥山; http://miyajima-ropeway.info; ropeway one-way/return ¥1000/1800; ⏲ ropeway 9am-5pm) Covered with primeval forest, the sacred, peaceful Misen is Miyajima's highest mountain (530m), and its ascent is the island's finest walk. You can avoid most of the uphill climb by taking the two-stage ropeway, which leaves you with a 20-minute walk to the top. There are monkeys and deer around the cable-car station, and some fantastic views – on clear days you can see across to the mountain ranges of Shikoku. Close to the summit is a temple where Kōbō Daishi meditated for 100 days following his return from China in the 9th century. Next to the main temple hall close to the summit is a flame that's been burning continually since Kōbō Daishi lit it 1200 years ago. From the temple, a path leads down the hillside to Daishō-in and Itsukushima-jinja. The descent takes a little over an hour, or you can take the ropeway down.

The ropeway station (Momiji-dani Station), is about a 10-minute walk on from Momiji-dani-kōen (p423), or a few minutes on the free shuttle bus, which runs every 20 minutes from a stop near Iwasō Ryokan. A four-hour hike of Misen is detailed in Lonely Planet's *Hiking in Japan*.

Sea Kayaking

KAYAKING

(⏲ 50-4340; www.paddlepark.com; half-/full-day course ¥6000/10,000) For a different perspective on the floating torii, try a kayaking tour. Paddle Park offer half- and full-day courses, or a night-time tour, heading out from the mainland near Maezora Station, which is one stop from Miyajima-guchi. Depending on the conditions on the day, you may even get to kayak through the torii itself.

🎏 Festivals & Events

⭐ Kangen-sai

SHINTŌ

This Shintō ritual sees decorated wooden boats float by to the sound of traditional drums and flutes. It's held in summer, starting early evening on the 17th of the sixth lunar-calendar month (late July/early August). Check with the tourist office for exact dates for the year you're here.

Hiwatarishiki

FIRE-WALKING

The island's monks walk across fire on 3 November. You can join in if you're keen.

🛏 Sleeping

It's well worth staying on the island as you'll be able to enjoy the evening quiet after the day trippers have left. The Miyajima Hotel Directory (www4.ocn.ne.jp/~miyayado) has a list of the island's accommodation.

Backpackers Miyajima

HOSTEL ¥

(バックパッカーズ宮島; ⏲ 56-3650; www.backpackers-miyajima.com; 1-8-11 Miyajima-guchi; dm ¥2300; ⏲ @ ⏲) Not actually on the island, but a good budget base just a short walk from the mainland ferry terminal in Miyajima-guchi. Cash only.

⭐ Guest House Kikugawa

RYOKAN ¥¥

(ゲストハウス菊がわ; ⏲ 44-0039; www.kikugawa.ne.jp; 796 Miyajima-chō; s/tw from ¥6500/11,600; ⏲ @ ⏲) This charming inn is built in traditional style and has lovely wooden interiors. There are Western- and Japanese-style rooms, all with attached bathrooms. The tatami rooms are slightly larger and one has a loft-like bedroom. Meals are available. Heading inland from the ferry terminal, you'll walk through a tunnel; turn right after this and look for Kikugawa on the left opposite Zonkō-ji (存光寺) temple.

Iwasō Ryokan

RYOKAN ¥¥¥

(岩惣; ⏲ 44-2233; www.iwaso.com; Momiji-dani Miyajima-chō; per person with 2 meals ¥20,100-42,150; @) The Iwasō, open since 1854, offers the grand ryokan experience in exquisite gardens. It's especially stunning in autumn when Momiji-dani (Maple Valley) explodes with colour. There are three wings: a stay in a lovely 'Hanare' cottage will set you back the most. Not all rooms have private bathrooms, but you can soak in the onsen in the main building. It's about 15 minutes to walk from the ferry port, or call and they will pick you up.

🍴 Eating & Drinking

There are plenty of places to eat along and around the main strip, where you can try the local oysters, as well as eel in various guises (on rice, or perhaps in a steamed bun). It's often very busy and at some places you may have to wait to get a seat. Just one street back from the main strip is the much quieter Machiya-dōri, with a few cafes and eateries. Most restaurants shut down after the crowds go home.

Sarasvati CAFE ¥

(http://sarasvati.jp; 407 Miyajima-chō; coffees ¥350-550, lunch ¥1280; ⏰8.30am-8pm; 📱) The aroma of roasting coffee beans lures people into this cafe inside a former storehouse building from the early 1900s. Bare wooden floors and tables match a simple menu of traditional coffees (no frappuccinos here), cakes, and the one pasta-set option for lunch.

★Yakigaki-no-hayashi OYSTERS ¥¥

(焼がきのはやし; 📱44-0335; www.yakigaki-no-hayashi.co.jp; 505-1 Miyajima-chō; dishes ¥700-1400; ⏰10.30am-5pm, closed Wed; 📱) The oysters in the tank and on the barbecue outside are what everyone is eating here. Try a plate of *nama-gaki* (raw oysters) or *kaki-furai* (crumbed, fried oysters) for ¥1300. It's not all about the slimy shell-dwellers, however. There are other meals, such as *udon* sets, on offer too.

Mame-tanuki IZAKAYA ¥¥

(まめたぬき; 📱44-2131; 1113 Miyajima-chō; ⏰11am-3.30pm & 5-11pm, closed dinner Tue; 📱) At this friendly place there's a floor-level wooden counter, with a space to dangle your legs underneath. By day there are lunch sets, such as *anago meshi* (steamed conger eel with rice; ¥1575) and fried oysters, and at night Mame-tanuki is one of the few places open late, serving drinks and *izakaya*-style dishes. There's no smoking in the evening. Look for the large blue sign with white writing.

Kaki-ya OYSTERS

(牡蠣屋; 📱44-2747; www.kaki-ya.jp; 539 Miyajima-chō; oysters ¥1000-2000; ⏰10am-6pm) Kaki-ya is a sophisticated oyster bar on the main street. It serves delicious local oysters freshly grilled on the barbecue by the entrance, along with beers and wines by the glass.

ℹ️ Information

Tourist Information Counter (宮島観光案内所; 📱44-2011; www.miyajima.or.jp; ⏰9am-5pm) Inside the ferry terminal.

ℹ️ Getting There & Away

Miyajima is accessed by ferry, and is often visited as a day trip from Hiroshima.

The mainland ferry terminal is a short walk from Miyajima-guchi Station on the JR San-yō line, halfway between Hiroshima (¥400, 27 minutes) and Iwakuni.

The ferry terminal can also be reached by tram 2 from Hiroshima (¥270, 70 minutes), which runs from Hiroshima Station, passing Genbaku Dome on the way. Ferries shuttle regularly across to the island from Miyajima-guchi (¥170, 10 minutes). JR Pass holders should use the one operated by JR.

SAIJŌ SAKE

A short train ride east of Hiroshima is the town of Saijō (西条), home to 10 sake breweries, eight of which are clustered within easy walking distance of the station. The brewers here know their stuff – Saijō has been producing sake for around 300 years – and most open up their doors to curious and thirsty visitors.

Heading down the road leading south from the station, you'll find the **tourist office** (⏰10am-4pm, closed Mon) on the left, where you can pick up an English map of the breweries. Go left from here to well-known **Kamotsuru** (賀茂鶴; www.kamotsuru.jp), which has a large tasting room screening a DVD about the district. Nearby is one of Saijō's oldest breweries, **Hakubotan** (白牡丹; www.hakubotan.co.jp), with a lovely broad-beamed display and tasting room with Munakata woodblock prints on the wall. In the area west of the station you'll find **Kamoki** (賀茂輝; ⏰cafe 10.30am-5pm, closed Mon), the smallest brewery here – try the tasty chiffon cake in their attached Sakagura Cafe. When you're done sake tasting, you can pay your respects to the god of sake at Matsuo-jinja, a short walk to the north of Saijō Station.

If you're in the area in the second weekend of October, don't miss the **Saijō Sake Matsuri** (http://sakematsuri.com), when crowds descend on the town for hours of sampling and events. For more on the town, breweries and history, check out http://saijosake.com.

Saijō is 35 minutes by train from Hiroshima (¥570).

High-speed ferries (¥1800, 30 minutes, six to eight daily) operate direct to Miyajima from Hiroshima's Ujina port. Another option is to take a ferry directly from Peace Memorial Park in central Hiroshima (¥1900, 45 minutes, eight to 12 daily; the return trip costs ¥1500). These boats cruise under the bridges of Kyūota-gawa before coming out into the bay towards Miyajima. No reservation is required.

ℹ Getting Around

Everywhere on the island is within easy walking distance. For **bicycle hire** (per hour ¥100; ◷ 9am-5pm), go to the JR office in the ferry terminal. There are also taxis on the island – ask at the tourist office for details should you require one.

Iwakuni 岩国

◷ 0827 / POP 143,800

About an hour away from Hiroshima by train or bus, Iwakuni makes for a worthwhile half-day trip, or a stop-off en-route between Yamaguchi and Hiroshima. The main reason to come here is to see the five-arched Kintai-kyō bridge and take a walk around the Kikkō-kōen area to which it leads.

◉ Sights

Kintai-kyō BRIDGE
(錦帯橋; admission ¥300, combination ticket incl cable car & castle ¥930; ◷ 24hr) Iwakuni's chief claim to fame is the graceful Kintai-kyō, built in 1673 during the rule of feudal lord Kikkawa Hiroyoshi. It has been restored several times since then, but its high arches remain an impressive sight over the wide river, with Iwakuni-jō atop the green hills behind. In the feudal era only members of the ruling class were allowed to use the bridge, which linked the samurai quarters on the west bank of Nishiki-gawa with the rest of the town. Today, anyone can cross over for a small fee.

Kikkō-kōen PARK
(吉香公園) What remains of the old samurai quarter now forms pleasant Kikkō-kōen on the west bank of the river, across Kintai-kyō bridge. Within it are old residences, a pavillion, a couple of museums and spots for picnicking. Worth a look is the **Mekata Family Residence** (旧目加田家住宅; ◷ 9.30am-4.30pm, closed Mon) FREE, the former home of a middle-ranking samurai family from the mid-Edo period. Reptile enthusiasts and kids might want to pop next door to the small **White Snake Viewing Facility** (白蛇観覧所; admission ¥100; ◷ 9am-5pm), where several of the bizarre albino snakes unique to Iwakuni are on display.

Iwakuni-jō CASTLE
(岩国城; admission ¥260; ◷ 9am-4.45pm, closed mid-end Dec, cable car 9am-5pm) The original Iwakuni-jō was built by Hiroie, the first of the Kikkawa lords, between 1603 and 1608. Just seven years later, the Tokugawa shogunate passed a law limiting the number of castles *daimyō* were allowed to build, and the castle at Iwakuni was demolished. It was rebuilt not far from its original setting in 1960. There is nothing much of interest inside, but there are good views from the hilltop setting.

You can get to the castle by **cable car** (one-way/return ¥320/540, every 20 minutes), or you can walk up to the castle among the greenery and birdlife on a pathway that leads up from the west side of the park. The walk takes about 45 minutes.

Cormorant Fishing FISHING
(Ukai; ◷ 28-2877; boat rides per person ¥3500; ◷ 6.30pm Jun-Aug) Watch from the riverbank at Kintai-kyō as fishermen and their feathered workers hunt by torchlight, or take a boat ride. Daily in summer, except when rain makes the water muddy, or on nights with a full moon.

✕ Eating

There are small eateries in the park and stalls down along the riverside. Local specialities include *iwakuni-zushi,* a sushi made in large square molds, and *renkon* (lotus root) cooked in *korokke* (croquette) form.

Midori-no-sato SUSHI, NOODLES ¥
(緑の里; 1-4-10 Iwakuni; meals ¥580-1050; ◷ 10am-6pm; ☻) This restaurant has set menus including an *iwakuni-zushi* set (¥1050) that comes with *renkon* noodles, and *udon* dishes from ¥580. From the bus centre near Kintai-kyō, walk towards the bridge and take the left opposite the bridge entrance. It's on the right.

ℹ Information

Tourist Information (www.iwakuni-kanko.com; ◷ 10am-5pm, closed Mon) Inside JR Iwakuni Station. There is another office at Shin-Iwakuni Station (◷ 10.30am-3.30pm, closed Wed).

ℹ Getting There & Away

The bridge and park are a 15-minute bus ride (¥240) from JR Iwakuni Station. There are also buses to the bridge (¥280, 20 minutes) from

Shin-Iwakuni. Buses leave regularly. JR Iwakuni Station is on the San-yō line, west of Hiroshima (¥740, 50 minutes). Shin-Iwakuni is on the San-yō *shinkansen* line, linking to Hiroshima (¥1570, 15 minutes) and Shin-Yamaguchi (¥3300, 38 minutes).

If coming from Hiroshima without a JR pass, you may find it more convenient to get the Iwakuni bus from Hiroshima bus centre, as it handily drops you at Kintai-kyō (¥900, 50 minutes to an hour, hourly).

Tomo-no-ura 鞆の浦

🎧 084 / POP 5000

Perfectly situated in the middle of the Inland Sea coast, Tomo-no-ura flourished for centuries as a stopping-off point for boats travelling between western Japan and the capital, until the arrival of steam put an end to the town's glory days. The town is not completely unspoilt, but the old harbour and the cobbled streets that surround it retain much of the flavour of the Edo-period heyday, and it's good for a few hours of strolling. Inland from the harbour there are a dozen or so temples, and stone steps lead up the hillside to views of the Inland Sea.

The town is small enough to be seen in half a day. If you're interested in spending the night, it's worth staying on nearby island Sensui-jima. Alternatively, nearby Fukuyama has a bunch of decent hotels in the station area. The Fukuyama Station tourist office and the Tomo-no-ura tourist office can help with local accommodation bookings.

◎ Sights

Fukuzenji BUDDHIST TEMPLE
(福禅寺) Close to the waterfront, this temple dates back to the 10th century. Adjoining the temple is **Taichōrō** (対潮楼; admission ¥200; ⊙8am-5pm), a reception hall built in the 1690s. This is where you go for a classic view out across the narrow channel to the uninhabited island of Benten-jima and its shrine.

Jōyatō LANDMARK
(常夜燈) The main harbour area in Tomo-no-ura is dominated by this large stone lantern, which used to serve as a lighthouse.

★ Ōta Residence HISTORIC BUILDING
(太田家住宅; admission ¥400; ⊙10am-5pm, closed Tue) Just back from the harbour area, the former Ōta residence is a fine collection of restored buildings from the mid-8th cen-

tury. Guided tours take you through the impressive family home and workplace. There is an English pamphlet.

Tomo-no-Ura Museum of
History & Folklore MUSEUM
(鞆の浦歴史民俗資料館; www.tomo-rekimin. org; admission ¥150; ⊙9am-5pm, closed Mon) This museum sits at the top of the hill behind the harbour, with exhibits relating to local industry and craft. Nearby is the site of the **old castle**, of which nothing remains but a few foundation stones. There are good views across the water from here.

Iō-ji BUDDHIST TEMPLE
(医王寺) **FREE** Up a steep hill to the west of the harbour, Iō-ji was reputedly founded by Kōbō Daishi in the 900s. A path leads from the temple to the top of a bluff, from where there are fabulous views.

Amo Chinmi Processed
Seafoods Company FACTORY
(阿藻珍味; www.amochinmi.com; 1567-1 Ushiroji Tomo-chō) Amo Chinmi has its factory at the far western end of the harbour, about 10 minutes walk from the town centre. In the factory premises, **Uonosato** (うをの里; ⊙9am-5pm, closed Mon & Tue) **FREE** processes much of the locally caught fish and it's interesting to watch the workers making prawn *sembei* (rice crackers) and *chikuwa* (tube-shaped processed fish).

Sensui-jima ISLAND
(仙酔島) The small island of Sensui-jima is just five minutes across the water from town by ferry (¥240 return), which leaves every 20 minutes from early morning to 9.30pm. There's a walking path around the island and lovely views, especially at sunset. After a stroll, drop into **Kokuminshukusha Sensui-jima** (国民宿舎仙酔島; 🎧970-5050; www.tomonoura. co.jp/sen/02shukusha.html; 3373-2 Ushiroji Tomo-chō; per person with 2 meals from ¥8850; ❄), where non-guests can take a soak in their range of baths for ¥525 (from 10am to 9pm).

✕ Eating

Tomo-no-ura @Cafe CAFE ¥
(Jōyatō-mae, Tomo-chō; meals ¥600-1500; ⊙11am-6pm, closed Wed) This friendly, modern cafe is in a 150-year-old building beside the stone lighthouse on the harbour. There's a small menu consisting of pasta dishes (a pasta lunch set is ¥1500) and sandwiches. There's usually some basic English on the chalkboard menu outside.

Tabuchiya
CAFE, JAPANESE ¥

(田渕屋; www.tomonoura-tabuchiya.com; Tomo-chō-tomo; dishes from ¥1000; ⊙11.30am-5pm, closed Wed) Come to this cosy former merchant building for coffee and light meals, including their speciality *hayashi raisu* (beef in sauce on rice). Walk past the Ōta Residence away from the harbour and look for the small white sign with a green leaf on it.

ⓘ Information

Brochures and maps are also available at JR Fukuyama Station.

Tomo-no-ura Tourist Information Centre
(鞆の浦観光情報センター; ☑982-3200; http://tomonoura-kanko.info; 416-1 Tomo-chō-tomo; ⊙9am-5pm) Located opposite the Tomo-no-ura bus stop, attached to a souvenir shop. It has a handy English map, and rents out audio guides (¥500), which give explanations and background info for numerous sites around town.

ⓘ Getting There & Around

Buses run to Tomo-no-ura every 15 minutes from outside JR Fukuyama Station (¥510, 30 minutes). Note that it's ¥530 to stay on the bus another 450 metres or so to the Tomo-kō stop (Tomo Port), which is closest to the central harbour area, but the tourist office is located at the Tomo-no-ura stop. JR Fukuyama Station is a main hub and *shinkansen* stop on the San-yō line.

It's easy and most convenient to get around the town on foot. Bikes can be hired (¥300 for two hours) from a booth next to the terminal where the ferries leave for Sensui-jima.

Onomichi
尾道

☑0848 / POP 145,200

Onomichi is a gritty, old-timey seaport town whose hills are full of temples and literary sites. Film director Ōbayashi Nobuhiko was born in Onomichi, and the town has featured in a number of Japanese movies, notably Ozu's *Tokyo Story*. It's also known for its *rāmen,* and you'll find plenty of places dishing it up. For many travellers, Onomichi is the base from which to cycle the Shimanami Kaidō, the system of road bridges that allows people to island-hop their way across the Inland Sea to Shikoku.

⊙ Sights

The modern town stretches east from the station along a thin corridor between the railway tracks and the sea. Most of the places of interest are on the other side of the tracks, in the series of steep flagstoned streets that ladder the hillside. There are also some interesting sights on the islands accessible by ferry and/or bike from Onomichi; nearby Ikuchi-jima is a popular half-day trip.

★ Historical Temple Walk
TEMPLES

(古寺めぐり) FREE This well-signed trail takes in 25 old temples in the hills behind the town, following narrow lanes and steep stone stairways, where cats laze about here and there in the sunshine.

About a third of the way along the route is a **ropeway** (千光寺山ロープウェイ; one-way/return ¥280/440; ⊙every 15min 9am-5.15pm) that whisks you up to a hilltop observation tower and park area (Senkō-ji-kōen). Here also is **Senkō-ji** (千光寺), the best known and most impressive of Onomichi's temples. Among its features is the *kyō-onrō*, a bell tower whose bell always rings in the new year – the sound of this bell is registered as one of the '100 soundscapes of Japan'. You can walk or take the ropeway back down.

The walk starts just east of the station: take the inland road from the station and cross the railway tracks by the statue of local author Hayashi Fumiko. To walk the whole trail takes a couple of hours. You can cut back down into town at various points along the way.

Onomichi City Museum of Art
GALLERY

(尾道市立美術館; 17-19 Nishi Tsuchidō-chō; admission varies by exhibition; ⊙9am-5pm, closed Mon) In Senkō-ji-kōen, downhill from the observation tower, is this museum with changing exhibitions of local and Western art. The building, which has fine views, was remodelled by architect Andō Tadao. There is a bright attached cafe.

Maneki-neko Museum
MUSEUM

(招き猫美術館, Beckoning Cat Museum; admission ¥200; ⊙11am-5pm, from 10am weekends, closed Thu) Not far from the lower ropeway station on Onomichi's temple walk is this quirky museum, housing a few thousand of the ornamental beckoning cats that wave you into shop entrances all over Japan.

Onomichi Literature Museum
MUSEUM

(文学記念室; 13-28 Tsuchidō; admission with Shiga Naoya residence ¥300; ⊙9am-5pm Nov-Mar, to 6pm Apr-Oct, closed Tue Dec-Feb) Close to Hōdo-ji, the fourth temple along Onomichi's temple walk, this museum features displays on the lives and works of Hayashi Fumiko and

CYCLING THE SHIMANAMI KAIDŌ

The **Setouchi Shimanami Kaidō** (瀬戸内しまなみ海道, Shimanami Sea Route) is a chain of bridges linking Onomichi in Hiroshima Prefecture with Imabari in Ehime Prefecture on Shikoku, via six Inland Sea islands. Besides being remarkable feats of engineering (the monster Kurushima-kaikyō trio at the Imabari end are among the longest suspension bridges in the world), the bridges make it possible to cycle the whole way across. Breezing along 50m or more above the island-dotted sea is an amazing experience, and a highlight of a trip to this part of Japan.

The Route

The route begins on Mukai-shima (a quick boat ride from Onomichi) and crosses Innoshima, Ikuchi-jima, Ōmi-shima, Hakata-jima and Ōshima, before the final bridge to reach Imabari. The 'recommended' route is well marked and signed with information boards and maps, but there's nothing stopping you from taking detours and plotting your own course from bridge to bridge. Much of the recommended route is fairly flat, with the odd minor hill, but there are long, thigh-burning inclines leading up to each bridge entrance.

Distance & Time

The total recommended route from Onomichi to Imabari is roughly 70km, and could be done in eight or so hours, depending on your fitness and propensity to stop and take pictures. You could take the ferry part of the way, such as to Ikuchi-jima, and bike the rest. Or, a good day trip from Onomichi is to cycle to Ikuchi-jima (about 30km) and return to Onomichi on the ferry in the afternoon. Some cyclists opt to spend a night on one of the islands on the way across.

Information

The tourist office in Onomichi, and those on each of the islands, can help with all the information you need, including an excellent map in English showing the routes, distances, sights and locations of bike terminals along the way. There's some information in English at www.go-shimanami.jp, as well as a downloadable map in Japanese. You'll also find basic maps, plus bus and ferry schedules, at www.city.onomichi.hiroshima.jp.

If you need to get luggage across, try **Kuroneko Yamato** (ヤマト運輸; www.kuronekoyamato.co.jp/en), whose *takkyūbin* service will deliver it for you by the next business day (from around ¥1000 depending on size). It picks up from many convenience stores.

Bikes & Costs

Bike hire is ¥500 per day, plus ¥1000 deposit. You don't get the deposit back if you return the bike to a different rental place along the route. There are bike-hire terminals in Onomichi and in Imabari, and on each island in between. It's not necessary to reserve a bike, though it's possible to do so and you may want to consider it if you're planning to cycle on a major holiday.

Cyclists also need to pay bridge tolls. These are between ¥50 and ¥200 per bridge – no one is actually collecting this money; you're trusted to drop the coins into the box at the bridge entrances. To take your bike on a ferry costs up to ¥150.

other writers connected with Onomichi. It's interesting for fans of Japanese literature, and if you can speak or read some Japanese, but there are no English explanations.

Sleeping

Fuji Hostel HOSTEL ¥

(フジホステル; ☎36-6215; http://nora-t.p-kit.com; 3-30 Toyohimoto-machi; dm ¥2500; @ 📶) Simple, small and cosy, Fuji Hostel has two bedrooms (six bunks in each), one shared bathroom, a kitchen and living area. There's not a lot of cushioning on the beds, but they're comfortable enough. The easy-going owner, who lives on site, speaks very little English but manages. Note the stairs up to the rooms are steep and narrow.

Green Hill Hotel Onomichi HOTEL ¥¥

(グリーンヒルホテル尾道; ☎24-0100; http://gho.hotwire.jp/index_e.html; 9-1 Higashi Gosho-machi; s/tw from ¥7875/15,750; 🚭 @) Directly above the ferry port and a minute's walk from the station, this well-appointed hotel could hardly be better located. Pay a little more for a room on the sea-view side.

Uonobu Ryokan   RYOKAN ¥¥¥
(魚信旅館; ☑37-4175; www.uonobu.jp; 2-27-6 Kubo; per person with meals from ¥16,800) Right on the waterfront, this elegantly old-fashioned place is renowned for its seafood. Nonguests can eat here too, but you'll need to reserve by 5pm the previous day. It's a good 20-minute walk east from the station. Look for the traditional building on the right just after the city hall (市役所).

🍴 Eating

Go east from the station to find eateries along the waterfront and in the arcade one block inland.

Onomichi Rāmen Ichibankan   RĀMEN ¥
(尾道ラーメン壱番館; www.f-ichibankan.com; 2-9-26 Tsuchidō; noodles ¥530-890; ⊙11am-7pm, closed Fri) Opposite the Sumiyoshi shrine on the waterfront, a 15-minute walk from the station, this popular noodle shop is a good place to try Onomichi *rāmen,* characterised by thick slabs of juicy pork. Its best seller is the *kaku-ni rāmen* (noodles with eggs and tender cuts of fatty pork) for ¥890.

Yamaneko Cafe   CAFE, RESTAURANT ¥
(やまねこ; 2-9-33 Tsuchidō; dishes ¥700-1000; ⊙11.30am-10pm, to midnight Fri & Sat, closed Mon) Retro furnishings, battered-looking walls decorated with local artwork, and a mellow playlist add up to a relaxed spot for a drink or light meal. The menu includes pasta and curry lunch sets, pizza, plus cakes and coffees. Find it on a corner along the waterfront road, a 15-minute walk from the station.

Yasuhiro Sushi   SUSHI, SASHIMI ¥¥
(保広寿司; http://yasuhiro.co4.jp; 1-10-12 Tsuchidō; dishes from ¥1600; ⊙11.30am-3pm & 5-9pm, closed Mon) Enjoy excellent, fresh local seafood in this cosy, traditional black-and-white building on the seafront, about five minutes' walk from the station and on the left. Try the *sashimi teishoku* (¥1600) at lunchtime. Prices are higher in the evening.

ℹ️ Information

The city website, www.city.onomichi.hiroshima.jp, is a a good source of information on sights, accommodation and transport links.
Tourist Information Office (☑20-0005; www.ononavi.jp; ⊙9am-6pm) Supplies local maps,

information on the Shimanami Kaidō, and can help with accommodation. It's inside JR Onomichi Station.

ℹ️ Getting There & Around

BICYCLE

Onomichi Port Rent-a-Cycle (☑22-5332; per day ¥500, deposit ¥1000; ⊙7am-6pm) Located in the car park next to the ferry terminal, with multiple bikes. Bikes with gears and electric-assist bikes are available.

BUS

Regular buses run to Imabari (¥2200), in Shikoku, from Onomichi Station (some originating in Shin-Onomichi Station), all with a transfer at Inno-shima. It takes up to two hours, depending on the connection.

FERRY

Ferries travel from Onomichi to Setoda port on Ikuchi-jima (¥800, 40 minutes, nine daily), stopping at Shigei port on Inno-shima (¥400, 20 minutes) on the way. There are frequent ferries to Mukai-shima (¥100, five minutes). There are no ferries directly linking Onomichi with Ōmi-shima. It is up to an additional ¥150 to take a bicycle on the ferries.

TRAIN

Onomichi is on the main JR San-yō line, east of Hiroshima (¥1450, 1½ hours). The Shin-Onomichi *shinkansen* station is 3km north. Regular buses (¥180, 15 minutes) connect the two.

Islands on the Shimanami Kaidō

Six islands are connected by the Shimanami Kaidō bridge system between Onomichi and Imabari. They're accessible by bike (p429) or car, and by ferries from Onomichi.

Inno-shima 因島

Famed for its flowers and fruit, Inno-shima is connected by bridge to Mukai-shima, facing Onomichi, and Ikuchi-jima to the west. The Inland Sea was once a haven for pirates, and Inno-shima was the base of one of the three Murakami pirate clans. Today you can get a taste for that time at the modern-replica **pirate castle** (因島水軍城; admission ¥310; ⊙9.30am-5pm, closed Thu), which has some displays of weaponry. Worth cycling (or driving) up to is **Shirataki-yama** (白滝山), a collection of sculptures of the 500 Rakan disciples of the Buddha.

Ikuchi-jima 生口島

Ikuchi-jima is known for its citrus groves and beaches, including **Sunset Beach** on the west coast.

There's very little doing in the main port town of **Setoda**, but it does have the remarkable temple complex of **Kōsan-ji** (耕三寺; admission ¥1200; ⊘ 9am-5pm). Shortly after the death of his beloved mother in 1934, local steel-tube magnate and arms manufacturer Kanemoto Kōzō became a Buddhist priest and sank his fortune into a series of garishly coloured temple buildings. The result is a chaos of over-the-top Buddhist kitsch, consisting of some 2000 exhibits. Don't miss the **1000 Buddhas Cave** and its series of graphically illustrated hells. Just past Kōsan-ji is the **Ikuo Hirayama Museum of Art** (平山郁夫美術館; www.hirayama-museum.or.jp; admission ¥700; ⊘ 9am-5pm), dedicated to the life and work of the well-travelled, famous Setoda-born artist. The collection here includes several striking works inspired by Ikuo's journeys in India and along the Silk Road.

Ikuchi-jima is a good place to overnight if you're cycling the Shimanami Kaidō. The friendly **Setoda Private Hostel** (瀬戸田垂水温泉; Setoda Tarumi Onsen; ☑ 27-3137; ww7.enjoy.ne.jp/~ymdymd777/shimanami.html; 58-1 Tarumi Setoda-chō; per person with/without meals ¥4600/3000) on Sunset Beach and has its own onsen, with accommodation in individual tatami rooms; payment is by cash only. If you're not arriving on two wheels, a pick-up can be arranged from Setoda ferry port.

Ōmi-shima 大三島

The mountainous island of Ōmi-shima is connected by bridge to Ikuchi-jima to the east and Ō-shima to the west. It is home to one of the oldest Shintō shrines in western Japan, **Ōyamazumi-jinja** (大山祇神社; admission Treasure Hall & Kaiji Museum ¥1000; ⊘ 8.30am-5pm), near Miyaura port. The deity enshrined here is the brother of Amaterasu, the sun goddess. The present structure dates from 1378, but in the courtyard is a 2600-year-old camphor tree, and the treasure hall contains the most important collection of ancient weapons found anywhere in Japan. Heading past the shrine, make your way back to the present with a look at the modern sculpture in the **Tokoro Museum** (ところミュージアム大三島; http://museum.city.imabari.ehime.jp/tokoro; admission ¥300; ⊘ 9am-5pm, closed Mon), from where there are also fabulous views.

OKAYAMA & AROUND

Okayama Prefecture (岡山県; Okayama-ken) is known for its rural character, and the villa at Hattōji offers one of Japan's great countryside getaways. The area is also home to Kurashiki and its well-preserved merchant quarter, the Kibiji district cycling route, and a coastline that provides jumping-off points for some of the most popular islands in the Inland Sea, including Naoshima.

Okayama 岡山

☑ 086 / POP 709,600

The most many travellers see of Okayama is the blur of colour as they fly through on the *shinkansen* to Hiroshima. But it's worth stepping off the train, if only to spend a few hours strolling around Kōraku-en, one of Japan's top three gardens, which is overlooked by the city's crow-black castle. If you have a few days up your sleeve, make Okayama your base for day trips to other attractions in the region.

The city is proud of its connection to Momotarō, the demon-quelling boy hero of one of Japan's best-known folk tales. You'll spot his face beaming out at you all over town.

⊙ Sights

★**Kōraku-en**   GARDEN

(後楽園; www.okayama-korakuen.jp; 1-5 Kōraku-en; admission ¥400; ⊘ 7.30am-6pm Apr-Sep, 8am-5pm Oct-Mar) Kōraku-en draws the crowds with its reputation as one of the three most beautiful gardens in Japan. Built on the orders of *daimyō* Ikeda Tsunemasa, it was completed in 1700 and, despite suffering major damage during floods in the 1930s and air raids in the 1940s, remains much as it was in feudal times. It was opened to the public in 1884.

Unusually for a Japanese garden, it is mostly expansive lawns (though, as usual, you can't walk on them). The garden is broken up by ponds, teahouses and other

---

ⓘ DISCOUNT TICKETS

Save a few yen with a **combination ticket** (¥560) covering entry to both Kōraku-en and Okayama-jō. Passes including other local museums are also available. Buy combination tickets at whichever site you visit first.

Okayama

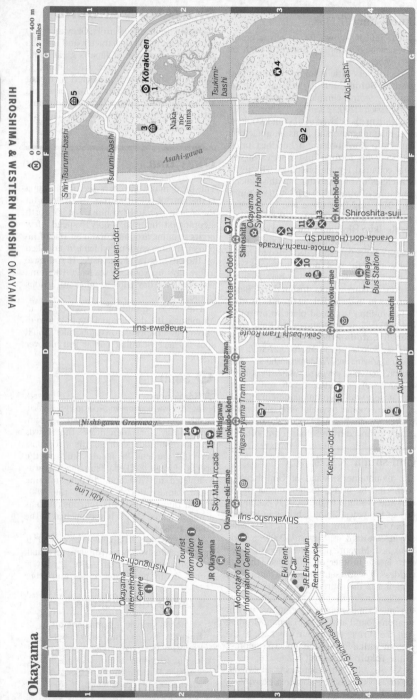

Kōraku-en
1

3

Naka-no-shima

Asahi-gawa

Tsukimi-bashi

4

5

2

Shin-Tsurumi-bashi

Tsurumi-bashi

Tsurumi-bashi

Aioi-bashi

Kōrakuen-dōri

Okayama
Symphony Hall

Shiroshita-suji

17

Shiroshita

13

Kenchō-dōri

Momotarō-Ōdori

12

11

Oranda-dōri (Holland St)

Omote-machi Arcade

10

9

8

Tenmaya
Bus Station

Yūbinkyoku-mae

Yanagawa-suji

Seiki-bashi Tram Route

Tamachi

Yanagawa

Higashi-yama Tram Route

Akura-dōri

7

16

6

Nishi-gawa Greenway

14

15

Nishigawa-
ryokudō-kōen

Sky Mall Arcade

Okayama-eki-mae

Kenchō-dōri

Kibi Line

Nishiguchi-suji

Tourist
Information
Counter

JR Okayama

Shiyakusho-suji

Momotarō Tourist
Information Centre

Okayama
International
Centre

9

Eki Rent-
a-Car

JR Eki-Rinkun

Rent-a-cycle

San-yō Shinkansen Line

400 m
0.2 miles

N

0
0

Okayama

Edo-period buildings, including a stage for nō, and even has a small tea plantation and rice fields. The highlights change with the seasons – in spring the groves of plum and cherry blossoms are stunning, white lotuses unfurl in summer, and in autumn the maple trees are a delight for photographers. There are also seasonal events (fancy some harvest-moon viewing?).

From Okayama Station, take the Higashi-yama tram to the Shiroshita stop (¥100) then follow the signs. Alternatively, it's a 20-minute walk up Momotarō-Ōdōri.

Okayama-jō CASTLE
(岡山城; 2-3-1 Marunouchi; admission ¥300, additional charge for special exhibitions; ⊙9am-5pm) Nicknamed U-jō (烏城; Crow Castle) because of its colour, the striking black Okayama Castle was built by *daimyō* Ukita Hideie and completed in 1597. Much of the castle was dismantled after the Meiji Restoration and most of what remained burnt down during WWII air raids. The castle was rebuilt in 1966.

The imposing exterior – its gilded fish-gargoyles flipping their tails in the air – is the castle's most impressive aspect, and you can enjoy it for nix from the grounds, or looking from across the river. Inside the *donjon* (main keep) museum, modern finishes and an elevator mar the 16th-century feel, but there are a few interesting displays and views from the top floor.

Yumeji Art Museum GALLERY
(夢二郷土美術館; www.yumeji-art-museum.com; 2-1-32 Hama; admission ¥700; ⊙9am-5pm, closed Mon) Prominent Taishō-era artist and poet Takehisa Yumeji (1884–1934) is particularly known for his *bijin-ga* (images of beautiful women), and various wistfully posed ladies feature among the paintings, prints and

screens on display at this small museum. It's just across the river on the northeast side of Kōraku-en.

Okayama Prefectural Museum MUSEUM
(岡山県立博物館; www.pref.okayama.jp/kyoiku/kenhaku/hakubu.htm; 1-5 Kōraku-en; admission ¥250; ⊙9am-6pm, closed Mon) Exhibits a range of historical artefacts from the region, including documents, tools, armoury and Bizen pottery. The museum is near the entrance to Kōraku-en.

Hayashibara Museum of Art MUSEUM
(林原美術館; www.hayashibara-museumofart.jp; 2-7-15 Marunouchi; admission ¥300; ⊙9am-5pm, closed Mon) This is a small museum with exhibits of scrolls, armour and paintings that were once the property of the Ikeda clan (who ruled Okayama for much of the Edo period). It's near the back entrance of the castle.

🛏 Sleeping

Modern midrange and budget hotels dominate the scene in Okayama. For a more traditional ryokan experience, consider staying in nearby Kurashiki.

Saiwai-sō HOTEL ¥
(ビジネスホテル幸荘; ☑254-0020; http://w150.j.fiw-web.net; 24-8 Ekimoto-chō; s/tw ¥4200/7600; ⊖🛜📶) This 'happy house' declares itself Okayama's first business hotel but it's not typical of that genre, having mostly tatami rooms (go for one of these) in a warren-like building. Some rooms have shared bathrooms. Groups and families are welcomed (up to six people from ¥3600 per person), and what other business hotel has an old-school video-game table in the hotel lounge? The affable owners don't speak English.

MOMOTARŌ, THE PEACH BOY

Okayama Prefecture and Kagawa Prefecture, on the island of Shikoku, are linked by the legend of Momotarō, the Peach Boy, who emerged from the stone of a peach and, backed up by a monkey, a pheasant and a dog, defeated a three-eyed, three-toed people-eating demon. The island of Megi-jima, off Takamatsu in Shikoku, is said to be the site of the clash with the demon. Momotarō may actually have been a Yamato prince who was deified as Kibitsuhiko. His shrine, Kibitsu-jinja, lies along the route of the Kibiji bicycle ride.

There are statues of Momotarō at JR Okayama Station, he and his sidekicks feature on manhole covers, and the city's biggest street is named after him. One of the most popular souvenir treats from Okayama is also Momotarō's favoured sweet, *kibi-dango*, a soft *mochi*-like dumpling made with millet flour. And if you can sing the first couple of lines of the well-known old children's tune, Momotarō's Song, you'll impress the locals no end. All together now: *Momotarō-san, Momotarō-san, o-koshi ni tsuketa kibi-dango*...

★ Kōraku Hotel HOTEL ¥¥
(後楽ホテル; ☑ 221-7111; www.hotel.kooraku.co.jp; 5-1 Heiwa-chō; s/tw from ¥7500/15,000; ⊜@🛜) Kōraku has classy touches such as local museum pieces displayed on each floor, and stylish rooms with plenty of breathing space. Corner rooms, with large curved windows, are especially luxurious. Staff members speak English, as does the enthusiastic manager, who you may bump into mingling with guests in the lobby. Rates are significantly lower if you book online.

Central Hotel Okayama HOTEL ¥¥
(セントラルホテル岡山; ☑ 222-2121; www.c-hotelokayama.co.jp; 1-10-28 Tamachi; s/tw from ¥4800/8000; ⊜@) Behind the rather pedestrian name are thoughtfully designed wood-hued rooms with neatly hidden amenities, friendly service, and a hotel with an interesting history (ask about the room at the top). There is a good restaurant attached, where you can also have breakfast (¥600).

Okayama View Hotel HOTEL ¥¥
(岡山ビューホテル; ☑ 224-2000; www.okaview.jp; 1-11-17 Naka-sange; s/tw from ¥6300/10,500; ⊜@🛜) Blonde-wood fittings and beds on the floor in the 'concept' rooms here make this an attractive modern Japanese option. Rooms are small but the hotel is in a good spot between the station and the garden.

Eating

★ Okabe TOFU ¥
(おかべ; 1-10-1 Omote-chō; dishes ¥800-850; ⏱11.30am-2pm, closed Sun) This street-corner tofu restaurant is recognisable by the big illustration of a heavily laden tofu seller in a straw hat. Squeeze in at the counter and watch the team of women chopping and frying as you wait. There are only two things on the menu: an *okabe teishoku* (set meal with several types of tofu) and a *namayuba-don teishoku* (dried 'tofu skin' on rice, with soup).

Tori-soba Ōta NOODLES ¥
(とりそば太田; www.torisoba.com; 1-7-24 Omote-chō; dishes ¥650-990; ⏱11am-8pm, closed Mon; ⊜🍴) The name of this little countertop restaurant is also its trademark dish: *tori-soba* (steaming bowls of noodles packed with chicken and served in a tasty broth). Other options are variations on the chicken, noodle and spring onion theme and even the small serve is a decent feed. Look for the blue sign with white writing.

Quiet Village Curry Shop CURRY ¥
(クワイエットビレッジカレーショップ; 1-6-43 Omote-chō; dishes ¥780-880; ⏱11.30am-7.30pm, closed Mon; 🍴) This cosy restaurant consists of one long table and counter, where the welcoming owners serve up Bengali-style curries and tasty cups of chai. Some English is spoken and there are vegetarian and vegan options.

Padang Padang ITALIAN, FRENCH ¥¥
(パダンパダン; ☑ 223-6665; www.padangpadang.jp; 1-7-10 Omote-chō; dishes ¥1000-2000; ⏱6pm-midnight, closed Tue; 🍴) Despite its name, this mellow, lamp-lit restaurant focuses on French and Italian dishes, deftly whipped up in the small open kitchen. There is occasional live music and it's a good spot for a glass of wine after a day of sightseeing.

🍷 Drinking & Nightlife

Izayoi no Tsuki
IZAKAYA

(いざ酔いの月; 1-10-2 Ekimae-chō; ⏰5pm-midnight) A convivial atmosphere, walls decorated with sake labels, and an enormous drink menu – just what you want from a local *izakaya*. There are numerous sakes from Okayama Prefecture and beers from local microbreweries – try the Doppo pilsner or a Kibi Doteshita Bakushu ale. Izoyoi is just off the Sky Mall arcade. The bar's name is written across a yellow moon.

Saudade na Yoru
BAR, CAFE

(サウダーヂな夜; www.saudade-ent.com/saudade; 2nd fl Shiroshita Bldg, 10-16 Tenjin-chō; ⏰6pm-3am Mon-Fri, 3pm-3am Sat & Sun) This 2nd-floor lounge bar overlooking the Symphony Hall building makes all the right retro-chic moves, with a rough concrete floor, mismatched furniture and ornate-glass lighting. It has a good drinks list (most priced around ¥700), coffees and a limited food and snacks menu. A ¥300 cover charge applies after 9pm.

Marugo Deli
JUICE BAR

(マルゴ・デリ; 1-1-11 Tamachi; juices ¥400; ⏰9am-11pm Mon-Fri, 10am-11pm Sat, 10am-9pm Sun) Funky little bar with a good range of fresh juices and coffee and a couple of seats outside. Its sign is a number 5 in a circle.

Aussie Bar
PUB

(オージーバー; 1-10-21 Ekimae-chō; ⏰7pm-3am) An expat-run watering hole popular with the city's English-speaking population.

ℹ Information

ATMs at 7-Eleven stores accept international cards.

Comic Buster (コミックバスター; www.comicbuster.jp/kameiten/33_okayama; 4th fl Chūgoku Kōtsū Bldg, 2-1 Honmachi; internet 1hr/3hr ¥300/780; ⏰24hr) Internet access near the station.

Momotarō Tourist Information Centre (ももたろう観光センター; ☏222-2912; www.okayama-japan.jp/en/; ⏰9am-8pm) Large office with maps and information on Okayama and the region. The helpful staff speak some English. It's in the basement complex below the station – come out of the station's east exit, then go down the stairs to the right.

Okayama Central Post Office (岡山中央郵便局; 2-1-1 Naka-sange; ⏰9am-7pm Mon-Fri, to 5pm Sat, to 12.30pm Sun; ⏰ATM 7am-11pm Mon-Fri, 9am-9pm Sat, 9am-7pm Sun) Has ATMs accepting international cards.

Okayama International Centre (岡山国際交流センター; ☏256-2914; www.opief.or.jp/english; 2-2-1 Hōkan-chō; ⏰9am-5pm, closed Sun) Information and resources for foreign residents. Booking service for the Hattōji and Shiraishi International Villas. Free internet access (30 minutes).

Tourist Information Counter (観光案内所; ⏰9am-6pm) In the station, by the entrance to the *shinkansen* tracks.

ℹ Getting There & Away

BUS

Highway buses connect Okayama with major cities across the region. There are also buses betwen Okayama and Kansai International Airport (3¼ hours, ¥4500).

Buses to Shin-Okayama port (¥480, 40 minutes, one or two per hour) leave from Okayama Station, stopping at Tenmaya bus station in the city centre on the way.

FERRY

Ferries run to Shōdo-shima and Naoshima from Shin-Okayama port and Uno port respectively.

TRAIN

Okayama is on the JR San-yō line and *shinkansen* line, connecting to Osaka (¥5350, 45 minutes) in the east and Hiroshima (¥5350, 35 minutes) to the west. Other destinations from Okayama:

Takamatsu (Shikoku) ¥1470, one hour

Yonago (Tottori Prefecture) ¥4620, two hours

DON'T MISS

NAKED FESTIVAL

If you're in the area on the third Saturday in February, head to Saidai-ji for the **Saidai-ji Eyō**, also known as the Hadaka Matsuri (Naked Festival). It takes place at the Kannon-in temple, where a chaotic crowd of around 10,000 men in loincloths and *tabi* (split-toe socks) fight over two sacred *shingi* (wooden batons) while freezing water is poured over them and crowds around the temple look on. The fun kicks off at 10pm, though there's also a version for elementary-school boys earlier in the evening. Sorry, ladies, only the guys are allowed to strip off and fight for the *shingi*, but anyone can watch. Regular trains run to Saidai-ji from Okayama, about 20 minutes away.

ⓘ Getting Around

Okayama can be seen on foot or with a couple of short tram rides. The Higashi-yama line takes you to the main attractions, going all the way up Momotarō-Ōdōri, then turning right. The Seiki-bashi line turns right earlier, passing the Central Post Office. Travel within the central city area costs ¥100 and you pay as you get off the tram. Okayama is also a good city for cycling.

JR Eki-Rinkun Rent-a-cycle (レンタサイクル駅リンくん; ☑ 223-7081; per day ¥300; ⊙ 7am-9pm)

Eki Rent-a-Car (駅レンタカー; ☑ 224-1363; www.ekiren.co.jp; per day from ¥5770; ⊙ 8am-8pm)

Bizen 備前

☑ 0869 / POP 37,800

The Bizen region has been renowned for its ceramics since the Kamakura period (1185–1333). The pottery produced here tends to be earthy and subdued, and has been prized by dedicated tea-ceremony aficionados for centuries. Travellers with an interest in pottery will find the gritty Bizen town of **Imbe** (伊部) and its kilns a worthwhile side trip from Okayama.

Most places of ceramic interest are within easy walking distance of Imbe Station. The **information counter** (☑ 64-1001; www.touyu-ukai.jp; ⊙ 9am-6pm, closed Tue), inside the souvenir shop on the left as you exit the platform, has a handy *Inbe Walk* map, in English, showing the locations of kilns, shops and other sites.

On the 2nd floor of the station building is a gallery run by the **Friends of Bizen-yaki Ceramics Society** (岡山県備前焼陶友会; www.touyuukai.jp; ⊙ 9.30am-5.30pm, closed Tue) **FREE**, selling a wide range of ceramics by contemporary potters.

The sombre-looking concrete building to the right as you exit the station is the **Okayama Prefectural Bizen Ceramics Art Museum** (岡山県備前陶芸美術館; admission ¥800; ⊙ 9.30am-5pm, closed Mon), with pieces from the Muromachi (1333–1568) and Momoyama (1568–1600) periods, plus work by several modern artists who have been designated 'Living National Treasures'.

The station area is pretty uninspiring, but walking up the road leading north you begin to spot the smoking chimneys and the bamboo groves of the hills behind the town. There are several galleries and shops on this road and many more along the road

that forms a T-intersection at the end. Lanes running uphill from here are dotted with potters' workshops, some selling their wares directly to the public.

Go right at the T-intersection then left up a lane to glimpse the large kiln ruins of **Tempogama** (天保窯), dating from c 1832, now fenced off for protection. Look for the red iron roof. You can continue up from here to the understated and pretty wooden shrine **Imbe-jinja** (忌部神社). Further along is **Amatsu-jinja** (天津神社), decorated with Bizen-yaki figures of the animals of the Chinese zodiac.

Several kilns in the area offer the chance to try your hand at making your own masterpiece. Try **Bishūgama** (備州窯; ☑ 64-1160; www.gift.or.jp/bisyu; 302-2 Imbe, Bizen-shi; ⊙ 9am-3pm), where making a piece will cost ¥2625 or ¥3675, depending on the type of firing you choose. The information counter in the station has a list of other kilns and costs.

There is one direct train an hour to Imbe from Okayama (¥570, 40 minutes) on the Akō line (赤穂線), bound for Banshū-Akō (播州赤穂) and Aioi (相生).

Kibiji 吉備路

The largely rural Kibiji district around Okayama is best explored on two wheels, following a popular **cycling route** across the Kibi plain. It takes in several interesting temples and shrines, an ancient burial mound and an old sake brewery, passing through rice fields along the way.

To get to the starting point, take a local JR Kibi line train from Okayama to Bizen Ichinomiya (備前一宮; ¥200, 11 minutes, about every half-hour). From here, the mostly flat cycling route runs west for roughly 15km to the station at Sōja (総社), where you can drop off your bike and take a train back to Okayama. It can take as little as a couple of hours if you're just peddling on through, but allow three or four if you want to wander around the sights (or take a few detours (or get lost) here and there.

Uedo Rent-a-Cycle (レンタサイクルウエド; ☑ 086-284-2311; per day ¥1000; ⊙ 9am-6pm) is on the right at the front of Bizen Ichinomiya Station. It occasionally closes in bad weather. If no one is around, try asking the guard at the nearby bike parking lot, who may be able to call and get it opened up for you. Bike rental is ¥1000 if you're returning the bike at Sōja.

WORTH A TRIP

HATTŌJI

As you head up through the hills past the farms and thatched-roof houses to Hattōji (八塔寺), the crowds and vending-machine-packed streets of big-city Japan begin to feel delightfully out of reach.

The chief reason to journey out here is to stay at the **Hattōji International Villa** (八塔寺国際交流ヴィラ; Kagami Yoshinaga-chō, Bizen-shi; per person ¥3500; ☻🚲), a restored farmhouse that is one of two remaining places established by the prefectural government in the late 1980s as accommodation for foreigners. This is an excellent option for those weary of the fast lane, and a great opportunity to get a sense of Japan outside the well-touristed urban centres.

The house itself has four large tatami rooms separated by sliding doors, a shared bathroom and kitchen, and bicycles that are free to use. There's an open hearth in the common area, where you can burn charcoal for the full olden-days effect, and near the villa you'll find hiking tracks, shrines and temples (where it's possible to join morning meditation). There are a couple of eateries in the area but hours are irregular – stock up on groceries in Okayama or Yoshinaga before you come to Hattōji. You can also pay ¥25,000 (for up to eight people) or ¥40,000 (up to 13 people) to have exclusive use of the house. For reservations, contact the **International Villa Group** (☎086-256-2535; www.international-villa.or.jp; ☺phone reservations 9am-noon & 1-5pm Mon-Fri) in Okayama by phone or via the website. Payment is cash only.

Buses (¥200, 30 minutes, five to six daily Monday to Saturday) run to Hattōji from Yoshinaga (吉永) on the JR San-yō line, accessible by train (¥570, 33 minutes, roughly every hour) from Okayama. The bus drops you near the villa entrance. See the International Villa Group website for the latest schedule.

While you're near Yoshinaga Station, it's worth visiting the historic Edo-period **Shizutani Gakko** (閑谷学校, Shizutani School; http://shizutani.jp; admission ¥300; ☺9am-5pm), the first public school in Japan, its wood interiors and Bizen-yaki roof tiles now beautifully preserved. The school is about 3km from the station. There are infrequent buses but it's walkable; ask at the station for directions.

From here, follow the route map you receive with the bike, and the blue 'Kibiji District' road signs along the course. If you wander off track, locals will be able to set you straight – just ask them for the Kibiji *jitensha dōro* (Kibiji bike path).

The first shrine you'll pass is the **Kibitsuhiko-jinja** (吉備津彦神社), fronted by a pond near the start of the bicycle path. Not far from here is the **Kibitsu-jinja** (吉備津神社). This major shrine is dedicated to an ancient warrior who subdued a local bandit/demon called Ura and brought the area under central control. Many people believe that these exploits were the ultimate source of the Momotarō legend. You'll see Momotarō's peachy features looking out at you from the votive tablets in front of the shrine.

Pedalling on, you'll pass the **Koikui-jinja** (鯉喰神社), located slightly off the main route by the river, and the 5th-century **Tsukuriyama-kofun** (造山古墳). The fourth-biggest *kofun* tomb in Japan, this is thought to mark the final resting place of a local king who ruled the Kibi region when this area was a rival power to the Yamato court (which eventually came to rule all of Japan).

The next major stop on the route is the **Bitchū Kokobun-ji** (備中国分寺), a temple with a picturesque five-storey pagoda. The oldest buildings here date from the Edo period, but the first temple on this site was built in the 8th century. Across the main road from the temple is the **Miyake Sake Brewery Museum** (三宅酒造資料館; ☎0866-92-0075; admission ¥400; ☺10am-4pm Tue-Fri & 1st & 3rd Sat of month). Look for the large white building. The brewery has been in the same family for over 100 years, and there is a small museum of old brewing paraphernalia, as well as opportunities to taste and buy. It's worth calling to let them know if you're dropping in.

From here, it's a few kilometres to Sōja, where you can return your bicycle at **Araki Rent-a-Cycle** (荒木レンタサイクル; ☎0866-92-0233; ☺9am-6pm), at the side of the bus area in front of the station. You can, of course, start from Sōja and head in the other direction.

Kurashiki 倉敷

♫ 086 / POP 475,400

Kurashiki's main attraction is its atmospheric Bikan quarter (美観地区), an area of historic buildings by an old willow-edged canal, where a picturesque group of black-and-white warehouses has been converted into museums.

In the feudal era the warehouses were used to store rice brought by boat from the surrounding countryside. Later, the town became an important textile centre, under the Kurabō Textile Company. Owner Ōhara Magosaburō built up a collection of European art and opened the Ōhara Museum of Art in 1930, which today draws many Japanese tourists.

⊙ Sights

★ Ōhashi House HISTORIC BUILDING
(大橋家住宅; http://ohashi-ke.com; 3-21-31 Achi; admission ¥500; ⊗9am-5pm, closed Fri Dec-Feb) Between the station and the canal area is the beautifully restored Ōhashi House, built in 1793. The house belonged to one of Kurashiki's richest families and was built at a time when prosperous merchants were beginning to claim privileges that had previously been the preserve of the samurai.

★ Ōhara Museum of Art GALLERY
(大原美術館; www.ohara.or.jp; 1-1-15 Chūō; admission ¥1300; ⊗9am-5pm, closed Mon except summer) This is Kurashiki's premier museum, housing the predominantly Western art collection amassed by local textile magnate Ōhara Magosaburō (1880–1943), with the help of artist Kojima Torajirō (1881–1929). The varied assemblage of paintings, prints and sculpture features works by Picasso, Cézanne, El Greco and Matisse, and one of Monet's water-lilies paintings (said to have been bought from the man himself by Torajirō while visiting Monet's home in 1920). While no rival to the major galleries of Europe, it's an interesting collection and one of the town's biggest attractions for Japanese tourists.

The valid-all-day ticket gets you into the museum's **Craft & Asiatic Art Gallery**, the **contemporary Japanese collection** housed in an annexe behind the main building, plus the **Kojima Torajirō Memorial Hall** (児島虎次郎記念館).

Japan Rural Toy Museum MUSEUM
(日本郷土玩具館; 1-4-16 Chūō; admission ¥400; ⊗9am-5pm) Four rooms are crammed with displays of wooden toys, masks, dolls and spinning tops (including a world record breaker), and a colourful array of kites just beckoning to be put on a breeze. You can purchase a new toy of your own in the attached **shop**, which also sells crafts and regional artwork.

Ivy Square SQUARE
(アイビースクエア) Present-day Ivy Square was once the site of Ōhara's Kurabō textile factories. The company moved into more modern premises a long time ago, and the red-brick factory buildings (dating from 1889) now house a hotel, restaurants, shops and yet more museums, including the **Kurabō Memorial Hall** (倉紡記念館; www.kurabo.co.jp/kurabo_kinenkan; 7-1 Honmachi; admission ¥350; ⊗9am-5pm), where you can learn all about the history of the Japanese textile industry.

Kojima Torajirō Memorial Hall MUSEUM
(児島虎次郎記念館; www.ivysquare.co.jp/cultural/torajiro.html; 7-2 Honmachi; admission ¥500; ⊗9am-5pm, closed Mon) Kojima Torajirō was the European-style painter who went above and beyond in helping Ōhara build up his art collection; head to this museum to immerse yourself in his life. Entry is included in the ticket for the Ōhara Art Museum.

Kurashiki Museum of Folk-craft MUSEUM
(倉敷民芸館; 1-4-11 Chūō; admission ¥700; ⊗9am-5pm Mar-Nov, to 4.15pm Dec-Feb, closed Mon) Housed in an attractive complex of rice warehouses dating from the late 18th century, with interesting exhibits of ceramics, glassware, textiles and furniture.

🛏 Sleeping

Kurashiki is a good place to spend a night in a ryokan so you can soak up the olde-worlde atmosphere. There are also plenty of Western-style business hotels around the station and along Chūō-dōri, but if you're considering one of these you might be better off staying in Okayama, where you'll get similar digs for less money.

Guesthouse U-Rin-An HOSTEL ¥
(倉敷ゲストハウス有鄰庵; ♫426-1180; www.u-rin.com; 2-15 Honmachi; dm ¥3500; ⊜ 🕸) Friendly U-Rin-An has shared tatami rooms in a traditional old house near the Bikan quarter. It offers a kitchen and cafe, and the guesthouse also hosts events. For stays of more than one night, the rate is discounted. Note that it takes cash only.

Kurashiki

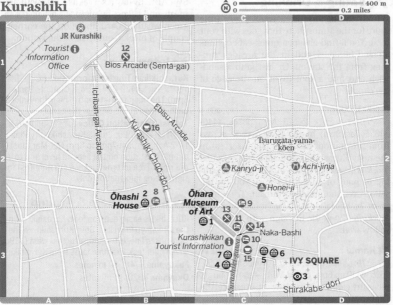

N 0 — 400 m
0 — 0.2 miles

Kurashiki

◎ Top Sights
1 Ōhara Museum of Art	C3
2 Ōhashi House	B2

◎ Sights
3 Ivy Square	D3
4 Japan Rural Toy Museum	C3
5 Kojima Torajirō Memorial Hall	C3
6 Kurabō Memorial Hall	C3
7 Kurashiki Museum of Folk-craft	C3

🛏 Sleeping
8 Dormy Inn Kurashiki	B2
9 Guesthouse U-Rin-An	C2
10 Ryokan Kurashiki	C3
11 Ryokan Tsurugata	C3

🍴 Eating
12 Bukkake Udon	B1
13 Kamoi	C3
14 Mamakari-tei	C3

🍷 Drinking & Nightlife
15 Kurashiki Coffee-Kan	C3
16 SWLABR	B2

Ryokan Tsurugata   RYOKAN ¥¥
(鶴形; ☎424-1635; www.turugata.jp; 1-3-15 Chūō; per person with two meals ¥14,800-33,600) This welcoming ryokan in a converted building right in the historic area has tatami rooms overlooking a garden, and meals featuring local seafood. Prices vary according to room size and most have shared bathrooms. A little English is spoken.

Dormy Inn Kurashiki   HOTEL ¥¥
(ドーミーイン倉敷; ☎426-5489; www.hotespa. net/hotels/kurashiki; 3-21-11 Achi; s/tw from ¥5000/8000; ❄@) The pick of the Western-style chains, this relatively new hotel is

not far from the historic district and has a little something extra to tip the scales in its favour – an onsen on the top floor.

★Ryokan Kurashiki   RYOKAN ¥¥¥
(旅館くらしき; ☎422-0730; www.ryokan-kurashi ki.jp; 4-1 Honmachi; per person with two meals from ¥28,000) By the canal in the heart of the historic district, this ryokan, which incorporates several beautifully restored Edo-period buildings, is probably the best in town. The spacious suites all have tatami lounge areas with attached twin-bed rooms and bathrooms. Dinner is a multicourse *kaiseki* affair with Inland Sea delicacies. Some English spoken.

✕ Eating & Drinking

Within the historic area you'll pay a little more for the atmosphere that goes with your food. You'll find cheaper, quick-eats options along Chūō-dōri and in the arcades running from the station. Or just grab a sandwich and find a spot to sit on the edge of the canal.

Bukkake Udon NOODLES ¥
(ぶっかけうどん; 2-3-23 Achi; dishes ¥440-840; ⏱7am-9pm) In the Bios Arcade across from the station, this local chain serves up the tasty Kurashiki *udon* speciality – called *bukkake udon* (from *bukkakeru,* meaning to pour or splash) because you tip the sauce over the noodles yourself. Try a *tempura bukkake* or a *niku* (meat) *kimuchi bukkake.* Look for the sign with a ぶ in a yellow oval.

★ Kamoi SUSHI, SASHIMI ¥¥
(カモ井; ☑422-0606; 1-3-17 Chūō; dishes ¥1050-2625; ⏱10am-6pm, closed Mon; ⊜▣) A large, pleasant canal-side restaurant opposite the Ōhara Museum, serving sashimi set meals, seafood-and-rice dishes, and some desserts (from ¥525). You can get the local sardine-like speciality here in *mamakari-zushi* form for ¥1050. Cash only.

Mamakari-tei SEAFOOD ¥¥
(ままかり亭; ☑427-7112; www.hamayoshi-kurashiki.jp; 3-12 Honmachi; dishes ¥840-3150; ⏱11am-2pm & 5-10pm, closed Mon) This traditional eatery, in a 200-year-old warehouse with chunky beams and long wooden tables, is famed for the sardine-like local speciality. The tasty fish is supposed to induce bouts of uncontrollable feasting, so that people are obliged to *kari* (borrow) more *mama* (rice) from their neighbours in order to carry on with their binge. Lunchtime-only set meals include a *mamakari teishoku* for ¥2625.

Kurashiki Coffee-Kan CAFE
(倉敷珈琲館; www.kurashiki-coffeekan.com; 4-1 Honmachi; coffees ¥500-850; ⏱10am-5pm) The low-ceilinged, wood-and-brick interior of this caffeine-lovers' paradise is thick with the aroma of freshly roasted beans. The menu features coffee and coffee only, though you can choose hot or cold. It's on the canal next to Ryokan Kurashiki.

SWLABR CAFE, BAR
(2-18-2 Achi; ⏱11.30am-3am) After the Bikan area closes down, relax with the good music and friendly staff at the slightly scruffy SWLABR. By day it serves as a cafe with light meals and cakes; by night it's a bar. It's the green weatherboard house on the corner, a couple of blocks southeast of the station.

ℹ Information

Kurashikikan Tourist Information (倉敷館観光案内所; ☑422-0542; 1-4-8 Chūō; ⏱9am-6pm) The main tourist centre, near the Naka-bashi bridge at the bend in the canal.

Tourist Information Office (倉敷駅前観光案内所; ☑424-1220; 2nd fl, Kurashiki City Plaza, 1-7-2 Achi; ⏱9am-7pm, to 6pm Oct-Mar) Just out of the station on the second level and to the right. Free internet access (15 minutes) for sightseeing information only.

ℹ Getting There & Around

Kurashiki is easily seen on foot. Kurashiki is on the JR San-yō main line. Shin-Kurashiki, on the *shinkansen* line, is two stops further west (¥190, seven minutes). Example fares from Kurashiki:

Fukuyama ¥740, 40 minutes

Okayama ¥320, 14 minutes

Shōdo-shima 小豆島

☑0879 / POP 31,200

Famed for its olive groves and as the setting of the classic film *Nijūshi-no-hitomi* (Twenty-four eyes; it tells the story of a village school teacher and her young charges), Shōdo-shima makes an enjoyable day trip or overnight escape from big-city Japan. It has a smattering of sights but is mainly appealing for its mountainous landscape, scenic coastal roads and Inland Sea vistas. Tonoshō is the main town and port, and also where you can see the 'world's narrowest navigable strait' (Dobuchi Strait), which runs through the centre of town. The island is popular during summer and when the autumn leaves are at their peak in October and November. Come out of season and you'll find a sleepy isle with very few fellow travellers.

◉ Sights & Activities

◉ Around the Coast

Shōdo-shima Olive Park PARK, ONSEN
(小豆島オリーブ公園; www.olive-pk.jp; Nishimura-misaki 1941-1; ⏱8.30am-5pm) FREE
This park is where the island's olive-growing activities are celebrated with several white-washed buildings, some fake Grecian ruins, a museum, and opportunities to buy olive-

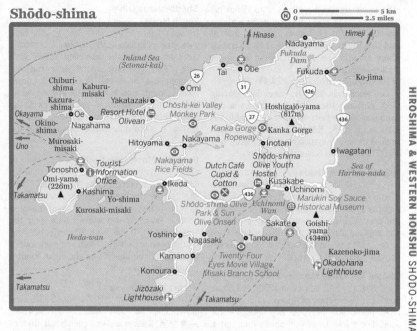

themed souvenirs. It's worth tolerating the kitsch for the **Sun Olive Onsen** (サン・オリーブ温泉; admission ¥700; ☺ noon-9pm), where you can enjoy fabulous views of the Japanese Aegean from a variety of herbal baths.

★ Marukin Soy Sauce Historical Museum   MUSEUM

(マルキン醤油記念館; www.marukin-chuyu.com /kodawari/shoyu/kinenkan.html; admission ¥210; ☺ 9am-4pm) Shōdo-shima was famous for its soy beans long before olives arrived, and several old soy-sauce companies are still in business here (as frequent whiffs around the island will remind you). Marukin has a small museum with displays of the sauce-making process, old implements, photos, and interesting facts you never knew about the ubiquitous brown stuff. There are good English explanations, and you can try the surprisingly tasty soy-sauce-flavoured ice cream. It's on the main road between Kusakabe and Sakate.

Twenty-Four Eyes Movie Village   MUSEUM

(二十四の瞳映画村; www.24hitomi.or.jp; admission ¥700, combined ticket with the old school ¥790; ☺ 9am-5pm) Just north of Sakate is the turn-off to the picturesque fishing village of **Tanoura** (田ノ浦), site of the village school that featured in the film *Twenty-Four Eyes*.

The film was based on a novel by local writer Tsuboi Sakae and was a huge hit in postwar Japan. The set used in the 1980s remake of the original 1954 B&W film is now open to the public as this movie village, where busloads of tourists gather to wallow in nostalgia.

Misaki Branch School   HISTORIC BUILDING

(岬の分教場; www.24hitomi.or.jp; admission ¥200, combined ticket with the movie village ¥790; ☺ 9am-5pm) Worth visiting in Tanoura is this perfectly preserved 1902 school, setting for the *Twenty-Four Eyes* story and the 1954 film. It's a short walk from the movie village on the road back to Sakate.

⊙ Central Mountains

★ Kanka Gorge   GORGE

(寒霞渓; www.kankakei.co.jp; ropeway one-way/return ¥700/1250; ☺ ropeway 8.30am-5pm, to 4.30pm late Dec–late Mar) The **cable car** (寒霞渓ロープウエイ) is the main attraction at Kanka-kei in the central mountains, making a spectacular trip through the gorge, particularly when it is ablaze with autumn colours (though be warned that many others have the same idea). Of course, you could just take in the breathtaking views of the Inland Sea from the area around the upper cable-car station without taking the ride. An alternative for keen walkers is to climb between the lower and upper cable-car stations via the **Omote 12 Views** (表12景; 2.3km) and **Ura Eight Views** (裏8景; 1.8km) tracks. There are other scenic walks from the upper station, including a hike to the eastern peak of **Hoshigajō-yama** (星ヶ城東峰; 817m).

On weekends, and on weekdays during peak periods, there are four buses a day from Kusakabe port to the lower cable-car station (紅雲亭; Kōuntei), with additional sevices during the autumn leaf-viewing season. There are no buses during winter.

Nakayama Rice Fields
RICE TERRACES

(中山千枚田; Nakayama Senmaida) About 4km inland from the Ikeda ferry terminal are Nakayama's 'thousand rice fields'. The terraces are pretty in any season but are especially picturesque after rice planting in late April or early May, when the water-filled fields become a hillside of mirrors.

Chōshi-kei Valley Monkey Park
MONKEY PARK

(銚子渓お猿の国; admission ¥370; ☉8.20am-5pm) Large troupes of monkeys will come right up to you here as they squabble for food. For a less intense monkey encounter, look out for them on the way up to the park area, where they're sometimes found lazing on the road.

☆☆ Festivals & Events

Nōson Kabuki
KABUKI

Shōdo-shima was famous during the Edo period for its tradition of rural kabuki (stylised Japanese theatre), and two 17th-century thatched theatres survive in the mountain villages east of Tonoshō. Performances are held on 3 May at the Rikyū Hachiman Shrine in Hitoyama (肥土山) and on the second Sunday in October at the Kasuga Shrine in Nakayama (中山).

🛏 Sleeping & Eating

Tonoshō offers a variety of hotels and simple places to eat, particularly along the road running straight back from the waterfront in Tonoshō.

Minshuku Maruse
MINSHUKU ¥

(民宿マルセ; ☎62-2385; http://new-port.biz/maruse/1.htm; per person from ¥3700; 🛜) This welcoming, neatly kept place next to Tonoshō's post office is a short walk from the ferry terminal. It has Japanese-style rooms with shared bathrooms. Meals are available and feature local seafood.

Shōdo-shima Olive Youth Hostel
HOSTEL ¥

(小豆島オリーブユースホステル; ☎82-6161; www.jyh.gr.jp/shoudo; 1072 Nishimura, Uchinomichō; dm members/nonmembers ¥3255/3885; 😊🛜) This pleasant hostel near the waterfront has bunk-bed dorms and tatami rooms. Meals and bike rental are available. Buses stop in front of the hostel (at the Shōdoshimi Orību-Yūsu-mae stop), or it's about a 20-minute walk from Kusakabe port.

Business Hotel New Port
HOTEL ¥¥

(ビジネスホテル・ニューポート; ☎62-6310; www.new-port.biz; s/tw from ¥3980/7400; 📧) Run by the same friendly management as at Minshuku Maruse, this small business hotel is handy if you want a base near the Tonoshō port. It has both Western-style and tatami rooms. Go right when you come out of the ferry terminal – it's on the right about a minute's walk away.

Resort Hotel Olivean
RESORT ¥¥¥

(リゾートホテルオリビアン; ☎65-2311; www.olivean.com; tw with meals from ¥24,600; 😊📧🛜💧) This grand complex has it all: tennis courts, open-air onsen, swimming pool, restaurants and sunset views from spacious Western- and Japanese-style accommodation. There are courtesy buses to the resort from Tonoshō.

★ Dutch Café Cupid & Cotton
CAFE

(ダッチカフェキューピッドアンドコトン; ☎82-4616; lunch set ¥850; ☉11am-5pm, closed Wed & Thu; 📧) Inside a cosy knick-knack-filled windmill on a hillside, Dutch Cafe serves savoury and sweet 'real Dutch' pancakes. Turn right at the top of the Olive Park complex and look for the small sign pointing up a narrow road on the left. The owners also have a campsite nearby, but this was temporarily closed at the time of writing.

ℹ BUS & FERRY COMBO

If you're going to Shōdo-shima from Okayama, pick up a *Kamome bus kippu* (one-way ¥1200), a discounted combination ticket covering the bus from Okayama Station to Shin-Okayama port plus the ferry to Shōdo-shima. They're sold at the booth in the bus terminal of Okayama Station, and in the Tonoshō ferry terminal.

SHŌDO-SHIMA FERRIES

ORIGIN	DESTINATION	FARE (¥)	DURATION	FREQUENCY (PER DAY)
Himeji	Fukuda	1480	1hr 40min	7
Shin-Okayama	Tonoshō	1000	70min	13
Takamatsu	Tonoshō (regular)	670	1hr	15
Takamatsu	Tonoshō (high speed)	1140	30min	16
Takamatsu	Ikeda	670	1hr	8
Takamatsu	Kusakabe (regular)	670	1hr	5
Takamatsu	Kusakabe (high speed)	1140	45min	5
Uno	Tonoshō (via Teshima)	1200	1½hr	7

ⓘ Information

Tonoshō, at the western end of the island, is the biggest town and the usual point of arrival from Takamatsu or Okayama. Check www.town.shodoshima.lg.jp for more information.

Tourist Information Booth (☑62-5300; ⊙8.30am-5.15pm) Inside the Tonoshō ferry terminal.

ⓘ Getting There & Away

There are several ferry routes to and from Shōdo-shima's ports.

ⓘ Getting Around

The most convenient way to see the island is by car and it's definitely worth hiring one for the day to take in all the scenic routes. Buses do not go everywhere and services are infrequent.

BICYCLE

Cycling can be enjoyable around the coast if you have plenty of time, but you'd want to be very keen to venture inland as there are some serious climbs. Bikes can also be rented at the youth hostel near Kusakabe.

Asahiya Rent-a-Cycle (旭屋レンタサイクル; ☑62-0162; gearless bikes per hr ¥300; ⊙8.30am-5pm) Inside the Asahiya hotel, opposite the post office in Tonoshō, a short walk from the ferry terminal.

Ishii Rent-a-Cycle (石井レンタサイクル; ☑62-1866; www7.ocn.ne.jp/~ishii-c/rental. htm; Olive-dōri; gearless bikes per day ¥1000, mountain & electric bikes ¥2000; ⊙8.30am-5pm) It's worth the walk here to get a bicycle with gears. It's about 2km from Tonoshō port. Ask at the ferry terminal for a town map with directions.

BUS

Shōdo-shima Olive Bus (小豆島オリーブバス; ☑62-0171; www.shodoshima-olive-bus. com) operates services around the island. The most frequent bus, at one or two per hour, runs between Tonoshō and Kusakabe ports, passing Ikeda and Olive Park. Some continue on to Sakate port, passing the Marukin Soy Sauce Historical Museum; some head north to Fukuda port. There are infrequent services along the north coast, inland to Nakayama, and to Tanoura. There are no services to the Monkey Park. A one-/two-day pass is ¥2000/2500, though if you're only taking the bus a couple of times it's cheaper to pay the individual fares as you go.

CAR

There are a handful of car-rental places. Note you can bring a car on some ferries, but it can cost more than hiring one on the island.

Orix Rent-a-Car (オリックスレンタカー小豆島; ☑62-4669; http://car.orix.co.jp; 6hr from ¥4725; ⊙8.30am-6pm) Has a basic touring map in English. Walk about two minutes along the road heading right out of the Tonoshō ferry terminal.

Naoshima   直島

☑087 / POP 3300

Until not too long ago, the arty isle of Naoshima was no different from many others in the Inland Sea: home to a dwindling population subsisting on the joint proceeds of a dying fishing industry and the old-age pension. Today, as the location of the Benesse Art Site Naoshima, the island is one of the area's biggest tourist attractions, offering a unique opportunity to see some of Japan's best contemporary art in gorgeous natural settings.

The project started in the early '90s, when the Benesse Corporation chose Naoshima as the setting for its growing collection of modern art. Naoshima now has a number of world-class art galleries and installations, and has attracted creative types from all over the country to set up home here.

In addition to the main sites, numerous works of outdoor art are situated around the coast, including the pumpkin sculpture by Kusama Yayoi that has become a symbol of the island.

◉ Sights & Activities

During holiday seasons the museums can become quite crowded and you may find you have to queue. At peak times at Chichū Art Museum, a 'timed ticket' system may be in place, designating the time you are able to purchase a ticket and enter.

★ Art House Project ART INSTALLATION
(家プロジェクト; www.benesse-artsite.jp/art-house; combined ticket ¥1000; ⊘10am-4.30pm, closed Mon) In the old fishing village of Honmura (本村), half a dozen traditional buildings have been restored and turned over to contemporary artists to use as the setting for creative installations. Highlights include Ōtake Shinrō's shacklike **Haisha** house, its Statue of Liberty sculpture rising up through the levels; James Turrell's experiment with light in **Minami-dera**, where you enter in total darkness...and wait; and Sugimoto Hiroshi's play on the traditional **Go'o Shrine**, with a glass staircase, and underground 'Stone Chamber' (those who are claustrophobic or wide of hip will want to give this a miss).

The sites are within walking distance of each other. Take the Naoshima bus to the Nōkyō-mae stop, where you can buy your Art House Project ticket from the tobacco shop and start exploring. Or buy a ticket at the first site you visit.

Benesse House Museum GALLERY
(ベネッセハウス; www.benesse-artsite.jp/benessehouse-museum; admission ¥1000; ⊘8am-9pm) Award-winning architect Andō Tadao designed this stunning museum and hotel on the south coast of the island. Among the works here are pieces by Andy Warhol, David Hockney, Jasper Johns, and Japanese artists such as Ōtake Shinrō.

Chichū Art Museum GALLERY
(地中美術館; www.benesse-artsite.jp/chichu; admission ¥2000; ⊘10am-6pm, to 5pm Oct-Feb, closed Mon) A short walk from Benesse House is this Andō Tadao creation. A work of art itself, the museum consists of a series of cool concrete-walled spaces sitting snugly underground. Lit by natural light, it provides a remarkable setting for several Monet water-lily paintings, some monumental sculptures by Walter de Maria and installations by James Turrell. Outside is the Chichū garden, created in the spirit of Monet's garden in Giverny.

Lee Ufan Museum GALLERY
(李禹煥美術館; www.benesse-artsite.jp/lee-ufan; admission ¥1000; ⊘10am-6pm, to 5pm Oct-Feb, closed Mon) The most recent addition to Benesse's suite of museums is yet another design from the irrepressible Andō. It houses works by the renowned Korean-born artist (and philosopher) Lee Ufan, who was a leading figure in the Mono-ha movement of the 1960s and 1970s.

★ Naoshima Bath – I Heart Yū PUBLIC BATH
(直島銭湯; www.naoshimasento.jp; admission ¥500; ⊘2-9pm Tue-Fri, 10am-9pm Sat & Sun, closed Mon) For a unique bathing experience, take a soak at this colourful fusion of Japanese bathing tradition and contemporary art, designed by Ōtake Shinrō. It's a couple of minutes' walk inland from Miyanoura port. Look for the building with the palm trees out front.

☆ Festivals & Events

Setouchi Triennale FESTIVAL
(瀬戸内国際芸術祭; Setouchi International Art Festival; http://setouchi-artfest.jp) This festival of art, music, drama and dance comes around every three years and has a packed calendar of events occurring on multiple Inland Sea islands, many on Naoshima. In 2013, the events were spread across three seasons, the last from October 5 to November 4. Check the website for the lowdown on event and ferry passes. It's highly recommended you book your accommodation well in advance if you plan on staying during the festival. And mark your diaries for the next one in 2016.

⌂ Sleeping

The accommodation scene is dominated by privately run *minshuku* (guesthouses). Not a lot of English is spoken, but locals are becoming increasingly used to foreign guests. If you prefer hotel-style facilities, Benesse House hotel is your only real option. Alternatively, stay in Okayama or Uno port on the mainland, or Takamatsu in Shikoku, and visit as a day trip. The Tourist Information Centre in Miyanoura has a complete list of lodgings. Rates increase during high season.

★**Tsutsuji-sō**   CAMPGROUND ¥

(つつじ荘; ☎892-2838; www.tsutsujiso.com; tents per person from ¥3675; ➲) Perfectly placed on the beachfront not far from the Benesse Art Site area is this encampment of Mongolian-style *pao* tents. The cosy tents sleep up to four, have a small fridge and heater (but no air-con), and shared bathroom facilities. The tent-averse can opt instead for one of the caravans or cottages. Meals are available if reserved in advance. Cash only.

Gallery Inn Kuraya   GUESTHOUSE ¥

(ギャラリーインくらや; ☎892-2253; http:// kuraya-naoshima.net; per person with/without breakfast from ¥4500/4000; ➲) Kuraya Gallery offers accommodation when it's not occupied by visiting artists. There's a tatami room in the house, or you can sleep in the small wood-floored gallery room opposite. Both share the bathroom. The lovely owner speaks very good English and there is a small cafe attached (irregular hours). Kuraya is near Honmura port, on the left if you're walking towards the Art House Project's 'Ishibashi'.

Minshuku Oyaji-no-Umi   MINSHUKU ¥

(民宿おやじの海; ☎090-5261-7670; http:// yopopo.moo.jp; per person incl breakfast ¥4200; @🛜) This is a good option for friendly, family-style lodgings, with tatami rooms (separated by sliding doors) and shared bathroom, in an old house close to the Art House Project in Honmura. Owners don't speak English; it's best to book via email if you don't speak Japanese. The entrance is next to the Cat Cafe.

Dormitory in Kūron   HOSTEL ¥

(ドミトリーin九龍; ☎892-2424; http://kaw-loon.gozaru.jp; dm ¥2800; @🛜) Basic dormitory accommodation just back from the ferry port in Miyanoura. Note that you'll pay ¥3500 if you show up without a reservation. Some English is spoken.

★**Benesse House**   BOUTIQUE HOTEL ¥¥¥

(☎892-3223; www.benesse-artsite.jp/en/benesse-house; tw/ste from ¥30,000/50,000; ➲) A stay at this unique Andō-designed hotel-museum is a fabulous experience for art and architecture enthusiasts. Take the monorail to the hilltop 'Oval' wing, where rooms are arranged around a pool of water open to the sky, stay by the sea at a 'Beach' suite, or stick close to the art in the 'Museum' lodgings.

Rooms have a clean, modern design and feature artworks from the Benesse collection. Best of all, you can roam around the Benesse House museum whenever the mood takes you.

✖ **Eating & Drinking**

There are a few cafes in the Art House Project area and near the port at Miyanoura. Not many places open in the evenings and hours can be irregular.

★**Shioya Diner**   CAFE ¥

(シオヤダイナー; dishes ¥400-1000; ⊙9am-9pm, closed Mon; 🛜📖) With rock n roll music, retro furniture and kitsch knick-knacks, Shioya is an odd mix of American diner and grandma's kitchen. The menu features tacos and chilli dogs, and they sometimes charcoal-grill Cajun chicken on the barbecue out front. It's a great place to relax over a coffee or a meal near Miyanoura port.

Cafe Salon Naka-Oku   CAFE, RESTAURANT ¥

(カフェサロン中奥; ☎892-3887; www.naka-oku.com; lunch from ¥650, dinner ¥380-750; ⊙11.30am-9pm, closed Tue; 📖) Up on a small hill at the rear of a farming plot, Naka-Oku is a good option in the Honmura area, and one of only a couple of places open in the evenings here. It's all wood-beamed warmth and cosiness, with homey specialities like *omuraisu* at lunchtime, and small dishes with drinks in the evening.

Genmai-Shinshoku Aisunao   CAFE ¥

(玄米心食あいすなお; http://aisunao.jp; meals ¥600-900; ⊙11am-5.30pm; ➲🍴) 🌱 A tranquil rest stop within the Art House Project area, Aisunao has seating on raised tatami flooring, and a decidedly health-conscious menu – try the tasty Aisunao lunch set, with local brown rice, soup and vegies. Desserts (such as soy-milk ice cream), juices and fairtrade coffees are also on offer. It's around the corner from 'Gokaisho'. Look for the sign with a picture of a bowl of rice.

Cin.na.mon   CURRY, BAR ¥

(シナモン; www.cin-na-mon.jp; meals ¥600-1000; ⊙11am-3pm & 5-10pm, closed Mon; 📖) The laid-back team here serve curries, cakes and smoothies by day, and open up the bar (with some light meals and snacks) at night. It's a short walk from the Miyanoura port. It also has **accommodation** (シナモン; ☎840-8133; www.cin-na-mon.jp; per person incl breakfast ¥4000).

TESHIMA

If there's not enough to inspire you on Naoshima, get yourself across to Teshima (豊島), a small island between Naoshima and Shōdo-shima. It has the curvacious concrete-shell **Teshima Art Museum** (admission ¥1500; ⏱10am-5pm, 10.30am-4pm Oct-Feb, closed Tue, also closed Wed & Thu Dec-Feb), and the oddly fascinating **Les Archives du Cœur** (admission ¥500; ⏱10am-5pm, to 4pm Oct-Feb, closed Tue, also closed Wed & Thu Dec-Feb), where you can listen to recordings of human heartbeats; for ¥1500 you can record your own and get a keepsake. Three ferries a day go from Naoshima to Teshima (not every day in low season), eight go from Uno port on the mainland (bound for Shōdo-shima), and three or four go from Takamatsu.

Museum Restaurant Issen   KAISEKI ¥¥¥
(日本料理一扇; ☎892-3223; www.benesse-artsite.jp/en/benessehouse/restaurant_cafe.html; breakfast & lunch from ¥2000, dinner courses from ¥6000; ⏱7.30-9.30am, 11.30am-2.30pm & 6-9.45pm; ⊖🔲) The artfully displayed *kaiseki* dinners at this Benesse House basement restaurant are almost too pretty to eat. Courses feature seafood, but there is a veg-dominated option (request a couple of days ahead), and the menu changes with the seasons. Breakfast and lunch are also served. Reservations are recommended.

❶ Information

The ATMs at the post offices in Miyanoura and Honmura take international cards. Ask at the tourist office for directions.

Tourist Information Centre (☎892-2299; www.naoshima.net; ⏱8.30am-6pm) In the Marine Station at the Miyanoura ferry port. Has a comprehensive bilingual map of the island (also downloadable from the website), a walking map, and a full list of accommodation options.

❶ Getting There & Away

Naoshima can be visited as a day trip from Okayama or Takamatsu, and it makes a good stopover if you're travelling between Honshū and Shikoku.

From Okayama, take the JR Uno line to Uno (¥570, about an hour); this usually involves a quick change of trains at Chayamachi. Ferries go to Naoshima's main port of Miyanoura from the port near Uno Station (¥280, 15 to 20 minutes, 13 daily). There are also ferries from Uno to the port of Honmura (¥280, 20 minutes, five daily).

From Takamatsu, ferries run to the port of Miyanoura (¥510, one hour, six to eight daily).

Ferry timetables are on the Naoshima map available on the tourist website, at www1.biz.biglobe.ne.jp/~shikoku (in Japanese), or as at the tourist offices in Okayama and Takamatsu.

❶ Getting Around

It's possible to get around the main sights on foot. For example, it's just over 2km from Miyanoura port to Honmura and the Art House Project area.

BICYCLE

Naoshima is great for cycling. **Cafe Ōgiya Rent-a-Cycle** (☎892-3642; per day ¥500; ⏱9am-7pm, to 6pm Dec-Feb) is inside the Marine Station at the Miyanoura ferry port. A few electric bikes are also available (per day ¥2000).

BUS

Minibuses run between Miyanoura, Honmura and Tsutsuji-sō once or twice an hour. It costs ¥100 per ride. From Tsutsuji-sō, there's a free Benesse shuttle, stopping at all the Benesse Art Site museums. In busy seasons buses can fill up quickly, especially towards the end of the day when people are returning to the port to catch ferries. Be sure to check the timetables and allow yourself enough time.

Kasaoka Islands   笠岡諸島

Located between Kurashiki and Fukuyama, the port of Kasaoka is the jumping-off point for six small islands connected to the mainland only by boat. In particular, the islands of Shiraishi-jima and Manabe-shima are worth visiting to enjoy the slower pace of life as it used to be lived all over the Inland Sea.

Kasaoka is 40 minutes west of Okayama and 25 minutes west of Kurashiki on the JR San-yō line. From the station, it's a five-minute stroll down to the port and the ferry terminal, from where eight **Sanyō Kisen** (三洋汽船; ☎0865-62-2866; www.sanyo-kisen.com) boats a day run to Shiraishi-jima (¥650 or ¥1130, 35 minutes or 22 minutes) and on to Manabe-shima (¥990 or ¥1710, one hour and 10 minutes or 44 minutes). Five of these are express services, which cost almost double but don't save that much time.

Shiraishi-jima 白石島

0865 / POP 750

Sleepy Shiraishi-jima is popular in the summer for its beaches and there are some good walking paths. Go-everywhere Buddhist saint Kōbō Daishi stopped off here on his way back from China in 806; the temple associated with him, **Kairyū-ji** (開龍寺), incorporates a trail of small shrines leading to a huge boulder on top of the hill.

Visitors can stay at the great-value **International Villa** (per person ¥3500). The villa is a large house atop a hill, with spacious living areas and kitchen, and an outdoor deck with views of the sea. There are five bedrooms and amenities are shared. It's particularly good for groups or families. For reservations, contact International Villa Group (p437) in Okayama. Alternatively, there are several *minshuku* on the beach, including **San-chan** (民宿さんちゃん; ☑68-3169; http://fhp.jp/sanchan; per person with/without two meals ¥6000/3000), with no-frills Japanese-style rooms with shared bathrooms.

During summer, resident expat Amy Chavez runs the **Mooo! Bar** (http://daily-moooo.blogspot.com.au; ☺summer) on the beach and can also arrange sailing trips to other islands. It's also possible to rent windsurfs and sea kayaks (per person per hour ¥1000).

There are a handful of eateries on the island, including San-chan, though hours are irregular outside of summer. If you're staying at the Villa, make sure you bring groceries along with you.

Manabe-shima 真鍋島

☑0865 / POP 300

Manabe-shima is home to more cats than people, and its one small town is an atmospheric maze of old wooden houses, a solitary village shop that has been in business since the Meiji period, and an old-fashioned school with fewer than 10 pupils at last count. As with everywhere in this part of Japan, Kōbō Daishi got here first – the great man spent time at the **Enpukuji** (円福寺) temple. More recently, the island and all its characters have been wonderfully captured in Florent Chavouet's illustrated book *Manabé Shima*. The locals are sure to show you a copy (and point themselves out in it).

A good reason to venture out here is to stay at the waterfront ryokan **Santora** (島宿三虎; ☑68-3515; www.kcv.ne.jp/~santora; per person with two meals from ¥10,500; ☎🖥) 🖊 so you can laze about in its outdoor salt-water bath while watching boats sail by. The rooms are spacious, the shared indoor bathroom has sea views, and the meals feature local seafood and vegies grown by the friendly owners. Those on a tighter budget can ask for the 'easy plan' (¥7000 per person), which gets you a pared-down supper and light breakfast. Or upgrade and go for one of the *hanare* (separate) cabins (from ¥12,600 per person with meals), which have private bathrooms and huge balconies looking out to sea.

There are few places to eat out on the island (most with irregular hours) – the helpful staff at the ferry-terminal office can give you some tips.

YAMAGUCHI & AROUND

Yamaguchi 山口

☑083 / POP 196,600

During the 100 years of civil war that bedevilled Japan until the country was reunited under the Tokugawa in the early 17th century, Yamaguchi prospered as an alternative capital to chaotic Kyoto. In 1550 Jesuit missionary Francis Xavier paused for two months here on his way to the imperial capital, and quickly returned when he was unable even to find the emperor in Kyoto. Yamaguchi today is a surprisingly small prefectural capital with a handful of sights.

⦿ Sights & Activities

St Francis Xavier Memorial Church   CHURCH
(ザビエル記念聖堂; www.xavier.jp; donation ¥100, ☺9am-5pm) Yamaguchi was a major centre of Christian missionary activity before the religion was outlawed in 1589. This church has the look of a large tent, and sits above the town in Kameyama-kōen. Built in 1952 in honour of St Francis Xavier, it burned down in 1991 and was rebuilt in 1998. The ground-floor **Christian museum** (admission ¥300; ☺9am-5pm, closed Wed) contains exhibits on the life of Xavier and the early history of Christianity in Japan, most of it in Japanese only. Steps opposite the church lead up the hill to views of Yamaguchi.

Yamaguchi

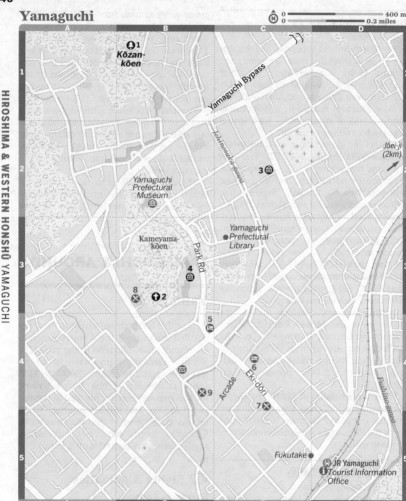

Yamaguchi Prefectural Art Museum GALLERY
(山口県立美術館; www.yma-web.jp; 3-1 Kameyama-chō; admission ¥300; ⏰9am-5pm, closed Mon) This interesting gallery focuses on art of the region, with three rooms showing work from their varied permanent collection, leafy grounds featuring modern sculpture, and regular special exhibitions (admission extra).

Yamaguchi Furusato Heritage Centre HISTORIC BUILDING
(山口ふるさと伝承総合センター; www.c-able.ne.jp/~denshou; 12 Shimotatekōji; ⏰9am-5pm) **FREE** The ground floor of the 1886 sake

merchant building (the Manabi-kan; まなび館) has a small display of local crafts, including some Ōuchi dolls, and the building itself is interesting. Go upstairs to get a closer look at the large dark-wood beams, and look in the garden for the delightful tea-ceremony room made from old sake-brewing barrels. In the modern learning centre behind the old building you can see lacquerware being made.

★Kōzan-kōen PARK, TEMPLES
(香山公園) North of the town centre is Kōzan Park, where the five-storey pagoda of **Rurikō-ji** (瑠璃光寺), a National Treasure dating from 1404, is picturesquely situated

Yamaguchi

beside a small lake. The park is also the site of the **Tōshun-ji** (洞春寺) and the graves of the Mōri lords.

Jōei-ji   TEMPLE, GARDEN
(常栄寺; 2001 Miyano-shimo; garden admission ¥300; ⊙ garden 8am-5pm, to 4.30pm Oct-Mar) About 4km northeast of JR Yamaguchi Station, temple Jōei-ji is notable for its simple, stone-dotted Zen garden, **Sesshutei**, designed by the painter Sesshū. From the garden, a trail leads uphill through the woods to several more temples. You can reach the temple by bicycle or taxi (about ¥1250) from central Yamaguchi. Or take the train two stops to Miyano and from there it's about 1km to walk.

Yuda Onsen   ONSEN
(湯田温泉; http://yudaonsen.com) Just west of Yamaguchi city is the 800-year-old Yuda Onsen. The area is covered in a rash of hotels and bathing facilities, mostly along a busy main road, which isn't really a place for tottering between baths in your *yukata*. Still, a soak here is a nice way to spend a few hours.

You can take a dip in the indoor and outdoor baths of **Yu-no-Machi Club** (湯の町倶楽部; admission ¥600; ⊙ 11am-10pm), use the baths at the large **Hotel Kamefuku** (ホテルかめ福; www.kamefuku.com; admission ¥800; ⊙ 11.30am-10pm) or, for a taste of luxury and a peaceful garden setting, head to **Sansuien** (山水園; www.yuda-sansuien.com; admission ¥1600; ⊙ 10am-9pm). For a full list and map of the baths and hotels, drop in first at the **tourist information office** (☑ 901-0150; 2-1-23 Yuda Onsen; ⊙ 9am-7pm) on the main road.

Buses run regularly to Yuda Onsen bus stop from Yamaguchi Station (¥190, 10 minutes). They drop you on the main strip, Yuda Onsen-dōri, a short walk from the tourist office (just keep walking in the direction of the bus). Yuda Onsen also has a station, one stop on the local train line from Yamaguchi (¥140). From the station, follow the red road for about 1km to get to the busy main T-intersection and turn right for the tourist office.

★ Festivals & Events

Gion Matsuri   TRADITIONAL DANCE
On 20, 24 and 27 July, during the Gion Matsuri, the *Sagi-mai* (Egret Dance) is held at Yasaka-jinja.

Tanabata Chōchin Matsuri   LANTERN FESTIVAL
From 6 to 7 August, thousands of decorated lanterns illuminate the city.

🛏 Sleeping

There's not a great deal of choice in central Yamaguchi, but nearby Yuda Onsen is a good base, especially if you like the idea of an on-site onsen with your accommodation. There are also some good-value Western-style chain hotels clustered around Shin-Yamaguchi Station, including the **Comfort Hotel** (コンフォートホテル新山口; ☑ 974-2511; www.choice-hotels.jp/cfyamagu; 1255-1 Ogori-Shimogo; s/tw inc breakfast from ¥5500/8600; ⊙ @ 🖥), where rates include a buffet-style breakfast.

Taiyō-dō Ryokan   RYOKAN ¥
(太陽堂旅館; ☑ 922-0897; fax 922-1152; 2-3 Komeya-chō; per person from ¥3000) The Taiyō-dō is a friendly old ryokan in the shopping arcade just off Eki-dōri. The tatami rooms are quite a good size, and there are large communal bathrooms (which you may have private use of, depending on how busy they are). It helps to be able to speak some Japanese here.

Yu Bettō Nohara   RYOKAN ¥¥
(湯別当野原; ☑ 922-0018; www.yubettou-nohara.com; 7-8 Yuda Onsen; per person with 2 meals ¥9000-19,000; ⊙) You'll be welcomed by keen staff at this centrally located ryokan in Yuda Onsen. Most rooms are of the traditional tatami variety; some have both tatami and an area with two single beds. Not all have private bathrooms. Meals are *kaiseki*-style with a seafood focus, and you can stay without meals or with breakfast only.

Sunroute Kokusai Hotel HOTEL ¥¥
(サンルート国際ホテル山口; ☎923-3610; www.hsy.co.jp; 1-1 Nakagawara-chō; s/tw from ¥6825/12,180; ❀@) This modern hotel has stylish, neutral-toned rooms, and is in a good location in the centre of town at the base of tree-lined Park Rd.

★**Matsudaya Hotel** RYOKAN ¥¥¥
(ホテル松田屋; ☎922-0125; www.matsudaya hotel.co.jp; 3-6-7 Yuda Onsen; per person with two meals from ¥18,000; @☎) At this centuries-old, now modernised, ryokan, you can bathe in the tub where once dipped the plotters of the Meiji Restoration. The ryokan's garden setting and excellent service will likely ease any present-day rebellious thoughts. Matsudaya is on the main drag in Yuda Onsen.

✕ Eating & Drinking

★**Sabō Kō** CAFE ¥
(茶房幸; 1-2-39 Dōjōmonzen; dishes ¥600-900; ❀11.30am-6pm, closed Tue; ❀) A cosy atmosphere prevails in this low-ceilinged little eatery, where customers perch on wooden stools sipping coffee. The speciality on the Japanese-only menu is the generous, rustic *omuraisu*, but there are also curries and *soba*. Look for the small wood-covered place with ceramic pots sticking out of the exterior plasterwork.

Frank RESTAURANT, BAR ¥¥
(フランク; 2nd fl, 2-4-19 Dōjōmonzen; meals ¥880-1200; ❀11.30am-6pm, to 1am Fri, Sat & Sun) Overlooking the main shopping street, this stylish cafe-restaurant serves Asian-style rice dishes, pastas and curries, and is a relaxing space for a late-night wine or cocktail. Look for 'Frank' painted on the wall at the entrance, just off Eki-dōri.

La Francesca ITALIAN ¥¥¥
(ラフランチェスカ; ☎934-1888; http://la-francesca.com/restaurant.html; 7-1 Kameyama; lunch/dinner sets ¥1890/5250; ❀11.30am-2.30pm & 5.30-9pm; ❀▥) Excellent Italian food is the main attraction at this elegant Tuscan-style villa, on the left as you head up the hill to the St Francis Xavier Memorial Church. There are set-course options for lunch and dinner, and an à la carte evening menu with dishes from ¥1470. The menu changes seasonally.

ℹ Information

Central Post Office (中央郵便局; ❀9am-7pm, to 5pm Sat, to 12.30pm Sun, ATM 7am-11.30pm Mon-Fri, 9am-9pm Sat, 9am-7pm Sun) Postal and currency exchange services. ATM accepting international cards.

Tourist Information Office (山口観光案内所; ☎933-0090; http://yamaguchi-city.jp; ❀9am-6pm) Inside Yamaguchi Station. There is also an office at Shin-Yamaguchi (☎972-6373; 2nd fl, Shin-Yamaguchi Station; ❀9am-6pm), at the *shinkansen* exit side.

ℹ Getting There & Away

BUS

Chūgoku JR Bus (www.chugoku-jrbus.co.jp) runs nine to 11 buses daily to Hagi (Higashi-Hagi Station; ¥1680, one hour and 10 minutes) from Yamaguchi Station, some originating at Shin-Yamaguchi. **Bōchō Bus** (www.bochobus.co.jp) runs buses to Higashi-Hagi Station (¥1970, 1½ hours, at least hourly) from Shin-Yamaguchi.

TRAIN

Yamaguchi Station is on the JR Yamaguchi line. Shin-Yamaguchi station is 10km southwest in Ogōri on the San-yō *shinkansen* line, which connects to Shimonoseki, Hiroshima, and to Osaka in the east. The Yamaguchi local service connects the Shin-Yamaguchi and Yamaguchi stations (¥230, 25 minutes).

ℹ Getting Around

It's possible to walk to the central sights from Yamaguchi Station, but it's handy to hire a bicycle for the outlying temple areas. Jōei-ji, for example, is about 4km away (closer to Miyano Station). A taxi might be an easier option if you don't want to walk or cycle. For bikes, try **Fukutake** (福武; ☎922-0915; Eki-dōri 1-4-6; per day ¥700; ❀8am-7pm) just across from the station.

Yuda Onsen is served by bus or train from Yamaguchi and Shin-Yamaguchi.

Akiyoshi-dai 秋吉台

Within the **Akiyoshi-dai Quasi-National Park**, the rolling Akiyoshi-dai tablelands are dotted with curious rock spires, beneath which are hundreds of limestone caverns. One of these is **Akiyoshi-dō** (秋芳洞; admission ¥1200; ❀8.30am-4.30pm), the largest limestone cave in Japan.

It is size that makes the cave impressive. It extends about 10km, at some points 100m wide (though public access is limited to a 1km section), and a river flows through it. The watery reflection of the towering cave walls at times gives the dizzying impression you're walking over a deep ravine. But you can leave the spelunking gear at home – there's a paved route, regular push-button information points that belt out explanations in various languages, and an elevator in the middle that takes you up to a lookout. Despite the development, Akiyoshi-dō is a good side trip from Yamaguchi or Hagi, or a stop en route between the two.

For more on the cave and the surrounding plateau region, a great area for nature walks, go to www.karusuto.com. Information is also available at tourist offices in Yamaguchi and Hagi.

ℹ️ Getting There & Away

Buses go to the cave from major stations in the region. Buses leaving from Yamaguchi Station also stop at Yuda Onsen. JR pass holders coming from Yamaguchi should get the JR bus from Yamaguchi Station.

Yamaguchi ¥1130, 55 minutes, 10 daily

Shin-Yamaguchi ¥1140, 45 minutes, nine daily

Higashi-Hagi ¥1760, one hour and 10 minutes, 10.50am and 1.15pm; returning 1pm and 3.40pm

Shimonoseki (via Mine) ¥1730, two hours, eight daily

Tsuwano 津和野

☑ 0856 / POP 8400

A highlight of this region, Tsuwano is a quiet, 700-year-old mountain town with an important shrine, a ruined castle, and an evocative samurai quarter. It also has a wonderful collection of carp swimming in the roadside water channels – in fact, there are far more carp here than people.

◉ Sights & Activities

◉ Tonomachi District

Only the walls and some fine old gates from the former samurai quarter of Tonomachi (殿町) remain, but it's an attractive area for strolling. The water channels that run alongside the picturesque Tonomachi road are home to numerous carp, bred to provide food in the case of emergency. As you're walking, look out for *sugidama* (cedar balls) hanging outside a few old sake breweries.

Catholic Church   CHURCH
(津和野カトリック教会; Tonomachi; ◷8am-5.30pm Apr-Nov, to 5pm Dec-Mar) The church here is a reminder of the town's Christian history. Hidden Christians from Nagasaki

were exiled here in the early Meiji period. It's interesting to peep inside to see tatami mats instead of pews.

Anno Art Museum   GALLERY
(安野光雅美術館; 60-1 Ushiroda; admission ¥800; ◷9am-5pm, closed 2nd Thu in Mar, Jun, Sep & Dec) Tsuwano-born Anno Mitsumasa is famous for his wonderfully detailed illustrated books, including *Anno's Alphabet* and *Anno's Journey*. You can see his work at this traditional-looking white building near the station, where the large collection is rotated throughout the year.

Katsushika Hokusai Art Museum   MUSEUM
(葛飾北斎美術館; 254 Ushiroda-guchi; admission ¥500; ◷9.30am-5pm, closed Tue, closed Dec & Jan) This museum features a small collection by the Edo-period artist and his disciples, and has an interesting display showing the wood-block process plate by plate.

◉ Around Town

★**Taikodani-Inari-jinja**   SHINTŌ SHRINE
(太鼓谷稲成神社; ◷8am-4.30pm) Just above the castle chairlift station, Taikodani-Inari-jinja, built in 1773 by the seventh lord Kamei Norisada, is one of the five major Inari shrines in Japan. Walk up the hillside to it through a tunnel created by hundreds of torii. At night the torii are lit up, creating a beautiful sight from the town. There are fabulous views of the valley and mountains from the top.

Tsuwano-jō   CASTLE
(津和野城; chairlift ¥450; ◷chairlift 9am-5pm, irregular hours winter) The broken walls of Tsuwano-jō brood over the valley. A slightly rickety chairlift takes you slowly up the hillside, and there's a further 15-minute walk through the woods to the castle ruins. There's nothing here but the walls and, of course, great views.

Morijuku Museum   MUSEUM
(杜塾美術館; 542 Morimura; admission for foreigners ¥300; ◷9am-5pm) This museum is housed in a 150-year-old building that once served as the home of a *shōya* (village headman). Downstairs is a collection of soft-edged scenes painted by local-born artist Nakao Shō, a roomful of bullfight sketches by Goya, and a framed set of beautifully embroidered Taishō-era kimono collars. The caretaker will gladly point out the features of the building, including the pinhole camera hidden away upstairs.

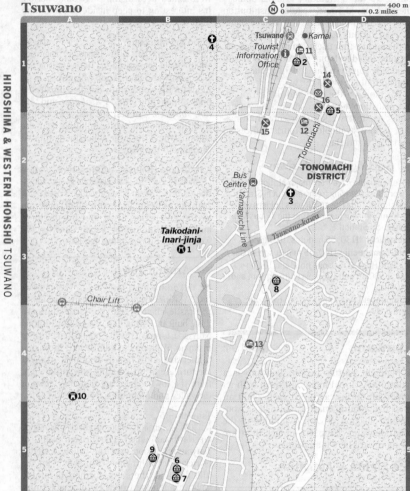

Tsuwano

◎ Top Sights

1 Taikodani-Inari-jinja B3

◎ Sights

2 Anno Art Museum C1
3 Catholic Church C2
4 Chapel of St Maria B1
5 Katsushika Hokusai Art Museum D1
6 Mori Ōgai Former Residence B5
7 Mori Ōgai Memorial Museum B5
8 Morijuku Museum C3
9 Nishi Amane Former Residence B5

10 Tsuwano-jō A4

🛏 Sleeping

11 Hoshi Ryokan C1
12 Noren Yado Meigetsu C2
13 Wakasagi-no-Yado C4

🍴 Eating

14 Pommes Soufflées D1
15 Tsurube C2
16 Yūki D1

Chapel of St Maria
CHAPEL

(マリア聖堂) The tiny Maria-dō dates from 1951. More than 150 'hidden Christians' were imprisoned in a Buddhist temple on this site in the early years of the Meiji Restoration; 36 died before a law allowing freedom of religion was passed in 1873. A procession is held here on 3 May.

👁 South of Town

Nishi Amane
Former Residence
HISTORIC BUILDING

(西周旧居; ⊘9am-5pm) **FREE** It's a pleasant walk down the river from Tsuwano town centre to see the peaked-roof former residence of Nishi Amane (1829–97), a philosopher and political scientist prominent in the Meiji government.

Mori Ōgai
Former Residence
HISTORIC BUILDING

(森鴎外旧宅; www.town.tsuwano.lg.jp/shisetsu/ougai.html; admission ¥100; ⊘9am-5pm, closed Mon Dec–early Mar) Across the river from the Nishi Amane house is the old residence of Mori Ōgai (1862–1922), a highly regarded novelist who served as a physician in the Imperial Japanese Army. It's next to the **Mori Ōgai Memorial Museum**.

Nagomi-no-sato
ONSEN

(なごみの里; www.nagomi-nosato.com; 256 Washibara; admission ¥600; ⊘10am-9pm, closed Thu) After a day of sightseeing, take a soak at this onsen complex. It's about 2.5km from the centre of town, or a 15-minute walk from the Mori Ōgai Memorial Museum. Buses do travel there from the station, but there are only three a day (¥200, eight minutes).

🎊 Festivals & Events

★ Yabusame
ARCHERY

At Washibara Hachiman-gū (鷺原八幡宮), south of town about 4km from the station, crowds gather to watch archery contests on horseback on the second Sunday in April.

Sagi-mai Matsuri
TRADITIONAL DANCE

The Heron Dance Festival sees processions of dancers dressed as herons, on 20 and 27 July.

🛏 Sleeping

You could see Tsuwano in a day trip from Yamaguchi, but staying the night gives you the chance to enjoy one of the town's *minshuku* or ryokan, and a walk through the quiet lamp-lit streets in the evening. For information in English online, go to www.gambo-ad.com/english and click on 'Tsuwano' – a few of the local ryokan are listed.

★ Hoshi Ryokan
MINSHUKU ¥

(星旅館; ☎72-0136; fax 72-0241; 53-6 Ushiroda; per person with/without meals ¥7000/5000) You'll get a warm, family welcome at this big, creaky *minshuku* located a minute from the station. The tatami rooms are spacious and there's a shared family-style bathroom.

Wakasagi-no-Yado
MINSHUKU ¥

(民宿わかさぎの宿; fax 72-1146; 98-6 Morimuraguchi; per person with/without 2 meals ¥7500/4500) This well-kept *minshuku* is on the main road between Tonomachi and the Mori Ōgai house. Bathrooms are shared. Walking from the station, look for the building with a diamond-pattern tile design on the facade and a curtain with a picture of a heron.

Noren Yado Meigetsu
RYOKAN ¥¥

(のれん宿明月; ☎72-0685; fax 72-0637; 665 Ushiroda-guchi; per person with two meals from ¥10,000) This is a traditional ryokan on a narrow lane in the Tonomachi area. *Fusuma* (sliding screen doors) slide open in the rooms to reveal a garden, and there are soothing, wood-panelled shared bathrooms. Some rooms have private bathrooms. Look for the old-fashioned gate with a red-tiled roof.

🍴 Eating & Drinking

There are a few cafes and eateries on the main Tonomachi street, and more along the (less picturesque) street that runs directly south from the station. Not many places open at night, as people tend to eat at their accommodation. If you're looking for something in the evening, try the road that runs south from the station. Restaurants may also close if it's quiet, especially during winter.

★ Tsurube
NOODLES ¥

(つるべ; 384-1 Ushoroda-guchi; dishes ¥525-900; ⊘11am-4pm, closed Fri; 📶) The speciality here is fresh wheat noodles handmade on the premises, going into filling dishes like *sansai udon* (noodles with wild vegetables) and *umeboshi udon* (noodles with dried plum). For a little extra, have a side of *omusubi* (rice ball). Tsurube is next to a small graveyard.

Yūki
FISH ¥¥

(遊亀; ☎72-0162; 271-4 Ushiroda; meals ¥1300-3000; ⊘11am-3pm) The *tsuwano teishoku* (a carp-themed sampler of local dishes) is recommended at this elegantly rustic restaurant,

OFF THE BEATEN TRACK

CHŌMON GORGE

If you're travelling between Yamaguchi and Tsuwano, consider a stop at Chōmon-kyō (長門峡), a gorge with a walking track, waterfalls, swimming pools and beautiful colours in autumn. The gorge entrance is just near Chōmon-kyō station on the JR Yamaguchi line.

which has wooden tables and the sound of running water. There are *koi* (carp) in a pool in the floor here, and more on the menu. Look for the old-fashioned building with a small pine tree outside. Dinner by appointment only.

Pommes Soufflées ITALIAN ¥¥
(ポンム・スフレ; ☎72-2778; www.tsuwano. ne.jp/pomme; 284 Ushiroda; dishes ¥850-1700; ◷10am-9pm, closed Thu; ◉) The menu at this modern cafe-restaurant includes pastas and pizzas, plus there's a range of sweet bready items you can have with your coffee. Dinner course menus are from ¥2000. Reservations are recommended in the evening.

ⓘ Information

Post Office (◷9am-4pm Mon-Fri, ATM 8.45am-6pm Mon-Fri, 9am-5pm Sat, 9am-1pm Sun) Has an ATM accepting international cards.
Tourist Information Office (津和野町観光協会; ☎72-1771; www.tsuwano.ne.jp/kanko; ◷9am-5pm) Immediately to the right as you exit the station. Audio sightseeing guides are available for rent (per day ¥300). Also has a computer for internet access (per 30 minutes ¥100).

ⓘ Getting There & Around

Most attractions are within walking or cycling distance of the station. There is a local bus service but it's not of much use to travellers and runs only a few times a day. Rent bikes at **Kamai** (貸自転車かまい; bike hire per 2hr/day ¥500/800; ◷8am-sunset), across from the station.

BUS

Long-distance buses go to Hagi (¥2130, one hour and 45 minutes, five daily). There are also overnight buses to Kōbe/Osaka and Tokyo.

TRAIN

Tsuwano is on the JR Yamaguchi line, which runs from Shin-Yamaguchi and Yamaguchi in the south, to Masuda on the Japan Sea coast (which con-nects to the San-in line). There are a few direct trains from Shin-Yamaguchi, otherwise there's a change at Yamaguchi. The *super oki* service from Yamaguchi will shave about 20 minutes off the trip, but costs more than double the standard fare.
Yamaguchi ¥950, one hour and 10 minutes
Shin-Yamaguchi ¥1110, one hour and 15 minutes (direct)
Masuda ¥570, 40 minutes

STEAM TRAIN

The **SL Yamaguchi** (www.c571.jp; adult/child ¥1620/800) steam train trundles through the scenic valleys from Shin-Yamaguchi to Tsuwano between mid-March and late November on weekends and holidays. It's a fun way to travel and is very popular; check the latest schedules and book well ahead at JR and tourist information offices.

Shimonoseki 下関

☎083 / POP 280,900

At the extreme western tip of Honshū, Shimonoseki is separated from Kyūshū by a narrow strait, famous for a decisive 12th-century clash between rival samurai clans. The expressway crosses the Kanmon Straits (Kanmon-kaikyō) on the Kanmon-bashi, while another road, the *shinkansen* railway line and the JR railway line all tunnel underneath. You can even walk to Kyūshū through a tunnel under the water. Shimonoseki is also an important connecting point to South Korea. The town is famous for its seafood, particularly *fugu,* the potentially lethal pufferfish.

◉ Sights & Activities

Kyūshū is just across the water and a good side trip from Shimonoseki is a visit to the 'retro' port town of Mojikō (p654).

★**Karato Ichiba** MARKET
(唐戸市場; www.karatoichiba.com; 5-50 Karato; ◷5am-1pm Mon-Sat, 9am-3pm Sun) A highlight of a trip to Shimonoseki is an early-morning visit to the Karato fish market. It's a great opportunity to try sashimi for breakfast or lunch, and the fish doesn't get any fresher – a fair bit of it will still be moving. The best days to come are Friday to Sunday, when stallholders set up tables selling *bentō* of sashimi and cooked dishes made from the day's catch. You can take away or eat at the counters on the mezzanine level. Note that the market is closed on some Wednesdays.

Buses to Karato (¥190) leave from outside the station and take about seven minutes.

Shimonoseki Kaikyō-kan AQUARIUM

(海響館; www.kaikyokan.com; 6-1 Arukapōto; adult/child ¥2000/900; ⏱9.30am-5.30pm) In Karato, Shimonoseki's aquarium has penguins, dolphins, and sea-lion shows, plus a blue-whale skeleton and tanks of *fugu*.

Akama-jingū SHINTŌ SHRINE

(赤間神宮; 4-1 Amidaiji-chō; ⏱24hr) Bright vermilion, Akama-jinjū is a shrine dedicated to the seven-year-old emperor Antoku, who died in 1185 in the battle of Dan-no-ura. At the left side of the shrine is a statue of Mimi-nashi Hōichi (Earless Hōichi), the blind bard whose musical talents get him into trouble with ghosts in a story made famous by Lafcadio Hearn.

The shrine is between Karato and Hinoyama, about a five-minute walk from the Karato market area. From the station, get off the bus at the Akama-jingū-mae bus stop (¥230, 10 minutes).

Hino-yama Park PARK

(火の山公園) About 5km northeast of Shimonoseki Station, there are superb views over the Kanmon Straits from the top of 268m-high Hino-yama. To get to the ropeway (火の山ロープウエイ; one-way/return ¥300/500; ⏱10am-5pm Mar-Nov, closed Tue & Wed), get off the bus at Mimosusōgawa (御裳川; ¥230). From here it's a steep 10-minute walk to the ropeway entrance. There are buses that drop you at the entrance (Hino-yama ropeway stop), which run hourly from the station.

Dan-no-ura Memorial MEMORIAL

(壇ノ浦銅像) This memorial marks the spot where the decisive clash between the Minamoto and Taira clans took place in 1185. Here, Taira no Tokiko plunged into the sea with the young emperor Antoku in her arms, rather than surrender to the enemy. The statues depict Yoshitsune (the victorious Minamoto general) and Taira no Tomomori, who tied an anchor to his feet and leapt into the sea at Dan-no-ura when it became clear that his side had lost. Local legend holds that the Heike crabs that live in these waters and have strange face-like patternings on their shells are the reincarnations of angry Taira warriors. It's across the road from the Mimosusōgawa bus stop.

Kanmon Tunnel TUNNEL

(関門トンネル人道; bike admission ¥20; ⏱6am-10pm) FREE This is where you come to get that picture of yourself with one foot in Honshū and the other in Kyūshū.

For the 780m submarine walk to Kyūshū, head down to the tunnel via the lifts by the Mimosusōgawa bus stop.

Kaikyō Yume Tower TOWER

(海峡ゆめタワー; www.yumetower.jp; 3-3-1 Buzenda-chō; observatory ¥300; ⏱9.30am-9.30pm) This 153m tower looks like a midget skyscraper topped by a futuristic billiard ball. Head to the observatory for 360-degree views.

◉ Chōfu 長府

Chōfu, east of Shimonoseki Station along the coastal road, is home to the old castle town area. While little remains of the castle itself, there are earth walls and samurai gates, several temples and shrines, and inviting narrow streets, making it an atmospheric spot for a wander.

The **Shimonoseki City Art Museum** (下関市立美術館; www.city.shimonoseki.yamaguchi.jp/bijutsu; Chōfu-Kuromon Higashi-machi 1-1; admission ¥200, extra during special exhibitions; ⏱9.30am-5pm, closed Mon) is on the main road at the edge of the old area. It houses an eclectic collection of local art, which is rotated based on changing themes. There are regular temporary exhibits, sometimes of international artists. Across the road from the museum is pretty **Chōfu-teien** (長府庭園; admission ¥200; ⏱9am-5pm), a garden set around a pond and famous for its flowers in spring and autumn.

A few minutes' walk along the main road from the garden, turn inland to enter the castle-town area. Follow the signs and the small river, Dangu-gawa (壇具川), to walk up to National Treasure **Kōzan-ji** (功山寺; ⏱9am-5pm). This is the family burial temple of the local Mōri lords, which has a Zen-style hall dating from 1327. The narrow streets in the area near the temple feature old walls and gates, and close by is the impressive **Chōfu Mōri Residence** (長府毛利邸; admission ¥200; ⏱9am-5pm), a well-preserved 100-year-old home and garden.

There are a few cafes dotted around Chōfu; a good lunch stop is cafe Antiques & Oldies (p457).

Chōfu is about 20 minutes by bus from Shimonoseki Station. Buses run regularly along the main coastal road, stopping at Karato along the way. For the art museum and garden, get off at Bijutsukan-mae (¥350); for the castle-town area, get off at Jōkamachi-Chōfu (¥370), a couple of stops further along.

Shimonoseki

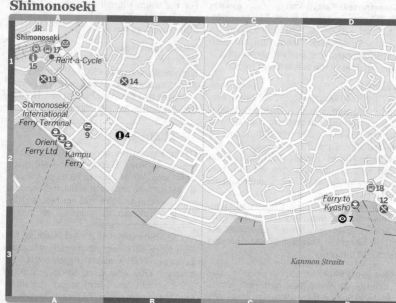

🎎 Festivals & Events

Sentei Festival   TRADITIONAL FESTIVAL
Held at Akama-jingū 2 to 4 May to remember the Heike women who worked as prostitutes to pay for rites for their fallen relatives. On 3 May women dressed as Heian-era courtesans form a colourful procession at the shrine.

Kanmon Straits Fireworks Festival
                              FIREWORKS
(Hanabi Taikai) A spectacular fireworks display occurring on both sides of the straits at the same time. Held on 13 August.

🛏 Sleeping

⭐ Hinoyama Youth Hostel   HOSTEL ¥
(火の山ユースホステル; ☎ 222-3753; www. e-yh.net/shimonoseki; 3-47 Mimosusogawa-chō; dm ¥3200; ☀@🛜) Amazing views and welcoming service make this one of the best youth hostels in Western Honshū. Take a bus (¥230, 25 minutes, hourly) from the station to Hinoyama, from where it's a short walk. Note that the caretakers are sometimes pop – let them know if you're coming to drop off your bags.

Kaikyō View Shimonoseki   HOTEL ¥¥
(海峡ビューしものせき; ☎ 229-0117; www. kv-shimonoseki.com; 3-58 Mimosusogawa-chō; per person with two meals from ¥9975) Perched up on Hino-yama, Kaikyō View has professional service and the choice of Japanese- or Western-style rooms. Some of the Japanese-style rooms don't have private bathrooms. The hotel has a fabulous onsen with sea views – nonguests can also use it from 11am to 3pm (entry ¥700), except Wednesday.

Dormy Inn Shimonoseki   HOTEL ¥¥
(ドーミーイン下関; ☎ 223-5489; www.hotespa. net/hotels/shimonoseki; 3-40 Shinmachi; s/d from ¥6300/9800; ☀@) This modern hotel gets a vote for having a top-floor onsen, where you can look out over the straits and bathe under a *fugu*-shaped lantern. Rooms are stylish, though small, and it's a good central location. There's a courtesy shuttle to the station in the morning, and from the station in the evening (though it's not far to walk).

🍴 Eating

Close to the fish market is the **Kamon Wharf** area with eateries and shops specialising in local goodies. Seekers of only-in-Japan cuisine can look out for the *uni*-flavoured ice cream (うにソフトクリーム; sea urchin) and *fugu* burgers (ふぐバーガー). Note that whale meat (*kujira*) is on the menu at many seafood places in Shimonoseki. Check for くじら or クジラ if you'd rather avoid it.

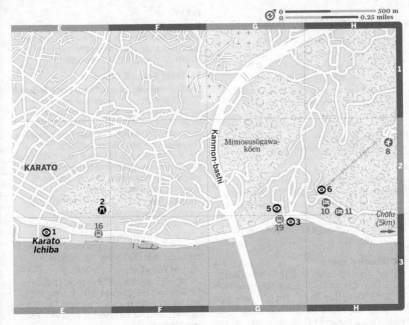

Shimonoseki

For easy eating near the station, head to the upper floors of the **Sea Mall Shimonoseki** shopping complex, where there are restaurants serving local and international food, all with menus and displays in the windows.

Kaiten Karato Ichiba Sushi　SUSHI, SASHIMI ¥
(海転からと市場寿司; www.kaitenkaratoichiba-zusi.com; 2nd fl, 5-50 Karato; per plate ¥105-525; ⊘11am-3pm & 5-9pm; 🅿) This conveyor-belt sushi restaurant on the 2nd floor, right

above the fish market, is a great place to get your hands on the freshest fish without needing to know what they're all called. It's closed when the market closes on some Wednesdays. Cash only.

Antiques & Oldies　CAFE ¥
(アンティーク＆オールディーズ; www. aando-since1993.com; 2-3-22 Chōfu-Kawabata; dishes ¥650-1200; ⊘11am-7pm, closed Tue & every 3rd Mon; 🅿) At the back of a charming antique shop in Chōfu's castle-town area is this

DISCOUNT BUS PASS

If you're taking more than a couple of bus rides in Shimonoseki, pick up a **one-day bus pass** (*ichi-nichi furī jōsha-ken*; ¥700) from the booth at the bus terminal outside the station or at the Karato bus terminal. It's good value – a trip to Chōfu and back alone normally costs more than ¥700 – and it saves you the hassle of paying coins each time you get off the bus.

small cafe, serving up bagel sandwich sets, coffees, juices and cakes. There are just a few tables inside and a shady outdoor terrace. It's near the bend of the river, not far from the entrance to Kōzan-ji. Look for the red signboard.

★ **Yabure-Kabure**   FUGU ¥¥¥
(やぶれかぶれ; ☑234-3711; http://820.jp; 2-2-5 Buzenda-chō; lunch/dinner set menu from ¥3150/5250; ⊙11am-10pm) There's only one thing on the menu in this boisterous spot: pick from a range of *fugu* sets, such as the Ebisu course (¥5250), which features the cute little puffer in raw, seared, fried and drowned-in-sake incarnations. A lunchtime *tetsuyaki setto* (set meal with grilled *fugu*) is ¥3150. You can also order individual dishes. Look for the blue-and-white puffer fish outside.

Information

Note that at the time of writing, JR Shimonoseki Station was undergoing major redevelopment work. The location of the tourist office, and of other places in the station area, may have changed by the time you read this.

Shimonoseki Post Office (下関郵便局; 2-12-12 Takezaki-chō; ⊙9am-7pm Mon-Fri, to 5pm Sat, to 12.30pm Sun, ATM 9am-9pm Mon-Fri, to 7pm Sat & Sun) Currency exchange and ATMs.

Shimonoseki Station Tourist Information Office (下関駅観光案内所; ☑232-8383; www.city.shimonoseki.lg.jp; ⊙9am-7pm) Inside Shimonoseki Station. There is another office at the shinkansen station (☑256-3422; ⊙9am-7pm).

Getting There & Around

The main sights outside of the city centre are accessible by regular buses from the station. Shimonoseki is also great for cycling. Bikes (per day ¥500; ⊙8am-8pm) can be hired from outside the station from a booth in the car park beside the bus terminal area.

FERRY

Kanmon Kisen (☑222-1488; www.kanmon-kisen.co.jp) ferries run about every 20 minutes from the Karato wharf area of Shimonoseki to Mojikō in Kyūshū (¥390, five minutes).

To/From Korea & China

The **Shimonoseki International Ferry Terminal** (下関港国際ターミナル; www.shimonoseki-port.com) is the boarding point for ferries to Busan, Korea, and Qīngdǎo, China. Check the ferry company websites for the latest schedules. They also have their offices inside the terminal. The port website also has some information, but this doesn't always seem to be updated. There are currently no passenger ferry services to Shànghǎi (cargo sevices only).

Kampu Ferry (関釜フェリー; ☑224-3000; www.kampuferry.co.jp) operates the Shimonoseki–Busan ferry. There are daily departures at 7pm from Shimonoseki, arriving in Busan at 8am the following morning. One-way fares start at ¥9000 from Shimonoseki.

Orient Ferry Ltd (オリエントフェリー; ☑232-6615; www.orientferry.co.jp) operates the Shimonoseki–Qīngdǎo ferry, leaving noon Wednesday and Saturday, arriving at 4pm the following day. One-way fares start at ¥15,000 from Shimonoseki.

In addition to the ticket costs, there is fuel surcharge (¥2300) and terminal fee (¥600; payable by cash only). Tickets for Qīngdǎo can't be purchased at the terminal on the day of sailing; make reservations via travel agencies in Japan (such as JTB). See the Orient Ferry website for more details.

TRAIN

JR Shimonoseki is the end of the San-yō line. Shin-Shimonoseki *shinkansen* station is two stops from JR Shimonoseki (¥190, 10 minutes). Shimonoseki also connects to the San-in line, which runs north to Nagato and beyond along the Japan Sea coast.

Hagi   萩

☑0838 / POP 53,700

The quiet town of Hagi is known for producing some of the finest ceramics in Japan, and has a well-preserved old samurai quarter. During the feudal period, Hagi was the castle town of the Chōshū domain, which, together with Satsuma (corresponding to modern Kagoshima in southern Kyūshū), was instrumental in defeating the Tokugawa government and ushering in a new age after the Meiji Restoration. Hago also has a good beach, which is at its best in the summer months.

Get off at JR Higashi-Hagi for the main sights. Western and central Hagi are effectively an island created by the two rivers Hashimoto-gawa and Matsumoto-gawa; eastern Hagi (with the major JR station Higashi-Hagi) lies on the eastern bank of the Matsumoto-gawa.

◉ Sights

The main area of interest is the old samurai residential district of Jōkamachi (城下町), and surrounds, where there are many streets lined with whitewashed walls, enclosing old houses. Nearby is the beach and pretty bay views. There are also a few sights further afield on the edges of town.

★ Kikuya Residence HISTORIC BUILDING
(菊屋家住宅; 1-1 Gofuku-machi; admission ¥500; ◷ 9.30am-5.30pm) The Kikuya family were merchants rather than samurai. As official merchants to the *daimyō* their wealth and connections allowed them to build a house well above their station. This house dates from 1604 and has a fine gate and attractive gardens, and numerous interesting displays of items used in daily life, including an old public phone box. Don't miss the large old maps of Hagi, which show just how little has changed in the town layout.

Shizuki-kōen PARK
(指月公園) Within this park, there's not much of the old **Hagi-jō** (萩城; admission with Asa Mōri House ¥210; ◷ 8am-6.30pm Apr-Oct, to 4.30pm Nov-Feb, to 6pm Mar) to see, apart from the typically imposing outer walls and the surrounding moat. The castle was built in 1604 and dismantled in 1874 following the Meiji Restoration. But the grounds are a pleasant park, with the **Shizuki-yama-jinja** (志都岐山神社), the **Hanano-e Tea House** (花江茶亭) from the mid-19th century, and other buildings. From the castle ruins you can climb the hillside to the 143m peak of Shizuki-yama.

Hagi-jō Kiln KILN
(萩城窯; 2-5 Horiuchi; ◷ 8am-5pm) *Hagi-yaki* is noted for its fine glazes and delicate pastel colours, and connoisseurs of Japanese ceramics rank it as some of the best. At a number of shops and kilns you can see *hagi-yaki* being made, and browse the finished products, including this one within the walls of the old castle ruins. The tourist office has a complete list of kilns in the area.

Hagi Uragami Museum MUSEUM
(山口県立萩美術館・浦上記念館; www.hum. pref.yamaguchi.lg.jp; 586-1 Hiyako; admission ¥300; ◷ 9am-5pm, closed Mon) In this appealing modern building you'll find a superb collection of ceramics and wood-block prints, with fine works by Katsushika Hokusai and Utamaro Kitagawa. There are also regular special exhibitions.

Shōin-jinja SHINTŌ SHRINE
(松陰神社; treasure house ¥500) This shrine, with a garden and small complex, was founded in 1890 and is dedicated to Meiji

---

TAWARAYAMA ONSEN

Nestled in the mountains, Tawarayama Onsen (俵山温泉) is a small village that has a reputation as a favoured hidden spa for *tōji* (curative bathing). The story goes that an injured monkey once healed itself in the waters here, but the only monkeys you'll see these days are the ones painted on the street and peering at you from the tasty *manjū* sold around town. While Tawarayama draws local tourists, it sees relatively few international travellers.

There is a narrow main strip lined with a mix of old and newer ryokan, none of which has its own bath. Instead, guests go out to bathe in the two public baths: **Machi-no-yu** (町の湯; admission ¥390; ◷ 6am-10pm) and the newer **Hakuen-no-yu** (白猿の湯; admission ¥700, early morning & late evening ¥500; ◷ 7am-9pm). If you're looking for a place to stay, try popular **Izumiya** (泉屋; ☏ 0837-29-0231; www.tabi-izumiya.com; per person with two meals from ¥8925), a well-maintained old inn with wooden floors and a garden. The friendly managers can pick up guests at Nagato-Yumoto Station. See www.tawarayamaonsen.com (in Japanese) for more information. There is also an Australia-based English blog: www.tawarayama-onsen.com.

Tawarayama is not especially convenient to anywhere, which for some is part of its appeal. There's a direct bus from Shimonoseki (¥1630, one hour and 50 minutes, eight daily). Or get to Nagato-Yumoto Station (two stops south of Nagato on the JR Mine line), from where there is one bus an hour (¥510, 25 minutes).

Hagi

Restoration movement leader Yoshida Shōin. His old house and the school where he agitated against the shōgunate in the years leading up to the revolution are also here, as well as a treasure house (宝物館). The shrine is located southeast of Higashi-Hagi Station. The circle bus drops you out the front.

Itō Hirobumi House   NOTABLE BUILDING
(伊藤博文旧宅; admission ¥100; ⊙9am-5pm) About 200m from Shōin-jinja is the thatched early home of the four-term prime minister,

who was a follower of Yoshida Shōin, and who later drafted the Meiji Constitution. It's interesting to see the contrast between this humble place and the impressive mansion he lived in during his years in Tokyo, which is next door, having been moved to Hagi after his death.

★ Tōkō-ji   BUDDHIST TEMPLE
(東光寺; 1647 Chintō; admission ¥300; ⊙8.30am-5pm) East of the river, near Shōin-jinja, stands pretty Zen Tōkō-ji, built in 1691 and home to the tombs of five Mōri lords. The stone walk-

ways on the hillside behind the temple are flanked by almost 500 stone lanterns, which were erected by the lords' servants.

Kasa-yama
MOUNTAIN

(笠山) About 5km northeast of the town is the 112m dormant volcano Kasa-yama. The pond at the mountain's base, **Myōjin-ike** (明神池), is connected to the sea and shelters a variety of saltwater fish. When in this area, listen and look out for the birdlife in the surrounding trees.

About five minutes' walk up the mountain from the pond is **Hagi Glass** (萩ガラス工房; ☑ 26-2555; www.hagi-glass.jp; ⏰ 9am-6pm, demonstrations 9am-noon & 1-4.30pm) **FREE**, where quartz basalt from the volcano is used to make extremely tough Hagi glassware. There is a showroom and a shop with some beautiful coloured-glass vases and cups, and you can watch the glass-blowing in process. Next door is Hagi's own beer and citrus-juice factory, **Yuzuya Honten** (柚子屋本店; www.e-yuzuya.com; ⏰ 9am-5pm) **FREE**. Stop in here to see the very small team at work, taste juice in the attached shop, or have a refreshing mikan-flavoured soft cream.

The road continues to the top of Kasa-yama, from where there are gorgeous views and a tiny 30m-deep crater. There is also a walking track around the coast. From late February to late March a beautiful grove of camellias here is in bloom.

Buses go to Kasa-yama from Higashi-Hagi Station once every hour to 1½ hours (¥270, 15 minutes); get off at the Koshi-ga-hama stop, about eight minutes' walk from the base of the mountain and Myōjin-ike.

☆ Activities

Jōzan
POTTERY MAKING

(城山; ☑ 25-1666; 31-15 Horiuchi Nishi-no-hama; lessons ¥1680; ⏰ 8am-4pm) You can try your hand at making pottery in this large workshop; once fired, items can be shipped anywhere in Japan. Look for the building next to the large kiln.

🛏 Sleeping

Hagi doesn't see many foreign tourists and you can't assume all staff at hotels will speak English. The tourist office can help with bookings.

Hotel Hagi-no-Hama
HOTEL ¥¥

(ホテル萩の浜; ☑ 21-7100; http://hotel-hagi.com; 485 Kiku-ga-hama; s/tw inc breakfast ¥7500/13,600; ⊛ @) At this large, light ho-

tel on the beach you can have clear views over the bay from your room balcony, and from the on-site onsen. The Japanese-style tatami rooms are clean and spacious, and are recommended over the somewhat tired-looking Western-style ones. Do yourself a favour and book a room on the beach side of the building.

Hagi Royal Intelligent Hotel
HOTEL ¥¥

(萩ロイヤルインテリジェントホテル; ☑ 21-4589; http://hrih.jp; 3000-5 Chintō; s/tw incl breakfast ¥5900/7400; ⊛ @) Walk out of Higashi-Hagi Station and straight into this modern hotel. The large rooms have some quirky features – the magnetic dartboard and puzzles will keep you entertained – plus spacious showers that spray you at all angles. There's an onsen on site and some staff members speak English.

Hagi no Yado Tomoe
RYOKAN ¥¥¥

(萩の宿常茂恵; ☑ 22-0150; www.tomoehagi.jp; 608-53 Kōbō-ji Hijiwara; per person from ¥17,850; ⊛ @) The finest inn in Hagi, the historic Tomoe has gorgeous Japanese rooms with garden views, beautifully prepared cuisine and luxurious baths. Prices vary according to season, and there are discounted plans on the website (if you don't read Japanese, it may be easier to reserve via email). Cross the bridge from the station and take the road along the river.

🍴 Eating & Drinking

★ Hotoritei
CAFE ¥

(畔亭; http://hotoritei.com; 62 Minami-Katakawa; meals from ¥1000; ⏰ 11am-5pm, closed Thu & Jan 4-Feb) A tranquil rest stop near the Jōkamachi area, Hotoritei is within a large house surrounded by gardens. It mainly serves coffees, teas and cakes – try the fluffy, cream-filled *matcha* (green-tea) roll. There are a few lunch sets; the menu has some pictures. Look for the entrance set back from the road, next to Sam's Irish pub.

POTTED HISTORY

During his Korean peninsula campaigns in 1592 and 1598, Toyotomi Hideyoshi abducted whole families of potters as growing interest in the tea ceremony generated desire for the finest Korean ceramics. The firing techniques brought over all those centuries ago live on in Japanese ceramics today.

Cafe Tikal
CAFE ¥

(長屋門珈琲・カフェティカル; http://hagi-nagayamoncoffee.jimdo.com; 298-1 Hijiwara; coffee from ¥250; ⊙9.30am-8pm, to 6pm Sun, closed Mon) Through the old gate of the Kogawa family residence is this small cafe with large windows looking on to a pleasingly unkempt garden. Sit among the games and books at one of the wooden tables and choose from a range of coffees, including a hilly cappuccino. Cakes are also served.

Don Don Udonya
NOODLES ¥

(どんどん; 377 San-ku Hijiwara; dishes ¥350-700; ⊙9am-9pm; 🛈) A popular spot serving tasty *udon* and rice dishes, with set meals are *donburi* standards like *oyako-don* (chicken and egg on rice). There's a cheaper morning selection. It's in a big black-and-white building on the right across the bridge from the station.

Hagi Shinkai
SEAFOOD ¥¥

(萩心海; ☑26-1221; 370-71 Hijiwara; set meals ¥3150-6000; ⊙11am-2.30pm & 5-9pm) Seating here is arranged around a large open tank, so you can watch as the doomed fish are plucked out by the staff while you eat. There are various set-meal options, or ask for the manager-recommended *Shinkai teishoku* (¥1050/1890 at lunch/dinner), which includes sashimi, tempura and *chawanmushi* (steamed savoury egg custard) and isn't on the menu. Look for the white building with the lighthouse.

Maru
IZAKAYA ¥¥

(まる; 78 Yoshida-chō; dishes from ¥500; ⊙5-11pm, closed Sun) A relaxed, modern *izakaya*, Maru features the local beef, *kenran-gyū* (見蘭牛), available as sashimi, sushi or as a sizzling garlic steak. It also serves all the usual *izakaya* favourites. Try the *Hagi no kuramoto udedameshi setto* (¥1000) for a tasting set from six local sake breweries. Look for the large wooden door marked with a circle.

❶ Information

Hagi City Library (萩市立萩図書館; 2nd fl, 552-26 Emukai; ⊙9.30am-5.30pm, to 7pm Wed & Sat, closed Mon) Free internet access on 2nd floor. You may need to show ID.

Tourist Information Office (萩市観光案内所; ☑25-3145; ⊙9am-5.45pm, to 5pm Dec-Feb) Located inside Higashi-Hagi Station. Has a good English cycling and walking map. There's another tourist office near Hagi Station.

❶ Getting There & Away

BUS

Long-distance bus connections from Higashi-Hagi Station, via Hagi Bus Centre:

Shin-Yamaguchi ¥1970, 1½ hours, at least hourly

Tsuwano ¥2130, one hour and 45 minutes, five daily

Yamaguchi ¥1680, one hour and 10 minutes, nine to 11 daily; this is a JR bus

TRAIN

Hagi is on the JR San-in line, which runs along the coast from Tottori and Matsue. Local services between Shimonoseki and Higashi-Hagi (¥1890) take up to three hours, depending on transfers. If you're going to Tsuwano and have a JR Pass, you'll want to go by train up the coast to Masuda (¥950, one hour and 10 minutes), then change to the JR Yamaguchi line for Tsuwano.

❶ Getting Around

It's easy to walk around central Hagi and the Jōkamachi area. Some sights are on the edges of town and Hagi is a good place to explore by bicycle or bus if you're not keen on walking.

BICYCLE

Hagi Rainbow Cycles (萩レインボーサイクル; ☑080-2909-1666; hire per hr/24hr ¥150/800; ⊙8am-5pm) Allows you to take bikes overnight and return them at different locations for no extra charge. It's the small place directly to the left as you exit Higashi-Hagi Station.

BUS

The handy *maru basu* (まぁーるバス; circle bus) takes in all of central Hagi's main attractions. There are east- (東回り) and west-bound (西回り) loops, with two services per hour at each stop. One trip costs ¥100, and one-/two-day passes cost ¥500/700. Both routes stop at Higashi-Hagi Station.

MATSUE & AROUND

Along the San-in coastline on the Sea of Japan is Shimane Prefecture (島根県; Shimane-ken), of which Matsue is the capital. It may be off the beaten track, but there is no shortage of reasons to visit. Cities are few and far between, the pace of life is decidedly slower than on the San-yō coast and the people are particularly friendly towards visitors.

JAPAN'S ADOPTED SON

Born to a Greek mother and an Anglo-Irish army surgeon on the island of Lefkada in the Ionian Sea, Patrick Lafcadio Hearn (1850–1904) grew up in Dublin and studied in England before being packed off at 19 with a one-way ticket to America. He worked as a journalist in Cincinnati, and in New Orleans wrote about voodoo and developed the taste for the exotic that would characterise his writing on Japan. After two years in the French West Indies, Hearn accepted an assignment from *Harper's* magazine to travel to Japan.

Hearn soon became famous for his articles and books about his new home. Eager to stay on after his contract with *Harper's* ran out, he took a job teaching English. For 15 idyllic months he lived in Matsue, where he married Koizumi Setsu, the daughter of a local samurai family. After stints elsewhere, he finally settled in Tokyo ('the most horrible place in Japan') where he was appointed professor of English Literature at Tokyo Imperial University.

Although Japan has changed almost beyond recognition since Hearn lived here, his best pieces are still well worth reading today. His first Japan-themed collection, *Glimpses of Unfamiliar Japan* (1894), contains his famous essay on Matsue – 'Chief City of the Province of the Gods', as well as an account of his trip to Izumo, where he was the first European allowed inside the gates of the ancient shrine.

Matsue 松江

☑ 0852 / POP 193,300

With its fine castle and crowd-pleasing sunsets over Shinji-ko (Lake Shinji), Matsue is an appealing city with some interesting historical attractions. The city straddles the Ōhashi-gawa, which connects Shinji-ko with Nakanoumi, a saline lake. Most of the main attractions are in a compact area in the north, where you'll find the castle, a rare original. Matsue is also a good base for sojourns to other places in Shimane Prefecture and you could easily spend a few lazy days here.

◉ Sights

★ Matsue-jō CASTLE

(松江城, Matsue Castle; www.matsue-tourism.or.jp/m_castle; 1-5 Tonomachi; admission ¥550, foreigners with ID ¥280; ☺ 8.30am-6.30pm Apr-Sep, to 5pm Oct-Mar) Dating from 1611, picturesque Matsue-jō is known as Plover Castle for the graceful shape of its gable ornaments. As one of only 12 original keeps left in Japan, it is well worth a look at its wooden interior, where treasures of the Matsudaira clan are showcased. It has dioramas of the city, plus armoury displays, including a helmet collection. Each helmet's design is said to have reflected its wearer's personality. The top of the castle offers great unobstructed views.

It's pleasant to walk around the castle grounds (free entry) and along the surrounding moat, with its charming bridges and pines reaching out across the water. A good way to see the castle area is a trip on a Horikawa Sightseeing Boat (p465).

Matsue History Museum MUSEUM

(松江歴史館; www.matsu-reki.jp; 279 Tono-machi; admission ¥500, foreigners with ID ¥250; ☺ 8.30am-6.30pm, to 5pm Oct-Mar, closed 3rd Thu of month) Matsue's excellent new museum gives a broad-ranging introduction to the history of the region clans, and development of local industry and crafts. Among the displays are old town maps, ceramics, letters and the local speciality Matsue *wagashi* (sweets) – you can taste modern versions in the attached shop. The free English audio guide is very good.

Koizumi Yakumo (Lafcadio Hearn) Memorial Museum MUSEUM

(小泉八雲記念館; www.matsue-tourism.or.jp/yakumo; 322 Okudani-chō; admission ¥300, foreigners with ID ¥150; ☺ 8.30am-6.30pm Apr-Sep, to 5pm Oct-Mar) This memorial museum has displays on the life and work of the well-travelled Lafcadio Hearn, as well as some of the man's personal effects – including his dumb-bells, spectacles, and a stack of Japanese newspapers on which he wrote words and phrases to teach English to his son. Hearn enthusiasts should pop round next door to have a look at his **old residence** (小泉八雲旧居; admission ¥300, foreigners with ID ¥150; ☺ 8.30am-6.30pm Apr-Sep, to 5pm Oct-Mar).

Buke Yashiki Samurai Residence HISTORIC BUILDING

(武家屋敷; www.matsue-tourism.or.jp/buke; 305 Kitahori-chō; admission ¥300, foreigners with ID ¥150; ☺ 8.30am-6.30pm Apr-Sep, to 5pm Oct-Mar) Built for a middle-ranking samurai family during the early 18th century, Buke Yashiki is an immaculately preserved house and garden.

Matsue

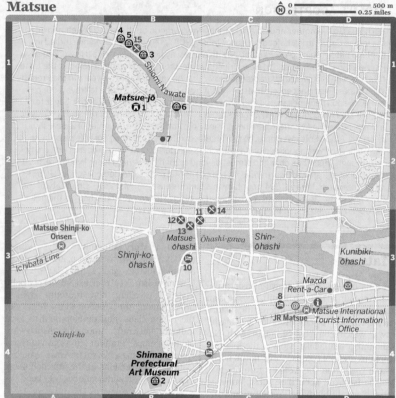

Matsue

⊙ Top Sights
1 Matsue-jō	B1
2 Shimane Prefectural Art Museum	B4

⊙ Sights
3 Buke Yashiki Samurai Residence	B1
4 Koizumi Yakumo (Lafcadio Hearn) Memorial Museum	B1
5 Lafcadio Hearn Old Residence	B1
6 Matsue History Museum	B1

☺ Activities, Courses & Tours
7 Horikawa Sightseeing Boat	B2

⊜ Sleeping
8 Green Rich Hotel Matsue Minamikan	C3
	(see 12)
9 Terazuya	C4
10 Young Inn Matsue	B3

⊗ Eating
11 Kawa-kyō	B3
12 Nakria	B3
13 Naniwa	B3
14 Tsurumaru	C3
15 Yakumo-an	B1

⊙ Drinking & Nightlife
Cafe Bar EAD	(see 13)

★ **Shimane Prefectural Art Museum** GALLERY
(島根県立博物館; www1.pref.shimane.lg.jp/contents/sam; 1-5 Sodeshi-chō; admission ¥300, foreigners with ID ¥150; ☺10am-6.30pm, to 30min after sunset Mar-Sep, closed Tue) With its white undulating roof and huge glass windows facing the lake, the museum building itself is an impressive sight. Inside, it displays rotating exhibits from its collection of wood-block

prints (there are some Hokusai among them), as well as European paintings and contemporary art. The sunset views from the museum's 2nd-floor platform or outside by the water also draw crowds here. The museum is a 15-minute walk west of the station.

👉 Tours

Horikawa Sightseeing Boat   BOAT TOUR

(¥1200, foreigners with ID ¥800; ⊙ every 15-20min 9am-5pm) The characterful boatmen circumnavigate the castle moat and then zip around the city's canals and beneath a series of bridges. There are a few boarding points; the main one is near the castle entrance.

🛌 Sleeping

★ Terazuya   RYOKAN ¥

(旅館寺津屋; ☎ 21-3480; www.mable.ne.jp/~terazuya; 60-3 Tenjin-machi; per person with/without breakfast ¥4800/4200; @🛜🐾) You'll find a warm welcome and simple tatami rooms at this family-run inn, opposite a shrine. A little English is spoken, and the owners can collect you from the station. A canal runs behind the ryokan, as does the JR line – fortunately there's little traffic at night in these parts. The bathroom is shared, there's a 10pm curfew, and coffee and toast is included if you haven't paid for the full breakfast. They only take cash.

Young Inn Matsue   GUESTHOUSE ¥

(ヤングイン松江; ☎ 25-4500; http://younginn.net; 5 Uo-machi; dm/s/tw ¥2000/2500/4800; ⊜@🛜) Basic budget accommodation in a good location. The dorms are tatami rooms with futons; private rooms have beds. Shower rooms are shared and there's a lounge-bar. It's not a bad option if you just need a place to sleep.

Green Rich Hotel Matsue   HOTEL ¥¥

(グリーンリッチホテル松江駅前; ☎ 27-3000; www.gr-matsue.com; 493-1 Asahi-machi; s/tw from ¥5950/11,950; ⊜@🛜) A modern chain hotel going for a designer look with dark-toned furnishings and back-lit headboards. Most inviting is the large, sunken public bath and sauna. A buffet breakfast is an additional ¥500.

★ Minamikan   RYOKAN ¥¥¥

(皆美館; ☎ 21-5131; www.minami-g.co.jp/minamikan; 14 Suetsugu Hon-machi;; per person with breakfast/two meals from ¥15,000/23,000) A refined inn on the edge of the lake, Minamikan has a choice of 'modern', 'retro' and 'classic' rooms, all with broad views across the water. The top-end 'modern' has a tatami room with twin beds and private cypress-wood onsen. The cheaper 'classic' has seen the likes of literary great Kawabata Yasunari pass through. There is also an excellent restaurant. The ryokan entrance is set back from the road.

🍴 Eating & Drinking

★ Yakumo-an   NOODLES ¥

(八雲庵; www.yakumoan.jp; 308 Kita-Horiuchi; dishes ¥700-1150; ⊙10am-3pm; 🚗) Next door to the samurai house, this busy *soba* (buckwheat noodle) restaurant and its beautiful grounds are an excellent place to sample the local *warigo soba*. Try the tasty *soba kamo nanban* (noodles with slices of duck in broth). Look for sign on a piece of wood outside.

★ Kawa-kyō   IZAKAYA ¥

(川京; 65 Suetsugu Hon-machi; dishes ¥800-1575; ⊙6-10.30pm, closed Sun; ⊜🚗) You can count on a friendly welcome at this small *izakaya*, which specialises in the 'seven delicacies' from Shinji-ko and is a good place to try some local sake. The daughter of the owners speaks English. Look bamboo-roofed menu display outside.

Tsurumaru   SEAFOOD ¥

(鶴丸; www.tsurumaru2.net; 1-79 Higashi Hon-machi; dishes ¥500-1250; ⊙12-2pm & 5.30-10.30pm, closed Sun; 🚗) The smell of fish grilling over coals permeates this restaurant, which specialises in the cuisine of the Oki Islands. The menu features meals like *eri-yaki konabe* (hot spicy soup cooked over

---

LAKE DELICACIES

Matsue's *kyōdo ryōri* (regional cuisine) includes the 'seven delicacies' from Shinji-ko.

➡ *suzuki* – bass, paper-wrapped and steam-baked

➡ *shirauo* – whitebait, as tempura or sashimi

➡ *amasagi* – smelt, as sweet tempura or teriyaki

➡ *shijimi* – freshwater clams, usually in miso soup

➡ *moroge ebi* – shrimp, steamed

➡ *koi* – carp, baked in sauce

➡ *unagi* – freshwater eel, grilled

DON'T MISS

ADACHI MUSEUM OF ART

Adachi Museum of Art (足立美術館; www.adachi-museum.or.jp; 320 Furukawa-chō, Yasugi-shi; admission ¥2200, foreigners with ID ¥1100; ⊙ 9am-5.30pm, to 5pm Oct-Mar) East of Matsue in Yasugi is this excellent museum, founded by local businessman and art collector Adachi Zenkō. The collection includes more than 100 paintings by Yokoyama Taikan (1868–1958) and a good selection of works by other major Japanese painters of the 20th century. There's also a delightful 'pictures for children' gallery. But for many the real attraction is the stunning **gardens**, regularly voted among the best in Japan. Sit and contemplate the perfectly clipped mounds of the Dry Landscape Garden – in the distance, mountains rise up as though part of the garden itself. From Matsue, take the JR line to Yasugi (安来; ¥400, 25 minutes), where there's a free shuttle bus to the museum (11 daily from 9.05am).

a flame at your table) and sashimi. You'll know it by the *noren* with the crane on it, and the rustic folk-singing that drifts into the street. There's a limited English menu.

Nakria   JAPANESE, INTERNATIONAL ¥¥
(菜厨; ☑ 33-7702; http://hwsa8.gyao.ne.jp/nakria; 2nd fl Matsuya Bldg, 13 Suetsugu Hon-machi; lunch/dinner sets from ¥850/1000; ⊙ 11am-2.30pm & 6-10pm, closed Mon; 🗷 🖩) Stylish Nakria specialises in a range of steamed meat, seafood and vegetable dishes, and also serves pasta and curry sets. Try the deliciously dark and hot sesame curry. Vegetarians are catered for – let the staff know what you don't eat. There are also plenty of drinks and cocktails on the menu.

Naniwa   JAPANESE ¥¥
(なにわ; ☑ 21-2835; http://honten.naniwa-i.com; 21 Suetsugu Hon-machi; meals ¥2100-10,500; ⊙ 11am-9pm) Next to Matsue-ōhashi bridge, this bright, wood-themed restaurant is a tranquil spot for *unameshi* (eel and rice; ¥2625). Or opt for one of the delicately prepard *kaiseki* spreads, such as the Shinji-ko course (¥4200).

Cafe Bar EAD   BAR, CAFE
(カフェバーEAD; 36 Suetsugu Hon-machi; drinks/food from ¥525/735; ⊙ 9pm-1am, closed Tue & Wed) Low lighting, sofas, and a broad terrace with a river view make this relaxed bar-cafe a nice place to end your evening. Snacks include homemade pizzas. It's on the 3rd floor of a building just near the bridge.

❶ Information

There's free wi-fi in the lobby area of the large Matsue Terrsa building (松江テルサ) near the station. It's open from 9am to 9pm, and to 8pm on weekends.

Matsue Central Post Office (松江中央郵便局; ⊙ 9am-7pm, to 5pm Sat, to 12.30pm Sun, ATM 7am-11pm Mon-Fri, 9am-9pm Sat, 9am-7pm Sun) Has ATMs accepting international cards.

Matsue International Tourist Information Office (松江国際観光案内所; ☑ 21-4034; www.kankou-matsue.jp; 665 Asahi-machi; ⊙ 9am-6pm) Excellent, friendly assistance directly in front of JR Matsue Station. Internet access available.

❶ Getting There & Away

Matsue is on the JR San-in line, which runs along the San-in coast. You can get to Okayama via Yonago on the JR Hakubi line. It's ¥480 to Yonago (35 minutes), then ¥4620 to Okayama by *tokkyū* (2¼ hours). Highway buses operate to Japan's major cities from the terminal in front of the station.

❶ Getting Around

It's possible to walk around the sights. Matsue is also a good place to explore by bicycle; these can be rented close to Matsue station at **Mazda Rent-a-Car** (マツダレンタカー; 466-1 Asahi-machi; per day ¥300; ⊙ 8am-7pm).

There is a handy city-loop bus: the red streetcar-like Lake Line buses follow a set route around the attractions every 20 minutes. One ride costs ¥200; a day pass is available for ¥500.

Oki Islands   隠岐諸島

POP 21,700

North of Matsue in the Sea of Japan are the remote and spectacular Oki-shotō, within the **Oki Islands Geopark**, and with coastal areas that are part of the **Daisen-Oki National Park**. These islands were once used to exile officials (as well as two emperors) who came out on the losing side of political squabbles. Four of the islands are inhabited: the three Dōzen islands – Nishino-shima,

Chiburi-jima and Nakano-shima – and the larger Dōgo island. Being cut off from the mainland, there are cultural and religious practices preserved here that aren't observed elsewhere in Japan, the pace of life is decidedly slower, and there's a refreshing lack of development at the tourist spots. Allow at least a couple of days to visit, and keep in mind that ferry services are subject to change or halt in bad weather.

The biggest island, **Dōgo** (島後) is notable for its giant, wisened old cedar trees: the 800-year-old Chichi-sugi tree is believed to be the home of a deity; and the Yao-sugi tree at Tamakawasu-no-mikoto-jinja is thought to be 2000 years old, its gnarled sprawling branches propped up with posts. There are nature and coastal walks, and boat tours in the Saigō port area and the northern Shirashima coast. Bull sumō is an attraction throughout the year – not big guy versus bull, but bull versus bull.

West of Dōgo, **Nishino-shima** (西ノ島) boasts the stunning rugged Kuniga coastline, with the sheer 257m Matengai cliff. The coastal hike here is a must do. The island is also home to interesting shrines, such as Yurahime-jinja, near a small inlet. Legend has it that squid come en-masse to this inlet every year in autumn/winter as a way to ask forgiveness from the deity (there are pictures at the shrine to prove it). Nishino-shima is also known for horses, and you'll see them roaming the hillsides.

The small **Chiburi-jima** (知夫里島), where the local slogan is *nonbiri Chiburi* (carefree Chiburi), is home to more impressive coastline, featuring the striking Sekiheki, an expanse of rust-coloured cliffs. You can also see stone-wall remains on the island – what is left of a crop-rotation practice that began here in the middle ages. The Akiya coast and Oki-jinja are draws on **Nakano-shima** (中ノ島), also known locally as Ama.

A great choice for accommodation on Chiburi-jima is **Hotel Chibu-no-Sato** (ホテル知夫の里; ☑08514-8-2500; http://tibuno-sato.com; per person with two meals from ¥11,000), where the balconied rooms have fabulous sea views and there's an open-air bath. On Nishino-shima, **Oki Seaside Hotel Tsurumaru** (隠岐シーサイドホテル鶴丸; ☑08514-6-1111; http://oki-tsurumaru.com; per person with two meals from ¥10,500) has a pleasant waterfront location and runs regular cruises. You'll find more accommodation options on Dōgo, particularly in Saigō port. Outside of Saigō is

Hotel Uneri (ホテル海音里; ☑08512-5-3211; www.oki-island.jp/uneri; cabins ¥13,900-18,500), which has self-catering log cabins. All the islands also have ryokan and *minshuku* (from around ¥5000 up to around ¥8000 with meals), and there are campgrounds.

The **Nishino-shima Tourism Office** (☑08514-7-8888; www.nkk-oki.com) in Beppu port is an excellent source of information and can book accommodation. For more on the natural and cultural features of the islands, the **Oki Islands Geopark Promotion Committee** (☑08512-2-9636; www.oki-geopark. jp) produces a very good English guide and map. The tourist office in Matsue is also very helpful.

It's possible to get to some of the main attractions by bike, but to see all of the islands it's best to hire a car or make use of a taxi or eco-tour guide service. There's a local bus on Nishino-shima that goes to the Kuniga coast, though it's infrequent. Ferries go to the Oki Islands from Shichirui and Sakai-minato ports, northeast of Matsue. They are operated by **Oki Kisen** (☑08512-2-1122; www.oki-kisen.co.jp), calling at the main ports, including Saigō (¥3150, 2½ hours; high speed ¥6000, 70 minutes). There's also an inter-island ferry service. Buses go to Shichirui port from Matsue Station (¥1000, 40 minutes) and Yonago Station (¥850, 40 minutes). Sakai-minato is at the end of the JR Sakai train line, which connects with the JR San-in line at Yonago.

Izumo 出雲

☑0853 / POP 143,800

Just west of Matsue, Izumo has one major attraction – the great Izumo Taisha shrine, which ranks with Ise-jingū as one of the most important shrines in Japan. The shrine and surrounding area can be visited as a day trip from Matsue.

Izumo Taisha is 8km northwest of central Izumo. The shrine area is basically one street, lined with eateries and shops, that leads up to the shrine gates. The Ichibata-line Izumo Taisha-mae Station is at the foot of the street.

⊙ Sights

★ **Izumo Taisha**   SHINTŌ SHRINE
(出雲大社; ⊙6am-8pm) **FREE** Perhaps the oldest Shintō shrine of all, Izumo is second in importance only to Ise-jingū, the home of the sun goddess Amaterasu. The shrine is as

old as Japanese recorded history – there are references to Izumo in the *Kojiki,* Japan's oldest book – and its origins stretch back into the age of the gods. Impressive as the structure is today, it was once even bigger. Records dating from AD 970 describe the shrine as the tallest building in the country; there is evidence that the shrine towered as high as 48m above the ground during the Heian period. It may well have been too high for its own good – the structure collapsed five times between 1061 and 1225, and the roofs today are a more modest 24m.

The current appearance of the main shrine dates from 1744. The main hall has recently undergone one of its periodic rebuildings, ending in May 2013, to be done again in another 60 years.

The shrine is dedicated to Ōkuninushi, who, according to tradition, ceded control over Izumo to the sun goddess' line – he did this on the condition that a huge temple would be built in his honour, one that would reach as high as the heavens. Long revered as a bringer of good fortune, Ōkuninushi is worshipped as the god of marriage, and visitors to the shrine summon the deity by clapping four times rather than the usual two.

Huge *shimenawa* (twisted straw ropes) hang over the entry to the main buildings. Those who can toss and lodge a coin in them are said to be blessed with good fortune. Visitors are not allowed inside the main shrine precinct, most of which is hidden behind huge wooden fences. Ranged along the sides of the compound are the *jūku-sha,* which are long shelters where Japan's myriad deities stay when they come for their annual conference.

Shimane Museum of Ancient Izumo
MUSEUM

(島根県立古代出雲歴史博物館; 99-4 Kizuki Higashi Taisha-chō; admission ¥600, foreigners with ID ¥300; ◷9am-6pm, to 5pm Nov-Feb, closed 3rd Tue of month) Just to the right of the shrine's front gate, this museum contains exhibits on local history. These include reconstructions of the shrine in its pomp, and recordings of the annual ceremonies held to welcome the gods to Izumo. There is also a superb collection of bronze from the ancient Yayoi period.

🎎 Festivals & Events

Kamiari-sai
SHINTŌ

The 10th month of the lunar calendar is known throughout Japan as Kan-na-zuki (Month without Gods). In Izumo, however, it is known as Kami-ari-zuki (Month with Gods), for this is the month when all the Shintō gods congregate at Izumo Taisha.

The Kamiari-sai is a series of events to mark the arrival of the gods in Izumo. It runs from the 11th to the 17th of the 10th month according to the old calendar; exact dates vary from year to year.

🛈 Information

Tourist Information Office (☑30-6015; ◷9am-5.30pm) Not far from Izumo Taisha-mae Station on the main street.

🛈 Getting There & Away

The private, old-fashioned Ichibata line starts from Matsue Shinjiko-onsen Station in Matsue and trundles along the northern side of Shinji-ko to Izumo Taisha-mae Station (one-way/return ¥790/1500, one hour, with a transfer at Kawato, 川跡).

The JR line runs from JR Matsue Station to JR Izumo-shi Station (¥570, 42 minutes), where you can transfer to an Ichibata train to Izumo Taisha-mae (¥480, 30 minutes), or to a bus to the shrine (¥510, 25 minutes).

Long-distance buses run from a few major cities in the region, including Hiroshima, Okayama and Kyoto.

Iwami Ginzan   石見銀山

About 6km inland from Nima Station on the San-in coast west of Izumo is the old Iwami Ginzan silver mine, a Unesco World Heritage Site. In the early 17th century, the mine produced as much as 38 tonnes of silver annually, making it the most important mine in the country at a time when Japan was producing around a third of the world's silver every year. The Tokugawa shōgunate had direct control over the 500 or so mines in the area.

The site is spread along a valley, with the small town of Ōmori at its centre. The main streets and the walking path along the river roughly form a long narrow loop, with mine shafts, temples, historic residences and ruins dotted along it and in the wooded hillsides. From one end to the other is about 2km; allow at least four or more hours to do the loop on foot and see the various sites at leisure.

Among the highlights is the the **Iwami Ginzan Museum** (石見銀山資料館; admission ¥500; ◷9am-5pm, to 4pm Dec-Feb), containing various documents, tools and silver-related items. It's inside the Ōmori Daikansho Ato, near the Daikansho Ato bus stop. Nearby is the **Kigami-jinja** (城上神社), with a colourful dragon mural on its ceiling – to hear the dragon 'roar', stand underneath it and clap. Not far from here up the old road is the lovingly restored **Kumagai Residence** (熊谷家住宅; admission ¥500; ⏰9.30am-5pm, closed Mon), rebuilt in 1801 after an earthquake destroyed most of the town the previous year. The house belonged to a merchant family who made their fortune as officials in the silver trade. Further along is an interesting temple, **Rakan-ji** (羅漢寺; admission incl Gohyakurakan ¥500; ⏰9am-5pm). Opposite is the wonderful **Gohyakurakan** (五百羅漢) where, crowded into two small caves, there are 500 diminutive stone statues of the Buddha's disciples, each showing a different expression – some smiling, some turning their head to chat to their neighbour. The collection was completed in 1766, after 25 years of work. South of Rakan-ji, the **Iwami Ginzan World Heritage Centre** (石見銀山世界遺産センター; admission ¥300; ⏰8.30am-6pm, to 5.30pm Dec-Feb) has exhibits on the history of the mines and the surrounding area.

Further along the road, don't miss the detour to see the **Shimizudani Refinery Ruins** (清水谷製錬所跡) and, at the far end of the site, the **Ryūgenji Mabu Shaft** (龍源寺間歩; admission ¥400; ⏰9am-5pm), which has been widened substantially from its original size. One glance at the original tunnel that stretches beyond the fence at the end of the accessible area should be enough to make most people glad they weren't born as 17th-century miners. Past the Ryūgenji mine shaft, a hiking trail leads 12km to Yunotsu, following the old route along which silver was hauled to port.

There are a few cafes along the old road in town. For a drink and a sweet treat, stop in at **Yamabuki** (やまぶき; ⏰closed Wed), where the speciality is sweet-potato doughnuts. It's near Seisui-ji.

Iwami Ginzan could be visited on a (very long) day trip from Matsue. Alternatively, it's good to combine a trip here with a stay in nearby Yunotsu. Another great option for accommodation is near Nima Station, at the **Jōfuku-ji Youth House** (城福寺ユースハウス; ☎0854-88-2233; www14.plala.or.jp/joufukuji; 1114 Nima-machi, Nima-chō; per person with/without meals ¥4500/3000; @). Accom-

OFF THE BEATEN TRACK

SANBE-SAN 三瓶山

About 20km inland from Ōda is Sanbe-san, an old volcano with grassy slopes that reaches 1126m. It takes about an hour to climb from **Sanbe Onsen** (三瓶温泉) and five hours to walk around the caldera. You can have a dip in the onsen on your return. Day trippers can try the outdoor baths at **Kokuminshuku-sha Sanbesō** (国民宿舎さんべ荘; ☎83-2011; www.sanbesou.jp; Shigaku Sanbe-chō, Ōda-shi; per person with meals from ¥8500, baths ¥500; ⏰10.30am-9pm), where accommodation is available. The area is a popular ski centre in winter. Buses run between Ōda-shi Station and Sanbe Onsen (¥830, 45 minutes, seven or eight daily).

modation is in comfortable tatami rooms in a Buddhist temple. Meals are available, and the owners can collect you from the station.

There is a booth near the Ōmori Daikansho Ato stop where you can pick up a map and audio guide (¥500), also available at the **tourist information office** (☎0854-89-0333; ⏰9am-5pm, to 4pm Oct-Apr) by the car park close to Rakan-ji. Buses run to the Ōmori Daikansho Ato stop about every half-hour from Ōda-shi Station (¥610, 25 minutes), and from Nima Station (¥390, 15 minutes, four or five per day). There is also a long-distance bus to Hiroshima. Within the mine area, shuttle buses connect Ōmori Daikansho-ato and the World Heritage Centre every 15 minutes (¥200). There are also bikes for rent (¥500 for three hours; ¥700 for an electric-assist bike for two hours).

Yunotsu 温泉津

☎0855

Three stations south of Nima is the coastal onsen town of Yunotsu, one of the ports from where silver from the Iwami Ginzan mines was shipped to the capital and beyond. Now a protected historic area, it consists of a couple of narrow streets of well-preserved wooden buildings and two atmospheric public baths where you can soak up the mineral-rich waters with the locals.

On the main street of the town, recognisable by the statue outside and the large blue sign, **Motoyu Onsen** (元湯温泉; admission ¥300; ⊙ 5.30am-9pm) traces its history back 1300 years, to when an itinerant priest came across a *tanuki* (racoon) nursing its wounded paw in the waters here. There are no fancy shower heads and racks of shampoo in the wash area here – just grab a wooden bucket, run the tap and give yourself a good splash down. Just a short walk away on the other side of the street is the relatively modern **Yakushinoyu Onsen** (薬師湯温泉; admission ¥350; ⊙ 5am-9pm), which was discovered when hot water bubbled up from the ground after an earthquake in 1872.

There are a number of places to stay, including the 100-year-old **Ryokan Masuya** (旅館ますや; ☑ 65-2515; www.ryokan-masuya. com; per person with 2 meals from ¥10,600), down the street towards the sea from the two public baths. A little English is spoken, and accommodation is in tatami rooms (a Western-style room is available, but go for the Japanese-style ones). Or try **Yoshidaya** (吉田屋; ☑ 65-2014; www.lets.gr.jp/yoshidaya; per person with/without two meals from ¥8400/4500; 🖥) 🍴, a creaky 80-year-old building with spacious tatami rooms. The staff here do various works in the community, including with local elderly women farmers, who sell *mottainai* vegetables (imperfect-looking vegies that wouldn't normally sell in a store) to use in the meals here. Rooms are available Friday to Sunday only and payment is by cash. Yoshidaya is a few doors down from Motoyu Onsen.

Yunotsu is on the San-in line, down the coast from Matsue (¥1450, 1½ hours to two hours), a few stops from Nima and Ōda-shi stations, where there is access to Iwami Ginzan silver mine. When you exit Yunotsu Station, go left, then follow the road around to the right along the waterfront to reach the main street of ryokan. It's a 10- to 15-minute walk.

TOTTORI & AROUND

Although Tottori Prefecture (鳥取県; Tottori-ken) is the least populous of Japan's 47 prefectures, it has a wealth of coastal scenery, sand dunes, onsen and volcanoes. The snag is it takes time and a bit of planning to get to some areas – this is a good place to hire a car. Summer is the best time to visit to get the most out of the beaches.

Tottori　鳥取

📞 0857 / POP 197,300

Tottori is a medium-sized city that attracts crowds of Japanese tourists coming to take pictures of each other next to camels on the famous sand dunes. There's not a lot to keep you here once you've made the obligatory trip to the sand, but it's a decent base for exploring the nearby coastal areas.

◉ Sights & Activities

There are beaches and scenic stretches of coastline within the San-in Coast National Park, a good side trip from Tottori city. The tourist office also has informaton in English about the local beaches.

★ **Tottori-sakyū (The Dunes)**　SAND DUNES
(鳥取砂丘) Used as the location for Teshigahara Hiroshi's classic 1964 film *Woman in the Dunes,* the Tottori sand dunes are on the coast about 5km from the city. There's a viewing point on a hillside overlooking the dunes, along with a car park and the usual array of tourist schlock. The dunes stretch for over 10km along the coast and, at some points, can be about 2km wide. You can even get a 'Lawrence of Arabia' photo of yourself accompanied by a camel. There are maps and pamphlets at the Sand Pal Tottori Information Centre (p472).

Buses to the dunes also stop at the Sakyū-Sentā (砂丘センター; Dunes Centre), on the hillside, where you can take a **cable car** (one-way ¥200; ⊙ 8.30am-4.30pm) down to the sand.

★ **Sand Museum**　MUSEUM
(砂の美術館; www.sand-museum.jp; admission ¥600; ⊙ 9am-8pm Apr-Jan) You came to see sand? They've got truckloads at this impressive museum of sand sculptures, where sand aficionados from all over the world are invited to created huge, amazingly detailed works based on a particular theme. The exhibition changes each year: check at the tourist office for this year's theme and opening months. The museum is near the sand dunes.

Kannon-in　TEMPLE, GARDEN
(観音院; 162 Ue-machi; admission ¥500; ⊙ 9am-5pm) The main attraction at this 17th-century temple is its beautiful **garden**, built around a pond. Gather your thoughts and contemplate the arrangement of stones and trees while sipping a cup of *matcha*, which is included in the admission. The city loop bus passes near the temple.

TOTTORI ONSEN

There are several onsen areas dotted across Tottori Prefecture. With a bit of time, why not put together your own tour of the springs.

Hawai Onsen West of Tottori city and just north of Kurayoshi (倉吉) Station is Tōgō-ike, with **Hawai Onsen** (はわい温泉) on its western side. Among the many hotels with baths here, you'll find friendly local *sentō* **Hawai Yūtown** (ハワイゆーたうん; www.supersentou.com/4_chugoku/05_hawai.htm; admission ¥350; ☺ 9am-9pm, closed Thu). You can pick up a map of the other baths in the area from the information centre. Buses to Hawai Onsen run from Kurayoshi Station. For more information on the area, see www.hawai-togo.jp.

Hamamura Onsen Take a dip in the delightful indoor and outdoor baths at Hamamura (浜村), further east along the train line from Kurayoshi. From Hamamura Station, walk straight and take the first major turning on the right. **Hamamura Onsen Kan** (浜村温泉館; admission ¥420; ☺ 10am-10pm, closed 1st Wed of month) is on the left, a seven-minute walk from the station.

Iwai Onsen East of Tottori city is Iwai Onsen (岩井温泉), said to be the oldest onsen in the region and known for its curative waters. This small collection of ryokan is about eight minutes by bus from Iwami Station along Rte 9. Day trippers can relax at modern *sentō* **Iwai Yukamuri Onsen** (岩井ゆかむり温泉; http://yukamuri.net; admission ¥300; ☺ 6am-10pm). It's right by the bus stop and has an old-fashioned, white-and-blue exterior.

Tottori-jō & Jinpū-kaku Villa CASTLE, MUSEUM
(鳥取城跡・仁風閣; 2-121 Higashi-machi; villa admission ¥150; ☺ 9am-5pm, closed Mon) Tottori's castle once overlooked the town, but now only the foundations remain. It's a pleasant walk up the hillside to see them and views over the city. Below is the elegant Jinpū-kaku Villa, built as accommodation for the Taishō emperor when he visited as Crown Prince in 1907, and now used as a museum.

Hinomaru Onsen SENTŌ
(日乃丸温泉; 401 Suehiro Onsen-chō; admission ¥350; ☺ 6am-midnight, closed 2nd Mon of month except Jan & Aug) There are a number of inner-city onsen within a short walk of the station. If you can brave the scorching hot waters, try soaking with the locals at this public bath in the heart of the entertainment district.

🛏 Sleeping

Matsuya-sō GUESTHOUSE ¥
(松屋荘; ☎ 22-4891; 3-814 Yoshikata Onsen; s/tw ¥3500/6000) This *minshuku*-style lodging has no mod cons but simple, clean tatami rooms and shared bathrooms. From the station, go straight up the main street and turn right onto Eiraku-dōri (永楽通り). Look for Matsuya-sō on the left after a few blocks; it's about a 15-minute walk from the station. The welcoming owner doesn't speak English.

Green Hotel Morris HOTEL ¥¥
(グリーンホテルモーリス; ☎ 22-2331; www.hotel-morris.co.jp/tottori; 2-107 Ima-machi; s/tw from ¥5460/11,550; ➖@🛜) Stylish, neutral-toned rooms, large spa baths and a sauna make Morris a good-value modern option. It's close to the station, and there's a buffet breakfast for ¥550.

✗ Eating & Drinking

Tottori-ya YAKITORI ¥
(とっ鳥屋; 585-1 Yamane; skewers from ¥80; ☺ 5pm-midnight) This bustling *yakitori* (skewers of grilled chicken) place has a large menu of individual sticks and rice dishes. Get an assortment of six for ¥580 or 12 for ¥1150. As well as chicken there are grilled veg options. It's on Suehiro-dōri, east of the intersection with Eki-mae-dōri. Look for the rope curtain hanging over the door.

Caffe Piace CAFE ¥
(カフェピアーチェ; coffees ¥390-600, dishes from ¥450; ☺ noon-10pm, to 8pm Sun, closed Mon) A casual, light cafe with an extensive coffee menu, desserts, and a few small meals. Beer and wine are also served. It's on Suehiro-dōri, just near the corner of Eki-mae-dōri.

Jujuan GRILL, SEAFOOD ¥¥

(ジュジュアン; www.jujuann.com; 751 Suehiro Onsen-chō; meals ¥2000-10,000; ⏰11am-3pm & 5-7pm) Fresh seafood and local beef *sumibi-yaki* (charcoal grilled) are the specialities in this airy restaurant. It does *shabu shabu*, and set courses, such as the *kaisen gozen* (grilled seafood and vegetables with sides), with a seasonal menu that may include crab and other locally sourced goodies. It's on Suehiro-dōri, east of the intersection with Eki-mae-dōri.

ⓘ Information

Tourist Information Office (鳥取市観光案内所; ☑22-3318; www.torican.jp; ⏰9.30am-6.30pm) To the right as you exit the station, with English-language pamphlets and maps. Staff can help book accommodation.

ⓘ Getting There & Away

Tottori is on the coastal JR San-in train line. Major destinations:

Matsue ¥2210, 2¼ hours; express service ¥3470, 1½ hours

Okayama Express via Yonago ¥4270, two hours

Toyooka Local service ¥1450, 2½ hours

There are also long-distance buses to major cities in the region.

ⓘ Getting Around

BUS

The *Kirinjishi* loop bus (¥300/600 per ride/day pass) operates on weekends, holidays and between 20 July and 31 August. It passes the main sights and goes to the dunes. Red- and blue-roofed *Kururi* minibuses (¥100 per ride) ply inner-city loops from the station every 20 minutes, passing by the main city attractions. Regular city buses depart from the station and travel to the dunes area (¥360, 20 minutes). There are maps and timetables available at the information office.

BICYCLE

Rent-a-Cycle (per day ¥500; ⏰8am-6.30pm) Outside the station. You can also rent bikes at the Sand Pal Tottori Information Centre (サンドパルとっとり; 083-17 Yūyama, Fukube-chō; ⏰9am-6pm) near the dunes.

CAR

Cal Rent-a-Car (☑24-0452; http://cal-rent.net; 1-88 Tomiyasu; 24hr from ¥3800; ⏰8am-8pm) Take the main road leading straight out from the south side of the station, then take a left turn at the first major intersection. Cal Rent-a-Car is in a petrol station on the right.

Daisen 大山

☑0859

Although it's not one of Japan's highest mountains, at 1729m Daisen looks impressive because it rises straight from sea level – its summit is only about 10km from the coast. Daisen is part of the **Daisen-Oki National Park**.

The popular climb up the volcano is a five- to six-hour return trip from **Daisen-ji temple** (大山寺). From the summit, there are fine views over the coast and, in perfect conditions, all the way to the Oki Islands. Lonely Planet's *Hiking in Japan* has detailed information on the hike.

Even if you're not planning to hike to the summit, there's plenty to keep you occupied. Temples, ruins and forest walking tracks surround Daisen-ji, and you can walk up the stone path to shrine **Ōgamiyama-jinja** (大神山神社), the oldest building in western Tottori-ken. Further along the Daisen Park Way is the **Masumizu Plateau** (Masumizu-kōgen), where a gondola lift takes you up to an obsevation point and hiking trails. At the park's edge is **Shōji Ueda Museum of Photography** (植田正治写真美術館; www.japro.com/ueda; 353-3 Sumura, Hōki-chō; admission ¥800; ⏰9am-5pm, closed Tue & Dec-Feb), showcasing the work of Tottori-Prefecture photographer Shōji Ueda (1913–2000), in a large minimalist concrete building with fabulous views across to the mountain.

The mountain catches the northwest monsoon winds in the winter, bringing lots of snow to what is western Japan's top skiing area. Among the slopes are **Daisen White Resort** (大山ホワイトリゾート; ☑52-2315; www.daisen-resort.jp) and **Daisen Masumizu-kōgen Ski Resort** (大山ますみず高原スキー場; ☑52-2420; www.masumizu.net/ski).

The closest station to Daisen is Yonago, about 30 minutes from Matsue and an hour to 90 minutes from Tottori on the San-in line. The Daisen Loop bus (one-/two-day pass ¥1000/2000) runs to Daisen-ji from Yonago Station on weekends, holidays and during peak seasons. It stops at all the main sights around the mountain. Regular buses run to the temple from Yonago (¥800, 50 minutes, five daily) with **Nihon Kōtsu** (www.nihonkotsu.co.jp). At the temple is the large **Daisen-ji Information Centre** (☑52-2502; ⏰8.30am-6pm), with brochures, maps and hiking information. Staff can arrange bookings at the local ryokan. For info online in English, check out http://en.go-to-japan.jp/daisenguide.

San-in Coast National Park 山陰海岸国立公園

The coastline east from the Tottori dunes stretching all the way to the Tango-hantō in Kyoto-fu is known as the San-in Kaigan Kokuritsu-kōen – the San-in Coast National Park. There are sandy beaches, rugged headlands and pines jutting into the blue sky. To get the most out of your travels here, having a car is the best option. However, it is possible to get to some sites via train and bus.

Near the edge of Hyōgo Prefecture is **Uradome Kaigan** (浦富海岸), a scenic stretch of islets and craggy cliffs with pines clinging precariously to their sides. Forty-minute **Uradome Kaigan Cruises** (浦富海岸・島めぐり遊覧船; ☑ 0857-73-1212; www.you-run1000.com; cruises ¥1200-2100; ⊙ every 20min 9.10am-4.10pm Mar-Nov) leave from the fishing port of Ajiro, 35 minutes east of Tottori by bus. From Tottori Station, take a bus bound for Iwami Station (岩美駅) and Iwai Onsen (岩井温泉) and get off at the Tōmeguri Yūransen Noriba-mae stop, which is right outside the cruise ticket office and boarding point. The bus goes via the dunes, so it's possible to visit the dunes and do the cruise as a day trip from Tottori. Note that cruises are sometimes cancelled due to rough conditions; get the tourist office to call and check before you go.

Uradome (浦富) and **Makidani** (牧谷), two popular beaches, are a few kilometres east. The closest station is Iwami on the JR San-in line, where there's a **tourist information office** (☑ 0857-72-3481; ⊙ 9am-6pm, closed Mon). You can take a bus to the beach, rent bicycles, and arrange accommodation in the area. **Higashi-hama** (東浜) is a among the best of the swimming beaches along the coast, and is easily accessed by train from Tottori – it's just near Higashi-hama Station (¥400, 30 minutes).

Along this stretch of coast are walking tracks that are part of the **Chūgoku Shizen Hodō** (中国自然歩道; Chūgoku Nature Walking Path), linking to tracks in neighbouring prefectures.

Northern Honshū (Tōhoku)

Why Go?

'The rough sea, stretching out towards Sado, the Milky Way.'
Matsuo Bashō, The Narrow Road to the Deep North (1689)

In the days of Matsuo Bashō, the famous travelling poet, a trip to Northern Honshū was synonymous with walking to the ends of the earth. Tōhoku (東北; literally 'northeast') is still very much the rugged north, a land of hulking volcanic massifs and remote hot springs, of ancient folk beliefs and unique customs born of centuries of isolation.

In a sense, nothing has changed, and yet everything has changed. In 2011, an enormous earthquake and tsunami destroyed a long stretch of coastline. The recovery effort, happening at both government and grassroots levels, faces huge challenges, but this shouldn't stop you from visiting. The vast majority of Northern Honshū was spared significant damage and remains as attractive as ever to those seeking, as Bashō was, an off-the-beaten-track adventure.

Best Onsen

➡ Tsuru-no-yu Onsen (p515)
➡ Aoni Onsen (p511)
➡ Sukayu Onsen (p506)
➡ Zaō Onsen (p527)
➡ Naruko Onsen (p492)

Best Hikes

➡ Dewa Sanzan (p522)
➡ Hakkōda-san (p505)
➡ Akita Komaga-take (p513)
➡ Iwaki-san (p512)
➡ Oirase-gawa (p506)

When to Go

Aomori

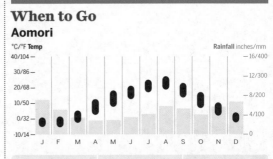

Dec–Feb Siberian cold, but great skiing and *yukimiburo* (snow viewing from an onsen).

Jun–Aug Mild summers come to life with spirited festivals and magnificent greenery.

Sep–Oct A brief but intense autumn is marked by spectacular displays of foliage.

Northern Honshū (Tōhoku) Highlights

1 Following the footsteps of the *yamabushi* (mountain priests) through the sacred peaks of **Dewa Sanzan** (p522)

2 Soaking your worries away at rustic **Nyūtō Onsen** (p515), in the mountains above Tazawa-ko

3 Cycling through the **Tōno Valley** (p496), the land that time forgot

4 Getting away from the mainland crush on **Sado-ga-shima** (p530), a former island of exile

5 Experiencing one of Tōhoku's legendary festivals, like the Tanabata Matsuri in **Sendai** (p483)

6 Dodging ice-covered trees known as 'ice monsters' at **Zaō Onsen** (p527)

7 Making a pilgrimage to the mountaintop temples of **Yamadera** (p526), just as the poet Matsuo Bashō did

8 Exploring the apocalyptic landscape of Ozore-san on the **Shimokita Peninsula** (p508)

9 Reliving the glory of **Hiraizumi** (p494), the 11th-century Buddhist paradise on earth

10 Traipsing around the verdant shores of **Towada-ko** (p506), Honshū's largest crater lake

History

Tōhoku has been populated since at least the Jōmon period (13,000–400 BC), but first entered historical records when, in the 8th century, the newly formed central government in Nara enlisted generals to subjugate the indigenous Emishi people. By the mid-9th century the land, then known as Michinoku (literally 'the land beyond roads') was, if only tenuously, under imperial control.

In the 11th century the Ōshu Fujiwara clan established a short-lived settlement at Hiraizumi that was said to rival Kyoto in its opulence. However it was the warrior and leader Date Masamune, in the 17th century, who would bring lasting notoriety to the region. Masamune transformed the fishing village of Sendai into the capital of a powerful domain. His descendants ruled until the Meiji Restoration brought an end to the feudal system, and an end to Tōhoku's influence, by restoring imperial control.

Although from the outside Tōhoku seems like a cohesive region, there are historic differences within the area. Blessed with rich alluvial plains, the coast along the Sea of Japan became an agricultural centre supplying rice to the imperial capital and, as a result, picked up more influence from Kyoto. Farming was less productive on the Pacific side, and the coastline rocky, wind-battered and difficult to navigate, resulting in a strong culture of perseverance born of hardship and isolation.

National Parks

Sprawling over Fukushima, Niigata and Yamagata Prefectures, **Bandai-Asahi National Park** (磐梯朝日国立公園), at 1,870 sq km, is the third-largest protected area in Japan. The region is defined to the south by

the Bandai-Azuma mountain range and to the north by the holy peaks of Dewa Sanzan.

The **Rikuchū-kaigan National Park** (陸中海岸国立公園) runs 180km along the Pacific coast, from Kuji in Iwate Prefecture to Kesennuma in Miyagi Prefecture. It is characterised by sheer cliffs, crashing waves and, to the south, deep inlets and rocky beaches.

Further north, the 855-sq-km **Towada-Hachimantai National Park** (十和田八幡平国立公園) is a vast wilderness area of beech forests, volcanic peaks, crater lakes and alpine plateaus that straddles Akita and Aomori Prefectures.

The Unesco-protected **Shirakami-sanchi** (白神山地) is a primeval beech forest, also on the Akita–Aomori border. One of the last of its kind in East Asia, it harbours a number of protected species, such as the Asiatic black bear and the golden eagle.

🛈 Getting There & Around

CAR & MOTORCYCLE

Exploring the more remote parts of Tōhoku is possible with local train and minor bus connections, but renting a car is preferable – it offers more flexibility than established public transport routes allow, and you can even get off the grid entirely.

Shimokita Peninsula and Sado-ga-shima are two destinations where having a car can make all the difference. They have some stunning vistas where you'll want the freedom to linger, and driving those winding coastal roads is just plain fun. Towada-ko and Tazawa-ko also offer wonderful scenic drives.

Tōhoku has a solid network of expressways, signposted in romaji (Japanese roman script), and well-maintained prefectural roads. Traffic is much lighter here than in central Honshū, although facilities are often few and far between. Be advised, however, that roads can be severely affected by winter weather. If you're travelling between November and April, check in with a tourist information centre (or call ahead to your destination) for the latest road conditions; road closures caused by snow are not uncommon.

TRAIN

The JR Tōhoku *shinkansen* (bullet train) line travels as far as Aomori. From there, limited-express and local trains run further north to Hokkaidō. The Akita and Yamagata *shinkansen* branches run through central Tōhoku to the Sea of Japan coast.

The JR Tōhoku main line follows roughly the same route as the Tōhoku *shinkansen*, but with regular local and express trains and only as far as Morioka, after which private lines take over. A combination of JR and private lines runs along the east and west coasts.

> ℹ **JR EAST PASS**
>
> The **JR East Pass** (www.jreast.
> co.jp/e/eastpass) offers unlimited
> rail travel around Tokyo and eastern
> Honshū (including all of Tōhoku, plus
> Niigata and Nagano). It's cheaper
> than the full JR Pass and good for four
> flexible days, or five or 10 consecu-
> tive days. Passes can be purchased
> in Japan at both Narita and Haneda
> airports or at major JR train stations.
> They are only valid for foreign passport
> holders on a temporary visitor visa;
> you will need to show your passport
> and visa when you purchase the pass.
> Note that this pass does not cover
> travel on JR buses.

FUKUSHIMA PREFECTURE

Fukushima-ken （福島県）, Japan's third-largest prefecture, serves as the gateway to Tōhoku. Here, the mountains that characterise the north begin to pick up. Come this far and you've left the Tokyo day trippers behind; the wild, varied terrain of the Bandai Plateau attracts hikers and skiers who are keen on deeper exploration. Outside the few cities, the largest of them the capital Fukushima, development is sparse. Fukushima's top cultural attraction is the medieval capital of Aizu-Wakamatsu, a town with a dramatic and disturbing past.

Aizu-Wakamatsu 会津若松

📞 0242 / POP 125,000

Aizu-Wakamatsu, a pilgrimage destination for Japanese history buffs, is a former feudal capital with a story to tell. It's a sprawling city really, but the downtown area where the sights are plays up its history well. Nanoka-machi-dōri, in particular, has a number of old-fashioned shops selling local crafts. Aizu is also famous for its sake, and there are a number of breweries around town that do tours and tastings.

History

Aizu-Wakamatsu was once the capital of the Aizu clan, whose reign came to an end in the Bōshin civil war of 1868, when the clan sided with the Tokugawa shōgunate against the imperial faction. The fall of Aizu is famous throughout Japan on account of the *Byak-kotai* (White Tigers). This group of teenage samurai committed *seppuku* (ritual suicide by disembowelment) when they saw Tsu-ruga Castle shrouded in smoke. In reality, it was the surrounding area that was ablaze and it took weeks before defeat was final, but the White Tigers emerged as a powerful symbol of loyalty and fraternity.

👁 Sights

The main sights in Aizu are conveniently arrayed around the fringes of downtown, and a surprising amount of English signage makes it easy to get around on foot. Alternatively, the retro Classic Town Bus (p480) loops around the city.

Tsuruga-jō CASTLE
（鶴ヶ城; Crane Castle; 📞27-4005; Ōte-machi; museum & teahouse admission ¥500; ⊗8.30am-4.30pm) The towering 1965 reconstruction of Tsuruga-jō sits in sprawling grounds framed by the original moat and some ruins of the old castle walls. Inside is a museum with historical artefacts from battles and daily life, but the real drawcard is the view from the 5th-floor lookout. There's also an evocative, 400-year-old teahouse, rescued by a local family when the castle was destroyed and returned here in 1990.

Iimori-yama HISTORIC SITE
（飯盛山） On the eastern edge of Aizu is Iimori-yama, the mountain where the White Tiger samurai killed themselves. You can take an escalator or walk to the top to visit their graves. There are also some creepy old monuments here, gifted by the former fascist regimes of Germany and Italy, in honour of the samurai's loyalty and bravery.

At the foot of the mountain the **White Tigers Memorial Hall** （白虎隊記念館; Byak-kotai Kinenkan; 📞24-9170; 33 Bentenshita, Ikki-machi; admission ¥400; ⊗8am-5pm Apr-Nov, 9am-4pm Dec-Mar) tells the story of the dramatic suicides and houses the departed samurai's personal possessions.

On the way down, don't miss the **Sazae-dō** （さざえ堂; 📞22-3163; admission ¥400; ⊗8.15am-sunset Apr-Oct, 9am-sunset Nov-Mar), a rare 18th-century wooden hall (that has nothing to do with the White Tigers). It has a fabulous spiral staircase that, Escher-esque, allows you to walk up and down without retracing your steps.

Aizu Bukeyashiki
HISTORIC BUILDING

(会津武家屋敷; ☑28-2525; Innai Higashiyama-machi; admission ¥850; ☺8.30am-5pm Apr-Oct, 9am-4.30pm Nov-Mar; ℗) This is a superb reconstruction of the *yashiki* (villa) of Saigō Tanomo, the Aizu clan's chief retainer. Wander through the 38 rooms, which include a guestroom for the Aizu lord, a tea-ceremony house, quarters for the clan's judge and a rice-cleaning mill, presented here in full, noisy working order.

Aizu Sake Brewing Museum
MUSEUM

(会津酒造歴史館; ☑26-0031; 8-7 Higashi-sakae-machi; admission ¥300; ☺8.30am-5pm Apr-Nov, 9.30am-4.30pm Dec-Mar) This museum, depicting the sake-making process, shares space with a real working brewery. You can sample the house tipple in the gift shop.

🎎 Festivals & Events

Aizu Aki Matsuri
PARADE

(会津秋祭り; Autumn Festival; ☺21-23 Sep) This three-day festival culminates on 23 September with an extravagant procession that threads through the city to Tsuruga-jō, accompanied by a drum-and-fife band, a children's parade and an evening lantern parade.

🛌 Sleeping

Aizuno Youth Hostel
HOSTEL ¥

(会津野ユースホステル; ☑55-1020; www.aizuno.com; 88 Kaki-yashiki, Terasaki, Aizu-Takada-chō; dm ¥3200-3800, s 4000-4600, 3200/4000; ℗☺@) One of the best budget options in the region, Aizuno thrives amid a pleasant rural setting far from the congestion of central Aizu. The spick-and-span hostel, which has Western-style rooms, is located about 20 minutes by foot from Aizu-Takada Station along the Tadami line from Aizu-Wakamatsu (¥230, 20 minutes). If you don't want to walk, call ahead for pick-up from Aizu-Takada.

Minshuku Takaku
MINSHUKU ¥

(民宿多賀来; ☑26-6299; www.naf.co.jp/takaku; 104 Innai Higashiyama-machi; r per person/with 2 meals ¥4200/6300; ℗☺@) This Japanese-style inn offers modest tatami rooms, a pleasant *o-furo* (bath) and an attractive dining area framed by hardwood furnishings. It's located just east of the Aizu Bukeyashiki bus stop; from there, continue along the road, turn left at the post office and it's just behind, on the left.

Aizu Wakamatsu Washington Hotel
BUSINESS HOTEL ¥¥

(会津若松ワシントンホテル; ☑22-6111; www.aizu-wh.com; 201 Byakko-dōri; s/d from ¥8159/14,333; ℗☺@☎) The rooms in this hotel have been updated and are well priced for privacy seekers. It is a three-minute walk from the station's east exit along Byakkotai-dōri; look for the tall beige building.

🍽 Eating

Aizu is famous for *wappa meshi,* steamed fish or vegetables over rice, prepared in a round container made from tree bark, which adds a woody fragrance. Alternatively, head over to neighbouring Kitakata for some serious *rāmen* (egg noodles).

Mitsutaya
JAPANESE ¥

(満田屋; ☑27-1345; 1-1-25 Ōmachi; skewers from ¥120; ☺10am-5pm, closed 1st & 3rd Wed of each month & every Wed Jan-Mar; 🍴) A former bean-paste mill dating from 1834, this is an Aizu landmark. The speciality here is *dengaku,* bamboo skewers of tofu, *mochi* (pounded rice cake) or vegetables basted in sweet miso paste and baked over charcoal. Just point at what you want, or go for the *dengaku cōsu* (tasting course; ¥1150 for seven skewers). Walking west down Nanoko-machi-dōri, take the second left and the restaurant is just around the corner; look for the black banners out front.

★ Takino
JAPANESE ¥¥

(田季野; ☑25-0808; www.takino.jp/frame.html; 5-31 Sakae-machi; wappa meshi from ¥1420; ☺11am-9pm; 🍴🅿) One of the most famous places to try the sublime *wappa meshi,* Takino offers several versions including salmon, crab and wild mushroom. There's a picture menu and dining is on tatami mats under polished wooden beams. Head east on Nanoko-machi-dōri and turn right at the first light; go left at the second alleyway, and you'll see an old, ivy-covered farmhouse on the right – that's it.

ℹ Information

Aizu Wakamatsu Post Office (会津若松郵便局; 1-2-17 Chūō; ☺post 9am-7pm Mon-Fri, to 3pm Sun; ATM 8.45am-7pm Mon-Fri, 9am-5pm Sat & Sun) Located on the main street, with an international ATM.

Police Box (☑22-1877, main office 22-5454) Situated in front of the train station.

THE GREAT EAST JAPAN EARTHQUAKE

At 2.46pm (JST) on 11 March 2011, a magnitude 9.0 earthquake struck off the eastern coast of Tōhoku. The Higashi-Nihon Dai-Shinsai (東日本大震災), or Great East Japan Earthquake, was the most powerful quake to hit Japan since record-keeping began in the early 20th century, and among the five strongest ever recorded in the world. However, it was the tsunami that followed just 20 minutes later that brought the most devastation, levelling coastal communities and taking the death toll to nearly 20,000 people.

Travelling in the Region

All of Tōhoku's major tourist destinations are open and accessible. Sendai, the capital of Miyagi Prefecture, was hit hard on the coast, but the downtown looks unchanged; in fact, as the de facto headquarters of the reconstruction effort, the city is booming. Matsushima, the famously beautiful bay further up the coast, sustained some damage but remains unspoilt. However, some off-the-beaten track destinations, like the island of Kinkasan, are not yet ready for visitors. It's possible to visit others, like Ishinomaki and Oku-Matsushima, but you'll have to work a little harder to get there.

Rail travel remains suspended along some coastal routes; alternative bus routes are provided for affected destinations. For an updated list of JR line closures, see www. jreast.co.jp/e/eastpass/index.html. For closures along the private Sanriku Tetsudō line, which serves the coast of Iwate Prefecture, see www.sanrikutetsudou.com.

Be aware that in some smaller towns along the northeast coast, accommodation is routinely filled with construction workers, and if you're planning to explore this area, make sure to call ahead.

The Road to Recovery

Areas that were damaged by the earthquake but spared by the tsunami were quick to rebound, making the necessary repairs and returning to life as usual. It is a different story for the areas in Miyagi and Iwate Prefectures, where the tsunami hit hardest. Optimistic estimates put recovery at five years, while more realistic ones suggest at least 10 to 15 years. For the most part, the rubble has been cleared, although what to do with it remains unresolved. The devastation is now more apparent in what is missing: large swathes of coastal land are populated with nothing but knee-high grass.

It is time to begin rebuilding, but the question is where? Given the risk of future tsunami, should the coastline even be rebuilt at all? Smaller, more nimble communities have simply opted to pull up their roots and rebuild further inland. Larger ones, with diverse interests, find it harder to reach consensus and move on.

And then follows the question of whether rebuilding should replicate the past or aim for something new. Before the disaster, Miyagi and Iwate Prefectures were among the poorest and least developed in the country. Especially among the younger generation, there is a push for a new approach. But what would that look like and who should decide, the government or the people? These are the kind of questions being raised within the affected communities and, to a certain degree, all over Japan.

The Fukushima Question

Following the earthquake and tsunami, the Fukushima Dai-ichi nuclear power plant experienced a meltdown in three of its reactors, resulting in a Level 7 nuclear disaster, considered the worst since Chernobyl in the Ukraine in 1986. A 20km exclusion zone remains around the plant, which is on the coast 58km from the capital city of Fukushima and 80km from Sendai; however, radioactive contamination exists outside the zone as well. For most travellers, this is the biggest question mark. It's a good idea to look at the maps compiled by Safe Cast (www.safecast.org), an independent group of volunteers who have been collecting data with Geiger counters around the country, to get an idea of contamination levels. Keep in mind that the risks faced by long-term residents far outweigh those encountered by short-term travellers.

WORTH A TRIP

KITAKATA 喜多方

An old Kitakata saying goes: 'A man is not a man unless he has built at least one *kura* (mud-walled storehouse)'.

Scattered around this area, not far from Aizu-Wakamatsu, are literally thousands of these *kura*, constructed between the late 18th and early 20th centuries; there are dozens within walking distance of the station alone. Some have been turned into tourist facilities like galleries and souvenir shops; others house ordinary businesses like drug stores. While each is unique, they share a few common elements, such as thick plaster walls and tile roofs.

Step inside the **Yamatogawa Sake Brewing Museum** (大和川酒蔵北方風土館; 4716 Teramachi; ⏰9am-4.30pm) to peek inside a *kura* that dates from 1790 and, until 20 years ago, functioned as a sake brewery. It's a 15-minute walk north of the station. East of the museum and across the river, Otazukikura-dōri has a cluster of pretty *kura* that are a drawcard for photographers. **Mamemaru** (マメマル; 2854 Minami-machi; coffee & dessert ¥600; ⏰10am-4pm), once a miso storehouse, is now a cafe that serves sweets like ice cream and pudding spiked with the fermented bean paste. Look for the wooden sign on the pale yellow (yes, miso-coloured) *kura*.

Where the quest for storehouses leaves off, the quest for noodles begins: Kitakata is just as famous for its *rāmen* (egg noodles) as for its *kura* obsession. Kitakata's signature noodles are thick and curly, and served up in a hearty pork and fish broth that makes use of the local spring water, soy sauce and sake. Delicious. Of the 100-plus *rāmen* shops in town, **Genraiken** (源来軒; ☎22-0091; 7745 Ippongi-ue; bowls from ¥600; ⏰10am-7.30pm Wed-Mon) is the oldest and most famous. Find it one block north and one block east of the station, with a red facade and a queue.

Kitakata can be reached from Aizu-Wakamatsu by frequent trains along the JR Ban-etsu-saisen line (¥320, 25 minutes). For drivers, Rte 121 runs between Aizu and Kitakata. Bicycle rentals are available across the street from the station for ¥500 per day.

The **Tourist Information Center** (⏰8.30am-5pm), just outside the train station, can provide English maps.

Tourist Information Center (☎33-0688; ⏰9am-5.30pm) Helpful staff and English maps; inside the JR station.

❶ Getting There & Away

BUS

Highway buses connect Aizu-Wakamatsu and Tokyo (¥4800, 4½ hours).

CAR & MOTORCYCLE

The **Tōhoku Expressway** (東北自動車道) runs between Tokyo and Kōriyama, while the **Ban-etsu Expressway** (磐越自動車道) connects Kōriyama and Aizu-Wakamatsu.

TRAIN

The JR Tōhoku *shinkansen* runs hourly between Tokyo and Kōriyama (¥7970, 1¼ hours). Kōriyama is connected to Aizu-Wakamatsu by the JR Banetsu-saisen line; hourly *kaisoku* (rapid) trains (¥1110, 1¼ hours) ply this scenic route.

There are a couple of daily *kaisoku* on the JR Ban-etsu and Shin-etsu lines between Aizu-Wakamatsu and Niigata (¥2210, 2¾ hours); you'll need to change trains at Niitsu.

❶ Getting Around

The retro **Classic Town Bus** (まちなか周遊バス; single/day pass ¥200/500) departs from outside the train station and does a slow loop of the main sights. Bicycle rental is available at several points around town for ¥500 per day; enquire at the Tourist Information Center.

Bandai Plateau 磐梯高原

☎0241 / POP 4000

The Bandai Plateau is part of the **Bandai-Asahi National Park** (磐梯朝日国立公園) and its spectacular scenery and vast potential for independent exploration attract hikers, climbers, fishing enthusiasts, skiers and snowboarders. In the centre is **Bandai-san** (磐梯山; 1819m), a once-dormant volcano that erupted suddenly in 1888, spewing forth a tremendous amount of debris that's said to have lowered the mountain's height by 600m. The eruption destroyed dozens of villages and completely rearranged the landscape, resulting in the vast, lake-dotted plateau now known as Bandai-kōgen.

🏃 Activities

Goshiki-numa
WALKING

(五色沼) The most popular walk in the area follows a 3.7km nature trail around a dozen or so pools known collectively as the **Five Colours Lakes**. Mineral deposits from the 1888 eruption imparted various hues to the waters, including cobalt blue, emerald green and reddish brown, which change with the weather.

There are trailheads located at the Goshiki-numa Iriguchi and Bandai-kōgen bus stops, which are the main transport hubs on the edge of Hibara-ko, the largest of the lakes in Ura-Bandai. This route is serviced by buses that depart from the town of Inawashiro. In April, the Goshiki-numa trail may still be covered in packed snow, and November marks the start of the long Tōhoku winter.

Bandai-san
HIKING

(磐梯山) Bandai-san can be climbed in a day with an early start, and the view from the top takes in the surrounding mountain ranges and Inawashiro Lake to the south. There are six trails up the mountain. The one from the **Ura-Bandai Tozan-guchi** (裏磐梯登山口) is the easiest to reach by public transportation – and the most challenging, at seven hours up and back. From Inawashiro Station, take a bus to Bandai-kōgen. After a climb through ski grounds, the path meets up with the one starting from **Happō-dai** (八方台), the shortest and most popular route. Pick up a *tozan mappu* (trail map) at the Tourist Information Center. Note that the summit is only accessible from mid-May to late October.

Snow Paradise Inawashiro
SNOW SPORTS

(猪苗代スキー場; ☑ 0242-62-5100; www.g-jmt.com/inawashiro/eng/index.php; 7105 Hayama, Inawashiro-machi; 1-day lift ticket adult/child ¥4400/3600; ⊙ Dec–Mar) The original ski area on Bandai-san, Inawashiro has 16 runs, all but two of them beginner and intermedi-ate. Wide slopes, a slow-speed lift and scant weekday crowds particularly suit this resort to novice skiers and families with small children. Seasoned veterans may quickly grow bored with the lack of options, though it's worth pointing out that the signature black diamond run is a 1.5 km chute that frequently stages national competitions.

English signage is adequate, and there are a number of restaurants on the premises. Full equipment rental is available for ¥3900 per day. The slopes are located in the hills above Inawashiro town and during the ski season, frequent shuttle buses run between Inawashiro Station and the resort.

🛏 Sleeping

Urabandai Youth Hostel
HOSTEL ¥

(裏磐梯ユースホステル; ☑ 32-2811; http://homepage3.nifty.com/urabandai/indexe.html; 1093 Kengamine, Hibara, Kita-Shiobara; camping from ¥1000, dm/with 2 meals from ¥3600/5100, YHA discount ¥3000/4500; cabin from ¥5000; ⊙ May–Oct; [P] [@] [🛜] [🐾]) One of the region's classic mountaineering institutions, this hostel is supremely located next to the Goshiki-numa trailhead, a seven-minute walk from the Goshiki-numa Iriguchi bus stop (there are signs). Choose one of the dorm rooms for a social atmosphere, grab a camping spot if you want to rough it, or share a romantic cabin in the woods with your better half.

An English Inn
PENSION ¥¥

(アン・イングリッシュ・イン; ☑ 0242-63-0101; http://aei.inawasiro.com; 3449-84 Higashi-Nakamaru, Osada, Inawashiro-machi; r per person with 1/2 meals from ¥6500/8700; [P] [😊] [🛜] [🐾]) An English-Japanese couple run this pension in Inawashiro, convenient to the slopes. They're happy to share their local knowledge and help guests arrange their visit. With flowered wallpaper and sloping ceilings reminiscent of attic bedrooms, the Western-style rooms have a country-house feel, with the added bonus of an onsen. Ask about family rates.

ℹ Information

Tourist Information Center (☑ 0242-62-2048; ⊙ 8.30am–5pm) Located to the left outside Inawashiro Station.

Ura-Bandai Visitors Center (裏磐梯ビジターセンター; ☑ 32-2850; 1093–697 Kengamine, Hibara; ⊙ 9am–5pm Wed-Mon Apr-Nov, to 4pm Dec-Mar) Near the Goshiki-numa Iriguchi trailhead.

BEST SKIING

➡ Zaō Onsen (p527)

➡ Naeba (p538)

➡ Tazawa-ko (p512)

➡ Myōkō Kōgen

➡ GALA Yuzawa (p536)

Bandai Plateau & Around

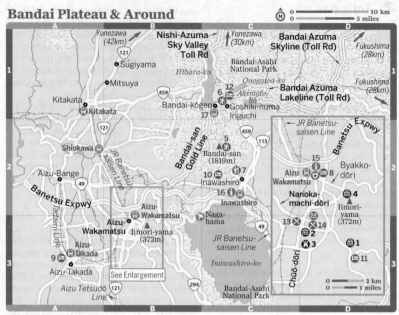

Bandai Plateau & Around

ⓘ Getting There & Away

BUS

From outside Inawashiro Station, frequent buses depart from stop 3 for the Goshiki-numa Iriguchi trailhead (¥750, 25 minutes), before heading on to the Bandai-kōgen stop (¥870, 30 minutes).

TRAIN

Several express *kaisoku* run daily along the JR Banetsu-saisen line (¥480, 30 minutes) between Aizu-Wakamatsu and Inawashiro.

MIYAGI PREFECTURE

Miyagi-ken (宮城県) is something of a transition zone between the rural hinterlands of the far north and the massive urban development that typifies much of central Honshū. Its capital, Sendai, has excellent tourist infrastructure, unique culinary offerings and plenty of cultural attractions to boot. Of course, if you want to escape the urban trappings and get back to the nature that most likely brought you up this way, then don't miss the healing waters of Naruko Onsen and Matsushima, a worthy contender for the title of Japan's most beautiful bay.

Sendai 仙台

🎵 022 / POP 1,060,000

Despite being the largest and most commercially vibrant city in Tōhoku, Sendai is fairly compact, with well-ordered, tree-lined streets that front a ruined castle. Japanese are quick to associate the city with its samurai benefactor, Masamune Date, and its spectacular Tanabata Matsuri, one of Japan's most famous festivals.

Sendai's downtown lies far enough inland to have been spared by the 2011 tsunami; it's as lively as ever, with the best nightlife you'll find in the north. With good transportation connections, it makes a convenient base for exploring some of the more scenic areas of Miyagi and neighbouring prefectures.

History

Sendai, or the 'city of a thousand generations', was established by Date Masamune in 1600. A ruthless, ambitious *daimyō* (domain lord), Masamune turned Sendai, then a fishing village, into a feudal capital that controlled trade routes, salt supplies and grain milling throughout much of Tōhoku. The Date family ruled the Sendai-han until the Meiji Restoration brought an end to the feudal era in 1868. Yet Masamune's presence can still be felt: the roof of Miyagi Stadium's west stand is modelled after the unique crescent symbol the *daimyō* wore on his helmet.

⊙ Sights

It is possible to tour the city on foot, though you'd have to burn a fair amount of shoe leather to hit all the sights. Alternatively, you can take a spin on the Loople tourist bus.

Zuihō-den Mausoleum HISTORIC BUILDING
(瑞鳳殿; ☎ 262-6250; 23-2 Otamaya-shita, Aoba-ku; admission ¥550; ⊙ 9am-4.30pm Feb-Nov, to 4pm Dec & Jan; 🚌 Loople stop 4) Sendai's largest tourist drawcard is the mausoleum of Date Masamune, which sits majestically atop the summit of a tree-covered hill by the Hirose-gawa. Built in 1637, destroyed by Allied bombing during WWII and eventually reconstructed in 1979, the present building is an exact replica of the original. It's faithful to the ornate and sumptuous Momoyama style: a complex, interlocking architecture, characterised by multicoloured woodcarvings. Also atop the hill are the mausoleums of Masamune's second and third successors, Date Tadamune and Date Tsunamune.

VOLUNTEERING IN THE TSUNAMI ZONE

With the clean-up mostly finished, local aid groups have turned to helping communities rebuild. This is delicate work that differs from community to community and, for the most part, requires volunteers with a reasonable degree of Japanese-language skill. Here are a few organisations that are *gaijin* (foreigner)-friendly.

Oga for Aid (www.ogaforaid.org/en) needs volunteers to work on a farming project that aims to provide a steady stream of fresh veggies and extra income to a community whose fishing industry was completely wiped out by the tsunami. Run by an international, multilingual lot, Oga accepts volunteers with no Japanese-language ability. It's based in Minami-Sanriku, up the coast from Ishinomaki.

Earth Camp (www.earthcamp.net) is a new organisation aiming to revitalise the devastated area along Miyagi's Sanriku coast by turning it into an outdoor and education hub. It needs English-speaking volunteers to lead English-language immersion events, hiking trips and the like. Check the website for dates.

Peace Boat (http://peaceboat.jp/relief/volunteer) accepts volunteers with Japanese language ability to work on projects in Ishinomaki or Onagawa for two days or more. This could mean tying nets to help *hoya* (sea squirt) cultivators get back to work or helping with preparations for a local festival. Work starts each Monday, Wednesday or Saturday after a brief orientation session at the Peace Boat Ishinomaki Center.

All organisations can provide volunteers with basic accommodation for a small fee (though you'll need your own sleeping bag and other supplies). You need to apply in advance, and ideally as soon as possible.

Miyagi Prefecture

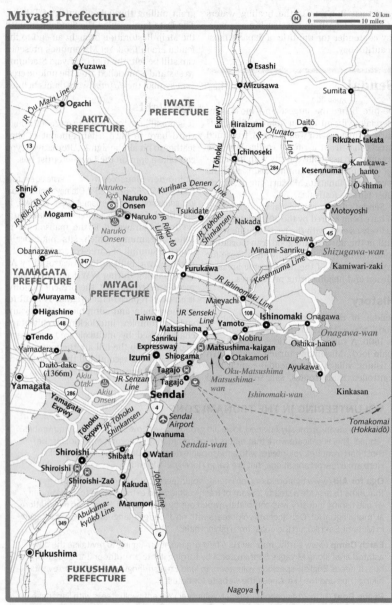

0 ———————— 20 km
0 ———————— 10 miles

Yuzawa

Esashi

Mizusawa

Sumita

JR Ōu Main Line

Ogachi

IWATE PREFECTURE

AKITA PREFECTURE

13

Tōhoku Expwy

Hiraizumi

Daitō

JR Ōfunato Line

Ichinoseki

Rikuzen-takata

284

Karukawa-hantō

Kesennuma

Ō-shima

Shinjō

Naruko-kyō

Naruko Onsen

Naruko Onsen

Kurihara

Denen Line

JR Rikū-tō Line

Mogami

Tsukidate

JR Tōhoku Shinkansen

Motoyoshi

Nakada

JR Rikū-tō Line

45

Naruko Onsen

Shizugawa

Obanazawa

Minami-Sanriku

Shizugawa-wan

347

Furukawa

Kamiwari-zaki

YAMAGATA PREFECTURE

MIYAGI PREFECTURE

47

JR Ishinomaki Line

Kesennuma Line

Murayama

Maeyachi

Higashine

Taiwa

JR Senseki Line

108

Ishinomaki

Onagawa

48

Yamoto

Onagawa-wan

Tendō

Matsushima

Sanriku Expressway

Nobiru

Oshika-hantō

Yamadera

Izumi

Shiogama

Matsushima-kaigan

Oku-Matsushima

Ayukawa

Daitō-dake (1366m)

Akiu Ōtaki

JR Senzan Line

Tagajo

Otakamori

Matsushima-wan

Yamagata

Akiu Onsen

Tagajo

Sendai

Ishinomaki-wan

Kinkasan

286

Yamagata Expwy

4

Sendai Airport

Tomakomai (Hokkaidō)

Tōhoku Expwy

JR Tōhoku Shinkansen

Iwanuma

Sendai-wan

Shiroishi

Shibata

Watari

Shiroishi

Jōban Line

Shiroishi-Zaō

Kakuda

Abukuma-kyūkō Line

Marumori

349

6

Fukushima

FUKUSHIMA PREFECTURE

Nagoya

Sendai Castle Ruins　　　　　　CASTLE
(仙台城跡 | Sendai-jō Ato; 🚌 Loople stop 6, regular bus stop 'Sendai Jō Ato Minami') Built on Aoba-yama in 1602 by Date Masamune and destroyed during Allied bombing, Sendai-jō, also called Aoba-jō (Green Leaves Castle),

still looms large over the city. Giant moss-covered walls, as imposing as they are impressive, are still intact and the grounds offer sweeping views over the city. There's also a larger-than-life statue of Masamune on horseback.

Sendai City Museum
MUSEUM
(仙台市博物館 | Sendai-shi Hakubutsukan; ☎ 225-3074; 26 Kawauchi, Aoba-ku; admission ¥400; ⏰ 9am-4.45pm Tue-Sun; 🚌 Loople stop 5) If you're interested in learning more about Masamune, the city museum offers a comprehensive account of the samurai's epic life, as well as more than 13,000 artefacts on loan from the Date family. There are plenty of explanations in English, too. Interestingly, although Masamune was blind in one eye, which earned him the nickname 'One-Eyed Dragon', he is nearly always depicted in his portraits as having two eyes!

Sendai Mediatheque
LIBRARY
(せんだいメディアテーク; www.smt.city.sendai.jp; 2-1 Kasuga-machi, Aoba-ku; ⏰ 9am-10pm; gallery hours vary) FREE Housed in an award-winning structure designed by Japanese architect Itō Toyō, this cultural hub includes a library, art galleries and event space. Check the website to see if anything is going on when you're in town.

✪ Festivals & Events

Donto-sai
FESTIVAL
(どんと祭; ⏰ 14 Jan) Men brave subzero weather to don loincloths and pray for good fortune for the new year.

Aoba Matsuri
PARADE
(青葉祭り; www.aoba-matsuri.com; ⏰ 3rd weekend in May) Following a 350-year tradition, dancers and floats take to the streets to celebrate spring.

Sendai Tanabata Matsuri
FESTIVAL
(仙台七夕まつり | Star Festival; www.sendaitanabata.com; ⏰ 6-8 August) Sendai's biggest event celebrates a Chinese legend about the stars Vega and Altair. Vega was the king's daughter who fell in love with and married Altair, a common herder. The king disapproved, so he formed the Milky Way between them. Once a year magpies are supposed to spread their wings across the universe so that the lovers can meet – traditionally on 7 July (on the old lunar calendar). Sendai celebrates in grand style by decorating the main streets with bamboo poles festooned with multicoloured streamers, and holding afternoon parades on Jōzenji-dōri. A million visitors ensure that accommodation is booked solid at this time of year.

Jōzenji Street Jazz Festival
LIVE MUSIC
(定禅寺ストリートジャズフェスティバル; www.j-streetjazz.com; ⏰ 2nd weekend in September) Hundreds of buskers from across Japan perform in Sendai's streets and arcades. Book your accommodation way, way in advance.

Sendai Pageant of Starlight
FESTIVAL
(SENDAI光のページェント; ⏰ mid to late Dec) About 600,000 festive lights illuminate Aoba-dōri and Jōzenji-dōri.

🛏 Sleeping

★ Dōchū-an Youth Hostel
HOSTEL ¥
(道中庵ユースホステル; ☎ 247-0511; www.jyh.or.jp/yhguide/touhoku/dochuan; 31 Kita-yashiki, Ōnoda, Taihaku-ku; dm ¥3750, YHA discount ¥3150; P ⊕ @) This evocative former farmhouse has cosy Japanese-style rooms, genial managers, bike rental, free internet and a fantastic old cedar bath to soak in. Its only drawback is being quite a way south of the city centre. The closest station is Taishidō (¥180, eight minutes from Sendai Station) on the JR Tōhoku line, from where

---

DON'T MISS

TŌHOKU'S FAMOUS FESTIVALS

Tōhoku is known throughout Japan for its traditional festivals, which number among the most elaborate – and raucous – in the country. While every town has its own signature celebration (or two or three), these are the 'big three' not to miss. You'll need to plan ahead though: huge crowds mean the accommodation is booked solidly months in advance.

Sendai Tanabata Matsuri (p485) Thousands of coloured streamers around the downtown area honour a tale of star-crossed lovers.

Aomori Nebuta Matsuri (p503) Local artists outdo themselves in creating elaborate floats, and merrymakers take to the streets in throngs.

Akita Kantō Matsuri (p518) Stunning acrobatics are performed with towering bamboo poles hung with lanterns.

Central Sendai

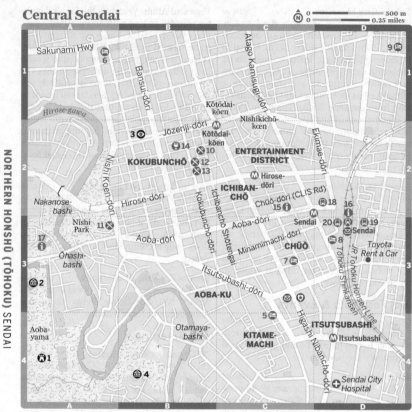

it's a six-minute walk; ask for a map at the station or print one from the website.

Sendai Chitose Youth Hostel
HOSTEL ¥
(仙台千登勢ユースホステル; ☎222-6329; www.jyh.or.jp/yhguide/touhoku/sendai/index.html; 6-3-8 Odawara, Aoba-ku; dm ¥3855, YHA discount ¥3255; ☻@☎) For budget digs within walking distance of the city centre, this hostel has snug Japanese-style rooms in a residential area north of the train station. From the east exit, walk straight through the bus pool and take a left on the main road, walking for 15 minutes until you see a drug store, then take a left, followed by the second right onto a narrow street.

Aisaki Ryokan
RYOKAN ¥
(相崎旅館; ☎264-0700; http://aisakiryokan.com; 5-6 Kitame-machi, Aoba-ku; s/tw ¥3990/7350; ☻☎) If you're not intimidated by cramped spaces, this budget inn offers simple yet functional Japanese- and Western-style

rooms with clean and modern furnishings; cheaper rooms have shared facilities. It's also within easy walking distance of the station. Aisaki is one block over from the main post office; look for the sign indicating the entrance down a narrow side street

.Bansuitei Ikoisō
RYOKAN ¥¥
(晩翠亭いこい荘; ☎222-7885; www.ikoisouryokan.co.jp; 1-8-31 Kimachi-dōri, Aoba-ku; r per person/with 2 meals from ¥4725/7350; ☻☎) One of the few traditional inns remaining in central Sendai, Ikoisō manages to feel peaceful even within walking distance of downtown. The tatami rooms are spotless and the owners friendly and accommodating. It's a seven-minute walk from the Kita-yoban-chō subway station.

Hotel Central Sendai
BUSINESS HOTEL ¥¥
(ホテルセントラル仙台; ☎711-4111; www.hotel-central.co.jp/08englis01.html; 4-2-6 Chūō, Aoba-ku; s/d from ¥7140/12,600; ☻@☎) As its

Central Sendai

name implies, Hotel Central Sendai is located smack dab in the centre of town, just two blocks west of Sendai Station. While fairly standard as far as business hotels go, it's a good choice for privacy seekers and a much cheaper alternative to Sendai's more famous brand-name accommodation options.

Hotel Metropolitan Sendai HOTEL ¥¥¥
(ホテルメトロポリタン仙台; ☎ 268-2525; www.s-metro.stbl.co.jp/english/index.html; 1-1-1 Chūō, Aoba-ku; s/d ¥12,705/23,100; ❄@🛜🖥) For comfort and convenience, you can't beat the Metropolitan, which is part of the Sendai Station complex. Rooms here are smart, well appointed and comfortably plush.

🍴 Eating

Gyūtan (charcoal-grilled cow's tongue) is a much-loved local delicacy.

Gengo Chaya TEAHOUSE ¥
(源吾茶屋; 1-1 Sakuragaoka-kōen, Aoba-ku; snacks from ¥350; ⏰ 11am-6pm; 🚗🅿) In business for 130 years, this teahouse is known for its *zunda-mochi*, pounded rice cakes topped with a jam made from fresh soybeans – a Sendai speciality. You can get meals here, too, but the *mochi* alone is incredibly filling. The teahouse is on the eastern edge of Sakuragaoka Park, with white *noren* (sunshade) curtains out front.

Hosoya BURGERS ¥
(ほそや; 2-10-7 Kokubunchō, Aoba-ku; burgers from ¥330; ⏰ noon-10pm, to 8pm Sun; 🚗) This vintage burger counter has grilled more than a million patties since opening in 1950,

and still serves up old-school soda fountain treats like ice-cream floats. There are also a few options for vegetarians, like egg and cheese sandwiches. Look for the English sign out front.

★ Aji Tasuke JAPANESE ¥¥
(味太助; ☎ 225-4641; www.aji-tasuke.co.jp; 4-4-13 Ichiban-chō, Aoba-ku; meals from ¥1400; ⏰ 11.30am-10pm Wed-Mon; 🅿) At this landmark restaurant it's not what you order, but how much. Everyone is here to sample the famous *gyūtan*, served with a side of pickled cabbage and tail soup. Grab a seat at the counter to watch – and smell – the grilling in action. The restaurant is next to a small torii (shrine gate) and usually has a queue.

Jiraiya IZAKAYA ¥¥
(地雷也; ☎ 261-2164; www.jiraiya.com/pc; Basement fl, 2-1-15 Kokubunchō, Aoba-ku; dishes from ¥1050; 🅿) Local seafood and sake are the drawcards here. Seating is elbow-to-elbow at the counter, but the atmosphere is warm and jovial. If you can splurge, try the charcoal-grilled *kinki* (also called *kichiji*, or rockfish), the house speciality. Jiraiya's entrance is on a side street, marked by a giant red lantern. Reservations are recommended on weekends, especially for groups.

🍷 Drinking & Nightlife

The Kokubunchō area is Tōhoku's largest entertainment district. It's noisy, slightly chaotic and bright, with everything from hole-in-the-wall bars and British-styled pubs to raging dancing clubs and seedy strip shows. Note that there are a fair

WORTH A TRIP

AKIU ONSEN

Akiu Onsen (秋保温泉) was the Date clan's favourite therapeutic retreat, with a natural saltwater spring that's said to be a curative for back pain and arthritis. There are dozens of inns here that offer up their baths to day trippers.

You can also stretch your legs along the rim of **Rairai Gorge** (磊々峡; Rairai-kyō), a 20m-deep gorge that runs through the village. Pick up maps and a list of bathhouses at the **Tourist Information Center** (☑398-2323; akiuonsenkumiai.com/en/index.html; ☺9am-6pm) at the Akiu Sato Center (two bus stops before the terminus at Akiu Onsen Yumoto).

In the hills west of town is **Akiu Falls** (秋保大滝; Akiu Ōtaki), a 6m-wide, 55m-high waterfall designated as one of Japan's three most famous waterfalls (Japanese do love those famous sets of three!). View the falls from a scenic outlook or hike down 20 minutes to the bottom.

Buses leave hourly for Akiu Onsen from stop 8 at Sendai Station's west bus pool (¥780, 50 minutes). On weekends there are two buses daily that continue to Akiu Ōtaki (¥1070, 1½ hours). Otherwise, catch one of the few buses for the falls from the Akiu Sato Center (¥630, 20 minutes).

number of hostess and host clubs here, as well as seemingly ordinary bars, that levy steep cover charges; it's a good idea to check before ordering.

Gallo
BAR

(http://gallo-bar.jimdo.com; 2-12-23 Kokubunchō, Aoba-ku; cover charge ¥500; ☺7pm-2am, closed irregularly) Bucking the trend for flash and brashness in Kokubunchō, this tiny basement bar has a mellow vibe and retro-pop soundtrack. The menu features fruit-infused spirits from around Japan. Our pick is the lemon and ginger-spiked *umeshū* (plum wine; ¥650). Look for the hand-painted English sign.

Club Shaft
DANCE CLUB

(☑722-5651; www.clubshaft.com; 4th fl, Yoshiokaya Dai 3 Bldg, 2-10-11 Kokubunchō, Aoba-ku; ☺8pm-late Mon-Thu, from 10pm Fri & Sat) This perennial venue spins a shuffled playlist of hip-hop, house and J-pop. You'll have a great time here, and most likely regret it once the hangover kicks in.

ⓘ Information

EMERGENCY

Sendai Central Police Station (仙台中央警察署; ☑222-7171; 1-3-19 Itsutsubashi, Aoba-ku)

MEDICAL SERVICES

Sendai City Hospital (仙台市立病院; ☑266-7111, 24-hr emergency hotline 216-9960; http://hospital.city.sendai.jp; 3-1 Shimizu-kōji, Wakabayashi-ku; ☺outpatient service 8.30am-11.30am Mon-Fri)

MONEY & POST

Sendai Central Post Office (仙台中央郵便局; ☑267-8035; 1-7 Kitame-machi, Aoba-ku; ☺post 9am-9pm Mon-Fri, to 5pm Sat & Sun; ATM 7am-11pm Mon-Fri, 9am-9pm Sat, to 7pm Sun) There's an international ATM here.

TOURIST INFORMATION

Sendai City Information Center (☑222-4069; www.sentabi.jp/1000/10000000.html; 2nd fl, JR Sendai Station; ☺8.30am-7pm) Pick up English maps and brochures here.

Sendai International Centre (仙台国際センター; ☑265-2471; www.sira.or.jp/icenter/english/index.html; Aoba-yama, Aoba-ku; ☺9am-8pm) English-speaking staff, plus an international newspaper library and bulletin board.

TRAVEL AGENCIES

IACE Travel (☑211-0489; www.iace.co.jp; 2-2-1 Chūō, Aoba-ku; ☺10am-7pm Mon-Fri, 10am-5pm Sat) For international travel arrangements.

View Plaza (びゅうプラザ; 2nd fl, JR Sendai Station; ☺10am-7pm) For domestic travel arrangements, including ferry tickets.

ⓘ Getting There & Away

AIR

From Sendai airport, 18km south of the city centre, flights head for Tokyo, Osaka, Nagoya, Hiroshima, Sapporo and many other destinations.

The Sendai Kūkō Access line leaves for the airport from Sendai Station roughly every 20 minutes (¥630, 25 minutes).

BOAT

From Sendai-kō port, **Taiheyo Ferry** (☎ 263-9877; www.taiheyo-ferry.co.jp/english/index.html) has one daily ferry to Tomakomai on Hokkaidō (from ¥7000, 15 hours), and three to four ferries per week to Nagoya (from ¥6500, 22 hours).

Buses leave from stop 34 at Sendai Station for Sendai-kō (¥490, 40 minutes), but only until 6pm.

BUS

Highway buses depart from outside the east exit of the train station, and connect Sendai to major cities throughout Honshū. Purchase tickets at the **JR Tōhoku Bus Center** (☎ 256-6646; www.jrbustohoku.co.jp; ⏰ 6.50am-7.30pm), next to bus stop 42.

CAR & MOTORCYCLE

The **Tōhoku Expressway** (東北自動車道) runs between Tokyo and the greater Sendai area.

Toyota Rent a Car (☎ 293-0100; http://rent.toyota.co.jp/en/index.html; 1-5-3 Tsutsujigaoka, Miyagino-ku; ⏰ 8am-8pm) has an office a few blocks east of the station.

TRAIN

The JR Tōhoku *shinkansen* runs hourly between Tokyo and Sendai (¥10,590, two hours), and between Sendai and Morioka (¥6290, 45 minutes).

There are several daily *kaisoku* on the JR Senzan line between Sendai and Yamagata (¥1110, 1¼ hours), via Yamadera (¥820, one hour). Local trains on the JR Senseki line connect Sendai and Matsushima-kaigan (¥400, 35 minutes); make sure to get one going all the way to Takagi-machi, or you'll have to transfer at Higashi-Shiogama.

❶ Getting Around

The **Loople** (one ride/day pass ¥250/600) tourist trolley leaves from the west bus pool's stop 15-3 every 30 minutes from 9am to 4pm, making a useful loop around the city in a clockwise direction.

Sendai's single subway line runs from Izumi-chūō in the north to Tomizawa in the south, but doesn't cover any tourist attractions; single tickets cost ¥200 to ¥350.

---

❶ SENDAI MARUGOTO PASS

The **Sendai Marugoto Pass** (仙台まるごとパス; adult/child ¥2600/1300) covers unlimited travel for two days on the Loople tourist bus, Sendai subway and area trains and buses going as far as Matsushima-kaigan, Akiu Onsen and Yamadera (in Yamagata Prefecture). Pick one up at JR Sendai Station.

Matsushima 松島

☎ 022 / POP 15,800

Matsushima's glorious bay, studded with some 260 pine-covered islands, is one of Japan's *Nihon Sankei* (Three Great Sights). Over the centuries, the trees have been slowly twisted by the winds, while their rocky bases have been eroded by the lapping waves. The result is a spectacular monument to nature's dramatic powers.

The poet Matsuo Bashō, who filled his journal with apprehensions about the journey northward, frequently dreamed of moonlit nights over Matsushima. More recently, locals credit the islands – which served as a natural breakwater – with mostly sparing Matsushima from the devastation experienced elsewhere along the coast in the 2011 tsunami.

Matsushima is the most popular tourist destination on the northeast coast and can get very crowded, especially on summer weekends. Still, its charms are undeniable.

◉ Sights

Matsushima-kaigan, where the sights are, is essentially a small village, easily navigated on foot.

Zuigan-ji　　　　　　　　　　TEMPLE
(瑞巌寺; admission ¥700; ⏰ 8am-5pm Apr-Sep; closes earlier Oct-Mar) Tōhoku's finest Zen temple, Zuigan-ji was established in 828 AD. The present buildings were constructed in 1606 by Date Masamune to serve as a family temple. Zuigan-ji is undergoing a major restoration project that will take until 2019 to complete. As a result, some buildings are closed and others are sheathed in tarps, though it is possible to enter them. Still open is the excellent Seiryūden (temple museum), which has a number of well-preserved relics from the Date family, including National Treasures.

Kanran-tei　　　　　　　　　PAVILION
(観瀾亭; admission ¥200; ⏰ 8.30am-5pm Apr-Oct, to 4.30pm Nov-Mar) This pavilion was presented to the Date family by the *daimyō* Toyotomi Hideyoshi in the late 16th century. It served as a genteel venue for tea ceremonies and moon-viewing parties – the name means 'a place to view ripples on the water'. Today it's a peaceful spot for sipping a bowl of whisked *matcha* (powdered green tea).

Godai-dō
TEMPLE

(五大堂) Date Masamune constructed this small wooden temple in 1604. Although it stands on an island in the bay, connected to the mainland by a short bridge, it was miraculously untouched by the 2011 tsunami. The temple doors open to the public only once every 33 years (next in 2039). Come instead for the sea views and to see the 12 animals of the Chinese zodiac carved on the eaves.

Fuku-ura-jima
ISLAND

(福浦島; admission ¥200; ⊙8am-5pm Mar-Oct, to 4.30pm Nov-Feb) Connected to the mainland by a 252m-long red wooden bridge, Fuku-ura-jima puts you right in the bay. The shady trails here, which wind along the coast through native pines and a botanic garden, make for a pleasant hour-long stroll.

🏃 Activities

Matsushima-wan
CRUISE

(松島湾; www.matsushima.or.jp; adult/child ¥1400/700; ⊙9am-3pm) To get a sense of the scale of the bay and its dense cluster of pine-topped islands, which sit like so many bonsai floating in a giant's backyard pond, you need to get out on the water. Cruise boats depart hourly, year-round, from the central ferry pier, completing a 50-minute loop. A running commentary, most of it translated into English, provides trivia about some of the more famous islands. Between April and October, you can opt for a longer course (¥2500, 1¾ hours) that goes all the way to Oku-Matsushima.

🎎 Festivals & Events

Matsushima Kaki Matsuri
FESTIVAL

(松島牡蠣祭り | Matsushima Oyster Festival) Bivalve aficionados will appreciate this festival, held on the first weekend in February, where you can purchase oysters and cook them on a 100m-long grill.

Zuigan-ji Tōdō
FESTIVAL

(瑞巌寺灯道; ⊙6 to 8 Aug) The approach to Zuigan-ji is lit with candlesticks to honour the ancient shrine.

Matsushima Ryūtōe Umi-no-bon
FESTIVAL

(松島流灯会海の盆; http://uminobon.jp; ⊙mid-Aug) The souls of the departed are honoured with the O-Bon (Festival of the Dead) ritual, when lighted lanterns are floated out to sea.

🛏 Sleeping & Eating

Bistro Abalon
PENSION ¥¥

(びすとろアバロン; ☎354-5777; www.bistro abalon.com/06/index.html; 26-21 Sanjugari; s/d ¥6300/10,500, r per person with 2 meals ¥12,000; P🐕🍴📶) 🍴 This pension looks like a little chateau perched on a hill. Inside, however, are dark-wood beams, rattan furniture and bamboo shades. The nicer rooms have balconies and views of the sea. Meals are a feast of locally sourced seafood, beef and produce. The inn is a seven-minute walk up the hill behind Matsushima-kaigan Station.

Hotel Ubudo
LUXURY HOTEL ¥¥¥

(ホテル海風土; ☎355-0022; www.ubudo.jp; 5-3 Higashi-hama; r per person with 2 meals from ¥18,000; P@📶) Fancy catching the sunrise over the bay from your window, or perhaps from the bath? This onsen hotel gets top billing for its fabulous *rotemburo* (outdoor bath), which faces out towards the bay; when the hotel is not too crowded, guests can reserve it for private use. The spacious rooms are either Japanese or Western style; the priciest ones have private baths on the balcony. Meals are lavish *kaiseki* (Japanese haute cuisine), showcasing the rich variety of local seafood. The hotel is away from the fray, past the bridge to Fukuura-jima but still within walking distance of the main sights.

OKU-MATSUSHIMA

On the eastern curve of the bay, remote Oku-Matsushima (奥松島) saw far more tsunami damage than Matsushima. At the time of researching this edition, little had been rebuilt. It is still possible to visit **Ōtakamori** (大高森), a hill in the middle of Miyato Island that offers stunning views of the bay; however, you will have to work to get here. The Tourist Information Centre in Matsushima can help you arrange a taxi there and back for about ¥6000. Otherwise, it's an hour's walk from the closest bus stop at Nobiru (¥230, 20 minutes). Cross the bridge in front of the bus stop and head to the coast, turning right on the newly paved road and continuing until you see the sign for the trailhead and a small parking lot. From here, it's a 15-minute walk to the top of Ōtakamori. There are no facilities (or street lights) along the way, so pack water and make sure you can make it back before dark.

THE DELICACIES OF THE DEEP NORTH

Eating in Tōhoku is all about simple pleasures: the bounty of the land and sea where and when it exists, and making the most of what you've got.

Gyū-tan (牛タン; cow tongue), grilled over charcoal and served with a side of tail soup, is much loved by Sendai locals. Apparently the tradition derived from hard times (as so many Tōhoku traditions do). For good times, there's **Yonezawa-gyū** (米沢牛), the premium grade beef of Yonezawa.

You can't leave Akita Prefecture without sampling its most famous dish, **kiritanpo** (きりたんぽ), which is kneaded rice wrapped around bamboo spits and then barbecued over a charcoal fire. More often than not it's served in a chicken and soy-sauce broth with vegetables to make a hotpot called **kiritanpo-nabe** (きりたんぽ鍋). Another Akita specialty is **inaniwa udon** (稲庭うどん), thinner-than-usual wheat noodles.

Morioka is all about noodles: there's the all-you-can-eat noodle extravaganza that is **wanko-soba** (わんこそば) and **jaja-men** (じゃじゃ麺), flat wheat noodles topped with sliced cucumber, miso paste and ground meat. When it comes to *rāmen* (egg noodles), the little Fukushima town of Kitakata punches above its weight.

With a coastline that stretches from the Pacific to the Sea of Japan, Aomori Prefecture is known for fresh seafood like **uni** (うに; sea urchin roe) and **hotate** (ホタテ; scallops). The village of Ōma, at the tip of the Shimokita Peninsula, is said to have the finest tuna in the country.

Santori Chaya JAPANESE ¥
(さんとり茶屋; 24-4-1 Senzui; meals from ¥980; ☉11.30am-3pm & 5-10pm Thu-Tue) Perennial local favourites from land and sea such as *kaisen-don* (mixed sashimi on rice) and *gyūtan* (cow tongue) are on the menu here, along with seasonal specialities like Matsushima's famous oysters. Seating is on floor cushions on the 2nd floor; try to get a table by the window. The restaurant is in a beige building with an indigo banner and has a picture menu.

ℹ️ Information

Tourist Information Center (☎354-2263; www.matsushima-kanko.com; ☉9.30am-4.30pm Mon-Fri, 8.30am-5pm Sat & Sun) Get English brochures, accommodation bookings and the latest info on Oku-Matsushima here.

ℹ️ Getting There & Away

CAR & MOTORCYCLE
By road, Matsushima can be reached from Sendai via the **Sanriku Expressway** (三陸自動車道).

TRAIN
Frequent trains on the JR Senseki line connect Sendai and Matsushima-kaigan (¥400, 35 minutes).

Due to tsunami damage, the rail service is disrupted between Takagi-machi (one stop after Matsushima-kaigan) and Rikuzen-Ono. A bus runs along this route instead, leaving from Matsushima-kaigan Station and travelling to Yamoto (one stop after Rikuzen-Ono). It stops near all the train stations along the way, including Nobiru (¥230, 20 minutes), the closest stop for Oku-Matsushima. Buy a regular JR ticket at the train station to use on the bus. Pick up the Senseki line for Ishinomaki in Yamoto.

Ishinomaki 石巻

☎0225 / POP 152,000
This seaside city's singular tourist attraction is one that matters big to manga fans: **Ishinomaki Mangattan Museum** (石ノ森萬画館; ☎96-5055; www.man-bow.com/manga; 2-7 Nakase; adult/child ¥800/200; ☉9am-6pm Mar-Nov, to 5pm Wed-Mon Dec-Feb, closed 3rd Tue Mar-Nov). Looking like an otherworldly spaceship, this museum is packed with tributes to influential *manga-ka* (cartoonist) and local hero Shōtarō Ishinomori, most famous for creating the *Cyborg 009* and *Kamen Rider* series.

The museum, and Ishinomaki, were heavily damaged by the 2011 tsunami. At the time of researching this edition, the museum was still undergoing reconstruction, but had reopened. From the train station it's about a 20-minute walk; pick up a map at the **Tourist Information Center** (☎93-6448; www.i-kanko.com; ☉9am-5.30pm), just outside the station. Along the way you'll spot a few statues of Ishinomori's characters, a teaser for what's to come.

LOCAL KNOWLEDGE

ISHINOMAKI 2.0

Cachet may not be up there with infrastructure, but it can certainly help a city attract a young, vibrant population. Ishinomaki was devastated by the earthquake and tsunami, but even before that it was on its way to becoming a city of shuttered storefronts. **Ishinomaki 2.0**, a collective of creative types from Sendai and Tokyo, NPO workers and local merchants, is working to 'upgrade' the city by taking abandoned damaged buildings and turning them into something, well, cool. So far they've got a workshop to brand 'made in Ishinomaki' goods, a bar and a guesthouse, where dorm beds costs just ¥2000 a night. Stop by the hub, **Irori** (☑0225-25-4953; http://ishinomaki2.com/v2/english; 2-10-2 Chūō; ⊙10am-7pm; 🐦), to see what else is going on; you're welcome to hang out and use their wi-fi for the price of a cup of coffee. It's in the town centre, a 10-minute walk from Ishinomaki Station.

Most travellers just come for the afternoon, but if you'd like to spend more time getting to know the city, now in the process of rebuilding, you can bed down for the night at the guesthouse run by Ishinomaki 2.0.

The JR Senseki line, connecting Sendai and Ishinomaki was suspended between Takagi-machi and Rikuzen-Ono at the time this edition was produced. Travellers coming from Matsushima-kaigan should take a bus to Yamoto and connect with the Senseki line there for Ishinomaki (¥480, 1½ hours). Direct highway buses leave for Ishinomaki roughly twice an hour from stop 33 in front of Sendai Station (¥800, 1½ hours).

Naruko Onsen   鳴子温泉

☑ 0229 / POP 8500

Come to Naruko Onsen to hear the clip-clop of *geta* (Japanese clogs) as bathers wearing *yukata* (light, cotton kimonos) saunter between spring-fed baths. Breathe in and smell the sulphurous steam as it rises from street culverts. Stop and soak tired feet in the (free!) *ashiyu* (foot baths), or go for the full wash in one of the town's onsen ryokan. Naruko Onsen is famous for having nine distinct springs, whose waters have a different composition of minerals and thus different healing qualities. Take advantage of the Yumeguri Ticket (¥1200), which you can buy at the Tourist Information Center, to visit the baths at several different inns.

⊙ Sights & Activities

Taki-no-yu   ONSEN

(滝の湯; admission ¥150; ⊙7.30am-10pm) This fabulously atmospheric wooden bathhouse has hardly changed in 150 years and is a sheer delight. Water gushes in from *hinoki* (cypress) channels, carrying various elements and minerals including sulphur, sodium bicarbonate and sodium chloride. This onsen is particularly famous for its therapeutic relief of high blood pressure and hardened arteries.

Naruko Gorge   HIKING

(鳴子峡 | Naruko-kyō) Northwest of Naruko town, this 100m-deep gorge is particularly spectacular in the fall when the leaves change colour. At the time of research, the trail leading to the gorge from town was closed for repairs. An alternative course, taking about an hour to loop around two bridges, can be reached from Nakayamadaira Onsen Station (¥180, seven minutes). The path also intersects with a 10km stretch of the old foot highway, walked by the haiku poet Matsuo Bashō, which is now a hiking trail. Pick up maps and the latest trail info at the Tourist Information Center.

🛏 Sleeping

Yusaya Ryokan   RYOKAN ¥¥

(ゆさや旅館; ☑83-2565; www.yusaya.co.jp; 84 Yumoto; r per person with 2 meals from ¥13,800; 🅿@) Among the many charms of this country inn is the chance to bathe in three different baths, which take their waters from different springs. The particularly impressive *rotemburo*, which may be used privately, is in an isolated building surrounded by a dense thicket of trees. The main building, dating to 1936, has tatami-lined sleeping quarters separated from Western-style sitting areas by sliding *shoji* (rice paper screens). Meals are elegant banquets of river fish and mountain vegetables.

Bentenkaku   RYOKAN ¥¥

(弁天閣; ☑83-2461; www.bentenkaku.jp; 87 Kuruma-yu; r per person/with 2 meals from ¥6300/

11,025) This homly, though slightly worn, ryokan is popular with foreign visitors. The tatami rooms are plenty comfortable, but best of all are the twin *rotemburo*, set in a landscaped garden fenced off with bamboo and available for private use. The inn is at the edge of town overlooking the Arao-gawa. Call for pick-up from the station; otherwise it's a 20-minute walk.

Shopping

Naruko Onsen is famous for its *kokeshi* (traditional wooden dolls). Originally toys for children, they became a popular souvenir of onsen towns in the early 20th century.

Kokeshi-no-Ōnuma CRAFTS
(こけしの大沼; 93-1 Yumoto; ⏲8am-8pm) This father-and-son team represents the 5th and 6th generation, respectively, in a line of well-regarded *kokeshi* makers. The workshop is behind the store – ask if you can take a peek.

ⓘ Information

Tourist Information Center (鳴子観光・旅館案内センター; ☎83-3441; www.naruko.gr.jp; ⏲8.30am-6pm) Located just outside the train station.

ⓘ Getting There & Away

There is an hourly service on the JR Tōhoku *shinkansen* between Sendai and Furukawa (¥3040, 15 minutes). Hourly trains run on the JR Rikū-tō line between Furukawa and Naruko Onsen (¥650, 45 minutes).

IWATE PREFECTURE

Japan's second-largest prefecture, Iwate-ken (岩手県) is a quiet place, largely characterised by sleepy valleys, rugged coastline and some pretty serious mountain ranges. Although the region once played host to warring states and feudal rule, there are few remnants of this

Iwate Prefecture

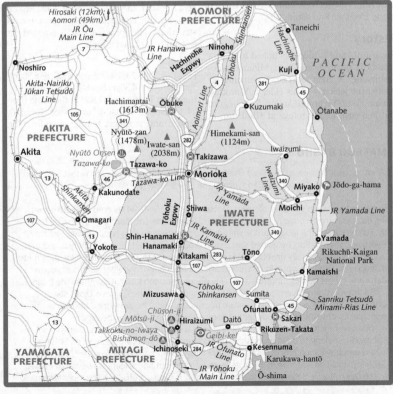

turbulent past, aside from the magnificent temples at Hiraizumi. Indeed, Iwate feels more provincial – in the best of ways – and stopping in places like the Tōno valley, which influenced a rich collection of folk tales, can feel almost like turning back time.

Hiraizumi 平泉

☑ 0191 / POP 8000

'Summer grass, all that remains of warrior dreams.'

Matsuo Bashō, *The Narrow Road to the Deep North* (1689)

Hiraizumi's grandeur once rivalled that of Kyoto. From 1089 to 1189, three generations of the Ōshu Fujiwara clan used their gold-mining wealth to create a living paradise devoted to the principles of Buddhism. However, feudal strife brought these ambitions to an abrupt, tragic end. Today only a few sights bear testament to Hiraizumi's former glory, yet this pleasantly rural town remains one of Tōhoku's premier cultural attractions. Hiraizumi's sights were added to the Unesco World Heritage Site list in 2011.

History

Hiraizumi's fate is indelibly linked to that of Japan's favourite tragic hero, Minamoto-no-Yoshitsune. A great warrior, Yoshitsune attracted the jealousy of his elder half-brother Minamoto-no-Yoritomo (Japan's first shōgun) and fled east, taking refuge at Hiraizumi in 1187. This gave Yoritomo the perfect excuse to attack, resulting in both the defeat of the Ōshu Fujiwara and the death of Yoshitsune. Yoritomo was said to be so impressed with the temples of Hiraizumi that he allowed them to remain, and it was the Kamakura shōgunate (military government) that later sponsored the construction of the first wooden hall to protect the Konjiki-dō mausoleum.

👁 Sights & Activities

★ **Chūson-ji** BUDDHIST TEMPLE
(中尊寺; ☑ 46-2211; admission to Konjiki-dō & Sankōzō ¥800; ⊙8am-5pm Apr-Oct, 8.30am-4.30pm Nov-Mar) Chūson-ji was established in AD 850 by the priest Ennin, although it was the Ōshu Fujiwara family who expanded the complex in the 12th century. A total of 300 buildings with 40 temples was constructed. Ironically, in the face of the family's grand scheme to build a Buddhist utopia, Hiraizumi was never far from tragedy: a massive fire ravaged nearly everything in 1337. Only two of the original constructions, the **Konjiki-dō** (金色堂; Golden Hall; ⊙8am-4.30pm Apr-Oct, to 4pm Nov-Mar) and **Kyōzō** (経蔵; Sutra Repository), remain alongside more recent reconstructions. The sprawling site is reached via a steep cedar-lined avenue.

Mōtsū-ji GARDENS
(毛越寺; ☑ 46-2331; admission ¥500; ⊙8.30am-5pm Apr-Oct, to 4.30pm Nov-Mar) Established by the priest Ennin in AD 850 at the same time as Chūson-ji, Mōtsū-ji was once Tōhoku's largest and grandest temple complex. The

---

MATSUO BASHŌ

'Another year is gone, a traveller's shade on my head, straw sandals at my feet.'
Matsuo Bashō, *Account of Exposure to the Fields* (1685)

Regarded as Japan's master of haiku, Matsuo Bashō (1644–94) is credited with elevating its status from comic relief to Zen-infused enlightenment. Born into a samurai family, Bashō served the feudal lord Yoshitada into his late teenage years. Moving first to Kyoto and then to Edo, he gained success as a published poet, but ultimately found the acclaim to be spiritually unsettling. He eventually turned to Zen, and the philosophy had a deep impact on his work. In fact, comparisons have been made between his haiku and Zen *kōan* (short riddles), intended to bring about a sudden flash of insight in the listener.

Bashō was also influenced by the natural philosophy of the Chinese Taoist sage Chuangzi, and began to examine nature uncritically. Later he developed his own poetic principle by drawing on the concept of *sabi*, a kind of spare, lonely beauty.

When he reached his 40s, Bashō abandoned his career in favour of travelling throughout Japan, seeking to build friendships and commune with nature as he went. He published evocative accounts of his travels, including *The Records of a Weather-Beaten Skeleton* and *The Records of a Travel-Worn Satchel,* but his collection *The Narrow Road to the Deep North,* detailing his journey throughout Tōhoku in 1689, is the most famous.

Hiraizumi

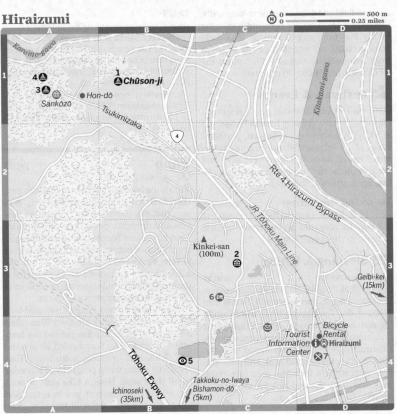

buildings are all long gone, but the enigmatic 12th-century 'Pure Land' gardens, designed with the Buddhist notion of creating an earthly paradise, remain.

Takkoku-no-Iwaya Bishamon-dō　　TEMPLE
(達谷窟毘沙門堂; ☑ 46-4931; admission ¥300; ⏰ 8am-5pm, varies by season) Located 6km outside town, this temple built into a cave is dedicated to Bishamon, the Buddhist guardian of warriors. It was built by the general Sakanoue-no-Tamuramaro in 801 CE after his victory against a local warlord. You can cycle here from Mōtsū-ji along a paved path in about 30 minutes.

**Hiraizumi Cultural
Heritage Center**　　MUSEUM
(平泉文化遺産センター; 44 Hanadate; ⏰ 9am-5pm) FREE This new museum charts Hiraizumi's rise and fall, with English explanations throughout.

Geibi Gorge　　CRUISE
(厳美渓; Geibi-kei; 90-minute cruise ¥1500; ⏰ 8.30am-4pm) Singing boatmen on flat-bottomed wooden boats steer passengers down the Satetsu River, which cuts through

a ravine flanked by towering limestone walls. Geibi-kei is 15km east of Hiraizumi; take the hourly bus from stop 7 outside Ichinoseki Station (¥620, 40 minutes) or the *kaisoku* from Ichinoseki to Geibi-kei Station on the JR Ōfunato line (¥480, 30 minutes).

✿✿ Festivals & Events

Haru-no-Fujiwara Matsuri　　　TRADITIONAL
(春の藤原まつり | Spring Fujiwara Festival; ◷1 to 5 May) A costumed procession, performances of nō (classical dance-drama), traditional *ennen-no-mai* (longevity dance) and an enormous rice cake–carrying competition are features of this festival.

Aki-no-Fujiwara Matsuri　　　TRADITIONAL
(秋の藤原まつり | Autumn Fujiwara Festival; ◷1 to 3 Nov) Parades and performances similar to those in the spring festival.

🛏 Sleeping & Eating

Hotel Musashibō　　　HOTEL ¥¥
(ホテル武蔵坊; ☑46-2241; www.musasibou.co.jp; 15 Hiraizumi-ōsawa; r per person with 2 meals from ¥9600; P @) The Musashibō is within walking distance of the main sights. Considering that it also comes with spacious tatami rooms, an attractive onsen bath and formal, sit-down dinners, it's a pretty good deal. From the station, walk straight for 500m then turn right, walk another 500m and look for the hulking concrete building on the left.

O-shokuji-dokoro Sakura　　　JAPANESE ¥
(お食事処さくら; 73-4 Hiraizumi-ya; snacks/meals from ¥100/700; ◷8.30am-7pm; 📖) Sakura looks more like a local lunch counter than a tourist restaurant and, fittingly, the menu is packed with tasty home-style dishes. The speciality here is the handmade *hatto gozen* (wheat dumplings) – try them with the sweet sesame sauce. It's right by the train station; look for the orange awning out front.

ⓘ Information

Tourist Information Center (☑46-2110; ◷8.30am-5pm) Located next to the train station, with English pamphlets available. Bicycles can be hired from the adjacent kiosk (per day ¥1000; ◷9am-4pm, closed irregularly Dec-Mar).

ⓘ Getting There & Away

CAR & MOTORCYCLE
The **Tōhoku Expressway** (東北自動車道) runs between Sendai and Hiraizumi.

TRAIN
Hourly *shinkansen* run along the JR Tōhoku line between Sendai and Ichinoseki (¥3720, 30 minutes). Local trains (¥1620, 1¼ hours), running every hour or two, ply the same route on the JR Tōhoku main line and also connect Ichinoseki and Hiraizumi (¥190, 10 minutes).

Ichinoseki is connected to Morioka by the JR Tōhoku *shinkansen* (¥3720, 40 minutes) and the JR Tōhoku main line *futsū* (local trains; ¥1620, 1½ hours).

Tōno　　　遠野

☑ 0198 / POP 29,300

Tōno is the heartland for some of Japan's most cherished folk tales. A comparatively poor area that has suffered from devastating famines and droughts throughout the centuries, Tōno has always been subject to the unforgiving whims of nature. Superstitious residents, in turn, developed a healthy mix of fear and admiration for the natural world, which led to the creation of a whole assortment of *yōkai* or ghosts, demons, monsters and spirits.

If you have a vivid imagination and long for some clean country air, then Tōno offers a wonderful place to leave behind the trappings of urban life. Surrounded by verdant rice fields and dramatic mountains, Tōno speaks to a time when people lived intimately, off their land. Here, a bike ride through the woods can transport you to a mythical 'Lost Japan', where the wild things roamed free and were left to their own devices, however devious they might be.

◉ Sights

◉ Tōno Town

Tōno Municipal Museum　　　MUSEUM
(遠野市立博物館; 3-9 Higashidate-chō; admission ¥310, combined entrance to Tōno Folk Village ¥520; ◷9am-5pm) With its smattering of English text, artefacts of village life and videos depicting some of Tōno's famous legends, this museum provides a good measure of background information and context for what's to come in the valley beyond.

Tōno Folk Village　　　MUSEUM
(とおの昔話村; Tōno Mukashibanashi-mura; ☑62-7887; 2-11 Chūō-dōri; admission ¥310, combined entrance to Tōno Municipal Museum ¥520; ◷9am-5pm) Housed in the restored ryokan where Yanagita Kunio penned his famous work *Legends of Tōno,* this evocative muse-

Tōno Valley

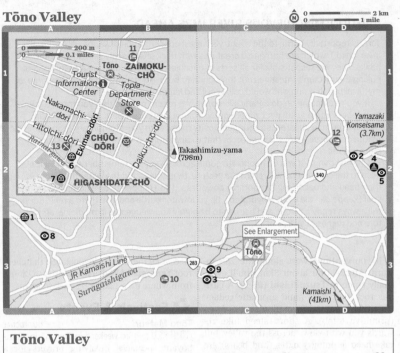

Tōno Valley

um has audiovisuals of some of the tales and memorabilia pertaining to Yanagita. Several times a day, local storytellers regale visitors with *mukashi-banashi* (old-time stories); however, given the heavy country dialect, even Japanese visitors may have trouble understanding them.

⊙ Around Tōno

The best way to see the countryside is by bicycle, made all that much easier by a fantastic trail that runs alongside the river. The Tōno Valley opens up into some beautiful terrain, particularly if you head far enough east.

What follows is a rough circuit, taking in Tōno's landmark sights to the west and east of the town. This could be completed in a long day or split into two. The valley is fairly

well signposted in English, but don't let that deter you from setting off down unmarked roads. Getting lost is part of the fun, and there are many small discoveries to be made if you keep your eyes peeled. Rest assured that it's fairly easy to right yourself – just be warned that you never really know what manner of creature lies waiting in the hills and streams around you...

About 2.5km southwest of Tōno Station is **Unedori-sama** (卯子酉様), the matchmaking shrine. According to legend, if you tie a strip of red cloth around one of the pines, using only your left hand, you'll meet your soul mate. In the hills above are **Gohyaku Rakan** (五百羅漢), the eerie, moss-covered rock carvings of 500 disciples of Buddha that were fashioned by a priest to console the spirits of those who died in a 1754 famine.

CAUTION: MISCHIEVOUS RIVER IMPS AHEAD

Tōno is reportedly home to the country's largest concentration of *kappa* (河童; literally 'river-child'), which are humanoid creatures with thick shells, scaly skin and pointed beaks. They are responsible for all sorts of mischief and grief, and have a nasty habit of pulling their victim's intestines out through their bum in order to feed on *shirikodama*, a mythical ball that humans would call a soul and *kappa* would call delicious.

If you're planning on doing any swimming, it's recommended that you throw a few cucumbers into any suspect water source. *Kappa* love cucumbers, even more than they love human children, so your generosity might earn you a temporary reprieve. Astute connoisseurs of sushi will note that a *kappa-maki* is none other than a cucumber hand roll.

One last thing – if you do happen to come across a *kappa*, remember to bow. Japanese to the core, *kappa* will return the gesture, thus spilling out the water they store in their head and becoming temporarily powerless. If you happen to be a compassionate soul (*kappa* can die if not rehydrated), tip your water bottle and give them a refill. *Kappa* will always repay a favour, and happen to be highly knowledgeable in medicine, agriculture and games of skill.

If you continue west along Rte 283 towards Morioka for about 8km, you'll eventually come to **Tsuzuki-ishi** (続石). A curious rock that rests amid aromatic cedars, it's either a natural formation or a *dolmen* (primitive tomb). A short, steep hike rewards you with views across the valley, but take heed as hungry ogres (and bears) are reported to lurk in these parts. One kilometre past Tsuzuki-ishi is the **Chiba Family Magariya** (南部曲り家千葉家; ⊙9am-4pm), a grand 200-year-old farmhouse in the traditional L-shaped Tōno style.

Turning to the other side of town, about 5km east of the town centre is **Denshōen** (伝承園; admission ¥310; ⊙9am-4pm), another traditional farmhouse, now housing a small cultural museum. The highlights here are the thousand Oshira-sama deities fashioned from mulberry wood.

A few hundred metres southeast of Denshōen is **Jōken-ji** (常堅寺), a peaceful temple dedicated to the deity image of Obinzuru-sama. Behind the temple is the **Kappa-buchi** (カッパ淵) pool, where Tōno's famous water sprites lurk. It is said that if pregnant women worship at the shrine on the riverbank, they'll produce plenty of milk, but only if they first produce a breast-shaped offering. The tiny altar is filled with small red or white cloth bags, most replete with nipple.

About 5km east of Denshōen is the turn-off for **Yamazaki Konseisama** (山崎のコンセイサマ), a shrine to the god of birth, favoured by women hoping to conceive. If you cycle back to the main road, you can contin-ue east all the way to the nostalgic thatched-roof **Yamaguchi Waterwheel** (山口の水車), from where it's a 12km ride back to town.

✦ Festivals & Events

Tōno Matsuri   TRADITIONAL
(遠野祭り; ⊙3rd weekend in Sep) This flamboyant spectacle, involving prayers for a bountiful harvest, is deeply connected with the legends of Tōno. There are *yabusame* (horseback archery, in this case a 700-year-old event), traditional dances and costume parades through the city.

🛏 Sleeping & Eating

⭐ **Tōno Youth Hostel**   HOSTEL ¥
(遠野ユースホステル; ☑62-8736; www1.odn.ne.jp/tono-yh/index-e.htm; 13-39-5 Tsuchibuchi, Tsuchibuchi-chō; dm from ¥3900, YHA discount ¥3300, breakfast/dinner ¥550/1150; P 🐾 @ 🛜)
🍃 Fronted by rice fields, this remote farmhouse-turned-hostel pays homage to the Tōno of yesteryear. The amicable manager, who speaks a decent smattering of English, is well versed in the local lore and captivates imaginations with nightly reports on rumoured sightings. Accommodation is in simple dorms that share open-air baths, while meals are built around seasonal produce and served communally. Bicycle rental is available. From Tōno Station, take a bus bound for Saka-no-shita to the Nitagai stop (¥290, 12 minutes). From there, it's a 10-minute walk, with the hostel clearly signposted along the way (look for the small wooden signs at knee-level).

Minshuku Tōno   MINSHUKU ¥

(民宿とおの; ☎62-4395; www.minshuku-tono.
com; 2-17 Zaimoku-chō; r per person/with 2 meals
from ¥3500/6500; P) There are several convenient places to bed down in Tōno village,
but this dignified *minshuku* (Japanese
guesthouse) behind the station is the best.
It's a quiet spot, with comfortable tatami
rooms, and the owners are keen on serving
up their home-brewed *doburoku* (unfiltered
sake) in generous portions.

Minshuku Magariya   MINSHUKU ¥¥

(民宿曲り屋; ☎62-4564; 30-58-3 Niisato, Ayaori-
chō; r per person with 2 meals from ¥8190; P)
🏮 If you came to Tōno to experience rural
Japan, you couldn't do much better than
this 120-year-old farmhouse up in the hills
surrounded by apple orchards and woods.
At its centre is a large hearth where guests
congregate for hearty country cooking. The
old-fashioned tatami rooms look like time
capsules, and when the sun sets and the
shadows lengthen it's easy enough to con-
jure up images of nefarious *yōkai*. Magariya
is located about 3km southwest of the train
station off Rte 283 and atop a steep, gravelly path – if you don't have a car, take a taxi
(about ¥1000).

Itō-ke   NOODLES ¥

(伊藤家; 2-11 Chūō-dōri; mains from ¥600; ☺11am-
5pm) All of the standard *soba* (buckwheat

noodles) dishes are on the menu here, but
the one to try is *hittsumi* (ひっつみ), a local
dish of thick, hand-cut noodles and chicken
in hot broth. The restaurant is in a traditional (but new-looking) dark-wood building adjacent to the Tōno Folk Village; look for the
wooden sign over the sliding doors.

ℹ Information

Tōno Post Office (遠野郵便局; ☎62-2830;
6-10 Chūō-dōri; ☺post 9am-5pm Mon-Fri; ATM
8.45am-7pm Mon-Fri, 9am-5pm Sat & Sun) An
international ATM is available here.

Tourist Information Center (☎62-1333;
www.city.tono.iwate.jp; ☺8am-6pm Apr-Oct,
8.30am-5.30pm Nov-Mar; @ 🕿) Across
from the train station, with bicycle rentals (¥1000 per day), English maps and free
internet.

ℹ Getting There & Away

Trains run hourly on the JR Tōhoku line between
Hiraizumi and Hanamaki (¥820, 45 minutes).
The JR Kamaishi line connects Hanamaki to
Tōno (¥1330, one hour), while the JR Tōhoku
line connects Hanamaki to Morioka (¥650, 45
minutes).

   If you're coming from Sendai, take the Tōhoku
shinkansen to Shin-Hanamaki (¥5550, one
hour) and transfer to the JR Kamaishi line for
Tōno (¥1250, 45 minutes). The *shinkansen* line
connects Shin-Hanamaki to Morioka (¥2950, 15
minutes).

LEGENDS OF TŌNO

At the beginning of the 20th century, writer and scholar Yanagita Kunio (1875–1962)
published *Tōno Monogatari* (遠野物語; *Legends of Tōno*), a collection of regional folk
tales. The stories were based on interviews with Sasaki Kyōseki, an educated man born
into a Tōno peasant family who had committed to memory more than 100 *densetsu*
(local legends). What Yanagita and Sasaki unearthed captured the nation's imagination,
bringing into sharp focus the oral storytelling traditions of a region that previously had
been almost completely ignored. The collection has been translated into English and is
well worth a read before – or better yet, while – visiting.

   The cast of characters and situations is truly weird and wonderful, and draws heavily
on the concept of animism, a system of belief that attributes a personal spirit to everything that exists, including animals and objects. Of particular importance to Tōno is the
story of Oshira-sama. It begins with a farm girl who develops a deep affection for her
horse; eventually the two marry, though not with her father's permission. One night, the
girl's father finds her sleeping in the stables and, outraged, drags the horse out to the
garden and hangs the poor beast from a mulberry tree. Distraught, the daughter clings
to the horse's head and together they are spirited up to the heavens, becoming the *kami*
(deity) Oshira-sama.

   There are also shape-shifting foxes; impish water sprites called *kappa* (see boxed text
opposite); *zashiki-warashi* spirits, who live in the corners of houses and play tricks on the
residents; and *oni* (ogres) who live in the hills and eat lost humans. Throughout all of the
stories is a common theme: the struggle to overcome the everyday problems of rural life.

Morioka 盛岡

♪ 019 / POP 300,000

Morioka is an old castle town framed by three flowing rivers and a brooding volcano. Once the seat of the Nanbu domain, it is now the prefectural capital and a regional transportation hub. Though the castle itself is long gone, the park in its place and surrounding area make for a pleasant stroll. Morioka is also famous for its cast-iron artisan work.

◉ Sights

Iwate-kōen PARK

(岩手公園) If you head east on foot from the station along Kaiun-bashi for about 20 minutes, you'll eventually come to this landscaped park, where Morioka-jō once stood. All that remains of the castle, completed in 1633 and destroyed in 1874, are its moss-covered stone foundation walls. Still, you can get a sense of its scale.

Rock-Splitting Cherry Tree LANDMARK

(石割桜 | Ishiwari-zakura) A few blocks north of Iwate-kōen, in front of the Morioka District Court, is this much-loved local attraction: a 300-year-old cherry tree, which sprouted from the crack in a huge granite boulder. Some claim that it has pushed its way through over time, and while that's clearly an impossible feat it's nevertheless a sight to behold.

🎎 Festivals & Events

Chagu-Chagu Umakko PARADE

(チャグチャグ馬コ; ⊙ 2nd Sat in Jun) A parade of brightly decorated horses and children in traditional dress.

Sansa Odori DANCE

(さんさ躍り; ⊙ 1 to 4 Aug) In Morioka's most famous festival, thousands of dancers take to the streets, celebrating the banishment of an evil ogre that once upon a time plagued the city.

Morioka Aki Matsuri FESTIVAL

(盛岡秋祭り; ⊙ 14 to 16 Sep) Portable shrines and colourful floats are paraded to the rhythm of *taiko* (Japanese drums).

🛏 Sleeping

Kumagai Ryokan RYOKAN ¥¥

(熊ヶ井旅館; ♪ 651-3020; http://kumagairyokan. com; 3-2-5 Ōsawakawara; s/d from ¥4200/8000; ❀@🛜) Set in a garden and with folk crafts scattered about, Kumagai has a homely vibe and is very welcoming of foreign guests. The tatami rooms, surprisingly spacious, are well maintained, and there's a wonderful *iwa-buro* (rock bath) for evening soaks. All rooms have shared facilities. The inn is located about eight minutes on foot east of the station (behind the large church).

Morioka New City Hotel BUSINESS HOTEL ¥¥

(盛岡ニューシティホテル; ♪ 654-5161; www. moriokacityhotel.co.jp; 13-10 Eki-mae-dōri; s/tw from ¥5670/9800; 🛜) Conveniently located across the road from the station, this relaxed business hotel caters primarily for single travellers. Rooms are slightly cramped, but more than adequate.

🍴 Eating

Fans of noodles should take note that Morioka has some seriously delicious, and unusual, ways of serving them. *Wanko-soba* (わんこそば), buckwheat noodles served by the mouthful in tiny wooden bowls, is more like a competition between you and the waitress, who tries to top up your bowl faster than you can say you're full. Prefer to savour at your own pace? Try *jaja-men* (じゃじゃめん), udon-like noodles heaped with cucumber, miso paste and ground meat – mix all this up and add vinegar, spicy oil and garlic to taste.

★ Pairon Honten NOODLES ¥

(白龍本店; 5-15 Uchi-maru; noodles from ¥400; ⊙ 11.30am-9pm Mon-Sat) Loved by locals, this hole-in-the wall serves up super-tasty *jaja-men* and nothing else. Ordering is a breeze: just ask for *shō* (small), *chū* (medium) or *dai* (large). When you're finished, crack a raw egg (¥50) into the bowl and the staff will add hot soup and more of that amazing miso paste. The restaurant is down the narrow lane directly across from **Sakurayama-jinja**; look for the white *noren* curtains on your left.

Azumaya Honten NOODLES ¥¥

(東屋本店; ♪ 622-2252; www.wankosoba-azumaya.co.jp; Naka-no-hashi-dōri; wanko-soba from ¥2625; ⊙ 11am-8pm; 📖) Famished? This 100-year-old shop specialises in the all-you-can-eat noodle binge that is *wanko-soba*, a Morioka tradition. Fifteen of these tiny bowls, which the waitress will refill with *soba* as soon as you've put the last one down, is equivalent to one ordinary bowl – but the average customer will put away 50

Morioka

N 0 ——— 400 m
0 ——— 0.2 miles

(and 100, or 200, is not unheard of). You can also order ordinary single servings of noodles downstairs. The restaurant is in a traditional building two blocks east of the Nakatsu-gawa.

Fukakusa CAFE
(ふかくさ; 1-2 Konya-chō; coffee ¥350, beer ¥450; ⏱11.30am-3pm, 5pm-11pm Mon-Sat, noon-5pm Sun) This little hideaway on the banks of the Nakatsu-gawa is the perfect place to stop for a pick-me-up or to unwind after a long afternoon. Look for the ivy out front.

🛍 Shopping

Gozaku, the area just east of the Nakatsu-gawa, is the old merchants' district, now home to craft studios and cafes.

Kamasada Honten HOMEWARES
(釜定本店; 2-5 Konya-chō; ⏱9am-5.30pm Mon-Sat) Morioka is known for its *nanbu tekki* (cast ironware), notably tea kettles. There are some beautiful examples at this venerable old shop, along with more affordable items, like windchimes and incense holders.

ℹ Information

Iwate Medical University Hospital (岩手医科大学附属病院; ☎24hr emergency hotline 651-5111; www.iwate-med.ac.jp/hospital/index.html; 19-1 Uchi-maru; ⏱outpatient services 8.30am-11am, 1pm-4pm Mon-Fri)

Morioka Central Post Office (盛岡中央郵便局; ☎624-5353; 1-13-45 Chūō-dōri; ⏱post 9am-7pm Mon-Fri, to 5pm/12.30pm Sat/Sun; ATM 7am-11pm Mon-Fri, 9am-9pm Sat, to 7pm Sun) An international ATM is available here.

Northern Tōhoku Information Center (☎625-2090; ⏱9am-5pm) Located on the 2nd floor of Morioka Station, with English speakers and help available to book accommodation.

Tourist Information Center (☎604-3305; www.hellomorioka.jp; 2nd fl, Odette Plaza, 1-1-10 Naka-no-hashi-dōri; ⏱9am-6pm, closed 2nd Tue each month; 📶) English-speaking staff and free internet are available here.

ℹ Getting There & Away

BUS

Regional buses depart from outside the west exit of the train station, and connect Morioka with Sendai (¥2850, 2½ hours) and Hirosaki (¥2930, 2¼ hours). Night buses depart for Tokyo (¥7800, 7½ hours) from the east exit.

CAR & MOTORCYCLE

If you're driving, the **Tōhoku Expressway** (東北自動車道) runs between Tokyo and the greater Morioka area.

TRAIN

There are hourly *shinkansen* on the JR Tōhoku line between Tokyo and Morioka (¥13,640, 2½ hours), and Morioka and Shin-Aomori (¥5770, 1¼ hours).

Frequent trains run on the JR Akita *shinkansen* line between Morioka and Akita (¥4300, 1½ hours) via Tazawa-ko (¥1780, 30 minutes) and Kakunodate (¥2570, 50 minutes). The local Tazawa-ko line covers the same route in about twice the time for around half the price; you may need to transfer at Ōmagari.

ⓘ Getting Around

The charmingly named **Dendenmushi** (one ride/day pass ¥250/600) tourist trolley (*dendenmushi* literally means 'electric transmission bug') makes a convenient loop around town, departing in a clockwise direction from stop 15 in front of Morioka Station (anticlockwise from stop 16) between 9am and 7pm.

Bicycles can be rented from **Sasaki Jitensha Shōkai** (佐々木自転車商会; 10-2 Morioka Eki-mae-dōri; per hour/day ¥200/1000; ⓧ 8.30am-6pm), near Morioka Station.

AOMORI PREFECTURE

Aomori-ken (青森県), at the curious northern tip of Honshū, is split in the middle by Mutsu-wan, the bay cradled in the arm of the axe-shaped Shimokita Peninsula. This is a prefecture where having a rental car will really open up some of Japan's most remote and wildly exotic areas. The ethereal volcanic landscapes around Osore-zan are where Aomori's people come to commune with the dead. The old cultural centre of Hirosaki and the verdant nature clinging to the shores of Towada-ko are definitely more rooted in this world.

Aomori　　　青森

♫ 017 / POP 301,000

Aomori, the prefectural capital, is a stopover point for travellers on their way to Hokkaidō and a regional transportation hub. In 2010 the Tōhoku *shinkansen* line was extended to Aomori, giving the city reason to spruce itself up, including new development along the harbour. There are several worthwhile

museums scattered around the city, but Aomori's most famous attraction is its Nebuta Matsuri.

◉ Sights

Sannai Maruyama Site　　ARCHAEOLOGICAL SITE
(三内丸山遺跡 | Sannai Murayama Iseki; http://sannaimaruyama.pref.aomori.jp; Sannai Maruyama 305; ⓧ 9am-5.30pm Jun-Sep, to 4.30pm Oct-May; ⓐ) FREE Excavation of this site turned up an astonishing number of intact artefacts from Japan's Jōmon era (10,000–2,000 years ago), which are on display at the museum here. The actual archaeological site, along with some reconstructed dwellings, form the grounds out back. Sannai Maruyama is approximately 5km west of Aomori Station. City buses leaving from stop 6 for Menkyō Center stop at Sannai Maruyama Iseki-mae (¥300, 20 minutes).

Aomori Museum of Art　　MUSEUM
(青森県立美術館; www.aomori-museum.jp/en/index.html; 185 Chikano, Yasuta; admission ¥500; ⓧ 9am-6pm Jun-Sep, 9.30am-5pm Oct-May, closed 2nd & 4th Mon of month) Artists from Aomori Prefecture feature heavily in the permanent collection here, including pop icon Yoshitomo Nara, master print maker Munakata Shikō and Tohl Narita, who designed many of the monsters from the iconic *Ultraman* television show. The museum is about 5km west of Aomori Station, adjacent to the Sannai Maruyama Site; city buses leaving from stop 6 for Menkyō Center stop at Kenritsu-bijyutskan-mae (¥270, 20 minutes).

Nebuta no Ie Wa Rasse　　MUSEUM
(ねぶたの家ワ・ラッセ; www.nebuta.or.jp/warasse/index.html; 1-1-1 Yasukata; adult/child ¥600/250; ⓧ 9am-7pm May-Aug, to 6pm Sep-Apr; ⓐ) Even if you missed the festival, you can still gawk at the awesome craftsmanship of the Nebuta floats displayed at this new museum on the waterfront. On weekends there are performances of dancing and drumming as well.

Munakata Shikō Memorial Hall　　MUSEUM
(棟方志功記念館 | Munakata Shikō Kinenkan; http://munakatashiko-museum.jp/schedule_e.html; 2-1-2 Matsubara; admission ¥500; ⓧ 9.30am-5pm Tue-Sun) A collection of prints, paintings and calligraphy by Munakata Shikō (1903–1975), an Aomori native who won international fame in his lifetime, is housed in this museum 3km east of the station. Catch the city shuttle bus (¥200, 20 minutes).

Aomori Prefecture

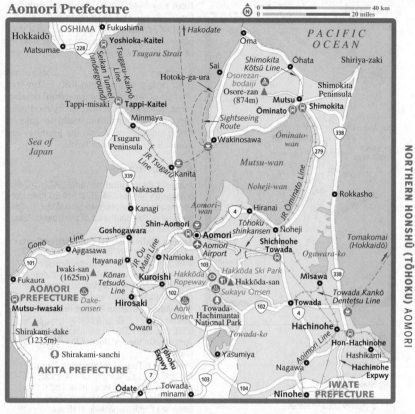

✿ Festivals & Events

Aomori Nebuta Matsuri   PARADES
(青森ねぶた祭り; www.nebuta.or.jp/english/
index_e.htm; ☺ 2 to 7 August) The Nebuta Matsuri has parades of spectacular illuminated
floats, accompanied by thousands of rowdy,
chanting dancers. The parades start at sunset and last for hours; on the final day, the
action starts at about noon. As this is one of
Japan's most famous festivals, you'll need to
book accommodation way in advance.

🛏 Sleeping

Aomori Moya Kōgen Youth Hostel   HOSTEL ¥
(青森雲谷高原ユースホステル; ☎764-2888;
http://moya.jp; 9-5 Yamabuki, Moya; dm/with 2 meals
¥3900/5600, YHA discount ¥3300/5000; P 🌐 @)
This homely hostel lies 12km south of the city
on the road to Hakkōda. Rooms are standard,
but the owners add personal touches, including garden-fresh herbal tea brewed nightly.
Buses for Moya Hills from stops 1 or 4 out-

side Aomori Station can drop you off at Moya
Kōgen (¥590, 40 minutes, last bus 6.40pm
weekdays, 4.30pm weekends), from where
you can see the hostel (a yellow building).

Aomori Center Hotel   HOTEL ¥¥
(青森センターホテル; ☎762-7500; www.ao-
moricenterhotel.jp/index2.htm; 1-10-9-1 Furukawa;
s/d from ¥4780/6900; 🌐 @) Besides being excellent value, this business hotel is attached to an
onsen complex that guests may use for free.
Rooms in the brand new *bekkan* (annexe) are
the nicest. The hotel (not to be confused with
the Aomori Central Hotel) is a 10-minute walk
from Aomori Station. Rates include breakfast.

Aomori Grand Hotel   HOTEL ¥¥
(青森グランドホテル; ☎723-1011; www.agh.
co.jp; 1-1-23 Shin-machi; s/d from ¥6500/10,000;
🌐 @ 📶) A step up from a business hotel, the
Grand is two minutes from the train station
and a good bet if you're making an early connection in the morning.

Aomori

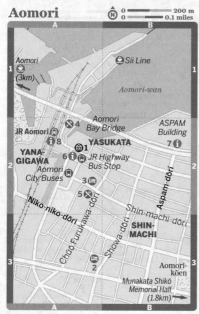

N
0 — 200 m
0 — 0.1 miles

Aomori
(3km)

Sii Line

Aomori-wan

Aomori
Bay Bridge

ASPAM
Building

JR Aomori

YASUKATA

YANA-
GIGAWA

JR Highway
Bus Stop

Aomori
City Buses

Chuo-Furukawa-dori

Niko-niko-dori

Aspam-dori

Shin-machi-dori

Showa-dori

SHIN-
MACHI

Aomori-
koen

Munakata Shikō
Memorial Hall
(1.8km)

Aomori

✕ Eating

★ Shinsen Ichiba

MARKET ¥

(新鮮市場; Basement fl, Auga Building, 1-3-7 Shinchō; meals from ¥580; ⊙5am-6.30pm) Aomori is famous for a number of speciality items, including scallops, codfish, apples, pickled vegetables and many, many other foods that are all laid out at this seafood and produce market. There are also a handful of counter restaurants where you can get a fresh *sanshoku-don* (rice topped with scallops, fish roe and sea urchin roe) or a hot bowl of *rāmen*. Open early, it's also a good place to stock up on snacks for the next leg of your journey.

A-Factory

FOOD COURT ¥

(1-4-2 Yanagigawa; meals from ¥880; ⊙11am-8pm; 🖥) Part of the city's new waterfront development, A-Factory is a bright, airy food court serving everything from sushi to galettes. Apple cider is brewed on the premises and available by the glass or bottle.

ℹ Information

Aomori City Hospital (青森市民病院; ☎24hr emergency hotline 734-2171; 1-14-20 Katsuda; ⊙outpatient services 9am-5pm Mon-Fri) The hospital is 3km southeast of the train station, off of Rte 103.

Aomori Station Tourist Information Center (青森市観光交流情報センター; ☎723-4670; www.city.aomori.aomori.jp/contents/english/index.html; internet ¥100/10 minutes; ⊙8.30am-7pm; 🖥) English-language pamphlets, bus schedules and a city map.

Shin-Aomori Station Tourist Information Center (あおもり観光情報センター; ☎752-6311; internet ¥100/10 minutes; ⊙8.30am-7pm; 🖥) On the 2nd floor of the *shinkansen* station.

Prefectural Tourist Information Counter (青森県観光総合案内所; ☎734-2500; http://en.aptinet.jp/index.html; 2nd fl, ASPAM Bldg, 1-1-40 Yasukata; ⊙9am-6pm; ☎) English-speaking staff are available here.

ℹ Getting There & Away

AIR

From Aomori Airport, 11km south of the city centre, there are flights to and from Tokyo, Osaka, Nagoya and many other destinations. Airport buses are timed for flights and depart from stop 11 in front of Aomori Station (¥680, 40 minutes).

BOAT

Sii Line (シィライン; ☎722-4545; www.sii-line.co.jp) ferries depart twice daily for Wakinosawa (¥2540, one hour) from Aomori-kō Ryokyaku Fune Terminal (青森港旅客船ターミナル).

Tsugaru Kaikyō (津軽海峡; ☎766-4733; www.tsugarukaikyo.co.jp) operates eight ferries daily between Aomori and Hakodate (from ¥2700, four hours), year-round. Ferries depart from Aomori Ferry Terminal (青森フェリーターミナル) on the western side of the city, a 10-minute taxi ride from Aomori Station (about ¥1500).

BUS

JR highway buses connect Aomori to Sendai (¥5700, five hours) and Tokyo (from ¥8500, 9½ hours).

Buses depart from stop 11 for Hakkōda (¥1070, 50 minutes) and Towada-ko (¥3000, three hours); schedules are highly seasonal and infrequent during winter.

CAR & MOTORCYCLE

The **Tōhoku Expressway** (東北自動車道) runs between Tokyo and greater Aomori.

There's a handy **Toyota Rent a Car** (トヨタレンタカー; ☑ 782-0100; http://rent.toyota.co.jp/en/index.html; 104-79 Takama, Ishie; ☺ 8am-10pm) outside the west exit of the Shin-Aomori *shinkansen* station.

TRAIN

The Tōhoku *shinkansen* runs roughly every hour from Tokyo Station, by way of Sendai and Morioka, to the terminus at Shin-Aomori Station (¥16,370, 3½ hours).

Futsū trains on the JR Ōu main line connect Aomori with Shin-Aomori (¥180, five minutes) and Hirosaki (¥650, 45 minutes). A few JR Tsugaru *tokkyū* (limited-express) trains run daily between Aomori and Akita (¥5450, 2¾ hours) on the same line.

Hourly *tokkyū* trains run on the JR Tsugaru-Kaikyō line between Aomori and Hakodate on Hokkaidō (¥5340, two hours), via the Seikan Tunnel.

One daily *kaisoku* express train on the JR Ōminato line connects Aomori and Shimokita (¥2120, 1½ hours). Alternatively, you can take a *futsū* train on the private Aoimori Tetsudō line and transfer at Noheji for the JR Ōminato line.

ⓘ NIGHT TRAIN TO AOMORI

The JR Akebono sleeper train leaves Ueno Station in Tokyo every evening at 9.15pm and arrives in Aomori at 9.55am the next morning, after passing through Niigata and Akita. The return leaves Aomori at 6.22pm and pulls into Ueno at 6.58am. One-way fare for a basic sleeper berth (called *goron-to-shiito*) without pillows or blankets is ¥14,160 and is covered by both the JR Pass and JR East Pass; you can pay extra to upgrade to something cushier. Akebono is one of just a handful of old-school sleeper trains still running in Japan, and books out quickly. Tickets can be reserved up to one month in advance.

ⓘ Getting Around

Shuttle buses (one ride/day pass ¥200/500) circle the city, connecting Shin-Aomori Station, Aomori Station, Aomori Ferry Terminal and most city sights. They may be less direct than regular municipal buses, but they are the most economical way to get around the city.

Hakkōda-san 八甲田山

🎧 017

Hakkōda-san, which translates as 'many peaks and marshlands', is a region of intense natural beauty with a dark history. In 1902 a regiment of 210 Japanese soldiers training in the winter weather were caught in a sudden and severe snow storm. All but 11 men perished, carving out a place for Hakkōda-san in the collective Japanese psyche.

Today, most hikers tackle Honshū's northernmost volcanic range between May and October. However, the biting winter months are a great time for skiing and snowboarding. Even if you do catch a chill, take comfort in the fact that Hakkōda-san is home to one of Tōhoku's best onsen, Sukayu.

◉ Sights

Hakkōda Ropeway   ROPEWAY
(八甲田山ロープウェー; www.hakkoda-ropeway.jp; 1-12 Kansuizawa, Arakawa; one-way/return ¥1150/1800; ☺ 9am-4.20pm; ℗) For anyone who wants a taste of the alpine without having to brave the steep ascent, this scenic ropeway quickly whisks you up to the summit of Tamoyachi-dake (田茂萢岳; 1324m). From there, you can follow an elaborate network of hiking trails, although purists prefer the magnificent one-day loop that starts and finishes in Sukayu Onsen Ryokan.

🏃 Activities

★**Hakkōda-san**   HIKING
(八甲田山) Hakkōda-san's quintessential hike covers 12km and can be completed in a gruelling but highly rewarding day. The trailhead is right around the corner from Sukayu Onsen Ryokan. Things start out relatively flat as you wind through marshlands, but eventually the pitch starts to increase in the shadow of Ōdake (大岳; 1584m). The ridge trail continues to Ido-dake (井戸岳; 1550m) and Akakura-dake (赤倉岳; 1548m) before connecting with Tamoyachi-dake (田茂萢岳; 1326m).

After stopping at the ropeway terminal for a quick pick-me-up, follow the descending trail through wildflower-filled marshes and rolling pasturelands. Arriving back at Sukayu Onsen Ryokan before nightfall, it's time to indulge in a post-hike beer and the obligatory muscle-relaxing soak.

Hakkōda Ski Park
SNOW SPORTS

(八甲田スキー場; www.hakkoda-ropeway.jp; 5-time pass ¥4900; ⊙9am-4.20pm) Compared with other ski mountains across Tōhoku and Hokkaidō, Tamoyachi-dake is fairly modest in scope. The plus side is that you can expect frozen fir trees, piles of wet snow and scant to no crowds. There are just two official runs from the top of the Hakkōda Ropeway, both winding intermediate trails. The longer of the two, the 5km Forest Course, cuts through the treeline and has a few steep and speedy pitches.

At its heart, however, Hakkōda is a destination for hardcore skiers and boarders: come spring, it's possible to explore a network of unofficial trails that extend to some of the nearby peaks. Weather conditions can be severe, though, and getting lost is easy, so even experienced alpinists should go with a local; most accommodations in the area can arrange guides.

There are limited goods and services at the ropeway building, aside from equipment rental (¥3500 per day).

🛏 Sleeping

Sukayu Camping Ground CAMPGROUND ¥

(酸ヶ湯キャンプ場; ☑738-6566; www.sukayu. jp/camp; per person ¥500, campsite from ¥500; ⊙late Jun-late Oct; ℗) A good spot to pitch a tent, with clean facilities and rental supplies, located at the end of a small access road immediately south of Sukayu Onsen Ryokan.

★Sukayu Onsen RYOKAN ¥¥

(酸ヶ湯温泉; ☑738-6400; www.sukayu.jp; r per person with 2 meals from ¥10,650, day bathing ¥600; ⊙day bathing 7am-5.30pm; ℗) Plucked right out of an *ukiyo-e* (woodblock print), Sukayu's cavernous bathhouse is a delight for the senses. Look at the dark wood, milky water and steam; listen to the gurgle of the water; feel its penetrating heat or knead tired shoulders with its *utase-yu* (massaging stream of water); and smell the sulphur. On a cold day, relaxing here is hard to beat. Shy bathers should note that the main bath is *konyoku* (mixed bathing), save for a lady's hour in the morning and evening. Rooms in the sprawling old-fashioned inn are simple but comfortable, with shared facilities.

Hakkōda-sansō LODGE ¥¥

(八甲田山荘; ☑728-1512; www.hakkoda-sanso. com; 1-61 Kansuizawa, Arakawa; r per person/with 2 meals ¥5250/9450; ℗ ⊙ 🐕) Right at the bottom of the Hakkōda Ropeway, this lodge with Japanese-style rooms caters to skiers and snowboarders. The dining area, with picture windows facing the mountain, does hot lunches as well.

ℹ Getting There & Away

JR buses leave from stop 11 outside Aomori Station, stopping at Hakkōda Ropeway-eki (¥1070, 50 minutes) and the next stop, Sukayu Onsen (¥1300, one hour). The bus continues to Towada-ko-eki (¥2020, 1½ hours). Bus schedules are highly seasonal, with infrequent departures during winter months.

Towada-ko 十和田湖

☑0176 / POP 6000

Formed by a series of violent volcanic eruptions, Towada-ko is a roughly circular caldera lake hemmed in by rocky coastlines and dense forests. Part of the Towada-Hachimantai National Park, it is the largest crater lake in Honshū (52km in circumference).

It is rivalled in beauty by the Oirase-gawa, the winding river that drains Towada-ko into the Pacific Ocean. The recent extension of the *shinkansen* to Aomori Prefecture put the area within easy striking distance, yet development around the lake remains sparse, save for the main tourist hub of Yasumiya.

◉ Sights & Activities

★Oirase-gawa HIKING

(奥入瀬川) This meandering river is marked by cascading waterfalls, carved-out gorges and gurgling rapids. Casual hikers can follow its path for a 14km stretch connecting Nenokuchi, a small tourist outpost on the eastern shore of the lake, to Yakeyama, from where relatively frequent buses return to either Nenokuchi (¥660, 30 minutes) or the main tourist hub of Yasumiya (¥1100, one hour). The entire hike should only take you about three hours. Set out in the early morning or late afternoon to avoid slow-moving coach parties.

Towada-ko CRUISE

(十和田; ⊙8am-4pm) To get a sense of the lake's enormous scale, you really need to leave the shoreline. From the docks in Yasumiya, there are a couple of options for scenic cruises, the best of which is the one-hour circuit between Yasumiya and Nenokuchi (one-way ¥1400). From April to early November, boats leave approximately every hour. A loop circuit (¥1400, 40 minutes) operates year-round.

You can also rent rowboats and paddleboats next to the dock. Note that inconsistent water temperatures (warm patches followed by frigid ones) make swimming in the lake dangerous.

🛏 Sleeping

Hotel rates can increase dramatically during August, the peak travel period for Japanese tourists, and late October, when the leaves blaze red.

Towada-ko Oide Camping Ground
CAMPGROUND ¥

(十和田湖生出キャンプ場; ☑ 75-2368; www.bes.or.jp/towada/camp.html; 486 Yasumiya, Towada-kohan; per person ¥300, campsite ¥200; ⊙ 25 Apr–5 Nov; 🅿) Well-maintained facilities, with rental supplies available.

★ Towada Hotel
HOTEL ¥¥

(十和田ホテル; ☑ 75-1122; www.towada-hotel.com; Namariyama, Towada-ko, Kosaka-machi; r per person with 2 meals from ¥14,700; 🅿) The Towada Hotel is a pre-WWII construction defined by its dramatic lobby of hulking timbers rising to a chandelier-lit cathedral ceiling. The historic main building has elegantly refurbished Japanese-style rooms (with and without baths). The Western-style rooms in the newer annexe, however, are comparatively lacking in character. All rooms offer lake views and there are communal baths which look out over the water as well. A path leads from the hotel to the lake's secluded southwestern shore. While having a car out here would certainly be helpful, a hotel shuttle (timed for check-in and check-out) runs to and from the bus station in Yasumiya; reserve a seat when you reserve a room.

Oirase Keiryū Hotel
HOTEL ¥¥

(☑ 74-2121; www.oirase-keiryuu.jp; 231 Tochikubo, Oirase; r per person with 2 meals from ¥12,000; 🅿🛜) This large hotel, which caters to the package crowds, lies near the trailhead for the Oirase-gawa hike. There are both Japanese- and Western-style rooms, in addition to a string of hot springs along the river. The standout feature is the cavernous dining hall, with picture windows edging the

forest and sloping eaves of panelled hardwood. The hotel offers free transfer from Shin-Aomori Station (once daily; reserve in advance).

Himemasu Sansō
MINSHUKU ¥¥

(ひめます山荘; ☑ 75-2717; www.aominren.jp/minsyuku/58himemasu.html; 16-15 Yasumiya, Towada-kohan; r per person/with 2 meals ¥4400/6500; 🅿) A number of the *minshuku* in Yasumiya have seen better days, but not this one. It has eight spotless tatami rooms, an onsen bath and filling spreads of home-cooked food. It's a 15-minute walk from the lake.

❶ Information

Tourist Information Center (十和田湖総合案内所; ☑ 75-2425; ⊙ 8am-5pm) Next to the bus station in Yasumiya, with English-language pamphlets available.

❶ Getting There & Away

JR buses run from Aomori, through Yakeyama (¥2240, two hours) to Towada-ko-eki in Yasumiya (¥3000, three hours); departures are highly seasonal and infrequent in winter.

A limited network of local buses runs around the lakeside. Infrequent connections are reason enough to bring your own wheels.

Rte 103 runs south of Aomori to Towada-ko.

NORTHERN HONSHŪ (TŌHOKU) TOWADA-KO

Shimokita Peninsula
下北半島

☎ 0175 / POP 100,000

Remote, axe-shaped Shimokita-hantō is centred on Osore-zan (恐山; 874m), a barren volcano that is regarded as one of the most sacred places in all of Japan. Osore, which means fear or dread, is an appropriate name, given that the peak is the stage for Buddhist purgatory. With flocks of jet-black ravens swarming about and sulphur-infused tributaries streaming by, it's not too hard to make the metaphysical leap.

◉ Sights & Activities

★ Osorezan-bodaiji   TEMPLE

(恐山菩提寺; admission ¥500; ⊙6am-6pm May-Oct; 🅿) This holy shrine at the top of Osore-zan is a somewhat terrifying, strangely atmospheric place that attracts people in mourning or those seeking to commune with the dead. Several stone statues of the child-guardian deity Jizō overlook hills of craggy, sulphur-strewn rocks and hissing vapour. According to ritual, visitors are encouraged to help lost souls with their underworld penance by adding stones to the cairns. You can even bathe on hell's doorstep at the free onsen off to the side as you approach the main hall.

Hotoke-ga-ura   CRUISE

(仏ヶ浦) The western edge of the peninsula is a spectacular stretch of coastline dotted with 100m-high wind-carved cliffs, which are said to resemble images of Buddha. Boats depart for sightseeing round trips from Wakinosawa to Hotoke-ga-ura between April and October at 10.45am and 2.55pm (¥3800, two hours). Services are often suspended in poor weather.

⚑ Festivals & Events

Osore-zan Taisai   SPIRITUAL

(恐山大祭; ⊙20 to 24 Jul & 9 to 11 Oct) These two annual festivals attract huge crowds of people, who come to consult *itako* (mediums) in order to contact deceased family members.

⏾ Sleeping

★ Wakinosawa Youth Hostel   HOSTEL ¥

(脇野沢ユースホステル; ☎44-2341; www.wakinosawa.com; 41 Senokawame, Wakinosawa, Mutsu; dm ¥3900, YHA discount ¥3300, breakfast/dinner ¥525/945; 🅿🔁❄🛜) 🏴 This standout hostel is perched on a hillside at Wakinosawa village, about 15 minutes west of the ferry pier – call ahead for a pick-up if you don't have a car. Both Western- and Japanese-style dormitory rooms are available, all of which are adorned with rich hardwoods and country furnishings. While it helps to speak a bit of Japanese, the owners are extremely accommodating. They're also dedicated naturalists who unofficially catalogue the movements of the local macaques. With the right bit of luck, they can help you find a few furry little snow monkeys.

Plaza Hotel Mutsu   HOTEL ¥¥

(プラザホテルむつ; ☎23-7111; www.0175.co.jp/plaza; 2-46 Shimokita-chō, Mutsu; s/tw from ¥5500/11,600; ❄@🛜) A bit dated, but com-

---

LOCAL KNOWLEDGE

ŌMA TUNA

Ōma, at the tip of the Shimokita Peninsula, may look like the end of the earth, but it's the centre of the universe when it comes to tuna. The frigid waters of the Tsugaru Strait directly off the coast are said to yield the tastiest *maguro* (bluefin tuna) in Japan. At the height of the season, a prize catch can sell for ¥25,000/kg.

Ōma's fishing co-ops catch fish the old-fashioned way, with hand lines and live bait (and a lot of muscle – these fish are enormous). It's a way of life that sets them squarely against large-scale commercial interests and in favour of greater regulation to protect the bluefin population.

Here in Ōma, tuna is served literally sea-to-table, and you can see the locals barbecuing fish heads on the street. **Kaikyōsō** (海峡荘; ☎37-3691; 17-734 Ōma-taira, Ōma; maguro-don ¥1000-2500; ⊙11am-3pm late Apr-early Nov), in the bright green building, does a *maguro-don* (tuna sashimi over rice) with thick melt-in-your-mouth cuts of *akami* (lean red meat), *chū-toro* (medium-grade fatty tuna) and *ō-toro* (top-grade fatty tuna).

Tuna is caught fresh between late August and January, although most shops close up by mid-November when the cold winds turn fierce.

fortable enough, this hotel is a two-minute walk from Shimokita Station. Look for the brick-coloured (but not brick) building. Book online for a discounted rate; breakfast is an extra ¥200.

ⓘ Getting There & Away

BOAT

Sii Line (p504) operates two daily ferries between Wakinosawa and Aomori (¥2540, one hour).

Tsugaru Kaikyō (p504) runs two to three ferries daily from Ōma to Hakodate on Hokkaidō (¥2200, 1¾ hours).

BUS

From May to October, there are up to five buses departing from Shimokita Station for Osore-zan (¥750, 45 minutes). Year-round, buses connect Shimokita and Ōma (¥1990, two hours). There are a few buses each day to Wakinosawa from Ōminato Station (¥1800, 70 minutes).

TRAIN

The JR Ōminato line runs several times a day and connects Aomori and Ominato (¥2120, two hours), stopping at Shimokita (¥2120, 1½ hours); you may need to transfer at Noheji.

Hirosaki 弘前

♪ 0172 / POP 181,000

Established in the feudal era by the Tsugaru clan, the historic town of Hirosaki remains one of Tōhoku's principal cultural centres. Although it faded in prominence after political power shifted to Aomori, Hirosaki remains elegant and graceful, with many older structures still intact. The town is centred around castle grounds, complete with keeps and towers, and highlighted by canopies of majestic cherry trees. Hirosaki also serves as a convenient jumping-off point for the spiritual trek up Iwaki-san.

⊙ Sights

★ Hirosaki-kōen   PARK

(弘前公園; ⓘ) This expansive public park has been shaped over the centuries by three castle moats, and landscaped with overhanging cherry trees (more than 5000 in total) that bloom in late April or early May. It's a 20-minute walk from Hirosaki Station, or take the Dote-machi Loop Bus (¥100, 20 minutes), which stops in front of the park. The remains of Hirosaki-jō (弘前城; admission ¥300; ⊙9am-5pm Apr-Nov) lie at the heart of the park; the castle burnt to the ground just 16 years after it was built in 1611.

Chōshō-ji   TEMPLE

(長勝寺; 1-23-8 Nishi-Shigemori; admission ¥300; ⊙9am-4pm) A 10-minute walk southwest of the castle ruins brings you to an atmospheric temple district redolent of feudal times. The focus here is on Chōshō-ji, the largest temple, which harbours the oldest wooden building in Aomori Prefecture and rows of mausoleums built for the rulers of the Tsugaru clan.

Neputa Mura   CULTURAL BUILDING

(ねぷた村; 61 Kamenoko-machi; admission ¥500; ⊙9am-5pm) Come here to see some of Hirosaki's Neputa floats and try your hand at the giant *taiko*. There are also exhibitions of local crafts. It's a short walk from the Bunka Center stop on the Dote-machi Loop Bus.

✷ Festivals & Events

Hirosaki Neputa Matsuri   FLOATS

(弘前ねぷたまつり; ⊙1 to 7 Aug) Hirosaki's Neputa Matsuri is famous for the illuminated floats that parade each evening to the accompaniment of flutes and drums. The festival is considered to signify ceremonial preparation for battle, expressing sentiments both of the bravery required to face what lies ahead and of the heartache for what lies behind.

⨳ Sleeping

Hirosaki Youth Hostel   HOSTEL ¥

(ひろさきユースホステル; ♪33-7066; www.jyh.or.jp/english/touhoku/hirosaki/index.html; 11 Mori-machi; dm ¥3645, YHA discount ¥3045) Tucked away on a side street two blocks south of the castle's outer moat, this hostel is identifiable by the large 'YH' sign on the outside. Although it lacks personality, the price is right and you're smack in the middle of the town's main sights.

★ Ishiba Ryokan   RYOKAN ¥¥

(石場旅館; ♪32-9118; www.ishibaryokan.com; 55 Mototera-machi; r per person/with meals ¥4725/7740; Ⓟ) With its labyrinthine, late 19th-century wooden building, this ryokan has both the setting and the history to go upmarket. Yet the well-maintained tatami rooms, most of which overlook a small garden, are priced reasonably and the owners offer a casual, warm vibe. English and French are spoken here and there are bicycles for rent as well. Enquire about trekking and cultural tours.

Hirosaki

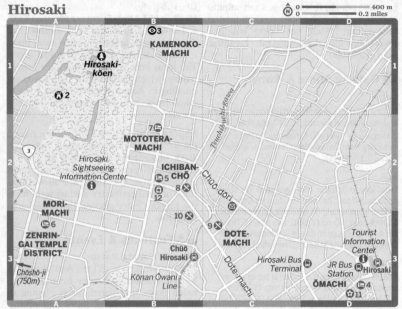

Hirosaki

Hirosaki Grand Hotel HOTEL ¥¥
(弘前グランドホテル; ☎32-1515; http://breez
bay-group.com/hirosaki-gh; 1 Ichiban-chō; s/d from
¥4300/6980; 🅿😊@) A very affordable business hotel with good service, free breakfast
and medium-sized rooms, the Hirosaki
Grand is within easy walking distance of the
castle. It's a fairly nondescript grey building –
look for the large 'G' sign.

**Best Western Hotel
New City Hirosaki** HOTEL ¥¥¥
(ベストウェスタンホテルニューシティ弘
前; ☎37-0700; www.bestwestern.co.jp/hirosaki;
1-1-2 Ōmachi; s/d from ¥9000/16,000; 🅿😊@
📶🐾) Not your typical instalment of the

international franchise, this Best Western is
surprisingly stylish. It's also conveniently attached to Hirosaki Station and has an excellent fitness centre.

✖ Eating & Drinking

Kikufuji JAPANESE ¥
(菊富士; ☎36-3300; www.kikufuji.co.jp; 1
Sakamoto-chō; meals ¥880-2300; ⏱11am-3.30pm,
5pm-9pm) A variety of set meals and a picture
menu make sampling the local cuisine a piece
of cake. There's also an extensive list of Aomori sake, which you can try in an *otameshi*
(sampler) set of three. Paper lanterns and folk
music add atmosphere without being kitschy.
Look for the vertical white sign out front.

★**Kadare Yokochō** FOOD COURT ¥¥
(かだれ横丁; www.kadare.info; 2-1 Hyakkoku-machi; ◷11am-2am; 🖊) You wouldn't expect much from this nondescript office building (marked by the lanterns out front), but inside are a dozen food stalls dishing up everything from fried noodles to Nepalese curry. It's a lively local hangout. **Hinata-bokko** (日向ぼっこ), with the orange *noren* curtains, is particularly recommended; its mother and daughter team turn out excellent renditions of local dishes like *hotate misoyaki* (grilled scallops in miso; ¥600) and *ikamenchi* (minced squid battered and fried; ¥400).

Manchan CAFE ¥
(万茶ン; ☑35-4663; 36-6 Dote-machi; coffee & dessert ¥800; ◷11am-6.30pm) Among Hirosaki's numerous coffee shops, this one has the longest history. In business since 1929, it's said to be the oldest in Tōhoku. Once a hangout for the local literati, it's now a lovely spot to sample another Hirosaki speciality, apple pie. Look for the bifurcated cello out front.

☆ Entertainment

★**Live House Yamauta** LIVE MUSIC
(ライブハウス山唄; ☑36-1835; 1-2-4 Ōmachi; music ¥800, dinner from ¥3000; ◷5-11pm, closed alternate Mon) Come here to listen to the distinct twang of the *shamisen* (three-stringed lute) from Tsugaru – the old name for western Aomori. Nightly performances include traditional folk songs and spirited solo improvisation. The dinner course is a good deal, but you can also just sit at the counter with a drink. There's an English sign out front and the staff caters well for foreign guests. Call ahead for reservations.

🛍 Shopping

Tanaka-ya CRAFTS
(田中屋; www.tugarunuri.jp; Ichibanchō-kado; ◷10am-7pm) Tanaka-ya deals in high-grade works by local artisans. The prices aren't cheap, but even if you're not looking to buy it's worth stopping in for a peek at the boldly coloured *tsugaru-nuri* (lacquerware of the Tsugaru region), produced in-house.

ℹ Information

Hirosaki Sightseeing Information Center (弘前市立観光館; ☑37-5501; www.en-hirosaki.com; 2-1 Shimo-Shirogane-chō; ◷9am-6pm) Situated inside the Kankōkan (tourism building).
Hirosaki Post Office (弘前郵便局; 18-1 Kita Kawarake-chō; ◷post 9am-7pm Mon-Fri, to 3pm Sat; ATM 8am-9pm Mon-Fri, 9am-7pm Sat & Sun) An international ATM is available here.
Tourist Information Center (弘前市観光案内所; ☑26-3600; ◷8.45am-6pm; 🕾) Offers free internet access. On the ground floor of Hirosaki Station.

OFF THE BEATEN TRACK

AONI ONSEN 青荷温泉

A seriously atmospheric, but seriously isolated hot spring, Aoni Onsen has just one inn. It's the ultimate escape, not just from civilisation but also from the present day.

★**Rampu-no-yado** (ランプの宿; ☑0172-54-8588; www.yo.rim.or.jp/~aoni/index.html; 1-7 Aoni-sawa, Taki-no-ue, Okiura, Kuroishi; r per person with 2 meals from ¥9600, day bathing ¥500; ◷day bathing 10am-3pm; 🅿) 🖉, literally 'lamp inn', exists in another time, using oil lamps instead of electric bulbs to light its rooms and wooden corridors. The proprietors here work hard to suspend your reality and transport you back to a simpler age. As the sun goes down and the stars come out over the valley, the effect is magical.

The guest rooms and baths are spread over several small wooden buildings along both sides of a stream, crossed by a footbridge. There are four baths in all, including a stone *rotemburo* (outdoor bath). Winters are snowy, yet particularly ambient (and the cold is nothing that a good long soak can't fix).

Aoni Onsen is located alongside Rte 102 between Hirosaki and Towada-ko. If you don't have a car, you're going to have to work to get out here. By public transport, take the private Kōnan Tetsudō line from Hirosaki to Kuroishi (¥420, 30 minutes, six daily); Kōnan buses connect with arriving passengers for Niji-no-ko (¥750, 30 minutes), from where shuttle buses run to Aoni (free, 30 minutes, four daily). From December through March, the narrow lane that winds down to Aoni Onsen is closed to private vehicles; if you're coming by car, park at the Niji-no-ko bus station and catch the free shuttle bus. Advance reservations are a must.

WORTH A TRIP

IWAKI-SAN & SHIRAKAMI-SANCHI

Hirosaki is the gateway to some of Tōhoku's most remote, and spectacular, landscapes. Soaring above the city is the sacred volcano of **Iwaki-san** (岩木山; 1625m). In mid-September, area farmers gather for the Oyama-Sankei, an annual moonlit pilgrimage up to the peak, where they pray for a bountiful harvest.

Tradition dictates that summit-bound travellers should first make an offering to the guardian god at **Iwaki-san-jinja** (岩木山神社). After peaking at the summit, you can follow a different trail down, past the smaller peak of **Tori-no-umi-san** (鳥ノ海山) and eventually reaching the village of **Dake-onsen** (岳温泉). The entire 9km hike should take you about 6½ hours, which means you can easily summit Iwaki-san on a day trip from Hirosaki if you get an early enough start.

Southwest of Iwaki-san is the isolated **Shirakami-sanchi** (白神山地), a Unesco-protected virgin forest of Japanese beech trees. From the bus stop at Anmon Aqua Village, an hour-long trail leads into the woods to the three **Anmon Falls** (暗門の滝; Anmon-no-taki), the longest of which is 42m. This is part of the park's 'buffer zone', which is open to the public without permit.

From early April to late October up to eight buses depart each day from platform 6 of the Hirosaki Station bus stop for Iwaki-san-jinja (¥690, 40 minutes). From Dake-onsen, there are up to eight buses back to Hirosaki daily (¥1010, one hour). From May through October, there are two buses in the morning for Anmon Aqua Village (one-way/return ¥1600/2400, 1½ hours), leaving from platform 6 at the Hirosaki Station bus stop; two buses make the return trip in the afternoon.

❶ Getting There & Around

Tokkyū trains on the JR Ōu main line run hourly between Aomori and Hirosaki (¥1460, 35 minutes), and Hirosaki and Akita (¥2520, three hours).

The **Tsugaru free pass** (adult/child ¥2000/1000) covers area buses and trains, including those out to Iwaki-san and Shirakami-sanchi, for two consecutive days. Enquire at the Tourist Information Center.

The **Dote-machi Loop Bus** (¥100 per ride), which circuits the downtown area, leaves from in front of Aomori Station.

Bicycle rental (¥300, 9am–4pm) is available at either tourist information centre from May through November.

AKITA PREFECTURE

Japan's sixth-largest prefecture, Akita-ken (秋田県) is shaped by the Ōu-sanmyaku and Dewa mountain ranges. These soaring peaks have long kept the region isolated, and even today development is sparse. Mountains, of course, are good news for hikers and skiers, but also for those with more idle pursuits: Akita's peaks shelter remote, rustic hot springs that are among the best in the country. Paired with neighbouring Tazawa-ko, Nyūtō Onsen is an unrivalled retreat. At lower altitudes, towns and cities have sprung up in fertile valleys, including the prefectural capital of Akita and the feudal city of Kakunodate, a storehouse of samurai culture. The region is also said to have the most beautiful women in Japan, the so-called *Akita-bijin* (Akita beauties).

Tazawa-ko   田沢湖

🎵 0187 / POP 12,900

At 423m, Tazawa-ko is Japan's deepest lake. Its convenient *shinkansen* access makes it a popular summertime escape. The nearby mountains offer excellent views of the lake and four seasons of activity, including skiing.

◉ Sights

Tazawa-ko   LAKE

(田沢湖) Tazawa-ko has a sandy beach, **Shirahama** (白浜), yet swimming is a frigid proposition outside the balmy summer months. You can rent all manner of boats in the town of Tazawa Kohan during the spring, summer and autumn. A stroll by the lake at sunset is a treat at any time of year and the preferred activity for romance-seeking Japanese couples. On the eastern shore is Tazawa-ko's landmark, a bronze statue of the legendary beauty Tatsuko, sculpted by Funakoshi Yasutake.

A 20km road wraps around the lake, perfect for a slow drive or vigorous cycle – bike rentals are available in Tazawa Kohan (¥400 per hour). There are also a few buses each day from Tazawa-ko Station or Tazawa Kohan that loop around the lake, stopping for 15 minutes to admire the statue of Tatsuko.

🏃 Activities

⭐ Akita Komaga-take   HIKING
(秋田駒ヶ岳) Straddling the border with Iwate Prefecture, this mountainous area is admired for its summer wildflowers, autumn foliage and rare prevalence of both dry and wet plant species. If you have two days to spare, you can pursue a 17km course that takes in three peaks, overnights in a picturesque mountain hut and finishes up with a rewarding soak in the healing waters of Nyūtō Onsen.

You can access the trailhead at Komaga-take Hachigōme (eighth station) by taking one of seven daily buses (all departing before 1.30pm) from Tazawa-ko Station (¥1000, one hour). From the eighth station, it should take you an hour or two to reach the summit of Oname-dake (男女岳; 1637m).

From here, you should press on to the eastern edge of the oval-shaped pond below and claim your space at the **Amida-ike Hinan Goya** (阿弥陀池避難小屋) unmanned mountain hut; it's recommended that you leave a small tip (¥1000). You can also double back for 20 minutes or so and scale O-dake (男岳; 1623m).

On the second day, it will take you about seven hours to descend to Nyūtō Onsen, including first summiting Yoko-dake (横岳; 1583m). The descending trail follows the ridgeline most of the way and eventually winds through expansive marshlands that harbour all manner of avian life. The circuit ends at the Nyūtō Onsen bus stop, from where it is just a short walk to a hot bath.

Tazawako Ski Park   SNOW SPORTS
(たざわ湖スキー場; www.snowjapan.com/e/spotlight/tazawako.html; 73-2 Shimo-Takano; 1-day lift ticket adult/child ¥3800/2600; ⊙Dec-Apr) Akita's largest winter-sports destination, Tazawako Sukī-jō is just a little more than a three-hour *shinkansen* ride from Tokyo. The powder accumulates here over 13 runs that wind down Akita Komaga-take and overlook the nearby shores of Tazawa-ko.

Trails are evenly divided between beginner, intermediate and advanced levels. However, they tend to be a bit on the shorter side,

with the exception of the 1.6km Kokutai and Shirakaba runs. Six lifts do a reasonable job of keeping the queues to a minimum, but it can get busy here on high-season weekends.

You'll find English-language signs on the mountains and in the restaurants. There are three large cafeteria-style eateries serving the usual fast-food-style staples in addition to local specialities such as ginger *rāmen* and Tazawa-ko microbrews. Full equipment rental is available for ¥3500 per day.

In the winter months, buses leaving Tazawa-ko Station for Nyūtō Onsen stop at Tazawako Sukī-jō (¥530, 30 minutes).

🛏 Sleeping

You can also elect to bed down in one of Nyūtō Onsen's excellent ryokan.

Tazawa-ko Youth Hostel   HOSTEL ¥
(田沢湖ユースホステル; ☎43-1281; www.jyh.or.jp/yhguide/touhoku/tazawako/index.html; 33-8 Kami-Ishigami; dm ¥3890, YHA discount ¥3290, breakfast/dinner ¥650/1050; P📶) A few minutes' walk from the lake, this rambling hostel has clean, functional tatami rooms, an onsen bath and filling home-cooked meals.

ℹ Information

Folake (☎43-2111; ⊙8.30am-5.30pm; @) Inside the train station, with tourist information and free internet available.

ℹ Getting There & Away

BUS
Frequent local buses run between JR Tazawa-ko Station and Tazawa Kohan (¥350, 10 minutes), the tourist hub on the eastern shore of the lake.

Buses also run to Nyūtō Onsen (¥650, 45 minutes). Note that these services terminate after sunset.

LOCAL KNOWLEDGE

THE LEGEND OF TATSUKO

Rumour has it that a local beauty, Tatsuko, inhabits the lake in the form of a dragon. Believing that the spring water would make her youthful looks last forever, she imbibed so much of it that she was transformed into a water dragon. One version of the story adds another dragon, formerly a prince, as her lover. Their passionate nocturnal antics are said to be the reason why Tazawa-ko doesn't freeze in winter!

Akita Prefecture

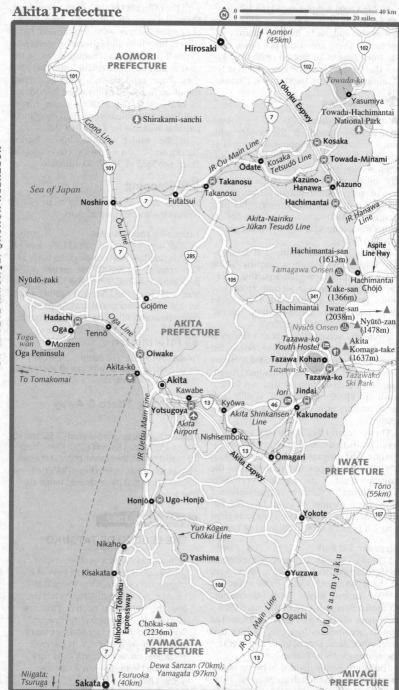

0   40 km
0   20 miles

AOMORI
PREFECTURE

Hirosaki

*Aomori
(45km)*

Towada-ko

101

102

102

Tōhoku Expwy

Shirakami-sanchi

7

Yasumiya
Towada-Hachimantai
National Park

JR Ōu Main Line

Kosaka

Gonō Line

Odate

Kosaka
Tetsudō Line

Towada-Minami

Takanosu

Takanosu

**Kazuno-
Hanawa**

Kazuno

Noshiro

Futatsui

7

Ōu Line

Hachimantai

JR Hanawa
Line

Sea of Japan

*Akita-Nairiku
Jūkan Tesudō Line*

285

**Hachimantai-san
(1613m)**

Aspite
Line Hwy

101

7

Nyūdō-zaki

105

Tamagawa Onsen

**Yake-san
(1366m)**

**Hachímantai
Chōjō**

341

Gojōme

Hachimantai

**Iwate-san
(2038m)**

**Nyūtō-zan
(1478m)**

Hadachi

Oga

Tennō

Nyūtō Onsen

AKITA
PREFECTURE

*Tazawa-ko
Youth Hostel*

**Akita
Komaga-take
(1637m)**

*Toga-
wan*

Monzen
Oga Peninsula

Oga Line

Oiwake

Tazawa Kohan

Tazawa-ko

Akita-kō

To Tomakomai

Akita

Kawabe

Tazawa-ko

*Tazawako
Ski Park*

Iori

Jindai

46

Yotsugoya

JR Uetsu Main Line

13

Kyōwa

*Akita Shinkansen
Line*

Kakunodate

*Akita
Airport*

Nishisemboku

**IWATE
PREFECTURE**

13

Akita Expwy

Omagari

*Tōno
(55km)*

107

Honjō

Ugo-Honjō

7

*Yuri Kōgen
Chōkai Line*

Yokote

Nikaho

Yashima

Ōu-sanmyaku

Nihonkai-Tōhoku
Expressway

Kisakata

108

Yuzawa

JR Ōu Main Line

**Chōkai-san
(2236m)**

Ogachi

YAMAGATA
PREFECTURE

7

*Niigata;
Tsuruga*

*Tsuruoka
(40km)*

*Dewa Sanzan (70km);
Yamagata (97km)*

13

**MIYAGI
PREFECTURE**

Sakata

CAR & MOTORCYCLE

If you're driving, Rte 46 connects the **Akita Expressway** (秋田自動車道) with Tazawa-ko.

TRAIN

JR Tazawa-ko Station is located a few kilometres southeast of the lake and serves as the area's main access point.

Shinkansen on the Akita line run several times an hour between Tazawa-ko and Tokyo (¥15,240, three hours) and between Tazawa-ko and Akita (¥3280, 55 minutes) via Kakunodate (¥1560, 15 minutes).

Nyūtō Onsen　乳頭温泉

This is one of Japan's choicest hot springs and a must-visit for any aspiring onsen aficionado. While *nyūtō* literally means 'nipple', the name comes from the mammary-shaped Nyūtō-sanroku, or Nyūtō Foothills, where the onsen is located (although some springs do have milky-white waters).

The area is home to no fewer than seven rustic ryokan, each with a different character. All offer healing waters that are great for an away-from-it-all soak. Many also have *konyoku* or mixed-sex baths (when it comes to bathing, the Japanese certainly aren't shy!).

🛏 Sleeping

For a complete list of ryokan in Nyūtō, see www.nyuto-onsenkyo.com/english/index.html.

★**Tsuru-no-yu Onsen** RYOKAN ¥¥
(鶴の湯温泉; ☑0187-46-2139; www.tsurunoyu.com/english.html; 50 Kokuyurin, Sendatsui-zawa; r per person with 2 meals ¥8500-15,900, day bathing ¥500; ⊙day bathing 10am-3pm Tue-Sun; P) The most-storied onsen in Nyūtō, Tsuru-no-yu has been in the business for almost four centuries. The reason for its enduring fame is its mineral-rich spring containing sulphur, sodium, calcium chloride and carbonic acid, which combine to produce a distinctive milky-white colour. According to local lore, a hunter once saw a *tsuru* (crane) healing its wounds in the spring and reported the fortuitous discovery to his lord. The hot spring was soon designated as the official bathhouse of the Akita clan's ruling elite.

Today it's open to commoners and nobles alike. The mixed *rotemburo* is positively jubilant, although shyer folk can take refuge in the indoor sex-segregated baths. Accommodation is extremely varied, ranging from tiny six-mat tatami rooms that share bathrooms to compartmentalised suites opening up to the forest. Regardless of where you bed down, the evening hours are a nostalgic affair, distinguished by hearty meals cooked over the sunken *irori* (hearth) and guests in *yukata* dining and socialising by lantern light. Given the onsen's fame, it is recommended that you book well in advance.

Taenoyu RYOKAN ¥¥
(妙乃湯; ☑0187-46-2740; www.taenoyu.com; 2-1 Komagatake; r per person with 2 meals from ¥12,855, day bathing ¥700; ⊙day bathing 10am-3pm Wed-Mon; P🛜) 🌊 What Taenoyu lacks in history, it more than makes up for in style. This boutique ryokan specialises in sophisticated refinement: sleeping quarters are framed by rich hardwoods and elaborate furnishings, and locavore meals are based on wild plants foraged for on the grounds. Bathing options are comprehensive, including private family onsen, reclining cypress tubs, mixed *rotemburo,* rock-lined springs and indoor relaxation pools.

Kuroyu Onsen RYOKAN ¥¥
(黒湯温泉; ☑0187-46-2214; www.kuroyu.com; 2-1 Kuroyu-zawa; r per person with 2 meals from ¥11,700, day bathing ¥500; ⊙day bathing 9am-4pm May-Nov; P) At the streamside Kuroyu, you'll feel as though you've stepped into a Japanese woodblock print. With a bathing tradition dating back more than 300 years, Kuroyu is famous for its hydrogen-sulphide spring that is reputed to ease high blood pressure, diabetes and arteriosclerosis. Don't miss the waterfall jets, which send cascades of water onto your shoulders and back. Japanese-style rooms are fairly standard, though the forest setting is the stage for a relaxing retreat.

❶ Getting There & Away

Buses run from JR Tazawa-ko Station to Nyūtō Onsen (¥650, 45 minutes).

DAY BATHING

Many ryokan open their baths for a few hours in the afternoon to visitors who aren't staying the night. Called *higaeri onsen* (literally 'day-trip hot spring'), this practice is a great way to get a luxurious soak, without having to pay ryokan prices – a bath usually costs ¥500 to ¥1000, but you'll have to bring your own towel or pay to rent one.

TAMAGAWA ONSEN

Its remote location in the heart of Hachimantai, Tōhoku's central volcanic plateau, makes Tamagawa Onsen a bastion of a different sort of onsen culture. People don't come here to relax and enjoy the mountain scenery; it's a barren, rocky wilderness stained egg-yolk yellow in patches. Instead, they come for the purported healing properties of the water – it's the most acidic in the country, with a pH of just 1.1 – and to undergo strict bathing regimens that can last a week or longer. Far from a resort, the **Tamagawa Onsen Ryokan** (玉川温泉旅館; ☑0187-58-3000; www.tamagawa-onsen.jp; Shibukurosawa, Tamagawa; r per person with 2 meals from ¥8300, baths ¥600; ☉day bathing 7am-5pm; ℙ) is downright institutional.

Steam literally rises from the ground here, which is a big part of the draw: in between soaks, bathers stretch out fully clothed on reed mats on rocks heated by the underwater springs and sweat it out under blankets – a natural *ganbanyoku* (stone sauna). Lying head-to-toe with strangers, breathing in the heady, sulphuric air, you can feel your body temperature gradually rise to near feverish in about half an hour (at which point it is time to take a break).

From late April through November, buses leave from Tazawa-ko Station for Tamagawa Onsen (¥1420, 1¼ hours). You can purchase reed mats (required for the *ganbanyoku*) at the ryokan.

Kakunodate 角館

☑0187 / POP 13,000

Established in 1620 by Ashina Yoshikatsu, the lord of the Satake clan, Kakunodate is known as 'Little Kyoto' and presents a thoughtful, immersive experience for anyone interested in catching a glimpse of the samurai era. While the castle that once guarded the feudal town is no more, the *buke yashiki* (samurai district) is splendidly preserved. A veritable living museum of Japanese culture and history, the *buke yashiki* consists of orderly mansions surrounded by cherry trees and manicured gardens.

◉ Sights

Half a dozen villas are open to the public, lining a street shaded by cherry trees a 20-minute walk northwest of the train station. The more elaborate ones are set up like miniature museums; others are simply left as they were and are free for visitors to peek inside.

Aoyagi Samurai Manor Museum   MUSEUM
(角館歴史村青柳家 | Kakunodate Rekishi-mura Aoyagi-ke; www.samuraiworld.com/english/index.html; 3 Omote-machi; admission ¥500; ☉9am-5pm Apr-Oct, to 4pm Nov-Mar) The Aoyagi family compound is impressive in its own right, but inside each well-maintained structure is a fascinating exhibition of family heirlooms. The collection spans generations and includes centuries-old samurai weaponry, folk art and valuable antiques, along with gramophones and classic jazz records.

Bukeyashiki Ishiguro-ke   HISTORIC BUILDING
(武家屋敷石黒家; 1 Omote-machi; admission ¥300; ☉9am-5pm) Built in 1809 as the residence of the Isihiguro family, advisers to the Satake clan, this is one of the oldest buildings in the district. A descendant of the family still lives here, but some rooms are open to the public. In addition to samurai gear, don't miss the weathered maps and the precision scales for doling out rice.

Andō Brewery   BREWERY
(安藤醸造; 27 Shimo-Shinmachi; ☉8.30am-6pm) A centuries-old brewery, Andō makes soy sauce and miso (sorry, tipplers, it's not that kind of brewery!) in a beautiful, brick storehouse from the late 19th century. You can tour a few of the rooms and sample some pickles and miso soup (for free!) in the cosy cafe.

Kakunodate Cherry-Bark Craft Center   ARTS CENTRE
(角館樺細工伝承館 | Kakunodate Kabazaiku Denshōkan; 10-1 Omote-machi; admission ¥300; ☉9am-5pm Apr-Oct, to 4.30pm Nov-Mar) Inside are exhibits and demonstrations of *kabazaiku,* the craft of covering household or decorative items in fine strips of cherry bark. This pursuit was first taken up by lower-ranking and masterless samurai in times of hardship.

🎎 Festivals & Events

Kakunodate Sakura   CULTURE
(角館の桜; ⏱mid-Apr to early May) On the river embankment, a 2km stretch of cherry trees becomes a tunnel of pure pink during the *hanami* (blossom viewing) season. Some of the *shidare-zakura* (drooping cherry) trees in the *buke yashiki* are up to 300 years old.

Kakunodate O-matsuri   TRADITIONAL
(角館のお祭り; ⏱7 to 9 Sep) As they have done for 350 years, festival participants haul around enormous 7-tonne *yama* (wooden carts) to pray for peaceful times, accompanied by folk music and dancing.

🛏 Sleeping

Note that rates rise during high seasons, such as when the cherry blossoms bloom.

Tamachi

Bukeyashiki Hotel   BOUTIQUE HOTEL ¥¥
(田町武家屋敷ホテル; ☑52-1700; www.bukeyashiki.jp; 23 Tamachi; r per person with 1/2 meals from ¥11,125/15,750; 🅿@) Though it's only been in business for a few decades, you can easily imagine travel-worn samurai passing through the wooden gate of this hotel. The structure resembles a traditional villa, but is fully stocked with modern amenities. Rooms, both Japanese and Western style, are simply elegant, with dark wooden beams and paper lanterns; in comparison, meals are lavish affairs.

Folkloro Kakunodate   BUSINESS HOTEL ¥¥
(フォルクローロ角館; ☑53-2070; www.folkloro-kakunodate.com; Nakasuga-zawa 14; s/tw from ¥6615/11,340; 🅿⊜@🛜) This standard but nicely maintained business hotel gets points for its convenient location next to the train station and its free breakfast spread; it loses a few for charging nearly ¥2000 extra for a nonsmoking room.

🍴 Eating

Kosendō   NOODLES ¥
(古泉洞; ☑53-2902; 9 Higashi-katsuraku-chō; noodles from ¥1050; ⏱10am-4pm) Kakunodate's most historic lunch spot is in this Edo-era wooden schoolhouse. The house speciality is *buke-soba* served with *takenoko* (bamboo) and tempura-fried *ōba* (large perilla leaf). The eatery is in the middle of the *buke yashiki*; look for the wooden sign above the entrance.

Nishi-no-miyake
Restaurant Kita-kura   SHOKUDŌ ¥
(西宮家レストラン北蔵; ☑52-2438; 11-1 Kami-chō, Tamachi; meals from ¥1050; ⏱11am-5pm; 📶) This sprawling former residence houses a restaurant in a century-old warehouse towards the back of the complex. Here, diners sit under hulking wooden rafters, tucking into classic *yōshoku* (Japanese-style Western food) dishes like *hayashi raisu* (hashed beef on rice) that would have been in vogue when the structure was built. Nishi-no-miyake is halfway between the station and the sightseeing district.

ℹ Information

Tourist Information Center (角館町観光協会; ☑54-2700; ⏱9am-6pm mid-Apr–Sep, to 5.30pm Oct–mid-Apr) Pick up English maps outside the station in a small building shaped like a *kura* (traditional Japanese storehouse).

OFF THE BEATEN TRACK

FARMHOUSE INNS

If you want to get away from the tourist crowds, consider staying in a *nōka minshuku* (farmhouse inn). **Iori** (☑0187-55-2262; www.akita-gt.org/stay/minshuku/iori.html; 65 Maeda, Ogata, Kakunodate-machi; r per person/with 2 meals ¥4500/6000), 3km north of Kakunodate Station, is part of a working family farm. It's a spare building, really, which the owners have turned into a comfortable cabin. The look is pure Japanese country, with whitewashed walls and dark-wood beams, fresh tatami mats and indigo floor cushions. How much you take part in life on the farm is up to you: Iori can be your base for exploring Kakunodate, a peaceful retreat or a chance to get your hands dirty in the kitchen or fields. It helps to have your own wheels, but you can arrange pick-up from Kakunodate Station.

Akita's countryside has dozens of *nōka minshuku*. For a complete list, see www.akita-gt.org/stay.

ⓘ Getting There & Around

Several of the *shinkansen* on the Akita line run hourly between Kakunodate and Tazawa-ko (¥1560, 15 minutes), and between Kakunodate and Akita (¥2940, 45 minutes).

Local trains also run infrequently on the JR Tazawako line between Kakunodate and Tazawa-ko (¥320, 20 minutes), and between Kakunodate and Akita (¥1280, 1½ hours), with a change at Ōmagari to the JR Ōu main line.

Bicycle rentals are available across from the train station for ¥300 per hour.

Akita   秋田

♪ 018 / POP 336,000

The northern terminus of the Akita *shinkansen,* this sprawling commercial city and prefectural capital is one of the region's principal transport hubs. Like most contemporary cities, it was once a castle town, in this case the seat of power of the Satake clan.

◉ Sights

Akita's few sights are in the city centre near the train station, so you can easily get around on foot.

Senshū-kōen   PARK

(千秋公園) Originally constructed in 1604, Akita's castle was destroyed with other feudal relics during the Meiji Restoration. The moat still guards the entrance to this leafy park; though hardly sinister, it becomes choked with giant waterlilies in summer. There are also a few pieces of the castle foundation remaining, along with plenty of grassy patches and strolling paths. A reconstruction of a guard tower in the north corner offers views over the city.

Akita Museum of Art   MUSEUM

(秋田県立美術館; http://common.pref.akita.lg.jp /art-museum; 1-4-2 Naka-dōri; ◷10am-6pm) Akita's most famous painting, Tsuguharu Fūjita's *Events of Akita,* is also reputed to be the world's largest canvas painting. It measures 3.65m by 20.5m and depicts traditional Akita life through the seasons. This work and others from the former Hirano Masakichi Bijutsukan (museum) were scheduled to move into their sleek new home, this Andō Tadao–designed museum in the Naka-Ichi centre, in September 2013. Visitors can rest in the 2nd-floor cafe, from where the reflecting pool seems to run directly into the palace moat.

Akarenga-kan Museum   MUSEUM

(赤れんが郷土館 | Akarenga Kyōdokan; www. city.akita.akita.jp/city/ed/ak; 3-3-21 Ō-machi; admission ¥200; ◷9.30am-4.30pm) Once the opulent headquarters of Akita Bank, this brick structure built in 1912 is now a folk museum. Inside, you'll find fascinating woodblock prints of traditional Akita life by self-taught artist Katsuhira Tokushi.

✱✲ Festivals & Events

Akita Kantō Matsuri   LANTERN

(秋田竿燈まつり; www.kantou.gr.jp/english/index.htm; ◷3 to 6 August) At summer's height, Akita celebrates its visually stunning Pole Lantern Festival. As evening falls on the city centre, more than 160 men skillfully balance giant poles, weighing 60kg and hung with illuminated lanterns, on their heads, chins, hips and shoulders, to the beat of *taiko* groups.

🛏 Sleeping

Naniwa Hotel   HOTEL ¥

(ホテルなにわ; ☑832-4570; www.hotel-naniwa. jp; 6-18-27 Naka-dōri; r per person/with 2 meals from ¥2625/5250; P✷@) This small family-run hotel has a variety of tatami rooms (some teeny tiny, others with private sinks and toilets). It also outdoes itself with extras: a beautiful 24-hour *hinoki* bath, massage chairs and filling meals that use the owners' home-grown rice. Look for the red building with a wooden entrance.

Richmond Hotel
Akita Eki-mae   BUSINESS HOTEL ¥¥

(リッチモンドホテル秋田駅前; ☑884-0055; www.richmondhotel.jp/en/akita/index.php?lang=en; 2-2-26 Naka-dōri; s/d from ¥5600/7800; ✷@☎) Remarkably stylish for a business hotel, and conveniently located between the station and the sights. Prices can vary wildly so it's a good idea to book ahead online.

Akita Castle Hotel   HOTEL ¥¥

(秋田キャッスルホテル; ☑834-1141; www. castle-hotel.co.jp; 1-3-5 Naka-dōri; s/d from ¥7500/11,000; P✷@☎) It may not look much from the outside, but this is the classiest hotel in town. If you can lock in a discount rate online, it's not a bad deal either. The rooms recently got a stylish makeover; the nicest ones overlook the castle moat.

✗ Eating & Drinking

Kawabata-dōri, lined with restaurants and bars both classic and seedy, is the city's main nightlife strip. For a picnic lunch, stop by the supermarket in the Naka-Ichi centre.

Kanbun Gonendō
NOODLES ¥

(寛文五年堂; www.kanbun5.jp; 1-4-3 Naka-dōri; noodles from ¥900; ⊘11am-10.30pm; ☑) Sample delicate, fresh *inaniwa udon* (thin wheat noodles) at this popular speciality shop. They're particularly refreshing on a hot day served cold with soy sauce and sesame dipping sauces. Vegetarian dishes are available; ask before ordering. The restaurant is part of the Naka-Ichi shopping centre.

Otafuku
JAPANESE ¥¥

(お多福; ☑862-0802; http://akitaotafuku. com; 4-2-25 Ō-machi; hotpot dishes from ¥2520; ⊘11.30am-2pm & 5-10.30pm Mon-Fri, 5-10.30pm Sat) This upmarket traditional restaurant does good renditions of classic local dishes like *kiritanpo nabe*, a filling hotpot of kneaded and grilled rice (the *kiritanpo*) and vegetables in a chicken and soy-sauce broth. Though pricey, courses simplify ordering and include Otafuku's famous pickles.

Spica Ryokōsha Cafe & Bar
CAFE

(スピカ旅行社カフェ＆バー; http://spica-travel.com/cafe_bar/cafe_bar.html; 5-4-18 Naka-dōri; drinks from ¥500; ⊘11.30am-11pm Tue-Thu, to 1am Fri & Sat, to 6pm Sun) By day, this colourful cafe serves tasty smoothies and lunch plates. Come night, it morphs into a hip little bar. During happy hour (5pm to 7pm), Heartland beer sells for just ¥390.

ℹ Information

Akita Eki-mae Post Office (秋田駅前郵便局; 4-11-14 Naka-dōri; ⊘post 9am-6pm Mon-Fri, ATM 9am-4pm Mon-Fri, to 12.30pm Sat)

Akita Red Cross Hospital (秋田赤十字病院; ☑24hr emergency hotline 829-5000; www. akita-med.jrc.or.jp; 222-1 Nawashirosawa; ⊘outpatient services 8am-11.30am Mon-Fri) The hospital is 5km southeast of the train station, off of Rte 41.

Tourist Information Center (秋田市観光案内所; ☑832-7941; www.akitafan.com/language/ en/index.html; ⊘9am-7pm) Opposite the *shinkansen* tracks on the 2nd floor of Akita Station.

ℹ Getting There & Away

AIR
From Akita Airport, 21km south of the city centre, flights go to/from Tokyo, Osaka, Nagoya, Hiroshima, Sapporo and many other destinations.

Akita

Frequent buses leave for the airport from platform 1 in front of Akita Station (¥900, 40 minutes).

BOAT
From the port of Akita-kō, **Shin Nihonkai** (新日本海; ☑880-2600; www.snf.jp) has ferries to Tomakomai on Hokkaidō (from ¥4400, 10 hours), departing at 7am on Tuesday, Wednesday, Friday, Saturday and Sunday.

One bus leaves at 6.05am from platform 11 outside Akita Station for Akita-kō (¥420, 30 minutes), 8km northwest of the city.

NORTHERN HONSHŪ (TŌHOKU) AKITA

BUS

Highway buses depart from the east exit of the train station, and connect Akita to major cities throughout Honshū.

CAR & MOTORCYCLE

If you're driving, the **Akita Expressway** (秋田自動車道) runs east from Akita until it joins with the Tōhoku Expressway. The **Nihonkai-Tōhoku Expressway** (日本海東北自動車道) runs south along the coast.

You can pick up a car at **Toyota Rent a Car** (トヨタレンタカー; 833-0100; 4-6-5 Naka-dōri; ☺8am-10pm), a few minutes' walk west from Akita Station.

TRAIN

The JR Akita *shinkansen* runs hourly between the northern terminus of Akita and the southern terminus of Tokyo (¥16,810, four hours) via Tazawa-ko (¥3280, one hour) and Kakunodate (¥2940, 45 minutes).

Infrequent local trains also run on the JR Ōu main line between Akita and Kakunodate (¥1280, 1½ hours), with a change at Ōmagari to the JR Tazawako line. There are a few *tokkyū* each day on the JR Uetsu line, connecting Akita with Niigata (¥7020, 3¾ hours).

YAMAGATA PREFECTURE

As its name (literally 'mountain shape') suggests, Yamagata-ken (山形県) is a land of mountains. Its most famous peaks are the three sacred ones that make up Dewa Sanzan, revered by *yamabushi* (mountain priests) and hikers alike. But it is also a land of hot springs, like Zaō Onsen, with its dramatic caldera lake and challenging ski slopes. Yamadera, the temple perched atop a cliff, has been enchanting visitors for centuries, among them the legendary travelling poet Matsuo Bashō.

Tsuruoka   鶴岡

☎0235 / POP 136,000

Tsuruoka, in the middle of the Shōnai plain, was established by the Sakai clan, one of feudal Yamagata's most important families. Today, it's the second-largest city in the prefecture and the jumping-off point for the mountains of Dewa Sanzan. Downtown is pretty sleepy; if you need a bite to eat or snacks for the road, try the S-Mall shopping centre, a few minutes on foot from the station.

◉ Sights & Activities

Chidō Museum   MUSEUM

(致道博物館 | Chidō Hakubutsukan; 10-18 Kachū-shinmachi; admission ¥700; ☺9am-4.30pm; Ⓟ) Founded in 1950 by the former Lord Shōnai in order to preserve local culture, this museum features Sakai-family artefacts, two Meiji-era buildings, a traditional storehouse and a *kabuto-zukuri* (farmhouse with a thatched roof shaped like a samurai helmet).

The museum is on the southwest corner of Tsuruoka-kōen, the site of the former Sakai castle. You can either walk for about 15 minutes southwest from Tsuruoka Station, or take a bus from stop 1. Frequent buses bound for Yunohama Onsen pass by the Chidō Hakubutsukan-mae stop (¥260, 10 minutes).

✯ Festivals & Events

Tenjin Matsuri   MASKS

(天神祭) On 25 May each year, people stroll around in masks and costumes, serving sake and keeping an eye out for friends and acquaintances. The object is to make it through the festival without anyone recognising you. Manage this feat three years running and local lore claims you'll have good luck for the rest of your life!

🛏 Sleeping

Narakan   INN ¥

(奈良館; ☎22-1202; 2-35 Hiyoshi-machi; r per person/with 2 meals from ¥3885/6300; Ⓟ☎) A travellers' favourite for years, Narakan has both simple tatami rooms with shared bath and Western-style rooms with bath. The home-cooked meals are filling and delicious. Head five minutes south along the main street leading out from the station; the inn, distinguished by a tall chimney, will be on your left.

Tokyo Daiichi Hotel Tsuruoka   BUSINESS HOTEL ¥¥

(東京第一ホテル鶴岡; ☎24-7662; www.tdh-tsuruoka.co.jp; 2-10 Nishiki-machi; s/d from ¥8662/12,075; Ⓟ@) A cut above the other business hotels around the station, this one has comparatively spacious and stylish rooms. Even better is the rooftop onsen, complete with sauna and *rotemburo*, perfect for a post-hike soak. It's the huge yellow-brick building connected to the S-Mall shopping centre.

Yamagata Prefecture

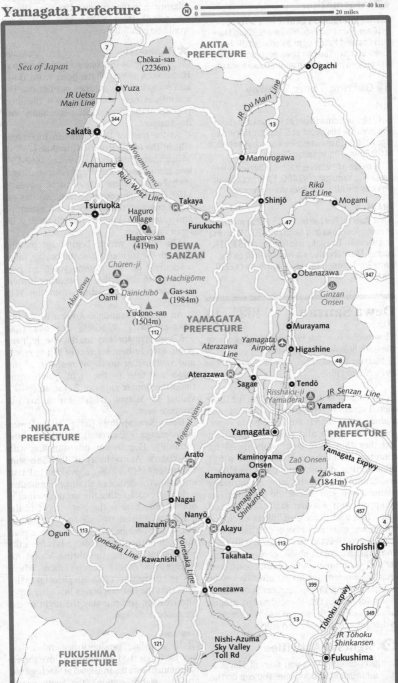

N
0   40 km
0   20 miles

AKITA
PREFECTURE

Sea of Japan

Chōkai-san
(2236m)

Ogachi

Yuza

*JR Uetsu
Main Line*

Sakata

JR Ōu Main Line

Mamurogawa

Amarume

Mogami-gawa

Rikū West Line

*Rikū
East Line*

Takaya

Shinjō

Mogami

Tsuruoka

Haguro
Village

Furukuchi

Haguro-san
(419m)

DEWA
SANZAN

Chūren-ji

Hachigōme

Obanazawa

Dainichibō

Ōami

Gas-san
(1984m)

*Ginzan
Onsen*

Aka-gawa

Yudono-san
(1504m)

YAMAGATA
PREFECTURE

Murayama

*Yamagata
Airport*

Higashine

*Aterazawa
Line*

NIIGATA
PREFECTURE

Aterazawa

Sagae

Tendō

JR Senzan Line

*Risshaku-ji
(Yamadera)*

Yamadera

Mogami-gawa

Yamagata

MIYAGI
PREFECTURE

Yamagata Expwy

Arato

Kaminoyama
Onsen

Zaō Onsen

Kaminoyama

Zaō-san
(1841m)

Nagai

*Yamagata
Shinkansen*

Nanyō

Imaizumi

Akayu

Oguni

Yonesaka Line

Yonesaka Line

Shiroishi

Kawanishi

Takahata

Yonezawa

Tōhoku Expwy

*IR Tōhoku
Shinkansen*

Nishi-Azuma
Sky Valley
Toll Rd

FUKUSHIMA
PREFECTURE

Fukushima

ℹ️ Information

Tourist Information Center (☎ 25-7678; ⏰ 10am-5pm Nov-Feb, 9.30am-5.30pm Mar-Oct) Located to the right as you exit JR Tsuruoka Station. You can book accommodation and pick up information about Dewa Sanzan.

ℹ️ Getting There & Away

BUS

Buses leave from in front of Tsuruoka Station and from the bus depot at S-Mall for Haguro village (¥800, 35 minutes). Pick up a bus schedule at the Tourist Information Center.

There are a few buses each day between Tsuruoka and Yamagata (¥2400, 1¾ hours), though services are often cut back during winter.

TRAIN

A few daily *tokkyū* run on the JR Uetsu main line between Tsuruoka and Akita (¥3820, 1¾ hours) and between Tsuruoka and Niigata (¥4330, 1¾ hours). There are also a few daily *futsū* on the same line between Tsuruoka and Akita (¥2210, 2¾ hours).

Dewa Sanzan 出羽三山

☎ 0235

'How cool it is, a pale crescent shining, above the dark hollow of Haguro-san.'

Matsuo Bashō, *The Narrow Road to the Deep North* (1689)

Dewa Sanzan is the collective title for three sacred peaks – Haguro-san, Gas-san and Yudono-san – which are believed to represent birth, death and rebirth respectively. Together they have been worshipped for centuries by followers of Shugendō, a folk religion that draws from both Buddhism and Shintō. During the annual pilgrimage seasons, you can see white-clad pilgrims equipped with wooden staff, sandals and straw hat, and fleece-clad hikers equipped with poles, waterproof boots and bandana.

Of course, it is the *yamabushi,* with their unmistakable conch shells, chequered jackets and voluminous white pantaloons, that keep the ancient traditions alive. Whether stomping along precipitous trails or sitting under icy waterfalls, these devoted mountain men undertake severe ascetic exercises to discipline both body and spirit.

👁 Sights & Activities

Tradition dictates that you start at Haguro-san and finish at Yudono-san. You can do the pilgrimage in the opposite direction, though the ascent from Yudono-san to Gas-san would be painfully steep.

★ Haguro-san   SPIRITUAL

(羽黒山) The 2446 stone steps to the top of Haguro-san (419m) have been worn down and smoothed by centuries of pilgrims. The mountain's easy access makes it the most popular of the three peaks, particularly with day trippers.

At the base of the mountain in Haguro village, the **Ideha Bunka Kinenkan** (いでは文化記念館 | Ideha Bunka Kinenkan; ☎ 62-4727; www.tsuruokakanko.com/haguro/kankou/ideha.html; 7-2 Injū-minami, Haguro-machi; admission ¥400; ⏰ 9am-4pm, closed Tue Sep-Jun) has exhibits covering the history of the mountain and *yamabushi* culture, though there is little in English.

The climb, which begins by passing through the torii and over the bridge, takes a leisurely hour. En route you'll go past **Gojū-no-tō** (五重塔), a weather-beaten, five-storey pagoda dating from the 14th century.

An ancient teahouse known as **Ni-no-saka-chaya** (二の坂茶屋; tea sets ¥700; ⏰ 8.30am-5pm Apr-Nov) marks the halfway point. Stop in here for sets of filling *mochi* and revitalising bowls of *matcha*. If you make a detour to the right, you'll come upon the temple ruins of **Betsu-in** (別院), visited by Matsuo Bashō during his pilgrimage here.

Dewa Sanzan-jinja (出羽三山神社; www.dewasanzan.jp; ⏰ dawn-dusk) sprawls over the summit of Haguro-san, intermingling with the cedars. At its heart is the **San-shin Gōsaiden** (三神合祭殿), a vivid red hall that enshrines the deities of all three mountains.

If you're completing the circuit, your only option from here is the bus – most of the old 20km pilgrim trail along the ridgeline to Gas-san became overgrown after a road was built in the 1960s. Catch a bus from the parking lot beyond the shrine bound for **Hachigōme** (八合目; eighth station), where the trail to the top of Gas-san picks up again. Note that the last bus leaves just after 2pm. Alternatively, you can stay the night at the atmospheric Saikan.

Gas-san   SPIRITUAL

(月山) Accessible from July to September, Gas-san (1984m) is the highest of the three sacred mountains. From the trail head at **Hachigōme** (八合目; eighth station), the route passes through an alpine plateau to **Kyūgōme** (九合目; ninth station) in 1¾ hours, and then grinds uphill for another 1¼ hours.

Perched on the summit is the tiny, yet deeply spiritual **Gassan-jinja** (月山神社; admission ¥500; ⊘ 5am-5pm, Jul–mid-Sep). To enter the shrine, you'll first need to undergo a ritual purification: bow your head to receive the priest's benediction, then brush yourself from head to toe with the slip of paper, placing it afterwards in the fountain. Beyond the gate, visitors traditionally make a circuit of the inner shrine. Note that photography is not permitted inside.

From here, the pilgrimage route presses on towards the steep descent to Yudono-san. This takes another three hours or so, and you'll have to carefully descend rusty ladders chained to the cliff sides and pick your way down through a slippery stream bed at the end of the trail.

Yudono-san
SPIRITUAL

(湯殿山) Accessible from May to October, Yudono-san (1504m) is the spiritual culmination of the Dewa Sanzan trek. Coming from Gas-san, it's just a short walk from the stream bed at the end of the descent to **Yudono-san-jinja** (湯殿山神社; admission ¥500; ⊘ 6am-5pm, closed Nov-Apr). This sacred shrine is not a building, but something else... It's taboo to discuss it with the uninitiated, so you'll just have to find out for yourself! Trust us, though, we've never seen anything like it.

Yudono-san-jinja has the strictest rituals of the three. Take off your shoes at the entrance, bow your head before the priest for the purification rites and then follow the other pilgrims inside; no photos are allowed.

To finish the pilgrimage, it's a mere 10-minute hike further down the mountain to the trailhead at **Yudono-san Sanrōsho** (湯殿山参籠所), which is marked by a torii and adjacent to the **Sennin-zawa** (仙人沢) bus stop.

From here, you have a number of options: spend the night at Yudono-san Sanrōsho, catch a direct bus back to Tsuruoka, or take a detour to Dainichibō and Chūren-ji.

🎎 Festivals & Events

The peak of Haguro-san is the site of several major festivals.

Hassaku Matsuri
TRADITIONAL

(八朔祭; ⊘ 31 Aug) *Yamabushi* (mountain priests) perform ancient fire rites throughout the night to pray for a bountiful harvest.

Shōrei-sai
RELIGIOUS

(松例祭; ⊘ 31 Dec) On New Year's Eve, *yamabushi* perform similar rituals to those of the mountain priests at the Hassaku Matsuri, competing with each other after completing 100-day-long austerities.

🥾 Courses

If you haven't yet found your calling, you might consider becoming a *yamabushi*.

Autumn Peak
RELIGIOUS

(秋の峰入 Aki-no-mine; ☑ 62-2355; fax 62-2352) At the end of August, ascetics-in-training undergo a week-long course of austerities at Dewa Sanzan-jinja. It's for men only, but women can join a four-day 'shrine maiden' training course (神子修行; *miko shūgyō*) in early September. Neither are for the faint of heart and some command of Japanese is useful.

Reservations begin on the last day of May; sign up early to reserve a spot. The course fee is ¥40,000 for men, and ¥35,000 for women.

Yamabushi Study Experience
CULTURAL

(山伏修行体験塾 Yamabushi Shūgyō Taiken Jyuku; ☑ 62-4727; kankoshoko@city.tsuruoka. yamagata.jp) For those who are happy being just a *yamabushi* apprentice, the Ideha Bunka Kinenkan (p522) in Haguro village runs a three-day mini-course for both sexes in September that includes fasting, mountain sprints and morning wake-up calls. Phone ahead to enquire about dates and book at least a month in advance. The course fee is ¥29,800.

🛌 Sleeping & Eating

Sleeping options are listed in order from start to finish of the Haguro-san–Yudono-san pilgrimage route; reservations are a must.

★ Saikan
TEMPLE LODGE ¥¥

(斎館; ☑ 62-2357; 7 Tōge, Haguro-machi; r per person with 2 meals ¥7350; Ⓟ) 🅿 Located at the top of Haguro-san, this is the most famous *shukubō* (temple lodging) at Dewa Sanzan. The approach skirts past towering trees and through an imposing gate before arriving at a secluded temple. The grounds overlook a grand sweep of valleys below, while the building itself has been weathered by the ages and is imbued with an air of stoic grandeur.

Meals are *shōjin-ryōri* (vegetarian Buddhist cuisine) with foraged mushrooms and mountain vegetables. Saikan can also prepare *shōjin-ryōri* lunch spreads (from ¥1575); reserve in advance.

Midahara Sanrōsho   HUT ¥¥
(御田原参籠所; ☑ mobile 090-2367-9037; r per person with 2 meals ¥7350; ⊙ closed Oct-Jun) At the eighth station on Gas-san, this mountain hut is a convenient place to break up the long three-mountain hike. Futons are laid out in one big communal room and there's no shower, but the vegetarian meals are filling and the close quarters conducive for swapping stories. Wake up to catch the sunrise and you'll be on your way to the peak before the tour buses arrive.

Hot dishes like *soba* and curry rice can also be ordered here, until around 3pm.

Yudono-san Sanrōsho   LODGE ¥¥
(湯殿山参籠所; ☑ 54-6131; 7 Rokujuri-yama, Tamugimata; r per person with 2 meals from ¥7350; ⊙ closed Nov-Apr; Ⓟ) This airy mountain lodge at the bottom of Yudono-san has a hot bath and is full of jovial pilgrims celebrating the completion of their multiday circuit. Meat and fish are on offer in case you've been missing it, as are plenty of beer and sake.

Lunch sets (from ¥1575), with river fish and mountain vegetables, are served here as well.

ℹ Information

Theoretically, if you hiked at a military pace and timed the buses perfectly, you might be able to cover all three peaks in one day. However, this would leave you no time to enjoy the scenery and the chances of missing a key bus connection are very high. If you want to tackle all three mountains, which is possible from June through September, it's best to devote two days.

Before setting out, it's recommended that you book accommodation and stock up on maps at the Tourist Information Office in Tsuruoka. Note that transport can grind to a halt once the snow starts to pile up.

ℹ Getting There & Around

Directions are given in the same sequence as the trek.

During the summer climbing months, there are up to 10 buses daily (the earliest leaving at 6am) from Tsuruoka to Haguro village (¥800, 35 minutes), most of which then continue to Haguro-sanchō (Haguro summit; ¥1150, 50 minutes). Outside the high season, the schedule is greatly reduced.

From early July to late August, and then on weekends and holidays until late September, there are up to four daily buses from Haguro-sanchō to Gas-san as far as Hachigōme (¥1520, one hour).

Between early June and early November, there are up to four daily buses from the Yudono-san Sanrōsho trailhead at Yudono-san to Tsuruoka (¥1770, 1¼ hours), which also pass by Ōami (¥1100, 35 minutes).

Yamagata   山形

☑ 023 / POP 255,000

Yamagata is a thriving industrial centre with a sizeable student population, making for a more youthful vibe than in comparable *inaka* (rural) cities. While it's a bit short on sights, Yamagata is an excellent base for day trips to Yamadera and Yonezawa, and serves as a transit point for Zaō Onsen and Ginzan Onsen.

◎ Sights & Activities

**Hirashimizu
Pottery District**   ARTS & CRAFTS
(平清水陶器地域) The fiery kilns lining the Hazukashi-kawa (Embarrassed River) turn out beautiful blueish-grey mottled pieces known as *nashi-seiji* (pear skin). In the 19th century there were dozens of workshops here, but now only a few remain. **Shichiemon-gama** (七右エ門窯; 153 Hirashimizu; ⊙ 8.30am-5.30pm, pottery making 9am-3pm) is the largest of them and offers you the best chance to see master potters at work.

You can also try your hand at making your own pottery here. Lessons (which are in Japanese) are 90 minutes and priced according to the amount of clay you use (¥2000 per kilogram; shipping fee extra). No reservations are necessary and kids are welcome, too. Note that finished pieces ship to an address in Japan one month later. You can also pick up professional pieces in the studio's shop.

Buses bound for Nishi-Zaō or Geikō-dai run hourly or half-hourly from stop 5 outside Yamagata Station to the Hirashimizu stop (¥280, 15 minutes).

🎏 Festivals & Events

Hanagasa Matsuri   TRADITIONAL
(花笠まつり; www.hanagasa.jp/en; ⊙ early Aug) Large crowds of dancers wear *hanagasa* (flower-laden straw hats) and sing folk songs.

THE LIVING BUDDHAS OF YAMAGATA

It is believed that there are some 20 *sokushinbutsu* (living Buddhas) in Japan, and that half of them are in Yamagata Prefecture. Becoming a *sokushinbutsu* takes years – even decades – of ascetic determination. It involves extreme fasting, literally lacquering one's insides by drinking *urushi* (the sap of the lacquer tree) and eventually being buried alive to meditate until death. After 1000 days the body – now mummified – is disinterred and enshrined. The practice was outlawed during the 19th century, but folk beliefs still attribute great spiritual power to these 'living Buddhas'.

There are two *sokushinbutsu* near Dewa Sanzan, at the temples of **Dainichibō** (大日坊; www.dainichibou.or.jp; 11 Nyūdō, Ōami; admission ¥500; ☺8am-5pm) and **Chūren-ji** (注連寺; www2.plala.or.jp/sansuirijuku/index.html; 92-1 Nakadai, Ōami; admission ¥500; ☺8am-5pm). Both can be viewed by the public, though seeing the one at Dainichibō involves first kneeling for a purification ritual. The Danichibō *sokushinbutsu* is the older of the two by nearly half a century, having entered the earth at age 96 in 1783. Taking photographs is not permitted.

Both temples are in the village of Ōami, off Rte 112 halfway between Yudono-san and Tsuruoka. To get to Dainichibō, walk uphill from the bus stop to the village, turning left at the post office and then left again onto the main road; look for the sign with the red arrow and the temple up the hill on the left. For Chūren-ji, head north from the bus stop and follow the curving road for about 20 minutes, keeping an eye out for the blue-and-white signs on the telephone poles. Buses are spaced about two hours apart, which allows time to look around and still make your connection back to Tsuruoka.

Yamagata International Documentary Film Festival
FILM

(www.yidff.jp; ☺Oct) This biennial event takes place over one week in October and screens films from all over the world, along with retrospectives, symposiums and a Japanese panorama.

🛏 Sleeping & Eating

Guesthouse Mintaro Hut
GUESTHOUSE ¥

(ゲストハウスミンタロハット; 📱mobile 090-2797-1687; www.mintarohut.com; 5-13 Ōtemachi; s/d ¥3500/6000; 🅿@🛜) English-speaking Sato-san turned his childhood home into this comfortable guesthouse just off the northeast corner of the central park. The common area is built around a radiant stove, which ensures a warm and familial atmosphere conducive to chatting with fellow travellers, and the kitchen is stocked with supplies for self-caterers.

Tōyoko Inn Yamagata Eki Nishiguchi
BUSINESS HOTEL ¥¥

(東横イン山形駅西口; 📱644-1045; www.toyoko-inn.com/hotel/00097; 1-18-13 Jōnan-machi; s/d ¥5480/7770; ➖@🛜) Business hotels cluster around JR Yamagata Station, but this one is the best value for money: clean, efficient rooms, with complimentary breakfast, just minutes on foot from the station's west exit.

Kitanosuisan
IZAKAYA ¥¥

(北野水産; 📱624-0880; www.kitanosuisan.com; 2nd fl, 1-8-8 Kasumicho; table charge ¥500, dishes ¥300-1500; ☺5pm-midnight) Come here to sample local Yamagata specialities (on the wooden board, with pictures) and sake. Take the first left outside the station's east exit and look for the blue sign across the 2nd floor.

ⓘ Information

Tourist Information Center (山形市観光案内センター; 📱647-2266; ☺9am-5.30pm) On the 2nd floor of Yamagata Station, in a small glass booth.

ⓘ Getting There & Away

BUS

Buses leave for Zaō Onsen approximately once an hour from stop 1 outside Yamagata Station (¥980, 40 minutes). JR highway buses make an overnight trip between Yamagata and Tokyo (one-way/return ¥6300/11,500, 6½ hours each way).

TRAIN

There are hourly trains on the Yamagata *shinkansen* between Tokyo and Yamagata (¥11,030, 2¾ hours).

There are also hourly *kaisoku* on the JR Senzan line between Yamagata and Yamadera (¥230, 20 minutes).

WORTH A TRIP

YONEZAWA 米沢

Carnivores should head here to chow down on Yonezawa beef, famous for its tenderness and flavour, and arguably rivalling Kobe's own. There are dozens (perhaps hundreds) of places in town to try yonezawa-gyū. Of these, the 100-year-old **Tokiwa** (登起波; ☑24-5400; www.yonezawabeef.co.jp/info/eng.html; 7-2-3 Chūō; meals from ¥4200; ⊙11am-9pm, closed Tue) is the most famous. Ask the staff at the Tourist Information Centre in Yonezawa Station to mark the location on a map – it's a bit out of the way.

Yonezawa is also home to the ruined 17th-century castle of the Uesugi clan. The foundations of the castle now form the boundaries of Matsugasaki-kōen (松ヶ崎公園), an attractive park framed by a placid moat. Inside, there's a shrine and a treasury, the **Keishō-den** (稽照殿; 1-4-13 Marunouchi; admission ¥400; ⊙9am-4pm Apr-Nov), which displays armour and works of art belonging to several generations of the Uesugi family.

To really see the feudal era in action, visit on 3 May, when more than a thousand participants in full samurai regalia act out the epic battle of Kawa-naka-jima during the annual **Uesugi Matsuri** (上杉祭り; http://uesugi.yonezawa.info).

Yonezawa is a stop on the Yamagata shinkansen (bullet train); alternatively, regular futsū (local) trains run on the JR Ōu main line between Yonezawa and Yamagata (¥820, 45 minutes).

Yamadera　　　　山寺

☑ 023 / POP 1500

'Stillness, seeps into the stones, the cry of cicadas.'

　　Matsuo Bashō, *The Narrow Road to the Deep North* (1689)

A favourite destination of the itinerant haiku master, Yamadera is an atmospheric cluster of temples perched precariously on lush and wooded slopes. The town was founded in AD 860 by priests who carried with them the sacred flame from Enryaku-ji near Kyoto, and supposedly the same flame is still alight today. It is believed that Yamadera's rock faces are the boundaries between this world and the next.

Sights

The sights are fairly well signposted from the train station. Souvenir and noodle shops line the main street.

★ Risshaku-ji
BUDDHIST

(立石寺; admission ¥300; ⊙8am-5pm) The 'Temple of Standing Stones', more commonly known as Yamadera, rests atop a rock-hewn staircase weathered over the centuries by unrelenting elements. At the foot of the mountain, guarded by a small lantern, is the sacred flame **Konpon-chūdō** (根本中堂; admission ¥200) said to have been transported from Kyoto many centuries ago.

The **San-mon** (山門) gate marks the start of the climb, some 1000 steps that take you past carvings so mossy and worn they appear to be part of the landscape. It's a steep ascent – a sort of walking meditation – but one that makes the views from the top, of the surrounding mountains and bucolic countryside below, that much more spectacular. During the summer months, the electric whir of the cicadas is almost overpowering.

Past the **Nio-mon** (仁王門), through which only those with pure souls may enter (be honest now!), the path splits, heading in one direction to the **Oku-no-in** (奥の院; Inner Sanctuary) and in the other to the **Godaidō** (五大堂). The latter, an 18th-century pavilion perched on the cliffside, has the most arresting views.

For a better shot at a measure of the meditative bliss that so inspired Bashō, visit early in the morning or late in the afternoon. It's possible to visit Yamadera during the winter, although if you arrive just after a snowfall the paths may not yet be shovelled.

Bashō Kinenkan
MUSEUM

(山寺芭蕉記念館; 4223 Yamadera; admission ¥400; ⊙9am-4.30pm, closed Mon Dec-Feb) In the village near the train station, this biographical museum exhibits scrolls and calligraphy related to poet Bashō's famous northern journey.

Getting There & Away

There are hourly kaisoku on the JR Senzan line between Yamadera and Yamagata (¥230, 20 minutes) and, in the other direction, to Sendai (¥820, one hour).

Zaō Onsen 蔵王温泉

♪ 023 / POP 14,000

Zaō Onsen is a small hot-springs town with some big skiing. Even bigger are its *juhyō* (ice monsters), conifers that have been frozen solid by harsh Siberian winds. Skiing or snowboarding through fields of lurking ice monsters is a surreal experience unique to Zaō. During the rest of the year, Zaō attracts visitors with great hiking and the chance to soak in any number of tubs filled with milky, sulphurous water.

⊙ Sights & Activities

★ Zaō Onsen Ski Resort   SNOW SPORTS
(蔵王温泉スキー場; www.zao-spa.or.jp; 1-day lift tickets ¥4800; ⊙ Dec-Apr) Zaō is arguably home to the best slopes in Northern Honshū. In comparison to heavyweight Hokkaidō, you shouldn't come here expecting spine-tingling chutes, but rather a huge breadth of beginner and intermediate runs. In fact, it's possible to ski all the way from the highest point of the mountain right down to the base without ever turning down a black diamond or getting stuck in a field of moguls.

But don't come expecting boring bunny slopes. On the contrary, Zaō is distinguished by its broad and winding courses, some of which are nearly 10km long! With 40 ropeways and ski lifts spanning 14 spidery courses with multiple offshoots, it's almost impossible to swish down the same route twice. Of course, you might want to have a second go at the Juhyō Kōgen (樹氷高原; Ice Monster Plateau), which reaches its peak ferocity in frigid February. At this time, blizzards are particularly severe, so dress appropriately.

English signage is excellent, and full equipment rental is available at various locations throughout the village. Zaō Onsen also has a full complement of bars, cafes, restaurants and onsen, making for a truly memorable *après-ski*. There is nothing quite like the sensation of stripping off your ski-wear, sliding into an onsen bath and uncorking a bottle of microbrewed sake.

Zaō Sanroku Ropeway   ROPEWAY
(蔵王山麓ロプウェー; one-way/return ¥1400/2500; ⊙ 8.30am-5pm Apr-Nov) This succession of cable cars whisks you over the conifers and up **Zaō-san** (蔵王山) to within spitting distance of **Okama** (御釜), a crater lake of piercing cobalt blue. The walk to the lake passes Buddhist statues and monuments hidden among the greenery, before the terrain breaks up into a sunset-coloured crumble of volcanic rock. You can extend the hike (and save money) by taking one of the other two shorter ropeways, the Zaō Chūō Ropeway or the Zaō Sky Cable, up or down.

WORTH A TRIP

GINZAN ONSEN

With its century-old inns forming mirror images on either side of the peaceful Obanazawa, **Ginzan Onsen** (銀山温泉) looks curiously like a movie set. It was – Japanese know it as the setting for *Oshin*, an enormously popular historical drama from the 1980s – but it wasn't designed to be. It's just a fortunate collection of ryokan in the classic Taisho-era style, which adds romantic Western flourishes like turrets and stained glass to traditional wooden structures. It's most popular in the winter, when snow adds a dreamy touch to the wooden eaves and surrounding mountains. Several ryokan open up their baths to day trippers; pick up a list outside the tourist information centre.

Of course, Ginzan is most romantic in the evening. Should you decide to stay the night, **Notoya Ryokan** (能登屋旅館; ♪ 0237-28-2327; www.notoyaryokan.com; 446 Ginzan Shin-Hata, Obanazawa; r per person with 2 meals from ¥18,000; P), one of the grandest in Ginzan, is a fine choice. The three-storey structure, complete with balconies, elaborate woodwork and a curious garret tower, dates from 1922, although piecemeal renovations have been completed inside. Make sure you get a room in the main building overlooking the river.

Ginzan Onsen is in easy striking distance of Yamagata. Take the Yamagata *shinkansen* (bullet train) to its terminus in Oishida (¥1890, 30 minutes), then transfer to one of up to five daily buses leaving for Ginzan Onsen (¥690, 40 minutes) from the west exit bus pool.

Zaō Onsen Dai-rotemburo　ONSEN

(蔵王温泉大露天風呂; admission ¥450; ⊙ 6am-7pm May-Oct) Follow the wooden steps down the mountainside to this huge open-air hot-spring pool. The sulphur-stained rocks set the stage for the spectacle that is dozens of complete strangers bathing naked together in joyful unison.

Shinzaemon-no-Yu　ONSEN

(新左衛門の湯; ☎ 693-1212; www.zaospa.co.jp; 905 Kawa-mae; ¥700; ⊙ 10am-6.30pm Mon-Fri, to 9pm Sat & Sun, closed irregularly) An upmarket bathing option, this modern hot-spring complex has several pools. The nicest are outside, set in stone and with wooden canopies.

🛏 Sleeping & Eating

Accommodation abounds, but reservations are essential if you're visiting during the ski season or on weekends in summer.

Lodge Chitoseya　LODGE ¥

(ロッジちとせや; ☎ 694-9145; www.lodge-chitoseya.com; r per person/with 2 meals from ¥3675/6090; P 🛜) Thanks to its budget-friendly prices and delicious home-style meals, Chitoseya attracts a youthful crowd of skiers and hikers. The tatami rooms are fresh looking and unfussy; facilities are shared. The lodge is between the bus station and Chūo Ropeway.

Pension Boku-no-Uchi　PENSION ¥¥

(ペンションぼくのうち; ☎ 694-9542; www.bokunouchi.com; 904 Zaō Onsen; r per person with 2 meals from ¥3500/7200; P 🛜) This is a skiers' lodge through and through, from the posters on the dining-room wall to the location right in front of the Chūo Ropeway. The owner is a former member of Japan's national ski team and speaks English and French. Rooms are Japanese-style with communal facilities, including a 24-hour sulphur bath.

Yoshida-ya　RYOKAN ¥¥

(吉田屋; 13 Zaō Onsen; r per person from ¥4650, breakfast/dinner ¥800/2000; P 🛜) Yoshida-ya has a following among foreign travellers, no doubt because the friendly, helpful proprietress speaks flawless English. It's a modern building, five minutes from the Zaō Sky Cable, with basic tatami rooms, communal facilities and an onsen bath.

Takamiya　RYOKAN ¥¥¥

(高見屋; ☎ 694-9333; www.zao.co.jp/takamiya; 54 Zaō Onsen; r per person with 2 meals from ¥16,950; P 🛜) Among the upmarket ryokan in town, Takamiya is our pick for its emphasis on the classics. After all, it's been in business for nearly three centuries! There are several beautiful baths here, both indoor and outdoor, made of stone or aromatic cedar. Meals are traditional *kaiseki ryōri* (formal banquets served in multiple courses), with top-grade local beef as the headliner. The spacious rooms have tatami sitting areas and fluffy *wa-beddo* (thick futons on platforms).

Oto-chaya　ECLECTIC ¥

(音茶屋; http://otochaya.com; 935-24 Zaō Onsen; meals from ¥850; ⊙ 11am-9pm Thu-Tue; 🛜) Oto-chaya is all things for all people (at almost all hours): hearty stews and casseroles, elaborate Chinese tea sets and a stocked bar. It's also a popular hangout with a mellow vibe. Look for the wooden sign with the teapot, on the main road beyond the Chūo Ropeway.

ℹ Information

Tourist Information Center (☎ 694-9328; www.zao-spa.or.jp; 708-1 Zaō Onsen; ⊙ 9am-6pm) Next to the bus terminal; it has English maps available.

ℹ Getting There & Away

Buses run hourly between the bus terminal in Zaō Onsen and JR Yamagata Station (¥980, 40 minutes).

At the height of the ski season, private companies run overnight shuttles between Tokyo and Zaō. Prices can be as low as ¥7000 return. Enquire at travel agencies in Tokyo for more information.

NIIGATA PREFECTURE

Niigata-ken (新潟県) isn't just the setting for Kawabata Yasunari's acclaimed novel *Snow Country,* it *is* snow country. The prefecture receives some of the country's highest snowfalls, burying villages and bewitching powder fiends. Top ski destinations include Myōkō Kōgen, Naeba and Echigo-Yuzawa Onsen; at the latter, sultry baths sweeten the deal. For those who prefer to get away from it all, there's the persimmon-peppered island of Sado-ga-shima. While the prefecture technically isn't part of Tōhoku proper, its capital city, Niigata, serves as the gateway to lands further north.

Niigata 新潟

🎵 025 / POP 811,600

The prefectural capital of Niigata serves as a transit hub and a springboard to nearby Sado-ga-shima. Japan's longest river, the Shinano-gawa, runs through the centre of the city; if you have time to spare, join the locals for a stroll along the riverbank.

🛏 Sleeping & Eating

Dormy Inn Niigata HOTEL ¥¥
(ドーミーイン新潟; 🎵 247-7755; www.hotespa. net/hotels/niigata; 1-7-14 Akashi, Chūō-ku; s/d from ¥5500/7500; 😔@) While the Dormy Inn skimps on interior design – no carpet in the hallways here – it splurges on its baths, which include a sauna and *rotemburo*. The rooms, small but well-maintained, fall somewhere in between.

Ueda Ryokan RYOKAN ¥¥
(植田旅館; 🎵 225-1111; www.uedaryokan.com; 2120 Yon-no-chō, Ishizuechō-dōri, Chūō-ku; r per person/with 2 meals from ¥3780/7350; @) This pleasant Japanese-style inn occupies a quiet spot just beyond the river.

Pia Bandai MARKET ¥¥
(ピアBandai; 2-10 Bandai-shima, Chūō-ku; meals from ¥1000; 🕘9am-9pm) Conveniently located

Niigata Prefecture

on the way to the Sado Kisen Ferry Terminal, this outdoor complex includes markets and eateries – so you can gawk at the bounty of Niigata's coast and sample it, too. Our pick: **Benkei** (弁慶), an upmarket *kaiten-sushi* (conveyor-belt sushi) restaurant that specialises in fish from the seas around Sado-ga-shima.

ⓘ Information

Niigata Central Post Office (新潟中央郵便局; 2-6-26 Higashi Ōdori , Chūō-ku; ☺post 9am-7pm Mon-Fri, to 5pm Sat, to 12.30pm Sun; ATM 7am-11pm Mon-Fri, 9am-7pm Sat, Sun & holidays)

Niigata University Medical & Dental Hospital (新潟大学医歯学総合病院; ☏227-2460, after-hours 227-2479; www.nuh.niigata-u.ac.jp/index_e.html; 1-757 Asahimachi-dōri, Ichiban-chō, Chūō-ku; ☺outpatient service 8.30-11.30am Mon-Fri)

Tourist Information Center (新潟駅万代口観光案内センター; ☏241-7914; ☺9am-6pm) English maps and information about Sado-ga-shima are available, to the left of Niigata Station's Bandai exit.

ⓘ Getting There & Away

AIR

From Niigata Airport, 13km north of the city centre, there are flights to/from Tokyo, Osaka, Nagoya, Hiroshima, Sapporo and many other destinations.

Buses to the airport run from stop 5 outside Niigata Station's south exit roughly every half-hour from 6.30am to 6.40pm (¥400, 25 minutes); a taxi should cost about ¥2500.

BOAT

From the port of Niigata-kō, **Shin-Nihonkai** (新日本海; ☏273-2171; www.snf.jp) ferries depart at 10.30am daily, except Monday, for Otaru on Hokkaidō (from ¥6300, 18 hours). To get to Niigata-kō, take any bus bound for Rinko-nichōme from stop 6 at the Bandai exit bus pool in front of Niigata Station and get off at Suehiro-bashi (¥200, 25 minutes). A taxi should cost about ¥1500.

Sado Kisen (佐渡汽船; ☏245-1234; www.sadokisen.co.jp) runs frequent ferries and hydrofoils to Ryōtsu on Sado-ga-shima. Buses to the ferry terminal (¥200, 15 minutes) leave from stop 5 at the Bandai exit bus pool 45 minutes before sailing. A taxi should cost about ¥1000; alternatively, you can walk there in about 40 minutes.

BUS

Highway buses depart from the **Bandai Bus Center** (万代シティバスセンター), a big yellow building 1km northwest of the train station, and connect Niigata to major cities throughout Honshū.

CAR & MOTORCYCLE

If you're driving, the **Kan-Etsu Expressway** (関越自動車道) runs between Tokyo and the greater Niigata area. The **Nihonkai-Tōhoku Expressway** (日本海東北自動車道) connects Niigata with Akita.

TRAIN

Shinkansen on the Jōetsu line run approximately twice an hour between Niigata and Tokyo (¥10,270, 2¼ hours), via Echigo-Yuzawa Onsen (¥5240, 50 minutes).

There are a few *tokkyū* each day on the JR Uetsu line between Niigata and Tsuruoka (¥4330, two hours), and between Niigata and Akita (¥7020, 3¾ hours).

To access the port of Naoetsu-kō, where you can grab a ferry or hydrofoil to the town of Ogi on Sado-ga-Shima, there are a few *tokkyū* each day on the JR Shinetsu line between Niigata and Naoetsu (¥2720, 1¾ hours). There are also a few buses leaving daily from the Bandai exit bus pool at Niigata Station for Naoetsu (¥1950, 2½ hours). From Naoetsu Station, it's a 10-minute bus ride (¥200) or about ¥1000 for a taxi to the port.

Sado-ga-shima 佐渡島

☏0259 / POP 62,000

Despite being Japan's sixth-largest island, Sado-ga-shima is relatively undeveloped and is characterised by rugged natural beauty and eccentric reminders of its rich and evocative past. There are more persimmon trees than people here, and the island's sandy coves are fronted by campgrounds instead of concrete. Crowds peak during the third week in August for the Earth Celebration, headlined by the world-famous Kodo Drummers. Outside of the summer holiday season, it's blissfully quiet.

History

Sado has always been something of a far-flung destination, just not always a voluntary one. During the feudal era, the island was a notorious penal colony where out-of-favour intellectuals were forever banished. The illustrious list of former prisoners includes Emperor Juntoku, nō master Ze-Ami and Nichiren, the founder of one of Japan's most influential Buddhist sects. When gold was discovered near the village of Aikawa in 1601, there was a sudden influx of miners, who were often vagrants press-ganged from the mainland and made to work like slaves.

Sado-ga-shima

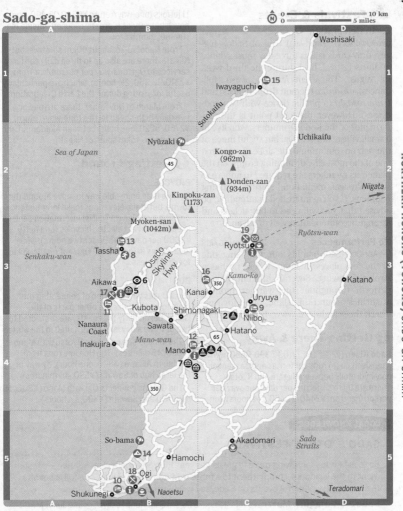

Sado-ga-shima

✨ Festivals & Events

Earth Celebration
FESTIVAL

(www.kodo.or.jp; ⊙mid-Aug) One of Sado's biggest drawcards is this three-day music, dance and arts festival, held during the third week in August. The event features *okesa* (folk dances), *onidaiko* (demon drum dances) and *tsuburosashi* (a phallic dance with two goddesses). However, the focal point is the performance of the Kodo Drummers, who live in a small village north of Ogi but spend much of the year on tour around the globe. Considered one of the most elite drumming groups on the planet, its members are required to adhere to strict physical, mental and spiritual training regimens. If you're interested in attending, be advised that you will need to buy tickets and arrange accommodation well in advance.

Nō Performances
PERFORMING ARTS

(⊙Apr-Oct) Sado stands out for being one of the few places in Japan where nō has a strong following. Several different groups perform throughout the warmer months at shrines around the island, often for free. Check the schedule at www.visitsado.com.

ℹ Getting There & Away

Sado Kisen (佐渡汽船; ☎03-5390-0550; www.sadokisen.co.jp) runs car ferries and passenger-only hydrofoils between Niigata and Ryōtsu. There are up to six ferries per day (one-way per person/car from ¥2440/11,460, 2½ hours) and 11 jetfoils (one-way/return ¥6340/11,490, one hour), but service is greatly reduced outside the summer months.

From Naoetsu-kō, about 90km southwest of Niigata, there are also up to three daily car-ferry services to Ogi (one-way per person/car from ¥2310/12,360, 2½ hours), which are particularly useful for visiting during the Earth Celebration.

From March to November, there are one or two daily high-speed ferries (one-way/return, ¥2760/5020, one hour) between Akadomari and Teradomari, 45km south of Niigata.

ℹ Getting Around

BICYCLE

Cycling is an enjoyable way to move around the towns, but steep elevations make long-distance cruising a challenge. Tourist information centres in each town rent electric bicycles for a hefty ¥2000 per day (or ¥500 for two hours), while local shops in Ryōtsu and Ogi rent regular bikes for slightly less.

BUS

Local buses do a good job of connecting the main towns. Services to other parts of the island, particularly the coasts, are restricted to two or three a day, and often halted in the winter.

The Minami line connects Ryōtsu with Mano (¥650, 45 minutes). The Hon line runs from Ryōtsu to Aikawa (¥800, one hour), by way of the large hub of Sawata (¥590, 40 minutes).

The Ogi line connects Ogi with Mano (¥800, 55 minutes) and Sawata (¥800, 1¼ hours).

LOCAL KNOWLEDGE

SADO'S 'OTHER' FESTIVALS

Sado is famous for having more festivals per year than anywhere else in Japan – a testament to the islanders' commitment to a more traditional way of life. For a full list of all the weird and wonderful events on Sado, see www.visitsado.com.

Sado Hon-maguro Matsuri (佐渡本まぐろ祭り | Sado Tuna Festival; ⊙late June) Midsummer is the high season for catching tuna in the Sea of Japan. Fresh fish is on the menu all over the island, and tuna-cutting exhibitions take place in Ryōtsu.

Wataru from Ryōtsu

Asari-sagashi Dai-kai (アサリさがし大会 | Clam Search Convention; ⊙mid-July) My kids love this one! They get to splash around in the ocean while searching for clams. We bring them home, and cook them in a big pot with miso, *dashi* (fish stock) and leeks.

Eriko from Sawata

Sazae Matsuri (さざえ祭り | Turban Shell Festival; ⊙late July) Have you ever eaten a turban shell? We look for them at night while holding flaming torches. Their insides are delicious when grilled with soy and sake, and you can keep the shell as a unique souvenir.

Akira from Ogi

Chinowa Matsuri (茅の輪まつり | Straw Circle Festival; ⊙30 June) We celebrate summer by passing through a straw circle and casting off six months of uncleanliness. Then we eat delicate dumplings made with steamed iris petals.

Akiko from Ogi

DON'T MISS

NIIGATA SAKE

Niigata Prefecture is one of Japan's top sake-producing regions, known in particular for a crisp, dry style called *tanrei karakuchi*. The long, cold winters produce plenty of fresh mountain snow melt for the valleys below, which translates into delicious rice and then delicious sake. Tipplers should be sure to treat themselves while passing through.

In March, a mammoth bacchanal in Niigata city, called **Sake-no-jin** (酒の陣; www.niigata-sake.or.jp/index.html), highlights more than 90 varieties of sake from around the prefecture.

Another convenient, and unlikely, place to get a sampling of the local brew is the Echigo-Yuzawa *shinkansen* (bullet train) station, where a tasting bar on the 2nd floor lets you sample five different kinds (from a selection of nearly a hundred) for ¥500. *Kampai!*

Along the northern coast, a few buses run on the Kaifu line each day between Aikawa and Iwayaguchi (¥800, one hour). The Uchikaifu line connects Iwayaguchi and Ryōtsu (¥800, 1½ hours).

There's an English-language timetable available at the Tourist Information Centre. The unlimited-ride bus pass (two weekdays/weekend ¥2500/2000) is good value if you plan to cover a lot of ground.

CAR & MOTORCYCLE

A car is the best way to access the island's most scenic parts, and a good number of the best accommodation options are located far from bus stops.

Ferries from Honshū can accommodate cars for a substantial fee, though it's usually cheaper to pick up a rental in Ryōtsu or Ogi. Expect to pay ¥6000 to ¥10,000 per day, depending on size and availability.

The tourist information offices at either port can help arrange rentals. Note that gas stations are few and far between outside the main towns.

Ryōtsu & Around 両津

Sado's main hub, Ryōtsu is a low-key port town. The main street is lined with amenities for travellers, but there is little in the way of sights. Head inland, however, and the townscape gives way to rice fields sprinkled with wooden farmhouses and ancient temples. With buses running from Ryōtsu to most other areas on the island, this is a convenient place to base yourself.

⊙ Sights

Konpon-ji　　　　　　　BUDDHIST TEMPLE
(根本寺; 1837 Niibo Ōno; admission ¥300; ⊙ 8am-5pm; **P**) This rustic wooden temple, with its thatched roof and pleasant gardens, is where the Buddhist monk Nichiren was first brought when exiled to Sado in 1271. Any bus on the Minami line from Ryōtsu can drop you off at the Konpon-ji-mae bus stop.

🛏 Sleeping & Eating

★ Green Village　　　　　HOSTEL **¥**
(グリーンヴィレッジ; 📞22-2719; www.e-sadonet.tv/~gvyh/eng/index.html; 750-4 Niibo Uryuya; dm/s ¥3600/4200, breakfast/dinner ¥700/1500; **P** ⊝ @ 🛜) One of our favourite lodgings is this adorable little Western-style cottage plopped down in the middle of Sado. The wonderfully accommodating hosts, who speak basic English, can help you arrange all manner of activities and will stuff you full of home-baked apple pie before sending you on your way. Accommodation is in six-person dormitories or a handful of private rooms with shared facilities. From Ryōtsu, regular buses on the Minami line can drop you off at Niibo Yubinkyoku-mae, a hundred yards past the turn-off for the hostel.

Tōkaen　　　　　　　　MINSHUKU **¥¥**
(桃華園; 📞63-2221; www.on.rim.or.jp/~toukaen; 1636-1 Kanai-Shinbo; r per person/with 2 meals from ¥4200/8400; **P** 🛜) 🍽 This rambling *minshuku* has an attractive but isolated location in the middle of the central plains. It's a great escape, especially considering that the owners are avid outdoors folk who know every trail on the island and will heat up their *shiogama-buro* (salt sauna) for you if you give them a week's notice. Any bus travelling on the Hon line from Ryōtsu can drop you off at Undōkōen-mae, from where it's another 3km north on foot. If you tell the driver you're going to Tōkaen, they will drop you off a bit closer.

Uohide　　　　　　　　SUSHI **¥¥**
(魚秀; 136 Ryōtsu-ebisu; meals ¥1000-2200; ⊙11am-2pm & 4-7pm) Get a taste of Sado's seas at this counter shop, directly across from the ferry terminal. The *jizakana* (local fish) set is a sampling of the day's catch. Look for the red lobster logo on the front of the building.

ℹ️ Information

Tourist Information Center (📞27-5000; www.visitsado.com/en; 2nd fl, Sado Kisen Ferry Terminal; ⏰8.30am-6pm) There's an excellent selection of English maps and pamphlets here, including walking and cycling guides for all of the island's main areas. The helpful English-speaking staff can help you arrange car rental.

Ryōtsu Post Office (両津郵便局; 2-1 Ryōtsu-ebisu; ⏰post 9am-5pm Mon-Fri; ATM 8.45am-7pm Mon-Fri, 9am-5pm Sat & Sun) One block behind the main road running in front of the port, with an international ATM. Another branch inside the ferry terminal has shorter opening hours.

Mano & Around 真野

Although Mano was the provincial capital and cultural centre of the island from early times until the 14th century, it has since been dwarfed by the heavily populated administrative capital to the north, Sawata. Good for Mano, which gets to keep its village feel and its main street lined with wooden buildings and weeping willows.

◎ Sights

A peaceful 7km nature trail east of town winds through paddy fields and past Mano's top attractions. The entrance is near the Danpū-jō bus stop, along the Minami bus route between Ryōtsu and Sawata. From the trailhead, it's a short walk to **Myōsen-ji** (妙宣寺; ⏰dawn-dusk) **FREE**, which was founded by one of the Buddhist monk Nichiren's disciples and features a distinctive five-storey pagoda.

From Myōsen-ji, it's a 10-minute walk through farmland and up old wooden steps set into the hillside to **Kokubun-ji** (国分寺; 113 Kokubun-ji; ⏰dawn-dusk) **FREE**, Sado-ga-shima's oldest temple, dating from AD 741. Another 3km takes you past marvellous lookout points to **Mano Go-ryō** (真野御陵), the tomb of Emperor Juntoku. From there, it's a short walk down to **Sado Rekishi Densetsukan** (佐渡歴史伝説館; 655 Mano; admission ¥700; ⏰8am-5.30pm; 🅿️), the island's museum, where tireless animatrons act out scenes from Sado's dramatic past.

🛏️ Sleeping

Itōya Ryokan RYOKAN ¥¥
(伊藤屋; 📞55-2019; www.itouyaryokan.com; 278 Mano Shin-machi; r per person/with 2 meals ¥5250/8400; 🅿️🛜) At the heart of Mano village is the peaceful Itōya Ryokan, just 50m southwest of the Shin-machi traffic signal. This historic house is full of handicrafts from across the island, and evening dishes feature fish and shellfish from the deep sea. Rooms are spotless, the sheets are crisp and there's an inviting *hinoki* bath that's perfect for cool evenings.

ℹ️ Information

Tourist Information Center (📞55-3589; ⏰8.30am-5.30pm, closed Wed & Sun May-Oct, closed Sat & Sun Nov-April) Has information about hikes and temples in the vicinity, as well as rental bicycles. Located in front of the Mano Shin-machi bus stop.

Ogi 小木

Although the area is home to the famed Kodo Drummers, Ogi is little more than a minor port that sees much less ferry traffic than Ryōtsu. During the Earth Celebration, Ogi does become something of a heaving metropolis, but for the rest of the year it's a drowsy village.

◎ Sights & Activities

For Japanese visitors, Ogi is famous for its *taraibune*, round boats made from huge barrels designed for collecting shellfish in the many coastal inlets. Today, they're mainly used by women in traditional fisher-folk costumes to give **rides** (¥450, 10 minutes, 8.30am-4.30pm) to tourists. Tickets are available at the marine terminal, to the west of the ferry pier.

If you want to cover a bit more ground, you can take a **sightseeing boat** (¥1400, 45 minutes, 8.30am-4.30pm, April to November) on a circle tour that runs from the marine terminal to the Sawa-zaki lighthouse and back.

For travellers with their own wheels (two or four will do), the coast west of Ogi is riddled with caves and coves ripe for exploring. You could also visit the small village of **Shukunegi** (宿根木), which is just 5km from Ogi. A medieval port town that peaked in the early 19th century, Shukunegi retains its historic atmosphere, with weathered wooden merchant houses, narrow alleyways and stone staircases snaking up and down the hillside.

On the other side of the point, the rocky coast gives way to sandy beaches, like **Sobama** (素浜), along Mano-wan.

🛏 Sleeping & Eating

So-bama Campground CAMPGROUND ¥
(素浜キャンプ場; ☑ 86-2363; per person/tent from ¥300/600; ☺ May-Oct; 🅿) Right across the road from a tempting stretch of sand and only 6km from Ogi, this campground is an attractive option for festival-goers. During the Earth Celebration, shuttle buses run several times a day between the campground and Ogi.

★ Hana-no-ki RYOKAN ¥¥
(花の木; ☑ 86-2331; www.sado-hananoki.com; 78-1 Shukunegi; r per person/with 2 meals from ¥5500/9450; 🅿😊🛜) To create this enchanting ryokan, the owners painstakingly took apart and reassembled a 150-year-old farmhouse, setting it down among rice paddies along the road to Shukunegi. Accommodation is in Japanese-stye rooms in the main building or detached cottages in the garden. Call ahead for pick-up from Ogi.

★ Uohara SEAFOOD ¥¥
(魚晴; 415-1 Ogi-machi; meals from ¥1050; ☺ 11am-5pm, closed irregularly) When a restaurant is attached to a fishmonger, it's always a good sign. Order at the shop counter from the picture menu, then settle onto a floor cushion upstairs while your lunch is prepared from the morning's catch. The speciality here is *awabi* (abalone), grilled as a steak (at market rate) or, more affordably, barbecued with a sweet soy-sauce marinade and served over rice. Follow the shop-lined road snaking up the hill behind the tourist information centre for about five minutes, until you see a white building with red and blue writing on the side.

ℹ Information

Tourist Information Center (☑ 86-3200; 1935-26 Ogi-machi; ☺ 8.30am-5.30pm) English maps and bicycle rentals, a few minutes' walk west of the bus and ferry terminals.

Aikawa 相川

From a tiny hamlet, Aikawa grew almost overnight into a 50,000-person boom town when gold was discovered nearby in 1601. Mining amid some incredibly rough and rugged conditions continued throughout the Edo period, a sufficient length of time to associate Sado with hardship and suffering. Today, the town is dwindling with each passing generation, but the scars of its mining past remain up in the hills.

👁 Sights

From Aikawa bus terminal, it's a 40-minute walk (or a much shorter drive) up a steep mountain to **Sado Kinzan** (佐渡金山; ☑ 74-2389; www.sado-kinzan.com/en; 1305 Shimo-Aikawa; admission 1/2 courses ¥800/1200; ☺ 8am-5pm Apr-Oct, 8.30am-4.30pm Nov-Mar; 🅿). This is the infamous 'Golden Mountain' which, in the 17th century, was one of the most bountiful gold mines in the world. Mining only officially stopped here in 1989. The main tourist route descends into the chilly depths of the mine, where you'll encounter robots that dramatise the perilous existence of former miners. A second route takes you through century-old hauling tunnels and leads a further 300m up the mountain to the original opencast mine, where you can still see the remains of the workings.

It takes about 30 minutes to return on foot down the mountain road to Aikawa. On the way you'll pass several temples and the **Sado Hangamura Museum** (佐渡版画村美術館; 38-2 Aikawa Komeyamachi; ¥400; ☺ 9am-5pm Mar-Nov; 🅿), an old wooden house where local artists display woodblock prints depicting country life in Sado.

🛏 Sleeping & Eating

Hotel Oosado HOTEL ¥¥
(ホテル大佐渡; ☑ 74-3300; www.oosado.com; 288-2 Aikawa-kabuse; r per person with 2 meals from ¥12,750; 🅿😊🛜) Along the town's southern waterfront is this grand hotel, where you can watch the sun set over the Sea of Japan while you sprawl in the *rotemburo*. Accommodation is available in either Western- or Japanese-style rooms, the best of which face the sea.

Isonoya NOODLES ¥
(磯の家; 16 Aizawa Edozawa-machi; noodles ¥350-850; ☺ 11am-8pm Fri-Wed, to 1pm Thu) This little *soba* shop, a few minutes' walk up the coast from the bus stop, is popular for its *isonoya teishoku* (a crisp assortment of tempura with a side of noodles). Turn right in front of the police station and look for the indigo *noren* curtain where the road bends.

ℹ Information

Tourist Information Center (☑ 74-2220; 15 Aikawa Haneda-machi; ☺ 8.30am-6pm Apr-Oct) A five-minute walk from the bus stop, behind the police station.

Sotokaifu 外海府

Sado's rugged northern coast is a dramatic landscape of sheer sea cliffs dropping off into deep blue waters. Roads are narrow and windy, which lead to harrowing but exhilarating coastal drives. Indeed, this is one area of Sado where having a rental car will make a big difference.

⊙ Sights & Activities

In order to truly appreciate the beauty of the region, you're going to have to head out into the bay. From May to October, **glass-bottomed boats** (¥1000; ⊘8am-5pm) depart every 15 minutes from the village of **Tassha** (達者) on a 15-minute cruise of **Senkaku-wan** (尖閣湾).

🛏 Sleeping

Sado Belle Mer Youth Hostel　HOSTEL ¥
(佐渡ベルメールユースホステル; ☑75-2011; http://sado.bellemer.jp; 369-4 Himezu; dm ¥3360-¥3960, breakfast/dinner ¥760/1260; Ｐ🐾) This modern hostel is scenically perched near the shore about five minutes on foot from the Minami-Himezu bus stop. It's run by a knowledgeable Japanese family, who can give you some good outdoor tips for exploring Sado's wildest stretch of coastline. Rooms are basic dorms, almost all of which have sea views.

Sotokaifu Youth Hostel　HOSTEL ¥
(外海府ユースホステル; ☑78-2911; www.jyh.or.jp/yhguide/hokushinestu/sotokaif/index.html; 131 Iwayaguchi; dm ¥3960, YHA discount ¥3360, breakfast/dinner ¥760/1260; Ｐ🐾) Tucked away in a tiny fishing hamlet, this cosy hostel may be just the ticket for solitude-seekers. It's in a traditional Sado house, complete with central hearth, refitted with shared and private rooms. Filling meals include fresh seafood. The hostel is right in front of the Iwayaguchi (岩谷口) bus stop.

Echigo-Yuzawa Onsen
越後湯沢温泉

☑025 / POP 8330

If Kawabata Yasunari's famous novel *Yukiguni* (*Snow Country*), set here, is to be believed, Echigo-Yuzawa was once a louche hotspring retreat where geisha competed for guests' affection. Then came skiing and the *shinkansen*. Now most visitors head directly to the convenient slopes of GALA Yuzawa and then back home. But you needn't pick your pleasure – there are still plenty of onsen inns here, and a long soak is the perfect end to a day on the mountain.

⊙ Sights & Activities

GALA Yuzawa　SNOW SPORTS
(ガーラ湯沢; www.galaresort.jp/winter/english; day lift tickets ¥4500; ⊘Dec-Apr) Just 200km north of Tokyo, GALA Yuzawa's claim to fame is its own *shinkansen* stop, right at the base of the mountain. It is entirely possible to wake up early in the morning in Tokyo, hit the slopes after breakfast and be home for dinner and a movie. With such incredible ease of access, GALA Yuzawa is predictably packed, especially on weekends and holidays, but you can't beat the convenience.

GALA Yuzawa is divided into three areas (northern, central and southern), which together offer 15 runs. Most trails are intermediate and beginner level, though with the reopening of the southern area in 2012 there are a few more advanced runs. Courses from top to bottom are moderate in length, with the longest stretching 2.4km. Three quad lifts alongside six triple and double lifts help to thin the crowds, but expect queues at peak times.

Given its proximity to Tokyo, GALA Yuzawa draws all types, although it is particularly popular with students and novices. English is spoken everywhere, and you'll see plenty of other foreigners. Full equipment rental is available for a somewhat pricey ¥4800 per day. Tokyo travel agents can often arrange cheap packages that include lift and train fare, especially if you're planning to head up on a weekday.

Yuzawa Town History Museum　MUSEUM
(雪国館 | Yukiguni-kan; 354-1 Yuzawa; admission ¥500; ⊘9am-4.30pm Thu-Tue) This wonderful little museum displays memorabilia from the life of Kawabata Yasunari, the first Japanese recipient of the Nobel Prize for Literature, in addition to interesting displays about life in snow country that bring his classic book to life. From the west exit of Echigo-Yuzawa Station, the museum is a 10-minute walk to the right.

🛏 Sleeping

Most visitors are day trippers from the capital, but you can spend the night to take advantage of the hot springs and aim to be the first one on the slopes the following day.

ECHIGO-TSUMARI ART FIELD

North of Echigo-Yuzawa Onsen lie some of the country's most fertile paddy fields. It's an enchanting scene of brilliant green fields and wooden farmhouses, some still with thatched roofs. It's also typical of agricultural communities everywhere around Japan: as younger generations leave the farms in favour of careers in the city, the region and its way of life are slowly dying.

In 2000 the **Echigo-Tsumari Art Field** (越後妻有大地の芸術祭の里; www.echigo-tsumari.jp/eng) was conceived as a way to bring people back, if only for a day or two. Here, spread out over some 77,000 hectares, are a hundred installations by both Japanese and international artists, set as naturally as possible in the surrounding landscape. The area really comes to life during the summer-long **Echigo-Tsumari Triennale** (next up in 2015).

Information is available at the contemporary art centre **Kinare** (キナーレ; ☑ 761-7767; http://kinare.jp/; 6 Honchō, Tōkamachi; admission ¥1000; ☺10am-5pm Thu-Tue), a few minutes from Tōkamachi Station. The Hokuhoku line connects Echigo-Yuzawa Onsen with Tōkamachi (¥610, 30 minutes) and other stations within the region; however, given the scope, a car really is necessary to get around.

⭐Hatago Isen
INN ¥¥

(HATAGO井仙; ☑ 784-3361; http://hatago-isen.jp; 2455 Yuzawa; r per person with 1/2 meals from ¥8400/12,075; Ⓟ) 🍴 Hatago Isen manages the aesthetic of an old-time travellers' inn – with dim lighting and plenty of dark wood – without skimping on modern amenities. Rooms vary from a humble six-mat space to rest your head, to deluxe suites with private *rotemburo*. There's a communal onsen bath, too. Meals make the most of local ingredients and are unusually flexible: you can choose from three different dinner courses and even elect to swap breakfast for lunch and a later checkout.

Hakuginkaku Hana-no-yoi
RYOKAN ¥¥

(白銀閣華の宵; ☑ 784-3311; www.hakugin.com/English.html; 2-1-10 Yuzawa; r per person/with 2 meals from ¥10,500/13,650; Ⓟ🛜) Right outside the station's east exit is this traditional ryokan and secluded refuge from the madding crowds. After a day on the slopes, you'll relish the opportunity to soak contemplatively in the outdoor *hinoki* tub or indoor marble bath. Dinner is served in the room, so you can stretch your legs out on the tatami.

NASPA New Ōtani
HOTEL ¥¥

(NASPAニューオータニ; ☑ 780-6111; www.naspanewotani.com; 2117-9 Yuzawa; r per person with breakfast & lift pass from ¥11,000; Ⓟ♨@🛜❄🐾) This family- and foreigner-friendly resort has its own backyard ski park that is particularly suited to beginners and small children. Rooms are Western-style and

reasonably spacious, and there's a whole range of resort facilities, including an onsen. Free shuttles take just five minutes to run between Echigo-Yuzawa Station and the resort.

ⓘ Getting There & Around

BUS

Echigo-Yuzawa Onsen is connected to Naeba by regular local buses (¥640, 40 minutes). A free shuttle runs between Echigo-Yuzawa Station and GALA Yuzawa.

TRAIN

There are several hourly *shinkansen* on the Jōetsu line from Tokyo to Echigo-Yuzawa (¥6490, 1¼ hours) and GALA Yuzawa (¥6900, 1½ hours). Trains continue from Echigo-Yuzawa to Niigata (¥5240, 50 minutes).

Naeba
苗場

♫ 025

Naeba is a little town with a lot going on. Not only does it (along with adjacent Kagura) offer some of the most challenging skiing and snowboarding in the whole of Tōhoku, it's also the setting for Japan's biggest outdoor music festival, Fuji Rock Festival.

🏃 Activities

Naeba Ski Resort
SNOW SPORTS

(苗場スキー場; www.princehotels.co.jp/ski/naeba; 202 Mikuni, Yuzawa; day lift ticket/combined Naeba & Kagura ¥4500/5000; ☺Dec-Apr) Naeba is an impressive resort, with 20 courses fairly evenly divided among skill levels. The longest run (4km) starts at the top of the mountain and winds through birch forests and mogul fields prior to dropping a full kilometre. The snow tends to be dry and light, and there are plenty of ungroomed areas where you can carve up some serious powder.

There's a snow park and sledding hill where the little ones can roam free, as well as a freestyle snowboarding course complete with rails, half pipes and kickers. English is widespread, and you definitely won't be the only foreigner on the slopes. At the bottom of the hill, you'll find the N-Plateau, a massive complex with full food court, onsen, convenience store and ski shop. You can also rent equipment here for ¥4300 per day.

Six- and eight-person gondolas do a decent job of keeping the crowds in check at peak times. But if you find the lines a little too long for your liking, you can always jump on the awesomely named Dragondola (ドラゴンドラ). Covering a distance of 5.5km, this is reportedly the longest gondola in the world and whisks you away to the neighbouring Kagura resort in just 15 minutes.

Kagura Ski Resort SNOW SPORTS
(かぐらスキー場; www.princehotels.co.jp/ski/kagura; 742 Mitsumata, Yuzawa; day lift ticket/combined Naeba & Kagura ¥4200/5000; ☉Nov-May) Naeba is an even more attractive winter destination when you consider that it's contiguous with Kagura, an impressive mountain in its own right. Divided into the Tashiro, Kagura and Mitsumata areas, this resort offers up an additional 23 runs that are divided 45/35/20 among beginner, intermediate and advanced.

But don't let the numbers fool you – Kagura has a lax policy on back-country skiing, which means that experienced alpinists can really have an extreme adventure up here. For those who feel more comfortable sticking to the trails, fret not, as one of the courses here reaches an impressive 6km. With the combined pass, you can return to Naeba by the Dragondola at any time, or take one of the free shuttle buses that depart from the bottom of the Mitsumata area.

★ Festivals & Events

Fuji Rock Festival LIVE MUSIC
(www.fujirockfestival.com; ☉late July) Fuji Rock Festival is three days of musical madness – like Woodstock, only with toilets and (usually) less mud – where up to 100,000 people show up to hang out, listen to great bands and enjoy the party atmosphere. Headliners include top overseas and domestic acts in a variety of genres.

🛏 Sleeping

Naeba gets its fair share of day trippers. Bedding down here or in Yuzawa Onsen helps you get the most out of your ski holiday.

Prince Hotel Naeba HOTEL ¥¥
(プリンスホテル苗場; ☎789-2211; www.princehotels.co.jp/naeba; 202 Mikuni, Yuzawa; r per person from ¥8000; P❄@☎⊛) All of the ski action in Naeba centres on this monolithic resort at the base of the mountain. On offer is a range of Western-style rooms and suites that vary considerably in size, amenities and price – check online for specials – in addition to a slew of bars, cafes, restaurants and health and fitness facilities.

Wadagoya Mountain Hut HUT
(和田小屋; ☎789-2211; www.princehotels.com/en/ski/mtnaeba/accommodation.html; r per person/with 2 meals ¥4500/7000; ☉Dec-May) The Prince Hotel runs this mountain hut up on Kagura. Sleeping on futons in a communal room, but you'll get to cut first tracks in the morning. Note that you have to arrive in Naeba by 3pm in order to catch the sequence of lifts up to the hut.

ℹ Getting There & Away

Echigo-Yuzawa Onsen is connected to Naeba by regular local buses (¥640, 40 minutes). Free shuttle buses to the Prince Hotel also run this route, though you need to be a registered guest to take advantage of the service.

At the height of the ski season, **Seibu Travel** (http://bus.seibutravel.co.jp/en) runs a shuttle bus between the Shinagawa Prince Hotel in Tokyo and Naeba (¥3500, four hours).

Myōkō Kōgen 妙高高原
☎0255

This up-and-coming skiing and snowboarding destination comprises a sprawling collection of powder-rich winter resorts that line the Myōko mountain range. On the whole, the region is much less developed for mass tourism than neighbouring areas, but its off-the-beaten-path appeal is precisely why you should visit. Myoko's location near the sea means that it gets snow before anywhere else does – upwards of 13m per season.

🏃 Activities

Akakura Onsen Ski Park
SNOW SPORTS

(赤倉温泉スキー場; ☎87-2169; www.akakura-ski.com; day lift ticket ¥3900; ☺ Dec-Apr) Akakura Onsen Sukī-Jō is one of the more popular resorts, especially among travellers with small children. All but two of the 20 runs were laid out with the needs of novice skiers in mind, and even the black diamonds are little more than short chutes. But the high-quality powder and picturesque setting ensure a good time for everyone. Family restaurants, many drawing inspiration from European chalets, are scattered around the slopes. English signage is generally available.

Dancing Snow
SNOW SPORTS

(ダンシングスノー; ☎ mobile 090-1433-1247; www.dancingsnow.com) For off-piste excitement, check out these local experts for guided tours through the backwoods terrain and snowshoe treks, as well as personalised one-on-one instruction – all in English. Prices depend on the length and type of tour, so contact the ski school for more information.

🛏 Sleeping

Akakura Onsen, a cosy mountain village with plenty of restaurants, is the perfect base for a long stay.

Hotel Alp
INN ¥¥

(ホテルアルプ; ☎87-3388; www.alp-myoko.com/english/index.html; 585-90 Akakura Onsen; r per person with 1/2 meals from ¥10,000/13,000; ⓟ🚭@🛜♨) The tranquil Hotel Alp lies at the base of the slopes and is extremely conducive to a ski-in, ski-out holiday. There are fewer than 20 rooms on the premises, allowing for a sense of intimacy not found at the resort hotels. Be sure to spend some quality time in the therapeutic sauna and hot-spring bath, perfect for thawing out your joints.

ℹ Information

Tourist Information Center (☎86-3911; http://myoko.tv/english/index.html; 291-1 Taguchi; ☺9am-5pm) Enquire here about multiple mountain and monthly passes especially for overseas travellers, as well as info about accommodation, rentals and ski schools in English. The office is located to the right of Myōkō Kōgen Station, past the bus stop.

ℹ Getting There & Away

The Nagano *shinkansen* runs once or twice every hour between Tokyo and Nagano (¥7770, 1¾ hours). Nagano is connected to Myōkō Kōgen by the JR Shinetsu line; hourly *kaisoku* (¥960, 45 minutes) ply this route. From Myōkō Kōgen Station, shuttle buses and taxis run to Akakura Onsen Sukī-Jō and other ski resorts.

Sapporo & Hokkaidō

Why Go?

Hokkaidō (北海道) defies the image of Japan as a crowded nation. It's a whole different world up here, or at least it feels like it, with 20% of Japan's land area but only 5% of its population. Japanese identify this northern land with its wildlife and mountains, greenery and agriculture, snowy winters, temperate summers and long arrow-straight roads disappearing into the horizon.

But there's more to it than the scenery. The Ainu, Hokkaidō's indigenous people, are making a determined return after a century of forced assimilation. Sapporo is a bustling modern city that can meet all your urban needs before you head out to explore. And the island is winning a reputation as a haven for thrill-seeking travellers wanting to ski and hike in its mountains, explore its magnificent national parks, relax in its hidden onsen, and to experience its offerings at their own pace. Enjoy it at your leisure.

Best Hikes

➡ Rishiri-zan (p588)
➡ Asahi-dake (p579)
➡ Yōtei-zan (p572)
➡ Shiretoko Traverse (p593)
➡ Poroshiri-dake (p605)

Best Brewery Pubs

➡ Sapporo Beer Garden (p555)
➡ Abashiri Bīru-kan (p592)
➡ Taisetsu Ji-bīru-kan (p574)
➡ Hakodate Beer (p560)
➡ Otaru Sōko No 1 (p563)

When to Go
Sapporo

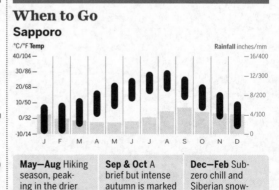

May–Aug Hiking season, peaking in the drier months of June and July.

Sep & Oct A brief but intense autumn is marked by the changing leaves.

Dec–Feb Sub-zero chill and Siberian snow-falls herald the ski season.

History

Hokkaidō was connected to north Asia via Sakhalin and the Kuril islands during the glacial age 30,000 to 40,000 years ago. The native peoples who settled in these northern lands called them Ainu Moshiri – Ainu meaning 'human' and Moshiri meaning 'world'.

Remarkably, the Ainu and the Japanese had relatively little contact until 1590, when Toyotomi Hideyoshi granted the Matsumae clan land at the southwestern tip of Hokkaidō and charged them with defending Japan from the 'barbarians' to the north. At this time, Hokkaidō and the people who lived there were known to the Japanese as Ezo (or Yezo). As well as building up exclusive trade relations with the people now known as the Ainu over the next few centuries, the Matsumae also had Japan's first tentative relations with Russians in the 1700s.

By the end of the Edo period in 1868, trade and colonisation had begun in earnest. With the Meiji Restoration, the new government introduced the name of Hokkaidō in 1869, and established a Development Commission with the primary purpose of colonising the northern islands to prevent the Russians furthering their expansion in the region. One of Hokkaidō's sub-divisions created at this time was Chishima (meaning '1000 islands'; now part of the Kuril islands and still in dispute with Russia). Mainland Japanese with little future at home – such as second sons and the newly unemployed samurai class – started to head north, much in the way that Americans were heading west at about the same time in history.

By the start of the 20th century, the mainland Japanese population on the island topped one million, and when the Meiji period ended, the Ainu had become de facto second-class citizens in their own land. Many Ainu customs were banned, women were forbidden to get tattoos, and men were prohibited from wearing earrings. An 1899 Japanese government act effectively forced assimilation. The Ainu's land was taken and they were granted Japanese citizenship, denying them the status of an indigenous group. Many Ainu even hid their ethnicity out of fear of discrimination in housing, schools and employment.

After the 1904–5 Russo-Japanese war, won by Japan, Karafuto (now Sakhalin; before 1905 known to Japanese as Kita-Ezo) was added to Japanese territory and by 1940, 400,000 Japanese were living there as part of a continuing colonial policy.

The 'northern territories', which included Hokkaidō, expanded, but by the end of WWII they were contracting. Both Karafuto and Chishima (now the disputed Kuril islands) were captured by Russia and remain Russian to this day.

World attention briefly focused on Hokkaidō in 1972 when Sapporo hosted the Winter Olympics, only eight years after the Summer Olympics were held in Tokyo.

In 1998 the act that had forced assimilation on the Ainu peoples was replaced with one that recognised that there are ethnic minority groups in Japan. Finally, in 2008, the Japanese government recognised the Ainu people as 'an indigenous people with a distinct language, religion and culture'. Today, the Ainu are proudly continuing their traditions while still fighting for further recognition of their unique culture.

Geography & Climate

Shaped a bit like the squashed head of a squid, Hokkaidō is a very big island and is far and away Japan's largest prefecture. In terms of area, it is almost exactly the same size as Ireland. However, many will find it surprising to hear that in terms of latitude, Hokkaidō is closer to the equator than Ireland.

Surprisingly, Sapporo, at about 43° N, is about the same latitude as Marseille in the south of France. It's not that far north!

Hokkaidō's winter weather, however, is affected by its proximity to Siberia and cold northwesterly winds. That means frigid weather and significant snowfall, especially on the Sea of Japan side of the island – the kind of powdery snow that excites winter sports enthusiasts! On the Sea of Okhotsk side of Hokkaidō, winter brings drift ice from the north, which clogs up the sea.

Hokkaidō supposedly misses out on *tsuyu*, the rainy season in June and July that brings rain, humidity and a stickiness to the rest of Japan – but in these days of climate change, there are claims that Hokkaidō is getting hotter and more humid. Summer is generally warm and pleasant, cooler in the mornings and evenings.

Another bonus – *taifu* (typhoons) seldom make it as far north as Hokkaidō, usually petering out after pounding southern Japan, and/or heading out to sea.

Sapporo & Hokkaidō Highlights

1 Drinking beer straight from the source in **Sapporo** (p546)

2 Staring down a Hello Kitty snow-woman at the **Sapporo Snow Festival** (p550)

3 Carving up the slopes at **Niseko** (p564) or **Furano** (p575)

4 Charting a path through the wilderness in **Daisetsuzan National Park** (p578)

5 Saying goodbye to stress as you steam at **Noboribetsu Onsen** (p572)

6 Discovering enormous, ancient *marimo* (balls of algae) in **Akan National Park** (p597)

7 Dining on fresh *uni* (sea-urchin roe) and *ikura* (salmon eggs) in **Otaru** (p562)

8 Strolling through 19th-century streetscapes in historic **Hakodate** (p557)

9 Heading to the 'end of the world' in the Unesco World Heritage site of **Shiretoko National Park** (p593)

10 Taking a ferry out to the remote islands of **Rishiri-Rebun-Sarobetsu National Park** (p585) to climb Rishiri-zan

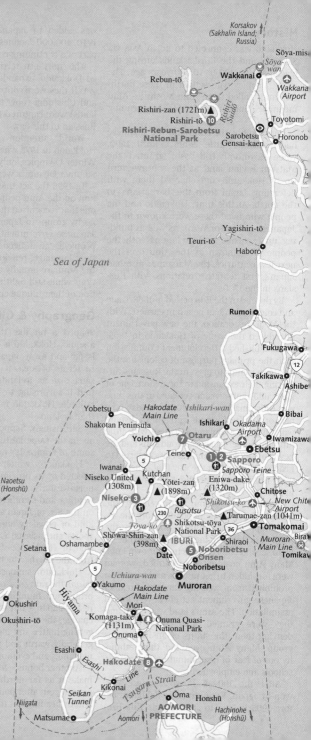

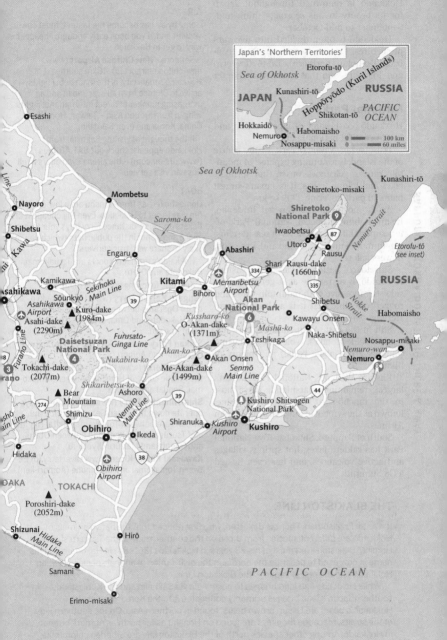

Japan's 'Northern Territories'

Sea of Okhotsk

Etorofu-tō

JAPAN   Kunashiri-tō   Hoppōryōdo (Kuril Islands)   RUSSIA

Shikotan-tō   PACIFIC
                                                OCEAN

Hokkaidō   Habomaisho
        Nemuro   Nosappu-misaki

0 ————— 100 km
0 ————— 60 miles

Sea of Okhotsk

Esashi

Nayoro

Shibetsu

Mombetsu

Saroma-ko

Kunashiri-tō

Shiretoko-misaki

Shiretoko
National Park   9

Iwaobetsu   87
Utoro
        Rausu

Engaru

Abashiri

Kamikawa

Sekihoku
Main Line

Asahikawa

Asahikawa
Airport

Kuro-dake
(1984m)

Asahi-dake
(2290m)

39

Kitami

Bihoro

Memanbetsu
Airport

Shari   Rausu-dake
            (1660m)

334

Akan
National Park

335

Shibetsu

Kawayu Onsen

Nemuro Strait

Etorofu-tō
(see inset)

RUSSIA

Habomaisho

Nosappu-misaki

Nokke Strait

Daisetsuzan
National Park

4

Kussharo-ko
O-Akan-dake
(1371m)

6

Mashū-ko

Naka-Shibetsu

Furusato-
Ginga Line

Akan-ko

Teshikaga

Nemuro-wan

Nemuro

Tokachi-dake
(2077m)

rano

Nukabira-ko

Me-Akan-dake
(1499m)

Akan Onsen

Senmō
Main Line

44

8

Furano Line

274

Bear
Mountain

Shimizu

Shikaribetsu-ko

Ashoro

39

Kushiro Shitsugen
National Park

Obihiro

Ikeda

Shiranuka

Kushiro
Airport

Kushiro

Hidaka

38

Obihiro
Airport

DAKA

TOKACHI

Poroshiri-dake
(2052m)

Shizunai

Hidaka
Main Line

Hirō

Samani

PACIFIC OCEAN

Erimo-misaki

N   0 ————— 100 km
     0 ————— 60 miles

Autumn brings gorgeous fall colours and Hokkaidō is renowned throughout Japan for its beauty in this season – think mid-September to mid-October.

Hokkaidō is often divided into five sub-prefectures: Dō-nan (southern), Dō-ō (central), Dō-hoku (northern), Dō-tō (eastern) and Tokachi – and that is how this chapter is organised.

National Parks

Hokkaidō boasts some of Japan's oldest and most beautiful national parks.

Daisetsuzan National Park, in the centre of the island, is a stunning expanse of mountain ranges, volcanoes, onsen (hot springs), lakes and hiking tracks. It is Japan's largest national park, covering 2309 sq km.

As far north as you can get in Japan, Rishiri-Rebun-Sarobetsu National Park offers superb hiking and views of seaside cliffs, a mammoth Fuji-like volcano and, in season, flowers galore!

Shiretoko National Park, in eastern Hokkaidō, is as remote as it gets: a peninsula so impressive with mountain wilds and rugged coastline that it is a Unesco World Heritage Site.

Still in the east, Akan National Park has onsen, caldera lakes, volcanoes, marimo (famous green algae balls!) and plenty of hiking.

Kushiro Wetlands National Park, Japan's largest remaining marshland, plays host to the tanchō-zuru, the Japanese crane, known as the symbol of longevity...and Japan Airlines.

South of Sapporo, Shikotsu-Tōya National Park has caldera lakes, hot springs villages and active volcanoes, and has even hosted a G8 Summit!

ⓘ Getting There & Away

AIR

Going by air has become the fastest, most convenient and, if you book early enough, cheapest way to get to Hokkaidō.

Sapporo's **New Chitose Airport** (www.new-chitose-airport.jp), 40km southeast of Hokkaidō's main city, is the main hub. Flights arrive in Chitose from all over Japan and an increasing number of direct international flights wing in from around Asia – Taiwan, Hong Kong, China, Korea and even Sakhalin.

If the thought of visiting Sakhalin from Hokkaidō appeals, check out **SAT Airlines** (www.uts-air.com) – the airline even offers a full Russian visa service.

BOAT

Domestic ferries from Honshū are a low-cost, fun way to get to Hokkaidō. Even the cheapest of tickets on a long-distance ferry buys your tatami space and a spot in the public bath (which you're likely to share with truck drivers!).

Hokkaidō's main ferry ports are Tomakomai, Hakodate and Otaru.

Keep the following options in mind:

Tsugaru Kaikyō Ferry (www.tsugarukaikyo.co.jp) Operates between Hakodate and Aomori, and Hakodate and Ōma, at the northernmost tip of Honshū.

Seikan Ferry (www.seikan-ferry.co.jp) Between Hakodate and Aomori.

Taiheiyō Ferry (www.taiheiyo-ferry.co.jp) Down the Pacific coast of Honshū, between Tomakomai, Sendai and Nagoya.

Shin-Nihonkai Ferry (www.snf.jp) These guys operate down the Japan Sea side of Honshū. Options are between Tomakomai, Akita, Niigata and Tsuruga (Fukui-ken); and between Otaru and Niigata and Maizuru (Kyoto-fu).

Kawasaki Kinkai Kisen (www.silverferry.jp) Between Tomakomai and Hachinohe (Aomori-ken).

THE BLAKISTON LINE

It was an Englishman, Thomas Blakiston, who first noticed that the native animals of Hokkaidō are different species from those on the southern side of the Tsugaru straits on Honshū. Blakiston lived most of his 23 years in Hokkaidō (1861–84) in Hakodate and his name is now used to describe the border in the distribution of animal species between Hokkaidō and the rest of Japan – 'the Blakiston Line'.

While Hokkaidō had land bridges to north Asia via Sakhalin and the Kuril islands, southern Japan's land bridges primarily connected it to the Korean peninsula. Hokkaidō's bears are Ussuri brown bears, found in northern Asia. On the southern side of the straits, macaque monkeys are found on Honshū as far north as Aomori, but not in Hokkaidō. Among other species north of the Blakiston line are Siberian chipmunks, Hokkaidō red squirrels, the ezo-jika (Hokkaidō deer), kita-kitsune (northern fox), northern pika and Blakiston's Fish Owl.

Shosen Mitsui Ferry (www.sunflower.co.jp) Operates between Tomakomai and Ōarai (Ibaraki-ken).

An intriguing international ferry route from Hokkaidō operates from Wakkanai to Sakhalin. See the boxed text, p585.

TRAIN

If you have a JR Pass, getting to Hokkaidō is relatively simple. Take a Tohoku *shinkansen* (bullet train) from Tokyo to Aomori, then change to a limited express to Hakodate – this train heads through the Seikan Tunnel to Hokkaidō. The *shinkansen* is expected to have a service to Hakodate in 2015 and has plans for a service all the way to Sapporo in 2035!

For some interesting overnight train options for getting to Sapporo, see p556.

ⓘ Getting Around

AIR

While it's possible to get around Hokkaidō by air, it's definitely not the cheapest way to do things and the number of flights are limited.

ANA (www.ana.co.jp) Offers a number of options, especially seasonal ones such as New Chitose Airport to Rishiri-tō from 1 June to 30 September.

Hokkaidō Air System (HAC; www.hac-air.co.jp) Operates a number of routes in Hokkaidō, mainly from Sapporo's secondary airport, Okadama. Also flies direct to Rishiri-tō.

BICYCLE

For fans of greener ways to get around, Hokkaidō is a great place to tour by bike. Cyclists are a common sight all over the island, especially in summer.

Rider houses or cycling terminals are cheap, and great places to meet other cyclists and bikers.

BUS

Within cities, buses are convenient and usually cheap. Ask about a *norihōdai* (all-day) pass if you're going to use them a lot – there's often a substantial discount.

Between cities, there are a lot of bus options. Here are a few:

Chūō Bus (www.chuo-bus.co.jp) Operates between Sapporo and Hakodate, Asahikawa, Obihiro, Kitami, Abashiri, Shiretoko and Kushiro, among others. These guys go everywhere.

Dōnan Bus (www.donanbus.co.jp) Operates mainly between Sapporo and points south, including Hakodate, New Chitose Airport, Tomakomai, Niseko, Rusutsu, Jōzankei, Tōya-ko Onsen and Noboribetsu Onsen.

Sōya Bus (www.soyabus.co.jp) Between Sapporo and Wakkanai.

Dōhoku Bus (www.dohokubus.com) Between Asahikawa and Obihiro, Kushiro and Sapporo.

ⓘ ROAD TRIP

Hokkaidō's highlights are its national parks, magnificent mountains, hidden hot springs, remote gorges and capes – and basically, public transport struggles to get you to where you want to be. Trains and buses give limited access and you won't get the chance to explore.

We heartily recommend that if you really want to see what Hokkaidō has to offer, get your own wheels and take a road trip.

CAR & MOTORCYCLE

In general, car-rental rates vary, but if you walk in off the street expect to pay between ¥7000 and ¥10,000 per day, plus the cost of fuel. The best Hokkaidō rental-car deal is with **Toyota Rent-a-Car** (www.toyotarentacar.net/english). These days, as with budget airlines, book online and in English before you go. Other options include **Nippon Rent A Car Hokkaido** (www.nrh.co.jp/foreign) and **Nissan Rent a Car** (www.nissan-rentacar.com/english/shop/hokkaido).

If you are flying into New Chitose Airport, there is a shuttle that takes you direct to the airport car depot, where friendly English-speaking staff help to get you on your way.

Roads & Driving

➤ Hokkaidō's roads are very well maintained.

➤ There is an expanding pay-your-way expressway system (高速道路; *kōsoku-dōro*) which is relatively expensive and you won't need to use unless you're in a hurry.

➤ Major roads are dotted with *michi-no-eki* (道の駅; road stations), which usually have toilets, refreshments for sale, and often house a small tourist information office.

➤ Rules are not made to be broken in Japan. Do your best not to exceed what may seem like exasperatingly slow speed limits (even when the road is as straight as a billiard cue!) and don't park illegally.

TRAIN

Trains run frequently on the trunk lines, but there aren't that many lines and reaching remote locations involves infrequent connections. Hokkaidō is a big island with a low population density, so coverage isn't particularly good, especially when compared to the rest of Japan.

In addition to the country-wide JR Rail Pass, there is also a Hokkaidō Rail Pass: a three-/ flexible four-/five-/seven day pass costs ¥15,000/19,500/19,500/22,000.

Check out your options at www.jrhokkaido.co.jp.

SAPPORO 札幌

☑ 011 / POP 1.90 MILLION

Japan's fifth-largest city, and the prefectural capital of Hokkaidō, Sapporo is a surprisingly dynamic and cosmopolitan urban centre that pulses with energy. Designed by European and American architects in the late 19th century, Sapporo is shaped by its wide grid of tree-lined streets and ample public-park space, which contribute to the city's surprising level of liveability. Even if you get cold easily, you can always get your energy back over a hot meal, a great proposition given Sapporo's wholly deserved gastronomic reputation.

As the island's main access point and transport hub, Sapporo serves as an excellent base for striking out into the wilds. But don't check out too quickly: Sapporo is a major tourist destination in itself, especially for those partial to the delicious liquid gold that is Sapporo beer. If you're planning long periods of time hiking in isolation, you might want to first indulge in a bit of the raucous nightlife of the Susukino district. And, of course, if the calendar month happens to read February, don't miss out on the Sapporo Snow Festival (Yuki Matsuri), a winter carnival highlighted by frozen sculptures of everything from brown bears and *tanuki* (racoon dogs) to Godzilla and Doraemon.

History

Sapporo is one of Japan's newest cities, and lacks the temples and castles found in its more southerly neighbours. However, it has a long history of occupation by the Ainu, who first named the area Sari-poro-betsu ('a river which runs along a plain filled with reeds').

The present-day metropolis was once nothing but a quiet hunting and fishing town in the Ishikari Plain of Hokkaidō. While the Ainu were left alone until 1821, everything changed when the Tokugawa *shōgunate* (military government) created an official trading post that would eventually become Sapporo. The city was declared the capital of Hokkaidō in 1868, and its growth was carefully planned.

In the 20th century, Sapporo emerged as a major producer of agricultural products. Sapporo Beer, the country's first brewery, was founded in 1876, and quickly became synonymous with the city itself. In 1972, Sapporo hosted the Winter Olympics, and the city's annual Sapporo Yuki Matsuri, begun in 1950, attracts more than two million visitors.

In recent years, Sapporo has experienced something of a cultural and spiritual renaissance, especially as more and more youths are choosing to flee their lives in the Tokyo and Osaka areas in search of a new start.

ⓘ Orientation

Sapporo, laid out in a Western-style grid pattern, has to be one of the easiest cities in the world to navigate.

Blocks are labelled East or West and North or South in relation to a central point near the TV Tower in the city centre.

The grass-covered park Ōdōri Kōen divides the city into its north–south halves. The address is either north or south of Ōdōri Kōen.

The east–west divider is officially the canal-like Sōsei-gawa (創成川). Addresses are either west or east of the river. Most of the central city and its points of interest are west.

Sitting almost perfectly on the intersecting points is Sapporo Terebi-tō, just to the west of the river. As the TV Tower can be easily seen, everyone takes their bearings off the TV Tower.

It's all very simple. For example, the famous landmark Tokei-dai (Clock Tower) is in the block of North 1, West 2 (Kita Ichi-jo, Nishi Ni-chōme) – N1W2.

JR Sapporo Station is at N6W3. South of Ōdōri is the downtown shopping district with shops and arcades. Susukino, the club and entertainment district, is located mainly between the South 2 and South 6 blocks.

⦿ Sights

Sapporo is a very walkable city for much of the year. The gridded streets (a rarity in Japan) make for very simple navigation, and most of the major sights are clustered together in the city centre.

We're not going to lie to you though – Sapporo can be bitterly cold in winter, especially when the Arctic winds are blowing and the snow is piling up. Dress appropriately – and maybe get a beer or two into your system – if you're planning to walk in winter.

Of course, if your body starts to go numb, you can always take advantage of the city's super-efficient subway, tram and bus lines. There is also a 520m underground walkway under Ekimae-dōri linking JR Sapporo Station with Ōdōri subway station.

Hours for attractions listed are for high season (generally April to October); most of them have reduced hours the rest of the year.

★ Ōdōri Kōen
PARK

(大通公園) Ōdōri Kōen is the long block-wide park that splits Sapporo into its north–south grid. Fully 13 blocks (1.5km) long, with the TV Tower at its eastern end, the park plays host to the city's major events and festivals. Beautifully manicured flower gardens match the green lawns, overhanging trees and the plentiful artwork, fountains, statues and benches to relax on. A true haven in the heart of the city. The park is a 10-minute walk south from JR Sapporo Station along Ekimae-dōri.

Sapporo TV Tower
TOWER

(さっぽろテレビ塔; Sapporo Terebi-tō; www.tv-tower.co.jp/en; Ōdōri-nishi 1-chōme; admission ¥700; ⊙9am-10pm) There's no way you'll miss this 147m-high Eiffel Tower–shaped affair at the eastern end of Ōdōri kōen, which stands alongside Tokyo Tower in the category of misplaced monuments. Still, the views from the observation deck at 90m are very impressive, especially when the sun drops below the horizon and Sapporo lights up for the night.

Old Sapporo Court of Appeals Building
MUSEUM

(札幌市資料館; ☎251-0731; www.s-shiryokan.jp/; W13 Ōdōri; ⊙9am-7pm) FREE At the western end of Ōdōri Kōen stands this impressive brick building that was built in 1926 as the Sapporo High Court. While the grounds and gardens seem like an extension of the park, the building houses a free museum of Sapporo's history.

JR Tower
TOWER

(JRタワー; ☎209-5500; www.jr-tower.com; admission ¥700; ⊙10am-11pm) Opened in 2003, the 38-floor JR Tower (173m) offers the best views of Sapporo. It's easy, all indoor, and there are shopping, eating and drinking options galore in the huge complex that surrounds JR Sapporo Station.

Sapporo Clock Tower
CLOCK TOWER

(札幌市時計台; Sapporo Tokei-dai; www15.ocn.ne.jp/~tokeidai/english.html; N1W2 Chūō-ku; admission ¥200; ⊙8.45am-5pm) No Japanese tourist can leave Sapporo without snapping a photo of the city's signature landmark, the clock tower. Built in 1878, the clock has not missed tolling the hour for more than 130 years. That's impressive, but these days Sapporo's encroaching urban metropolis somewhat dwarfs the small building. The clock tower is just two minutes on foot from Ōdōri station, or a 10-minute walk from JR Sapporo Station.

Old Hokkaidō Government Office Building
BUILDING

(北海道庁旧本庁舎; ☎204-5019; N3W6 Chūō-ku; ⊙8.45am-6pm) FREE Known as Akarenga (red bricks), this magnificent neo-baroque building (1888) is surrounded by lovely lawns and gardens. It has various historical exhibits and art on show. While Akarenga closes at 6pm, the gardens are open until 9pm and are a popular place for a stroll.

Sapporo Winter Sports Museum
MUSEUM

(札幌ウィンタースポーツミュージアム; www.sapporowintersportsmuseum.com; 1274 Miyano-mori Chūō-ku; admission ¥600; ⊙8.30am-6pm) Housed in the ski-jump stadium built for the Sapporo Olympics west of the central city, this highly amusing museum includes a computerised ski-jump simulator that allows you to try your skills without potentially breaking every bone in your body. Even if you do land a few virtual jumps, a chairlift ride to the launch point of the actual ski jump used in the 1972 games should serve as a quick reality check. To reach the museum, take the Tozai subway line to Maruyama (円山), and then take exit 2 for the Maruyama bus terminal. Next, take bus 14 to Ōkurayama-kyōgijō-iriguchi (大倉山競技場入り口; ¥200, 15 minutes); from here, it's a 10-minute walk uphill to the stadium.

Moiwa-yama Ropeway
ROPEWAY

(藻岩ロープウェイ; ☎561-8177; www.sapporo-dc.co.jp/eng; one-way/return ¥900/1700; ⊙10.30am-10pm) Panoramic views of Sapporo can be had from this scenic ropeway and cable-car system, which runs up to the top of Moiwa-san (531m) to the southwest of the central city. You are on the gondola (ropeway) for five minutes, then on the cable car for two more to reach the top where there is a large tourist complex and magnificent views. You can easily access the ropeway by taking the tram to the Rōpuwei-iriguchi stop, and then hopping on the free shuttle bus.

Hokkaidō University
UNIVERSITY

(北海道大学; Hokkaidō Daigaku; www.hokudai.ac.jp/en/index.html; ⊙dawn-dusk) Established in 1876, this scenic university has a number of unique buildings. The Furukawa Memorial Hall and the Seikatei are noteworthy, and several campus museums are open to the public. The bust of William S Clark, the university's founding vice-president, is a well-known landmark. Upon his departure, Professor Clark famously told his students: 'Boys, be ambitious!'

Sapporo

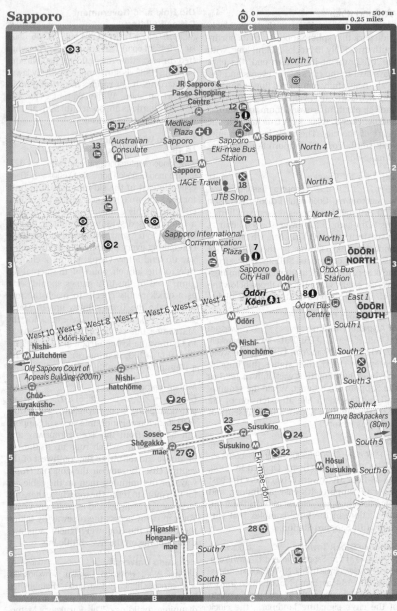

North 7

North 4

North 3

North 2

North 1

ŌDŌRI NORTH

Chūō Bus Station

East 1

ŌDŌRI SOUTH

South 1

South 2

South 3

South 4

Jimmyz Backpackers (80m)

South 5

Hōsui Susukino South 6

JR Sapporo & Paseo Shopping Centre

Medical Plaza Sapporo

Australian Consulate

Sapporo

Sapporo Eki-mae Bus Station

Sapporo

IACE Travel

JTB Shop

Sapporo International Communication Plaza

Sapporo City Hall

Ōdōri

Ōdōri Kōen

Ōdōri Bus Centre

Ōdōri

Ōdōri

Ōdōri-kōen

Nishi-yonchōme

Nishi-Juitchōme

Old Sapporo Court of Appeals Building (200m)

Chūō-kuyakusho-mae

Nishi-hatchōme

Soseo-Shōgakkō-mae

Susukino

Susukino

Eki-mae-dōri

Higashi-Honganji-mae

South 7

South 8

West 10 West 9 West 8 West 7 West 6 West 5 West 4

Hokkaidō University Botanical Garden

GARDENS

(北大植物園; Hokudai Shokubutsuen; ☏ 221-0664; www.hokudai.ac.jp/fsc/bg; N3W8; admission ¥400; ◷ 9am-4.30pm Tue-Sun) 🍃 One of Sapporo's must-sees, this beautiful outdoor garden is the botanical showpiece of Hokkaidō University. Here you'll find more than 4000 plant varietals, all attractively set on a meandering 14-hectare plot just 10 minutes on foot southwest of the station. Of particular note is the small section

Sapporo

dedicated to Ainu wild foods and medicinal plants, though English-language signage is sadly in short supply.

Ainu Association of Hokkaidō   CULTURAL CENTRE
(北海道アイヌ協会; Hokkaidō Ainu Kyōkai; ☎221-0462; www.ainu-assn.or.jp/english/eabout01.html; 7th fl, Kaderu 2.7 Community Centre, N2W7 Chūō-ku; ⊙9am-5pm Mon-Sat) **FREE** Across the street from the botanical gardens, this cultural centre offers an interesting display room of robes, tools and historical information on the Ainu.

Hokkaidō Jingu   SHRINE
(北海道神宮; www.hokkaidojingu.or.jp/eng/index.html) **FREE** This temple is nestled in a forest to the west of the city that is so dense it's easy to forget that Sapporo is just beyond the grounds. Dating back to 1869, this is one of the oldest shrines in Hokkaidō. Attention has been paid to labelling the natural surroundings: a large plaque lists a number of local birds and the largest trees have identification signs. The temple lies a few blocks west of Maruyama-kōen station (円山公園).

Hokkaidō Museum of Modern Art MUSEUM
(北海道立近代美術館; Hokkaidō Ritsukindaibijutsukan; www.aurora-net.or.jp/art/dokinbi; N1W17 Chūō-ku; admission ¥450; ⊙9.30am-5pm Tue-Sun) A comprehensive collection of modern works by primarily Japanese artists. The museum is a few blocks north of Nishi-18-chōme station (exit 4) on the Tōzai line.

Hokkaidō Museum of Literature MUSEUM
(北海道立文学館; Hokkaidō Ritsubun-gakukan; ☎511-7655; www.h-bungaku.or.jp; Nakajima-kōen 1-4 Chūō-ku; admission ¥400; ⊙9.30am-5pm) This museum offers the opportunity to see the private side of many of Japan's famous novelists, primarily those with a Hokkaidō connection. Letters, memorabilia, books and short films all help viewers understand why these writers have earned a place in the canon of Japanese literature. The museum is scenically located in Nakajima park (中島公園) in the southern district.

Moerenuma-kōen SCULPTURE PARK
(モエレ沼公園; www.sapporo-park.or.jp/moere/english.php; 1-1 Moerenuma-kōen; ⊙7am-10pm) **FREE** Completed in 2005, this former wastetreatment plant to the northeast of the central city is now a reclaimed green belt full of modern sculptures, originally designed by the legendary Noguchi Isamu before his death in 1988. Taking pride of place is the Glass Pyramid. To reach the park, take bus 69 or 79 from the Kanjo-dōri Higashi subway stop.

🏃 Activities

Sapporo Teine SKIING, SNOWBOARDING
(サッポロテイネ; ☎223-5830; www.sapporoteine.com/snow; day passes ¥4800; ⊙9am-4pm) With Niseko so close, many alpine enthusiasts aren't too keen on spending any more time in Sapporo than they have to. But you can't beat Teine for convenience, as the slopes lie quite literally on the edge of the city.

Teine has two zones: the lower more beginner- and family-oriented Olympia Zone including the Pandaruman Kids' Park; and the more challenging Highland Zone. There are 15 runs and nine lifts. Highlights include a 4km-long beginner trail that undulates from the Highland Zone down to the village, and then continues into a low-lying valley. There is also an exhilarating 700m black-diamond chute that was featured in the downhill rotation at the 1972 Sapporo Winter Olympics.

Cafeteria-style restaurants are located at each level, offering winter warmers such as *udon* (thick white wheat noodles), *rāmen* (egg noodles) and curry rice. Skiers/snowboarders can rent equipment (per day ¥4950). English signage is a bit limited, and there are less foreigners than in Niseko.

Just 15 minutes from Sapporo by local train, Teine can get very crowded, particularly on weekends and school holidays. Frequent trains on the JR Hakodate line run between Sapporo and Teine (¥260). From JR Teine Station, shuttle buses conveniently whisk you back and forth to the slopes.

A good option is the Bus Pack, which gets you a return bus trip from Sapporo central city hotels and a seven-hour lift ticket for ¥4500/2800 per adult/child. This deal requires prebooking by a week, but is perfect if you are heading to Sapporo with your family. Check the website (in English) for a list of hotels and timetables.

Sapporo Dome STADIUM
(札幌ドーム; ☎ 850-1020; www.sapporo-dome. co.jp) Built for the 2002 FIFA World Cup, the Sapporo Dome was tested early, hosting the hotly contested England vs Argentina match. This intriguing stadium, with a fixed roof, is interesting in that it switches surfaces depending on the sport being played. Sapporo is home to baseball's **Hokkaidō Nippon Ham Fighters** (www.fighters.co.jp), who play on an artificial surface. The local soccer team is **Consadole Sapporo** (www. consadole-sapporo.jp), and for their matches, a natural grass pitch is slid into the stadium. The Fighters have been doing well of late, and with extremely boisterous crowds, a trip to the Sapporo Dome is a great way to see parochial Japan in action. Check out the website for schedules. You can also take tours of the Dome on the hour from 10am to 4pm for ¥1000 – it pays to make a booking.

The Dome is a 10-minute walk from Fukuzumi Station (福住) on the Tōho subway line (地下鉄東豊線).

Hokkaidō Chūō Bus Tours BUS TOUR
(北海道中央バス; ☎ 231-0500; www.chuo-bus. co.jp/sightseeing.en) Chūō Bus runs all sorts of tours – morning, afternoon and night tours as well as full-day tours – to many top Hokkaidō visitor spots mentioned in this chapter. As well as half- and full-day tours to Sapporo's attractions, you can take day tours to Furano, Biei, Asahi-dake Onsen, Asahiyama Zoo, Sōunkyō Onsen, Shikotsuko and Tōya-ko, Niseko, Jozankei and Otaru to name just a few. There are flower tours, onsen tours, market tours... Take a look at the English website and take your pick.

NAC Sapporo CLIMBING WALL
(ＮＡＣ札幌; ☎ 812-7979; www.nac-web.com/ sapporo; Īas Shopping Centre A Town 1 Fl, イーアス札幌Ａタウン１Ｆ; day pass ¥1800; ◷ 10am-8pm) Sapporo's version of the Niseko Adventure Centre (NAC) features Japan's largest indoor climbing wall, covering a whopping 1200 sq metres, inside a shopping centre! You can take '1st step' lessons or aim higher once experienced. On-site is another NAC institution, Jojo's Café, where you can chill out between climbs. Īas Shopping Centre A Town is a three-minute walk from Higashi-Sapporo (東札幌) Station on the Tōzai subway line (東西線).

✿❀ Festivals & Events

Sapporo hosts a lot of festivals and there is always something going on throughout the year.

★ Sapporo Snow Festival SNOW
(さっぽろ雪まつり; Sapporo Yuki Matsuri; www. snowfes.com/english) Drawing more than two million visitors, the annual Sapporo Yuki Matsuri takes place in early February, and is arguably one of Japan's top festivals. Its humble origins go back to 1950, when local high-school students built six snow statues in Ōdōri Kōen. By 1974, the event had grown into an international contest attracting teams from more than a dozen countries. Taking weeks and weeks to carve, past snow sculptures have included life-sized statues of Hideki Matsui, entire frozen stages for visiting musical acts, ice slides and mazes for the kiddies and – of course – a cutesy-cool Hello Kitty statue or two. You can view these icy behemoths in Ōdōri Kōen as well as in other locations around the city. The festival also highlights the best in regional food and drink from across the island, and you can expect all kinds of wild and drunken revelry,

particularly once the sun sets (at these latitudes, it's quite early!). Finding reasonably priced accommodation can be extremely difficult, so book as far in advance as possible.

Sapporo Beer Festival BEER

(札幌ビールまつり) The summer beer festival is held in Ōdōri Kōen from mid-July to mid-August. Sapporo, Asahi and microbrewers set up outdoor beer gardens, offering a variety of beers and other beverages, as well as food and snacks. A whole month of beer drinking in the sun!

Sapporo Autumn Fest FOOD

(さっぽろオータムフェスト; www.sapporo-autumnfest.jp/english) A new kid in terms of Sapporo festivals, Autumn Fest has been going since 2008 and is proving extremely popular. It runs for the last two weeks of September and is based on that great Japanese enthusiasm for consuming exquisite food and drink. Stalls are set up with vendors from all over Hokkaidō selling every kind of consumable product imaginable. A must for foodies!

🛏 Sleeping

Sapporo offers a diverse range of accommodation ranging from budget crash pads to lavish escapes. Advance reservations are necessary during Sapporo Yuki Matsuri, and potentially on weekends during peak winter snowfall and peak summer wildflowers.

If you're looking for a place to crash in an emergency, internet cafes across the city are open 24 hours, offer reclining chairs and hot showers, and are often cheaper than even the cheapest of hotels.

Love hotels in Susukino are another colourful (if slightly promiscuous) option, and are as clean as (or cleaner than!) budget hostels and hotels. Check in after 11pm for the lowest rates.

Ino's Place HOSTEL ¥

(イノーズプレイス; ☑832-1828; http://inos-place.com/e; dm/s/d from ¥2900/4300/7600; @ 🛜) Ino's Place is a true backpackers' spot with all the fixings – friendly and bilingual staff are on hand to make your stay warm and welcome, while clean rooms, private lockers, free internet, free coffee and tea, no curfew, a Japanese bath, laundry facilities, a kitchen and a communal lounge space sweeten the deal. To reach Ino's, take the Tōzai subway line to the Shiroishi stop (白石; don't go to JR Shiroishi Station); take exit 1 and walk straight for a few minutes

along the main street in the direction of the Eneos petrol station. Turn right at the fourth traffic light and you'll see a detached two-storey white building – you've arrived!

Jimmyz Backpackers HOSTEL ¥

(☑206-8632; www.jimmyzbp.com/english; S5E3 Chūo-ku; per person ¥2950; 🛜) With only 10 beds (six in a mixed dorm and four in a female dorm), Jimmyz isn't huge. In a normal Japanese house converted into a homely backpackers, it's conveniently only a few blocks east of Susukino. It's simple, but everything you could want is here, from free tea and coffee to free internet and ¥200 laundry facilities. There's a good English website.

**Sapporo International
Youth Hostel** HOSTEL ¥

(札幌国際ユースホステル; ☑825-3120; www.youthhostel.or.jp/kokusai; 6-5-35 Toyohira-ku; dm/r per person from ¥3200/3800; @ 🛜) Housed in a surprisingly modern and stylish building that could give most business hotels a run for their money, this well-conceived youth hostel has perfected the basics by offering simple rooms to budget travellers. Both Western- and Japanese-style private rooms are available, as well as 'dorm rooms' featuring four full-sized beds. The closest subway stop is Gakuen-mae (学園前; exit 2) on the Tōhō line; the hostel is just two minutes from the station behind the Sapporo International Student Centre.

Capsule Inn Sapporo HOTEL ¥

(カプセル・イン札幌; ☑251-5571; www.capsuleinn-s.com/english; S3W3-7 Chūo-ku; r per person ¥2800; @ 🛜) If you're a man of simple needs who doesn't get scared easily by small spaces, this XY-chromosome-only capsule hotel offers your standard berth plus a sauna, large bathroom, coin laundry and even a 'book corner' with reclining chairs. It's located a stone's throw from the main Susukino crossing right in the heart of the action. Check-in from 1pm; check out by 10am.

Sapporo House Youth Hostel HOSTEL ¥¥

(札幌ハウスユースホステル; ☑726-4235; http://yh-sapporo.jp/english/accommo/index.html; N6W6-3-1 Kita-ku; dm/tw from ¥3360/7770; @ 🛜) Only five minutes on foot west of JR Sapporo Station, just north of the train tracks, the Sapporo House Youth Hostel is in an excellent location. Though it looks like an office building and is slightly sterile, this hostel is a good option for those wanting a cheap place to lay their head.

★ Nakamuraya Ryokan
RYOKAN ¥¥

(中村屋旅館; ☎ 241-2111; www.nakamura-ya.com/english.html; N3W7-1 Chūō-ku; r per person high season from ¥7875, low season ¥7350; @ 🛜) Located on a small side street near the entrance to the botanical gardens, this charming little Japanese-style inn is a wonderful introduction to the pleasures of the island. A variety of different plans are available, featuring tatami rooms of varying shapes and sizes, as well as lavish feasts incorporating the unique flavours of Hokkaidō. All guests can also relax in the on-site bath, and the owner-managers are well equipped to deal with the needs of foreigner travellers. It's a 10-minute walk from JR Sapporo Station.

Marks Inn Sapporo
HOTEL ¥¥

(マークスイン札幌; ☎ 512-5001; www.marks-inn.com/sapporo/english.html; S8W3 Chūō-ku; s/d from ¥4500/6000; @ 🛜) If you want private accommodation, you really can't get cheaper than this business hotel on the edge of the Susukino entertainment district, right across from the canal. Rooms are a bit cramped, but the feathery beds are soft, and become even softer if you party too hard in Susukino and stumble back in the wee hours of the morning. Free breakfast is a bonus too!

Cross Hotel Sapporo
HOTEL ¥¥

(クロスホテル札幌; ☎ 272-0010; www.cross-hotel.com/eng_sapporo; N3W2 Chūō-ku; s/d from ¥6000/9600; @ 🛜) This shimmering modernist tower is located about five minutes south of the JR Sapporo Station on foot. The interior is a veritable designer's showcase, with chic rooms categorised according to three thematic styles: urban, natural and hip. As an added bonus, there is a steel- and glass-enclosed onsen that allows you to stare out at the city while you soak in a steaming tub. The best deals are online and early.

Hotel Gracery Sapporo
HOTEL ¥¥

(ホテルグレイスリー札幌; ☎ 251-3211; www.gracery.com/en/sapporo/index.html; N4W4-1 Chūō-ku; s/d from ¥8000/14,000; @ 🛜) The former Sapporo Washington Hotel has been completely remodelled and subsequently relaunched as a stylish yet affordable boutique hotel. The design is minimalist meets industrial with a splash of colour. Rooms vary in price depending on the design and layout, and there are even specially designated executive and women's-only floors. The prop-erty is connected to the JR Sapporo Station by an underground shopping passage, which comes in handy when the mercury drops.

Sapporo Grand Hotel
HOTEL ¥¥¥

(札幌グランドホテル; ☎ 261-3311; www.grand1934.com/english/index.html; N1W4 Chūō-ku; r from ¥19,000; @ 🛜) Established in 1934 as the first European-style hotel in Sapporo, this grand old dame now occupies three adjacent buildings that lie at the southeast corner of the former Hokkaidō government building. Fairly subdued rooms vary considerably in price and style, though all guests are seemingly treated to VIP service from arrival to checkout.

Keiō Plaza Hotel Sapporo
HOTEL ¥¥¥

(京王プラザホテル札幌; ☎ 271-0111; www.keioplaza-sapporo.co.jp/english/index2.html; N5W7 Chūō-ku; r from ¥20,000; @ 🛜 ☎) At the northeast corner of the botanical gardens, Sapporo's Keiō Plaza Hotel offers all the upmarket amenities you would expect as a member of the Keiō Plaza group. Very convenient for checking out the city.

JR Tower Hotel Nikko Sapporo
HOTEL ¥¥¥

(ＪＲタワーホテル日航札幌; ☎ 251-2222; www.jrhotelgroup.com/eng/hotel/eng101.htm; N5W2 Chūō-ku; s/d/tw from ¥20,000/29,000/36,000; @ 🛜) You can't beat the location at this lofty hotel, which is firmly attached to the JR Sapporo Station. Taking advantage of such great heights, the Hotel Nikko Sapporo offers plush rooms priced by floor, a spa with a view on the 22nd floor, and both Western and Japanese restaurants perched on the 35th floor. The views from the top are some of the best in the city, so be sure to stop by for dinner (Mikuni Sapporo), a drink (Sky J) or even a beauty treatment at the on-site holistic spa.

✕ Eating

In addition to its namesake beer, Sapporo is famous for its miso-based *rāmen* (egg noodles), which makes use of Hokkaidō's delicious butter and fresh corn. The city also serves up some truly incredible seafood, winter-warming stews and *jingisukan,* an easy-to-love dish of roasted lamb that pays tribute to everybody's favourite Mongol warlord, Genghis Khan.

★ Rāmen Yokochō
RAMEN ¥

(元祖さっぽろラーメン横丁; Rāmen Alley; www.ganso-yokocho.com; ⊙ 11am-3am) This famous alleyway in the Susukino entertain-

A FOOD LOVER'S GUIDE TO HOKKAIDŌ

From a gourmand's perspective, it is something of a tragedy that little tangible evidence remains of Hokkaidō's indigenous cuisine. In 1878, a Yorkshire woman by the name of Isabella Bird dined with Ainu, and wrote the following lip-smacking account: 'Soon, the evening meal was prepared by the chief's principal wife, who tipped into a soot pot swinging over the flames a mixture of wild roots, beans, seaweed, shredded fish, dried venison, millet paste, water and fish oil, and left the lot to stew for three hours.'

Of course, the frontier spirit is still alive and well on the island, and Hokkaidō does remain a foodie's paradise. One Ainu dish that has survived the passage of time is *ruibe* (ルイベ), which is simply a salmon that has been left out in the Hokkaidō midwinter freeze, sliced up sashimi style, and then served with high-grade soy sauce and water peppers.

The Ainu tradition of hotpots is also being fostered by modern Japanese, and you'll find winter-warming *nabemono* (鍋物) all across the island. A particularly delicious variant of this dish is *ishikari-nabe* (石狩鍋), a rich stew of cubed salmon, miso, mirin, potatoes, cabbage, tofu, leek, kelp, wild mushrooms and sea salt. Sapporo-ites are also fond of their original *sūpu-karē* (スープカレー), which is quite literally a soupy variant of Japanese curry.

In addition to salmon, another cold-water speciality is *kani-ryōri* (かに料理; crab cuisine). The long-legged crabs of Wakkanai and Kushiro fetch the highest prices, though anything from Hokkaidō's icy waters will be packed with flavour. Crab appears in a variety of manifestations on the menu, though we're partial to boiled crustaceans served alongside a dish of melted butter.

Dairy cows flourish in the island's wide open expanses, which is reason enough to add a bit of lactose to your diet. Hokkaidō milk is used in everything from ice cream and cappuccinos to creamy soups and sauces, while Hokkaidō butter is best served atop a bowl of **rāmen** (ラーメン).

There are variants on everybody's favourite soup-noodle dish across the island, though the most famous is the miso-based Sapporo *rāmen*. If you want to be a purist, wash down your bowl with a pint of the legendary lager that is Sapporo *bīru* (札幌ビール).

And finally, no culinary account of Hokkaidō is complete without mention of Sapporo's beloved *jingisukan* (ジンギスカン), which was perhaps best summed up by British writer Alan Booth: 'I ordered the largest mug of draught beer on the menu and a dish of mutton and cabbage, which the Japanese find so outlandish that they have dubbed it *jingisukan* (Ghenghis Khan) after the grandfather of the greatest barbarian they ever jabbed at. The beer, as always, was about one-third froth, but a single portion of Ghenghis was so huge that it took an hour to eat – compensation for the loss of fluid ounces...'

ment district is crammed with dozens of *rāmen* shops. Anyone with a yen for *rāmen* shouldn't miss it, but it can be tricky to find. From the main Susukino crossroads, walk south to the first crossroad. Turn left (east); Rāmen Yokochō is halfway down on the right, running parallel to Ekimae-dōri. If you can't find it just ask – it's one place people *will* know. Hours vary for different shops, though prices are consistently cheap, with a bowl of noodles setting you back no more than ¥1000. This is the original Rāmen Yokochō, and they are keen to distance themselves from all imposters!

Rāmen Kyōwakoku
RAMEN ¥

(らーめん共和国; Rāmen Republic; www.sapporo-esta; 10th fl, ESTA Bldg, JR Sapporo Station; ⏰11am-10pm) If Rāmen Yokochō is the original Rāmen Alley with history and atmosphere on its side, then these guys are the shameless copycats. The only thing is, Japan is renowned for copying things and improving them. Rāmen Kyōwakoku is a 'clean', touristy version of the original, but it is also very good. It's all here in eight different shops – Sapporo *miso-rāmen*, Asahikawa *shōyu-rāmen* and Hakodate *shio-rāmen*. A Hokkaidō *rāmen* odyssey! No early morning noodles here after a hard night's drinking though. It all closes down with the department stores!

Ni-jō Ichiba
MARKET ¥

(二条市場; S3E1&2 Chūō-ku; ⏰7am-6pm) Buy a bowl of rice and select your own sashimi toppings, gawk at the fresh delicacies or sit down at a shop in Ni-jō, one of Hokkaidō's best fish markets. Sea urchin and crab are favourites; as is Hokkaidō's version of 'Mother and Child' (oyakodon), a bowl of rice topped with salmon and roe. Get there early for the freshest selections and the most variety; individual restaurants have their own hours. The market is just over the Sōsei-gawa at the eastern end of the Tanuki-kōji shopping arcade.

Yosora-no-Jingisukan
JINGISUKAN ¥¥

(夜空のジンギスカン; ☎219-1529; www.yozojin.com; S4W4 Chūō-ku, 9th & 10th fl; plates from ¥850; ⏰5pm-2.30am) Genghis Khan is on the menu everywhere, though at this speciality restaurant, located on the 9th & 10th floors of the My Plaza building, you can grill up tender slices of locally raised lamb, as well as more exotic cuts from around the world. There is no English, though the handy picture menu makes ordering a breeze. The 10th floor features jingisukan-with-a-view, while the 9th floor has jingisukan-with-special-sauce. If you're really hungry, go for the two-hour, ¥3000, eat-all-you-can plan on the 9th floor. It's at the opposite end of the same block as McDonald's at Susukino Crossing.

Sushi-no-uo-masa
SUSHI ¥¥

(鮨の魚政; ☎644-9914; www.asaichi-maruka.jp; Chūō Oroshi-uri-ichiba Maruka Centre 1F, N12W21, 中央卸売市場マルカセンター 1F; ⏰5am-11am) This is something very special – sushi for breakfast out among the fish markets. It's going to take a bit of effort to get here, but the sushi is the best and you can wander around the Sapporo fish markets before and after eating. It's out at N12W21, a 10-minute walk from JR Sōen Station (桑園) or a 10-minute drive from Sapporo Station. Sushi-no-uo-masa is smack in the middle of the stalls on the ground floor of the Maruka Centre. If you're asking locals for directions, ask for the Chūō Oroshi-uri-ichiba.

Kushidori
YAKITORI ¥¥

(串鳥; ☎758-2989; www.sapnet.ne.jp/kushidori; N7W4-8-3 Kita-ku; skewers from ¥150; ⏰4.30pm-12.30am) A famous Sapporo chain serving a variety of yakitori (skewers of grilled chicken) and grilled vegetables, Kushidori is usually packed with boisterous college kids and 20-somethings. While there is no English menu, you can simply point at what you want, and the chef will grill it for you – choose from either tare (sauce) or shio (salt). There are locations all around the city, including one just a few blocks north of JR Sapporo Station (look for the English sign).

★Kani-honke
SEAFOOD ¥¥¥

(札幌かに本家; ☎222-0018; N3W2 Chūō-ku; set courses from ¥4000; ⏰11.30am-10pm; 🚇) The frigid seas surrounding Hokkaidō are extremely bountiful and yield some of the tastiest crustaceans on the planet. There is no better place to dine on all manner of exotic crab than at the famous Kani-honke, which serves up elaborate kaiseki ryōri (Japanese cuisine following strict rules of etiquette) centred on these juicy little critters. Seasonal set courses are priced according to the size and rarity of the crab, so simply choose depending on how much you want to spend. Don't miss the opportunity to sample the tarabagani (red king crab), which is considered to be the most expensive yet most delicious decapod known to humankind.

🍷 Drinking & Nightlife

Sapporo-ites are famous for their love of the drink, though you can hardly blame them as the beer here really does seem to taste better. (If you want to drink delicious Sapporo lager straight from the source, don't miss Sapporo Beer-En.) While there are literally hundreds of bars and clubs scattered throughout the city, all of the action and nightlife revolves around Susukino, the largest entertainment district north of Tokyo.

The places listed are all within easy stumbling distance of the Susukino subway station, and are some of Sapporo's party landmarks, though you can always simply follow the crowds to whatever is new and trendy. Some bars and most clubs have a cover charge of ¥1000 to ¥3000 on Friday and Saturday nights, which often includes one or two drinks.

★TK6
BAR

(☎272-6665; www.tk6.jp; S2W6 Chūō-ku; ⏰4pm-late; 📶) Sapporo's top sports bar, TK6 keeps everybody bubbling with Happy Hour from 4pm to 7pm daily, free wi-fi for all patrons, and international sports events on the big screen. Get some tips on what to do in town from the locals, both Japanese and foreign. The bar food is as good as the beer.

DON'T MISS

SAPPORO BEER

Let's face it: 'Sapporo' means beer. After visiting Germany (and being favourably impressed), Kihachirō Ōkura returned and selected Sapporo as the lucky place to start what would become Japan's first beer brewery, founded in 1876.

⭐ **Sapporo Beer Garden** (サッポロビール園; www.sapporo-bier-garten.jp/foreign/english.php; N7E9 Higashi-ku; ◎beer garden 11.30am-10pm, tours 9am-3.40pm) **FREE**, part museum, part beer garden, is located in the original Sapporo Beer brewery, almost due east of JR Sapporo Station. Visitors wanting to belly up to the trough should take the free one-hour tour (recorded English commentary provided), which includes a tasting (¥200 per beer) and most likely a slight buzz! The adjoining beer garden has four restaurants spanning a variety of cuisines – purists should note that pints of Sapporo were meant to be enjoyed with the local grilled-lamb speciality, *jingisukan* (Genghis Khan). There is also a great gift shop selling beer memorabilia.

Take the Tōhō subway to the Higashi-Kuyakusho-mae stop (exit 4), or Chūō Bus Higashi 63 and get off at the Kitahachi Higashinana (N8E7) stop. While tour reservations aren't essential, they're not a bad idea – if you don't speak Japanese, ask tourist information or your hotel staff to phone ahead for you.

Hokkaidō Brewery (サッポロビール北海道工場; ☑011-748-1876; www.sapporobeer.jp; Toiso 542-1; ◎tours 9.15am-3.45pm) **FREE**, which is the current brewing and bottling facility, is a 40-minute train ride from Sapporo. A must for diehard fans of Sapporo beer, the mammoth production plant seems more like something out of a James Bond movie rather than a place where beer is made. Technicians in white lab coats peer into test tubes; immaculate stainless-steel tanks are covered with computerised gauges and dials; and video cameras monitor the bottles as they whizz by. The 40-minute tour is self-guided and English is minimal, but you'll be rewarded with a refreshing 20 minutes to tipple at the end. Admission is free, but you need to make reservations by 5pm the day before.

Take the JR Chitose line towards the airport, and get off at the Sapporo Beer Teien Station.

buddhabar 280
BAR

(☑261-2806; www.buddha-bar280.com; S3W6 Chūō-ku; ◎6pm-2am) Buddhabar 280 is one of those bars that anyone can appreciate. A relaxed, convivial atmosphere, tasty Chinese dishes and surfing videos in the background. Needless to say, there's a buddha or two keeping an eye on things. Hata-san runs a great bar and his staff are having as much fun as the patrons.

500 Bar
BAR

(ファイブハンドレッドバー; S4W2 Chūō-ku, 1st fl, Hoshi Bldg; ◎6pm-5am Mon-Sat, to 2am Sun & holidays) It's usually packed, even on weekdays, with a mix of foreign and local clientele. Every drink on the menu here is ¥500, hence the name (pronounced *'gohyaku-baa'*). This is one of the franchise's several locations in Sapporo, not far from the Susukino subway station's Nanboku line.

Booty
CLUB

(ブーティー; www.booty-disco.com; S7W4 Chūō-ku; ◎8pm-close) There's always plenty of booty at this discotheque and lounge bar, which serves up Western-style fast food alongside urban beats. The rotating schedule – which you can check out online – incorporates the best in hip-hop, R&B and reggae, and attracts a young, clubby crowd.

alife
CLUB

(エーライフ; www.alife.jp/pc; S4W6 Chūō-ku, B1F Tailki Bldg; ◎8pm-close) This well-heeled club brings a bit of the Tokyo high life to the far north. Although the thermometer might be dropping outside, it's always hot and heavy in this cavernous joint, so dress to impress!

ⓘ Information

CONSULATES

Australian Consulate (☑242-4381; www.australia.or.jp/en/consular/sapporo; N5W6 Chūō-ku Sapporo Centre Bldg F17)

Russian Consulate (☑561-3171; http://sapporo.rusembassy.org; S14W12 Chūō-ku)

US Consulate (☑641-1115; http://sapporo.usconsulate.gov/; N1W28 Chūō-ku)

MEDICAL SERVICES

If you have a medical emergency, dial ☑119.

For good advice on health in Hokkaidō, visit www.healthhokkaido.com.

Medical Plaza Sapporo (メディカルプラザ札幌; ☑209-5410; www.medical-plaza.jp; N5W2 Chūō-ku) Conveniently located on the 7th and 8th floors of the JR Tower in JR Sapporo Station.

Sapporo City General Hospital (市立札幌病院; ☑726-2211; www.city.sapporo.jp/hospital; N11W13 1-1 Chūō-ku; ☺24hr) Offers 24-hour emergency care.

POST

Sapporo Central Post Office (札幌中央郵便局; Sapporo Chūō Yūbinkyoku; N6E1-2-1 Higashi-ku) This branch is located just east of JR Sapporo Station. Take the north exit, turn right, walk towards the giant white bowling pin, and the building is right across the first major intersection. Like many larger post offices, it is open evenings and weekends. The ATMs stay open longer than the window.

TOURIST INFORMATION

Hokkaidō-Sapporo Food & Tourist Information Centre (北海道さっぽろ「食と観光」情報館; ☑213-5088; www.welcome.city.sapporo.jp/english; JR Sapporo Station; ☺8.30am-8pm) Located on the ground floor of Sapporo Stellar Pl, inside JR Sapporo Station. This is the island's mother lode of tourist information, so stock up on maps, timetables, brochures and pamphlets, and be sure to make use of the friendly and helpful bilingual staff. JR also has English-speaking staff in here to answer your train questions.

Sapporo International Communication Plaza (札幌国際プラザ; ☑211-3678; www.plaza-sapporo.or.jp/english/index_e.html; N1W3 Chūō-ku, 3rd fl, MN Bldg; ☺9am-5.30pm Mon-Sat) Directly opposite the Sapporo Clock Tower (Tokei-dai), this place is set up to cater for the needs of foreign residents and visitors. There is an extensive list of English resources, free internet access and helpful, friendly staff.

TRAVEL AGENCIES

IACE Travel (IACE トラベル; ☑219-2796; www.iace.co.jp/english/sapporo; N3W3 Chūō-ku, 9th fl, Kita San Jō Bldg; ☺10am-7pm Mon-Fri, to 4pm Sat, closed Sun) A popular Japanese travel agency that also caters to foreigners, and is useful for making international travel arrangements.

JTB Shop (JTB ショップ; ☑241-6201; N3W3 Chūō-ku; ☺10am-7pm) This popular Japanese travel agency is useful for making domestic travel arrangements, including plane and train bookings.

ⓘ Getting There & Away

AIR

Sapporo's main airport is New Chitose Airport, about 40km southeast of the city. Domestic destinations include Tokyo, Osaka, Nagoya, Hiroshima and many others.

There's a smaller airport at **Okadama** (丘珠空港; Okadama Kūkō), about 10km north of the city, which has limited service to cities in Hokkaidō.

BUS

Highway buses connect Sapporo with the rest of Hokkaidō, and are generally cheaper than trains and even time-competitive on some routes. **Sapporo Eki-mae Bus Station** (札幌駅前バスターミナル) is the main terminal, just southeast of JR Sapporo Station, beneath Esta. The **Chūō Bus Station** (中央バスターミナル) and **Ōdōri Bus Centre** (大通バスターミナル) are also departure spots. At all three departure points you will find ticket booths from where you can purchase tickets to major cities throughout Hokkaidō.

Some sample destinations, which have frequent daily departures from Sapporo Eki-mae:

Asahikawa ¥2000, two hours

Furano ¥2100, three hours

Niseko ¥2300, three hours

Noboribetsu Onsen ¥2100, two hours

Tōya-ko Onsen ¥2700, 2¾ hours

Wakkanai ¥6000, six hours

From Chūō bus station there are a few departures a day to Abashiri (¥6210, 6¼ hours) and Obihiro (¥3670, 4¼ hours).

Buses to Hakodate depart from both the Chūō and Ōdōri bus stations (¥4680, 5¼ hours).

Discounted round-trip tickets are available for most routes.

CAR & MOTORCYCLE

The best place in Hokkaidō to pick up a rental car is at the New Chitose Airport. There are a dozen different companies located in the arrivals area on the 1st floor.

TRAIN

Getting to Sapporo by train is relatively easy. If you're coming from Honshū, the easiest way is to get to Aomori, the northern terminal for the Tohoku *shinkansen*. Once there, transfer to the JR Tsugaru Kaikyō line – trains run through the Seikan Tunnel between Aomori and Hakodate (¥5340, two hours), and then change to the JR Hakodate line between Hakodate and Sapporo (¥8590, 3½ hours).

The following are interesting overnight options for getting to Sapporo from Honshū:

➡ From Tokyo, the sleeper train **Hokutosei** (www2.jrhokkaido.co.jp/global/english/train/

tr017_01.html), taking 16 hours. One departure in both directions every evening.

➡ From Tokyo, the more luxurious (and costly!) sleeper **Cassiopeia** (www2.jrhokkaido.co.jp/global/english/train/tr016_01.html), taking 16 hours. Three evening departures in each direction every week.

➡ From Osaka, Japan's longest train route, the **Twilight Express** (www2.jrhokkaido.co.jp/global/english/train/tr018_01.html), taking 21 hours and covering 1500km.

Reservations for these overnight trains can be made at any JR ticket counter or travel agency. These trains are very popular and often booked solid, particularly in the summer months, so make a reservation as far in advance as possible. Additional payments are required for JR Pass holders.

ⓘ Getting Around

TO/FROM THE AIRPORT

New Chitose Airport is accessible from Sapporo by *kaisoku* train (¥1340, 35 minutes) or bus (¥1000, 1¼ hours). There are also convenient bus services connecting the airport to various Hokkaidō destinations including Niseko.

For Okadama airport, buses leave every 20 minutes or so from in front of the ANA ticket offices, opposite JR Sapporo Station (¥400, 30 minutes).

BUS & TRAM

JR Sapporo Station is the main terminus for local buses. From late April to early November, tourist buses loop through major sights and attractions between 9am and 5.30pm; a one-day pass costs ¥750, single trips are ¥200 (basic fee).

There is a single tram line in Sapporo that heads west from Ōdōri, turns south, then loops back to Susukino (すすきの). The fare is a flat ¥170.

SUBWAY

Sapporo's three subways are efficient. Fares start at ¥200 and one-day passes cost ¥800 (weekend-only passes are ¥500 per day). There are also ¥1000 day passes that include the tram and buses as well. The pay-in-advance non-rechargeable With You card (various denominations available) can be used on subways, buses, trams, and Jōtetsu and Chūō buses; unlike the one-day passes, it does not expire at midnight. There is also a rechargeable SAPICA card for subways only.

TAXI

Taxis are a quick and comfortable way to move around the city, but you'll pay substantially for the convenience factor. Flagfall is ¥650, which gives you 2km (1.5km after 11pm), after which the meter starts to clock an additional ¥90 for every 300m, or two minutes in traffic.

SOUTHERN HOKKAIDŌ

Southern Hokkaidō (道南; Dō-nan) is often bypassed entirely by Sapporo-bound travellers. That's a shame as Hakodate, a prominent Meiji-era port, is one of the most atmospheric cities in Hokkaidō and is certainly worth a visit. Dō-nan is also home to a couple of small but historically significant towns, which bear striking architectural reminders of the Edo period.

Hakodate 函館

📋 0138 / POP 288,000

Built on a narrow strip of land between Hakodate Harbour to the west and the Tsugaru Strait to the east, hourglass-shaped Hakodate is the southern gateway to the island of Hokkaidō. Under the Kanagawa Treaty of 1854, the city was one of the first ports to open itself up to international trade and, as such, hosted a small foreign community. Much of that influence can still be observed in the Motomachi district, a steep hillside that is sprinkled with wooden buildings and brick churches. You can also get a sense of the city's history by riding nostalgic trams through its orderly streets, or by watching the squid boats, with their traditional lantern lights, bob gently in the bay.

◉ Sights & Activities

Motomachi HISTORIC DISTRICT
(元町) On Mt Hakodate's lower slopes, this area is home to the lion's share of 19th-century sites, and commands stunning panoramic views of the bay.

To get to Motomachi, take tram 5 from the station and get off at the Suehiro-chō stop, then walk uphill for 10 minutes.

★ Old Public Hall of Hakodate Ward MUSEUM
(旧函館区公会堂; Kyū-Hakodate Kukōkaidō; 11-13 Motomachi; admission ¥300; ⊘9am-7pm) The old Public Hall of Hakodate Ward, built in 1910, is an ornate mansion awash in pale blues and yellows that reigns regally over the district. Inside are items of historical interest relating to the city, although the main appeal is the wonderful colonial-style architecture.

Old English Consulate MUSEUM
(旧イギリス領事館; Kyū-Igirisu Ryōjikan; 33-14 Motomachi; admission ¥300, afternoon tea from

Central Hakodate

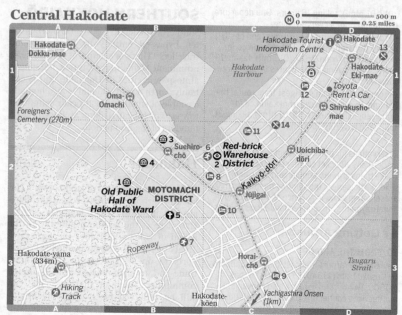

Central Hakodate

¥550; ⊙9am-7pm) From 1913 to 1934, this whitewashed mansion served as the British consulate, though today it's primarily used as a tea salon for sightseers in need of some bergamot-scented afternoon respite.

Russian Orthodox Church   CHURCH
(函館ハリストス正教会; Hakodate Harisutosu Seikyōkai; 3-13 Motomachi; admission ¥200; ⊙10am-5pm Mon-Fri, 10am-4pm Sat, 1-4pm Sun) Dating from 1916, this beautiful old Russian Orthodox church is adorned with distinctive copper domes and spires.

Foreigners' Cemetery   CEMETERY
(外国人墓地; Gaikokujin Bochi; ⊙dawn-dusk) The Foreigners' Cemetery, an interesting slice of local history, has the graves of sailors, clergy and others who unfortunately died far away from their homelands. Many of the graves are marked with English, Russian or French inscriptions.

**Hakodate Museum of
Northern Peoples**   MUSEUM
(函館市北方民族資料館; Hakodate-shi Hoppō-minzoku Shiryōkan; ☎22-2148; 21-7 Suehiro-chō;

admission ¥300; ⏱9am-7pm) The Hakodate City Museum of Northern Peoples is a recommended place to learn about the Ainu and their material culture. English signs have been added to some exhibits.

Hakodate-yama   MOUNTAIN

(函館山) This small mountain (334m) offers a memorable view of Hakodate, especially at night when the twinkling city lights contrast the dark waters. A **ropeway** (ロープウェイ; ☑23-3105; www.334.co.jp/eng; one-way/return ¥640/1160; ⏱10am-10pm) whisks you to the top in a few minutes.

Take tram 2 or 5 to the Jūjigai stop, and walk up to the ropeway platform. Alternatively, a summit-bound bus (¥360, 30 minutes) leaves directly from the station, and stops at several viewing places as it winds to the top. Those wanting to rough it can take the **hiking track** (from May to late October).

★Hakodate Morning Market   MARKET

(函館朝市; Hakodate Asa-ichi; ⏱5am-noon) **FREE** Located just to the south of JR Hakodate Station, this market is a great place for hungry seafood lovers. Like tightly packed ammo,

freshly caught squid glisten in ice-stuffed Styrofoam. Most of the live commerce is over by 8am, but you can still pick up snacks and souvenirs during closing hours.

★Red-brick Warehouse District   DISTRICT

(赤レンガ倉庫) Hakodate's red-brick warehouses were built around 1907, and after renovation now house food markets, cafes, shops and galleries. This extremely popular part of town sits on the waterfront between JR Hakodate Station and Motomachi. If your feet get a tad tired, give them a rest in the *ashi-yu* (foot-bath) out the back of La Vista Hakodate Bay Hotel.

Bluemoon Cruises   CRUISE

(函館ベイクルーズ・ブルームーン; ☑26-6161; www.hakodate-factory.com/bluemoon) Based in a wharf in the Red-brick Warehouse District, Bluemoon Cruises offers 30-minute cruises (¥1600) that visit the historic harbour, and one-hour night cruises (¥2500).

Goryō-kaku Fort   FORT

(五稜郭) **FREE** Japan's first Western-style fort was built in 1864 in the shape of a five-pointed star (*goryō-kaku* means 'five-sided

---

> **WORTH A TRIP**
>
> ## MATSUMAE & ESASHI
>
> On this interesting day trip you can visit the only castle on Hokkaidō, explore the regal dwellings of the island's former fishing barons, and be back in Hakodate with enough time to watch the sunset from atop Hakodate-yama.
>
> ### Matsumae
>
> Prior to the start of the Meiji era, this town was the stronghold of the Matsumae clan and the centre of Japanese political power in Hokkaidō. As a result, Matsumae (松前) is home to the only castle on the island. **Matsumae-jō** (松前城; admission ¥270; ⏱9am-5pm mid-Apr–Dec) dates from the 19th century, and currently houses feudal relics and a small collection of Ainu items. Around 10,000 cherry trees blossom in the park around the castle for about a month from late April to mid-May.
>
> Frequent *tokkyū* (limited express) on the JR Esashi line run between Hakodate and Kikonai (¥1620, 35 minutes). Regular buses run between JR Kikonai Station and Matsumae (¥1220, 1½ hours).
>
> ### Esashi
>
> If Matsumae was Hokkaidō's Edo-period political centre, then Esashi (江差) was its economic lifeblood. Prior to the depletion of fishing stocks in the early 20th century, a number of *nishingoten* (herring barons' homes) dominated the shoreline. Today several of these buildings remain – **Yokoyama-ke** (横山家; admission ¥300; ⏱9am-5pm) and **Nakamura-ke** (中村家住宅; admission ¥300; ⏱9am-5pm) in particular are well preserved. The **Hiyama District Office Building**, designed by a Russian architect and constructed in 1887, is also distinctive.
>
> Frequent *tokkyū* on the JR Esashi line run between Hakodate and Kikonai (¥1620, 35 minutes). Kikonai is connected to Esashi by the JR Esahi line – a few daily *kaisoku* (rapid express trains) ply this route (¥900, one hour).

fort'), and was designed to trap attackers in deadly crossfire. Nothing remains of the actual fort structure, but the landscaped grounds and moat are picturesque, and 1600 cherry trees make this a great spot in spring. The 98m **Goryō-kaku Tower** (☑51-4785; www.goryokaku-tower.co.jp; admission ¥840; ⊙8am-7pm) was opened in 2006 so that the five-storied star can be viewed from above. Take tram 2 or 5 to the Goryōkaku-kōen-mae stop.

Yachigashira Onsen　　　　ONSEN
(谷地頭温泉; 20-7 Yachigashira; admission ¥390; ⊙6am-9.30pm, closed every 2nd & 4th Tue) On the southern edge of Hakodate-yama is this enormous hot spring, one of Hokkaidō's oldest, with dark iron-laden water. To get here, take tram 2 to Yachigashira, the final stop. On foot, continue to the first intersection and then turn right – you'll see the public bathhouse complex on the left shortly after you turn.

🎎 Festivals & Events

Hakodate Goryō-kaku Matsuri　　HISTORY
(函館五稜郭祭り) Held on the third weekend in May, this festival features a parade of townsfolk dressed in the uniforms of the soldiers who took part in the Meiji Restoration battle of 1868.

Hakodate Port Festival　　　　PORT
(函館港祭り; Hakodate Minato Matsuri) During the Hakodate Port Festival in early August, groups of seafood-fortified locals (reportedly 10,000 of them) move like waves doing an energetic squid dance.

🛏 Sleeping

Hakodate Youth Guesthouse　　HOSTEL ¥
(函館ユースゲストハウス; ☑26-7892; www12.ocn.ne.jp/~hakodate; 17-6 Hōraimachi; dm Oct-Jun ¥3800, Jul & Sep ¥4200, Aug ¥4500; @ 🖶) This guesthouse is a relaxed and affordable base for budget travellers. It's conveniently located near the Hōrai-chō tram stop – after getting off the tram, turn left at the first light, then go past two more lights and turn right. The guesthouse is across the street from a supermarket and car park.

B&B Hakodate-mura　　　　PENSION ¥¥
(Ｂ＆Ｂペンションはこだて村; ☑22-8105; www.bb-hakodatemura.com; 16-12 Suehiro-chō; s/d incl breakfast ¥6280/11,800; @ 🛜) In a great location near the corner of the harbour, everything is close here. Expect a friendly welcome and English speakers at this B&B which has restaurant and lounge on the ground floor, and rooms upstairs. Plenty of room options – check out the website.

Tōyoko Inn Hakodate Eki-mae Asaichi　　　　HOTEL ¥¥
(東横イン函館駅前朝市; ☑23-1045; www.toyoko-inn.com/e_hotel/00063/index.html; 22-7 Ōtemachi; s/d Nov-May ¥4210/6825, Jun-Oct ¥5460/7980; @ 🛜) Hakodate's version of the Tōyoko Inn is an affordable choice for budget-conscious travellers in need of private space. It's located just steps away from the morning market, and only three minutes on foot from JR Hakodate Station.

★**La Vista Hakodate Bay Hotel**　HOTEL ¥¥¥
(ラビスタ函館ベイ; ☑23-6111; www.hotespa.net/hotels/lahakodate/english_room.html; 12-6 Toyokawacho; r from ¥13,300; @ 🛜) This excellent upmarket hotel benefits from its waterfront district location. Rooms are smallish but attention to detail is excellent. There is a rooftop onsen and spa complex, complete with soaking tubs overlooking the mountains and the bay.

La Villa Concordia　　　　HOTEL ¥¥¥
(ヴィラ・コンコルディア; ☑24-5300; http://villa-concordia.com; 3-5 Suehiro; r from ¥42,000; @ 🛜) Although it operates as a full-service resort and spa, La Villa Concordia is packaged as a boutique hotel, with customised attention throughout your stay – even if Japanese isn't your first language. Rooms range in size from deluxe studios with kitchenettes to full-on suites overlooking the harbour. Round out your stay with a pampering beauty treatment and a proper meal of Italian-French fusion. The property is located one block from the Suehiro-chō 3 traffic light; look for the white neoclassical structure.

🍴 Eating & Drinking

Daimon Yokochō　　　FOOD STALLS ¥
(大門横丁; ☑24-0033; 7-5 Matsukaze-chō) Head east from JR Hakodate Station for five minutes – two blocks past Wako – to find this collection of food stalls with all sorts of cuisine on offer. Hakodate is known for its *shio-rāmen* with a clear, salty soup. There are plenty of opportunities to try it here.

★**Hakodate Beer**　　　　PUB ¥¥
(はこだてビール; ☑23-8000; www.hakodate-factory.com/beer; 5-22 Ōtemachi; dishes from ¥650; ⊙11am-10pm; ⓓ) Scan the English menu at Hakodate Beer and choose from

a variety of microbrews – from cold ales and golden wheat beers to dark stouts – to complement homemade pizzas and various items from the grill including fresh-caught squid and locally made sausages.

Bluemoon Diner BUFFET ¥¥
(ブルームーンダイナー; ☑24-8104; lunch ¥1500, dinner ¥1980; ☺lunch 11.30am-2pm, dinner 5-8pm) Head down to the Red-brick Warehouse district to find Hakodate's top buffet right next to the Bluemoon Cruise boats. Enjoy yourself all the more with a ¥1200 drink-all-you-like deal!

ℹ Information

Hakodate Tourist Information Centre (函館市観光案内所; ☑23-544; ☺9am-7pm Apr-Oct, to 5pm Nov-Mar) Inside JR Hakodate Station, the information centre has plenty of English brochures and maps.

ℹ Getting There & Away

AIR

From Hakodate Airport, just a few kilometres east of the city centre, there are international flights to Seoul, and domestic flights to various destinations including Sapporo, Tokyo and Kansai.

Frequent buses run direct between Hakodate Airport and JR Hakodate Station (¥300, 20 minutes), or you can simply take a taxi (¥2000).

BOAT

Tsugaru Kaikyō Ferry (津軽海峡フェリー; www.tsugarukaikyo.co.jp/global/english/) operates ferries (departing year-round) between Aomori and Hakodate (from ¥2700, 3¾ hours), and between Hakodate and Ōma (¥2200, 1¾ hours) on the Shimokita Peninsula. The ferry terminal, where you also buy your tickets, is on the northeast corner of Hakodate Harbour.

Regular shuttle buses (¥250, 15 minutes) and taxis (¥1500) run between the ferry terminal and the train station.

BUS

There are daily buses between JR Hakodate Station and Sapporo's Chūō bus station and Ōdōri bus centre (¥4680, 5¼ hours).

CAR & MOTORCYCLE

If you've just arrived in Hokkaidō, Hakodate is a good place to pick up a rental car and start your road-tripping adventure across the island. **Toyota Rent-a-Car** (トヨタレンタカー函館駅前; ☑26-0100; www.rent.toyota.co.jp; 19-2 Ōtemachi; ☺8am-8pm) has a branch office a few blocks southwest of the station. **Nippon Rent a Car** (www.nrh.co.jp) is right outside the station.

SEIKAN TUNNEL

A modern marvel of Japanese engineering, this railway tunnel travels beneath the Tsugaru Strait, connecting the islands of Honshū and Hokkaidō. With a total length of 53.85km, including a 240m-deep and 23.3km-long undersea portion, the Seikan Tunnel (青函トンネル) is the deepest and longest undersea tunnel in the world.

TRAIN

The JR Tsugaru Kaikyō line runs between Hakodate and Aomori (¥5340, two hours) via the Seikan Tunnel. The JR Hakodate line runs between Hakodate and Sapporo (¥8590, 3½ hours).

A combination of *tokkyū* (limited express) and *kaisoku* (rapid express) trains run on the JR Hakodate line between Hakodate and Niseko via Oshamambe (¥5410, 3½ hours).

ℹ Getting Around

Single-trip fares on trams and buses are generally between ¥200 and ¥250, and are determined by how long you ride. One-day (¥1000) passes offer unlimited rides on both trams and buses (¥600 for tram alone), and are available at the tourist information centre or from the drivers. These passes are also good for the bus to the peak of Hakodate-yama.

Ōnuma Quasi-National Park 大沼国定公園

Only about 25km north of Hakodate, Ōnuma Kōen is the coastal city's version of a mountain and lake playground. Sitting beneath the impressive volcano, **Komaga-take** (駒ケ岳; 1131m) are the three lakes, **Ōnuma** (大沼), **Konuma** (小沼) and **Jun-sainuma** (じゅんさい沼), easily accessed by train or car.

International visitors have been enjoying Ōnuma since the early Meiji era when Hakodate was one of the few Japanese ports open for foreign trade. Members of the Italian and German royal families turned up in the late 1800s, but things really took off when the Emperor Meiji came for a look in 1881, attracting national attention.

These days visitors show up to cruise on the lakes, cycle around them and explore Ōnuma's many small islands on bridged footpaths. The park is perfect for a family fun day out.

Ōnuma Cruises (大沼遊船; ☎0138-67-2229; www.onuma-park.com; cruise ¥960) runs pleasant popular 30-minute cruises out on the lake and also rents out rowing dinghies, Swan-shaped pedalboats and fishing boats.

Rental bicycles (¥500 per hour; ¥1020 per day) are available outside JR Ōnuma Kōen Station and cycling the 14km around Ōnuma is a good option. Rental Segway are also available. A series of linked walking paths around Ōnuma's small islands start not far from the train station.

While it is possible to hike up Komagatake on the Akaigawa Tozan-dō (赤井川登山道), the high peaks are off limits because of ongoing volcanic activity.

For those who get a bit hot and thirsty, a five-minute walk from JR Ōnuma Kōen Station will bring you to Ōnuma Beer (大沼ビール; ☎0138-67-1611; www.onumabeer.co.jp; ⊙9am-4pm), a top spot to relax and try the highly recommended local brews.

In the yellow building right next to JR Ōnuma Kōen Station is B&B Chairo-tori (B&B茶色い鳥; ☎0138-67-2231; per person without/with breakfast ¥3800/4500), a good place to stay. The owner speaks English and greets international visitors enthusiastically. Rooms are Japanese-style with shared facilities. There are eating options around the station.

The Ōnuma Tourist Information Centre (大沼観光案内所; ☎0138-67-2170; www.onuma-guide.com; ⊙8.30am-6pm), next to the station, has helpful staff and good English information.

JR Ōnuma Kōen Station is on the JR Hakodate line. Trains head south to Hakodate (¥1440, 20 minutes) and north to Sapporo (¥7870, three hours). If you've got your own wheels, Rte 5 runs right through the park.

CENTRAL HOKKAIDŌ

Central Hokkaidō (道央; Dō-ō) is where Hokkaidō garners its deserved reputation for stunning national parks, world-class ski slopes and rustic hot spring villages. Although the scenic port town of Otaru is the largest population centre, the focus in winter is on Niseko, where legendary powder attracts skiers and snowboarders from across the globe. Shikotsu-Tōya National Park offers up caldera lakes, a towering Fuji-san look-alike and steaming onsen towns.

Otaru 小樽

☎0134 / POP 140,000

One of Hokkaidō's most popular tourist destinations for Japanese visitors, Otaru is a romantic port town steeped in a rich history that dates back to its glory days as a major herring centre. Otaru was the terminal station for Hokkaidō's first railroad, and today nostalgic warehouses and buildings still line the picturesque canal district. There are great options for foodies, and if you're into music boxes or any kind of glass object imaginable, you'll go gaga in Otaru.

JR Otaru Station is up the hill and inland from the canal and port. Head out the main doors and straight down Chūo-dōri for 10 minutes to get to the canal.

⊙ Sights

★ Otaru Canal   CANAL
(小樽運河) Walk beneath the old Victorian-style gas lamps lining this historic canal, and admire the charismatic warehouses dating from the late 19th and early 20th centuries.

Nihon Yūsen Building   BUILDING
(旧日本郵船株式会社小樽支店; admission ¥300; ⊙9.30am-5pm Tue-Sun) Lying behind the park at the northern end of the canal is the old Nihon Yūsen Company Building. Before the collapse of the herring industry, much of Hokkaidō's shipping orders were processed here. The interior of the building has been restored to its former grandeur, and provides a revealing look at the opulence of the era.

Otaru Museum   MUSEUM
(小樽市総合博物館; admission ¥300; ⊙9.30am-5pm Tue-Sun) This small but engaging museum is housed in a restored warehouse dating from 1893, and has displays on Hokkaidō's natural history, some Ainu relics, and various special exhibitions on herring, ceramics and literature.

Nichigin-dōri   STREET
(日銀道り) Once known as the 'Wall Street of the North', Nichigin-dōri is lined with elegant buildings that speak to Otaru's past life as a prominent financial centre.

Old Bank of Japan Building   BUILDING
(日本銀行旧小樽支店金融資料館; ⊙9.30am-5pm Tue-Sun) FREE Don't miss the old Bank of Japan (日本銀行), a classic brick building that was designed by the same architect responsible for Tokyo Station. The exterior is

marked by owl keystones, which pay homage to the Ainu guardian deity, while an impressive 100m-high ceiling highlights the interior.

Otaru Music Box Museum MUSEUM
(小樽オルゴール堂; ☎21-3101; www.otaruorgel.co.jp; ⊙9am-6pm) **FREE** At the Marchen Crossroads (メルヘン交差点), a 15-minute walk east of the canal, the main music box museum is mind-boggling. So is the fact that they've got another five buildings about town! There are over 25,000 music boxes and if you're really keen, you can make your own.

🛏 Sleeping

Otarunai Backpackers'
Hostel Morinoki HOSTEL ¥
(おたるないバックパッカーズホステル杜の樹; ☎23-2175; www.infotaru.net; 4-15 Aioi-chō; dm ¥3200; @ 🛜) This is a great little backpacker spot that is worlds apart from your usual Japan YH offerings. Accommodation is in fairly simple male and female dormitories, though guests are treated to kitchen, laundry and internet facilities, as well as bilingual staff, communal lounges, and a laidback and congenial vibe. The hostel is about a 20-minute walk from JR Otaru Station.

★ **Hotel Vibrant Otaru** HOTEL ¥¥
(ホテルヴィブラントオタル; ☎31-3939; www.vibrant-otaru.jp/en/index.html; s/d from ¥5500/6500, vault r from ¥10,500; @ 🛜) A stylish renovation of a historic Otaru bank resulted in this justifiably 'vibrant hotel', which is located across the road from the main post office. The lobby is very attractive with period-piece furniture, including wrought-iron tables. For a memorable night's stay, shell out a bit of extra cash and bed down in the old bank vault!

Hotel Nord Otaru HOTEL ¥¥
(ホテルノルド小樽; ☎24-0500; www.hotelnord.co.jp/en/index.php; 1-4-16 Ironai; s/d from ¥7350/12,600; @ 🛜) The Hotel Nord is a European-style hotel that fronts the warehouses along Otaru Canal. Rooms are priced according to size and view – the larger, canal-facing rooms are by far the most atmospheric.

Ginrinsō RYOKAN ¥¥¥
(銀鱗荘; ☎54-7010; www.ginrinsou.com; 1-1 Sakura; s/d with meals from ¥68,295/105,3000; @ 🛜) Part of the Luxury Ryokan Collection, this is one of Hokkaidō's most spectacular accommodation options, and a worthwhile splurge if you want to experience a living piece of history. Ginrinsō was originally constructed in 1873 as a herring estate, though in 1938 it began a new life as a top-end ryokan. Perched high on a bluff in Otaru Chikko, Ginrinsō stands like a sentry guarding the rocky coastline. The property is located south of Otaru proper in close proximity to Otaru Chikko Station, but the staff can arrange transport from either Sapporo or Otaru with advance notice.

🍴 Eating

★ **Kita-no-aisukurīmu Yasan** ICE CREAM ¥
(北のアイスクリーム屋さん; ☎23-8983; 1-2-18 Ironai; ice cream from ¥350; ⊙9.30am-7pm; 🍴) Housed in a converted warehouse just back from the canal (look for the ice-cream banner), this legendary Otaru ice-cream parlour scoops up some seriously stomach-turning flavours. If you're up to the challenge, you can sample *nattō* (fermented soy beans), tofu, crab, sea urchin, beer and even a jet-black scoop of squid ink.

Uminekoya SEAFOOD ¥¥
(海猫屋; ☎32-2914; 2-2-14 Ironai; dishes from ¥750; ⊙lunch & dinner; 🍴) Housed in a crumbling brick warehouse laced with vines of ivy, this famous bar-restaurant across from the museum has been the setting for several novels of Japanese literary fame. The English menu helps with the ordering, though it's best to ask the waiter for their *osusume* (recommendation), as the catch of the day and some local sake is generally what you're after here.

Otaru Sushi-kō SUSHI ¥¥
(小樽すし耕; ☎21-5678; 2-2-6 Ironai; sushi set from ¥1470; ⊙noon-8.30pm; 🍴) For Japanese travellers, eating in Otaru is *all* about sushi. Local specialities include *sake* (salmon), *ikura* (salmon roe), *uni* and *kani*. This tiny grey-brick warehouse is a block and a half back and one west from the Canal Plaza Information Centre.

🍷 Drinking

★ **Otaru Sōko No 1** BREW PUB
(小樽倉庫 No.1; 5-4 Minato-machi; dishes from ¥800; ⊙11am-10pm) Housed in a converted warehouse on the harbour side of the canal, Sōku No 1 offers a nice selection of microbrewed drafts, plus German culinary fare to complement its Bavarian decor. Look for the 'Otaru Beer' sign.

🛍 Shopping

Kitaichi Glass　　　　　　　　GLASS

(北一硝子; www.kitaichiglass.co.jp; ⊙8.45am-6pm) A 15-minute walk east of the canal area, the Kitaichi Glass area virtually fills a street with 16 shops, galleries, cafes and museums with everything imaginable made of glass.

ℹ Information

Otaru Station Tourist Information Centre

(小樽駅観光案内所; ☑29-1333; ⊙9am-6pm) If coming by train, drop in here and pick up good maps and information in English.

Canal Plaza Tourist Information Centre (運河プラザ観光案内所; ☑33-1661; ⊙9am-6pm) A 10-minute walk straight down Chūō-dōri from JR Otaru Station will bring you to the canal. On the corner at the bottom, this place is housed in Otaru's oldest warehouse. All sorts of information is available here.

ℹ Getting There & Away

BOAT

Shin-Nihonkai Ferries (新日本海フェリー; ☑22-6191; www.snf.jp) run between Otaru and Niigata, Tsuruga (Fukui-ken) and Maizuru (Kyoto-fu). Check the website for the latest details. These ferries, which operate on the Japan Sea side of Japan, are good options for getting between Hokkaidō and Honshū.

To get to the ferry terminal, take the bus from stop 4 in front of JR Otaru Station (¥210, 30 minutes).

TRAIN

There are hourly *kaisoku* on the JR Hakodate line between Otaru and Sapporo (¥620, 40 minutes). Trains also continue on the same line to Niseko (¥1410, two hours).

Niseko　　　　　　ニセコ

☑0136 / POP 4650

Hokkaidō is dotted with world-class ski resorts, but the reigning prince of powder is unquestionably Niseko. There are four interconnected resorts here, offering more than 800 skiable hectares along the eastern side of the mountain Niseko Annupuri. Soft and light powdery snow and an annual average snowfall of more than 15m make Niseko extremely popular with international skiers. Many own second homes here – resulting in a diverse dining and nightlife scene that is atypical of far-flung rural Japan.

But Niseko is not just about winter. Growing efforts to turn the area into a year-round resort are reaping rewards and visitors are also turning up for the hiking, biking, rafting, canoeing, fishing and other outdoor opportunities. Think of Niseko as Japan's version of Whistler, Aspen or Queenstown.

The first thing you'll be struck by in Niseko is the perfect conical volcano Yōtei-zan (羊蹄山; 1898m), which looms ominously across the valley and provides a dramatic backdrop unlike any other.

👁 Sights & Activities

★ **Niseko United**　　　SKIING, SNOWBOARDING

(ニセコユナイテッド; www.niseko.ne.jp/en; 8hr/1-day pass ¥4900/5900; ⊙8.30am-9.30pm Nov-Apr) Niseko United is the umbrella name for four resorts, namely Niseko Annupuri, Niseko Village, Grand Hirafu and Hanazono. What makes Niseko United stand out from the competition is that you can ski or snowboard on all four slopes by purchasing a single all-mountain pass. This electronic tag gives you access to 18 lifts and gondolas, 60 runs, as well as free rides on the inter-mountain shuttle bus. If you're planning on skiing for several days, a week or even the season, you can also buy discounted multi-day passes.

Rental equipment is of very high quality, and can be picked up virtually everywhere at affordable prices. Rental shops also typically have a few foreign staff on hand to help English-speaking customers. A high percentage of visitors to Niseko are from Australia, which means that English is everywhere you look and listen.

At the base, most of the après-ski action is in Hirafu, though luxury seekers harbour in the Hilton at Niseko Village, and locals tend to stick to Annupuri.

Communal bathing in an onsen after a day on the slopes is your chance to jump into Japanese culture. The scene is even more surreal during a blizzard when frozen flakes melt mid-air into steamy vapour clouds. Most hotels either have an onsen on the premises, or can point you in the direction of the nearest bathhouse.

Niseko Adventure Centre (NAC)　　OUTDOORS

(ニセコアドベンチャーセンター; ☑23-2093; www.nac-web.com/e_index.htm) These guys are the innovators in Japan, following examples set in other mountain resorts throughout the world. In winter they offer everything from ski and snowboard lessons

RUSUTSU

Compared to neighbouring Niseko, Rusutsu (ルスツ; population 2000) is much less developed, and pales in size and scope. On the flip side, however, the slopes aren't nearly as crowded, and the lack of foreigners results in a decidedly more traditional ambience.

There is some serious powder waiting for you at the **Rusutsu Resort** (ルスツリゾート; ☑0136-46-3111; http://en.rusutsu.co.jp; lift tickets day/night ¥5300/2200; r from ¥9500; ⊘day 9am-5pm, night 4-9pm Nov-Apr), which boasts well-groomed trails and fantastic tree runs. The resort caters equally to skiers and snowboarders, has trails of all difficulty levels, 18 lifts, more than two dozen runs, a 100m half pipe and numerous off-piste options. The lodge offers Western-style rooms, while larger suites overlook the slopes in the modern tower.

The resort website is easy to follow in English and gives you all the options. Book in advance as discounted packages including room, lift ticket and meal plan are often available.

If you're staying in Niseko, Rusutsu is only a 20- to 30-minute drive away. Various operators offer Rusutsu day trips if you don't have your own wheels.

During the ski season, several companies run highway buses from Sapporo and New Chitose Airport to Niseko via Rusutsu (¥1990, two hours). If you're driving, Rte 230 runs between Sapporo and Tōya-ko via Rusutsu.

to snowshoe and backcountry tours. In summer they offer rafting, hiking, sea kayaking and canyoning tours...plus more! Based in a massive purpose-built building in Hirafu, there's even an 11m indoor climbing wall and Jojo's Café & Restaurant on the top floor. Definitely check it all out online before you go.

Niseko Annupuri Gondola   GONDOLA
(ニセコアンヌプリゴンドラ; ☑58-2080; http://annupuri.info; one-way/return ¥720/1200; ⊘9am-4.30pm) The gondola at Annupuri doesn't just run in winter. Summer visitors can ride it up to the 1000m viewing platform in 10 minutes from the skifield base. The views are brilliant, plus energetic types can go hiking from there. One option is to hike over to the Hirafu Summer Gondola and use the round-trip portion of your ticket to take that down.

Niseko Circuit Hike   HIKING
(ニセコサーキットハイキング) Summer is the best time of year to tackle some of the area's challenging wilderness hikes. The 16km Niseko Circuit that starts around the back of Niseko Annupuri at Goshiki Onsen is a good one. Fully described in Lonely Planet's *Hiking in Japan*, it takes six to seven hours, and the trailhead is accessible by local bus lines. From Goshiki Onsen (五色温泉), it climbs Nitonupuri (ニトヌプリ; 1080m), Chisenupuri (チセヌプリ; 1134m), then rounds the ponds Chō-numa (長沼) and Ō-numa (大沼) and finishes back at Goshiki Onsen.

From Goshiki Onsen, you can also hike up the back of Niseko Annupuri (ニセコアンヌプリ; 1308m) in 1½ to two hours. If it's a clear day, the panorama at the top will be very impressive, looking across the valley to Yōtei-zan. You can then hike down to the top of the Annupuri or Hirafu summer gondolas or down into Hirafu itself.

Onsen Options   ONSEN
Niseko has a brochure with 25 onsen options in the area, be they for use in winter or summer. Prices are generally around ¥500 to ¥700 per person. Winter visitors may like to opt for luxury at the Hilton Niseko Village (¥1000) or at the Niseko Grand Hotel (¥700), while those with their own wheels in summer will love Niimi Onsen (¥500) and Goshiki Onsen (¥600), both away in the mountains to the west of Niseko Annupuri and its skifields.

Niseko Green Bikes   CYCLING
(ニセコグリーンバイク; ☑44-2121; ⊘9am-6pm Apr-Oct) 🚲 FREE Enjoy cycling around Niseko on a free bicycle for the day! Pick up a bike at JR Niseko Station and return it at any of six 'Green Bike Stations' while following recommended courses.

Milk Kōbō (Milk Factory)   GALLERY
(ミルク工房; ☑44-3734; www.milk-kobo.com; ⊘9.30am-6pm) On the road up to Niseko Village, this complex of milk-related shops and galleries is a popular spot. What they're selling is made on-site – there's the Cake Corner, Ice-cream Corner, Yoghurt factory,

Coffee Shop (using local milk of course!) and they've expanded out into vegetables, souvenirs and the Prativo Restaurant. All under the gaze of Yotei-zan.

🛏 Sleeping

Niseko proper is spread out along the base of the four slopes. The closer you get to the slopes themselves, the more options you'll have. Hirafu and Annupuri host the vast majority of accommodation, while Niseko Village is centred on the upmarket Hilton. Most places provide pick-up and drop-off for the slopes in winter, or you can take buses and shuttles. It's strongly recommended that you book well in advance in winter.

Youth Hostel Karimpani Niseko   HOSTEL ¥
(ユースホステルカンパリ・ニセコ藤山; ☑/fax 44-1171; http://karimpani-niseko.jimdo.com/english/; 336 Aza Niseko; dm ¥3300, breakfast/dinner ¥500/1200; P@🌐) In an 80-year old converted schoolhouse, Max and Yūko's place is super-friendly and clean. Old classrooms now house dorms and concerts are held regularly in the gymnasium. The meals are first class! The family lived in New Zealand for five years and they speak excellent English. They'll do transfers for free – a five-minute drive to the Annupuri slopes.

Eki-no-yado Hirafu   MINSHUKU ¥
(駅の宿ひらふ; ☑22-1956; hirafu-eki.com; per person with/without 2 meals ¥5500/3500; @) An excellent budget choice with character in an operating JR train station! Yes, that means trains rolling through every hour or so. Shared rooms are upstairs in the station building while downstairs is a compact dining room. The bath is a big hollowed-out log – if you leave the door open you can lie back and watch the trains pass by 5m away! They do skifield transfers for ¥150. And, of course, you can come by train!

Niseko Annupuri Youth Hostel   HOSTEL ¥
(ニセコアンヌプリユースホステル; ☑58-2084; www.annupuri-yh.com; 470-4 Niseko; dm with/without 2 meals ¥5380/3360; P🌐) This mountain lodge constructed entirely from hardwood sits conveniently close to the Annupuri ski grounds. Guests congregate in front of the fire, swapping ski tips and tucking into delicious meals.

Jam Garden   PENSION ¥¥
(ジャムガーデン; ☑22-6676; www.jamgarden.com; 37-89 Kabayama; r per person incl 2 meals ¥8000; P🌐) Not far from the ski lifts at Hirafu, this deluxe farmhouse comes complete with its own Jacuzzi and sauna. Western-style rooms and country cooking are also on offer once you pry yourself away from the nearby slopes of Hirafu.

Yumoto Niseko Prince Hotel   HOTEL ¥¥¥
(湯元ニセコプリンスホテルひらふ亭; ☑23-2239; http://hirafutei.info/en; per person incl 2 meals from ¥11,760; P@🌐) If you're after comfort and convenience in the heart of Hirafu, this is it. You can virtually ski in the front door, there are both Western- and Japanese-style rooms, and the onsen is tops. Excellent buffet meals will keep you more than happy.

Hilton Niseko   RESORT ¥¥¥
(ニセコヒルトンヴィレジ; ☑44-1111; www.placeshilton.com/niseko-village; r from ¥20,000; P@🌐📶) There is no shortage of resort hotels in Niseko, though the Hilton enjoys the best location of all – it is quite literally attached to the Niseko Gondola. As you might expect from the name, spacious Western-style rooms at the Hilton are complemented by a whole slew of amenities spread out across a self-contained village. Check the website before arriving as special deals are usually available, which combine discounted room rates with breakfast and dinner buffets.

Annupuri Village   CHALET ¥¥¥
(アンヌプリ・ヴィレジ; ☑59-2111; www.annupurivillage.com; Niseko Annupuri; chalets for 2-10 people from ¥21,000-110,000; P@🌐) If you're travelling with a large group of friends, consider giving the resort hotels a pass and renting an immaculate ski chalet in Annupuri Village, located at the base of the Annupuri ski slopes. Natural hardwoods and picture windows are featured prominently from floor to ceiling, while rich stone fireplaces, spa-quality bathroom fixtures, professional kitchens and plasma TVs add a touch of modern class.

🍴 Eating & Drinking

Many of the lodges and ryokan offer great meals cooked to order, and the slopes have plenty of snacks, pizza, *rāmen* and other goodies. After hours, things are tricky because lodging is spread out and buses are inconvenient, but there are plenty of watering holes in Hirafu.

⭐ **Graubunden**   CAFE ¥
(グラウビュンデン; ☑23-3371; www.graubunden.jp; ⊗8am-7pm Fri-Wed) Seriously good

sandwiches, cakes, cookies and drinks in Hirafu East Village. A local favourite that has been open 20 years, Graubunden is the perfect spot to chill out with good service, tastes and a relaxed atmosphere.

Jojo's Café & Restaurant CAFE ¥
(ジョジョズカフェ; ☑ 23-2220; www.nac-web.com/niseko/cafe.html; mains from ¥750; ⊘ lunch & dinner; ▣) Excellent casual dining to be had at the Niseko Adventure Centre (NAC). We're talking burgers, salads, pasta and tacos, and stupendous views of Yotei-zan from out on the terrace on a good day.

Restaurant Prativo INTERNATIONAL ¥¥
(レストランプラテイーヴォ; ☑ 55-8852; www.milk-kobo.com/prativo/e; buffet ¥1500; ⊘ 11am-2.30pm) Part of the extremely popular Milk Kōbō complex on the road to Niseko Village, Prativo offers a salad buffet with meat, fish or pasta main dishes at lunchtime. Locals believe it's the best!

The Barn FRENCH ¥¥
(ザ・バーン; ☑ 55-5553; 188-9 Aza-Yamada; lunch/dinner courses ¥1800/4300; ⊘ 11.30am-2pm & 6-11pm, closed Mon summer; ▣) Housed in a modernist rendition of an old Hokkaidō barn, this self-described French Alpine Bistro sets the bar on the Hirafu dining scene. You can order up a bottle of Boyer-Gontard, which comes from the owner's personal vineyard in Burgundy, France. The visually striking steel-and-glass barn is located two blocks south of the Seicomart in Hirafu.

ⓘ Information

At the base of the ski slopes lie several towns and villages that compose Niseko's population centre. Most of the restaurants and bars are clustered together in Hirafu (ひらふ), while Annupuri (アンヌプリ), Niseko Village (ニセコビレッジ) and Hanazono (花園) are much quieter and less developed. Further east are Kutchan (倶知安) and Niseko (ニセコ) proper, which are more permanent population centres that remain decidedly Japanese.

Niseko Tourist Information (ニセコ観光案内所; ☑ 44-2468; www.nisekotourism.com; ⊘ 9am-6pm) Has offices at JR Niseko Station and at the View Plaza Michi-no-Eki on Rte 66 heading into town. It has pamphlets, maps, bus timetables and staff can help with bookings.

Information Centre Plat (☑ 22-3344; www.town.kutchan.hokkaido.jp; ⊘ 10am-7pm) If you head straight down the street outside JR Kutchan Station, on the left hand side after

200m you'll find the very helpful Information Centre Plat, with English brochures and maps.

Hirafu Welcome Centre (ひらふウエルカムセンター; ☑ 22-0109; www.grand-hirafu.jp/winter/en/index.html; ⊘ 8.30am-9pm) To meet the winter crush, the Hirafu Welcome Centre (which is where direct buses to/from New Chitose Airport originate and terminate) also provides English-language information.

ⓘ Getting There & Away

BUS

During the ski season, both **Chūō Bus** (☑ 011-231-0500; www.chuo-bus.co.jp) and **Dōnan Bus** (☑ 0123-46-5701; www.donanbus.co.jp) run regular highway buses from JR Sapporo Station and New Chitose Airport to Niseko. The trip takes around three hours depending on road conditions, costs ¥2300 (return ¥3850) and drops off at the welcome centre in Hirafu before continuing on to the Hilton and Annupuri. Reservations are necessary, and it's recommended that you book well ahead of your departure date. If you don't speak Japanese, ask the staff at the tourist information centres or your accommodation to make a reservation for you.

CAR & MOTORCYCLE

Scenic Rte 5 winds from Sapporo to Otaru around the coast, and then cuts inland through the mountains down to Niseko. Having a car will make it easier to move between the various ski slopes, though drive with extreme caution as fatalities have tragically occurred here in the past. In the summer (low season), public transport services drop off, which provides more incentive to pick up a car in Sapporo or at New Chitose Airport.

TRAIN

While there is a JR Hirafu Station, it is far from the town itself, and is not well serviced by local buses. From JR Niseko and JR Kutchan Stations, you will need to switch to local buses to access the villages at the base of the ski slopes. For these reasons, it's recommended that you travel to Niseko via highway bus or car. If, however, the bus lines are fully booked, trains run on the JR Hakodate line between Sapporo and Niseko (¥2400, two hours) via Kutchan (¥2090, 1¾ hours).

ⓘ Getting Around

There are twice-hourly local buses linking JR Kutchan and JR Niseko Stations to Hirafu, Niseko Village, Annupuri and Hanazono. Pick up a schedule from the tourist information centres so that you don't miss your connection. Also, if you've purchased an all-mountain pass, you can ride the free hourly shuttle bus between the villages.

Shikotsu-Tōya National Park 支笏洞爺国立公園

To the south and southwest of Sapporo, Shikotsu-Tōya National Park (993 sq km) is very spread out and largely mountainous wilderness. It is marked by two picturesque caldera lakes, two of Hokkaidō's top hot-spring towns, and Yotei-zan, also known as Ezo-Fuji (the Fuji-san look-alike of Hokkaidō!).

Shikotsu-ko 支笏湖

Directly south of Sapporo and surrounded by soaring volcanoes, Shikotsu-ko is the second-deepest lake in Japan. While it is 250m above sea level, its deepest spot is 363m, 113m below sea level! Not easy to reach without your own wheels, it's a superb spot for independent exploration and excellent for campers.

On the northwestern side of the lake, **Eniwa-dake** (恵庭岳; 1320m) is a pointed mountain with a crater on its eastern side. Allow five to six hours for the rewarding return hike. Downhill Ski racing for the 1970 Winter Olympics was held on a course on its southwestern side.

Directly below Eniwa-dake is **Marukoma Onsen Ryokan** (丸駒温泉旅館; ☎ 0123-25-2341; www.marukoma.co.jp; per person incl 2 meals from ¥9800; P @), a marvellous place to stay with lakeside *rotemburo* (outdoor baths; ¥1000; 10am to 3pm) you can relax in even if you're not staying.

There is a lakeside **camping area** at Okotan to the southwest of Eniwa-dake just off Rte 78. Other camping areas are at Morappu in the east and Bifue in the west, both off Rte 276.

On the southern side of the lake is **Tarumae-zan** (樽前山; 1041m), an active volcano that is the area's most popular hike. The crater itself is usually closed, but you can reach and go around the rim from the seventh station (650m; only accessible by private car). Allow 1½ hours for the return hike to the rim.

From the same trailhead you can also climb **Fuppushi-dake** (風不死岳; 1102m) in five to six hours return, which offers excellent views of the lake and park. Locals suggest a bear-bell is essential for this hike.

Shikotsu-ko Onsen (支笏湖温泉), on the eastern side of the lake, is the only town. This compact little resort village has some nice short walks, including a nature trail for bird-watchers. Sightseeing boats head out onto the lake and there are rental boats and canoes.

A top spot to stay, **Log Bear** (ログベアー; ☎ 0123-25-2738; http://logbear.moto-nari.com/shikotsu; r per person ¥5000; 🛜) is right in the middle of the village, and is run by a real character called Robin. Log Bear is also a coffee shop and restaurant and you're likely to be sent to the youth hostel for your onsen, but it's a very fun place.

Also at Shikotsu-ko Onsen is the **Shikotsu-ko Visitor Centre** (支笏湖ビジターセンター; ☎ 0123-25-2404; www15.ocn.ne.jp/~sikotuvc/; ⊙ 9am-5.30pm Apr-Nov, 9am-4.30pm Dec-Mar), with good displays and helpful staff.

Tōya-ko 洞爺湖

At the southwestern side of the park, Tōya-ko is an almost classically round caldera lake with a large island (Naka-jima) sitting in the middle.

On the southern side of the lake are two active volcanoes, **Shōwa-Shin-zan** (昭和新山; 398m) and **Usu-zan** (有珠山; 729m). The former, which popped up out of a wheat field in 1944 and was given the name meaning 'the new mountain of the Shōwa period', regularly belches sulphurous fumes, while the latter has quieted somewhat since erupting in 2000 and covering the region in ash. That eruption made television news worldwide – as did the G8 Summit that was held at Tōya-ko in 2008.

Tōya-ko Onsen (洞爺湖温泉) is a sizeable town with an attractive waterfront that is keen to attract visitors. It has 12 free hand- and foot-baths throughout town (think of it as an onsen treasure hunt!), a fireworks display on the lake every night from April until October at 8.45pm, and paddle steamers running lake cruises. The 50km circumference of the lake features 58 statues in an outdoor art gallery that can be rounded by car or bicycle!

The **Usu-zan Ropeway** (有珠山ロープウェイ; www.wakasaresort.com; return ¥1450; ⊙ 8.30am-5pm) runs up from between the active volcanoes to a couple of viewing platforms and some stunning views of the lake and the steaming crater.

The **Volcano Science Museum** (火山科学館; ☎ 0142-75-2555; www.toyako-vc.jp; admission ¥600; ⊙ 9am-5pm) is a must for anyone interested in the spectacular landforms of the national park. You can even 'experience' an eruption in the Volcanic Eruption Theatre. The museum is attached to the **Tōya-ko Visitor Centre** (洞爺湖ビジターセンター; ☑ 0142-75-2555; www.toyako-vc.jp) **FREE**, which has excellent displays. They are together a short walk west from the bus station.

From town, if you look up west to the rim of the surrounding mountains you'll see a cruise ship–shaped resort! This is the **Windsor Hotel International** (ザ・ウィンザーホテル洞爺; ☑ 0120-29-0500; www.windsor-hotels.co.jp; r from ¥33,600; P @ 🖘 🏊), which hosted the 2008 G8 Summit. As you'd expect, you need a fat wallet to stay here!

Two blocks east of the bus station is **Daiwa Ryokan** (大和旅館; ☑ 0142-75-2415; http://daiwa-ryokan.gogo.tc/index.html; r per person 1/2/4 people ¥4350/3825/3300; P @), more likely to fit the budget. Nonguests can use the onsen here for ¥400.

In the bus station, the **Tōya-ko Tourist Information Centre** (洞爺湖観光情報センター; ☑ 0142-75-2446; www.laketoya.com; ⊙ 9am-5pm) is incredibly helpful with an unbelievable number of brochures and maps in English.

JR Tōya Station is 25 minutes away by bus (¥320) on the south coast. Trains on the JR Muroran line link JR Tōya with Hakodate (¥5340, 1¾ hours), Sapporo (¥5760, 1¾ hours) and Noboribetsu (¥2650, 35 minutes).

Buses run frequently between Tōya and Sapporo (¥2700, 2¾ hours).

AINU RENAISSANCE

Although Ainu culture was once declared 'dead' by the Japanese government, the past few decades have seen people of Ainu descent assert their ethnicity both politically and culturally. For some background on Hokkaidō's indigenous people, see p541. If you're interested in learning more about the Ainu, we recommend the following.

Head to **Shiraoi**, between Tomakomai and Noboribetsu on the south coast in central Hokkaidō. Shiraoi's **Poroto Kotan** (ポロトコタン) is a lakeside village of reconstructed traditional Ainu buildings, anchored by the **Ainu Museum** (アイヌ民族博物館; www.ainu-museum.or.jp/en/; admission ¥750; ⊙ 8.45am-5pm). Museum exhibits are labelled in both Japanese and English, and in the village you might catch demonstrations of Ainu crafts and cultural performances. The JR Muroran line runs between Shiraoi and Sapporo (¥3200, one hour).

In the village of **Nibutani** (in the northern outskirts of Biratori village on Rte 237, north of Tomikawa, also on the south coast of central Hokkaidō), **Nibutani Ainu Culture Museum** (二風谷アイヌ文化博物館; www.town.biratori.hokkaido.jp/biratori/nibutani; admission ¥400; ⊙ 9am-5pm mid-Apr–mid-Nov, 9am-5pm Tue-Sun mid-Nov–mid-Apr, closed mid-Dec–mid-Jan) has arguably better collections and more attractive displays, although most information is in Japanese only. Visitors could easily spend half a day watching documentary videos about Ainu folk crafts, traditional dances, epic songs and traditional ceremonies. Across Nibutani's main street, amid some traditional huts, the **Kayano Shigeru Ainu Memorial Museum** (萱野茂二風谷アイヌ資料館; admission ¥400; ⊙ 9am-5pm Apr-Nov, by appointment Dec-Mar) houses the private collection of Kayano Shigeru, the first person of Ainu descent to be elected to the Japanese Diet. You'll need your own wheels to get to Nibutani.

If you are heading to **Akan National Park**, make sure to visit the Ainu Village (p600) in Akanko Onsen. There are Ainu handcraft shops, restaurants and cultural performances in the theatre Ikor (p600). Further east in the park, on the shores of Kussharo-ko, is the Museum of Ainu Folklore (p598).

In Sapporo itself, head to the Ainu Association of Hokkaidō (p549). Forty minutes by car, southwest of Sapporo at Kogane-yu on Rte 230, is the **Sapporo Pirka Kotan** (アイヌ文化交流センター[サッポロピリカコタン]; ☑ 011-596-5961; www.city.sapporo.jp/shimin/pirka-kotan/en/index.html; Kogane-yu 27; admission ¥200; ⊙ 9am-5pm Tue-Sun), a new Ainu culture promotion centre with displays and an excellent exhibition room. Well worth a visit.

Other useful sources of information include the **Foundation for the Research & Promotion of Ainu Culture** (アイヌ文化振興研究推進機構; ☑ 011-271-4171; www.frpac.or.jp/eng/index.html) in Sapporo and the **Ainu Culture Centre** (アイヌ文化交流センター; Ainu Bunka Kōryū Centā; ☑ 03-3245-9831) in Tokyo.

Shikotsu-Tōya National Park

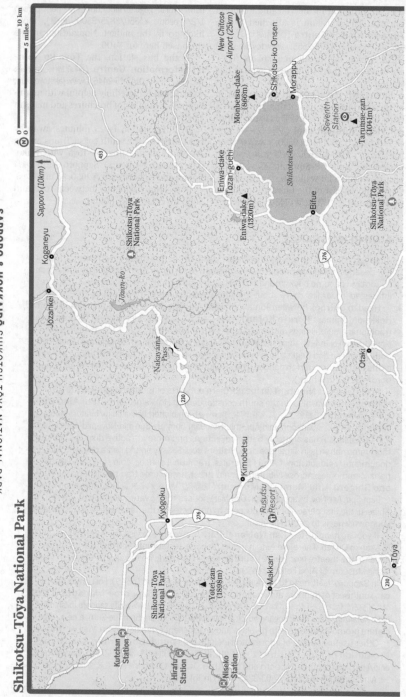

New Chitose Airport (25km)

Shikotsu-ko Onsen

Morappu

Monbetsu-dake (866m)

Seventh Station

Tarumae-zan (1041m)

Shikotsu-ko

453

Sapporo (10km)

Koganeyu

Eniwa-dake Tozan-guchi

Eniwa-dake (1320m)

Bifue

Shikotsu-Tōya National Park

Jozanke

Shikotsu-Tōya National Park

Jozan-ko

276

Shikotsu-Tōya National Park

Nakayama Pass

Otaki

230

Kimobetsu

Rusutsu Resort

Kyogoku

276

Tōya

Makkari

230

Shikotsu-Tōya National Park

Yotei-zan (1898m)

Kutchan Station

Hirafu Station

Niseko Station

10 km

5 miles

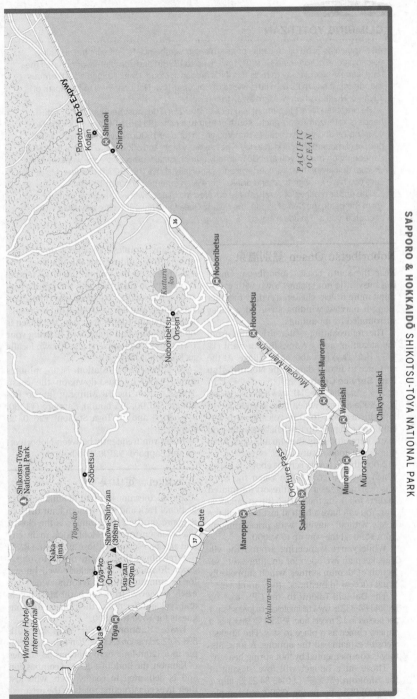

WORTH A TRIP

CLIMBING YŌTEI-ZAN

Also known as Ezo-Fuji, because of its striking resemblance to Fuji-san, the stunning volcanic cone of Yōtei-zan (羊蹄山) towers up to 1898m and completely dominates the landscape. The only way to miss it is if it's hidden in cloud. One of Japan's 100 Famous Mountains, it sits in its own little island of Shikotsu-Tōya National Park to the north of Tōya-ko. Niseko is barely 10km away to the west.

Be prepared for a big climb if you tackle Yōtei-zan. The most popular of four trailheads is Yōtei-zan Tozan-guchi, south of Kutchan near JR Hirafu Station at 350m. Do your maths and you'll calculate that you are in for over 1500m of vertical climb. Most people climb and descend in a day – get an early start and allow six to nine hours return, depending on how fit you are! Be mentally and physically prepared – the weather can change quickly on this exposed volcano, especially above the 1600m tree line. Make sure you have enough food and drink. There is an emergency hut at 1800m.

The upper reaches of Yōtei-zan are covered in alpine flowers during the summer. From the peak, the Sea of Japan, the Pacific Ocean and Lake Tōya are all visible – unless, of course, you are inside a cloud!

Noboribetsu Onsen 登別温泉

Near the south coast, Noboribetsu Onsen is a busy little hot springs town with everything more or less clustered tightly together along a narrow, winding street in a valley surrounded by mountains.

The rejuvenating water originates from the steaming and hissing **Jigoku-dani** (地獄谷; Hell Valley) just above the village. At the entrance to Jigoku-dani is the **Noboribetsu Park Service Centre** (登別パークサービスセンター; ☑ 0143-84-3141; www.noboribetsu-spa.jp; ◷ 8.30am-5pm), which does a good job of introducing you to this volcanic wonderland. You can pick up English brochures and maps here, and it is the starting spot for a number of good nature trails.

Noboribetsu is very serious about its baths, which received great fame when the town was designated as a health resort for injured soldiers following the 1904–5 Russo-Japanese War. You can have a bath at just about all the hotels without staying, with prices ranging from ¥390 all the way up to ¥2000.

While you're wandering around the village, keep an eye open for an interesting selection of 'demon statues' which supposedly bring success in business, study and love!

The **Dai-ichi Takimoto-kan** (第一滝本館; ☑ 0143-84-3322; www.takimotokan.co.jp/english; r per person incl 2 meals from ¥9150; @ 🛜 🏠) is a superb choice as a place to stay. The English website explains all the options. A long history is complemented by 'hot spring heaven'.

Those on a budget will love staying at the **Shōkōin** (聖光院; ☑ 0143-84-2359; http://jodo.jp/01-063/; per person ¥3300; 🛜) temple.

Not many temples look like a three-storey green office building, but this one does! The entrance is on the ground floor, the temple rooms are on floor two, and the priest's wife runs a *minshuku* (Japanese guesthouse) on floor three. You'll have to head out for meals, but the tatami rooms are clean, the onsen is open 24 hours and there is wi-fi. Bring your own towel. The temple is also known locally as Kannon-ji (観音寺).

JR Noboribetsu Station is 15 minutes away (¥330) by bus, down on the coast. Trains run on the JR Muroran line to Hakodate (¥6700, 2½ hours), Sapporo (¥4360, 1¼ hours) and JR Tōya Station (¥2650, 35 minutes).

Buses run frequently between Noboribetsu and Sapporo (¥2100, two hours).

Jōzankei 定山渓

At the northernmost extent of Shikotsu-Tōya National Park and less than an hour drive to Sapporo on Rte 230, Jōzankei is the closest major onsen town to Hokkaidō's main city and an easy escape for those after some R&R.

Stretching along a gorge of the Toyohiragawa, Jōzankei is particularly well known for its stunning autumn colours, which can easily be viewed from the bath! Most hotels and ryokan offer use of their onsen for nonguests for ¥500 to ¥1500.

Iwato Kannon-dō (岩戸観音堂; ☑ 011-598-2012; admission ¥300; ◷ 7am-8pm) is a temple in a 120m-long cave that has 33 statues of Kannon, the Buddhist deity of compassion and is dedicated to roadworkers who lost their lives constructing roads in the area.

A good spot to stay is the **Jōzankei View Hotel** (定山渓ビューホテル; ☑ 011-598-3339; http://karakami-kankou.jp/en/jv/; r from ¥8000; P @ ♨), especially if you're with children. This monster complex (647 rooms) may look as if it has seen better days, but it more than meets most needs and there are some good deals to be had, especially if booking online. There are underground and rooftop onsen, a family-fun 'Water Kingdom', restaurants, an all-purpose shop and loads of parking.

Buses run regularly between Sapporo and Jōzankei (¥750, 1¼ hours).

Tomakomai   苫小牧

Just as New Chitose Airport acts as the airport hub for Sapporo and Hokkaidō, the industrial port town of Tomakomai, 20km south of Chitose, is the main port of entry for long-distance ferries. Most people are there because they're getting on or off a ferry. There are a few options for arriving in Hokkaidō (or departing!) by ferry via Tomakomai:

Taiheiyō Ferry (www.taiheiyo-ferry.co.jp) Operates down the Pacific coast of Honshū, between Tomakomai, Sendai and Nagoya.

Shin-Nihonkai Ferry (www.snf.jp) Operates on the Japan Sea side of Honshū.between Tomakomai, Akita, Niigata and Tsuruga (Fukui-ken); and between Otaru and Niigata and Maizuru (Kyoto-fu).

Kawasaki Kinkai Kisen (www.silverferry.jp) Between Tomakomai and Hachinohe (Aomori-ken).

Shosen Mitsui Ferry (www.sunflower.co.jp) Operates between Tomakomai and Ōarai (Ibaraki-ken).

There really is no reason to stay in Tomakomai unless your ferry arrives or departs at a very nasty hour. If you do decide to stay, right next to the station is **Toyoko Inn Tomakomai Eki-mae** (東横イン苫小牧駅前; ☑ 0144-32-1046; www.toyoko-inn.com/e_hotel/00108/index.html; s/d from ¥4980/6480; P @ ☎), part of the Japan-wide chain of Toyoko Inns. While there mightn't be a lot of character on hand, there is free internet, breakfast and supper – plus you are guaranteed spotless rooms.

Getting to or away from Tomakomai is relatively easy. **Hokkaidō Chūō Bus** (www.chuo-bus.co.jp) runs highway buses between Tomakomai Ferry Terminal and Sapporo Eki-mae Bus Station (¥1270; 1¾ hours). **Dōnan Bus** (www.donanbus.co.jp) runs between the ferry terminal and JR Tomakomai Station (¥240; 15 minutes). JR Tomakomai Station is on the JR Muroran Line, 45 minutes from Sapporo (¥3020).

NORTHERN HOKKAIDŌ

Northern Hokkaidō (道北; Dō-hoku) is where the majestic grandeur of the natural world takes over. Southeast of Asahikawa, the second-largest city on the island, Daisetsuzan National Park is a raw virgin landscape of enormous proportions. West of Wakkanai, in the shadow of Siberia, Rishiri-Rebun-Sarobetsu National Park is a dramatic island-scape famous for its wildflowers. And, in case you still need a few reminders of human settlement, Furano is one of Hokkaidō's most famous ski resorts, and home to one of the world's only belly-button appreciation festivals!

Asahikawa   旭川

☑ 0166 / POP 355,000

Asahikawa carries the dual honour of having the most days with snowfall in all of Japan, as well as the record for the coldest temperature (-40°C). It is mainly used by travellers as a transit point for Wakkanai to the north, Daisetsuzan National Park to the southeast, and Biei and Furano to the south, but is also a pleasant city in which to spend a day or two.

⊙ Sights

Asahiyama Zoo   ZOO
(旭山動物園; ☑ 36-1104; www5.city.asahikawa.hokkaido.jp/asahiyamazoo/zoo/English/top.html; admission ¥800; ☺ 9.30am-5.15pm May-Oct, 10.30am-3.30pm Nov-Apr) Known Japan-wide, the country's northernmost zoo attracts visitors with its stars from cold climates, polar bears and penguins. It's well done and extremely popular. Buses 41, 42 or 47 run between bus stop 5 in front of the station and the entrance to the zoo (¥400, 40 minutes).

Otokoyama Sake Brewery Museum   SAKE BREWERY
(男山酒造り資料館; ☑ 47-7080; www.otokoyama.com/english/index.html; 2-7 Nagayama; ☺ 9am-5pm) **FREE** If you want a free tipple, take the 30-minute tour of this legendary brewery, which appears in old *ukiyo-e* (woodblock prints) and historic literature. These guys export all over the world. Take bus 67, 70,

71, 667 or 669 from bus stop 18 in front of the station, and get off at Nagayama 2-jō 6-chōme (¥200, 20 minutes).

Kawamura Kaneto Ainu Memorial Hall
MUSEUM

(川村カネトアイヌ記念館; ☎51-2461; 11 Kitamonchō; admission ¥500; ⏱9am-5pm) Kaneto Kawamura, an Ainu chief, became a master surveyor and helped to lay the tracks for several of Hokkaido's railways. In 1916, after eye problems forced him to retire, he used his accumulated wealth to create the first Ainu museum. Take bus 23 or 24 from bus stop 14 in front of the station to the Ainu Kinenkan-mae stop (¥170, 15 minutes).

Hokkaidō Folk Arts & Crafts
MUSEUM

(北海道伝統美術工芸村; www.yukaraori.co.jp; 3-1-1 Minamigaoka; combined tickets ¥1200) Located 5km southwest of the train station, this collection of three museums provides an overview of the island's traditional folk arts. A free shuttle runs every hour or two between the village and the Kureyon Parking, next to the Asahikawa Washington Hotel.

✻ Festivals & Events

Winter Festival
WINTER FESTIVAL

(冬祭り; Fuyu Matsuri) Held every February and into its sixth decade, this is one of Japan's top winter festivals. The International Ice Sculpture Competition is a highlight, along with local food and fun seasonal events.

Kotan Matsuri
TRADITIONAL

(コタン祭り) Held on the autumn equinox in September on the banks of the Chubestugawa, south of the city. There are traditional Ainu dances, music and prayer ceremonies offered to the deities of fire, the river, kotan (the village) and the mountains.

🛏 Sleeping

Guest House Asahikawa
GUESTHOUSE ¥

(ゲストハウス旭川; ☎73-8269; www.guest-houseasahikawa.jp; Rokujō-dōri 7-chōme 31-10 ; dm ¥3000; @🤶) On the 2nd floor of what used to be an office building, this guesthouse has been crafted with loving care. It's a bit squashy, but the owners are enthusiastic, there's free coffee and internet, a kitchen, games and a book exchange. It's about a 10-minute walk from the station.

Tōyoko Inn Asahikawa Ekimae
HOTEL ¥¥

(東横イン旭川駅前; ☎27-1045; www.toyoko-inn.com/e_hotel/00069/index.html; 9-164-1 Ichijō-dōri; s/d incl breakfast from ¥5980/7480; P@🤶)

This popular chain's clean and convenient Asahikawa hotel is a short walk from JR Asahikawa Station. There is free breakfast and wi-fi.

Loisir Hotel Asahikawa
HOTEL ¥¥¥

(ロワジールホテル旭川; ☎25-8811; fax 25-8200; www.solarehotels.com; s/d from ¥8000/10,000; P@🤶) An easy-to-spot white tower block, the Loisir is Asahikawa's top hotel. First-class amenities include a large gym and spa as well as four fine restaurants, one of which is a 15th-floor bistro with a view. Book early on the internet for good deals.

🍴 Eating & Drinking

Asahikawa is famous for its shōyu (soy sauce) rāmen, and there are rāmen shops on virtually every street in the city. **Furarīto Alley** (ふらりーと小路 Alley; www.furari-to.com) is a rambling collection of 18 restaurants running the length of an alley between Yonjō-dōri and Gojō-dōri, about a 10-minute walk north of the station. Very popular with locals, it's the place to go. Stroll along (loosely translated, furarīto means wander) and see what looks good. Virtually everything is on offer.

★ Taisetsu Ji-bīru-kan
BREWERY

(大雪地ビール館; ☎25-0400; www.ji-beer.com; 1604-1 Miyashita-dōri 11-chōme; ⏱11.30am-10pm) To try the local award-winning brew, walk east of the station for five minutes to Taisetsu Ji-bīru-kan. Taisetsu Beer is good! You can drink it, buy it, try beer jelly and, of course, sit down and consume it with a plate of jingisu-kan or a bowl of rāmen. Highly recommended.

ℹ Information

By the time this book comes out, Asahikawa's brand-new JR Station should be up and running. A large pedestrian avenue extends north of it for eight blocks, and most of the hotels and restaurants listed here are within easy walking distance of the station.

Tourist Information Counter (旭川観光案内所; ☎26-6665; www.asahikawa-daisetsu.jp/e/index.html; ⏱8.30am-7pm Jun-Sep, 9am-7pm Oct-May) Inside JR Asahikawa Station, everyone is very helpful and friendly; there are English speakers, English maps and brochures.

Asahikawa International Centre (旭川国際交流センター; ☎25-7491; Feeeal Asahikawa 7F, Ichijō-dōri 8-chōme; ⏱10am-7.30pm) A useful spot a few minutes north of the station on the 7th floor of the Feeeal Building. Information on Asahikawa, Hokkaido as a whole and free internet use. Take some time out and relax here.

BIEI

More or less halfway between Asahikawa and Furano, with the dramatic mountains of Daisetsuzan National Park in the background, Biei (美瑛; population 11,000) is an artist's and nature-lover's mecca. With the freedom of a rental car, you can cruise for hours along blissful country roads lined with fields of sunflowers, lavender and white birch. The so-called Patchwork Road to the west of town will get you lost for sure.

Whether you arrive by train or car, however, a visit to Biei's lovely old stone station should be on your agenda. It has been voted one of Japan's 100 top train stations! Next door is the **Biei tourist information office** (美瑛観光案内所; ☑ 0166-92-4378; www.biei-hokkaido.jp; ◷ 8.30am-7pm May-Oct, 8.30am-5pm Nov-Apr) with enthusiastic English-speaking staff, English maps and brochures, and even map codes for Biei highlights for your car navigation system. Rental bicycles are available for ¥200 per hour.

★ **Biei Potato-no-Oka** (美瑛ポテトの丘; ☑ 0166-92-3255; www.potatovillage.com/eng/top.html; dm/r per person from ¥4960/6100, 4-person cottages ¥22,000, 3-/5-person log houses ¥13,650/21,000; P @ 🛜) 🍴 is an endearing place perched at the top of a field of potatoes. A variety of accommodation options are available in dormitories, rooms with private bathrooms, and adorable cottages and log houses. Guests congregate at night for hearty dinners (extra cost) featuring local produce, most notably potatoes. Staff will pick you up at Biei station if you book ahead.

Rte 237 runs between Asahikawa, Biei and Furano, but the real appeal of Biei is simply exploring the detours, getting lost and stopping to enjoy the rural flavour – so get off the main road. If you don't have a car, there are *kaisoku* on the JR Furano line between Biei and Asahikawa (32 minutes) and Biei and Furano (36 minutes).

ℹ Getting There & Around

AIR

Asahikawa Airport is 10km southeast of the city. Among the domestic-flight destinations are Tokyo, Nagoya, Osaka. Buses between the airport and JR Asahikawa Station (¥570, 30 minutes) are timed to connect with arrivals and departures.

BUS

There are frequent daily departures from bus stops in front of JR Asahikawa Station to Sapporo (¥2000, two hours), Wakkanai (¥4700, 4¾ hours), Furano (¥860, 1½ hours) and Biei (¥520, 50 minutes).

CAR & MOTORCYCLE

If you want to pick up a car before heading either north, south or east, **Toyota Rent a Car** (トヨタレンタカー; ☑ 23-0100; http://www.toyotarentacar.net/english/; 9-396-2 Miyashitadōri; ◷ 8am-8pm Apr-Oct, to 7pm Nov-Mar) has a branch office at Asahikawa Airport and one right outside the city JR station. **Nippon Rent A Car** (www.nrh.co.jp) also has locations at the airport and station.

TRAIN

Super Kamui *tokkyū* run twice an hour between Asahikawa and Sapporo (¥4480, 1½ hours). There are just a couple of *tokkyū* on the JR Sōya line each day between Asahikawa and Wakkanai (¥7870, 3¾ hours), and on the JR Sekihoku line between Asahikawa and Abashiri (¥7750, four

hours). Finally, there are regular *kaisoku* on the JR Furano line between Asahikawa and Furano (¥1040, 1¼ hours) via Biei (¥530, 35 minutes).

Furano　　富良野

☑ 0167 / POP 26,000

Furano is a delight in all seasons. One of Japan's most inland towns, it receives extreme amounts of powdery snow, and is ranked as one of the country's top skiing and snowboarding destinations. Somewhat surprisingly, a continental climate descends on the area outside the winter months, fostering a burgeoning wine industry, producing award-winning cheeses and enabling sprawling fields of lavender to spring to life. For Japanese tourists who can't manage the time and money to summer in the south of France, Furano is regarded as something of a close second.

The centre of town and the station are in the valley, while the ski district is a couple of kilometres west at the base of the mountains.

⊙ Sights

The real appeal of Furano is simply exploring and getting lost in the beautiful nature surrounding the town, but there are also a number of attractions worth checking out. Having the luxury of your own wheels will greatly enhance your visit.

★ **Ningle Terrace**   ARTS CENTRE
(ニングルテラス; ☎ 22-1111; www.princehotels.
co.jp/newfurano; ◷ noon-8.45pm Sep-Jun, 10am-
8.45pm Jul-Aug) **FREE** Anyone into arts, crafts
and shopping should not miss visiting Ningle Terrace at the New Furano Prince Hotel,
5km southwest of JR Furano Station. With 15
log cabins all specialising in different crafts
connected by boardwalks in the forest, there
is everything from wooden toys to glass-
blowing to candles to paper products. The
mini-woodwind instruments shop is captivating. Everything is being made on-site.

★ **Farm Tomita**   FLOWER FARM
(ファーム富田; www.farm-tomita.co.jp/en; ◷ 9am-
4.30pm Oct-late Apr, 8.30am-6pm late Apr-Sep)
FREE You really have to see Farm Tomita to
believe it, though try to imagine huge fields
of brightly coloured flowers blooming like
a rainbow. The Japanese tend to go wildest
over the lavender, but the seasonal fields tend
to produce just as many squeals of delight.
The cafe and gift shop sell lavender-infused
products including soft creams, puddings,
jellies, pastries and soft drinks. This place
is so popular that from June to September,
JR actually opens up a temporary station
known as Lavender Batake (ラベンダー畑;
Lavender Farm) to accommodate the influx
of visitors. Otherwise, the closest station is JR
Naka-Furano.

Furano Winery   WINERY
(ふらのワイン工場; www.furanowine.jp; ◷ 9am-
4.30pm Sep-May, 9am-6pm Jun-Aug) **FREE** About
4km northwest of JR Furano Station, this
place gives tours explaining the wine-making
process and obliges visitors with a complimentary tipple.

Furano Cheese Factory   CHEESE FACTORY
(富良野チーズ工房; Furano Chīzu Kobō; www.
furano-cheese.jp; ◷ 9am-5pm Apr-Oct, to 4pm Nov-
Mar) **FREE** Foodies should continue on to
the cheese factory, about 2km south of JR
Furano Station – try the squid-ink brie. This
complex also has other Furano milk products such as ice cream...and even a pizza
restaurant. There's the opportunity to try
your hand at making things, such as cheese
and ice cream, but you need to book ahead.
Check out the website.

🏃 Activities

Furano Ski Area   SKIING, SNOWBOARDING
(富良野スキー場; Furano Skī-Jō; www.princeho-
tels.co.jp/ski/furano_e/index.html; lift tickets full
day/night only ¥4200/1500; ◷ day 8.30am-5pm,
night 5-8pm) Lying between two Prince hotels, this world-class winter-sports resort
has hosted numerous FIS World Ski and
Snowboarding events, yet remains relatively
undiscovered by foreign visitors compared
to Niseko. While Furano does not allow for
off-piste skiing, there is plenty here to take
your fancy.

Open from late November until early May,
the slopes are predominantly beginner and
intermediate, but there is a handful of steep,
ungroomed advanced runs. The novice-
friendly courses, all with perfect powder,
can run up to 3km in length. They also wind
scenically through pristine birch forests, and

PARK GOLF

If you do much driving around Hokkaidō, it won't take long until you run into a meticulously manicured Park Golf course (パークゴルフ) – every town and village in Hokkaidō
has got at least one!

This version of golf – about halfway between real golf and putt-putt golf – was invented
in Hokkaidō, and has really taken off. There are 18 holes covering an area of about three
or four football fields. The holes vary in length from about 40m to 80m – just like real golf,
par 3s are shorter and par 5s are longer – with bunkers and greens. You are, however, only
allowed one club and the ball is hard and sized halfway between a golf ball and a baseball.

It's really fun, you can wear what you like, and etiquette is very relaxed – it's perfectly
OK to laugh at your opponent's poor shots!

If you feel like a bit of fun, stop your car and take a look. Most local courses charge
from ¥300 to ¥500 to play; it should take around 1½ hours for a round. With a bit of luck
there'll be a rental club and ball you can use.

There is thought to be 700,000 'parkers' in Japan, mostly retirees. Many take their
park golf very seriously, having town-wide tournaments and competitions. Most towns
are very proud of their courses, which are absolutely immaculate – and whoever is running the course will be most impressed if foreign visitors turn up to play. Give it a go!

open up in sections to tremendous views. Eleven lifts, including the fastest gondola in Japan, help to keep the crowds in check.

The two Prince hotels provide a wonderful après-ski atmosphere of fine dining, lively drinking and curative onsen soaking. Full equipment rental is available for ¥4500 per day. English signage is adequate.

✸ Festivals & Events

Heso Matsuri
BELLY BUTTONS

Humorously known as Heso-no-machi (Belly-Button Town), Furano is in the centre of Hokkaidō. This geographic distinction gave rise to the town's famous navel festival on 28 and 29 July, held rain or shine. If you're in town, strip off, have a humorous face painted on your midriff and join the Belly-button Dance plus other inventive events.

Furano Wine Festival
WINE

This harvest festival on the third Sunday in September offers all kinds of drink and food tastings along with other events. In an effort towards sustainability, organisers ask revellers to bring their own chopsticks!

🛏 Sleeping

Alpine Backpackers
HOSTEL ¥

(アルパインバックパッカーズ; ☑22-1311; www.alpn.co.jp/english/index.html; dm per person ¥2500, tw/q ¥5000/10,000; ℗@🛜) Conveniently located just a few minutes' walk from the lifts, this is a great spot for skiers and active types. Backpackers are well catered for with cooking facilities, laundry facilities, and a boiling onsen that gets the aches and pains out after skiing. There are also all sorts of activities from rafting to fishing to hot-air ballooning on offer. Check out the website.

Furano Youth Hostel
HOSTEL ¥

(富良野ユースホステル; ☑44-4441; www4.ocn. ne.jp/~furanoyh/english.htm; 3-20 Okamati Naka-Furano-Cho; dm incl breakfast & dinner ¥3360; ℗@) Five minutes' walk west of JR Naka-Furano Station (not JR Furano Station!), the Furano Youth Hostel occupies a big farmhouse complete with an expansive deck overlooking the countryside. Breakfast and dinner is on the house (except Sunday night – the chef takes a break!). Meals are simple, tasty and feature local produce. Private rooms may be available for an extra ¥2100 per person.

★ New Furano Prince Hotel
HOTEL ¥¥

(新富良野プリンスホテル; ☑22-1111; www. princehotels.com/en/newfurano; s/d incl breakfast & lift tickets from ¥15,000/18,000; ℗@🛜🏠) Lying at opposite ends of the ski slopes near the gondolas, both Prince hotels are snazzy places with a variety of restaurants, bars and lounge areas. While the rooms themselves are nothing more than standard issue here at the New Prince, the service is impeccable, and the convenience factor helps to maximise your slope time. Note that the cheapest prices are available if you book online well in advance.

Furano Prince Hotel
HOTEL ¥¥

(富良野プリンスホテル; ☑23-4111; www. princehotels.com/en/furano; s/d incl breakfast & lift tickets from ¥12,500/15,000; ℗@🛜🏠) Somewhat akin to an oversized chalet, the Furano Prince Hotel is the older sibling that has aged gracefully, thanks to a number of interior makeovers. You're paying for convenience, amenities and service, though costs can be kept at a reasonable level if you book well in advance.

Furano Natulux Hotel
BOUTIQUE HOTEL ¥¥¥

(富良野ナチュラクスホテル; ☑22-1777; www.natulux.com/en/index.html; s/d from ¥15,850/21,000; ℗@🛜) Located directly across from JR Furano Station, this boutique hotel has style. Rooms are on the small side, but there is a spa with bath and sauna. The cafe is a great place to indulge in a wine and cheese fondue set – both locally sourced, of course!

🍴 Eating

★ Chīzu Rāmen-no-mise Karin
RĀMEN ¥

(チーズラーメンの店かりん; ☑22-1692; 9-12 Moto-machi; dishes from ¥1000; ⏰11am-8pm) Furano is famous for its cheese and one-way the locals eat it is shredded over a bowl of *rāmen*. This excessively high-calorie indulgence can be found in a nondescript brown-and-white building (look for the red curtain) a few minutes' walk southwest of JR Furano Station. There is no English menu, but just say *'cheezu rāmen'*.

Kunen-kōbō Yamadori
CURRY ¥

(くんえん工房 YAMADORI; ☑39-1810; 4-14 Asahi-machi; dishes from ¥1000; ⏰lunch Fri-Wed; 🍴) Furano is famous for its omelette curries known as *omu-karē* (オムかれー) and Yamadori tops off that dish with a sliced sausage for ¥1000. You'll find this neat little treat in a cutesy-cool pink farmhouse with white trim a couple of minutes' walk from JR Furano Station.

ℹ️ Information

Tourist Information Office (富良野観光案内所; ☎23-3388; www.furanotourism.com; ⏰9am-6pm) Stock up on English maps and pamphlets, get some last-minute help booking accommodation, rent bicycles and even check your internet for free at JR Furano Station. There is also an office below the Kitanomine Gondola station in the ski district. The website is very good.

ℹ️ Getting There & Away

BUS

Frequent buses run between Furano and Sapporo (¥2200, 2½ hours), as well as between Furano and Asahikawa (¥860, 1½ hours).

CAR & MOTORCYCLE

Rte 237 runs between Asahikawa, Biei and Furano. It is 59km to Asahikawa by road, and 142km to Sapporo. Be extremely careful in winter as roads in this area can be icy and treacherous.

TRAIN

There are frequent *kaisoku* on the JR Furano line between Furano and Asahikawa (¥1040, 1¼ hours). For Sapporo (¥4030, 2½ hours), take a *futsū* (local train) on the JR Nemuro line to Takikawa, and then change to the hourly Super Kamui *tokkyū*.

Daisetsuzan National Park 大雪山国立公園

Known as 'Nutakukamushupe' in Ainu, Daisetsuzan or 'Big Snow Mountain' is Japan's largest national park, designated in 1934 and covering more than 2300 sq km. A vast wilderness area of soaring mountains, active volcanoes, remote onsen, clear lakes and dense forests, Daisetsuzan is the kind of place that stressed-out workers in Tokyo and Osaka dream about on their daily commute.

Virtually untouched by human hands, the park has minimal tourism, with most visitors basing themselves in the hot-spring villages on the periphery. The three main access points into the park are **Asahidake Onsen** in the northwest, **Sōunkyō Onsen** in the northeast and **Tokachi-dake Onsen** in the southwest.

Asahidake Onsen 旭岳温泉

☎ 0166

This forested hot-springs village, at 1100m above sea level, has a few small inns at the base of Asahi-dake, Hokkaido's tallest peak. There are plenty of hiking options and healing onsen for afterwards.

Most onsen, even at the higher-end hotels, are open for day use to the general public. Prices range from ¥500 up to ¥1500.

Be prepared. There are no ATMs, shops or restaurants at Asahidake Onsen, so you'll need to have cash, and food sorted out if you are going camping or contemplating taking on the Grand Traverse. If you are staying, order meals at your accommodation house when you book.

🏃 Activities

Asahidake Ropeway   ROPEWAY
(旭岳 ロープウェイ; ☎68-9111; http://wakasaresort.com/eng/; one-way/return 1 Jun-20 Oct ¥1600/2800, 21 Oct-31 May ¥1100/1800; ⏰6am-5.30pm Jul–mid-Oct, 9am-4pm mid-Oct–Jun) This ropeway runs from Asahidake Onsen (1100m) up to Sugatami (姿見) at 1600m, making **Asahi-dake** (旭岳; 2290m) a very feasible day hike. There are all sorts of hiking options. The ropeway runs year-round and the area is popular with backcountry types and with hardcore skiers and snowboarders through winter.

DON'T MISS

FUKIAGE ONSEN 吹上温泉露天の湯

If you like sitting naked in small pools of hot steaming water surrounded by pristine forest, then head to Fukiage Onsen Roten-no-yu. This semi-secret spot is about 5km from Tokachi-dake Onsen – head down on Rte 291, then right on Rte 966 – easy to get to if you have a good map and your own wheels.

There's a big sign on the downhill side of the road, a parking area and a 200m track down through the forest. There's nothing there except two hot pools. The one higher up is hotter than the other.

It's not for the shy! Strip off and hop in! There's no charge...and this place is *konyoku*, meaning men and women bathe together. You might like to take a small 'modesty towel' if you've got one.

ℹ️ HIKING IN DAISETSUZAN NATIONAL PARK

There are a lot of options for hiking in the national park ranging from half-day trips to the Daisetsuzan Grand Traverse, a hardcore five- to seven-day, 55km hike the length of the park.

Get a copy of Shōbunsha's *Yama-to-Kōgen Chizu Map 3: Daisetsuzan* (昭文社山と高原地図３大雪山), be prepared, and check the weather forecast. Visitor centre staff will be more than happy to update you on conditions.

From Asahidake Onsen – from the top of the ropeway at 1600m...

➡ There is a very nice short loop walk around Sugatami-daira (姿見平) that will take less than an hour.

➡ Alternatively, climb the well-trodden track to **Asahi-dake** (旭岳), at 2290m Hokkaidō's highest point and one of Japan's 100 Famous Mountains, for amazing views and an excellent day trip of four to five hours hiking (return).

➡ If you are really keen and organised, get an early start and hike from Asahi-dake all the way over to Kuro-dake, then take the chairlift and ropeway down to Sōunkyō Onsen. You'll need to check ropeway start and finish times and allow six to eight hours for the hike across between the ropeway stations. This is an excellent hike!

From Sōunkyō Onsen – from the top of the ropeway and chairlift at 1520m...

➡ Kuro-dake (黒岳; 1984m) is only an hour or so climb away on a rocky trail renowned for its alpine flowers. Allow a couple of hours walking for the return trip.

➡ From Kuro-dake you could carry on over to Asahi-dake and take the ropeway down to Asahidake Onsen. Allow six to eight hours for this mission, a reversal of the Asahi-dake to Kuro-dake hike mentioned above.

➡ Another good day hike from Sōunkyō Onsen involves taking the bus to Ginsendai (銀泉台; 1400m; check bus times at the visitor centre) and climbing Aka-dake (赤岳; 2078m). This is a lovely track. Allow four to five hours and make sure you're back in time for the return bus.

From Tokachi-dake Onsen – as well as being the end point for the Grand Traverse, a couple of excellent full-day hikes can be tackled from here. Tokachi-dake Onsen is at 1200m.

➡ A return trip up Tokachi-dake (十勝岳; 2077m), one of Japan's Hyakumeizan (100 Famous Mountains) will take six to eight hours return and reveal some marvellous volcanic landscapes.

➡ Alternatively, head south and climb Furano-dake (富良野岳; 1912m) for great views out over Furano and the valley. A return trip up here will take four to six hours.

Daisetsuzan Grand Traverse – you will need to be seriously prepared for this extremely rewarding five- to seven-day hike the length of the park. This is anything but a walk in the park!

The season for this hike runs from early July to October. A tent and camping gear may be preferable to the extremely bare-bones huts. You'll need to carry in your own food and cooking supplies. This is also bear country, so be smart and tie a bell to your rucksack.

You could start at either Asahidake Onsen or Sōunkyō Onsen and you'll finish at Tokachi-dake Onsen. Pick up a copy of Lonely Planet's *Hiking in Japan*, do your homework before you go, and make the most of this adventure!

🛏️ Sleeping

Daisetsuzan Shirakaba-sō　　　INN ¥
(大雪山白樺荘; ☎ 97-2246; http://park19.wakwak.com/~shirakaba/english.html; incl 2 meals, dm from ¥5530, r per person ¥7940; Ⓟ ⓐ) A cross between a youth hostel and a ryokan, this mountain lodge near the ropeway's lower terminal offers comfortable Japanese- and Western-style rooms and hot-spring baths. There is a large kitchen available if you're self-catering, but it's worth going for the meal plan. Lots of options, so check out the website.

Daisetsuzan National Park

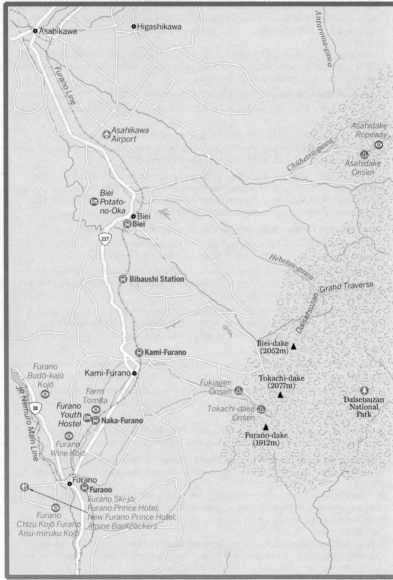

★**Lodge Nutapukaushipe**   LODGE ¥¥
(ロッジ・ヌタプカウシペ; ☎97-2150; r per person incl 2 meals from ¥7500) ⓟ This log cabin–style accommodation is an excellent choice, run by a real character who has hand-crafted most of the furniture and fittings from local timber. The onsen is superb, as are the meals. You'll have to make a bit of an effort, though, as there isn't a website. Pick up the phone. You won't be disappointed.

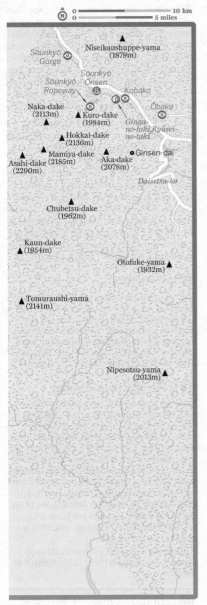

Modelled on alpine chalets, it combines elegant rooms (some with polished wooden floors) and a stunning onsen which offers both indoor and outdoor rock tubs. Prices vary with the season, and it can be quite full at times; calling ahead is a good plan. Visiting the bath only is possible for ¥1500.

ℹ Information

Hikers should pay a visit to the **Asahidake Visitors Centre** (旭岳ビジターセンター; ☎ 97-2153; www.town.higashikawa.hokkaido.jp/vc; ⏱ 9am-5pm Jun-Oct, 9am-4pm Nov-May), which has excellent maps that the staff will mark with daily track conditions. If you're heading out on a long hike, inform them of your intentions. An onsen map is also available here, which lists the locations, prices and hours of the various baths.

ℹ Getting There & Away

There are three buses in both directions daily between bus stop 4 in front of JR Asahikawa Station and Asahidake Onsen (¥1320, 1½ hours). The first bus leaves Asahikawa at 9.25am, returning from Asahidake Onsen at 11am.

Sōunkyō Onsen 層雲峡温泉

☎ 01658

The national park's second major gateway is Sōunkyō Onsen on its northeastern edge. Sōunkyō is a nice base for forays into the park's interior, and there are some impressive natural attractions in the area that are worth seeking out between dips in the hot springs.

The town has ATM facilities, restaurants and a couple of convenience stores, though if you are heading out into the backcountry, you'd be better to organise supplies before coming. There is no petrol station.

◉ Sights

Sōunkyō (層雲峡; Layer Cloud Gorge) is a string of gorges 15km long formed by the Ishikari River, the very same Ishikari River that empties out into the Sea of Japan just north of Sapporo.

Popular with visitors are the waterfalls **Ryūsei-no-taki** (流星の滝; Shooting Stars Falls) and **Ginga-no-taki** (銀河の滝; Milky Way Falls). Also noteworthy are **Ōbako** (大箱; Big Box) and **Kobako** (小箱; Little Box), two unique sections of perpendicular rock formations, though getting to see them is difficult.

If you don't have a rental car, a number of shops along the main street rent out **mountain bikes** (¥2000 per day).

Hotel Beamonte   HOTEL ¥¥¥

(ホテルベアモンテ; ☎ 97-2321; www.bearmonte.jp; r per person incl 2 meals from ¥10,650; 🅿 @ 🛜) Across from the visitors centre, this is Asahidake's most upmarket accommodation.

In summer, one bus a day goes to **Ginsendai** (銀泉台), where the trailhead for **Akadake** (赤岳; 2078m) is located. Check departure times at the visitors centre.

After a hard day of play, **Kurodake-no-yu** (黒岳の湯; ☑5-3333; www.sounkyo.com/kurodakenoyu.html; admission ¥600; ⊘10am-9pm) offers handsome hot-spring baths including a 3rd-floor *rotemburo* – it's on the town's main pedestrian street. You can also soothe your aching feet in the free footbath next to the Ginsenkaku Hotel.

🏃 Activities

Sōunkyō Ropeway
ROPEWAY
(大雪山層雲峡・黒岳ロープウェイ; www.rinyu.co.jp/kurodake/; ⊘8am-7pm Jul-Aug, closed intermittently in winter) This combination ropeway-chairlift provides fast and easy access to Kuro-dake. From Sōunkyō Onsen at 670m, the ropeway will fly you up to 1300m for ¥1000/1850 (one-way/return). From there, the chairlift can take you up to 1520m for ¥400/600 (one-way/return). The peak of Kuro-dake is at 1984m. Hiking up here is a favourite with alpine plant and flower enthusiasts. Backcountry skiers and snowboarders also enjoy this area in winter.

🎿 Festivals & Events

Ice Waterfall Festival
ICE
(層雲峡ひょうばくまつり) Hyōbaku Matsuri runs from the end of January to the end of March and features ice sculptures, caves, tunnels and domes with extensive colourful lighting.

Gorge Fire Festival
FIRE
(峡谷火まつり) Kyōkoku Hi Matsuri, on the last weekend in July, is meant to purify the hot springs and appease the mountain and fire deities. Revellers perform traditional Ainu dances and drumming, climaxing with archers shooting flaming arrows into the gorge.

🛏 Sleeping

Sōunkyō Youth Hostel
HOSTEL ¥
(層雲峡ユースホステル; ☑5-3418; www.youthhostel.or.jp/sounkyo2012/e-index2012.html; dm per person with/without 2 meals ¥4830/3150; ⊘Jun-Oct; P@) Expect a warm welcome at this humble wooden hostel, a 10-minute walk uphill from the bus station. Offering bunk-bed accommodation, as well as basic but filling meals, this is a great place to meet other hikers before tackling the trails in the park. Only open for the summer season.

★ Pension Yama-no-ue
PENSION ¥¥
(ペンション山の上; ☑5-3206; www.p-yamanoue.jp; r with/without 2 meals ¥8800/5800; P@) 🍴 This friendly family-run place is in the middle of the village, straight down from the ropeway terminal. The meals are prepared with great care. Rooms are tatami-style with shared facilities. The owner is a mine of knowledge on the area. Kurodake-no-yu Onsen is next door.

Ginsenkaku
RYOKAN ¥¥
(銀泉閣; ☑5-3003; www.ginsenkaku.com; r per person incl 2 meals high/low season from ¥15,900/10,500; P🐕) A Japanese-style inn with European architectural flourishes, Ginsenkaku is a very professional operation located in the centre of the village. Tatami rooms are the scene of lavish nightly feasts, though not before you give yourself a good scrub down in the steamy common baths, including a *rotemburo* with a view.

ℹ Information

There is an excellent **Sōunkyō Visitor Centre** (層雲峡ビジターセンター; ☑9-4400; http://sounkyovc.net; ⊘8am-5.30pm Jun-Oct, 9am-5pm Nov-May) near the bottom of the Kuro-dake ropeway. It features interactive displays, short videos, photos and maps of the park. Definitely worth a visit. English brochures available here.

ℹ Getting There & Away

There are up to seven buses a day in both directions between Sōunkyō Onsen and Asahikawa (¥1950, 1¾ hours) via Kamikawa. JR Rail Pass holders travel free between Asahikawa and Kamikawa, and then catch the bus between Kamikawa and Sōunkyō Onsen (¥800, 35 minutes). These buses also run between Sōunkyō Onsen and Akan Kohan (¥3260, 3½ hours) in Akan National Park.

There are also a couple of buses a day to Kushiro (¥4790, 5¼ hours) via Akan Kohan (¥3260, 3½ hours). Finally, there are two buses a day to Obihiro (¥2200, 80 minutes), which follow a scenic route via Nukabira-ko.

If you're driving, Rte 39 connects Sōunkyō Onsen to Asahikawa in the west and Abashiri in the east.

Tokachi-dake Onsen 十勝岳温泉

The third gateway to the national park is in the south, northeast of Furano and east of Biei.

The remote hot-spring village of Tokachi-dake Onsen is not only the end point for the Grand Traverse hike, but is also a great spot for starting day hikes into the park (see p579).

It is much less crowded than Asahidake and Sōunkyō Onsen. There are no shops, ATMs or petrol stations so come prepared.

A decent place where you can unwind after hiking is the **Kamihoro-sō** (カミホロ荘; ☑ 0167-45-2970; http://tokachidake.com/kamihoro; s/d incl 2 meals from ¥12,000/18,000; ℗ @) with pleasant Japanese-style rooms and hot-spring baths fronting the distant mountains. Nonguests can use the bath for ¥600.

If coming by bus, get off at Kokuminshukusha-mae, which is almost right in front of Kamihoro-sō. Look out for Kon-chan, a slightly crippled semi-pet *kita-kitsune* (northern fox) who lives around the lodge.

Frequent *futsū* run on the JR Furano line between Furano and Kami-Furano (¥350, 20 minutes). Kami-Furano Station is connected to Tokachi-dake Onsen by regular buses (¥500, 20 minutes).

Wakkanai 稚内

☑ 0162 / POP 41,000

Wakkanai, Japan's most northern city, changes wildly with the seasons. From November to March, it's something akin to a remote Siberian outpost, home to hearty fishermen, kelp farmers and a harp-seal colony. Outside the winter months, it's a pleasantly mild port city that serves as a departure point for ferries to Rishiri-tō and Rebun-tō, two dramatic wildflower-dotted islands that rank among Hokkaidō's highlights, and – assuming you have your visa in order – a trip across the border to the Russian island of Sakhalin. And yes...those translations on the street signs about town are in Russian!

While it may seem at the northerly end of the world, Wakkanai is actually 45° North in latitude, about the same as Portland, Oregon, and Milan, Italy.

◉ Sights

If you think that the huge breakwater protecting Wakkanai harbour from pounding waves from the north looks a bit odd, take a closer look. It was first built in 1936 to look like a straightened version of the Colosseum in Rome. Around 427m long, it has 70 columns that are 13.6m high! It's a popular spot for a stroll.

★ **Fukukō-ichiba** MARKET
(副港市場; ☑ 29-0829; www.wakkanai-fukukou.com) About a 10-minute walk south of JR Wakkanai Station, this complex houses everything from a food market to souvenir shops to restaurants to the **Minato-no-yu Onsen** (港の湯温泉; ☑ 22-1100; admission ¥700; ⊙ 10am-10pm). A bit like a living museum, fascinating historical corners show photos and videos of the history of Wakkanai and Karafuto (Sakhalin – when it was still part of Japan before 1945).

Wakkanai Centennial Memorial Tower TOWER
(稚内開基百年記念塔; ☑ 24-4019; admission ¥400; ⊙ closed Nov-Apr) Atop a grassy hill a few blocks (but a big climb) from the train station is the town's centennial memorial tower, the Shikai Hyaku-nen Kinen-tō. On a clear day you can see Russia and get great views of Japan's northernmost points. If you turn up around dusk, you're likely to run into a surprisingly bold band of *ezo-jika* (Hokkaidō deer).

Noshappu-misaki CAPE
(ノシャプ岬) On a good day, this cape, the second most northern point in mainland Japan, is a nice place for a picture or a picnic. It's a pleasant walk (45 minutes) or bike ride (20 minutes) north from town. Along the way, look out for the kelp-drying yards along the shoreline. If the weather is good, look out to the west for Rishiri-tō.

Sōya-misaki CAPE
(宗谷岬) Off to the east and 30km from Wakkanai, Sōya-misaki is the real thing: mainland Japan's most northern point. Birdwatchers will love the seagulls and terns, while people-watchers will enjoy the stream of tour buses and groups being photographed before the 'northernmost point' monument. This is where length-of-Japan walkers or cyclists either start or finish, so if there's person getting their photo taken in front of the monument, go up and shake their hand. Buses depart regularly from JR Wakkanai Station (¥2430, one hour each way).

Sarobetsu Genya MARSHLANDS
(サロベツ原野) While technically part of Rishiri-Rebun-Sarobetsu National Park, these marshlands are best accessed from Wakkanai. Approximately 35km south of town, Sarobetsu Genya is full of colour every year, best in June and July, with dramatic wildflower blooms. Frequent *futsū* on the JR Sōya line run between Wakkanai and Toyotomi (¥900, 45 minutes). Toyotomi is connected to the park entrance by regular local buses (¥430, 15 minutes).

🏃 Activities

Harp Seals
WILDLIFE WATCHING

FREE There's some wonderful wildlife-watching in Bakkai (抜海), where harp seals arrive each year and stay from November to May. A basic viewing hut provides shelter, a toilet and some information on the seals. Frequent *futsū* run on the JR Sōya line between Wakkanai and Bakkai (¥260, 15 minutes). Dress warmly! It's a 30-minute walk from the station to the port where the seals are.

🎊 Festivals & Events

Japan Cup Dogsled Race
DOGSLED RACE

In February, the city hosts the Zenkoku Inuzori Wakkanai Taikai, the biggest dogsled race in Japan at Wakkanai Airport Park. The track winds through some truly inhospitable frozen terrain, though everyone warms up back in the city where festivities carry on well into the night.

🛏 Sleeping

Wakkanai Youth Hostel
HOSTEL ¥

(稚内ユースホステル; ☑23-7162; www7.plala.or.jp/komadori-house; 3-9-1 Komadori; dm/r from ¥3150/4200; P@) The Wakkanai Youth Hostel is perched on top of a hill, and has a commanding view of the surrounding town and ocean. While still a youth hostel, it feels more homely and it sources everything locally. Its location is a tad inconvenient, unless you have your own wheels – a 15-minute walk from Minami-Wakkanai Station.

Wakkanai Moshiripa Youth Hostel
HOSTEL ¥

(稚内モシリパユースホステル; ☑24-0180; www.moshiripa.net; 2-9-5 Chūō; dm/r from ¥3960/4800; @) Conveniently located a few blocks north of JR Wakkanai Station, this dark-blue, three-storey building offers functional unfussy dormitories and private rooms. But the management is warm and friendly, even if the temperatures outside are cold and unforgiving.

Wakkanai Sun Hotel
HOTEL ¥¥

(稚内サンホテル; ☑22-5311; www.sunhotel.co.jp; s/d from ¥5000/8000; @) The beauty of this simple business hotel is its location right next to JR Wakkanai Station. It's standard stuff, but everything in town is close, including the ferry terminal.

ANA Hotel Wakkanai
HOTEL ¥¥

(稚内全日空ホテル; ☑23-8111; www.ana-hotel-wakkanai.co.jp; s/d from ¥8000/12,000; P@📶) Tall, sleek and stylish, this place seems a bit out of place in downtown Wakkanai – walk to the waterfront and you can't miss it. Book early online and you'll be surprised how reasonable prices can be.

🍴 Eating

★ Pechika
RUSSIAN ¥

(ペチカ; ☑23-7070; www.w-kenki.com/pechika; Fukakō-ichiba; set menu from ¥1000; ◷5-11pm) This Russian restaurant in the Fukakō-ichiba complex is a joy, proudly displaying friendship on a local level between Wakkanai and its neighbour. There's Russian beer, Russian music and the place is packed with locals. The Saharin Course (Sakhalin Course; サハリンコース) is popular for ¥1500.

Takechan
SEAFOOD ¥¥

(竹ちゃん; ☑22-7130; 2-8-7 Chūō; dishes from ¥1000; ◷11am-2pm & 5-11pm) This is a famous Wakkanai restaurant where you can sample *tako-shabu* (¥1575), an octopus variant of traditional *shabu-shabu*. Steady your chopsticks, and then slowly dip slices of tentacle into steaming broth. A five-minute walk from the station.

Narazushi
SUSHI ¥¥

(なら鮨; ☑23-6131; 2-13 Chūō; set menu from ¥1300; ◷lunch & dinner) This sushi spot a five-minute walk from the station is easily identified by the giant shrimp stamped on the exterior curtain. From the picture menu, you can choose between a variety of house specialities, each featuring various combinations of coldwater fish, crustaceans and echinoderms (think: sea urchins) from Japan's northern seas.

ℹ Information

JR's new Wakkanai Station is right next to the bus terminal, and both are just 10 minutes on foot from the ferry port. You can pick up maps and get your bearings at the **tourist information counter** (☑22-2384; www.welcome.wakkanai.hokkaido.jp/en; ◷10am-6pm) located inside the train station.

ℹ Getting There & Around

AIR

From Wakkanai Airport, about 10km east of the city centre, there are year-round daily flights to Sapporo and Tokyo, plus seasonal flights to Nagoya and Osaka. Regular buses run between JR Wakkanai Station and the airport (¥590, 35 minutes).

FERRY TO RUSSIA

From June to September, an unusual excursion from Wakkanai is a ferry trip to the city of Korsakov on Sakhalin Island in Russia. Most Japanese tourists, many of whom are actually travelling to see where they were born or to visit *ohaka* (family gravesites), make this journey with a tour group, but with a little planning, it's fairly easy to go on your own.

In order to qualify for a Russian tourist visa, you will need to obtain an invitation letter from a hotel or tourist agency in the country. With a reservation, this letter can usually be emailed to you without any hassle.

You can then apply for the visa at the Russian embassy (p830) in Tokyo or at the **Russian consulate** (在札幌ロシア連邦総領事館; ☑ 011-561-3171~2; www.rusconsul.jp; 2-5 12-chōme Nishi, Minami 14-jo, Sapporo; ⏰ 9.30am-12.30pm Mon-Fri) in Sapporo. Exact requirements are detailed on the website. Note that fees vary considerably depending on your nationality, and it pays to apply well before your intended departure date.

From Wakkanai Harbour, Heartland Ferry (p585) operates five to nine monthly ferries (June to September) in both directions between Wakkanai and Karsakov (7½ hours). A 2nd-class one-way/return ticket costs ¥25,000/40,000. If you are not returning to Japan, you may be asked to show an onward ticket at customs in Russia.

BUS

There are a couple of daily buses in either direction between JR Wakkanai Station and Sapporo (¥6000, six hours), as well as Asahikawa (¥4700, 4¾ hours).

BOAT

Heartland Ferry (ハートランドフェリー; ☑ 011-233-8010; www.heartlandferry.jp/english/index.html) has sailings to Rishiri-tō and Rebun-tō as well as Russia.

CAR & MOTORCYCLE

Long and lonely Rte 40 runs between Asahikawa and Wakkanai. If you're heading out to Rishiri-to or Rebun-to, parking is available at the ferry terminal for ¥1000 per night.

TRAIN

There are just a couple of *tokkyū* each day on the JR Sōya line between Asahikawa and Wakkanai (¥8070, 3¾ hours).

Rishiri-Rebun-Sarobetsu National Park
利尻礼文サロベツ国立公園

While the remote islands of Rishiri-tō and Rebun-tō (off the coast of Wakkanai to the west) are virtually abandoned in winter, from May to August they burst to life with wildflower blooms, drawing visitors by the boatload. This is also the best time to summit Rishiri-zan (1721m), a near-perfect cone rising like a miniature Mt Fuji from the surrounding sea. The national park includes the flower-filled marshlands of Sarobetsu Genya, best accessed from Wakkanai.

Rishiri-tō 利尻島
☑ 0163 / POP 5000

Author and alpinist Fukada Kyūya did Rishiri-tō a favour in 1962, ensuring its prosperity when he named it as one of his Nihon Hyakumeizan, Japan's '100 Famous Mountains'. These days, every Japanese hiker has it on his bucket list, meaning a steady supply of visitors throughout the northern summer. While hikers head to Rishiri-tō, flower enthusiasts flock to Rebun-tō.

It's not just hikers though. This is far-flung Japan at its best.

🏃 Activities

Rishiri-Fuji Onsen　　　　　ONSEN
(利尻富士温泉; ☑ 82-2388; admission ¥600; ⏰ 11am-9pm Jun-Aug, noon-9pm Sep-May) Could there be a better place to go to recover from climbing Rishiri-zan? We don't think so. The onsen is on the road from Oshidomari to the trailhead. Pick it out on your way to the climb in the morning so you know where to go on the way back.

🛏 Sleeping

Hokuroku Campground　　CAMPGROUND ¥
(利尻北麓野営場; ☑ 82-2394; campsites per person ¥500, cabins ¥5000; ⏰ 15 May-15 Oct; Ⓟ) Located right near the start of the Rishiri-zan track, this campground is a good spot to stay if you want to get an early start to the hike. There are four other campgrounds on the island. Check at the tourist information booth when you get off the ferry.

Rishiri-Rebun-Sarobetsu National Park

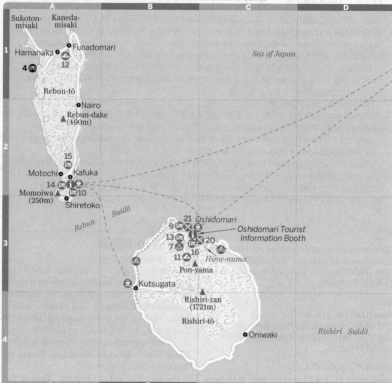

Rishiri-Rebun-Sarobetsu National Park

B&B Rishiri Green Hill B&B¥
(B&B 利尻グリーンヒル; ☎82-2507; http://
katy.jp/rishiri-greenhill; dm from ¥3960; ☺ Jun-
Sep; @) About 25 minutes' walk from Oshidomari port or a short bus ride to the Gurīn-
Hiru-mae stop, this former youth hostel is a
sociable spot with dormitories. A bit out of
the way, but a decent budget option.

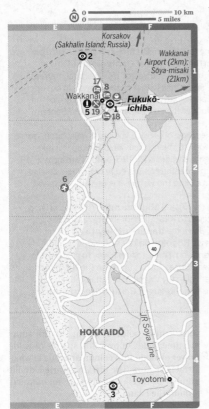

but comfortable rooms of varying shapes and styles as well as full resort amenities and sit-down dinners.

✖ Eating

There are not a lot of restaurants on the island, so eating where you stay is a good option. There are a couple of good spots serving seafood down by the ferry terminal in Oshidomari.

★ Sunset Dream Cafe

CAFE ¥

(サンセットドリームカフェ; ☑ 82-2033; www.hi-ho.ne.jp/m-1949; ⊙ 11am-5pm May-Sep) This place perched above the port may be your salvation in horrible weather when hiking is out of the question. There are tasty coffees, teas and snacks, soothing jazz, plus the wonderful photos of Matsui Hisayuki on display in the attached gallery. A perfect port in a storm!

Shokudō Satō

SEAFOOD ¥

(食堂さとう; ☑ 82-1314; ⊙ 7am-6pm May-Oct) Opposite the ferry terminal, this place stays open until the last ferry has gone and serves that seafood delicacy that every Japanese visitor must try when they come to Rishiri-tō – *unidon* (sea urchin on rice; ¥1500). There are plenty of other options if sea urchin doesn't appeal.

ⓘ Information

Oshidomari Tourist Information Booth
(☑ info 82 2201; www.rishiritou.com; ⊙ 8am-5.30pm 15 Apr-15 Oct) Plans are for the info booth to be in the new terminal, providing English maps and details about transport, sights and hiking. Staff can also help you book accommodation and/or ferry services.

ⓘ Getting There & Around

AIR

From Rishiri-tō Airport, just a few kilometres west of Oshidomari, there are a couple of flights a day to Sapporo, more in the summer tourist season. Check out ANA (www.ana.co.jp) and Hokkaidō Air System (HAC; www.hac-air.co.jp).

Local buses run infrequently by the airport; a taxi into town costs around ¥1200.

BICYCLE

Cycling is a great way to see the island – rent a bike from shops near the Oshidomari ferry terminal. A leisurely circuit of the island (56km) takes anywhere from five to seven hours. There is also a 25km cycling path that runs through woods and coastal plains from Oshidomari past Kutsugata.

★ **Maruzen Pension Rera Mosir** PENSION ¥¥
(マルゼンペンションレラモシリ; ☑ 82-2295; www.maruzen.com/tic/oyado; r per person with/without 2 meals from ¥9450/6300; P @ 🛜) Open year-round, this new place is set up to cater for all needs. With a lovely design, stylish rooms and restaurant, outdoor baths and terrace, this is THE place to stay. It does free port pick-ups, can arrange rental cars and will drop off at the trailhead. The owner is a mountain guide and also runs nature tours.

Rishiri Fuji Kankō Hotel HOTEL ¥¥
(利尻富士観光ホテル; ☑ 82-1531; www15.plala.or.jp/fujikan; r per person incl 2 meals from ¥15,900; ⊙ closed Dec-Feb; P @) Just two minutes on foot from the port, Oshidomari's ageing upmarket offering is a firm favourite for package holiday makers and large tour groups. Although the Fuji Kankō can be positively swamped during the crowded summer months, it offers low-key

WORTH A TRIP

CLIMBING RISHIRI-ZAN

Also known as Rishiri-Fuji for its resemblance to Fuji-san, **Rishiri-zan** (利尻山) is a big climb. The main trailhead is about 4km from the ferry port at **Oshidomari** (鴛泊) at 220m above sea level. The peak is at 1721m, meaning you've got 1500 vertical metres to climb. While this can be an incredibly rewarding hike with amazing views, do not underestimate the fitness required to make such a climb or the changeable nature of the weather on this exposed volcano poking up out of the sea. Between June and September is best.

Limited bus service runs to the start of the track; otherwise you must walk, hitch, taxi or ask staff at your lodging if they can drop you off. The return hike to the top will take eight to 10 hours. At 1230m, just past the eighth station, is **Rishiri-dake Yamagoya** (利尻岳山小屋), an unstaffed mountain hut that perches on the edge of a precipice, and provides the bare minimum of a roof over your head (no water). It is possible to spend the night here.

There are actually two peaks, **Kita-mine** (北峰) and **Minami-mine** (南峰), the latter just 2m higher. You may only be allowed to climb to Kita-mine for safety reasons.

For the descent, it's also possible to head down the trail to **Kutsugata** (杏形) on the island's west coast. The track, which passes **Rōsoku-dake** (ローソク岩; Candle Rock) near the top, runs into road at 430m and you'll have to find a way to get down to Kutsugata from there, probably using your feet. Buses run regularly on the 18km road between Kutsugata and Oshidomari. Alternatively, stay the night in Kutsugata.

Get a copy of Shobunsha's excellent map, *Yama-to-kōgen Chizu 1 Rishiri; Rausu* (昭文社 山と高原地図 1 利尻；羅臼).

BOAT

By the time you read this, Rishiri's brand-new ferry terminal **Oshidomari** should be all go. From Wakkanai Harbour, **Heartland Ferry** (ハートランドフェリー; ☑ 011-233-8010; www.heartlandferry.jp) operates two to four daily ferries (year-round) between Wakkanai and Oshidomari (from ¥2180, 1¾ hours). Slightly less frequent ferries run in both directions from Oshidomari and Kutsugata Harbours to Kafuka (¥880, 45 minutes) on Rebun-tō. All ferry tickets are available for purchase at the various ports.

BUS

Regular local buses run in both directions around the island's perimeter, completing a circuit in about two hours (¥2200). The trip from Oshidomari to Kutsugata (¥730) takes 30 to 50 minutes, depending on whether the bus stops at the airport. Pick up a bus schedule at the Tourist Information booth.

CAR & MOTORCYCLE

Rental cars are available down by the port.

Rebun-tō 礼文島

☑ 0163 / POP 3200

Rebun is a naturalist's dream. While Rishiri-tō is a volcanic cone towering out of the sea to 1721m, Rebun-to is completely different, shaped like a long dried squid with a high point of 490m. In the summertime, fields of over 300 species of wildflower explode into colour, and this is what attracts visitors. The terrain is varied, and a number of excellent tracks are maintained around the island.

🏃 Activities

Most people come to Rebun-tō to hike, whether it is an eight-hour length of the island version or a shorter two- to four-hour option.

For starters, it's a good idea to take a bus to the northern tip of the island, **Sukoton-misaki** (スコトン岬). Keep your eyes open for harp seals, which can be seen year-round here, in **Funadomari Bay** (船泊湾) and at Kaneda-misaki (金田岬).

From Sukoton-misaki, you can hike your way back south to **Sukai-misaki** (澄海岬) in 2½ hours. From here, either turn east and inland for 45 minutes to reach the bus stop at **Hamanaka** (浜中), or alternatively, you can continue south and hike the entire length of the island.

Another popular hike is from **Nairo** (内路), halfway down the east coast, to the top of **Rebun-dake** (礼文岳; 490m). It's a pleasant four-hour return journey, and the view from the summit helps to give perspective on the shape of Rebun.

Near the port in **Kafuka** (香深) there is a wildflower trail leading across a backbone of spectacular highlands to **Momoiwa** (桃岩; Peach Rock). The track then winds down through more flowers and bamboo to the lighthouse at **Shiretoko** (知床). Take the bus back to Kafuka. It's a great two-hour taste for those without a lot of time.

Usuyuki-no-yu Onsen　　　　ONSEN
(うすゆきの湯; ☏86-2345; admission ¥600; ⏰noon-10pm) This impressive onsen is right on the waterfront in Kafuka, a couple of minutes' walk from the ferry terminal. A great place for a soak after a day's hiking.

🛏 Sleeping

⭐Guesthouse Nonno　　　　GUESTHOUSE ¥
(ゲストハウスのんの; ☏86-2350; yanaman1025@gmail.com; r per person ¥3150; P@🛜) A top budget option with Japanese-style rooms and shared facilities. Nonno is a 10-minute walk south of the ferry terminal. Rooms are clean and simple, there's internet, a laundry and kitchen, and if you use your own sleeping bag, the price drops to ¥2700 per person. Free transfer from the ferry terminal.

Momoiwa-sō Youth Hostel　　　HOSTEL ¥
(桃岩荘ユースホステル; ☏86-1421; www.youthhostel.or.jp/n_momoiwaso.htm; dm ¥3600, breakfast/dinner ¥600/1000; ⏰Jun-Sep; @) This eclectic youth hostel (located in an old herring house) has a devoted cult following. Beds are a combination of Japanese-style dorms (on tatami mats) and bunks. Staff can pick you up when the ferry docks: look for the flags. Keep in mind that it's a hardcore youth hostel – no booze or smoking.

Kushu-kohan Campground　　CAMPGROUND ¥
(久種湖畔キャンプ場; ☏87-3110; campsites per person/tent ¥600/500, 4-person cabins ¥2000; ⏰May-Oct) Kushu-kohan campground offers attractive lakeside camping and woodsy cabins beside Lake Kushu at the northern end of the island. You'll need to take the bus to get there (¥1030; 45 minutes). There is another campground at Midori-ga-oka Kōen, near Kafukai, 5km north of Kafuka.

Nature Inn Hanashin　　　　HOTEL ¥¥
(はな心; ☏86-1648; www16.plala.or.jp/hanasin; r per person incl 2 meals from ¥8800; @🛏) 🏖 The Nature Inn is something of an ecolodge divided into two wings, offering the choice between functional tatami rooms with shared

bathrooms and slightly larger rooms with private facilities. Guests congregate in the cafeteria for country-style meals prepared by an attentive family. The property is a 25-minute walk north from Kafuka-kō. By bus, head in the Shimadomari direction and get off at 'Youth Iriguchi'.

Hana Rebun　　　　　　HOTEL ¥¥¥
(花れぶん; ☏86-1177; www.hanarebun.com; r with 2 meals from ¥17,850; @🛜) This upmarket spot in the middle of Kafuka packs in the crowds during the busy summer months. You might want to consider elsewhere if you're searching for peace and calm. There is an excellent *rotemburo* here that overlooks Rishiri-zan, and sumptuous banquet dinners that are attended to by a professional staff.

🍴 Eating

⭐Robata Chidori　　　　SEAFOOD ¥
(炉ばたちどり; ☏86-2130; ⏰11am-10pm) Chidori is a lovely little intimate spot along the waterfront in Kafuka, about five minutes' walk from the ferry terminal. This is real *robata-yaki*, with a small grill in each table that you cook your food on. The speciality of the house is *Hokke Chanchan-yaki* for ¥1400. *Hokke* is a local fish similar to a mackerel, and you grill it yourself over charcoal.

ℹ Information

Tourist Information Counter (☏86-2655; www.rebun-island.jp; ⏰8am-5pm mid-Apr–Oct) In the ferry terminal; helpful English-speaking staff who can assist with transport, sights, hiking and accommodation. Open until the last ferry departs.

ℹ Getting There & Around

AIR
Rebun-tō Airport has recently closed.

BICYCLE
Rental bicycles can be found outside the Kafuka ferry terminal.

BOAT
From Wakkanai Harbour, Heartland Ferry (p588) operates two to five daily ferries (year-round) between Wakkanai and Kafuka (from ¥2400, two hours). Less frequent ferries run in both directions from Kafuka to Oshidomari and Kutsugata Harbours (¥830, 45 minutes) on Rishiri-tō. All ferry tickets are available for purchase at the various ports.

ℹ️ DRIVING THE OKHOTSK LINE

If the name Okhotsk doesn't sound very Japanese to you, you're dead right! The Japanese never had a name for the sea that borders the eastern coast of Hokkaidō, so they've adopted (and adapted!) the Russian name.

Take a look at a map and you'll see that the Okhotsk Sea falls between Sakhalin (formerly known as Karafuto and part of Japan from 1905 to 1945), a long stretch of eastern Siberia, the Kamchatka Peninsula, the Kuril Islands (including the Northern Territories still in dispute between Japan and Russia) and Hokkaidō.

The name Okhotsk may even make you shiver – it just sounds cold. With 80% covered in ice flows in winter and the scene of countless Cold War operations, the Okhotsk Sea just doesn't seem to be the most inviting place.

Strange then, considering the history and ongoing territorial disputes, that the Japanese have called that region of Hokkaidō that faces the Okhotsk Sea the Okhotsk Region (オホーツク地方; Ohōtsuku-chihō). Not only that, the long and lonely road that runs the length of the coast is known as the Okhotsk Line, Monbetsu Airport is named Monbetsu Okhotsk Airport and the region revels in its Okhotsk connection. The region has a very different feel to the rest of Japan.

If you're driving around Hokkaidō in a rental car and you've been up to Wakkanai and Rishiri-Rebun-Sarobetsu National Park, we heartily recommend driving back south by the Okhotsk Line. After rounding Sōya-misaki, the northernmost point in mainland Japan, and turning south, you'll be stunned at the nothingness. No towns, no traffic lights, few cars and only wind-battered coastline. For Tokyo drivers this is a dream come true and will shatter any thoughts you had that Japan is a densely populated, crowded country. The closer to Abashiri you get, the more farming you'll run into, but savour the remoteness.

If you want to break up the drive, stay the night in Esashi, 100km south of Sōya-misaki, at the **Hotel New Kohrin** (ホテルニュー幸林; ☏ 0163-62-4040; www.esashi.biz; r per person from ¥3000; 🅿 @). Right on the main road, this place features a big onsen in which to sit and contemplate your remote Hokkaidō adventure.

BUS

Buses run along the island's main road from Kafuka in the south to Sukoton-misaki in the north (¥1180, 70 minutes). There are also bus routes from Kafuka to Shiretoko (¥280, 15 minutes) and Motochi (¥440, 20 minutes) – pick up a timetable at Tourist Information at the Kafuka ferry terminal on arrival.

CAR & MOTORCYCLE

Scooters and cars are readily available outside the Kafuka ferry terminal. Having your own wheels gives the opportunity to explore Rebun to the max.

EASTERN HOKKAIDŌ

Eastern Hokkaidō (道東; Dōtō) is a harsh yet hauntingly beautiful landscape that has been shaped by volcanoes and vast temperature extremes. In the winter months, dramatic ice floes off the coast of Abashiri in the Okhotsk Sea can be seen from the decks of ice-breakers. Both Akan and Shiretoko National Park, the latter a World Heritage Site, are best explored during the mild summers when there are great hiking opportunities.

Kushiro Wetlands National Park offers the chance to see the red-crested white crane, the symbol of longevity in Japan.

Abashiri　　網走

📶 0152 / POP 40,000

To the Japanese, Abashiri is as synonymous with the word 'prison' as Alcatraz is to Westerners. Winters here are as harsh as they come, and the mere mention of the prison (still in operation) sends chills through the spines of even the most hardened individuals. Abashiri is also famous for its frozen seas, which can be explored on ice-breakers, and its coral-grass blooms, which burst into life every September. Throughout the warmer months, Abashiri serves as a jumping-off point for both Akan National Park and Shiretoko National Park.

🔘 Sights

From June to October, a tourist-loop bus connects the bus and train stations to the three museums mentioned here, all of which are a few kilometres southwest of town.

Abashiri Prison Museum
MUSEUM
(網走監獄博物館; www.kangoku.jp/world/index.htm; admission ¥1050; ⊙8am-6pm Apr-Oct, 9am-5pm Nov-Mar) Housed in the remains of the original Meiji-era structure, the dark and foreboding Kangoku Hakubutsukan details the reasons that this historic prison was so feared.

Okhotsk Drift Ice Museum
MUSEUM
(オホーツク流氷館; www.ryuhyokan.com; admission ¥520; ⊙8am-6pm Apr-Oct, 9am-4.30pm Nov-Mar) The Ryūhyō-kan sits atop a hill with great viewing platforms, interesting displays and the tiny *kurione* (sea angel), a funky relative of the sea slug that has become the de facto Abashiri mascot.

Hokkaidō Museum of Northern Peoples
MUSEUM
(北海道立北方民族博物館; www.hoppohm.org/english/index.htm; admission ¥450; ⊙9.30am-4.30pm Tue-Sun) The Hoppō-minzoku Hakubutsukan, southwest of town, is dedicated to northern cultures. A state-of-the-art place, it has numerous exhibits of Ainu, Native American, Aleutian and other indigenous cultures.

🏃 Activities

⭐ Aurora
CRUISE
(MSおーろら; http://ms-aurora.com/abashiri/en; cruises ¥3300; ⊙9am-6pm) From roughly late January to late March, the ice-breaker *Aurora* departs four to six times a day from Abashiri port for one-hour cruises into the frozen Sea of Okhotsk. Dress warmly!

Abashiri Nature Cruise
CRUISE
(網走ネイチャークルーズ; ☎44-5849; cruises ¥8000; ⊙Apr-Oct) Once the ice disappears from the Sea of Okhotsk, usually by April, popular three-hour nature cruises depart twice daily and head out looking for whales, dolphins and seabirds.

Sango Sōgunraku
CORAL-GRASS VIEWING
(サンゴ草群落) Known as salt pickle or glasswort in other parts of the world, the humble marsh plant of coral glass gets its 15 minutes of fame in September, when it turns bright red. There are a few viewing spots about 10km west of town at Lake Notoro (能取湖).

Ryūhyō Norokko-gō
TRAIN RIDE
(流氷ノロッコ号) Running concurrently with the *Aurora* in winter is this sightseeing train, puttering along twice a day from Abashiri to Shiretoko-shari Station (¥810, one hour) through a field of utterly white snow.

Stare out at this frozen landscape while eating dried *surume* (squid) and nursing a can of Sapporo lager.

Cycling Road
CYCLING
Running for 25km west from Abashiri to Lake Saroma (サロマ湖), it takes in the coral-grass-viewing areas and features beautiful views of lakes, forests and pumpkin fields.

🎎 Festivals & Events

Okhotsk Drift Ice Festival
ICE
(オホーツク流氷まつり; ⊙mid-Feb) An opportunity to celebrate the cold! Ice sculptures and statues, illuminated at night, plus lots of warm sake to keep your blood flowing.

Orochon-no-hi Festival
FIRE
(オロチョンの火祭り) Held on the last Saturday in July, this fire festival prays for a good harvest and consoles the spirits of those who have past.

🛏 Sleeping

Minshuku Lamp
MINSHUKU ¥
(民宿ランプ; ☎43-3928; r per person ¥2800; P@) A 10-minute walk from JR Abashiri Station, this is the best budget option in town, with simple Japanese-style rooms with shared facilities. It has a coin laundry and rental bicycles on-site. Book ahead or ask the tourist information office to call for you.

Abashiri Gensei-kaen Youth Hostel
HOSTEL ¥
(網走原生花園ユースホステル; ☎46-2630; www7.plala.or.jp/genseikaen/; dm per person incl 2 meals ¥5200; ⊙May-Oct; P@) 🍽 This rural farmhouse turned youth hostel is located four stops east of Abashiri near Kitahama on the JR Senmō line. The hostel is a 10-minute walk from there, at the western end of the Koshimizu Gensei-kaen (p593), a coastal wildflower garden 20km long and 700m wide and boasting more than 300 species.

Toyoko Inn Okhotsk Abashiri Eki-mae
HOTEL ¥¥
(東横インオホーツク網走駅前; ☎45-1043; www.toyoko-inn.com; s/d ¥4980/6980; P@🛜) Directly opposite the station, Abashiri's Toyoko Inn may be a simple business hotel, but it is clean, convenient and keen to attract business. At the time of research, buffet breakfasts and curry-rice dinners were free for guests!

Hotel Route Inn Abashiri Eki-mae
HOTEL ¥¥
(ホテルルートイン網走駅前; ☎44-5511; www.route-inn.co.jp; s/d ¥6050/10,450; @🛜) Conveniently located across from JR Abashiri

DON'T MISS

A BEER WITH THE INNOVATORS

While in Abashiri, all beer lovers should take the opportunity to visit the innovators at Abashiri Beer – the guys who brought you Bilk. This amazing concoction, made up of 70% beer and 30% Hokkaidō milk, may not have survived its first season in the bottles (for lack of sales!), but these guys keep trying.

On offer now is the most mind-bogglingly colourful range of beers on the planet: the Ryūhyō (drift ice) Draft, representing winter, is a startlingly bright blue; the Hamanasu Draft, developed for summer in the colour of the *hamanasu* flower, is cherry red; the Jaga (potato) Draft is somewhat surprisingly shocking pink; and the Shiretoko Draft nicely represents the colours of the national park by being alarmingly green!

Traditionalists should put aside all preconceptions and visit the **Abashiri Biru-kan** (網走ビール館; www.takahasi.co.jp/beer/yakiniku/index.html; Minami-ni-jō-nishi, Yon-chōme; meat plates from ¥780, beers from ¥500; ⊙ lunch & dinner), on the main drag about a 10-minute walk east of the station. All beers are up for tasting with brilliant *yaki-niku* (grilled meat) meals. Think of it as a Japanese version of beers around the BBQ – even if the beers are the colours of the rainbow! You may also find the brews for sale in bottles in supermarkets and convenience stores in the region.

Station, this instalment of the Route Inn chain offers the usual; however, a nice perk is the large winter-warming onsen.

Eating & Drinking

Izakaya Ishikawa IZAKAYA ¥
(食事処いしざわ; ☑ 43-4661; Minami 5 Nishi 1; ⊙ 11am-11.30pm Wed-Mon) This *izakaya* in the old downtown area east of the station specialises in local seafood including crab, sea urchins, scallops and mackerel. Popular with locals.

Kandō Asa-ichi MARKET ¥
(感動朝市; ☑ 43-7670; ⊙ 6.30-9.30am Mon-Fri, to 10.30am Sat & Sun Jul-Sep) Head to the morning market for a seafood breakfast. Local farmers and fishermen turn up to sell their wares; there are plenty of hearty '*ohayō gozaimasu*'s and tasty eating options.

Information

The **tourist information office** (☑ 44-5849; http://abashiri.jp/tabinavi/en/index.html; ⊙ 9am-5pm) inside JR Abashiri Station has English-language maps and a wide offering of pamphlets on Eastern Hokkaidō.

There's another office at the *michi-no-eki* (road station) on Rte 23 at the port. Both can help with accommodation bookings.

Getting There & Away

AIR
From Memanbetsu Airport, about 15km south of the city centre, there are domestic flights to various destinations including Sapporo, Tokyo

and Osaka. Airport buses (¥880, 30 minutes) are approximately timed to flights and run from the bus station via JR Abashiri Station to the airport.

BICYCLE
Rental bicycles are readily available next to the station.

BUS
There are highway buses each day in both directions between the bus terminal in Abashiri (1km east of the train station), and the Chūō bus station in Sapporo (¥6210, 6¼ hours). Between June and mid-October there are three daily buses from Memanbetsu Airport via Abashiri bus terminal and Shari to Utoro in Shiretoko National Park (¥3200, 2½ hours). Finally, there are buses linking Abashiri and Shari (¥1120, 1¼ hours).

CAR & MOTORCYCLE
Hiring a car is the best option for those who want to get to the more remote sections of Shiretoko and Akan National Parks. Various car-rental agencies, including **JR Hokkaido Rent-a-Lease** (ジェイアール北海道レンタリース; www.jrh-rentacar.jp; ⊙ 8am-6pm Jan-Apr & Nov-Dec, to 8pm May-Oct), are located in front of the station.

TRAIN
The JR Sekihoku line runs between Abashiri and Asahikawa (¥7750, four hours). One-way to Akan National Park is to catch the train to Bihoro (¥1440, 25 minutes), then catch an onward bus into the park.

The JR Senmō main line runs between Abashiri and Kushiro (¥3570, 3½ hours). On the way it passes through Shiretoko-Shari (¥810, 40 minutes), the closest station to Shiretoko National Park, and through Kawayu Onsen (¥1600, 1½ hours) in Akan National Park.

Shari 斜里

☑ 0152 / POP 13,000

The town of Shari sits on the coast about 40km east of Abashiri and acts as a gateway to Shiretoko National Park. JR Shiretoko-Shari is the closest train station to the World Heritage Site, but you're still about an hour by bus or car from the entrance to the national park.

Koshimizu Gensei-kaen (小清水原生花園; ⊙ closed Nov-Apr) **FREE** is a 20km stretch of wildflowers along the coast between Abashiri and Shari. Visit in early summer and catch it at its peak, with over 40 species of flowers simultaneously blooming. Gensei-kaen has its own tiny JR station with an information centre plus short walks through the flora and dunes out to the sea. There are also rental bicycles.

If you stay in Shari, right outside the station and dwarfing everything else around is **Hotel Grantia** (ホテルグランティア斜里; ☑ 22-1700; ⊙ r from ¥7800; P @ 🛜) with free internet and onsen. A 20-minute walk from the station is **Minshuku Yumoto-kan** (民宿湯元館; ☑ 23-6489; www.yumotokan.info; r per person ¥3300, plus dinner & breakfast ¥1200; P @). Nonguests can use the onsen here for ¥400.

There is a useful **tourist information counter** (☑ 23-2424; ⊙ 8.30am-5.30pm Apr-Oct) inside JR Shiretoko-Shari Station with maps, bus timetables and brochures.

Trains run on the JR Senmō main line between Shiretoko-Shari and Abashiri (¥810, 50 minutes), and between Shiretoko-Shari and Kushiro (¥2730, 2½ hours). Between Shari and Kushiro is Kawayu Onsen (¥900, one hour) in Akan National Park.

There are between five and nine buses daily between Shari and Utoro (¥1490, 1¼ hours) in Shiretoko National Park.

Shiretoko National Park 知床国立公園

Shiretoko-hantō, the peninsula that makes up Shiretoko National Park, was known in Ainu as 'the end of the world'. As remote as it gets, this magnificent stretch of land has limited vehicle access. Unless you're a keen hiker, you'll be limited to viewing the park from a cruise boat or seeing minimal parts of it from a bus. The rewards of a visit, however, are obvious. Shiretoko, a Unesco World Heritage Site, is Japan's last true wilderness.

The park has two access points, at Utoro (ウトロ) on its northwestern side, and at Rausu (羅臼) on its southeastern side. Chances are that if you're using public transport, you'll be bussing from Shari to Utoro.

◎ Sights & Activities

★ Shiretoko Traverse   HIKING

The classic traverse is a two-day hike that stretches for 25km from Iwaobetsu Onsen (岩尾別温泉) to Kamuiwakka-yu-no-taki (カムイワッカ湯の滝). You'll need to be properly equipped to tackle this route. You'll climb Rausu-dake (羅臼岳; 1661m), traverse along the tops to Iō-zan (硫黄山; 1563m), then descend to Kamuiwakka-no-taki, a 'waterfall onsen'. There are four camping areas along the top that have steel food bins (think bears!). Don't underestimate the difficulty of the terrain.

The last bit of this track has recently been reopened. Whatever you do, make sure you drop in at the Shiretoko Nature Centre and advise them of your intentions.

Rausu-dake Hike   HIKING

(羅臼岳) One of Japan's 100 Famous Mountains, Rausu-dake (1661m) makes a great

SAPPORO & HOKKAIDŌ SHARI

WORTH A TRIP

CLIMBING SHARI-DAKE

Shari township has a magnificent mountain that it can call its own directly to the south. Shari-dake (斜里岳), at 1547m, is a spectacular volcanic cone that casts a big shadow and is one of Japan's 100 Famous Mountains.

It is a great hike: either use your own wheels to get to the trailhead at the Kiyodake-sō (清岳荘) hut at 650m, or hop off the train at JR Kiyosato (清里町) station and take a taxi to the trailhead (¥4000, 30 minutes).

Allow seven to eight hours for the return hike, which involves plenty of stream crossings plus spots with ropes and chains to help you. The views from the top are superb. If you get stuck, you can stay at the Kiyodake-sō for ¥2000 but there are no meals or drinking water. Go between June and October and use a bear-bell!

Shiretoko National Park

day hike, best tackled from Iwaobetsu Onsen (岩尾別温泉; 340m). Allow six to eight hours of hiking for the return trip. From the top there are stunning views of Kunashiritō, one of the disputed Kuril islands. These days there are no buses up to Iwaobetsu Onsen so you'll either need your own wheels, or you'll have to hitch or walk the last 4km up to the trailhead from the Iwaobetsu bus stop. The good news is that the Iwaobetsu Onsen *rotemburo* are sitting waiting for you when you come down!

Shiretoko-go-ko Nature Trail NATURE TRAIL
(知床五湖; www.goko.go.jp/english; ⏱7.30am-6pm late Apr-late Nov) This little group of five lakes (*go-ko*) is well worth a visit, but unfortunately it's trapped in a bureaucratic quagmire! Fourteen kilometres north from Utoro, a short walk of 800m on an elevated boardwalk (40 minutes return) from the entrance to the rather unromantically named Ichi-ko (Lake 1) is free and requires no applications.

If you want to go on to Lakes 2 to 5, however, you need to submit applications, pay the right fee and attend a lecture first! Between 10 May and 31 July you can only walk as part of an authorised tour party with a registered guide. See the website for exact requirements.

Nature Cruises from Utoro CRUISES
A number of companies operate nature cruises along the northwestern side of the peninsula from Utoro. Cruises on offer range from 90-minute return trips as far as Kamui-wakka-no-taki (around ¥3000 per person) to 3½-hour trips all the way out to the cape and back (around ¥7000 per person).

Aurora Cruises (おーろら; ☎0152-24-2147; http://ms-aurora.com/shiretoko/en/), operating ice-breakers that do drift ice trips out of Abashiri in winter, offers both options.

Godzilla-Iwa Cruises (ゴジラ岩観光; ☎0152-24-3060; http://kamuiwakka.jp/) does too, with smaller, faster and more flexible boats. It also runs winter cruises from Utoro among the ice from January to April.

Nature Cruises from Rausu CRUISES
Nature cruises operate out of Rausu on the southeastern side of the peninsula. **Marumi Cruises** (まるみ観光船; ☎0153-88-1313; shiretoko-rausu.com) has daily 9am departures in both summer and winter that see local wildlife such as whales, dolphins, seals, seabirds and eagles.

Shiretoko Pass Lookout LOOKOUT
(知床峠展望台) If hiking isn't your thing, you can still obtain dramatic views by driving Rte 334 between Utoro and Rausu and stopping at the Shiretoko Pass Lookout (740m). The pass sits just to the southwest of Rausu-dake (1661m) and Rte 334 winds through magnificent forest. Keep your eyes open for deer.

🛏 Sleeping

Oyado Kiraku MINSHUKU ¥
(お宿来羅玖; ☎0152-24-2550; http://travel.rakuten.com/hotelinfo/33/130733; r per person with/without 2 meals ¥7350/4000; @) A short walk from the *michi-no-eki* (road station) in Utoro, Kiraku is a bargain with tatami rooms, shared facilities, tasty meals and a convenient location. The staff at the information counter at the *michi-no-eki* will call for you, but it will pay to book ahead in summer.

Shiretoko Iwaobetsu Youth Hostel HOSTEL ¥
(知床岩尾別ユースホステル; ☎0152-24-2311; www4.ocn.ne.jp/~iwayh/english/e-top.html; dm from ¥3900, breakfast/dinner from ¥700/1260; ⏱Mar-Nov; 🅿@) 🍽 At the Iwaobetsu bus stop, 5km north of Utoro, this is a popular base for hikers. The hostel also provides numerous chances to spot wildlife, as bears, deer and foxes live in the surrounding woods. A sea-kayak tour is run by the hostel on demand. The road up to Iwaobetsu Onsen and the trailheads starts here.

★ Marumi RYOKAN ¥¥
(羅臼の宿まるみ; ☎88-1313; www.shiretoko-rausu.com; r per person with/without 2 meals from ¥12,600/8900; 🅿@♨) Eight kilometres southwest of Rausu township on Rte 335, Marumi has more than everything you need. There is an onsen, sauna, restaurant,

SAPPORO & HOKKAIDŌ SHIRETOKO NATIONAL PARK

ℹ WARNING: BEAR ACTIVITY

The peninsula of Shiretoko-hantō is home to around 600 *higuma* (brown bears), the highest density in Hokkaidō. *Higuma* are a whole different story to the smaller black bears on Honshū – they're much bigger and much more aggressive. Take all precautions, especially in the early morning and at dusk, and avoid hoofing it alone. Make a lot of noise; like Japanese hikers, tie a *kuma-yoke* (bear-bell) to your rucksack! Remember, the bears want to avoid you just about as much as you want to avoid them and if they hear you coming, they'll take evasive action.

If you're camping, use the steel food bins or tie up your food and do not bury your rubbish. Bear activity picks up noticeably during early autumn when the creatures are actively foraging for food ahead of their winter hibernation. Be especially cautious at this time. For more information on Hakkaidō's *higuma*, see p605.

GETTING INTO HOT WATER

The Shiretoko peninsula offers some great opportunities to get into hot water. The following onsen are those spots sought out by onsen connoisseurs – free pools of hot water that you can just strip off and hop into. They are not for the timid! Some are in the forest, some by the sea. They are free because, in most cases, there is nothing there except hot water. You'll need your own wheels to reach most of these spots.

Iwaobetsu Onsen (岩尾別温泉) At the end of the road. While there is also an onsen in the hotel, head down the trail at the back end of the car park to find three hidden hotpools in the forest. The third, and smallest, is 100m after the first two.

Kamuiwakka-yu-no-taki (カムイワッカ湯の滝) This is a popular warm waterfall that is at the end of the road on the northwestern side of the peninsula. Most wear bathing suits here. Unfortunately, the hot water further upstream has been made off-limits for safety reasons by the bureaucrats.

Kuma-no-yu (熊の湯) A few kilometres up and inland from Rausu, this pair of steaming pools on the far side of the steaming river is superb. Park by the road and cross the bridge. Some locals come every day – plead with them to let you put some cold water in if it's too hot. The onsen is segregated by sex and has changing facilities.

Seseki Onsen (セセキ温泉) A man-made rockpool by the sea. The heat of the water in here is determined by whether the tide is in or not! Soak it in while staring out to sea. Made famous by a popular television drama.

Aidomari Onsen (相泊温泉) This little boiler, almost at the end of the road on the southeastern side of the peninsula, has two little pools, side by side, segregated by sex and a makeshift shed during the busy summer season – but freely accessible the rest of the year. You'll want to look out to sea because it backs onto the road and a fair bit of concrete.

internet and simple but clean tatami rooms overlooking the sea. This friendly place also runs the daily nature cruises out of Rausu year-round.

Rausu Dai-Ichi Hotel HOTEL ¥¥
(羅臼第一ホテル; ☏0153-87-2259; http://rausu-daiichi-hotel.jp; r from ¥12,000; P🛜) This upmarket place is a couple of kilometres inland from Rausu township in the valley on Rte 334. There is a large onsen with *rotemburo*, restaurant and parking on-site. Rooms are Japanese-style with private facilities. A great spot from which to explore the national park with your own wheels.

ℹ Information

There are information centres left, right and centre. There are simple information desks at the *michi-no-eki*, the big roadside drive-ins in both Utoro and Rausu.

Shiretoko Nature Centre (知床ネイチャーセンター; ☏24-2114; www.shiretoko.or.jp; ⏰8am-5.40pm mid-Apr–mid-Oct, 9am-4pm mid-Oct–mid-Apr) Run by the Shiretoko Nature Foundation, this is effectively the National Park Visitor Centre. Be sure to register here before heading off hiking into the wilds. Tell staff what you are up to and they will bring you up-to-

date with the latest weather, track and bear conditions. You can pick up maps and English brochures here.

Rausu Visitor Centre (羅臼ビジターセンター; ☏0153-87-2828; ⏰9am-5pm Tue-Sun) On the Rausu side of the peninsula on Rte 334, this place has displays, explanations, maps and information, much of it in English. Worth a visit. Take a look out the back and spot some deer.

Rusa Field House (ルサフィールドハウス; ☏0152-24-4354; http://shiretoko-whc.jp; ⏰9am-5pm May-Oct, 10am-4pm Feb-Apr, closed Tue) This excellent log-house-type facility at the park entrance on Rte 87, 13km northeast of Rausu, is very good. Displays are informative, as is the staff. Every year in summer around 100 to 200 hardy souls walk from Aidomari to Shiretoko-misaki (Cape Shiretoko) – this 50km round-trip hike is not recommended except for the highly intrepid and well prepared – and you must check in and out here. Same for adventurous sea-kayakers heading out to the cape.

ℹ Getting There & Around

BUS

There are buses daily between Shari and Utoro (¥1490, 50 minutes); from Utoro, buses continue on as far as Shiretoko Go-ko (¥690, 25 minutes).

A shuttle bus operates from the Nature Centre to Kamuiwakka-yu-no-taki from 1 to 25 August and 15 to 24 September (¥1300). The road from Shiretoko Go-ko to Kamuiwakka-yu-no-taki is closed to private traffic in these periods.Outside of these dates, you can drive to the road end.

There are buses daily between Utoro and Rausu (¥1310, 55 minutes) via the dramatic Shiretoko-Toge pass. Daily buses also run between Rausu and Kushiro (¥4740, 3½ hours).

CAR & MOTORCYCLE

Having your own wheels will greatly enhance your visit.

Akan National Park
阿寒国立公園

One of Japan's first groups of national parks, Akan National Park was designated in 1934 and covers 905 sq km of volcanic peaks, large caldera lakes, thick forests and rejuvenating onsen. A marvellous place to explore!

If you are using trains, the eastern part of the park will be easiest to get to. The JR Senmō line runs between Abashiri and Kushiro and has useful stops in the park at JR Kawayu Onsen Station and at JR Mashū Station in the town of Teshikaga, a little further south. You'll need to hit the road, either by bus or car, to get to Akanko Onsen and western parts of the park. Rental wheels will be very useful here.

Kawayu Onsen 川湯温泉

♪ 015

Kawayu is a quiet onsen town that is home to more than two dozen hot-spring hotels, but it's the surrounding area where Akan National Park really comes to life.

Kawayu Onsen township is a five-minute bus ride from JR Kawayu Onsen Station.

◉ Sights & Activities

Kawayu Eco-Museum Centre   MUSEUM

(川湯エコミュージアムセンター; ☎ 483-4100; www6.marimo.or.jp/k_emc; ☺ 8am-5pm May-Oct, 9am-4pm Nov-Apr) FREE This museum cum visitors centre in Kawayu Onsen has impressive displays, handy hiking maps and helpful staff. Check out how the volcanic landscape was formed. A number of short nature trails start here.

Kusshoro-ko   LAKE

(屈斜路湖) The park's biggest lake is famous for its swimming, boating, volcanically warmed sands and its own version of

the Loch Ness monster, Kusshi. Roads run around its southern and eastern shores that are fun for exploring.

Wakoto Peninsula Nature Trail   NATURE TRAIL

(和琴半島ネイチャートレイル) FREE At the southern end of Kussharo-ko, the Wakoto Peninsula was created by a volcanic eruption much later than that which formed the lake. A circular 'island' is connected to the mainland by a narrow neck of land and has a lovely 2.5km nature trail around it. The walk will take about an hour. Relax in the free onsen at the trailhead after your walk. There is also a campground here next to the car park on the 'mainland'.

★ Mashū-ko   LAKE

(摩周湖) Considered by many to be Japan's most beautiful lake, Mashū-ko once held the world record for water clarity! The island in the middle was known by the Ainu as the Isle of the Gods. A road runs along the western rim of this impressive caldera lake. You can't get down to lake level, but there are two official viewing points called Viewpoint 1 and Viewpoint 3.

★ Mashū-dake Hiking   HIKING

(摩周岳) The trailhead for this excellent hike is at Mashū-ko Viewpoint 1 at 400m at the southern end of the lake. You can bus, drive or hitch to this point. The walk to the top of Mashū-dake (857m) takes you around the lake to its eastern side and back in four to six hours, and you will be rewarded with amazing volcanic views for much of the hike.

Iō-zan   VOLCANO

(硫黄山) This steaming, hissing mountain (512m), a couple of kilometres south of Kawayu Onsen, comes complete with sunshine-yellow sulphur and onsen-steamed eggs. You'll hear the sellers calling *Tamago! Tamago! Tamago!* (Eggs!) even before you reach the car park.

Tsutsuji-ga-hara Nature Trail   NATURE TRAIL

(つつじヶ原ネイチャートレイル) This nature trail connects the Kawayu Eco-Museum Centre and Iō-zan with a very pleasant 2.5km walkway. While climbing Iō-zan is prohibited for safety reasons, the nature trail allows you to get up and close with volcanic activity and smell the sulphur!

Kawayu Sumō Museum   MUSEUM

(川湯相撲記念館; ☎ 483-2924; admission ¥400; ☺ 9am-9pm Jun-Sep, 9am-5pm Oct-May) Sumō

Akan National Park

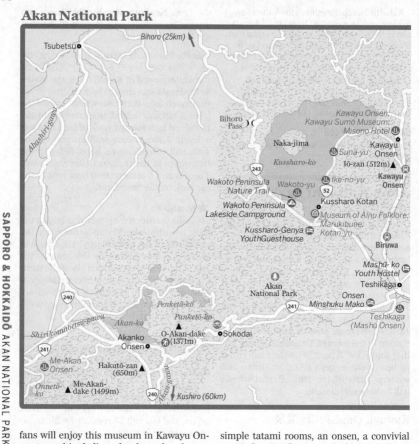

fans will enjoy this museum in Kawayu Onsen township dedicated to legendary hometown hero, Taihō (大鵬; 1940–2013). He was born on Karafuto (Sakhalin) to a Ukrainian father and Japanese mother, brought up in Kawayu Onsen, and went on to become one of the greatest *yokozuna* (grand champions) of all time. Taihō retired in 1971.

Museum of Ainu Folklore   MUSEUM
(コタンアイヌ民族資料館; ☑482-2340; admission ¥400; ⊙9am-5pm mid-Apr-Oct) In the village of Kussharo Kotan on the southern shores of the lake; displays traditional Ainu tools and crafts.

🛏 Sleeping

Onsen Minshuku Mako   MINSHUKU ¥
(温泉民宿摩湖; ☑482-5124; www.onsen-mako.com; r per person with/without 2 meals ¥4800/3300; P@) A 20-minute walk from JR Mashū Station, this family-run place has

simple tatami rooms, an onsen, a convivial atmosphere and serves meals. A good option, especially if you have your own wheels.

Mashū-ko Youth Hostel   HOSTEL ¥
(摩周湖ユースホステル; ☑482-3098; www.masyuko.co.jp; dm ¥3000-3500; s ¥4500-7400, d ¥5000-9000, breakfast/dinner ¥760/1260; P@) A 10-minute drive from Teshikaga on the road to Mashū-ko, this youth hostel offers dorms and Western-style rooms with shared facilities. There is a restaurant on-site and if you don't have a car, the English-speaking staff will pick you up at JR Mashū Station with an advance reservation.

Wakoto Peninsula Lakeside Campground   CAMPGROUND ¥
(和琴半島湖畔キャンプ場; ☑484-2350; campsites ¥500, cabins ¥4500; ⊙mid-May-Oct; P) There's a number of camping areas in the vicinity. This one is at the Wakoto Peninsula on the southern shores of Kussharo-ko.

Kushiro (53km)

Kussharo-Genya Youth Guesthouse HOSTEL ¥
(屈斜路原野ユースゲストハウス; ☑484-
2609; www.gogogenya.com/intro/e-intro.htm; dm/
r per person from ¥4300/5200, breakfast/dinner
¥600/1300; [P][@][🛜]) On a backroad off Rte
243 on the southern shores of Kussharo-ko,
this wonderfully designed youth hostel is
an architectural treat, with vaulted ceilings,
lofty skylights and polished wooden floors.
If you don't have a car, the English-speaking
staff will pick you up from JR Mashū Station
provided you make an advance reservation.

★**Misono Hotel** HOTEL ¥¥
(御園ホテル; ☑483-2511; www.misonohotel.com;
r from ¥7000; [P][@][🛜]) This big hotel with a
massive onsen complex in Kawayu Onsen
can have amazing online deals. From tatami
rooms to Western-style rooms to restaurants
and souvenir shop, it's all here. Don a *yukata*
and stroll to the bath at this friendly and welcoming spot. Check out the English website.

✖ Eating

Marukibune AINU CUISINE ¥
(丸木舟; ☑484-2644; dishes from ¥650; ☉11am-
7.30pm) Positioned between the Museum
of Ainu Folklore and the *rotemburo* in
Kussharo Kotan, this popular restaurant
specialises in Ainu food. Try the sashimi of
parimono (a local river fish; ¥1000).

ⓘ Information

JR Mashū Station Tourist Information
(☑482-2642; www.masyuko.or.jp; ☉9am-
5pm May-Oct, 10am-4pm Nov-Apr) In JR
Mashū Station, this helpful counter can give
you English maps and brochures and help with
accommodation bookings. Two stations south
of Kawayu Onsen.

ⓘ Getting There & Around

BUS

In the high season, daily buses run by **Akan Bus**
(阿寒バス; ☑0154-37-8651; www.akanbus.
co.jp; 4-day pass ¥4000; ☉mid-Jul–Oct) connect Abashiri and Kushiro, travelling through the
park via Kawayu Onsen, Mashū-ko, JR Mashū
Station and Akanko Onsen.

CAR & MOTORCYCLE

Your own wheels will let you fully explore the
park. Between Mashū Station and Akanko Onsen
on Rte 241 is a particularly scenic stretch with an
outstanding lookout at Sokodai that overlooks
Penketō-ko and Panketō-ko.

TRAIN

Trains run north on the JR Senmō main line
between Kawayu Onsen and Shiretoko-shari
(¥900, 45 minutes), and south between Kawayu
Onsen and Kushiro (¥1790, 1¾ hours) via Mashū
(¥350, 20 minutes).

JR Kawayu Onsen Station is a five-minute bus
ride from the town centre (¥280); buses are
timed to meet most of the trains.

Akanko Onsen 阿寒湖温泉

☑0154

The resort town of Akanko Onsen, which
is in the western part of the park, is on the
southern shores of Akan-ko (Lake Akan).
It has one of the largest Ainu *kotan* in
Hokkaidō, and is recommended for anyone
interested in this ancient culture. Here you
can also catch a glimpse of *marimo,* the
most famous algae ever to bob to the surface – then you can quickly leave behind the
tourist throngs on a hike into the national
park.

👁 Sights

Akan Kohan Eco-Museum Centre MUSEUM
(阿寒湖畔エコミュージアムセンター; http://business4.plala.or.jp/akan-eco; ⊙ 9am-5pm Wed-Mon) **FREE** At the eastern edge of town, this place has well-maintained exhibits with lots of photographs, and a number of *marimo* in aquarium tanks. It also has hiking maps and displays about the local flora and fauna. The *bokke* (bubbling clay pools) walk starts from the museum, and makes a shaded, breezy loop out to the lake and back through some pine forest, with views of obliging tufted-eared squirrels, chipmunks and birds.

★ Ainu Village VILLAGE
(アイヌコタン; Ainu Kotan) While it's definitely tourist-oriented, the *kotan* on the western edge of Akanko Onsen is inhabited by one of the largest remaining Ainu communities in Hokkaidō. There are Ainu shops selling woodcrafts, leatherwork and other handmade items, and restaurants offering traditional Ainu food.

Ikor THEATRE
(イコロ; www.marimo.or.jp/~akanainu/) A new theatre back over the hill in the Ainu Kotan, Ikor (meaning 'treasure') gives local Ainu the chance to share their culture. There are daily Ainu dance performances (¥1000) and puppet plays, and you can try making and playing *mukkuri* (similar to a mouth harp), wood carving and embroidery. Book at least a day in advance for the three craft experiences. Check out the website for more.

Ainu Folklore Museum MUSEUM
(アイヌ生活記念館; Ainu Seikatsu Kinenkan; admission ¥300; ⊙ 10am-10pm May-Oct) At the top of the hill in the Ainu *kotan*, this tiny museum celebrates Ainu lifestyles of yesteryear.

🏃 Activities

As an onsen town, a number of hotels offer use of their baths to nonguests. This can cost anywhere from ¥500 to ¥1500. **Marimo-yu** (まりも湯; ☑ 67-2305; admission ¥500; ⊙ 9am-9pm) is a public onsen back from the sightseeing boat docks.

★ Me-Akan-dake Hiking HIKING
(雌阿寒岳; Female Mountain) The highest mountain in the park at 1499m, Me-Akan-dake is an active volcano that is one of Japan's 100 Famous Mountains. It can be climbed from Akanko Onsen (430m) in five to seven hours return, but if you've got your own wheels, head around to the trailhead at Me-Akan Onsen (720m), from where you can do a return climb in three to four hours. The best option, though, is to climb from Me-Akan Onsen to the peak, descend to Onneto and complete the loop back to your vehicle in four to five hours. Make sure to pick up a map.

O-Akan-dake Hiking HIKING
(雄阿寒岳; Male Mountain) O-Akan-dake is the big volcano (1371m) to the east of Akanko Onsen. The return hike to the top from the Takiguchi trail entrance at 450m takes five to six hours. From the peak there are great views of Penketō-ko and Panketō-ko, two small lakes formed when O-Akan's eruption separated them from the rest of Akan-ko.

WORTH A TRIP

A BIT OF ROTEMBURO RELAXING

If you just can't get enough of onsen in the open air, try these beauties. They are all free, but don't forget, that means few or no facilities.

Kawayu Onsen Ashi-no-yu (川湯温泉足の湯) This one is just for the feet. Smack in the middle of town, this 'footbath' has seating and is covered by a roof for when it's raining. Right beside the steaming stream running through the township.

Suna-yu (砂湯) On Kussharo-ko's eastern side, hot water comes up through sand at the side of the lake. Bury your feet in it or dig your own hole and wallow. There's no privacy.

Ike-no-yu (池の湯) You'll need a car navi or be good with maps to find this huge rock-pool of hot water on the eastern side of Kussharo-ko. It's worth the effort though.

Kotan-yu (コタン湯) On the southern shores of Kussharo-ko, in the Ainu *kotan*, this *rotemburo* offers great views out to the lake. It's one pool with a big rock in the middle splitting it into male and female sides.

Wakoto-yu (和琴湯) At the base of the Wakoto Peninsula at the south of Kussharo-ko, this big rockpool is easy to find at the start of the Nature Trail. Changing rooms here.

MARIMO VIEWING

Akan-ko is famous for its *marimo* (まりも; *Cladophora aegagropila*), spheres of green algae that are both biologically intriguing – it takes as long as 200 years for them to grow to the size of a baseball – and very, very *kawaii* (cute). The *marimo* became endangered after being designated a national treasure: suddenly, everyone in Japan wanted to have one.

The Ainu came to the rescue by starting the **Marimo Matsuri** (まりも祭り), held in mid-October, which returns *marimo* to Akan-ko.

The best way to actually get up close and personal with *marimo* is to take a **sightseeing cruise** (☏67-2511; www.akankisen.com; trips ¥1850), which makes an 85-minute loop around the lake. Included in the trip is a brief 15-minute stop at a small observation centre where you can hopefully spot a few balls of algae photosynthesising on the surface of the water.

There are also some on display at the Akan Kohan Eco-Museum Centre.

Hakutō-zan HIKING
(白湯山) The shorter climb to the observation platform on Hakutō-zan (650m) affords fine views of the lake, township and O-Akan-dake. Get a map and allow two to three hours return from Akanko Onsen.

Onneto Nature Trail NATURE TRAIL
(オンネトーネイチャートレイル) This extremely picturesque little lake to the west of Me-Akan-dake can be circumnavigated on foot. There are viewing platforms, toilets, parking, a restaurant and a number of short nature trails. Allow an hour to circle the lake and less than that return to the Yu-no-taki (湯の滝) waterfall. There is also a campground at the southern end of the lake.

🛏 Sleeping

★Minshuku Kiri MINSHUKU ¥
(民宿桐; ☏67-2755; www10.plala.or.jp/kirimin syuku; r per person with/without breakfast ¥4000/3500; 🛜) Expect tiny rooms and shared facilities at this great-value *minshuku* above a souvenir shop a couple of minutes' walk from the Ainu *kotan*. The rooms may be small but you'll enjoy your stay. There is a wooden onsen, excellent meals and a friendly welcome here.

Akanko Onsen Campground CAMPGROUND ¥
(阿寒湖温泉キャンプ場; ☏67-3263; 5-1 Akan Onsen; campsites per person ¥630; 🕓 Jun-Sep; ℗) About a five-minute walk west of the village centre, across Rte 241 from the Ainu theatre; has shady pitches, and even an *ashiyu* (footbath) for relaxing tired feet.

Gosensui Hotel HOTEL ¥¥
(ホテル御前水; ☏67-2031; www.akanko.co.jp/gozensui-top.html; 4-5-1 Akan Onsen; r per person from ¥7500; ℗@🛜) One of the big hotels along the waterfront, Gosensui is good value and right in the middle of town. Both tatami and Western-style rooms are on offer, along with an attractive onsen complex.

Akan Ykyū-no-sato Tsuruga RYOKAN ¥¥¥
(あかん遊久の里鶴雅; Lake Akan Tsuruga Resort Spa; ☏67-2531; www.tsuruga-g.com/english/01tsuruga/01tsuru-facility.html; 4-6-10, Akan Onsen; r per person incl 2 meals from ¥23,000; ℗@🛜🚼) If you're looking for a worthwhile splurge, this stunner of a *ryokan* offers refined elegance in the truest Japanese sense. A variety of tatami rooms are on offer, some of which feature private soaking tubs, rocking chairs in front of picture windows and silk cushions strategically strewn about hewn-wooden floors. Regal meals are built around neverending courses of edible art, while two floors of onsen bliss run the gamut from ceramic tubs to open-air rock-garden baths.

🍴 Eating

★Poronno AINU CUISINE ¥
(ポロンノ; ☏67-2159; www.poronno.com; 🕓10am-9.30pm May-Oct, noon-8.30pm Nov-Apr) If you're interested in Ainu culture, head to this tiny place in the *kotan*. Lovingly run, Poronno will have you admiring both Ainu handcraft and culinary skills. Try the *yukku-don* (venison on rice; ¥1000).

ℹ Information

Tourist Information Office (☏67-3200; www.lake-akan.com/en/index.html; 🕓9am-6pm) This big new building in the middle of town has parking and can help with your needs in Akanko Onsen. There are English brochures and maps, along with helpful staff.

ⓘ Getting There & Away

There are daily buses in both directions between Asahikawa and Akanko Onsen (¥5210, 4½ hrs) via Sōunkyō Onsen (¥3260, 3½ hours) in Daisetsuzan National Park. There are also buses between Akanko Onsen and Kushiro (¥4790, 5¼ hrs).

If you're driving, Akanko Onsen is on Rte 240, which (of course!) has been renamed Marimo Highway (まりも国道).

Kushiro Wetlands National Park
釧路湿原国立公園

Kushiro Shitsugen National Park, at 269 sq km, is Japan's largest expanse of undeveloped wetland. Sitting directly north of the coastal city of Kushiro, it was designated a national park in 1987 to combat urban sprawl and protect the wetland habitat of numerous different species of wildlife, but chiefly the *tanchō-zuru* (red-crested white crane), the traditional symbol of both longevity and Japan.

In the early 20th century, Japanese cranes were thought to be extinct due to overhunting and habitat destruction. In 1926, however, a group of about 20 birds was discovered in the marshes around Kushiro, and with concentrated conservation efforts, they now number more than 1000 birds. The cranes can be seen year-round, but the best time is in winter when they gather at feeding spots. Popular with Japanese photographers, the cranes often dance exotically in pairs.

While it is difficult to get out into the middle of the park, the JR Senmō line that links Kushiro with Kawayu Onsen, Shiretoko-Shari and Abashiri, runs up its eastern fringes. Similarly, Rte 53 runs up the park's western fringes.

On the western side, the **Akan International Crane Centre** (阿寒国際ツルセンター; ☏0154-66-4011; www.tecs.jp/photobook/tancho/; admission ¥460; ◷9am-5pm) is accessible by the Kushiro to Akanko bus (¥1410, one hour) that travels on Rte 240. Attached is the **Crane Observation Centre** (◷daily Nov-Mar). This is a winter feeding ground and your best chance to see cranes.

If you have your own wheels, you can explore the park at length, including the **Kushiro Marsh Observatory** (釧路市湿原展望台; admission ¥400; ◷8.30am-6pm May-Oct, 9am-5pm Nov-Apr) with exhibits about the surrounding marshlands and a number of boardwalks. This is a 10-minute drive north of Kushiro on Rte 53.

Train users can ride from Kushiro to JR Kushiro Shitsugen Station (¥350, 20 minutes), then walk uphill for 15 minutes to the **Hosooka Observatory** (細岡展望台) from where you can easily appreciate the grand scale of this wetland preserve.

Two stations further north, **Kushiro Shitsugen Tōro Youth Hostel** (釧路湿原とうろユースホステル; ☏87-2510; www.sip.or.jp/~tohro/sub1.htm; dm from ¥3360, breakfast/dinner ¥630/1050; 🅿@) is a couple of minutes' walk from JR Tōro (塘路) Station. This is an extremely friendly and efficient place with bunk-style rooms and a great viewing deck from which you can survey the national park. From May to November the hostel runs canoe tours and offers a guiding service, while from December to March there are tours to see the cranes.

Kushiro   釧路
☏0154 / POP 190,000

Kushiro is a large, rather unattractive port city with little to offer visitors. It is, however, potentially an important transport hub or stopover should you be heading to or from eastern Hokkaidō's spectacular national parks.

Trains on the JR Senmō line run north to JR Kushiro Shitsugen, for Kushiro Wetlands National Park. These same trains continue on to JR Mashū and JR Kawayu Onsen stations for Akan National Park, and then on to JR Shiretoko-Shari, the station closest to Utoro, northern gateway for Shiretoko National Park.

Buses run from here to Rausu, the southern gateway for Shiretoko National Park.

Best advice is to get into Kushiro early enough in the day to make onward connections, but if you do find yourself stuck here, there are a number of business hotels near the station.

We're not talking tons of character here, but you can't go wrong with the **Toyoko Inn Kushiro Juji-gai** (東横イン釧路十字街; ☏23-1045; www.toyoko-inn.com/e_hotel/00084/index.html; s/d ¥4980/6980; 🅿@📶) hotel. Kushiro's version of the Toyoko Inn is a five-minute walk south of the station, offers free breakfast, internet and the standard spotless rooms.

Opposite the station on the southern side, **Washō Market** (和商市場; www.washoichiba.com; ◷8am-6pm Mon-Sat) features every kind of seafood imaginable and a food court.

NORTHERN TERRITORIES DISPUTE

To glimpse Russia, head to Nemuro (根室; population 3100), at the end of the JR Nemuro line and take a bus to Nosappu-misaki (納沙布岬; one-way/return ¥1040/1900, 50 minutes), the easternmost point of mainland Japan and as close to Russia as you can get!

At the cape, you will find the **Nosappu-misaki Memorial Peace Tower** (納沙布岬平和の塔; admission ¥900; ⊙8.30am-15min after sunset), a 100m-tall viewing tower that overlooks the disputed **Chishima Retto** (千島列島; Kuril Islands). The Habomai islets, uninhabited apart from a Russian border guard outpost, are barely 10km away.

The Kurils are a volcanic archipelago that stretches for 1300km northeast to Kamchatka, Russia, and separate the Sea of Okhotsk from the Pacific Ocean.

After tit for tat squabbles in the early 1800s, the first agreed demarcation line between Japan and Russia was set at the 1855 Treaty of Shimoda, which divided the chain into the Japanese-controlled South Kurils and the Russian-controlled North Kurils.

The subsequent 1875 Treaty of St Petersburg awarded Japan control of the entire chain in return for giving up claims to Sakhalin. It all got a bit heated and messy after Japan trounced the Russians in the 1904–5 Russo-Japanese War. Japan grabbed Sakhalin back and started colonising Karafuto (Sakhalin) and continued setting up in the Kurils.

It got even messier at the end of WWII. While Japan agreed to the terms of surrender in the Potsdam Declaration and the war finished on 15 August 1945, Russia was not party to that agreement and had only just declared war on Japan on 9 August. Russian military forces started their invasion of the Kuril islands on 18 August, three days after Japan had surrendered! Russia then expelled the Japanese inhabitants two years later.

The ongoing dispute over control arose from ambiguities in the 1945 Yalta Treaty and the 1951 Treaty of San Francisco.

The Japanese contend that the San Francisco treaty renounced their control of the North Kurils but secured their right to the South Kurils. The former USSR, however, did not sign this treaty. The Russians contend that Yalta protects their WWII land acquisitions. The Japanese counter that this treaty did not specify territorial claims in the Kurils.

Although sparsely populated, the Kurils have valuable mineral deposits, possibly oil and gas reserves, and are surrounded by rich fishing grounds. In 2010 Russian President Dmitry Medvedev landed here and promised residents development assistance. Medvedev later called the islands an 'inseparable' part of the country and a strategic Russian region.

The Northern Territories continue to be a hot topic in Hokkaidō and if you are driving around, particularly in eastern Hokkaidō, you may be surprised at roadside signs calling for the islands to be returned to Japan.

🛈 Getting There & Away

AIR

Kushiro's airport is located about 10km northwest of the city. From here, there are domestic flights to various destinations including Tokyo, Osaka, Nagoya. Buses between the airport and JR Kushiro Station (¥910, 45 minutes) are timed to connect with arrivals and departures.

BUS

Buses run daily between Sōunkyō Onsen and Kushiro (¥4790, 5¼ hours) via Akanko Onsen (¥1530, 2¼ hours). There are also daily buses between Rausu and Kushiro (¥4740, 3½ hours).

TRAIN

Kushiro is on the JR Nemuro line, which runs all the way from Sapporo (¥8920, four hours) to Kushiro, and on to Nemuro (¥2420, 2¼ hours).

Heading north, the JR Senmō main line runs between Kushiro and Abashiri (¥3570, 3½ hours) via Shiretoko-shari (¥2730, 2½ hours), Kawayu Onsen (¥1790, 1½ hours) and Kushiro Shitsugen (¥350, 20 minutes).

TOKACHI

The name Tokachi (十勝) is as synonymous with wine in Japan as Beaujolais is for Westerners. While its name doesn't fit in neatly with the cardinal monikers of Hokkaidō's other subprefectures, Tokachi was a historic but short-lived province that was established in the late 19th century. Today, the region is largely agricultural and has few major tourist draws, though it does boast some lively wine-scented countryside.

Obihiro 帯広

☎ 0155 / POP 170,000

A former Ainu stronghold, the modern city of Obihiro was founded in 1883 by the Banseisha, a group of colonial settlers from Shizuoka Prefecture in Central Honshū. Squeezed in between the Hidaka and Daisetsuzan mountain ranges, Obihiro is a friendly, laid-back city without much for tourists.

A great place to break for the night is the **Toipirka Kitaobihiro Youth Hostel** (トイピルカ北帯広ユースホステル; ☎ 30-4165; http://homepage1.nifty.com/TOIPIRKA/english/main_eng.htm; dm from ¥3200, breakfast/dinner ¥600/1000; P@🖭), with Western-style beds, a pool table and nightly tea time. It's near a cluster of resort-style onsens and hotels along the Tokachi-gawa, about 15-minutes east of the city – if you phone ahead, staff can pick you up from the station.

ℹ Getting There & Away

AIR

Obihiro's airport is 25km southwest of the city. There are flights to Tokyo, Osaka and Nagoya, among others. Buses between the airport and JR Obihiro Station (¥1000, 45 minutes) are timed to connect with arrivals and departures.

BUS

Buses run between Obihiro and the Chūō bus station in Sapporo (¥3670, 4¼ hours). Regular buses also run between Obihiro and Sōunkyō Onsen (¥2200, 80 minutes).

TRAIN

The JR Nemuro line runs between Obihiro and Sapporo (¥7220, 2½ hours), and between Obihiro and Kushiro (¥4880, 1½ hours).

Ikeda 池田

☎ 015 / POP 8500

Located amid the grape fields of the eastern Tokachi plain, Ikeda is a small farming town that became famous in the 1960s when the municipal government started experimenting with winemaking. While conservative oenophiles might not consider Japanese wines in the same league as more traditional producers, pull out a bottle of Ikeda and decide for yourself. Judging by the giant corkscrew sculpture and the wineglass fountain at the station, the folks here hope you will.

Getting around the various sights will be much easier if you have your own wheels. Pick up a map and cruise.

Some perfectly quaffable wines are made at the **Ikeda Wine Castle** (ワイン城 Wain-jō; www.tokachi-wine.com; ⊙ factory tours 9am-5pm) **FREE**, set on a hillside overlooking the town not far south of the station. There are tours and tastings, along with a souvenir shop and an excellent restaurant. The Tokachi Lunch for ¥680 is unbelievably good value, using products from all over the Tokachi region.

What goes well with wine? Cheese, of course! **Happiness Dairy** (ハッピネスデーリィ; http://happiness-dairy.com; ⊙ 9.30am-5.30pm Mon-Fri, to 6pm Sat, Sun & holidays summer, to 5pm Mon-Fri, to 5.30pm Sat, Sun & holidays winter) **FREE** takes you through the entire process, from walking in the wheat fields with the milk cows to tasting the final product, be it fresh cheese or rum-raisin gelato. It's a two-minute drive northeast from the Wine Castle.

There is also a burgeoning artists' community in Ikeda that produces some lovely craft goods. The **Moon Face Gallery & Cafe** (画廊喫茶ムーンフェイス; ⊙ 10am-6pm Wed-Mon) **FREE** displays works by locals while serving up tasty cappuccinos and espressos. The **Spinner's Farm Tanaka** (スピナーズファーム・タナカ; www12.plala.or.jp/spinner; ⊙ 10am-6pm Apr-Oct, to 5.30pm Nov-Mar) 🧶 **FREE** is a wool-weaving workshop.

Friendly management and delicious dinners, including a complimentary glass of local wine, make **Ikeda Kita-no-Kotan Youth Hostel** (池田北のコタンユースホステル; ☎ 572-3666; www11.plala.or.jp/kitanokotan; dm incl 2 meals from ¥5600; P@🖭) a real treat. It's walking distance from Toshibetsu Station, one stop west of Ikeda (¥200, five min).

Trains run on the JR Nemuro line between Obihiro and Ikeda (¥440, 30 minutes) and Kushiro and Ikeda (¥4160, 70 minutes).

Erimo-misaki 襟裳岬

☎ 01466

This remote cape poking out south into the Pacific is far off the beaten path, but with its windswept cliffs and dramatic ocean vistas, it's a good day trip for anyone with their own wheels and some extra time.

The cape, a magnet for wind, even has its own museum dedicated to wind, namely **Kaze-no-Yakata** (風の館; www9.ocn.ne.jp/~kaze; admission ¥300; ⊙ 8.30am-6pm May-Sep, 9am-5pm Oct-Apr, closed Dec-Feb). There are plenty of weather-related films and displays, but the undisputed highlight is being blasted by gale-force winds inside an artificial wind tunnel.

DON'T MISS

BEAR MOUNTAIN

Hokkaidō is bear country and, let's face it, these aren't those small black bears that inhabit Honshū. These are *higuma* (Ussuri brown bear), thought to be the ancestor of the North American grizzly bear. And they are every hiker's nightmare.

If you are going to do any hiking in Hokkaidō, make sure you have a *kuma-yoke* (bear repeller) in the form of a small bell tied to your backpack. The theory goes that a bear wants to meet you face to face about as much as you want to meet him face to face and if he hears you coming, he'll avoid you. This is a good theory...

So while hikers want to avoid meeting a bear in the wild at all costs, there is a certain fascination with these massive, potentially ferocious creatures. Everyone wants to see one up close, but in most cases, without putting their life on the line. It's similar to that 'shark in the water' phenomena.

Bear Mountain (ベアマウンテン; ☏ 0156-64-7007; www.bear-mt.jp; per person with/without bus option ¥2785/1785; ☉ 9am-6pm late Apr-Oct), a 15ha enclosure at the Sahoro Resort in northern Tokachi, meets this requirement perfectly. Thirteen male *higuma* roam the forested enclosure, which has very clever viewing facilities. For the cheaper entrance price you can stroll along a 370m boardwalk 5m above ground level and look down on the bears. For the more expensive entrance price you get to ride a heavily fortified bus that looks like it's going into a war zone. In either case, you're virtually guaranteed a close-up with a massive (300kg to 400kg) *higuma*. There's an observation point at ground level where your only separation from the bears is a very thick window. It is a very sobering experience...and an absolute must. Highly recommended!

You'll need your own wheels to get to Bear Mountain. It's part of the **Sahoro Resort** (サホロリゾート) complex on Rte 38, 54km northeast of Obihiro and 66km southeast of Furano. Bear Mountain is closed in the winter as all the bears are hibernating.

Kuril seals, which bask all year round on the rocks below, are called *zenigata-azarashi* (money-shaped) because the white spots on their black bodies are reminiscent of old Japanese coins.

At the tip of the cape, just around the corner from the wind museum, you will find the **Ryokan Misaki-sō** (旅館みさき荘; ☏ 3-1316; www.goodinns.com/misakiso; r per person with/without 2 meals ¥6300/4200; P @), a surprisingly homely option in this lonely part of the world.

Seemingly abandoned Rte 34 hugs the coastline, and provides an incredibly scenic drive for anyone who has no other pressing engagements elsewhere in the world.

Poroshiri-dake   幌尻岳

Take a look at any map of Hokkaidō and you'll see that there is a large gap with virtually nothing marked to the west of the Tokachi region.

Actually, this gap is filled with the 130km-long Hidaka mountain range, surely the least-penetrated region and most remote area in Japan. From the township of Hidaka almost all the way to the tip of Erimo-misaki there is nothing but forested tectonically-uplifted mountains. Road penetration and signs of human habitation are minimal.

Highest of the Hidaka peaks is Poroshiri-dake (2052m), one of Japan's Hyakumeizan, the 100 Famous Mountains. For those trying to conquer the 100, Poroshiri is legendary as the hardest to get to and the one where you're bound to get your feet wet – there are 23 crossings of the Nukabira-gawa! There is a hut, however, after those 23 crossings, offering the chance to dry out.

Access is from the township of Furenai (振内) on Rte 237 to the west of the mountains. Allow two days for the 40km loop hike that starts at Torisui Dam (取水ダム), climbs Poroshiri-dake and Tottabetsu-dake (1959m; トッタベツ岳) and ends back at the dam. You can stay at the Poroshiri-sansō hut or camp beside it for one or two nights.

Get a copy of Lonely Planet's *Hiking in Japan*, a map called *Shōbunsha's Yama-to-kōgen Chizu 3* (昭文社山と高原地図 3), and a Japanese-reader to check out www5.ocn.ne.jp/~biratori for the latest in information on getting to the trailhead.

This is a great hike, but do not attempt it after heavy rains or if they are forecast, as the river will be uncrossable.

Shikoku

Includes ➡

Best Outdoor Adventures

➡ Rafting Yoshino-gawa (p617)

➡ Hiking Ishizuchi-san (p640)

➡ Hiking Tsurugi-san (p621)

➡ Surfing Tokushima (p622)

➡ Cycling the Shimanami Kaidō (p639)

Best Temples

➡ Zentsū-ji (p641)

➡ Konpira-san (p641)

➡ Ishite-ji (p634)

➡ Kongōfuku-ji (p629)

➡ Yashima-ji (p646)

Why Go?

The birthplace of revered Buddhist ascetic Kōbō Daishi (774–835), Shikoku (四国) is synonymous with natural beauty and the pursuit of spiritual perfection. It's home to the 88 Temple route, Japan's most famous pilgrimage, even if some *henro* (pilgrims) today make the trek in air-conditioned comfort.

Yet this is not merely a place for passive soul-searching. The stunning Iya Valley, a rugged and ancient Pacific Ocean coastline, gorgeous free-flowing rivers and mountain ranges all beckon to be explored firsthand. If the inner demons are restless, there's also Takamatsu, Kōchi and Matsuyama, attractive and youthful cities with excellent regional cuisine and all the trappings of 'mainland' modernity.

Travellers are quietly heralding the virtues of the island where 12th-century Heike warriors disappeared into the mountains to escape their Genji pursuers. Easy to access from Honshū via two glorious feats of engineering, Shikoku offers an adventurous retreat from the outside world.

When to Go
Takamatsu

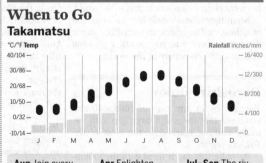

Aug Join every man, woman and *oka-san* for Awa Odori, the wildest dance party in Japan.

Apr Enlightenment may know no weather, but any pilgrimage is best taken in spring.

Jul–Sep The rivers are running, the surf is rolling, and the sun is shining.

ⓘ Getting There & Around

This chapter follows the same clockwise loop that most visitors have used to travel around Shikoku over the past 1000 years. Most visitors arrive on the island by train from Okayama or by highway bus from Osaka, Kyoto or Tokyo. The Iya Valley and the two southern capes are probably best explored by car, as many towns there have tricky bus and train connections.

AIR

All Nippon Airways (www.ana.co.jp) and **Japan Airlines** (www.jal.co.jp) services connect Matsuyama, Kōchi, Takamatsu and Tokushima in Shikoku with Tokyo, Osaka and other major centres.

BOAT

Nankai Ferry (南海フェリー; ☑ 636-0750; www.nankai-ferry.co.jp) Runs daily connections between Tokushima and Wakayama (¥2500, two hours, eight daily).

Ocean Tōkyū Ferry (オーシャン東九フェリー; ☑ 662-0489; www.otf.jp) Departs once daily to/from Tokyo (¥9310, 18 hours).

Setonaikai Kisen Ferry (☑ 253-1212, Matsuyama booking office 953-1003; www.setonaikaikisen.co.jp; ☺ 9am-7pm) Has regular hydrofoil connections between Matsuyama and Hiroshima (¥6900, 1¼ hours, 13 daily).

Jumbo Ferry (ジャンボフェリー; ☑ 811-6688) Runs between Takamatsu and Kōbe (¥1800, three hours and 40 minutes, five daily).

BUS

Three bridge systems link Shikoku with Honshū. In the east, the Akashi Kaikyō-ōhashi connects Tokushima with Kōbe in Hyōgo-ken via Awaji-shima (Awaji Island). The Shimanami Kaidō is an island-hopping series of nine bridges (with bike paths!) leading from Imabari in Ehime-ken to Onomichi near Hiroshima.

TRAIN

The Seto-ōhashi (Seto Bridge) runs from Okayama to Sakaide, west of Takamatsu. This is the only one of the bridges to carry trains. JR and private Kotoden trains run to all regions, except the tips of the two southern capes.

ⓘ INTERNATIONAL DRIVING PERMIT

If you plan on renting a car to explore Shikoku's more out-of-the-way destinations – such as the Iya Valley and the southern surf beaches – be sure to procure an International Driving Permit before leaving your home country.

TOKUSHIMA PREFECTURE

The traditional starting point for generations of pilgrims, Tokushima Prefecture (徳島県) is home to the first 23 of Shikoku's 88 Temples. Notable attractions in this region include the lively Awa-odori Matsuri (Awa-odori Festival), which takes place in Tokushima in August; the mighty whirlpools of the Naruto Channel between Tokushima and Awaji-shima; the dramatic scenery of the Iya Valley; and the surf beaches of the southern coast.

Tokushima　　　徳島

☑ 088 / POP 270,000

With Mt Bizan looming in the west, and the Shinmachi-gawa cutting a gentle swathe through the middle, Tokushima is an appealing modern city and, with a number of nearby temples, makes a popular starting point for pilgrims.

Every August, the Awa-odori Matsuri, a traditional dance festival, attracts thousands of Japanese from across the country. At other times, the Naruto whirlpools have visitors in a spin.

◉ Sights & Activities

★**Bizan**　　　　　　　　　　SITE
(眉山) At the foot of Bizan, the 280m-high summit at the southwestern end of Shinmachibashi-dōri, **Awa Odori Kaikan** (阿波おどり会館; ☑ 611-1611; www.awaodori-kaikan.jp; 2-20 Shinmachibashi; admission ¥300; ☺ 9am-5pm, closed 2nd & 4th Wed of each month) features extensive exhibits relating to the Awa-odori Matsuri and dance. The dance is performed at 2pm, 3pm and 4pm daily (with an additional performance at 11am on weekends), with a nightly performance at 8pm (afternoon/evening performances ¥500/700). From the 5th floor, a **cable car** (☑ 652-3617; one-way/return Nov-Mar ¥600/1000; ☺ 9am-5:30pm Nov-Mar, to 9pm Apr-Oct & during cherry-blossom season) whizzes you to the top of Bizan for fine views over the city. A combined ticket covering the museum, cable car and dance show is ¥1500.

Awa Jūrobei Yashiki Puppet Theatre　　　　　THEATRE
(阿波十郎兵衛屋敷; ☑ 665-2202; http://joruri.info/jurobe; 184 Miyajima Motoura, Kawauchi-chō; museum admission ¥400; ☺ 9.30am-5pm) For

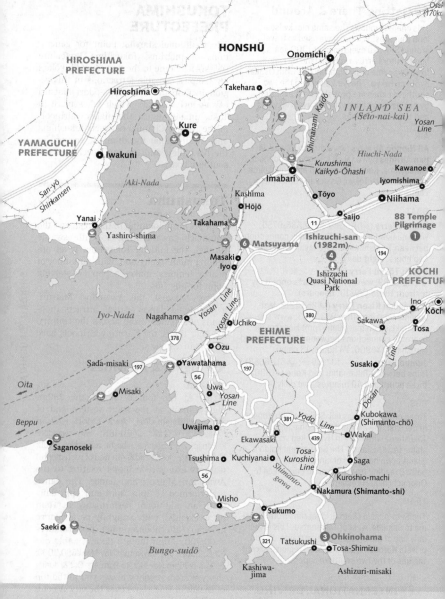

Shikoku Highlights

① Walking the time-worn route of the **88 Temple pilgrimage** (p617)

② Finding seclusion, if not enlightenment, like Kōbō Daishi did at **Muroto-misaki** (p623)

③ Surfing prime waves or snorkelling pristine streams at **Ohkinohama** (p629)

④ Hiking up sacred **Ishizuchi-san** (p640), one of Japan's most gripping ascents

⑤ Picking your way across swaying vine bridges and rafting the white-water of Yoshino-gawa in the gorgeous isolation of the **Iya Valley** (p616)

hundreds of years, puppet theatre thrived in the farming communities around Tokushima. The traditional dramas can still be seen at Awa Jūrobei Yashiki, in the former residence of Bandō Jūrobei, a samurai who allowed himself to be executed for a crime he didn't commit in order to preserve the good name of his master. The tale provided inspiration for the drama *Keisei Awa no Naruto*, first performed in 1768. Sections from the play are performed at 11am daily, and at 11am and 2pm on weekends. More puppets can be seen at nearby **Awa Deko Ningyō Kaikan** (阿波木偶人形会館; ☑ 665-5600; 1-226 Miyajima Motoura, Kawauchichō; admission ¥400; ⊙ 9am-5pm, closed 1st & 3rd Wed of each month). To get to the museum, take a bus for Tomiyoshi Danchi (富吉団地) from bus stop 7 at Tokushima Station and get off at the Jūrobei Yashiki-mae stop (¥270, 25 minutes).

Chūō-kōen PARK
(中央公園) Northeast of the train station, on the slopes of Shiroyama, is Chūō-kōen, where you'll find the scant ruins of Tokushima-jō (Tokushima Castle). Built in 1585 for Hachisuka Iemasa after he was granted the fiefdom of Awa by Toyotomi Hideyoshi, most of the castle was destroyed in 1875 following the Meiji Restoration. If you're having problems imagining the former grandeur of the site, **Tokushima Castle Museum** (徳島城博物館; 1-8 Jōnai; admission ¥300; ⊙ 9am-5pm Tue-Sun) contains an impressive reconstruction of the castle town at its peak, as well as the *daimyō's* (domain lord's) boat, some displays of armour, and letters to the local lord from Hideyoshi and the first Tokugawa shōgun, Ieyasu. The displays are all in Japanese. The beautiful **Senshūkaku-teien** (千秋閣庭園; admission ¥50, incl in museum ticket) is an intimate 16th-century garden featuring rock bridges and secluded ponds.

☞ Tours

Boats (ひょうたん島一周遊覧船) cruise around the 'gourd-shaped' Hyōtan-jima (Hyōtan Island) in central Tokushima. The tours cost ¥100 and leave from Ryōgoku-bashi (両国橋; Ryōgoku Bridge) on the Shin-machi-gawa every 20 minutes from 1pm to 3.40pm on Saturday and Sunday from mid-March to mid-October, and daily from 20 July to 31 August. In July and August there are additional departures every 40 minutes from 5pm to 7.40pm.

☆ Festivals & Events

Every August Tokushima is the location for one of the biggest parties in Japan, when the fabulous **Awa-odori Matsuri** takes place to mark the O-bon holidays.

🛏 Sleeping

Sakura-sō MINSHUKU
(さくら荘; ☑ 652-9575; fax 652-2220; 1-25 Terashima-honchō-higashi; r per person without bathroom ¥3300) The delightful older lady in charge readily welcomes lost foreigners to her charming *minshuku* (Japanese guesthouse), which has large, good-value tatami rooms. It's a few blocks east of the train station, just before the NHK TV studio. Look for the sign on the right in Japanese.

Agnes Hotel Tokushima BOUTIQUE HOTEL ¥¥
(アグネスホテル徳島; ☑ 626-2222; www.agneshotel.jp; 1-28 Terashima-honchō-nishi; s/d with breakfast from ¥6300/12,600; P ⊖ @ 🛜) Hip little Agnes lies 200m west of the station and offers a more sophisticated aesthetic than the usual business hotel. The rooms have stylish interiors, and the foyer pastry cafe is a destination in its own right. There's internet access in the lobby, and LAN access in all rooms.

Hotel Four Season Tokushima BOUTIQUE HOTEL ¥¥
(☑ 622-2203; www.fshotel.jp; 1-54-1 Terashima-honchō-nishi; s/tw with breakfast from ¥5800/11,600; ⊖ @ 🛜) It's not *quite* the famous chain, but the 23 rooms are stylish nonetheless, à la their sister hotel, the Agnes, just down the road. The streetside cafe downstairs is a great spot for afternoon coffee and pastry.

AWA-ODORI MATSURI

The Awa-odori is the largest and most famous *bon* (Japanese Buddhist custom that honours one's ancestors) dance in Japan. Every night from 12 to 15 August, men, women and children don *yukata* (light cotton kimono) and straw hats and take to the streets to dance to the samba-like rhythm of the theme song 'Awa Yoshikono', accompanied by the sounds of *shamisen* (three-stringed guitars), *taiko* (drums) and *fue* (flutes). More than a million people descend on Tokushima for the festival every year, and accommodation is at a premium.

Tokushima

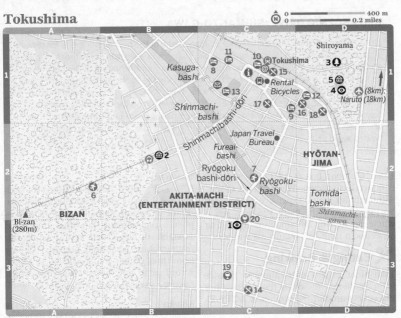

Tokushima

⊙ Sights
1 ACTY 21	C3
2 Awa Odori Kaikan	B2
3 Chūō-kōen	D1
4 Senshūkaku-teien	D1
5 Tokushima Castle Museum	D1

⊕ Activities, Courses & Tours
6 Bizan Ropeway	A2
7 Hyōtan-jima Boats	C2

⊜ Sleeping
8 Agnes Hotel Tokushima	C1
9 Hotel Astoria	C1
10 Hotel Clement Tokushima	C1
11 Hotel Four Season Tokushima	C1
12 Sakura-sō	D1
13 Tokushima Tōkyū Inn	C1

⊗ Eating
14 Kisuke	C3
15 Masala	C1
16 Saffron	D1
17 Sawaragi	C1
18 YRG Café	D1

⊙ Drinking & Nightlife
19 Ingrid's International Lounge	C3
20 Leaf Bar	C3

Hotel Astoria   HOTEL ¥¥
(ホテルアストリア; ☎653 6151; fax 653-6350; 2-26-1 Ichiban-cho; s/tw ¥6300/8400; 🅿⊝@🛜) An informal vibe pervades this neat family hotel tucked off the main drag. The narrow rooms are well appointed, with spacious bathrooms and firm beds. There is LAN internet access in rooms, and a popular cafe-restaurant in the lobby. It's across the road and down a block from the giant Tōyoko Inn signage.

Tokushima Tōkyū Inn   HOTEL ¥¥
(徳島東急イン; ☎626-0109; www.tokyuhotels.co.jp; 1-24 Motomachi; s/d from ¥7600/12,600;

🅿⊝@🛜) A step up in comfort and class from more cramped business hotels, the Tōkyū Inn offers clean, relatively spacious rooms and is conveniently located across the plaza from the JR Tokushima Station. Find the hotel entrance on the river side of the Sogō department store building. Book online for more competitive rates.

Hotel Clement Tokushima   HOTEL ¥¥¥
(ホテルクレメント徳島; ☎656-3111; www.hotelclement.co.jp; 1-61 Terashima-honchō-nishi; s/d from ¥10,200/19,700; 🅿⊝@) Directly on top of the station building, the luxurious

BEST SCENIC DRIVE: SHIMANTO-GAWA

Little traffic and stunning scenery make Shikoku one of the best destinations for driving in Japan. There's also a lack of regular public transport services in some areas, namely around the two southern capes and the Iya Valley, so your International Driving Permit can at last come in handy. Our favourite drive is along the banks of the Shimanto-gawa on Rte 381. Here you vie with the odd truck for single-lane access to some of the narrowest, bendiest, prettiest roads in the country. Travelling on these winding roads, boxed in by rocky cliffs on one side and the shimmering Shimanto-gawa on the other, you'll feel like you're in a rally driving video game where the animated cars just know how to avoid you.

Hotel Clement boasts 18 floors and 250 comfortable, spacious Western-style rooms. Although it's more expensive than other business hotels, the extra yen gets you a whole smattering of amenities including a spa and a range of restaurants and bars.

✖️ Eating & Drinking

Tokushima's main entertainment district is in Akita-machi across the river, along the streets around the landmark **ACTY 21 building**.

YRG Café
CAFE ¥

(☑ 656-7899; 1-33-4 Terashima Honchō Higashi; meals ¥700-1500; ☺ 11am-3pm & 8pm-late; 📶) This adorable coffee shop down by the train tracks is run by super-talented, English-speaking Takao. 'Yellow, Red, Green' sells hip jewellery and postcards and mix CDs, not to mention whopping cups of chai latte and nutritious, comforting meals that change weekly.

Saffron
CAFE ¥

(☑ 656-0235; 2-10-2 Ichiban-cho; meals ¥800-1000; ☺ 10am-4pm) The huge Japanese *omuraisu* (fried and folded egg filled with spiced rice and covered in sweet, brown sauce) at this very cosy lunch spot make delicious hangover food. Linger for a scoop of homemade ice cream and hang out with the friendly owner. Look for the English sign propped outside.

Masala
INDIAN ¥

(マサラ; ☑ 654-7122; Terashima-honchō-nishi; dishes ¥480-680; ☺ 11am-9.30pm; 📶) Sometimes all you need is a good, authentic curry. The Indian staff at Masala serve veggie curries and a range of enormous, piping hot naan. This branch of the small Shikoku-based chain is on the 5th floor of the Clement Plaza.

Sawaragi
JAPANESE ¥¥

(さわらぎ; ☑ 625-2431; 5-3 Ichiban-chō; lunch ¥980; ☺ 11.30am-1.30pm & 5.30-10pm) Its beige facade looks unremarkable, and its atmosphere unassuming, but the traditional Japanese dishes served at this family-run restaurant are beautifully prepared. Choose from three dinner courses (¥3150 to ¥5250, according to how hungry you are), which feature a variety of seasonal dishes.

Kisuke
IZAKAYA ¥¥

(喜助; ☑ 652-1832; dishes ¥500-800; ☺ 6pm-midnight, closed some Sun) Named after an anime character who always arrives in the nick of time, Kisuke has built a reputation for imaginative seafood dishes. Get a recommendation for the freshest specials by asking, *'Osusume wa arimasu ka?'* To find it, take Ryōgoku-bashi south through Akita-machi. Turn left just before the big Kyoei supermarket, and look for Kisuke's striking, modern exterior on the next corner.

Ingrid's International Lounge
KARAOKE BAR

(☑ 626-0067; www.ingridsinternational.com; 2-19 Sakae-machi 2 Chome; ☺ 6pm-late) Filipina Ingrid is Tokushima's go-to-girl for expatriate gossip and all-night karaoke. The lounge is hard to find, tucked among the hostess clubs in the southwest of Akita-machi, but there's nothing duplicitous about this Tokushima travellers' institution. Beware: Ingrid never forgets a face!

Leaf Bar
BAR

(☑ 652-3547; 6F, Konpa Bldg, 1-47 Akitamachi; cover charge ¥500; ☺ 5pm-3am) This small 6th-floor bar diagonally opposite the ACTY 21 building is a gamer's fantasy with manga posters, Tekken on the big screen, groups of dolled-up Japanese girls drinking cocktails and squealing over the top of mainstream American R&B. Food is available and a (very) small beer costs ¥350.

ℹ️ Information

There are coin lockers at the station, and the ATMs at the post office accept international cards.

Japan Travel Bureau (JTB; ☏ 623-3181; 1-29 Ryōgoku Honmachi; ⊙ 10am-6pm Thu-Tue)

Tokushima Prefecture International Exchange Association (徳島県国際交流協会; TOPIA; ☏ 656-3303; www.topia.ne.jp; 6F, Clement Plaza, 1-61 Terashima Honchō-nishi; ⊙ 10am-6pm) English-speaking staff. Internet access is available (¥50 for 10 minutes).

Tourist Information Office (徳島総合観光案内所; ☏ 622-8556; ⊙ 9am-8pm) In a booth on the plaza outside the station.

ℹ️ Getting There & Around

TO/FROM THE AIRPORT

Tokushima's **airport** (徳島阿波おどり空港; ☏ 699-2831; www.tokushima-airport.co.jp/english) is reached by bus (¥430, 30 minutes, buses timed to coincide with flights) from bus stop 1 in front of the station.

BUS

JR highway buses connect Tokushima with Tokyo (¥10,000, nine hours) and Nagoya (¥6600, 4½ hours); there are also buses to Takamatsu (¥1600, 1½ hours), Hiroshima (¥6000, 3¾ hours, two daily) and Kansai airport (¥4000, 2¾ hours).

BIKE

Rental Bicycles (貸し自転車; per half/full day ¥270/450, deposit ¥3000; ⊙ 9am-5pm) are available from the underground bike park to the left as you leave the station.

TRAIN

Tokushima is just over an hour by train from Takamatsu (¥2560 by *tokkyū* – limited express). For the Iya Valley and Kōchi, change trains at Awa-Ikeda (阿波池田, ¥2730, 1½ hours).

Around Tokushima

Naruto Whirlpools 鳴門のうず潮

At the change of tides, seawater whisks through the narrow channel between Shikoku and Awaji-shima at such speed that ferocious whirlpools are created. The Naruto-no-Uzushio are active twice a day. Check www.uzusio.com for a timetable or visit the tourist office.

For an up-close and personal view of the whirlpools, you can venture out into the Naruto Channel on one of the **tourist boats** that depart from the waterfront in Naruto. **Naruto Kankō Kisen** (鳴門観光汽船; ☏ 088-687-0101; per person ¥1530-2530; ⊙ every 20 minutes from 9am-4.20pm) is one of several companies making regular trips out from the port, next to the Naruto Kankō-kō (鳴門観光港) bus stop. For a bird's-eye view, you can walk out along **Uzu-no-michi** (渦の道; ☏ 088-683-6262; admission ¥500; ⊙ 9am-6pm, to 5pm Oct-Feb), a 500m-long walkway underneath the Naruto-ōhashi, which puts you directly above the action.

To get to the whirlpools, take a bus bound for Naruto-kōen (鳴門公園) from bus stop 1 in front of Tokushima Station (¥690, one hour, hourly from 9am).

If you want to stare into the abyss a bit longer, **Mizuno Ryokan** (旅館公園水野; ☏ 088-772-0013; s/d from ¥10,000/15,000) has beautiful, spacious Japanese-style rooms with fabulous sea views and efficient, foreigner-friendly service.

The First Five Temples: Ryōzen-ji to Jizō-ji

Naruto is the starting point for Shikoku's 88 Temple pilgrimage. The first five temples are all within easy walking distance of each other, making it possible to get a taste of the *henro* trail on a day trip from Tokushima.

To get to Temple 1, **Ryōzen-ji** (霊山寺), take a local train from Tokushima to Bandō (板東; ¥260, 25 minutes). The temple is a 10- to 15-minute walk (about 700m) along the main road; the map at Bandō Station should point you in the right direction. From Ryōzen-ji it's a short walk along the main road from the first temple to the second, **Gokuraku-ji** (極楽寺), and another 2km from here to Temple 3, **Konsen-ji** (金泉寺). There are more-or-less regular signposts (in Japanese) pointing the way. Look for the signs by the roadside marked *henro-michi* (へんろ道 or 遍路道), often decorated with a red picture of a *henro* in silhouette. From here, it's about 5km along an increasingly rural path to **Dainichi-ji** (大日寺), and another 2km to **Jizō-ji** (地蔵寺), where there's an impressive **collection of statues** (admission ¥200) of the 500 Rakan disciples of the Buddha. From the Rakan (羅漢) bus stop on the main road in front of the temple you can catch a bus to Itano Station (板野), where a train will take you back to Tokushima (¥350, 30 minutes).

88 Temples of Shikoku

SHIKOKU

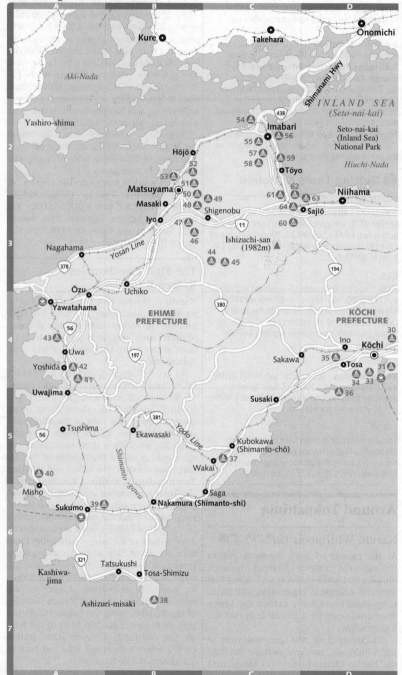

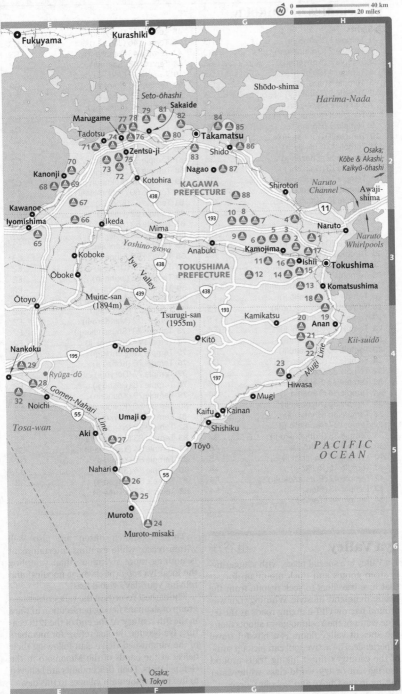

0   40 km
0   20 miles

Fukuyama
Kurashiki

Shōdo-shima

Harima-Nada

Seto-ōhashi
79   81   **Sakaide**
Marugame   77 78   82   84   85
Tadotsu   74   76   80   **Takamatsu**   86
71   **Zentsū-ji**   75   83   Shido
70   73   **Nagao**   87   Shirotori
Kanonji   72   Kotohira   *Osaka;*
68   69   **KAGAWA**   *Kōbe & Akashi;*
67   **PREFECTURE**   88   *Kaikyō-ōhashi*
Kawanoe   438   *Naruto*
Iyomishima   66   Ikeda   193   10 8   *Channel*   *Awaji-*
65   Mima   9   7   4   11   *shima*
Yoshino-gawa   Anabuki   6   5   3   **Naruto**
Koboke   **TOKUSHIMA**   **Kamojima**   2   1   *Naruto*
Iya Valley   **PREFECTURE**   11 16   17   *Whirlpools*
Ōboke   438   12   14   15   **Ishii**   ● **Tokushima**
Ōtoyo   439   13   **Komatsushima**
Muine-san   438   18
(1894m)   195   *Tsurugi-san*   Kamikatsu   20   19   **Anan**
(1955m)   Kitō   21   *Kii-suidō*
Nankoku   Monobe   22   *Mugi Line*
29   *Ryūga-dō*   197   23
28   Hiwasa
32   Noichi   Kaifu   Mugi
55   **Umaji**   Kainan
Tosa-wan   Shishiku   *PACIFIC*
Aki   27   Tōyō   *OCEAN*
55
Nahari   26
25
Muroto   24
Muroto-misaki

Osaka;
Tokyo

SHIKOKU

88 Temples of Shikoku

Iya Valley　祖谷渓

Iya Valley is a special place, with staggeringly steep gorges and thick mountain forests that lure travellers to seek respite from the hectic 'mainland' lifestyle. Winding your way around narrow cliff-hanging roads as the icy blue water of the Yoshino-gawa shoots along the ancient valley floors is a blissful travel experience. The active soul can pick up some of the country's finest hiking trails around Tsurugi-san or try world-class white-water rafting in the Ōboke and Koboke Gorges.

Three top-notch onsen are also well within reach, while evening entertainment is nothing more strenuous than sampling the local Iya *soba* (buckwheat noodles) and reliving your day's visual feast.

The earliest records of the valley describe a group of shamans fleeing persecution in Nara in the 9th century. At the end of the 12th century, Iya became the last refuge for members of the vanquished Heike clan following their defeat at the hands of the Minamoto in the Gempei Wars. Their descendants are believed to live in the mountain villages to this day.

Ōboke & Koboke 大歩危・小歩危

Ōboke and Koboke are two scenic gorges on the Yoshino-gawa, which fluctuates from languid green waters to Class IV rapids. Driving through these rural river valleys provides the first verdant glimpse into the magic of Iya.

Spectacular scenery abounds in the deep canyons along Old Rte 32 – infrequent public buses (¥880, 55 minutes, 7.15am, 10.15am and 12:15pm) ply this narrow route between Awa-Ikeda and the Iya Valley.

To orient yourself in this maze of valleys, stop by **Lapis Ōboke** (ラピス大歩危; ☑ 0883-84-1489; www.yamashiro-info.jp/lapis; admission ¥500; ⊙ 9am-6pm Apr-Nov, to 5pm Dec-Mar) for basic tourist information. Its primary role is as a geology and local *yōkai* (ghost) museum – skip the rocks, but get acquainted with the folkloric apparitions, colourfully represented in a hall of delightful horrors (explained with some English signage).

Stop by the tourist complex **River Station West-West** (☑ 0887-84-1117; www.west-west.com) for river gear at the Mont Bell shop, road snacks and pit stops at the *conbini* (convenience store) and excellent *soba* at the restaurant **Momiji-tei** (もみじ亭; ☑ 0883-84-1117; meals ¥900-2000; ⊙ 10am-5.30pm Thu-Tue) – try the *tempura soba* set (¥1400), either hot or cold.

🏃 Activities

Happy Raft RAFTING
(ハッピーラフト; ☑ 0887-75-0500; www.happyraft.com) South of Ikeda on Rte 32 between

---

WALKING PILGRIMS

The *henro* (pilgrim on the 88 Temple walk) is one of the most distinctive sights of any trip to Shikoku. They're everywhere you go, striding along busy city highways, cresting hills in remote mountain valleys – solitary figures in white, trudging purposefully through heat haze and monsoonal downpour alike on their way from temple to temple. Who are these people, and what drives them to make a journey of more than 1400km on foot?

Although the backgrounds and motives of the *henro* may differ widely, they all follow in the legendary footsteps of Kōbō Daishi, the monk who established Shingon Buddhism in Japan and made significant contributions to Japanese culture. Whether or not it is true that Kōbō Daishi actually founded or visited all 88 sacred sites, the idea behind making the 88-temple circuit is to do so accompanied by the spirit of Kōbō Daishi himself – hence the inscription on so many pilgrims' backpacks and other paraphernalia: 同行二人 (*dōgyō ninin*), meaning 'two people on the same journey'.

Regardless of each *henro's* motivations, the pattern and routine of life on the road is very similar for everyone who undertakes the trail. The dress is uniform, too: *hakue* (white garments) to signify sincerity of purpose and purity of mind; the *sugegasa* (straw hat) that has protected pilgrims against sun and rain since time immemorial; and the *kongōzue* (colourful staff). The routine at each temple is mostly the same, too: a bang on the bell and a chant of the Heart Sutra at the Daishi-dō (one of the two main buildings in each temple compound), before filing off to the *nōkyōsho* (desk), where the pilgrims' book is inscribed with beautiful characters detailing the name of the temple and the date of the pilgrimage.

If you're eager to become an *aruki henro* (walking pilgrim) yourself, you'll need to budget around 60 days (allowing for an average distance of 25km a day) to complete the circuit. To plan your pilgrimage, the website www.shikokuhenrotrail.com and the guidebook *Shikoku Japan 88 Route Guide* (Buyodo Publishing) are both excellent English-language resources; the book can also be purchased at Temple 1, Ryōzen-ji.

Travellers who don't have the time or inclination for the whole thing can get a taste of what it's all about by following one of the *henro*-for-a-day minicircuits. Aside from Naruto, cities with concentrations of temples within easy reach of each other include Matsuyama in Ehime Prefecture and Zentsū-ji in Kagawa Prefecture.

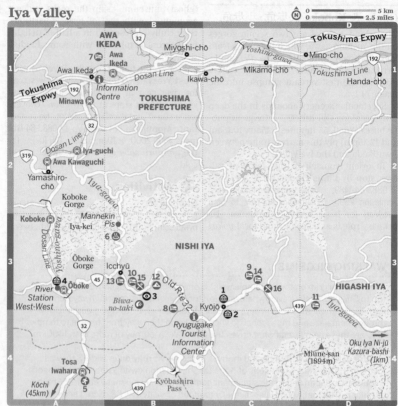

Iya Valley

Koboke and Ōboke, around 20 companies run white-water rafting and kayaking trips from April to late November. Happy Raft, steps from JR Tosa Iwahara Station, operates sensational daily trips with English-speaking guides (half-day ¥5500 to ¥7500, full day ¥10,000 to ¥15,500).

Iya Onsen ONSEN
(祖谷温泉; ☏ 0883-75-2311; www.iyaonsen.co.jp; Matsuo Matsumoto 367-2; admission ¥1500; ☉ 7am-9pm, to 7pm Jan-Feb) On Old Rte 32, this is a great place to warm up after a chilling plunge through white-water. A cable car descends a steep cliff-face to some sulphurous open-air

baths overlooking the river, and accommodation (per person with meals from ¥15,270) is available.

🛏 Sleeping

Happy Guest House GUESTHOUSE ¥
(☑ 0887-75-0500; per person ¥3000; P) A group of small guesthouses that can each accommodate up to 10. The original guesthouse is a self-contained and fully restored farmhouse, with a tatami room overlooking the Yoshino Valley.

Ku-Nel-Asob GUESTHOUSE ¥
(空音遊; ☑ 090-9778-7133; www.k-n-a.com; dm with breakfast/dinner/breakfast & dinner ¥5000/

6000/7000; P) Simple but attractive accommodation in communal tatami rooms; the house itself perches on a beautiful bluff overlooking the river. The friendly English-speaking owners can provide free pick-ups/drop-offs at JR Ōboke Station, 3km away. Since the house doesn't have a bath, a ride to nearby Iya Onsen is offered for ¥500, including entry to the onsen.

Midori no Tokeidai GUESTHOUSE ¥
(みどりの時計台; ☑ 0887-72-0202; http://midorinotokeidai.com; per person ¥3500; P) A delightfully decorated former school building that houses many 'in-the-know' Japanese and foreign guests.

CHIIORI: A RURAL RETREAT

High on a mountainside in the remote Iya Valley, looking out over forested hillsides and plunging gorges, is one of Japan's most unusual places to stay.

Chiiori (☑ 0883-88-5290; www.chiiori.org; per person ¥10,000-20,000, depending on group size) – 'The Cottage of the Flute' – is a once-abandoned 18th-century thatched-roof farmhouse that has been painstakingly restored towards its original brilliance. Unlike many such examples of cultural heritage in Japan, where concrete and plastic have wrecked the architectural aesthetic, here glistening red-pine floorboards surround open-floor hearths under soaring rafters. Set amid steep hillsides dotted by thatched houses and forests strewn with narrow mountain paths, Iya was for centuries an example of an untouched coexistence of man and nature, albeit one that offered residents little hope of wealth and comfort.

In recent decades, however, the locals' traditional lifestyle and the balance with the environment have been rapidly upset; employment moved from agriculture to government-subsidised and frequently pointless construction, the effects of which – eg paved riverbeds – can be seen from almost any roadside. Part of the project's mission has been working with residents to promote sustainable, community-based tourism and realise the financial potential of traditional life – which until recently many locals saw as backward and valueless. It is a work in progress – many thatched roofs in the area are still hidden by corrugated tin sheets – but by adding to the growing number of tourists visiting the area, largely because of the work of those involved in Chiiori, staying here helps to encourage those conservation efforts.

The house was bought as a ruin by the author and aesthete Alex Kerr in the early 1970s, and he went on to romanticise the Iya Valley in his award-winning book *Lost Japan*. Chiiori remains a beautiful and authentic destination for sensitive travellers, with its *shōji* (movable screens), antique furnishings and *irori* (traditional hearths) – all complemented by a gleaming, fully equipped modern kitchen and gorgeous bathroom, complete with *hinoki* (Japanese cypress) tub. Since the establishment of the nonprofit Chiiori Trust in 2005, the local government has approached the Trust to help restore smaller traditional houses in the area (called **Fusho**, **Seiko** and **Udoku**). These houses have been renovated to a similarly high standard and aesthetic as Chiiori and are also available as accommodations. All are outfitted with modern kitchens and bathrooms, and even washing machines.

To stay in these extraordinary environs, you must reserve in advance through **Chiiori Trust** (www.chiiori.org). Because guests are required to check in at the **Ryugugake Tourist Information Center** (龍宮崖観光案内所; ☑ 0883-88-5120; 96-3 Wada, Higashi-Iya; ◷ 9am-6pm) before heading to Chiiori (4.5km away), and because of the remote locations of Chiiori and the other houses, the Chiiori Trust strongly recommends that guests bring their own vehicles.

Awa Ikeda Youth Hostel HOSTEL ¥
(阿波池田ユースホステル; ☎0883-72-5277; dm ¥3600, breakfast/dinner ¥525/1050; P) An isolated hostel with huge communal tatami rooms and a do-it-yourself vibe, set alongside the serene Mitsugon-ji mountain temple. Make sure you book ahead if you need to be picked up at JR Awa-Ikeda Station, 5km away, and if you require meals.

Nishi Iya 西祖谷

The extravagant greenery and river-smoothed stones along the Iya-gawa form a verdant backdrop to the Nishi Iya's famous vine bridge. Rte 32 follows the river valley to connect with Higashi Iya to the east.

◉ Sights

Kazura-bashi BRIDGE
(かずら橋; admission ¥500; ☺7am-5pm) This remarkable vine bridge is one of only three left in the valley (the other two are further east in Higashi Iya). Stepping onto the creaking vine bridge, with the river sparkling between the gaps, is worth the slightly depressing approach via the monstrous car park. Check out the nearby Biwa-no-taki, an impressive, 50m-high waterfall.

🛏 Sleeping & Eating

Kazura-bashi Camping Village CAMPGROUND ¥
(かずら橋キャンプ村; ☎090-1571-5258; campsite ¥500, plus per person ¥200, 4-5-person bungalow from ¥5200; ☺Apr-Nov) This rustic but well-maintained campground lies 500m upriver from the vine bridge. Showers are free, and rental equipment – from tents to kitchenware – is available at reasonable rates. The friendly but non–English speaking caretaker asks that guests have a Japanese speaker call for a reservation, and to check in between 9am and 5pm.

★**Hotel Kazura-bashi** RYOKAN ¥¥¥
(ホテルかずら橋; ☎0883-87-2171; www.kazura-bashi.co.jp; per person with two meals from ¥15,900; P) At the base of a steep hillside about a kilometre north of the bridge, this lovely hotel offers spacious, comfortable Japanese-style rooms with mountain views. Beautifully prepared traditional meals are served in the tatami dining room by the unobtrusively attentive staff. A funky cable car ferries guests up to the hotel's highlight: a gorgeous, open-air onsen on the hill. Nonguests are welcome to use the onsen (¥1000) between 10am to 4pm.

Iya Bijin Keikoku-ten SOBA ¥
(祖谷美人渓谷店; ☎0883-87-2009; 9-3 Zentoku; meals ¥600-1000; ☺8am-5pm) For a taste of local Iya *soba*, try Iya Bijin Keikoku-ten, in an attractive black-and-white building with lanterns out the front. A plate of *zaru soba* (cold noodles with seaweed strips) is ¥700.

Higashi Iya 東祖谷

About 30km east of Nishi Iya, Rte 439 winds deeply into the green gulches of Higashi Iya (also known as Oku Iya).

◉ Sights & Activities

Oku Iya Ni-jū Kazura-bashi BRIDGE
(奥祖谷二重かずら橋; admission ¥500; ☺7am-5pm) The spectacular Oku Iya Ni-jū Kazura-bashi are secluded vine bridges hanging side by side high over the river. A self-propelled, three-seated wooden cable-cart is another fun way to cross the river; there's a small public camping area on the other side.

Higashi Iya History & Folk Museum MUSEUM
(東祖谷歴史民俗資料館; ☎0883-88-2286; admission ¥400; ☺8:30am-5pm) This folk museum is in a large red building in Kyōjō, displaying historic artefacts and daily-use tools, as well as items relating to the Heike legend.

VINE BRIDGES

The wisteria vine bridges of the Iya Valley are glorious remnants of a remote and timeless Japan. Crossing the bridges has for centuries been notoriously difficult, which well suited the bandits and humbled warriors who took refuge in the secluded gorges. The bridges are feats of ancient engineering, undertaken roughly a thousand years ago, and were formed by tying together the wild vines that hung on either side of the 45m-wide valley. Only in recent years have the bridges been reinforced with side rails, planks and wire. But it's not only the acrophobic among us who will get the wobbles.

Only three *kazura-bashi* survive, one heavily touristed bridge at Nishi Iya and another pair of 'husband and wife' bridges at Higashi Iya, which is a further 30km east – the secluded, deep gorge setting is worth the extra effort.

Buke Yashiki   HISTORIC BUILDING

(武家屋敷喜多家; ☑0883-88-2040; admission ¥300; ☺9am-5pm, closed Tue & Dec-Mar) Several kilometres up a narrow, winding road near Kyōjō, Buke Yashiki is a thatched-roof samurai-house museum commanding spectacular views of the valley. Beside the house is a Shintō shrine that is home to a massive cedar tree dating back more than 800 years.

🍴 Sleeping & Eating

Iyashi no Onsen-kyō   HOTEL ¥¥

(いやしの温泉郷; ☑0883-88-2975; www.sobano yado.jp; per person with meals from ¥13,800; ☺10am-10pm) Off the main road between Kyōjō and the Higashi Iya vine bridges is this lovely, unpretentious hotel and hot-springs complex with six Japanese-style and six Western-style rooms, an onsen and a restaurant. Nonguests can use the onsen for ¥800.

Soba Dōjō   SOBA ¥

(そば道場; ☑0883-88-2577; ☺11am-5pm Fri-Wed) At Soba Dōjō on Rte 439, you can sample a bowl of *zaru soba* (¥800) and even make your own (¥2500; reservation required). The restaurant has a reddish roof, and a yellow curtain hanging over the door.

Tsurugi-san   剣山

At 1955m, Tsurugi-san is the second-highest mountain in Shikoku and provides excellent and challenging hiking opportunities, as well as some fairly basic snowboarding from December to February. A **chairlift** (return/one-way ¥1800/1000; ☺9am-5pm, last return 4.45pm) goes most of the way up, after which it is a leisurely 30-minute walk to the summit. If you decide to climb all the way, you'll pass the Tsurugi-jinja (Tsurugi Shrine) en route, which is close to a natural spring of drinkable water.

Just below the peak, **Unkaisō Bekkan** (雲海荘別館; ☑0886-23-4533, 0883-68-2028; with meals ¥7000) offers basic lodgings in this mountaintop sea of clouds. For more info on ascending Tsurugi-san and Miune-san, check out Lonely Planet's *Hiking in Japan*.

ⓘ Getting There & Around

Access to the area is via Ōboke Station, reached by train from Takamatsu (¥3000) or Tokushima (¥3170) with a change at Awa-Ikeda, or from Kōchi (¥2390). From Honshū, Nanpū limited express trains depart hourly from Okayama (¥4410, 1¾ hours); Okayama is on the Sanyō *shinkansen* (bullet train) line.

Getting around the valley itself involves some planning because Iya's sights are widespread, and public transport is sporadic at the best of times. Four buses per day travel between Ōboke and Iya (¥640, 40 minutes). **Ikeda DK Taxi** (☑0883-76-0011) and **Ōboke Taxi** (☑0883-84-1225) are among several companies filling the gaps in the bus schedule.

The best way to explore the region is with your own wheels; you will thank the Daishi for the freedom and flexibility a car offers here. Rental cars are available in Shikoku's larger cities.

SOUTHERN TOKUSHIMA PREFECTURE 徳島県南部

The slow-paced highway running south from Tokushima-shi (Tokushima City) passes through prosperous little agricultural towns fronted by lazy surf beaches and marine industry machinery, and is flanked by hidden temples and spectacular rocky bluffs.

The JR Mugi line runs down the coast as far as Kaifu, just short of the border. From Kaifu, the private Asa Kaigan railway runs two stops further to Kannoura, just across the border. From here, you can continue by bus to the cape at Muroto-misaki and on to Kōchi city. Coming the other way, trains run from Kōchi as far as Nahari – but you'll have to rely on buses to get you around the cape.

Hiwasa   日和佐

☑0884

The major attraction in the small coastal town of Hiwasa is **Yakuō-ji** (薬王寺), Temple 23, and the last temple in Tokushima Prefecture. Yakuō-ji dates back to the year 726, and is famous as a *yakuyoke no tera* (a temple with special powers to ward off ill fortune during unlucky years). The unluckiest age for men is 42; for women, 33 is the one to watch out for. Kōbō Daishi is said to have visited in 815, the year of his own 42nd birthday. The long set of stone steps leading up to the main temple building comes in two stages: 33 steps for the women, followed by another 42 for the men. The tradition is for pilgrims to put a coin on each step – when it's busy, you may find the steps practically overflowing with one-yen coins. Make your way to the pagoda at the top, and fork over ¥100 to view the basement gallery – to see the (figuratively) dark artwork of this underworld, you'll need to creep along the wall of a (literally) pitch-dark hall.

SURFING TOKUSHIMA

Southern Tokushima is a surfer's paradise, with world-class river mouths, consistent barrels and relatively few surfers in the water. Despite the prevalence of concrete on the shoreline, this region has mostly gorgeous white-sand beaches and relaxed, friendly locals.

Surfboards are available for hire (around ¥3000 for 24 hours) at numerous places in the one-street beach-bum town of **Ikumi** (生見), where you'll find most of the best places to stay. For money, there is a post office with an international ATM in Kaifu, and another in Kannoura.

Road-weary pilgrims will find refreshment at the **rest stop** in the middle of town, which, in addition to the usual food stalls, immaculate restrooms and small market, also has a free foot bath.

About 1.5km from the centre of town is **Ōhama beach** (大浜), a long stretch of sand where sea turtles come to lay their eggs from May to August each year.

The best accommodation option is at Yakuō-ji's **shukubō** (temple lodgings; ☎ 77-1105; fax 77-1486; per person with meals ¥7300; P), the white building with blue trim opposite the temple. The tatami rooms here are spacious and well kept, and filling meals are served.

South to Muroto-misaki

A short train ride south from Hiwasa is the sleepy fishing town of **Mugi** (牟岐), where the winding streets of the old fishing port make an interesting stopover. A 45-minute (3km) walk along the coast past the fishing port is **Mollusc Mugi Shell Museum** (貝の資料館モラスコむぎ; ☎ 0884-72-2520; admission ¥400; ⊙ 9am-4.30pm Tue-Sun), where there's an impressive collection of shells and tropical fish in an idyllic setting on a quiet beach. There is an old Hachiman shrine in the centre of the town, and boats run out to the island of Teba-jima (出羽島).

Blue Marine (ブルーマリン; ☎ 0884-76-1401, 0884-76-3100; www.bluemarine.v-town.jp; cruises ¥1800, guided kayaking trips ¥2500-3000; ⊙ 8am-5pm Wed-Mon) operates glass-bottomed boats tours around Takegashima Island near Shi-shikui, plus guided sea-kayaking tours.

🛏 Sleeping & Eating

There are plenty of places to stay along the coast at Kannoura, Shishikui and Ikumi.

Minshuku Ikumi   MINSHUKU ¥
(民宿いくみ; ☎ 0887-24-3838; www.ikumiten.com; r per person with breakfast ¥4400; P) This cosy, family-run *minshuku* sits right alongside the highway in Ikumi. It's a popular surfer's choice, thanks to the well-presented rooms and the helpful, knowledgeable owner, Ten.

South Shore   INN ¥
(サウスショア; ☎ 0887-29-3211; www.south-shore-ikumi.com in Japanese; r per person with/without meals ¥5250/3675; P) A sunny, simple inn with shared bathrooms, South Shore sits about a block from the beach in Ikumi and has a relaxed Hawaiian-esque vibe. The cute attached cafe and tiny pool area are convivial spots to hang out après surf.

Ikumi White Beach Hotel   HOTEL ¥
(生見ホワイトビーチホテル; ☎ 0887-29-3018; www.wbhotel.net; r per person with breakfast ¥5000; P) This clean, laid-back Ikumi beachfront hotel has Japanese- and Western-style rooms with big beach views. It also runs an inexpensive restaurant called Olu-Olu (オルオル; meals ¥800-1000; ⊙ 7am-2pm & 5-8pm), featuring a picture menu and shelves of dog-eared Japanese surf mags.

★ Pension Shishikui   PENSION ¥¥
(ペンションししくい; ☎ 0884-76-2130; www.p-shishikui.com; r per person with meals from ¥9000; P) Perfect for families or romantic getaways, charming Pension Shishikui occupies a snug cove with a private crescent of beach (protected by a seawall). All rooms, whether in the main house or free-standing log cabins, have ocean views and private bathrooms. The English-speaking owner rents surfboards, kayaks and bikes, and guests can also use the tennis court and two communal baths. To get there, look for the sign pointing you off the highway as you pass through Shishikui.

Hotel Riviera   HOTEL ¥¥
(ホテルリビエラししくい; ☎ 0884-76-3300; www.hotel-riviera.co.jp; r per person with meals from ¥13,000; P) In Shishikui, this large hotel has upmarket Western- and Japanese-style rooms. Nonguests can use the sea-view onsen (¥600; from 6.30am to 9am and 11am to 10pm).

Aunt Dinah   CURRY ¥

(☎ 0887-29-2080; meals ¥750-1500; ⊙ 9.30am-9.30pm Wed-Mon) Japanese country music and a range of curries are available at this old-timey spot near the main crossroad in Kannoura.

ℹ Getting There & Away

Trains run as far south as Kannoura. There are also buses from Mugi to Kannoura (¥770, 45 minutes, 14 per day), stopping at Kaifu and Shishikui on the way. Seven buses a day run from Kannoura to Muroto-misaki, via Ikumi (¥1390, 40 minutes). Buses run as far as Aki (安芸; ¥2880, two hours), where you can transfer to a train to Kōchi. On the last 40km to the cape, the road hugs the coast, hemmed in by mountains and sea.

KŌCHI PREFECTURE

The largest of Shikoku's four prefectures, Kōchi Prefecture spans the entire Pacific coastline between the two capes of Muroto-misaki and Ashizuri-misaki. Cut off from the rest of Japan by the mountains and sea, the province once known as Tosa was traditionally regarded as one of the wildest and remotest places in the country.

Although the trip through Tosa makes up more than a third of the pilgrimage, only 16 of the 88 Temples are located in the province. In fact, there is a journey of 84km from the last temple in Tokushima Prefecture at Hiwasa before you get to the first temple in Kōchi Prefecture at Muroto-misaki. The longest distance between temples is also in Kōchi: a crippling 87km from Temple 37 (岩本寺; Iwamoto-ji) in Kubokawa to Temple 38 (金剛福寺; Kongōfuku-ji) at Ashizuri-misaki.

Kōchi Prefecture is a good place for outdoor types. Whale-watching, rafting, hiking and camping are all options here. Kōchi Prefecture brims with scenic spots, especially along the Shimanto-gawa, one of the last undammed rivers in Japan.

Tokushima to Kōchi

Continuing further south, you'll pass more pretty fishing villages tucked away along a painfully slow-paced oceanside highway. It's a beautiful, desolate coastal drive, and all the more remarkable for its proximity to the bright lights of Kōchi.

Muroto Cape 室戸岬

☑ 0887

Kōbō Daishi found enlightenment on this gorgeous, wild cape (Muroto-misaki; 室戸岬), and it's easy to ponder why as you reach the 'doorway to the land of the dead'. Visitors can explore Kōbō Daishi's rather murky bathing hole among the rock pools, and the Shinmeikutsu cave (神明窟) where he meditated.

A huge white statue of the saint stares out to sea just north of the cape. Temple 24, **Hotsumisaki-ji** (最御崎寺; also known as Higashi-dera), was founded by Kōbō Daishi in the early 9th century. It's at the top of a steep hill directly above the point. Next to the temple, accommodation is available at the peaceful **shukubō** (☑ 23-0024; r per person with/without meals ¥5775/3885), a modern building with spotless tatami rooms.

For something different, **Hoshino Resort Utoco Auberge & Spa** (星野リゾートウトコオーベルジュ＆スパ; ☑ 22-1811; www.utocods.co.jp; d from ¥33,600; 🅿 ➤) is a remarkable concept hotel founded by the late cosmetics giant Uemura Shū. Pumping water from 1000m below the surface, the spa and resort aim to harness the restorative powers of mineral-rich, deep-sea water. The design is elegant and minimalist, each room a spacious retreat with sea-view bathtubs and beds precisely placed so that the occupant's gaze rests parallel to the horizon. A whole menu of massage and salt-water spa therapy is available, with day courses that include lunch and two deep-sea water treatments for ¥10,000. Utoco is located on the shoreline, 100m before Daishi's statue and adjacent to another day spa with attached restaurant.

Seven buses a day run west from the cape to Nahari or Aki (安芸; ¥1300, 1½ hours), where you can change to the JR line for a train to Kōchi (one hour). Trains between Aki and Kōchi take anywhere between 45 minutes and 1½ hours, depending on connections at Gomen (tickets cost between ¥1150 and ¥1460). There are also buses up the east coast to Kannoura and Mugi in Tokushima Prefecture.

Ryūga-dō 龍河洞

☑ 0887

Accessible by bus from Tosa-Yamada Station on the Dosan line is the limestone cave **Ryūga-dō** (龍河洞; ☑ 53-2144; www.ryugadou.or.jp; admission ¥1000; ⊙ 8.30am-5pm, to 4.30pm Dec-Feb). The cave has some interesting stalactites and stalagmites, and traces of pre-historic habitation. The route gets quite steep in places. Visitors on a standard ticket will see about 1km of the 4km cave. Advance reservations and an additional ¥1000 are required for the *bōken kōsu* (adventure course; 冒険コース), where you get to don helmet and overalls and follow a guide for a 90-minute exploration of the inner reaches of the cave.

There are five buses a day to Ryūga-dō from Tosa-Yamada Station (¥440, 20 minutes). Tosa-Yamada Station is 30 minutes from Kōchi by local train (¥350), or 15 minutes by *tokkyū* (¥600).

Kōchi 高知

✓088 / POP 335,000

Kōchi is a smart, compact city with a deserved reputation for enjoying a good time. The castle here is largely undamaged, and remains a fine example of Japanese architecture. Excellent access to the Ashizuri-misaki, Iya Valley and southern Tokushima, and easy day trips to caves, beaches and mountains make Kōchi perhaps the perfect base for travels around the island. The town also boasts a samurai of great national significance. During the Meiji Restoration, Sakamoto Ryōma was instrumental in bringing down the feudal government.

⊙ Sights & Activities

★ Kōchi-jō   CASTLE
(高知城; 1-2-1 Marunouchi; admission ¥400; ⊙9am-5pm) Kōchi-jō is one of just a dozen castles in Japan to have survived with its original *tenshu-kaku* (keep) intact. The castle was originally built during the first decade of the 17th century by Yamanouchi Katsutoyo, who was appointed *daimyō* by Tokugawa Ieyasu after he fought on the victorious Tokugawa side in the Battle of Sekigahara in 1600. A major fire destroyed much of the original structure in 1727, and the castle was largely rebuilt between 1748 and 1753.

The castle was the product of an age of peace – it never came under attack, and for the remainder of the Tokugawa period it was more like a stately home than a military fortress.

Godaisan   PARK
(五台山) Several kilometres east of the town centre is the mountain of Godaisan, where there are excellent views out over the city from a **lookout point** (展望台) in a park.

A short walk away at the top of the hill is **Chikurin-ji** (竹林寺), Temple 31 of the 88, where the main hall was built by the second Tosa *daimyō*, Yamanouchi Tadayoshi, in 1644. The extensive grounds also feature a five-storey pagoda and thousands of statues of the Bodhisattva Jizō, guardian deity of children and travellers. The **Treasure House** (宝物館; admission ¥400; ⊙9am-5pm) hosts an impressive collection of Buddhist sculpture from the Heian and Kamakura periods; the same ticket gets you into the lovely late-Kamakura-period garden opposite. Descending the steps by the Treasure House brings you to the entrance gates of the **Kōchi Prefectural Makino Botanical Garden** (高知県立牧野植物園; ☑882-2601; www.makino.or.jp; admission ¥700; ⊙9am-5pm), a beautiful network of gardens and parkland featuring more than 3000 different plant species. These gardens are named for Makino Tomitarō, the 'Father of Japanese Botany'.

The **My-Yū** circular bus stops at Godaisan on its way to Katsura-hama from Kōchi Station (all-day ticket ¥1000, 25 minutes).

Katsura-hama   BEACH
(桂浜) Katsura-hama is a popular beach 13km south of central Kōchi at the point where Kōchi's harbour empties out into the bay. Unfortunately, strong currents prohibit swimming. Just before you get to the beach itself is **Sakamoto Ryōma Memorial Museum** (坂本龍馬記念館; ☑841-0001; 830 Jōsan; admission ¥400; ⊙9am-5pm), where the exhibits are dedicated to the life of a local hero who was instrumental in bringing about the Meiji Restoration in the 1860s. Born in Kōchi in 1835, Ryōma brought about the alliance between the Satsuma (modern Kagoshima) and Chōshū (Yamaguchi) domains that eventually brought down the Tokugawa shōgunate. He was killed in Kyoto in 1867, aged 32.

There is an **aquarium** (桂浜水族館; ☑841-2437; admission ¥1100; ⊙9am-5.30pm) on the beach, and a small shrine on the hillside. Public buses run to Katsura-hama from Kōchi Station (¥610, 35 minutes, six daily) and Harimaya-bashi (¥560, 25 minutes, frequent). The My-Yū bus also makes a stop in Katsura-hama.

Sunday Market   MARKET
(日曜市; ⊙5am-6pm Sun Apr-Sep, 6am-5pm Sun Oct-Mar) Our favourite street market in Shikoku, 300 years old, takes place every Sunday along the main road leading to the

castle. Colourful stalls sell fresh produce, tonics and tinctures, knives, flowers, garden stones and wooden antiques.

Ino Japanese Paper Museum   MUSEUM
(いの町紙の博物館; ☑893-0886; admission ¥500; ◎9am-5pm Tue-Sun) Make your own Japanese paper for ¥300 at this museum, about 10km west of Kōchi. From the Harimayabashi tram stop, take a tram to the last stop in Ino. From there, walk westward until the next main intersection, turn right and find the museum 100m ahead.

✿🎎 Festivals

Kōchi's lively **Yosakoi Matsuri** (よさこい祭り; Yosakoi Festival) on 10 and 11 August perfectly complements Tokushima's Awa-odori Matsuri (12 to 15 August). There's a night-before event on 9 August and night-after effort on 12 August, but 10 and 11 August are the big days.

🛏 Sleeping

★ **Kochi Youth Hostel**   HOSTEL ¥
(高知ユースホステル; ☑823-0858; www.kyh-sakenokuni.com; 4-5 Fukuigashi-machi; dm/s with breakfast ¥2415/3150; ℗@) This charming wood-panelled hostel sits along a canal near Engyōjiguchi (円行寺口) Station. The tatami rooms are simple and comfortable, shared facilities are immaculate, and the food is excellent quality and value. The friendly host Kondo Tomio, a former sake company rep, is very welcoming to foreign guests and offers sake sampling courses for ¥500. Find detailed directions on the website.

Tosa Bekkan   MINSHUKU ¥
(とさ別館; ☑883-5685; fax 884-9523; 1-11-34 Sakura-chō; r per person ¥3800; ℗) One of the most relaxed and economical *minshuku* on the island is set in a quiet residential area 15 minutes' walk (900m) from the station. To get here, follow the tramlines straight ahead from the station and turn left when you see Green Hotel on your right. Look out for signs on the telephone posts with the name in Japanese.

Petit Hotel   BUSINESS HOTEL ¥¥
(プチホテル高知; ☑826-8156; www.phk.jp; 1-8-13 Kitahon-machi; s/d ¥5000/8000; ℗🚭@🛜) This excellent business hotel near Kōchi Station is an astute alternative to the larger chains. Service is efficient and friendly, and the rooms are reasonably spacious, particularly the sparkling clean bathrooms.

Richmond Hotel   HOTEL ¥¥¥
(リッチモンドホテル高知; ☑820-1122; www.richmondhotel.jp/en/kochi; 9-4 Obiyamachi; s ¥11,000, d ¥16,000-20,000; ℗🚭@🛜) Kōchi's classiest hotel has the spotless, modern rooms and professional service expected for a hotel of this class, plus it's located just off the main shopping arcade in the heart of the city. There are public consoles with free internet access; rental laptops are also available and LAN access is in all rooms.

Sansuien   HOTEL ¥¥¥
(三翠園; ☑822-0131; www.sansuien.co.jp; 1-3-35 Takajō-machi; per person with meals from ¥13,800; ℗🚭@) Three blocks south of the castle along Kenchō-mae Dōri is this classy multi-storey hotel with luxurious onsen baths and a garden incorporating a series of buildings that once formed part of the *daimyō's* residence. The Japanese tatami rooms far outweigh their Western counterparts for both size and comfort. Nonguests can use the baths from 10am to 4pm (¥900).

🍴 Eating

Kōchi's main entertainment district is in the area around the Obiyamachi arcade and the Harimaya-bashi junction where the tramlines meet. Local specialities include *katsuo tataki* (lightly seared bonito fish). After a night of drinking, head to **Green Rd**, a small street lined till late with open-air noodle stalls.

★ **Hirome Ichiba**   JAPANESE ¥
(ひろめ市場; ☑822-5287; 2-3-1 Obiyamachi; dishes ¥300-900; ◎8am-11pm, from 7am Sun; 📷) Some hundred or so mini restaurants specialising in everything from *gomoku rāmen* (seafood noodles) to *takoyaki* (octopus balls) surround communal tables; this is the hub of Kōchi's cheap eats scene. On weekends, it positively heaves with young people drinking hard and happy. It's at the end of the main arcade, just before the castle.

Uofuku   IZAKAYA ¥¥
(魚福; ☑824-1129; 2-13 Nijūdai-chō; dishes ¥600-1500; ◎5.30am-11pm, closed Sun) Uofuku is a fabulous curb-side *izakaya* (pub-eatery) on a quiet backstreet behind the arcade. Fish is the order of the day, hand-picked from the tank by the door. The menu is a mess of kanji; try the *katsuo tataki* (around ¥1200) or ask for *osusume* (a recommendation). This is a good place for adventurous eaters to try *shutō* – the pickled and fermented innards of the bonito fish (¥450), which locals regard as a delicacy.

Kōchi

SHIKOKU KŌCHI

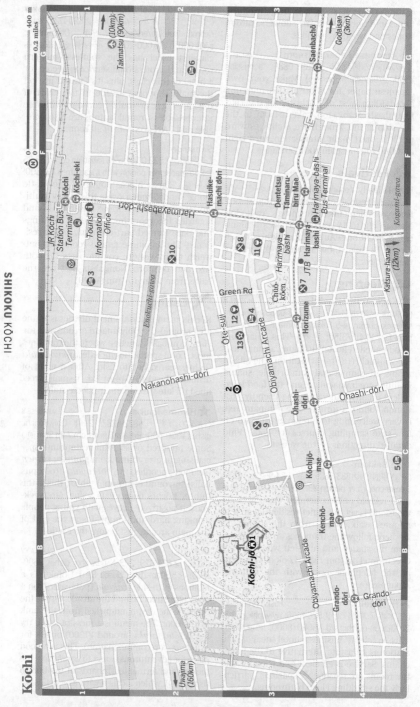

400 m
0.2 miles

(10km)
Takmatsu (90km)

Godaisan (3km)

Saenbachō

6

Hasuike-machi dōri

Dentetsu Tāminaru-biru Mae

Harimaya-bashi Bus Terminal

JR Kōchi Station Bus Terminal

Kōchi

Kōchi-eki

Tourist Information Office

Harimayabashi-dōri

8

10

11

Harimaya-bashi

Harimaya-bashi

Kagami-gawa

Enokuchi-gawa

3

JTB

7

Green Rd

Chūō-kōen

Katsura-hama (12km)

Horizume

Ōte-suji

12

4

13

Obiyamachi Arcade

Nakanohashi-dōri

2

Ōhashi-dōri

Ōhashi-dōri

9

Kōchijō-mae

Kenchō-mae

5

Obiyamachi Arcade

Kōchi-jō 1

Kōchi-jō

Grando-dōri

Grando-dōri

Uwajima (160km)

Kōchi

Habotan IZAKAYA ¥

(葉牡丹; ☑872-8686; 2-21 Sakai-machi; dishes ¥150-1100; ⊙11am-11pm) Red lanterns mark out this locals' *izakaya* that opens at the shockingly early hour of 11am. The menu, plastered over the walls, is in Japanese, but the food is under glass on the counter, so you can always point. *Sashimi moriawase* (a selection of sashimi) is ¥1050. Local booze includes Tosa-tsuru sake and Dabada Hiburi, a *shōchū* (distilled grain liquor) made from chestnuts.

Hakobe OKONOMIYAKI ¥

(はこべ; ☑823-0084; 1-2-5 Obiyamachi; dishes ¥600-1000; ⊙11am-midnight) This is one of the few remaining cook-it-yourself *okinomiyaki* joints in Kōchi serving cheap and cheerful Japanese pancakes (¥630), with good English spoken by the waiters. The 'mix' of *ika* (squid) and *ebi* and *tori* (chicken) is heavenly. Other alternatives include *buta* (pork) and *yasai* (vegetables). It's slap bang in the heart of the arcade.

🍷 Drinking & Entertainment

Love Jamaican NIGHTCLUB

(☑872-0447; 3rd fl, 1-5-5 Obiyamachi; ⊙7pm-3am) This fully legit reggae and hip-hop club is a hive of after-hours mayhem thanks to a classy sound system, generous drink deals and a manicured young crowd.

Amontillado PUB

(アモンティラード; ☑875-0899; 1-1-17 Obiyamachi; ⊙5pm-1am) When you're *izakaya*'d out and crave fish-and-chips with a pint of Guinness (¥900), pop into this Irish pub off Obiyamachi Arcade.

Boston Cafe Bar BAR

(ボストンカフェ; ☑875-7730; 1-7-9 Ôte-suji; ⊙5.30pm-2am, later on Sat & Sun) Across the alley from the backside of the Hotel Richmond, this is a friendly, American-themed neighbourhood bar.

ℹ Information

Coin lockers and a left-luggage office are in the station, and international ATMs are available at the **post office** down the street from the station.
JTB (☑823-2321; 1-21 Sakai-chō; ⊙10am-6pm Thu-Tue) Close to the Harimayabashi intersection.
Kōchi International Association (高知県国際交流協会; ☑875-0022; www.kochi-kia.or.jp; 2F, 4-1-37 Honmachi; ⊙8.30am-5.15pm Mon-Sat, closed Sat in Aug) Free internet access, a library and English newspapers.
Tourist Information Office (高知市観光案内所; ☑826-3337; ⊙9am-6pm) The helpful tourist information pavilion in front of JR Kōchi Station provides English-language maps and Kōchi mini-guidebooks.

ℹ Getting There & Around

TO/FROM THE AIRPORT
Kōchi's Ryōma airport, about 10km east of the city, is accessible by bus (¥700, 40 minutes) from the station. There are daily flights to/from Tokyo (¥31,570, 1½ hours, four daily), Osaka (¥17,500, 45 minutes, seven daily) and Fukuoka (¥23,700, 45 minutes, three daily).

BUS
The My-Yū circular bus runs to Godaisan and Katsura-hama from Kōchi Station; one-day passes cost ¥1000.

TRAIN
Kōchi is on the JR Dosan line, and is connected to Takamatsu (*tokkyū* ¥4760, two hours and 10 minutes) via Awa-Ikeda (*tokkyū* ¥2730, 70 minutes). Trains also run west to Kubokawa (*tokkyū* ¥2560, one hour), where you can change for Nakamura (for the Shimanto-gawa).

SHIKOKU KŌCHI

TRAM

Kōchi's colourful tram service (¥190 per trip) has been running since 1904. There are two lines: the north–south line from the station intersects with the east–west tram route at the Harimaya-bashi (はりまや橋) junction. Pay when you get off, and ask for a *norikae-ken* (transfer ticket) if you have to change lines.

Kōchi to Ashizuri-misaki

The quiet stretch of coast between Kōchi and Ashizuri-misaki offers a number of interesting diversions. Tosa-wan (Tosa Bay) was once a major whaling centre; today, whale-watching is increasingly popular along the coast. There are kayaking opportunities along the Shimanto-gawa, one of the last free-flowing rivers in Japan, and an exquisite beach at Ohkihama. At the cape itself, there's some rugged scenery and Temple 38 on the Shikoku pilgrim trail.

The train line from Kōchi parts at Wakai. The JR Yodo line heads northwest through the mountains to Uwajima in Ehime-ken, while the private Tosa-Kuroshio line heads around to Nakamura and ends at Sukumo. There is also a bus service to Ashizuri-misaki from Nakamura Station (¥1930, one hour and 40 minutes, nine daily).

🏃 Activities

Ōgata Whale Watching WHALE-WATCHING
(大方遊漁船主会; ☑ 0880-43-1058; http://nita-rikujira.com; adult/child ¥5000/1000; ⏲ 8.30am-5pm) In the town of Kuroshio-machi, not far from Nakamura, Ōgata Whale Watching runs three four-hour trips daily between late April and October, leaving at 8am, 10am and 1pm. Tosa Irino and Tosa Kamikawaguchi are the closest stations to Kuroshio-machi on the Tosa-Kuroshio railway line.

🛏 Sleeping

★ **Shimanto-gawa Youth Hostel** HOSTEL ¥
(四万十川ユースホステル; ☑ 0880-54-1352; nonmembers per person with 2 meals ¥5980; ☺) A charming place and reason enough to get upstream. A friendly couple oversee excellent accommodation in shared bedrooms and run regular canoeing trips on the river (¥8400 for a regular day's touring; cheaper introductory courses are available for beginners). It's 4.5km away from Kuchiyanai (口屋内), accessible by (infrequent) buses from Ekawasaki Station and Nakamura. Given

enough notice, the manager will pick you up from Kuchiyanai. The hostel closes from mid-December to late January.

Kawarakko CAMPGROUND ¥
(かわらっこ; ☑ 0880-31-8400; www.kawarakko.com; campsite from ¥3150) A neatly maintained riverside campground run by an adventure company. Canoes, mountain bikes and even tents are available to hire should you fancy a spontaneous night under the stars.

Nakamura 中村

☑ 0880 / POP 37,900

Nakamura, recently renamed Shimanto-shi, is a good place to organise trips on the beautiful **Shimanto-gawa** (四万十川). Staff at the **Tourist Information Office** (四万十市観光協会; ☑ 35-4171; ⏲ 8.30am-5.30pm), located on the right side of the highway as you enter town from the north, can provide information on kayaking and canoe trips, and camping and outdoor activities. A number of companies offer **river cruises** on traditional fishing boats called Yakata-bune (¥2000 for 50 minutes) and kayak rental (half-/full day from ¥3500/5000); the Tourist Information Office has a full list. Bike rental is available here (per five hours/one day ¥600/1000) too, allowing you to scoot out to the river under your own steam.

In front of the station, decent Western-style rooms are available at the **Dai-ichi Hotel Nakamura** (中村第一ホテル; ☑ 0880-34-7211; http://park18.wakwak.com/~nd-h; s/d ¥5300/10,500). A post office with international ATM is a short walk away.

Ashizuri Cape 足摺岬

☑ 0880

Like the Muroto Cape, the Ashizuri Cape (Ashizuri-misaki; 足摺岬) is a rugged, picturesque promontory that's famous for its other-worldly appearance and violent weather.

On a bluff at Ashizuri-misaki there's an imposing statue of locally born hero John Manjirō. Born in 1836 as Nakahama Manjirō, the young fisherman was swept onto the desolate shores of Tori-shima, 600km from Tokyo Bay, in 1841. Five months later, he and his shipmates were rescued by a US whaler passing by, and granted safe passage to Hawaii. After moving to Massachusetts and learning English, 'John' finally

OHKINOHAMA

About 40 minutes south of Nakamura, on the bus to Ashizuri-misaki, is **Ohkinohama** (大岐の浜), Shikoku's most magnificent sandy white beach. The only souls to frequent this unspoilt 2km stretch shielded by neat rows of pine trees are the pick of the region's surfers, some egg-laying turtles and the odd, grinning clam diver. Facing east means you can watch the sun and moon rise from your beach towel, and warm currents ensure swimming is possible year-round.

Most travellers shoot through en route to the cape, but a stay at **Kaiyu Inn** (海癒; ☑ 0880-82-8500; www.kaiyu-inn.jp; s from ¥7000, extra person ¥2500; P ⊝ ☎ 🐕) 🐾 is itself worth the visit to Shikoku. The accomplished owner, Mitsu, studied agriculture in the USA before serving a hotel apprenticeship in Bali. Here he has redesigned a white concrete 1960s conference centre into a sublime yet affordable contemporary retreat. Each self-contained apartment has been designed by a different emerging Japanese architect and, coupled with Mitsu's keen aesthetical eye and extensive designer furniture collection, has created spaces worthy of Condé Nast covers, each with Pacific Ocean views. The communal meals are inventive, super fresh and organic, and feature famed local clams, catch-of-the-day fish, and loads of fruit and vegetables.

While the Kaiyu concept is about slowing down and savoring the area's rivers and ocean (long-term stays are the norm here), visitors are also welcome for one-night stays and day visits to the boiler-fired luxury **onsen** (guests/nonguests ¥700/950; ⊙ 1-7pm Wed-Mon) – advance reservations recommended. This ecofriendly day spa is itself a day-trip destination, with tranquil views of Ohkinohama from the stylish baths, featuring imported heat-conducive stone and adjustable temperature gauges. Never has the word 'wellness' felt so apt.

returned to Japan and later played a leading role in diplomatic negotiations with the USA and other countries at the end of the Tokugawa period.

Ashizuri-misaki is also home to Temple 38, **Kongōfuku-ji** (金剛福寺), which has breathtaking views of the promontory and the Pacific Ocean. A short walk back towards civilisation is **Ashizuri Youth Hostel** (足摺ユースホステル; ☑ 88-0324; dm ¥3360), run by a cute older couple, who provide large, well-cared-for tatami rooms. With advance notice, meals are available. More upmarket is **Ashizuri Kokusai Hotel** (足摺国際ホテル; ☑ 88-0201; www.ashizuri.co.jp; r per person with meals from ¥13,650), which has onsen baths overlooking the sea. It's located along the main road into town.

EHIME PREFECTURE

Occupying the western region of Shikoku, Ehime Prefecture (愛媛県) has the largest number of pilgrimage temples – 27 of them, to be precise. Like Tosa, the southern part of the prefecture has always been considered wild and remote; by the time pilgrims arrive in Shikoku's largest city, Matsuyama,

they know that the hard work has been done. There are large clusters of temples around Matsuyama and the Shimanami Kaidō bridge system, which links Shikoku with Honshū and makes for a spectacular bike ride (p639).

Prefectural highlights are the immaculately preserved feudal castle and historic Dōgo Onsen in Matsuyama, and the sacred peak of Ishizuchi-san (1982m), the tallest mountain in western Japan.

Uwajima 宇和島

☑ 0895 / POP 62,000

An unhurried castle town, Uwajima draws a steady trickle of titillated travellers to its academically inclined sex museum and attached Shintō fertility shrine. Though most travellers bypass it en route to Matsuyama, the town makes a pleasant stop and retains some noteworthy traditions, such as pearl farming, terraced agriculture and bloodless bullfighting.

⊙ Sights & Activities

Taga-jinja & Sex Museum SHRINE, MUSEUM
(多賀神社 & 凸凹神童; ☑ 22-3444; www3.ocn. ne.jp/~dekoboko; admission ¥800; ⊙ 8am-5pm)
Once upon a time, many Shintō shrines had

Uwajima

a connection to fertility rites. Of those that remain, Taga-jinja is one of the best known. The grounds of the shrine are strewn with tree-trunk phalluses and numerous statues and stone carvings. Inside, the museum is packed with anthropological erotica from all corners of the procreating world – you can pay for the privilege of photographing it with a scant ¥20,000.

Uwajima-jō   CASTLE
(宇和島城; admission ¥200; ⊙9am-4pm) Dating from 1601, Uwajima-jō is a small three-storey castle on an 80m-high hill in the centre of town. The present structure was rebuilt in 1666 by the *daimyō* Date Munetoshi. The *donjon* (main keep) is one of only 12 originals left in Japan; there is nothing much to see inside. The surrounding park, **Shiroyama-kōen** (城山公園), is open from sunrise to sunset, and is a pleasant place for a stroll.

Date Museum   MUSEUM
(伊達博物館; 9-14 Goten-machi; admission ¥500; ⊙9am-4.30pm Tue-Sun) The well-presented exhibits at the excellent Date Museum are dedicated to the Date family, who ruled Uwajima from the castle for 250 years during the Tokugawa period. The explanations are mostly in Japanese, but a lot of the stuff on display – swords, armour, palanquins and lacquerware – is pretty self-explanatory.

Municipal Bullfighting Ring   BULLFIGHTING
(宇和島市営闘牛場; admission ¥3000) *Tōgyū* (闘牛) could probably be described as a type of bovine sumō. Victory is achieved when one animal forces the other to its knees, or when one turns tail and flees from the ring. Fights are held on 2 January, the first Sunday of April, 24 July, 14 August and the fourth Sunday of October. Directions to the bullfighting ring are available at the Tourist Information Office.

Uwajima

Temples 41-42   TEMPLE

A great way to get a taste of the 88 Temple pilgrimage without having to slog it out along busy main roads is to take a bus from Uwajima Station direct to Temple 42, **Butsumoku-ji** (仏木寺; admission ¥510, 40 minutes). After admiring the thatched bell-house and the statues of the seven gods of good fortune, follow the clearly marked *henro* trail back through picturesque farming villages and rice paddies to Temple 41, **Ryūkō-ji** (龍光寺). Here, a steep staircase leads up to a pleasant temple and shrine overlooking the fields. It's a little over 5km in all. From outside Ryūkō-ji there are signs to Muden Station (務田駅), a 15-minute (800m) walk away. From here, you can catch a train or bus back to Uwajima.

🛏 Sleeping & Eating

Mori-no-Yado Uwajima Youth Hostel   HOSTEL ¥

(森の宿うわじまユースホステル; ☑22-7177; www2.odn.ne.jp/~cfm91130/eigo.htm; 166-11 Daichojioku Hei; dm/s/tw ¥2100/3500/7000; P◎◎@) 🌀 This friendly, low-key hostel is hidden away in the forest 2.5km uphill from the station. The dorm rooms and showers are spotless, bike rentals are free and trips to surrounding islands can be arranged. Look for the directions to Uwatsuhiko-jinja (English sign) and the small white and green 'YH' sign. From here, a small path leads up the hill to the hostel. Be sure to call ahead for reservations, as the hostel occasionally closes.

Uwajima Oriental Hotel   BUSINESS HOTEL ¥

(宇和島オリエンタルホテル; ☑23-2828; www.oriental-web.co.jp/uwajima; 16-10 Tsurushima-chō; s/d ¥5500/10,500; P@) North of the sta-tion, this friendly business hotel has clean, typically small rooms with unobstructed views of the city from the upper floors. Perks include a pillow menu, a *conbini* on the first floor and bike rentals.

★ Kiya Ryokan   RYOKAN ¥¥¥

(木屋旅館; ☑22-0101; http://kiyaryokan.com; per night ¥21,000, additional ¥5250 per person with breakfast) A rare opportunity to rent an en-tire house where literary greats have stayed, Kiya Ryokan offers a compelling reason for an Uwajima stop. Though not a strictly tradi-tional ryokan experience – no in-house staff nor elaborate *kaiseki* (Japanese haute cui-sine) dinners here – its modern quirks add to the unique appeal. A glass floor between the entry and a second-storey room create an unexpected, harmonious view of the house's architectural lines. Coloured LED lights and remote-controlled screens allow guests to create their own ambience. The house surrounds an inner courtyard garden, and bathing facilities are a beautifully integrated combination of modern and traditional. Best enjoyed and most economical for a larger group (the house sleeps up to eight).

Wabisuke   SEAFOOD ¥¥

(和日輔; ☑24-0028; 1-2-6 Ebisu-machi; dishes ¥1000-1500; ◎lunch & dinner) This restaurant, washed by the gentle sounds of running wa-ter, is an elegant spot to try the local *tai* (sea bream) specialities, available here as a *tai-meshi gozen* (sea bream set course; ¥1880). There is a picture menu, and the young staff speak some English.

Hozumi-tei   IZAKAYA ¥¥

(ほづみ; ☑22-0041; 2-3-8 Shinmachi; dishes ¥750-1500; ◎11am-1.30pm & 5-10.30pm, closed some Sun) This formal *izakaya* has been serving up local food for over 70 years. The menu is all in Japanese, but if you say the words '*Kyōdo ryōri*' (郷土料理) – meaning 'local cuisine' – the friendly owner should unlock his secrets. A course of the local *tai-meishi* is ¥2100.

Boulangerie Riz   BAKERY ¥

(ブランジュリリズ; ☑22-8800; 1-4-22 Ebisu-machi; pastries ¥50-250; ◎8am-4pm Fri-Wed) Heavenly, light and crisp pastries and breads made with rice flour are the house speciality at this bakery along the Gintengai shopping arcade. Enjoy a simple breakfast at the coun-ter while watching the bakers expertly turn-ing out handmade treats, such as croissants flecked with local mandarin, and rolled *matcha* (powdered green tea) cake.

SHIKOKU UWAJIMA

ⓘ Information

There are coin lockers at the station and international ATMs at the post office across from the station.

Tourist Information Office (宇和島市観光協会; ☑22-3934; ⊙8.30am-5pm Mon-Fri, 9am-5pm Sat & Sun) At Kisaya Hiroba at the port; find a more conveniently located information booth (☑23-5530; ⊙9am-6pm) at the JR station.

ⓘ Getting There & Around

Uwajima is on the JR Yosan line, and can be reached from Matsuyama (*tokkyū* ¥2900, 1½ hours) via Uchiko (*tokkyū* ¥2210, one hour). You can hire **bicycles** (per hour ¥100; ⊙9.30am-5pm) at the station, in the corner office on the left after you exit the building.

Uwajima to Matsuyama

There are several worthwhile stops along the western coast between Uwajima and Matsuyama, including Ōzu, with its recently reconstructed castle, and Uchiko, a town that grew rich on wax in the 19th century and is home to several elegant old buildings. From Uwajima, the JR Yodo line runs to Kubokawa and Kōchi; the JR Yosan line heads north to Matsuyama.

Yawatahama 八幡浜

☑0894 / POP 41,200

Throughout the centuries, pilgrims from Kyūshū traditionally arrived in Yawatahama by ferry, and then started and ended their pilgrimage at nearby Temple 43, **Meiseki-ji** (明石寺).

Take the **Uwajima Unyu Ferry** (宇和島運輸フェリー; ☑23-2536; www.uwajimaunyu.co.jp) from Yawatahama to Beppu (¥3020, three hours, six daily) and Usuki (¥2250, 2½ hours, six or seven daily) on Kyūshū. Yawatahama port is a five-minute bus ride (¥150) or taxi ride (around ¥630); because buses are so infrequent, the 20-minute (1.5km) walk from Yawatahama Station is often faster than waiting for a bus. To walk there, turn left out of the station and head straight until you hit the sea.

If you need to stay overnight, **Harbor Plaza Hotel** (ハーバープラザホテル; ☑22-0007; www.harbor.or.jp; 1 Nakano-machi; s/tw from ¥6825/11,550; [P]), just off the main north–south thoroughfare, is the best choice.

Ōzu 大洲

☑0893 / POP 50,000

On the Yosan line northeast of Yawatahama is Ōzu, where traditional **ukai** (鵜飼; cormorant river fishing) takes place on the Hiji-kawa from 1 June to 20 September. **Sightseeing boats** (☑24-2664; per person ¥3000; ⊙depart 6.30pm, return 9pm) follow the fishing boats down the river as the cormorants catch fish. Reservations are required. Less strenuous **cruises** (¥100; ⊙10am-4pm) run across the river during April and May.

◎ Sights

Ōzu-jō　　　CASTLE
(大洲城; ☑24-1146; ¥500; joint ticket with Garyū-sansō ¥800; ⊙9am-5pm) One of Japan's most authentically reconstructed castles. Other buildings in the grounds are original survivals from the Edo period. The castle is an impressive sight above the river, especially at night.

Garyū-sansō　　　GARDEN
(臥龍山荘; ☑24-3759; admission ¥500, or joint ticket with Ōzu-jō ¥800; ⊙9am-5pm) Across town from Ōzu-jō, Garyū-sansō is an elegant Meiji-period teahouse and garden in an idyllic spot overlooking the river. On Sundays from April to October, you can partake in the tea ceremony (from 10am to 4pm; ¥400).

🛏 Sleeping

Ōzu Kyōdokan Youth Hostel　　HOSTEL ¥
(大洲郷土館ユースホステル; ☑24-2258; http://homepage3.nifty.com/ozuyh; dm per person ¥3200) A delightful place to stay at the foot of Ōzu-jō, with a modernist garden below it. The tatami rooms are fit for an army, and the hostel doubles as a museum, featuring interesting curios and antique ceramics from the town's boom years as a Tokugawa-period castle town.

Uchiko 内子

☑0893 / POP 20,300

Uchiko is undergoing a mini-renaissance, with a growing number of domestic travellers taking interest in this handsome town with its prosperous past. During the late Edo and early Meiji periods, Uchiko boomed as a major producer of wax, resulting in a number of exquisite houses that still stand today along a street called Yōkaichi.

⊙ Sights

Uchiko-za
THEATRE
(内子座; ☎44-2840; admission ¥400; ⊙9am-4.30pm) About halfway between the station and Yōkaichi is Uchiko-za, a magnificent traditional kabuki theatre. Originally constructed in 1916, the theatre was completely restored in 1985, complete with a revolving stage. Performances are still held at the theatre; call ahead for a schedule.

Museum of Commerce & Domestic Life
MUSEUM
(商いと暮らし博物館; ☎44-5220; admission ¥200; ⊙9am-4.30pm) A few minutes' walk further north along the main road from Uchiko-za is this museum, which exhibits historical materials and wax figures portraying a typical merchant's home of the early 20th century. If you understand Japanese, the recorded voicing of various characters in the house is campy and entertaining; otherwise, there's a basic English flyer.

Yōkaichi Historic District
HISTORIC DISTRICT
(八日市) Uchiko's picturesque main street has a number of interesting buildings, many now serving as museums, souvenir stalls, craft shops and charming teahouses. The old buildings typically have cream-coloured plaster walls and 'wings' under the eaves that serve to prevent fire spreading from house to house.

On the left as you walk up the street, look for Ōmori Rōsoku (大森ろうそく; ⊙9am-5pm, closed Mon & Fri), Uchiko's last remaining candle manufacturer. The candles are still made by hand here, according to traditional methods, and you can watch the candlemakers at work.

As the road makes a slight bend, several well-preserved Edo-era buildings come into view, including Ōmura-tei and Hon-Haga-tei, the latter of which is a fine example of a rich merchant's home. The Hon-Haga family established the production of fine wax in Uchiko, winning awards at World Expositions in Chicago (1893) and Paris (1900).

Further on, the exquisite Kamihaga-tei is a wax merchant's house within a large complex of buildings related to the wax-making process. The adjacent Japanese Wax Museum (木蝋資料館; admission ¥500; ⊙9am-4.30pm) has good English explanations on wax-making and the town's prosperous past.

Finally, at the end of the historic district, you'll see signs pointing to Kōshō-ji (高昌寺; ⊙9am-4.30am) FREE, the shrine up the hill. It's just a few minutes' walk up to see the large reclining Buddha in front of the shrine.

🛏 Sleeping & Eating

Matsunoya Ryokan
RYOKAN ¥¥
(松乃屋旅館; ☎44-5000; www.dokidoki.ne.jp/home2/matsunoya; s/d ¥7500/12,600; P🏠😊@) Still the best place to stay in town, this smart, central ryokan has neatly kept tatami rooms and a lovely communal bath. The management is not the warmest you'll encounter in Shikoku, but polite and welcoming to foreign guests. The attached Poco a Poco restaurant serves delicious pasta. Set meals (including crème brulée!) start at ¥1000.

Auberge Uchiko
INN ¥¥¥
(オーベルジュ内子; ☎44-6565; www.orienthotel.jp/uchiko; 485-2 Otsu Ikazaki, Uchiko-cho; r per person with two meals ¥25,000) Worth a splurge if you've got your own wheels and can speak Japanese. Five free-standing modern cubes in the hills above Uchiko have glass walls affording views of the surrounding woods and town below. 'Nouvelle Uchiko' cuisine is the order of the day, and there's an onsen that nonguests can use for ¥1000.

Uchiko Fresh Park Karari
MARKET ¥¥
(内子フレッシュパークからり; ☎43-1122; ⊙11am-8pm) Above the Oda River, this farmers market offers fresh, locally-grown produce, prepared *bentō* (boxed meals), regional specialities and a restaurant serving good *teishoku* meals. Try the Karari set (¥1200) and choose a main from the picture menu, served with bread or rice.

Mother Restaurant
CAFE ¥
(洋食マザー; ☎44-5463; lunch ¥800-1000; ⊙11:30am-9pm Tue-Sun) Near the turn-off to Yōkaichi St is this friendly Japanese diner that prepares a tasty two-choice lunch menu and good, strong coffee.

ⓘ Information

There are coin lockers at the station.

Tourist Information Booth (☎43-1450; ⊙9.30am-5pm Thu-Tue) You can pick up an English map at this booth, located on your right as you leave JR Uchiko Station.

ⓘ Getting There & Around

Uchiko is 25 minutes from Matsuyama by *tokkyū* (¥1250, hourly) and by *futsū* (local train; ¥740, one hour). Yōkaichi is 1km north of Uchiko Station, and is well signposted in English.

SHIKOKU UWAJIMA TO MATSUYAMA

Matsuyama 松山

📻 089 / POP 513,000

Located in a lush river basin, Shikoku's largest city is both handsome and refined, with just a hint of 'mainland' hustle. Matsuyama is famed across Japan for Dōgo Onsen Honkan, a luxurious 19th-century public bathhouse built over ancient hot springs. The finest castle on the island towers above the stylish trams criss-crossing the city streets and the harbour glistening in the distance. Matsuyama is also home to seven of the 88 Temples, including Ishite-ji, one of the most famous stops on the pilgrimage.

⊙ Sights

★ Matsuyama-jō   CASTLE

(松山城; admission ¥500; ⊙9am-5pm, to 5.30pm Aug, to 4.30pm Dec & Jan) Perched on top of Mt Katsuyama in the centre of town, the castle dominates the city, as it has for centuries. Matsuyama-jō is one of Japan's finest surviving castles, and one of the very few with anything interesting to peruse inside: the castle has a treasure trove of artefacts with excellent English-language displays.

A ropeway (one-way/return ¥260/500) is on hand to whisk you up the hill, though there is a pleasant pathway if you prefer to walk. It's worth walking down via the back slopes of the castle and stopping off at **Ninomaru Shiseki Tei-en** (二之丸史跡庭園; admission ¥100; ⊙9am-5pm, to 5.30pm Aug, to 4.30pm Dec & Jan) in the outer citadel of the fort, consisting of old gardens and modern water features.

Ishite-ji   TEMPLE

(石手寺) East of Dōgo Onsen is Ishite-ji, 51st of the 88 Temples, and one of the largest and most impressive in the circuit. *Ishite* means 'stone hand' and comes from a legend associated with Kōbō Daishi. A statue of Kōbō Daishi overlooks the temple from the hillside.

Shiki Memorial Museum   MUSEUM

(松山市立子規記念博物館; 📞931-5566; http://sikihaku.lesp.co.jp; 1-30 Dōgo-kōen; admission ¥400; ⊙9am-6pm May-Oct, to 5pm Nov-Apr) This memorial museum celebrates the life and work of Matsuyama-born poet Masaoka Shiki (1867–1902), as well as the history of Matsuyama. Shiki initiated the reform of *haiku* and *tanka* (two forms of traditional poetry), and influenced a generation of poets after him. The museum has some English-language signage but also offers English-speaking guides with advance reservations.

Dōgo-kōen   PARK

(道後公園; www.dogokouen.jp) This small park contains the site of Yuzuki-jō, which is the former residence of the Kōno clan that ruled Iyo province in feudal times. Articles unearthed during recent excavations of the site are on display in **Yuzuki-jō Museum** (湯築城資料館; 📞941-1480; Dōgo-kōen; ⊙9am-5pm Tue-Sun) **FREE**, near the west entrance of the park.

Isaniwa-jinja   SHINTŌ SHRINE

(伊佐爾波神社) Designated a National Treasure, this shrine was modelled on Kyoto's Iwashimizu-Hachimangū and was built in 1667. It's located a short walk east of Dōgo Onsen.

🛏 Sleeping

★ Sen Guesthouse   GUESTHOUSE ¥

(泉ゲストハウス; 📞961-1513; www.senguesthouse-matsuyama.com; 4-14 Dōgo-takōchō; dm/s/d ¥2700/4500/7000; 🅿☺@🛜🚲) This welcoming new guesthouse is *the* place in Shikoku to get the lowdown on all things pilgrimage. Run by a super-friendly young American/Japanese couple, Sen has spacious tatami rooms with shared facilities, a roomy and well-equipped kitchen, a small bar and a tidy, homely communal area. The rooftop is a great place to catch the sunset over Matsuyama. The guesthouse is a five-minute walk from Dōgo Onsen, and the owners rent bicycles and happily share local info on Matsuyama and advice on undertaking a pilgrimage.

Guest House Matsuyama   GUESTHOUSE ¥

(ゲストハウスまつやま; 📞934-5296; www.sophia-club.net/guesthouse; 8-3-3 Okaido-chō; dm/s/tw ¥2000/2500/4000, apartment ¥8000; 🛜) Community-minded Tamanoi-san welcomes foreign guests to her neat guesthouse in a cool strip by the ropeway. Formerly an international-student liaison, she offers long-term stays and creates customised language and cultural classes (think aikido, tea ceremony, cooking) for her guests at very reasonable rates. She offers Japanese and Western rooms, complimentary wi-fi and bicycle hire. Email ahead for reservations.

AN INSIDER'S GUIDE TO DŌGO ONSEN

According to legend, Dōgo Onsen (道後温泉) was discovered during the age of the gods when a white heron was found healing itself in the spring. Since then, Dōgo has featured prominently in a number of literary classics, and won itself a reputation for the curative powers of its waters. The mono-alkaline spring contains sulphur, and is believed to be particularly effective at treating rheumatism, neuralgia and hysteria.

Dōgo Onsen Honkan (5-6 Dōgo-yunomachi), the main building, was constructed in 1894, and designated as an important cultural site in 1994. The three-storey, castle-style building incorporates traditional design elements, and is crowned by a statue of a white heron to commemorate its legendary origins. Although countless famous people have passed through its doors, Dōgo Onsen Honkan is perhaps best known for its inclusion in the famous 1906 novel *Botchan* by Natsume Sōseki, the greatest literary figure of Japan's modern age, who based his novel on his time as a school teacher in Matsuyama in the early 20th century.

Even if you're well versed in onsen culture, Dōgo can be a bit confusing as there are two separate baths (and four pricing options) from which to choose. The larger and more popular of the two baths is *kami-no-yu* (神の湯; water of the gods), which is separated by gender and adorned with heron mosaics. A basic bath costs ¥400, while a bath followed by tea and *senbei* (rice crackers) in the 2nd-floor tatami room costs ¥800, and includes a rental *yukata* (light cotton kimono). A rental towel and soap will set you back a further ¥50. The smaller and more private of the two baths is the *tama-no-yu* (魂の湯; water of the spirit), which is also separated by gender and adorned with simple tiles. A bath followed by tea and *botchan dango* (sweet, skewered rice dumplings) in the 2nd-floor tatami room costs ¥1200, while the top price of ¥1500 allows you to enjoy your snack in a private tatami room on the 3rd floor.

Although there are English-language pamphlets on hand to clarify the correct sequence of steps, Dōgo Onsen can be a bit intimidating if you don't speak Japanese. After paying your money outside, you should enter the building and leave your shoes in a locker. If you've paid ¥400, go to the *kami-no-yu* changing room (signposted in English), where you can use the free lockers for your clothing. If you've paid ¥800 or ¥1200, first go upstairs to receive your *yukata,* and then return to either the *kami-no-yu* or *tama-no-yu* (also signposted in English) changing room. After your bath, you should don your *yukata* and retire to the 2nd-floor tatami room to sip your tea and gaze down on the bath-hoppers clip-clopping by in *geta* (traditional wooden sandals). If you've paid top whack, head directly to the 3rd floor, where you will be escorted to your private tatami room. Here, you can change into your *yukata* before heading to the *tama-no-yu* changing room, and also return after your bath to sip tea in complete isolation.

Regardless of which option you choose, you are allowed to explore the building after taking your bath. On the 2nd floor, there is a small **exhibition room** displaying artefacts relating to the bathhouse, including traditional wooden admission tickets. If you've taken one of the pricier upstairs options, you can also take a guided tour (in Japanese) of the private **imperial baths**, last used by the royal family in 1950. On the 3rd floor, the corner tatami room (which was the favourite of Natsume Sōseki) has a small **display** (in Japanese) on the life of the writer.

Dōgo can get quite crowded, especially on weekends and holidays, although at dinner time it's usually empty, because most Japanese tourists will be dining at their inns. If you want to escape the crowds, one minute on foot from the Honkan (through the shopping arcade) is **Tsubaki-no-yu** (椿の湯; admission ¥360; ⊙ 6.30am-11pm), Dōgo Onsen's hot-spring annexe, frequented primarily by locals. If you don't want a full bath, there are also nine free **ashi-yu** (足湯; foot baths) scattered around Dōgo Onsen where you can take off your shoes and socks and warm your feet. The most famous one is located just opposite the station at the start of the arcade. Here, you can also check out **Botchan Karakuri Clock** (坊ちゃんからくり時計), which was erected as part of Dōgo Onsen Honkan's centennial in 1994. It features figures based on the main characters from *Botchan,* who emerge to take a turn on the hour from 8am to 10pm.

Matsuyama

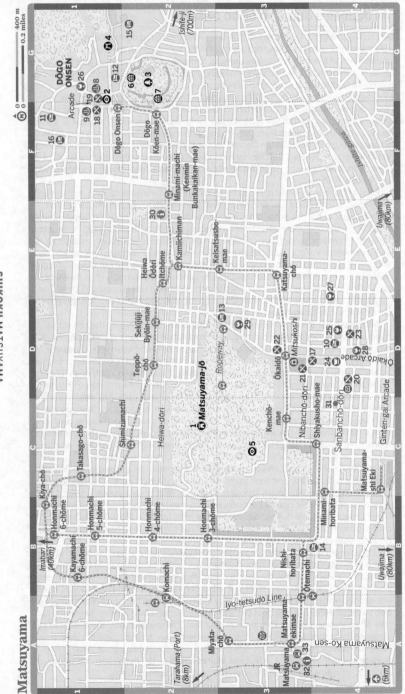

400 m
0.2 miles

DŌGO ONSEN

Matsuyama-jō

Matsuyama

SHIKOKU MATSUYAMA

Matsuyama Youth Hostel HOSTEL ¥
(松山ユースホステル; ☏ 933-6366; www.
matsuyama-yh.com/english; 22-3 Dōgo-himezuka;
dm ¥2625, r per person ¥3360; P ☀ @) ✔ The
health-conscious, communal atmosphere
at this hilltop hostel makes it a great base
for multiple visits to Dōgo Onsen, since it's
only a 10-minute walk up the hill east of the
complex. It's a good idea to make reservations in advance. Meals are also available
(buffet breakfasts are ¥525; dinners cost
¥1050).

Check Inn Matsuyama HOTEL ¥¥
(チェックイン松山; ☏ 998-7000; www.checkin.
co.jp/matsuyama; 2-7-3 Sanban-chō; s/tw from
¥4980/7700; P ☀ @) This business hotel
is excellent value for money, offering well-
equipped and modern rooms, chandeliers
in the lobby and an onsen on the roof. A
short walk from the Ōkaidō arcade (大
街道), the hotel is convenient to the city's
nightlife and restaurants. LAN internet is
in all rooms and there are consoles in the
lobby.

Hotel JAL City HOTEL ¥¥
(☏ 913-2580; www.jalhotels.com/matsuyama; 1-10-
10 Otemachi; s/tw from ¥7100/11,000; P @) The
No 5 tram runs right past the door of the

best business hotel in Matsuyama. JAL City
is a tasteful offering with near five-star service and exemplary dining. The rooms are a
bit bland, but very spacious and comfortable. The castle is a short walk away.

Dōgo Kan HOTEL ¥¥
(道後舘; ☏ 941-7777; www.dogokan.co.jp; 7-26
Dōgo-takōchō; r per person with meals Mon-Fri
from ¥15,000, Sat & Sun from ¥21,000) The Ki-
shi Kurokawa–designed Dōgo Kan lies on
a slope behind the Tsubaki-no-yu public
baths. Indoor ponds and supremely gracious
staff complement the grand tatami rooms
and an elaborate series of communal baths.
The Western rooms are appreciably cheaper,
but lack any real 'Dōgo-ness'.

Funaya RYOKAN ¥¥¥
(ふなや; ☏ 947-0278; www.dogo-funaya.co.jp;
1-33 Dōgo-yunomachi; r per person with meals
from ¥22,050) Natsume Sōseki took refuge
here from his writer's block and aching
limbs, and so should you if you can afford
it. The beauty lies on the inside, from the
central garden and private onsen to the exquisite surrounding tatami rooms fit (and
fitted) for Japanese royalty. It's a short walk
from the Dōgo Onsen tram station along
the road that leads up to Isaniwa-jinja.

✖ Eating

The area around the Ginten-gai and Ōkaidō shopping arcades in central Matsuyama is full of places to eat and drink.

Dōgo-no-machiya   CAFE ¥

(道後の町屋; ☑ 986-8886; www.dogonomachiya. com; meals ¥650-1000; ⊙ 9am-10pm; ⊛) With a traditional shopfront along the Dōgo arcade, this former teahouse now offers burgers and sandwiches. Its shotgun-style layout leads through beautifully preserved dark-wood rooms to a Japanese garden out back. Run by a young crew, it's an excellent spot for a Western breakfast – the toast set with scrambled eggs, bacon, salad and coffee costs ¥630.

Café Bleu   CAFE ¥

(☑ 907-0402; 4F, 2-2-8 Ōkaidō; meals ¥600-900; ⊙ 11am-11pm) This lovely little music cafe on the edge of the Ōkaidō arcade serves tasty, simple lunches to a bookish clientele (there's a picture menu and daily specials). The decor includes album covers, music photography and vintage typewriters. Beer (including Guinness on draught) and generous cocktails are also available.

Ohana Cafe   BURGERS ¥

(オハナカフェ; ☑ 993 3668; 2-2-8 Ōkaidō; burgers from ¥600; ⊙ 11.30am-3pm & 6-11pm) This Hawaiian burger joint in the heart of Matsuyama is a happening little business. The four-seater lunch counter and one comfy booth are permanently packed during happy lunch hours, and the tiny, many varied burgers are sweet and delicious. The fruity enchiladas are pretty good too. It's off the Ōkaidō arcade.

Goshiki Sōmen Morikawa   NOODLES ¥¥

(五色そうめん森川; ☑ 933-3838; 3-5-4 Sanbanchō; meals ¥780-2000; ⊙ 11am-10.30pm, occasionally closed 3-5pm; 📖) Next to the central post office is this elegant Matsuyama institution, which specialises in *goshiki sōmen* (thin noodles in five different colours). You'll recognise it by the piles of colourful noodles in the window waiting to be snapped up and taken home as souvenirs. Set meals are around ¥1500; there is a picture menu.

Tengu no Kakurega   IZAKAYA ¥

(てんぐの隠れ家; ☑ 931-1009; 2-5-17 Sanbanchō; dishes ¥400-1200; ⊙ 5pm-midnight, to 1am Fri & Sat) A chic young people's *izakaya* serving *yakitori* and other dishes in a pleasant setting; try the *omakase* (chef's choice) set of grilled, skewered carnivorous delights (¥1260). Paper screens give onto a little garden at the back. Heading away from the post office, look for the *tengu* (long-nosed goblin) hung above the doorway, to the right in the second block after the Ōkaidō arcade.

Takizawa   JAPANESE ¥¥

(たきざわ; ☑ 931-9377; 3-4-4 Ōkaidō; meals ¥850-2500; ⊙ 11.30am-2pm & 5-10pm) Near the castle ropeway, this restaurant serves straightforward, well-balanced Matsuyama-style food at reasonable prices. Rice lunch sets (¥850) change daily but are invariably skillfully prepared with subtle flavours and nods to local specialities. Try the *tai kamameshi* (kettle-steamed rice with snapper; ¥1000).

Futaba   JAPANESE ¥

(ふたば; ☑ 945-9508; 13-22 Dōgo-yunomachi; dishes ¥800-2000; ⊙ lunch & dinner) Excellent noodles and *nabe* (Japanese hotpot) for your post-onsen replenishment, in a small, traditional establishment.

🍷 Drinking

The bulk of drinking establishments are concentrated in Ichiban-chō and Niban-chō amid the network of neon-lit streets either side of the Ōkaidō arcade.

Sala Sol   BAR

(3rd fl, Ciel Bldg, 2-3-5 Sanbanchō; drinks from ¥600; ⊙ 8.30pm-3am, closed Mon) The town's most popular bar with foreigners is surprisingly cool, with excellent music and generous drink specials. It's also one of the few places in town where people dance... all night long. You'll have to look closely for the little sandwich board pointing out the stairwell.

Dōgo Bakushukan   BREWERY

(道後麦酒館; ☑ 945-6866; 20-13 Dōgo-yunomachi; ⊙ 11am-10pm) Right by Dōgo Onsen Honkan, this place brews its own beer, and is a good spot for a drink and a bite to eat after a relaxing soak. The names of the beers are allusions to novelist Natsume Sōseki and his famous novel, *Botchan*. There's also a decent range of food available from a picture menu (such as *iwashi no karaage* – fried sardines).

Peggy Sue Saloon   BAR

(ペギー・スー; 2nd fl, 1-2-9 Nibanchō; drinks from ¥700; ⊙ 8.30pm-3am, closed Mon) Run by a music nut with a fondness for country music, this friendly bar is a treasure trove of cowboy-themed Americana. There's a Wurlitzer jukebox, and several guitars and mandolins on the walls that are just waiting for someone to take them down and start picking. The 2nd-floor sign is visible from street level. It's in a cluster of bars just east of Ōkaidō arcade.

Underground Cafe
BAR

(☑998-7710; 3-6-6 Ōkaidō; ☺6pm-4am) A local and expat secret bar hang-out that feels more Honshū than Shikoku and serves Japanese-style Mexican food on the side. It's off the street leading to the ropeway; look for the Union Jack flag, so coolly out of context.

Chocobar
BAR

(☑933-2039; 2-2-6 Sanbanchō; drinks from ¥700; ☺5pm-late) This tiny shot bar located on a busy road has a regular hip-hop soundtrack and colourful decor. It's one of the few places in Matsuyama where passers-by can watch you get drunk.

Cafe BC
CAFE

(☑945-9295; 2-2-20 Ōkaidō; ☺9am-10pm Mon-Thu & Sun, to 11pm Fri & Sat) The best coffee in town. The lady of the house also makes killer sandwiches (lunch sets cost ¥630 to ¥730).

ℹ Information

ATMs accepting international cards can be found at the central post office and at the post office that's a couple of minutes' walk north of JR Matsuyama Station.

Ehime Prefectural International Centre (愛媛県国際交流協会; EPIC; ☑917-5678; www. epic.or.jp; 1-1 Dōgo Ichiman; ☺8.30am-5pm Mon-Sat) Provides advice, internet access and bike rental. EPIC is near the Minami-machi or Kenmin Bunkakaikan-mae (南町) tram stop. Look for the red question mark.

JTB (☑931-2281; 4-12-10 Sanbanchō; ☺10am-6pm Mon-Sat) In the centre of town.

Tourist Information Office (☑931-3914; ☺8.30am-8.30pm) The main office is located inside JR Matsuyama Station, while a branch office (☑info 943-8342; ☺8am-8pm; 🖥near terminus for Dōgo Onsen) is opposite the tram terminus for Dōgo Onsen.

ℹ Getting There & Away

BOAT

The superjet hydrofoil, run by the Setonaikai Kisen ferry (p607), has regular hydrofoil connections between Matsuyama and Hiroshima (¥6900, 1¼ hours, 13 daily). The Hiroshima–Matsuyama ferry (¥3500, 2½ hours, 10 daily) is also a popular way of getting to/from Shikoku.

Ferry Sunflower (フェリーさんふらわあ; ☑951-0167; www.ferry-sunflower.co.jp) runs between Matsuyama and Kokura port, near Kitakyūshū (¥5600, seven hours, one daily).

ℹ A CYCLING PILGRIMAGE

For *henro* who wish to start or finish their pilgrimage on two wheels, a fantastic way to travel between Shikoku and Hiroshima Prefecture is via the **Shimanami Kaidō**, a bicycle route that crosses a series of bridges across six Inland Sea islands. **Sunrise Itoyama** (サンライズ糸山; ☑0898-41-3196; www.sunrise-itoyama. jp; 2-8-1 Sunaba-chō, Imabari; ☺8am-8pm Apr-Sep, to 5pm Oct-Mar) in Imabari is the most convenient starting point on the Shikoku side. It's also a good idea to send heavy luggage ahead with a courier service like Yamato; many guesthouses and convenience stores can help you with the paperwork. See also p429.

BUS

There are JR Highway buses that run to/from Osaka (¥6700, 5½ hours, five daily) and Tokyo (¥12,100, 12 hours, one daily), and there are frequent buses to major cities in Shikoku.

TRAIN

The JR Yosan line connects Matsuyama with Takamatsu (*tokkyū* ¥5500, 2½ hours), and there are also services across the Seto-ōhashi to Okayama (*tokkyū* ¥6530, 2¾ hours) on Honshū.

ℹ Getting Around

AIRPORT

Matsuyama's airport, 6km west of the city, is easily reached by bus (¥330, 20 minutes, hourly) from the front of the JR Matsuyama Station.

BICYCLE

JR Matsuyama Rental Bicycles (per day ¥300; ☺9am-6pm Mon-Sat) Available at the large bicycle park to the right as you exit JR Matsuyama Station.

TRAM

Tickets cost a flat ¥150 for each trip (pay when you get off). A day pass costs ¥400. Lines 1 and 2 are loop lines, running clockwise and anticlockwise around Katsuyama (the castle mountain). Line 3 runs from Matsuyama-shi Station to Dōgo Onsen, line 5 goes from JR Matsuyama Station to Dōgo Onsen, and line 6 from Kiya-chō (木屋町) to Dōgo Onsen. You can also ride the vintage Botchan Ressha (坊ちゃん列車), small trains that were imported from Germany in 1887. Named for Natsume Sōseki's famous novel, they ran up and down Matsuyama's streets for 67 years, and they're back in occasional use. Combo tickets for the Botchan Ressha plus a one-day tram pass cost ¥500.

Ishizuchi-san 石鎚山

☑ 0897

At 1982m, Ishizuchi-san is the highest peak in western Japan, and was traditionally considered to be a holy mountain. Ishizuchi attracts pilgrims and climbers alike, particularly during the July and August climbing season. During the winter (late December to late March) skiing is possible.

To get to the Nishi-no-kawa cable-car station (on the northern side of the mountain), take the direct bus (¥990, 55 minutes, four daily) from Iyo-Saijo Station. The **cable car** (石鎚登山ロープウェイ; ☑ 59-0331; one-way/return ¥1000/1900; ⏰ 8am-5pm Mon-Fri, to 6pm Sat & Sun) carries hikers to an elevation of 1300 metres; from here, plan on about a five-hour round-trip hike to the summit.

You can climb up one way and down the other or make a complete circuit from Nishi-no-kawa to the summit, down to Tsuchi-goya and then back to Nishi-no-kawa. Allow all day and an early start for the circuit. For detailed information on hiking Ishizuchi-san, see Lonely Planet's *Hiking in Japan*.

Accommodation is available at **Ishizuchi Fureai-no-Sato** (石鎚ふれあいの里; ☑ 59-0203; 1-25-1 Nakaoka, Saijo-shi; r per person ¥1170, cabins from ¥2920), where the cabins are cosy and the complex includes a small on-site restaurant, *ofuro* (public bath) and outdoor cooking area. Reserve accommodation and meals in advance, as it's a destination for school groups.

KAGAWA PREFECTURE

Formerly known as Sanuki, Kagawa Prefecture (香川県) is the smallest of Shikoku's four regions, and the second smallest of the country's 47 prefectures. It has plenty to offer, including the site of a celebrated shrine of Kompira-san at Kotohira, reached via a stirring stair climb, and the handsome port city of Takamatsu with its world-renowned Japanese garden.

The region's hospitable weather and welcoming people have always been a comfort to pilgrims as they come to the end of their journey. Today, it's an important point of arrival, too, since the only rail link with Honshū is via the Seto-ōhashi bridge to Okayama. Equally importantly, it's a short ferry ride to the remarkable Inland Sea island of Naoshima.

Matsuyama to Takamatsu

The JR Yosan line runs around the coast between Takamatsu and Matsuyama. At Tadotsu, the JR Dosan line splits off and runs south to Zentsū-ji and Kotohira, through the Iya Valley and then heading eventually to Kōchi.

Kanonji 観音寺

☑ 0875 / POP 65,000

Coming east from Ehime-ken, the first town of consequence in Kagawa Prefecture is Kanonji, notable as the only spot on the pilgrimage trail to have two of the 88 Temples within the same grounds: Temple 68, **Jinne-in** (神恵院), and Temple 69, **Kanon-ji** (観音寺).

It's also known for the odd **Zenigata** (銭形), a 350m-circumference coin-shaped sculpture in the sand which dates from 1633. The coin and its inscription are formed by huge trenches dug in the sand, and are said to have been dug overnight by the local population as a welcome present to their feudal lord. To get the best views of the sculpture, you'll need to climb the hill in Kotohiki-kōen, 1.9km northwest of Kanonji Station (not far from the two temples). A small **Tourist Information Office** (☑ 25-3839), over the bridge from the station, has maps. Kanonji is considerably closer to Takamatsu (*tokkyū* ¥2210, 48 minutes) than Matsuyama (*tokkyū* ¥4130, 1¾ hours).

Marugame 丸亀

☑ 0877 / POP 110,700

An interesting detour from the 88 Temple circuit is in Marugame, home to **Marugame-jō** (丸亀城; admission ¥200; ⏰ 9am-4.30pm). The castle dates from 1597, and is one of only 12 castles in Japan to have its original wooden *donjon* intact.

At **Uchiwa-no-Minato Museum** (うちわの港ミュージアム; ☑ 24-7055; ⏰ 9.30am-5pm, closed Mon) **FREE** there are displays and craft demonstrations showing how *uchiwa* (traditional paper fans) are made. The museum is at the harbour, a few minutes' walk from the station.

Across from the station, **bike hire** (☑ 25-1127; per day ¥200, deposit ¥500) is available from the bicycle park . By bike, it is less than an hour from Marugame to Zentsū-ji. Marugame is easily covered as a day trip from Takamatsu (*tokkyū* ¥1050, 25 minutes).

Zentsū-ji 善通寺

☑ 0877 / POP 34,000

If you only have time for one temple, then make it **Zentsū-ji** (善通寺) `FREE`, number 75 of the 88 Temples and the place where Kōbō Daishi was born. It is also the largest temple – most of the other 88 could fit comfortably into the car park here. The temple boasts a truly magnificent five-storey pagoda and giant camphor trees that are said to date back as far as Daishi's childhood. Visitors can venture into the basement of the **Mie-dō** (御影堂; admission ¥500; ⊙ 8am-5pm) building and traverse a 100m-long passageway (戒壇めぐり) in pitch darkness: by moving carefully along with your hand pressed to the wall (painted with mandalas, angels and lotus flowers), you are said to be safely following Buddha's way. If you're on a bike, there are several other pilgrimage temples within easy reach of this one, including Temple 73, **Shusshaka-ji** (出釈迦寺) `FREE`.

The temple is about 1km from the JR Zentsuji Station, straight ahead as you exit. On the right you'll find a number of well-priced, casual restaurants.

Kotohira 琴平

☑ 0877 / POP 10,900

The small mountain village of Kotohira is home to one of Shikoku's most famous tourist attractions, Kompira-san, a Shintō shrine dedicated to the god of seafarers. The 1368 steep stone steps are a rite of passage for many Japanese, with plenty of interesting enroute distractions.

◎ Sights

★ Kompira-san   SHINTŌ SHRINE

(金刀比羅宮; Hōmotsu-kan admission ¥500, Shoin admission ¥500; ⊙ Hōmotsu-kan 8.30am-5pm, Shoin 8.30am-4.30pm) Kompira-san or, more formally, Kotohira-gū, was originally a Buddhist and Shintō temple dedicated to the guardian of mariners. It became exclusively a Shintō shrine after the Meiji Restoration.

A lot of fuss is made about how strenuous the climb (1368 steps) to the top is, but if you've made it this far in Japan, you've probably completed a few long ascents to shrines already.

The first notable landmark on the long climb is **Ō-mon** (大門), a stone gateway that leads to **Hōmotsu-kan** (宝物館; Treasure House), where the collection of treasures is pretty underwhelming for such a major

shrine. Nearby you will find five traditional-sweets vendors at tables shaded by large white parasols. A symbol of ancient times, the vendors (the Gonin Byakushō – Five Farmers) are descendants of the original families that were permitted to trade within the grounds of the shrine. Further uphill is **Shoin** (書院; Reception Hall), a designated National Treasure that dates from 1659 and has some interesting screen paintings and a small garden.

Continuing the ascent, you eventually reach large **Asahino Yashiro** (旭社; Shrine of the Rising Sun). Built in 1837, this large hall is dedicated to the sun goddess Amaterasu, and is noted for its ornate wood-carving. From here, the short final ascent, which is the most beautiful leg of the walk, brings you to **Gohonsha** (御本社; Gohon Hall) and **Ema-dō** (絵馬堂; Ema Pavilion). The latter is filled with maritime offerings ranging from pictures of ships and models to modern ship engines. From this level, there are spectacular views that extend right down to the coast and over the Inland Sea.

Incurable climbers can continue for another 500 or so steps up to Oku-sha (Inner Shrine), which features stone carvings of tengu on the cliff.

★ Kanamaru-za   THEATRE

(金丸座; ☑ 73-3846; admission ¥500; ⊙ 9am-5pm) Japan's oldest kabuki playhouse, though it had a lengthy stint as a cinema before falling out of use. The restorations are superb; wander backstage and see the revolving-stage mechanism, basement trapdoors and a tunnel out to the front of the theatre. The playhouse is 200m east of the main approach to Kompira-san. English-speaking volunteer guides are sometimes on hand.

Kinryō-no-Sato   MUSEUM

(金陵の郷; ☑ 73-4133; admission ¥310; ⊙ 9am-4pm Mon-Fri, to 6pm Sat & Sun) This sake museum, located along the main approach to the shrine, is in the old premises of a brewery that has owned the building since 1789. At the end of the tour you can try three different Kinryō sakes for ¥100 a glass.

🛏 Sleeping & Eating

Kotobuki Ryokan   RYOKAN ¥¥

(ことぶき旅館; ☑ 73-3872; 245-5 Kotohira-chō; s/d with 2 meals ¥6825/12,600; ℗) This welcoming ryokan with comfortable tatami rooms and warm hospitality is conveniently

Kotohira

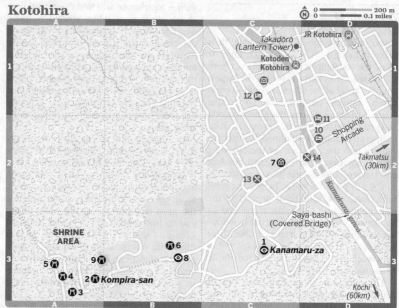

situated by the riverside. Umbrellas, internet access and spotless shared bathrooms are all available. Turn left for the arcade and some small restaurants; turn right for the shrine.

Kotohira Riverside Hotel　HOTEL ¥¥
(琴平リバーサイドホテル; ☎75-1800; 246-1 Kotohira-chō; s/d with breakfast ¥7950/14,900; 📶) This well-run business hotel has comfortable Western-style rooms. There's an in-house bath, but guests also receive discounted rates at its sister property's onsen nearby.

Kotosankaku　RYOKAN ¥¥¥
(琴参閣; ☎75-1000; www.kotosankaku.jp; 685-11 Kotohira-chō; r per person Mon-Fri from ¥9600, Sat & Sun from ¥17,850; 🅿️🉐) One of the biggest ryokan in Shikoku, this well-designed

grand dame has superlative Japanese- and Western-style rooms and a summer-time pool. The onsen complex is open to non-guests (¥900, from 11am to 4pm).

Kompira Udon　UDON ¥
(こんぴらうどん; ☎73-5785; meals ¥500-950; ⊙8am-5pm) Just short of the first set of steps leading up Kompira-san, this is one of dozens of *Sanuki udon* joints in Kotohira. You can't miss it, as the front window shows off the busy *udon*-makers rolling out dough and slicing noodles by hand. Try the *kake udon* (¥500), simply hot or cold noodles in broth.

New Green　CAFE ¥
(ニューグリーン; ☎73-3451; meals ¥850-1600; ⊙8.30am-8.30pm; 🅿️) A cute neighbourhood

spot where the local ladies cackle over coffee, New Green is also one of the few restaurants in town open for dinner. If the salads, *kaki-furai* (breaded, fried oysters) and *omuraisu* leave you wanting, there's cake as well.

ℹ Information

There are coin lockers and tourist brochures at the JR station. The ATMs at the post office accept international cards.

ℹ Getting There & Away

You can travel to Kotohira on the JR Dosan line from Kōchi (*tokkyū* ¥3810, one hour and 38 minutes) and Ōboke. For Takamatsu and other places on the north coast, change trains at Tadotsu. The private Kotoden line has regular direct trains from Takamatsu (¥610, one hour).

Takamatsu 高松

📞 087 / POP 425,000

Takamatsu is a sparkling port city with a spectacular garden, solid nightlife and efficient transport links with the mainland by rail, road and sea. There's an air of prefectural capital among the well-heeled locals and wide boulevards, which all lead to wonderful Ritsurin-kōen. The city also serves as a base for a number of unique day trips, notably to the olive groves of Shōdo-shima and the island of Naoshima in the Inland Sea.

◉ Sights

★ Ritsurin-kōen   PARK

(栗林公園; 📞 833-7411; 1-20-16 Ritsurin-chō; admission ¥400; ◐ sunrise-sunset) One of the most beautiful gardens in the country, Ritsurin-kōen dates from the mid-1600s and took more than a century to complete. Designed as a walking garden for the *daimyō's* enjoyment, the park winds around a series of ponds, tearooms, bridges and islands. To the west, Shiun-zan (Mt Shiun) forms an impressive backdrop to the garden. The classic view of Engetsu-kyō bridge with the mountain in the background is one of the finest in Japan.

Enclosed by the garden are a number of interesting sights, including **Sanuki Folkcraft Museum** (讃岐民芸館; ◐ 8:45am-4:30pm) FREE, which displays local crafts dating back to the Tokugawa dynasty. There are a number of teahouses in the park, including 17th-century **Kikugetsu-tei** (掬月亭; matcha ¥710; ◐ 9am-4pm), where you can sip *matcha* with a traditional sweet and enjoy various garden tableaux from the tatami rooms. Or try the lovely thatched-roof **Higurashi-tei**, which dates from 1898.

The easiest way to reach Ritsurin-kōen is by taking the frequent direct bus (¥230, 15 minutes) from JR Takamatsu Station.

Takamatsu-jō   CASTLE

(高松城; 2-1 Tamamo-chō; admission ¥200; ◐ sunrise-sunset) The site of Takamatsu's castle now forms delightful Tamamo-kōen, a park where the walls and seawater moat survive, along with several of the original turrets. Each spring a swimming race is held in the moat to honour an age-old chivalrous tradition. The original castle was built in 1588 for Itoma Chikamasa, and was the home of the region's military rulers until the Meiji Restoration, which happened nearly 300 years later. Reconstruction of the main keep is slated for completion in 2015; watch this space.

Takamatsu City Museum of Art   MUSEUM

(高松市美術館; 📞 823-1711; 10-4 Konya-machi; admission ¥200; ◐ 9.30am-7pm Mon-Fri, to 5pm Sat & Sun) This impressive inner-city gallery is testament to Takamatsu's quality art scene. The light and spacious refitting of a former Bank of Japan building is a stroke of curatorial genius, well served by interesting exhibitions on rotation from across Japan and the world.

🛏 Sleeping

Budget lodgings in Takamatsu are virtually nonexistent, but it's worth spending up if you can – the midrange hotels in town represent great value.

Hotel Sakika   HOTEL ¥

(ホテルサキカ; 📞 822-2111; 6-9 Hyakken-machi; r per person from ¥3900) The hallways are dark and the doors are metal, but rooms here are perfectly OK if you're desperate to save ¥1000 on accommodations. Opt for a Japanese-style room. Guests can use the onsen at the Hotel Mimatsu around the corner. Ask a Japanese speaker to help you book ahead.

Dormy Inn Takamatsu   HOTEL ¥¥

(さぬきの湯ドーミーイン高松; 📞 832-5489; www.hotespa.net/hotels/takamatsu; 1-10-10 Kawaramachi; s/d ¥7000/9000; ☉ @) The Dormy is a little bit different from the usual big hotel fare, with its keen eye for design and a location at the heart of the entertainment district. The rooms are sleek and spacious, while the service is top notch for the price.

Takamatsu

SHIKOKU TAKAMATSU

The onsen and *rotemburo* (outdoor bath) on the top floor are welcome additions. There's LAN access in all rooms.

Area One Hotel   BUSINESS HOTEL ¥¥
(☑823-7801; 2-23 Nishinomaru-chō; s/tw from ¥5000/7600; ℙ ⊖ @ 🛜) Opposite the JR station is this no-fuss business hotel from a reliable, design-focused chain. Rooms are relatively spacious and represent excellent value. Useful extras such as desk lamps, laptops and humidifiers are available for rent in the lobby. The restaurant next door serves a delicious, cheap breakfast (¥500) for hotel guests.

Hotel No 1 Takamatsu   BUSINESS HOTEL ¥¥
(ホテルNo.1高松; ☑812-2222; www.hotelno1. jp/takamatsu; 2-4-1 Kankō-dōri; s/d ¥5140/7870; ℙ ⊖ @) Three blocks east and three blocks south of Kotoden Kawaramachi Station, this is a sparkling business hotel with standard rooms and a rooftop men-only *rotemburo* with sweeping views of the city (the women's baths are on the 2nd floor). There is internet access in the lobby, and there are LAN connections in all rooms.

JR Hotel Clement Takamatsu   HOTEL ¥¥¥
(JRホテルクレメント高松; ☑811-1111; www.jrclement.co.jp; 1-1 Hamano-chō; s/d from ¥12,474/20,790; ℙ ⊖ @ 🛜) This eye-catching ultramodern hotel is one of the first buildings you see as you exit JR Takamatsu Station. The rooms are spacious, and there's a good selection of bars and restaurants with sweeping views of the Inland Sea.

✗ Eating

Restaurants and bars are clustered in the covered arcades and entertainment district to the west side of the tracks between Kotoden Kataharamachi and Kawaramachi stations. People in Takamatsu are serious about their *udon*, and no trip here would be complete without at least one bowl of the famous speciality, *Sanuki udon*. Look for the words *te-uchi udon* (手打ちうどん), meaning 'handmade noodles'.

Kawafuku
UDON ¥

(川福; ☎822-1956; 2-1 Daiku-machi; udon lunch set ¥600; ⊗11am-midnight) One of Takamatsu's best-known *udon* shops, Kawafuku serves its silky *Sanuki udon* in a variety of ways. Choose from the plastic food models outside. Look for the red-and-white striped lanterns in front, along Lion-dōri.

Kanaizumi
UDON ¥

(かな泉; ☎822-0123; 9-3 Konyamachi; medium serving of noodles with 2 toppings ¥500; ⊗9:30am-5pm) A self-service, self-explanatory noodle joint that is ideal for famished victims of culture shock. You can choose between *shō* (small), *chū* (medium) or *dai* (large) helpings of *kake udon* (*udon* in broth) or *zaru udon* (cold *udon*, with a dipping sauce), and then help yourself to a wide variety of toppings.

Tsurumaru
UDON ¥

(鶴丸; ☎821-3780; 9-34 Furubaba-chō; curry udon ¥700; ⊗8pm-4am Mon-Sat) Sit at the counter and watch the noodles being pounded by hand in this popular spot, which is busy with the bar-hopping crowd until late into the night. The delicious *karē udon* (curry *udon*) is the most popular choice here. Look for the curtain over the door with a picture of a crane on it.

Ofukuro
IZAKAYA ¥

(おふくろ; ☎862-0822; 1-11-12 Kawara-machi; dishes ¥500-1500; ⊗5-10pm Mon-Sat; 📵) This fabulous *washofu* (local eating house) in the heart of the entertainment district offers a well-priced and hearty dining experience. A number of delicious, pre-prepared vegetarian and fish dishes sit on the counter, served with complimentary salad and miso soup. Find it east of Minami-shinmachi.

Bijin-tei
IZAKAYA ¥¥

(美人亭; ☎861-0275; 2-2-10 Kawara-machi; dishes ¥700-1500; ⊗5-10pm Mon-Sat) Smiling *mama-san* sees all at this discreet seafood *izakaya*.

Point to the menu items already plated – the pickled *tako* (octopus) is a mouthful – or ask for an *osusume* (recommendation). It's on the ground floor of a building containing several snack bars and karaoke joints. Look for the sign with the shop's name on it in kanji.

Tokiwa Saryō
SEAFOOD ¥¥¥

(ときわ茶寮; ☎861-5577; 1-8-2 Tokiwa-chō; dishes ¥1200-3600; ⊗11am-3pm & 5-10pm) An old Japanese inn with a pond and excellent sashimi and tempura sets; there's a clear photo menu. It's off the Tokiwa arcade from Ferry Dōri, take the second left; it's the building on the right with the big white lantern.

🍸 Drinking

★ King's Yawd
BAR

(☎837-2660; 1-2-2 Tokishin-machi; ⊗6pm-2am Mon-Sat) The chilled-out, dreadlocked Sato-san holds court over a diverse crew that hangs out at this Jamaican bar. She slings authentic Jamaican food (think jerk chicken and ackee), while her staff pours generous cocktails, all to a background of reggae and red, gold and green decor. The legendary weekend parties are popular with both locals and expats.

Anbar Bar
BAR

(アンバー; 1st fl, Dai-ichi Bldg, 8-15 Furubaba-chō; ⊗8pm-midnight Wed-Tue) The company of surreal feline imagery is an interesting companion to a fine whisky. There's an English sign outside, and plenty of hip weirdos inside.

Cancun Bar
BAR

(カンクン; 6-23 Furubaba-chō; ⊗6pm-3am, closed Sun) A hodge-podge of bric-a-brac and bad lighting, Cancun is about as far from Mexico as you can get without leaving Kagawa. There's a wide range of drinks (most ¥700 to ¥800), and the friendly young bar staff speak some English and know the party scene well.

ℹ Information

There are coin lockers and a left-luggage office at JR Takamatsu Station, and international ATMs at the central post office (located near the northern exit of Marugamemachi Arcade).

e-TOPIA (e-とぴあかがわ; 5th fl, Takamatsu Symbol Tower; ⊗10am-8pm Tue-Sun) Free internet access in a large, sunny facility; in the Sunport complex between the JR station and the port.

JTB (☎851-2117; 7-6 Kajiyamachi; ⊙10am-6pm Mon-Sat)

Kagawa International Exchange (アイパル香川国際交流会館; I-PAL Kagawa; ☎837-5901; www.i-pal.or.jp; 1-11-63 Banchō; ⊙9am-6pm Tue-Sun) In the northwest corner of Chūō-kōen, this international exchange association has a small library, satellite TV and internet access.

Tourist Information Office (高松市観光案内所; ☎851-2009; ⊙9am-6pm) In the plaza outside the station.

❶ Getting There & Around

BICYCLE

Takamatsu is flat, and excellent for biking. The city offers a great deal on its 'blue bicycles' (¥100 per 24 hours; photo ID is required), which can be picked up at **Takamatsu-shi Rental Cycles** (高松駅前広場地下レンタサイクルポート; ☎821-0400; ⊙7am-10pm) in the underground bicycle park outside JR Takamatsu Station.

BOAT

Jumbo Ferry (ジャンボフェリー; ☎811-6688) runs between Takamatsu and Kobe (¥1800, three hours 40 minutes). Free buses shuttle passengers from the port to JR Takamatsu Station.

BUS

There are bus services to/from Tokyo (¥10,000, 9½ hours, three daily), Nagoya (¥6800, 5½ hours, two daily), Kyoto (¥4800, three hours and 40 minutes, six daily) and most other major cities.

TRAIN

Takamatsu is the only city in Shikoku with regular rail links to Honshū. There are frequent trains to Okayama (¥1470, 55 minutes, every half-hour), where you can connect to *shinkansen* services that will whizz you to any of the major cities in just a few hours.

From Takamatsu, *tokkyū* trains on the JR Kōtoku line run southeast to Tokushima (¥2560, one hour and seven minutes, hourly); the JR Yosan line runs west to Matsuyama (¥5500, 2½ hours, hourly); and the JR Dosan line runs to Kōchi (¥4760, 2½ hours, hourly). The private Kotoden line also runs direct to Kotohira (¥830, one hour, frequent).

Around Takamatsu

Takamatsu is a great stepping-off point for the olive groves of Shōdo-shima and the wonderful art of Naoshima in the Inland Sea, both less than an hour by boat from the ferry port close to Takamatsu Station.

Yashima 屋島

About 5km east of Takamatsu is the 292m-high tabletop plateau of Yashima, where you'll find **Yashima-ji** (屋島寺), number 84 of the 88 Temples. This was the site of a decisive battle between the Genji and Heike clans in the late 12th century, and the temple's **Treasure House** (admission ¥500; ⊙9am-5pm) exhibits artefacts relating to the battle. Just behind the Treasure House is the **Pond of Blood**, where victorious Genji warriors washed the blood from their swords.

At the bottom of Yashima, about 500m north of the station, is **Shikoku-mura** (四国村; ☎843-3111; www.shikokumura.or.jp; 91 Yashima-nakamachi; admission ¥800; ⊙8.30am-5pm Apr-Oct, 8.30am-4.30pm Nov-Mar), an excellent village museum that houses old buildings transported here from all over Shikoku and neighbouring islands. The village's fine kabuki stage came from Shōdo-shima, which is famous for its traditional farmers' kabuki performances. There is also an excellent **restaurant** serving, you guessed it, *Sanuki udon* (from ¥450) in an old farmhouse building down a stone staircase to the right.

Yashima is six stops from Kawaramachi on the private Kotoden line (¥240). Shuttle buses run from the station to the top of the mountain (¥100) every half an hour from 9.30am to 4.30pm, but it's a very pleasant hour-long hike up the forested back side of the plateau to the temple.

Isamu Noguchi Garden Museum イサム・ノグチ庭園美術館

It's worth considering an excursion to the town of Murechō, east of Takamatsu, to witness the fascinating legacy of noted sculptor Isamu Noguchi (1904–88). Born in Los Angeles to a Japanese poet and an American writer, Noguchi set up a studio and residence here in 1970. Today the **complex** (イサムノグチ庭園美術館; ☎870-1500; www.isamunoguchi.or.jp; 3-5-19 Murechō; tours ¥2100; ⊙tours 10am, 1pm & 3pm Tue, Thu & Sat, by appointment) is filled with hundreds of Noguchi's works, and holds its own as an impressive art installation. Inspiring sculptures are on display in the beautifully restored Japanese buildings and in the surrounding landscape.

Visitors should fax or email ahead for reservations, preferably two weeks or more in advance (see the website for reservations and access details).

Kyūshū

Includes ➡

Best Places to Eat

➡ Zauo (p657)

➡ Kawashima Tōfu (p663)

➡ Hamakatsu (p675)

➡ Takamori Dengaku-no-Sato (p690)

➡ Miyachiku (p706)

Best Places to Stay

➡ Garden Terrace Nagasaki (p674)

➡ Hakusuikan (p703)

➡ Yoyōkaku (p663)

➡ With the Style (p655)

➡ Yamada Bessou (p714)

Why Go?

Japan's southern- and westernmost main island is its warmest, friendliest and (we're partial) most beautiful, with active volcanic peaks, rocky, lush and palmy coastlines, and onsen virtually everywhere. Much Japanese history was made in Kyūshū (九州). Jōmon ruins, Shintō's sun goddess, wealthy trading ports, cloistered foreigners, samurai rebels and one of the earth's greatest wartime tragedies all loom large.

Today, burgeoning Fukuoka is a multicultural metropolis. In picturesque Nagasaki, tragedy contrasts deftly with a colourful trading history, Kumamoto's castle is one of Japan's finest, and the volcanic Aso caldera is the world's largest. Saga Prefecture boasts *three* legendary pottery centres. Steam pours from the earth in Beppu, and lightly populated Kagoshima and Miyazaki Prefectures have wide open vistas and mountainous terrain outside their laid-back capitals. Peppered throughout are relaxing hot-spring towns and hiking opportunities.

When to Go
Fukuoka

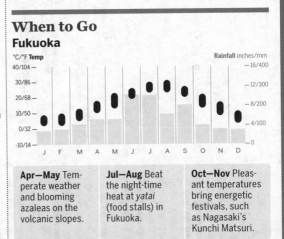

Apr–May Temperate weather and blooming azaleas on the volcanic slopes.

Jul–Aug Beat the night-time heat at *yatai* (food stalls) in Fukuoka.

Oct–Nov Pleasant temperatures bring energetic festivals, such as Nagasaki's Kunchi Matsuri.

Kyūshū Highlights

1 Joining the night owls for beer and *yakitori* skewers at a *yatai* food stall in **Fukuoka** (p656)

2 Being moved – and charmed – by the unique history of **Nagasaki** (p665)

3 Soaking in an onsen au naturel in **Beppu** (p712)

4 Seeing where the last samurai made their last stand at **Kumamoto Castle** (p683)

5 Marvelling at Japan's unique ceramics traditions in **Arita** (p664), **Imari** (p664) and **Karatsu** (p662)

6 Communing with Shintō's sun goddess in **Takachiho** (p710)

7 Recharging in a riverside *rotemburo* (outdoor baths) in

tranquil **Kurokawa Onsen** (p691)

8 Getting buried in warm volcanic sand in **Ibusuki** (p702)

9 Chilling out in **Aoshima** (p708) and the **Nichinan coast** (p710)

10 Sipping sweet-potato *shōchū* in **Kagoshima** (p692) as the Sakurajima volcano puffs away across the bay

MIYAZAKI PREFECTURE

JR Nippo Line

- Hyuga
- Tsuno
- Takanabe
- Saito
- Sadowara
- Kizaki-hama
- Miyazaki Airport
- Aoshima
- Miyazaki
- *Sea of Hyūga*
- *Saitobaru Burial Mounds*

Ichifusa-yama (1721m)

Ichifusa-yama (1739m)

- Yunomae
- Taragi
- Hitoyoshi
- Ashikita
- Minamata
- Okuchi
- Ebino
- Ebino-kogen
- Kobayashi
- Karakuni-dake (1700m)
- *Senmu-taki Waterfall*
- Takazaki
- Kirishima
- Kirishima-jingū
- Hayashida
- Miyakonojō
- *Udo-jingū*
- Obi
- Nichinan
- **Aoshima and Nichinan Coast** (p710)
- Nangō
- Kushima
- Kojima
- *Ishinami-kaigan*
- *Koigaura-hama*
- Toi-misaki
- Osumi
- Shibushi
- *Shibushi-wan*

MIYAZAKI PREFECTURE

- Hayato
- Aira
- Kokubu
- Uenohara
- Kagoshima Airport
- Naka-dake (1060m)
- Sakurajima
- Tarumizu
- Kanoya
- Ōsaki
- *Ōsumi Peninsula*
- Nejime
- Nagasaki-bana
- Sata
- Sata-misaki Sata
- *Ōsumi Straits*
- *Tanegashima (35km)*
- *Kinki-wan*

KAGOSHIMA PREFECTURE

JR Kagoshima Line

JR Kagoshima Shinkansen Line

- Izumi
- Akune
- Sendai
- Miyanojō
- Ijuin
- Kushikino
- Fukiage
- *Satsuma Peninsula*
- Fukiage-hama
- Kaseda
- Bōnotsu
- Makurazaki
- Chiran
- JR Makurazaki-Ibusuki Line
- Kiire
- Yamakawa
- **Ibusuki**
- Kaimon-dake (924m)
- *Ikeda-ko*
- **Kirishima-Yaku National Park**
- *Yakushima (60km)*
- **Kagoshima**
- Nagashima
- *Koshiki Islands*
- Kami-jima
- Hondo
- Shimo-jima
- Amakusa Archipelago
- Ushibuka
- *Unzen-Amakusa National Park*
- *Yatsushiro-kai*

Sea of Amakusa

EAST CHINA SEA

PACIFIC OCEAN

Kirishima-Yaku National Park

History

Excavations dating to around 10,000 BC indicate that southern Kyūshū was the likely entry point of the Jōmon culture, which gradually crept north.

Japan's trade with China and Korea began in Kyūshū, and the arrival of Portuguese ships in 1543 initiated Japan's at-times thorny relationship with the West and heralded the beginning of its 'Christian Century' (1549–1650). With Christianity, the Portuguese also brought gunpowder weaponry, heralding the ultimate decline of the samurai tradition.

In 1868 rebels from Kyūshū were instrumental in carrying through the Meiji Restoration, which ended the military shōgunate's policy of isolation, marking the birth of modern Japan. During the ensuing Meiji era (1868–1912), rapid industrialisation caused profound social, political and environmental change.

Sadly, this historically rich region is best known for one event – the 9 August 1945 atomic bombing of Nagasaki.

ⓘ Getting There & Away

AIR

Fukuoka Airport is Japan's third largest, servicing destinations in Asia and Japan. In addition to frequent domestic connections, Ōita (Beppu), Kagoshima, Kumamoto, Miyazaki and Nagasaki airports all have flights to Seoul, and Kagoshima, Nagasaki and Kitakyūshū airports serve Shanghai and Miyazaki Taipei, but not always daily. Upstart carrier Solaseed Air has space-available Visit Japan Fares of ¥10,000 for foreign visitors, connecting many Kyūshū airports to Tokyo and Naha (Okinawa).

BOAT

There are sea connections to Kyūshū from Osaka and Okinawa. High-speed ferries shuttle between Fukuoka and Busan, in South Korea.

TRAIN

The opening of the Kyūshū shinkansen (bullet train) in March 2011 brought high-speed rail travel directly from Shin-Osaka to Kagoshima, via Hakata Station (Fukuoka) and Kumamoto.

ⓘ Getting Around

BUS

Kyūshū's extensive highway bus system is often the most efficient and cheapest way around the island. See www.rakubus.jp/english for routes and reservations.

CAR

Outside the cities, car rental is the best way to reach many of the best-preserved and least-known landscapes, particularly in rural southern and northeastern Kyūshū and around Aso-san. Car-rental agencies are conveniently located all over Kyūshū.

TRAIN

Kyūshū shinkansen lines run north–south through western Kyūshū between Hakata and Kagoshima, and other major Kyūshū cities are connected by tokkyū (limited express) train services.

FUKUOKA PREFECTURE

Fukuoka

✔ 092 / POP 1,495,000

Fukuoka is Kyūshū's largest city (and Japan's sixth largest). It's still growing. It's made up of two former towns, the Fukuoka castle town on the west bank of the Naka-gawa and Hakata on the east. The two towns merged in 1889 as Fukuoka, though the name Hakata is still widely in use (for instance, it's Fukuoka Airport but Hakata Station).

Whatever you call it, this youthful, user-friendly metropolis in Fukuoka Prefecture (福岡県) has a cosmopolitan charm, particularly after dark, peppered with the flavours of its Asian neighbours. Hakata traces its trading history back some 2000 years, which continues today with visitors from Seoul and Shanghai. Among Japanese, the city is famed for its 'Hakata bijin' (beautiful women), SoftBank Hawks baseball team and hearty Hakata rāmen (egg noodles).

If Fukuoka doesn't burst with sights like Tokyo or Kyoto, its friendly atmosphere, warm weather and contemporary attractions – art, architecture, shopping and cuisine – make up for it, and it's a good base for regional excursions.

ⓘ Orientation

For visitors, Fukuoka can be divided into three main districts. Hakata, the old shitamachi (downtown), is now dominated by Fukuoka's shinkansen stop, the busy JR Hakata Station. Three subway stops away and across the river Naka-gawa is Fukuoka's beating heart, the Tenjin district, bursting with department stores, boutiques, eateries and nightlife. Above ground, Tenjin centres around Watanabe-dōri, paralleled underground by Tenjin Chikagai, a long shopping arcade with mood lighting and cast-ironwork ceilings that make it a cool refuge from the summer heat. West of Tenjin is trendy Daimyō, Fukuoka's homage to Tokyo's Harajuku, minus the crowds, heading towards Fukuoka's former castle grounds.

The coastal neighbourhoods, best reached by bus or taxi, have many attractive sights, restaurants and hotels.

⊙ Sights & Activities

⊙ Hakata Area

⭐**Fukuoka Asian Art Museum**   MUSEUM
(福岡アジア美術館; http://faam.city.fukuoka.lg.jp; 7th & 8th fl, Riverain Centre Bldg, 3-1 Shimokawabata-machi; adult/child/student ¥200/free/¥150; ⊙10am-8pm, closed Wed; ☒Nakasu-Kawabata) On the upper floors of the large Hakata Riverain Centre (博多リバレイン), this large museum houses the world-renowned **Asia Gallery** and additional galleries for special exhibits (admission fee varies) and artists in residence. Changing exhibits cover contemporary works from 23 countries, from East Asia to Pakistan.

⭐**Hakata Machiya Furusato-kan**   MUSEUM
(博多町家ふるさと館; www.hakatamachiya.com; 6-10 Reisen-machi; admission ¥200; ⊙10am-6pm; ☒Gion) Spread over three *machiya* (traditional townhouses), this folk museum re-creates a Hakata *nagare* (neighbourhood unit) from the late Meiji era. The replica buildings house historical photos and displays of traditional Hakata culture, festivals, crafts and performing arts, as well as recordings of impenetrable Hakata-ben (dialect). Artisans are frequently on hand offering demonstrations.

Canal City   NOTABLE BUILDING
(キャナルシティ; www.canalcity.co.jp/eg; 1-2 Sumiyoshi; ⊙shops 10am-9pm, restaurants 11am-11pm) Once-futuristic Canal City shopping centre may be showing its age (it opened in 1996), but it still attracts crowds with its artificial canal with illuminated fountain symphony, hotels, multiplex cinema, playhouse, and about 250 boutiques, bars and bistros. It was designed by Jon Jerde, who later created Tokyo's Roppongi Hills. A new east building features international brands.

⊙ Tenjin Area

Fukuoka-jō & Ōhori-kōen   HISTORIC SITE
(福岡城・大濠公園) Only the walls of Fukuoka-jō (Fukuoka Castle) remain, but the castle's hilltop site (Maizuru-kōen) provides good views of the city.

Ōhori-kōen, the park adjacent to the castle grounds, has the traditionally styled **Nihon-teien** (日本庭園; Japanese Garden; 1-7 Ōhori-kōen; admission ¥240; ⊙9am-5pm Sep-May, to 6pm Jun-Aug, closed Mon; ☒Ōhori-kōen). It's a more recent construction (1984) around a pond with stone gardens and a teahouse.

Nearby, the **Fukuoka Art Museum** (福岡市美術館; ☎714-6051; www.fukuoka-art-museum.jp/english; 1-6 Ōhori-kōen; admission ¥200; ⊙9.30am-5pm Tue-Sun Sep-May, to 7pm Tue-Sat, to 5pm Sun Jul & Aug; ☒Ōhori-kōen) has ancient pottery and Buddhist guardians on one floor; works by Basquiat, Brancusi, Rothko and Warhol upstairs; and galleries pairing Western artists with Japanese contemporaries. Most exhibits change every few months.

SHRINES & TEMPLES

The intimate **Kushida-jinja**, municipal Shintō shrine of Hakata, traces its history to AD 757 and sponsors the Hakata Gion Yamakasa Matsuri, in which storeys-high floats make their way through the streets. A one-room **local history museum** (櫛田神社; 1-41 Kamikawabata; admission ¥300; ⊙10am-5pm, closed Mon; ☒Gion or Nakasu-Kawabata) covers the festival, plus swords, ancient pottery and more.

Sumiyoshi-jinja (住吉神社; 2-10-7 Sumiyoshi) is said to be the original *taisha* (grand shrine) of Shintō's Sumiyoshi sect. On its north side is **Rakusuien** (楽水園; http://rakusuien.net; admission/tea ¥100/300; ⊙9am-5pm, closed Tue), a pretty garden and teahouse built by a Meiji-era merchant, which offers an outdoor tea ceremony.

Tōchō-ji (東長寺; 2-4 Gokushō-machi; ☒Gion) has Japan's largest wooden Buddha (10.8m high, 30 tonnes, created 1992) and some impressively carved Kannon (Goddess of Mercy) statues. The temple is said to date from AD 806 and to have been founded by Kūkai, founder of the Shingon school of Buddhism.

Shōfuku-ji (聖福寺; 6-1 Gokushō-machi; ☒Gion) is a Zen temple founded in 1195 by Eisai, who introduced Zen and tea to Japan; it's said that the nation's first tea plants were planted here. The buildings are closed to the public, but tree-lined stone paths make a nice ramble.

Central Fukuoka

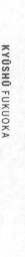

Central Fukuoka

Chūō-kōen PARK
(中央公園) Some attractive historic Western architecture populates this park by City Hall, most notably the French Renaissance–styled **Former Prefectural Hall & Official Guest House** (旧福岡県公会堂貴賓館; 6-29 Nishi-nakasu; admission ¥240; ⏰9am-5pm Tue-Sun, closed 29 Dec-3 Jan; 🚉Nakasu-Kawabata or Tenjin), dating from 1910 and with a French cafe where you can watch the scene. A couple of blocks north, the copper-turreted **Akarenga Bunka-kan** (福岡市赤煉瓦文化館; Red Brick Cultural Centre; ⏰9am-9pm Tue-Sun) **FREE** was built in 1909 by the same architect who designed Tokyo Station and now hosts simple historical exhibits.

◎ Coastal Fukuoka

Fukuoka's northwest coast is a modern mix of corporate headquarters, hotels, large shopping and entertainment venues and apartment blocks, easiest reached by bus from Tenjin or Hakata.

Fukuoka Tower OBSERVATORY
(福岡タワー; www.fukuokatower.co.jp; 2-3-26 Momochi-hama; adult/child/student & senior ¥800/200/500; ⏰9.30am-10pm Apr-Sep, to 9pm Oct-Mar; 🚉) Standing above the Momochi district is the 234m-tall Fukuoka Tower, a symbol of the city and mostly hollow (its main purpose is as a broadcast tower). There's an observation

MOJIKŌ & YAHATA

Most visitors don't get to the industrial city of Kitakyūshū at the island's far north, but two enclaves there can be combined for a worthwhile day trip from Fukuoka.

Mojikō (門司港), Kyūshū's closest point to Honshū, has been a port since 1889, and its harbourside 'Retro Town' is a trove of Meiji- and Taishō-period architecture, handsome brick buildings that once housed shipping companies and customs houses, and a drawbridge for pedestrians. A bit further on, you can walk under the Gempei Strait via the tunnel to Shimonoseki on Honshū. A row of shops along the waterfront serves Mojikō's signature dish, *yaki-curry* (curry rice topped with melted cheese and grilled).

Yahata (八幡) is a one-time industrial town that has cleaned up its act with inspirational results. **Kitakyūshū Kankyō Museum** (北九州市環境ミュージアム; Kitakyūshū Environment Museum; 2-2-6 Higashida Yahata; admission ¥100; ◷9am-5pm, closed Mon;) tells of the environmental degradation of Kyūshū in the early industrial period (including the notorious Minamata disease that struck near Kumamoto in the 1950s) via 'radioramas' with sound available in English. Interactive exhibits illustrate the effects of pollution. Steps away, the futuristic **Kitakyūshū Innovation Gallery & Studio** (北九州イノベーションギャラリー; www.kigs.jp; 2-2-11 Higashida Yahata; ◷9am-7pm Tue-Fri, to 5pm Sat & Sun;) offers changing special exhibits (¥500) and an excellent chronology of technological innovation. Across the road is a towering **steel foundry** from 1901, now cleaned up and a great place for a *bentō* (boxed meal) picnic.

From Hakata, transfer at Kokura (*shinkansen* ¥3100, 15 minutes; *tokkyū* limited express ¥2050, 45 minutes). From Kokura local trains cost ¥270 to either Mojikō (15 minutes) or Space World Station (for Yahata, 10 minutes).

deck at 123m and a cafe for soaking up the views, especially at dusk. While you're here, drop into Robosquare nearby.

Fukuoka City Museum   MUSEUM
(福岡市博物館; http://museum.city.fukuoka.jp; 3-1-1 Momochi-hama; admission ¥200; ◷9.30am-5.30pm Tue-Sun Sep-Jun, to 7.30pm Tue-Sat, to 5.30pm Sun Jul & Aug) This smart museum displays artefacts from local history and culture, and the pride of the museum is an ancient 2.3 sq cm, 109g golden seal with an inscription proving Japan's historic ties to China.

Yahoo! Japan Dome   STADIUM
(ヤフードーム; www.hawkstown.com) This monolithic, retractable-roof stadium is the home field of Fukuoka's much-loved Soft-Bank Hawks baseball team. Tours (in Japanese) are offered and there's a museum of the life of Oh Sadaharu, the world's all-time home-run king (best for die-hard fans).

Nearby Islands   ISLANDS
A quick ferry ride from Fukuoka, pretty **Nokonoshima** mixes natural and man-made parks. The latter, called **Island Park** (アイランドパーク; www.nokonoshima.com; adult/child ¥1000/500), gets the most visitors, with a swimming beach, fields of seasonal

wildflowers, huts selling crafts, and sweeping ocean views. Bicycle rental (per hour/day ¥300/1000) and English maps are available at Noko Market, by the ferry dock. Buses 300 and 301 depart frequently from Nishitetsu Tenjin bus terminal (¥360, 20 minutes) for Meinohama Municipal Ferry Port (not to be confused with Meinohama on the subway line).

Ferries to delightfully rural **Shikanoshima** (志賀島), where fresh seafood restaurants line the harbourside streets, depart hourly (¥650, 33 minutes) from Bayside Place, along with seasonal sightseeing cruises around Hakata Bay. Shikanoshima also has a **fishing shrine** (志賀海神社), decorated with deer antlers, and a popular **beach** about 5km east of the shrine.

✸ Festivals & Events

Hakozaki-gū Tamaseseri   TRADITIONAL
On 3 January, two groups of young men clad in loincloths raucously chase a wooden ball in the name of good fortune, at Hakozaki-gū shrine.

Hakata Dontaku Minato Matsuri   TRADITIONAL
Tracing its roots to the port festival, on 3 and 4 May, Fukuoka's Meiji-dōri vibrates to the percussive shock of *shamoji* (wooden

serving spoons) being banged together like castanets, with *shamisen* (three-stringed banjo) accompaniment.

Hakata Gion Yamakasa Matsuri TRADITIONAL
The city's main festival is held from 1 to 15 July, climaxing at 4.59am on the 15th, when seven groups of men converge at Kushida-jinja to race along a 5km-long course carrying huge portable shrines called *yamakasa* that require 30 people to carry them. According to legend, the festival originated after a 13th-century Buddhist priest was carried aloft, sprinkling holy water over victims of a plague.

Kyūshū Bashō Sumō Tournament SUMŌ
Held over two weeks at the Fukuoka Kokusai Centre during mid-November. Spectators start lining up at dawn for limited same-day tickets (*tōjitsu-ken*; ¥3400 to ¥15,000).

🛏 Sleeping

Fukuoka is a destination for both business and pleasure, with plenty of quality accommodation at all budgets. Stay near JR Hakata Station for convenience if railing around, but Tenjin is a better bet if you plan to spend a few days shopping and playing.

🛏 Hakata Area

Khaosan International
Hostel Fukuoka HOSTEL ¥
(☏ 404-6035; www.khaosan-fukuoka.com; 11-34 Hiemachi; dm/s/tw from ¥2400/3500/5200; ☷@☎; ☐Hakata) This 19-room hostel offers bare-bones accommodation and a communal TV and DVDs, plus roof deck for meeting other travellers. From Hakata Station, head down Chikushi-dōri and turn left at Hotto Motto *bentō* shop.

Hotel New Simple HOTEL ¥
(ホテルニューシンプル; ☏ 411-4311; www.hotel-newsimple.jp; 1-23-11 Hakata-ekimae; dm/s/tw from ¥3000/4200/8190; ☐Gion) A boxy, inexpensive yet modern lodging. Neat and clean dorms sleep six people (comfortably) to 12 (tightly), while single and twin rooms have private bath. 'Family' rooms sleep up to four people at ¥3300. Guests in single and twin rooms get a simple Japanese breakfast. Enter the street across from Family Mart.

★Ryokan Kashima Honkan RYOKAN ¥¥
(和風旅館 鹿島本館; ☏ 291-0746; fax 271-7995; 3-11 Reisen-machi; s/d Sun-Thu ¥4000/7000, Fri & Sat ¥6300/10,000; @☎; ☐Gion) This charmingly creaky, unpretentious Taishō-era ryokan

is a historic landmark, pleasantly faded and focused around a small garden with a stone lantern. Oozing atmosphere, it's a great place to sample traditional Japan. The friendly owners communicate well in English. No private bathroomss, but a Japanese/Western breakfast is available for ¥800/700.

Nishitetsu Inn Hakata HOTEL ¥¥
(西鉄イン博多; ☏ 413-5454; www.n-inn.jp; 1-17-6 Hakata-ekimae; s/tw from ¥7500/14,000; ☷@☎; ☐Hakata) Across from the station, this shiny, spotless 503-room hotel has decent-sized rooms but really scores points for its common baths and sauna (in addition to en-suite facilities). Visit them in a spiffy waffle-pattern *yukata* (light cotton kimono).

Dormy Inn Premium BUSINESS HOTEL ¥¥
(ドーミーインプレミアム; ☏ 272-5489; www.hotespa.net; 9-1 Gionmachi; s/d from ¥11,000/16,000; ℙ☷@☎) Rates are not the cheapest in town and rooms are pretty cramped, but that doesn't tell the whole story. The Dormy Inn is Fukuoka's only hotel with natural onsen (hot springs) in addition to in-room showers, and rates include nightly bowls of *rāmen*. Plus, the location next to Canal City is hard to beat.

Its 122 rooms (all nonsmoking) are done up in warm earth tones and bold Hakata-ori weaving patterns, and sliding doors keep corridor noise at bay. Look for discounts on the website.

Grand Hyatt Fukuoka HOTEL ¥¥¥
(グランドハイアット福岡; ☏ 282-1234; http://fukuoka.grand.hyatt.com; 1-2-82 Sumiyoshi; s/d from ¥28,000/34,000; ℙ☷@☎⛱) Ensconced amid the fountains of Canal City, this massive yet sumptuous property's warm, light-filled rooms synthesise traditional Japanese aesthetics (*shoji* screen room dividers) with contemporary baths (separate shower and tub) and top restaurants.

★With the Style HOTEL ¥¥¥
(ウィズザスタイル福岡; ☏ 433-3900; www.withthestyle.com; 1-9-18 Hakataeki-minami; r with breakfast, minibar & welcome drinks from ¥39,270; ☷@; ☐Hakata) We don't know what the name means, but 'style' is indeed the byword at this sleek designer hotel. You could easily imagine yourself poolside in Hollywood around the fountain courtyard. Each of the 16 rooms exude rock-star cool, and guests can reserve complimentary private use of the rooftop spa or penthouse bar. With a sushi bar and steakhouse on-site, it's an inner-city retreat to savour.

Tenjin Area

Hotel Etwas Tenjin
HOTEL ¥¥

(ホテルエトワス天神; ☎737-3233; www.ho-teletwas.co.jp; 3-5-18 Tenjin; s/d incl light breakfast ¥5800/7800; ☯@; ⓡTenjin) Recently refurbished and good value. Its 84 rooms are tiny, but at these prices and with lively Oyafuko-dōri around the corner, it's hard to complain.

Hotel Ascent
BUSINESS HOTEL ¥¥

(ホテルアセント福岡; ☎711-1300; www.hotel-ascent.com; 3-3-14 Tenjin; s/d from ¥7245/13,650; ☯@☎; ⓡTenjin) This hotel has 263 compact rooms in the heart of Tenjin, with contemporary decor in the public spaces and a chic Italian restaurant.

Plaza Hotel Premier
HOTEL ¥¥

(プラザホテルプルミエ; ☎734-7600; www.plaza-hotel.net; 1-14-13 Daimyō; s/tw from ¥7800/15,000; ℗☯@☎; ⓡTenjin or Akasaka) Location, location and location are the main reasons to stay here, in trendy Daimyō, yet business hotel–size rooms rival far pricier hotels. The night vibe on the street outside is ubercool and its ground floor trattoria AW Kitchen looks like it belongs on a fashionable Tokyo side street.

La Soeur Hotel Monterey
HOTEL ¥¥

(ホテルモントレ ラ・スール福岡; ☎726-7111; www.hotelmonterey.co.jp/en; 2-8-27 Daimyō; s/d from ¥13,860/23,100; ☯@; ⓡTenjin) A popular wedding spot, this 182-room property has a prime location and well-appointed rooms with contemporary French touches and parquet floors. Check the website for bargains.

Il Palazzo
HOTEL ¥¥¥

(☎716-3333; www.ilpalazzo.jp; 3-13-1 Haruyoshi; s/d from ¥22,050/28,350; ☯@; ⓡNakasu-Kawabata) Don't be put off by the windowless, colonnaded facade of burnt orange and obsidian, by Uchida Shigeru, whose work also includes boutiques for fashion's Yohji Yamamoto. The lobby is as glossy as black lipstick, the 62 rooms are slick and soothing, staff couldn't be sweeter, and you're just steps from Nakasu-gawa and Tenjin hot spots (yet hidden on a quiet street).

Coastal Fukuoka Area

Hilton Fukuoka Sea Hawk
HOTEL ¥¥¥

(ヒルトン福岡シーホーク; ☎844-8111; www.hilton.com; 2-2-3 Jigyohama; s/d from ¥8500/14,000; ℗☯@☎☜) If you want to make an impression, you can hardly do better anywhere in Ja-pan. The lobby restaurant of this César Pelli-designed hotel soars like its namesake bird, and at 1052 rooms it's Asia's largest Hilton.

Eating

To most Japanese, Hakata means *tonkotsu rāmen* – noodles in a distinctive broth made from pork bones. Other specialities include *yakitori* (grilled chicken on skewers), *yaki-niku* (Korean-style grilled beef) and fresh seafood.

The Fukuoka way to eat is at *yatai* (屋台), mobile hawker-style food stalls with simple counters and seats; Fukuoka claims about 150 *yatai*, more than in the rest of Japan combined! Let the aromas and chatty conversation lead you to the best cooking and the best companions. For a more local experience, try the **yatai** (☉dusk) around Tenjin or Nagahama. Get there early as most seats are soon taken.

For other restaurant browsing, greater Tenjin is a good bet, or try the spanking new restaurants on the 9th and 10th floors of JR Hakata City (the Hakata Station building). Or grab some takeaway from the *depachika* (food hall) of Hankyu department store next door.

Curry Honpo
CURRY ¥

(伽哩本舗; ☎262-0010; www.curry-honpo.com; 6-135 Kami-kawabata; curry from ¥650; ☉11am-9.30pm; ☑🅿; ⓡNakasu-Kawabata) Can't make it to Mojikō? Try the Kawabata Shōtengai location of the famous shop for some *yaki-curry* (curry rice topped with melted cheese), disturbingly described in the English menu as 'combustion curry'. The standard is pork combustion curry (¥870). It's the wood-panelled and faux brick storefront in the arcade.

Murata
NOODLES ¥

(信州そばむらた; ☎291-0894; 2-9-1 Reisen-machi; soba from ¥700; ☉11.30am-9pm, closed 2nd Sun of month; ☑🅿; ⓡGion) Down the street from the Hakata Machiya Furusato-kan, this lovely eatery makes homemade *soba* (buckwheat noodles) from the Shinshū area of central Japan (around Nagano), prepared in a variety of ways including *kake-soba* (in hot broth; ¥700), *zaru-soba* (cold with dipping sauce; ¥850) and *oroshi-soba* (cold, topped with grated daikon; ¥1000).

Taigen Shokudō
KOREAN ¥

(☎752-5589; 1-1-5 Akasaka; dishes from ¥780; ☉lunch & dinner; ⓡAkasaka) Locally popular for Korean BBQ of Kagoshima beef, served from behind the counter on sizzling *teppan* (steel plates). A great bargain at lunchtime. There's no English menu, but order the *yakiniku teishoku* (set meal with salad, soup and rice; ¥880) or *Taigen teishoku* (*yakiniku* set meal plus hamburger, beef cutlet and sausage; ¥1200). It's next to Plaza pachinko parlour.

★**Fish Man** IZAKAYA ¥¥
(Sakana Otoko; 魚男; ☎717-3571; 1-4-23 Imaizumi; teishoku ¥680-1500; ⊙lunch & dinner; ⑧Tenjin-minami) Fish Man's decor is all post-industrial minimalism with lacquered plywood and big windows, all the better to show off the deft, unconventional presentations of seafood fresh from the Nagahama market across town: *kaidan-zushi* (sushi served on a wooden spiral staircase; ¥1500), *tsubotai no misoyaki* (miso-grilled snapper; ¥880) or a *maguro* hamburger served on a steel plate (¥980). There's no English menu, but English-speaking staff can help explain. Look for the banner outside reading 'No Fish, No Life'.

Afterwards, stop for dessert at Fish Man's adorable affiliated cake shop **Henry & Cowell** (☎741-7888; 1-3-11 Imaizumi; ⊙10am-9pm), just down the street. It also has a small selection of takeaway foods.

★**Zauo** SEAFOOD ¥¥
(ざうお; www.zauo.com/contents/zauo_tenjin.html; 1-4-15 Nagahama; catch your own fish from ¥3360; ⊙5-11pm Mon-Fri, 11.30am-11pm Sat & Sun; ⊛) Staff equip you with fishing rods, bait and nets to fish your own *tai* (sea bream), *hirame* (flounder) and more, from giant

tanks surrounding tables on boat-shaped platforms. When you make a catch, they'll bang drums, cheer and applaud before taking the fish away to prepare to your taste: sashimi, grilled, fried etc. Kitschy, sure, but also lots of fun. There are other *izakaya*-style dishes if fish isn't your thing.

Sushikō Honten SUSHI ¥¥
(すし幸本店; ☎761-1659; 2-11-18 Minatomachi; meals from ¥1050; ⊙10am-10pm) Sushi here can be two completely different experiences: elegant and dignified on the 2nd floor, or served together with other dishes in a rollicking upstairs beer garden that's open year-round for dinner only and covered in inclement weather (all you can eat and drink for women/men from ¥2500/3150).

Tenjin Nobunaga YAKITORI ¥¥
(☎721-6940; 2-6-21 Tenjin; skewers ¥105-¥263; ⊙dinner; ⑧Tenjin) Nobunaga is raucous and rowdy, and that's just the chefs. There's no English menu but it's easy to choose from the skewers behind the counter. Another house speciality is *potato-mochiage* (¥420), a fried dumpling of mashed potato, cheese and *mochi* (pounded rice). Look for the red lanterns just to the right of Big Echo karaoke hall.

No No Budo BUFFET ¥¥
(野の葡萄; ☎714-1441; IMS Bldg, 1-7-11 Tenjin; lunch/dinner ¥1680/2200; ⊙lunch & dinner; ⑧Tenjin) The IMS building (天神イムズ) has prime skyline views from its 12th- and 13th-floor restaurants, including No No Budo. The

KYŪSHŪ FUKUOKA

HAKATA'S RĀMEN KINGS

Not unlike Pavlov's dogs, Fukuokans salivate at the mention of Hakata *rāmen* (egg noodles). The distinctive local style is called *tonkotsu rāmen*, noodles in a hearty broth made from pork bones. You can find it all over town, but two chains have national reputations.

★**Ippudō** (一風堂; ☎781-0303; 1-12-61 Daimyō; rāmen ¥700-800; ⊙11am-2am Sun-Thu, 10.30am-4am Fri & Sat; ⓓ; ⑧Tenjin) has workmanlike and always bustling branches in Tenjin, serving the best-selling Akamaru Modern (with black sesame oil and a fragrant *umami-dama*, or flavour ball), Shiromaru Classic (with thin noodles) and Karaka (spicy *rāmen*). There's also a second branch **Ippudō** (☎413-5088; 10th fl, JR Hakata City, 1-1 Hakata-eki-chūō-gai; rāmen ¥700-800; ⊙11am-midnight) on the 10th floor of JR Hakata City shopping centre.

Ichiran (☎713-6631; 2-1-57 Daimyō; rāmen from ¥690; ⊙10am-7am; ⓓ; ⑧Tenjin) is an entirely different experience, with multiple branches around town. Purchase tickets from a vending machine at the entrance, sit at one of the individual booths and fill out a form (available in English) detailing your order: noodle tenderness, level of spice, thickness of broth etc. Then enjoy in peace (or dislocation, depending on your perspective).

And if for some reason Hakata-style *rāmen* doesn't satisfy, in Canal City there's **Rāmen Stadium** (ラーメンスタジアム; ☎282-2525; 5th fl, Canal City; rāmen from ¥550; ⊙11am-10.30pm), an entire floor of eight *rāmen* vendors imported from the length and breadth of Japan.

busy self-serve gourmet buffet has good-for-you Japanese and Western fish and meat dishes, noodles, salads, soups and nice pastries. An extra ¥1300 buys all-you-can-drink beer, wine and cocktails.

🍷 Drinking & Nightlife

The weekend starts on Thursday in multicultural, party-friendly Fukuoka. Tenjin and Daimyō's streets are safe, easy to explore and great for people-watching. The main drag, Oyafuko-dōri, roughly translates to 'street of unruly children' because of the cram schools that once lined it. In a way, the cap still fits. Nakasu Island, while one of Japan's busiest entertainment districts, is often sleazy.

International Bar   BAR

(インターナショナルバー; 4th fl, Urashima Bldg, 3-1-13 Tenjin; ®Tenjin) There's free karaoke on Tuesdays at this tiny bar. Like the name implies, it's one of the original places in Fukuoka for locals and *gaijin* (foreigners) to connect, in a time warp of red velvet seating with hip-hop beats.

Mitsubachi   BAR

(ミツバチ; 5th Hotel East, 3-4-65 Haruyoshi; ®Nakasu-Kawabata) Enjoy views of Hakata and Canal City across the Naka-gawa through giant windows in this pretty dining bar. Inside it's like a contemporary log cabin.

Craic & Porter Beer Bar   PUB

(http://craic.mine.nu; 3-5-16 Tenjin; ®Tenjin) A tiny taste of Ireland with open windows and about 10 premium import beers on tap. Owner Mike is a friendly character, with plenty of experience in Japan. It's above ABC flower shop on Oyafuko-dōri.

Morris   PUB

(7th fl, Stage 1 Nishidōri Bldg, 2-1-4 Daimyō; ⊗from 5pm; @; ®Tenjin) One of the better pubs in Japan, it attracts a nice mix of Japanese and *gaijin*. Begin the evening with happy-hour cocktails (¥250; 5pm to 7pm) on the awesome patio perched high above trendy Daimyō. There's a good beer selection and tasty food.

Small Spaces   BAR

(1-13-12 Daimyō; ®Tenjin or Tenjin-Minami) While this corner bar may be a little tricky if you can't speak Japanese, it's worth a look. Small Spaces is all about young Japanese doing their own thing. The cool glow spills out onto the street through the open door and white-shuttered windows of this little wooden shack. Peace, man.

Club X   CLUB

(クラブX; ☑741-3800; http://clubxfukuoka.com/; 6th fl, 1-8-38 Maizuru; ®Tenjin) This foreign-run club has the urban vibe covered, with serious DJs spinning hip-hop to rock and a stripper pole should you need it.

Juke Joint   BAR

(ジュークジョイント; ☑762-5596; http://juke-records.net/jukejoint; 2nd fl, 1-9-23 Maizuru; ⊗closed irregularly; ®Tenjin) Funsters can select the tunes at this Fukuoka original DJ lounge. The eclectic music collection is the work of record-shop owner 'Kinky' Ko Matsumoto. Drinks start at ¥500, plus there's no cover charge.

Dark Room   BAR

(ザ・ダークルーム; ☑725-2989; www.thedarkroom.biz; 8th fl, Tenjin Bacchus-kan, 3-4-15 Tenjin; ⊗6pm-2am; ®Tenjin) Dark, rocky and loud, this is a cool urban rock oasis with a killer sound system, pool table, foosball, friendly dudes behind the bar and a spiral staircase leading to a fun, summer-only rooftop patio.

🛍 Shopping

Big department stores dominate the skyline of Tenjin and around Hakata Station. Fukuoka's department stores occupy a three-block gauntlet of Watanabe-dōri in Tenjin. **Tenjin Core** (天神コア; ☑tel, info 721-7755), **Mitsukoshi** (三越; ☑724-3111), **Daimaru** (大丸; ☑712-8181), **Solaria Plaza** (ソラリアプラザ; ☑733-7004), the **IMS Building** (天神イムズ; Tenjin 1-7-11) and **mina tenjin** are all favourites, as is the subterranean **Tenjin Chikagai** (天神地下街; ☑721-8436).

For contemporary fashion, low-rise boutiques in the Daimyō district show off local designers, and lining the avenue Keyaki-dōri are intimate shops for antiques, design items and foreign crafts.

Shōgetsudō   ARTS & CRAFTS

(松月堂; ☑291-4141; 5-1-22 Nakasu; ⊗9am-7pm; ®Nakasu-Kawabata) White-faced clay Hakata *ningyō* (Hakata dolls) depicting women, children, samurai and geisha are a popular Fukuoka craft. This place sells them and offers painting workshops (¥1575 to ¥3150).

Hakata-ori no Sennen Kōbō   KIMONO

(博多織の千年工房; B1 fl, Hakata Riverain, 3-1 Shimo-Kawabata-machi; ⊗10.30am-7.30pm; ®Nakasu-Kawabata) Hakata's is also renowned for its weaving tradition, called Hakata-ori, and this elegant shop offers obis, kimonos and accessories from business-card holders to handbags in the distinctive style. None of it's cheap (silk obi start at around ¥10,000), but it's meant to last generations. Hakata-ori is also available at Tenjin's department stores.

Mandarake MANGA
(まんだらけ; 5-7-7 Tenjin; ☺noon-8pm; ℝTenjin) The Fukuoka branch of Mandarake is Kyūshū's largest manga store with several storeys of games, comic books and DVDs.

Robosquare ELECTRONICS
(ロボスクエアー; 2nd fl, TNC Bldg, 2-3-2 Momochihama; ☺closed 2nd Tue) Near Fukuoka Tower, Robosquare sells robotics and offers demonstrations, robot performances and small exhibits of current technology.

Junkudō Fukuoka BOOKS
(ジュンク堂書店; 1st-4th fl, Media Mall; ☺10am-8.30pm; ℝTenjin) Sells foreign paperbacks.

Maruzen BOOKS
(丸善; 8th fl, Hakata Station Bldg, Hakata-eki; ☺10am-9pm; ℝHakata) Huge selection of Japanese- and English-language books, magazines and DVDs.

ⓘ Information

INTERNET ACCESS
Fukuoka is wired and getting more so. Free public wi-fi is available at city hall, major train and subway stations, tourist information centres and in the Tenjin Chikagai (Underground Arcade).

Cybac Café (サイバックカフェ; www.cybac.com; 2nd fl, 3-2-22 Tenjin; registration fee ¥300, per 1st 30min/subsequent 15min ¥300/100; ☺24hr; ℝTenjin)

Kinko's Branches at Akasaka (キンコーズ赤坂店; 2-12-12 Daimyō; ☺24hr; ℝAkasaka), Chikushiguchi (キンコーズ筑紫口店; 2-5-28 Hakata-eki higashi; ☺24hr) and Hakata-ekimae (キンコーズ博多駅前店; 2-19-24 Hakata-ekimae; ☺8am-10pm; ℝHakata). Ten minutes' access for ¥210.

Media Café Popeye (www.media-cafe.net) Branches at Hakata-ekimae (メディアカフェポパイ博多駅前; 8th fl, Fukuoka Kōtsū Centre Bldg; ☺24hr; ℝHakata), Nakasu (メディアカフェポパイ中州店; 8th fl, Spoon Bldg, 5-1-7 Nakasu; ☺24hr; ℝNakasu-kawabata) and Tenjin (メディアカフェポパイ天神店; 2nd fl, Nishitetsu Imaizumi Bldg, 1-12-23 Imaizumi; ☺24hr; ℝTenjin-minami). Each has a free soft-drink bar, massage chairs and couples' booths. Offers ¥510 for the first 60 minutes, then ¥80 per subsequent 10 minutes.

MEDIA
Fukuoka Now (www.fukuoka-now.com) Indispensable monthly English-language street mag with detailed city maps.

Yokanavi.com (www.yokanavi.com/eg) A comprehensive Fukuoka/Hakata tourist information site.

MEDICAL SERVICES
International Clinic Tojin-machi (☎717-1000; http://internationalclinic.org; 1-4-6 Jigyo; ℝTōjin-machi, exit 1) Multilingual clinic for general medical services and emergencies. It's two blocks from the station.

MONEY
In addition to the post office and Seven Bank ATMs, banks and ATMs offer currency exchange at Fukuoka Airport, there's a 24-hour Citibank ATM (シティバンク ATM) in Tenjin, and most banks around JR Hakata Station and Tenjin handle foreign-exchange services.

POST
The **central post office** (福岡中央郵便局) is one block northeast of Tenjin subway station, and **Hakata post office** (博多郵便局) is just outside JR Hakata Station's Hakata-guchi.

TOURIST INFORMATION
Fukuoka City Tourist Information Counters (福岡市観光案内所) at Fukuoka Airport, **JR Hakata Station** (福岡市観光案内所JR博多駅支店; 431-3003; ☺8am-9pm) and **Nishitetsu Bus Centre** (福岡市観光案内所天神支店; ☎751-6904; Nishitetsu Tenjin Bus Centre; ☺10am-6.30pm) in Tenjin dispense maps, coupons and the helpful *City Visitor's Guide*, and can help with lodging, transport and car-rental information. Information centres at **ACROS Fukuoka** (アクロス福岡; ☎725-9100; www.acros.or.jp/r_facilities/information.html; Cultural Information Centre, 2nd fl, ACROS Bldg, 1-1-1 Tenjin; ☺10am-6pm, closed 29 Dec-3 Jan; ℝNakasu-Kawabata or Tenjin) and **Rainbow Plaza** (レインボープラザ; ☎733-2220; www.rainbowfia.or.jp; 8F, IMS Bldg, 1-7-11 Tenjin; ☺10am-8pm, closed 3rd Tue most months) are targeted mostly at foreign residents.

TRAVEL AGENCIES
HIS Travel (☎415-6121; 1st fl, 2-6-10 Hakata-ekimae; ☺10am-6.30pm Mon-Fri, 11am-4.30pm Sat; ℝHakata) Discount international and domestic arrangements can be made at the Hakata branch of this international chain.

JR Kyūshū Travel Agency (☎431-6215; 1-1 Chuo-gai; ☺10am-8pm Mon-Fri, to 6pm Sat & Sun; ℝHakata) Provides bookings and advice for travel within Kyūshū and Japan. Located within JR Hakata Station.

No 1 Travel (ナンバーワントラベル; ☎761-9203; www.no1-travel.com/fuk/index.html; 3rd fl, ACROS Fukuoka Bldg, 1-1-1 Tenjin; ☺10am-6.30pm Mon-Fri, 11am-4.30pm Sat; ℝNakasu-Kawabata or Tenjin) For discount international airfares and reliable information in English.

KYŪSHŪ FUKUOKA

ⓘ Getting There & Away

AIR

Fukuoka Airport (☎ domestic terminal 621-6059, international terminal 621-0303; ⏱ 6.20am-10.20pm; 🚇 Fukuoka Airport) is an international hub serving carriers from east and Southeast Asia, as well as many domestic routes including Tokyo (from Haneda/Narita airports ¥36,870/36,700, 1½ hours), Osaka (¥21,900, one hour) and Okinawa (Naha; from ¥27,500, 1½ hours).

Cut-rate carrier **Skymark** (☎ 736-3131, in Tokyo 03-3433-7026; www.skymark.co.jp/en) flies to Haneda/Narita Airports (from ¥16,000/19,190).

BOAT

Ferries from Hakata connect to Okinawa and other islands off Kyūshū. **Beetle** (☎ in Japan 092-281-2315, in Korea 051-469-0778; www.jrbeetle.co.jp/english) high-speed hydrofoils connect Fukuoka with Busan in Korea (one-way/round trip ¥13,000/24,000, three hours, at least four daily). The **Camellia line** (☎ in Japan 092-262-2323, in Korea 051-466-7799; www.camellia-line.co.jp) has a regular ferry service from Fukuoka to Busan (one-way/return ¥9000/17,000, six hours, daily at noon). Both ships dock at Chūō Futō (Hakata Port Ferry Terminal) via bus 88 from JR Hakata Station (¥220), or bus 80 from Tenjin (Solaria Stage-mae; ¥180).

BUS

Long-distance buses (Nishitetsu Bus Information Centre; ☎ 0570-00-1010, ask operator for English interpreter 303-3333) depart from the **Fukuoka Kōtsū Centre** (福岡交通センター) next to JR Hakata Station (Hakata-gate) and also from the **Nishitetsu Tenjin Bus Terminal** (西鉄天神バスセンター). Destinations include Tokyo (economy/business ¥8000/15,000, 14½ hours), Osaka (from ¥10,000, 9½ hours), Nagoya (¥10,500, 11 hours) and many towns in Kyūshū; ask about discounted round-trip fares.

TRAIN

JR Hakata Station (JR博多駅; ☎ English information 471-8111, JR English info line 03-3423-

ⓘ CHEAP TRANSPORT

There are discounted all-you-can-ride passes on JR Kyūshū and Kyūshū buses, from ¥8000/10,000 for three days in northern Kyushu/all of Kyushu, or a four-day all Kyushu Pass for ¥14,000. For further information visit http://www.sunqpass.jp/english/pass/index.html.

0111) is a hub in northern Kyūshū. *Shinkansen* services operate to/from Tokyo (¥22,520, five hours), Osaka (¥15,090, 2½ hours), Hiroshima (¥9100, 65 minutes), Kumamoto (¥5190, 40 minutes) and Kagoshima-Chūō (¥10,370, one hour and 20 minutes).

Within Kyūshū, non-*shinkansen* trains run on the JR Nippō line through Beppu to Miyazaki; the Sasebo line runs from Saga to Sasebo; and the Nagasaki line runs to Nagasaki. You can also travel by subway and JR train to Karatsu and continue to Nagasaki by train.

ⓘ Getting Around

TO/FROM THE AIRPORT

The subway takes just five minutes to reach JR Hakata Station (¥250) and 11 minutes to Tenjin (¥250). Shuttle buses connect domestic and international terminals.

Taxis cost around ¥1600 to Tenjin/Hakata.

BUS

City bus services operate from the Fukuoka Kōtsū Centre adjacent to JR Hakata Station and from the Nishitetsu Tenjin Bus Terminal (西鉄天神バスセンター). Many stop in front of the station (Hakata-guchi). Specially marked buses have a flat ¥100 rate for city-centre rides, or a one-day pass costs ¥600/1000 for one/two adults.

TRAIN

Fukuoka has three **Subway Lines** (http://subway.city.fukuoka.lg.jp; ⏱ 5.30am-12.25am), of which visitors will find the Kūkō (Airport) line most useful, running from Fukuoka Airport to Meinohama Station via Hakata, Nakasu-Kawabata and Tenjin stations. Fares start at ¥200 (¥100 if going just one stop); a one-day pass costs adult/child ¥600/300.

Dazaifu　太宰府

☎ 092 / POP 70,245

Dazaifu, former governmental centre of Kyūshū, has a beautiful cluster of temples, a famous shrine and a striking national museum, making for a popular day trip from Fukuoka. The **tourist information office** (太宰府市立観光案内所; ☎ 925-1880; ⏱ 9am-5.30pm) at Nishitetsu Dazaifu Station has helpful staff and an English-language map.

◎ Sights

★ **Kyūshū National Museum**　　MUSEUM
(九州国立博物館; www.kyuhaku.com; 4-7-2 Ishizaka; adult/student ¥420/210; ⏱ 9.30am-5pm, closed Mon) Built into the tranquil hills of Dazaifu and reached through a colour-

TACHIARAI

From 1919 to 1945, the isolated farm village of Tachiarai (大刀洗) hosted a training school for Japanese fighter pilots, including some on kamikaze suicide missions. Expanded in 2009, **Tachiarai Heiwa Kinenkan** (大刀洗平和記念館; Tachiarai Peace Memorial Museum; ☎ 0946-23-1227; admission ¥500; ⏱ 9.30am-5pm) shows the rigorous training these men endured. English signage is basic, but the artefacts are evocative (uniforms, medals, gold-plated sake cups etc). The centrepiece is a jet fighter shot down during the war and recovered from Hakata Bay in 1996. The museum also memorialises kamikaze pilots and townspeople who died during a USAF B-29 bombing on 27 March 1945.

The museum is across from Tachiarai Station. From Fukuoka, take the Nishitetsu line to Nishitetsu Ogōri (¥500, 30 minutes); from Dazaifu (¥330) it takes 25 minutes plus transfer time at Nishitetsu Futsukaichi. Then walk to Ogōri Station on the Amagi Railway for the trip to Tachiarai (¥280, 15 minutes). JR passengers can transfer to the Amagi Railway at Kiyama (¥330, 20 minutes).

shifting tunnel, this striking structure (built in 2005) resembles a massive space station for the arts. Highlights include a fascinating exhibit of the relationship between Japanese arts and culture and those of the rest of Asia, stone carvings of AD 1st-century women with spears on horseback and a delicate 13th-century oil-spot *tenmoku* tea bowl. Self-guided audio tours and HD video theatre are free, and there's a wonderful 'please touch' section for the youngest visitors.

★ **Tenman-gū Shrine**   SHINTŌ SHRINE
(天満宮; www.dazaifutenmangu.or.jp; 4-7-1 Saifu) Poet and scholar Sugawara-no-Michizane was a distinguished figure in the Kyoto court until he fell afoul of political intrigue and was exiled to distant Dazaifu, where he died two years later. Subsequent disasters that struck Kyoto were blamed on his unfair dismissal, and he became deified as Tenman Tenjin, god of culture and scholars. Among the countless visitors to the grand, sprawling Tenman-gū, his shrine and burial place, are students hoping to pass college entrance exams. The *hondō* (main hall) was rebuilt in 1591.

Behind the shrine is the **Kankō Historical Museum** (菅公歴史館; admission ¥200; ⏱ 9am-4.30pm Wed-Mon), with dioramas showing Tenjin's life (an English leaflet provides explanations).

Across the grounds, the **Daizifu Tenman-gū Treasure House** (太宰府天満宮宝物殿; admission ¥300; ⏱ 9am-4.30pm, closed Mon) has artefacts from his life including some excellent swords.

Every second month the shrine hosts an *omoshiro-ichi* (market).

Kōmyōzen-ji   BUDDHIST TEMPLE
(光明禅寺; admission ¥200; ⏱ 9am-4.30pm) Secreted away on the southern edge of Dazaifu, this small temple has an exquisite jewel of a Zen garden. It's a peaceful contrast to the crowds at the nearby shrine.

Kaidan-in   MONASTERY
(戒壇院) Across town, nestled among rice paddies and reachable by bus (¥100), Kaidan-in dates from 761 and was one of the most important Buddhist ordination monasteries in Japan.

Kanzeon-ji   BUDDHIST TEMPLE
(観世音寺) Adjacent to the monastery, this temple dates from 746 but only the great bell (said to be Japan's oldest) remains from the original construction. Its **treasure hall** (宝蔵; admission ¥500; ⏱ 9am-4.30pm) has an impressive collection of statuary, most of it wood, dating from the 10th to 12th centuries. Many of the items show Indian or Tibetan influence.

Dazaifu Exhibition Hall   MUSEUM
(大宰府展示館; admission ¥150; ⏱ 9am-4.30pm, closed Mon) Dazaifu Exhibition Hall displays finds from local archaeological excavations. Nearby are the **Tofurō ruins** (都府楼) of ancient government buildings.

Enoki-sha (榎社) is where Sugawara-no-Michizane died. His body was transported to Tenman-gū on the ox cart that appears in so many local depictions.

ⓘ Getting There & Around

The private Nishitetsu train line connects Nishitetsu Fukuoka (in Tenjin) with Dazaifu (¥390, 25 minutes). Change trains at Nishitetsu Futsukaichi Station. Bicycles can be rented (per three hours/day ¥300/500) at Nishitetsu Dazaifu Station.

KYŪSHŪ DAZAIFU

SAGA PREFECTURE

Occupying Kyūshū's northwestern corner, Saga-ken (佐賀県) is chiefly known for three towns: Karatsu, Imari and Arita. The towns were central to Japan's historic pottery trade.

Karatsu 唐津

📞 0955 / POP 130,000

Karatsu is at the base of the scenic Higashi-Matsūra Peninsula, an ideal location for its historic pottery trade. Korean influences elevated the town's craft from useful ceramics to art.

Even if Karatsu isn't as busy as it once was, pottery fanatics will be in their element. For everyone else, there's a hilltop castle, historic buildings, a homely Shōwa-era town centre and a pretty seaside cycling trail. Outside of town, the coastline was pounded into shape by the roiling Sea of Genkai, making for dramatic vistas.

At JR Karatsu Station, the **tourist information office** (📞72-4963; ⊙9am-6pm) has a selection of English-language tourist maps and brochures, and some enthusiastic English-speaking staff who can book accommodation.

👁 Sights & Activities

It's about 25 minutes' walk from JR Karatsu Station to the sea, and around town are **kilns and studios** where you can see local potters at work, and ceramic shops.

A **walking and cycling path** cuts through the pine trees planted behind the 5km-long Niji-no Matsubara Beach.

Nakazato Tarōemon MUSEUM
(中里太郎右衛門; 3-6-29 Chōda; ⊙9am-5.30pm) FREE This kiln-gallery is dedicated to the life and work of the potter (1923–2009) responsible for the revival of Karatsu ware. His work is in the inner gallery.

Karatsu Ware
Federation Exhibition Hall GALLERY
(唐津焼総合展示場; 2nd fl, Arpino Bldg; ⊙9am-6pm) FREE Adjacent to Karatsu Station, this exhibition hall displays and sells (from ¥500) local potters' works.

Kyū-Takatori-tei HISTORIC BUILDING
(旧高取邸; 5-40 Kita-jōnai; adult/child ¥500/250; ⊙9.30am-5pm Tue-Sun) Kyū-Takatori-tei is a fabulously restored late Meiji Period villa of a local trader, built in a mix of Japanese and Western styles, with lantern-filled gardens, a Buddhist altar room, a wealth of paintings on cedar boards and an indoor Noh stage. An English audio guide rents for ¥300.

Karatsu-jō CASTLE
(唐津城; 8-1 Higashi-jōnai; adult/child ¥400/200; ⊙9am-5pm) This 1608 castle (rebuilt 1966) is picturesquely perched on a hill overlooking the sea, houses antique ceramics, samurai armour and archaeological displays. To avoid the climb through the park Maizuru-kōen, an outdoor elevator charges ¥100/50 per adult/child per ride.

KYŪSHŪ POTTERY TOWNS

In mountainous Kyūshū, many villages had difficulty growing rice and looked towards other industries to survive. Access to good clay, forests and streams made pottery-making a natural choice, and a number of superb styles can be found here.

Karatsu, Arita and Imari are the major pottery towns of Saga-ken. From the early 17th century, pottery was produced in this area by captive Korean potters, experts who were zealously guarded so that neither artist nor the secrets of their craft could escape. When trade routes opened up to the West, potters in Japan began imitating the highly decorative, Chinese-style ware popular in Europe. Pottery styles are often called by the suffix -*yaki* (pottery) added to the town name.

➡ **Arita** Highly decorated porcelain, often with squares of blue, red, green or gold.

➡ **Imari** Fine porcelain, originally blue and white, bursting into vibrant colours in the mid-Edo period.

➡ **Karatsu** Marked by subtle earthy tones, prized for its use in the tea ceremony.

In southern Kyūshū, Kagoshima Prefecture is known for Satsuma-yaki (Satsuma is the feudal name for that region). Styles vary from crackled glazes to porcelains painted with gleaming gold, and rougher, more ponderous 'black Satsuma' ware.

YOBUKO

A colourful **morning market** (朝市; ⊘7.30am-noon) for squid, fish and produce animates the quaint, dwindling fishing port of Yobuko (呼子) each day, drawing visitors from all over the region. At the far end of the market is the **Nakao Mansion** (中尾家屋敷; adult/child ¥200/100; ⊘9am-5pm, closed Wed), opened in 2011, the painstakingly refurbished home and processing house of a whaling family, filled with historical exhibits explained in English and excellent architectural details; whales were hunted in nearby waters until 1877.

Buses connect from Karatsu's Ōteguchi Bus Centre (Shōwa bus; ¥730, 30 minutes).

An overnight stay at one of the ryokan across the road from the waterfront (from around ¥10,500 including meals) will allow you to watch the flickering lights of fishing boats heading out to sea.

Hikiyama Festival
Float Exhibition Hall   MUSEUM
(6-33 Nishi-jōnai; admission ¥300; ⊘9am-5pm)
Contains the 14 amazing floats used in the annual Karatsu Kunchi Matsuri. Floats include the Aka-jishi (Red Lion, constructed 1819), samurai helmets, and the auspicious phoenix and sea bream. There's good signage in English, and a video shows festival scenes. It's near scenic **Karatsu-jinja** (3-13 Minami-jōnai), the shrine that sponsors the festival.

🎊 Festivals & Events

Doyō-yoichi   NIGHT MARKET
Held in the town centre over four consecutive Saturdays from late July.

Karatsu Kunchi Matsuri   TRADITIONAL
From 2 to 4 November, Karatsu comes to life in this spectacular festival, designated a festival of national cultural importance, and dating from 1592. The highlight is a parade of massive, exquisitely decorated *hikiyama* (floats).

🛏 Sleeping & Eating

Karatsu Dai-Ichi Hotel   HOTEL ¥¥
(☎74-1000; www.kugimoto.co.jp/dai-ichi.info.htm; 488-1 Nishi-Teramachi; s/d/tw from ¥6100/10,000/ 11,100; Ⓟ⊜@) About five minutes on foot from Karatsu Station, rooms don't break any style barriers, but they're spotless and the staff are accommodating. Some singles are nonsmoking. Rates include a simple breakfast buffet.

★ **Yōyōkaku**   RYOKAN ¥¥¥
(洋々閣; ☎72-7181; www.yoyokaku.com; 2-4-40 Higashi-Karatsu; r per person incl 2 meals from ¥15,750; Ⓟ@⊙) In a word: gorgeous. Here

are some more words: rambling, minimalist, woodwork, pine garden and Karatsu-yaki pottery for your in-room seafood meals. A real getaway, yet under 10 minutes' walk from the castle. Can't stay here? Visit the on-site gallery of Nakazato family pottery.

★ **Kawashima Tōfu**   TOFU ¥¥
(川島豆腐店; ☎72-2423; www.zarudoufu.co.jp; Kyōmachi 1775; set meals lunch ¥1575-2675, dinner ¥3675-10,000; ⊘8am-6.30pm, meal seatings at 8am, 10am & noon, kaiseki dinner 5.30-10pm) On the shopping street near the station, this renowned tofu shop has been in business since the Edo period and serves set meals starring tofu plus other seasonal specialities (reservations required) around the 10-seat counter in a jewel box of a back room. For a snack, try frozen tofu 'soft cream' for ¥300.

ℹ Getting There & Around

From Fukuoka, take the Kūkō (Airport) subway line from Hakata or Tenjin to the end of the line at Meinohama. Many trains continue directly (or you may need to switch) to the JR Chikuhi line to reach Karatsu (¥1110, 70 minutes).

From Karatsu to Nagasaki (¥3620, three hours) take the JR Karatsu line to Saga, and the Kamome *tokkyū* on the JR Nagasaki line from there.

From Karatsu's **Ōteguchi Bus Centre** (☎73-7511), highway buses depart for Fukuoka (¥1000, 70 minutes) and Yobuko.

At the **Arpino** (☎75-5155) building, next to the station, are a few loaner bicycles for day trips. There are also electric-powered bikes available for rent at the station (two/four hours/full day ¥300/600/900 for JR ticket holders, ¥500/1000/1500 for those without a JR ticket).

Imari 伊万里

☑ 0955 / POP 57,700

Quiet Imari lies near the border of Nagasaki Prefecture. Tourist brochures are available at **Imari City Information** (伊万里市観光協会; ☑ 23-3479; ☺ 9am-6pm) at Imari Station on the regional Matsūra Railway, across the street from JR Imari Station.

The pottery kilns are concentrated on photogenic **Ōkawachiyama** (大川内山), a 20-minute bus ride from the station. Thirty or so workshops and public galleries make for a lovely ramble uphill alongside streams, cafes and a bridge covered with local shards. Arrive by midday to allow for exploring and shopping. About five buses per day (¥150) make the trip. Alternatively, the taxi fare is approximately ¥1700 each way.

Back in the town centre, near the river Imari-gawa, **Imari City Ceramic Merchant's Museum** (伊万里市陶器商家資料館; ☑ 22-7934; ☺ 10am-5pm, closed Mon) **FREE** houses some priceless pieces of Koimari (as old Imari ware is known) from the 18th and 19th centuries, inside the handsomely preserved home of a merchant family; there's an excellent English leaflet.

A few hundred metres from the station area, family-run **Kippō** (吉峰; ☑ 23-3563; 196 Tatemachi; lunch set menus from ¥1,260; ☺ lunch & dinner, closed Wed) serves up super-fresh tempura, some on Imari ware dishes. No English is spoken, so just say '*setto o kudasai*' (set menu please).

Imari is connected to Karatsu (¥630, 50 minutes) by the JR Chikuhi line, and also to Arita by the private Matsūra-tetsudō line (¥410, 25 minutes).

Arita 有田

☑ 0955 / POP 21,390

Kaolin clay was discovered here in 1615 by Ri Sampei, a naturalised Korean potter, enabling the manufacture of fine porcelain in Japan for the first time. By the mid-17th century, the porcelain was being exported to Europe.

The town of Arita is a beautiful example of how tourism can support the preservation of history and culture. The staff at the tiny **tourist information desk** (☑ 42-4052; www.arita.or.jp/index_e.html; ☺ 9am-5pm) inside Arita Station can assist with maps in English, timetables and accommodation, predominantly small private *minshuku* (guesthouses).

Arita's streets fill with vendors for the annual **pottery market**, held from 29 April to 5 May.

Between the station and Kyūshū Ceramic Museum is the **Yakimono Sanpo-michi** (Pottery Promenade) of around 16 galleries. The tourist office has a map that's in Japanese but is easy enough to follow.

Out of the town centre, two of Arita-yaki's prime practitioners have been at it for 14 generations. The **Imaemon Gallery** (今衛門ギャラリー; ☑ 42-5550; admission ¥300; ☺ 9.30am-4.30pm, closed Mon) and **Kakiemon Kiln** (柿右衛門窯; ☑ 43-2267; ☺ 9am-5pm) **FREE** both have museums in addition to sales shops. **Genemon Kiln** (源衛門窯; ☑ 42-4164; ☺ 8am-5.30pm Mon-Sat) **FREE** makes and sells more contemporary styles. These can be reached by a short taxi ride (about ¥1000), or infrequent community bus from the station.

Taxi or Arita bus (¥150, four daily) can also take you out to the **clay mines** (磁石場; *jisekiba*). From here you can walk back to the station in about an hour, via a route lined with numerous old houses with left-over pottery used in the bricks, as well as many galleries.

A short train ride east of Arita, **Takeo Onsen** (武雄温泉) is a modern hot-springs town with about a dozen onsen hotels. For a quick dip, the original **Takeo Onsen** (武雄温泉; admission ¥400; ☺ 6.30am-midnight) has a 1300-year history and is said to have refreshed the armies of Toyotomi Hideyoshi. Its impressive lacquered Chinese-style entrance gate was built without nails, and the oldest existing bathing building (Moto-yu) is a wooden hall from 1870. It's a 15-minute walk west of the station's north exit.

You can also stay among hot-spring baths at the simple but comfortable, 14-room **Takeo Onsen Youth Hostel** (武雄温泉ユースホステル; ☑ 0954-22-2490; fax 0954-20-1208; 16060 Nagashima; dm incl breakfast member/non-member ¥3300/3900). The friendly owners don't speak English but make a good go of it. Since it's a few kilometres from the station and up a hill, ring ahead to request a pick-up after the 4pm check-in time. A few loaner bikes are available. Rates include a simple breakfast of *onigiri* (rice balls) and coffee, but no dinner is served, so if you're not dining in a local restaurant, the shuttle can stop at local shops for provisions.

The private Matsūra-tetsudō line connects Arita with Imari (¥410, 25 minutes).

KYŪSHŪ CERAMIC MUSEUM

The best ceramics museum in the region, about five minutes on foot from Arita Station, is the large, hilltop **Kyūshū Ceramic Museum** (九州陶磁文化館; admission charge for special exhibits; ⏰9am-5pm, closed Mon) `FREE`. The Shibata Collection comprehensively showcases the development and styles of Kyūshū's many ceramic arts, with excellent English signage.

JR *tokkyū* trains between Hakata (¥2690, 80 minutes) and Sasebo (¥1050, 30 minutes) stop at Arita and Takeo Onsen. Takeo Onsen is also connected to Arita by local trains (¥270, 20 minutes). Infrequent community buses (¥150) cover most sights, but you'll save time by taking taxis (about ¥1000 to most sights). Arita Station rents out bicycles (¥300 per day).

NAGASAKI PREFECTURE

History

Nagasaki Prefecture's multilayered role in Japanese history started when an off-course Chinese ship landed in Kagoshima Prefecture in 1543, carrying guns and Portuguese adventurers. Catholic missionaries arrived soon thereafter, ushering in Japan's 'Christian Century' (1549–1650) centered in Nagasaki, Hirado and other local communities.

By 1570 Nagasaki was a wealthy, fashionable port, as Portuguese traders shuttled between Japan, China and Korea and missionaries converted Japanese. In 1580 the *daimyō* (domain lord) briefly ceded Nagasaki to the Society of Jesuits.

The shōgun then reclaimed Nagasaki, expelled the Jesuits and, in 1597, crucified 26 European and Japanese Christians. Portuguese and Spanish traders were replaced with the Protestant Dutch, thought to be more interested in trade than religion. Christianity was officially banned altogether in 1613, yet some 'hidden Christians' continued to practise.

After a peasant uprising at Shimabara in 1637–38, the shōgunate forbade all foreigners from Japan and Japanese travelling overseas, beginning a period called *sakoku* (national seclusion), which lasted two centuries

(see p772). The single exception was Dejima, a man-made island in Nagasaki harbour where Dutch traders lived under close scrutiny.

When Japan reopened its doors to the West in the 1850s, Nagasaki was uniquely positioned to become a major economic force, particularly in shipbuilding, the industry that ultimately led to its tragic bombing on 9 August 1945.

Nagasaki 長崎

📞 095 / POP 443,400

How ironic it is that the name Nagasaki conjures up the tragic destruction of war, as for much of its history the city of Nagasaki was Japan's only link to the outside world; other parts of Nagasaki Prefecture (長崎県) served a similar role. A visit to the scenes of atomic devastation is a must, but beyond them you'll find that this one-of-a-kind, embracing city boasts a colourful trading history, alluring churches, shrines, temples and an East-meets-West culinary scene, prettily set within hills around a gracious harbour. Schedule a few days here to meet the people and get a sense of Nagasaki's spirit.

ℹ️ Orientation

Nagasaki's sights are scattered over a broad area, but once you're in a district it's easy to walk from one location to the next. The atomic bomb hypocentre is in the suburb of Urakami, about 2.5km north of JR Nagasaki Station. Central and southern Nagasaki are where you'll find sights related to its history of trade and foreign influence. Main enclaves are around JR Nagasaki Station and about 2km south: Shinchi Chinatown, the Dutch slopes and Glover Garden. Near Shinchi Chinatown, Shianbashi is the main nightlife and shopping district. Parts of Nagasaki are quite hilly, so bring good walking shoes.

◉ Sights

◉ Urakami (Northern Nagasaki)

Urakami, the hypocentre of the atomic explosion, is today a prosperous, peaceful suburb. While nuclear ruin seems comfortably far away seven decades later, many sights here keep the memory alive.

⭐ **Nagasaki Atomic Bomb Museum** MUSEUM
(長崎原爆資料館; Map p666; www1.city.nagasaki.nagasaki.jp/peace/English.abm; 7-8 Hirano-machi; admission ¥200, audio guide ¥150; ⏰8.30am-

Nagasaki

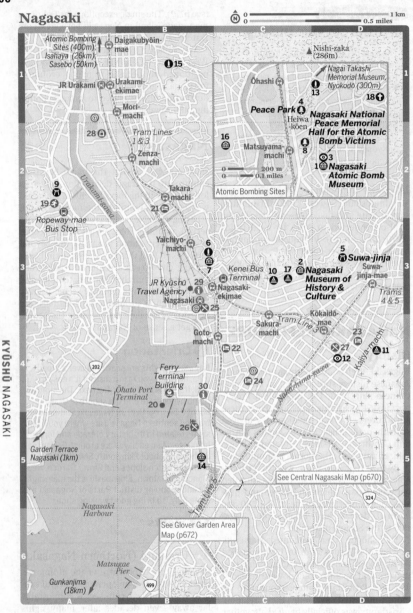

See Central Nagasaki Map (p670)

See Glover Garden Area Map (p672)

5.30pm Sep-Apr, to 6.30pm May-Aug; Matsuyama-machi) An essential Nagasaki experience, this sombre place recounts the city's destruction and loss of life through photos and artefacts, including mangled rocks, trees, furniture, pottery and clothing, a clock stopped at 11.02 (the hour of the bombing), first-hand accounts from survivors and stories of heroic relief efforts. Exhibits also include the post-bombing struggle for nuclear disarmament, and conclude with a chilling illustration of which nations bear nuclear arms.

Nagasaki

★ Nagasaki National Peace Memorial Hall for the Atomic Bomb Victims   MEMORIAL

(国立長崎原爆死没者追悼平和祈念館; Map p666; www.peace-nagasaki.go.jp; 7-8 Hirano-machi; ⊙8.30am-5.30pm Sep-Apr, to 6.30pm May-Aug; 🚇Matsuyama-machi) FREE Adjacent to the Atomic Bomb Museum and completed in 2003, this minimalist memorial by Kuryū Akira is a profoundly moving place. It is best approached by quietly reading the carved inscriptions and walking around the sculpted water basin. In the hall below, 12 glass pillars, containing shelves of books of the names of the deceased, reach skyward.

★ Peace Park   PARK

(平和公園; Map p666; Heiwa-kōen; 🚇Ōhashi) FREE North of the hypocentre, the Peace Park is presided over by the 10-tonne bronze **Nagasaki Peace Statue** (平和記念像), designed in 1955 by Kitamura Seibo. It also includes the dove-shaped Fountain of Peace (1969) and the Peace Symbol Zone, a sculpture garden with contributions on the theme of peace from around the world. On 9 August, a rowdy antinuclear protest is held within earshot of the more respectful official memorial ceremony for those lost to the bomb.

Atomic Bomb Hypocentre Park   PARK

(長崎爆心地公園; Map p666; 🚇Matsuyama-machi) FREE The park has a smooth, black stone column marking the point above which the bomb exploded. Nearby are bomb-blasted relics, including a section of the wall of the Urakami Cathedral.

Urakami Cathedral   CHURCH

(浦上天主堂; Map p666; 1-79 Motō-machi; ⊙9am-5pm, closed Mon) FREE Once the largest church in Asia (1914), the cathedral took three decades to complete and three seconds to flatten. This smaller replacement cathedral was completed in 1959 on the ruins of the original. Walk around the side of the hill to see a belfry lying in state where the original building fell after the blast.

Nagai Takashi Memorial Museum   MUSEUM

(永井隆記念館; off Map p666; 22-6 Ueno-machi; admission ¥100; ⊙9am-5pm) This small but quietly moving museum celebrates the courage and faith of one man in the face of overwhelming adversity. Already suffering from leukaemia, Dr Nagai survived the atomic explosion but lost his wife to it. He immediately devoted himself to the treatment of bomb victims until his death in 1951. In his final days, he continued to write prolifically

THE ATOMIC EXPLOSION

When USAF B-29 bomber *Bock's Car* set off from the Marianas on 9 August 1945 to drop a second atomic bomb on Japan, the target was Kokura on Kyūshū's northeastern coast. Due to poor visibility, the crew diverted to the secondary target, Nagasaki.

The B-29 arrived over Nagasaki at 10.58am amid heavy cloud. When a momentary gap appeared and the Mitsubishi Arms Factory was sighted, the 4.57-tonne 'Fat Man' bomb, with an explosive power equivalent to 21.3 kilotonnes of TNT (almost twice that of Hiroshima's 'Little Boy'), was released over Nagasaki.

The bomb missed the arms factory, its intended target, and exploded at 11.02am, at an altitude of 500m almost directly above the largest Catholic church in Asia (Urakami Cathedral). In an instant, it annihilated the suburb of Urakami and 74,000 of Nagasaki's 240,000 people. Ground temperatures at the hypocentre were estimated between 3000°C and 4000°C, and as high as 600°C 1.5km away. Everything within a 1km radius of the explosion was destroyed, and searing winds estimated at over 1000km/h (typhoons generally top out at 150km/h) swept down the valley of the Urakami-gawa towards the city centre. With able-bodied men at work or at war, most victims were women, children and senior citizens, as well as 13,000 conscripted Korean labourers and 200 allied POWs. Another 75,000 people were horribly injured (and it is estimated that as many people died as a result of the after-effects). After the resulting fires burned out, a third of the city was gone.

Yet the damage might have been even worse had the targeted arms factory been hit. Unlike in the flatlands of Hiroshima or the Nagasaki port itself, the hills around the river valley protected outlying suburbs from greater damage.

and secure donations for survivors and orphans, earning the nickname 'Saint of Nagasaki'. Ask to watch the video in English.

Next door is **Nyokodō** (如己堂), the simple hut from which Dr Nagai worked – its name comes from the biblical commandment 'love thy neighbour as thyself'.

Shiroyama Elementary School
HISTORIC BUILDING

(城山小学校; Map p666; ☎861-0057; 23-1 Shiroyama-chō; ⊘8.30am-4.30pm Mon-Fri) FREE This was the closest school to the nuclear blast, up a hill a mere 500m away, and it's hard not to be moved by the very ordinariness that exists here today. Except for one building that still stands as it did following the bombing (to the right at the top of the stairs), this functioning school looks much like any other, albeit with the addition of sculptures, monuments and memorials commemorating the loss of life, the latter laden with strands of 1000 origami cranes, the traditional children's prayer for peace.

One-Pillar Torii
MONUMENT

(一本柱鳥居; Map p666; ☐Daigakubōyin-mae or Urakami Eki-mae) FREE The blast knocked down half of the stone entrance arch to the Sanno-jinja, 800m southeast of the hypocentre. The other pillar remains, a quiet testimony to the power of strength and resilience.

⊙ Central Nagasaki

★ Dejima
HISTORIC SITE

(出島; Map p670) In 1641, the Tokugawa shōgunate banished all foreigners from Japan, with one exception: Dejima, a fan-shaped, man-made island 560m in circumference (15,000 sq m) in Nagasaki harbour. From then until the 1850s, this small Dutch trading post was the sole sanctioned foreign presence in Japan; about the only local contact for the Dutch segregated here was with trading partners and courtesans, and an annual official visit to Edo, which took 90 days!

These days the city has filled in around the island and you might walk right past it. Don't. Seventeen buildings, walls and structures (plus a miniature Dejima) have been painstakingly reconstructed based on pictorial representations into the **Dejima Museum** (出島資料館; www1.city.nagasaki.nagasaki.jp/dejima; 6-1 Dejima-machi; admission ¥500; ⊘8am-7pm; ☐Dejima). Restored and reopened in 2006 and constantly being upgraded, the buildings here are as instructive inside as they are good-looking outside, with exhibits covering the spread of trade, Western learning and culture, archaeological digs, and rooms combining Japanese tatami (woven floor matting) with Western wallpaper. There's excellent English signage. Allow at least two hours.

★ Nagasaki Museum of History & Culture   MUSEUM

(長崎歴史文化博物館; Map p666; www.nmhc. jp; 1-1-1 Tateyama; admission ¥600; ⊗8.30am-7pm, closed 3rd Tue of month; ☐Sakura-machi) This large museum with attractive displays opened in 2005 to focus on Nagasaki's proud history of international exchange. The main gallery is a fabulous reconstruction of a section of the Edo-period Nagasaki Magistrate's Office, which controlled trade and diplomacy. Detailed English-language explanations were in the works at the time of writing.

★ Suwa-jinja   SHINTŌ SHRINE

(諏訪神社; Map p666; 18-15 Kaminishiyama-machi; ⊗24hr; ☐Suwa-jinja-mae) Situated on a forested hilltop and reached via multiple staircases, this enormous shrine was established in 1625. Around the grounds are statues of *komainu* (protective dogs), including the *kappa-komainu* (water-sprite dogs), which you pray to by dribbling water onto the plates on their heads. The *gankake komainu* (turntable dog) was often called on by prostitutes, who prayed that storms would arrive, forcing the sailors to stay at the port another day. Between 7 and 9 October each year, the shrine comes to life with the dragon dance of Kunchi Matsuri (p673), Nagasaki's most important annual festival.

Nagasaki Station Area   NEIGHBOURHOOD

The **26 Martyrs Memorial** (日本二十六聖人殉教地; Map p666) features reliefs commemorating the six Spanish and 20 Japanese crucified in 1597, when authorities cracked down on practising Christians. The youngest killed were boys aged 12 and 13. Behind the memorial is a simple Christianity-related **museum** (☐822 6000; 7-8 Nishisaka-machi; admission ¥250).

Fukusai-ji Kannon (福済寺[長崎観音; Map p666; Nagasaki Universal Kannon Temple; 2-56 Chiku-go-machi; admission ¥200; ⊗8am-4pm; ☐Sakura-machi) is shaped like a huge turtle carrying an 18m-high figure of the goddess Kannon. Inside, a Foucault pendulum, demonstrating the rotation of the earth, hangs from the top.

Nearby, the gardens of the temple **Shōfuku-ji** (聖福寺; Map p666; 3-77 Tamazono-machi; ⊗24hr; ☐Sakura-machi) contain an arched stone gate dating from 1657. It's worth the significant uphill climb to reach the palm-filled inner court and main building, dating from 1715. Also note the interesting *onigawara* (ogre-covered wall) and sacred kiln used for the ceremonial burning of disused Buddhist scriptures.

Nagasaki Prefectural Art Museum   MUSEUM

(長崎県美術館; Map p666; ☐833-2110; www. nagasaki-museum.jp/english; 2-1 Dejima-machi; admission ¥400; ⊗10am-8pm, closed 2nd & 4th Mon each month) ✏ Designed by Kuma Kengō (the architect behind Tokyo's Nezu Museum), this museum straddles a canal in an environmentally friendly building (note the roof garden). The permanent collection covers both Nagasaki-related art and Spanish art, and special exhibits are eclectic, from Chinese to Chagall. There's a lovely cafe in the bridge over the canal.

Teramachi   NEIGHBOURHOOD

(寺町) Between the Shianbashi shopping and nightlife area and Nakashima-gawa (the smaller of the city's two rivers), the Teramachi district is anchored at either end by Nagasaki's two best-known temples.

Sōfuku-ji (崇福寺; Map p670; 7-5 Kajiya-machi; admission ¥300; ⊗8am-5pm; ☐Shōkakuji-shita) was built in 1629 by Chinese monk Chaonian. Its red entrance gate (Daiippo-mon) exemplifies Ming-dynasty architecture. Inside the temple is a huge cauldron that was used to prepare food for famine victims in 1681, and a statue of Maso, goddess of the sea.

From here, it's a relaxing walk of about 1.2km to **Kōfuku-ji** (興福寺; Map p666; 4-32 Tera-machi; admission ¥300; ⊗8am-5pm; ☐Kōkaidō-mae), along a side street lined with temples, stone walls and shops selling Buddhist articles, crafts and dolls. The temple dates from the 1620s and is noted for the Ming architecture of the main hall. Like Sōfuku-ji, it is an Ōbaku Zen temple – and the oldest in Japan.

Nakashima-gawa   RIVER

(中島川; Map p666; ☐Kōkaidō-mae or Nigiwai-bashi) **FREE** Parallel to Teramachi, the Nakashima-gawa is crossed by a picturesque collection of 17th-century stone bridges. Once, each bridge was the distinct entranceway to a separate temple. Best known is the double-arched **Megane-bashi** (めがね橋; Spectacles Bridge), originally built in 1634 and so called because the reflection of the arches in the water looks like a pair of Meiji-era spectacles. Six of the 10 bridges, including Megane-bashi, were washed away by flooding in 1982 and restored using the recovered stones.

Shinchi Chinatown   NEIGHBOURHOOD

(新地中華街; Map p670; ☐Tsuki-machi) During Japan's long period of seclusion, Chinese traders were theoretically just as restricted as the Dutch, but in practice they were relatively free. Only a couple of buildings

Central Nagasaki

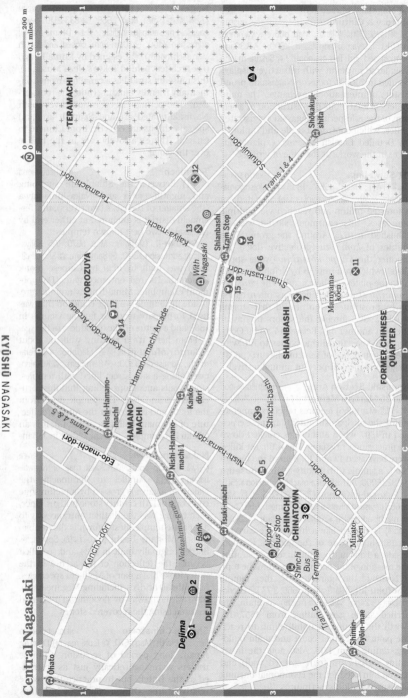

KYŪSHŪ NAGASAKI

remain from the old area, but Nagasaki still has an energetic Chinese community, evident in the city's culture, architecture, festivals and cuisine. Visitors come from far and wide to eat here and shop for Chinese crafts and trinkets.

Inasa-yama   LANDMARK
(稲佐山; Map p666) West of the harbour, a **cable car** (長崎ロープウェイ; www.nagasaki-ropeway.jp; return ¥1200; ⊙9am-10pm; 🚌Kōkaidō-mae) ascends every 20 minutes to the top of 333m-high Inasa-yama, offering superb views over Nagasaki, particularly at night. Buses 3 and 4 leave from outside JR Nagasaki Station going towards Shimo-Ōhashi; get off at the **Ropeway-mae bus stop** (ロープウェイ前) and walk up the steps through the grounds of **Fuchi-jinja** (淵神社).

Elsewhere on the mountainside is **Onsen Fukunoyu** (温泉ふくの湯; 451-23 Inasa-chō; admission ¥800; ⊙9.30am-1am). In addition to wet baths, try the *gabanyoku* stone baths (additional ¥700), with temperatures from a balmy 38°C to the *are-you-nuts?* 70°C. There's a free shuttle from JR Nagasaki and Urakami stations (20 minutes, twice per hour).

◎ Southern Nagasaki

Glover Garden   GARDENS
(グラバー園; Map p672; ☎822-8223; www.glover-garden.jp; adult/student ¥600/300; ⊙8am-9.30pm 29 Apr–mid-Jul, to 6pm mid-Jul–28 Apr; 🚌Ōura Tenshudō-shita) Some former homes of the city's Meiji-period European residents have been reassembled in this hillside garden. Glover Garden is named after Thomas Glover (1838–1911), the Scottish merchant who built Japan's first railway, helped establish

the shipbuilding industry and whose arms-importing operations influenced the course of the Meiji Restoration.

The best way to explore the garden is to take the moving walkways to the top of the hill then walk back down. The **Mitsubishi No 2 Dock building** (旧三菱第2ドックハウス; ☎tel, info 822 8223; 8-1 Minami-yamatemachi; adult/student ¥600/300; ⊙8am-9.30pm 27 Apr-9 Oct, to 6pm 10 Oct-26 Apr) is highest, with panoramic views of the city and harbour from the 2nd floor. Next highest is **Walker House** (旧ウォーカー住宅), filled with artefacts donated by the families, followed by **Ringer House** (旧リンガー住宅), **Alt House** (旧オルト住宅) and finally **Glover House** (旧グラバー住宅; ☎822 8223; 8-1 Minami-yamatemachi; adult/student ¥600/300; ⊙8am-9.30pm 27 Apr-9 Oct, to 6pm 10 Oct-26 April). Halfway down is the **Madame Butterfly Statue** of Japanese opera singer Miura Tamaki, inspiration of the famous opera by Puccini – the story took place here in Nagasaki. Exit the garden through the **Nagasaki Traditional Performing Arts Museum** (☎tel, info 822 8223; 8-1 Minami-yamatemachi; adult/student ¥600/300; ⊙8am-9.30pm 27 Apr-9 Oct, to 6pm 10 Oct-26 April), which has a display of dragons and floats used in Nagasaki's colourful Kunchi Matsuri.

Ōura Catholic Church   CHURCH
(大浦天主堂; Map p672; ☎823-2628; admission ¥300; ⊙8am-6pm; 🚌Ōura Tenshudō-shita) This hilltop church, Japan's oldest (1865), is dedicated to the 26 Christians who were crucified in Nagasaki in 1597. It's more like a museum than a place of worship, with an ornate Gothic altar and bishop's chair, and an oil painting of the 26 martyrs. To pray for free, use the regular church across the street.

KYŪSHŪ NAGASAKI

Glover Garden Area

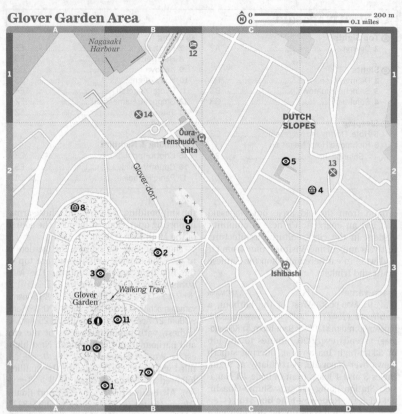

Glover Garden Area

Dutch Slopes　　　　　　　　HISTORIC SITE
(オランダ坂; Oranda-zaka; 🚋Ishibashi) The gently inclined flagstone streets known as the Dutch Slopes were once lined with wooden **Dutch houses**. Several buildings here have been beautifully restored and offer glimpses of Japan's early interest in the West. The quiet **Ko-shashin-shiryōkan**
(古写真資料館; Map p672; Museum of Old Photographs; 6-25 Higashi-yamatemachi; combined admission ¥100; ☺9am-5pm, closed Mon) and **Maizō-shiryōkan** (埋蔵資料館; Map p672; Museum of Unearthed Artefacts; 6-25 Higashi-yamatemachi; combined admission ¥100; ☺9am-5pm, closed Mon) showcase the area's history (note that most signage is in Japanese).

KYŪSHŪ NAGASAKI

Kōshi-byō & Historical Museum of China
SHRINE, MUSEUM

(孔子廟・中国歴代博物館; Map p672; ☑824-4022; 10-36 Ōuramachi; shrine & museum admission ¥600; ⊙8.30am-5.30pm; ⊟Ishibashi) The jauntily painted Kōshi-byō shrine claims to be the only Confucian shrine built by and for Chinese outside China, and the statues of sages in its courtyard certainly make you feel like you've journeyed across the sea. The original 1893 building was destroyed by fire following the A-bomb explosion.

Behind it, a glossy museum of Chinese art spans jade artefacts and Neolithic archaeological finds to terracotta warriors and Qing-dynasty porcelain. There's also a large gift shop with Chinese trinkets, from classy to kitschy.

⚐ Tours

One-hour **Nagasaki Harbour Cruises** (長崎港めぐりクルーズ; Map p666; ☑822-5002; Nagasaki Harbour Terminal Bldg; adult/child ¥1300/650) are a great way to glimpse picturesque Nagasaki. Check at the ferry terminal for up-to-date schedules.

✿ Festivals & Events

Peiron Dragon Boat Races
DRAGON BOATS

Colourful boat races were introduced by the Chinese in the mid-1600s, and held to appease the god of the sea. They still take place in Nagasaki Harbour in late July.

Shōrō-nagashi
TRADITIONAL

On 15 August lantern-lit boats are floated on the harbour to honour ancestors. The boats are of many sizes and handcrafted from a variety of materials (bamboo, wood, rice stems etc). Eventually they float out to sea and are destroyed by waves. The best viewpoint for the procession is at the Ōhato ferry terminal.

Kunchi Matsuri
TRADITIONAL

Held from 7 to 9 October, this energetic festival features Chinese dragons dancing all around the city but especially at Suwa-jinja. The festival is marked by elaborate costumes, fireworks, cymbals and giant dragon puppets.

🛏 Sleeping

For ease of transport and access to restaurants and nightlife, we recommend staying near JR Nagasaki Station or Shianbashi.

Nagasaki Kagamiya
HOSTEL ¥

(長崎かがみや; ☑895-8250; www.n-kagamiya.com; 1-12-9 Hongouchi; dm ¥2300, s/d from ¥4000/5600; ⊙check-in 3-8pm; ⊟@🛜; ⊟Hotaru-jaya) Away from the action in a hilly residential neighbourhood, this new, neat, six-room hostel has personality to spare and a cosy mix of Japanese and Western (we prefer Japanese) rooms. A *hanare* (annexe) sleeps up to eight. The innkeepers keep over 400 kimono and *yukata* for guests to try on (kimono/yukata ¥4200/3200). Continental breakfast is ¥400 and towel rental is ¥100.

From Hotaru-jaya tram stop (end of the line), walk uphill, turn left after Royal Host restaurant and through the Shintō shrine.

Hostel Akari
HOSTEL ¥

(ホステルあかり; Map p666; ☑801-7900; www.nagasaki-hostel.com; 2-2 Kajiya-machi; dm/s from ¥2500/3900, d & tw from ¥5900; ⊙reception 8am-8pm; ⊟@🛜; ⊟Kōkaidō-mae) This commendably friendly 28-bed hostel sets the standard, with bright, clean Japanese-style rooms with Western-style bedding and bathrooms, uber-helpful staff, an open kitchen and a dedicated crew of local volunteers who lead free walking tours around the city. It's by the lovely Nakashima-gawa. Towel rental is ¥100.

KYŪSHŪ NAGASAKI

WORTH A TRIP

GUNKANJIMA

Gunkanjima means 'battleship island', a name that captures the eeriness of this abandoned cluster of buildings rising out of the Pacific. Yet 'battleship' refers to its outline when viewed from afar, and not its purpose, which was harvesting coal from mines below the ocean floor beginning in 1890. When supplies ran out, the island was abandoned in 1974 and began gradually decaying. Now visitors can ramble on walkways among the long-disused skyscrapers, concrete remnants of conveyor belts and impressive fortified walls. It looks like it comes straight out of an apocalyptic manga, so much so that it was the backdrop for the villian's lair in the 2012 James Bond film *Skyfall*.

Three-hour cruises (¥4300, including one hour on the island) are by reservation (conditions permitting), running twice daily from April to October, with fewer departures November to March. Contact Nagasaki Harbour Cruises (p673).

Hotel Dormy Inn Nagasaki   BUSINESS HOTEL ¥¥

(☑820-5489; Map p670; www.hotespa.net/hotels/nagasaki; 7-24 Dōza-machi; s/d from ¥9500/13,000; ⊕@; ⊟ Tsuki-machi) Adjacent to Chinatown, this hotel would be worth it just for the location. Rooms are crisp and neat as a pin with quality mattresses. There are large gender-separated common baths and saunas in addition to in-room facilities. The breakfast buffet (¥1100) includes *sara udon*, and there's free soba served from 9.30pm to 11pm. Look for online discounts.

Richmond Hotel
Nagasaki Shianbashi   HOTEL ¥¥

(リッチモンドホテル長崎思案橋;   Map p670; ☑832-2525; www.richmondhotel.jp; 6-38 Motoshikkui-machi; s/d/tw from ¥8000/11,000/14,000; ⊕@⊜; ⊟ Shianbashi) You can't be closer to the heart of Shianbashi than this travellers' favourite. Completed in 2007, rooms are ultramodern with dark tones and flat-screen TVs. Deluxe rooms are large by Japanese standards. The hotel has cheerful, English-speaking staff, as well as a terrific breakfast buffet (¥1000) which includes Nagasaki specialities.

Hotel Monterey Nagasaki   HOTEL ¥¥

(ホテルモントレ長崎; Map p672; ☑827-7111; www.hotelmonterey.co.jp/nagasaki; 1-22 Ōura-machi; s/tw from ¥12,000/16,500; ⊕@) At this Portuguese-themed hotel near the Dutch Slopes and Glover Garden, rooms are spacious and light filled, beds are comfy, and staff are courteous and used to the vagaries of foreign guests. Look for online discounts.

ANA Crowne Plaza
Nagasaki Gloverhill   HOTEL ¥¥

(ANAクラウンプラザ長崎グラバーヒル; ☑818-6601; www.anacrowneplaza-nagasaki.jp; 1-18 Minami-yamate-machi; s/d/tw from ¥8500/13,000/16,000; P⊕@⊜; ⊟ Ōura-Tenshudō-shita) Near Glover Garden, Ōura Cathedral and the Dutch Slopes, this old-school hotel was getting a slick renovation at the time of writing, with separate showers and baths, and plush bedding and clean, contemporary lines. About the only downside: no view to speak of.

Chisun Grand Nagasaki   BUSINESS HOTEL ¥¥

(チサングランド長崎; Map p666; ☑826-1211; www.solarehotels.com/english; 5-35 Goto-machi; s/d/tw ¥12,000/16,000/18,000; ⊕@⊜; ⊟ Goto-machi) On the main drag, look for 153 sleek rooms with dark wood panelling, separate shower, tub and vanity. Staff are used to

foreign guests, and there's a coin laundry. Discounted rates are listed on the website.

★ Garden Terrace Nagasaki   HOTEL ¥¥¥

(ガーデンテラス長崎; ☑864-7777; www.gt-nagasaki.jp; 2-3 Akizuki-machi; r from ¥42,000; P⊕@⊜⊠) If money is no object, this hillside hotel is a design masterpiece, clad in the unvarnished wood planks of architect Kuma Kengo. Generous rooms (50 sq m plus) feature minimalist style, angular sofas and armchairs, fabulous baths and sweeping views. Non-staying guests can visit for high-flying French or teppanyaki meals.

About the only disadvantage: distance, across the harbour from the city centre. If you miss the hotel shuttle from JR Nagasaki Station, a taxi costs about ¥1500.

Sakamoto-ya   RYOKAN ¥¥¥

(料亭旅館坂本屋; Map p666; ☑826-8211; www.sakamotoya.co.jp; 2-13 Kanaya-machi; r per person incl 2 meals from ¥15,575; P@; ⊟ Goto-machi) This magnificent old-school ryokan has been in business since 1894. Look for art-filled rooms, hallways lined with Arita-yaki pottery, postage-stamp-sized gardens off 1st-floor rooms, *kaiseki* meals (Japanese haute cuisine) and only 10 rooms for personal service. From Goto-machi tram stop, walk past Chisun Grand Hotel and turn left. It's diagonally across from the TV broadcast tower.

Best Western
Premier Hotel Nagasaki   HOTEL ¥¥¥

(ベストウエスタンプレミアホテル長崎; Map p666; ☑821-1111; www.bestwestern.co.jp/english/nagasaki; 2-26 Takara-machi; s/d from ¥15,000/23,000; P⊕@⊜; ⊟ Takara-machi) The city centre's top hotel has a vast marble lobby, comfortably elegant rooms with marble-countered bathrooms and panoramic views from the top-floor steakhouse and buffet restaurant, where a Japanese–Western buffet breakfast is served (¥2000).

✗ Eating

Nagasaki is a culinary crossroads and one of Japan's most interesting dining scenes. *Champon* is a nationally famous local take on *rāmen* featuring squid, octopus, pork and vegetables in a cloudy white, salt-based broth. *Sara-udon* nests the same toppings in a thick sauce over crispy fried noodles. Chinese and Portuguese influences converge in *shippoku ryōri*, Nagasaki-style *kaiseki*. *Kakuni-manju* is a Chinese import, a slab of pork belly in a thick, sweet sauce, served in a steamed wheat bun and often found at street stalls. And *chirin-chirin* (ding ding) flavoured shaved ice is sold from tiny carts around town in warmer months.

The Mirai Nagasaki Cocowalk (p676) features some 20 restaurants on its 4th and 5th floors. **Aletta** (Map p666; ☑ 801-5245; lunch/dinner ¥1580/1980; ⏱ lunch & dinner) is an airy buffet restaurant on the 4th floor, with a different national theme each month. On the 5th floor, **Big Man** (Map p666; ☑ 865-8600; sandwiches ¥350-850; ⏱ 10am-9pm; ➌ 🖩 🖪) serves burgers that are popular in nearby Sasebo, where a US naval base has brought yet another cultural influence. Some burgers have a Japanese twist, such as bacon-egg burgers or Kyūshū's *kurobuta* (black pork) sandwiches.

Other good places for restaurant browsing include the restaurant floors of the shopping mall **Amu Plaza** (アミュプラザ長崎; Map p666) and **Dejima Wharf** (出島ワーフ; Map p666), a picturesque, harbourside collection of open-air restaurants (seafood to Italian) at a variety of price points, plus bars and galleries, just west of Dejima.

Hōuntei
IZAKAYA ¥

(Map p670; ☑ 821-9333; 1-8 Motoshikkui-machi; dishes ¥360-520; ⏱ 5-11pm; 🖪 Shianbashi) Patrons have been ordering the *hito-kuchi gyōza* (one-bite *gyōza;* ¥360 for 10) at this rustic hole-in-the-wall since the 1970s. Also try *butaniratoji* (pork and shallots cooked omelette style; ¥520). There's a picture menu. Look for the lantern and brown *noren* (door curtain) across from With Nagasaki.

Shikairō
CHINESE ¥

(四海楼; Map p672; ☑ 822-1296; 4-5 Matsugae-machi; champon or sara-udon ¥997; ⏱ lunch & dinner; ➌ 🖩; 🖪 Oura-Tenshudō-shita) This huge, freestanding Chinese restaurant (look for the giant red pillars) near Glover Garden is credited as the creator of *champon* and has been in operation since 1899. There are harbour views and a small *champon* museum.

Kadoya
IZAKAYA ¥

(かど屋; Map p670; ☑ 823-0273; 10-9 Dōzamachi; dishes ¥150-750; ⏱ 6pm-midnight Sun-Thu, 6pm-3am Fri & Sat; 🖩) The English-language signage outside may be a little wacky ('Be skilled the world of a wonderful scorch bird' etc), but inside the youthful staff at this local chain clearly know what they're doing, from *izakaya* classics like edamame and yakitori to avocado and seafood salad, to roast loin of Saga beef. There's plenty of choice of alcohol to wash them down for a darn good time.

Tsuru-chan
CAFE ¥

(ツル茶ん; Map p670; ☑ 824-2679; 2-47 Aburaya-machi; Toruko rice ¥980-1180; ⏱ 9am-10pm; 🖪 Shianbashi) Despite the name 'Toruko (Turkish) rice', there's nothing much Turkish about this hearty Nagasaki signature dish: pork cutlet in hearty, curry-flavoured gravy over pasta and rice (¥980). Established in 1925, this unabashedly retro *kissaten* (coffee shop) claims to have invented it. Creative recent preparations include chicken, beef and even cream sauce.

★ Shippoku Hamakatsu
KAISEKI ¥¥

(卓袱浜勝; Map p670; ☑ 826-8321; www.sippoku.jp; 6-50 Kajiya-machi; lunch/dinner menus from ¥1500/2940; ⏱ lunch & dinner; 🖩; 🖪 Shianbashi) Come here if you would like to experience *shippoku ryōri* and still afford your airfare home. Course menus are filling and varied (the Otakusa Shippoku is served on a dramatic round tray). In addition, there is a choice of either Japanese- or Western-style seating.

Yosso
JAPANESE ¥¥

(吉宗; Map p670; ☑ 821-0001; 8-9 Hama-machi; set meals from ¥1260; ⏱ 11am-8pm; 🖪 Shianbashi) People have been coming to eat *chawan-mushi* (Japanese egg custard) since 1866. Look for the traditional shopfront festooned with red lanterns. The Yosso *teishoku* (¥1260) adds fish, *soboro* (sweetened, ground chicken over rice), *kakuni* (stewed pork belly), dessert and more. There's no English menu, but a display case makes ordering easy.

Kairaku-en
CHINESE ¥¥

(会楽園; Map p670; ☑ 822-4261; 10-16 Shinchi-chō; dishes ¥700-1600; 🖩) At this Shinchi Chinatown standby, cheerful staff dressed in black with white aprons have been serving southern Chinese cuisine since the Shōwa Era. The

KYŪSHŪ NAGASAKI

WORLD FOODS WEEKLY

In the Dutch Slopes, the 'World Foods Restaurant' inside **Higashi-yamate Chikyū-kan** (東山手「地球館」; Map p672; ☑ 822-7966; www.h3.dion.ne.jp/~chikyu; 6-25 Higashiyamate-machi; ⏱ cafe 10am-5pm Thu-Tue, restaurant noon-3pm Sat & Sun) operates most weekends; each week a different chef comes to prepare inexpensive meals from their home country, some 70 nations and counting. This little gem is what cultural exchange – and Nagasaki – is all about.

¥800 lunch set meals (noodle dishes, sweet and sour pork etc) are a good deal, or for a splurge, try Peking duck (¥5000).

Ryōtei Kagetsu

KAISEKI ¥¥¥

(史跡料亭花月; Map p670; ☑822-0191; www.ry-outei-kagetsu.co.jp; 2-1 Maruyama-machi; set lunch/dinner from ¥10,080/13,860; ☺lunch & dinner, closed most Tue; ☒Shianbashi) A sky-high *shippoku* restaurant dating to 1642 when it was a high-class brothel. If you have Japanese skills or a chaperone, dining companions and a love of food, you might not flinch at the price.

Drinking & Nightlife

Nagasaki doesn't bustle after dark, but little nightspots punctuate the narrow lanes around Hamano-machi and Shianbashi.

Chotto-Ippai

BAR

(Map p670; Ken's Bar; 2-17 Motoshikkui-machi; ☺6pm-3am, closed Sun; ☒Shianbashi) Known as Ken's bar, for the American owner who holds court in both English and prodigious Nagasaki dialect, this cheerful bar has big windows onto the narrow lane behind the main street, and a great selection of *shōchū*. Look for the US flag and the sign reading 'Kendall' in English.

Panic Paradise

BAR

(パニックパラダイス; Map p670; basement, 5-33 Yorozuya-machi; drinks from ¥600; ☺9pm-late; ☒Kankō-dōri) Cool but friendly, this dark basement bar is a bit of a local icon, cluttered with rock memorabilia. There's a huge collection of tunes, cosy booths with dim lamps and the staff has pride in the environment.

Country Road

BAR

(カントリーロード; Map p670; 7-34 Maruyama-machi; ☺6pm-midnight; ☒Shianbashi) This cosy family-run country-music bar oozes Americana with a Japanese twist. You'll feel welcome here and the Western bar snacks tempt. It's off the main street before the steps to Maruyama.

Inokuchiya

WINE BAR

(猪ノ口屋; ☑821-0454; 4-11 Sakae-machi; ☺5.30-11pm Mon-Sat; ☒Nigiwaibashi) Away from Shianbashi but worth the trip, this cool spot has a wine store fronting a warren of rooms for sampling wines, *shōchū* and Nagasaki *sake*, alongside delectable small plates of pâté, carpaccio and salads. Not much English on the menu, but you can usually make yourself understood.

Shopping

Local crafts and products are sold around and opposite JR Nagasaki Station, as well as in shops along busy Hamano-machi shopping arcade near Shianbashi tram stop. Try to ignore tortoiseshell crafts (べっ甲) sold around town: turtles actually need their shells.

For mall shopping, Amu Plaza (p675) at the station is nice and easy, and you can't miss **Mirai Nagasaki Cocowalk** (みらい長崎ココウォーク; Map p666; www.cocowalk.jp; 1-55 Morimachi; ☺10am-9pm; ☒Mori-machi, ☒JR Urakami), a massive shopping, dining and cinema complex with a rooftop Ferris wheel (¥500).

Information

INTERNET ACCESS

Nagasaki offers free wi-fi in many public places including JR Nagasaki Station, Dejima Wharf and Shinchi Chinatown. Visit www.ninjin-area.net/sites/map to find locations, and look for ninjin.net in your browser to sign on (there's an option in English).

Chikyū-shimin Hiroba (地球市民ひろば; ☑842-3783; www1.city.nagasaki.nagasaki.jp/kokusai/exchange/plaza.html; 2nd fl, Nagasaki Brick Hall, 2-38 Morimachi; per hr ¥100; ☺9am-8pm; ☒Mori-machi) Also offers Japanese-language and other cultural classes; behind Mirai Nagasaki Cocowalk.

Cybac Café (サイバックカフェ; ☑818-8050; 3rd & 4th fl, Hashimoto Bldg, 2-46 Aburaya-chō; registration fee ¥300 then 1st 30/subsequent 15min ¥300/100; ☒Shianbashi) This enormous internet cafe has showers, darts and drinks.

Kinko's (キンコーズ; ☑818-2522; 1st fl, Amu Plaza, 1-1 Onoue-machi; per 10min ¥210; ☺8am-10pm Sat-Mon, 24hr Tue-Fri; ☒JR Nagasaki) Next to 18-Bank, a convenient internet option.

MONEY

In addition to postal and 7-Eleven ATMs, several branches of **18 Bank** (十八銀行) handle foreign-currency exchange.

TOURIST INFORMATION

In addition to tourist brochures available at locations following, look for the free English-language magazine *Nagazasshi*, published by local expats, containing events, sightseeing tips and features. A new multilingual call centre (☑825-5175) caters to English-speaking visitors.

Nagasaki City Tourist Information Centre (長崎市総合観光案内所; Map p666; ☑823-3631; www.at-nagasaki.jp/foreign/english; 1st fl, JR Nagasaki Station; ☺8am-8pm) Can assist with finding accommodation and has brochures and maps in English.

Woe to the traveller who does not return from Nagasaki with a box of **castella** as an *omiyage* (travel gift). These Portuguese-style sponge cakes have been an exotic Nagasaki treat for four centuries, as Japanese homes did not have ovens for most of that time.

The yellow, brick-shaped castella remains ubiquitous here even now. Two of the finer shops are **Fukusaya** (福砂屋; Map p670; www.castella.co.jp; 3-1 Funadaiku-machi; ◷8.30am-8pm; 🚊Shianbashi), making the cakes since 1624; and **Shōkandō** (匠寛堂; Map p666; 🚻826-1123; www.shokando.jp; 7-24 Sakana-no-machi; ◷9am-7pm; 🚊Kōkaidō-mae), across from Megane-bashi, supplier to the Japanese imperial family.

Nagasaki Prefectural Convention and Visitors Bureau (🚻828-7875; 8th fl, 14-10 Motofuna-machi; ◷9am-5.30pm, closed 27 Dec-3 Jan) Has detailed information on the city and prefecture.

TRAVEL AGENCIES

JR Kyūshū Travel Agency (🚻822-4813; JR Nagasaki Station; ◷10am-5.30pm) Handles domestic travel and hotel arrangements.

Getting There & Away

AIR

There are flights between Nagasaki and Tokyo (Haneda; JAL & ANA/Solaseed Air ¥39,070/33,670), Osaka (Itami; ¥25,700), Okinawa (¥25,500) and Nagoya (¥31,900).

BOAT

Ferries sail from a few places around Nagasaki, including Ōhato terminal, south of JR Nagasaki Station.

BUS

From the Kenei bus station opposite JR Nagasaki Station, buses depart for Unzen (¥1900, 1¾ hours), Sasebo (¥1450, 1½ hours), Fukuoka (¥2500, 2¼ hours), Kumamoto (¥3600, 13¼ hours) and Beppu (¥4500, 3½ hours). Night buses for Osaka (¥11,000, 10 hours) leave from both the **Kenei bus terminal** (県営バスターミナル) and the **Shinchi bus terminal** (新地バスターミナル).

TRAIN

JR lines from Nagasaki head for Sasebo (for Hirado; *kaisoku*; ¥1600, 1¾ hours) or Fukuoka (Hakata Station; *tokkyū*; ¥4080, two hours). Most other destinations require a change of train. Nagasaki is not currently served by *shinkansen*.

Getting Around

TO/FROM THE AIRPORT

Nagasaki's airport is located about 40km from the city. Airport buses (¥800, 45 minutes) operate from stand 4 of the Kenei bus terminal opposite JR Nagasaki Station and outside the Shinchi bus terminal. A taxi to the airport costs about ¥9000.

BICYCLE

Bicycles can be rented (40% discount for JR Pass holders) from JR Nagasaki Station at the **Eki Rent-a-Car** (🚻826-0480; per 2hr/day ¥500/1500). Some are even electric powered.

BUS

Buses cover a wider area than trams do, but they're less user-friendly for non-Japanese speakers.

TRAM

The best way of getting around Nagasaki is by tram. There are four colour-coded routes numbered 1, 3, 4 and 5 (route 2 is for special events) and stops are signposted in English. It costs ¥120 to travel anywhere in town, but you can transfer for free at the Tsuki-machi (築町) stop only (ask for a *noritsugi*, or transfer pass), unless you have a ¥500 all-day pass for unlimited travel, available from tourist information centres and many hotels. Most trams stop running around 11.30pm.

Hirado 平戸

🚻0950 / POP 36,000

Tucked away in Nagasaki-ken's northwest corner, the secluded little island of Hirado played a big role in Japan's early opening to the West. Portuguese ships – and missionaries – landed here in 1550. In 1584 a trading post followed, and Hirado grew wealthy off trade as the entry point for Japan's first tobacco, bread and beer. The Dutch and British soon followed, and by 1618 the Japanese had to restore law and order on the island! There are many reminders of early Western involvement, particularly of *kakure-Kuris-utan* (hidden Christians) who populated this region (see p772). It's also a popular beach getaway.

ℹ️ Orientation

The island's main town, Hirado, is small enough to navigate on foot, but you'll need your own transport for points elsewhere. The tourist information centre located near the bus terminal has lots of English-language materials and can book accommodation.

◎ Sights & Activities

★ Ji-in to Kyōkai no Mieru Michi   STREET

(寺院と協会の見える道; Street for Viewing Temples & Churches) Rising up a steep hill from town is this street, one of the most photogenic vantage points in all of Kyūshū. The Buddhist temples and large Christian church are testimony to the island's history.

★ Oranda Shōkan   HISTORIC BUILDING

(オランダ商館; ☎26-0636; 2477 Okubo; admission ¥300; ⊙8.30am-5pm, closed 3rd Tue, Wed & Thu of June) Across from the waterfront, this was the **trading house of the Dutch East India Company**. Shōgunal authorities took the Gregorian date on the front of the building (1639) as proof of forbidden Christianity, ordered it destroyed and used it to justify confining Dutch traders to Dejima (p668). It has just been rebuilt according to the original plans and now houses displays of textiles, pewter ware, gin and pottery traded.

Hirado-jō   CASTLE

(平戸城; ☎22-2201; 1458 Iwanoue-machi; admission ¥500; ⊙8.30am-5.30pm) Hirado-jō presides over the town, with an enormous number of rebuilt structures. Inside you'll see traditional armour and clothing, and photos and models of old Hirado.

Matsūra Historical Museum   MUSEUM

(松浦史料博物館; ☎22-2236; www.matsura. or.jp; 12 Kagamigawa-chō; admission ¥500; ⊙8am-5.30pm) Across the bay, the historical museum is housed in the stunning residence of the Matsūra clan, who ruled the island from the 11th to the 19th centuries. Among the treasures you'll find armour that you can don to pose for photos, *byōbu* (folding screen) paintings and the thatched-roof **Kanun-tei**, a *chanoyu* (tea ceremony) house for the unusual Chinshin-ryū warrior-style tea ceremony (¥500) that is still practised on the island.

Kawachi Pass   HIKING

(川内峠) FREE West of central Hirado, this series of grassy hilltops offers views of both sides of the island – east towards the Japanese mainland and west towards the East China Sea – and above the tiny islands that populate the waters. Paths are lined with eulalia and azaleas, and the occasional condor flies overhead.

Cape Shijiki   BEACH

(🚶) From Hirado, it's about a 40km (one-hour) drive to the island's southern tip at Cape Shijiki, from where there are views of the Gotō-rettō archipelago. En route, **Hotel Ranpū** (ホテル蘭風; ☎23-2111; per day ¥1000) rents out fishing equipment.

Long **Neshiko Beach** on Hirado's lovely west coast is popular for swimming.

Hirado Christian Museum   MUSEUM

(平戸切支丹資料館; ☎28-0176; admission ¥200; ⊙9am-5.30pm, closed Wed) Across the middle of the island, this small museum displays items including a Maria-Kannon statue that the hidden Christians used in place of the Virgin Mary.

🎎 Festivals & Events

Hirado's famous **Jangara Matsuri** folk festival, held on 18 August, is particularly colourful, reminiscent of Okinawa or Korea. Arrive in Hirado by late morning for the afternoon events. From 24 to 27 October, the **Okunchi Matsuri** has dragon and lion dancing at Kameoka-jinja.

🛏️ Sleeping & Eating

While there are sleeping and eating options throughout Hirado, two of the best choices are on the mainland side.

Grass House Youth Hostel   HOSTEL ¥

(平戸ユースホステル・グラスハウス; ☎57-1443; www.grass-house.com; 1111-3 Ōkubo, Tabira-chō; dm ¥3510, d per person incl 2 meals ¥8550; P@) In Hirado-guchi, the closest mainland town, is this unexpectedly awesome hostel with koi pond, hilltop water views, two lovely *rotemburo* (outdoor baths) and a sprawling grassy campground (ring ☎22-4111 for camping permits). There are also private rooms and a restaurant. A taxi from Tabira-Hirado-guchi Station costs about ¥560.

Samson Hotel   RESORT ¥¥

(サムソンホテル; ☎57-1110; www.samson-hotel.jp; 210-6 Nodamen, Tabira-chō; r per person incl 2 meals from ¥12,000, capsule ¥3150; P⊙@) This 10-storey hot-spring hotel on the mainland reopened in 2012 after an expansion and renovation. Public baths are like lookouts over the water, and pricey giant suites contain multiple rooms, some with balconies. By contrast, capsule hotel beds are as simple as you can get (meals not included), and there's a summertime beer garden. We'll overlook the occasional kitsch decor.

Shunsenkan
SEAFOOD ¥
(旬鮮館; ☑22-4857; 655-13 Miyanomachi; Kaisen-don ¥700) Across from the tourist information office and operated by local fishing families, this cooperative is basically a market with picnic tables, where staff will prepare meals. Ask for *sashimi moriawase* (assorted sashimi; ¥400), *kaisendon* (seafood over rice) or just point.

Ichiyama
STEAKHOUSE ¥¥
(市山; ☑22-2439; 529 Tsukiji-machi; set meals ¥2630-7600; ⊙lunch & dinner, closed Tue) Hirado beef compares well in taste with other *wagyu* varieties. Try it at this spacious and comfy spot for *yakiniku* (Korean-style grilled beef). Multicourse set menus are a good deal.

❶ Getting There & Around

Hirado is closer to Saga-ken than to Nagasaki city, joined to Kyūshū by a mini Golden Gate–lookalike bridge from Hirado-guchi. The closest train station, Tabira-Hirado-guchi on the private Matsūra-Tetsudō line (to Imari ¥1090, 67 minutes; Sasebo ¥1190, 80 minutes), is Japan's westernmost; and local buses cross the bridge to the island (¥260, 10 minutes). From Nagasaki, journey to Sasebo by JR/express bus (¥1600/1450, both 1½ hours), continuing to Hirado by bus (¥1300, 1¼ hours).

Rental bikes are available at the tourist information centre for ¥500 per four hours. Rental cars start at ¥6000 per day.

SHIMABARA PENINSULA

The hilly Shimabara Peninsula (島原半島) along the calm Ariake Sea is a popular route between Nagasaki and Kumamoto, via ferry from Shimabara.

The 1637–38 Shimabara Uprising led to the suppression of Christianity in Japan and the country's subsequent two centuries of seclusion from the West. Peasant rebels made their final stand against overwhelming odds (37,000 versus 120,000 people) and held out for 80 days before being slaughtered.

More history was made on 3 June 1991, when the 1359m peak of **Unzen-dake** erupt-ed after lying dormant for 199 years, taking the lives of 43 journalists and scientists. Over 12,000 people were evacuated from nearby villages before the lava flow reached the outskirts of Shimabara.

Unzen 雲仙
☑0957

In **Unzen-Amakusa National Park**, Japan's first, Unzen boasts dozens of onsen and woodsy walks through volcanic landscapes. Unzen village (population 1089) is easily explored in an afternoon, and once the day trippers clear out it's a peaceful night's stay in some great hot-spring accommodation. For town maps and accommodation bookings, consult **Unzen Tourist Association** (雲仙観光協会; ☑73-3434; 320 Unzen; ⊙9am-5pm).

◉ Sights & Activities
Hot Springs

A path just outside the village winds through the bubbling *jigoku* (meaning 'hells'; boiling mineral hot springs). Unlike the touristy *jigoku* of Beppu, these natural wonders are broken up only by stands selling *onsen tamago* (onsen-steamed hard-cooked eggs). A few centuries ago, these *jigoku* lived up to their name, when some 30 Christian martyrs were plunged alive into Oito Jigoku.

Onsen

Check at Unzen Tourist Association for which lodgings accept visitors during your stay. The following public facilities are open regularly:

Unzen Spa House
ONSEN
(雲仙スパハウス; ☑73-3131; admission ¥800; ⊙10am-7pm) This large bathing complex also has glass-blowing workshops (lessons ¥2000 to ¥3000 per 10 to 15 minutes).

Kojigoku
ONSEN
(小地獄温泉館; 500-1 Unzen; admission ¥400; ⊙9am-9pm) A super-rustic wooden public bath, a few minutes' drive or about 15 minutes on foot from the village centre.

Shin-yu
ONSEN
(新湯共同浴場; 320 Unzen; admission ¥100; ⊙9am-11pm, closed Wed) Simple *sentō* (public bath) style with lots of local colour.

Yunosato
ONSEN
(湯の里温泉; 303 Unzen; admission ¥100; ⊙9am-11pm, closed 10th & 20th each month) *Sentō* style, known for its distinctive round stone bathtubs.

KYŪSHŪ UNZEN

Hiking

From the town, popular walks to Kinugasa, Takaiwa-san and Yadake are all situated within the national park. The **Mt Unzen Visitors Centre** (雲仙お山の情報館; ☑73-3636; ⊙9am-7pm 20 Jul-Aug, to 5pm 1 Sep-19 Jul, closed Thu) has displays on volcanoes, flora and fauna, and information in English.

Nearby, via Nita Pass, is **Fugen-dake** (1359m), part of the Unzen-dake range. Its hiking trail has incredible views of the lava flow from the summit. A shared **Heisei Taxi** (☑73-2010; per person each way ¥430) ride takes you to the Nita-tōge parking area, starting point for the Fugen-dake walk. A **cable car** (Ropeway; ☑73-3572; ticket each way ¥610; ⊙8.55am-5.23pm) gets you close to a shrine and the summit of **Myōken-dake** (1333m), from where the hike via **Kunimi-wakare** takes just under two hours return. Walk 3.5km back from the shrine to Nita via the village and valley of Azami-dani.

For a longer excursion (three hours), detour to **Kunimi-dake** (1347m) for a good glimpse of Japan's newest mountain, the smoking lava dome of **Heisei Shinzan** (1483m), created in November 1990, when Fugen-dake blew its stack.

🛏 Sleeping & Eating

Unzen has numerous hotels, *minshuku* and ryokan, with nightly rates from around ¥9500 including dinner and breakfast.

Shirakumo-no-Ike Camping Ground
CAMPGROUND ¥

(白雲の池キャンプ場; ☑73-2543; http://www.dango.ne.jp/unzenvc/camp.html; campsites from ¥400; ⊙27 Apr-6 May & 20 Jul-Sep) This picturesque summertime campground next to Shirakumo Pond is about a 600m walk downhill from the post office, then a few hundred metres from the road. Tent hire is available (¥3000) or you may pitch your own tent (one/two people ¥600/2000).

Unzen Sky Hotel
HOTEL ¥

(雲仙スカイホテル; ☑73-3345; www.unzen-skyhotel.com; r per person with/without 2 meals from ¥8555/5400; P🅿☎) Ignore the exterior and the lobby; the well-maintained rooms (mostly Japanese-style) are a great deal. The *rotemburo* is in an attractive garden.

Unzen Kankō Hotel
HOTEL ¥¥¥

(雲仙観光ホテル; ☑73-3263; www.unzenkanko-hotel.com; s/d & tw from ¥13,860/23,300; P🅿☎@🅿) Designers of this grand 1936 edifice in stone and timber clearly had Yosemite in mind. A destination in itself, it has a charming library, woody billiard room, decadent onsen baths and large, ornate but not overdone rooms with clawfoot tubs. Dinners start at ¥9800.

Kyūshū Hotel
HOTEL ¥¥¥

(九州ホテル; ☑73-3234; www.kyushuhtl.co.jp/language/en; r per person incl 2 meals from ¥16,950; P🅿☎@) Unzen's *jigoku* make a dramatic backdrop for this five-storey, mid-century property, updated with plush fabrics and a splash of Zen. There's a variety of tempting room types (Japanese and Western, some with open-air baths and balconies), lovely indoor-outdoor common baths, East-West meals, and rates sometimes lower if you just walk in.

ℹ Getting There & Away

Three buses run daily between Nagasaki and Unzen (¥1900, one hour and 40 minutes). Unzen is also a stop on the more frequent bus route from Shimabara (¥730, 45 minutes) to Isahaya (¥1300, one hour and 20 minutes), with train connections to Nagasaki (¥450, 35 minutes) and Sasebo (for Hirado; ¥1250, 1¼ hours).

Shimabara   島原

☑0957 / POP 48,815

This relaxed castle town (and ferry gateway to Kumamoto) flows with springs so clear that koi-filled waterways line the street. The springs first appeared following the 1792 eruption of nearby Mt Unzen, and the town still vividly recalls the deadly 1991 eruption, commemorated with a harrowing museum. Other attractions to note include the reconstructed Shimabara castle, a samurai street and a reclining Buddha. The **Tourist Information Office** (島原温泉観光協会; ☑62-3986; Shimokawashiri-machi; ⊙8.30am-5.30pm) is located inside the ferry-terminal bus station.

👁 Sights

★ Shimabara-jō
CASTLE

(島原城; ☑62-4766; ⊙9am-5pm) Built between 1618 and 1625, the five-storey, hilltop Shimabara Castle was ruled mostly by the Matsudaira Clan since the 1660s, played a part in the Shimabara Rebellion and was rebuilt in 1964. Amid carp ponds, tangled gardens, almost 4km of mossy walls, picturesque pines and staff dressed in period costumes, the grounds house four **museums** (combined admission adult/child ¥520/260). Most notable is the main castle, displaying arms, armour and items relating to the Christian uprising with English explanations; and **Seibō Kinenkan** (西望記念館), dedicated to the work of native son Kitamura Seibō, sculptor of the Nagasaki Peace Statue.

Samurai Houses
NOTABLE BUILDINGS

(武家屋敷) **FREE** In the Teppō-machi area, northwest of the castle, are *bukeyashiki* (samurai houses) set along a pretty, 450m-long gravel road with a stream down the middle. Most of the houses are currently inhabited, but three are open to the public.

Nehan-zō
STATUE

(ねはん像) **FREE** In the cemetery of Kōtō-ji Buddhist temple (江東寺) is this tranquil Nirvana statue, dating from 1957. At 8.6m, it's the longest reclining Buddha in Japan.

Gamadas Dome Mt Unzen Disaster Memorial Hall
MUSEUM

(がまだすドーム雲仙岳災害記念館; www.udmh.or.jp; 1-1 Heisei-machi; admission ¥1000; ◎9am-6pm) About 3km south of the town centre, this excellent high-tech museum about the 1991 eruption and vulcanology in general is plonked eerily at the base of the lava flow. Get the free English audio guide, and visit the disturbingly lifelike simulation theatre.

🎊 Festivals & Events

The town's **water festival** is held in early August.

🛏 Sleeping & Eating

Shimabara Youth Hostel
HOSTEL ¥

(島原ユースホステル; ☑62-4451; 7938-3 Shimokawashiri-machi; dm HI member/nonmember ¥2950/3450; 🅿😊) Steps from Shimabara-Gaikō Station, this 10-room hostel looks like a misplaced ski chalet. There are both bunk beds and futons.

Hotel & Spa Hanamizuki
BUSINESS HOTEL ¥¥

(花みずき; ☑62-1000; 548 Nakamachi; s/tw ¥5800/10,000; 🅿😊@) Near Shimabara Station, this kindly 42-room tower has communal baths with wooden tubs (in addition to in-room baths), sauna and Japanese-style breakfast (¥800).

Himematsu-ya
JAPANESE ¥

(姫松屋; ☑63-7272; 1-1208 Jōnai; dishes ¥550-1180, set meals ¥750-2100; ◎10am-8pm; 📖) This polished restaurant across from the castle serves Shimabara's best-known dish, *guzōni*

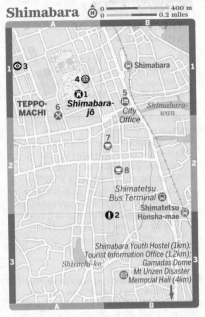

(¥980), a clear broth with *mochi* (pounded rice dumplings), seafood and vegetables. There's more standard Japanese fare too, and Unzen-raised *wagyu* beef goes for ¥1600.

🛈 Getting There & Around

JR trains from Nagasaki to Isahaya (*futsū/tokkyū* ¥450/750, 30/15 minutes) connect with hourly private Shimabara-tetsudō line trains to Shimabara/Shimabara-gaikō Stations (¥1390/1470, one hour), respectively by the castle/port.

KYŪSHŪ SHIMABARA

THE TEAHOUSES OF SHIMABARA

With all the clear water flowing through the town, Shimbara is known for its teahouses. For a quick break, the city-owned former villa **Shimeisō** (四明荘; 2-125 Shinmachi; ⊙9am-5pm) **FREE** sits on stilts over a spring-fed pond and serves tea for free. Off Shimabara's central arcade, the delightful, Meiji-era **Shimabara Mizuyashiki** (しまばら水屋敷; ☑62-8555; www.mizuyashiki.com; 513 Yorozumachi; tea & sweets ¥315-683; ⊙11am-5pm) has a lovely garden, spring-fed pond and collection of *maneki-neko* (lucky cat) figurines from all over Japan, some for sale. The enthusiastic owner has created a detailed walking map of sights and restaurants in town.

Ferries to Kumamoto Port depart frequently from Shimabara Port (7am to 7pm), both fast **Ocean Arrow ferries** (オーシャンアロー; adult/child ¥800/400, 30 minutes) and slower **Seagull ferries** (シーガル; ☑65-4044; adult/child ¥500/250, 45 minutes) and car ferries (adult/child ¥680/340, one hour). From Kumamoto Port, buses take you to the city (¥480, 30 minutes).

Local buses shuttle between Shimabara Station and the port (¥100). Bikes can also be rented at Shimabara-gaikō Station (per hour ¥150).

KUMAMOTO PREFECTURE

Kumamoto-ken (熊本県) is the crossroads of Kyūshū. Chief draws are the city of Kumamoto, whose castle played a key role in Japanese history, and Mt Aso (Aso-san), the gigantic and mysterious volcanic crater at the island's centre.

Kumamoto 熊本

☑096 / POP 730,000

Kumamoto is deeply proud of its castle and greatest landmark, Kumamoto-jō, and the city radiates around it both physically and spiritually. There's a tempting collection of restaurants, bars and shopping around the busy arcades east of the castle. Kumamoto is also the gateway to the Aso-san region, which is fortunate indeed since in summer Kumamoto is one of the warmest cities in Japan.

◉ Sights

Former Hosokawa Gyōbutei NOTABLE BUILDING
(旧細川刑部邸; 3-1 Furukyō-machi; admission with/without castle ¥640/300; ⊙8.30am-5.30pm Apr-Oct, to 4.30pm Nov-Mar) North of the castle, down paths of immaculately raked gravel, is the large villa and garden built for the Hosokawa clan. Inside are displays of furniture and art pieces.

Kumamoto Prefectural Traditional Crafts Centre GALLERY
(熊本県伝統工芸館; 3-35 Chibajō-machi; admission ¥200; ⊙9am-5pm, closed Mon & 28 Dec-4 Jan) Near the prefectural art museum annexe, this large facility displays local Higo inlay, Yamaga lanterns, porcelain and woodcarvings, many for sale in the excellent museum shop (free entry). Sakuranobaba Johsaien (p685) and the **Kumamoto Prefectural Products Centre** (熊本県物産館; NTT Bldg, 3-1 Sakura-machi) also sell craft items (plus food and *shōchū* liquor).

Honmyō-ji TEMPLE
(本妙寺) On the grounds of this sprawling hillside temple complex northwest of the castle, over 150 steps lined with hundreds of lanterns lead to the mausoleum of Katō Kiyomasa (加藤清正公のお墓; 1562–1611), *daimyō* and architect of Kumamoto castle. The mausoleum was designed at the same height as the castle's *tenshūkaku* (central tower). A **treasure house** (宝物館; 4-13-20 Hanazono; admission ¥300; ⊙9am-5pm Sat & Sun) exhibits Kiyomasa's crown and other personal items.

Shimada Museum of Art MUSEUM
(島田美術館; 4-5-28 Shimazaki; admission ¥700; ⊙10am-6pm Thu-Tue) Through the winding backstreets south of Honmyō-ji (about 20 minutes on foot), this quiet museum displays the calligraphy and scrolls of Miyamoto Musashi (1584–1645), samurai, artist and strategist. Current artists' work is on display in adjoining galleries.

Lafcadio Hearn's House HISTORIC BUILDING
(小泉八雲熊本旧居; 2-6 Ansei-machi; admission ¥200; ⊙9.30am-4.30pm, closed Mon & 29 Dec-3 Jan) Irish-Greek immigrant Lafcadio Hearn (aka Koizumi Yakumo; 1850–1904) became one of the foremost interpreters of Japanese culture to the outside world (see p463). He lived in town from 1891 to 1894, in this house dating from 1877.

Sōseki Memorial Hall　　　HISTORIC BUILDING

(夏目漱石内坪井旧居; 4-22 Tsuboi-machi; admission ¥200; ☺ 9.30am-4.30pm, closed Mon) Meiji-era novelist Natsume Sōseki (1867–1916) is honoured at the pretty 1870s home where he lived during his four years teaching English in Kumamoto. The home has some fine architectural details, and in the garden you can stroll in the master's footsteps. It's about a 100m walk west of the river, Tsuboi-gawa.

Suizenji Park　　　GARDENS

(水前寺公園; Suizenji-kōen; www.suizenji.or.jp; 8-1 Suizenji-kōen; admission ¥400; Kokindenju-no-ma Teahouse tea & Hosokawa sweets ¥500-600; ☺ 7.30am-6pm Mar-Nov, 8.30am-5pm Dec-Feb) Southeast of the city centre, this photogenic lakeside garden represents the 53 stations of the Tōkaidō (the old road that linked Tokyo and Kyoto). The miniature Mt Fuji is instantly recognisable, though much of the rest of the analogy is often lost in translation.

🎎 Festivals & Events

Takigi Nō　　　TRADITIONAL

Traditional performances at Suizenji-kōen take place by torchlight on the first Saturday in August (from 6pm).

Hi-no-kuni Festival　　　TRADITIONAL

Kumamoto lights up with fireworks and dancing for the Land of Fire Festival in mid-August.

Autumn Festival　　　TRADITIONAL

From mid-October to early November, Kumamoto-jō stages its grand festival, including *taiko* drumming and cultural events.

🛏 Sleeping

Youth PIA Kumamoto　　　HOSTEL ¥

(ユースピア熊本[熊本県青年会館]; ☎ 381-6221; www.ks-kaikan.com; 3-17-15 Suizenji; dm HI member ¥3150, nonmember ¥3780-4515; P ☺ @) Away from the town centre, seven minutes' walk from JR Suizen-ji Station, this institutional-style hostel has dorms and private rooms (Japanese and Western style) and a 10pm curfew. A simple restaurant serves *shokudō* standards.

Minshuku Kajita　　　INN ¥

(民宿梶田; kajita@titan.ocn.ne.jp; 1-2-7 Shinmachi; s/d without bathroom ¥3800/7000; ☺ @) This 10-room, wooden inn is ageing but clean, quiet, friendly and around the back of the castle. Breakfast/dinner is available from ¥700/2000. The catch: hard to find. Ask the owners to pick you up from Kumamoto Station.

DON'T MISS

KUMAMOTO CASTLE

Dominating the skyline, Kumamoto's robust **castle** (熊本城; Kumamoto-jō; admission ¥500; ☺ 8.30am-6pm Apr-Oct, to 5pm Nov-Mar) is one of Japan's best, built in 1601–07 by *daimyō* Katō Kiyomasa, whose likeness is inescapable around the castle (look for the distinctive tall pointed hat). From 1632, it was the seat of the powerful Hosokawa clan.

Although it's a reconstruction, it's unique in that the original building was destroyed honourably, in a battle among Japanese, rather than dismantling by shōgunal decree or imperial edict, or WWII bombings.

Historically, Kumamoto-jō is best known as the scene of the story of the last samurai (see p775). During the 1877 Satsuma Rebellion, rebels against the new imperial order held out for a 50-day siege here before the castle was burned, leaving the Meiji government to rule unfettered.

The castle's massive curved stone walls, 5.3km in circumference, are crammed with 13 photogenic buildings, turrets, keeps and the soaring black **Tenshūkaku** (main building, 29.5m tall), today a historical museum with 6th-storey lookouts. Next door, the 2008 reconstruction of the **Honmaru Palace** (Honmaru Goten) fairly gleams with fresh wood and gold leaf paintings, particularly in the **Sho-kun-no-ma** receiving room. Free castle tours are offered in English; call ☎ 322-5900 to check availability.

Within the castle walls, the **Kumamoto Prefectural Museum of Art** (熊本県立美術館; 2 Ninomaru; admission ¥260; ☺ 9.30am-4.30pm, closed Mon & 25 Dec-4 Jan) has ancient Buddhist sculptures and modern paintings. Across the castle park, the museum's postmodern **Chibajo Annexe** (2-18 Chibajō-machi; ☺ 9.30am-6.30pm, closed Mon & 25 Dec-4 Jan) **FREE**, built in 1992 by the Spanish architects Elias Torres and José Antonio Martínez-Lapeña, is an architectural landmark.

Central Kumamoto

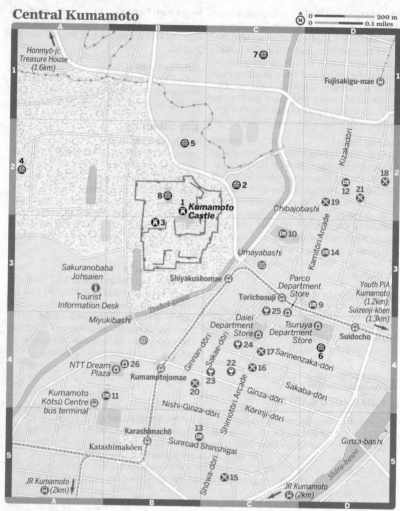

★ **Kumamoto Hotel Castle**   HOTEL ¥¥
(熊本ホテルキャッスル; ☎ 326-3311; www.hotel-castle.co.jp; 4-2 Jōtō-machi; s/d/tw from ¥9817/17,315/18,480, Japanese-style r ¥34,650; P ⊛ @) Overlooking the castle, this upmarket hotel has professional, friendly staff (who wear Hawaiian shirts in the hot summers), a beamed ceiling inspired by its namesake, and rooms with slick renovations in muted browns and whites. Request a castle-view room.

Maruko Hotel   RYOKAN ¥¥
(丸小ホテル; ☎ 353-1241; www.maruko-hotel.jp; 11-10 Kamidōri-machi; r per person with/without 2 meals from ¥12,600/6300; @) Kindly, old-school Japanese-style rooms, a top-storey *o-furo* (common bath) and tiny ceramic *rotemburo* and some English-speaking staff, just outside the covered arcade.

JR Kyūshū
Hotel Kumamoto   BUSINESS HOTEL ¥¥
(JR九州ホテル熊本; ☎ 354-8000; www.jrhotel-group.com/eng/hotel/eng150.htm; 3-15-15 Kasuga; s/tw ¥6900/12,600; P ⊛ @) The best stay among the hotels around JR Kumamoto Station, this 150-room tower has a comfortably contemporary design, some English-

Central Kumamoto

speaking staff and larger-than-usual rooms for a business hotel. Thick-paned glass minimises train noise, but request a room away from the tracks if sensitive.

Kumamoto Kōtsū Centre Hotel
BUSINESS HOTEL ¥¥
(熊本交通センターホテル; ☑326-8828; www.kyusanko.co.jp/hotel; 3-10 Sakuramachi; s/tw from ¥7800/13,000; ℗ ❷ @ 🛜) In a prime location above the main bus terminal, this hotel has a mid-century Japanese look and pleasant staff. Look for discounted rates online or by phone. An extra ¥800 gets you a large breakfast buffet.

Wasuki
HOTEL ¥¥
(和数奇; ☑352-5101; www.wasuki.jp; 7-35 Kamitōri-machi; s/d/tw from ¥8400/12,600/16,800; ℗ @ 🛜) A mid-20th-century building redone in the style of Kumamoto Castle. It has a charcoal exterior, white plaster, dark beams and brooding *tansu*-style furniture in generously sized rooms, most combining tatami, hardwood floors and Western-style bedding. So what if the water pressure is a bit weak and the doorways a bit low? It's well located for eating and nightlife, and has common baths on the top floor (plus in-room facilities).

Richmond Hotel Kumamoto Shinshigai
HOTEL ¥¥¥
(リッチモンドホテル熊本新市街; ☑312-3511; www.richmondhotel.jp; 6-16 Shinshigai; s/d/tw from ¥13,000/19,000/23,000; ❷ @ 🛜) There's

no view to speak of, but you can't beat the location or the standard of this crisp hotel near the south end of the Shimotōri Arcade, with great-looking rooms in blonde woods and chocolate browns, and some English-speaking staff. Breakfast (¥800) features local specialities. Look for discounted rates online.

Hotel Nikko Kumamoto
HOTEL ¥¥¥
(ホテル日航熊本; ☑211-1111; www.nikko-kumamoto.co.jp; 2-1 Kamitōri-chō; s/d/tw from ¥17,325/46,200/31,185; ℗ ❷ @ 🛜) The classic Japanese hotel experience, Kumamoto's premier hotel offers staff in crisp uniforms, fine-grained woods, soothing marble, and spacious rooms with big bathrooms and views to the castle or Aso-san.

✖ Eating

The Kamitōri and Shimotōri arcades and surrounding lanes are happy grazing grounds for Japanese and foreign cuisines, from gourmet extravaganzas to fast food. Kumamoto is famous for *karashi-renkon* (fried lotus root with mustard) and *Higo-gyū* (Higo beef) and the Chinese-inspired *taipien*, bean vermicelli soup with seafood and vegetables. However, the most popular dish seems to be *basashi* (raw horsemeat). Other menus include whale meat (*kujira*; 鯨), which we hope you'll avoid.

To sample many foods in one place, visit **Sakuranobaba Johsaien** (桜の馬場城彩

苑), a tourist complex near the castle, with many stalls and restaurants serving local specialities.

Ramen Komurasaki
RĀMEN ¥

(熊本ラーメンこむらさき; ☑ 325-8972; 8-16 Kamidōri; rāmen ¥550-1000; ⊙ 11am-10pm, closed Mon; 🔊) This popular and fast *rāmen* joint is next to Yoshinoya near the north end of the Kamitōri Arcade. The signature 'king *rāmen'* (¥600) is garlicky, cloudy Kumamoto-style *tonkotsu* (pork) broth with bamboo shoots, julienned mushrooms and *chashū* (roast pork) so lean you'd think it had been working out.

Chocolat
CAFE, FRENCH ¥

(ショコラ; ☑ 355-3157; 2-5-10 Shimotōri; crêpes ¥650-1000; ⊙ noon-11pm, closed Mon) A couple of blocks south of the Shimotōri Arcade, amid sidestreets reminiscent of Tokyo's trendy Omote-Sando, this charming shop has mottled walls like a Parisian boudoir and specialises in sweet and savoury crêpes like ham, cheese and vegetables. Galettes are crêpes made with soba flour. There's no English menu (only French or Japanese), but staff are eager to please.

★ Kome no Kura
IZAKAYA

(米の蔵; ☑ 212-5551; 2nd fl, 1-6-27 Shimotōri; dishes ¥250-950; ⊙ dinner; 🔊) This black-walled, quietly chic *izakaya*, with cosy private booths and *hori-kotatsu* (well in the floor for your feet) seating, has a whole menu of share-plates of Kumamoto specialities in addition to more standard fare. *Tsukune* (ground chicken) is served pressed around a bamboo pole. Look for 'dynamic kitchen' on its sign.

★ Yokobachi
IZAKAYA ¥¥

(☑ 351-4581; 11-40 Kaminoura; small plates ¥480-1200; ⊙ 5pm-midnight) It's quiet on this backstreet, but energetic in Yokobachi's leafy courtyard and rangey suite of rooms around an open kitchen. There's no English menu, but standout small plates include spicy *tebasaki* (chicken wings), an inventive Caesar salad with sweet potato and lotus root chips, delicately fried *mābō-nasu* (eggplant in spicy meat sauce) and, if you dare, *basashi* (¥1200). There are about a dozen *shōchū* liquors to choose from.

Kōran-tei
CHINESE ¥¥

(紅蘭亭; ☑ 352-7177; 5-26 Ansei-machi; meals from ¥750; ⊙ 11.30am-9pm Mon-Sat, 11am-9pm Sun; ⊙ ⊛ 🔊 ⊞) On the 2nd storey above a Swiss pastry shop on the Shimotōri Arcade,

this glossy restaurant has an endless menu. Enjoy the action on the arcade as you tuck into *taipien* ('bean noodle with vegetable' on the English menu; ¥750), daily lunch specials (¥787) or a six-course feast for a mere ¥1575.

Las Margaritas
MEXICAN ¥¥

(ラス・マルガリータス; ☑ 352-7121; 2-20 Minami-Tsuboi-machi; mains ¥550-1500; ⊙ 6pm-midnight, closed Mon) Chef Alex from Mexico City rules at this intimate *cantina* northeast of Kamitōri. Best hits include guacamole, *molcajetes* (hot stone bowls) teeming with chicken, onion, capsicum, chillies and cheese, and tortillas imported all the way from, er, Tokyo. Wash them down with a couple dozen tequila varieties.

Second Sight
INTERNATIONAL ¥¥

(www.s-sight.com; 12-10 Hanahata-chō; per person around ¥2500; ⊙ 11.30am-3am, to 2am Sun) Restaurants in this trendy dining building and date spot include Italian (Giardino), Chinese (Jang Jan Go, dinner only) and Swiss (Konditorei bakery cafe).

🍷 Drinking & Nightlife

The laneways off Shimotōri Arcade and the hip Namikizaka-dōri area at the north end of Kamidōri Arcade are lively after dark.

Sanctuary
CLUB

(サンクチュアリー; ☑ 325-5853; 4-16 Tetori Honmachi; cover ¥0-500) The city's biggest night club is five (count 'em!) storeys of bars, food, darts, billiards, karaoke, dancing, lounges and DJs spinning alt-rock to hip-hop for an international crowd. Food and drinks are cheap (from ¥300), and if there's a cover charge, it includes a drink ticket. Fridays and Saturdays are busiest.

Jeff's World Bar
BAR

(ジェフズワールドバー; 2nd fl, 1-4-3 Shimotōri) Predominantly *gaijin* expats and local Japanese frequent this sometimes friendly, sometimes sleazy 2nd-floor pub with satellite TV, sofas and a good selection of beers. There's dancing some weekends.

Good Time Charlie
BAR

(5th fl, 1-7-24 Shimotōri) Charlie Nagatani earned the rank of Kentucky Colonel for his contributions to the world of country music (he runs the Country Gold Festival near Aso-san), and this bar is his home base. Look for live music, a tiny dance floor and thousands of pictures on the walls.

Days
BAR

(www.rockbar-days.com; 3rd fl SMILE Bldg, 1-7-7 Shimotōri; drinks around ¥600) An incredible cross-genre collection of CDs adorns the wall of this grungy rock bar. Dance if there's space, or make friends at the bar or in comfy chairs.

ℹ️ Information

Visit www.kumamoto-icb.or.jp/english for city information.

Higo Bank (肥後銀行) Currency exchange; also has conveniently located postal ATMs.

Kumamoto City International Centre (熊本市国際交流会館; ☑ 359-2121; 4-18 Hanabata-chō; ⊙ 9am-8pm Mon-Sat, to 7pm Sun & holidays; @ 🕾) Has free 30-minute internet use, BBC news and English-language magazines.

Tourist Information Desks (熊本駅総合観光案内所) Branches at JR Kumamoto Station (熊本駅総合観光案内所; ☑ 352-3743; ⊙ 8.30am-7pm) and Sakuranobaba Johsaien (桜の馬場城彩苑総合観光案内所; ☑ 322-5060; ⊙ 8.30am-5.30pm). Both locations have English-speaking assistants and accommodation listings.

ℹ️ Getting There & Away

Flights connect Aso-Kumamoto Airport with Tokyo (from ¥36,870, 1½ hours) and Osaka (¥23,500, 1¼ hours)

JR Kumamoto Station is an inconvenient few kilometres southwest of the centre (though an easy tram ride). It's a stop on the Kyūshū *shinkansen* with destinations including Kagoshima-Chūō (¥6250, 45 minutes), Fukuoka (Hakata Station; ¥4480, 40 minutes), Hiroshima (¥12,460, 1¾ hours) and Shin-Osaka (¥17,510, 3¼ hours). Flooding in July 2012 washed out tracks on the JR Hōhi line heading east to Beppu; until it is repaired, the fastest way to get to eastern Kyūshū is via Fukuoka.

Highway buses depart from the Kumamoto Kōtsū Centre (熊本交通センター) bus terminal. Routes include Fukuoka (¥2000, two hours), Kagoshima (¥3650, 3½ hours), Nagasaki (¥3600, 3¼ hours) and Miyazaki (¥4500, three hours).

ℹ️ Getting Around

TO/FROM THE AIRPORT

Buses to and from the airport (¥670, 50 minutes) stop at Kumamoto Kōtsū Centre and JR Kumamoto Station.

BUS

City buses are generally hard to manage without Japanese skills, with one exception: the Castle Loop Bus (per ride/day pass ¥130/300) connecting the bus centre with most sights in the castle area at least every half-hour, between 8.30am and 5pm daily.

CAR & MOTORCYCLE

Renting a car is recommended for trips to Aso and beyond, from about ¥5250 per 12 hours. Rental services line the street across from JR Kumamoto Station.

TRAM

Kumamoto's tram service (Shiden) reaches the major sights for ¥150 per ride. One-/two-day passes (¥500/800) can be bought onboard, offer discounted admission to sights and can be used on city buses.

Aso-san Area
阿蘇山

☑ 0967 / POP 30,000

Halfway between Kumamoto and Beppu lies the Aso-san volcanic caldera. It's the world's largest (128km in circumference), so big that it's hard at first to get a sense of its scale, and strikingly beautiful. Formed through a series of eruptions over the past 300,000 years, the current outer crater is about 90,000 years old and now accommodates towns, villages and train lines.

Aso-san is still active, and the summit is frequently off-limits due to toxic gas emissions or wind conditions. Check with the tourist information centre or www.aso.ne.jp/~volcano/eng/ for updates in English.

ℹ️ Orientation

Best explored by car, the region offers fabulous drives, diverse scenery and peaceful retreats. Routes 57, 265 and 325 encircle the outer caldera, and the JR Hōhi line runs across the northern section from Kumamoto. If you're driving, **Daikanbō Lookout** (大観峰) is one of the best places to take it all in, but it's often crowded with tour buses. **Shiroyama Tembōdai** (Yamanami Hwy) is a nice alternative. Aso is the main town, but Takamori, to the south, is more intimate and charming.

⦿ Sights

★ **Aso-gogaku**
MOUNTAINS

(阿蘇五岳) The **Five Mountains of Aso** are the smaller mountains within the outer rim: Eboshi-dake (1337m), Kijima-dake (1321m), Naka-dake (1506m), Neko-dake (1408m), furthest east, and the highest, Taka-dake (1592m).

Naka-dake is the active volcano: *very* active in recent years, with fatal eruptions occurring in 1958 and 1979, and other significant eruptions in 1989, 1990 and 1993.

If **Naka-dake** is behaving, a **cable car** (Ropeway; one-way/round trip ¥600/1000; ⊙ 8.30am-6pm mid-Mar–Oct, 8.30am-5pm Nov,

Aso-san

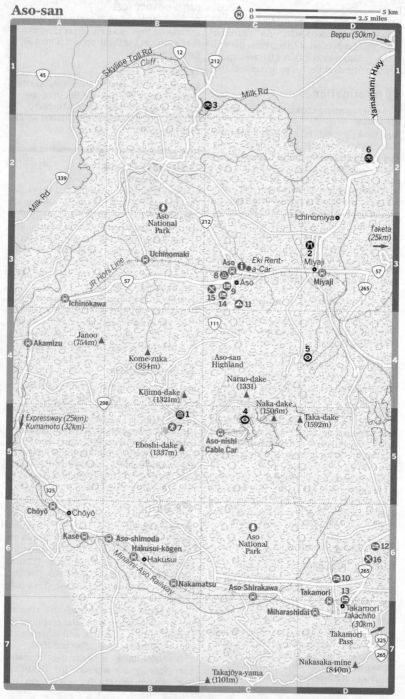

Aso-san

◎ Sights		◉ Sleeping	
1 Aso Volcano Museum	B5	9 Aso Base Backpackers	C3
2 Aso-jinja	D3	10 Bluegrass	D6
3 Daikanbō Lookout	C1	11 Bōchū Kyampu-jo	C3
4 Naka-dake Crater	C5	12 Kyūkamura Minami-Aso	D6
5 Sensui Gorge	D4	13 Murataya Ryokan Youth Hostel	D6
6 Shiroyama Tembōdai Lookout	D2	14 Shukubō Aso	C3
◉ Activities, Courses & Tours		◉ Eating	
7 Kusasenri	B5	15 Sanzoku-Tabiji	C3
8 Yume-no-yu Onsen	C3	16 Takamori Dengaku-no-Sato	D6

9am–5pm Dec–mid-Mar) whisks you up to the crater's edge in just four minutes, or it's ¥600 in tolls and parking if driving yourself. The cable car is 3km from the Aso Volcano Museum. From there, the walk to the top takes less than 30 minutes. The 100m-deep crater, with pale green waters bubbling and steaming below, varies in width from 400m to 1100m, and there's a walk around the southern edge of the crater rim. Arrive early in the morning to glimpse a sea of clouds hovering inside the crater, with Kujū-san (1787m) on the horizon.

Aso Volcano Museum　　　　　　　MUSEUM
(阿蘇火山博物館; ☑34-2111; www.asomuse.jp; 1930-1 Akamizu; admission ¥840, parking per car ¥410; ☺9am-5pm) This unique museum has a real-time video feed from inside the active crater, informative English-language brochures and audio guides (free), and a video presentation of Aso friends showing off.

Opposite the museum, **Kusasenri** (草千里) is a grassy meadow with two 'lakes' in the flattened crater of an ancient volcano. It's postcard-perfect on a clear day. Just off the road from the museum to Aso town is the perfectly shaped cone of **Kome-zuka** (954m), another extinct volcano.

Aso-jinja　　　　　　　　SHINTŌ SHRINE
(阿蘇神社) **FREE** Dedicated to the 12 gods of the mountain, this shrine is about a 1.3km walk north of JR Miyaji Station, and is one of only three shrines in Japan with its original gate. The drinking water here is so delicious that visitors fill canteens to take home.

✦ Activities

From the top of the cable-car run you can **walk** around the crater rim to the peak of Naka-dake and on to Taka-dake. Trails to some of the other higher peaks were badly damaged after flooding in 2012, so ask at tourist information offices before setting out

for **Sensui Gorge** (Sensui-kyō), which blooms with azaleas in mid-May; or between Taka-dake and Neko-dake and on to Miyaji, the next train station east of Aso.

Shorter walks include the easy ascent of Kijima-dake from the Aso Volcano Museum, about 25 minutes to the top. You can then return to the museum or take the branch trail to the Naka-dake ropeway in about 30 minutes. The walk around Kusasenri takes about one hour, and can be combined with a climb to the top of Eboshi-dake (about 80 minutes).

Yume-no-yu Onsen　　　　　　　ONSEN
(阿蘇坊中温泉夢の湯; 1538-3 Kurokawa; admission ¥400; ☺10am-10pm, closed 1st & 3rd Mon of the month) After a long hike, this welcoming onsen, just in front of JR Aso Station, has wonderful indoor and outdoor pools, a large sauna and private 'family' bath (¥1000 per hour).

✦✦ Festivals & Events

A spectacular fire festival, **Hi-furi Matsuri**, is held at Aso-jinja in mid-March.

🛏 Sleeping & Eating

Most accommodation is in Aso or Takamori. Away from the towns, restaurants and lodgings are scattered and hard to reach by public transport. Stocking up on snacks is suggested, and there's a cluster of eateries on Hwy 57 near JR Aso Station.

🏨 Aso Town

Bōchū Kyampu-jo　　　CAMPGROUND ¥
(阿蘇坊中キャンプ場; ☑34-0351; 810 Kurokawa Yoshinokubo; campsites per person ¥500, plus per tent or tarp ¥500; ☺Apr-Oct) Easiest to reach by car, this sprawling campground off the highway en route to the mountain has lovely mountain views, good facilities and tent rentals (from ¥3000) in tube-shaped platform tents. Bathe at the nearby onsen.

Aso Base Backpackers
HOSTEL ¥

(阿蘇ベースバックパッカーズ; ☑34-0408; www.aso-backpackers.com; 1498 Kurokawa; dm/s/ tw/d without bathroom ¥2800/5500/6000/6600; ☺closed mid-Jan–mid-Feb; ℗@☺☎) A quick walk from JR Aso Station, this clean, 30-bed hostel has English-friendly accommodation, a balcony with mountain views, the aroma of cedar in the bedrooms, coin laundry, warm staff, and an excellent local guide to transport and sights. There are showers on-site, and many guests like to bathe in the nearby onsen.

★Shukubō Aso
RYOKAN ¥¥

(宿坊あそ; ☑34-0194; www.aso.ne.jp/syukubo-aso; 1076 Kurokawa; r per person with/without 2 meals from ¥11,000/5000; ℗) This lovely, rustic ryokan in a reconstructed 300-year-old samurai house has modern touches and a tree-lined setting, less than 500m from Aso Station. Its 12 rooms have private toilet and shared bath, and a dinner of local meats and fish is served around an *irori* hearth. It's near pretty Saiganden-ji temple, which dates from AD 726.

Sanzoku-Tabiji
JAPANESE ¥

(山賊旅路; ☑34-2011; 2127-1 Kurokawa; meals ¥650-1500; ☺11am-6.30pm, closed Wed; ☑☺☺) Cute shop known for *dangojiru* (miso soup with thick-cut noodles) and *takana ryōri* (dishes using mustard greens), beneath a ceiling strung with traditional ceramic bells. It's on Hwy 57, opposite the Villa Park Hotel, 10 minutes' walk west from JR Aso Station.

🛏 Takamori

Murataya Ryokan Youth Hostel
HOSTEL ¥

(ユースホステル村田家旅館; ☑62-0066; www13.ocn.ne.jp/~okuaso; 1672 Takamori; dm per person HI member/nonmember ¥2940/3540, ryokan incl 2 meals ¥8000) This 1930s building in central Takamori feels like a private home. Its seven rooms are identical and have shared facilities, but at the ryokan rate you'll have a better grade of services (like laying out of futons) and meals. It's about 800m from the station. At the youth hostel rate, dinner/breakfast cost ¥945/575 extra.

Bluegrass
INN ¥

(ブルーグラス; ☑62-3366; www.aso-bluegrass.com; 2814 Takamori; r per person with/without 2 meals ¥7000/3000; ℗☎) This cowboy ranch house and inn has attractive clean tatami rooms and a Jacuzzi! The restaurant serves burgers, steaks and local cuisine (lunch and dinner from ¥1150, closed 1st and 3rd Wednesday of the month) from a picture menu. It's on Hwy 325, about a 20-minute hike from the station. Look for the US flags.

Kyūkamura Minami-Aso
HOTEL ¥¥

(休暇村南阿蘇; ☑62-2111; www.qkamura.or.jp/ aso; 3219 Takamori; r per person incl 2 meals from ¥9800; ℗☺@☎) This modern, national vacation village is beautifully maintained, and the views of the three main peaks are magnificent. Rates vary by facilities: Japanese or Western room, with or without bath etc, and all have access to onsen and *rotemburo*. It's easiest to reach by car, and crowded in July and August.

★Takamori Dengaku-no-Sato
GRILL ¥¥

(高森田楽の里; ☑62-1899; 2685-2 Ōaza-Takamori; set meals ¥1680-2500; ☺10am-7.30pm; ☺) In this fantastic thatch-roofed former farmhouse, around your own *irori* (hearth) embedded in the floor, staff use oven mitts to grill hot skewers of your choice of sets of vegetables, meat, fish and tofu, some covered in the namesake *dengaku* (sweet miso) paste. Expect too much food, but this is one of the few places we've encountered in Japan that lets you take away leftovers. It's a few minutes by car or taxi (about ¥500) from Takamori Station.

ℹ Information

Next to JR Aso Station, the helpful **Tourist Information Centre** (阿蘇駅道の駅案内所; ☑35-5077; 1440-1 Kurokawa; ☺9am-6pm; ☎) offers free road and hiking maps and local information in English, and coin lockers. A postal ATM is 100m south, across Hwy 57.

ℹ Getting There & Around

Aso is on the JR Hōhi line between Kumamoto (*tokkyū*; ¥1680, 70 minutes) and Ōita; train services to Ōita (connecting to Beppu) were suspended at the time of writing, as some train lines were washed out due to flooding. Some buses from Beppu (¥2950, three hours) continue to the Aso-nishi cable-car station (an extra ¥540).

For Takamori, transfer from the JR Hōhi line at Tateno (¥360, 30 minutes) to the scenic Minami-Aso private line, which terminates at Takamori (¥470, 30 minutes). Buses from Takamori continue southeast to Takachiho (¥1280, 70 minutes, two daily).

Buses operate approximately hourly from JR Aso Station via the volcano museum to Aso-nishi cable-car station (¥540, 40 minutes), stopping at Kusasenri (¥470).

Rent bikes at JR Aso Station (two hours ¥300), or cars at **Eki Rent-a-Car** (駅レンタカー; ☑ 0800-888-4892; www.ekiren.co.jp; per half-/full-day from ¥4720/5790), adjacent to the train station (reserve in advance).

Kurokawa Onsen 黒川温泉

☑ 0967 / POP 302

Along a steep gorge about one hour northeast of Aso Town, tranquil Kurokawa Onsen is one of Japan's prettiest hot-spring villages. Safely secluded from the rest of the world, it's the perfect spot to experience a ryokan.

For day trippers, a *nyūtō tegata* (onsen passport; ¥1200) allows access to three baths from Kurokawa's 24 ryokan (open 8.30am to 9pm). Buy one at the **tourist information desk** (Ryokan Association; 旅館組合; ☑ 44-0076; Kurokawa-sakura-dōri; ⊙ 9am-6pm), and ask which locations are open during your visit. Favourites include Yamamizuki, Kurokawa-sō and Shimmei-kan, with cave baths and riverside *rotemburo* (Kurokawa is especially famous for its *rotemburo*). Many places offer *konyoku* (mixed bathing).

🛌 Sleeping

Kurokawa's onsen ryokan aren't cheap, but this isn't an experience you'll have every day. English is spoken at the two recommended here, which can arrange pick-up from Kurokawa Onsen bus stop.

Chaya-no-Hara Campground CAMPGROUND ¥
(茶屋の原キャンプ所; ☑ 44-0220; 6323 Manganji; campsite per person from ¥600, plus ¥600 per tent) About 5km before Kurokawa Onsen is this place, which is essentially a sloping lush green paddock with inspirational views.

Aso Kujū-Kōgen Youth Hostel HOSTEL ¥
(阿蘇くじゅう高原ユースホステル; ☑ 44-0157; www.asokujuuyh.sakura.ne.jp; 6332 Ogunimachi Senohara; dm HI member/nonmember from ¥2000/2600) About 1km further from Kurokawa Onsen, this friendly hostel has English information about hiking Kujū-san and other high peaks in the area, which can be viewed from the property; there's also a couple of log cabins. Breakfast and dinner (¥500 and ¥1000) are available.

Sanga Ryokan RYOKAN ¥¥
(山河旅館; ☑ 44-0906; www.sanga-ryokan.com; r per person incl 2 meals from ¥13,800; 🅿) Deep in the gorge, about 1.5km from the town centre, this romantic ryokan has 15 deluxe rooms, 15 of which have private onsen at-

tached. Exquisite *kaiseki* meals, attention to detail and heartfelt service make this a place to experience the Japanese art of hospitality.

Okyakuya Ryokan RYOKAN ¥¥
(御客屋旅館; ☑ 44-0454; www.okyakuya.jp; r per person incl 2 meals from ¥13,800; 🅿) At Kurokawa Onsen's oldest ryokan (in its seventh generation of the same family) all 10 rooms have river views, plus sink and toilet, and share common onsen baths; the riverside *rotemburo* is worth it by itself.

ℹ Getting There & Away

Experiencing this area is most enjoyable by car, but several daily buses connect Kurokawa Onsen with Kumamoto/Aso (¥2000/960, 2½ hours/one hour) and a couple continue on to Beppu (¥2900, 2½ hours) via Yufuin (¥2300). Check timetables if you intend to make this a day trip.

KAGOSHIMA PREFECTURE

Shaped like a southward-facing dragon with a pearl in its mouth, Kagoshima-ken (鹿児島県) is mainland Japan's southernmost prefecture, and one of the nation's most beautiful and relaxed. Kagoshima city lies in the shadow of the highly active Sakurajima volcano (the pearl, in the middle of Kinkō-wan), with the fertile coastal plains of the Satsuma Peninsula to the south. To the north is the striking Kirishima-Yaku National Park, with its own string of volcanoes.

SHŌCHŪ

Other Japanese regions are known for their fine sake, but the drink of choice throughout Kyūshū is *shōchū*, a strong distilled liquor (sometimes nicknamed Japanese vodka). Kagoshima-ken claims the highest consumption in Japan, which may well explain why everyone's so friendly! Each prefecture is known for its own particular variety. In Kumamoto, *shōchū* is usually made from rice; in Oita, it's barley, and here it's *imo-jōchū* from sweet potatoes. Drink it straight, with soda or over ice, but the most traditional way is *oyu-wari*, with water heated in a stone pot over glowing coals, until you begin to glow yourself.

Kagoshima 鹿児島

🎵 099 / POP 605.640

Japan's southernmost metropolis, sunny Kagoshima has a personality to match its climate, voted Japan's friendliest city in national polls. Its backdrop is Sakurajima, a very much living volcano *just* across the bay. Unfazed, locals raise their umbrellas against the mountain's recurrent eruptions, when fine ash coats the landscape like snow and obscures the sun like fog – creepy, yet captivating.

ℹ Orientation

Kagoshima spreads north–south beside the bay and has two JR stations, the main one being Kagoshima-Chūō to the south. The centre of the action is about 1km north where the Tenmonkan-dōri shopping arcade crosses the tramlines.

History

For much of its history, the region was called Satsuma province, ruled by the Shimazu clan for a remarkable 700 years. Satsuma's location helped it grow wealthy through trade, particularly with China. Contact was also made with Korea, whose pottery methods were influential in the creation of Satsuma-yaki. St Francis Xavier arrived here in 1549, making Kagoshima (like Nagasaki) one of Japan's earliest gateways to Christianity and the West.

When Japan opened to the world in the mid-19th century, Satsuma's government competed with the shōgunate, engaging in war with Britain and hosting a Satsuma pavilion – independent from the Japanese pavilion – at the 1867 Paris Expo. Satsuma's best known samurai, the complicated and (literally) towering figure of Saigō Takamori, played a key role in the Meiji Restoration. There's a **statue of Saigō Takamori** in central Kagoshima.

◉ Sights & Activities

Sengan-en (Iso-teien) GARDENS
(仙巌園[磯庭園]; ☎ 247-1551; 9700-1 Yoshinochō; admission with/without guided villa tour & tea ceremony ¥1500/1000; ⏱ 8.30am-5.30pm) In 1658, the 19th Shimazu lord laid out this hilly, rambling bayside property of groves, gardens, hillside trails and one of Japan's most

---

ISN'T IT RYŌMANTIC?

Saigō Takamori may be Kyūshū's most famous historical figure, but **Sakamoto Ryōma** (坂本龍馬; 1836–67) is the most beloved. In a 2009 survey of candidates in Japanese national elections, Ryōma was cited as the second-most inspirational political figure (Abraham Lincoln was first). A 2010 historical drama series on NHK TV, *Ryōmaden*, increased his popularity among younger Japanese, as both rebel and romantic hero. Some formative incidents in his life took place here in Kagoshima, and you'll see his dashing likeness all over town, in both sculpture and manga form.

Born to a samurai family on Shikoku, Ryōma grew skilful at both swordsmanship and business. As Japan cracked open to the West with the arrival of the Black Ships in 1853, he became inspired by the American ideal that 'all men are created equal', and thus that Japan needed to end its feudal system. Having lost his enthusiasm for the shōgunate, he quit his samurai post and became a *rōnin* (masterless samurai).

Losing his patron left him poorer but free to live by his own principles. An apocryphal story has Ryōma going to assassinate an official of the Tokugawa regime, but after hearing him out and realising that they shared common goals, they instead became allies, working together to bring change.

In 1864 Ryōma came to Kagoshima and used his negotiation skills to unite the mighty Satsuma and Chōshū clans (of present-day Kagoshima and Yamaguchi Prefectures, respectively) towards unseating the Tokugawa regime.

In 1866, while Ryōma was staying at a Kyoto inn, intruders came to assassinate him, and a bathing chambermaid sprang naked from her tub to warn him. He survived but was injured, and the maid Oryo and Ryōma soon married. At Saigō Takamori's invitation, they went to recuperate in the onsen of Satsuma, on what's said to be Japan's first honeymoon.

Although the Satsuma and Chōshū armies eventually succeeded, Ryōma did not live to see the Meiji Restoration. In 1867 assassins completed the job they had failed the year before, bringing to mind Ryōma's legendary saying, 'Even if you die in a ditch during battle, you should die moving forward'.

THE WONDERS OF SAKURAJIMA

Kagoshima's iconic symbol (which even has its own plush toys), Sakurajima, has been spewing an almost continuous stream of smoke and ash since 1955 and it's not uncommon to have over one thousand (mostly) small eruptions per year. The most violent recent eruption was in 1914, when over three billion tonnes of lava swallowed numerous island villages – over 1000 homes – and joined Sakurajima to the mainland to the southeast.

Despite its volatility, Sakurajima is currently friendly enough to get fairly close. Among the volcano's three peaks, only Minami-dake (South Peak; 1040m) is active. Climbing the mountain is prohibited, but there are several lookout points.

On the mainland, Kagoshima residents speak reverently of Sakurajima. It is said to have *nanatsu-no-iro* (seven colours) visible from across Kinkō-wan, as the light shifts throughout the day on the surface of the mountain.

The volcanic island is best enjoyed by car; the drive around takes a couple of hours, depending on stops. A drive along the tranquil north coast and then inland will lead you to **Yunohira Lookout**, for views of the mountain and back across the bay to central Kagoshima. On the east coast, the top of a once-3m-high **torii** emerges from the volcanic ash at Kurokami, the rest buried in the 1914 eruption.

Before you head off, stop first at the **Sakurajima visitors centre** (⌨293-2443; ⏰9am-5pm), near the ferry terminal, with exhibits about the volcano including a model showing its growth, with English signage.

South of the visitors centre is **Karasujima Observation Point**, where the 1914 lava flow engulfed a small island that had once been 500m offshore. There's now an *ashi-yu* (footbath), Japan's second longest. Continuing along the south coast, **Arimura Lava Observatory** is one of the best places to observe the smoky Minami-dake and the lava flow.

There are several places to stay on the island.

About 650m from the ferry terminal, the large, ageing **Sakurajima Youth Hostel** (fax 293-2150; 189 Yokoyama-chō; P ☺ @) has dorm and Japanese bunk-bed rooms, plus onsen baths with brown waters. Curfew is 10pm.

Adjacent to the ferry terminal, the light-filled **Rainbow Sakurajima Hotel** (⌨293-2323; www.rainbow-sakurajima.com; 1722-16 Yokoyama-chō; d & tw per person incl 2 meals from ¥9285; P ☺) faces the puffing volcano in one direction, and central Kagoshima across the bay in the other. Most rooms are Japanese style. There's an onsen open to the public (¥300) from 10am to 10pm, and a bayside beer garden over summer.

Sakurajima Island View Buses (one-way ¥110-430, day pass ¥500, eight per day, 9am to 5.30pm) loop around Sakurajima. Alternatively, try **Sakurajima Rentacar** (⌨293-2162; 2hr from ¥4500), which also rents out bikes, though biking is not recommended since, if the volcano erupts during your ride, you may find yourself unprotected from breathing noxious fumes.

Frequent passenger and car ferries shuttle around the clock between Kagoshima and Sakurajima (¥150, 15 minutes). Reach the ferry terminal, near the aquarium, via City View Bus or other buses headed for Suizokukan-mae, or by tram to Suizokukan-guchi. The **Yorimichi Cruise** (よりみちクルーズ船; ⌨223-7271; http://sakurajima-ferry.jp; adult/child ¥500/250; ⏰11.05 daily) takes the circuitous route from Kagoshima Port to Sakurajima Port in about 50 minutes. Purchase a regular ferry ticket back from Sakurajima to Kagoshima.

impressive pieces of 'borrowed scenery': the fuming peak of Sakurajima. It was a place of pleasure and a strategically important lookout for ships entering Kinkō-wan.

Allow at least 30 minutes for a leisurely stroll, 20 minutes more to tour the 25-room Goten, a former villa of the Shimazu clan

(traditional tea and sweets provided). Shops around the garden sell *jambo-mochi* (pounded rice cakes on a stick) and Kiriko cut glass.

The adjacent **Shōko Shūseikan** (尚古集成館; admission free with garden ticket; ⏰8.30am-5.15pm) museum once housed Japan's first

Central Kagoshima

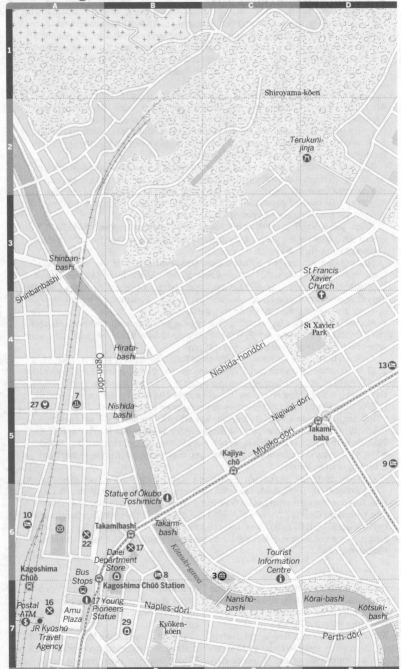

Shiroyama-kōen

Terukuni-jinja

Shinban-bashi

Shinbanbashi

St Francis Xavier Church

St Xavier Park

Ogon-dōri

Hirata-bashi

Nishida-hondōri

13

Nishida-bashi

27

7

Nigiwai-dōri

Takami-baba

Kajiya-chō

Miyako-dōri

9

Statue of Ōkubo Toshimichi

10

Takamibashi

Takami-bashi

Kōtsuki-gawa

22

Daiei Department Store

17

Tourist Information Centre

Kagoshima Chūō

Bus Stops

Kagoshima Chūō Station

8

3

Nanshū-bashi

Kōrai-bashi

Postal ATM

16

17 Young Pioneers Statue

Naples-dōri

Kōtsuki-bashi

Amu Plaza

JR Kyūshū Travel Agency

29

Kyōken-kōen

Perth-dōri

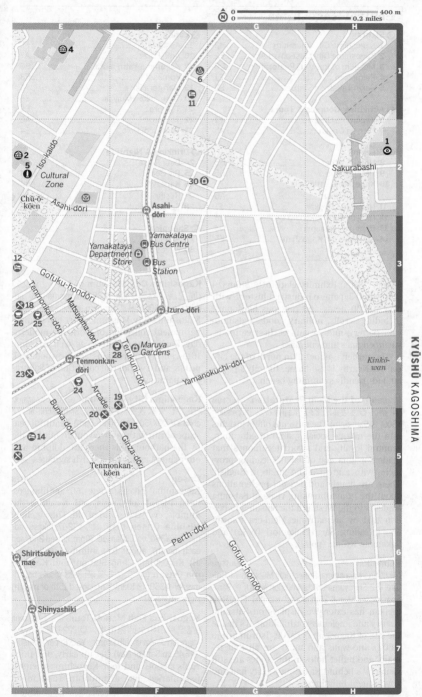

N 0 ——————— 400 m
0 ——————— 0.2 miles

4

6

11

Iso-kaidō

2
5
Cultural
Zone

30

Chū-ō-
kōen

Asahi-dōri

Asahi-
dōri

Yamakataya
Bus Centre

Yamakataya
Department
Store

12

Gofuku-hondōri

Bus
Station

Tenmonkan-dōri

Matsuyama-dōri

Izuro-dōri

18

26 **25**

28

Maruya
Gardens

Terukuni-dōri

Tenmonkan-
dōri

Yamanokuchi-dōri

23

24

Arcade

19

Bunka-dōri

20

15

14

Ginza-dōri

21

Tenmonkan-
kōen

Perth-dōri

Gofuku-hondōri

Shiritsubyōin-
mae

Shinyashiki

Sakurabashi

1

Kinkō-
wan

KYŪSHŪ KAGOSHIMA

Central Kagoshima

factory (1850s). Exhibits relate to the Shimazu family and Japanese industrial history, with over 10,000 items and precious heirlooms, including scrolls, military goods, Satsuma-yaki pottery, and Japan's earliest cannons, steam engines and cut glass.

The garden is about 2km north of the city centre. Nearby is Iso-hama, the city's popular, kid-friendly swimming beach.

Museum of the Meiji Restoration   MUSEUM
(維新ふるさと館; 23-1 Kajiya-chō; admission ¥300; ⊙9am-5pm) The museum offers insights into the unique social system of education, samurai loyalty and sword techniques that made Satsuma one of Japan's leading provinces, with a great audio guide in English. There are hourly audio-visual presentations about the groundbreaking visits of Satsuma students to the West and the Satsuma Rebellion told by animatronic Meiji-era reformers, including Saigō Takamori (p775) and Sakamoto Ryōma (p692).

Reimeikan   MUSEUM
(黎明館; Kagoshima Prefectural Museum of Culture; 7-2 Shiroyama-chō; admission ¥300; ⊙9am-6pm, closed Mon & 25th of each month) The Reimeikan has extensive displays on Satsuma history and ancient swordmaking. It's inside the site of Kagoshima's castle, Tsurumaru-jō (1602); the walls and moat are all that remain, and bullet holes in the stones are still visible. It's behind Kagoshima's city hall and government buildings.

Kagoshima City Museum of Art   MUSEUM
(鹿児島市立美術館; 4-36 Shiroyama-chō; admission ¥300; ⊙9.30am-6pm, closed Mon) The Kagoshima City Museum of Art has a small, permanent collection of works by modern-day Kagoshima painters, as well as some 16th-century porcelains and woodblock prints, and a wonderful collection of Sakurajima paintings.

Kagoshima City Aquarium   AQUARIUM
(かごしま水族館; 3-1 Honkō Shinmachi; adult/child ¥1500/750; ⊙9.30am-6pm) Beautiful seascapes brim with your favourite marine life by the harbour, plus there are dolphin and otter shows and great English signage.

Onsen   ONSEN
Kagoshima boasts some 50 bathhouses, most meant for locals and recalling the humble, everyday *sentō* of old. They include **Nishida Onsen** (西田温泉; 12-17 Takasu; admission ¥360; ⊙5.30am-10.30pm, closed 2nd Mon each month), about five minutes' walk from JR Kagoshima-Chūō Station; and **Kagomma Onsen** (かごつま温泉; 3-28 Yasui-chō; admission ¥360; ⊙10am-1am, closed 15th of month) near city hall.

Kagoshima Fish Market Tour   TOUR
(鹿児島市中央卸売市場; ☑222-0180; www.kagoshimasakanaichiba.com; ¥800 per person; ⊙6.45am Sat Apr-Nov) Get up early, don thick rubber boots and tour Kagoshima's central fish market, like a miniature (and much more accessible) version of Tokyo's Tsukiji

Market. Pick-up is offered from many hotels in town. Reserve well in advance if you'll need English translation. After the tour (about 8am), tour guides can introduce you to restaurants in the market for a sushi breakfast (from about ¥1000).

🎏 Festivals & Events

Sogadon-no-Kasayaki TRADITIONAL
One of Kagoshima's more unusual events is the Umbrella Burning Festival in late July. Boys burn umbrellas on the banks of Kōtsuki-gawa in honour of two brothers who used umbrellas as torches in one of Japan's oldest revenge stories.

Isle of Fire Festival TRADITIONAL
Held in late July on Sakurajima.

Ohara Festival DANCE
A festival featuring folk dancing in the streets on 3 November; visitors are invited to join in.

🛏 Sleeping

Kagoshima has plenty of good-value places to sleep. The station is a bit far from the action, so aim to stay towards Tenmonkan.

Kagoshima Little Asia Guesthouse HOSTEL ¥
(鹿児島リトルアジア; ☎251-8166; www.cheaphotelasia.com; 2-20-8 Nishida; dm/s/tw ¥1500/2500/4000; ❀@🛜; ⛩ JR Kagoshima-Chūō) Good luck finding cheaper accommodation anywhere in Japan. This very basic but clean, chill and friendly hostel is a stone's throw from the station. Private rooms have air-con and TV, there's a free washing machine, and bikes rent for ¥500 per day.

Nakazono Ryokan RYOKAN ¥
(中薗旅館; ☎226-5125; 1-18 Yasui-chō; s/d/tr without bathroom ¥4200/8400/11,970; ❀@🛜; ⛩ Shiyakusho-mae) Creaky, kindly and over half a century old, this friendly Japanese Inn Group member will give you a taste of Kagoshima hospitality. Plus, it's filled with the personality of its keeper. Baths are down the hall. Look for the sign in English, near the footpath across from city hall.

Sun Days Inn Kagoshima BUSINESS HOTEL ¥
(サンデイズイン鹿児島; ☎227-5151; www.sundaysinn.com; 9-8 Yamanokuchi-chō; s/tw ¥5400/8900; Ⓟ❀@🛜; ⛩ Tenmonkan-dōri) Good value at the heart of Tenmonkan. Rooms are compact, but the beds, showers and warm decor make up for it, and the hotspots are steps away. Rates are cheaper

booked online (in Japanese). The breakfast buffet (some 30 choices including local specialities) is a bargain at ¥500.

Hotel Gasthof HOTEL ¥
(ホテルガストフ; ☎252-1401; www.gasthof.jp; 7-1 Chūō-chō; s/d & tw/tr ¥5500/8900/12,600; Ⓟ❀@🛜; ⛩ JR Kagoshima-chuō) Old-world Europe meets urban Japan at this unusual 48-room hotel, with good-sized rooms, hardwood paneling and stone- and brick-wall motifs. Near the station and with triple and interconnecting rooms, it's a good choice for families.

★ Onsen Hotel Nakahara Bessō HOTEL ¥¥
(温泉ホテル中原別荘; ☎225-2800; www.nakahara-bessou.co.jp; 15-19 Terukuni-chō; r per person with/without 2 meals from ¥12,600/8400; Ⓟ@; ⛩ Tenmonkan-dōri) Just outside Tenmonkan and across from a park, this family-owned inn traces its history to 1904. Ignore its boxy exterior; inside are a modern *rotemburo*, spacious Japanese-style rooms with private bath, traditional artwork and a good *Satsuma-ryōri* restaurant.

Hotel Lexton HOTEL ¥¥
(ホテル・レクストン鹿児島; ☎222-0505; www.nisikawa.net/lexton/english; 4-20 Yamanokuchi-chō; s/d/tw from ¥7900/12,800/13,800; Ⓟ❀@; ⛩ Tenmonkan-dōri) Popular with wedding parties, this smart 155-room hotel in Tenmonkan was recently refurbished with a minimalist design and occasional Japanese touches like *ranma* (carved wooden panels). Decent-sized rooms encircle a light-filled atrium.

Remm Kagoshima HOTEL ¥¥
(レム鹿児島; ☎224-0606; www.hankyu-hotel.com; 1-32 Higashi-sengoku-chō; s/d/tw from ¥9450/12,075/13,650; ❀@✉; ⛩ Tenmonkan-dōri) At this new hotel in Tenmonkan, rooms are business-hotel sized but futuristic in style and amenities: custom-designed beds, fluffy white duvets, massage chairs, rain showers and glass windows in the bathrooms for natural light (and, thoughtfully, curtains). The public spaces' ageless design incorporates ancient stones and hardwoods, and it's worth springing for the extensive breakfast buffet (¥1000) in Minohachi restaurant.

🍴 Eating

Kagoshima's regional cuisine, *Satsuma-ryōri,* is prized for dishes like *kurobuta* shabu-shabu (black pork hotpot), *tonkotsu* (pork ribs) seasoned with miso and brown sugar, *kurodori* (black chicken), *katsuo* (bonito, locally called *buen*) and *Satsuma-age* (deep-fried fish cake). Other produce includes *Satsuma-imo* (purple sweet potatoes) and *Satsuma-mikan* (oranges).

JR Kagoshima-Chūō Station area, the backstreets of Tenmonkan and the Dolphin Port shopping centre near the ferry terminals all abound with restaurants. Local friends will think you're really in the know if you venture into the narrow lanes of the Meizanbori neighbourhood southeast of City Hall, crammed with tiny, yet often chic purveyors of everything from *yakitori* and curry rice to French and Spanish cuisine.

★ Yamauchi Nōjō — IZAKAYA ¥

(山内農場; ☑ 223-7488; 2nd fl, 1-26 Higashi-sengoku-chō; dishes ¥390-1250; ⊙ 5pm-midnight Sun, until 2am Mon-Thu, until 3am Fri & Sat; ⃣ Tenmonkan-dōri) *Kuro Satsuma-dori* (black Satauma chicken) is the name of bird served here, and also what it looks like after being grilled *sumibi-yaki* style over open charcoal. Other local dishes: marinated *katsuo* (bonito) sashimi (¥770), *kurobuta* (black pork) salad (¥680) and *tsukune* (chicken meatballs; ¥490) with cheese or raw egg. Decor is modern meets rustic. Enter around the corner from Remm Kagoshima Hotel.

Tenmonkan Mujyaki — SWEETS ¥

(天文館むじゃき; ☑ 222-6904; 5-8 Sennichi-chō; large/small shirokuma ¥683/483; ⊙ 11am-10pm, from 10am Jul & Aug & Sat & Sun year-round; ⃣ Tenmonkan-dōri) Slake Kagoshima's steamy summers with highly refreshing *kakigori* (shaved ice with condensed milk, fruits and beans). Go for the *shirokuma*, with toppings arranged to look like its namesake polar bear. Look for the polar bear outside.

Tontoro — RĀMEN ¥

(豚とろ; rāmen dishes from ¥650; ⃣) Tontoro's two locations are local institutions for *rāmen* in thick *tonkotsu* pork broth, finished with scallion (shallots) and a hint of garlic. The branch at **Yamanokuchi** (☑ 222-5857; 9-41 Yamanokuchi; ⊙ 11am-3.30am; ⃣ Tenmonkan-dōri), in the corner house with the red trim, is rather workaday; while the one near JR Kagoshima-Chūō Station, on **Chūō-machi** (☑ 258-9900; 3-3 Chūō-machi; ⊙ 11am-1am; ⃣ JR Kagoshima-Chūō), is more polished.

Marutora Ikka — IZAKAYA ¥

(○虎一家; ☑ 219-3948; 2nd fl, 14-17 Sennichi-chō; dishes from ¥300; ⊙ dinner, closed Mon; ⃣; ⃣ Tenmonkan-dōri) This happy spot is festooned with an eclectic collection of Shōwa-period (1926–89) pop-culture memorabilia, where young Japanese come to hang out over a few rounds of beer and comfort food like bite-sized black pork *hitokuchi-gyōza* (10 pieces for ¥350!). Look for the dark wooden street frontage and staircase leading upstairs, down the block from 7-Eleven.

Kagomma Yatai-mura — FOOD STALLS ¥

(かのつま屋台村; ☑ 255-1588; 6-4 Chūō-chō; prices vary; ⊙ lunch & dinner, individual stall hours vary) Yatai-mura means 'food stall village', and some two dozen stalls near Kagoshima-chūō Station offer a taste of Kagoshima of old. Follow your nose to your favourite stalls for *sumibi-yaki* (coal-fired chicken), sashimi, teppanyaki beef and fish dishes.

Amu Plaza — FAST FOOD

(アミュプラザ鹿児島; ⊜) Amu Plaza at JR Kagoshima-Chūō Station has good seated dining options on the upper floors and a variety of stalls, takeaway and fast food in the basement-level food court.

★ Kumasotei — JAPANESE ¥¥

(熊襲亭; ☑ 222-6356; 6-10 Higashi-Sengoku-chō; set meals lunch/dinner from ¥1500/3000; ⊙ lunch & dinner; 🛜 ⃣; ⃣ Tenmonkan-dōri) This atmospheric multistorey restaurant near central Tenmonkan covers all your *Satsuma-ryōri* needs: *Satsuma-age, tonkotsu, kurobuta* shabu-shabu, and lots of fresh fish and seafood.

Ajimori — JAPANESE ¥¥

(あぢもり; ☑ 224-7634; 13-21 Sennichi-chō; shabu-shabu courses from ¥4200; ⊙ lunch & dinner, closed Tue; ⃣; ⃣ Tenmonkan-dōri) This classy multistorey shop claims to have invented *kurobuta* shabu-shabu. Set meals come with handmade udon noodles and side dishes depending on the price. There are also *tonkatsu* (deep-fried pork cutlet) meals (from ¥650 at lunchtime, except Sunday). It's just north of the arch with giant eyeglasses on it.

🍷 Drinking & Nightlife

Tenmonkan is where most of the action happens – shot bars, clubs and karaoke boxes. Most dance clubs don't get going until around 11pm and many bars charge admission (average ¥500 to ¥1000).

Kanezyō — CAFE, BAR

(☑ 223-0487; 2nd fl, 7-20 Higashi-sengoku-chō; ⊙ cafe noon-9pm, closed Mon; bar 7pm-2am, closed Sun; ⃣ Tenmonkan-dōri) This chill, cool spot with wood-beamed ceiling and concrete walls hung with Chinese textiles is a great place to sample *shochū*, malt whiskies, cocktails or teas from China and Taiwan.

Recife

BAR

(レシフェ; ☎258-9774; 2-1-5 Takashi; ☺closed Tue; ☒JR Kagoshima-Chūō) Closer to Kagoshima-chūō Station than Tenmonkan, this arty, mellow bar-restaurant also has DJ decks and hosts occasional parties. It's popular with locals and expat groovers, and has Latin-American eats.

Big Ben

PUB

(☎226-4470; Basement, 8-23 Higashi-Sengoku-chō; ☒Tenmonkan-dōri) This basement meeting spot has dozens of beers, footy and memorabilia from around the world, and patrons from – wait for it – around the world. Meals include *kurobuta* burgers and steamed mussels, alongside fish and chips.

Beer Reise

BAR

(ビアライゼ; ☎227-0088; Hirata Bldg, 9-10 Sennichi-chō; ☺5pm-3am; ☒Tenmonkan-dōri) This cheery narrow bar has Guinness and Hoegaarden, a variety of German and Belgian beers, and ¥100-off happy hour from 5pm to 7pm.

Salisbury Pub

BAR

(ソールズベリーパブ; ☎223-2386; 2nd fl, 1-5 Gofuku-chō; ☺6pm-3am, closed Tue; ☒Tenmonkan-dōri) This classy, quiet bar appeals to a 30-something crowd and stocks a good selection of foreign beers and wines and a few single malts. Food is available, but the menu is in Japanese.

🛍 Shopping

Regional specialities include Satsuma Kiriko cut glass, Tsumugi silk, bamboo and wood products, and Satsuma-yaki pottery (most typically in austere black and white). Some are for sale at Sengan-en and the **Kagoshima Brand Shop** (鹿児島ブランドショップ; 1st fl, Sangyo Kaikan bldg, 9-1 Meizan-chō; ☺9am-6pm) near Tenmonkan. Pick up the English-language *A Guide to Kagoshima Products* (free).

Fun shopping experiences include the **Asa-ichi** (朝市; Morning Market; ☺6am-noon Mon-Sat) just south of JR Kagoshima-Chūō Station.

ℹ Information

Tourist information is available on the prefectural site, www.kagoshima-kankou.com/for. The city website (www.city.kagoshima.lg.jp) has detailed info on transit, sights and living in town. For sightseeing info and arts and entertainment listings, see www.kic-update.com.

Central Post Office (鹿児島中央郵便局) near JR Kagoshima-Chūō Station has an ATM.

Tourist Information Centre (鹿児島中央駅総合観光案内所; ☎253-2500; inside JR Kagoshima-Chūō Station; ☺8.30am-7pm) Has plenty of information in English and the handy *Kagoshima* visitor's guide. Near the Museum of the Meiji Restoration, the Tourism Exchange Centre (観光交流センター; ☎298-5111; 1-1 Uenosono-chō; ☺9am-7pm) has pamphlets and can make hotel reservations.

JR Kyūshū Travel Agency (JR九州旅行鹿児島支店; ☎253-2201; inside JR Kagoshima-Chūō Station; ☺10am-7pm Mon-Sat, 10am-6pm Sun) Can assist with domestic travel bookings.

ℹ Getting There & Away

AIR

Kagoshima Airport has connections to Shanghai and Seoul, and convenient domestic flights include to Tokyo (¥36,770, 1¾ hours), Osaka (¥25,400, 1¼ hours) and Okinawa (Naha; ¥25,400, 85 minutes).

BOAT

Ferries depart from Minami-futō pier to Yakushima (jetfoil ¥7700, one hour and 45 minutes; regular ferry ¥4600, four hours). From Kagoshima Shin-kō (Kagoshima New Port), **Queen Coral Marix Line** (☎225-1551) has ferries to Naha (Okinawa) via the Amami archipelago (¥14,800, 25 hours)

KYŪSHŪ KAGOSHIMA

WORTH A TRIP

UENOHARA JŌMON-NO-MORI

Archaeology enthusiasts will want to detour to this **museum** (上野原縄文の森; ☎0995-48-5701; 1-1 Uenohara Jōmon-no-mori, Kokubu; admission ¥300; ☺9am-5pm, to 7pm Jul & Aug, closed Mon), on the site where the oldest authenticated Jōmon-era pottery shards were discovered during excavations for nearby office parks. Based on these findings, anthropologists began to conclude that the first humans may have come to Japan from the south rather than the north, via canoes or rafts along the Ryūkyū island chain. Look also for a re-created village of Jōmon-era dwellings, demonstrations, tools and artefacts. The museum can be reached by train from Kagoshima to Kokubu, from where it's about 8km by taxi or private car.

BUS

Long-distance buses depart from the Express bus centre located opposite the east exit of Kagoshima-Chūō Station and from streetside stops nearby and near Yamakataya department store in Tenmonkan.

Routes include Miyazaki (¥2700, 2¾ hours), Fukuoka (¥5300, 3¾ hours), Oita (¥5500, 5½ hours), Nagasaki (¥6500, 5½ hours) and overnight to Osaka (¥12,000, 12 hours).

TRAIN

JR Kagoshima-Chūō Station is the terminus of the Kyūshū *shinkansen*, with stops including Kumamoto (¥6960, 45 minutes), Hakata (¥10,370, 1¾ hours), Hiroshima (¥17,200, 2¼ hours) and Shin-Osaka (¥21,800, 3¾ hours). Also stopping at Kagoshima Station, the JR Nippō line goes to Miyazaki (*tokkyū*; ¥4120, two hours) and Beppu (¥9460, five hours).

ⓘ Getting Around

TO/FROM THE AIRPORT

Express buses depart every five to 20 minutes to and from JR Kagoshima-Chūō Station/Tenmonkan (¥1200, one hour/ 55 minutes).

BICYCLE

Bikes can be rented (two hours/day ¥500/1500, 40% discount for JR pass holders) at JR Kagoshima-Chūō Station.

BUS

Hop-on, hop-off City View Buses (¥180, every 30 minutes, 9am to 6.30pm) loop around the major sights in two routes. A one-day pass (¥600) is also valid on trams and city bus lines and offers discounted admission to many attractions. Otherwise, local buses tend to be inconvenient, particularly if you don't speak Japanese (you're better off with trams).

CAR & MOTORCYCLE

Many outlets around JR Kagoshima-Chūō Station rent cars for trips around the region.

ⓘ CUTE TRANSIT CARDS

Visitors with passports can take advantage of the Cute transit card (one/ two days ¥1200/1800) covering city buses (including the City View and Sakurajima Island View buses), trams, Sakurajima ferries and the Yorimichi Cruise. Cardholders can also get 20% discounted admission to many attractions. Pick it up at tourist information offices.

TRAM

If you're doing only a limited amount of sightseeing, trams are the easiest way around town. Route 1 starts from Kagoshima Station and goes through the centre into the suburbs. Route 2 diverges at Takami-baba (高見馬場) to JR Kagoshima-Chūō Station and terminates at Korimoto. Either pay the flat fare (¥160) or buy a one-day travel pass (¥600) from the tourist information centre or onboard.

Kirishima-Yaku National Park 霧島屋久国立公園

This mountainous park straddling northern Kagoshima-ken and western Miyazaki-ken has excellent hikes of many lengths, although lava flows and noxious gases following volcanic activity in January 2011 have dramatically cut back accessibility. The area is known for its wild azaleas, hot springs and the 75m waterfall, **Senriga-taki**.

Monitor the weather before setting out. Thunderstorms and fog are common during the rainy season (mid-May to June); otherwise, the vistas are superb.

◎ Sights

Kirishima-jingū   SHINTŌ SHRINE
(霧島神宮; 2608-5 Kirishima-Taguchi; ⊙24hr) Picturesque, tangerine Kirishima-jingū has a good vantage point. Though the original dates from the 6th century, the present shrine was built in 1715. It is dedicated to Ninigi-no-mikoto, who, according to *Kojiki* (a book compiled in 712), led the gods from the heavens to the Takachiho-no-mine summit. The shrine is accessible by bus (¥240, 15 minutes) from JR Kirishima-jingū Station.

There's a small village with inns and restaurants at the foot of the shrine.

🏃 Activities

The **Ebino-kōgen circuit** is a relaxed 4km stroll around a series of volcanic lakes – **Rokkannon Mi-ike** is intensely cyan in colour. Across the road from the lake, **Fudō-ike**, at the base of Karakuni-dake, is a steaming *jigoku*. The stiffer climb to the 1700m summit of **Karakuni-dake** skirts the edge of the volcano's deep crater before arriving at the high point on the eastern side. The panoramic view southwards is outstanding, taking in the perfectly circular caldera lake of Ōnami-ike, **Shinmoe-dake** (the one that erupted in January 2011; it remains inaccessible) and the perfect cone of **Takachiho-no-mine**. On a clear day, you can see Kagoshima and the smoking cone of Sakurajima. Friendly wild deer roam freely through the town of **Ebino-kōgen** and are happy to be photographed.

Two buses per day connect Kirishima-jingū area with Ebino-kōgen.

🛏 Sleeping & Eating

Lodgings are clustered near Kirishima-jingū or in Ebino-kōgen village, with good accommodation options, but few eateries. Most village shops close by 5pm.

Kirishima Jingū-mae Youth Hostel HOSTEL ¥
(霧島神宮前ユースホステル; ☑0995-57-1188; 2459-83 Kirishima-Taguchi; dm HI member/nonmember ¥3200/3800, minshuku rates per person incl 2 meals ¥7350; ℙ@) A few minutes from Kirishima-jingū, this neat, comfy youth hostel has Japanese rooms and mountain views from its onsen baths. Breakfast/dinner costs ¥500/1000. It also operates as a more expensive *minshuku,* with better meals and amenities.

Minshuku Kirishima-ji MINSHUKU ¥
(民宿きりしま路; ☑0995-57-0272; 2459 Kirishima-Taguchi; r per person with/without 2 meals ¥7350/4500; ℙ) This spartan but friendly eight-room inn, just across the gorge from the shrine, has forest views and shared onsen baths. Day visitors can stop here for a lunch of house-made soba dishes (¥400 to ¥850) including Nagasaki-style *champon.*

Ebino-Kōgen

Campground & Lodge CAMPGROUND ¥
(えびの高原キャンプ村; ☑0984-33-0800; 1470 Ōaza Suenaga; campsites/tent rental/lodge cabins per person from ¥800/1100/1600; ⊙ midwinter closing dates vary; ℙ) A pretty stream runs through the middle of this delightful campground with onsen baths (open 5pm to 8pm), 500m from the Eco-Museum Centre. Rates rise in July and August.

★**Ebino-Kōgen Sō** HOTEL ¥¥
(えびの高原荘; ☑0984-33-0161; www.ebinokogenso.com; 1489 Ōaza Suenaga; r per person incl 2 meals with/without bathroom from ¥10,800/9800; ℙ⊜) This friendly onsen hotel has recently been spiffed up and boasts some excellent new facilities including mountain-view rooms and coin laundry. The lovely *rotemburo* is open to the public from 11.30am to 8pm (¥500), and there's a mixed-bathing bath deep in the forest. The location, near Ebino-Kōgen village, is superb and the res-

> ### ⓘ ERUPTION OF SHINMOE-DAKE
>
> On 26 January 2011, the massive eruption of Shinmoe-dake, in the centre of the mountainous park, shut down roads and air travel and blanketed much of the region in a thick layer of ash. It also left impassible a popular 15km hiking route along the summit of the park's other volcanic peaks: Karakuni-dake (1700m) via Shishiko-dake, Naka-dake and Takachiho-gawara to the summit of Takachiho-no-mine (1574m). Check with local authorities in case of a change of conditions.

taurant makes tasty meals. There's a shuttle bus to JR Kirishima-Jingū and JR Kobayashi Stations; ring ahead to reserve.

ⓘ Information

Nature centres at each end of the volcano walk have bilingual maps and hiking information, and exhibits on local wildlife.

Ebino-kōgen Eco Museum Centre (えびのエコミュージアムセンター; ☑0984-33-3002; ⊙9am-5pm)

Takachiho-gawara Visitors Centre (高千穂河原ビジターセンター; ☑0995-57-2505; ⊙9am-5pm)

ⓘ Getting There & Away

The main train junctions are JR Kobayashi Station, northeast of Ebino Plateau, and Kirishima-Jingū Station to the south.

Satsuma Peninsula
薩摩半島

The peninsula south of Kagoshima city has fine rural scenery, samurai houses, a haunting kamikaze museum and sand baths. While buses operate to Chiran and trains to Ibusuki, renting a car from Kagoshima will save time and hassles. You'll also find wonderful views along Ibusuki Skyline Rd of Kinkō-wan and the main islands' southernmost mountains.

Chiran 知覧

☑0993 / POP 40,391 (MINAMI-KYŪSHŪ CITY)

A river runs through Chiran, 34km south of Kagoshima, parallel to a collection of restored samurai houses. On the town's edge is a fascinating memorial to WWII's kamikaze pilots.

Seven of the mid-Edo period residences along Chiran's 700m street of **samurai houses** (武家屋敷; 6198 Chiran-chō; combined admission to all houses ¥500; ⏱9am-5pm) have gardens open to the public, in which water is usually symbolised by sand, *shirasu* (volcanic ash) or gravel. Allow up to one leisurely hour to view them all.

Just off the samurai street, **Taki-An** (高城庵; ☎83-3186; 6329 Chiran-chō; soba ¥630; ⏱10.30am-4.30pm) is a lovely restaurant in another traditional house where you can sit on tatami and admire the garden over a bowl of hot *soba* (¥630) or Satsuma specialities such as *tonkotsu teishoku* (pork set meal; ¥1575) and Chiran's famous green tea. Picture menu available.

Having tea in the English-style tearoom of **Chiran Eikoku-kan** (知覧英国館; Tea World; ☎83-3963; 13746-4 Chiran-chō; tea from ¥530; ⏱10am-6pm, closed Tue), across the main road from the samurai houses, entitles you to take the tour of the tiny one-room collection of newspaper accounts, photos and memorabilia of the **Anglo-Satsuma Museum**. It commemorates the 1862 war between Britain and Satsuma, which started when British visitors refused to bow to a samurai of the Shimazu clan. Eikoku-kan's Yumefuki loose tea, made with Chiran leaves, has won Britain's Great Taste Award for several years running.

Around 2km west of town, Chiran's air base was the point of departure for 1036 WWII kamikaze pilots *(tokkō)*, the largest percentage in the Japanese military. On its former site, the large, thought-provoking **Kamikaze Peace Museum** (知覧特攻平和会館; ☎83-2525; 17881 Chiran-chō; admission ¥500; ⏱9am-5pm; 🚌Kamon-iriguchi) presents aircraft, mementos and photographs of the fresh-faced young men selected for the Special Attack Corps. It's worth investing in the English-language audio guide (¥100), which harrowingly tells individual pilots' stories.

Kagoshima Kōtsū (鹿児島交通) buses to Chiran (samurai houses/Peace Museum ¥890/930, 80/85 minutes, hourly) run from the Yamakataya bus centre (山形屋バスセンター) in Tenmonkan and JR Kagoshima-Chūō Station. From Chiran, buses run five times daily to Ibusuki (¥940, 65 minutes).

Ibusuki 指宿

☎0993 / POP 44,200

In southeastern Satsuma Peninsula, around 50km from Kagoshima, the hot-spring resort of Ibusuki is quiet, particularly in the low sea-son, and more especially after dark. Ibusuki Station is located about 1km from the beach-front and most accommodation, but the few eateries are near the station. The station **information desk** (指宿観光案内所; ☎22-4114; ⏱9am-6pm) has basic maps and can assist with directions and accommodations.

Wi-fi access is at Ibusuki Information Plaza. Rent bikes at Eki-Rent-a-Car (with/without JR ticket from ¥300/500), adjacent to Ibusuki Station.

⊙ Sights & Activities

Ibusuki's biggest attraction is sand baths, in which onsen steam rises through natural sand, reputedly with blood-cleansing properties.

Ibusuki Sunamushi Kaikan Saraku　　　　　　SAND BATH
(いぶすき砂むし会館「砂楽」; ☎23-3900; 5-25-18 Yunohama; admission ¥900; ⏱8.30am-9pm, closed noon-1pm Mon-Fri) Pay at the entrance, change into the provided *yukata* and wander down to the beach where, under a canopy of bamboo slat blinds, women with shovels bury you in hot volcanic sand. Reactions range from panic to euphoria. It's said that 10 minutes will get rid of impurities, but many stay longer. When you're through, head back up to soak in the onsen.

Yaji-ga-yu　　　　　　　　　　　　SENTŌ
(弥次ヶ湯; 1068 Jūcchō; admission ¥270; ⏱7am-9pm, closed 2nd & 4th Thu) There's loads of atmosphere in this historic wooden *sentō* (1892) away from the town centre, so old it has no showers; you wash by dipping buckets in the tub.

Yoshi-no-yu　　　　　　　　　　　　SENTŌ
(吉乃湯; 4-2-41 Yunohama; admission ¥300; ⏱2-9pm, closed Thu) Up-to-date *sentō* with a pretty *rotemburo* in a garden.

🛏 Sleeping & Eating

Tamaya Youth Hostel　　　　　　　HOSTEL ¥
(圭屋ユースホステル; ☎22-3553; 5-27-8 Yunohama; dm incl 2 meals/breakfast/no meals ¥4140/3195/2725; ⏱@🛜) This 25-bed, three-storey hostel is rather plain, but it's located diagonally across from the sand baths and has kayaks for rent in summer. There's both Japanese- and Western-style bedding.

Tsukimi-sō　　　　　　　　　　　RYOKAN ¥¥
(月見荘; ☎22-4221; www.tsukimi.jp; 5-24-8 Yunohama; r per person with 2 meals from ¥12,750; 🅿🛜) Rooms at this spotless seven-room

ryokan across from the sand baths have private facilities, in addition to pretty indoor and outdoor baths and meals featuring *Satsuma-ryōri* such as *tonkotsu* and sashimi. There's not much English spoken, but amenable staff make it work.

Ryokan Ginshō
RYOKAN ¥¥

(旅館吟松; ☑ 22-3231; www.ginsyou.co.jp; 5-26-27 Yunohama; r per person incl 2 meals from ¥15,750; P@⌂) The exquisite 2nd- and 9th-floor *rotemburo* of this upmarket beachfront ryokan have broad views and a lovely relaxation garden. Ocean-facing rooms start from ¥17,850 and rooms with baths on the balcony are available. There's an onsen vent right in your dinner table, as genteel servers cook *Satsuma-age* before your eyes.

★ Hakusuikan
HOTEL ¥¥¥

(白水館; ☑ 22-3131; www.hakusuikan.co.jp/en/; 12126-12 Higashi-kata; r per person incl 2 meals from ¥15,900; P@⌂) Visiting dignitaries might stay in one of the stratospheric-priced rooms in the sumptuous, 41-room Rikyū wing, but we of more modest means can splurge on the less expensive of its 205 rooms. The opulent onsen/*rotemburo*/sand baths are worth the stay by themselves. The Fenice restaurant in the Denshōkan building is as tasty as it is attractive.

Iwasaki Hotel
HOTEL ¥¥¥

(いわさきホテル; ☑ 22-2131; http://ibusuki.iwasakihotels.com/en; 3775 Jūni-chō; tw from ¥15,015; P⌂⌂⌂) Straight out of 1980s Hawaii, this kid-friendly pink tower has a putting green, onsen, pools and acres of lush, palm-filled gardens. Even if decor is showing its age, all rooms face the ocean and have balconies, and there are sports equipment rentals including bikes and tennis courts. Sand baths cost ¥1050. Look for evening Hawaiian dance shows in summer.

Aoba
IZAKAYA ¥

(青葉; ☑ 22-3356; 1-2-11 Minato; dishes from ¥480; ⌚ lunch & dinner, closed Wed) Behind the yellow *noren* (door curtain) a minute's walk left of the station, this cheery shop serves satisfying *kurobuta rōsukatsu* (black pork cutlet) *teishoku* (¥1360) or, if you dare, *Satsuma jidori sashimi* (raw sliced chicken; ¥980). Picture menu available.

ⓘ Getting There & Around

Ibusuki is about 1¾ hours from Kagoshima by bus (¥930) or about half that by train (*kyūko/tokkyū* ¥970/2070, 55/50 minutes). Train geeks

SATSUMA DENSHŌKAN

The **Satsuma Denshōkan** (薩摩伝承館; www.satsuma-denshokan.com; 12131-4 Higashikata; admission ¥1500; ⌚9am-6pm) museum is the prefecture's – if not Kyūshū's – most striking, offering a history of the Satsuma region, plus jaw-dropping displays of Chinese ceramics and gleaming, golden Satsuma-yaki, in a temple-style building that seems to float on its own lake. There's an English-language audio guide. It's about 3.5km (taxi ¥1000, 10 minutes) from Ibusuki Station, on the grounds of the Haku-suikan onsen hotel.

and sightseers will love the second wood-panelled Ibutama *tokkyū* with specially angled seats for breathtaking bay views. Rent bikes from Eki Rent-a-Car (from ¥300/500 for JR ticket holders/nonticket holders) and there are car-rental locations near the station.

Around Satsuma Peninsula

Ikeda-kō is a volcanic caldera lake west of Ibusuki, inhabited by giant eels kept in tanks by the parking lot. South of the lake is **Cape Nagasaki-bana**, from where you can see offshore islands on a clear day.

In a gorge near Ikeda-kō, **Tōsenkyō Sōmen Nagashi** (唐船峡そうめん流し; ☑ 32-2143; 5967 Jūchō; sōmen ¥550; ⌚9.30am-5pm, later in summer) is a pilgrimage for many Japanese (an estimated 200,000 annual visitors) as the 1967 birthplace of *nagashi-sōmen* (flowing noodles). *Sōmen* (vermicelli) spin around tyre-shaped tabletop tanks of swiftly flowing 13°C water; catch the noodles with chopsticks and dip in sauce to eat. It's fun, and ultra-refreshing on hot days. *Teishoku* (from ¥1300) come with *onigiri* (rice balls), miso soup and grilled *masu* (trout).

The beautifully symmetrical 924m cone of **Kaimon-dake**, nicknamed 'Satsuma Fuji', dominates the southern skyline and can be climbed in two hours. An early start may reward you with views of Sakurajima, Cape Sata, and Yakushima and Tanegashima islands.

At the southwestern end of the peninsula, about one hour from Ibusuki, is **Makurazaki**, a port famous for *katsuo* (bonito). By the port, the workmanlike **Sakana Centre** has

CAPE SATA

Collectors of 'mosts' will want to journey around Kinkō-wan to Cape Sata (佐多岬, Sata-misaki), southernmost point in the Japanese main islands, at the tip of the Ōsumi Peninsula and site of Japan's oldest lighthouse. **Sata-Day-Go Boats** (さたでい号; ☑0994-27-3355; Sata-Misaki; 30min tours adult/child ¥2000/1000) offer day cruises to see coral, sea turtles, *fugu* (pufferfish), dolphins and sharks. Cape Sata is best reached by car.

a dozen or so vendors, souvenir shops and a simple restaurant, but for the real deal, head to humble **Daitoku** (だいとく; ☑0993-72-0357; 17 Origuchi-chō; funajin meshi ¥750; ◷11am-9pm, closed irregularly) on the main drag, for award-winning *katsuo funado meshi*, a *donburi* (dish served over rice) with fresh bonito, bonito flakes, green onion, nori strips and rice crisps in katsuo broth. Makurazaki is the terminus of the train line from Kagoshima.

MIYAZAKI PREFECTURE

Miyazaki-ken (宮崎県) is best known for its palmy, balmy coastline from the city of Miyazaki southwards. Surfing, fishing boats and picturesque coastal drives here may remind you of California or the Italian Riviera. At the prefecture's northern reaches (easier accessed from Kumamoto) is lovely Takachiho, mythical home of the sun goddess Amaterasu.

Although there are train and bus services, the most rewarding way to explore this diverse prefecture is by car.

Miyazaki   宮崎

☑0985 / POP 398,100

The prefectural capital makes a convenient base for forays around the region, with a friendly, low-key vibe and fun, unique restaurants and night spots in the Nishitachi nightlife district, about 700m from the station.

◉ Sights

Miyazaki-jingū & Museum   SHRINE
(宮崎神宮・宮崎総合博物館; 2-4-1 Jingū) This shrine honours the Emperor Jimmu, the semi-mythical first emperor of Japan and founder of the Yamato court. Spectacu-

lar 600-year-old wisteria vines cover the thickly forested grounds. It's a 500m walk from Miyazaki-jingū Station, one stop (¥160, three minutes) north of Miyazaki Station.

Just north of the shrine, **Miyazaki Prefectural Museum of Nature & History** (宮崎県立総合博物館; 2-4-4 Jingū; admission free; ◷9am-5pm, closed Tue) FREE exhibits items on local history, archaeology, festival artefacts and folkcrafts. Behind the museum, **Minka-en** (民家園; admission free) FREE hosts four traditional-style Kyūshū farmhouses and other outbuildings.

Heiwadai-kōen   PARK
(平和台公園; Peace Park) The park's centrepiece is the 37m-high **Peace Tower** monument constructed in 1940, a time when peace in Japan was about to disappear. Its timeless design may remind you of ancient Inca or Khmer monuments, and it's made of stones from all over the world. The **Haniwa Garden** is dotted with reproductions of clay *haniwa* (earthenware figures found in Kōfun-period tombs) excavated from the Saitobaru burial mounds (710), set among mossy hillocks.

Heiwadai-kōen is about 1km north of Miyazaki-jingū. Buses from Miyazaki Station stop along Tachibana-dōri (¥290, 20 minutes, at least two per hour).

Miyazaki Science Centre   MUSEUM
(宮崎科学技術館; 38-3 Miyawakichō; admission with/without sky show ¥730/520; ◷9am-4.30pm, closed Mon; ⊞) Steps away from Miyazaki Station, this interactive science museum boasts one of the world's largest planetariums; some exhibits include English translations.

✿ Festivals & Events

Yabusame   ARCHERY
Witness samurai-style horseback archery at Miyazaki-jingū on 2 and 3 April.

Fireworks   FIREWORKS
Kyūshū's largest fireworks show lights up the summer sky over the Oyodo-gawa in early August.

Erekocha Matsuri   TRADITIONAL
Miyazaki's newest festival with dancers and *taiko* drummers filling Tachibana-dōri in mid-August.

Miyazaki-jingū Grand Festival   TRADITIONAL
In late October, this festival brings in the autumn with horses and *mikoshi* (portable shrines) being carried through the streets.

🛏 Sleeping

Sunflower Miyazaki Youth Hostel　HOSTEL ¥
(☎24-5785; 1-3-10 Asahi; dm ¥2900; ☷@) Near
the prefectural office, this institutional-style,
20-bed hostel has both Japanese and Western-style rooms and doubles as a community
centre during the day. There's a giant kitchen,
loaner bikes (first two hours free), coin laundry, a restaurant and a nominal 10pm curfew.

Hotel Route Inn　BUSINESS HOTEL ¥¥
(ホテルルートイン宮崎;　☎61-1488; www.
route-inn.co.jp; 4-1-27 Tachibana-dōri-nishi; s/d/tw
incl breakfast ¥5900/9500/10,000;　P☷@☎)
Across from the Nishitachi district, this
200-plus-room hotel is excellent value with
a great breakfast buffet, spacious, decently
appointed rooms, free coffee in the granite
lobby and common baths (in addition to private bathrooms).

**Richmond Hotel
Miyazaki Ekimae**　BUSINESS HOTEL ¥¥
(リッチモンドホテル宮崎駅前;　☎60-0055;
www.richmondhotel.jp; 2-2-3 Miyazaki-eki-higashi;
s/d/tw incl breakfast from ¥7000/9000/12,500;
P☷@) Behind Miyazaki Station, this light-
filled business hotel has clean, modern furnishings, larger-than-average rooms and a
breakfast buffet including local specialities.

Miyazaki Kankō Hotel　HOTEL ¥¥
(宮崎観光ホテル;　☎27-1212; www.miyakan-h.
com; 1-1-1 Matsuyama; s/tw from ¥7150/13,300,
Japanese-style r from ¥9075; P☷@) This hotel
towers next to the river with two buildings;
the east wing is snappier, although the west
wing was in the process of renovation as we
went to press (expect to pay ¥3000/5000
more per renovated single/twin room). All
are relatively spacious. There's an on-site
onsen with *rotemburo,* plus a baby grand
piano in the lobby.

Sheraton Grande Ocean Resort　RESORT ¥¥¥
(シェラトン・グランデ・オーシャン・
リゾート;　☎21-1133; www.starwoodhotels.com;
Hamayama, Yamazaki-cho; s/tw from ¥13,000/
18,000; P☷@☒➊) A true five-star Western-
style hotel with excellent leisure facilities,
this 743-room, 43-storey oceanfront tower
adjoins the SeaGaia entertainment complex. Oversized rooms are well appointed,
although internet access costs ¥1575. The
onsen and Thai spa induce flights of fancy.
Look for discounted rates online. The only
downside: distance from the city centre.
From Miyazaki take a bus for SeaGaia (25
minutes) or drive yourself.

🍴 Eating

Miyazaki is famous for *chikin nanban*
(sweet fried chicken with tartar sauce),
hiya-jiru (cold summer soup made from
baked tofu, fish, miso paste and cucumbers,
served over rice), *jidori* (local chicken) and
kama-age udon (wheat noodles boiled in
a cauldron). Miyazaki *gyū* (beef) has won
national competitions. Snack foods include
nikumaki onigiri (rice balls wrapped in
marinated pork) and *chiizu manjū* (cream-
cheese-filled dumplings). Local produce includes mango and *yuzu* (citron), sometimes
mixed with pepper for spicy *yuzu-kōshō*
paste.

The Nishitachi neighbourhood is great
for restaurant browsing, although don't
expect many English menus. For takeaway
food, try the basement marketplaces at **Bon
Belta** (ボンベルタ橘) and **Yamakataya** (山
形屋) department stores, or pick up a *shiitake ekiben* (mushroom boxed lunch) at Miyazaki Station.

★ Ogura Honten　JAPANESE ¥
(おぐら本店;　☎22-2296; 3-4-24 Tachibana-
higashi; chikin nanban ¥980; ⊙lunch & dinner
Wed-Mon) *Chikin nanban* was invented here
over half a century ago, and crowds still
flock to Ogura's red and white awning in
the alley just behind Yamakataya department store. For shorter queues, try the
larger, kitsch-filled crosstown **branch** (おぐ
ら瀬頭店; ☎23-5301; 2-2-23 Segashira; ⊙11am-
10pm; ➊).

★ Togakushi　NOODLES ¥
(戸隠; ☎24-6864; 7-10 Chūō-dōri; noodles ¥600-
900; ⊙6pm-2am) Workmanlike Togakushi
has no English menu, but ordering is easy:
delicate, thin *kama-age-udon* (¥600) for
dipping in tangy sauce of *negi* (green onion), *tempura-ko* (tempura crispies) and
refreshing *yuzu* (Japanese citron); pour
the water from the noodles into the sauce
to make soup. It's what locals crave after a
bender. Look for the giant red lantern. Dur-
ing the day, there's another **branch** (戸隠|市
役所前支店; 1-3-3 Tachibana-nishi-dōri; ⊙11am-
5pm, closed Sun) near city hall.

Nikumaki Honpō　SNACKS ¥
(にくまき本舗; ☎20-2900; 3-8-7 Tachibana-
nishi; nikumaki onigiri ¥300; ⊙6pm-3am Mon-Fri,
from 11am Sat & Sun) Corner stand that invented *nikumaki onigiri.* Sauces on top include cheese, Indonesian sambal, fried egg
and more.

Miyazaki

Okashi no Hidaka
SWEETS ¥

(お菓子の日高; ☎25-5300; 2-7-25 Tachibana-nishi-dōri; sweets from ¥105; ◷9.30am-9.30pm) Peruse, if you will, the refrigerator case of luscious-looking Japanese and Western pastries, but order the giant *nanjakō-daifuku* (dumpling of sweet bean paste, strawberry, chestnut and cheese in a wrapper of airy *mochi*; ¥336). Cheese *manju* (dumplings; ¥157) are another signature taste of Miyazaki.

Izakaya Seoul
KOREAN ¥¥

(韓国居酒屋ソウル; ☎29-8883; 1st fl, 7-26 Chūōmachi; most mains ¥1000-1200; ◷6pm-2am; ▣) This Korean restaurant does a brisk business in barbecue made with Miyazaki *gyū*, *bibimba* (rice hotpot) and *pajeon* (savoury pancakes).

Maruman Honten
YAKITORI ¥¥

(丸万本店; ☎22-6068; 3-6-7 Tachibana-dōri-nishi; grilled chicken ¥1100; ◷dinner, closed Sun)

This homely shop serves *jidori*, full of flavour but tougher and cooked rarer than you may be used to. The standard is *momoyaki* (grilled chicken leg), but *tataki* (seared; ¥600) and *sashimi* (what you think it is; ¥650) are also popular, and meals come with a light and delicious chicken broth. For more thorough cooking, say '*yoku yaite kudasai*'. Basic English spoken. Look for the red marble facade.

Bosco
ITALIAN ¥¥

(ぼすこ; ☎23-5462; 1st fl, 7-22 Chūōmachi; mains ¥950-1260; ◷6pm-midnight, closed alternate Sun; ▣) Just outside the covered arcade (look for the pink lit signs), this cosy trattoria has an open kitchen, two large tables and a long counter. The shrimp and avocado spaghetti in cream sauce has legions of fans.

★ Miyachiku
STEAK ¥¥¥

(みやちく; ☎62-1129; 2nd fl, Miyazaki Kankō Hotel, 1-1-1 Matsuyama; lunch set menu from ¥2000,

Miyazaki

dinner set menu from ¥4500; ☺lunch & dinner) If you're going to splurge on Miyazaki *gyū*, make it at this gracious teppanyaki house with river views. Lunch set menus are a nice deal with appetizer, salad, beef, vegetables, dessert and coffee.

🍷 Drinking & Nightlife

Miyazaki also plays to the wee hours, especially in the summer, with hundreds of tiny bars. Most of the action is in Nishitachi.

The Bar
BAR
(ザ・バー; www.thebarmiyazaki.com; 3rd fl, Paul Smith Bldg, 3-7-15 Tachibana-dōri-higashi; ☺8pm-3am) This hub of the expat community and its local friends draws a cheery mixed crowd who are proud of their city and keen to welcome visitors over a few cold beers. There's even a full-sized billiard table.

Brick
BAR
(ブリック; ☎83-0339; www.brick.jp; 3-10-2 Tachibana-dōri Nishi) Forty multinational beers slake the thirst of a multinational clientele at this hopping new beer hall in the heart of Nishitachi. Sausages and spare ribs are popular snacks, and on warm summer nights there's nothing quite like Brick's 'frozen beer' (from ¥600).

One Coin Bar
BAR
(ワンコインバー; 8-21 Chūō-dōri; ☺6pm-3am, closed Tue) All drinks are ¥500 (one coin!) at this smart eight-stool hole-in-the-wall with a regular clientele who return for the conversation. The well-mannered 'master' speaks English and dispenses pizzas and spaghetti from the world's tiniest kitchen.

Lifetime
JAZZ BAR
(ライフタイム; 2nd fl, 2-3-8 Hiroshima; admission Fri ¥500; ☺11.45am-2pm & 5pm-12.30am, closed Sun) Modern jazz is alive and well in Miyazaki with near-nightly jams held in this upstairs bistro-bar. Drinks start at ¥600, with coffee, snacks and steaks on the menu.

Suntory Shot Bar 4665
BAR
(サントリーショットバー4665; 1-12 Chūōdōri; ☺closed Mon) Drink a highball at nightfall at this subdued art deco–styled spot with many malt whiskies on offer, and hand-carved ice for cocktails. The owner speaks some English.

Anbai
BAR
(あんばい; 3-1-24 Tachibana-dōri-nishi; ☺6pm-1am, closed Sun) Located on Tachibana-dōri, just south of Janjan-yokochō alley and across from UFJ Bank, this sophisticated *izakaya* has more than 350 varieties of *shōchū*, Guinness on tap, well-chosen local dishes and cool jazz background music.

🛍 Shopping

Miyazaki Prefectural Products Promotion Exhibition Hall
ARTS & CRAFTS
(みやざき物産館; 1-6 Miyata-chō; ☺9.30am-7pm Mon-Fri, 9.30am-6.30pm Sat & Sun) This place sells local wood crafts and clay *haniwa*, as well as lots of snacks and a wall of *shōchū* liquors.

ⓘ Information

Located inside JR Miyazaki Station, the helpful **tourist information centre** (宮崎市観光案内所; ☎22-6469; ☺9am-6pm) has maps of the city and its surroundings. There are international ATMs both at the station and at the **central post office**, five minutes' walk west along Takachiho-dōri. Opposite the post office, the **Miyazaki Prefectural International Plaza** (宮崎県国際交流協会; ☑ 32-8457; 8th fl, Carino Bldg; ⏰ 10am-7pm Tue-Sat) has satellite TV as well as various foreign-language newspapers and magazines.

Near the station's west exit is the internet cafe **E-Planet** (2-12-20 Hiroshima; ⏰ 24hr).

ⓘ Getting There & Away

AIR

Miyazaki is connected by air with Tokyo (ANA & JAL/Solaseed ¥36,870/30,670, 1½ hours), Osaka (¥23,500, 1½ hours), Okinawa (¥25,500, 1½ hours) and Fukuoka (¥19,700, 50 minutes), plus a few flights weekly to Seoul and Taipei.

BOAT

Miyazaki Car Ferry (宮崎カーフェリー; ☑ 29-5566; www.miyazakicarferry.com; from 2nd class ¥11,200) links Miyazaki with Osaka; it's a 13-hour trip.

BUS

Routes include Kagoshima (¥2700, 2¾ hours), Kumamoto (¥4500, 3¼ hours), Nagasaki (¥6500, 5½ hours) and Fukuoka (¥3300, four hours). Phone the **Miyazaki Ekimae Bus Centre** (宮崎交通; ☑ 51-5153).

TRAIN

The JR Nippō line runs down to Kagoshima (*tokkyū*, ¥4090, two hours) and up to Beppu (*tokkyū*, ¥6070, 3¼ hours).

ⓘ Getting Around

Miyazaki's airport is connected to the city centre by bus (¥430, 30 minutes) or train (¥340, 10 minutes) from JR Miyazaki Station. Most city bus services use the Miyazaki Ekimae Bus Centre opposite the station.

Car rental is the most convenient way to explore the coastal region outside the city. There are many agencies outside the station's west exit (12 hours from ¥4725).

ⓘ VISIT MIYAZAKI BUS CARD

For budget travellers not in a hurry, this bus pass (¥1000 per day) is a fabulous deal, covering city and regional buses including to Aoshima and Nichinan Coast. Buy it at tourist counters and some hotels.

Aoshima & Kaeda
青島・加江田
☑ 0985

Aoshima is a tiny palm-covered island (1.5km in circumference), and also the name of the adjacent mainland town, one of Japan's more relaxed, alternative communities. Together with Kaeda, on a forested stretch west of town, it's great for surrendering to the summer heat and a good alternative to staying in central Miyazaki.

◉ Sights & Activities

The first thing you'll notice as you cross the water to the island of Aoshima is the unique geological feature surrounding it. Called the **devil's washboard** (*oni no sentaku-ita*, 鬼の洗濯板), it looks as if a giant sandbar has turned to stone. On the island, the photogenic Shintō shrine **Aoshima-jinja** (青島神社) is reputedly good for matchmaking, and the **Legend of Hyūga Hall** (日向神話館; ⏰ 8am-5pm, until 6pm Jul & Aug) tells the story of Amaterasu, Emperor Jimmu and the founding of Japan in wax museum-style dioramas with English explanations. An estimated 200 species of plants and animals can be found in its small circumference.

On the landside, the **Prefectural Subtropical Plant Garden** (青島亜熱帯植物園; admission free, greenhouse ¥200; ⏰ 9am-5pm) boasts 64 different species of fruit trees.

West of town, an 8km-long, well-maintained **hiking path** winds through **Kaeda Gorge** (加江田渓谷) following the Kaedagawa, a refreshingly clear stream filled with boulders and excellent swimming holes. Lush foliage includes banana palms and mountain cedars. Your own transport is helpful to get here; turn off Rte 220 onto prefectural road 339.

✿ Festivals & Events

On the second Monday in January, loincloth-clad locals dive ceremoniously into the ocean at Aoshima-jinja. At the end of July there's more splashing as *mikoshi* are carried through the shallows to the shrine.

🛏 Sleeping & Eating

Log Cabin House Rashinban CHALET ¥
(丸太小屋羅針盤; ☑ 65-0999; dm ¥3500; Ⓟ) If it's time for a tree change, head to this owner-builder-created chalet on the banks of a soothing stream. You'll probably want

directions or a taxi from town. There's little English spoken, but this distinctive accommodation in a tranquil setting is great if you want to get away; there's a barbecue area and swimming is permitted in the stream. Note: no air-con, and showers only available in warmer months.

Hotel Grantia Aoshima Taiyokaku HOTEL ¥
(ホテルグランティアあおしま太陽閣; ☑ 65-1531; www.route-inn.co.jp/english; s/d from ¥5500/10,000; P ⊖ @) On the hillside midway between Aoshima and Kodomo-no-kuni stations, this hot-spring property offers excellent value. Day use of onsen, *rotemburo* and *ganbanyoku* (stone bath) is from ¥650.

Miyazaki Cocona Shirahama Drive-in Campsite CAMPGROUND ¥
(宮崎白浜オートキャンプ場ココナ; ☑ 65-2020; tent hire ¥1570, campsites from ¥2940, cabins for up to 4 people ¥9970; 🅿) Opposite Shirahama beach, this modern complex has plenty of room and some nice rustic cabins set back from the main area.

Aoshima Palm Beach Hotel HOTEL ¥¥
(青島パームビーチホテル; ☑ 65-1555; www.palmbeach-h.com; 1-16-1 Aoshima; tw from ¥13,400; P @ 🛜 ≋ 🅿) This shiny white, semi-cylindrical, beachfront tower with glass elevators has ocean-view rooms and onsen baths (day use ¥1000). The Japanese restaurant, **Shizuku** (set menus from ¥1500, kaiseki dinners from ¥3000), serves great tempura and sashimi from local waters.

Ao & Sounders CAFE, INTERNATIONAL ¥
(パンcafeao; バー・サウンダース; ☑ Ao 080-5253-9812, Sounders 65-0767; 1-6-23 Aoshima; set meals from ¥650, bakery ¥300-600; ⊙ Ao 9am-5pm, closed Tue & 3rd Sun of month; Sounders 6-10pm Wed-Sat; 🅐 🅿) This laid-back surf shack by the railroad tracks does double duty as Ao, a friendly bakery-cafe by day; and the Hawaiian-inspired Bar Sounders by night. Chill over Ao's coffee and muffins, or Sounders' *loco moco* bowl (burger with fried egg, gravy and rice) or avocado pizza.

Tenkū Café Zeal ORGANIC ¥¥
(天空カフェ・ジール; ☑ 65-1508; 6411 Kaeda; buffet adult/child Wed-Fri ¥1000/500, Sat & Sun ¥1500/800; ⊙ 11am-4pm Wed-Fri, 11am-6pm Sat & Sun; 🅿) This wonderful hillside macrobiotic lunch spot, in a greenhouse-style building with sunny al-fresco dining, offers a constantly changing menu from produce

grown on-site. This is as delightfully hippie as it gets in Japan; some staff speak English, and the food couldn't be better for you.

🛈 Getting There & Around

Aoshima is on the JR Nichinan line from Miyazaki (¥360, 30 minutes). Buses from Miyazaki Station stop at Aoshima (¥700, 40 minutes, hourly) en route to Udo-jingū. It's about 800m to the island from the station.

Udo-jingū 鵜戸神宮

Reached via a coastal path, this brightly painted **Shintō shrine** (☑ 0987-29-1001; 3232 Ōaza Miyaura) occupies an open cavern overlooking unusual rock formations in the cove below. It's protocol to buy five *undama* (luck stones; ¥100), make a wish and try to hit the shallow depression on top of the turtle-shaped rock. Wishes are usually related to marriage, childbirth and lactation, because the boulders in front of the cavern are said to represent Emperor Jimmu's grandmother's breasts.

Hourly buses from Aoshima (¥1020, 40 minutes) and Miyazaki (¥1470, 1½ hours) stop on the highway. From the bus stop, it's about a 700m walk to the shrine past interesting rock formations and picturesque fishing boats.

Obi 飫肥

In this quaint town nicknamed 'Little Kyoto', the wealthy Ito clan ruled from Obi castle for 14 generations beginning in 1587, somehow surviving the 'one kingdom, one castle' ruling in 1615.

Only the walls of the original **Obi-jō** (飫肥城; ☑ 0987-25-4533; combined admission ¥600; ⊙ 9.30am-4.30pm) are intact, but the grounds have six important buildings, including the impressive, painstakingly reconstructed **Ōtemon gate** and **Matsuo-no-maru**, the lord's private residence. The **museum** has a collection relating to the Itō clan's long rule over Obi. **Yōshōkan**, formerly the residence of the clan's chief retainer, stands just outside the castle entrance and has a large garden with Mt Atago (Atago-san) as 'borrowed scenery'.

Once you've seen these sights, rent bikes (¥300 for three hours) to explore the rest of the town, with some photogenic streetscapes, shrines and a historic shopping street; your admission ticket has a simple map.

By the castle, **Obiten** (おび天; ☑0987-25-5717; 9-1-8 Obi; mains ¥850-1150; ◷9am-4pm) serves a local version of *Satsuma-age* (fried cakes of fish paste and vegetables, here called *tempura*). The signature Obiten with udon is ¥850.

The JR Nichinan line connects Obi with Miyazaki (*kaisoku;* ¥910, 65 minutes) via Aoshima. From Obi Station, it's a 10-minute walk to the castle. Buses from Miyazaki (¥2020, 2¼ hours, last return bus 3.40pm) stop below the castle entrance.

Nichinan-kaigan & Cape Toi   日南海岸・都井岬

The palm-lined stretch of coastal road from Aoshima to Cape Toi via the town of Nichinan is a rewarding drive, with seaside cliffs and views of the islands reminiscent of gumdrops and camels.

Just off the coast from **Ishinami-kaigan**, the tiny island of **Kō-jima** is home to a group of monkeys that apparently rinse their food in the ocean before eating, but they're a fickle bunch, and hard to spot. Boats shuttle visitors back and forth for ¥3000 per person return.

From here to the south, the road was washed away in 2012 storms. If and when it reopens, it's about another 7km to **Cape Toi**, famed for wild horses and a dramatic fire festival on the last weekend in September. En route is **Koigaura Beach**, where the *surf-zoku* (surf tribe) hang out.

For a laid-back stay, the palm-filled seaside **Hadashi** (ハダシ; ☑0985-67-0444; 7516 Ōzono, Uchiumi; per person ¥500, plus per tent/trailer/cottage up to 3 people ¥1000/2000/5000) offers campgrounds, cabins and simple cottages. Activities run the gamut from barbecues to hula classes, and Hadashi rents out snorkelling, windsurfing and paddleboarding equipment (use them elsewhere due to dangerous undersea rock formations). It's in Uchiumi, at about the 25.5km mark of Rte 220 or reachable by train from Aoshima to Kouchiumi (¥220, 12 minutes, hourly) and an almost 1km walk (use caution along the busy road).

Saitobaru   西都原
☑0983

North of Miyazaki, the **Saitobaru Burial Mounds Park** looks like a golf course at first glance, but the hillocks dotting the several square kilometres of fields and forests are actually more than 300 *kofun* (tumuli, or burial mounds). These mostly keyhole-shaped mounds, dating from AD 300 to 600, served much the same function as Egyptian pyramids for early Japanese nobility.

The large **Saitobaru Archaeological Museum** (西都原考古博物館; ◷10am-6pm, closed Mon) FREE displays excavated items like Jōmon pottery, ancient swords, armour and *haniwa*. Rent the English audio guide (¥400); signage is in Japanese. A hall nearby is built around an excavation site.

Buses run frequently to Saitobaru from Miyakō City bus terminal (¥1040, one hour), but you'll need your own transport if you want to explore the tomb-strewn countryside. Saitobaru is not on the Visit Miyazaki Bus Card.

In the nearby town of Saito, drummers wear odd pole-like headgear for the unique **Usudaiko dance festival** in early September. A harvest festival lasts from 12 to 16 December, highlighted by **Shiromi Kagura** performances on the 14th and 15th.

Takachiho   高千穂
☑0982 / POP 14,000

In far northern Miyazaki-ken, this pretty mountain town is a remote but rewarding destination, as the site where legend says Japan's sun goddess brought light back to the world. As if that weren't reason enough to visit, there's a deep and dramatic gorge through the town centre. The **Town Centre Information Office** (街中案内所; ☑72-3031; 802-3 Mitai; ◷8.30am-5.30pm) is across from the bus centre.

◉ Sights

★ **Ama-no-Iwato-jinja**   SHINTŌ SHRINE
(天岩戸神社; 1073-1 Iwato; ◷24hr, office 8.30am-5pm) One of Shintō's loveliest shrines honours the cave where Amaterasu hid. The cave itself is off-limits, but Nishi Hongū (the shrine's main building) sits right across the river Iwato-gawa. If you have a Japanese speaker, ask a staff member to show you the viewpoint behind the *honden* (main hall). Buses leave approximately hourly (¥300, 20 minutes) from Takachihō's Miyakō bus centre.

A seven-minute walk beside a picturesque stream takes you to **Ama-no-Yasuka-wara**, a deep cave where tradition says that thousands of other deities discussed how to lure Amaterasu from the cave. Modern-

Takachiho

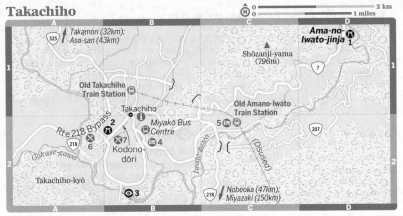

day visitors have left innumerable stacks of stones in tribute, imparting a sort of Indy Jones feeling.

Takachiho-kyō GORGE
(高千穂峡) Takachiho's magnificent gorge, with its waterfall, overhanging rocks and sheer walls, was formed over 120,000 years ago by a double volcanic eruption. There's a 1km-long nature trail above the gorge. Or view it up close from a **rowboat** (☑73-1213; per 30min ¥2000; ⊙8.30am-5pm), though during high season it can be as busy as rush hour.

Takachiho-jinja SHINTŌ SHRINE
(高千穂神社) Takachiho-jinja, about 10 minutes' walk from the bus centre, is dramatically set in a grove of cryptomeria pines, including one that's over 800 years old. Some of the buildings here look like they could be almost as old.

✨ Festivals & Events

Takachiho's artistic claim to fame is **kagura** (sacred dance). In May, September and November (the dates change annually), performances are held at Ama-no-Iwato-jinja from 10am to 10pm, while hour-long performances of **yokagura** (Night-Time Kagura; tickets ¥500; ⊙8pm) take place nightly at Takachiho-jinja.

There are also all-night performances *(satokagura)* in farmhouses on 19 nights from November to February. In all, 33 dances are performed from 6pm until 9am the next morning. If you brave the cold until morning, you'll be caught up in a wave of excitement. Contact the tourist information office for details.

🛏 Sleeping & Eating

Takachiho has about 30 hotels, ryokan, *minshuku* and pensions, which all typically book out during the autumn foliage season.

Takachiho Youth Hostel HOSTEL ¥
(高千穂ユースホステル; ☑72-3021; 5899-2 Mitai; dm HI member/nonmember ¥2800/3400; P⊝@) This large hostel is far from the sights but clean, efficient and deep in the woods. Rooms are Japanese style, and breakfast/dinner (¥500/900) are available, as are laundry machines and pick-up from the bus centre.

Folkcraft Ryokan Kaminoya RYOKAN ¥¥
(民芸旅館かみの家; ☑72-2111; www.kaminoya.jp; 806-5 Mitai; r with/without 2 meals from ¥12,600/7350; P⊝@☎) In central Takachiho, this beautifully kept, eight-room ryokan has folkcraft pieces, wood beams and a whitewashed facade. It has a *hinoki* (cypress) bath as well as in-room facilities.

SUN GODDESS DISAPPEARS! WORLD GOES DARK!

According to Shintō legend, the sun goddess Amaterasu, angered by the misbehaviour of her brother, exiled herself into a cave sealed by a boulder, plunging the world into darkness. Alarmed, other gods gathered at another nearby cave to discuss how to get her to re-emerge. Eventually the goddess Ama-no-Uzume performed a bawdy dance which aroused Amaterasu's curiosity, and she emerged from the cave and light was restored to earth. *Iwato kagura* dances performed in Takachiho today re-enact this story.

Chiho-no-ie NOODLES ¥
(千穂の家; ☑ 72-2115; 62-2 Ojimukoyama; meals from ¥500; ⊙ 9am-5pm) At the base of the gorge (though, sadly, with no water views), this simple building serves seasonal regional treats and *nagashi-sōmen* (¥600) – have fun catching tasty noodles with your chopsticks as they float by in halved bamboo shafts.

Gamadase Ichiba MARKET
(がまだせ市場; ☑ Nagomi 73-1109; 1099-1 Mitai; Nagomi lunch set menus ¥1400-2500, dinner set menus ¥1650-3800; ⊙ 9am-6pm, Nagomi lunch & dinner closed 2nd Wed each month) Operated by the local agricultural collaborative, this facility has markets for local produce and the **Nagomi** (和) restaurant for local beef set menus.

ⓘ Getting There & Around

Takachiho is most easily reached by car from the Aso-san area in Kumamoto Prefecture. Two buses daily serve Takachiho's **Miyakō Bus Centre** (宮交バスセンター) from Kumamoto (¥2300, 2¾ hours) via Takamori (¥1280, 1¼ hours). From the bus centre it's walkable to the gorge and Takachiho-jinja, but you'll need transport to reach other sights. The town centre information office rents out bicycles for ¥300/1500 per hour/day.

ŌITA PREFECTURE

Beppu 別府

☑ 0977 / POP 120,536
You don't have to look far in Beppu, in Ōita Prefecture (大分県), to see the reason for its popularity: steam rising from vents in the earth means onsen bathing opportunities galore. Beppu is at turns quaint, touristy, modern, traditional, solid and rickety, but the charm of this hilly, hospitable city grows on visitors as sure as the waters are warm.

⊙ Sights & Activities

Hot Springs

Beppu has two types of hot springs, collectively pumping out more than 100 million litres of hot water every day. *Jigoku* (hells) are for looking at; onsen are for bathing.

Jigoku Meguri HOT SPRINGS
(Hell Circuit; each hell/combination ticket ¥400/2000; ⊙ 8am-5pm) Beppu's most hyped attraction is the jigoku meguri. Unlike Unzen, where the geothermal wonders are unadorned, the circuit's eight stops have become mini amusement parks, each with a theme and some loaded with tourist kitsch; consider yourself warned.

Six hells are at **Kannawa** (Map p716), over 4km northwest of Beppu Station, and two are about 2.5km further north. In the Kannawa group are steaming blue **Umi Jigoku** (海地獄; Sea Hell), **Oni-bōzu Jigoku** (Demon Monk Hell), where bubbling mud looks like a monk's shaved head, **Shira-ike Jigoku** (白池地獄; White Pond Hell) and **Kamado Jigoku** (かまど地獄; Oven Hell), named because it was once used for cooking. At **Oni-yama Jigoku** (鬼山地獄; Devil's Mountain Hell) and **Yama Jigoku** (山地獄; Mountain Hell), a variety of animals are kept in enclosures that look uncomfortably small. Take a bus from Beppu Station to Umi-Jigoku-mae (¥320).

The smaller group of hells has **Chi-no-ike Jigoku** (血の池地獄; Map p713; Blood Pool Hell), with photogenic red water, and **Tatsumaki Jigoku** (龍巻地獄; Map p713; Tornado Hell), where a geyser shoots off about every 35 minutes.

Onsen

Beppu has eight onsen districts, **Beppu Hattō** (www.city.beppu.oita.jp/01onsen/english/index.html). Onsen aficionados spend their time in Beppu moving from one bath to another and consider at least three baths a day *de rigueur*; bathing costs from ¥100 to ¥1000. Bring your own soap, washcloth and towel, as some places don't rent them.

Beppu

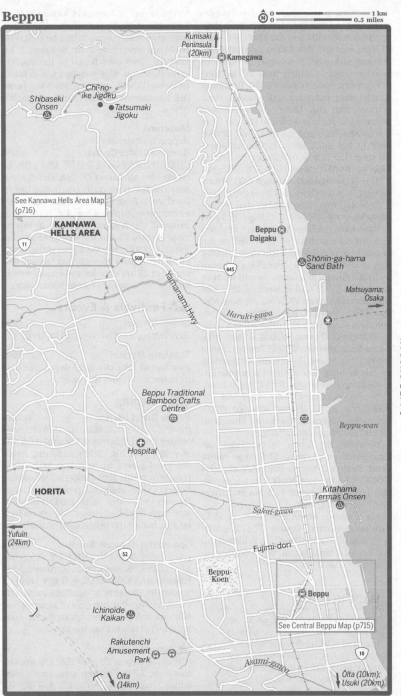

0 — 1 km
0 — 0.5 miles

Kunisaki
Peninsula
(20km)

Kamegawa

Chi-no-
ike Jigoku

Shibaseki
Onsen

Tatsumaki
Jigoku

See Kannawa Hells Area Map
(p716)

**KANNAWA
HELLS AREA**

11

500

Beppu
Daigaku

Shōnin-ga-hama
Sand Bath

Matsuyama;
Osaka

645

Yamanami Hwy

Haruki-gawa

Beppu Traditional
Bamboo Crafts
Centre

Beppu-wan

Hospital

HORITA

Kitahama
Termas Onsen

Sakai-gawa

Yufuin
(24km)

52

Fujimi-dori

Beppu-
Koen

Beppu

See Central Beppu Map (p715)

Ichinoide
Kaikan

Rakutenchi
Amusement
Park

10

Ōita
(14km)

Asami-gawa

Ōita (10km);
Usuki (20km)

KYŪSHŪ BEPPU

In central Beppu, the *very* hot **Takegawara Onsen** (竹瓦温泉; Map p715; 16-23 Motomachi; admission ¥100, sand bath ¥1000; ⊙ 6.30am-10.30pm, sand bath 8am-9.30pm, sand bath closed 3rd Wed each month) occupies a fabulous wooden building dating back to the Meiji era (present building from 1938). Bathing is simple; scoop out water with a bucket, wash yourself, then soak. There's also a sand bath where a *yukata* is provided so you can lie in a shallow trench and get buried up to your neck in hot sand; arrive earlier for warmest sand. The simple half-timber building of **Ekimae Kōtō Onsen** (駅前高等温泉; Map p715; 13-14 Ekimae-machi; admission ¥200; ⊙ 6am-midnight) is just a short walk from the station.

Downhill from Kannawabus stop is **Kannawa Mushi-yu** (鉄輪蒸し湯; Map p716; 1-gumi Kannawa-kami; ⊙ 6.30am-8pm), where wrapped in a *yukata* you steam at 65°C (ow!) on top of Japanese rush leaves. Eight to 10 minutes here is said to have the detoxifying power of up to 30 minutes in a sauna. Nearby **Hyōtan Onsen** (ひょうたん温泉; Map p716; 159-2 Kannawa; admission/yukata ¥700/200, admission after 6pm ¥550; ⊙ 9am-1am) has multiple pools, *rotemburo,* sand baths and private baths.

Shibaseki Onsen (柴石温泉; Map p713; 4-kumi Noda; admission ¥210; ⊙ 7am-8pm, closed 2nd Wed of each month) is en route to the smaller pair of hells. You can rent a private *kazoku-buro* (family bath) for ¥1570 per hour.

Nearby, popular **Onsen Hoyōland** (温泉保養ランド; 5-1 Myōban; admission ¥1050; ⊙ 9am-8pm) has giant mud baths, plus open-air and mixed-gender bathing.

Between JR Beppu Station and the Kamegawa onsen area, **Shōnin-ga-hama sand bath** (上人ヶ浜; Map p713; admission ¥1000; ⊙ 8.30am-6pm Apr-Oct, 9am-5pm Nov-Mar) has a great beach location and some English-speaking staff.

For a seaside onsen experience, head to **Kitahama Termas Onsen** (北浜温泉テルマス; Map p713; admission ¥500; ⊙ 10am-8pm). You'll need a bathing suit, as the outside *rotemburo* mixes it up.

The owner of **Ichinoide Kaikan** (いちのいで会館; Map p713; 14-2 Uehara-machi; ⊙ 11am-5pm) loves onsen so much that he built three pool-sized *rotemburo* in his backyard. It has fabulous views over Beppu to the sea. The general deal is that you order a delicious *teishoku* (¥1300), prepared while you bathe. Ask for directions at the tourist information offices.

Museums

Beppu Traditional Bamboo Crafts Centre   MUSEUM
(別府市竹細工伝統産業会館; Map p713; 8-3 Higashi-sōen; admission ¥300; ⊙ 8.30am-5pm Tue-Sun) The hands-on crafts centre displays refined works from Edo-period masters as well as current examples of uses for this versatile material, which grows copiously in this region. If you'd like to try your own hand at the craft (¥300), request a reservation a couple of days ahead. From Beppu Station, take bus 22 or 25 to Dentō Sangyō-kaikan-mae or bus 1 to Minami-haru (about 200m away).

✷ Festivals & Events

Onsen Festival   ONSEN
Held during the first weekend in April.

Tanabata Matsuri   TRADITIONAL
In adjacent Ōita city, held over three days from the first Friday in August.

🛌 Sleeping

Beppu Guest House   HOSTEL ¥
(別府ゲストハウス; Map p715; ☎ 76-7811; www.beppu-g-h.net; 1-12 Ekimae-chō; dm/s ¥1500/2500; P ⊜ @ 🛜) The big kitchen and living rooms are great places to hang out with fellow travellers at this arty, funky and welcoming hostel. Other positives: free loaner bikes, laundry machines and English-speaking staff with local knowledge. There's no bath on-site, but a ¥100 public bath is nearby.

Spa Hostel Khaosan Beppu   HOSTEL ¥
(スパホステルカオサン別府はまゆう; Map p715; ☎ 23-3939; www.khaosan-beppu.com; 3-3-10 Kitahama; dm/s ¥2000/3000; P ⊜ @ 🛜) Beppu's newest backpackers is excellent value with clean, renovated rooms (mix of Japanese and Western styles) and hot-spring baths. Look for the Thai *tuk-tuk* out the front.

★ Yamada Bessou   RYOKAN ¥¥
(山田別荘; Map p715; ☎ 24-2121; http://yamad-abessou.jp; 3-2-18 Kitahama; r per person with/without 2 meals from ¥10,650/5400; P ⊜ @ 🛜 🚌)

Central Beppu

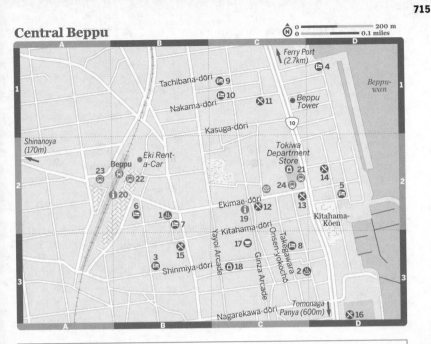

Central Beppu

KYŪSHŪ BEPPU

Step back in time at this sprawling family-run 1930s inn with wonderfully well-preserved rooms and fabulous art deco features. The onsen and private *rotemburo* are so lovely you'll hardly mind that only a couple of its eight rooms have full bath and toilet.

Yōkōsō RYOKAN ¥¥
(陽光荘; Map p716; ☎66-0440; www.coara.or.jp/~hideharu/EngSmry.html; 3-kumi, Kannawa Ida; r per

person ¥3300-3800) This creaky 27-room inn has been in business since 1944, and feels like it hasn't been much updated since (three storeys with no elevator, surcharges for air-con and TV, and one pokey internet terminal?). Still, a stay here can be delightfully retro. Cook your meals over onsen steam and bathe in onsen baths. It's near the hells of Kannawa, away from the main action, with an 11pm curfew.

Kannawa Hells Area

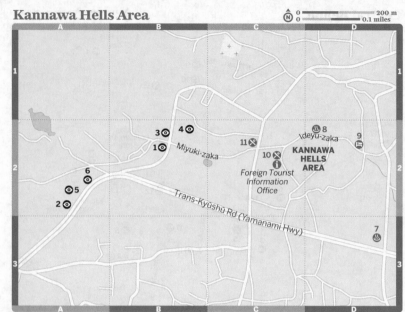

Kokage International Minshuku
MINSHUKU ¥¥

(国際民宿こかげ; Map p715; ☎ 23-1753; ww6.tiki.
ne.jp/~kokage; 8-9 Ekimae-chō; s/d ¥4350/7650;
🅿 @ 🛜) Off an alley near Ekimae-dōri, this
cosy 10-room inn is old and friendly, chock-
full of atmospheric woodwork, antiques and
trinkets. There's a lovely stone onsen, and
toast and coffee for breakfast. Rooms over
the entrance are quietest.

Nogami Honkan Ryokan
RYOKAN ¥¥

(野上本館; Map p715; ☎ 22-1334; www.yukemuri.
net; 1-12-1 Kitahama; r per person with/without breakfast ¥5000/4000; 🅿 @ 🛜) In a classic 1950s
building near Takegawara Onsen, most of
the 25 rooms don't have private bathrooms,
but three small baths can be reserved. Owner
Ken is a knowledgeable and gracious host.

Hotel Seawave Beppu
BUSINESS HOTEL ¥¥

(ホテルシーウェーブ別府; Map p715; ☎ 27-1311;
www.beppuonsen.com; 12-8 Ekimae-chō; s/tw/ste
from ¥5800/8400/17,800; 🅿 ➔ @ 🛜) For late arrivals or early getaways, this hotel with small
rooms is right across from the station. There
are in-room baths, but for onsen you'll need to
head to its sister property a few doors down.

Hotel Aile
BUSINESS HOTEL ¥¥

(ホテル エール; Map p715; ☎ 21-7272; 2-14-35 Kitahama; s/d/tw ¥6240/9540/10,800; 🅿 ➔ @ 🛜)
A rooftop *rotemburo*, 10th-storey common
baths with sweeping city views and spacious
guest rooms make this a better than average
business hotel. Breakfast (¥840) is a Japanese-Western buffet. Ignore the music-box
soundtrack in the hallways.

★ Beppu Hotel Umine
HOTEL ¥¥¥

(別府ホテルうみね; Map p715; ☎ 26-0002; www.
umine.jp; 3-8-3 Kitahama; r per person with breakfast

from ¥15,750; (P @ @) In-room onsen baths with water views, gorgeous common baths, savvy contemporary design, excellent restaurants and oodles of personal service make this Beppu's top stay. Rates are high but include drinks and snacks in the library lounge.

Suginoi Hotel
HOTEL ¥¥¥

(杉乃井ホテル; ☎24-1141; www.suginoi-hotel.com/english; 1 Kankaiji; r per person incl 2 meals from ¥15,900; P @ @) On a hillside above town, Suginoi offers the tiered rooftop Tanayu *rotemburo,* the Aqua Garden onsen swimming pool (combined day use ¥1300, bathing suit required) and high standards indoors. Japanese-style rooms are more alluring than Western ones, but the 15 Ceada Floor rooms are slick and special.

✖ Eating & Drinking

Beppu is renowned for *toriten* (chicken tempura), freshwater fish, *Bungo-gyū* (local beef), *fugu* (pufferfish), wild mountain vegetables and *dango-jiru* (miso soup with thick-cut noodles). On the 1st floor of the **You Me Town shopping mall** (ゆめタウン別府; Map p715), English-friendly restaurants include conveyor-belt sushi, noodles and a buffet.

★ Gyoza Kogetsu
GYŌZA ¥

(餃子湖月; Map p715; ☎21-8062; 3-7 Ekimae-honmachi; gyōza ¥600; ⊙2-9.30pm, closed Tue) This seven-seat counter shop with manic local following has only two things on the menu, both ¥600 – generous plates of *gyōza* fried to a delicate crunch, and bottles of beer. It's in the tiny alley behind the covered arcade; look for the display case filled with cat figurines.

Tomonaga Panya
BAKERY ¥

(友永パン屋; off Map p715; ☎23-0969; Chiyo-machi 2-29; pastries from ¥90; ⊙8.30am-5.30pm Mon-Sat) This charming, historic bakery has been in business since 1916, and people still queue for its ever-changing selection of oven-fresh breads and pastries. The *wanchan*

(doggie) bun (¥110) is filled with custard cream and uses raisins for the eyes and nose. Note: the shop closes when sold out.

Ureshi-ya
SHOKUDŌ ¥

(うれしや; Map p715; ☎22-0767; 7-12 Ekimae-honmachi; dishes from ¥200-850; ⊙5pm-2am, closed Mon) You'll get your money's worth at this friendly and busy *shokudō* with *donburi* (dishes served over rice), sashimi, *oden* (hotpot), noodle dishes and more, displayed for you to choose.

Shinanoya
CAFE, NOODLES ¥

(信濃屋; off Map p715; ☎25-8728; 6-32 Nishinoguchi; mains ¥600-1300; ⊙9am-9pm, until 6pm Tue & Wed) A few minutes from the station's west exit and dating back to 1926, this kindly *kissaten* also serves a renowned *dango-jiru* loaded with veggies and best enjoyed while viewing the piney garden. It's the traditional building just before Family Mart.

Jin Robata & Beer Pub
IZAKAYA ¥

(ろばた仁; Map p715; ☎21-1768; 1-15-7 Kitahama; dishes ¥300-840; ⊙5pm-midnight) A neon fish sign directs you to this welcoming international pub. To go with your booze, pick from the rows of fresh fish on display (get it sashimi or cooked) or sample *toriten* and local beef.

★ Toyotsune
JAPANESE ¥¥

(とよ常; Map p715; ☎22-2083; mains ¥630-1580; 🈯) Toyotsune nails the Beppu specialities: *toriten, Bungo-gyū* and lots of fresh fish, plus tempura. The **main branch** (☎22-3274; 2-13-11 Kitahama; ⊙lunch & dinner, closed Wed) is on the corner behind Jolly Pasta. The second branch is across from Beppu Station.

Mitsuboshi
FRENCH ¥¥

(三ツ星; Map p716; ☎67-3536; 284 Kannawa; mains ¥1050-1260, set meals ¥1575-5250; ⊙lunch & dinner Wed-Mon; 🈯) By the Kannawa bus terminal (look for the rose-coloured awnings), cosy, slightly kitschy Mitsuboshi has been serving up country French cooking for

KYŪSHŪ BEPPU

DON'T MISS

JIGOKU MUSHI KŌBŌ

Ingenious! Amid the hells of Kannawa, you can cook your own meal in onsen steam in this **workshop** (地獄蒸し工房; Map p716; Hell Steaming Workshop; ☎66-3775; 5-kumi Furomoto; dishes from ¥600-1300, steamers ¥500 per 30min; ⊙9am-9pm, closed 3rd Wed of month). Purchase ingredients on the spot (or bring your own), and steam them in *kama* (vats) roiling from the onsen below. It shares a building with the Foreign Tourist Information Office, so there's usually an English speaker on hand to help until 5pm. It can be crowded at peak times such as weekend lunch.

years. The chef-owner trained and worked in Europe and Canada and speaks English. There are also refined versions of *yōshoku* (Japanese interpretations of Western cooking) such as *om-rice* (rice omelette), *hayashi rice* (hashed rice) and burgers of local Bungō beef.

Fugu Matsu
FUGU ¥¥¥

(ふぐ松; Map p715; ☑21-1717; 3-6-14 Kitahama; fugu set meals from ¥7350; ◷ lunch & dinner; 🖼) This friendly shop is the place to try *fugu* in simple style. Sit on *hori-kotatsu* seating and chow on sashimi, *karaage* (fried fugu) and *hiresake* (sake boiled with a fugu fin).

Natsume Kissa
CAFE

(喫茶なつめ; Map p715; 1-4-23 Kitahama; ◷10am-8.30pm, closed Wed) This retro snack and dessert spot in the covered arcade is best known for its own *onsen kōhī* (¥530), coffee made with hot-spring water. Look for the wooden barrel above the door.

🛍 Shopping

For over a century the must-have souvenir for Japanese holidaymakers in Beppu was everyday-use bamboo products (such as baskets); nowadays the trend is art pieces. Find them at shops like **Yamashō** (山正; Map p715; 4-9 Kusunoki-machi) in the central shopping arcades, although be forewarned that many pieces are Chinese imports. Ask '*Nihon-sei des[u] ka?*' (Is this made in Japan?) to check.

ℹ Information

International ATMs can be found at Beppu Station, **Kitahama post office** (別府北浜郵便局) and the nearby Cosmopia shopping centre. **Ōita Bank** (大分銀行) handles foreign-exchange services.

Foreign Tourist Information Offices (別府外国人観光客案内所; www.beppuftio.blogspot.com) Branches at Beppu International Plaza (☑21-6220; 12-13 Ekimae-machi; ◷9am-5pm), Beppu Station (別府外国人観光客案内所; ☑23-1119; cnr Ekimae-dōri & Ginza Arcade; ◷10am-5pm; 🖼) and Kannawa (☑66-3855; 5-kumi Furomoto; ◷9am-5pm; 🖼). Well equipped with helpful bilingual volunteers and an arsenal of local information and advice.

ℹ Getting There & Away

AIR

Flights go to Ōita Airport from Tokyo Haneda (ANA or JAL ¥35,700, Solaseed Air ¥29,670; 1½ hours) and Osaka (¥19,300, one hour). Flights also operate to Seoul.

BOAT

The **Ferry Sunflower Kansai Kisen** (☑22-1311) makes an overnight run between Beppu and Osaka and Kōbe (¥11,300, 11 hours), stopping at Matsuyama (4½ hours). The evening boat departs at 6.35pm to western Honshū and passes through the Inland Sea, arriving at 7.35am the next morning. For the port, take bus 20 or 26 from Beppu Station's west exit.

BUS

There's a Kyūshū Odan (Trans-Kyūshū) bus to Aso Station (¥3500, 3¼ hours) and Kumamoto (¥6450, five hours).

TRAIN

The Kyūshū *shinkansen* from Hakata (Fukuoka) connects with the JR Nippō line at Kokura (*shinkansen* and *tokkyū*; ¥5580, 90 minutes) to Beppu. The JR Nippō line continues to Miyazaki via Oita (*tokkyū*; ¥5330, 3¼ hours). Trains to Aso and Kumamoto were suspended at the time of writing, as tracks were washed away due to flooding.

ℹ Getting Around

TO/FROM THE AIRPORT

Beppu Airport buses to Ōita Airport stop outside Tokiwa department store (¥1450, 45 minutes) and Beppu Station.

BUS

Kamenoi is the main bus company. An unlimited 'My Beppu Free' pass comes in two varieties: 'mini' (adult/student ¥900/700), which covers Beppu city (and offers discounts); and the 'wide' (one/two days ¥1600/2400), which extends to Yufuin. Passes are available from foreign tourist information offices and some lodgings. From JR Beppu Station, buses 2, 5, 7, 41 and 43 go to Kannawa (15 to 25 minutes), and buses 16 and 26 serve Chi-no-ike and Tatsumaki *jigoku*.

Yufuin
由布院

☑0977 / POP 35,380

About 25km inland from Beppu, delightful Yufuin sits in a ring of mountains, with the twin peaks of Yufu-dake especially notable. The town lives for tourism and is a good place to see contemporary Japanese crafts; ceramics, clothing, woodworking and even interesting foods abound in its narrow lanes. However, Yufuin gets crowded on holidays and weekends. If staying overnight, arrive before dusk, when the day trippers leave and wealthier Japanese retreat to the sanctuary of their ryokan.

The **tourist Information office** (由布院温泉観光案内所; ☏84-2446; ◷9am-6.30pm) inside the train station has some information in English, including a detailed walking map showing galleries, museums and onsen. Bicycles are available for rent from 9am to 5pm.

As in Beppu, making a pilgrimage from one onsen to another is a popular activity. Most historic is **Shitan-yu** (下ん湯; admission ¥200, deposit money in slot outside; ◷9am-11pm), a one-room thatched bathhouse with mixed bathing only, on the northern shore of **Kinrin-ko** (Lake of Golden Fish Scales, named by a Meiji-era philosopher). Most local baths *are* separated by gender, such as nearby **Nurukawa Onsen** (ぬるかわ温泉; ☏84-2869; 1490-1 Kawakami Takemoto; admission ¥400; ◷8am-8.30pm), a cluster of small bathing rooms with with lots of character and mountain views.

Double-peaked **Yufu-dake** (1584m) volcano overlooks Yufuin and takes about 90 minutes to climb. Some buses from Yufuin stop at the base of Yufu-dake at Yufu-tozanguchi (由布登山口; ¥360, 16 minutes, hourly).

🛏 Sleeping & Eating

Most patrons have their meals while relaxing in their inn, but there's a handful of eateries by the station.

Yufuin Country Road Youth Hostel HOSTEL ¥ (由布院カントリーロードユースホステル; ☏84-3734; www4.ocn.ne.jp/~yufuinyh; 441-29 Kawakami; dm member/nonmember ¥2835/3435; 🅿@🛜) On a forested hillside overlooking the town and especially pretty at night, this first-rate 25-bed hostel has its own onsen and hospitable English-speaking owners. It's possible they may pick you up from the station if you aren't in time for one of the infrequent buses (¥200, Monday to Friday only). Two meals are available for an extra ¥1680.

Makiba-no-ie RYOKAN ¥¥ (牧場の家; ☏84-2138; 2870-1 Kawakami; r per person incl 2 meals from ¥9600; 🅿) There's atmosphere aplenty in these thatched-roof huts with sink and toilet around a *rotemburo*. The antique-filled garden restaurant offers *jidori* (local chicken) and *Bungō-gyū teishoku* meals from ¥1600. Visitors can use the *rotemburo* for ¥500.

★**Kamenoi Bessō** RYOKAN ¥¥¥ (亀の井別荘; ☏84-3166; www.kamenoi-bessou.jp; 2633-1 Kawakami; r per person incl 2 meals from

¥35,000; 🅿@) For the no-holds-barred Yufuin splurge, look no further. From Kinrin-kō, enter the *kayabuki* (thatched roof) gate down gravel paths to this campus of craftsman-style wooden buildings, encircling stone baths with peaked wooden roofs. Meals are sure to contain local specialities, and staff seem never to have heard the concept 'no'. Choose from Japanese, Western and combination Japanese-Western-style guest rooms.

Hidamari JAPANESE ¥ (陽だまり; ☏84-2270; 2914 Kamikawa; mains ¥735-1575; ◷lunch 11am-3pm, shop 8.30am-5.30pm) Operated by local farming families, this informal restaurant and produce market nails the local standards like *toriten, dangojiru* and local beef in *teishoku* (set meals); order from the picture menu. The rest of the day you can buy *bentōs*, local yoghurt and ice cream. It's about 150m from the station, at the intersection with the large stone *torii*.

Izumi Soba NOODLES ¥¥ (泉そば; ☏85-2283; 1599-1 Kawakami; soba from ¥1260; ◷11am-5pm) There are less expensive *soba* shops in town, but at this classy place with a view of Kinrin-ko you can watch the noodles being made in the window before you sit down. The standard is *seirō-soba* (on a bamboo mat); *oroshi-soba* comes topped with grated daikon.

ⓘ Getting There & Away

Trains connect Beppu with Yufuin (*futsū/tokkyū* ¥1080/2580, 1¼ hours/one hour) via Ōita.

Buses connect JR Beppu Station with Yufuin throughout the day (¥900, 50 minutes). Express buses serve Fukuoka (¥2800, 2¼ hours), Aso (¥2300, 2½ hours) and Kumamoto (¥3450, 4½ hours).

Usuki 臼杵

☏0972 / POP 41,500

Just outside Usuki are the thousand-year-old **Usuki Stone Buddhas** (臼杵石仏; Fukata; admission ¥530; ◷6am-6pm, to 7pm Apr-Sep). Four clusters comprising 60-plus images (59 are designated national treasures) lie in a series of niches in a ravine. Some are complete statues, whereas others have only the heads remaining. It's truly a spiritual place if it's uncrowded, although some of the magic can be lost in the tourist-trap ambience just outside.

Usuki has several temples and well-preserved traditional houses and a pretty downtown of historic wood and stucco homes and shops. On the last Saturday in August, the town hosts a **fire festival**, and other festivities are held throughout the year; ask for details at the **tourist information office** (臼杵市観光協会; ☑ 63-2366; Usuki Station; ⊙ 9am-3pm) adjacent to Usuki Station. There's free internet and some local history exhibits at the community centre **Sala de Usuki** (サーラデ臼杵; ☑ 64-7271; ⊙ 9am-7pm; @).

About a dozen local restaurants boast some of the best *fugu* in Japan; expect to pay from about ¥5000/8000 for a lunch/dinner set, including sake.

Usuki is 40km southeast of Beppu. Take the JR Nippō line to Usuki Station (*tokkyū/futsū* ¥1810/910, 45/60 minutes), usually involving a change in Ōita. From here infrequent buses take 20 minutes to the Buddha images, or it's about ¥2000 by taxi or 30 minutes via bike. You can rent bikes at the station (first two hours/subsequent hours ¥200/100).

Kunisaki Peninsula
国東半島

It would be easy to overlook this remote corner of Kyūshū north of Beppu, underserved as it is by public transport, but you'd be missing some of the most undisturbed *pawā spotto* (power spots, Japanese slang for spiritual places) in the nation. The town of Bungo-takada is nicknamed 'Buddha's Village' and the region is noted for its early Buddhist influence, including some rock-carved images linked to the more famous ones at Usuki. Your own car is useful for getting around the region efficiently.

The national treasure, 11th-century **Fuki-ji** (富貴寺; admission ¥200; ⊙ 8.30am-4.30pm) in Bungo-takada, is the oldest wooden structure in Kyūshū and one of the oldest wooden temples in Japan. Its overgrown grounds and moss-covered stupas complement the structure beautifully. Ōita Kōtsū buses from Usa Station go to Bungo-takada (¥810, 35 minutes); from there, it's a 10-minute taxi ride (around ¥1000).

In the centre of the peninsula, near the summit of Futago-san (721m), is **Futago-ji** (両子寺; 1548 Futago, Akimachi; admission ¥200; ⊙ 8am-5pm), founded in 718 and dedicated to Fudō-Myō-o, the ferocious, fire-enshrouded, sword-wielding deity, able to repel attacks while appearing calm. It's a lovely climb, especially in spring or autumn and there are plenty of subtemples to explore around its forested gorges.

Nearby **Taizō-ji** (admission ¥200; ⊙ 8.30am-5pm) is known for its famously uneven stone stairs. Local legend says that they are so random and haphazard that the Oni (devils) must have created them in a single night.

Around 2km south of **Maki Ōdō Hall**, and deep in a forest along a mossy riverbed, are two Heian-period Buddha images carved into a cliff, a 6m figure of the Dainichi Buddha and an 8m figure of Fudō-Myō-o. Known as **Kumano Magaibutsu** (熊野磨崖仏; admission ¥200; ⊙ 8.30am-5pm), these are the largest Buddhist images of this type in Japan. If you thought the few hundred steps to the carvings were tough, wait until the next few hundred to the shrine at the top.

The sprawling, wooded and water-crossed **Usa-jingū** (宇佐神社; 2859 Ōaza), the original of which dates back some 1200 years, is the chief shrine among some 40,000 in Japan dedicated to the warrior-god Hachiman. It's a 4km bus or taxi ride from Usa Station (get off at Usa-Hachiman-mae), on the JR Nippō line from Beppu.

Okinawa & the Southwest Islands

Best Beaches

➡ Ida-no-hama, Iriomote-jima (p756)

➡ Sunset Beach, Ishigaki-jima (p751)

➡ Sunayama Beach, Miyako-jima (p747)

➡ Nishibama Beach, Aka-jima (p745)

➡ Furuzamami Beach, Zamami-jima (p745)

Best Diving Destinations

➡ Yonaguni-jima (p759)

➡ Kerama Islands (p744)

➡ Ishigaki-jima (p750)

➡ Iriomote-jima (p756)

Why Go?

Japan's Southwest Islands (南西諸島; Nansei-shotō) are *the other Japan:* a chain of semitropical, coral-fringed islands that feels more like Hawaii or Southeast Asia.

They're a nature lover's paradise: in the northern Kagoshima Prefecture lush primeval forests hide among the craggy peaks of Yakushima, and the starfish-shaped Amami-Ōshima has fine beaches on its convoluted coastline. Heading south, Okinawa-hontō (沖縄本島) is the bustling main island of Okinawa Prefecture. The nearby Kerama Islands are tiny gems with white-sand beaches and crystal-clear waters. Miyako-jima boasts killer beaches and a laid-back scene. And furthest south, the Yaeyama Islands have Japan's best coral reefs, subtropical jungles and mangrove swamps.

But spectacular nature is only part of it – the Southwest Islands exude a peculiarly 'un-Japanese' culture. Indeed, they made up a separate country for most of their history, and the Ryūkyū cultural heart still beats strongly here.

When to Go
Naha

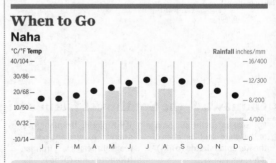

May & Jun Travel may coincide with the rainy season; while it's not too intense, sunshine may be scarce.

Jul–Sep This is the best time to enjoy the beaches, but expect some big crowds.

Oct–Mar The water is cooler but swimmable, and you'll have entire beaches to yourself.

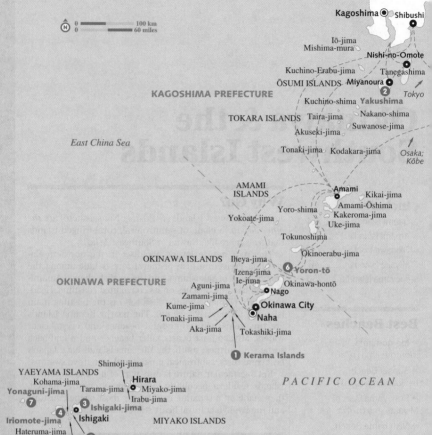

Okinawa & the Southwest Islands Highlights

❶ Soaking up the sun on one of the white-sand beaches of the **Kerama Islands** (p744)

❷ Hiking into the mountainous heart of **Yakushima** (p724) to commune with ancient *yakusugi* trees

❸ Diving with playful mantas off **Ishigaki-jima** (p750)

❹ Exploring the mangrove swamps, jungles and coral reefs of Japan's last frontier, **Iriomote-jima** (p756)

❺ Taking a ferry to a simpler time on the 'living museum' island of **Taketomi-jima** (p758)

❻ Chilling out on peaceful **Yoron-tō** (p735), with its blissful scenery of beaches and sugarcane

❼ Searching the horizon for Taiwan from **Yonaguni-jima** (p759), Japan's westernmost island, and diving its mysterious underwater ruins

History

For centuries ruled by *aji* (local chieftains), in 1429 Okinawa and the Southwest Islands were united by Sho Hashi of the Chūzan kingdom, which led to the establishment of the Ryūkyū dynasty. During this period Sho Hashi increased contact with China, which contributed to the flourishing of Okinawan music, dance, literature and ceramics. In this 'Golden Era', weapons were prohibited, and the islands were rewarded with peace and tranquillity.

But the Ryūkyū kingdom was not prepared for war when the Shimazu clan of Satsuma (modern-day Kagoshima) invaded in 1609. The Shimazu conquered the kingdom easily and established severe controls over its trade. The islands were ruled with an iron fist, and taxed and exploited greedily for the next 250 years.

With the restoration of the Meiji emperor, the Ryūkyūs were annexed to Japan as Okinawa Prefecture in 1879. However, life hardly changed for the islanders as they were treated as foreign subjects by the Japanese government. Furthermore, the Meiji government stamped out local culture by outlawing the teaching of Ryūkyū history in schools, and establishing Japanese as the official language.

In the closing days of WWII, the Japanese military made a decision to use the islands of Okinawa as a shield against Allied forces. Sacrificing it cost the islanders dearly: more than 100,000 Okinawan civilians lost their lives in the Battle of Okinawa.

Following the war, the occupation of the Japanese mainland ended in 1952, but Okinawa remained under US control until 1972. Its return, however, was contingent upon Japan agreeing to allow the Americans to maintain bases on the islands and some 30,000 American military personnel remain.

Climate

The Southwest Islands have a subtropical climate. With the exception of the peaks of Yakushima, which can be snowcapped between December and February, there's no real winter. You can easily travel the Southwest Islands any time of year, but swimming might be uncomfortable between late October and early May, unless you're the hardy sort.

The average daily temperature on Okinawa-hontō in December is 20°C, while in July is it is 30°C. The islands of Kagoshima Prefecture average a few degrees cooler, while those of the Yaeyama Islands and Miyako Islands are a few degrees warmer. The islands are most crowded during June, July and August and during the Golden Week holiday in early May. Outside of these times, the islands are often blissfully quiet.

The main thing to keep in mind when planning a trip to the Southwest Islands is the possibility of typhoons, which can strike any time between June and October. If you go then, build flexibility into your schedule, as typhoons often cause transport delays. Ideally, purchase tickets that allow changes without incurring a fee. The **Japan Meteorological Agency's website** (www.jma.go.jp/en/typh) has the latest details on typhoons approaching Japan.

Language

Although the Ryūkyū islands used to have their own distinctive language, this has by and large disappeared. Standard Japanese is spoken by almost every resident of the islands. That said, travellers who speak some standard Japanese might find the local dialects and accent a little hard to catch.

❶ Getting There & Away

There are flights between major cities in mainland Japan and Amami-Ōshima, Okinawa-hontō (Naha), Miyako-jima and Ishigaki-jima. Kagoshima has flights to/from all these islands and many of the smaller islands as well. Other islands such as Yonaguni-jima, Kume-jima and Zamami-jima can be reached from Naha or Ishigaki.

There are ferries between Tokyo, Osaka/Kōbe and Kagoshima to the Amami Islands and Okinawa-hontō, as well as plentiful ferries between Kagoshima and Yakushima and Tanegashima. Once you arrive in a port such as Amami (previously called Naze) on Amami-Ōshima or Naha on Okinawa-hontō, there are local ferry services to nearby islands. However, you cannot reach the Miyako Islands or Yaeyama Islands by ferry from mainland Japan or Okinawa-hontō; it's necessary to fly to these destination from mainland Japan.

If you are arriving in Japan by air, it is worth noting that Japan Airlines and All Nippon Airways both offer 'visit Japan'–type airfares for domestic flights within Japan – as long as they are bought outside Japan in conjunction with a ticket to Japan. Such tickets, if used to Okinawa, are an incredible saving from standard domestic airfares bought within Japan.

ALL-YOU-CAN-SAIL TICKET

A Line Ferry (☑ in Kagoshima 099-226-4141, in Tokyo 03-5643-6170; www.aline-ferry.com) sails from Kagoshima to Naha and offers a little-known but great deal in its *norihōdai kippu* (2nd-class sleeping rooms; ¥14,600), which lets you get on and off its south- or north-bound ferries freely within seven days; ferries stop at Amami-Ōshima, Tokunoshima, Okinoerabu-jima, Yoron-tō, and Motobu on Okinawa-hontō. On each leg of the trip, you must inform staff that you're hopping on and off, and you can travel in one direction only, but the savings on individual 2nd-class trips is more than ¥6000.

ℹ️ Getting Around

Aside from ferries, there are also reasonable air networks in the Amami Islands, Okinawa Islands and Yaeyama Islands, with airfields on most islands. While most islands have public bus networks, there are usually not more than a few buses per day on each route. We recommend bringing an International Driving Permit and renting a car or scooter, particularly on Yakushima, Ishigaki, Iriomote and Okinawa-hontō.

KAGOSHIMA PREFECTURE

The northern end of the Southwest Islands is part of Kagoshima Prefecture (鹿児島県; Kagoshima-ken), and contains three island groups (island groups are called 'shotō' or 'rettō' in Japanese). All are accessible by ferry or plane.

Northernmost are the Ōsumi Islands, which are home to the island of Yakushima, one of the most popular destinations in the Southwest Islands. Next are the Tokara Islands, consisting of 12 rarely visited volcanic islets; these are the most remote destinations in the region. Southernmost are the Amami Islands, which are home to the population centre of Amami-Ōshima as well as several more picturesque islands. Located 380km south of Kyūshū, this group has a pronounced tropical feel.

Ōsumi Islands 大隈諸島

The Ōsumi Islands comprise the two main islands of Yakushima and Tanegashima and the seldom-visited triumvirate of islands known as Mishima-mura. The all-star attraction in the group is Yakushima, a virtual paradise for nature lovers that attracts large numbers of both domestic and international travellers. Tanegashima, which is famous as the home of Japan's space program, sees few foreign travellers, though it is a popular surfing destination for Japanese. Finally, the most commonly visited island in the Mishima-mura group is tiny Iō-jima, a rarely visited gem of a volcanic island with excellent onsen (hot springs).

Yakushima 屋久島

♪ 0997 / POP 13,700

Designated a Unesco World Heritage Site in 1993, Yakushima is one of the most rewarding islands in the Southwest Islands. The craggy mountain peaks of the island's interior are home to the world-famous *yakusugi* (屋久杉; *Cryptomeria japonica*), ancient cedar trees that are said to have been the inspiration for some of the scenes in Miyazaki Hayao's animation classic *Princess Mononoke*.

Hiking among the high peaks and mossy forests is the main activity on Yakushima, but the island is also home to some excellent coastal onsen and a few sandy beaches.

Keep in mind that Yakushima is a place of extremes: the mountains wring every last drop of moisture from the passing clouds and the interior of the island is one of the wettest places in Japan. In the winter the peaks may be covered in snow, while the coast is still relatively balmy. Whatever you do, come prepared and don't set off on a hike without a good map and the proper gear. An International Driving Permit will also vastly increase your enjoyment here, as buses are few and far between.

⊙ Sights

Yakushima's main port is Miyanoura (宮之浦), on the island's northeast coast. This is the most convenient place to be based, as most buses originate from here. From Miyanoura, a road runs around the perimeter of the island, passing through the secondary port of Anbō (安房) on the east coast, and then through the hot-springs town of Onoaida (尾之間) in the south. Heading north from Miyanoura, the road takes you to the town of Nagata (永田), which has a brilliant stretch of white-sand beach.

Yakushima

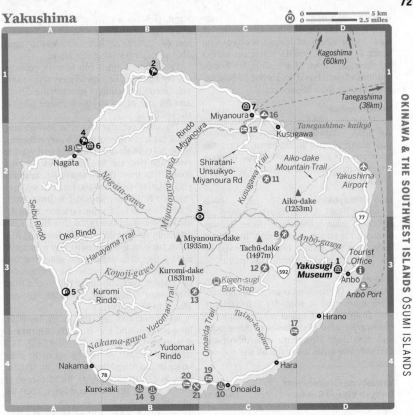

Yakushima

★ **Yakusugi Museum**   MUSEUM
(屋久杉自然館; ☏ 46-3113; admission ¥600; ⊙ 9am-5pm, closed 1st Tue) In a forested spot with sea views, the Yakusugi Museum has informative, beautifully designed exhibits about *yakusugi* and the history of the islanders' relationship to these magnificent trees. The museum offers an excellent audio guide in English. It's conveniently located on the road leading up to Yakusugi Land.

Nagata Inaka-hama   BEACH

(永田いなか浜) On the island's northwest coast in the village of Nagata is a beautiful beach for sunsets, and it's where sea turtles lay their eggs from May to July. It's beside the Inaka-hama bus stop, served by Nagata-bound buses from Miyanoura.

Umigame-kan   MUSEUM

(うみがめ館; ☑ 49-6550; 489-8 Nagata; admission ¥200; ◷ 9am-5pm Wed-Mon) About midway along Nagata Inaka-hama, along the main road, is this place which has displays and information about the turtles (mostly in Japanese).

Issō-kaisuiyokujō   BEACH

(一湊海水浴場) A fine beach, located on the north coast of the island, about midway between Miyanoura and Nagata. It's a short walk from the Yahazu bus stop (served by any Nagata-bound bus from Miyanoura).

Ōko-no-taki   WATERFALL

(大川の滝) On the west coast is Yakushima's highest waterfall at 88m. It's a five-minute walk from Ōko-no-taki bus stop, which is the last stop for some of the buses running south and west from Miyanoura and Anbo (note that only two buses a day run all the way out here).

Yakushima Environment Culture Village Center   MUSEUM

(屋久島環境文化村センター; ☑ 42-2900; admission & film ¥500; ◷ 9am-5pm Tue-Sun Sep-Jun, daily Jul & Aug) In Miyanoura at the corner of the ferry-terminal road. It has exhibits about the island's natural environment and history, with limited English signs. It screens a large-format 25-minute film (sparsely subtitled in English) at 20 minutes past the hour.

🏃 Activities

Hiking

Hiking is the best way to experience Yakushima's beauty. If you're planning anything more than a short stroll around Yakusugi

Land, pick up a copy of the Japanese-language guide *Yama-to-Kougen-no-Chizu-Yakushima* (山と高原の地図屋久島; ¥840), available at major bookshops in Japan.

Even though trails can be very crowded during holidays, be sure to alert someone at your accommodation of your intended route and fill in a *tōzan todokede* (route plan) at the trailhead.

The most popular hike is to **Jōmon-sugi** (縄文杉), a monster of a *yakusugi* estimated to be 3000 years old. There are two ways to reach the tree: the 19.5km, eight-to-10-hour round trip from the **Arakawa-tozanguchi** (荒川登山口) trailhead (604m). From March through November, in order to limit traffic congestion, all hikers must transfer to an Arakawa Mountain Bus (¥850; five departures and eight returns daily) at the Yakusugi Museum parking lot. You must buy a ticket at least a day in advance; also note that this fare is not covered by the one- or two-day bus passes. Two daily buses run to and from Miyanoura (¥930, one hour 20 minutes, March to November).

A shorter and arguably more beautiful hike is the round trip from the **Shiratani-unsuikyō-tozanguchi** (白谷雲水峡登山口) trailhead (622m), served by up to 10 daily buses to and from Miyanoura (¥530, 40 minutes, March to November). Budget three or four hours for this hike, and bring ¥300 for admission.

The granddaddy of hikes here is the day-long outing to the 1935m summit of **Miyanoura-dake**, the highest point in southern Japan. Fit climbers should allow about seven hours return from **Yodogawa-tozanguchi** (淀川登山口) trailhead (1370m). Yodogawa-tozanguchi is about 1.5km (about 30 minutes) beyond the Kigen-sugi bus stop, served by two buses a day to/from Anbo (¥910, one hour). The buses do not give you sufficient time to complete the round trip in a day – an early-morning taxi from Miyanoura (around ¥11,000) gives you time to make the second bus back to Anbō.

ℹ️ STAY DRY!

It rains *a lot* in Yakushima's interior. Be sure to be adequately prepared for hiking the rainforests. You may find yourself slogging through torrential rain for a whole day, so bring proper gear to protect yourself and whatever you're carrying. Mountain huts (*yama-goya*) have no staff, food or sleeping bags, so bring what you need. **Nakagawa Sports** (ナカガワスポーツ; ☑ 42-0341; http://yakushima-sp.com; 421-6 Miyanoura; rainwear rentals ¥1200-2400; ◷ 9am-7pm, closed every other Wed) in Miyanoura rents everything from rainwear (also in large sizes) to tents and baby carriers.

SEA TURTLES

Loggerhead sea turtles and green sea turtles come ashore on the beaches of Yakushima to lay their eggs. Unfortunately, human activity can significantly interfere with the egg-laying process. Thus we recommend that you keep the following rules in mind when visiting the beaches of Yakushima (particularly those on the northwest coast):

➡ Never approach a sea turtle that has come ashore.

➡ Do not start fires on the beach as the light will confuse the chicks (who use moonlight to orient themselves). Likewise, do not shine torches (flashlights) or car headlights at or near the beach.

➡ Do not walk on the beach at night.

➡ Be extremely careful when you walk on the beach, as you might inadvertently step on a newly hatched turtle.

➡ If you want to observe the turtles, enquire at Umigame-kan (p726).

Finally, it's possible to make a traverse of Miyanoura-dake with a stop at Jōmon-sugi en route. Do not attempt this in a day; you'll have to spend the night in one of the *yama-goya* (mountain huts) above Jōmon-sugi. Typical routes are between Yodogawa and Arakawa or Yodogawa and Shiratani-unsuikyō. A full traverse of the island is described in Lonely Planet's *Hiking in Japan*.

If you're feeling a little less adventurous, consider a visit to **Yakusugi Land** (ヤクスギランド; admission ¥300; ☺9am-5pm). This is a great way to see some *yakusugi* without a long trek into the forest. It offers shorter hiking courses over wooden boardwalks, and longer hikes deep into the ancient cedar forest. There are four buses a day to and from Anbō (¥720, 40 minutes).

Onsen

Yakushima has several onsen (hot springs), from beautifully desolate seaside pools to upmarket hotel facilities. The seaside onsen listed here are *konyoku* onsen (mixed sex baths) where swimsuits are not allowed; women traditionally wrap themselves in a thin towel for modesty.

Hirauchi Kaichū Onsen ONSEN
(平内海中温泉; admission ¥100; ☺24hr) Onsen lovers will be in heaven here. The outdoor baths are in the rocks by the sea and can only be entered at or close to low tide. You can walk to the baths from the Kaichū Onsen bus stop, but the next stop, Nishikaikon, is actually closer. From Nishikaikon, walk downhill towards the sea for about 200m and take a right at the bottom of the hill.

Yudomari Onsen ONSEN
(湯泊温泉; admission ¥100; ☺24hr) This blissfully serene onsen can be entered at any tide. Get off at the Yudomari bus stop and take the road opposite the post office in the direction of the sea. Once you enter the village, the way is marked. It's a 300m walk and you pass a great banyan tree en route.

Onoaida Onsen ONSEN
(尾之間温泉; 136-2 Onoaida; admission ¥200; ☺7am-9.30pm May-Oct, to 9pm Nov-Apr, from noon Mon) In the village of Onoaida is a rustic indoor bathhouse that is divided by gender. Expect to rub shoulders with the village elders here. The water is naturally, divinely hot. It's about 350m uphill from the Onoaida Onsen bus stop.

🛏 Sleeping

The most convenient place to be based is Miyanoura. You'll also find lodgings in larger villages and several bare-bones *yama-goya* in the mountains. In July and August and the spring Golden Week holiday, it's best to try to reserve ahead, since places fill up early.

★ Sankara Hotel & Spa HOTEL ¥¥¥
(サンカラ; ☎47-3488; www.sankarahotel-spa.com; r per person incl meals from ¥25,000; P @ ☒) Overlooking Yakushima's southeast coast, this stunning collection of luxury villas blends ocean views with Balinese floral design elements. The main restaurant's French fusion cuisine is created by Chef Takei Chiharu who trained at several three-Michelin-star establishments in France; the menu utilises as much local and organic produce as possible, much of which is grown expressly

for the hotel. All water used on the property comes directly from mountain run-off. Staff can pick you up, but if you have transport, look for the green signs in English along the road between Hirano and Hara. Guests 15 years and older only.

MIYANOURA

Ocean View Campground   CAMPGROUND ¥
(オーシャンビューキャンプ場; ☑42-0091; campsite per person ¥840) This campground is pretty much just a field for tents and a couple of showers and bathrooms, with a bit of rocky beach down the hill. It's just west of the Eneos petrol station. There are a few other campgrounds on the island, including one in Anbō and another on the Yahazu Cape.

Miyanoura Portside Youth Hostel   HOSTEL ¥
(宮之浦ポートサイドユースホステル; ☑49-1316; www.yakushima-yh.net; 278-2 Miyanoura; dm ¥3800, HI member ¥3200; ℗@🛜) This simple and clean youth hostel doesn't offer meals, but there are several good restaurants close by. It's a 10-minute walk from Miyanorua port – turn left off the main port road and veer left after passing the park; it's about 100m farther.

Lodge Yaedake-sansō   LODGE ¥¥
(ロッジ八重岳山荘; ☑42-1551; www17.ocn. ne.jp/~yakusima/lodge/index.html; r per person incl meals ¥7800; ℗) This secluded accommodation features Japanese- and Western-style rooms in rustic riverside cabins connected by wooden walkways. You can soak up the beauty of your surroundings in the communal baths, and children will enjoy splashing in the river. Meals served in the tatami dining room are simple, balanced and exquisite. The lodge is located inland on the Miyanoura-gawa; staff can pick you up in Miyanoura. If it's full, it also runs the **Minshuku Yaedake Honkan** (民宿八重岳本館; ☑42-2552; 208 Miyanoura; r per person incl meals ¥6300; ℗) in town.

ONOAIDA

⭐**Yakushima Youth Hostel**   HOSTEL ¥
(屋久島ユースホステル; ☑47-3751; www. yakushima-yh.net; 258-24 Hirauchi; dm with/without meals ¥5220/3540, HI member ¥4620/2940; ℗@🛜) This well-run youth hostel is about 3km west of Onoaida, nestled into the forest. Accommodation is in either Japanese- or Western-style dorms, and the shared kitchen and bathroom facilities are spotless. Get off

any southbound buses from Miyanoura at the Hirauchi-iriguchi bus stop and take the road towards the sea for about 200m.

Yakushima Iwasaki Hotel   HOTEL ¥¥¥
(屋久島いわさきホテル; ☑47-3888; http:// yakushima.iwasakihotels.com; 1306 Onoaida; d from ¥25,410; ℗@🛜🛝) This luxury hotel commands an impressive view from its hilltop location above Onoaida. Spacious Western-style rooms have either ocean or mountain views. The hotel has its own onsen and meals are available in two restaurants. Southbound buses from Miyanoura stop right in front.

NAGATA

⭐**Sōyōtei**   RYOKAN ¥¥
(送陽邸; ☑45-2819; http://soyote.ftw.jp/u44579. html; r per person incl meals ¥13,650; ℗) On the northwest coast near Nagata Inaka-hama, this gorgeous, family-run guesthouse has a collection of semidetached units that boast private verandahs and ocean views. The traditional structures feature rooftops unique to Yakushima, with stones serving as roof tiles – you'll recognise the place immediately. There is an outdoor bath overlooking the sea, but it's not always open. It's very close to the Inaka-hama bus stop.

🍴 Eating

There are a few restaurants in each of the island's villages, with the best selection in Miyanoura. If you're staying anywhere but Miyanoura, ask for the set two-meal plan at your lodgings. If you're going hiking, you can ask your lodging to prepare a *bentō* (boxed meal) the night before you set out.

If you need to stock up on supplies for camping or hiking, you'll find **Yakuden** (ヤクデン; ⊗9am-10pm) supermarket on the main street in Miyanoura, just north of the entrance to the pier area.

Naa Yuu Cafe   CAFE ¥
(なーゆーカフェ; ☑49-3195; lunch sets ¥800; ⊗11.30am-8pm Tue-Sun, closed 2nd & 4th Tue; 📶) Down a dirt road and facing a field of wild reeds, this cute cafe feels vaguely Hawaiian. The menu, however, leans more towards Thailand. Lunch sets range from red curry to Kagoshima black pork–sausage pizza. Look for a green sign in English, about 3km west of Onoaida.

Restaurant Yakushima   SHOKUDŌ ¥
(レストラン屋久島; ☑42-0091; 2nd fl, Yakushima Kankō Centre; dishes ¥1000; ⊗9am-4pm; 📶)

This simple restaurant serves a ¥520 morning set breakfast with eggs, toast and coffee and a tasty *tobi uo sashimi teishoku* (flying fish sashimi set meal; ¥980) for lunch. Look for the green, two-storey building on the main road, near the road to the pier.

Shiosai SEAFOOD ¥¥
(潮騒; ☑ 42-2721; dishes ¥1200; ☺ 11.30am-2pm & 5.30-10pm Fri-Wed) Find a full range of Japanese standards such as *sashimi teishoku* (sashimi set; ¥1700) or the wonderful *ebi-furai teishoku* (fried shrimp set; ¥1400). Look for the blue and whitish building with automatic glass doors along the main road through Miyanoura.

ⓘ Information

Tourist Information Centre (☑ 42-1019; ☺ 8.30am-5pm) Miyanoura's ferry terminal has a useful information centre in the round white building as you emerge from the ferry offices. It can help you find lodgings and answer all questions about the island.
Tourist Office (☑ 46-2333; ☺ 9am-6pm) In Anbō there's a smaller tourist office on the main road just north of the river.

ⓘ Getting There & Away

AIR

JapanAir Commuter has flights between Kagoshima and Yakushima (¥13,900, 35 minutes, five daily). Yakushima's airport is on the northeastern coast between Miyanoura and Anbō. Hourly buses stop at the airport, though you can usually phone your accommodation for a pick-up or take a taxi.

BOAT

Hydrofoil services operate between Kagoshima and Yakushima, some of which stop at Tanegashima en route. **Tane Yaku Jetfoil** (☑ in Kagoshima 099-226-0128, in Miyanoura 42-2003) runs four Toppy and Rocket hydrofoils per day between Kagoshima (leaving from the high-speed ferry terminal just to the south of Minamifutō pier) and Miyanoura (¥7700, one hour 45 minutes for direct sailings, two hours 40 minutes with a stop in Tanegashima). There are also two hydrofoils per day between Kagoshima and Anbō Port (2½ hours) on Yakushima.

The normal ferry *Yakushima 2* sails from Kagoshima's Minamifutō pier for Yakushima's Miyanoura port (one-way/return ¥4600/7900, once daily). It leaves at 8.30am and takes four hours.

The *Hibiscus* also sails between Kagoshima and Yakushima, leaving at 6pm, stopping overnight in Tanegashima, and arriving at Miyanoura at 7am the following day (one-way/return ¥3200/6400, once daily). Reservations aren't usually necessary for this ferry; it normally leaves from Kagoshima's Taniyama pier.

ⓘ Getting Around

Local buses travel the coastal road part way around Yakushima roughly every hour or two, though only a few head up into the interior. If you plan to get around the island by bus, we recommend buying a bus pass. Buses are expensive and you'll save a lot of money by purchasing a *Furii Jōsha Kippu*, which is good for unlimited travel on Yakushima Kotsu buses. One-/two-day passes cost ¥2000/3000 and are available at the Tane Yaku Jetfoil office in Miyanoura.

Hitching is also possible, but the best way to get around the island is to rent a car. **Toyota Rent-a-Car** (☑ 42-2000; up to 12hr from ¥5250; ☺ 8am-8pm) is located near the terminal in Miyanoura.

Tanegashima 種子島

☑ 0997 / POP 35,000

A long narrow island about 20km northeast of Yakushima, Tanegashima is a laid-back destination popular with Japanese surfers and beach lovers. Home to Japan's Space Centre, Tanegashima was where firearms were first introduced to Japan by shipwrecked Portuguese in 1543. Good ferry connections make this island easy to pair with a trip to Yakushima. Unfortunately, the relative lack of buses makes it difficult to enjoy this island without a rental car or scooter, or, at least, a good touring bicycle.

The island's main port of **Nishi-no-Omote** (西の表) is located on the northwest coast of the island, while the airport is about halfway down the island near the west coast. The best beaches and most of the surfing breaks are on the east coast of the island, which is also home to an onsen.

◉ Sights & Activities

Space Technology Museum MUSEUM
(宇宙科学技術館; ☺ 9.30am-5.30pm Tue-Sun, launch days) FREE Tanegashima's Space Centre, on the spectacular southeastern coast of the island, is a large parklike complex with rocket-launch facilities. Its Space Technology Museum details the history of Japan's space program, with some English labels. There are models of Japan's rockets and some of the satellites it has launched. Buses running from Nishi-no-Omote all the way to Tanegashima Space Center take two hours.

WORTH A TRIP

GET AWAY FROM IT ALL

Depending on when you go, the more remote Southwest Islands can be havens of tranquility with few other travellers. But if you really want to escape, it's just a question of hopping on the right ferry. In Kagoshima Prefecture, **Iō-jima** (硫黄島) is a tiny bamboo-covered island with a smouldering volcano and two brilliant seaside onsen. **Mishima Sonei Ferry** (☑ 099-222-3141) sails there from Kagoshima. The city is also home to **Ferry Toshima** (☑ 099-222-2101) which plies the **Tokara-rettō** (トカラ列島), a chain of seven inhabited and five uninhabited islands between Yakushima and Amami-Ōshima that offer plenty of hiking, fishing and onsen. Even for the Japanese, they seem like the end of the world.

Gun Museum MUSEUM
(種子島開発総総合センター・鉄砲館;
☑ 23-3215; 7585 Nishi-no-Omote; admission ¥420, combo ticket ¥550; ⊙ 8.30am-4.30pm) Though one focus is on the history of guns in Tanegashima, with an excellent collection of antique firearms, this is actually a cultural and natural-history museum as well. If you make as straight a beeline as possible up the hill from the port, you'll find it at a crossroads; the building looks like the stern of an old galleon. The combined ticket includes admission to an interesting **samurai house** (月窓亭; ☑ 22-2101; http://gessoutei.blogspot.com/p/english.html; 7528 Nishi-no-Omote; admission ¥200; ⊙ 9am-5pm) about 50m away.

Takesaki-kaigan BEACH
(竹崎海岸) Nearby to the Space Centre, this coastline is home to a beautiful stretch of white sand popular with surfers. The best spot to enjoy it is the beach in front of the Iwasaki Hotel (closest bus stop: Iwasaki Hotel), which has some impressive rock formations.

Nagahama-kaigan BEACH
(長浜海岸) The west coast of Tanegashima is also home to a 12km stretch of beach that is equally popular with surfers and egg-laying sea turtles.

Nakatane-chō Onsen Center ONSEN
(中種子町温泉保養センター; ☑ 27-9211; per person ¥300; ⊙ 11am-8pm Oct-Mar, to 9pm Apr-Sep, closed Thu) Hot springs at Kumanokaigan; the closest bus stop is Kumanokaisuiyokujō.

🛏 Sleeping & Eating

Nagareboshi MINSHUKU ¥
(流れ星; ☑ 23-0034; www.t-shootingstar.com; 7603-10 Nishi-no-Omote; r without bathroom, with/without breakfast ¥3000/2500; P @ 🛜) Run by a friendly, English-speaking woman, charm-

ing Nagareboshi has spotless, spacious rooms and a laid-back vibe. From the pier road, walk to the stoplight and jog around the right side of the post office, then walk uphill, bearing right at the top of the steps. Look for the sign up on the slope, and veer right towards a temple; it's on the left. Most travellers base themselves in the port town of Nishi-no-Omote. Listings in this section begin in Nishi-no-Omote, and end on Tanegashima's east coast.

Koryōri Shirō IZAKAYA ¥¥
(小料理しろう; ☑ 23-2117; 24-6 Higashi-chō; dishes from ¥500; ⊙ 5-11pm) Head to this friendly little *izakaya* in Nishi-no-Omote to sample tasty dishes such as the *sashimi teishoku* (sashimi set; ¥1200). There are plants out the front and blue-and-white *noren* (doorway curtains). It's along the main road east of the post office.

Izakaya Minshuku Sangoshō GUESTHOUSE ¥¥
(居酒屋民宿珊瑚礁; ☑ 23-0005; www6.ocn.ne.jp/~sangosyo/top.html; 201 Nishi-no-Omote; per person incl 2 meals from ¥8400; P 🛜) For something totally different, try this slice of Southeast Asia transported to Japan. It's a 'guesthouse-pub' with tons of cool features, including a brilliant rock-lined bathtub and a huge banyan tree out the front. Accommodation is in simple Japanese-style rooms. It's on the northwest coast, about five minutes' drive from Nishi-no-Omote.

Mauna Village BUNGALOWS ¥¥
(マウナヴィレッジ; ☑ 25-0811; www.mauna-village.com; 9668-40 Genna; r per person ¥4500-7300; P 🛜) On the east coast, this collection of cute, red-roofed cottages is popular with surfers and families. Some units have sea views and all have toilets, but bathing facilities are shared and meals are taken in a common dining room.

East Coast
BUNGALOWS ¥

(イーストコースト; 📞25-0763; www.eastcoast.
jp; Kanehama-kaigan; bungalow for 3 people ¥10,500-
12,600, per additional person ¥3150; 🅿) This
surf school–restaurant has two cosy, fully
equipped bungalows for those who want to
stay near the breaks. The owner is an English-
speaking Japanese surfer with a delightful
Aussie accent. As you might guess, it's on the
east coast of the island.

ⓘ Information

There is a helpful **information office** (種子島
観光案内所; 📞23-0111; ⊙9am-5.30pm) at the
pier in Nishi-no-Omote, inside the Cosmo ferry
office-waiting room.

ⓘ Getting There & Away

Tanegashima has five flights to and from Kagoshima (¥12,600, 30 minutes) on JapanAir
Commuter (JAC).

Tane Yaku Jetfoil (p729) has four daily high-
speed ferries (¥7000, 1½ hours) between Kagoshima and Yakushima, some of which stop at
Tanegashima. Finally, **Kashō Kaiun** (📞099-261-
7000) operates one normal ferry a day between
Kagoshima and Tanegashima (¥3500, three
hours and 40 minutes).

Amami Islands 奄美諸島

The islands of the Amami group are the
southernmost in Kagoshima Prefecture.
Amami-Ōshima, the largest and most popular island, lies at the northern end of the
group. It serves as the main transport hub
and boasts excellent beaches, as well as dense
jungle. The other islands in the chain are
dominated by sugarcane fields but also have
some good beaches. Heading south, Tokunoshima is famous for its 'bovine sumo', Okinoerabu-jima has intriguing caves and tiny
Yoron-tō is fringed with excellent beaches.

Amami-Ōshima 奄美大島

📞0997 / POP 68,600

Amami-Ōshima is Japan's third-largest
offshore island after Okinawa-hontō and
Sado-ga-shima. With a mild subtropical climate year-round, the island is home to some
unusual flora and fauna, including tree ferns
and mangrove forests. The coastline of the
island is incredibly convoluted – a succession of bays, points and inlets, punctuated
by the occasional white-sand beach – making the island an interesting alternative to
islands further south.

The main city and port, Amami (previously called Naze; 名瀬), is on the north
coast. The island's tiny airport is 55 minutes
away by bus (¥1100, almost hourly, buses are
timed to meet flights) on the northeast end
of the island. The best beaches are also at
the northeast end.

⊙ Sights & Activities

Amami-Ōshima is great to explore by touring bike or rental car. The coastal route to
Uken (宇検) on the west coast has some
lovely stretches. Another option is Rte 58
south to **Koniya** (古仁屋), from where you
can continue southwest to the **Honohoshi-
kaigan** (ホノホシ海岸), a rocky beach with
incredible coastal formations, or catch a ferry to **Kakeroma-jima** (加計呂麻島), a small
island with a few shallow beaches.

Ōhama-Kaihin-kōen
BEACH
(大浜海浜公園) The closest beach to Amami,
it's popular for swimming, snorkelling and sea
kayaking in summer. It can get crowded and
is not as nice as beaches further afield, but it's
convenient. Take an Ōhama-bound bus from
Amami and get off at the Ōhama stop (¥400).

Sakibaru Kaigan
BEACH
(崎原海岸) For a really stunning beach head
here, about 4.5km down a point of land just
north of Kise (about 20km northeast of Amami). Take a Sani-bound bus from Amami and
get off at Kiseura (¥950), and then walk. If
you're driving, it's marked in English off the
main road (be prepared for *narrow* roads).

Tomori Kaigan
BEACH
(土盛海岸) It's easy to get to this beach,
which also offers brilliant white sand and
some great snorkelling with a channel leading outside the reef. It's about 3km north
of the airport. Take a Sani-bound bus from
Amami and get off at Tomori (¥1210).

🛏 Sleeping

Minshuku Sango Beach
MINSHUKU ¥¥
(民宿さんごビーチ; 📞57-2580; sangobeach
0315@gmail.com; 68 Kuninao; r per person incl 2
meals from ¥6800; 🅿@) Overlooking a lovely
sand beach, this laid-back *minshuku* (Japanese guesthouse) offers peace in abundance.
Guests sleep in six semidetached units and
meals are taken overlooking the sea. Call
ahead for a pick-up from the ferry port or
from Amami. From the airport, take a bus
heading to Amami (¥800), and get off at the
West Court–mae stop.

Amami-Ōshima

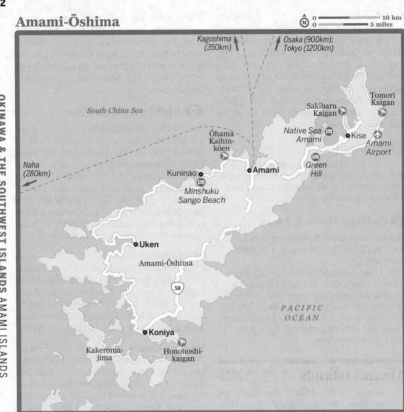

Pension Green Hill　　　GUESTHOUSE ¥¥
(ペンショングリーンヒル; ☎ 62-5180; www.
greenhill-amami.com; Tebiro; s/d incl two meals
¥8400/15,750; P @) A favourite among Japanese surfers, convivial Green Hill has ocean
views, Japanese- and Western-style rooms,
some with lofts. It's about 30 minutes from
the airport and a few minutes' walk to the
beach. Call ahead to ask for a pick-up.

Amami Sun Plaza Hotel　　BUSINESS HOTEL ¥¥
(奄美サンプラザホテル; ☎ 53-5151; 2-1 Minato-
machi; s/tw from ¥5900/8400; P ⊝ @) This
squeaky-clean and accommodating business
hotel is right in downtown Amami and a
five-minute taxi ride to the port. It's very convenient if you're leaving town on a 5am ferry.

Native Sea Amami　　　HOTEL ¥¥¥
(ネイティブシー奄美; ☎ 62-2385; www.native-
sea.com; 835 Ashitoku; r per person incl 2 meals
from ¥15,750; P @ ☎) About 28km east of
Amami (or 3km from the Akaogi bus stop),
this dive centre–resort has nice accommodation in a room block perched on a promontory over a lovely bay. There is a nice shallow
beach below the resort, and the dining room
and guest rooms have great views.

✗ Eating

Okonomiyaki Mangetsu　　OKONOMIYAKI ¥
(お好み焼き満月; ☎ 53-2052; 2-2 Irifune-chō;
dishes ¥1000; ☉ 11.30am-2.30am) Locals pile in
for the excellent *okonomiyaki* (batter and
cabbage cakes cooked on a griddle) at this excellent Amami eatery. For carnivores, we recommend the *kurobuta* mix (pork-shrimp-
squid mix; ¥1260), and for veggies, we recommend the *isobecchi* (*mochi* rice and nori
seaweed; ¥750). There's a picture menu.

ⓘ Information

Amami Tourist Service (奄美ツーリストサ
ービス; ☎ 53-3112; ☉ 8.30am-5.30pm) Can
help book flights and ferries, although some

Japanese skills will come in handy. Find it at the corner of the port entrance road and the main highway through town.

Tourist Information Counter (☑63-2295; ◷8.30am-6.45pm) In the airport arrivals hall; can help with maps and bus schedules.

ⓘ Getting There & Around

Amami-Ōshima has flights to/from Tokyo (¥48,570, 2½ hours, one daily), Osaka (¥38,400, one hour 45 minutes, one daily) and Kagoshima (¥21,200, one hour, four daily) on Japan Airlines (JAL) or JAC.

Ryukyu Air Commuter (RAC) operates a daily flight between Naha and Amami-Ōshima (¥24,400, one hour). There are also flights between Amami-Ōshima and the other islands in the Amami group.

Amami-Ōshima has a good bus system, but you will definitely appreciate a rental car if you have an International Driving Permit. **Matsuda Renta Car** (マツダレンタカー; ☑63-0240; ◷9am-6pm) on the main street in Amami has subcompacts from ¥4500. It also has a branch across from the airport.

A Line Ferry (☑in Kagoshima 099-226-4141; www.aline-ferry.com) operates four or five ferries a month running to/from Tokyo (¥20,500, 37 hours) and Osaka/Kobe (¥15,500, 29 hours), as well as daily ferries to and from Kagoshima (¥9400, 11 hours). Most of these ferries continue on to Naha (¥9540, 13 hours), so you can travel in the reverse direction from Naha to Amami-Ōshima as well.

Having joined forces commercially, **Marix Line** (マリックスライン; ☑53-3112, in Kagoshima 099-225-1551; www.marix-line.co.jp) and A Line still run their own ferries along the same routes, but on alternating days. If you find that one does not offer a route on the day you wish to travel, simply book with the other company.

Tokunoshima 徳之島

☑0997 / POP 25,500

Tokunoshima, the second-largest island of the Amami Islands, has some interesting coastal rock formations and a few good beaches. The island is famous for tōgyū (闘牛大会, bovine sumō), which has been practised on the island for more than 500 years. Attractions include decent diving and snorkelling and views that occasionally call to mind parts of Hawaii.

On the island's east coast is the main port of **Kametoku-shinkō** (亀徳新港) and the main town of **Kametsu** (亀津). Tokunoshima's airport is on its west coast, not far from the secondary port of **Hetono** (平土野).

◉ Sights & Activities

If the spectacle of bulls locking horns interests you (the animals are goaded on by human handlers), there are 13 official tōgyū (bovine sumō) venues on the island that stage tournaments. The three biggest fights are held in January, May and October – call the tourist office to confirm details.

Several good beaches are dotted around the coast, including the excellent **Aze Prince Beach** (畦プリンスビーチ), which is near the Aze/Fruits Garden bus stop on the northeast coast.

About 9km north of the airport at the northwestern tip of the island, **Mushiroze** (ムシロ瀬) is an interesting collection of wave-smoothed rocks that makes a great picnic spot. On a point on the southwest coast of the island, the **Innojō-futa** (犬の門蓋) is a collection of bizarrely eroded upthrust coral that includes a formation that resembles a giant pair of spectacles. Blink and you'll miss the sign on the main road about 10km south of the airport. From the turn-off into the maze of sugarcane fields, it's a bit poorly signed in kanji.

⌑ Sleeping

Aze Campground   CAMPGROUND ¥
(畦キャンプ場; campsites free; P) This fine little campground at Aze Prince Beach has showers, nice grassy campsites and a trail down to its own private beach.

★**Pension Shichifukujin**   MINSHUKU ¥
(ペンション七福神; ☑82-1126; s/d ¥3000/4000; P🐱📶) Run by the effusive Shikasa-san, this hillside minshuku has spacious, comfortable Japanese- and Western-style rooms in the main building and an additional block. There's a cheery kitchen area, and discounts are available for long-term stays. Add ¥1590 per person to include two meals in the deal. The family also runs a cheap **minshuku** (コーポ七福人; ☑82-2618; Kametsu; r per person ¥3000; P@) in town.

Kanami-sō   MINSHUKU ¥¥
(金見荘; ☑84-9027; www.kanamiso.com; r per person with/without meals ¥9980/4730; P@) In the village of Kanami at the very northeast tip of the island, this friendly divers' lodge has a great location overlooking a good snorkelling beach. Some of the upstairs rooms have sweeping views; cheaper rooms with shared bath are also available. The place specialises in ise ebi ryōri (Japanese lobster cuisine).

❶ Information

A small **tourist information office** (徳之島観光協会; ☎82-0575; ⊙9am-5:30pm Mon-Sat) at the ferry building has a detailed Japanese pamphlet and a simple English one about the island. It can help with accommodation, but book ahead.

❶ Getting There & Around

Tokunoshima has flights to/from Kagoshima (JAL; ¥29,000, one hour, four daily) and Amami-Ōshima (JAC; ¥13,300, 35 minutes, two daily).

Tokunoshima is served by Marix (p733) and A Line (p724) ferries, which run between Kagoshima (some originating in Honshu) and Naha, and Amami Kaiun ferries, which run between Kagoshima and Okinoerabu-jima.

There are bus stations at both ports, and a decent bus system to all parts of the island, but you'll definitely appreciate the convenience of a car, scooter or touring bicycle. **Toyota Renta Car** (トヨタレンタカー; ☎82-0900; ⊙9am-6pm) is right outside Kametoku-shinkō pier. There are also car-rental places near the airport.

Okinoerabu-jima 沖永良部島

☎0997 / POP 15,000

About 33km southwest of Tokunoshima, Okinoerabu is a sugarcane-covered island with some excellent beaches, interesting coastal formations and a brilliant limestone cave.

Wadomari (和泊), the island's main town, is decidedly retro. The airport is at the eastern tip of the island, with **Wadomari Port** (和泊港) in Wadomari, 6km away on the east coast.

◉ Sights & Activities

There are excellent beaches all around the island. You'll also find Japan's biggest banyan tree and several 'secret' little beaches off the coastal road between Fūcha and the airport.

The island's coast has many impressive geographical landforms. **Tamina-misaki** (田皆崎), at the northwest tip of the island, has ancient coral that has been upthrust to form a 40m cliff. At the island's northeast tip, **Fūcha** (フーチャ) is a blowhole in the limestone rock, which shoots water 10m into the air on windy days.

Okidomari Kaihin-kōen　　　　　BEACH

(沖泊海浜公園) Backed by green cliffs, the white sand and offshore coral formations make this beach a worthwhile stop; it's at the northwest end of the island.

Shōryū-dō　　　　　CAVE

(昇竜洞; ☎93-4536; admission ¥1000; ⊙9am-5pm) On the southwest slopes of Ōyama (the mountain at the west end of the island), you will find this brilliant limestone cave with 600m of walkways and illumination. It's a few kilometres inland from the southwest coastal road.

🛏 Sleeping & Eating

Okidomari Campground　　　　　CAMPGROUND

(沖泊キャンプ場; campsites free; ℗) This excellent beachfront campground at Okidomari Kaihin-kōen has showers and large grassy areas with trees for shade.

Business Hotel Ugurahama　　　　　HOTEL ¥¥

(ビジネスホテルうぐら浜; ☎92-2268; www.erabu.net/ugurahama; 6-1 Wadomari; r per person with/without meals from ¥6000/4300; ℗@) This friendly hotel has simple Japanese- and Western-style rooms. From the port, take a left on the main road and follow it over the bridge and through the town; look for the white building with blue trim on your right.

Mouri Mouri　　　　　IZAKAYA ¥¥

(もおりもおり; ☎92-0538; 582 Wadomari; meals from ¥1500; ⊙5pm-midnight, closed some Sun) This is a superfriendly place for dinner in Wadomari, with small dishes such as *gōyā champuru* (bitter melon stir-fry; ¥500). See if you can break the local beer-chugging record, which stands at under three seconds. It's a little hard to spot: from the Menshiori Shopping Street (when coming from port), take the first right then the first left and look for the small, dark-wood shopfront.

Sō　　　　　IZAKAYA ¥¥

(草; ☎92-1202; meals from ¥1800; ⊙6-11pm) Head towards the port from town, and on the main road after the bridge, you'll spy an ersatz water wheel in front of a corner restaurant. Step in the door and you'll find a friendly, cosy *izakaya* serving interesting local specialities like *yagi-jiru* (goat soup; ¥800) and *yachimochi* (rice cake made with black sugar; ¥650), as well as more typical *izakaya* items.

❶ Information

There is a small **tourist information booth** (☎92-2901; ⊙8.30am-5pm) at Wadomari port on the 2nd floor of the terminal building, which has maps of the island (the office is next to the ferry ticket window).

ⓘ Getting There & Around

Okinoerabu has flights to and from Kagoshima (¥29,500, one hour 15 minutes, three daily), Amami-Ōshima (from ¥16,800, 35 minutes, one daily) and Yoron-tō (from ¥10,000, 25 minutes, one daily) on JAC.

Okinoerabu-jima is served by Marix (p733) and A Line Ferry (p724), which run between Kagoshima (some originating in Honshu) and Naha, and Amami Kaiun ferries, which run between Kagoshima and Okinoerabu-jima.

The island has a decent bus system, but you'll definitely welcome the convenience of a car, scooter or touring bicycle. You'll find **Toyota Renta Car** (トヨタレンタカー; ☑ 92-2100; ⏱ 9am-6pm) right outside the airport.

Yoron-tō 与論島

☑ 0997 / POP 5500

Fringed with picture-perfect white-sand beaches and extensive coral reefs, Yoron-tō is one of the most appealing islands in the Southwest Islands chain. A mere 5km across, it is the southernmost island in Kagoshima Prefecture. On a good day, Okinawa-hontō's northernmost point of Hedo-misaki is visible 23km to the southwest.

The harbour is next to the airport on the western tip of the island, while the main town of **Chabana** (茶花) is 1km to the east.

◉ Sights & Activities

On the eastern side of the island, Yoron-tō's best beach is the popular **Oganeku-kaigan** (大金久海岸). About 500m offshore from Oganeku-kaigan is **Yurigahama** (百合ヶ浜), a stunning stretch of white sand that disappears completely at high tide. Boats (¥2000 return) putter back and forth, ferrying visitors out to it. Other good beaches include **Maehama-kaigan** (前浜海岸), on the southeast coast, and **Terasaki-kaigan** (寺崎海岸), on the northeast coast.

★ Yoron Minzoku-mura   MUSEUM
(与論民族村; 693 Higashi; admission ¥400; ⏱ 9am-6pm) At the island's southeastern tip, the excellent Yoron Minzoku-mura is a collection of traditional thatch-roof island dwellings and storehouses that contain exhibits on the island's culture and history. If at all possible, bring along a Japanese speaker, as the owner is an incredible source of information on the island.

Southern Cross Center   MUSEUM
(サザンクロスセンター; ☑ 97-3396; 3313 Ricchō; admission ¥300; ⏱ 9am-6pm) A short walk from the Ishini (石仁) bus stop, 3km south of Chabana, is a lookout that serves as a museum of Yoron-tō and Amami history and culture. Offering good views south to Okinawa, it celebrates the fact that Yoron-tō is the northernmost island in Japan from where the Southern Cross can be seen.

🛏 Sleeping

Shiomi-sō   MINSHUKU
(汐見荘; ☑ 97-2167; 2229-3 Chabana; r per person without bathroom incl meals from ¥5500; P @) This friendly and casual *minshuku* is popular with young people. Some Western-style rooms are available, though most are Japanese-style; all share bathrooms. Starting from Chabana harbour, take the main road north (uphill) out of town and look for it on the left after the turn; it looks like a private house. Staff will pick you up if you phone ahead.

★ Pricia Resort   HOTEL ¥¥
(プリシアリゾート; ☑ 97-5060; www.pricia.co.jp; 358-1 Ricchō; r per person incl breakfast from ¥7000; P @ ☀) These relaxing whitewashed cottages by the airport evoke Yoron-tō's sister island Mykonos in Greece. The best cottages are the beachfront 'B type' units. Breezy Western-style rooms and Jacuzzi baths are popular with Japanese divers and holidaying US servicemen from Okinawa. The hotel offers an entire menu of activities, including windsurfing, snorkelling and banana-boat rides.

🍴 Eating & Drinking

There's a large supermarket and two mini-markets in the centre of Chabana.

Umi Café   CAFE ¥
(海カフェ; ☑ 97-4621; 2309 Chabana; meals from ¥800; ⏱ 11am-6pm, from 1pm Sat; 🍴) This delightful terraced gallery-cafe with ocean views is something you'd expect to find perched on a Greek cliff; it's no surprise to find chicken gyros pitas (¥700) on the menu. Go to the village office at the top of the main drag, turn left and then right at the end of the street. Look for small signs along the road, or ask locals. The owner also runs a small hostel (dorm bed ¥1500).

Bar Natural Reef   BAR
(ナチュラルリーフ; 16-1 Chabana; snacks from ¥600; ⏱ 8.30pm to late) This tiki bar on Chabana's main drag is the best watering hole on the island, with plenty of *yū sen*, a local *shōchū* (strong distilled alcohol) made

LIVING LANGUAGES

If you spend a little time in Okinawa, you might hear bits of the Okinawan language: 'mensōre' ('welcome') instead of the standard Japanese 'yōkoso' – or 'nifei dēbiru' instead of 'arigatō'. What you may not realise is that besides Okinawan, there exists a colourful diversity of distinct dialects throughout the island chain – all considered Ryukyuan languages. Sadly, many of these dialects are dying out with older generations.

According to Unesco, of the existing 7000 or so languages spoken in the world, around 2500 are considered endangered. When Kiku Hidenori (owner of Yoron Minzoku-mura, p735, on Yoron-tō) heard this statistic several years ago, he was dismayed to find the Amami, Okinawa and Yoron dialects included among these endangered dialects. As someone who actively preserves traditional Yoron culture and grew up speaking Yoron-hōgen (Yoron dialect), he decided that he needed to help save his island's language from extinction.

Kiku explains, 'People of my generation – I'm 50 years old – can still speak Yoron-hōgen. Nowadays, there's a television in every house, broadcasting in standard Japanese. Children don't grow up in the same homes as their grandparents, so they just don't hear Yoron-hōgen. We are beginning to lose the dialect.'

Kiku has begun teaching Yoron-hōgen in local elementary schools, and bringing junior high school students to Yoron Minzoku-mura to give older kids a sense of pride in their unique heritage and dialect. His independent work has attracted the attention of Japanese language professors. 'Obviously, one must try one's very best individually, but I think that networking is crucial,' he says. Kiku actively liaises with other dialect preservationists in Japan to find the best strategies and methods for keeping dialects alive. With any luck, such grassroots efforts by him and others can bring these island tongues back from the brink.

from sugarcane, to keep everyone happy. Owner Kowaguchi-san has lots of tips about the best spots on Yoron-tō.

ⓘ Information

Beside the city office in Chabana is the useful **tourist information office** (ヨロン島観光協会; ☑ 97-5151; 32-1 Chabana; ☺ 8.30am-5.30pm), which provides maps, an English pamphlet and can make accommodation bookings.

ⓘ Getting There & Away

Yoron-tō has direct flights to/from Kagoshima (JAC; ¥31,000, one hour 20 minutes, one daily), Okinoerabu-jima (JAC; ¥10,000, 25 minutes, one daily) and Naha (RAC; ¥15,300, 35 minutes, one daily).

Yoron-tō is served by Marix (p733) and A Line Ferry (p724), which run between Kagoshima (some originating in Honshu) and Naha, and Amami Kaiun ferries, which run between Kagoshima and Okinoerabu-shima.

Yoron-tō has a bus system, but you'll definitely appreciate the convenience of a car, scooter or touring bicycle. **Yoron Rentacar** (与論レンタカー; ☑ 97-3633), located in Chabana, will meet car- or scooter-rental clients at the airport, and may offer you an energy drink when sending you on your way. If you don't opt for the convenient airport pick-up, find Yoron Rentacar on the road just east of the post office, off Chabana's main drag.

OKINAWA PREFECTURE

Japan's southernmost prefecture, Okinawa Prefecture (沖縄県; Okinawa-ken) makes up the southern half of the Southwest Islands. The prefecture stretches from the southern islands in Kagoshima Prefecture to within 110km of Taiwan. Three island groups make up the prefecture. From north to south, they are the Okinawa Islands, Miyako Islands and Yaeyama Islands.

The northernmost island group is the Okinawa Islands, which contains Okinawa-hontō (meaning 'Okinawa Main Island' in Japanese), home to the prefectural capital, Naha. This is the prefecture's transport hub, easily accessed by flights and ferries to/from the mainland. Plentiful ferries run between Naha and the Kerama Islands, which lie about 30km west of Okinawa-hontō.

Located 300km southwest of Okinawa-hontō, the Miyako Islands are home to the popular beach destination of Miyako-jima. There is no ferry access to this group; you must arrive via flights from the mainland, Naha or Ishigaki.

The Yaeyama Islands, a further 100km southwest, include the coral-fringed island of Ishigaki and the nearby jungle-clad Iriomote-jima. Like the Miyako Islands, you have to fly in.

Okinawa-hontō 沖縄本島

📀 098 / POP 1.39 MILLION

Okinawa-hontō is the largest island in the Southwest Islands, and the historical seat of power of the Ryūkyū dynasty. Although its cultural differences with mainland Japan were once evident in its architecture, almost all traces were completely obliterated in WWII. Fortunately, Allied bombing wasn't powerful enough to completely stamp out other remnants of Okinawan culture, and today the island is home to a unique culinary, artistic and musical tradition.

The island is also home to some excellent beaches, delicious food and friendly people, many of whom speak a little more English than their mainland counterparts. Of course, with US Air Force jets flying overhead from time to time, it's hard to forget the reality of the continuing American military presence on the island and the history behind that presence.

Prefectural capital Naha is a transportation hub for the other islands. War memorials are clustered in the south of the island, while there are some good beaches and other attractions on the Motobu peninsula. The north is relatively undeveloped.

Okinawa-hontō

It's worth noting that Okinawa-hontō has been somewhat overdeveloped for domestic tourism. If you seek Southeast Asian–style beaches and fewer big resorts, the majority of your time is best spent on Okinawa Prefecture's smaller islands.

Naha 那覇

POP 315,000

Flattened during WWII, the prefectural capital of Naha is now a thriving urban centre. The city sports a convenient elevated monorail and a rapidly expanding skyline of modern high-rise apartments, as well as the inevitable traffic jams.

The city plays host to an interesting mix of young Japanese holidaymakers, American GIs looking for off-base fun and a growing number of foreign tourists. The action centres on Kokusai-dōri (International Blvd), a colourful and energetic 2km main drag of hotels, restaurants, bars, clubs and just about every conceivable type of souvenir shop. And overlooking it all from a safe distance to the east is Shuri-jō, a wonderfully restored castle that was once the home of Ryūkyū royalty.

◎ Sights & Activities

Naha is fairly easy to navigate, especially since the main sights and attractions are located in the city centre. The main drag is Kokusai-dōri, while the Tsuboya pottery area is to the southeast via a series of covered arcades. The Shuri district is located about 3km to the east of the city centre.

The city's main artery, **Kokusai-dōri** (国際通り), is a riot of neon, noise, souvenir shops, bustling restaurants and Japanese young things out strutting their stuff. It's a festival of tat and tackiness, but it's a good time if you're in the mood for it.

Many people prefer the atmosphere of the three shopping arcades that run south off Kokusai-dōri roughly opposite Mitsukoshi Department Store: **Ichibahon-dōri** (市場本道り), **Mutsumibashi-dōri** (むつみ橋通り) and **Heiwa-dōri** (平和通り).

★ **Tsuboya Pottery Street**   NEIGHBOURHOOD
(壺屋やちむん道り; Tsuboya Yachimun-dōri) One of the best parts of Naha is this neighbourhood, a centre of ceramic production from 1682, when Ryūkyū kilns were consolidated here by royal decree. Most shops along this atmospheric street sell all the popular Okinawan ceramics, including *shiisā* (lion-dog roof guardians) and containers for serv-

ing *awamori*, the local firewater. The lanes off the main street here contain some classic crumbling old Okinawan houses. To get here from Kokusai-dōri, walk south through the Heiwa-dōri arcade for about 350m.

★ **Okinawa Prefectural Museum & Art Museum**   MUSEUM
(沖縄県立博物館・美術館; ☑ 941-8200; Omuromachi 3-1-1; admission ¥400; ⊙ 9am-6pm Tue-Thu & Sun, to 8pm Fri & Sat) Opened in 2007, this museum of Okinawa's history, culture and natural history is easily one of the best museums in Japan. Displays are well laid out, attractively presented and easy to understand, with excellent bilingual interpretive signage. The art museum section holds interesting special exhibits with an emphasis on local artists. It's about 15 minutes' walk northwest of the Omoromachi monorail station.

Tsuboya Pottery Museum   MUSEUM
(壺屋焼物博物館; ☑ 862-3761; 1-9-32 Tsuboya; admission ¥315; ⊙ 10am-6pm Tue-Sun) In Tsuboya, you will find the excellent Tsuboya Pottery Museum, which contains some fine examples of traditional Okinawan pottery. Here you can also inspect potters' wheels and *arayachi* (unglazed) and *jōyachi* (glazed) pieces. There's even a cross-section of a *nobori-gama* (kiln built on a slope) set in its original location, where crushed pieces of pottery that date back to the 17th century lay suspended in earth.

Daichi Makishi Kōsetsu Ichiba   MARKET
(第一牧志公設市場; 2-10-1 Matsuo; ⊙ 10am-8pm) Our favourite stop in the arcade area is the covered food market just off Ichibahon-dōri, about 200m south of Kokusai-dōri. The colourful variety of fish and produce on offer here is amazing, and don't miss the wonderful local restaurants upstairs. Keep in mind, however, that this is a working market, so please don't get in the way of shopkeepers and consider buying something as a souvenir.

Fukushū-en   GARDENS
(福州園; 2-29 Kume; ⊙ 9am-6pm Thu-Tue) FREE Garden fans should take a stroll through Chinese-style Fukushū-en. All materials were brought from Fuzhou, Naha's sister city in China, including the pagoda that sits atop a small waterfall.

Shikina-en   GARDENS
(識名園; 421-7 Aza Māji; admission ¥400; ⊙ 9am-5pm, closed Wed) Around 4km east of the city

centre is a Chinese-style garden containing stone bridges, a viewing pavilion and a villa that belonged to the Ryūkyū royal family. Despite its flawless appearance, everything was painstakingly rebuilt after WWII. To reach the garden, take bus 2, 3 or 5 to the Shikinaen-mae stop (¥220, 20 minutes).

Naha City Traditional
Arts & Crafts Center
ART GALLERY

(那覇市伝統工芸館; 3-2-10 Makishi; admission ¥300; ⊙9am-6pm) Right on Kokusai-dōri, this place houses a notable collection of traditional Okinawan crafts by masters of the media. Staff members demonstrate glass-blowing, weaving and pottery-making in the workshops.

SHURI DISTRICT 首里

The original capital of Okinawa, Shuri's temples, shrines, tombs and castle were all destroyed in WWII, but the castle and surrounding structures were rebuilt in 1992.

Shuri-jō
CASTLE

(首里城; admission ¥800; ⊙8.30am-7pm Apr-Jun & Oct-Nov, to 8pm Jul-Sep, to 6pm Dec-Mar) The reconstructed castle sits atop a hill overlooking Naha's urban sprawl. It was originally built in the 14th century and served as the administrative centre and royal residence of the Ryūkyū kingdom until the 19th century.

Enter through the Kankai-mon (歓会門) and go up to the Hōshin-mon (奉神門), which forms the entryway to the inner sanctum of the castle, dominated by the impressive **Seiden** (正殿). Visitors can enter the Seiden, which has exhibits on the castle and the Okinawan royals. There is also a small collection of displays in the nearby **Hoku-den**. To reach the complex, take the Yui-rail monorail to Shuri Station. Exit to the west, go down the steps, walk straight, cross one

big street, then a smaller one and go right on the opposite side, then walk about 350m and look for the signs on the left.

Irino-Azana
VIEWPOINT

(西のアザナ) While you're at the castle, visit the Irino-Azana, a viewpoint about 200m west of the Seiden that affords great views over Naha and as far as the Kerama Islands.

☆ Festivals & Events

Dragon-Boat Races
DRAGON BOATS

Held in early May, particularly in Itoman and Naha. These races (*hari*) are thought to bring luck and prosperity to fishermen.

Ryūkyū-no-Saiten
CULTURAL

Brings together more than a dozen festivals and special events celebrating Okinawan culture for three days at the end of October.

Naha Ōzunahiki
SPORTS

Takes place in Naha on Sunday around the national Sports Day Holiday in October, and features large teams that compete in the world's biggest tug of war, using a gigantic 1m-thick rope weighing over 40 tonnes.

🛏 Sleeping

Naha is the most convenient base for exploring Okinawa-hontō.

Stella Resort
GUESTHOUSE ¥

(ステラリゾート; ☎863-1330; www.stella-cg. com; 3-6-41 Makishi; dm ¥1300, s/d ¥3000/4600; ℗@⊛) Between Heiwa-dōri arcade and the Tsuboya pottery area, this tropical-themed guesthouse has private loft rooms, pool table, an aquarium room for zoning out and English-speaking staff. Look for the turquoise building at the end of the covered section of Heiwa-dōri and climb the stairs to the lobby. The

---

THREE-STRING HARMONY

Stroll through any Okinawa town and before long you'll likely hear the tinkly sound of the *sanshin*, a banjo-like precursor to the ubiquitous *shamisen* that is played on Japan's main islands. Typically constructed of a wooden frame covered with python skin, the *sanshin* has a long lacquered neck, a bamboo bridge and three strings that are struck with a plectrum, often carved from the horn of a water buffalo.

Introduced from China in the 16th century, the *sanshin* was used for court music during the Ryūkyū kingdom and later prized by commoners for its soothing sound; in the devastation after WWII, *sanshin* made of tin cans and nylon string cheered the exhausted survivors. Today, you can hear folksongs featuring *sanshin* all over Japan. Musicians such as Takashi Hirayasu and Yoriko Ganeko have helped popularise the sound in and out of Japan so you can even find *sanshin* groups overseas.

Naha

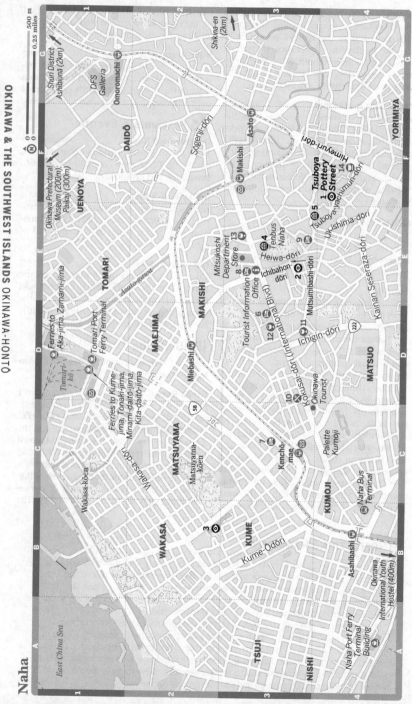

East China Sea

500 m
0.25 miles

Shuri District Ashibiuna (2km)
Shikina-en (2km)
DFS Galleria
Omoromachi

UENOYA
DAIDŌ

Sogenji-dōri

Asato

Makishi

Okinawa Prefectural
Museum (200m); Paikaji (300m)

TOMARI

Asato-gawa

Ferries to
Aka-jima, Zamami-jima

Tomari Port
Ferry Terminal

MAEJIMA

Ferries to Kume-
jima, Tonaki-jima,
Minami-daitō-jima,
Kita-daitō-jima

Tomari-
kō

Wakasa-kōen

WAKASA

Wakase-dōri

MATSUYAMA

Matsuyama-
kōen

58

Miebashi

KUME

Kume-Ōdori

TSUJI

NISHI

Naha Port Ferry
Terminal Building

Okinawa
International Youth
Hostel (400m)

Asahibashi

KUMOJI

Naha Bus
Terminal

Palette
Kumoji

Kenchō-
mae

7

Okinawa
Tourist

10

Kokusai-dōri (International Blvd)

Ichigin-dōri

MATSUO

222

Kainan Seseraza-dōri

Himeyuri-dōri

Tsuboya
1 Pottery
Street

5

Tsuboya-yachimun-dōri

Ukishima-dōri

Mutsumibashi-dōri

11

12

2

Ichibahon-
dōri

6

Tourist Information
Office

8 Store

Mitsukoshi
Department
Store

13

Heiwa-dōri

4

Tenbus
Naha

9

Maeshima

YORIMIYA

3

Naha

guesthouse also runs **Lohas Villa** (ロハスヴィラ; ☑ 867-7757; www.lohas-cg.com; 3rd fl, Breath Bldg, 2-1-6 Makishi; dm/s/d ¥1500/3500/5000; @🛜), just off of Kokusai-dōri.

Okinawa International Youth Hostel
HOSTEL ¥

(沖縄国際ユースホステル; ☑ 857-0073; www.oiyh.org; 51 Ōnoyama; dm ¥3360, r per person with/without bathroom ¥4620/4095; 🅿🚫@) This excellent youth hostel is located in Ōnoyama-kōen, a five-minute walk from the Tsubogawa Station; find detailed directions on the website. Prices are cheaper for Hostelling International members. Note that unmarried couples are not welcome to share rooms.

★ Hotel Sun Palace
HOTEL ¥¥

(ホテルサンパレス球陽舘; ☑ 863-4181; www.palace-okinawa.com/sunpalace; 2-5-1 Kumoji; r per person incl breakfast from ¥6500; 🅿🚫@) About three minutes' walk from Kokusai-dōri, the Sun Palace is a step up in warmth and quality from a standard business hotel. The fairly spacious rooms have interesting design touches and some have balconies; there's even a rooftop terrace, a refreshing bit of outdoor space laced with greenery.

Hotel JAL City Naha
HOTEL ¥¥

(ホテルJALシティ那覇; ☑ 866-2580; http://naha.jalcity.co.jp; 1-3-70 Makishi; s/d from ¥8000/10,000; 🅿🚫@🛜) Right on Kokusai-dōri, the modern JAL City has 304 swish, modern rooms, in which even the single beds are wide enough to serve as cosy doubles. Staff here have very limited English, but service is excellent.

✖ Eating & Drinking

Naha is the perfect spot to sample the full range of Okinawan cuisine.

Daichi Makishi Kōsetsu Ichiba
MARKET ¥

(第一牧志公設市場; 2-10-1 Matsuo; meals from ¥800; ⊙10am-8pm) We highly recommend a meal at one of the eateries on the 2nd floor of this food market. Just have a look at what the locals are eating and grab a seat.

Ashibiunā
OKINAWAN ¥

(あしびうなぁ; ☑ 884-0035; 2-13 Shuri-jō; dishes ¥900; ⊙11.30am-3.30pm & 5.30-midnight; 🈺) Perfect for lunch after touring Shuri-jō castle, Ashibiunā has a traditional ambience and serves staple set meals such as *gōyā champurū* (bitter melon stir-fry; ¥840) and *okinawa-soba* (thick white noodles served in a pork broth; ¥840) around a picturesque garden. Facing the entrance to Kankai-mon, turn left and follow the road until just before the intersection. It's on your right with a black-and-white sign and plants over the gate.

★ Yūnangi
OKINAWAN ¥¥

(ゆうなんぎい; ☑ 867-3765; 3-3-3 Kumoji; dishes ¥1200; ⊙noon-3pm & 5.30-10.30pm Mon-Sat) You'll be lucky to get a seat here, but if you do, you'll be treated to some of the best Okinawan food around, served in traditional but bustling surroundings. Try the *okinawa-soba* set (¥1400), or choose among the appealing options in the picture menu. On a sidestreet off Kokusai-dōri, look for the wooden sign above the doorway with white letters in Japanese.

★ Uchina Chaya Buku Buku
TEAHOUSE

(うちなー茶屋ぶくぶく; ☑ 861-2950; 1-28-3 Tsuboya; tea ¥800; ⊙10am-4.30pm Mon-Wed & Fri-Sat) This incredibly atmospheric teahouse near the east end of the Tsuboya pottery area is worth a special trip. It takes its name from the traditional frothy Okinawan tea served here: *buku buku cha* (¥800), jasmine tea topped with toasty rice foam and crushed peanuts. It's up a small lane just north of Tsuboya-yachimun-dōri and overlooks a historic 160-year-old house.

Baobab   BAR
(バオバブ; 2-12-7 Matsuo; ⊙ Tue-Sat) Tucked away on Ukishima-dōri, Baobab is an eccentric ode to Africa, with booths sculpted out of mock tree trunks, African wines and beer, and original cocktails (¥750) on offer.

Rehab   BAR
(3rd fl, 2-4-14 Makishi; ⊙ 7pm to late) This 3rd-floor international bar on Kokusai-dōri attracts a friendly, mixed crowd and has cosy nook seating, imported beer, and two-for-one drinks on Tuesdays. The cool bartenders here speak English.

Helios Pub   PUB
(ヘリオスパブ; ☑ 863-7227; 1-2-25 Makishi; beer ¥525; ⊙ 11.30am-11pm Sun-Thu, 11.30am-midnight Fri & Sat) Craft beer lovers who tire of Orion can perk up bored palates with a sample flight of three house brews (¥700) and pints for ¥525. Edibles cover the pub-menu gamut from fish and chips to taco rice, all very reasonably priced.

ⓘ Information

Post offices are scattered around town, including the **Miebashi post office** (美栄橋郵便局), on the ground floor of the Palette Kumoji building, the **Tomari-kō post office** (泊ふ頭郵便局; Port building), in the Tomari port building, and the **Kokusai-dōri post office** (国際通り郵便局), around the corner from Makishi Station.

Gera Gera (まんが喫茶グラゲラ; 2nd fl, 2-4-14 Makishi; per hr ¥480; ⊙ 24hr) A convenient net cafe on Kokusai-dōri. It's just a little east of the Family Mart convenience store.

Okinawa Tourist (沖縄ツーリスト; OTS; ☑ 862-1111; 1-2-3 Matsuo; ⊙ 9.30am-6.30pm Mon-Fri, to 5pm Sat) On Kokusai-dōri, a competent travel agency with English speakers who can help with all manner of ferry and flight bookings.

Tourist Information Counter (☑ 857-6884; 1F Arrivals Terminal, Naha International Airport; ⊙ 9am-9pm) At this helpful prefectural counter, we suggest picking up a copy of the *Naha Guide Map* before heading into town. If you plan to explore outside Naha, also grab a copy of the *Okinawa Guide Map*.

Tourist Information Office (那覇市観光案内所; ☑ 868-4887; 2-1-4 Makishi; ⊙ 8.30am-8pm Mon-Fri, 10am-8pm Sat & Sun) The city office has internet access and luggage storage for a small fee, and free maps and information. It's just off Kokusai-dōri (turn at Starbucks).

ⓘ Getting There & Away

AIR
Naha International Airport (OKA) has connections with Seoul, Taipei, Hong Kong and Shanghai. Connections with mainland Japan include Kagoshima (¥27,600, 1½ hours), Hiroshima (¥34,200, two hours), Osaka (¥36,400, 2¼ hours), Nagoya (¥41,100, 2½ hours) and Tokyo (¥43,070, 2¾ hours); significant discounts (*tabiwari* on All Nippon Airways and *sakitoku* on JAL) can sometimes be had if you purchase tickets a month in advance. Note that this is only a partial list; most large Japanese cities have flights.

Naha also has air connections with Kume-jima, Aka-jima, Miyako-jima, Ishigaki-jima and Yoron-tō, among other Southwest Islands.

BOAT
Naha has regular ferry connections with ports in Honshū (Tokyo and Osaka/Kōbe) and Kyūshū (Kagoshima).

Marix (p733) and **A Line** (☑ in Naha 861-1886, in Tokyo 03-5643-6170; www.aline-ferry.com) operate four to six ferries a month running to/from Tokyo (¥24,500, 47 hours) and Osaka/Kobe (¥19,600, 42 hours), as well as daily ferries to/from Kagoshima (¥14,600, 25 hours). Note that if you ask for a *norihōdai kippu* you can sail from Kagoshima to Naha and get on and off the ferries freely within seven days.

There are three ports in Naha, and this can be confusing: Kagoshima/Amami Islands ferries operate from Naha Port (Naha-kō); Tokyo/Osaka/Kōbe ferries operate from Naha Shin Port (Naha Shin-kō); and Kume-jima and Kerama Islands ferries operate from Tomari Port (Tomari-kō).

Note that there is no ferry service to the Miyako Islands or Yaeyama Islands from Naha.

ⓘ Getting Around

The Yui-rail monorail runs from Naha International Airport in the south to Shuri in the north. Prices range from ¥200 to ¥290; day passes cost ¥600. Kenchō-mae Station is at the western end of Kokusai-dōri, while Makishi Station is at its eastern end.

Naha Port is a 10-minute walk southwest from Asahibashi Station, while Tomari Port is a similar distance north from Miebashi Station. Bus 101 from Naha bus terminal (那覇バスターミナル) heads further north to Naha Shin Port (20 minutes, hourly).

When riding on local town buses, simply dump ¥200 into the slot next to the driver as you enter. For longer trips, take a ticket showing your starting point as you board and pay the appropriate fare as you disembark. Buses run from Naha to destinations all over the island.

A rental car makes everything easier when exploring Okinawa-hontō. The rental-car counter in the arrivals hall of Naha International Airport offers information on the dozen or so rental companies in Naha, allowing you to comparison shop.

Southern Okinawa-hontō
沖縄本島の南部

During the closing days of the Battle of Okinawa, the southern part of Okinawa-hontō served as one of the last holdouts of the Japanese military and an evacuation point for wounded Japanese soldiers. A visit to the area, a day or half-day trip from Naha, is highly recommended for those with an interest in wartime history.

Okinawa's most important war memorials are clustered in the **Memorial Peace Park** (平和祈念公園; ⊙ dawn-dusk), located in the city of Itoman on the southern coast of the island. The centrepiece of the park is the **Okinawa Prefectural Peace Memorial Museum** (沖縄県平和祈念資料館; ☑ 997-3844; 614-1 Mabuni, Itoman-shi; admission ¥300; ⊙ 9am-5pm), which focuses on the suffering of the Okinawan people during the invasion of the island and under the subsequent American occupation. The main exhibits are on the 2nd floor. The museum strives to present a balanced picture of the Pacific War and the history that led to the invasion, but there is plenty here to stir debate. Outside the museum is the **Cornerstone of Peace** (⊙ dawn-dusk), which is inscribed with the names of everyone who died in the Battle of Okinawa.

To reach the park, take bus 89 from Naha bus terminal to the Itoman bus terminal (¥560, one hour, every 20 minutes), then transfer to bus 82, and get off at Heiwa Kinen-dō Iriguchi (¥460, 30 minutes, hourly).

An interesting stop en route to the Peace Park is the **Himeyuri no Tō** (ひめゆりの塔; Himeyuri Peace Museum; ☑ 997-2100; 671-1 Ihara; admission ¥300; ⊙ 9am-5pm), located above a cave that served as an emergency field hospital during the closing days of the Battle of Okinawa. Here, 240 female high-school students were pressed into service as nurses for Japanese military wounded. As American forces closed in, the students were dismissed and the majority died. Bus 82 stops outside.

Directly south of Naha in Kaigungo-kōen is the **Former Japanese Navy Underground Headquarters** (旧海軍司令部壕; Kyūkaigun Shireibu-gō; ☑ 850-4055; 236 Tomigusu-ku; admission ¥420; ⊙ 8.30am-5pm), where 4000 men committed suicide or were killed as the battle for Okinawa drew to its bloody conclusion. Only 250m of the tunnels are open, but you can wander through the maze of corridors, see the commander's final words on the wall of his room, and inspect the holes and scars in other walls from the grenade blasts that killed many of the men. To reach the site, take bus 33 or 46 from Naha bus terminal to the Tomigusuku-kōen-mae stop (¥230, 20 minutes, hourly). From there it's a 10-minute walk – follow the English signs (the entrance is near the top of the hill).

Motobu Peninsula 本部半島

Jutting out to the northwest of Nago, the hilly peninsula of Motobu (Motobu-hontō) is home to some scenic vistas, islets and decent beaches, as well as an incredibly popular aquarium. Motobu peninsula is served by frequent loop lines from Nago – buses 66 and 65 respectively run anticlockwise and clockwise around the peninsula.

A couple of kilometres north of Motobu town is the **Ocean Expo Park** (海洋博公園), the centrepiece of which is the wonderful **Okinawa Chiraumi Aquarium** (沖縄美ら海水族館; http://oki-churaumi.jp; 424 Ishikawa, Motobu-chō; admission adult/child ¥1800/600; ⊙ 8.30am-6.30pm Oct-Feb, to 8pm Mar-Sep). The aquarium is built around the world's largest aquarium tank, which houses a fantastic variety of fish including whale sharks. Unfortunately, this place is on the checklist of every single tourist to the island, and it can be packed. From Nago, buses 65, 66 and 70 run directly to the park (¥860, 50 minutes).

About 1km north of the aquarium is the quaintly preserved village of **Bise** (備瀬), a leafy community of traditional Okinawan houses along a beach. An atmospheric lane lined with old garcinia trees (フクギ並木) is perfect for strolling, and a few shops sell sea-shell crafts. Near the lane's southern end, **Cahaya Bulan** (チャハヤブラン; ☑ 051-7272; 429-1 Bise; ⊙ noon-sunset Mon-Sat, closed Wed-Thu in winter; ☎ 🅟) is a relaxing cafe with noodle dishes such as *ajian-soba* (Asian-style *soba*; ¥800) and a patio with views of Ie-jima.

If you're after natural attractions and have your own wheels, we recommend a drive out to **Kōri-jima** (古宇利島) via **Yagaji-jima** (屋我地島). The bridge between the two islands is surrounded by picturesque turquoise water, and there's a decent beach on either side of the road as you reach Kōri-jima. The bridge to Yagaji-jima starts just north of the Motobu peninsula off Rte 58.

AMERICAN BASES IN OKINAWA

The US officially returned Okinawa to Japanese administration in 1972, but it negotiated a Status of Forces Agreement that guaranteed the Americans the right to use large tracts of Okinawan land for military bases, most of which are on Okinawa-hontō. These bases are home to approximately 24,000 American servicemen.

Although the bases have supported Okinawa's economic growth in the past, they now contribute to about 5% the Okinawa economy. The bases are a sore spot for islanders due in part to occasional crimes committed by American servicemen. Antibase feelings peaked in 1996, when three American servicemen abducted and raped a 12-year-old Okinawan girl. Similar incidents in recent years have perpetuated animosity, including several in 2012 alone.

In April 2010, 90,000 protesters gathered to call for an end to the bases, the biggest such demonstrations in 15 years. That year, then Prime Minister Yukio Hatoyama fell on his sword after breaking a promise to move Futenma air base off the island; he finally admitted it would stay.

Exacerbating local resentment towards the bases was the introduction of Osprey tilt-rotor aircraft in late 2012. Ahead of the deployment, around 100,000 residents, concerned about the safety of the aircraft, protested by blocking entrances to the Futenma military base. The US formally agreed in early 2012 to move 9000 Marines (amounting to around half of the Marines on Okinawa) to bases on Guam, Hawaii and elsewhere in the Pacific.

Tourists to Okinawa are surprised to find that servicemen keep a relatively low profile. Unless one ventures to the areas north of Naha, it is possible to visit Okinawa without even noticing their presence – until another American fighter jet goes screaming overhead.

Northern Okinawa-hontō
沖縄本島の北部

The northern part of Okinawa-hontō is largely undeveloped and comparatively wild and rugged. Since there is limited public transport in the north, you will probably need a rental car. Route 58 hugs the west coast all the way up to **Cape-misaki** (辺戸岬; Cape Hedo), which marks the northern end of Okinawa. The point is an incredibly scenic spot backed by hills, with rocks rising from the dense greenery. On a good day, Yoron-tō, the southernmost island in the Amami Islands, is easily seen only 23km to the northeast.

Islands Near Okinawa-hontō

Most travellers don't come this far just to shop for clay *shiisā* in Naha. Even if your time on Okinawa-hontō is limited, it's a short ferry ride from Naha to some of the most attractive isles in the entire Southwest Island chain – the clear azure waters and white-sand beaches of the Kerama Islands are only 30km offshore, and about 60km beyond the Keramas lies the rarely visited Kume-jima.

To fall even further off the map, venture out to the other nearby islands we don't cover in this guide: Ie-jima, Iheya-jima, Izena-jima, Aguni-jima, Kita-daitō-jima and Tonaki-jima. Naha's Tourist Information Office (p742) can help with the preliminaries.

Kerama Islands 慶良間諸島

The islands of the Kerama group are a world away from the hustle and bustle of Okinawa-hontō, though even these islands can get crowded during the summer holiday season. The three main islands here are Zamami-jima, Aka-jima and Tokashiki-jima. You can easily visit any of these as a day trip from Naha, but we recommend a few days in a *minshuku* on one of the islands to really savour the experience.

AKA-JIMA 阿嘉島
♩ 098 / POP 279

A mere 2km in diameter, tiny Aka-jima makes up for in beauty what it lacks in size. With some of the best beaches in the Keramas and an extremely peaceful atmosphere, it's easy to get stuck here for several days. There's also some great snorkelling and diving nearby.

If you keep your eyes open around dusk you might spot a **Kerama deer** (慶良間シカ), descendants of deer that were brought by the Satsuma from Kagoshima when they conquered the Ryūkyūs in 1609. The deer are smaller and darker than their mainland cousins, and have been designated a National Treasure.

There are great beaches on every side of the island, but for sheer postcard-perfect beauty, it's hard to beat the 1km stretch of white sand on the northeast coast known as **Nishibama Beach** (ニシバマビーチ). This beach can be crowded in summer; if you want privacy, there are quieter beaches on the other sides of the island.

Dive shop–hotel **Marine House Seasir** (ペンションシーサー; ☑ 0120-10-2737; www. seasir.com; r per person incl meals ¥7350) at the west end of the main village has good, clean Western- and Japanese-style rooms. Most of the guests are divers. It offers whale-watching tours (¥4800) from January to March.

Kawai Diving (☑ 987-2219; http://oki-zamami.jp/~kawai/; 153 Aka; r per person incl meals from ¥6510; P@🛜), located along Maehama Beach on the south coast, has simple rooms and a family atmosphere. English-speaking staff are happy to tell guests about the island and take them diving (one/two dives ¥6300/10,500, equipment rental ¥1260 per piece).

If you speak Japanese (or can charm the lady of the house into accommodating you), check out **West Coast** (ウエストコースト; ☑ 987-2533; dm incl 2 meals ¥7350; P🛜🛜), which has four-person dorms with shared bathrooms in a dark-wood A-frame. There's a *rotemburo* (outdoor bath) – swimsuit required – facing the beach, and a simple dining and lounge area across a small grassy courtyard.

Zamami Sonei Ferry (☑ 868-4567) has two or three fast ferries a day (¥3140, one hour, 10 minutes) and one regular ferry (¥2120, 1½ hours) to/from Naha's Tomari Port. A motorboat also makes four trips a day between Aka-jima and Zamami-jima (¥300, 15 minutes).

Due to its small size, the best way to get around the island is on foot.

ZAMAMI-JIMA 座間味島

🎵 098 / POP 586

A stone's throw from Aka-jima, Zamami-jima is *slightly* more developed, but also has some great beaches and a few rocky vistas. It's got some brilliant offshore islands and

great diving and snorkelling in the surrounding waters. There is a **tourist information office** (☑ 987-2277; ⏱ 9am-5pm) at the port.

★**Furuzamami Beach** (古座間味ビーチ), approximately 1km southeast from the port (over the hill), is a stunning 700m stretch of white sand that is fronted by clear, shallow water and a bit of coral. The beach is well developed for day trippers, and has toilets, showers and food stalls. You can also rent snorkelling gear here (¥1000).

If you fancy a little solitude, you'll find picturesque empty beaches in several of the coves on the other sides of the island. The best beaches, however, are on **Gahi-jima** (嘉比島) and **Agenashiku-jima** (安慶名敷島), which are located about a kilometre south of the port. Ringed by delightful white-sand beaches, they are perfect for a half-day *Robinson Crusoe* experience. One boat operator who can take you to these islands and arrange snorkelling trips is **Zamami Tour Operation** (☑ 987-3586). The tourist information office can also help arrange boat tours (pick-up/drop off ¥1500 per person round trip).

Whale-watching is possible between the months of December and April. For more information, either enquire at the tourist information office or call the **Zamami-mura Whale-Watching Association** (座間味村ホエールウォッチング協会; ☑ 896-4141; http://www.vill.zamami.okinawa.jp/whale; adult/child ¥5250/2625), which has one to two tours daily (two hours).

Zamami-jima makes a great day trip from Naha, but an overnight stay will be more relaxing. A good place to stay is **Joy Joy** (ジョイジョイ; ☑ 0120-10-2445, 987-2445; http://keramajoyjoy.com/index.html; 434-2 Zamami; r per person incl breakfast from ¥5250) in the northwest corner of the village. Accommodation is in a variety of rooms that surround a small garden. This pension also runs a dive shop, with beach and sea dive tours from ¥4730.

Minshuku Summer House Yū Yū (民宿サマーハウス遊遊; ☑ 987-3055; www.yuyu-okinawa.jp/index.html; 130 Zamami; r per person with/without meals from ¥6000/3500) is a friendly *minshuku* that is just up the street from Joy Joy in the main village. Both places are an easy walk from the pier.

Zamami Sonei (☑ 868-4567) has two or three fast ferries a day (¥3140, 50 minutes) and one regular ferry (¥2120, two hours) to/from Naha's Tomari Port. The ferries usually

IN DEEP WATER

The Southwest Islands have some excellent diving and an impressive variety of fish and coral species. There is also a healthy smattering of underwater wrecks, cavern systems and even the odd archaeological ruin.

Costs for diving in the Southwest Islands are higher than you might pay in Southeast Asia, but standards of equipment and guiding are fairly high. In order to dive around Okinawa and the Southwest Islands, you will need to be in possession of a valid diving certification. If you're renting equipment, you should know your weight in kilograms, your height in metres and your shoe size in centimetres.

Here are some English-speaking operators who welcome foreigners:

Ishigaki: Umicoza (海講座; ☑ 0980-88-2434; www.umicoza.com/english; 827-15 Kabira; 1/2 dives ¥9450/12,600, equipment rental ¥5250; ◷ 8am-6pm)

Okinawa Hontō: Piranha Divers (☑ 098-967-8487, 080-4277-1155; www.piranha-divers.jp; 2288-75 Aza-Nakama; full-day dives from ¥17,000, equipment rental ¥4000)

Okinawa Hontō: Reef Encounters (☑ 090-1940-3528, 098-995-9414; www.reefencounters.org; 1-493 Miyagi, Chatan-chō)

Yonaguni: Sou Wes (p760)

stop at Aka-jima en route from Naha to Zamami. A motorboat also makes four trips a day between Aka-jima and Zamami-jima (¥300, 15 minutes).

There are no buses or taxis on Zamami-jima, though nothing is too far away. Rental cars, scooters and bicycles are available near the pier.

TOKASHIKI-JIMA 渡嘉敷島

☑ 098 / POP 785

Tokashiki-jima, the largest island of the Kerama Islands, is a long, skinny, north–south island that has some great beaches. It's very popular with young Japanese holidaymakers, but is actually slightly less appealing than Aka-jima or Zamami-jima. Ferries arrive at the port of Tokashiki (渡嘉敷) on the east coast.

The island's most attractive beaches are **Tokashiku Beach** (トカシクビーチ) and **Aharen Beach** (阿波連ビーチ), both of which are located on the west coast. Both beaches are well developed for tourism, and have toilets, showers, food stalls and shops where you can rent snorkelling gear (¥1000).

You can easily visit Tokashiki as a day trip from Naha. If you prefer to spend the night, Aharen is the place to be. **Southern Cross** (サザンクロス; ☑ 987-2258, 090-1941-1232; r per person with/without meals from ¥8500/6500; ℗), a family-run inn with simple Western- and Japanese-style rooms, is practically on the beach. Rates are a little cheaper if you opt for shared bathrooms. A little further back in the village you'll find **Kerama-sō** (けら

ま荘; ☑ 987-2125; r per person with/without meals ¥4725/3675), which is a larger, more organised *minshuku* with basic Japanese-style rooms and reasonable rates. Staff will pick you up at the pier if you can get someone to make a reservation in advance in Japanese.

Marine Liner Tokashiki (マリンライナーとかしき; ☑ 987-3122) operates two or three fast ferries a day (¥2430, 40 minutes), while **Ferry Tokashiki** (フェリーとかしき; ☑ 868-7541) runs one regular ferry (¥1620, one hour 10 minutes) from Naha's Tomari Port.

Buses run from Tokashiki Port to the beaches on the west coast. Bicycles, cars and scooters are available in Tokashiki Port; **Kariyushi Rentasābisu** (かりゆしレンタサービス; ☑ 987-3311; http://kariyushi-kerama.com; ◷ 9.30am-6.30pm) is one rental spot just outside the port area.

Kume-jima 久米島

[TEL]098 / POP 8713

The furthest flung of the outer islands, Kume-jima is a quiet island that sees fewer visitors than the Keramas. It's mostly flat and covered with sugarcane, with a few good beaches and the mother of all sandbars off its east coast.

The airport is at the western extreme of the island, while the main port of Kaneshiro (兼城) is on the southwest coast. There is a **tourist information office** (☑ 985-7115) at the airport that opens to meet incoming flights in summer.

The most popular beach on the island is **Ifu Beach** (イーフビーチ), on the east coast. *Ifu* means 'white' in the local Kume dialect, and not surprisingly, the beach is known for its powdery white sand. Another attractive beach is **Shinri-hama** (シンリ浜), on the west coast near the airport, which is known for its sunsets over the East China Sea.

Kume-jima's most famous attraction is **Hate-no-hama** (はての浜), a 7km sandbar that extends from the eastern point of the island, pointing back towards Okinawa-hontō. If you arrive by air, you can't miss this coral-fringed strip of white framed by the turquoise waters of the East China Sea. The best way to get there is on an excursion with **Hatenohama Kankō Service** (☑ 090-8292-8854), which runs a three-hour tour to the sandbar for ¥3500. If you book in advance, staff members can pick you up from your accommodation.

On tiny **Ōjima** (奥武島), which is connected to Kume-jima's east coast by a causeway, you'll find the intriguing **Tatami-ishi** (畳石), a natural formation of flat pentagonal rocks that covers the seashore.

Ifu Beach is the place to stay, and there are plenty of choices along the 1.5km waterfront. Our pick is **Minshuku Nankurunaisā** (民宿なんくるないさぁ; ☑ 985-7973; 160-68 Higa; r per person from ¥5000; P @ 🛜), an excellent, friendly new *minshuku* set back just a bit from the beach. It's got Japanese- and Western-style rooms. For those with tents, there is a small campground on Ōjima, before the Tatami-ishi.

JTA and RAC operate five flights a day between Naha and Kume-jima (¥9000 to ¥12,300, 35 minutes), and seven daily flights from Tokyo to Kume-jima (¥52,070 to ¥55,370, 2½ hours). **Kume Shōsen** (☑ 868-2686) runs one or two daily ferries from Naha's Tomari Port to/from Kume-jima (¥3300, 3½ hours).

Kume-jima has an efficient bus system, and there are several rental-car companies at the port and airport.

Miyako Islands　宮古諸島

Located just north of the Tropic of Cancer, the Miyako lslands have some of the finest beaches in the Southwest Islands, and there is good diving and snorkelling in the waters offshore. It contains the main island of Miyako-jima, and the nearby islands of Ikema-jima, Irabu-jima, Shimoji-jima and Kurima-jima, as well as a scattering of tiny islets.

Miyako-jima　宮古島

☑ 0980 / POP 55,036

The main island in the Miyako group, Miyako-jima is a mostly flat expanse of sugarcane fringed by excellent beaches, with long fingers of land pointing out into the sea. Lying just offshore are four smaller islands, two of which are connected to the main island by bridges (another bridge is under construction that will allow road access to all the nearby islands).

Miyako-jima is a beach island and you can happily spend your days here hopping from one great beach to the next, with a spot of snorkelling at each one if you're so inclined. If you tire of that, a seaside drive to the various capes of the island is a great way to spend a few hours.

⊙ Sights & Activities

On the southeast corner of Miyako-jima are several attractions including **Boraga-hama** (保良泉ビーチ; Boraga Beach), which is a popular spot for snorkelling and kayaking (with a hair-raisingly steep access road). Around the cape to the north, you'll find **Yoshino-hama** (吉野海岸; Yoshino Beach) and **Aragusuku-hama** (新城海岸; Aragusuku Beach), two relatively shallow beaches with a lot of offshore coral (much of it dead).

If you've got a car, we recommend a drive out to the end of **Higashi Henna-zaki** (東平安名崎), a narrow finger of land that extends 2km into the Pacific Ocean. There are picnic tables, walking trails and a lighthouse at the point for you to explore.

Another good drive is across **Ikema-Ōhashi** (池間大橋) to **Ikema-jima** (池間島). The shallow turquoise water on either side of this 1.4km bridge is incredibly beautiful on a sunny day (just try to keep your eyes on the road). You'll find several **private pocket beaches** around the coast of Ikema-jima.

★ Sunayama Beach　BEACH

(砂山ビーチ) Just 4km north of Hirara you will find this excellent little beach, which lies at the bottom of a large sand dune (hence the name 'Sand Mountain Beach'). A cool stone arch at one side of the beach provides a bit of shade.

Yonaha-Maehama　BEACH

(与那覇前浜ビーチ) On the southwest coast, beautiful Yonaha-Maehama is a 6km stretch of white sand that attracts a lot of families and young folks due to its shallow waters.

Miyako Islands

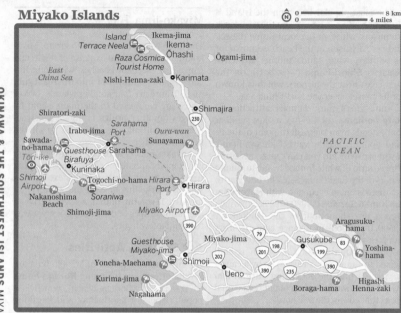

It's a lovely beach, but it can get crowded and the presence of the occasional jet-ski is a drawback. It's just before the Kurima-Ōhashi bridge, on the north side.

Nagahama
BEACH

(長浜) If you've had a look at the crowds at Yoneha-Maehama and decided you want something quieter, head across the Kurima-Ōhashi and drive to the northwest coast of **Kurima-jima** (来間島), where you will find the brilliant (and usually uncrowded) Nagahama.

Miyako Traditional Crafts Centre
ARTS CENTRE

(宮古伝統工芸品研究センター; Map p749; ⏰9am-6pm Mon-Sat) FREE If you can pry yourself away from the beaches for a moment, the Miyako Traditional Arts & Crafts Centre in Hirara has a 2nd-floor workshop where traditional *minsā* weaving is taught. It's up a small alley off Ichiba-dōri across from the Miyako Dai-ichi Hotel (宮古第一ホテル) – listen for the clack of wooden looms.

🛏 Sleeping

Most of the accommodation is located in the town of Hirara, but you'll also find places to stay closer to the beaches. There are free campgrounds at many beaches, including Yonaha-Maebama, Boraga and Aragusuku.

Hiraraya
GUESTHOUSE ¥

(ひららや; ☎75-3221; www.miyako-net.ne.jp/~hiraraya; 282 Higashi-nakasone; dm night/week ¥2000/12,000, r per person night/week ¥3000/18,000; P@) Located in central Hirara around the corner from Nakasone Super (look for the doorway curtain that says 'Hiraraya'), the genial, English-speaking Hiro presides over this laid-back spot where young neighbours and friends cruise in to hang out. Accommodation is available in a dorm with huge beds, or a Japanese-style private room; there are special rates available for longer-term stays.

Guesthouse Miyako-jima
GUESTHOUSE ¥

(ゲストハウス宮古島; ☎76-2330; www2.miyako-ma.jp/yonaha/index.html; 233 Yoneha; dm night/week ¥1800/11,200, r per person night/week ¥3500/21,000; P🛜) This bright and cheery guesthouse run by a kite-boarding enthusiast has a scenic location near Yoneha-Maehama beach. Accommodation is in cosy Western-style dorms and private rooms with shared facilities, and there are special rates available for long-term stays. Guests can also borrow bicycles and scooters.

★ **Raza Cosmica Tourist Home** HOTEL ¥¥
(ラザコスミカツーリストホーム; ☎75-2020; www.raza-cosmica.com; 309-1 Hirara-maezato; r per person incl breakfast ¥8000; 🅿🛜) This charming South Asian–themed inn sits above a lovely secluded beach on Ikemajima. Romantic Western-style rooms offer peace and quiet in truly lovely surroundings, which makes this the perfect destination for holidaying couples or honeymooners. Bathrooms are shared and children below 12 years of age are not permitted; owners ask that you reserve on their website. Look for the Shiva eyes on the door.

Island Terrace Neela BOUTIQUE HOTEL ¥¥¥
(アイランドテラス・ニーラ; ☎74-4678; www.neela.jp; 317-1 Hirara-maezato; s/d incl breakfast from ¥38,500/70,000; 🅿@🛜) Overlooking a serene white-sand beach on Ikema-jima, this intimate high-end resort looks like a whitewashed Mediterranean resort airlifted to Japan. The private villas would make a decadent honeymoon destination. Rates are moderately less expensive during slower seasons.

✗ Eating & Drinking

There are eateries scattered here and there across the island, but you'll find the best selection in the town of Hirara.

Moss Well CAFE ¥
(☎72-6991; 597-2 Shimozato; meals from ¥750; ⊙11.30am-2am) This Hirara corner cafe has a tiny slice of terrace seating, which is a great place to take the daily lunch set (¥750). On the menu are typical Japanese dishes – a little of this and that – using fresh island vegetables and seaweeds. The cosy interior also makes a pleasant spot to have some cake and coffee, or a beer in the evening.

Koja Shokudō Honten SOBA ¥
(古謝食堂本店; Map p749; ☎72-2139; 165 Nishizato; dishes ¥700; ⊙10am-8pm) One block northwest of the intersection between Ichiba-dōri and Nishizato-dōri, this nondescript noodle house is something of a local legend. For more than 50 years, Koja has been serving up steaming bowls of *sōki-soba* (¥650). It's across from a parking lot; look for the white tiles around the entryway. The owner speaks a bit of English.

★ **Pōcha Tatsuya** IZAKAYA ¥¥
(ぽうちゃたつや; ☎73-3931; 275 Nishizato; dishes ¥800; ⊙5.30-10.30pm Wed-Mon) Along an alley in the central restaurant district of Hirara, this hospitable *izakaya* serves delish

local fare such as *kobushime-yawaraka-ni* (steamed cuttlefish; ¥730) and *sūchiki* (vinegared pork with bitter melon; ¥630). From McCrum-dōri, go past the National store on your left. Look for the green latticework over the windows and a seahorse curled around the sign above the door.

Isla BAR
(イスラ; Map p749; 172 Nishizato) In an alley on the west side of Ichiba-dōri in Hirara, Isla is a Caribbean watering hole with relaxing grooves, plenty of rum and snacks such as Jamaican-style pizza (¥800). There are sometimes live bands on the small stage.

❶ Information

Hirara-Nishizato Post Office (平良西里郵便局; Ichiba-dōri, Hirara; ⊙9am-5pm Mon-Fri, ATMs open longer) The ATMs here accept foreign ATM cards.

Public Library (平良市立図書館; cnr McCrum-dōri & Chūō-dōri, Hirara) It's possible to access the internet for free on the 2nd floor.

Tourist Information Desk (☎72-0899; ⊙9am-6pm) In the arrivals hall of the airport, you can pick up a copy of the *Miyako Island Guide Map*. Travellers who can read Japanese should also pick up a copy of the detailed *Guide Map Miyako*.

Hirara

ⓘ Getting There & Away

Miyako-jima has direct flights to/from Tokyo's Haneda Airport (JTA; ¥57,870, three hours and 25 minutes, one daily), Naha (JTA/ANA; ¥13,800/18,600, 50 minutes, 13 daily) and Ishigaki (RAC/ANA; ¥8400/12,400, 20 minutes, four daily).

ⓘ Getting Around

Miyako-jima has a limited bus network that operates from two bus stands in Hirara. Buses run between the airport and Hirara (¥270, 10 minutes). Buses also depart from Yachiyo bus terminal for Ikema-jima (¥500, 35 minutes), and from the Miyako Kyōei bus terminal, 700m east of town, to Yoshino-hama/Boraga-hama (¥500, 50 minutes). Yet another line runs between Hirara and Yoneha-Maehama/Kurima-jima (¥390, 30 minutes).

The island's flat terrain is perfectly suited to biking; rent bicycles at the guesthouse Hiraraya in Hirara. If you want to move faster, there are rental-car counters at the airport and offices in Hirara.

Irabu-jima & Shimoji-jima
伊良部島・下地島

A 10-minute ferry ride from Hirara (on Miyako-jima) brings you to Irabu-jima and Shimoji-jima, two pleasantly rural islands covered with fields of sugarcane and linked by a series of bridges. Like Miyako, Irabu and Shimoji are a beach-lover's paradise. The islands are best visited as a day trip from Hirara, though there are guesthouses and free campgrounds.

The best swimming beach is **Toguchi-no-hama** (渡口の浜) on Irabu-jima's west coast. Easily the best snorkelling beach is **Nakanoshima Beach** (中の島ビーチ), protected by a high-walled bay on the west coast of Shimoji-jima. Look for the sign reading 'Nakano Island The Beach'.

An interesting site to stroll is **Tōri-ike** (通り池), two seawater 'ponds' on the west coast of Shimoji-jima that are actually sinkholes in the coral that formed the island. It's near **Shimoji Airport**, whose runway is used to practise 'touch-and-go' (landing and immediate takeoff) exercises by ANA pilots.

The chilled-out backpackers haven of **Guesthouse Birafuya** (ゲストハウスびらふやー; ☑78-3380, 080-5244-3955; www.birafuya.com; 1436-1 Irabusawada; dm/s/d ¥2000/2500/5000; ⊙closed Dec-Mar; ⓟ@🖂) is a few blocks inland from **Sawada-no-hama beach** (佐和田の浜). Run by a lovely young couple, Birafuya has a dorm and small Western-style rooms and is a great place to meet other travellers. If you phone ahead, staff will pick you up at the ferry terminal.

For a more secluded experience, opt for **Soraniwa** (そらにわ; ☑74-5528; www.soraniwa.org; 721-1 Irabu-azairabu; s/tw from ¥10,500/13,650; ⓟ@) on the south coast. This small, stylish cafe-hotel is also run by a young couple transplanted from the 'mainland.' In the restaurant (lunch ¥900-1200; ⊙11.30am-10pm), meals use local, organic ingredients, while the intimate, modern hotel features sumptuous beds, shelves made from repurposed wood and a rooftop Jacuzzi looking onto the sea.

Fast ferries (¥400, 15 minutes, 11 daily) and car ferries (¥350 per walking passenger, ¥2000 per car, 25 minutes, 13 daily) run between Hirara on Miyako-jima and Sarahama Port (佐良浜港) on Irabu-jima.

Yaeyama Islands
八重山諸島

At the far southwestern end of the Southwest Islands are the Yaeyama Islands, which include the main islands of Ishigaki-jima and Iriomote-jima as well as a spread of 17 isles. Located near the Tropic of Cancer, they are renowned for their lovely beaches, superb diving and lush landscapes.

The Yaeyama Islands are arguably the top destination in the Southwest Islands. They offer Japan's best snorkelling and diving, and some of Japan's last intact subtropical jungles and mangrove swamps (both on Iriomote-jima). Perhaps the best feature of the Yaeyamas is their variety and the ease with which you can explore them: plentiful ferry services run between Ishigaki City and nearby islands such as Iriomote-jima and Taketomi-jima, and you can easily explore three or four islands in one trip.

Ishigaki-jima 石垣島

☑0980 / POP 48,646

Blessed with excellent beaches and brilliant dive sites, Ishigaki-jima also possesses an attractive, rugged geography that invites long drives and day hikes. Located 100km southwest of Miyako-jima, Ishigaki is the most populated and developed island in the Yaeyama group. Some places around the island may seem reminiscent of Hawaii, but Ishigaki is tropical Japan through and through.

◉ Sights & Activities

Ishigaki City (石垣市) occupies the south-western corner of the island. You'll find most of the action in the two shopping arcades, which run parallel to the main street, Shiyakusho-dōri. The city is easily walkable, and can be explored in an hour or two.

A series of roads branch out from Ishigaki City and head along the coastline and into the interior. There are several settlements near the coast, though most of the interior is mountains and farmland.

Some of the best beaches on the island are found on the west coast. It's also worth spending a half-day exploring some of the city's sights to get a feel for its culture.

The sea around Ishigaki-jima is famous among the Japanese diving community for its large schools of manta rays, particularly from June to October. The most popular place is **Manta Scramble** (Map p752), off the coast of Kabira Ishizaki. Although you'll likely be sharing with a fair number of dive boats, you're almost guaranteed to see a manta (or four). There are a number of dive shops on Ishigaki-jima.

Ishigaki City Yaeyama Museum   MUSEUM
(石垣市立八重山博物館; Map p755; 4-1 Tono-shiro; admission ¥200; ◎9am-5pm Tue-Sun) This modest museum has exhibits on the culture and history of the island, which are quite well presented with English explanations. Notable among the more typical cultural artefacts are a few informational pages about some of Japan's oldest human remains (estimated, using carbon dating, to be 24,000 years old) that were discovered on Ishigaki in 2011, during construction of the new airport.

Miyara Dōnchi   HISTORIC BUILDING
(宮良殿内; Map p755; 178 Ōkawa; admission ¥200; ◎9am-5pm) The unique home of a Ryūkyū kingdom official dating from 1819; walk north along Sanbashi-dōri until you see signs in English. The house is still an actual residence, so you can only peer into the open rooms from the outside and enjoy the small garden.

Tōrin-ji   BUDDHIST TEMPLE
(桃林寺; Map p752; 285 Ishigaki; ◎9am-7pm) Founded in 1614, the Zen temple of Tōrin-ji, near the intersection of Shimin-kaikan-dōri and Rte 79, is home to the 18th-century guardian statues of Deva kings. Adjacent to the temple is **Gongen-dō** (権現堂; ◎9am-7pm), a small shrine rebuilt after being destroyed by a tsunami in 1771.

Yonehara Beach   BEACH
(米原海岸; Map p752) On the north coast of Ishigaki along Rte 79, Yonehara Beach is a nice sand beach with a good bit of reef offshore. You can rent snorkel gear (¥1000) at any of the shops along the main road.

Kabira-wan   BEACH
(川平湾; Map p752) Kabira-wan is a sheltered bay with white-sand shores and a couple of interesting clumplike islands offshore. This is more of a wading beach than a swimming beach and it's usually busy with boat traffic, which detracts somewhat from its beauty.

★ Sunset Beach   BEACH
(サンセットビーチ; Map p752) At the north end of the island, on the west coast, you will find a long strip of sand with a bit of offshore reef. As the name implies, this is a good spot to watch the sun set into the East China Sea.

🛏 Sleeping

★ Iriwa   GUESTHOUSE ¥
(イリワ; Map p752; ☑88-2563; http://iriwa.org; 599 Kabira; dm/r per person ¥2000/4500; P@🛜) Just above Kabira-wan on the north coast, Iriwa is a comfortable guesthouse with dorm beds, two large private rooms and a small self-contained cottage, all warmly decorated with a Hawaiian aesthetic. It's run by a super-chill, friendly young Korean/Japanese couple who like to share meals and snorkelling expeditions with guests. The main house has a communal lounge room and spacious, sunny kitchen – the roof, the highest point in Kabira village, offers excellent views of the sea during the day and stars at night.

Pension Yaima-biyōri   GUESTHOUSE ¥
(ペンションやいま日和; Map p755; ☑88-5578; http://yaimabiyori.com; 10-7 Miaski-chō; s/d from ¥2800/5000; P@) Centrally located in Ishigaki City two blocks north of the ferry and bus station, this welcoming pension offers appealing, spacious Western- and Japanese-style rooms with shared facilities or private bathrooms.

Rakutenya   GUESTHOUSE ¥
(楽天屋; Map p755; ☑83-8713; www3.big.or.jp/~erm8p3gi; 291 Ōkawa; r per person ¥3000; P@🛜) This quaint guesthouse is two blocks north of the covered markets in Ishigaki City, and has attractive Western- and Japanese-style rooms in a couple of rickety,

Yaeyama Islands

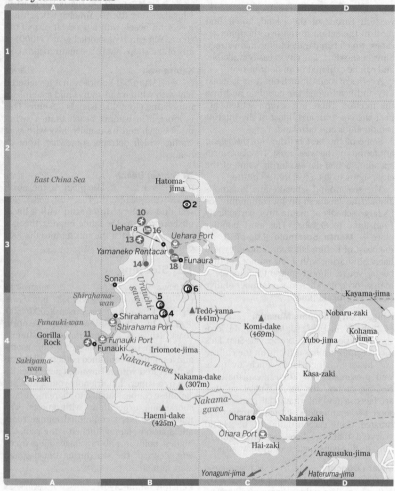

East China Sea

Hatoma-jima

10

Uehara 16

13 Uehara Port

Yamaneko Rentacar

14 18 Funaura

Sonai 6

Uchuchi-gawa

Shirahama-wan

5

4

Shirahama

Shirahama Port

Funauki-wan

11

Gorilla Rock

Funauki Port

Funauki Iriomote-jima

Nakara-gawa

Sakiyama-wan

Pai-zaki

Nakama-dake
(307m)

Tedō-yama
(441m)

Komi-dake
(469m)

Kayama-jima

Nobaru-zaki

Kohama-jima

Yubo-jima

Kasa-zaki

Nakama-gawa

Haemi-dake
(425m)

Ōhara

Nakama-zaki

Ōhara Port

Hai-zaki

Aragusuku-jima

Yonaguni-jima   Hateruma-jima

old wooden houses. The managers are a friendly Japanese couple who speak a little bit of English, and are a fantastic source of local information.

Hotel Patina Ishigaki-jima   HOTEL ¥¥
(ホテルパティーナ石垣島; ☏ 87-7400; www.patina.in; 1-8-5 Yashima-chō; s/tw incl breakfast from ¥6800/9800; P🅿️😊@🛜) Just a few minutes' walk from the port and central Ishigaki City, Hotel Patina is a small, friendly hotel that's far enough from downtown to be quiet at night. A French bakery across the way supplies snacks or a postbreakfast breakfast,

while the relaxed hotel offers bike and scooter rentals as well as free laundry (dryers are coin operated).

★Tsundara Beach Retreat   APARTMENT ¥¥¥
(つんだらビーチ・リトリート; Map p752; ☏ 89-2765, 090-7587-2029; http://tsundarabeach.com; 895-2 Nosoko; s/d incl breakfast ¥25,000/40,000; P🅿️) Truly a retreat, this spacious, fully equipped beach house affords privacy and peace in beautiful abundance. On Ishigaki's sparsely populated northern peninsula, the house sits on a 1-hectare grassy property with vegetable garden, trails to the gorgeous

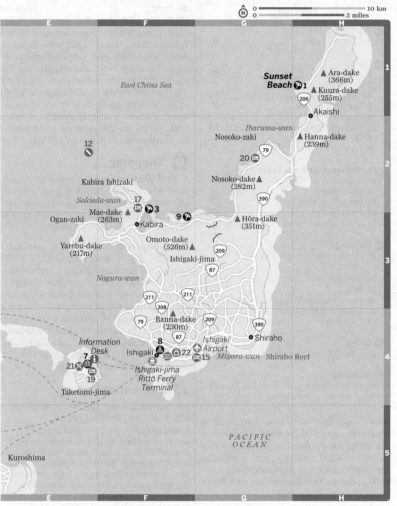

private beach and an enormous teepee. The pacifist American owners (who speak fluent Japanese and live on the premises) can organise ecotours such as **jungle zip-lining** and are extremely knowledgeable about Ishigaki. A stellar refuge for families, honeymooners or anyone wishing for quiet solitude.

**ANA Intercontinental
Ishigaki Resort** HOTEL ¥¥¥

(ANAインターコンチネンタル石垣リゾート; Map p752; ☑88-7111; www.anaintercontinental-ishigaki.com; 354-1 Maesato; r from ¥13,650; ⓟⓔ@🛜🏊) Right by the airport but not overwhelmed by plane noise, the Intercontinental has gorgeously refurbished rooms, all of which have wood floors and at least partial ocean views; rooms in the main building also have balconies. Our favourite rooms are the more spacious ones in the lower-scale Coral Wing, which features open-air hallways around a garden courtyard.

🍴 Eating & Drinking

Eifuku Shokudō SOBA ¥

(栄福食堂; Map p755; ☑82-5838; 274 Ōkawa; dishes ¥500; ⏰8.30am-midnight) This hole in the wall in Ishigaki City is a shrine to 1950s

Yaeyama Islands

actor Akagi 'Tony' Kei-ichirō. Tony Soba, as it's known, is one of the cheapest places on the island for *yaeyama-soba* (thin noodles in broth; ¥300), though we recommend the stinky (but tasty) *yagi-soba* (goat *soba*; ¥500). Look for the blue building with Tony's visage illustrating the wall.

Ishigaki-jima Kids
SOBA ¥

(石垣島キッズ; Map p755; ☑83-8671; 203-1 Ōkawa; meals ¥850; ☺noon-2pm & 6-9pm Thu-Tue) In one of the covered arcades this serves good Ishigaki-style cafe fare – *sōki-soba*, taco rice and the like – all detailed in a picture menu.

Mori-no-Kokage
IZAKAYA ¥

(森のこかげ; Map p755; ☑83-7933; 199 Ōkawa; dishes ¥800; ☺5pm-midnight Wed-Mon) This little Ishigaki City *izakaya* has warmth and natural ambience. Local treats are sliced steak of Ishigaki beef (¥1280) and the microbrew *ishigaki-jima-zake* (¥500). Look for the plants and tree trunks outside.

★ Paikaji
IZAKAYA ¥¥

(南風; Map p755; ☑82-6027; 219 Ōkawa; dishes ¥700; ☺5pm-midnight) No relation to Naha's Paikaji chain, this Ishigaki City favourite serves Okinawan and Yaeyama standards. Both the atmosphere and kitchen get top marks. Try the *ikasumi chahan* (squid ink fried rice; ¥650), the *gōyā champurū* (¥700) or the *sashimi moriawase* (sashimi assortment; ¥750 to ¥1800 depending on size). Look for the traditional front, coral around the entryway and a red-and-white sign.

🛍 Shopping

A good place to shop for *o-miyage* (souvenirs) is the main shopping arcade, which also has a public market. Shopkeepers start slashing prices in the hour or so before closing up shop in the early evening.

Minsā Kōgeikan
ART GALLERY

(みんさー工芸館; Map p752; ☑82-3473; 909 Tonoshiro; ☺9am-6pm) Minsā Kōgeikan is a weaving workshop and showroom with exhibits on Yaeyama Islands textiles. You can also try your hand at weaving – creating a coaster costs ¥1000, and you'll need to reserve ahead by phone. The building is located between the city centre and the airport, and can be reached via the airport bus (tell the driver you want to stop here).

ℹ Information

Information Counter (☑83-8384; Airport; ☺8.30am-9pm) Small but helpful.

Island Ishigaki (アイランド@ishigaki; ☑82-7848; www.island-ishigaki.jp; 3 Arakawa; 1hr internet ¥500; ☺24hr) A clean, well-lit place to surf the web or spend the night if you're in a bind, this *manga kissa* (comic-book coffee shop) is a short walk from the centre Ishigaki City.

Tourist Information Office (石垣市観光協会; ☑82-2809; 1st fl, Ishigaki-shi Shōkō Kaikan; ☺8.30am-5.30pm Mon-Fri) Has a friendly English-speaking staff and simple English maps of the island. Japanese readers should pick up the *Ishigaki Town Guide* and the *Yaeyama Nabi*.

Yaeyama Post Office (八重山郵便局; Sanbashi-dōri; ☺lobby 9am-7pm Mon-Fri, to 3pm Sat, ATM 8.45am-7pm Mon-Fri, 9am-7pm Sat, Sun & holidays) Has international ATMs.

ℹ Getting There & Away

AIR

Ishigaki-jima has direct flights to/from Tokyo's Haneda Airport (JTA; ¥36,470, three hours 35 minutes, two daily), Osaka's Kansai International Airport (JTA; ¥33,800, two

Ishigaki City

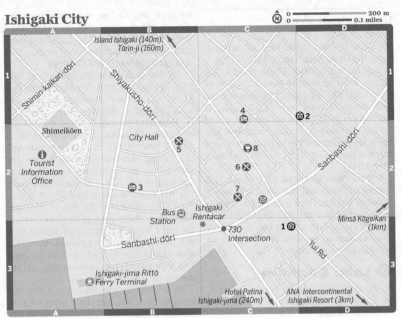

hours 55 minutes, one daily), Naha (JTA/ANA; ¥16,300/23,000, one hour, 17 daily), Miyako-jima (RAC/ANA; ¥9400/11,900, 35 minutes, three daily) and Yonaguni-jima (RAC; ¥11,800, 35 minutes, three daily).

BOAT

Ishigaki-jima Rittō Ferry Terminal (石垣港離島ターミナル) serves islands including Iriomote-jima, Kohama-jima, Taketomi-jima and Hateru-ma-jima. Departures are frequent enough that you can usually just turn up in the morning and hop on the next ferry departing for your intended destination (except during the summer high season). The three main ferry operators are:

Yaeyama Kankō Ferry (八重山観光フェリー; ☑82-5010; www.yaeyama.co.jp)

Ishigaki Dream Kankō (石垣島ドリーム観光; ☑84-3178; www.ishigaki-dream.co.jp)

Anei Kankō (安栄観光; ☑83-0055; www.aneikankou.co.jp)

To get to the ferry terminal, just head southwest along the waterfront from the 730 Intersection.

ⓘ Getting Around

The bus station is across the road from the ferry terminal in Ishigaki City. There are hourly buses to the airport (¥200, 20 minutes), as well as a few daily buses to Kabira-wan (¥700, 40 minutes), Yonehara Beach (¥800, one hour)

and Shiraho (¥400, 30 minutes). There's a five-day bus pass for the airport and Kabira routes (¥1000), or for all routes (¥2000); purchase directly from the driver.

Rental cars, scooters and bicycles are readily available at shops throughout the city centre. If you're comfortable on a scooter, it's a scenic four- to five-hour cruise around the island, though you should plan for longer if you want to spend some time relaxing on the island's beaches. **Ishigaki Rentacar** (石垣島レンタカー; ☑82-8840; ☺8am-7pm) is located in the city centre and has reasonable rates.

Iriomote-jima 西表島

☎ 0980 / POP 2276

Although it's just 20km west of Ishigaki-jima, Iriomote-jima could easily qualify as Japan's last frontier. Dense jungles and mangrove forest blanket more than 90% of the island, and it's fringed by some of the most beautiful coral reefs in all Japan. If you're super lucky, you may even spot one of the island's rare *yamaneko,* a nocturnal and rarely seen wildcat (they're most often seen crossing the road at night, so drive carefully after dark).

Several rivers penetrate far into the lush interior of the island and these can be explored by riverboat or kayak. Add to the mix sun-drenched beaches and spectacular diving and snorkelling, and it's easy to see why Iriomote-jima is one of the best destinations in Japan for nature lovers.

◉ Sights & Activities

The majority of the island's beaches are shallow due to the extensive coral reef that surrounds the island.

Tsuki-ga-hama   BEACH

(月ヶ浜; Moon Beach; Map p752) The best swimming beach on the island is Tsuki-ga-hama, a crescent-shaped yellow-sand beach at the mouth of the Urauchi-gawa on the north coast.

Hoshizuna-no-hama   BEACH

(星砂の浜; Star Sand Beach; Map p752) If you're looking to do a bit of snorkelling, head to this beach on the northwestern tip of the island. The beach is named after its star sand, which actually consists of the dried skeletons of tiny sea creatures. If you are a competent swimmer and the sea is calm, make your way with mask and snorkel to the outside of the reef – the coral and tropical fish here are spectacular.

★ Ida-no-hama   BEACH

(イダの浜; Map p752) From **Shirahama** (白浜), at the western end of the north coast road, there are four daily boats (¥500) to the isolated settlement of **Funauki** (船浮). Once there, it's a mere 10-minute walk on to the absolutely gorgeous Ida-no-hama.

Hiking

Iriomote has some great hikes, but do not head off into the jungle interior without notifying police and hiring a guide: the trails in the interior are hard to follow – many people have become lost and required rescue. We suggest that you stick to well-marked tracks like the one listed here. If you're more ambitious, your accommodation can help arrange a guide (at least ¥20,000).

At the back of a mangrove-lined bay called Funaura-wan a few kilometres east of Uehara, you can make out a lovely waterfall plunging 55m down the cliffs. This is **Pinaisāra-no-taki** (ピナイサーラの滝; Map p752), Okinawa's highest waterfall at 55m. When the tide is right, you can paddle a kayak across the shallow lagoon and then follow the Hinai-gawa (on the left) to the base of the falls. The short Māre-gawa (on the right) meets a trail where it narrows. This climbs to the top of the falls, from where there are superb views down to the coast. From the river, walk inland until you come to a pumping station, then turn around and take the right fork in the path. The walk takes less than two hours, and the river is great for a cooling dip.

Unfortunately, it is difficult to find a tour company that will rent you a kayak without requiring you to join a guided tour (half-/full days cost about ¥6000/10,000). If you have a foldable or inflatable kayak, we suggest bringing it. Otherwise, accommodation owners can arrange participation in a guided tour.

For another good hike, try the hikes along the Urauchi-gawa.

Diving

Much of the brilliant coral fringing Iriomote's shores is accessible to proficient snorkellers. Most of the offshore dive sites around Iriomote are served by dive operators based on Ishigaki.

One spot worth noting is the unusual **Barasu-tō** (Map p752), between Iriomote-jima and Hatoma-jima, which is a small island formed entirely of bits of broken coral. In addition to the island itself, the reefs nearby are in quite good condition and make for good boat-based snorkelling on a calm day.

↻ Tours

Iriomote's number-one attraction is a boat trip up the **Urauchi-gawa** (浦内川), a winding brown river reminiscent of a tiny stretch of the Amazon. From the mouth of the river, **Urauchi-gawa Kankō** (Map p752; ☎ 85-6154) runs boat tours 8km up the river (round trip ¥1800, 30 minutes each way, multiple departures daily between 8.30am and 5pm). At the 8km point, the boat docks and you can walk a further 2km to the scenic waterfalls of **Mariyudō-no-taki** (マリユドウの滝; Map p752), from where another 200m brings you to the **Kampire-no-taki** (カンピレーの滝; Map p752). The walk from the dock to Kampire-no-taki and back takes around two hours. Of course, you can just take the boat trip to the dock and back. The pier (浦川遊覧船乗り場) is about 6km west of Uehara.

From a pier on the south side of the river just east of the bridge in Ōhara, **Tōbū Kōtsū** (☑85-5304; ⊙8.30am-5.30pm) runs river cruises up Iriomote's second-largest river, the **Nakama-gawa** (仲間川). The one-hour tour (¥1500) passes through lush mangroves and thick vegetation.

🛏 Sleeping

Iriomote-jima's accommodation is spread out around the island. Most places will send a car to pick you up from the ferry terminal if you let them know what time you will be arriving.

Kanpira-sō   MINSHUKU ¥
(カンピラ荘; ☑85-6508; www.kanpira.com; 545 Uehara ; r per person with/without meals from ¥4500/3000, with meals & bathroom ¥5500; ℙ) Two minutes' walk from the ferry landing in Uehara, hospitable Kanpira has basic Japanese-style rooms and an informative manager who produces extraordinarily good, bilingual maps of the island. From the ferry, walk to the main road; you'll soon see it on the right.

Irumote-sō Youth Hostel   HOSTEL ¥
(いるもて荘; Map p752; ☑85-6255; 870-95 Uehara; dm with/without meals ¥5200/3500, HI member from ¥3300; ℙ@☎) Between Uehara Port (上原港) and Funaura Port (船浦港), this hillside hostel has comfortable dorms and simple Japanese-style private rooms (from ¥4600). Meals are served in the large communal dining room (breakfast/dinner ¥500/1200). We recommend calling for a pickup before you arrive since it's hard to find.

Coral Garden   PENSION ¥¥
(コーラルガーデン; Map p752; ☑85-6027; www.e-iriomote.com; 289-17 Uehara; s/d ¥7800/13,600; ℙ@☎☀) A five-minute drive from Uehara, this beachfront pension has simple Japanese- and Western-style rooms overlooking Hoshisuna-no-hama. There's a small pool, and a path leading down to the beach, which is a great spot for snorkelling. Call ahead for pick-up from the port.

🍴 Eating

With few restaurants on the island, most travellers prefer to take meals at their accommodation (or self-cater). However, if you want a meal out, we recommend the following.

Laugh La Garden   OKINAWAN ¥
(ラフラガーデン; ☑85-7088; 550-1 Uehara; dishes ¥900; ⊙11.30am-2pm & from 6.30pm Fri-Wed) Near the road from Uehara Port and beside the petrol station, this relaxed cafe-restaurant has sets such as *ishigakibuta-no-misokatsu teishoku* (miso-seasoned Ishigaki pork cutlets; ¥950) and oddities such as *inoshishi-sashimi* (wild boar sashimi; ¥600).

Shinpachi Shokudō   SOBA ¥
(新八食堂; ☑85-6078; 870 Uehara; dishes ¥700; ⊙11.30am-2pm & 5.30-8pm Tue-Sun) Just 200m south of the port in Uehara, this no-frills noodle shop is the perfect spot for a hot bowl of *sōki-soba* (¥700) or a *gōyā champuru* (¥800), washed down with a nice draught beer. Look for the blue front and the banners outside.

ℹ Getting There & Around

Iriomote-jima has a 58km-long perimeter road that runs about halfway around the coast. No roads run into the unspoiled interior.

Yaeyama Kankō Ferry (八重山観光フェリー; ☑82-5010; www.yaeyama.co.jp), **Ishigaki Dream Kankō** (石垣島ドリーム観光; ☑84-3178; www.ishigaki-dream.co.jp) and **Anei Kankō** (安栄観光; ☑83-0055; www.aneikankou.co.jp) operate ferries between Ishigaki City (on Ishigaki-jima) and Iriomote-jima. Ferries from Ishigaki sail to/from two main ports on Iriomote: Uehara Port (上原港; ¥1680, one hour, up to 20 daily), convenient for most destinations, and Ōhara Port (大原港; ¥1770, 40 minutes, up to 27 daily). Strong north winds will require Uehara-bound ferries to travel the safer route to Ōhara; in these cases, buses at the port will shuttle passengers to Uehara for free.

Six or nine buses daily run between Ōhara and Shirahama (¥1200, 1½ hours); raise your hand to get on anywhere. There's a 'free pass' for buses (one-/three-day passes ¥1000/1500) that also gives you 10% off attractions such as the Urauchi-gawa cruise.

If you have an International Driving Permit, try **Yamaneko Rentacar** (やまねこレンタカー; ☑85-6111; 584-1 Uehara; ⊙8am-6pm). Most of the island accommodation also rents bicycles to guests.

Taketomi-jima 竹富島

📞 0980 / POP 347

A mere 15-minute boat ride from Ishigaki-jima, the tiny islet of Taketomi-jima is a living museum of Ryūkyū culture. Centred on a flower-bedecked village of traditional houses complete with red *kawara* (tiled) roofs, coral walls and *shiisā* statues, Taketomi is a breath of fresh air if you're suffering from an overdose of modern Japan.

In order to preserve the island's historical ambience, residents have joined together to ban some signs of modernism. The island is criss-crossed by crushed-coral roads and free of chain convenience stores.

While Taketomi is besieged by Japanese day trippers in the busy summer months, the island remains blissfully quiet at night. This is true even in summer, as the island offers little in the way of after-dark entertainment. If you have the chance, it's worth spending a night here as Taketomi truly weaves its spell after the sun dips below the horizon.

⊙ Sights & Activities

There are a number of modest sights in Taketomi village, though it's best for simply wandering around and soaking up the ambience. Taketomi-jima also has some decent beaches. **Kondoi Beach** on the west coast offers the best swimming on the island. Just south is **Kaiji-hama**, which is the main *hoshi-suna* (star sand) hunting ground.

Nagomi-no-tō   MONUMENT

(なごみの塔; ⊙24hr; FREE) Roughly in the centre of the village, the modest lookout tower of Nagomi-no-tō has good views over the red-tiled roofs of the pancake-flat island.

Nishitō Utaki   SHRINE

(西塘御嶽) Near Nagomi-no-tō is a shrine dedicated to a 16th-century ruler of the Yaeyama Islands who was born on Taketomi-jima.

Kihōin Shūshūkan   MUSEUM

(喜宝院蒐集館; 📞85-2202; admission ¥300; ⊙9am-5pm) At the west of the village, this private museum houses a diverse collection of folk artefacts.

Taketomi Mingei-kan   ART GALLERY

(竹富民芸館; Map p752; 📞85-2302; 435 Taketomi; ⊙9am-5pm) FREE Where the island's woven *minsā* belts and other textiles are produced.

🍴 Sleeping & Eating

Many of the traditional houses around the island are Japanese-style ryokan serving traditional Okinawan cuisine. However, don't turn up on the last ferry expecting to find accommodation; Taketomi fills up quickly in the summer, so be sure to book ahead.

Takana Ryokan   HOSTEL ¥

(高那旅館; Map p752; 📞85-2151; www.kit.hi-ho.ne.jp/hayasaka-my; 499 Taketomi; dm with/without meals ¥4500/3100, r per person with meals from ¥8500) Opposite the tiny post office, Takana actually consists of a basic youth hostel and an attached upmarket ryokan. Basic Western-style dorms in the youth hostel are a great option if you're on a budget, though the Japanese-style tatami rooms in the ryokan are a bit more comfortable.

Ōhama-sō   MINSHUKU ¥¥

(大浜荘; 📞85-2226; fax 85-2226; 501 Taketomi; r per person with/without bathroom ¥6000/4000) Located beside the post office, this *minshuku* has a light and jovial atmosphere. Accommodation is in simple yet comfortable Japanese-style tatami rooms.

Soba Dokoro Takenoko   NOODLES ¥

(そば処竹の子; Map p752; 📞85-2251; 101-1 Taketomi; dishes ¥800; ⊙10.30am-4pm & 6.30-10pm) This tiny restaurant on the northwest side of the village (look for the blue banner and the umbrellas) serves up *sōki-soba* (¥800) and *yaki-soba* (fried *soba*; ¥800), and you can wash it all down with some Orion beer.

ⓘ Information

Ferries arrive at the small port (竹富港) on the northeast corner of the island, while Taketomi village is located in the centre of the island. There's a small **information desk** (📞84-5633; ⊙7.30am-6pm) in the port building.

ⓘ Getting There & Around

Yaeyama Kankō Ferry (📞82-5010), **Ishigaki Dream Kankō** (📞84-3178) and **Anei Kankō** (📞83-0055) operate ferries between Ishigaki City (on Ishigaki-jima) and Taketomi-jima (¥580, 10 minutes, up to 45 daily).

Rental bicycles are great for exploring the crushed-coral roads. Since the island is only 3km long and 2km wide, it is easily explored on foot or by bicycle. An assortment of bike-rental outfits meets arriving ferries at the port and runs free shuttles between their shops and the port. The going rate for bike rentals is ¥300 per hour or ¥1500 for the day. Another way to see the island is by taking a tour in a water buffalo cart. Two operators in the village offer 30-minute rides for ¥1200 per person.

Hateruma-jima 波照間島

🕿 0980 / POP 551

Forty-five kilometres south of Iriomote-jima is the tiny islet of Hateruma-jima, Japan's southernmost inhabited island. Just 15km around, Hateruma-jima has a couple of beauteous beaches and a seriously laid-back vibe.

Ferries arrive at the small port on the northwest corner of the island, while Hateruma village is in the centre.

Just to the west of the port is **Nishihama** (ニシ浜), a perfect beach of snow-white sand with some good coral offshore. Here you will find free public showers, toilets and a campground. At the opposite southeast corner of the island, directly south of the airport, is the impressive **Takanasaki** (高那崎), a 1km-long cliff of Ryūkyū limestone that is pounded by the Pacific Ocean. At the western end of the cliffs is a small monument marking **Japan's southernmost point** (日本最南端の碑), which is an extremely popular photo spot for Japanese visitors.

There are several *minshuku* on the island, including **House Minami** (ハウス美波; 🕿 85-8050; http://homepage2.nifty.com/minami85; 3138 Hateruma; r per person ¥3000-4500; 🅿) east of the town centre. Arranged around a cosy courtyard, these fully equipped, detached quarters sit in a village close to sugarcane fields. Though the proprietors don't speak English, they are very foreigner-friendly.

Another good choice is **Pension Sainantan** (ペンション最南端; 🕿 85-8686; 886-1 Hateruma; r per person from ¥8500; 🅿 @), which has Japanese-style rooms with small terraces downstairs and Western-style rooms with balconies upstairs. There's also a rooftop terrace with spectacular views of the beach and sea, and it's all three minutes' walk from Nishihama.

Anei Kankō (🕿 83-0055) and **Hateruma Kaiun** (🕿 82-7233) each have three ferries a day to Hateruma-jima from Ishigaki (¥3000 and ¥3050 respectively, one hour). There is no public transport on the island, but rental bicycles and scooters are readily available for hire.

Yonaguni-jima 与那国島

🕿 0980 / POP 1627

About 125km west of Ishigaki and 110km east of Taiwan is the islet of Yonaguni-jima, Japan's westernmost inhabited island. Renowned for its strong sake, small horses and marlin fishing, the island is also home to the jumbo-sized Yonaguni atlas moth, the largest moth in the world.

However, most visitors come to see what lies beneath the waves. In 1985, a diver discovered what appeared to be man-made 'ruins' off the south coast of the island. In addition, the waters off the west coast are frequented by large schools of hammerhead sharks. This makes the island perhaps the most famous single diving destination in Japan.

⊙ Sights

Just as Hateruma-jima has a monument to mark Japan's southernmost point, Yonaguni-jima has a rock to mark the country's **westernmost point** (日本最西端の碑) at **Irizaki** (西崎). If the weather is perfect, the mountains of Taiwan are visible far over the sea (this happens only about twice a year – so don't be disappointed if you can't make them out).

Yonaguni has an extremely rugged landscape, and the coastline is marked with great rock formations, much like those on the east coast of Taiwan. The most famous of these are **Tachigami-iwa** (立神岩), literally 'Standing-God Rock' (although another name might come to mind); the dramatic **Gunkan-iwa** (軍艦岩; Battleship Rock); and **Sanninu-dai** (サンニヌ台), all of which are off the southeast coast. At the eastern tip of the island, Yonaguni horses graze in the pastures leading out to the lighthouse at **Agarizaki** (東崎).

Higawa-hama   BEACH

(比川浜) On the south coast of the island is the pleasant little village of Higawa, which has a wide, sandy crescent of beach. The water here is clear and shallow, making it a great spot for swimming and snorkelling.

Ayamihabiru-kan   MUSEUM

(アヤミハビル館; 🕿 87-2440; admission ¥500; ⊙10am-4pm Wed-Sun) Displays on Yonaguni's giant Atlas moths, which have a wingspan of 25cm to 30cm and are affectionately known as Yonaguni-san, can be seen here, about 1km south of Sonai.

Kokusen Awamori   BREWERY

(国選泡盛; 🕿 87-2315; ⊙8am-5pm) If you want to sample Hanazake, the island's infamous local brew, head to Kokusen Awamori, which is located in Sonai and offers free tastings and sales on-site.

🏃 Activities

Local divers have long known about the thrills that await at **Irizaki Point** (西崎ポイント), off the coast of Cape Irizaki. In the winter months, the waters here are frequented by large schools of hammerhead sharks.

Kaitei Iseki
DIVING

(海底遺跡; Underwater Ruins) The Kaitei Iseki were discovered by chance in 1985 by marine explorer Kihachirou Aratake. Some claim that these ruins, which look like giant blocks or steps of a sunken pyramid, are the remains of a Pacific Atlantis, although there are equally compelling arguments that they are just the random result of geological processes. **Sou Wes** (☑87-2311; www.yonaguni.jp; 59-6 Yonaguni; 1/2 dives ¥8000/12,000, equipment rental ¥5000; ⊙8am-6pm) has English-speaking guides for diving. It also offers glass-bottomed boat tours over the ruins. If visibility is poor due to choppy water, passengers can watch a DVD about the ruins on board. **Mosura no Tamago** (もすらのたまご; ☑87-2112; per person ¥4000) also offers glass-bottomed boat tours.

Marlin Fishing
FISHING

The seas off Yonaguni are renowned for marlin, and the **All-Japan Billfish Tournament** is held here each year in June or July. If you're interested in trolling, boats in Kubura can be chartered from ¥55,000 a day. Call the **Yonaguni Fishing Co-operative** (☑in Japanese 87-2803) for information.

🛏 Sleeping & Eating

Although there are several sleeping options around the island, it's best to phone ahead as Yonaguni is quite a distance to travel without a reservation. The places reviewed here will pick you up at the airport or ferry terminal.

There is also a decent campground on the south coast near the village of Higawa, next to a nice beach called Kataburu-hama. If you want to self-cater, there are two simple supermarkets in the centre of Sonai.

Minshuku Yoshimarusō
MINSHUKU ¥

(民宿よしまる荘; ☑87-2658; www.yonaguniyds. com; 3984-3 Yonaguni; dm/r per person incl meals ¥5775/6825; P☎) Uphill from the port in Kubura, it is ideal for divers, as the friendly owners also operate the on-site, long-running Yonaguni Diving Service. Simple rooms have nice views of the nearby port and spacious communal bathing facilities. The real appeal of this *minshuku* is the owners' local diving expertise (two-dive boat trips cost ¥12,000).

Fujimi Ryokan
RYOKAN ¥

(ふじみ旅館; ☑87-2143; fax 87-2659; 71-1 Yonaguni; r per person incl 2 meals from ¥6000; P) This basic ryokan is a good choice if you're looking for more traditional accommodation. Coming from the airport, take the main road through Sonai and turn left at the stoplight, then make another left at the second alley thereafter. You'll see the sign on the right.

Ailand Resort Yonaguni
HOTEL ¥¥¥

(アイランドリゾート与那国; ☑87-2300; www.ailand-resort.co.jp; 4647-1 Yonaguni; tw per person incl breakfast from ¥12,500; P@☎) This spiffy hotel-resort is located on the north side of the island, between the airport and Sonai. It's got spacious, light, comfortable Western-style rooms and an on-site restaurant.

Dōurai
IZAKAYA ¥¥

(どぅーらい; ☑87-2909; 62 Yonaguni; dishes ¥800; ⊙11.30am-2pm & 6-11.30pm Mon-Sat) In the centre of Sonai is this delightful little Okinawan *izakaya* that serves local specialities such as *Ishigakigyū-sutēki* (Ishigaki-style steak; ¥1300) and *rafutē* (gingered, stewed pork; ¥700). It's about 100m southeast of the post office in Sonai. It's next door to a barber shop with a striped pole in front.

ℹ Information

The ferry port of Kubura (久部良) is at the island's western extreme. The main settlement is around the secondary port of Sonai (祖納) on the north coast. In between, on the northwest coast, you'll find the airport.

There is an **information counter** (☑87-2402; ⊙8.30am-noon, call after) in the airport, which can help you find accommodation. You can also pick up the Japanese-language *Yonaguni-jima* map, and an English-language version that includes set locations of the erstwhile TV drama *Dr Koto's Clinic*, which was set on Yonaguni.

ℹ Getting There & Around

RAC has flights between Yonaguni and Naha (¥18,750, one hour 40 minutes, one daily). RAC also operates flights between Yonaguni and Ishigaki-jima (¥11,800, 35 minutes, three daily).

Fukuyama Kaiun (☑82-4962) operates two ferries a week between Ishigaki-jima and Kubura Port on Yonaguni (¥3460, 4½ hours) – these are not for the faint of stomach.

There are public buses here, but they make only four trips around the island per day, so the best transport is rental car or scooter. **Yonehama Rentacar** (米浜レンタカー; ☑87-2148; ⊙8am-6pm) offers very reasonable rates and has a counter inside the airport terminal.

Understand Japan

Japan Today

The Great East Japan Earthquake and the ensuing tsunami and nuclear accident were inflection points for Japan. Shortly after the quake, optimists predicted that the disaster would usher in long-needed changes and revive the nation. Now more than two years on from that grim day, optimists are in short supply as Japan appears to be entering a period of economic stagnation, nationalist politics and inward-looking attitudes that hark back to days of sakoku (national seclusion).

Best in Print

The Chrysanthemum & the Sword (Ruth Benedict; 1946) Groundbreaking work on Japanese culture.

A Japanese Mirror: Heroes & Villains of Japanese Culture (Ian Buruma; 1984) A look into the Japanese psyche by one of the world's most astute commentators on Japan.

The Wages of Guilt: Memories of War in Germany and Japan (Ian Buruma; 1994) A fascinating comparison of postwar Japan and Germany.

The Anatomy of Dependence (Takeo Doi; 1971) A Japanese psychologist examines Japanese culture.

The Roads to Sata: A 2000-Mile Walk Through Japan (Alan Booth; 1985) A beautiful account of a walking journey through Japan.

Dogs and Demons: Tales from the Dark Side of Japan (Alex Kerr; 2002) Kerr reveals the hard truth about modern Japan. Read it on the way home.

Best on Film

Lost in Translation (2003) One of the few foreign films that manages to capture some of Japan's reality without condescending clichés.

Miyazaki Anime Director Miyazaki Hayao's animated films are classics. Start with My Neighbor Totoro (1988) or Castle in the Sky (1986).

The Future of Nuclear Power

The Great East Japan Earthquake and following tsunami, which struck on 11 March 2011, took the lives of almost 16,000 people and caused the second-worst nuclear disaster in history at the Fukushima Dai-Ichi nuclear power plant.

The nuclear disaster and the government's response to it caused a crisis of confidence in Japan. In a nation that otherwise prides itself on efficiency, technological expertise and clean government, questions were asked about the close ties between the nuclear industry and the ministries that regulate it. Concerns remain about radiation and the safety of food produced in local areas.

The anti-nuclear movement in Japan, previously a small fringe group, grew to be a political force. Anti-nuclear demonstrations, with protestors numbering in the tens and even hundreds of thousands, were held in several Japanese cities. Partially as a result of these demonstrations, nuclear power plants across the country were shut down one by one until, by May 2012, all of Japan's 54 nuclear plants were offline. However, less than two months later, the Oi nuclear plant in Fukui Prefecture was restarted and more restarts are scheduled.

Rebuilt but Still Recovering

With the exception of the Fukushima Dai-Ichi nuclear plant, which will take years or even decades to decommission, most of Tōhoku has been cleaned up and the main infrastructure has been largely rebuilt. Indeed, observers have been amazed at the pace of reconstruction in Tōhoku – proof of just how fast the Japanese can get things done when they work together.

Needless to say, rebuilding a vast area of the country costs money. Sadly, this was money that Japan could hardly afford to spend, with economic problems dating back to the Global Financial Crisis of 2008 and even to the 'lost decade' of the 1990s. In 2010 China surpassed Japan as the world's second-largest economy and countries like Korea and Malaysia are taking big bites out of industries that Japan used to dominate. In 2012 Japan's big three electronics giants, Sharp, Panasonic and Sony, reported losses of US$5.6 billion, US$9.6 billion and US$6.4 billion respectively. Meanwhile, Samsung, Korea's manufacturing giant, notched up nearly 100% year-on-year growth in the first quarter of 2012.

Neighbourhood Tensions

Given this backdrop of hard economic times, it's not surprising that nationalist politics have been enjoying something of a revival in recent years. Preaching the message that Japan can regain its former glory by returning to its 'Japanese roots', a number of politicians (including Ishihara Shintarō, the former governor of Tokyo, and Hashimoto Tōru, acting mayor of Osaka) formed nationalist political parties that garnered several seats in Japan's recent elections.

In 2012 Ishihara caused widespread outrage in China and Korea when he announced plans to purchase the disputed Senkaku Islands (known in China as the Daioyu Islands). The Japanese government intervened by purchasing and nationalising the islands, which further inflamed passions. As a result, the Japanese auto industry lost hundreds of millions of dollars as Chinese buyers avoided purchasing Japanese cars.

It's difficult to see Japan–China relations improving in the near future. In the December 2012 general election, the conservative Liberal Democratic Party (LDP) soundly defeated the ruling Democratic Party of Japan (DPJ). The LDP quickly installed the nationalist Abe Shinzō as prime minister. Abe wasted no time in ruffling Chinese feathers when he announced plans to replace earlier Japanese apologies for wartime atrocities with an unspecified 'forward-looking statement'.

Turning Inward

Given the grim economic realities in today's Japan, one might expect the youth of Japan to venture abroad in search of opportunities. However, between 2006 and 2009 the number of Japanese students studying at foreign colleges and universities fell by 23,000. While some of this drop can be directly attributed to Japan's declining economic fortunes, many commentators report that Japanese students are simply less interested in studying or living outside Japan. Others point out that Japanese companies are often unwilling to hire graduates who have studied abroad. Meanwhile, the number of resident foreigners in Japan has been dropping steadily for the last few years, with a 2% decline in 2012.

POPULATION: **127.5 MILLION**

GDP: **US$5.86 TRILLION**

GDP PER CAPITA: **US$36,200**

INFLATION: **-0.2%**

if Japan were 100 people

64 would be 15-64 years old
23 would be over 65 years old
13 would be 0-14 years old

belief systems
(% of population)

84 Shintoism
71 Buddhism
2 Christianity
8 Other

population per sq km

JAPAN   USA   UK

= 30 people

History

The history of Japan is greatly characterised by the distance of its islands from the mainland. Although over the centuries there has been contact between Japan and other parts of Asia, its separation from the mainland has been pivotal in Japan evolving into the unique country you find today. Japan's history may be broadly divided into five main periods: prehistory (ending in about 400 BC); pre-classical (until AD 710); classical (to 1185); medieval (to 1600); and pre-modern to modern (from 1600 on).

Jōmon pottery vessels dating back some 15,000 years are the oldest known pottery vessels in the world.

Ancient Japan:
From Hunter-Gatherers to Divine Rule

Once upon a time, the male and female deities Izanagi and Izanami came down to a watery world from Takamagahara (The Plains of High Heaven), to create land. Droplets from Izanagi's 'spear' solidified into the land now known as Japan, and Izanami and Izanagi then populated it with gods. One of these was Japan's supreme deity, the Sun Goddess Amaterasu (Light of Heaven), whose great-great grandson Jimmu became the first emperor of Japan, reputedly in 660 BC.

This is the seminal creation myth of Japan, but more certainly humans were present in Japan at least 200,000 years ago (though the earliest human remains go back only 30,000 years or so). Until the end of the last ice age about 15,000 years ago, a number of land bridges linked Japan to the continent – Siberia to the north, Korea to the west and probably present-day Taiwan to the south – so access was not difficult.

The first recognisable culture to emerge was the neolithic Jōmon (named after a 'rope-mark' pottery style), from about 13,000 BC. The Jōmon were mostly hunter-gatherers and preferred coastal regions, though agriculture developing from about 4000 BC brought more stable settlement and larger tribal communities. Northern Japan's indigenous Ainu people are of Jōmon descent.

From about 400 BC there were waves of immigrants, later known as Yayoi (from the earliest site of their reddish wheel-thrown pottery). They

TIMELINE	c 13,000 BC	c 400 BC	3rd Century AD
	First evidence of the hunter-gatherer Jōmon, ancestors of the present-day Ainu of northern Japan and producers of the world's earliest pottery vessels.	Yayoi people appear in southwest Japan (probably via Korea), practising wet rice-farming and using metal tools. They also promote inter-regional trade and a sense of territoriality.	Queen Himiko reigns over Yamatai (Yamato) and is recognised by Chinese visitors as 'over-queen' of Japan's more than 100 kingdoms. The Yamato clan remains dominant.

first arrived in the southwest, probably from the Korean Peninsula, and brought iron and bronze technology, and highly productive wet rice-farming techniques. The Yayoi's new technologies brought increased and more diverse production, and greater intertribal trade. At the same time, rivalry increased between regional tribal groups, often over resources, and there was greater social stratification.

The Jōmon were gradually forced north, although modern Japanese have significant amounts of Jōmon DNA, indicating some intermingling of the races. The Yayoi had spread to the middle of Honshū by the 1st century AD, but northern Honshū could still be considered Jōmon territory till at least the 8th century.

Yamato Clan

Agriculture-based settlement led to territories and boundaries being established. According to Chinese sources, by the end of the 1st century AD there were more than a hundred kingdoms in Japan, and by the middle of the 3rd century these were largely ruled by an 'over-queen' named Himiko, whose own territory was known as Yamatai (later Yamato). Its location is disputed, with some scholars favouring northwest Kyūshū, but most favouring the Nara region. The Chinese treated Himiko as sovereign of all Japan (with the name Yamato eventually applied to Japan as a whole) and, through tributes, she acknowledged her allegiance to the Chinese emperor.

HISTORICAL PERIODS

PERIOD	DATE
Jōmon	c 13,000 BC–c 400 BC
Yayoi	c 400 BC–c AD 250
Kofun/Yamato	250–710
Nara	710–94
Heian	794–1185
Kamakura	1185–1333
Muromachi	1333–1568
Azuchi-Momoyama	1568–1600
Edo/Tokugawa	1600–1868
Meiji	1868–1912
Taishō	1912–26
Shōwa	1926–89
Heisei	1989–present

Mid-5th Century	**Mid-6th Century**	**710**	**712 & 720**
Scholars from the Korean kingdom of Paekche introduce writing. Using Chinese characters to express spoken Japanese produces a highly complex writing system.	Scholars from Paekche introduce Buddhism. Its texts can be read by a now-literate elite, who use it to unify and control the nation.	Japan's first capital is established at Nara, based on Chinese models. Japan is arguably a nation-state by this stage.	The compilation of two major historical works, Kojiki (712) and Nihon Shoki (720), allow the imperial family to trace its 'divine' origins and, in this way, legitimise its right to rule.

Top Historic Sites

Nagasaki (Kyūshū)

Asuka (Kansai)

Nara (Kansai)

Kyoto

Tokyo

On her death in 248 Himiko is said to have been buried – along with 100 sacrificed slaves – in a massive barrow-like tomb known as a *kofun*, indicative of the importance of status. Other dignitaries chose burial in similar tombs, and so from this point on, till the establishment of Nara as a capital in 710, Japan is usually referred to as being in the Kofun or Yamato period.

The period saw the confirmation of the Yamato as the dominant – indeed imperial – clan in Japan. They appear to have consolidated their power by negotiation and alliance with (or incorporation of) powerful potential foes. This was a practice Japan was to continue through the ages where it could, though it was less accommodating in the case of perceived weaker foes.

The first verifiable emperor was Suijin (died c 318). He was likely a member of the Yamato clan, though some scholars think he led a group of 'horse-riders' believed to have entered Japan from the Korean Peninsula around the start of the 4th century. The period also saw the adoption of writing, based on Chinese but first introduced by scholars from the Korean kingdom of Paekche in the mid-5th century. Scholars from Paekche also introduced Buddhism a century later.

The Yamato rulers promoted Buddhism as a way to unify and control the land. Though Buddhism originated in India, the Japanese regarded it as a Chinese religion, and it was one of the 'things Chinese' they adopted to achieve recognition as a civilised country – especially by China. By copying China, Japan hoped it too could become powerful.

In 604 the regent Prince Shōtoku (573–620) enacted a constitution with a very Chinese flavour. Its 17 articles promoted harmony and hard work. In 645 major Chinese-style reforms followed, such as centralised government, nationalisation and allocation of land, and codes of law. Under Emperor Temmu (r 673–86) the imperial family had historical works compiled such as the *Kojiki* (Record of Old Things; 712) and *Nihon Shoki* (Record of Japan; 720), to legitimise their power by claiming divine descent. It had the desired effect, and despite a number of perilous moments Japan continues to have the world's longest unbroken monarchy.

Not all things Chinese were emulated. Confucianism, for example, condoned removing an unvirtuous ruler who had lost the 'mandate of heaven', but this idea was not promoted in Japan. Nor was the Chinese practice of achievement of high rank through examination, for the Japanese ruling class preferred birth over merit.

By the early 8th century, Japan, with its estimated five million people, had all the characteristics of a nation-state (with the exclusion of northern Japan). It was effectively unified, with a centralised government, systematic administration, legitimised power, social stratification, a written constitution and legal code, and external recognition.

740

Construction begins on the vast Tōdai-ji temple complex in Nara. It is thought the complex was built to provide a focus for the nation and to ward off smallpox.

700s

The classical age of Japanese religious sculpture, in which some of Japan's greatest works of Buddhist art are produced (some still visible in and around Nara).

➡ Tōdai-ji (p381)

The Age of Courtiers

In 710 a capital was established at Nara (Heijō-kyō). The influence of Buddhism is still seen today in the Tōdai-ji, which houses a huge bronze Buddha and is the world's largest wooden building (and one of the oldest).

Emperor Kammu (r 781–806) decided to relocate the capital in 784. His decision may have been prompted by a series of disasters following the move to Nara, including a massive smallpox epidemic that killed up to one-third of the population in 735–7. Then, in 794 the capital was transferred to nearby Kyoto (Heian-kyō) and remained Japan's capital for more than a thousand years, though it was not necessarily the centre of actual power.

Over the next few centuries courtly life reached a pinnacle of refined artistic pursuits and etiquette, captured famously in the novel *The Tale of Genji,* written by the court-lady Murasaki Shikibu in about 1004. It showed courtiers indulging in pastimes such as guessing flowers by their scent, building extravagant follies and sparing no expense for luxuries. On the positive side, it was a world that encouraged aesthetic sensibilities, such as *mono no aware* (the bitter-sweetness of things) and *okashisa* (pleasantly surprising incongruity), which have endured to the present day. But it was also a world increasingly estranged from reality and it lacked muscle. The court's effeteness was made worse by the weakness of the emperors, manipulated over centuries by the politically powerful Fujiwara family.

While the nobles immersed themselves in courtly pleasures and intrigues, out in provinces powerful military forces were developing. They were typically led by minor nobles, often sent on behalf of court-based major nobles to carry out 'tedious' local duties. Some were distant imperial family members, barred from succession claims – a practice known as 'dynastic shedding' – and hostile to the court. Their retainers included skilled warriors known as samurai (literally 'retainer').

The two main 'shed' families, the Minamoto (also known as Genji) and Taira (Heike), were enemies. In 1156 they were employed to help rival claimants to the Fujiwara leadership, but these figures soon faded into the background when a feud developed between the Minamoto and the Taira.

The Taira prevailed under their leader Kiyomori (1118–81), who was based in the capital. Over the next 20 years, he fell prey to many of the vices lurking there. In 1180 Kiyomori enthroned his two-year-old grandson. When a rival claimant requested the help of the regrouped Minamoto family, their leader, Yoritomo (1147–99), was more than ready to agree.

Both Kiyomori and the claimant died shortly afterwards, but Yoritomo and his younger half-brother Yoshitsune (1159–89), continued the campaign against the Taira – interrupted by a pestilence during the early 1180s. By 1185 Kyoto had fallen and the Taira had been pursued to the western tip of Honshū. A naval battle ensued, won by the Minamoto.

HISTORY ANCIENT JAPAN: FROM HUNTER-GATHERERS TO DIVINE RULE

TEA DRINKING

In 1191 the Zen monk Eisai is said to have brought tea leaves from China, starting Japan's tradition of tea drinking.

794	804	9th–12th Centuries	1156
In response to a series of misfortunes, including a smallpox epidemic, Japan's formal capital is relocated from Nara to Heian (present-day Kyoto), where it remains for more than a thousand years.	After travelling to China to study Buddhism, Kūkai (also known as Kōbō Daishi) founds Shingon (Esoteric) Buddhism in Japan and establishes the famous Kōya-san religious centre.	The court becomes culturally sophisticated but is increasingly effete and removed from the real world. Actual power is held by provincial military clans.	The major provincial families Taira and Minamoto are employed by rival court factions and engage in bitter warfare, with the Taira prevailing under its warrior-leader Kiyomori.

In a well-known tragic tale, Kiyomori's widow leapt into the sea with her grandson Antoku (now aged seven), rather than have him surrender. Minamoto Yoritomo, now the most powerful man in Japan, was to usher in a martial age.

The Age of Warriors

Yoritomo did not seek to become emperor, but wanted the new emperor to give him legitimacy by conferring the title of shōgun (generalissimo), which was granted in 1192. He left many existing offices and institutions in place and set up his base in his home territory of Kamakura rather than Kyoto. While in theory he represented the military arm of the emperor's government, in practice he was in charge of government. His 'shōgunate' was known in Japanese as the *bakufu*, meaning the tent headquarters of a field general, though it lasted almost 700 years as an institution.

The system of government became feudal, centred on a loyalty-based lord-vassal system. It was more personal and 'familial' than medieval European feudalism, particularly in the extended *oya-ko* relationship ('parent-child', in practice 'father-son'), which became another enduring feature of Japan.

But 'families' were not always happy, and the more ruthless powerseekers did not hesitate to kill family members they saw as threats. Yoritomo, apparently suspicious by nature, killed off so many of his own family that there were difficulties with the shōgunal succession when he died in 1199 (after falling from his horse in suspicious circumstances). His half-brother Yoshitsune, whom he had killed, earned an enduring place in Japanese literature and legend as the archetypical tragic hero.

Yoritomo's widow Masako (1157–1225) was a formidable figure, controlling the shōgunate for much of her remaining life. Having taken religious vows on her husband's death, she became known as the 'nun shōgun'. She was instrumental in ensuring that her own family, the Hōjō, replaced the Minamoto as shōguns. The Hōjō shōgunate continued to use Kamakura as the shōgunal base, and lasted till the 1330s.

Mongol Threats

It was during the Hōjō shōgunacy that the Mongols twice tried to invade, in 1274 and 1281. Under Kublai Khan (r 1260–94), the Mongol empire was close to its peak and after conquering Korea in 1259 he sent requests to Japan to submit to him, but these were ignored.

Kublai Khan's expected first attack came in November 1274, allegedly with about 900 vessels carrying 40,000 men, though these figures may be exaggerated. They landed near Hakata in northwest Kyūshū and, de-

The Tale of Genji, written by the courtesan Murasaki Shikibu in about 1004, is widely believed to be the world's first novel.

1185	1192	1199	1200–50
Minamoto Yoritomo topples the Taira and, as the most powerful man in the land, brings a level of unity. A suspicious man, he kills many of his own relatives.	Yoritomo takes the title shōgun (generalissimo) from a largely puppet emperor and establishes the *bakufu* (shōgunate) in his home territory at Kamakura, heralding the start of feudalism in Japan.	After Yoritomo's suspicious death, his formidable wife, Masako (the 'nun shōgun') becomes the most powerful figure in Japan, establishing her family, the Hōjō, as shōguns.	Hōnen and Shinran promote the 'Pure Land' schools of Buddhism, which remain the country's most popular Buddhist sects.

SAMURAI

The prime duty of a samurai – a member of the warrior class from about the 12th century onwards – was to give faithful service to his lord. In fact, the term 'samurai' is derived from a word meaning 'to serve'. Ideally, 'service' meant being prepared to give up one's life for one's lord, though, at least initially, it was typically only hereditary retainers who felt such commitment. At the other end of the ranks, samurai were professional mercenaries who were unreliable and often defected.

The renowned samurai code, *bushidō* (the way of the warrior), developed over centuries but was not formally codified until the 17th century, by which time there were no real battles to fight. The code was greatly idealised, with its intention appearing to have been to show samurai as moral exemplars, to counter criticism that they were parasitic.

Core samurai ideals included *gaman* (endurance), *isshin* (wholehearted commitment) and *makoto* (sincerity). Samurai were supposed to be men of Zen-like austerity who endured hardship without complaint. Even though samurai were often highly educated and sometimes paralleled European knights, their chivalry was not so dominant.

Samurai who became lordless were known as *rōnin* (wanderers or masterless samurai); they acted more like brigands and were a serious social problem.

Samurai who fell from grace were generally required to commit *seppuku* (ritual disembowelment) to show the purity of the soul, which was believed to reside in the stomach.

The samurai's best-known weapon was the *katana* sword, though in earlier days the bow also featured. Arguably the world's finest swordsmen, samurai were formidable opponents in single combat. During modernisation in the late 19th century, the government – itself comprising samurai – realised that a conscript army was more efficient as a unified fighting force and disestablished the samurai class. However, samurai ideals such as endurance and fighting to the death were revived through propaganda prior to the Pacific War, and underlay the determination of many Japanese soldiers.

HISTORY THE AGE OF WARRIORS

spite spirited Japanese resistance, made progress inland. However, for unclear reasons, they retreated to their ships and shortly afterwards a violent storm blew up, damaging about a third of the fleet. The remainder returned to Korea.

A more determined attempt was made from China seven years later. Kublai had a fleet of 4400 warships built to carry a force of 140,000 men – again, these are questionable figures. In August 1281 they landed once more in northwest Kyūshū and again met spirited resistance and had to retire to their vessels. Once more, the weather intervened – this time a typhoon – and half their vessels were destroyed. The survivors went back to China, and there was no further Mongol attempt to invade Japan.

1223	13th Century	1274 & 1281	1333
The monk Dōgen studies Chang Buddhism in China and later returns to found the influential Sōtō school of Zen Buddhism.	Zen Buddhism becomes established in Japan, especially among warriors, and also influences Japanese aesthetics. 'Mass-appeal' forms of Buddhism are also established.	Under Kublai Khan, the Mongols twice attempt to invade Japan, but fail due to poor planning, spirited Japanese resistance and, especially, the destruction of their fleets by typhoons.	General Ashikaga Takauji, initially allied with Emperor Go-Daigo, topples the unpopular Hōjō shōgunate. Takauji requests the title of shōgun, but Go-Daigo declines and a rift develops.

The typhoon of 1281 prompted the idea of divine intervention to save Japan, with the coining of the term kamikaze (literally 'divine wind'). Later this term was used about the Pacific War suicide pilots who, said to be infused with divine spirit, gave their lives to protect Japan from invasion. It also led the Japanese to feel that their land was indeed the Land of the Gods.

The kamikaze ('divine wind') of 1281 is said to have drowned 70,000 Mongol troops. If true, it would be the world's worst maritime disaster.

Demise of the Hōjō Shōgunate

Despite its successful defence of Japan, the Hōjō shōgunate suffered. Its inability to make promised payments to those involved in repelling the Mongols caused considerable dissatisfaction, while the payments it did make severely depleted its finances.

It was also during the Hōjō shōgunacy that Zen Buddhism was brought from China. The austerity and self-discipline of Buddhism appealed greatly to the warrior class, and it was also a factor in the appeal of aesthetic values such as *sabi* (elegant simplicity). More popular forms of Buddhism were the Jōdo (Pure Land) and Jōdo Shin (True Pure Land) sects.

Dissatisfaction towards the shōgunate came to a head under the unusually assertive emperor Go-Daigo (1288–1339). After escaping from exile imposed by the Hōjō, he started to muster anti-shōgunal support in western Honshū. In 1333 the shōgunate dispatched troops to counter this threat, under one of its most promising generals, the young Ashikaga Takauji (1305–58). However, recognising the dissatisfaction towards the Hōjō and that together he and Go-Daigo would have considerable military strength, Takauji threw in his lot with the emperor and attacked the shōgunal offices in Kyoto. Others also soon rebelled against the shōgunate itself in Kamakura.

Books and films such as *Letters from Iwo Jima* and *Memoirs of a Geisha* provide realistic historical context and can increase understanding of other eras and cultures.

This was the end for the Hōjō shōgunate, but not for the institution. Takauji wanted the title of shōgun, but his ally Go-Daigo feared that conferring it would weaken his own imperial power. A rift developed, and Go-Daigo sent forces to attack Takauji. However, Takauji emerged victorious and turned on Kyoto, forcing Go-Daigo to flee into the hills of Yoshino about 100km south of the city, where he set up a court in exile. In Kyoto, Takauji installed a puppet emperor from a rival line, who returned the favour by declaring him shōgun in 1338. The two courts coexisted until 1392 when the 'southern court' (at Yoshino) was betrayed by Ashikaga Yoshimitsu (1358–1408), Takauji's grandson and third Ashikaga shōgun.

Warring States

Takauji set up his shōgunal base in Kyoto, at Muromachi. With a few exceptions such as Takauji and his grandson Yoshimitsu (who had Kyoto's famous Kinkaku-ji (Golden Pavilion) built and once declared himself

1338–92	1400s–1500s	1543	1568
Takauji installs a puppet emperor who names him shōgun (1338), establishing the Ashikaga shōgunate at Muromachi. Two rival emperors exist till Go-Daigo's line is betrayed by Takauji's grandson Yoshimitsu (1392).	Japan is in almost constant internal warfare, including the particularly fierce Ōnin War of 1467–77. The era, especially from the late 15th to late 16th centuries, is known as the Sengoku (Warring States) period.	Portuguese, the first Westerners, arrive by chance in Japan, bringing firearms and Christianity. Firearms prove popular among warlords, while Christianity has a mixed reception.	The warlord Oda Nobunaga seizes Kyoto and becomes the supreme power, though he does not take the title of shōgun. He is noted for his massive ego and brutality.

'King of Japan'), the Ashikaga shōguns were relatively weak. Without strong, centralised government and control, the country slipped into civil war as regional warlords – who came to be known as *daimyō* (regional lords) – engaged in seemingly interminable feuds and power struggles. Starting with the Ōnin War of 1467–77 and for the next hundred years, the country was almost constantly in civil war. This time was known as the Sengoku (Warring States) era.

Ironically perhaps, during the Muromachi period a new flourishing of the arts took place, such as in the refined nō drama, ikebana (flower arranging) and *chanoyu* (tea ceremony). Key aesthetics were *sabi, yūgen* (elegant and tranquil otherworldliness, as seen in nō), *wabi* (subdued taste) and *kare* (severe and unadorned).

The first Europeans arrived in 1543, three Portuguese traders blown ashore on the island of Tanegashima south of Kyūshū. Soon other Europeans arrived, bringing with them Christianity and firearms. They found a land torn apart by warfare, ripe for conversion to Christianity – at least in the eyes of missionaries such as Francis Xavier, who arrived in 1549. The Japanese warlords, however, were more interested in the worldly matter of guns.

Reunification

Nobunaga Seizes Power

One of the most successful of the warlords using firearms was Oda Nobunaga (1534–82), from what is now Aichi Prefecture. Starting from a relatively minor power base, his skilled and ruthless generalship produced a series of victories over rivals. In 1568 he seized Kyoto and installed one of the Ashikaga clan (Yoshiaki) as shōgun, then drove him out in 1573 and made his own base at Azuchi. Although he did not take the title of shōgun, Nobunaga was the supreme power in the land.

Noted for his brutality, Nobunaga was not a man to be crossed. He hated Buddhist priests, and tolerated Christianity as a counterbalance to them. His massive ego led him to erect a temple where he himself could be worshipped, and to declare his birthday a national holiday. His stated aim was 'Tenka Fubu' ('A Unified Realm under Military Rule') and he went some way to achieving this by redistributing territories among the *daimyō*, having land surveyed and standardising weights and measures.

The Ambitions of Hideyoshi

In 1582 Nobunaga was betrayed by one of his generals and forced to commit suicide. However, the work of unification was continued by another of Nobunaga's generals, Toyotomi Hideyoshi (1536–98), a foot soldier who had risen through the ranks to become Nobunaga's favourite.

SHINTŌ DEITIES

The Japanese religion of Shintō is one of the few religions in the world with a female solar deity.

1582	Late 1500s
Nobunaga is betrayed and forced to commit suicide. Power transfers to one of his loyal generals, Toyotomi Hideyoshi, who becomes increasingly paranoid and anti-Christian. Hideyoshi takes the title of regent.	Sen-no-Rikyū lays down the form of the tea ceremony, the ritualised drinking of tea originally practised by nobility and later spreading to wealthy commoners.

➡ Cast-iron kettle for making tea

FRANK CARTER / GETTY IMAGES ©

HIDDEN CHRISTIANS

Japan's so-called 'Christian Century' began in 1549 with the arrival of Portuguese missionaries on the island of Kyūshū. Within decades, hundreds of thousands of Japanese, from peasants to *daimyō* (regional lords), were converted.

The rapid rise of Christian belief, as well as its association with trade, Western weaponry and control of Japanese territory, came to be viewed as a threat by the *bakufu* (military government) under Toyotomi Hideyoshi. With the expulsion of missionaries in 1587, an era of suppression of Christians began. Thousands of Christians were estimated to have been executed over the following six decades. The best-known execution was the 1597 crucifixion of 26 Japanese and Spanish Franciscans in Nagasaki. Many thousands of Christian peasants resisted in the 1637–38 Shimabara Rebellion, after which Christianity was outlawed completely.

Other persecution took the form of *fumi-e*, in which suspected Christians were forced to walk on images of Jesus. The Gregorian date on the Dutch trading house on the island of Hirado was taken as proof of the Dutch traders' Christianity and used to justify their exile to Nagasaki's Dejima, ushering in more than two centuries of *sakoku* (closure to the outside world).

Japanese Christians reacted by going undercover as *kakure Kirishitan* (hidden Christians). Without priests, they worshipped in services held in secret rooms inside private homes. On the surface, worship resembled other Japanese religions, including using Shintō *kamidana* altars and Buddhist *butsudan* ancestor-worship chests in homes, and ceremonial rice and sake. But *kakure Kirishitan* also kept hanging scrolls of Jesus, Mary and saints, as well as statues like the Maria-Kannon, depicting Mary in the form of the Buddhist deity of mercy holding an infant symbolising Jesus. The sounds of worship, too, mimicked Buddhist incantations. Scholars estimate there were about 150,000 hidden Christians.

It was not until 1865, 12 years after the arrival of the Black Ships, that Japan had its first large-scale church again, Oura Cathedral in Nagasaki, and missionaries began to return to Japan when it reopened in 1868. The Meiji government officially declared freedom of religion in 1871. Today, there are estimated to be between one and two million Japanese Christians (about 1% of the population).

Hideyoshi, too, was an extraordinary figure. Small and with simian features, he was nicknamed 'Saru-chan' ('Little Monkey') by Nobunaga, but his huge will for power belied his physical size. He disposed of any potential rivals among Nobunaga's sons, took up the title of regent, continued Nobunaga's policy of territorial redistribution and insisted that *daimyō* should surrender their families to him as hostages to be kept in Kyoto – his base being at Momoyama. He also banned weapons for all classes except samurai.

1592 & 1597–98	1600	1603	1638
Hideyoshi twice tries to conquer Korea as part of a plan to control Asia, the second attempt ending after his death in 1598. The invasions seriously damage relations between Japan and Korea.	The warlord Tokugawa Ieyasu breaks an earlier promise to the dying Hideyoshi to protect his young son and heir Hideyori, and seizes power at the Battle of Sekigahara.	Ieyasu becomes shōgun, with policies aimed at retaining power by maintaining the status quo and minimising threats.	Westerners have been expelled, except for a small Protestant Dutch population on a tiny island off Nagasaki. Shōgunal forces massacre Japanese Christians in the Christian-led Shimabara Rebellion.

In his later years, Hideyoshi became increasingly paranoid, cruel and megalomaniacal. He would saw in half messengers who gave him bad news, and had young members of his own family executed for suspected plotting. He also issued the first expulsion order of Christians (1587), whom he suspected were an advance guard for an invasion. In 1597 he crucified 26 Christians, nine of them Europeans. His grand scheme for power included a pan-Asian conquest, and as a first step he attempted an invasion of Korea in 1592, which failed amid much bloodshed. He tried again in 1597, but the campaign was abandoned when Hideyoshi died of illness in 1598.

Shōgun Ieyasu

On his deathbed, Hideyoshi entrusted one of his ablest generals, Tokugawa Ieyasu (1542–1616), with safeguarding the country and the succession of his young son Hideyori (1593–1615). Ieyasu betrayed that trust. In 1600, in the Battle of Sekigahara, he defeated those trying to protect Hideyori and effectively became the overlord of Japan. In 1603 his power was legitimised when the emperor gave him the title of shōgun and his Kantō base, the once tiny fishing village of Edo – later renamed Tokyo – became the real centre of power and government in Japan.

Through these three men, by fair means or more commonly foul, the country had been reunified within three decades.

A Time of Stability

Having secured power for the Tokugawa, Ieyasu and his successors were determined to retain it. Their basic strategy was to enforce the status quo and minimise any potential for challenge.

Their policies included tight control over military families, including requiring authorisation for castle-building and marriages. They continued to redistribute (or confiscate) territory and, importantly, required *daimyō* and their retainers to spend every second year at Edo, where their families were kept permanently as hostages.

The shōgunate also directly controlled ports, mines, major towns and other strategic areas. Movement was severely restricted by deliberately destroying many bridges, setting up checkpoints and requiring written authority for travel. Wheel transport was banned, potentially ocean-going vessels strictly monitored, and overseas travel for Japanese banned as well as the return of those already overseas.

Social movement was also banned, with society divided into four main classes: in descending order *shi* (samurai), *nō* (farmers), *kō* (artisans) and *shō* (merchants). Detailed codes of conduct including clothing, food, housing and even the siting of the toilet, applied to each of these classes

David Mitchell's *Thousand Autumns of Jacob de Zoet: A Novel* tells about the Dutch living on the island of Dejima during the period of *sakoku*.

1600s–1800s	1701–03	Mid- to Late 1700s	1808
The Tokugawa shōgunate is based at Edo (later renamed Tokyo). Life is tightly controlled, and the nation is shut off from most of the world. Nonetheless 'Edo merchant culture' emerges.	The mass suicide of the 'Forty-Seven Rōnin' after avenging their lord's death is seen by many as a model for samurai ethics.	Itō Jakuchū creates a flamboyant and seminaturalistic style of painting with hints of Western influence but retaining a Japanese heart. Jakuchū remains one of Japan's most famous painters.	The British ship HMS *Phaeton* captures several Dutch personnel at the island of Dejima and demands supplies. The British leave with the supplies before Japanese reinforcements arrive.

Though not greatly popular, Christianity threatened the shōgunate's authority, and missionaries were expelled in 1614. Following the Christian-led Shimabara Rebellion, Christianity was banned, several hundred thousand Japanese Christians were forced into hiding, and all Westerners except the Protestant Dutch were expelled by 1638.

The shōgunate found Protestantism less threatening than Catholicism (knowing that the Vatican could muster one of the biggest military forces in the world) and would have let the British stay on if the Dutch had not convinced it that Britain was a Catholic country. Nevertheless, the Dutch were just a few dozen men confined to a tiny trading base on the artificial island of Dejima near Nagasaki.

Retreat from the World

Japan entered an era of *sakoku* (closure to the outside world) that was to last for more than two centuries. Within the isolated and severely prescribed world of Tokugawa Japan, breaching even a trivial law could mean execution. Even 'rude behaviour', defined as 'acting in an unexpected manner', was a capital offence. Punishments could be cruel, such as crucifixion, and meted out collectively or by proxy, with for example a village headman punished for a villager's misdemeanour. Secret police reported on misdeeds.

As a result, people learned the importance of obedience to authority, collective responsibility and 'doing the right thing'. These are values still prominent in present-day Japan.

The disorienting collapse of the regimented Tokugawa world produced a form of mass hysteria called *Ee Ja Nai Ka* (Who Cares?), with traumatised people dancing naked and giving away possessions.

Merchants Rise as Samurai Decline

For all the constraints, the period had a considerable dynamism, especially among the merchants, who as the lowest class were often ignored by the authorities and had relative freedom. They prospered greatly from the services and goods required for *daimyō* processions to and from Edo, which were so costly that *daimyō* had to convert much of their domain's produce into cash. This boosted the economy in general.

A largely pleasure-oriented merchant culture thrived and produced the popular kabuki drama, with its colour and stage effects. Other entertainments included *bunraku* (classic puppet theatre), haiku, popular novels and *ukiyo-e* (woodblock prints), often of female geisha, who came to the fore during this time.

Samurai had no major military engagements. Well educated, most ended up fighting paper wars as administrators and managers. Ironically, it was during this period of relative inactivity that the renowned samurai code of *bushidō* (the way of the warrior) was formalised. Though largely idealistic, occasionally the code was put into practice, such as the loyalty shown in 1701–3 by the 'Forty-Seven Rōnin', masterless samurai who

1800–50

Ukiyo-e ('pictures of the floating world'), highly stylised woodblock prints depicting entertainment districts and landscapes, become popular. The movement is led by Hiroshige and Hokusai.

Early to Mid-1800s

The nation's isolation is threatened by increasing numbers of foreign whalers and other vessels entering Japanese waters. Treatment of those attempting to land is harsh.

FRANK CARTER / GETTY IMAGES ©

➜ *Ukiyo-e*, Kyoto Handicraft Center (p331)

THE REAL LAST SAMURAI

Saigō Takamori (1828–77) was a giant for his day, at about 180cm (6ft) tall, with a broad build, square head and large eyes. His importance in Japanese history is equally large.

Born to a samurai family in Kagoshima, Kyūshū (then called Satsuma Province, in the southwestern corner of the main islands), Saigō was an ardent supporter of the emperor Meiji and field commander of the imperial army against the forces of the Tokugawa shōgunate. A rebellion of Tokugawa loyalists quashed at Ueno in Tokyo in 1868 cemented the Meiji Restoration.

But things did not turn out as Saigō had hoped. The samurai system was abolished once Meiji ascended the throne, and by 1872 this system of professional warriors had given way to a Western model of military conscription. Saigō, by then part of the Meiji government, recommended invading Korea, and after this idea was rejected in 1873 he resigned and returned to Satsuma.

By 1874 the new army had put down small riots by former samurai that broke out around the country. Other former samurai rallied around Saigō and urged him to lead a rebellion against the imperial forces. The resulting 1877 siege of Kumamoto Castle lasted 54 days, with a reported force of 40,000 samurai and armed peasants arrayed against the imperial army. When the castle was incinerated and defeat became inevitable, it is said that Saigō retreated to Kagoshima and committed *seppuku* (ritual suicide by disembowlment).

The Satsuma Rebellion, as it came to be called, soon gained legend status among common Japanese. Capitalising on this fame, the Meiji government posthumously pardoned Saigō and granted him full honours, and today he remains an exemplar of the samurai spirit. Statues of his image can be found most prominently in Kagoshima and, walking his faithful dog, in Tokyo's Ueno-kōen. His most famous maxim, *keiten aijin*, translates to 'Revere heaven, love humankind'.

Fans of the 2003 movie *The Last Samurai* may recognise elements of this story in Katsumoto, the character played by Watanabe Ken. However, there is no evidence that any Western soldier, such as the one played by Tom Cruise, had any role in these events in Saigō's life.

waited two years to avenge the unfair enforced *seppuku* (ritual suicide by disembowlment) of their lord, killing the man responsible and then committing *seppuku* themselves.

A Time for Learning

Confucianism was officially encouraged, with the apparent aim of reinforcing the idea of hierarchy and status quo, but it also encouraged learning and literacy. By the end of the period, up to a third of the 30 million Japanese were literate – far ahead of Western populations of the time. However, a strong trend of nationalism, centred on Shintō and

1853–54	1854–67	1867–68	1870s–Early 1890s
US Commodore Matthew Perry uses 'gunboat diplomacy' to force Japan to open up for trade and reprovisioning. In response, many Japanese criticise the ineffective shōgunate.	Opposition to the shōgunate grows, led by samurai from the Satsuma and Chōshū domains. Initially hostile to foreigners, they soon realise Japan's defensive limitations.	The Meiji Restoration disestablishes the shōgunate and restores imperial authority, but 15-year-old emperor Mutsuhito is a puppet, and oligarchs rule. Japan's capital is moved to Edo, renamed Tokyo.	The oligarchs bring in policies of modernisation and Westernisation, such as creating a conscript army (1873), disestablishing the samurai (1876) and adopting a constitution (1889).

the ancient texts, also occurred. Its focus on the emperor's primacy was unhelpful to the shōgunate. Certainly, by the early to mid-19th century, there was considerable dissatisfaction with the shōgunate, fanned also by corruption and incompetence among officials.

It is questionable how much longer the Tokugawa shōgunate and its secluded world might have continued, but as it happened, external forces were to hasten its demise.

Modernisation

A number of Western vessels had appeared in Japanese waters since the start of the 19th century. Any Westerners who landed, even through shipwreck, were almost always expelled or even executed. This was not acceptable to Western powers. America in particular was keen to expand its interests across the Pacific, with its numerous whaling vessels in the northwest needing regular provisioning.

In 1853 and again the following year, US Commodore Matthew Perry steamed into Edo-wan with a show of gunships and demanded Japan open up to trade and provisioning. The shōgunate was no match for Perry's firepower and had to agree to his demands. Soon an American consul arrived, and other Western powers followed suit. Japan was obliged to give 'most favoured nation' rights to all the powers, and lost control over its own tariffs.

Meiji Restoration

Anti-shōgunal samurai, particularly in the outer domains of Satsuma (southern Kyūshū) and Chōshū (western Honshū), capitalised on the humiliation of the shōgunate, the nation's supposed military protector. A movement arose to 'revere the emperor and expel the barbarians' *(sonnō jōi)*.

Unsuccessfully skirmishing with the Western powers, the reformers realised that while expelling the barbarians was not feasible, restoring the emperor was. Their coup, known as the Meiji (Enlightened Rule) Restoration, in late 1867–early 1868, 'restored' the new teenage emperor Mutsuhito (1852–1912, later known as Meiji), following the convenient death of his father Kōmei (1831–67).

After some initial resistance, the last shōgun, Yoshinobu (1837–1913), retired to Shizuoka to live out his remaining years peacefully. The shōgunal base at Edo became the new imperial base and was renamed Tokyo (Eastern Capital).

Mutsuhito did as he was told by those who had restored him, though they would claim that everything was done on his behalf and with his sanction. His restorers, driven by both personal ambition and genuine concern for the nation, were mostly leading Satsuma or Chōshū samu-

The salaries of foreign specialists invited to Japan during the Meiji period are believed to have amounted to 5% of all government expenditure during the period.

1894–95	1902	1904–05	1910
Japan starts a war with China, at this stage a weak nation. Defeating China in the Sino-Japanese War (1895), Japan gains Taiwan and its territorial expansion begins.	Japan signs the Anglo-Japanese Alliance, the first-ever equal alliance between a Western and non-Western nation. Effectively, this means Japan has become a major power.	Japan wins the Russo-Japanese War. Antipathy towards Russia had developed after the Sino-Japanese War, when Russia pressured Japan to renounce Chinese territory that it then occupied.	Free of any Russian threat, Japan formally annexes Korea, in which it been increasingly interested since the 1870s. The international community makes no real protest.

rai aged in their early 30s, the most prominent of them Itō Hirobumi (1841–1909), who later became prime minister on no fewer than four occasions. Fortunately for Japan, they proved a very capable oligarchy.

Japan was also fortunate that the Western powers were distracted by richer and easier pickings in China and elsewhere, and did not seriously seek to occupy or colonise Japan. Nevertheless, the fear of colonisation made the reformers act with great urgency. Far from being colonised, they wanted to be colonisers and make Japan a major power.

Westernisation

Under the banner of *fukoku kyōhei* (rich country, strong army), the young men who now controlled Japan decided on Westernisation as the best strategy. Another slogan, *oitsuke, oikose* (catch up, overtake), suggests they even wanted to outdo their models. Missions were sent overseas to observe Western institutions and practices, and specialists were brought to Japan to advise in areas from banking to transport to mining.

In the following decades Japan Westernised quite substantially, not just in material ways such as telegraphs, railways and clothing, but also establishing a modern banking system and economy, a legal code, a constitution and Diet, elections and political parties, and a conscript army.

Where necessary, existing institutions and practices were disestablished. *Daimyō* were 'persuaded' to give their domain land to the government in return for governorships or other compensation, enabling a prefectural system to be set up. The four-tier class system was scrapped, and people were freed to choose their occupation and place of residence. Even the samurai class was phased out by 1876 to pave the way for a more efficient conscript army.

> The rickshaw was not developed until 1869, after the Tokugawa ban on wheeled transport was lifted.

New Ideologies

The ban on Christianity was lifted, though few took advantage of it. Nevertheless, numerous Western ideologies entered the country, one of the most popular being 'self-help' philosophy, which provided a guiding principle for a population newly liberated from a world in which everything had been prescribed for them. The government quickly realised that nationalism could usefully harness these new energies. People were encouraged to make a success of themselves and become strong, and in so doing show the world what a successful and strong nation Japan was.

Leaning Towards Democracy

The government took responsibility for establishing major industries and then selling them off at bargain rates to chosen 'government-friendly' industrial entrepreneurs – a factor in the formation of huge industrial combines known as *zaibatsu*. While the government's actions

1912	1914–15	1920s	1931
Emperor Meiji (Mutsuhito) dies, after seeing Japan rise from a remote pre-industrial nation to a world power in half a century. His mentally disabled son, Yoshihito, succeeds him.	Japan uses the involvement of Western countries in WWI in Europe to occupy German territory in the Pacific in 1914 (as Britain's ally), and in 1915 to present China with 'Twenty-One Demands'.	Japan becomes increasingly disillusioned with the West, feeling unfairly treated by decisions such as the Washington Conference naval ratios (1921–2) and the USA's immigration policies in 1924.	Increasingly defiant of the West, Japan invades Manchuria and then dramatically withdraws from the League of Nations in response to criticism. Japan's behaviour becomes more aggressive.

were not really democratic, this was typical of the day. Another example is the 'transcendental cabinet' that was responsible only to the emperor, who followed his advisers, who were members of the same cabinet! Meiji Japan was outwardly democratic but internally retained many authoritarian features.

The 'state-guided' economy was helped by a workforce that was well educated, obedient and numerous, and traditions of sophisticated commercial practices such as futures markets. In the early years Japan's main industry was textiles and its main export silk, but later in the Meiji period it moved into manufacturing and heavy industry, becoming a major world shipbuilder. Improvement in agricultural technology freed up farming labour to move into these manufacturing sectors.

The Coming of the Barbarians, by Pat Barr, is perhaps the most interesting account of the mid-19th-century opening of Japan.

The World Stage

A key element of Japan's aim to become a world power with overseas territory was the military. Following Prussian (army) and British (navy) models, Japan built up a formidable military force. Using the same 'gunboat diplomacy' on Korea that Perry had used on the Japanese, in 1876 Japan was able to force on Korea an unequal treaty of its own and increasingly interfered in Korean politics. Using Chinese 'interference' in Korea as a justification, in 1894 Japan manufactured a war with China, a weak nation at this stage despite its massive size, and easily emerged victorious. As a result, it gained Taiwan and the Liaotung Peninsula. Russia pressured Japan into renouncing the peninsula and then promptly occupied it, leading to the Russo-Japanese War of 1904–05, won by Japan. An important benefit was Western recognition of its interests in Korea, which it annexed in 1910.

Japan was arguably the first Asian nation to defeat a Western nation in a military conflict (the Russo-Japanese War of 1904–05).

By the time of Mutsuhito's death in 1912, Japan was recognised as a world power. In addition to its military victories and territorial acquisitions, in 1902 it had signed the Anglo-Japanese Alliance, the first-ever equal alliance between a Western and non-Western nation. The unequal treaties had also been rectified. Western-style structures were in place. The economy was world ranking. The Meiji period had been a truly extraordinary half-century of modernisation. But where to next?

Growing Dissatisfaction with the West

Mutsuhito was succeeded by his son Yoshihito (Taishō), whose mental deterioration led to his own son Hirohito (1901–89) becoming regent in 1921.

The Taishō period (Great Righteousness; 1912–26) saw continued democratisation, the extension of the right to vote and a stress on diplomacy. Until WWI Japan benefitted economically from the reduced presence of the Western powers and politically from its alliance with

1937	1941	1942	1945
During an attempted occupation of China, Japan commits an atrocity at Nanjing, torturing and killing many thousands of people, mostly innocent civilians.	Japan enters WWII by striking Pearl Harbor without warning on 7 December, destroying much of the USA's Pacific fleet and drawing that country into the war.	After early military successes, Japan's expansion is thwarted at the Battle of Midway in June, with significant losses. From this time, Japan is largely in retreat.	Following intensive firebombing of Tokyo in March, Hiroshima and Nagasaki become victims of an atomic bombing on 6 and 9 August, leading Japan's leader, Hirohito, to surrender on 15 August.

Britain, and was able to occupy German possessions in East Asia and the Pacific. However, Japan also used the reduced Western presence in 1915 to aggressively try to gain control of China, issuing its notorious 'Twenty-One Demands', which were eventually modified.

There was a growing sense of dissatisfaction in Japan towards the West, and a sense of unfair treatment. The Washington Conference of 1921–22 set naval ratios of three capital ships for Japan to five American and five British, which upset the Japanese despite being well ahead of France's 1.75. Around the same time, a racial-equality clause Japan proposed to the newly formed League of Nations was rejected. And in 1924 America introduced race-based immigration policies that effectively targeted Japanese.

This dissatisfaction intensified in the Shōwa period (Illustrious Peace), which started in 1926 with the death of Yoshihito and the formal accession of Hirohito. Not a strong emperor, he was unable to curb the rising power of the military, which pointed to a growing gap between urban and rural living standards and accused politicians and big businessmen of corruption. The situation was not helped by repercussions from the Great Depression in the late 1920s. The cause of these troubles, in Japanese eyes, was the West, with its excessive individualism and liberalism. According to the militarists, Japan needed to look after its own interests, which meant a resource-rich, Japan-controlled Greater East Asian Co-Prosperity Sphere that even included Australia and New Zealand.

Japan invaded Manchuria in 1931 and set up a puppet government. When the League of Nations objected, Japan promptly left the league. It soon turned its attention to China, and in 1937 launched a brutal invasion that saw atrocities such as the infamous Nanjing Massacre of December. Casualty figures for Chinese civilians at Nanjing vary from 340,000 to 20,000. Many of the tortures, rapes and murders were filmed and are undeniable, but even today, Japanese attempts to downplay this and other massacres in Asia remain a stumbling block in Japan's relations with many Asian nations.

The Yamato dynasty is the longest unbroken monarchy in the world, and Hirohito's reign from 1926 to 1989 the longest of any Japanese monarch.

WWII

Japan did not reject all Western nations, for it admired the new regimes in Germany and Italy and in 1940 entered into a pact with them. This gave it confidence to expand further in Southeast Asia, principally seeking oil. However, the alliance didn't lead to much cooperation, and since Hitler was openly talking of the Japanese as *untermenschen* (lesser beings) and the 'Yellow Peril', Japan was never sure of Germany's commitment. The USA was increasingly concerned at Japan's aggression, and applied sanctions. Diplomacy failed and war seemed inevitable.

1945–52

Japan undergoes USA-led occupation and a rapid economic recovery follows. Hirohito is spared from prosecution as a war criminal, angering many American allies.

1972

The USA returns administrative control of Okinawa to Japan, but keeps many bases in place, which is a continuing source of tension.

BRENT WINEBRENNER / GETTY IMAGES ©

➜ Peace Memorial Park (p414), Hiroshima

Japanese forces struck at Pearl Harbor on 7 December 1941, damaging much of the USA's Pacific fleet and apparently catching the USA by surprise (though some scholars believe Roosevelt and others deliberately allowed the attack, to overcome isolationist sentiment and bring the USA into the war against Germany). Whatever the reality, the USA certainly underestimated Japan's commitment, which led to widespread occupation of Pacific islands and parts of Asia. Most scholars agree that Japan never expected to beat the USA, but hoped to bring it to the negotiating table and emerge better off.

The tide started to turn against Japan from the Battle of Midway in June 1942, when much of its carrier fleet was destroyed. Japan had over-extended itself, and over the next three years was subjected to an island-hopping counter-attack. By mid-1945 Japan, ignoring the Potsdam Declaration calling for unconditional surrender, was preparing for a final Allied assault on its homeland. On 6 August the world's first atomic bomb was dropped on Hiroshima, killing 90,000 civilians. Russia, which Japan had hoped might mediate, declared war on 8 August. And on 9 August another atomic bomb was dropped, on Nagasaki, with another 50,000 deaths. The emperor formally surrendered on 15 August.

> Until Japan was occupied by the USA and other Allies following WWII, the nation had never been conquered or occupied by a foreign power.

The Modern Period

Japan's recovery from the war is now the stuff of legend. The American occupation officially ended in 1952, with the USA engaged in yet another war, this time on the Korean Peninsula. Many historians, both Japanese and American, say Japan's role as a forward base reignited the Japanese economy. Whatever the case, its growth from the 1950s on can only be termed miraculous. It wasn't until 1990, with the bursting of the 'Bubble Economy', that it finally came down to earth.

For details on the most significant event to happen in Japan in recent years – the Great East Japan Earthquake in 2011 and the resulting tsunami and nuclear disaster – see p479 and p824.

1990	2005	2010	2011
The so-called 'Bubble Economy', based on overinflated land and stock prices, finally bursts in Japan. By the end of the year, the stock market has lost 48% of its value.	Japan's population declines for the first year since WWII, and is a continuing trend.	China surpasses Japan as the world's second-largest economy after the USA.	On 11 March, the Great East Japan Earthquake strikes off the coast of northeast Japan (Tōhoku), generating a tsunami that kills many thousands and setting off a crisis at a nuclear powerplant in Fukushima Prefecture.

The People of Japan

The uniqueness and peculiarity of the Japanese is a favourite topic of both Western observers and the Japanese themselves. It's worth starting any discussion about the people of Japan by noting that there is no such thing as 'the Japanese'. Rather, there are 127 million individuals in Japan, each with their own unique character, interests and habits. Despite popular stereotypes to the contrary, Japanese people are as varied as any others on earth.

Defying Stereotypes

Why then the pervasive images of the Japanese as aloof or even bizarre? These stereotypes are largely rooted in language: few Japanese are able to speak English as well as, say, your average Singaporean, Hong Kong Chinese or well-educated Indian, not to mention most Europeans. This difficulty with English is largely due to the country's English-education system, and is compounded by cultural factors, including a natural shyness and a perfectionist streak, and the nature of the Japanese language itself, which contains fewer sounds than many other major languages (making pronunciation of other languages difficult). Thus, what appears to the casual observer to be a maddening inscrutability is more likely just an inability to communicate effectively. Outsiders who become fluent in Japanese discover a people whose thoughts and feelings are surprisingly – almost boringly – similar to those of folks in other developed nations.

All this said, the Japanese do collectively have certain cultural characteristics that reflect their unique history and interaction with their environment. First, Japan is an island nation. Second, until WWII, Japan was never conquered by an outside power, nor was it heavily influenced by Christian missionaries. Third, until the beginning of last century, the majority of Japanese lived in close-knit rural farming communities. Fourth, most of Japan is covered in steep mountains, so the few flat areas of the country are quite crowded – people literally live on top of each other. Finally, for almost all of its history, Japan has been a strictly hierarchical place, with something approximating a caste system during the Edo period.

All of this has produced a people who highly value group identity and social harmony – in a tightly packed city or small farming village, there simply isn't room for colourful individualism. One of the ways harmony is preserved is by forming consensus and concealing personal opinions and true feelings. Thus, the free-flowing exchange of ideas, debates and even heated arguments that one expects in the West are far less common in Japan. This reticence to share innermost thoughts may contribute to the Western image of the Japanese as somewhat mysterious.

Of course, there is a lot more to the typical Japanese character than just a tendency to prize social harmony. Any visitor to the country will soon discover a people who are remarkably conscientious, meticulous, industrious, honest and technically skilled. A touching shyness and sometimes almost painful self-consciousness are also undoubted features of many Japanese. These characteristics result in a society that is a joy for the traveller to experience.

It is thought that the modern Japanese population emerged from the mixing of early Jōmon people, who walked over to Japan via land bridges formed during an ice age, and later Yayoi people, who arrived from the Korean Peninsula in boats.

RELIGION

And let us say that any visit to Japan is a good opportunity to explode the myths about Japan and the Japanese. While you may imagine a nation of suit-clad conformists or enigmatic automatons, a few rounds in a local *izakaya* (pub-eatery) will quickly put all of these notions to rest.

Lifestyle

The way most Japanese live today differs greatly from the way they lived before WWII. As the birth rate has dropped and labour demands have drawn more workers to cities, the population has become increasingly urban. At the same time, Japan continues to soak up influences from abroad and the traditional lifestyle of the country is quickly disappearing in the face of a dizzying onslaught of Western material and pop culture. These days, the average young Tokyoite has a lot more in common with her peers in Melbourne or London than she does with her grandmother back in her *furusato* (home town).

In the City

The overwhelming majority of Japanese live in the bustling urban environments of major cities. These urbanites live famously hectic lives dominated by often gruelling work schedules and punctuated by lengthy commutes from city centres to more affordable outlying neighbourhoods and suburbs.

Until fairly recently, the nexus of all this activity was the Japanese corporation, which provided lifetime employment to the legions of blue-suited white-collar workers, almost all of them men, who lived, worked, drank, ate and slept in the service of the companies for which they toiled. These days, as the Japanese economy makes the transition from a manufacturing economy to a service economy, the old certainties are vanishing. On the way out are Japan's famous 'cradle to grave' employment and age-based promotion system. Now, a recent college graduate is just as likely to become a *furitaa* (part-time worker) as he is to become a salaryman. Needless to say, all this has wide-ranging consequences for Japanese society.

Most families once comprised a father who was a salaryman, a mother who was a housewife, kids who studied dutifully in order to earn a place at one of Japan's elite universities, and an elderly in-law who had moved in. Although the days of this traditional model may not be completely over, it has been changing fast in recent years. As in Western countries, *tomobataraki* (both spouses working) is now increasingly common.

The kids in the family probably still study like mad. If they are not yet in high school, they will be working towards gaining admission to a select high school by attending an after-school cram school, known as a *juku*. If they are already in high school, they will be attending a *juku* in the hopes of passing university admission exams.

As for the mother- or father-in-law, who in the past would have expected to be taken care of by the eldest son in the family, they may have found that beliefs about filial loyalty have changed substantially since the 1980s, particularly in urban centres. Now, more and more Japanese families are sending elderly parents and in-laws to live out their golden years in *rōjin hōmu* (literally 'old-folks homes').

In the Country

Only one in four Japanese live in the small farming and fishing villages that dot the mountains and cling to the rugged coasts. Mass postwar emigration from these rural enclaves has doubtless changed the weave of Japanese social fabric and the texture of its landscape, as the young continue their steady flight to the city, leaving untended rice fields to slide down the hills from neglect.

Most Japanese identify themselves as both Shintō and Buddhist, but many young Japanese get married in Christian ceremonies performed by foreign 'priests' (many of whom are not real Christian priests).

Today only 15% of farming households continue to make ends meet solely through agriculture, with most rural workers holding down two or three jobs. Though this lifestyle manages to make the incomes of some country dwellers higher than those of their urban counterparts, it also speaks clearly of the crisis that many rural communities are facing in their struggle to maintain the traditional way of life.

The salvation of traditional village life may well rely on the success of the 'I-turn' (moving from urban areas to rural villages) and 'U-turn' (moving from country to city, and back again) movements. Although not yet wildly successful, these movements have managed to attract young people who work at home, company workers who are willing to put in a number of hours on the train commuting to the nearest city, and retirees looking to spend their golden years among the thatched roofs and rice fields that symbolise a not-so-distant past.

Religion

Shintō and Buddhism are the main religions in Japan. Most Japanese practice some rites from both religions (though these are sometimes practiced without any particular religious fervour) and are likely to pay an annual visit to a shrine and a temple, particularly during important holidays like O-bon and New Year's.

Shintō, or 'the way of the gods', is the indigenous religion of Japan. Shintoists believe that *kami* (gods) are present in the natural world, or, at the very least, animate the natural world. Consisting of thousands of deities, the Shintō pantheon includes both local spirits and global gods and goddesses. Therefore, a devout Shintoist might worship the spirit of a nearby waterfall or that of a uniquely shaped rock, while simultaneously revering the most celebrated Shintō deity Amaterasu, the goddess of the sun. The majority of Japanese would say that their religion is Shintō, but what they would mean by this would vary widely from person to person.

Buddhism arrived from India via China and Korea sometime in the 6th century and has for the most part coexisted peacefully with Shintō. About 90 million people in Japan currently practice some form of Buddhism,

VISITING A SHINTŌ SHRINE

Entering a Japanese shrine can be a bewildering experience for travellers. In order to make the most of the experience, follow these guidelines and do as the Japanese do.

➡ Just past the torii (shrine gate), you'll find a chōzuya (trough of water) with long-handled ladles (*hishaku*) perched on a rack above. This is for purifying yourself before entering the sacred precincts of the shrine. Some Japanese forgo this ritual and head directly for the main hall. If you choose to purify yourself, take a ladle, fill it with fresh water from the tap, pour some over one hand, transfer the spoon and pour water over the other hand. Then pour a little water into a cupped hand and rinse your mouth, spitting the water onto the ground beside the trough, not into the trough.

➡ Next, head to the haiden (hall of worship), which sits in front of the honden (main hall) enshrining the kami (god of the shrine). Here you'll find a thick rope hanging from a gong, with an offerings box in front. Toss a coin into the box and ring the gong by pulling on the rope (to summon the deity). Then pray, clap your hands twice, bow and then back away from the shrine. Some Japanese believe that a ¥5 coin is the best for an offering at a temple or shrine and that the luck engendered by the offering of a ¥10 coin will come further in the future (since 10 can be pronounced tō in Japanese, which can also mean 'far').

➡ If photography is forbidden at a shrine, it will be posted as such. Otherwise, it is permitted and you should simply use your discretion when taking photos.

though most combine their practice with the exercise of periodic Shintō rites. Japanese Buddhism is mostly Mahayana Buddhism, which is notable for its belief in bodhisattva, beings who put off entry into nirvana in order to save all beings stuck in the corrupt world of time.

Japanese Buddhists often call on the assistance of these bodhisattva, usually by chanting mantras or otherwise invoking their names rather than meditating. Zen Buddhism, however, although being a Mayahana sect, places great emphasis on meditation.

Population

Japan has a population of approximately 127 million people (the ninth largest in the world) and, with 75% of it concentrated in urban centres, population density is extremely high. Areas such as the Tokyo–Kawasaki–Yokohama conurbation are so densely populated that they have almost ceased to be separate cities, running into each other and forming a vast coalescence that, if considered as a whole, would constitute the world's largest city.

One notable feature of Japan's population is its relative ethnic and cultural homogeneity. This is particularly striking for visitors from the USA, Australia and other multicultural nations. The main reason for this ethnic homogeneity lies in Japan's strict immigration laws, which have ensured that only a small number of foreigners settle in the country.

The largest non-Japanese group in the country is made up of 650,000 *zai-nichi kankoku-jin* (resident Koreans). For most outsiders, Koreans are an invisible minority. Indeed, even the Japanese themselves have no way of knowing that someone is of Korean descent if they adopt a Japanese name. Nevertheless, Japanese-born Koreans, who in some cases speak no language other than Japanese, were only recently released from the obligation to carry ID cards with their fingerprints at all times. Some still face discrimination in the workplace and other aspects of their daily lives. Aside from Koreans, most foreigners in Japan are temporary workers from China, Southeast Asia, South America and Western countries.

MINORITY CULTURES

The Ainu, of whom there are roughly 24,000 living in Japan, are the indigenous people of Hokkaidō and, some would argue, the only people who can claim to be natives of Japan. Due to ongoing intermarriage and assimilation, almost all Ainu consider themselves bi-ethnic. Today, fewer than 200 people in Japan can claim both parents with exclusively Ainu descent.

The *burakumin* are a largely invisible (to outsiders, at least) group of Japanese whose ancestors performed work that brought them into contact with the contamination of death – butchering, leatherworking and disposing of corpses. The *burakumin* were the outcasts in the social hierarchy (some would say caste system) that existed during the Edo period. While the *burakumin* are racially the same as other Japanese, they have traditionally been treated like an inferior people by much of Japanese society. Estimates put the number of hereditary *burakumin* in present-day Japan at anywhere between 890,000 and three million.

While discrimination against *burakumin* is now technically against the law, there continues to be significant discrimination against them in such important aspects of Japanese social life as work and marriage. It is common knowledge, though rarely alluded to, that information about any given individual's possible *burakumin* origin is available to anyone (generally employers and prospective fathers-in-law) who is prepared to make certain discreet investigations. Many Japanese consider this a very culturally sensitive issue and may prefer to avoid discussion of this topic with foreigners.

Indigenous groups such as the Ainu have been reduced to very small numbers, due to intermarriage with non-Ainu and government attempts to hasten their assimilation into general Japanese society. At present, Ainu are concentrated mostly in Hokkaidō, the northernmost of Japan's main islands.

The most notable feature of Japan's population is the fact that it is shrinking. Japan's astonishingly low birth rate of 1.3 births per woman is among the lowest in the developed world and Japan is rapidly becoming a nation of elderly citizens. The population began declining in 2005, and is predicted to reach 100 million in 2050 and 67 million in 2100. Needless to say, such demographic change will have a major influence on the economy in coming decades.

Women in Japan

Traditional Japanese society restricted the woman's role to the home where, as housekeeper, she wielded considerable power, overseeing all financial matters, monitoring the children's education and, in some ways, acting as the head of the household. Even in the early Meiji period (1868–1912), this ideal was rarely matched by reality: labour shortfalls often resulted in women taking on factory work and, even before that, women often worked side by side with men in the fields.

As might be expected, the contemporary situation is complex. There are, of course, women who stick to established roles. They tend to opt for shorter college courses, often at women's colleges, and see education as an asset in the marriage market. Once married, they leave the role of breadwinner to the husband. Part of the reason for this is the prevalence of gender discrimination in Japanese companies. Societal expectations, however, also play a role: Japanese women are often forced to choose between having a career and having a family. Not only do most companies refuse to hire women for career-track positions, many Japanese men are simply not interested in having a career woman as a spouse. This makes it very intimidating for a Japanese woman to step out of her traditional gender role and follow a career path.

Increasingly, however, Japanese women are choosing to forgo or delay marriage in favour of pursuing their own career ambitions. However, changing aspirations do not necessarily translate into changing realities, and Japanese women are still significantly underrepresented in upper management and political positions. There is a disproportionately high number of females employed as so called OLs (office ladies). OLs do a lot of the grunt work in many Japanese companies, with tasks often extending beyond secretarial work to include a lot of the day to day running of company affairs. In some conservative companies their duties also include making and serving tea to their male colleagues and visitors to the company.

Those women who do choose full-time work suffer from one of the worst gender wage gaps in the developed world: Japanese women earn only 66% of what Japanese men earn, compared to 76% in the USA, 83% in the UK and 85% in Australia (according to figures released by the respective governments). In politics, the situation is even worse: Japanese women hold only 10% of seats in the Diet, the nation's governing body.

THE PEOPLE OF JAPAN WOMEN IN JAPAN

Most Japanese babies are born with a Mongolian spot *(mōkohan)* on their lower backs. This harmless birthmark is composed of melanin-containing cells and usually fades by the age of five. It's common in several Asian populations and in Native Americans.

Japanese Cuisine

Those familiar with Japanese cuisine (nihon ryōri) know that eating is half the fun of travelling in Japan. Even if you've already tried some of Japan's better-known dishes, you're likely to be surprised by how delicious the original is when served on its home turf. More importantly, the adventurous eater will be delighted to find that Japanese food is far more than just sushi, tempura or sukiyaki. Indeed, it is possible to spend a month in Japan and sample a different speciality restaurant every day.

What's What in Japanese Restaurants: A Guide to Ordering, Eating and Enjoying (Robb Satterwhite) is a brilliant guide to Japanese restaurants. With thorough explanations of the various types of dishes and sample menus, this is a must for those who really want to explore and enjoy what's on offer.

Eating in a Japanese Restaurant

When you enter a restaurant in Japan, you'll be greeted with a hearty *irasshaimase* (Welcome!). In all but the most casual places, the waiter will next ask you *nan-mei sama* (How many people?). Answer with your fingers, which is what the Japanese do. You will then be led to a table, a place at the counter or a tatami room.

At this point you will be given an *o-shibori* (hot towel), a cup of tea and a menu. The *o-shibori* is for wiping your hands and face. When you're done with it, just roll it up and leave it next to your place.

Now comes the hard part: ordering. If you don't read Japanese, you can try using the romanisations and translations in this book to help you, or direct the waiter's attention to the Japanese script. If this doesn't work, there are two phrases that may help: *o-susume wa nan desu ka* (What do you recommend?) and *o-makase shimasu* (Please decide for me).

When you've eaten, you can signal for the bill by crossing one index finger over the other to form the sign of an X. This is the standard sign for 'Bill, please'. You can also say *o-kanjō kudasai*. Remember there is no tipping in Japan and tea is free of charge. Usually you will be given a bill to take to the cashier at the front of the restaurant. Only the bigger and more international places take credit cards, so cash is always the surer option.

Eating Etiquette

When it comes to eating in Japan, there are quite a number of implicit rules, but they're fairly easy to remember. If you're worried about putting your foot in it, relax – the Japanese don't expect you to know what to do and they are unlikely to be offended as long as you follow the standard rules of politeness from your own country. Here are a few major points to keep in mind:

Chopsticks in rice Do not stick your *hashi* (chopsticks) upright in a bowl of rice. This is how rice is offered to the dead in Buddhist rituals. On a similar note, do not pass food from your chopsticks to the chopsticks of someone else. This is another funeral ritual.

Polite expressions When eating with other people, especially when you're a guest, it is polite to say *itadakimasu* (literally 'I will receive') before digging in. This is as close as the Japanese come to saying grace. Similarly, at the end of the meal, you should thank your host by saying *gochisō-sama deshita,* which means 'It was a real feast'.

> **RESTAURANT PRICES**
>
> In this guide, restaurant listings are organised by price category, indicated by the symbols ¥ (budget), ¥¥ (midrange) or ¥¥¥ (top end). Budget options cost ¥1000 or less; midrange meals cost between ¥1000 and ¥4000; and top-end meals cost more than ¥4000.
>
> To assist you further, eating reviews in this book recommend specific dishes for restaurants in which no English menu is available. If there is an English menu, this is indicated in the review with the symbol 🔲.

Kampai It is bad form to fill your own glass. You should fill the glass of the person next to you and wait for them to reciprocate. Raise your glass a little off the table while it is being filled. Once everyone's glass has been filled, the usual starting signal is a chorus of *kampai,* which means 'Cheers!'.

Slurp When you eat noodles in Japan, it's perfectly OK, even expected, to slurp them. In fact, one of the best ways to find *rāmen* (egg noodle) restaurants in Japan is to listen for the loud slurping sound that comes out of them!

Restaurant Types & Sample Menus

With the exception of *shokudō* (all-round restaurants) and *izakaya* (pub-eateries), most Japanese restaurants concentrate on a particular speciality cuisine. In this chapter we discuss the main types of restaurants you are likely to encounter and we provide sample menus for each type. If you familiarise yourself with the main types of restaurants and what they serve, you'll be able to get the most out of Japan's incredible culinary scene.

Of course, you may baulk at charging into a restaurant where both the language and the menu are likely to be incomprehensible. Those timid of heart should take solace in the fact that the Japanese will go to extraordinary lengths to understand what you want and will help you order.

Shokudō

A *shokudō* is the most common type of restaurant in Japan, and is usually found near train stations, tourist spots and just about any other place where people congregate. Easily distinguished by the presence of plastic food displays in the window, these inexpensive places usually serve a variety of *washoku* (Japanese dishes) and *yōshoku* (Western dishes).

At lunch, and sometimes dinner, the easiest meal to order at a *shokudō* is a *teishoku* (set-course meal), which is sometimes also called *ranchi setto* (lunch set) or *kōsu* (course). This usually includes a main dish of meat or fish, a bowl of rice, *misoshiru* (miso soup), shredded cabbage and some *tsukemono* (Japanese pickles). In addition, most *shokudō* serve a fairly standard selection of *donburi-mono* (rice dishes) and *menrui* (noodle dishes). When you order noodles, you can choose between *soba* and *udon,* both of which are served with a variety of toppings. If you're at a loss as to what to order, simply say *kyō-no-ranchi* (today's lunch) and they'll do the rest. Expect to spend from ¥600 to ¥1000 for a meal at a *shokudō*.

katsu-don	かつ丼	rice topped with a fried pork cutlet
oyako-don	親子丼	rice topped with egg and chicken
ten-don	天丼	rice topped with tempura prawns and vegetables

Izakaya

An *izakaya* is the Japanese equivalent of a pub-eatery. It's a good place to visit when you want a casual meal, a wide selection of food, a hearty atmosphere and, of course, plenty of beer and sake. When you enter an *izakaya,* you are given the choice of sitting around the counter, at a table or on a tatami floor. You usually order a bit at a time, choosing from a selection of typical Japanese foods, such as *yakitori,* sashimi and grilled fish, as well as Japanese interpretations of Western foods like French fries and beef stew.

ŌTA KAZUHIKO ON JAPAN'S IZAKAYA

Ōta Kazuhiko is considered by many to be Japan's leading authority on *izakaya,* Japan's beloved pub-eateries. Ōta-san travels the length of Japan seeking out the best traditional *izakaya*. He has published his findings in more than a dozen books, including one titled *Ōta Kazuhiko no Izakaya Mishuran,* the 'Mishuran' in the title being a play on the famed Michelin restaurant guide series.

What is the definition of an izakaya? Simply put, an *izakaya* is a place where you can enjoy sake. More broadly, an *izakaya* is a place where you can enjoy sake and food. In addition, they are places that you can easily enter alone.

What is the history of the izakaya? Prior to the Meiji period, *saka-ya* (sake shops) would serve alcohol to customers who dropped by for a drink. The customers would stand around and drink their sake out of *masu* (square wooden boxes used to measure sake). Thus, these places were *tachi-nomiya* (stand-and-drink places). Later, some *saka-ya* turned the sake barrels into seats for their customers, so they could relax and enjoy their drink. Thus, they became *izakaya* (the *i* here means 'to be' which, added to *saka-ya,* forms *izakaya,* meaning a *saka-ya* where you can stay and drink). Later on, some places started to serve snacks to go with the sake, and this evolved into proper food to go with the sake.

What role did izakaya play in Japanese society? *Izakaya* played an important role in Japanese society. Traditionally, after men finished work at a company, they would go together to an *izakaya*. The older members of the group or the boss would often pay for the younger workers. While they drank, they could talk freely about work and also about things outside work, like their personal lives and their past. The older guys would teach the young ones how to drink, how to order and also about the ways of the world. Thus, the *izakaya* served as a place of human and social education, not just a drinking place.

What should you order in an izakaya? First of all, don't rush. Just have a look around. Maybe start with some *ginjō-shu* (a high-grade sake). Have the first one cold. Then, consider having some hot sake. As for food, seafood is the way to go: sashimi, stewed fish, grilled fish or shellfish. You can also try some chicken dishes. Have a look at what the other customers are eating or check out the specials board. If you can't speak or read Japanese, you can point at things or bring along a Japanese friend to help you order.

Where can you find good izakaya? Well, there are lots of chain *izakaya* near the train stations in most cities, but the best place to look for really good ones is in the old *hanka-gai* (entertainment district), which is usually not where the train station is. The best places have been run for generations by the same family, and the customers have also been coming for generations. So, the master might have watched his customers grow up. These are the places that take pride in their work and are the most reliable.

What is the best thing about izakaya? *Izakaya* are places where people show their true selves, their true hearts. The sake allows people to drop their pretensions and let their hair down. *Izakaya* are places where people show their individuality. They bind people together, whether strangers or friends. I think all countries have a place like this, but in Japan, if you want to see the way people really are, the *izakaya* is the place to go.

Izakaya can be identified by their rustic facades and the red lanterns outside their doors bearing the kanji for *izakaya* (居酒屋). Many also stack crates of beer and sake bottles outside. Since *izakaya* food is casual fare to go with drinking, it is usually fairly inexpensive. Depending on how much you drink, you can expect to get away with spending ¥2500 to ¥5000 per person.

agedashi-dōfu	揚げだし豆腐	deep-fried tofu in a *dashi* broth
hiyayakko	冷奴	a cold block of tofu with soy sauce and spring onions
jaga-batā	ジャガバター	baked potatoes with butter
niku-jaga	肉ジャガ	beef and potato stew
sashimi mori-awase	刺身盛り合わせ	a selection of sliced sashimi
shio-yaki-zakana	塩焼魚	a whole fish grilled with salt
yaki-onigiri	焼きおにぎり	a triangle of grilled rice with *yakitori* sauce

Yakitori

Yakitori (skewers of charcoal-grilled chicken and vegetables) is a popular after-work meal. *Yakitori* is not so much a full meal as an accompaniment for beer and sake. At a *yakitori-ya* (*yakitori* restaurant) you sit around a counter with the other patrons and watch the chef grill your selections over charcoal. The best way to eat here is to order several varieties, then order seconds of the ones you really like. Ordering in these places can be a little confusing since one serving often means two or three skewers (be careful – the price listed on the menu is usually that of a single skewer).

In summer, the beverage of choice at a *yakitori* restaurant is beer or cold sake, while in winter it's hot sake. A few drinks and enough skewers to fill you up should cost ¥3000 to ¥4000 per person. *Yakitori* restaurants are usually small places, often located near train stations, and are best identified by a red lantern outside and the smell of grilled chicken.

hasami/negima	はさみ/ねぎま	pieces of white meat alternating with leek
kawa	皮	chicken skin
piiman	ピーマン	small green capsicums (peppers)
rebā	レバー	chicken livers
sasami	ささみ	skinless chicken-breast pieces
shiitake	しいたけ	Japanese mushrooms
tama-negi	玉ねぎ	round white onions
tebasaki	手羽先	chicken wings
tsukune	つくね	chicken meatballs
yaki-onigiri	焼きおにぎり	a triangle of grilled rice with *yakitori* sauce

Sushi & Sashimi

Like *yakitori,* sushi is considered an accompaniment for beer and sake. Nonetheless, both Japanese and foreigners often make a meal of it, and it's one of the healthiest meals around. All proper sushi restaurants serve their fish over rice, in which case it's called sushi; without rice, it's called sashimi or *tsukuri* (or, politely, *o-tsukuri*).

There are two main types of sushi: *nigiri-zushi* (served on a small bed of rice – the most common variety) and *maki-zushi* (served in a seaweed roll).

Since 2000 there have been 23 cases of poisoning caused by improperly prepared *fugu* (globefish or pufferfish). Government sources, however, attribute these deaths to home, rather than restaurant, meals.

The Tsukiji Fish Market in Tokyo is the world's largest. It handles 2246 tonnes of marine products a day (more than 450 kinds of fish!).

Randy Johnson's 'Sushi a la Carte' (www.ease. com/~randyj/ rjsushi.htm) is a must for sushi lovers – it explains everything you need to know about ordering and enjoying sushi.

Sushi is not difficult to order. If you sit at the counter of a sushi restaurant you will be able to simply point at what you want, as most of the selections are visible in a refrigerated glass case between you and the sushi chef. You can also order à la carte from the menu (see the following sample menu). When ordering, you usually order *ichi-nin mae* (one portion), which normally means two pieces of sushi. Be careful, since the price on the menu will be that of only one piece.

If ordering à la carte is too daunting, you can take care of your whole order with just one or two words by ordering *mori-awase*, an assortment plate of *nigiri-zushi*. These usually come in three grades: *futsū nigiri* (regular *nigiri*), *jō nigiri* (special *nigiri*) and *toku-jō nigiri* (extra-special *nigiri*). The difference is in the type of fish used. Most *mori-awase* contain six or seven pieces of sushi.

Be warned that meals in a good sushi restaurant can cost upwards of ¥10,000, while an average establishment can run from ¥3000 to ¥5000 per person. One way to sample the joy of sushi on the cheap is to try an automatic sushi place, usually called *kaiten-zushi*, where the sushi is served on a conveyor belt that runs along a counter. Here you simply reach up and grab whatever looks good to you (which certainly takes the pain out of ordering). You are charged by the number of plates of sushi that you have eaten. Plates are colour-coded by their price and the cost is written either somewhere on the plate itself or on a sign on the wall. You can usually fill yourself up in one of these places for ¥1000 to ¥2000 per person.

Before eating the sushi, dip it very lightly in *shōyu* (soy sauce), which you pour from a small decanter into a low dish specially provided for the purpose. If you're not good at using *hashi* (chopsticks), don't worry – sushi is one of the few foods in Japan that is perfectly acceptable to eat with your hands. Slices of *gari* (pickled ginger) are served to refresh the palate. The beverage of choice with sushi is beer or sake (hot in winter, cold in summer), with a green tea at the end of the meal.

Note that most of the items on this sample sushi menu can be ordered as sashimi. Just add the words *no o-tsukuri* to get the sashimi version. So, for example, if you wanted some tuna sashimi, you would order *maguro no o-tsukuri*. Note that you'll often be served a different soy sauce to accompany your sashimi; if you like wasabi with your sashimi, you can add some directly to the soy sauce and stir.

ama-ebi	甘海老	sweet shrimp
awabi	あわび	abalone
ebi	海老	prawn or shrimp
hamachi	はまち	yellowtail
ika	いか	squid
ikura	イクラ	salmon roe
kai-bashira	貝柱	scallop
kani	かに	crab
katsuo	かつお	bonito
maguro	まぐろ	tuna
tai	鯛	sea bream
tamago	たまご	sweetened egg
toro	とろ	the choice cut of fatty tuna belly
unagi	うなぎ	eel with a sweet sauce
uni	うに	sea-urchin roe

TASTY TRAVEL

There's one word every food lover should learn before coming to Japan: *meibutsu*. It means 'speciality', as in regional speciality, and Japan has loads of them. In fact, it never hurts to simply ask for the *meibutsu* when you order at a restaurant or *izakaya* (pub-eatery). More often than not, you'll be served something memorable. Here are some of Japan's more famous local specialities, listed by region.

Hiroshima *kaki* (oysters); *Hiroshima-yaki,* which is Hiroshima-style *okonomiyaki* (batter and cabbage cakes cooked on a griddle)

Hokkaidō *kani-ryōri* (crab cuisine); salmon

Kyoto *kaiseki* (Japanese haute cuisine); *wagashi* (Japanese traditional sweets); *yuba* (the skim off the top of tofu, or soy-milk skin); *Kyō-yasai* (Kyoto-style vegetables)

Kyūshū *tonkotsu-rāmen* (pork-broth *rāmen*); *Satsuma-imo* (sweet potatoes)

Northern Honshū *wanko-soba* (eat-till-you-burst *soba*); *jappa-jiru* (cod soup with Japanese radish and miso)

Okinawa *gōya champurū* (bitter melon stir-fry); *sōki-soba* (*rāmen* with spare ribs); *mimiga* (pickled pigs' ears)

Osaka *tako-yaki* (battered octopus pieces); *okonomiyaki*

Shikoku *sansai* (wild mountain vegetables); *Sanuki-udon* (a type of wheat noodles); *katsuo tataki* (lightly seared bonito)

Tokyo sushi

Sukiyaki & Shabu-shabu

Restaurants usually specialise in both of these dishes. Popular in the West, sukiyaki is a favourite of most foreign visitors to Japan. Sukiyaki consists of thin slices of beef cooked in a broth of *shōyu*, sugar and sake, and accompanied by a variety of vegetables and tofu. After cooking, all the ingredients are dipped in raw egg before being eaten. When made with high-quality beef, such as Kōbe beef, it is a sublime experience.

Shabu-shabu consists of thin slices of beef and vegetables cooked by swirling the ingredients in a light broth, then dipping them in a variety of special sesame-seed and citrus-based sauces. Both of these dishes are prepared in a pot over a fire at your private table. Don't fret about preparation – the waiter will usually help you get started, and keep a close watch as you proceed. The key is to go slow, add the ingredients a little at a time and savour the flavours.

Sukiyaki and *shabu-shabu* restaurants usually have traditional Japanese decor and sometimes a picture of a cow to help you identify them. Ordering is not difficult. Simply say 'sukiyaki' or *shabu-shabu* and indicate how many people are dining. Expect to pay from ¥3000 to ¥10,000 per person.

Tempura

Tempura consists of portions of fish, prawns and vegetables cooked in a light batter. When you sit down at a tempura restaurant, you will be given a small bowl of *ten-tsuyu* (a light brown sauce) and a plate of grated *daikon* (Japanese radish) to mix into the sauce. Dip each piece of tempura into this sauce before eating it. Tempura is best when it's hot, so don't wait too long – use the sauce to cool each piece and dig in.

While it's possible to order à la carte, most diners choose to order *teishoku,* which includes rice, *misoshiru* and *tsukemono*. Some tempura restaurants offer courses that include different numbers of tempura pieces.

Expect to pay between ¥2000 and ¥10,000 for a full tempura meal. Finding these restaurants is tricky as they have no distinctive facade or decor. If you look through the window, you'll see customers around the counter watching the chefs as they work over large woks filled with oil.

kaki age	かき揚げ	tempura with shredded vegetables or fish
shōjin age	精進揚げ	vegetarian tempura
tempura moriawase	天ぷら盛り合わせ	a selection of tempura

Rāmen

The Japanese imported this dish from China and put their own spin on it to make what is one of the world's most delicious fast foods. *Rāmen* dishes are big bowls of noodles in a meat broth, served with a variety of toppings, such as sliced pork, bean sprouts and leeks.

In some restaurants, particularly in Kansai, you may be asked if you'd prefer *kotteri* (thick and fatty) or *assari* (thin and light) soup. Other than this, ordering is simple: just sidle up to the counter and say *rāmen,* or ask for any of the other choices usually on offer (a list follows). Expect to pay between ¥500 and ¥900 for a bowl. Since *rāmen* is derived from Chinese cuisine, some *rāmen* restaurants also serve *chāhan* or *yaki-meshi* (both dishes are fried rice), *gyōza* (dumplings) and *kara-age* (deep-fried chicken pieces).

Rāmen restaurants are easily distinguished by their long counters lined with customers hunched over steaming bowls. You can sometimes *hear* a *rāmen* shop as you wander by – it's considered polite to slurp the noodles and aficionados claim that slurping brings out the full flavour of the broth.

More than five billion servings of instant *rāmen* are consumed each year in Japan. The leading purveyors this snack are convenience stores, which also offer hot water to prepare them in.

chāshū-men	チャーシュー麺	*rāmen* topped with slices of roasted pork
miso-rāmen	みそラーメン	*rāmen* with miso-flavoured broth
rāmen	ラーメン	soup and noodles with a sprinkling of meat and vegetables
wantan-men	ワンタン麺	*rāmen* with meat dumplings

Soba & Udon

Soba (thin brown buckwheat noodles) and *udon* (thick white wheat noodles) are Japan's answer to Chinese-style *rāmen*. Most Japanese noodle shops serve both *soba* and *udon* in a variety of ways.

Noodles are usually served in a bowl containing a light, bonito-flavoured broth, but you can also order them served cold and piled onto a bamboo screen along with a cold broth to dip the noodles in (this is called *zaru soba*). If you order *zaru soba,* you will additionally receive a small plate of wasabi and sliced spring onions – you put these into the cup of broth and then eat the noodles by dipping them into this mixture. When you have finished your noodles, the waiter will give you some hot broth to mix with the leftover sauce, which you drink like a kind of tea. As with *rāmen,* you should feel free to slurp as loudly as you please.

The film *Tampopo* (Itami Jūzō, 1987) is essential preparation for a visit to Japan – especially if you intend to visit a *rāmen* shop while you're there! It's about two fellows who set out to help a *rāmen* shop owner improve her shop, with several food-related subplots woven in for good measure.

Soba and *udon* places are usually quite cheap (about ¥800 a dish), but some fancy places can be significantly more expensive (the decor is a good indication of the price).

kake soba/udon	かけそば/うどん	*soba/udon* noodles in broth
kitsune soba/udon	きつねそば/うどん	*soba/udon* noodles with fried tofu
tempura soba/udon	天ぷらそば/うどん	*soba/udon* noodles with tempura prawns
tsukimi soba/udon	月見そば/うどん	*soba/udon* noodles with raw egg

KŌBE BEEF

All meals involving Kōbe beef should come with the following label: warning, consuming this beef will ruin your enjoyment of any other type of beef. We're not kidding. It's that good.

The first thing you should know about Kōbe beef is how to pronounce it: 'ko-bay' (rhymes with 'no way'). In Japanese, Kōbe beef is known as *Kōbe-gyū*. Second, Kōbe beef is actually just one regional variety of *wagyū* (literally 'Japanese beef'). *Wagyū* can be any of several breeds of cattle bred for the extreme fatty marbling of their meat (the most common breed is Japanese black). Kōbe beef is simply *wagyū* raised in Hyogō-ken, the prefecture in which the city of Kōbe is located.

There are many urban legends about Kōbe beef – promulgated, we suppose, by the farmers who raise them or simply imaginative individuals who ascribe to cows the lives they'd like to lead. It is commonly believed that Kōbe-beef cattle spend their days drinking beer and receiving regular massages. However, in all our days in Japan, we have never seen a single drunk cow or met a cow masseur. More likely, the marbling pattern of the beef is the result of selective breeding and the cow's diet of alfalfa, corn, barley and wheat straw.

The best way to enjoy Kōbe beef, or any other type of *wagyū*, is cooked on a *teppan* (iron hotplate) at a *wagyū* specialist, known as *teppan-yaki-ya*. In the West, a giant steak that hangs off the side of the plate is generally considered a good thing. Due to the intense richness (and price) of a good *wagyū* steak, it is usually consumed in relatively small portions, smaller than the size of your hand. The meat is usually seared quickly, then cooked to medium rare – cooking a piece of good *wagyū* to well done is something akin to making a tuna-fish sandwich from the best cut of *toro* (fatty tuna belly) sashimi.

Although Kōbe beef and *wagyū* are all the rage in Western cities, like most Japanese food, the real thing consumed in Japan is far superior. And it can be cheaper to eat it in Japan than overseas. You can get a fine *wagyū* steak course at lunch for around ¥5000, and at dinner for around double that. Of course, the best place for Kōbe beef is Kōbe.

Unagi

Unagi (eel) is an expensive and popular delicacy in Japan. Even if you can't stand the creature when it's served in your home country – or if you've never tried it – you owe it to yourself to try *unagi* at least once while you're visiting Japan. *Unagi* is cooked over hot coals and brushed with a rich sauce of *shōyu* and sake. Full *unagi* dinners can be expensive, but many *unagi* restaurants also offer *unagi bentō* (boxed meals) and lunch sets for around ¥1500. Most *unagi* restaurants display plastic models of their set meals in their front windows, and may have barrels of live eels to entice passers-by.

kabayaki	蒲焼き	skewers of grilled eel without rice
una-don	うな丼	grilled eel over a bowl of rice
unagi teishoku	うなぎ定食	full-set *unagi* meal with rice, grilled eel, eel-liver soup and pickles
unajū	うな重	grilled eel over a flat tray of rice

The average Japanese person consumes 58kg of rice per year. The vast majority of this is made up of *shiro-gohan* (a white, steamed rice), but some health food enthusiasts prefer *genmai* (brown rice).

Tonkatsu

Tonkatsu is a deep-fried breaded pork cutlet that is served with a special sauce, usually as part of a set meal *(tonkatsu teishoku)*. *Tonkatsu* is served both at speciality restaurants and at *shokudō*. Naturally, the best *tonkatsu* is to be found at the speciality places, where a full set will cost ¥1500 to ¥2500. When ordering *tonkatsu,* you are able to choose between *rōsu* (a fatter cut of pork) and *hire* (a leaner cut).

hire katsu	ヒレかつ	*tonkatsu* fillet
tonkatsu teishoku	とんかつ定食	a set meal of *tonkatsu*, rice, *miso-shiru* and shredded cabbage

Okonomiyaki

Sometimes described as Japanese pizza or pancake, the resemblance is in form only. Actually, *okonomiyaki* are various forms of batter and cabbage cakes cooked on a griddle.

At an *okonomiyaki* restaurant you sit around a *teppan* (iron hotplate), armed with a spatula and chopsticks to cook your choice of meat, seafood and vegetables in a cabbage and vegetable batter.

Some restaurants will do most of the cooking for you and then bring the nearly finished product over to your hotplate where all you need to do is to season it with *katsuo bushi* (bonito flakes), *shōyu*, *ao-nori* (an ingredient similar to parsley), Japanese Worcestershire-style sauce and mayonnaise. Cheaper places, however, will simply hand you a bowl filled with the ingredients and expect you to cook it for yourself. If this happens, don't panic. First, mix the batter and filling thoroughly, then place it on the hotplate, flattening it into a pancake shape. After five minutes or so, use the spatula to flip it and cook for another five minutes. Then dig in.

Most *okonomiyaki* places also serve *yaki-soba* (fried noodles with meat and vegetables) and *yasai-itame* (stir-fried vegetables). All of this is washed down with mugs of draught beer.

One final word: don't worry too much about the preparation of the food – as a foreigner you will be expected to be a bit awkward, and the waiter will be keeping a sharp eye on you to make sure no real disasters occur.

gyū okonomiyaki	牛お好み焼き	beef *okonomiyaki*
ika okonomiyaki	いかお好み焼き	squid *okonomiyaki*
mikkusu	ミックスお好み焼き	*okonomiyaki* with a mix of fillings, including seafood, meat and vegetables
modan-yaki	モダン焼き	*okonomiyaki* with *yaki-soba* and a fried egg
negi okonomiyaki	ネギお好み焼き	thin *okonomiyaki* with spring onions

Kaiseki

Kaiseki is the pinnacle of Japanese cuisine, where ingredients, preparation, setting and presentation come together to create a dining experience quite unlike any other. Born as an adjunct to the tea ceremony,

Kaiseki is the pinnacle of Japanese cuisine, where ingredients, preparation, setting and presentation come together to create a dining experience

kaiseki is a largely vegetarian affair (although fish will often be served, meat never appears on the *kaiseki* menu). Diners usually eat *kaiseki* in the private room of a *ryōtei* (an especially elegant style of traditional restaurant), often overlooking a private, tranquil garden. The meal is served in several small courses, giving the participants an opportunity to admire the serving plates and bowls, which are carefully chosen to complement the food and season. Rice is eaten last (and is usually served with an assortment of pickles) and the drink of choice is sake or beer.

This experience comes at a steep price – a good *kaiseki* dinner costs upwards of ¥10,000 per person. A cheaper way to sample the delights of *kaiseki* is to visit a *kaiseki* restaurant for lunch. Most places offer a boxed lunch containing a sampling of their dinner fare for around ¥2500.

You can enter *kaiseki* places at lunchtime without a reservation, but you should ask your hotel or ryokan to call ahead to make arrangements for dinner.

bentō	弁当	boxed meal, usually of rice, with a main dish and pickles or salad
kaiseki	懐石	traditional, Kyoto-style haute cuisine
matsu	松	extra-special course
take	竹	special course
ume	梅	regular course

Sweets

Although most restaurants don't serve dessert (plates of sliced fruit are sometimes served at the end of a meal), there is no lack of sweets in Japan. Most Japanese sweets (known generically as *wagashi*) are sold in speciality stores for you to eat at home. Many of the more delicate-looking ones are made to balance the strong, bitter taste of the special *matcha* (powdered green tea) served during the tea ceremony.

Some Westerners find Japanese sweets a little challenging, due to the liberal use of a sweet, red *azuki*-bean paste called *anko*. This unusual filling turns up in even the most innocuous-looking pastries. The next main ingredient is often pounded sticky rice *(mochi)*, which has a consistency that is unfamiliar to many Westerners.

With such a wide variety of sweets, it's impossible to list all the names. However, you'll probably find many variations on the *anko*-covered-by-*mochi* theme.

Okashi-ya (sweet shops) are easy to spot; they usually have open fronts with their wares laid out in wooden trays to entice passers-by. Buying sweets is simple – just point at what you want and indicate with your fingers how many you'd like.

anko	あんこ	sweet paste or jam made from *azuki* beans
kashiwa-mochi	柏餅	pounded glutinous rice with a sweet filling, wrapped in an aromatic oak leaf
mochi	餅	pounded rice cakes made of glutinous rice
wagashi	和菓子	Japanese-style sweets
yōkan	ようかん	sweet red-bean jelly

Drinks

Drinking plays a big role in Japanese society, and there are few social occasions where beer or sake is not served. Alcohol (in this case sake) also plays a ceremonial role in various Shintō festivals and rites, including the marriage ceremony. As a visitor to Japan, you'll probably find yourself in lots of situations where you are invited to drink, and tipping back a few beers or glasses of sake is a great way to get to know the locals. However, if you don't drink alcohol, it's no big deal. Simply order *oolong cha* (oolong tea) in place of beer or sake. While some folks might put pressure on you to drink alcohol, you can diffuse this pressure by saying *sake o nomimasen* (I don't drink alcohol).

What you pay for your drink depends on where you drink and, in the case of hostess bars, with whom you drink. Hostess bars are the most expensive places to drink (up to ¥10,000 per drink), followed by upmarket traditional Japanese bars, hotel bars, beer halls and casual pubs. If you

The superb 'Tokyo Food Page' (www. bento.com) offers explanations of Japanese dishes, great places to eat in Tokyo and much, much more.

SAKE

The Insider's Guide to Sake (Philip Harper) offers a fine introduction to sake, including information on how to choose a good sake and the history of the drink.

SAKE

Despite being overtaken in recent years by beer and *shōchū* (distilled grain liquor), most Japanese still consider sake to be the national drink. The Japanese name reflects this: it's commonly known as *nihonshu* (the drink of Japan).

Sake has played an important part in Japanese culture for as long as there has been a Japanese culture. It plays an important part in a variety of Shintō rituals, including wedding ceremonies, and many Shintō shrines display huge barrels of sake infront of their halls (before you get any ideas, be aware that most of them are empty).

Although consumption has been on the wane in recent years, it is generally agreed that the quality of sake available is better than ever. Many of the best sakes have a complexity of flavours and aromas comparable to the fine wines and beers of Europe.

Not surprisingly, sake makes the perfect accompaniment to traditional Japanese food, and sake pubs (see *izakaya* p788) generally also serve excellent seasonal fish and other foods to go with the booze. Sake can be drunk chilled *(reishu)*, at room temperature *(jō-on)*, warmed *(nuru-kan)* or piping hot *(atsu-kan)*, according to the season and personal preference. The top-drawer stuff is normally served well chilled. Sake is traditionally served in a ceramic jug known as a *tokkuri*, and poured into tiny cups known as *o-choko* or *sakazuki*. A traditional measure of sake is one *gō* (一合) – a little over 180mL, or 6 fluid oz. In speciality bars, you will have the option of ordering by the glass, which will often be filled to overflowing and brought to you in a wooden container to catch the overflow. If you have company, the tradition is to pour your neighbour's drink and then wait for them to reciprocate. When they pour your drink, it's polite to lift your glass; women should place one hand underneath their glass when someone is pouring their drink.

Sake is always brewed during the winter, in the cold months that follow the rice harvest in September. The main ingredients of sake are rice and yeast. These are combined with a mould known as *kōji* that helps convert the starch in the rice into fermentable sugars. Sake is categorised by law into two main classes: *futsū-shu* (ordinary sake); and *tokutei-meishōshu* (premium sake). *Tokutei-meishōshu* is further broken into classes which are based on the extent to which the rice is refined before fermentation. This is generally shown on the label as the *seimai buai,* which expresses how much of the rice is polished away before being fermented. As a general rule, the lower this number, the better (or at least, the more expensive) the sake will be. Sake made from rice kernels with 40% to 50% of their original volume polished away is known as *ginjō*. Sake made from rice kernels with 50% or more of their original volume polished away is known as *dai-ginjō*. It is believed that sake made from the inner portion of the rice kernel is the smoothest and most delicious of all. Sake made only with rice and *kōji* (without the use of added alcohol) is known as *junmai-shu* (pure rice sake).

are not sure about a place, ask about prices and cover charges before sitting down. As a rule, if you are served a small snack (called *o-tsumami,* or 'charm') with your first round, you'll be paying a cover charge (usually a few hundred yen, but sometimes much more).

Izakaya and *yakitori-ya* are cheap places for beer, sake and food in a casual atmosphere resembling that of a pub. All Japanese cities, whether large or small, will have a few informal bars with reasonable prices. These are popular with young Japanese and resident *gaijin* (foreigners), who usually refer to such places as *gaijin* bars. In summer, many department stores and hotels in Japan's big cities open up beer gardens on the roof. Many of these places offer all-you-can-eat/drink specials for around ¥3000 per person.

Most of the nonalcoholic drinks you're used to at home will be available in Japan, with a few colourfully named additions like Pocari Sweat and Calpis Water. One convenient aspect of Japan is the presence of drink-vending machines on virtually every street corner and, at ¥120, refreshment is rarely more than a few steps away.

Sake is brewed in every prefecture in Japan – with the single exception of Kagoshima in southern Kyūshū, the traditional stronghold of the distilled drink known as *shōchū* – and there are more than 1500 breweries in operation today. Niigata and other parts of Northern Honshū are particularly famous for the quality of their sake, with Hiroshima and Nada-ku (in Kōbe) also major centres of the brewing industry. Almost everywhere you go in Japan you will have an opportunity to drink sake brewed just a few kilometres from where you are staying. A foreign visitor who shows an interest in the *jizake* (local brew) is likely to be treated to enthusiastic recommendations and the kind of hospitality that has been known to lead to sore heads the next morning.

ama-kuchi	甘口	sweet flavour
ama-zake	甘酒	sweet sake served at winter festivals
dai-ginjō	大吟醸	sake made from rice kernels with 50% or more of their original volume polished away
futsū-shu	普通酒	ordinary sake
genshu	原酒	undiluted sake, often with an alcohol content close to 20%
ginjō	吟醸	sake made from rice kernels with 40% to 50% of their original volume polished away
jizake	地酒	'local sake', often from small, traditional breweries
junmai-shu	純米酒	'pure rice sake', made from only rice, *kōji* and water
kara-kuchi	辛口	dry, sharp flavour
kōji	麹	the mould that helps to convert the starch in the rice into fermentable sugars
kura/saka-gura	蔵/酒蔵	sake brewery
nama-zake	生酒	fresh, unpasteurised sake
nigori-zake	濁り酒	milky-white 'cloudy sake', often rather sweet
nihonshu	日本酒	Japanese word for 'sake'
o-choko	お猪口	small cups traditionally used for sake
seimai buai	精米歩合	the percentage of the original size to which the grain is reduced by polishing before the brewing process starts
tokkuri	徳利	traditional ceramic serving vessel
tokutei-meishōshu	特定名称酒	premium sake

Beer

Introduced at the end of the 1800s, *biiru* (beer) is now the favourite tipple of the Japanese. The quality of Japanese beer is generally excellent and the most popular type is light lager, although some breweries have been recently experimenting with darker brews. The major breweries are Kirin, Asahi, Sapporo and Suntory. Beer is dispensed everywhere, from vending machines to beer halls, and even in some temple lodgings. A standard can of beer from a vending machine is about ¥250, although some of the gigantic cans cost more than ¥1000. At bars, a beer starts at ¥500 and the price climbs upwards, depending on the establishment. *Nama biiru* (draught beer) is widely available, as are imported beers.

biiru	ビール	beer
biniru	瓶ビール	bottled beer
nama biiru	生ビール	draught beer

Shōchū

For those looking for a quick and cheap escape route from the sorrows of the world, *shōchū* is the answer. It's a distilled spirit made from a variety of raw materials, including potato (in which case it's called *imo-jōchū*) and barley (in which case it's called *mugi-jōchū*). It's quite strong, with an alcohol content of about 30%. In recent years it has been resurrected from its previous lowly status (it was used as a disinfectant in the Edo period) to become a trendy drink. You can drink it *oyu-wari* (with hot water) or *chūhai* (in a highball with soda and lemon). A 720mL bottle sells for about ¥600, which makes it a relatively cheap option compared with other spirits.

The Japanese Ministry of Agriculture created a team a few years ago to assess the quality of Japanese restaurants abroad. The so-called 'Sushi Police' are intended to put a stop to third-rate restaurants serving poor imitations of real Japanese food. Does this spell the end of the California roll?

chūhai	チューハイ	*shōchū* with soda and lemon
oyu-wari	お湯割り	*shōchū* with hot water
shōchū	焼酎	distilled grain liquor

Coffee & Tea

Kōhii (coffee) served in a *kissaten* (coffee shop) tends to be expensive in Japan, costing between ¥350 and ¥500 a cup, with some places charging up to ¥1000. For a caffeine fix, a cheap alternative is one of the coffee-restaurant chains like Doutor or Pronto, or doughnut shops like Mr Donut (which offers free coffee refills). An even cheaper alternative than these is a can of coffee, hot or cold, purchased from a vending machine. Although unpleasantly sweet, at ¥120 the price is hard to beat.

When ordering coffee at a coffee shop in Japan, you will be asked whether you would like it *hotto* (hot) or *aisu* (cold). Black tea also comes hot or cold, and is served with *miruku* (milk) or *remon* (lemon). A good way to start a day of sightseeing in Japan is with a *mōningu setto* (morning set) of tea or coffee, toast and eggs, which generally costs around ¥400.

The highly prized Japanese *matsutake* mushroom can sell for up to US$2000 per kilogram. They are usually enjoyed in the autumn, sometimes in the form of a tea, at other times grilled or with rice.

American kōhii	アメリカンコーヒー	weak coffee
burendo kōhii	ブレンドコーヒー	blended coffee, fairly strong
kafe ore	カフェオレ	*café au lait,* hot or cold
kōcha	紅茶	black English tea
kōhii	コーヒー	regular coffee
orenji jūsu	オレンジジュース	orange juice

Japanese Tea

Unlike black tea, which Westerners are familiar with, most Japanese tea is green and contains a lot of vitamin C and caffeine. The powdered form used in the tea ceremony is called *matcha* and is drunk after being whipped into a frothy consistency. The more common form, a leafy green tea, is simply called *o-cha,* and is drunk after being steeped in a pot. In addition to green tea, you'll probably drink a lot of a brownish tea called *bancha,* which restaurants serve for free. In summer, a cold beverage called *mugicha* (roasted barley tea) is served in private homes.

bancha	番茶	ordinary-grade green tea, with a brownish colour
matcha	抹茶	powdered green tea used in the tea ceremony
mugicha	麦茶	roasted barley tea
o-cha	お茶	leafy green tea
sencha	煎茶	medium-grade green tea

Vegetarians & Vegans

Travellers who eat fish should have almost no trouble dining in Japan: almost all *shokudō*, *izakaya* and other common restaurants offer a set meal with fish as the main dish. Vegans and vegetarians who don't eat fish will have to get their protein from tofu and other bean products. Note that most *misoshiru* is made with *dashi* broth that contains fish, so if you want to avoid fish, you'll also have to avoid *misoshiru*.

Most big cities in Japan have vegetarian or organic restaurants which naturally serve a variety of choices that appeal to vegetarians and vegans. (See the Eating sections of the destination chapters for specific recommendations. Reviews that include the symbol 🖉 throughout this guide indicate places with a good vegetarian selection.)

In the countryside, you'll have to do your best to find suitable items on the menu, or try to convey your dietary preferences to the restaurant staff. Note that many temples in Japan serve *shōjin-ryōri* (Buddhist vegetarian cuisine), which is made without meat, fish or dairy products. A good place to try this is Kōya-san in Kansai.

Cooking Courses

If you enjoy the food in Japan, why not deepen your appreciation of Japanese cuisine by taking a cooking class? There are good cooking courses available in both Tokyo and Kyoto. Market tours can be arranged through Uzuki (p309) – reserve via the website – and you can learn how to cook typical Japanese dishes in a Kyoto home, or even request specific dishes, including Japanese sweets.

Arts & Architecture

Japan has a long history of receiving cultural imports from continental Asia and later the West, as well as a tendency to refine techniques and materials to an extreme degree. The result is an artistic tradition that is as varied, deep and rich as any on the planet. One cannot visit Japan without immersing oneself in its sublime artistic tradition, for it pervades every aspect of life from the presentation of food to the design of a room in a ryokan (traditional Japanese inn).

Hiroshige, noted for many collections of *ukiyo-e* prints including *One Hundred Famous View of Edo*, was a firefighter by trade, though he later retired to become a Buddhist monk.

Traditional Visual Art

Painting

From the Heian period (794–1185) up until the beginning of the Edo period (1600–1868), Japanese painting borrowed from Chinese and Western techniques and media, ultimately transforming them for its own aesthetic ends. By the Edo period, which was marked by the enthusiastic patronage of a wide range of painting styles, Japanese art had come completely into its own. The Kanō school, initiated more than a century before the beginning of the Edo era, continued to be in demand for its depiction of subjects connected with Confucianism, mythical Chinese creatures and scenes from nature. The Tosa school, which followed the *yamato-e* style of painting (often used on scrolls during the Heian period), was also kept busy with commissions from the nobility, who were eager to see scenes re-created from the classics of Japanese literature.

The Rimpa school (from 1600) not only absorbed the styles of painting that had preceded it, but progressed beyond well-worn conventions to produce a strikingly decorative and delicately shaded form of painting. The works of art produced by a trio of outstanding artists from this school – Tawaraya Sōtatsu, Hon'ami Kōetsu and Ogata Kōrin – rank among the finest of this period.

Calligraphy

Shodō (the way of writing) is one of Japan's most valued arts, cultivated by nobles, priests and samurai alike, and is still studied by Japanese schoolchildren today as *shūji*. Like the characters of the Japanese script, the art of *shodō* was imported from China. In the Heian period, a fluid, cursive, distinctly Japanese style of *shodō* called *wayō* evolved, though the Chinese style remained popular in Japan among Zen priests and the literati for some time.

In both Chinese and Japanese *shodō* there are three important types. Most common is *kaisho* (block-style script). Due to its clarity this style is favoured in the media and in applications where readability is key. *Gyōsho* (running hand) is semi-cursive and is often used in informal correspondence. *Sōsho* (grass hand) is a truly cursive style. *Sōsho* abbreviates and links the characters together to create a flowing, graceful effect.

Ukiyo-e (Woodblock Prints)

The term *ukiyo-e* means 'pictures of the floating world' and derives from a Buddhist metaphor for the transient world of fleeting pleasures. The subjects chosen by artists for these woodblock prints were characters and scenes from the tawdry, vivacious 'floating world' of the entertainment quarters in Edo (latter-day Tokyo), Kyoto and Osaka.

The floating world, centred on pleasure districts such as Edo's Yoshiwara, was a topsy-turvy kingdom, an inversion of the usual social hierarchies that were held in place by the power of the Tokugawa shōgunate. Here, money meant more than rank, while actors and artists were the arbiters of style, and prostitutes elevated their art to such a level that their accomplishments matched those of the women of noble families.

The vivid colours, novel composition and flowing lines of *ukiyo-e* caused great excitement in the West, sparking a vogue that one French art critic dubbed *japonisme*. *Ukiyo-e* became a key influence on Impressionists (for example, Toulouse-Lautrec, Manet and Degas) and post-Impressionists. Among the Japanese, the prints were hardly given more than passing consideration – millions were produced annually in Edo. They were often thrown away or used as wrapping paper for pottery. For many years, the Japanese continued to be perplexed by the keen interest foreigners took in this art form, which they considered of ephemeral value.

The screen paintings of Hasegawa Tohaku, created almost 400 years ago, are said to be the first examples of Impressionist art.

Ceramics

Ceramics are Japan's oldest art form: Jōmon pottery, with its distinctive cordlike decorative patterns, dates back up to 15,000 years. When the Jōmon people were displaced by the Yayoi people, starting around 400 BC, a more refined style of pottery appeared on the scene. While Jōmon pottery was an indigenous Japanese form, Yayoi pottery had clear continental Asian influences and techniques. Continental techniques and even artisans continued to dominate Japanese ceramic arts for the next millennium or more: around the 5th century AD Sue ware was introduced from Korea, and around the 7th century Tang Chinese pottery became influential.

WABI-SABI

No, it isn't the spicy green stuff you eat with your sushi. Rather, *wabi-sabi* is one of the fundamental visual principles governing traditional Japanese ideals of beauty. The idea of *wabi-sabi* is an aesthetic that embraces the notion of ephemerality and imperfection as it relates to all facets of Japanese culture.

The term *wabi-sabi* comes from the Japanese *wabi* and (you guessed it) *sabi* – both with quite convoluted definitions. *Wabi* roughly means 'rustic' and connotes the loneliness of the wilderness, while *sabi* can be interpreted as 'weathered', 'waning' or 'altered with age' (so it's no surprise that the Japanese word for 'rust' is also *sabi*). Together the two words signify an object's natural imperfections that arise during its inception and the acknowledgement that the object will evolve as it confronts mortality.

This penchant for impermanence and incompleteness transcends Japanese visual culture, from the fragrant cherry blossoms that bloom in spring to the slightly asymmetric *Hagi-yaki* pottery, but is perhaps most palpable in landscape design and traditional architecture. Japanese teahouses reflect *wabi-sabi* motifs with their natural construction materials, handmade ceramics and manicured gardens.

Although the origins of *wabi-sabi* can be traced back to ancient Buddhism, these aesthetic ideals are still present in modern Japan and can even be found throughout the imaginative cityscapes we see today.

In the medieval period Japan's great ceramic centre was Seto in Central Honshū. Here, starting in the 12th century, Japanese potters took Chinese forms and adapted them to Japanese tastes and needs to produce a truly distinctive pottery style known as Seto ware. One Japanese term for pottery and porcelain, *setomono* (literally 'things from Seto'), clearly derives from this still-thriving ceramics centre.

Today, there are more than 100 pottery centres in Japan, with scores of artisans producing everything from exclusive tea utensils to souvenir folklore creatures. Department stores regularly organise exhibitions of ceramics and offer the chance to see some of this fine work up close.

Shikki (Lacquerware)

The Japanese have been using lacquer to protect and enhance the beauty of wood since the Jōmon period (13,000–400 BC). In the Meiji era (1868–1912), lacquerware became very popular abroad and it remains one of Japan's best-known products. Known in Japan as *shikki* or *nurimono*, lacquerware is made using the sap from the lacquer tree *(urushi)*, a close relative of poison oak. Raw lacquer is actually toxic and causes severe skin irritation in those who have not developed immunity. Once hardened, however, it becomes inert and extraordinarily durable.

The most common colour of lacquer is amber or brown, but additives are used to produce black, violet, blue, yellow and even white lacquer. In better pieces, multiple layers of lacquer are painstakingly applied and left to dry, and finally polished to a luxurious shine.

Contemporary Visual Art

In the years that followed WWII, Japanese artists struggled with issues of identity. This was the generation that grappled with duelling philosophies: 'Japanese spirit, Japanese knowledge' versus 'Japanese spirit, Western knowledge'. They explored whether Western artistic media and methods could convey the space, light, substance and shadows of the Japanese spirit, or whether this essence could only truly be expressed through traditional Japanese artistic genres.

Today's emerging artists and movements have no such ambivalence. Gone is the anxiety about co-opting, or being co-opted by, Western philosophies and aesthetics; in its place is the insouciant celebration of the smooth, cool surface of the future articulated by fantastic colours and shapes. This exuberant, devil-may-care aesthetic is most notably represented by Takashi Murakami, whose work derives much of its energy from *otaku*, the geek culture which worships characters that figure prominently in manga, Japan's ubiquitous comic books (a good introduction to the art of manga is the Kyoto International Manga Museum, p284). Murakami's spirited, prankish images and installations have become emblematic of the Japanese aesthetic known as *poku* (a concept that combines pop art with an *otaku* sensibility), and his *Super Flat Manifesto*, which declares that 'the world of the future might be like Japan is today – super flat', can be seen as a primer for contemporary Japanese pop aesthetics.

Beyond the pop scene, artists continue to create works whose textures and topics relay a world that is broader than the frames of a comic book. Three notable artists to look for are Yoshie Sakai, whose ethereal oil paintings, replete with pastel skies and deep waters, leave the viewer unsure whether they are floating or sinking; Noriko Ambe, whose sculptural works with paper can resemble sand dunes shifting in the Sahara, or your high-school biology textbook; and the indomitable Hisashi Tenmyouya, whose work chronicles the themes of contemporary Japanese life, echoing the flat surfaces and deep impressions of woodblock prints, while singing a song of the street.

NŌ MASKS

The breathtakingly haunting masks of nō always depict female or non-human characters; adult male characters are played without masks.

TRADITIONAL JAPANESE GARDENS

Japanese gardens are worlds unto themselves, ranging from stark exercises in Zen minimalism to richly detailed grottoes that recapitulate the complexity of the natural world. For gardeners, touring some of Japan's best gardens is likely to be a revelation, as the Japanese have elevated the art of gardening from a mere hobby to the realm of fine art. In order to best appreciate Japanese gardens, it helps to arm yourself with a bit of basic background information. In this section, we'll introduce the major types of gardens you'll encounter: *funa asobi* (pleasure boat), *shūyū* (stroll), *kanshō* (contemplative) and *kaiyū* (varied pleasures).

Popular in the Heian period, *funa asobi* gardens featured a large pond used for pleasure boating. Such gardens were often built around noble mansions. The garden that surrounds Byōdō-in (p305) in Uji is a vestige of this style of garden.

The *shūyū* garden is intended to be viewed from a winding path, allowing the garden to unfold and reveal itself in stages and from different vantages. Popular during the Heian, Kamakura and Muromachi periods, *shūyū* gardens can be found around many noble mansions and temples from those eras. A celebrated example is the garden at Ginkaku-ji (p295) in Kyoto.

The *kanshō* garden is intended to be viewed from one vantage point. Zen rock gardens, also known as *kare-sansui* gardens, are an example of this type, which were designed to aid contemplation. Kyoto's Ryōan-ji (p300) is perhaps the most famous example of this type of garden. Although various interpretations of the garden have been put forth (the rocks represent a tiger and her cubs, for example), the garden's ultimate meaning, like that of Zen itself, cannot be expressed in words.

Lastly, the *kaiyū* features many small gardens with one or more teahouses surrounding a central pond. Like the stroll garden, it is meant to be explored on foot and provides the viewer with a variety of changing scenes, many with literary allusions. The imperial villa of Katsura Rikyū (p305) is the classic example of this type of garden.

ARTS & ARCHITECTURE TRADITIONAL THEATRE & DANCE

Traditional Theatre & Dance

Nō

Nō is a hypnotic dance-drama that reflects the minimalist aesthetics of Zen. The movement is glorious, the chorus and music sonorous, the expression subtle. A sparsely furnished cedar stage directs full attention to the performers, who include a chorus, drummers and a flautist. There are two principal characters: the *shite*, who is sometimes a living person but more often a demon, or a ghost whose soul cannot rest; and the *waki*, who leads the main character towards the play's climactic moment. Each nō school has its own repertoire, and the art form continues to evolve and develop.

Kabuki

The first performances of kabuki were staged early in the 17th century by an all-female troupe. The performances were highly erotic and attracted enthusiastic support from the merchant class. In true bureaucratic fashion, Tokugawa officials feared for the people's morality and banned women from the stage in 1629. Since that time, kabuki has been performed exclusively by men, giving rise to the institution of *onnagata*, or *ōyama* – male actors who specialise in female roles.

Over the course of several centuries, kabuki has developed a repertoire that draws on popular themes, such as famous historical accounts and stories of love-suicide, while also borrowing copiously from nō, *kyōgen* (comic vignettes) and *bunraku* (classical puppet theatre). Most kabuki plays border on melodrama, although they vary in mood.

Tokyo's main kabuki venue, Kabuki-za (p131), has recently undergone an extensive renovation and is once again the main place to enjoy kabuki in the capital.

Formalised beauty and stylisation are the central aesthetic principles of kabuki. The acting is a combination of dancing and speaking in conventionalised intonation patterns, and each actor prepares for a role by studying and emulating the style perfected by his predecessors. Kabuki actors are born into the art form, and training begins in childhood. Today, they enjoy great social prestige and their activities on and off the stage attract as much interest as those of popular film and TV stars.

Bunraku

Japan's traditional puppet theatre developed at the same time as kabuki, when the *shamisen* (a three-stringed instrument resembling a lute or banjo), imported from Okinawa, was combined with traditional puppetry techniques and *joruri* (narrative chanting). *Bunraku*, as it came to be known in the 19th century, addresses many of the same themes as kabuki; in fact many famous plays in the kabuki repertoire were originally written for puppet theatre. *Bunraku* involves large puppets – nearly two-thirds life-sized – manipulated by up to three black-robed puppeteers. The puppeteers do not speak; a seated narrator tells the story and provides character voices. One of the best places to see *bunraku* is at Osaka's National Bunraku Theatre (p353).

Rakugo

A traditional Japanese style of comic monologue, *rakugo* (literally 'dropped word') dates back to the Edo period. The performer, usually in kimono, sits on a square cushion on a stage. Props are limited to a fan and hand towel. The monologue begins with a *makura* (prologue), which is followed by the story itself and, finally, the *ochi* (punch line or 'drop', which is another pronunciation of the Chinese character for *raku* in *rakugo*). Many of the monologues in the traditional *rakugo* repertoire date back to the Edo and Meiji periods and, while well known, reflect a social milieu unknown to modern listeners. Accordingly, many practitioners today also write new monologues addressing issues relevant to contemporary life.

Contemporary Theatre & Dance

Contemporary theatre and dance are alive and well in Japan, though you'll quickly notice that most major troupes are based in Tokyo.

Underground Theatre

Theatre the world over spent the 1960s redefining itself, and it was no different in Japan. The *shōgekijō* movement, also called *angura* (underground), has given Japan many of its leading playwrights, directors and actors. It arose as a reaction to the realism and structure of *shingeki* (a 1920s movement that borrowed heavily from Western dramatic forms), and featured surrealistic plays that explored the relationship between human beings and the world. Like their counterparts in the West, these productions took place in any space available – in small theatres, tents, basements, open spaces and street corners.

The first generation of *shōgekijō* directors and writers often included speedy comedy, wordplay and images from popular culture in their works to highlight the lunacy of modern life. More recent *shōgekijō* productions have dealt with realistic and contemporary themes, such as modern Japanese history, war, environmental degradation and social oppression. Changing cultural perceptions have propelled the movement in new directions, notably towards socially and politically critical dramas.

Tokyo Art Beat (www.tokyoart-beat.com) is a bilingual art and design guide, with a regularly updated list of events.

Butoh

In many ways, butoh is Japan's most accessible – there are no words except for the occasional grunt – and exciting dance form. It is also its newest dance form, dating from only 1959, when Hijikata Tatsumi (1928–86) gave the first butoh performance. Butoh was born out of a rejection of the excessive formalisation that characterises traditional forms of Japanese dance. It also stems from the desire to return to the ancient roots of the Japanese soul, and is therefore also a rejection of the Western influences that flooded Japan in the postwar years.

Displays of butoh are best likened to performance-art happenings rather than traditional dance performances. During a butoh performance, one or more dancers use their naked or seminaked bodies to express the most elemental and intense human emotions. Nothing is sacred in butoh, and performances often deal with topics such as sexuality and death. For this reason, critics often describe butoh as scandalous, and butoh dancers delight in pushing the boundaries of what can be considered tasteful in artistic performance.

Butoh tends to be more underground than the more established forms of Japanese dance and, consequently, it is harder to catch a performance. The best way to see what's on while you're in town is to check the local English-language media, or to ask at a local tourist information office.

Literature

Interestingly, much of Japan's early literature was written by women. One reason for this was that men wrote in kanji (imported Chinese characters), while women wrote in hiragana (Japanese script). Thus, while the men were busy copying Chinese styles and texts, the women of the country were producing the first authentic Japanese literature. Among these early female authors is Murasaki Shikibu, who wrote Japan's first great novel, *Genji Monogatari* (The Tale of Genji). This detailed, lengthy tome documents the intrigues and romances of early Japanese court life and, although it is perhaps Japan's most important work of literature, its extreme length probably limits its appeal to all but the most ardent Japanophile or literature buff.

Most of Japan's important modern literature has been penned by authors who live in and write about cities. Though these works are sometimes celebratory, many lament the loss of a traditional rural lifestyle that has given way to the pressures of a modern, industrialised society. *Kokoro,* the modern classic by Sōseki Natsume, outlines these rural-urban tensions, as does *Snow Country,* by Nobel laureate Kawabata Yasunari. These works touch upon the tensions between Japan's nostalgia for the past and its rush towards the future, between its rural heartland and its burgeoning cities.

Although Mishima Yukio is probably the most controversial of Japan's modern writers and is considered unrepresentative of Japanese culture by many Japanese themselves, his work still makes for very interesting reading. *The Sailor Who Fell from Grace with the Sea* and *After the Banquet* are both compelling. For unsettling beauty, reach for the former; history buffs will want the latter tome, which was at the centre of a court case that became Japan's first privacy lawsuit.

Ōe Kenzaburo, Japan's second Nobel laureate, has produced some of Japan's most disturbing, energetic and enigmatic literature. *A Personal Matter* is the work for which he is most widely known. In this troubling novel, which echoes Ōe's frustrations at having a son with autism, a 27-year-old cram-school teacher's wife gives birth to a brain-damaged child. His life claustrophobic and his marriage failing, he dreams of escaping to Africa while planning the murder of his son.

Popular writer Murakami Haruki attended Waseda University and worked in a record shop, much like the main character of his novel *Norwegian Wood* (1987).

Of course, not all Japanese fiction can be classified as literature in highbrow terms. Murakami Ryū's *Almost Transparent Blue* is strictly sex and drugs, and his ode to the narcissistic early 1990s, *Coin Locker Babies,* recounts the toxic lives of two boys who have been left to die in coin lockers by their mothers. Like Murakami Ryū, Banana Yoshimoto is known for her ability to convey the prevailing Zeitgeist in easily, um, digestible form. In her novel *Kitchen,* she relentlessly chronicles Tokyo's fast-food menus and '80s pop culture, though underlying the superficial digressions are hints of a darker and deeper world of death, loss and loneliness.

Japan's internationally most celebrated living novelist is Murakami Haruki, a former jazz-club owner gone literary. His most noted work, *Norwegian Wood,* set in the late '60s against the backdrop of student protests, is both a portrait of the artist as a young man (as recounted by a reminiscent narrator) and an ode to first loves. The book was adapted into a movie in December 2010 and stars Kikuchi Rinko as the ill-fated Naoko.

Music

Japan has a huge, shape-shifting music scene supported by a local market of audiophiles willing to try almost anything. International artists make a point of swinging through on global tours, and the local scene surfaces every night in one of thousands of live houses. The jazz scene is enormous, as are the followings for rock, house and electronica.

More mainstream are the *aidoru,* idol singers whose popularity is generated largely through media appearances and is centred on a cute, girl-next-door image. These days, J-pop (Japan pop) is dominated by female vocalists who borrow heavily from American pop stars. The most famous of these is Utada Hikaru, whose great vocal range and English ability (she peppers her songs with English lyrics) make her a standout from the otherwise drab *aidoru* field.

Cinema

Japan has a vibrant film industry and proud, critically acclaimed cinematic traditions. Renewed international attention since the mid-1990s has reinforced interest in domestic films, which account for an estimated 40% of box-office receipts, nearly double the level in most European countries. Of course, this includes not only artistically important works, but also films in the science-fiction, horror and 'monster stomps Tokyo' genres, for which Japan is also known.

Early Japanese films were merely cinematic versions of traditional theatrical performances, but in the 1920s Japanese directors starting producing films in two distinct genres: *jidaigeki* (period films) and new *gendaigeki* films, which dealt with modern themes. The more realistic storylines of the new films soon reflected back on the traditional films with the introduction of *shin jidaigeki* (new period films). During this era, samurai themes became an enduring staple of Japanese cinema.

The golden age of Japanese cinema began with the release in 1950 of Kurosawa Akira's *Rashōmon,* winner of the Golden Lion at the 1951 Venice International Film Festival and the Oscar for best foreign film. The increasing realism and high artistic standards of the period are evident in such landmark films as *Tōkyō Monogatari* (Tokyo Story; 1953) by the legendary Ōzu Yasujirō; Mizoguchi Kenji's classics *Ugetsu Monogatari* (Tales of Ugetsu; 1953) and *Saikaku Ichidai Onna* (The Life of Oharu; 1952); and Kurosawa's 1954 masterpiece *Shichinin no Samurai* (Seven Samurai). Annual attendance at the country's cinemas reached 1.1 billion in 1958, and Kyoto, with its large film studios, such as Shōchiku, Daiei and Tōei, and more than 60 cinemas, enjoyed a heyday as Japan's own Hollywood.

AKB48

AKB48 is one of the inexplicably popular current crazes in Japan's pop scene – the ever-expanding group is made up of over 50 teenage girls who perform in rotation at their purpose-built theatre in Akihabara.

As it did elsewhere in the world, TV spurred a rapid drop in the number of moviegoers in Japan in the high-growth decades of the 1960s and '70s. But despite falling attendance, Japanese cinema remained a major artistic force. These decades gave the world such landmark works as Ichikawa Kon's *Chushingura* (47 Samurai; 1962) and Kurosawa's *Yōjimbo* (1961).

The decline in cinema-going continued through the 1980s, reinforced by the popularisation of videos, with annual attendance at cinemas bottoming out at just over 100 million. Yet Japan's cinema was far from dead: Kurosawa garnered acclaim worldwide for *Kagemusha* (1980), which shared the Palme d'Or at Cannes, and *Ran* (1985). Imamura Shōhei's heart-rending *Narayama Bushiko* (The Ballad of Narayama) won the Palme d'Or at Cannes in 1983. Itami Jūzō became perhaps the most widely known Japanese director outside Japan after Kurosawa, with such biting satires as *Osōshiki* (The Funeral; 1987), *Tampopo* (Dandelion; 1987) and *Marusa no Onna* (A Taxing Woman; 1987). Ōshima Nagisa, best known for controversial films such as *Ai no Corrida* (In the Realm of the Senses; 1976), scored a critical and popular success with *Senjo no Merry Christmas* (Merry Christmas, Mr Lawrence) in 1983.

In recent years, Japanese cinema has been enjoying something of a renaissance and foreign audiences and critics have taken note. In 1997 Japanese directors received top honours at two of the world's most prestigious film festivals: *Unagi* (Eel), Imamura Shōhei's black-humoured look at human nature's dark side, won the Palme d'Or at Cannes, making him the only Japanese director to win this award twice; and 'Beat' Takeshi Kitano took the Golden Lion in Venice for *Hana-bi*, a tale of life and death, and the violence and honour that links them. In 2009, Takita Yojiro's film *Okuribito* (Departures) won the Oscar for best foreign film.

The plots of most modern Japanese horror films can be traced back to the popular *kaidan* (traditional horror or ghost stories) of the Edo and Meiji periods.

Anime

The term anime, a contraction of the word 'animation', is used worldwide to refer to Japan's highly sophisticated animated films. Unlike its counterparts in other countries, anime occupies a position very near the forefront of the film industry in Japan. Anime films encompass all genres, from science fiction and action adventure to romance and historical drama.

Anime targets all age and social groups. The films include deep explorations of philosophical questions and social issues, humorous entertainment and bizarre fantasies. They offer breathtakingly realistic visuals, exquisite attention to detail, complex and expressive characters, and elaborate plots. Leading directors and voice actors are accorded fame and respect, while characters become popular idols.

Among the best-known anime is *Akira* (1988), Ōtomo Katsuhiro's psychedelic fantasy set in a future Tokyo inhabited by speed-popping biker gangs and psychic children. Ōtomo also worked on the interesting *Memories* (1995), a three-part anime that includes the mind-bending 'Magnetic Rose' sequence where deep-space garbage collectors happen upon a spaceship containing the memories of a mysterious woman. Finally, there is *Ghost in a Shell* (1995), an Ōishii Mamoru film with a sci-fi plot worthy of Philip K Dick – it involves cyborgs, hackers and the mother of all computer networks.

Of course, one name towers above all others in the world of anime: Miyazaki Hayao, who almost single-handedly brought anime to the attention of the general public in the West. See the boxed text on p808 for more information.

MIYAZAKI HAYAO – THE KING OF ANIME

Miyazaki Hayao, Japan's most famous and critically acclaimed anime director, has given us some of the most memorable images ever to appear on the silver screen. Consider, for example, the island that floated through the sky in his 1986 classic *Laputa*. Or the magical train that travelled across the surface of an aquamarine sea in *Spirited Away* (2001). Or the psychedelic dreamworlds that waited outside the doors of *Howl's Moving Castle* (2004). Watching scenes like this, one can only conclude that Miyazaki is gifted with the ability to travel to the realm of pure imagination and smuggle images back to this world intact and undiluted.

Miyazaki Hayao was born in 1941 in wartime Tokyo. His father was the director of a firm that manufactured parts for the famous Japanese Zero fighter plane. This early exposure to flying machines made a deep impression on the young Miyazaki, and one of the hallmarks of his films is skies filled with the most whimsical flying machines imaginable: winged dirigibles, fantastic flying boats and the flying wings of *Nausicaa of the Valley of the Winds* (to see one is to want one).

In high school, Miyazaki saw one of Japan's first anime, *Hakujaden,* and resolved to become an animator himself. After graduating from university in 1963, he joined the powerful Tōei Animation company, where he worked on some of the studio's most famous releases. He left in 1971 to join A Pro studio, where he gained his first directorial experience, working on the now famous (in Japan, at least) *Lupin III* series as codirector. In 1979 he directed *The Castle of Cagliostro,* another *Lupin* film and his first solo directorial credit.

In 1984 Miyazaki wrote and directed *Nausicaa of the Valley of the Winds*. This film is considered by many critics to be the first true Miyazaki film, and it provides a brilliant taste of many of the themes that run through his later work. The film enjoyed critical and commercial success and established Miyazaki as a major force in the world of Japanese anime. Capitalising on this success, Miyazaki founded his own animation studio, Studio Ghibli, through which he has produced all his later works.

In 1988 Studio Ghibli released what many consider to be Miyazaki's masterwork: *My Neighbor Totoro*. Much simpler and less dense than many Miyazaki films, *Totoro* is the tale of a young girl who moves with her family to the Japanese countryside while her mother recuperates from an illness. While living in the country, she befriends a magical creature who lives in the base of a giant camphor tree and is lucky enough to catch a few rides on a roving cat bus (a vehicle of pure imagination if ever there was one). For anyone wishing to make an acquaintance with the world of Miyazaki, this is the perfect introduction.

Serious Miyazaki fans will want to make a pilgrimage to his Ghibli Museum (p87), located in the town of Mitaka, a short day trip out of Tokyo.

Architecture

Most Nihon neophytes liken their first glimpses of Japan to touching down on an alien world. The sounds are different, the smells are different, but it's the sights that truly transport visitors to another planet – a place where glances out of the bullet-train window reveal an awe-inducing alternative universe bubbling over with bright lights and geometric shapes. From the wooden temples hidden in a bamboo forest, to the urban frenzies of metal and glass, Japan offers the ultimate feast of architectural eye candy.

Traditional Architecture

Upon glimpsing the visual chaos of Japan's urban centres, it's hard to believe that the local architectural aesthetic was once governed by a preference for understated, back-to-nature design. Long before the Japanese borrowed and bested Western design motifs, the island nation honed its craft and style during two centuries of self-inflicted isolation when Tokugawa Ieyasu defeated the last of his enemies and secured total control for the Tokugawa shōgunate.

Japan's flamboyant temples are undoubtedly the best examples of the nation's early architectural abilities. Important religious complexes were usually quite large and featured a great hall surrounded by smaller buildings like pagodas – the ancient version of the skyscraper – and structures that served as quarters for devotees.

Equally impressive was the country's collection of feudal castles, although most of the bastions we see today are concrete replicas of the original wooden structures destroyed by war, fire or decay. Initially, the feudal castles were simple mountain forts that relied more on natural terrain than structural innovation when defending the keep from invaders. Castle construction boomed during the 16th and 17th centuries, each one more impressive than the next; however, most were later razed by Edo and Meiji governments. The main castles in Osaka, Osaka-jō (p339), and Nagoya, Nagoya-jō (p204), are quite impressive and boast interactive museum spaces, but the country's must-see castle is Himeji-jō (p370), also known as the 'white heron', after its stately white form.

Principally simple and refined, the typical house was also constructed using post-and-beam timber, with sliding panels of wood or rice paper (for warmer weather) making up the exterior walls. *Shōji* (movable screens) would divide the interior rooms. In more densely populated areas, traditional housing took the form of *machiya* (traditional Japanese town houses), usually built by merchants. Although most of the neat, narrow rows of these structures have been replaced with flashier modern dwellings, one can still stumble across *machiya* in Kyoto. The reasoning behind the gossamer construction of domestic dwellings was twofold: light materials were favourable during boiling summer months, and heavier building products were inadvisable due to the abundance of earthquakes.

The most distinctive type of Japanese farmhouse was the thatch-roofed *gasshō-zukuri,* so named for the shape of the rafters, which resemble a pair of palms pressed together in prayer. While these farmhouses appear

TOP FIVE WOODEN WONDERS

Although Japan is currently known for its eye-popping alien architecture – like the buzzing metallic haze depicted in Sofia Coppola's film *Lost in Translation* – it was the almighty tree that dominated the nation's traditional construction materials. The following structures are among Japan's finest flourishes of timber.

Hōryū-ji (p389) Located in the ancient capital city of Nara, this temple complex is commonly believed to feature the two oldest wooden structures in the world: the pagoda (rising just over 32m) and the *kondō* (golden or main hall).

Tōdai-ji (p381) Tōdai-ji's original Daibutsu-den and giant bronze Buddha were constructed by more than two million people during the 8th century. The structure has been incinerated twice and the current incarnation dates back to 1709.

Chion-in (p293) This stunning temple complex is the centre of the Jōdo-shū, a sect of Pure Land Buddhism established by Hōnen, a Japanese monk who lived during the 12th century. Chion-in's main gate, known as San-mon, is the largest structure of its kind in Japan.

Kiyomizu-dera (p289) One of the most beloved temples in Kyoto, its pièce de résistance is the main hall with its signature verandah sitting atop a scaffolding-like structure.

Byōdō-in (p305) Its Amida-dō (Phoenix Hall; also known as Hōō-dō) is featured on the ¥10 coin. The Byōdō-in complex was duplicated on Hawaii's island of O'ahu.

NINJA-PROOFING

Long before lasers, padlocks and klaxons hampered trespassers, Japanese feudal lords employed a much simpler method of safeguarding their castles from stealth, black-masked assassins. Charged with the difficult task of protecting their masters from things that go bump in the night, court architects devised a straightforward security system known as *uguisubari* (nightingale floors). These special floorboards were rigged together with nails that would scratch against their clamps making a warbling noise when walked upon. Weathered timber planks usually creak on their own, but these special contraptions would sing like a songbird as people moseyed on by. The creaking floors of Nijō-jō (p288) are an excellent example of this melodic security technique. Tiptoe across the squeaky planks and see how far you can get before the ground starts to sing.

cosy and romantic, they were often home for up to 40 people and the occasional farm animal. The dark floorboards, soot-covered ceilings and lack of windows starkly contrasted with the breezy merchant houses in more populated areas.

Early Modern Architecture

When the Tokugawa shōgunate lost control of the island nation, the Meiji Restoration (1868) opened Japan's doors once more and architectural influences began to change. Josiah Conder, a British architect, was invited to Tokyo to design many structures that embodied the pillars of Western architecture. Conder erected numerous buildings in Gothic, Renaissance, Moorish and Tudor styles, energising Tokyo's heterogeneous cityscape. Conder was trying to develop an adaptation of Western architecture that could be understood as uniquely Japanese, but the adaptation of so many Western styles exhibited the difficulty of choosing and propagating a Japanese architecture. The Meiji administration was not pleased. They sought a ubiquitous Western aesthetic rather than a garish mishmash of colonial styles. Offended that Conder tried to impose a synthetic 'Japanisation' of the Western style, the Meiji administration rescinded his contract.

Several Japanese architects have won the Pritzker Prize, including Tange Kenzō, Maki Fumihiko, Andō Tadao, Sejima Kazuyo and Nishizawa Ryue.

This resistance to Western architecture continued until after WWI, when foreign architects such as Frank Lloyd Wright came to build the Imperial Hotel in Tokyo. Wright was careful to pay homage to local sensibilities when designing the Imperial's many elegant bridges and unique guest rooms (though he famously used modern, cubic forms to ornament the interiors of the hotel). The building was demolished in 1967 to make way for the current Imperial Hotel, which shows little of Wright's touch.

By the end of WWII, Tokyo was a veritable blank slate. The city had barely had time to regain its footing in the aftermath of the Great Kantō Earthquake (1923) before being bombed beyond recognition by the Allied forces. The other major metropolises in Japan suffered a similar fate. Through both geological and political phenomena, most of the country had been washed clean of the traditional Tokugawa aesthetic that had sustained the island nation through 200 years of forced isolation.

When TV was introduced as a Western marvel, Japan built its first broadcasting tower in the heart of Tokyo, known as Tokyo Tower. They didn't, however, just build an ordinary beacon; engineers constructed a duplicate of Paris' Eiffel Tower. True to the latent Japanese desire for importation and improvement, the orange-and-white behemoth was built to stand at 333m – 13m higher than the icon of modernity in the City of Light.

Contemporary Architecture

In 1964 all eyes were on Japan – the first time since WWII – for Tokyo's Summer Olympic Games. The newly founded Japanese government decided that the new Olympic centre would be built where the American occupation compound had once stood in Yoyogi, a southwestern district of the city. But choosing a site was the easy part. The Olympic planners were faced with the problems of identifying and exemplifying modern Japanese design. The architectural concept for the Olympics had to accomplish two things: first, it should demonstrate modernity through a unique architectural gesture, and second, it must reflect a distinctive sense of Japanese-ness. The Olympic complex would dictate the future language of Japanese design.

Capturing this inherent Japanese-ness and expressing it through architecture proved to be much more difficult than expected, even for native architects. A modern design by Japanese architect Tange Kenzō was ultimately chosen. Tange was a young architect whose ideas were highly influenced by the works of Le Corbusier. The designs for the two large stadiums were like swirling shells plucked from the depths of an alien ocean. The larger structure was shaped as though the hull of a majestic boat had been flipped upside down. The gracious gestures of the design masked the sheer volume required to house thousands of spectators. Indeed, the entire world was captivated by these inspired designs. Tange went on to have a very successful career, and would later design the Tokyo Metropolitan Government Offices (1991).

Also in the 1960s, architects such as Shinohara Kazuo, Kurokawa Kisho, Maki Fumihiko and Kikutake Kiyonori began a movement known as Metabolism, which promoted flexible spaces and functions instead of fixed forms in building. Shinohara came to design in a style he called Modern Next, incorporating both modern and postmodern ideas combined with Japanese influences. This style can be seen in his Centennial Hall at Tokyo Institute of Technology, an elegant and uplifting synthesis of clashing forms in a shiny metal cladding. Kurokawa's architecture blends Buddhist building traditions with modern influences; while Maki, the master of minimalism, pursued design in a modernist style while still emphasising the elements of nature – like the roof of his Tokyo Metropolitan Gymnasium (near Sendagaya Station), which takes on the form of a sleek metal insect. Another Maki design, the Spiral Building, built in Aoyama in 1985, is a favourite with Tokyo residents and its interior is also a treat.

Skip ahead a decade and Japan's second generation of architects began gaining recognition within the international architecture scene, including Andō Tadao and Toyo Ito. This younger group continued to explore both modernism and postmodernism, while incorporating a renewed interest in Japan's architectural heritage.

In 2010, SANAA (helmed by Sejima Kazuyo and Nishizawa Ryue) won the prestigious Pritzker Prize for their unwavering dedication to creating luminous form-follows-function spaces. They have dozens of impressive projects under their belt, including the 21st Century Museum of Contemporary Art (p260) in Kanazawa, and the New Museum of Contemporary Art in New York City.

TOKYO SKY TREE

Japan's newest contribution to superlative architecture is the Tokyo Sky Tree (p101), which stands at 634m. It is officially the tallest tower in the world, though not the tallest structure.

Traditional Japanese Accommodation

Let's face it: a hotel is a hotel wherever you go. And while some of Japan's hotels are very nice indeed, you're probably searching for something unique to the culture. If this is what you're after, you'll be pleased to learn that Japan is one of the last places in Asia where you can find truly authentic traditional accommodation: ryokan, minshuku and shukubō.

It is said that there are more than 80,000 ryokan in Japan, but that number decreases each year as modern Japanese find hotels to be more convenient.

Ryokan

Simply put, ryokan are traditional Japanese inns. Ryokan are where Japanese travellers stayed before they had heard the word *hoteru* (hotel). They are Japanese-style accommodation with tatami-mat rooms and futons instead of beds. Most serve Japanese-style breakfast and dinner, as well. However, this simple explanation doesn't do justice to ryokan.

A high-end ryokan is the last word in relaxation. The buildings themselves set the tone: they employ traditional Japanese architecture in which the whole structure is organic, made entirely of natural materials such as wood, earth, paper, grass, bamboo and stone. Indeed, a good ryokan is an extension of the natural world. And nature comes into the ryokan in the form of the Japanese garden, which you can often see from the privacy of your room or even your bathtub.

But more than the building, the service is what sets ryokan apart from even the best hotels. At a good ryokan, you will be assigned a personal maid who sees to your every need. These ladies seem to have a sixth sense: as soon as you finish one course of your dinner, you hear a knock on the door and she brings the next course. Then, when you stroll down the hall to take a bath, she dashes into your room and lays out your futon.

Many ryokan in Japan pride themselves on serving *kaiseki ryōri* (Japanese haute cuisine), which rivals that served in the best restaurants. Staying at one of these so-called *ryōri ryokan* (cuisine ryokan) is like staying at a three-star 'residential restaurant', where you sleep in your own private dining room.

Another wonderful variety is the onsen ryokan: a ryokan with its own private hot-spring bath. These places were like luxury spas long before anyone had heard the word 'spa'. Some of the top places have rooms with private en suite onsen baths, usually built overlooking gardens. When you stay at an onsen ryokan, your day involves a gruelling cycle of bathe-nap-eat-repeat. A night at a good onsen ryokan is the perfect way to get over your jet lag when you arrive in the country or a special treat to round out the journey in Japan.

Of course, it would be irresponsible to suggest that all ryokan fit this description. A lot of places that call themselves ryokan are really just hotels with Japanese-style rooms. Some places may not even serve dinner. That isn't to say they aren't comfortable: simple ryokan are often very friendly and relaxing and they may cost less than hotels in some places.

But if you can do it, we strongly recommend staying in a high-end ryokan for at least one night of your trip.

Note that ryokan may not have en suite bathtubs or showers, and at some simple places even the toilet facilities are shared. If this is an issue, be sure to enquire when you make a reservation.

Staying in a Ryokan

Due to language difficulties and unfamiliarity, staying in a ryokan is not as straightforward as staying in a Western-style hotel. However, it's not exactly rocket science and, with a little education, it can be a breeze, even if you don't speak a word of Japanese. Note that much of what we say here will also apply to staying at a *minshuku*.

Here's the basic drill. When you arrive, leave your shoes in the *genkan* (entry area or foyer) and step up into the reception area. Here, you'll be asked to sign in. Next, you'll be shown around the place and then to your room, where you will be served a cup of tea. You'll find that there is no bedding to be seen in your room – your futon is in the closet and will be laid out later. You can leave your luggage anywhere except the *tokonoma* (sacred alcove) that will usually contain some flowers or a hanging scroll. If it's early enough, you can then go out to do some sightseeing.

When you return, you'll change into your *yukata* (lightweight Japanese robe) and will be served dinner in your room or in a dining room. After dinner, it's time for a bath. If it's a big place, you can generally bathe anytime in the evening until around 11pm. If it's a small place, you'll be given a time slot. While you're in the bath, some mysterious elves will go into your room and lay out your futon so that it's waiting for you when you return all toasty from the bath.

Best Ryokan in Japan

Tawaraya (p312)

Hiiragiya Ryokan (p312)

Kayōtei (p274)

Nishimuraya Honkan (p409)

JAPANESE ACCOMMODATION MADE EASY

A number of foreign travellers have turned up unannounced in a ryokan or *minshuku* and been given a distinctly cold reception, then concluded that they have been the victim of discrimination. More than likely, they simply broke one of the main rules of Japanese accommodation: don't surprise them. With this in mind, here are a few tips to help you find a bed each night in Japan. Note that the following also goes for hotels, although these are generally a little more flexible than traditional accommodation.

Reservations Make reservations whenever possible, even if it's just a quick call a few hours before arriving.

Email or fax The Japanese are much more comfortable with written than spoken English. If you email or fax a room request with all your details, you will find a warm welcome. You can always follow it up with a phone call, once you're all on the same page.

The baton pass Get your present accommodation to call ahead and reserve your next night's lodging. This will put everyone at ease – if you're acceptable at one place, you'll be just fine at another.

Tourist information offices Even in the smallest hamlet or island in Japan, you'll find tourist information offices, usually right outside train stations or ferry terminals. These exist just to help travellers find accommodation (OK, they also give brilliant directions). They will recommend a place and call to see if a room is available, then they will tell you exactly how to get there. This is another form of introduction.

Lastly, there will be times when you just have to slide that door open and hope for the best. Even the surprise-averse Japanese have to resort to this desperate expediency from time to time. The secret here is to try to minimise the shock. Smile like you're there to sell them insurance, muster your best *konbanwa* (good evening) and try to convince them that you actually prefer futons to beds, green tea to coffee, chopsticks to forks, and baths to showers.

In the morning, you'll be served a Japanese-style breakfast (some places these days serve a simple Western-style breakfast for those who can't stomach rice and fish in the morning). You pay on check-out, which is usually around 11am.

Minshuku

A *minshuku* is usually a family-run private lodging, rather like a B&B in Europe or the USA. In some very simple *minshuku* you're really just staying with a Japanese family that has turned a few of the rooms in their house into guest rooms. Other places are purpose-built to serve as accommodation. In either case, the rooms will be Japanese style, with tatami mats and futons. Bathroom facilities are usually shared and meals are usually eaten in a common dining room. Unlike at a ryokan, in a *minshuku* you are usually expected to lay out and put away your own bedding.

The average price per person per night, including two meals, is around ¥5500. *Minshuku* are a little hard to find on your own if you don't speak and read Japanese. And, needless to say, owners are less likely to speak English than at hotels or popular ryokan. The best way to find a *minshuku* is to ask at a local tourist information office, where they will usually call ahead and make all arrangements for you.

Shukubō

Staying in a *shukubō* (temple lodging) is one way to experience another facet of traditional Japan. Sometimes you are allocated a simple room in the temple precincts and left to your own devices. At other places, you may also be allowed to participate in prayers, services or meditation. At some temples *shōjin-ryōri* (Buddhist vegetarian cuisine) is served.

The tourist information centres in Tokyo and Kyoto produce leaflets on temple lodgings in their regions. Kōya-san, a renowned religious centre, includes more than 50 *shukubō* and is one of the best places in Japan to try this type of accommodation (p397). Some youth hostels in Japan are also located in temple grounds, which make them a form of *shukubō*.

Staying at a *minshuku* can be like staying with your extended family over the holidays. If you've got a few boisterous relatives in the room next door, you'll probably hear what they're saying. Still, most guests are pretty good at observing quiet hours (midnight to 8am).

Onsen

Japan is in hot water. Literally. The stuff percolates up out of the ground from one end of the country to the other. The Japanese word for a hot spring is 'onsen', and there are more than 3000 of them here, more than anywhere else on earth. So if your idea of relaxation involves soaking your bones in a tub of bubbling water, you've come to the right place.

Some Japanese will tell you that the only distinctively Japanese aspect of their culture – that is, something that didn't ultimately originate in mainland Asia – is the bath. There are accounts of onsen bathing in Japan's earliest historical records, and it's pretty certain that the Japanese have been bathing in onsen as long as there have been Japanese.

Over the millennia, they have turned the simple act of bathing in an onsen into something like a religion. Today, the ultimate way to experience an onsen is to visit an onsen ryokan, a traditional Japanese inn with its own private hot-spring bath. At an onsen ryokan you spend all day enjoying the bath, relaxing in your room and eating sumptuous food.

Like many of the best things in life, some of the finest onsen in Japan are free. Just show up with a towel and your birthday suit, splash a little water on yourself and plunge in. No communication hassles, no expenses and no worries. And even if you must pay to enter, it's usually just a minor snip – averaging about ¥700 (US$6) per person.

Japan's Hidden Onsen by Robert Neff is a good guide to secluded onsen across the archipelago. It's a little out of date, but it still contains some fantastic finds.

Best Onsen Experiences

With so many onsen to choose from in Japan, it's a thankless task to pick favourites. That said, we're going to go way out on a limb here and recommend a few of our favourites, broken up into categories to help you choose.

Urban Onsen

Ōedo Onsen Monogatari (Tokyo; p103) Located on the artificial island of Odaiba in Tokyo Bay, this super-onsen is modelled on an Edo-period town. There's a huge variety of tubs, including outdoor tubs, as well as restaurants, relaxation rooms and shops.

Oceanside Onsen

Jinata Onsen (Shikine-jima, Izu Archipelago; p183) The setting of this onsen couldn't be more dramatic: it's located in a rocky cleft in the seashore of lovely little Shikine-jima. The pools are formed by the seaside rocks and it's one of those onsen that only works when the tide is right. You can spend a few lovely hours here watching the Pacific rollers crashing on the rocks. There are two other excellent onsen on the island.

Riverside Onsen

Takaragawa Onsen (Gunma Prefecture, Central Honshū; p166) Japanese onsen maniacs often pronounce this onsen to be the best in the country. Difficult for us to argue. 'Takaragawa' means 'treasure river', and its slate-floored pools sit along several hundred metres of riverbank. Most of the pools are mixed bathing, with one ladies-only bath. The alkaline waters are said to cure fatigue, nervous disorders and digestive troubles.

MINERALS

Onsen Town

Kinosaki (Kansai; p408) On the Sea of Japan coast in northern Kansai, Kinosaki is the quintessential onsen town. With seven public baths and dozens of onsen ryokan, this is the place to sample the onsen ryokan experience. You can relax in your accommodation taking the waters as it pleases you, and when you get tired of your ryokan's bath, you can hit the streets in a *yukata* (light cotton kimono) and *geta* (wooden sandals) and visit the public baths.

Hidden Onsen

Lamp no Yado (Noto Peninsula, Central Honshū; p273) Noto Peninsula is about as far as one can go in Central Honshū, and the seaside is about as far as one can go on this peninsula. A country road takes you to a narrow 1km-long path, from where you have to climb a switchback hill on foot. Sit in the *rotemburo* (outdoor bath) and enjoy the Sea of Japan views through craggy rocks.

Semitropical Onsen

Urami-ga-taki Onsen (Hachijō-jima, Izu Archipelago; p184) Even in a country of lovely onsen, this is a real standout: the perfect little *rotemburo* located next to a waterfall in lush semitropical jungle. It's what they're shooting for at all those resorts on Bali, only this is the real thing. Sitting in the bath as the late-afternoon sunlight pierces the ferns here is a magical experience. Did we mention that's it's free?

Be warned: the minerals in some onsen can discolour jewellery, particularly silver. But don't worry too much if you forget to take off your wedding ring before jumping in the tub – after a few hours, the discolouration usually fades.

Onsen-Beach Combination

Shirahama (Wakayama Prefecture, Kansai; p400) There's something peculiarly pleasing about dashing back and forth between the ocean and a natural hot-spring bath – the contrast in temperature and texture is something we will never tire of. At Shirahama, a beach town in southern Kansai, there is a free onsen right on the beach. The location of **Sakino-yu Onsen** (p400) is just spectacular – you can sit in the tubs and watch the rollers from the Pacific break over the rocks just a few metres away.

Do-it-Yourself Onsen

Kawa-yu Onsen (Wakayama Prefecture, Kansai; p403) If you like doing things your own way, you'll love this natural oddity of an onsen in southern Kansai. Here, the onsen waters bubble up through the rocks of a riverbed. You choose a likely spot and dig out a natural hotpot along the riverside and wait for it to fill with hot water and – voila! – your own private *rotemburo*. In the winter, it gets even better: they use bulldozers to turn the entire river into a giant 1000-person onsen. It doesn't hurt that the river water is a lovely translucent emerald colour.

TATTOO WARNING

Be warned that if you have any tattoos, you may not be allowed to enter Japanese onsen, or *sentō* (public bath). The reason for this is that Japanese *yakuza* (mafia) almost always sport tattoos. Banning people with tattoos is an indirect way of banning gangsters. Unfortunately, to avoid the appearance of unfairness (and because Japan is a country where rules are rigorously adhered to), the no-tattoo rule also applies to foreigners. If your tattoo is small enough, cover it up with Band-Aids and you'll have no problem. Otherwise, ask the people at the front desk if you can go in despite your tattoos. The phrase to use is, '*Irezumi wa daijōbu desu ka*' (Are tattoos okay?).

DO 'YU' SPEAK ONSEN?

JAPANESE	SCRIPT	ENGLISH
dansei-no-yu	男性の湯	male bath
josei-no-yu	女性の湯	female bath
kake-yu	かけ湯	rinsing one's body
kazoku-no-yu	家族の湯	family bath
konyoku	混浴	mixed bath
onna-yu	女湯	female bath (most commonly used)
otoko-yu	男湯	male bath (most commonly used)
o-yu	お湯	hot water (polite)
rotemburo	露天風呂	outdoor bath
soto-yu	外湯	public bath
uchi-yu	内湯	private bath
yu	ゆ/湯	hot water
yubune	湯船	bath tub

Onsen Ryokan

Nishimuraya Honkan (Kinosaki, Kansai; p409) If you want to sample the ultimate in top-end onsen ryokan, this is the place. With several fine indoor and outdoor baths and elegant rooms, your stay here will be a highlight of your trip to Japan, and will shed some light on why the Japanese consider an onsen vacation to be the utmost in relaxation.

Ski Town Onsen

Nozawa Onsen (Nagano Prefecture, Central Honshū; p245) What could be better than a day spent on the slopes, followed by a soak in a Jacuzzi? Well, how about a day on the slopes followed by a soak in a real natural hot spring? Best of all, the onsen here are scalding hot, which is a nice contrast to the snow outside and it feels wonderful on tired skier's legs.

Onsen Etiquette

First: relax. That's what onsen are all about. You'll be relieved to hear that there really is nothing tricky about taking an onsen bath. If you remember just one basic point, you won't go too far wrong. This is the point: the water in the pools and tubs is for soaking in, not washing in, and it should only be entered after you've washed or rinsed your body.

This is the drill: pay your entry fee, if there is one. Rent a hand towel if you don't have one. Take off your shoes and put them in the lockers or shelves provided. Find the correct changing room or bath for your gender (man: 男; woman: 女). Grab a basket, strip down and put your clothes in the basket. Put the basket in a locker and bring the hand towel in with you.

Once in the bathing area, find a place around the wall (if there is one) to put down your toiletries (if you have them), and wash your body or, at least, rinse your body. You'll note that some local men dispense with this step and just stride over to the tubs and grab a bucket (there are usually some around) and splash a few scoops over their 'wedding tackle'. Some miscreants can't even be bothered with this step and plunge right into the tubs unwashed and unrinsed. Frankly, we like to think that these people will be reincarnated into a world where there are only cold-water showers for their bathing needs.

I Love U Blog (http://kansaionsen.blogspot.com) is a useful source of information on Kansai onsen, with occasional reviews of onsen outside Kansai.

Living Art of the Geisha

No other aspect of Japanese culture is as widely misunderstood as the geisha. First – and let's get this out of the way – geisha are not prostitutes. Nor is their virginity sold off to the highest bidder. Nor do they have to sleep with regular patrons. To put it simply, geisha are highly skilled entertainers who are paid to facilitate and liven up social occasions in Japan.

Origins

Memoirs of a Geisha (1997) by Arthur Golden is an entertaining fictional account of the life of a Kyoto geisha.

The origins of geisha are subject to some debate, but most historians believe that the institution of the geisha started in the Edo period (1600–1868). At this time, there were various types of prostitutes who served men in the pleasure quarters of the large cities. Some of these ladies became very accomplished in various arts and it is said that some pleasure houses even employed male performers to entertain customers. Some believe that these male entertainers were the first to be dubbed 'geisha', which means 'artistic person'.

Eventually, there arose a class of young ladies who specialised exclusively in entertainment and who did not engage in sexual relations with clients. These were the first true female geisha, and over the years they became prized for the accomplishments in a wide variety of Japanese arts.

Geisha Central

Without a doubt, Kyoto is the capital of the geisha world. Confusingly, in Kyoto they are not called 'geisha'; rather, they are called *maiko* or *geiko*. A *maiko* is a girl between the ages of 15 and 20, who is in the process of training to become a fully fledged *geiko* (the Kyoto word for 'geisha'). During this five-year period, she lives in an *okiya* (geisha house) and studies traditional Japanese arts, including dance, singing, tea ceremony and *shamisen* (a three-stringed instrument).

During this time, she will also start to entertain clients, usually in the company of a *geiko*, who acts like an older sister.

Due to the extensive training she receives, a *maiko* or *geiko* is like a living museum of Japanese traditional culture. In addition to her skills, the kimono she wears and the ornaments in her hair and on her obi (kimono sash) represent the highest achievements in Japanese arts. It's therefore hardly surprising that both Japanese and foreigners consider a meeting with a geisha to be a magical occurrence.

While young girls may have been sold into this world in times gone by, these days girls make the choice themselves, often after coming to Kyoto to see one of the city's famous geisha dances. The proprietor of the *okiya* will meet the girl and her parents to determine if the girl is serious and if her parents are willing to grant her permission to enter the world of the geisha (the *okiya* makes a considerable investment in terms of training and kimonos, so they are loathe to take girls who may quit).

GEISHA MANNERS

There's no doubt that catching a glimpse of a geisha is a once-in-a-lifetime Japanese experience. Unfortunately, the sport of 'geisha-spotting' has really gotten out of hand in Kyoto's Gion district (the city's main geisha district). It's probably best to keep the following in mind if you join the ranks of geisha-spotters in Gion:

➡ The geisha you see in Gion are usually on the way to or from an appointment and cannot stop for photos or conversation.

➡ You shouldn't touch or grab a geisha, or physically block their progress.

➡ No one likes being mobbed by photographers or hounded as they walk down the street.

➡ If you really want to get close to a geisha, private tour agencies and high-end ryokan or hotels can arrange geisha entertainment.

➡ If you are intent on getting a few photos of geisha, you will find plenty of 'tourist geisha' in the streets of Higashiyama during the daytime. These are tourists who have paid to be made up as geisha. They look pretty much like the real thing and they are usually more than happy to pose for pictures.

Once a *maiko* completes her training and becomes a *geiko*, she is able to move out of the *okiya* and live on her own. At this point she is free to have a boyfriend, but if she gets married she has to leave the world of the geisha. It's very easy to spot the difference between a *maiko* and a *geiko*: *geiko* wear wigs with minimal ornamentation (usually just a wooden comb in the wig), while *maiko* wear their own hair in an elaborate hairstyle with many bright hair ornaments called *kanzashi*. Also, *maiko* wear elaborate long-sleeve kimonos, while *geiko* wear simpler kimonos with shorter sleeves.

Geisha Entertainment

Maiko and *geiko* entertain their clients in exclusive restaurants, banquet halls, 'teahouses' (more like exclusive traditional bars) and other venues. An evening of *maiko/geiko* entertainment usually starts with a *kaiseki* (Japanese haute cuisine) meal. While their customers eat, the *maiko/geiko* enter the room and introduce themselves in Kyoto dialect.

They proceed to pour drinks and make witty banter with the guests. Sometimes they even play drinking games, and we can tell you from experience that it's hard to beat geisha at their own games! If it's a large party with a *jikata* (*shamisen* player), the girls may dance after dinner.

As you might guess, this sort of entertainment does not come cheap: a dinner with one *maiko* and one *geiko* and a *jikata* might cost about US$900, but it's definitely worth it for a once-in-a-lifetime experience. Let's face it: 'I had dinner with a geisha' is a pretty good entry in any 'been-there-done-that' contest.

It's impossible to arrange private geisha entertainment without an introduction from an established patron. However, these days geisha entertainment can be arranged through top-end hotels, ryokan and some private tour operators in Kyoto.

Knowledgeable sources estimate that there are about 65 *maiko* and just over 185 *geiko* in Kyoto (the latter figure includes *jikata*). Geisha can also be found in other parts of the country, most notably Tokyo. However, it is thought that there are less than 1000 geisha or *geiko* and *maiko* remaining in all of Japan.

The best way to arrange private entertainment with a geisha in Kyoto is through a high-end travel agency or cultural organisation. Kyoto Culture.org (www.kyotoculture.org) can arrange dinners with geisha, as well as tea ceremonies and kimono fittings.

GEISHA DANCES

The best way to see geisha – a whole lot of geisha – is to attend one of Kyoto's spring or autumn geisha dances.

Environment

Stretching from the tropics to the Sea of Okhotsk, the Japanese archipelago is a fantastically varied place. Few countries in the world enjoy such a variety of climates and ecosystems, with everything from coral-reefed islands to snowcapped mountains. Unfortunately, this wonderful landscape is also one of the world's most crowded, and almost every inch of the Japanese mainland and coastline bears the imprint of human activity.

In 2005 the Ministry of the Environment launched 'Cool Biz', a campaign to cut CO_2 emissions by encouraging 'casual Fridays' in offices and using less air-con in summer. In one year it was estimated that annual CO_2 emissions were down by over 1 million tonnes – but makers of neckties complained of a decline in sales.

The Land

Japan was not always an island. As recently as the end of the last ice age, around 10,000 years ago, the level of the sea rose enough to flood a land bridge that had connected Japan to the Asian continent.

Today, Japan consists of a chain of some 3900 small islands along with its four major ones: Honshū (which is slightly larger than Britain), Hokkaidō, Kyūshū and Shikoku. Okinawa, the largest and most significant of Japan's many smaller islands, is situated about halfway along an archipelago that stretches from the western tip of Honshū almost all the way to Taiwan. Japan stretches from around 25°N at the southern islands of Okinawa to 45°N at the northern end of Hokkaidō. Cities at comparable latitudes are Miami and Cairo in the south and Montreal and Milan in the north. Japan's total land area is 377,435 sq km, and more than 80% of it is mountainous.

Japan has the dubious distinction of being one of the most seismically active regions of the world. In March 2011 the 9.0-magnitude Great East Japan Earthquake, one of the strongest in history, caused a tsunami that devastated coastal areas of northeast Honshū and killed thousands. Fortunately, most of the more than 1000 earthquakes that strike Japan every year are too weak to feel. Still, if you find yourself near a coastal area and you feel an earthquake, you should make for high ground immediately.

Japan is also rich with volcanoes, including the famous Mt Fuji. In February 2009 Mt Asama, northwest of Tokyo, sent smoke 2km into the air and scattered ash over the capital. Kyūshū, however, lays claim to being the most active volcano region in Japan and this is where most visitors will see volcanoes close up, including Aso-san.

Although Japan's environment has been manipulated and degraded by human activity over the centuries, there are still pockets of real beauty left, some quite close to heavily populated urban areas. Fortunately, environmental consciousness is on the rise in Japan, and more effort is being put into recycling, conservation and protection of natural areas. We can only hope that some of Japan's remaining areas of beauty will be preserved for future generations.

Some Japanese households recycle their bathwater in their laundry machines. Drying clothes in the sun is still favoured over dryers.

The Human Impact

Visitors to Japan are often shocked at the state of the Japanese landscape. It seems that no matter where you look, the hills, rivers, coastline and fields bear the unmistakable imprint of human activity. Indeed, it is only in the highest, most remote mountains that travellers will find nature untouched by human hands. Why is this?

Undoubtedly, population density is the crucial factor here. However, it is not just simple population pressure that accounts for Japan's scarred and battered landscape; misguided land-management policies and money-driven politics also play a role.

Almost 70% of Japan's total land area is forested. Of this area, almost 40% is planted (rather than natural) forest, most of it with uniform rows of conifers, known as *sugi* (cryptomeria). Even national forests are not exempt from tree farming, and these forests account for 33% of Japan's total lumber output. The end result of this widespread tree farming is a patchwork effect over most of Japan's mountains – monotonous stands of *sugi* interspersed with occasional swathes of bare, clear-cut hillside.

To make matters worse, the planting of monoculture forests and clear-cutting reduces the stability of mountain topsoil, resulting in frequent landslides. To combat this, land engineers erect concrete retaining walls over huge stretches of hillside, particularly along roads or near human habitations.

As if this weren't enough, it is estimated that only three of Japan's 30,000 rivers and streams are undammed. In addition to dams, concrete channels and embankments are built around even the most inaccessible mountain streams.

In Japan rural areas yield enormous power in national politics, as representation is determined more by area than by population. In order to ensure the support of their constituencies, rural politicians have little choice but to lobby hard for government spending on public-work projects, as there is little other work available in these areas. Despite the negative effects this has on the Japanese landscape and economy, Japanese politicians seem unable to break this habit.

The upshot of all this is a landscape that looks, in many places, like a giant construction site. Perhaps the writer Alex Kerr put it best in his book *Lost Japan*: 'Japan has become a huge and terrifying machine, a Moloch tearing apart its own land with teeth of steel, and there is absolutely nothing anyone can do to stop it.' For the sake of the beauty that remains in Japan, let's hope he is wrong.

Wildlife

The latitudinal spread of Japan's islands makes for a wide diversity of flora and fauna. The Nansei and Ogasawara archipelagos in the far south are subtropical, and flora and fauna in this region are related to those found on the Malay peninsula. Mainland Japan (Honshū, Kyūshū and Shikoku), on the other hand, shows more similarities with Korea and China, while Hokkaidō shares some features with nearby Sakhalin Island (part of Russia).

HONSHŪ BLOSSOM & FOLIAGE SEASONS

ENVIRONMENT WILDLIFE

Early February– mid-March

Whether white or pink, plums are the first sign that winter is loosening its grip.

March & April

Big, bold and coming in a variety of colours, camellias grace many fine gardens and temples in Japan and they often overlap nicely with the plums and cherries.

Mid-March–mid-April

Who hasn't heard of Japan's famous cherry blossoms (*sakura*)? Whether you're in Tokyo, Nara, Kyoto or some other spot, in a really good cherry-blossom year it can seem like Mother Nature has forgotten all her modesty and decided to put on her best party dress and go mad. This is obviously the most popular time to visit Japan, but don't expect to have it all to yourself!

April & May

Not headline grabbers like the cherries or plums, azaleas can be magnificent. Hikers should keep an eye out for some of the great wild varieties of these flowering shrubs that festoon the hills of Japan.

Late April–May

Only in Japan would they have a special word for that particularly fresh shade of green that typifies the new leaves of springtime: *shinryoku*. For about two or three weeks after budding, the broadleaved trees of Japan look absolutely magnificent. Photographers would call this 'oversaturation'.

CHOPSTICKS

Animals

Japan's land bridge to the Asian continent allowed the migration of animals from Korea and China. There are species that are unique to Japan, such as the Japanese giant salamander and the Japanese macaque. In addition, Nansei-shotō, which has been separated from the mainland for longer than the rest of Japan, has a few examples of fauna that are classified by experts as 'living fossils', such as the Iriomote cat.

Japan's largest carnivorous mammals are its bears. Two species are found in Japan – the *higuma* (brown bear) of Hokkaidō, and the *tsukinowaguma* (Asiatic brown bear) of Honshū, Shikoku and Kyūshū.

According to a 2009 report by the International Union for Conservation of Nature and Natural Resources (IUCN), there are 312 endangered animal species in Japan. Endangered species include the Iriomote cat, the Tsushima cat, Blakiston's fish owl and the Japanese river otter.

Plants

The flora of Japan today is not what the Japanese saw hundreds of years ago. This is not just because a lot of Japan's natural landscape has succumbed to modern urban culture, but also because much of Japan's flora is imported. It is thought that 200 to 500 plant species have been introduced to Japan since the Meiji period, mainly from Europe but also from North America.

A large portion of Japan was once heavily forested. The cool to temperate zones of Central and Northern Honshū and southern Hokkaidō were home to broad-leaf mixed deciduous forests. These days, however, you are much more likely to see monotonous stands of *sugi* (cryptomeria).

Fortunately, the sheer inaccessibility of much of Japan's mountainous topography has preserved some areas of great natural beauty – in particular the alpine regions of Central Honshū, the lovely national parks of Hokkaidō and the semitropical island of Iriomote.

According to a 2008 report in the *Proceedings of the Japan Academy,* there are 1690 endangered and threatened species of vascular plants in Japan. For more information, visit the website of the Biodiversity Center of Japan at www.biodic.go.jp/index_e.html.

Twenty-five billion pairs of *waribashi* (disposable chopsticks) are used in Japan annually – equivalent to the timber needed to build 17,000 houses.

SUSTAINABLE TRAVEL IN JAPAN

As a traveller, you can minimise your impact on the Japanese environment in several ways.

Refuse packaging The Japanese are nuts about packaging – some would say overpackaging. The solution to this is simply to refuse excess packaging. At the cash register, you can say: '*Fukuro wa irimasen*' (I don't need a bag), or simply '*Kekkō desu*' (That's alright).

Carry your own chopsticks Say no to *waribashi* (disposable chopsticks) provided in restaurants. Either keep the first nice pair of *waribashi* that you are given, or visit a convenience store or ¥100 shop and ask for *my hashi* – lacquered, washable chopsticks with a carrying case.

Less tuna, please When you go to a sushi place, try to stay away from species of fish that are endangered, such as *maguro* (tuna) – including *toro* (fatty tuna belly). We know, this one hurts!

Use public transport Japan's public transport system is among the best in the world, and using public transport is an environmental no brainer.

Hop on a bike Many of Japan's cities are perfect for cycling – join the legions of Japanese who commute on their *mama-charis* (shopping bikes).

National Parks

Japan has 29 *kokuritsu kōen* (national parks) and 56 *kokutei kōen* (quasi-national parks), ranging from the far south (Iriomote National Park) to the northern tip of Hokkaidō (Rishiri-Rebun-Sarobetsu National Park). Although these parks account for less than 1% of Japan's total land area, it is estimated that 14% of Japan's land is protected or managed for sustainable use.

Few of the parks have facilities that you might expect in national parks (ranger stations, campgrounds, educational facilities etc). More importantly, national park status doesn't necessarily mean that the area in question is free from residential, commercial or even urban development. For descriptions of Japan's parks, see www.env.go.jp/en/np/index.html.

Environmental Issues

Japan has spent a lot of time in the spotlight recently due to environmental issues. In 2009 the documentary film *The Cove* was released and went on to win an Academy Award. The film focuses on the town of Taiji (southern Kansai), where dolphins are killed or captured for sale to aquariums around the world. While the film received good reviews and was seen by millions around the world, few Japanese have seen it. Most of the cinema owners who considered screening the film gave up in the face of a campaign of intimidation by right-wing organisations (in the end only six cinemas in the whole country showed it). As for the Taiji fishermen themselves, they claim that they were lied to and misrepresented by the filmmakers.

Meanwhile, Japan remains under international criticism for continuing to hunt whales, despite a 1982 International Whaling Commission moratorium on commercial whaling. Japan claims that it is whaling for research purposes, but critics point out that killing more than 900 minke, 50 fin and 50 humpback whales per season is impossible to justify in the name of research. They also point out that the meat is widely sold as food in Japan (and is even served in some school cafeterias). In January 2010 the issue came to a head in the Southern Ocean when the antiwhaling organisation Sea Shepherd's vessel *Ady Gil* was rammed and sunk by Japanese whalers, who then turned their water cannons on the stricken crew. Anti-whaling activists both inside and outside Japan were further enraged when it was revealed in December 2011 that US$29 million of funds earmarked for tsunami recovery efforts had gone to shore up the whaling industry.

Unfortunately, the issues of whaling and dolphin hunting have become so politicised in Japan that meaningful dialogue is impossible. The domestic media seem to be so fearful of right-wing attacks that they cannot say anything critical about the practices, and most politicians and members of the public interpret any such criticism as 'Japan bashing'.

As if this weren't enough, Japan has also been criticised for its failure to join international efforts to protect tuna, which many biologists say could be driven extinct if commercial fishing is not banned. In 2010 Japan fought hard against the ban on tuna fishing proposed by the Convention on International Trade in Endangered Species (CITES), and many observers say that Japan's opposition was instrumental in the bill's defeat. Even if the bill had passed, Japan had long ago announced its intention not to comply.

In 2009, environmentalists were briefly cheered by the results of the general election in which the Democratic Party of Japan (DJP) took power from the Liberal Democratic Party of Japan (LDP). The DJP had promised

ENVIRONMENT NATIONAL PARKS

May
The purple blossoms of wisteria vines decorate many temple gardens and mountainsides in Japan. When they're really working, the forest can seem more purple than green.

Late October– early December
For many Japanophiles, autumn is the best season to visit Japan. When the leaves of the maples, ginkos and other broadleaved trees turn colour, the effect is truly magical, and nothing suits a beautiful Japanese temple like a backdrop of crimson *momiji* (maple leaves).

Under the 1997 Kyoto Protocol, Japan pledged to cut CO$_2$ emissions by 6% from 1990 levels, but emissions to 2007 rose by 8%. The government lets companies implement voluntary environmental action plans.

THE FUKUSHIMA NUCLEAR INCIDENT

When the Great East Japan Earthquake struck on 11 March 2011, it caused a tsunami that devastated coastal areas of northeast Honshū (the main island of Japan). This area is home to several of Japan's nuclear power plants, most of which were unscathed. But the Fukushima One nuclear power plant (Fukushima Dai-ichi), located about 240km northeast of Tokyo, suffered serious damage.

The tsunami easily breached the seawalls intended to protect the plant from such waves. At the time of the quake, three of the six nuclear reactors at the site were shut down for maintenance. The remaining three were automatically shut down ('scrammed') when the quake struck. However, even when scrammed, nuclear reactors and their spent fuel (stored in nearby pools) emit significant heat and require cooling. Fukushima One's emergency on-site generators were knocked out by the tsunami and backup battery power quickly ran out, resulting in a complete loss of cooling capability.

The three operational reactors quickly started overheating, along with the spent fuel rods stored at one of the nonoperational reactors. The Tokyo Electric Power Company (TEPCO), operator of the power plants, struggled to restore cooling to the plants. After heroic efforts and a variety of setbacks, the Japanese government finally announced in December 2011 that cold shutdown had been achieved at all of the affected reactors at Fukushima Dai-Ichi.

Despite initially denying the fact, in May 2011, the Japanese government confirmed that meltdowns had occurred at three of the reactors at Fukushima Dai-Ichi. While most of the radioactive materials remained within the containment vessels, a significant amount of radiation was released from the plant due to explosions, breaches in the reactor vessels and in water that was used to cool the plants. Most of this radiation either entered the sea or was dispersed in a plume that ran to the northwest of the plants (far from Japan's main tourist areas), but some hotspots have been found in other areas further afield.

At the time of writing, an exclusion zone with a radius of 20km exists around the plant. Travellers can find out the most recent status of the exclusion zone by checking the website of the British Foreign Office, which has excellent detail on present conditions (go to www.fco.gov.uk/en/travel-and-living-abroad/travel-advice-by-country/asia-oceania/japan). For maps of radiation hotspots, visit the Safecast site (http://blog.safecast.org/).

The safety of food in Japan remains a lingering concern after the disaster, especially after it was revealed that irradiated beef had entered the marketplace in April 2011. Bloomberg News reported in 2011 that Japan lacks a centralised system to screen food for radiation, leaving local municipalities and farmers to conduct voluntary checks. Fortunately, the private sector and towns and prefectures in the affected region have done their best to check locally produced foodstuffs and to meet the government's non-binding limits on acceptable levels of radiation in food (which were recently lowered to reassure nervous consumers).

In the wake of the disaster, all of the reactors in Japan that were still running (some were already shut down for scheduled maintenance) were shut down, with the last one going offline in May 2012. However, in July 2012, the first one (in the town of Oi in Fukui Prefecture) was restarted. It's a near certainty that more restarts will happen following the victory of the pro-nuclear Liberal Democratic Party in the December 2012 election.

to end the sort of unrestrained public-works projects that have left Japan littered with what many consider needless dams, bridges, concrete retaining walls and other eyesores. Soon after taking power, the DJP announced plans to cancel 48 large public-works projects. Unfortunately, they ran headlong into the power of the bureaucrats who are intimately tied to such projects, as well as the local communities that have become dependent on the so-called 'construction state'. The final nail in the coffin for efforts to rein in the 'construction state' came in December 2012, when the LDP retook power from the DJP after running on a platform promising a continuation of public-works projects and a restart of the country's nuclear power plants, many of which had been shut down in the aftermath of the Fukushima nuclear disaster of March 2011.

Survival Guide

Directory A–Z

Accommodation

Japan offers a wide range of accommodation, from cheap guesthouses to first-class hotels. In addition to the western-style hotels, you'll also find distinctive Japanese-style places such as ryokan and *minshuku*. We introduce ryokan, *minshuku* and *shukubō* in the Traditional Japanese Accommodation chapter (p812).

Reservations

It can be hard to find accommodation during high-season holiday periods (cherry blossom season, fall foliage season, Golden Week holiday and the Obon holiday period). If you plan to be in Japan during these periods, you should make reservations as far in advance as possible.

Tourist information offices at main train stations can usually help with reservations, and are often open until about 6.30pm or later. Even if you are travelling by car, the train station is a good first stop in town for information, reservations and cheap car parking.

Making phone reservations in English is usually possible at larger hotels and foreigner-friendly ryokan. Providing you speak clearly and simply, there will usually be someone around who can get the gist of what you want. **Japanese Inn Group** (http://japaneseinngroup. com/) is a collection of foreigner-friendly ryokan and guesthouses. You can book member inns via its website or phone/fax. Pick up a copy of its excellent guide to member inns at major tourist information centres in Japan.

Camping

Camping is possible at official campgrounds across Japan, some of which are only open during the summer high season of July and August. Camping is also possible year-round (when conditions permit) at campgrounds in the mountains or around certain mountain huts. 'Guerrilla' or unofficial camping is also possible in many parts of rural Japan, but we recommend asking a local person about acceptable areas before setting up your tent.

Cycling Terminals

Cycling terminals (*saikurin-gu tāminaru*) provide low-priced accommodation of the bunk-bed or tatami-mat variety and are usually found in scenic areas suited to cycling.

Cycling-terminal prices compare favourably with those of a youth hostel: at around ¥3000 per person per night, or ¥5000 including two meals.

Hostels

Japan has an extensive network of youth hostels, often located in areas of interest to travellers. The network is administered by **Japan Youth Hostels, Inc** (JYHA; ☑03-3288-1417; www.jyh.or.jp/english/index. html; 2-21-4 Yanagibashi Taito-ku Tokyo 111-0052). You can download a PDF of its English-language map and guide to member youth hostels at www.jyh.or.jp/english/ index.html.

The best way to find hostels is via the JYHA website or the PDF guide, both of which have details in English on all member hostels. The website allows online reservations. Another good resource is the *Youth Hostel Map of Japan*, which has one-line entries on each hostel. It's available for free from Japan National Tourism Organization (JNTO) and travel information centres (TICs) in Japan.

BOOK YOUR STAY ONLINE

For more accommodation reviews by Lonely Planet authors, check out http://hotels.lonelyplanet.com. You'll find independent reviews, as well as recommendations on the best places to stay. Best of all, you can book online.

SLEEPING PRICE RANGES

For all of Japan, where more than one accommodation is listed within a particular budget category, entries are organised by preference (most appealing options listed first).

The following price ranges refer to a double room for hotels, and per person double occupancy for ryokan (without meals). Unless otherwise stated, tax (ie the national 5% consumption tax) is included in the price, but note that some hotels quote exclusive of taxes.

¥ less than ¥8000 (Tokyo), less than ¥6000 (elsewhere)

¥¥ from ¥8000 to ¥20,000 (Tokyo), ¥6000 to ¥15,000 (elsewhere)

¥¥¥ more than ¥20,000 (Tokyo), more than ¥15,000 (elsewhere)

Accommodation tends to be more expensive in big cities than in rural areas. Likewise, in resort areas such as Izu Peninsula, accommodation is more expensive during the warm months, while in ski areas accommodation prices go up in winter and down in summer. Accommodation should be booked months in advance in Kyoto during the cherry-blossom season (late March to early April) and the autumn-foliage season (November).

Since air-conditioning is ubiquitous in Japan (due to its hot summers), we only mention air-con in reviews when a place does not have it.

MEMBERSHIP, PRICES & REGULATIONS

You can stay at youth hostels in Japan without being a member of either the JYHA or the International Youth Hostel Federation (IYHA). Sample hostel charges:

One-year membership ¥2800

One-night stay (dorm) ¥3000

One-night stay (private room) ¥4000

Breakfast ¥500

Dinner ¥900

Sheet rental ¥100

Hostellers are expected to check in between 3pm and 8pm to 9pm. There is usually a curfew of 10pm or 11pm. Checkout is often before 10am and dormitories are closed between 10am and 3pm. Bath time will normally be between 5pm and 9pm, dinner is between 6pm and 7.30pm, and breakfast is between 7am and 8am.

Hotels

You'll find a range of Western-style hotels in most Japanese cities and resort areas. So-called business hotels are efficient, utilitarian hotels that are geared to Japan's business travellers; while the rooms tend to be small,

they are usually perfectly adequate for a night's stay. Luxury hotels are what you'd find anywhere else in the world. Sample hotel charges:

Single room in a business hotel ¥8000

Twin room in a business hotel ¥12,000

Single room in a luxury hotel ¥17,000

Twin room in a luxury hotel ¥23,000

Capsule in a capsule hotel ¥3800

Twin room in a 'love hotel' (overnight) ¥6500

In addition to the 5% consumption tax that is levied on all accommodation in Japan, you may have to pay an additional 10% or more as a service charge at luxury hotels.

CAPSULE HOTELS

One of Japan's most famous forms of accommodation is the *capseru hoteru*. As the name implies, the 'rooms' in a capsule hotel consist of banks of neat white capsules stacked in rows two or three high. The capsules are about the size of a spacious coffin. Inside is a bed, a TV, a reading light, a radio and an alarm clock. Personal belongings

are kept in a locker room. Most capsule hotels have the added attraction of a sauna and a large communal bath.

Capsule hotels are common in major cities and often cater to workers who have partied too hard to make it home or have missed the last train. The majority of capsule hotels only accept male guests, but some also accept women. Given the fact that many of the guests at capsule hotels are inebriated salarymen, it's not entirely surprising that these aren't the most salubrious places to spend the night. The exceptions to this are the new breed of foreigner-friendly capsule hotels that have recently opened in places like Kyoto and Tokyo, which are very nice places to stay.

LOVE HOTELS

As the name implies, love hotels are used by Japanese couples for discreet trysts. You can use them for this purpose as well, but they're also acceptable for overnight accommodation.

To find a love hotel on the street, just look for flamboyant facades and signs clearly stating the rates. Love hotels are designed for maximum privacy: entrances and exits are kept separate; keys are provided through a small opening without contact between desk clerk and guest; and photos of the rooms are displayed to make the choice easy for the customer.

Most love hotels are comfortable with foreign guests, but travellers have reported being turned away at some places. Same-sex couples may have more trouble than heterosexual couples.

Kokumin-shukusha

Kokumin-shukusha (people's lodges) are government-supported institutions offering affordable accommodation in scenic areas. Private Japanese-style rooms are the norm, though some places offer Western-style rooms. Prices average ¥5500 to ¥6500 per person per night, including two meals.

Mountain Huts

Mountain huts (*yama-goya*) are common in many of Japan's hiking and mountain-climbing areas. While you'll occasionally find free emergency shelters, most huts are privately run and charge for accommodation. These places offer bed and board (two meals) at around ¥5000 to ¥8000 per person; if you prepare your own meal, that figure drops to ¥3000 to ¥5000 per person. It's best to call ahead to reserve a spot (contact

numbers are available in Japanese hiking guides and maps, and in Lonely Planet's *Hiking in Japan*), but you won't usually be turned away if you show up without a reservation.

Rider Houses

Catering mainly to touring motorcyclists, rider houses (*raidā hausu*) provide extremely basic shared accommodation from around ¥1000 per night. You should bring your own sleeping bag or ask to rent bedding from the owner. For bathing facilities, you will often be directed to the local *sentō* (public bath).

Rider houses are most common in Hokkaidō, but you'll also find them in places such as Kyūshū and Okinawa. If you can read some Japanese, spiral-bound *Touring Mapple* maps, published by Shobunsha and available in Japan, mark almost all of the rider houses in a specific region, as well as cheap places to eat along the way. Readers of Japanese will also find the **Rider House Database** (www.tabizanmai.net/rider/index_new.html) useful.

Toho

The **Toho network** (www.toho.net/eng.html) is a diverse collection of places that has banded loosely together to offer a more flexible alternative to youth

hostels. Most of the network's 90 members are in Hokkaidō, although there are a few scattered around Honshū and other islands further south. Prices average ¥4000 per person for dormitory-style accommodation, or ¥5000 with two meals. Private rooms are sometimes available for about ¥1000 extra.

Customs Regulations

Customs allowances:
Alcohol Up to three 760mL bottles.
Gifts/souvenirs Up to ¥200,000 in total value.
Perfume Up to 60mL.
Tobacco products Up to 100 cigars or 400 cigarettes or 500g.

You must be over the age of 20 to qualify for these allowances. Customs officers will confiscate any pornographic materials in which pubic hair is visible.

There are no limits on the importation of foreign or Japanese currency. The export of foreign currency is also unlimited but there is a ¥5 million export limit for Japanese currency.

Visit **Japan Customs** (www.customs.go.jp/english/index.htm) for more information on Japan's customs regulations.

ADDRESSES IN JAPAN

In Japan, finding a place from its address can be difficult, even for locals. The problem is twofold: first, the address is usually given by an area rather than a street; and, second, the numbers are not necessarily consecutive, as prior to the mid-1950s numbers were assigned by date of construction.

To find an address, the usual process is to ask directions. Have your address handy. The numerous local police boxes are there largely for this purpose. Businesses often include a small map in their advertisements or on their business cards to show their location.

Most taxis and many rental cars now have satellite navigation systems, which make finding places a breeze, as long as you can program the address or phone number into the system. Needless to say, you'll have to be able to read Japanese to input the address, but phone numbers should be no problem.

PRACTICALITIES

➡ **Newspapers & Magazines** There are three main English-language daily newspapers in Japan: the *Japan Times, Daily Yomiuri* and *Asahi Shimbun/International Herald Tribune*. In the bigger cities, these are available at bookstores, convenience stores, train-station kiosks and some hotels. In the countryside, you may not be able to find them anywhere. Foreign magazines are available in major bookshops in the bigger cities.

➡ **Radio** Recent years have seen an increase in the number of stations aimed specifically at Japan's foreign population. InterFM (76.1FM; www.interfm.co.jp/) is a favourite of Tokyo's expat community, and the Kansai equivalent is FM Cocolo (76.5FM; http://cocolo.jp/).

➡ **Electricity** The Japanese electric current is 100V AC. Tokyo and eastern Japan are on 50Hz, and western Japan, including Nagoya, Kyoto and Osaka, is on 60Hz. Most electrical items from other parts of the world will function on Japanese current. Japanese plugs are the flat two-pin type.

➡ **Video Systems** Japan uses the NTSC system.

➡ **Weights & Measures** Japan uses the international metric system.

Discount Cards

Hostel Cards

See p826 about obtaining a youth hostel membership card.

Museum Discount Card

The **Grutt Pass** (www.museum.or.jp/grutto/english.html) is a useful ticket that allows free or discounted admission to almost 50 museums in the Tokyo area. For more information, see p77

Senior Cards

Japan is an excellent destination for senior travellers, with discounts available on entry fees to many temples, museums and cinemas. To qualify for these widely available senior discounts, you have to be aged over 60 or 65, depending upon the particular place or company. In almost all cases a passport will be sufficient proof of age.

Japanese domestic airlines (JAS, JAL and ANA) offer senior discounts of about 25% on certain flights. See their individual websites for details.

Electricity

100v/50hz/60hz

Embassies & Consulates

Australian Embassy (☏03-5232-4111; www.australia.or.jp/en/; 2-1-14 Mita, Minato-ku)

Australian Consulate Fukuoka (☏092-734-5055; 7th fl, Tenjin Twin Bldg, 1-6-8 Tenjin, Chūō-ku); Osaka (☏06-6941-9448; 16th fl, Twin 21 MID Tower, 2-1-61 Shiromi, Chūō-ku)

Canadian Embassy (☏03-5412-6200; www.canadainternational.gc.ca/japan-japon/index.aspx; 7-3-38 Akasaka, Minato-ku)

Canadian Consulate Nagoya (☏052-972-0450; Nakatō Marunouchi Bldg, 6F, 3-17-6 Marunouchi, Naka-ku); Sapporo (☏011-281-6565; Nikko Bldg, 5F, Kita 4 Nishi 4, Chūō-ku); Hiroshima (☏082-246-0057; 4-33 Komachi, Naka-ku)

Dutch Embassy (☏03-5776-5400; http://japan.nlembassy.org/; 3-6-3 Shiba-kōen, Minato-ku, Tokyo)

Dutch Consulate (☏06-6944-7272; 33rd fl, Twin 21 MID Tower, 2-1-61 Shiromi, Chūō-ku, Osaka)

French Embassy (☏03-5798-6000; www.ambafrance-jp.org; 4-11-44 Minami Azabu, Minato-ku, Tokyo)

French Consulate (☏06-6131-5278; Manulife Place Dojima, 6F, Dojimahama 1-4-19, Kita-ku, Osaka)

German Embassy (☏03-5791-7700; www.japan.diplo.de/Vertretung/japan/ja/Startseite.html.html; 4-5-10 Minami Azabu, Minato-ku, Tokyo)

German Consulate (☏06-6440-5070; 35th fl, Umeda Sky Bldg Tower East, 1-1-88-3501 Ōyodonaka, Kita-ku, Osaka)

Irish Embassy (☎03-3263-0695; www.irishembassy.jp; Ireland House, 2-10-7 Kōji-machi, Chiyoda-ku, Tokyo)

New Zealand Embassy (☎03-3467-2271; www.nzembassy.com/japan; 20-40 Kamiyama-chō, Shibuya-ku, Tokyo)

New Zealand Consulate (☎06-6373-4583; Umeda Centre Bldg, 2-4-12 Nakazaki-nishi, Kita-ku, Osaka)

Russian Embassy (☎03-3583-4445; www.rusconsul.jp; 2-1-1, Azabudai, Tokyo)

Russian Consulate (☎011-561-3171~2; http://sapporo.rusembassy.org/; 2-5 12-chōme Nishi, Minami 14-jo, Chūō-ku, Sapporo)

South Korean Embassy (☎03-3455-2601; http://jpn-tokyo.mofat.go.kr/jpn/index.jsp; 1-7-32 Minami Azabu, Minato-ku, Tokyo)

South Korean Consulate (☎092-771-0461; 1-1-3 Jigyōhama, Chūō-ku, Fukuoka)

UK Embassy (☎03-5211-1100; http://ukinjapan.fco.gov.uk/en/; 1 Ichiban-chō, Chiyoda-ku, Tokyo)

UK Consulate (☎06-6120-5600; 19th fl, Epson Osaka Bldg, 3-5-1 Bakurōmachi, Chūō-ku, Osaka)

US Embassy (☎03-3224-5000; http://japan.usembassy.gov/; 1-10-5 Akasaka, Minato-ku, Tokyo)

US Consulate (☎06-6315-5900; http://osaka.usconsulate.gov/; 2-11-5 Nishitenma, Kita-ku, Osaka)

Food

For information on food in Japan see Eat & Drink Like a Local (p55) and Japanese Cuisine (p786).

Gay & Lesbian Travellers

With the possible exception of Thailand, Japan is Asia's most enlightened nation with regard to the sexual preferences of foreigners. Shinjuku-nichōme in Tokyo is an established scene where English is spoken and meeting men is fairly straightforward.

In provincial areas there may be one so-called 'snack' bar, where gay men meet. Snack bars can be found in the central entertainment districts of towns and cities. They are usually small places capable of seating only a dozen or fewer customers. They may appear like hole-in-the-wall bars. Note that most snack bars cater to heterosexual customers. Gay-friendly snack bars are extremely difficult to locate without an inside connection.

The lesbian scene is growing but is still elusive for most non-Japanese–speaking foreigners. Outside Tokyo you may find it difficult to break into the local scene unless you spend considerable time in a place or have local contacts who can show you around.

Staying in hotels is simple as most have twin rooms, but love hotels are less accessible; if you know someone Japanese and can overcome the language barrier, a stay in a love hotel may be possible, but some are not particularly foreigner friendly.

Utopia (www.utopia-asia.com) is the site most commonly frequented by English-speaking gays and lesbians.

For information about gay and lesbian venues in Tokyo, see p128.

There are no legal restraints to same-sex sexual activities of either gender. Public displays of affection are not really done, whether the couple be same-sex or heterosexual, but they are not usually a problem in cities. In the countryside, they may raise some eyebrows, but that's probably all.

Health

Japan is an advanced country with high standards of hygiene and few endemic diseases. There are no special immunisations needed to visit and, other than bringing prescription medications from home, no special preparations to make. Hospitals and clinics can be found all over the archipelago, and only the smallest outer islands lack medical facilities. That said, there are some things to keep in mind.

Insurance

A travel-insurance policy to cover theft, loss and medical problems is essential. Some policies will specifically exclude 'dangerous activities', which can include scuba diving, motorcycling and even trekking; if you plan to engage in such activities, you'll want a policy that covers them.

You may prefer a policy that pays doctors or hospitals directly rather than having you pay on the spot and claim later. If you have to claim later, make sure you keep all documentation. Some policies ask you to call (reverse charge) a centre in your home country where an immediate assessment of your problem is made. Check that the policy covers ambulances or an emergency flight home.

Be sure to bring your insurance card or other certificate of insurance to

---

EATING PRICE RANGES

Price ranges in this guide are for a main meal per person unless otherwise stated.

¥ less than ¥1000 (in Tokyo, less than ¥2000)

¥¥ from ¥1000 to ¥4000 (in Tokyo, ¥2000 to ¥5000)

¥¥¥ more than ¥4000 (in Tokyo, more than ¥5000)

MEDICAL CARE IN JAPAN

While the Japanese medical system is extensive and comprehensive, the level of care is very uneven. Here are some things to note if you need to seek medical attention:

➡ It is better to seek care at university hospitals or other large hospitals rather than clinics.

➡ Japanese doctors and hospitals are sometimes reluctant to treat foreigners. It helps to carry proof of insurance and be willing to show it. If a doctor or hospital seems reticent about giving care, you should insist on it (even though Japan has no Hippocratic oath, doctors can be told that they have to treat patients in need of care).

➡ Most hospitals and clinics have regular hours (usually in the mornings) when they will see patients.

➡ Hotels and ryokan that cater to foreigners will usually know the best hospitals in a particular area and will also know hospitals with English-speaking doctors.

➡ Most doctors speak some English. However, it helps to bring along a Japanese speaker if possible to help you explain your condition and to navigate the hospital.

Japan; Japanese hospitals have been known to refuse treatment to foreign patients with no proof of medical insurance.

Internet Access

Internet access in a nutshell:
Current 100V AC; 50Hz in east Japan, 60Hz in west Japan
Plugs flat two-pin type, identical to most ungrounded North American plugs
Connections LAN cable access more common than wi-fi
Internet-cafe rates ¥200 to ¥700 per hour

If you plan on bringing your laptop to Japan, make sure that it is compatible with the current and check to see if your plug will fit the wall sockets. Transformers and plug adaptors are readily available in electronics districts, such as Tokyo's Akihabara, Osaka's Den Den Town or Kyoto's Teramachi-dōri.

In this book, an internet symbol indicates that the accommodation option has at least one computer with internet for guests' use and/or LAN cable internet access in guest rooms. We also note where wi-fi is available. Note that wi-fi is far less common in Japanese hotels than in their Western counterparts. About a third of hotels in Japan have free wi-fi; another third charge for wi-fi; and a third have no wi-fi at all.

It is much more common to find LAN cable internet access points in hotel rooms (the hotels usually provide LAN cables, but you may want to bring your own to avoid having to ask for one everywhere you stay). These LAN connections usually work fine, but you may occasionally find it difficult to log on due to software or hardware compatibility issues or configuration problems – the front-desk staff *may* be able to help.

You'll find internet cafes and other access points in most major Japanese cities. As a rule, internet connections are fast (DSL, ADSL or optic fibre) and reliable.

Left Luggage

Only major train stations have left-luggage facilities, but almost all stations have coin-operated storage lockers (¥100 to ¥500 per day, depending on size). The lockers are rented until midnight (not for 24 hours). After that time you have to insert more money before your key will work. If your bag is simply too large to fit in the locker, ask someone *'tenimotsu azukai wa doko desu ka'* (Where is the left-luggage office?).

Legal Matters

Japanese police have extraordinary powers. They can detain a suspect for up to three days without charging them; after this time a prosecutor can decide to extend this period for another 20 days. Police can also choose whether to allow a suspect to phone their embassy or lawyer, though if you find yourself in police custody you should insist that you will not cooperate in any way until allowed to make such a call. Your embassy is the first place you should call if given the chance.

Police will speak almost no English; insist that a *tsūyakusha* (interpreter) be summoned. Police are legally bound to provide one before proceeding with any questioning. Even if you do speak Japanese, it's best to deny it and stay with your native language.

If you have a problem, call the **Japan Helpline** (☎0120-46-1997), a nationwide emergency number that operates 24 hours a day, seven days a week.

Maps

If you'd like to buy a map of Japan before arriving, both Nelles and Periplus produce reasonable ones. If you want something more detailed,

GETTING ONLINE IN JAPAN

Japan is one of the world's most technologically advanced countries, but if you're expecting to find free internet hot spots wherever you go, you're in for a surprise. Sure, wi-fi or mobile internet is everywhere, but most of it is available only to subscribers of various Japanese services, many of which are not easy for travellers to join (especially those who don't speak and read Japanese). **Freespot Map** (www.freespot.com/users/map_e.html) has a list of internet hot spots, but it's not exhaustive and the maps are in Japanese, but it's quite useful. Failing that, here are some ways to get online:

Starbucks All Starbucks stores in Japan offer free wi-fi to customers. You must register online to use the service (go to https://service.wi2.ne.jp/wi2net/SbjReg/2/?locale=en).

B-Mobile SIM cards If you bring an internet device that takes a SIM card, you can buy B-Mobile Visitor SIM cards from major electronics shops in big cities such as Tokyo, Osaka and Kyoto. You can also order them online (go to http://www.bmobile.ne.jp/english/) and have them delivered to your first night's lodgings or even to the post office at your arrival airport to hold for you. These will usually allow internet use for a specific length of time (a month is common). Note that the amount of data you can download is limited and your device must be unlocked and you must be able to input the APN settings. These are data-only (ie no voice) but you can use Skype with them.

Boingo Subscribers to Boingo's global plan (www.boingo.com) can use BB Mobilepoint wi-fi at McDonald's restaurants and some other spots.

Portable internet connections You can rent data cards, USB dongles or pocket wi-fi devices from various phone-rental companies. The most user-friendly option with English service is provided by **Rentafone Japan** (☎090-9621-7318, toll free within Japan 0120-746-487; www.rentafonejapan.com), which offers two types of pocket wi-fi from ¥3900 per week with unlimited use.

Free wi-fi in Kyoto The city of Kyoto has recently launched a free wi-fi access program for foreign travellers, with hotspots across the city. You must email to get the access code. Go to http://kanko.city.kyoto.lg.jp/wifi/en/ to find a map of hotspots and to get started. Note that access is limited to three hours, but you can get another access code for additional hours.

wait until you get to Tokyo or Kyoto, where you'll find lots of detailed maps in both English and Japanese.

The JNTO's free *Tourist Map of Japan*, available at JNTO-operated tourist information centres inside the country and JNTO offices abroad, is a reasonable English-language map that is suitable for general route planning.

The *Japan Road Atlas* (Shobunsha) is a good choice for those planning to drive around the country; unfortunately, it's out of print (you might be able to find a copy online, but it won't be cheap). Those looking for something less bulky should pick up a copy of the *Bilingual Atlas of Japan* (Kodansha). Of course, if you can

read a little Japanese, you'll do much better with one of the excellent *Super Mapple* road atlases published by Shobunsha.

Money

The currency in Japan is the yen (¥). The Japanese pronounce yen as 'en', with no 'y' sound. The kanji for yen is 円.

Yen denominations:

¥1 Coin; lightweight, silver colour
¥5 Coin; bronze colour, hole in the middle, value in Chinese character only
¥10 Coin; copper colour
¥50 Coin; silver colour, hole in the middle
¥100 Coin; silver colour
¥500 Coin; large, silver colour
¥1000 Banknote
¥2000 Banknote (rare)
¥5000 Banknote
¥10,000 Banknote

The Japanese postal system has recently linked its ATMs to the international Cirrus and Plus networks, and 7-Eleven convenience stores have followed suit, so getting money is no longer the issue it once was for travellers to Japan. Of course, it always makes sense to carry some foreign cash and credit cards. For those who don't have credit cards, it would be a good idea to bring some travellers cheques as a back-up.

ATMs

Automated teller machines are almost as common as vending machines in Japan.

Unfortunately, most of these do not accept foreign-issued cards. Even if they display Visa and MasterCard logos, most accept only Japan-issued versions of these cards.

Fortunately, Japanese postal ATMs accept cards that belong to the following international networks: Visa, Plus, MasterCard, Maestro, Cirrus, American Express, Diners Club, Discover and China Unionpay cards. Check the sticker(s) on the back of your card to see which network(s) your card belongs to. You'll find postal ATMs in almost all post offices, and you'll find post offices in even the smallest Japanese village.

Note that postal ATMs work with bank or cash cards – you cannot use credit cards, even with a pin number, in postal ATMs. That is to say, you cannot use postal ATMs to perform a cash advance.

Most postal ATMs are open 9am to 5pm Monday to Friday, 9am to noon on Saturday, and are closed on Sunday and holidays. Some postal ATMs in very large central post offices are open longer hours. The central post offices in major cities are open *almost* 24 hours a day.

In addition, 7-Eleven convenience stores across Japan have linked their ATMs to international cash networks, and these often seem to accept cards that for one reason or other will not work with postal ATMs. They are also open 24 hours. So, if you can't find an open post office or your card won't work with postal ATMs, don't give up: ask around for a 7-Eleven (pronounced like 'sebun erebun' in Japanese).

International cards also work in the ATMs at **Citibank Japan** (www.citibank.co.jp/en/banking/branch_atm/index.html). If you find that your card doesn't work in a postal or 7-Eleven ATM, this is a good last-ditch bet. Visit its site for a branch locator.

Finally, before leaving your home country, check that your ATM card can be used abroad and consider informing the issuing bank that you plan to use the card abroad – some banks will deactivate the card if it is suddenly used abroad as they may suspect it's been stolen.

CURRENCY WARNING

Exchange rates for the US dollar and euro are reasonable in Japan. All other currencies, including the Australian dollar and the currencies of nearby countries, fetch very poor exchange rates. If you want to bring cash to Japan, we suggest US dollars or euros. Or, if you must change other currencies into yen, we suggest doing so in your home country.

Credit Cards

Cash and carry is still very much the rule in Japan. If you do decide to bring a credit card, you'll find Visa the most useful, followed by Master-Card, Amex and Diners Club. Note also that Visa cards can be used for cash advances at Sumitomo Mitsui banks in Japan, but you might have to go to a specific branch to do this.

Exchanging Money

You can change cash or travellers cheques at most banks, major post offices, discount ticket shops, some travel agencies, some large hotels and most big department stores. Note that discount-ticket shops (known as *kakuyasu kippu uriba* in Japanese) often have the best rates. These can be found around major train stations. However, only US dollars and euros fetch decent exchange rates.

International Transfers

To make an international transfer you'll have to find a Japanese bank associated with the bank transferring the money. Start by asking at the central branch of any major Japanese bank. If it doesn't have a relationship with your bank, it can usually refer you to a bank that does. Once you find a related bank, you'll have to give your home bank the exact details of where to send the money: the bank, branch and location, and the bank's SWIFT code. A credit-card cash advance is a worthwhile alternative.

WARNING: JAPAN IS A CASH SOCIETY

Be warned that cold hard yen is the way to pay in Japan. While credit cards are becoming more common, cash is still much more widely used, and travellers cheques are rarely accepted. Never assume that you can pay for things with a credit card; always carry sufficient cash. The only places where you can count on paying by credit card are department stores, large hotels and at major JR ticket offices.

For those without credit cards, it would be a good idea to bring some travellers cheques as a back-up. As in most other countries, the US dollar is still the currency of choice in terms of exchanging cash and cashing travellers cheques.

USING A JAPANESE POSTAL ATM

Postal ATMs are relatively easy to use. Here's the drill: press 'English Guide', select 'Withdrawal', then insert your card, press 'Visitor Withdrawal', input your PIN, then hit the button marked 'Kakunin' (確認), then enter the amount, hit 'Yen' and 'Confirm' and you should hear the delightful sound of bills being dispensed.

Taxes

Japan has a 5% consumption tax (shōhizei). If you eat at expensive restaurants and stay in top-end accommodation, you will encounter a service charge that varies from 10% to 15%.

Tipping

There is little tipping in Japan. If you want to show your gratitude to someone, give them a gift rather than a tip. If you do choose to give someone (your maid at a ryokan, for instance) a cash gift, place the money in an envelope first.

Opening Hours

Business hours in Japan are fairly standard. Almost all museums, many other sights and many businesses close over the New Year period (30 or 31 December to 3 or 4 January). We do not list New Year closures in this guide in most instances because this is standard. Also, most museums in Japan are closed on Monday. Note that when a place is normally closed on a Monday, it will usually open on Monday if that Monday is a national holiday (in which case it will most likely be closed on the following Tuesday). The following is a list of typical business hours:

Banks Open 9am to 3pm Monday to Friday.

Bars Open 6pm to midnight or later, closed one day per week.

Department stores Open 10am to 7pm, closed one or two days per month. Often open for all or part of the New Year's holidays (making them good places to buy food during this time).

Museums Open 9am or 10am to 5pm, closed Monday.

Offices Open 9am to 5pm or 6pm Monday to Friday.

Post offices Local open 9am to 5pm Monday to Friday; central open 9am to 7pm Monday to Friday and 9am to 3pm Saturday (larger cities may have after-hours window open 24 hours a day, seven days a week).

Restaurants Open 11am to 2pm and 6pm to 11pm, closed one day per week.

Smaller shops Open 9am to 5pm, may be closed Sunday.

Post

The Japanese postal system is extremely reliable, efficient and, for regular postcards and airmail letters, not markedly more expensive than in other developed countries.

Postal Rates

The airmail rate for postcards is ¥70 to any overseas destination; aerograms cost ¥90. Letters weighing less than 25g are ¥90 to other countries within Asia, ¥110 to North America, Europe or Oceania (including Australia and New Zealand), and ¥130 to Africa and South America. One peculiarity of the Japanese postal system is that you will be charged extra if your writing runs over onto the address side (the right side) of a postcard.

Sending & Receiving Mail

The symbol for post offices is a red T with a bar across the top on a white background (〒).

Mail can be sent to, from or within Japan when addressed in English (Roman script).

Although any post office will hold mail for collection, the poste-restante concept is not well known and can cause confusion in smaller places. It is probably better to have mail addressed to you at a larger central post office. Letters are usually only held for 30 days before being returned to sender. When enquiring about mail for collection ask for kyokudome yūbin. Such mail should be addressed as follows:

➡ Name
➡ Poste Restante
➡ Central Post Office
➡ Tokyo, JAPAN

An alternative to poste-restante is to have letters sent to your lodgings with instructions to hold for you written below the address.

Public Holidays

Japan has 15 national holidays. When a public holiday falls on a Sunday, the following Monday is taken as a holiday. If that Monday is already a holiday, the following day becomes a holiday as well. And if two weekdays (say, Tuesday and Thursday) are holidays, the day in between also becomes a holiday.

Japan's national holidays:

Ganjitsu (New Year's Day) 1 January

Seijin-no-hi (Coming-of-Age Day) Second Monday in January

Kenkoku Kinem-bi (National Foundation Day) 11 February

Shumbun-no-hi (spring equinox) 20 or 21 March

Shōwa-no-hi (Shōwa Emperor's Day) 29 April

Kempō Kinem-bi (Constitution Day) 3 May

Midori-no-hi (Green Day) 4 May

Kodomo-no-hi (Children's Day) 5 May

Umi-no-hi (Marine Day) Third Monday in July

Keirō-no-hi (Respect-for-the-Aged Day) Second Monday in September

Shūbun-no-hi (autumn equinox) 22 or 23 September

Taiiku-no-hi (Health-Sports Day) Second Monday in October

Bunka-no-hi (Culture Day) 3 November

Kinrō Kansha-no-hi (Labour Thanksgiving Day) 23 November

Tennō Tanjōbi (Emperor's Birthday) 23 December

You will find transport crowded and accommodation bookings hard to come by during the following high-season travel periods:

Shōgatsu (New Year) 31 December to 3 January

Golden Week 29 April to 5 May

O-Bon mid-August

Safe Travel

The Great East Japan Earthquake of March 2011 and the following nuclear crisis made it unsafe to travel in certain parts of northeast Honshū (at the time of going to print, this was an area within 20km of the Fukushima One nuclear powerplant and some villages just to the north of this zone). Of course, the situation may change by the time you read this, so we strongly recommend that you check online sources and your government's travel warnings for the latest info. Here are a few resources (the British Foreign Office had the most information at the time of writing):

Australian Department of Foreign Affairs (www.smart-traveller.gov.au)

British Foreign Office (www.fco.gov.uk/en/travelling-and-living-overseas/travel-advice-by-country)

US State Department (http://travel.state.gov/travel/travel_1744.html)

Note: if you find yourself near a coastal area and you feel an earthquake, make for high ground immediately.

Solo Travellers

Japan is an excellent place for solo travellers: it's safe, convenient and friendly. Almost all hotels have single rooms, and business-hotel singles can cost as little as ¥4000. Ryokan usually charge by the person, not the room, which keeps the price down for the solo. The only hitch is that some ryokan owners baulk at renting a room to a single traveller, when they might be able to rent it to two people instead, especially during busy times.

Many restaurants have small tables or counters that are perfect perches for solo travellers. *Izakaya* (pub-eateries) are also generally welcoming to solo travellers, and you probably won't have to wait long before you're offered a drink and roped into a conversation, particularly if you sit at the counter. Finally, the '*gaijin* bars' in the larger cities are generally friendly, convivial places; if you're after a travel partner or just an English-speaking conversation partner, you'll find these are good places to start.

Telephone

Japanese telephone codes consist of an area code plus the number. You do not dial the area code when making a call in that area. When dialling Japan from abroad, dial the country code, 81, followed by the area code (drop the '0') and the number. The most common toll-free prefixes are 0120, 0070, 0077, 0088 and 0800. Directory-assistance numbers:

Local directory assistance 104 (¥60 to ¥150 per call)

Local directory assistance in English 0120-36-4463 (from 9am to 5pm Monday to Friday)

International directory assistance 0057

International Calls

The best way to make an international phone call from Japan is to use a prepaid international phone card.

Paid overseas calls can be made from grey international ISDN phones. These are usually found in phone booths marked 'International & Domestic Card/Coin Phone'. Unfortunately, these are very rare; try looking in the lobbies of top-end hotels and at airports. Some new green phones found in phone booths also allow international calls. Calls are charged by the unit, each of which is six seconds, so if you don't have much to say you could phone home for just ¥100. Reverse-charge (collect) overseas calls can be made from any pay phone.

You can save money by dialling late at night. Economy rates are available from 11pm to 8am. Note that it is also cheaper to make domestic calls by dialling outside the standard hours.

Useful international numbers:

International operator-assisted calls 0051 (KDDI; operators speak English)

Direct-dial international numbers KDDI 001 010, SoftBank Telecom 0041 010, NTT 0033 010

There's very little difference in the direct-dial rates. Dial one of the above numbers, then the international country code, the local code and the number.

PREPAID INTERNATIONAL PHONE CARDS

Because of the lack of pay phones from which you can make international phone calls in Japan, the easiest way to make a call is to buy a prepaid international phone card. Most convenience stores carry at least one of the following, which can be used with any regular pay phone:

➡ KDDI Superworld Card

➡ NTT Communications World Card

➡ SoftBank Telecom Comica Card

Local Calls

The Japanese public-telephone system is extremely reliable and efficient. Unfortunately, the number of pay phones is decreasing fast as more and more Japanese buy mobile phones. Local calls from pay phones cost ¥10 per minute; unused ¥10 coins are returned after the call is completed but no change is given on ¥100 coins.

In general it's much easier to buy a telephone card (terefon kādo) when you arrive rather than worry about always having coins on hand. Phone cards are sold in ¥500 and ¥1000 denominations (the latter earns you an extra ¥50 in calls) and can be used in most green or grey pay phones. Cards are available from vending machines (some of which can be found in public phone booths) and convenience stores. They come in myriad designs and are also a collectable item.

Mobile Phones

Japan's mobile networks use 3G (third generation) mobile-phone technology on a variety of frequencies. Thus, non-3G mobile phones cannot be used in Japan, which means that most foreign mobile phones will not work there. Furthermore, SIM cards are not commonly available. Thus, for most foreigners who want to use a mobile phone, the only solution is to rent one.

Several telecommunications companies specialise in short-term rentals including the following:

Rentafone Japan (☎090-9621-7318, toll free within Japan 0120-746-487; www.rentafonejapan.com) Rentals start at ¥3900 per week. Domestic calls cost ¥35 per minute.

Time

All of Japan is in the same time zone: nine hours ahead of Greenwich Mean Time (GMT). Sydney and Wellington are ahead of Japan (by one and three hours respectively), and most of the world's other big cities are behind: (New York by 14 hours, Los Angeles by 17 and London by nine). Japan does not have daylight savings time (also known as summer time).

Toilets

You will come across both Western-style toilets and Asian squat toilets. When you are compelled to squat, the correct position is facing the hood, away from the door. Take special care to ensure the contents of your pockets don't spill out! Toilet paper isn't always provided, so it is a good idea to carry tissues with you. You may be given small packets of tissues on the street, which is a common form of advertising.

In many bathrooms, separate toilet slippers are sometimes provided – usually located just inside the toilet door. These are for use in the toilet only, so remember to change out of them when you leave.

It's quite common to see men urinating in public – the unspoken rule is that it's acceptable at night time if you happen to be drunk. Public toilets are free. The katakana for 'toilet' is トイレ, and the kanji is お手洗い. You'll often also see these kanji signs:

➡ Female 女

➡ Male 男

Tourist Information

You'll find tourist information offices (kankō annai-sho; 観光案内所) in most cities and towns and even in some small villages. They are almost always inside or in front of the main train station. Staff may speak some English, but don't count on it. English-language materials are usually available. Naturally, places that get a lot of foreign visitors are more likely to have English-speaking staff and English-language materials. Nonetheless, with a little patience and a smile you will be able to get the information you need from even the smallest local tourist information office.

The **Japan National Tourism Organization** (JNTO; www.jnto.go.jp) is Japan's main English-language information service for foreign travellers. JNTO produces a great deal of useful literature, which is available from its overseas offices as well as its Tourist Information Center (p140) in Tokyo. Most of its publications are available in English and, in some cases, other European and Asian languages. The organisation's website is a very useful tool when planning your journey to Japan.

JNTO has overseas offices in Australia, Canada, France, Germany, the UK and the USA (see the JNTO website for exact locations and contact details).

Travellers with Disabilities

Japan gets mixed marks in terms of ease of travel for those with disabilities. On the plus side, many new buildings have access ramps, traffic lights have speakers playing melodies when it is safe to cross, train platforms have raised dots and lines to provide guidance for the visually impaired, and some ticket machines in Tokyo have Braille. Some attractions also offer free entry for disabled persons and one companion. However, many of Japan's cities are still rather difficult for disabled persons to negotiate, often due to a lack of normal sidewalks on narrow streets.

Train cars on most lines have areas set aside for people in wheelchairs. Those with other physical disabilities can use the seats near the train exits, called yūsen-zaseki. You will also find these seats near the front of buses; usually they're a different colour from the regular seats.

Useful organisations and services for travellers with disabilities:

Japanese Red Cross Language Service Volunteers (Map p70;☑3438-1311; http://accessible.jp.org/tokyo/en/index.html; 1-1-3 Shiba Daimon, Minato-ku, Tokyo) Has loads of useful information, and also produces an excellent guide, *Accessible Tokyo,* which can be requested by email, mail or telephone – or found on its website.

Accessible Japan (www.tesco-premium.co.jp/aj/index.htm) Details the accessibility of hundreds of sites in Tokyo, including hotels, sights and department stores, as well as general information about getting around Japan.

Eagle Bus Company (☑049-227-7611; www.new-wing.co.jp/english/english.html) Has lift-equipped buses and some English-speaking drivers who are also licensed caregivers. Offers tours of Tokyo and around for travellers with disabilities. The number of English-speaking driver-caregivers is limited, so reserve well in advance. Group bookings are possible. Also offers English-language tours of Kawagoe, a small town outside Tokyo, which is sometimes known as little Edo.

Visas

Generally, visitors who are not planning to engage in income-producing activities while in Japan are exempt from obtaining visas and will be issued a 90-day *tanki-taizai* (temporary-visitor) visa on arrival. Nationals of Australia, Canada, France, Ireland, Italy, the Netherlands, New Zealand, Spain, the UK and the USA are eligible for this visa.

Stays of up to six months are permitted for citizens of Austria, Germany, Ireland, Mexico, Switzerland and the UK. Citizens of these countries will almost always be given a 90-day temporary visitor visa upon arrival, which can usually be extended for another 90 days at immigration bureaux inside Japan.

Japanese law requires that visitors entering on a temporary-visitor visa possess an ongoing air or sea ticket or evidence thereof. In practice, few travellers are asked to produce such documents, but it pays to be on the safe side.

For additional information on visas and regulations, contact your nearest Japanese embassy or consulate, or visit the website of the **Ministry of Foreign Affairs of Japan** (www.mofa.go.jp). Here you can find out about the different types of visas available, read about working-holiday visas and find details on the Japan Exchange & Teaching (JET) program, which sponsors native English speakers to teach in the Japanese public school system.

On entering Japan, all short-term foreign visitors are photographed and fingerprinted.

Resident Card

Anyone who will stay in Japan longer than 90 days, which usually means those entering on various mid- to long-term visas rather than tourist visas, will be issued 'resident cards' ('在留カー'). These cards replace the old *gaikokujin torokusho* cards (commonly known as '*gaijin* cards'). If you're entering Japan on a visa that allows you to stay for longer than 90 days, you'll be issued one of these at the airport.

You must carry your card at all times as the police can stop you and ask to see it. If you don't have it, you may be taken back to the police station and will have to wait there until someone fetches the card for you.

Visa Extensions

With the exception of those nationals whose countries have reciprocal visa exemptions and can stay for six months, the limit for most nationalities is 90 days or three months. To extend a temporary-visitor visa beyond the standard 90 days or three months, apply at the

nearest immigration office. The **Japanese Immigration Bureau** (www.immi-moj.go.jp/english/soshiki/index.html) site lists the offices in Japan. You must provide two copies of an Application for Extension of Stay (available at the immigration office), a letter stating the reasons for the extension, supporting documentation and your passport. There is a processing fee of ¥4000.

Many long-term visitors to Japan get around the extension problem by briefly leaving the country, usually going to South Korea. Be warned, though, that immigration officials are wise to this practice and many 'tourist visa returnees' are turned back at the entry point.

Work Visas

Unless you are on a cultural visa and have been granted permission to work, or hold a working-holiday visa, you are not permitted to work without a proper work visa. If you have the proper paperwork and an employee willing to sponsor you, the process is straightforward, although it can be time consuming.

Once you find an employer who is willing to sponsor you, it is necessary to obtain a Certificate of Eligibility from the nearest immigration office. The same office can then issue you your work visa, which is valid for one or three years. The whole procedure usually takes two to three months.

Working-Holiday Visas

Citizens of Australia, Canada, Denmark, France, Germany, Hong Kong, Ireland, New Zealand, the Republic of Korea and the UK who are aged between 18 and 25 (the limit can be pushed up to 30 in some cases) can apply for a working-holiday visa. The program is also open to residents of Hong Kong and Taiwan.

This visa allows a six-month stay and two six-month extensions. It is designed to enable young people to travel extensively during their stay; although employment is supposed to be part-time or temporary, in practice many people work full time.

A working-holiday visa is much easier to obtain than a work visa and is popular with Japanese employers. Single applicants must have the equivalent of US$2000 of funds, a married couple must have US$3000 and all applicants must have an onward ticket from Japan. For details, enquire at the nearest Japanese embassy or consulate.

Volunteering

Japan doesn't have as many volunteer opportunities as some other Asian countries. However, there are positions out there for those who look. One of the most popular options is provided by **Willing Workers on Organic Farms Japan** (WWOOF Japan; www.wwoofjapan.com/main/index.php?lang=en; 6-7 3-chōme Honchō 2jō, Higashi-ku, Sapporo, Hokkaidō). This organisation places volunteers on organic farms around the country and provides participants with a good look at Japanese rural life and the running of an organic farm. It's also a great chance to improve your Japanese-language skills.

Alternatively, you can look for volunteer opportunities once you arrive. There are occasional ads for volunteer positions in the various English-language journals in Japan. Word of mouth is also a good way to search for jobs. Hikers, for example, are sometimes offered short-term positions in Japan's mountain huts.

Women Travellers

Japan is a relatively safe country for women travellers, though perhaps not quite as safe as some might think. Crimes against women are generally believed to be widely underreported, especially by Japanese women. Foreign women are occasionally sub-

jected to some forms of verbal harassment or prying questions. Physical attacks are very rare, but have occurred.

The best advice is to avoid being lulled into a false sense of security by Japan's image as one of the world's safest countries and to take the normal precautions you would in your home country. If a neighbourhood or establishment looks unsafe, then treat it that way. As long as you use your common sense, you will most likely find that Japan is a pleasant and rewarding place to travel as a woman.

Several train companies have recently introduced women-only cars to protect female passengers from *chikan* (men who feel up women and girls on packed trains). These cars are usually available during rush-hour periods on weekdays on busy urban lines. There are signs (usually in pink) on the platform indicating where you can board these cars, and the cars themselves are usually labelled in both Japanese and English (again, these are often marked in pink).

If you have a problem and you find the local police unhelpful, you can call the **Japan Helpline** (0120-46-1997), a nationwide emergency number that operates 24 hours a day, seven days a week.

Finally, an excellent resource available for any woman setting up in Japan is Caroline Pover's book *Being A Broad in Japan*, which can be found in bookstores and or ordered from www.being-a-broad.com.

Work

Japan is an interesting place to live and work for a year or two and you'll find expats in all the major cities doing just that. Teaching English is still the most common job for Westerners, but bartending, hostessing, modelling and various writing-editorial jobs are also possible.

Make sure to do your homework and present yourself properly. You'll definitely need a sharp outfit for interviews, a stack of *meishi* (business cards) and the right attitude. If you don't have a university degree, you won't be eligible for most jobs that qualify you for a work visa. Any qualification, such as an English-teaching certificate, will be a huge boost.

Outside of the entertainment, construction and English-teaching industries, you can't expect a good job unless you speak good Japanese (any more than someone could expect a job in your home country without speaking its language).

Bartending

Bartending doesn't qualify you for a work visa; most foreign bartenders in Japan are working illegally or are on another visa type. Some bars in big Japanese cities hire foreign bartenders; most are strict about visas. The best places to look are '*gaijin* bars', although a few Japanese-oriented places also employ foreign bartenders for 'ambience'. The pay is barely enough to survive on: usually about ¥1000 per hour. The great plus of working as a bartender (other than free drinks) is the chance to practise speaking Japanese.

English Teaching

Teaching English has always been the most popular job for native English speakers in Japan. A university degree is essential as you can't get a work visa without one (be sure to bring the actual degree with you). Teaching qualifications and some teaching experience will help when job hunting. Keep in mind that Japan is in the middle of a prolonged economic slump and the job market and wages are decreasing each year.

Consider lining up a job before you arrive. Some big schools now have recruitment programs in the USA and the UK. One downside to the big 'factory schools' that recruit overseas is that working conditions are often pretty dire compared with smaller schools that recruit internally.

Australians, New Zealanders, Canadians and British citizens, who can take advantage of the Japanese working-holiday visa, are in a slightly better position. Schools are happier about taking on unqualified teachers if they don't have to bother with sponsoring a teacher for a work visa.

There's a definite hierarchy among English teachers and teaching positions. At the bottom are the big chain *eikaiwa* (private English-language schools), followed by small local *eikaiwa*, in-house company language schools and private lessons. University and international-school positions are the most sought after. As you would expect, newcomers start at the lower rungs and work their way up the ladder.

ELT News (www.eltnews.com) is an excellent website with lots of information and want ads for English teachers in Japan.

PUBLIC SCHOOLS

The program run by **Japan Exchange & Teaching** (JET; www.jetprogramme.org) provides teaching-assistant positions for foreign teachers. It offers yearly contracts and must be organised in your home country. The program gets very good reports from many of its teachers.

Teachers employed by the JET program are known as Assistant Language Teachers (ALTs). Although you will have to apply in your home country in order to work as an ALT with JET, it's worth bearing in mind that many local governments in Japan are also employing ALTs for their schools. Such work can sometimes be arranged within Japan.

Visit the JET website or contact the nearest Japanese embassy or consulate for more details.

INTERNATIONAL SCHOOLS

Major cities with large foreign populations, such as Tokyo and Yokohama, have a number of international schools for the children of foreign residents. Work is available for qualified, Western-trained teachers in all disciplines; the schools will organise your visa.

PRIVATE SCHOOLS

Private language schools (*eikaiwa*) are the largest employers of foreign teachers and the best bet for job-hunting newcomers. The classifieds section of Monday's *Japan Times* is the best place to look. Some larger schools rely on direct enquiries from would-be teachers.

Tokyo is the easiest place to find teaching jobs; schools across Japan advertise or recruit in the capital. Heading straight to another of Japan's major population centres (say Osaka, Fukuoka, Hiroshima or Sapporo), where there are smaller numbers of competing foreigners, is also a good bet, but, as noted in this section, the hiring situation is tight these days and you cannot count on just showing up and finding work.

Proofreading, Editing & Writing

There is demand for skilled editors, copywriters, proofreaders and translators (Japanese to English and, less commonly, vice versa). And with the advent of the internet, you don't even have to be based in Japan to do this work. Unfortunately, as with many things in Japan, introductions and connections play a huge role, and it's difficult to simply show up in Tokyo or plaster your resume online and wind up with a good job.

You'll need to be persistent and do some networking to make much in this field. Experience, advanced degrees and salesmanship will all come in handy. And even if you don't intend to work as a translator, some Japanese-language ability will be a huge plus, if only for communicating with potential employers and clients. If you think you've got what it takes, check the Monday edition of the *Japan Times* for openings.

For more information about proofreading and editing in Japan, visit the website for the **Society of Writers, Editors & Translators** (SWET; www.swet.jp). The website has a job-listings section that is useful for those seeking work in this field.

Ski Areas

Seasonal work is available at ski areas, which is a popular option for Australians and New Zealanders who want to combine a trip to Japan with some skiing and the chance to earn money. A working-holiday visa makes this easier, although sometimes people are offered jobs without. The jobs are typical ski-town jobs – ski-lift attendants, hotel workers, bartenders and, for those with the right skills (language and skiing), ski instructors. You won't earn much more than ¥1000 per hour unless you're an instructor, but you'll get lodging and lift tickets. All told, it's a fun way to spend a few months in Japan.

Transport

GETTING THERE & AWAY

Entering the Country

While most travellers fly to Japan via Tokyo, there are several other ways of getting into and out of the country. For a start, there are many other airports, which can make better entry points than Tokyo's somewhat inconvenient Narita International Airport. It's also possible to arrive by sea from South Korea, China and Russia.

Flights, tours and rail tickets can be booked online at lonelyplanet.com/bookings.

Passport

A passport is essential. If your passport is within a few months of expiry, get a new one now. For information on visas, see p837.

Air

There are flights to Japan from all over the world, usually to Tokyo, but also to a number of other airports. Although Tokyo may seem the obvious arrival and departure point, for many visitors this may not be the case. For example, if you plan to explore western Japan or the Kansai region, it might be more convenient to fly into Kansai International Airport near Osaka.

Airports & Airlines

There are international airports situated on the main island of Honshū (Nagoya, Niigata, Osaka/Kansai, Haneda and Tokyo Narita), as well as on Kyūshū (Fukuoka, Kagoshima, Kumamoto and Nagasaki), Okinawa (Naha) and Hokkaidō (Sapporo).

The majority of international flights to/from Tokyo use **Narita** (NRT; www.narita-airport.jp/en/), about an hour from Tokyo by express train (¥2940); it's cheaper and more convenient to fly via Haneda Airport if you can.

Some international flights now go via **Tokyo International Airport** (HND; www.tokyo-airport-bldg.co.jp/en/), better known as Haneda Airport, about 30 minutes from Tokyo by monorail and thus more convenient than Narita. There's a new international terminal and runway; new international flights are being added all the time.

All of Osaka's international flights go via **Kansai International Airport** (KIX; www.kansai-airport.or.jp/en/index.asp), which serves the key Kansai cities of Kyoto, Osaka, Nara and Kōbe.

Near Nagoya, **Central Japan International Airport** (Centrair NGO; www.centrair.jp/en) has international connections with 12 countries.

Fukuoka, at the northern end of Kyūshū, is the main arrival point for western Japan. **Fukuoka International**

CLIMATE CHANGE & TRAVEL

Every form of transport that relies on carbon-based fuel generates CO_2, the main cause of human-induced climate change. Modern travel is dependent on aeroplanes, which might use less fuel per kilometre per person than most cars but travel much greater distances. The altitude at which aircraft emit gases (including CO_2) and particles also contributes to their climate change impact. Many websites offer 'carbon calculators' that allow people to estimate the carbon emissions generated by their journey and for, those who wish to do so, to offset the impact of the greenhouse gases emitted with contributions to portfolios of climate-friendly initiatives throughout the world. Lonely Planet offsets the carbon footprint of all staff and author travel.

BAGGAGE FORWARDING

If you have too much luggage to carry comfortably or just can't be bothered, you can do what many Japanese travellers do: send it to your next stop by *takkyūbin* (express shipping companies). Prices are surprisingly reasonable and overnight service is the norm. Perhaps the most convenient service is Yamato Takkyūbin, which operates from most convenience stores. Simply pack your luggage and take it to the nearest convenience store; staff will help with the paperwork and arrange for pick-up. Note that you'll need the full address of your next destination in Japanese, along with the phone number of the place. Alternatively, ask the owner of your accommodation to come and pick it up (this is usually possible but might cost extra).

Airport (FUK; www.fuk-ab. co.jp/english/frame_index.html), conveniently located near the city, has connections with nine countries, mostly in Asia.

On Kyūshū, **Kagoshima Airport** (KOJ; www.koj-ab. co.jp/english/index.html) has flights to/from Shanghai, Seoul and Taipei.

Located on Okinawa-hontō (the main island of Okinawa), **Naha Airport** (OKA; www.naha-airport.co.jp) has flights to/from Beijing, Hong Kong, Kaohsiung, Seoul, Shanghai and Taipei.

Central Honshū's **Niigata Airport** (KIJ; www.niigata-airport.gr.jp/?lang=en) has flights to/from Guam, Harbin, Irkutsk, Khabarovsk, Pyongyang, Seoul, Shanghai, Taipei and Yakutsk.

Kuŷshū's **Kumamoto Airport** (KMJ; www.kmj-ab.co.jp/eng/index.html) has flights to/from Seoul and Taipei.

Nagasaki Airport (NGS; www.nabic.co.jp/english) has flights to/from Shanghai and Seoul.

On Hokkaidō, **New Chitose Airport** (CTS; www.new-chitose-airport.co.jp/en/) has connections with 11 countries, mostly in Asia.

Tickets

Generally, high season for travel between Japan and Western countries is in late December (around Christmas and the New Year period) and late April to early May (around Japan's Golden Week holiday), as well as July and August. If you must fly during these periods, book well in advance.

Land

Trans-Siberian Railway

The main option for the Trans-Siberian Railway is via China, ie on Chinese Trans-Mongolia or Russian Trans-Manchuria routes, followed by ferry to/from Japan via Tientsin, Qingdao and Shanghai.

Sea

China

Japan China International Ferry Company (☑in China 021-6325-7642, in Japan 06-6536-6541; www.shinganjin.com/index_e.php) Shanghai–Osaka/Kōbe, 2nd class US$225, 48 hours.

Orient Ferry Ltd (☑in China 0532-8387-1160, in Japan 083-232-6615; www.orientferry.co.jp) Qingdao–Shimonoseki, US$170, 28 hours.

Russia

Heartland Ferry (☑in Japan 011-233-8010, in Russia 7-4242-72-6889; www.heartlandferry.

jp/english/index.html) Karsakov (Sakhalin Island, Russia)–Wakkanai (Hokkaidō), one-way/return US$277/444, 7½ hours, mid-May to late October.

South Korea

South Korea is the closest country to Japan and there are several ferry connections between them.

Beetle (☑in Japan 092-281-2315, in Korea 051-441-8200; www.jrbeetle.co.jp/internet/english/index.html) Busan–Fukuoka, US$145, three hours.

Camellia Line (☑in Japan 092-262-2323, in Korea 051-466-7799; www.camellia-line.co.jp) Busan–Fukuoka, from US$95, six hours from Fukuoka to Busan, six to 10 hours from Busan to Fukuoka.

Kampu Ferry (☑in Japan 083-224-3000, in Korea 82-2-730-2137, in Korea 463-3165(-8); www.kampuferry.co.jp) Busan–Shimonoseki, from US$100, 12 hours.

GETTING AROUND

Japan has one of the best public-transport systems in the world, which makes getting around the country an absolute breeze for travellers.

Air

Air services in Japan are extensive, reliable and safe. In many cases, flying is much faster than even *shinkansen* (bullet trains) and not that much more expensive. Flying is also an efficient way to travel from the main islands to the many small islands, particularly the Southwest Islands (the southern islands of Kagoshima and Okinawa Prefectures).

In most of Japan's major cities there are travel agencies where English is spoken. For an idea of the latest prices in Tokyo check the travel ads in the various local English-language publications, and in Kansai check *Kansai Scene*.

Airlines in Japan

Japan Airlines (JAL; ☎0570-025-121, 03-5460-0522; www.jal.co.jp/en) A major international carrier with an extensive domestic network.

All Nippon Airways (ANA; ☎0570-029-709, in Osaka 06-7637-6679, in Tokyo 03-6741-1120; www.ana.co.jp/eng) The other major Japanese international and domestic carrier.

Japan Trans Ocean Air (JTA; ☎0570-025-071, 03-5460-0522; www.jal.co.jp/jta) A smaller domestic carrier that mostly services routes in the Southwest Islands.

Shinchūō Kōkū (☎0422-31-4191; www.central-air.co.jp) Has light-plane flights between Chōfu Airport, outside Tokyo, and the islands of the Izu Archipelago.

SAT Airlines (UTSエアサービス株式会社; ☎011-222-1433; http://www.uts-air.com/) Has flights between Sakhalin (Russia) and Hokkaidō.

Tickets & Discounts

For domestic flights, return fares are usually around 10% cheaper than two one-way tickets. You can also get advance-purchase reductions: both ANA and JAL offer up to 50% discount on tickets purchased a month or more in advance, with smaller discounts for purchases made one to three weeks in advance. Seniors over 65 also qualify for discounts on most Japanese airlines, but these are sometimes only available if you fly on weekdays.

ANA also offers the Star Alliance Japan Airpass for foreign travellers. Provided you reside outside Japan, purchase your tickets outside Japan and carry a valid international ticket on any airline, you can fly up to five times within 60 days on any ANA domestic route for only ¥10,500 per flight (a huge saving on some routes). Visit www.ana.co.jp/wws/us/e/travelservice/reservations/special/airpass.html for more details.

Bicycle

Japan is a good country for bicycle touring, and several thousand local and foreign cyclists traverse the country every year. Favourite bike-touring areas include Kyūshū, Shikoku, the Japan Alps (if you like steep hills!), the Noto Peninsula and Hokkaidō.

There's no point in fighting your way out of big cities by bicycle. Put your bike on the train or bus and get out to the country before you start pedalling. To take a bicycle on a train you may need to use a bicycle-carrying bag, available from good bicycle shops.

A useful series of maps is *Touring Mapple* (Shōbunsha), which is aimed towards motorcyclists but is also very useful for cyclists.

For more information on cycling in Japan, check out the excellent website of **KAN-cycling** (www.kancycling.com).

Hire

You will find bicycle-rental shops outside the train or bus stations in most of Japan's popular tourist areas, as well as near the ferry piers on many of the country's smaller islands. Typical charges are around ¥200/1000 per hour/day. Kyoto, for example, is ideally suited to bicycle exploration and there are plenty of cheap hire shops to choose from.

Note that the bicycles for rent are not usually performance vehicles. More commonly they're what the Japanese call *mama chari* (literally 'mama's bicycles'): one- or three-speed shopping bikes that are murder on hills of any size. They're also usually too small for anyone more than 180cm in height.

Many youth hostels also have bicycles to rent.

Purchase

In Japan, prices for used bicycles range from a few thousand yen for an old shopping bike to several tens of thousands of yen for good mountain and road bikes. New bikes range from about ¥10,000 for a shopping bike to ¥100,000 for a flash mountain or road bike.

Touring cycles are available in Japan but prices tend to be significantly higher than you'd pay back home. If you're tall, you may not find any suitably sized bikes in stock. One solution for tall riders, or anyone who wants to save money, is to buy a used bike – in Tokyo, check the English-language publications; in Kyoto, visit the Kyoto International Community House and check the message board.

BUDGET AIRLINES IN JAPAN

Japan has opened up its skies to low-cost carriers and the result is a proliferation of budget airlines flying to various parts of the archipelago. This has brought previous expensive and distant destinations like Hokkaidō and Okinawa within the reach of even budget travellers. Keep in mind that budget airlines often come and go, so we cannot guarantee that all of these will be flying when you're in country, but we definitely recommend checking their fares online when making travel plans – you might save a bundle.

Skymark Airlines (www.skymark.co.jp)

Peach (www.flypeach.com)

Jetstar (www.jetstar.com)

Air Asia Japan (www.airasia.com)

FERRY FARES & DURATIONS

ROUTE	FARE (¥)	DURATION (HR)
Hokkaidō–Honshū		
Otaru–Maizuru	9300	21½
Otaru–Niigata	6300	19½
Tomakomai–Hachinohe	4500	8-9
Tomakomai–Ōarai	8500	19
From Tokyo		
Naha (Okinawa)	24,500	47-54
Shinmoji (Kitakyūshū)	15,070	35
Tokushima (Shikoku)	10,050	18-19½
From Osaka/Kōbe		
Beppu (Kyūshū)	10,600	12
Miyazaki (Kyūshū)	11,200	14
Naha (Okinawa)	19,600	38
Shibushi (Kyūshū)	12,700	15
Shinmoji (Kitakyūshū)	6600	12½
Kyūshū–Okinawa		
Kagoshima–Naha	14,600	25

Boat

Japan is an island nation and there are many ferry services between islands and between ports on the same island. Ferries can be an excellent way of getting from one place to another and for seeing parts of Japan you might otherwise miss. Taking a ferry between Osaka (Honshū) and Beppu (Kyūshū), for example, is a good way of getting to Kyūshū and – if you choose the right departure time – seeing some of the Inland Sea on the way.

On overnight ferries, 2nd-class travel means sleeping in tatami-mat rooms where you simply unroll your futon on the floor and hope that your fellow passengers aren't too intent on knocking back the booze all night. In this basic class, fares are usually lower than equivalent land travel, but there are also more-expensive private cabins. Bicycles can be brought along and most ferries also carry cars and motorcycles.

Information on ferry routes, schedules and fares is found in the *JR Jikokuhyō* and on information sheets from the **Japan National Tourism Organization** (JNTO; www.jnto.go.jp). Some ferry services and their lowest one-way fares appear in the table.

If you plan to explore Okinawa and the Southwest Islands by ferry, be sure to check out the 'all-you-can-sail' ticket offered by the A-Line ferry company. For more information see p724.

Bus

Japan has a comprehensive network of long-distance buses. These 'highway buses' are nowhere near as fast as the *shinkansen* but the fares are comparable with those of normal *futsū* (local) trains. For example, the trip between Tokyo and Kyoto takes just over 2½ hours by *shinkansen* and about eight hours by bus. Of course, there are many places in Japan where trains do not run and bus travel is the only public-transport option.

Bookings can be made through any travel agency in Japan or at the *midori-no-madoguchi* (green counters – look for counters with a green band across the glass) in large Japan Rail (JR) stations. The Japan Rail Pass is valid on some highway buses, but in most cases the *shinkansen* would be preferable (it's much faster and more comfortable).

Costs

Some typical long-distance fares and travel times out of Tokyo include the following (note that the cheapest fares on each route are shown).

Night Services

Night buses are a good option for those on a tight budget without a Japan Rail Pass. They are relatively cheap, spacious (allowing

BUS FARES & DURATIONS

DESTINATION	ONE-WAY (¥)	DURATION (HR)
Aomori	8500	9½
Hakata	8000	14½
Hiroshima	11,600	11½
Kōbe	7200	10
Kyoto	6700	8
Nagano	4000	4
Nagoya	5000	6
Nara	8400	9½
Osaka	7200	9

BARGAIN BUSES

Japan Railways (JR) operates the largest network of highway buses in Japan, and we quote its prices for most long-distance bus routes in this guide. However, several budget bus companies have recently sprung up in Japan and these are gaining popularity with backpackers. One such company is **Willer Express** (☏ from outside Japan 050-5805-0383; http://willerexpress.com/en/), which offers fares significantly cheaper than those of JR. It also offers three-/four-/five-day bus passes that are great value. Booking is possible in English online. Check the website for the latest details and pickup/drop-off points.

Another good deal is offered by a group of bus companies on Kyūshū, which have banded together to offer the **SUNQ Pass** (www.sunqpass.jp/english; 3/5 day ¥10,000/14,000, northern Kyūshū only ¥8000), which offers unlimited travel. Kyūshū buses reach many places trains don't.

room to stretch out and get some sleep) and they also save on a night's accommodation. They typically leave at around 10pm or 11pm and arrive the following day at around 6am or 7am.

Car & Motorcycle

Driving in Japan is quite feasible, even for just the mildly adventurous. The major roads are signposted in English; road rules are generally adhered to and driving is safer than in a lot of other Asian countries; and petrol, while expensive, is not prohibitively so. Indeed, in some areas of the country it can prove much more convenient than other forms of travel and, between a group of people, it can also prove quite economical.

In some parts of Japan (most notably Hokkaidō, the Noto Peninsula, some parts of Kyūshū and the Southwest Islands), driving is really the only efficient way to get around unless you have a good touring bicycle or fancy long waits for buses each time you need to make a move.

Automobile Associations

If you're a member of an automobile association in your home country, you're eligible for reciprocal rights with the **Japan Automobile Federation** (JAF; ☏ 0570-00-2811, 03-6833-9000; www.jaf.or.jp/e/index.htm; 2-2-17 Shiba, Minato-ku). Its office is near Onarimon Station on the Tōei Mita line.

Driving Licence

Travellers from most nations are able to drive in Japan with an International Driving Permit backed up by their own regular licence. The International Driving Permit is issued by your national automobile association and costs around US$5 in most countries. Make sure it's endorsed for cars and motorcycles if you're licensed for both.

Travellers from Switzerland, France and Germany (and others whose countries are not signatories to the Geneva Convention of 1949 concerning international driving licences) are not allowed to drive in Japan on a regular International Driving Permit. Rather, travellers from these countries must have their own licence backed by an authorised translation of the same licence. These translations can be made by their embassy or consulate in Japan or by the JAF. If you are unsure which category your country falls into, contact the nearest JNTO office for more information.

Foreign licences and International Driving Permits are only valid in Japan for six months. If you are staying longer, you will have to get a Japanese licence from the local department of motor vehicles.

Expressways

The expressway system is fast, efficient and growing all the time. Tolls cost about ¥24.6 per kilometre. Tokyo to Kyoto, for example, will cost ¥10,050 in tolls.

There are good rest stops and service centres at regular intervals. A prepaid highway card, available from tollbooths or at the service areas, saves you having to carry so much cash and gives you a 4% to 8% discount in the larger card denominations. You can also pay tolls with most major credit cards. Exits are usually fairly well signposted in English, but make sure you know the name of your exit as it may not necessarily be the same as the city you're heading towards.

Fuel

You'll find *gasoreen sutando* (petrol stations) in almost every town and in service stations along the expressways. The cost of petrol per litre ranges from ¥141 to ¥144 for regular and ¥152 to ¥155 for high octane.

Hire

You'll usually find car-rental agencies clustered around train stations and ferry piers. Typical rates for a small car are ¥5000 to ¥7000 per day, with reductions for rentals of more than one day. On top of the rental charge, there's about a ¥1000-per-day insurance cost.

Communication can sometimes be a major problem when hiring a car. Some of the offices will have a rent-a-car phrasebook, with questions you might need to ask in English. Otherwise, just speak as slowly as possible and hope for the best. A good way to open the conversation is to say 'kokusai menkyō wo motteimasu' (I have an international licence).

Toyota Rent-a-Car (☑in Japan 0800-7000-111, outside Japan 81-3-5954-8020; http://rent.toyota.co.jp/en/index.html) has the largest rental network and has a very informative website which allows reservations from overseas.

Parking

In most big cities, free curbside parking spots are almost nonexistent, while in rural areas you'll be able to park your car just about anywhere you want. In the cities you'll find that you usually have to pay ¥200 per hour for metered street parking, or anywhere from ¥300 to ¥600 per hour for a spot in a multistorey car park. You'll find car parks around most department stores and near some train stations. Fortunately, most hotels have free parking for guests, as do some restaurants and almost all department stores.

Road Rules

Driving is on the left. There are no unusual rules or interpretations of them and most signposts follow international conventions. JAF has a *Rules of the Road* book available in English and five other languages for ¥1000.

Maps & Navigation

If you can find a used copy of the *Road Atlas Japan* (Shōbunsha), grab it. It's all in English (romaji) with enough names in kanji to make navigation possible even off the major roads. Unfortunately, it's out of print and hard to find these days. If you're really intent on making your way through the back blocks, a Japanese map will prove useful even if your knowledge of kanji is nil. The best Japanese road atlases by far are the *Super Mapple* series (Shōbunsha), which are available in bookshops and some convenience stores.

There is a reasonable amount of signposting in romaji, so getting around isn't all that difficult, especially in developed areas. If you are attempting tricky navigation, use your maps imaginatively. For example, watch out for the railway line, the rivers, the landmarks. They're all useful ways of locating yourself when you can't read the signs. A compass will also come in handy when navigating.

These days, many rental cars come equipped with satellite navigation systems, making navigation a snap, provided you can figure out how to work the system; ask the person at the rental agency to explain it and be sure to take notes or, if you're just going from point A to point B, have them set it for you. With most of these systems, you can input the phone number of your destination, which is easy, or its address, which is just about impossible if you don't read Japanese. Even without programming in your destination, with the device on the default 'genzai-chi' (present location) setting, you will find it very useful.

Motorcycles

For citizens of most countries, your overseas driving licence and an International Driving Permit are all you need to ride a motorcycle

---

DRIVING IN JAPAN

Unless you plan on driving in central Tokyo or Osaka or forget that the Japanese drive on the left, you should have no major problems driving in Japan. In fact, driving here is remarkably sane compared to many countries (perhaps because it's so difficult to pass the test). Still, there are a few peculiarities that are worth keeping in mind.

Turn signals Some Japanese drivers have the annoying habit of turning on their turn signals only after they stop at a light or enter an intersection. This seems to defeat the purpose of a signal (ie to tell people *in advance* what you plan to do). This doesn't cause too many problems, but be ready for it.

Petrol stations While self-serve petrol stations are becoming popular, full-service stations are still the rule. And in Japan, when they say 'full service', they really mean it. They'll empty your ashtray, take any garbage you have, wipe your windshield and then wave you back into traffic. And if you're wondering how to say 'fill 'er up' in Japanese, it's 'mantan' (full tank).

Chains If you drive in mountain areas in winter, you might be required to put chains on your car. If you rent a car in these areas, it will probably come equipped. Petrol stations in mountain areas will usually put the chains on for a charge (¥1000 to ¥2000). There may be police stops in these areas to make sure that cars have chains.

in Japan. Crash helmets are compulsory. Touring equipment – panniers, carrier racks, straps and the like – is readily available from dealers.

Drivers in Japan tend to be relatively sane and safe, making Japan a good country for motorcycle touring.

HIRE & PURCHASE

Hiring a motorcycle for long-distance touring is not as easy as hiring a car, although small scooters are available in many places for local sightseeing.

Small motorcycles (those below 125cc) are banned from expressways and are generally not suitable for long-distance touring, but people have ridden from one end of Japan to the other on little 50cc scooters (taking the back roads, of course). An advantage of these bikes is that you can ride them with just a regular driving licence, so you won't need to get a motorcycle licence.

The best place to look for motorcycles in Japan is the Korin-chō motorcycle neighbourhood in Tokyo's Ueno district. There are more than 20 motorcycle shops in the area and some employ foreign salespeople who speak both Japanese and English. For used bikes in Kansai check *Kansai Flea Market* or the message board in the Kyoto International Community House.

Hitching

Hitching is never entirely safe in any country, and we don't recommend it. Travellers who decide to hitch should understand that they are taking a small but potentially serious risk. In particular, Japan is a dangerous place for women hitchhiking on their own; there have been cases of solitary female hitchers being attacked, molested and raped. People who do choose to hitch will be safer if they travel in pairs and let someone know where they are planning to go.

Provided you understand the risks and take appropriate precautions, Japan is known as a good country for hitchhiking. Many hitchhikers have tales of extraordinary kindness from motorists who have picked them up.

The rules for hitchhiking are similar to those anywhere else in the world. Dress neatly and look for a good place to hitch – expressway on-ramps and expressway service areas are probably your best bets.

Truck drivers are particularly good for long-distance travel as they often head out on the expressways at night. If a driver is exiting before your intended destination, try to get dropped off at one of the expressway service areas. The *Service Area Parking Area* (SAPA) guide maps are excellent for hitchhikers. They're available free from expressway service areas and show full details of each interchange (IC) and rest stop. These are important orientation points if you have a limited knowledge of Japanese.

For more on hitching in Japan, pick up a copy of the excellent *Hitchhiker's Guide to Japan* by Will Ferguson.

Local Transport

All the major cities offer a wide variety of public transport. In many cities you can get day passes for unlimited travel on bus, tram or subway systems. Such passes are usually called an *ichi-nichi-jōsha-ken*. If you're staying for an extended period in one city, commuter passes are available for regular travel.

Bus

Almost every Japanese city has an extensive bus service, but it's usually the most difficult public-transport system for foreign travellers to use. Destinations and stops are often written only in Japanese.

Fares are usually paid when you get off. In Tokyo and some other cities, there's a flat fare regardless of distance. In the other cities, you take a ticket (known as a *seiri-ken*) as you board that indicates the zone number at your starting point. When you get off, an electric sign at the front of the bus indicates the fare charged at that point for each starting zone number. You simply pay the driver the fare that matches your zone number (you put both the *seiri-ken* and the fare into the fare box). There is often a change machine near the front of the bus that can exchange ¥100 and ¥500 coins and ¥1000 notes.

Taxi

Taxis are convenient and can be found even in very small cities and on tiny islands; the train station is the best place to look. Fares are fairly uniform throughout the country. Flagfall (posted on the taxi windows) is ¥600 or ¥710 for the first 2km, after which it's around ¥100 for each 350m (approximately). There's also a time charge if the speed drops below 10km/h. A red light in the lower right corner of the windshield indicates if a taxi is available (it says 'vacant' in Japanese) – this can be difficult to spot during the day. At night, taxis usually have the light on their roof when they're vacant and off when they're occupied, but there are regional variations.

Don't open the door when you get into the taxi; the driver does that with a remote release. The driver will also shut the door when you leave the taxi.

Communication can be a problem with taxi drivers, but perhaps not as much as you fear. If you can't tell the driver where you want to go, it's useful to have the name written down in Japanese. At hotel front desks there will usually be business cards complete with name and location, which can be used for just this purpose.

Tipping is not necessary. A 20% surcharge is added after 11pm or for taxis summoned by radio. There may also be an added charge if you arrange the taxi by phone or reserve the taxi. Finally, taxis can usually take up to four adult passengers (one person can sit in the front). Drivers are sometimes willing to bend the rules for small children.

Train & Subway

Several cities, especially Osaka and Tokyo, have mass-transit rail systems comprising a loop line around the city centre and radial lines into the central stations and the subway system. Subway systems operate in Fukuoka, Kōbe, Kyoto, Nagoya, Osaka, Sapporo, Tokyo and Yokohama. They're usually the fastest and easiest way to get around.

For subways and local trains, you'll most likely have to buy your ticket from a machine. They're pretty easy to understand even if you can't read kanji as there is a diagram explaining the routes; from this you can find out what your fare should be. If you can't work the fare out, a solution is to buy a ticket for the lowest fare. When you finish your trip, go to the fare-adjustment machine (seisan-ki) or the staffed counter before you reach the exit gate and pay the excess. JR train stations and most subway stations have posted above the platform not only their names in kanji and romaji but also the names of the preceding and following stations.

Tram

Many cities have tram lines, in particular, Nagasaki, Kumamoto and Kagoshima on Kyūshū; Kōchi and Matsuyama on Shikoku; and Hakodate on Hokkaidō. These are excellent ways of getting around as they combine many of the advantages of bus travel (good views of the passing parade) with those of subways (it's easy to work out where you're going). Fares work on similar systems to bus travel and there are also unlimited-travel day tickets.

Train

Japanese rail services are among the best in the world: they are fast, frequent, clean and comfortable. The 'national' railway is Japan Railways, commonly known as 'JR', which is actually a number of separate private rail systems providing one linked service.

The JR system covers the country from one end to the other and also provides local services around major cities such as Tokyo and Osaka. JR also operates buses and ferries, and convenient ticketing can combine more than one form of transport.

In addition to JR services, there is a huge network of private railways. Each large city usually has at least one private train line that services that city and the surrounding area, or connects that city to nearby cities. These are often a bit cheaper than equivalent JR services.

Types of Trains

The slowest trains stopping at all stations are called futsū or kaku-eki-teisha. A step up from this is the kyūkō (ordinary express), which stops at only a limited number of stations.

A variation on the kyūkō trains is the kaisoku (rapid) service (usually operating on JR lines).

Finally, the fastest of the regular (non-shinkansen) trains are the tokkyū (limited-express) services, which are sometimes known as shin-kaisoku (again, usually operating on JR lines).

SHINKANSEN

The fastest and best-known services are JR's shinkansen, Japan's famed 'bullet trains'. Shinkansen lines operate on separate tracks from regular trains, and, in some places, the shinkansen station is a fair distance from the main JR station (as is the case in Osaka).

TRAIN TERMINOLOGY

PRONUNCIATION	SCRIPT	ENGLISH
futsū	普通	local
green-sha	グリーン車	1st-class car
jiyū-seki	自由席	unreserved seat
kaisoku	快速	JR rapid or express
kaku-eki-teisha	各駅停車	local
katamichi	片道	one-way
kin'en-sha	禁煙車	nonsmoking car
kitsuen-sha	喫煙車	smoking car
kyūkō	急行	ordinary express
ōfuku	往復	round trip
shin-kaisoku	新快速	JR special rapid train
shinkansen	新幹線	bullet train
shitei-seki	指定席	reserved seat
tokkyū	特急	limited express

On most *shinkansen* routes, there are two or three types of service: faster express services stopping at a limited number of stations, and slower local services stopping at more stations. There is no difference in fare, except for the Green Car (1st-class) carriages, which cost slightly more.

Most *shinkansen* cars are nonsmoking but there are also a limited number of smoking cars on each train. There are reserved and unreserved cars on all trains. If you're travelling outside peak travel periods, you can usually just show up and expect to get a seat in an unreserved car. If you're travelling during a peak period, it is a good idea to stop at a JR station to make a reservation a few days prior to your departure.

Classes

Most long-distance JR trains, including *shinkansen*, have regular and Green Car carriages. The seating is slightly more spacious in Green Car carriages (think of a typical business-class seat on an aircraft). The Green Car carriages also tend to be quieter and less crowded. However, all Green Car seats are reserved, so if you've got a Green Japan Rail Pass, you'll have to reserve every trip in advance (with a regular pass you just go through the turnstiles and get on the next available train).

Costs

JR fares are calculated on the basis of *futsū-unchin* (basic fare), *tokkyū-ryōkin* (an express surcharge levied only on express services) and *shinkansen-ryōkin* (a special charge for *shinkansen* services). Note that if you buy a return ticket for a trip that is more than 600km each way, you qualify for a 10% discount on the return leg.

The following are some typical fares from Tokyo or Ueno (prices given for *shinkansen* are the total price of the ticket):

DESTI-NATION	BASIC (¥)	SHINKAN-SEN (¥)
Hakata	13,440	21,720
Hiroshima	11,340	18,050
Kyoto	7980	13,220
Morioka	8190	14,340
Nagoya	6090	10,580
Niigata	5460	10,270
Okayama	10,190	16,360
Shin-Osaka	8510	13,750
Shin-Shimonoseki	12,810	20,570

SURCHARGES

Fares for reserved seats are slightly higher (5% to 10%) during peak travel seasons (21 March to 5 April, 28 April to 6 May, 21 July to 31 August and 25 December to 10 January).

Further surcharges apply for overnight sleepers, and these vary with the berth type. Japan Rail Pass users must still pay the sleeper surcharge.

The Nozomi super express has higher surcharges than other *shinkansen* services and cannot be used with a Japan Rail Pass. As a guideline, the Nozomi surcharge for Tokyo–Kyoto is ¥300; for Tokyo–Hakata it's ¥600.

Passes & Discount Tickets

JAPAN RAIL PASS

The **Japan Rail Pass** (www.japanrailpass.net/eng/en001.html) is a must for anyone planning to do extensive train travel within Japan. Not only will it save you a lot of money, it will save you from having to fish for change each time you board a train.

The most important thing to note about the pass is this: *the Japan Rail Pass must be purchased outside Japan*. It is available to foreign tourists and Japanese overseas residents (but not foreign residents of Japan). The pass cannot be used for the super express Nozomi *shinkansen* service but is OK for everything else (including other *shinkansen* services). Children between the ages of six and 11 qualify for child passes, while those aged under six ride for free. Japan Rail Pass costs are outlined in the following table:

DURA-TION	REGULAR (ADULT/CHILD)	GREEN (ADULT/CHILD)
7 day	¥28,300/14,150	¥37,800/18,900
14 day	¥45,100/22,550	¥61,200/30,600
21 day	¥57,700/28,850	¥79,600/39,800

Since a one-way reserved-seat Tokyo–Kyoto *shinkansen* ticket costs ¥13,220, you only have to travel Tokyo–Kyoto–Tokyo to make a seven-day pass come close to paying off. Note that the pass is valid only on JR services; you will still have to pay for private-train services.

In order to get a pass, you must first purchase an 'exchange order' outside Japan at a JAL or ANA office or a major travel agency. Once you arrive in Japan, you must bring this order to a JR Travel Service Centre (in most major JR stations and at Narita and Kansai International Airports). When you validate your pass, you'll have to show your passport.

The clock starts to tick on the pass as soon as you validate it. So don't validate it if you're just going into Tokyo or Kyoto and intend to hang around for a few days. Instead, validate when you leave those cities to explore the rest of the country.

For more information on the pass and overseas purchase locations, visit the Japan Rail Pass website.

JR EAST PASS

The **JR East Pass** (www.jreast.co.jp/e/eastpass/index.html) is a great deal for those who only want to travel in eastern Japan. The passes are good on all JR lines in eastern Japan (including Tōhoku, Yamagata, Akita, Jōetsu and Nagano *shinkansen*, but not including the Tōkaidō *shinkansen*). This includes the area around Tokyo and everything north of Tokyo to the tip of Honshū but doesn't include Hokkaidō. In addition to the normal five- and 10-day passes, four-day 'flexible' passes allow travel on any four consecutive or nonconsecutive days within any one-month period. Pass costs are outlined in the following table:

DURA-TION	REGULAR (ADULT/ YOUTH/ CHILD)	GREEN (ADULT/ CHILD)
5 day	¥20,000/ 16,000/ 10,000	¥28,000/ 14,000
10 day	¥32,000/ 25,000/ 16,000	¥44,800/ 22,400
flexible 4 day	¥20,000/ 16,000/ 10,000	¥28,000/ 14,000

For normal passes, 'adult' means anyone over 26, 'youth' means anyone between 12 and 25, and 'child' means anyone between six and 11. Strangely, for the Green passes, there are only adult passes (anyone over 12) and child passes (anyone between six and 11).

As with the Japan Rail Pass, this can only be purchased outside Japan (in the same locations as the Japan Rail Pass) and can only be used by those with temporary visitor visas (you'll need to show your passport).

JR WEST KANSAI AREA PASS

A great deal for those who only want to explore the Kansai area, the **Kansai Area Pass** (www.westjr.co.jp/global/en/travel-information/pass/kansai/) covers unlimited travel on JR lines between most major Kansai cities, such as Himeji, Kōbe, Osaka, Kyoto and Nara. It also cov-

ers JR trains to/from Kansai International Airport but does not cover any *shinkansen* lines. The pass also entitles holders to reserved seats at no extra charge (you'll have to reserve each trip before boarding the train). Passes are only good on consecutive days. Costs are outlined in the following table:

DURATION	REGULAR (ADULT/CHILD)
1 day	¥2000/1000
2 day	¥4000/2000
3 day	¥5000/2500
4 day	¥6000/3000

For these passes, 'child' means anyone between six and 11 (children aged under six travel free). The pass can be purchased at the same places as the San-yō Area Pass (both inside and outside Japan) and also entitles you to discounts at station car-hire offices. Like the San-yō Area Pass, this pass can only be used by those with a temporary visitor visa.

JR KANSAI WIDE AREA PASS

This is similar to the **JR West Kansai Area Pass** (www.westjr.co.jp/global/en/travel-information/pass/kansai_wide/), but it also allows travel on the Sanyō Shinkansen between Osaka and Okayama as well as trains going as far as Kinosaki in the north and Shingū in the south, including a variety of *tokkyū* (limited express trains). The pass is valid for four days and costs ¥7000/3500 per adult/child. For these passes, 'child' means anyone between six and 11 (children aged under six travel free). The pass can be purchased at the same places as the San-yō Area Pass (both inside and outside Japan) and also entitles you to discounts at station car-hire offices. Like the San-yō Area Pass, this pass can only be used by those with a temporary visitor visa.

JR WEST SAN-YŌ AREA PASS

Similar to the JR East Pass, the **San-yō Area Pass** (www.westjr.co.jp/global/en/travel-information/pass/san-yo/) allows unlimited travel on the San-yō *shinkansen* line (including the Nozomi super express) between Osaka and Hakata, as well as local trains running between the same cities. The pass is only good on consecutive days. Costs are outlined in the following table:

DURATION	REGULAR (ADULT/CHILD)
4 day	¥20,000/10,000
8 day	¥30,000/15,000

In the terms of this pass, 'child' applies to anyone between six and 11 years old (children aged under six travel free). The pass can be purchased both inside Japan (at major train stations, travel agencies and Kansai International Airport) and outside Japan (same locations as the Japan Rail Pass) but can only be used by those with a temporary visitor visa. The pass also entitles you to discounts at station rental-car agencies.

JR KYŪSHŪ RAIL PASS

JR Kyūshū (www.jrkyushu.co.jp/english/railpass.html) offers two passes: one that covers all JR lines in the northern part of Kyūshū and another that is good for all JR lines in Kyūshū (see the website for areas covered). Costs are outlined in the following table:

DURA-TION	ALL AREAS (ADULT/ CHILD)	NORTHERN KYŪSHŪ (ADULT/ CHILD)
3 day	¥14,000/ 7000	¥7000/ 3500
5 day	¥17,000/ 8500	¥9000/ 4500

For these passes, 'child' means anyone between six and 11 years old (children under six travel free). These passes can be purchased both inside Japan (at travel agencies in major train stations in Kyūshū) and outside Japan, at the same locations as the Japan Rail Pass. It can only be used by those on a temporary visitor visa. If you purchase an exchange order overseas, you can pick up your pass at major train stations in Kyūshū.

SEISHUN JŪHACHI KIPPU

If you don't have a Japan Rail Pass, one of the best deals going is a five-day **Seishun Jūhachi Kippu** (www.jreast.co.jp/e/pass/seishun18.html). It's name translates as 'Youth 18 Ticket'. Despite its name, however, the pass can be used by anyone of any age.

Basically, for ¥11,500 you get five one-day tickets valid for travel anywhere in Japan on JR lines.

The only catches are that you can't travel on *tokkyū* or *shinkansen* trains and each ticket must be used within 24 hours. However, even if you only have to make a return trip, say, between Tokyo and Kyoto, you'll be saving a lot of money.

Seishun Jūhachi Kippu can be purchased at most JR stations in Japan. Sale and validity periods are outlined in the following table:

SEASON	SALES PERIOD	VALIDITY PERIOD
Spring	20 Feb–31 Mar	1 Mar–10 Apr
Summer	1 Jul–31 Aug	20 Jul–10 Sep
Winter	1 Dec–10 Jan	10 Dec–20 Jan

Note that these periods are subject to change. For more information, ask at any JR ticket window. If you don't want to buy the whole book of five tickets, you can sometimes purchase separate tickets at the discount-ticket shops around train stations.

KANSAI THRU PASS

This pass allows unlimited travel on all non-JR private train lines and most bus lines in Kansai. For more information, see p338.

OTHER SPECIAL TICKETS & PASSES

There are a number of other special tickets, especially for travel in the Tokyo area. For more information on these passes, see the **JR East** (www.jreast.co.jp/e/eastpass/index.html) website's Fares & Passes section.

DISCOUNT-TICKET SHOPS

Discount-ticket shops are known as *kakuyasu-kippu-uriba* (格安切符売り場) or *kinken shoppu* (金券ショップ) in Japanese. These shops deal in discounted tickets for trains, buses, domestic plane flights, ferries, and a host of other things such as cut-rate stamps and phone cards. You can typically save between 5% and 10% on *shinkansen* tickets. Discount-ticket agencies are found around train stations in medium and large cities – ask at your lodgings for the nearest one.

Schedules & Information

The most-complete timetables can be found in the *JR Jikokuhyō* (Book of Timetables), which is available at all Japanese bookshops but is written in Japanese. JNTO, however, produces a handy English-language *Railway Timetable* booklet that explains a great deal about the services in Japan and gives timetables for the *shinkansen* services, JR *tokkyū* and major private lines. If your visit to Japan is a short one and you will not be straying far from the major tourist destinations, this booklet may well be all you need.

Major train stations all have information counters, and you can usually get your point across in simplified English.

TRAIN RESERVATIONS FROM ABROAD

First, keep in mind that you do not usually have to make reservations in advance for train travel in Japan. The only times you should consider reserving in advance are Golden Week, Obon (mid-August) and New Year.

Unfortunately, it is not possible to make reservations for JR trains online in English. However, most travel agents who handle the Japan Rail Pass can also make train reservations and sell you tickets in advance, but they will charge a fairly hefty surcharge to do this. A list of travel agents can be found at www.japanrailpass.net/eng/en001.html.

There's one more thing to keep in mind: if you've got a Japan Rail Pass, you will not be able to reserve travel through a travel agent outside Japan. The reason for this is that you must activate the pass in Japan and show the pass when you make reservations.

In all cases, if you're nervous about getting seats for your train travel in Japan, you can always walk into a JR office and book all your train travel immediately upon arrival or early in your stay (you can reserve travel up to a month in advance at JR ticket offices inside Japan).

If you need to know anything about JR, such as schedules, fares, fastest routes, lost baggage, discounts on rail travel, hotels and car hire, call the **JR East Infoline** (☎050-2016-1603; www.jreast.co.jp/e/customer_support/infoline.html; ⊗10am-6pm). Information is available in English, Korean and Chinese. More information can be found on the website. The website **Hyperdia** (www.hyperdia.com) is also a useful online source for schedules and is probably the most user-friendly English-language site.

Tickets & Reservations

Tickets for most journeys can be bought from train-station vending machines, ticket counters and reservation offices. For reservations of complicated tickets, larger train stations have *midori-no-madoguchi*. Major travel agencies in Japan also sell reserved-seat tickets, and you can buy *shinkansen* tickets through JAL offices overseas if you will be flying JAL to Japan.

On *futsū* services, there are no reserved seats. On the faster *tokkyū* and *shinkansen* services you can choose to travel reserved or unreserved. However, if you travel unreserved, there's always the risk of not getting a seat and having to stand, possibly for the entire trip. This is a particular danger at weekends, peak travel seasons and on holidays. Reserved-seat tickets can be bought any time from a month in advance to the day of departure.

Information and tickets can be obtained from travel agencies, of which there are a great number in Japan. Nearly every train station of any size will have at least one travel agency in the station building to handle all sorts of bookings in addition to train services. Japan Travel Bureau (JTB) is the big daddy of Japanese travel agencies. However, for most train tickets and long-distance bus reservations, you don't need to go through a travel agency – just go to the ticket counters or *midori-no-madoguchi* of any major train station.

Language

Japanese is spoken by more than 125 million people. While it bears some resemblance to Altaic languages such as Mongolian and Turkish and has grammatical similarities to Korean, its origins are unclear. Chinese is responsible for the existence of many Sino-Japanese words in Japanese, and for the originally Chinese kanji characters which the Japanese use in combination with the home-grown hiragana and katakana scripts.

Japanese pronunciation is easy to master for English speakers, as most of its sounds are also found in English – if you read our coloured pronunciation guides as if they were English, you'll be understood. Note though that in Japanese, it's important to make the distinction between short and long vowels, as vowel length can change the meaning of a word. The long vowels, shown in our pronunciation guides with a horizontal line on top of them (ā, ē, ī, ō, ū), should be held twice as long as the short ones. It's also important to make the distinction between single and double consonants, as this can produce a difference in meaning. Pronounce the double consonants with a slight pause between them, eg sak·ka (writer).

Note also that the vowel sound ai is pronounced as in 'aisle', air as in 'pair' and ow as in 'how'. As for the consonants, ts is pronounced as in 'hats', f sounds almost like 'fw' (with rounded lips), and r is halfway between 'r' and 'l'. All syllables in a word are pronounced fairly evenly in Japanese.

WANT MORE?

For in-depth language information and handy phrases, check out Lonely Planet's *Japanese Phrasebook*. You'll find it at **shop.lonelyplanet.com**, or you can buy Lonely Planet's iPhone phrase-books at the Apple App Store.

BASICS

Japanese uses an array of registers of speech to reflect social and contextual hierarchy, but these can be simplified to the form most appropriate for the situation, which is what we've done in this language guide too.

Hello.	こんにちは。	kon·ni·chi·wa
Goodbye.	さようなら。	sa·yō·na·ra
Yes.	はい。	hai
No.	いいえ。	ī·e
Please. (when asking)	ください。	ku·da·sai
Please. (when offering)	どうぞ。	dō·zo
Thank you.	ありがとう。	a·ri·ga·tō
Excuse me. (to get attention)	すみません。	su·mi·ma·sen
Sorry.	ごめんなさい。	go·men·na·sai

You're welcome.
どういたしまして。　dō i·ta·shi·mash·te

How are you?
お元気ですか?　o·gen·ki des ka

Fine. And you?
はい、元気です。　hai, gen·ki des
あなたは?　a·na·ta wa

What's your name?
お名前は何ですか?　o·na·ma·e wa nan des ka

My name is ...
私の名前は　wa·ta·shi no na·ma·e wa
…です。　... des

Do you speak English?
英語が話せますか?　ē·go ga ha·na·se·mas ka

I don't understand.
わかりません。　wa·ka·ri·ma·sen

Does anyone speak English?
どなたか英語を　do·na·ta ka ē·go o
話せますか?　ha·na·se·mas ka

ACCOMMODATION

Where's a ...?	…が ありますか?	... ga a·ri·mas ka
campsite	キャンプ場	kyam·pu·jō
guesthouse	民宿	min·shu·ku
hotel	ホテル	ho·te·ru
inn	旅館	ryo·kan
youth hostel	ユース ホステル	yū·su· ho·su·te·ru

Do you have a ... room?	…ルームは ありますか?	...rū·mu wa a·ri·mas ka
single	シングル	shin·gu·ru
double	ダブル	da·bu·ru

How much is it per ...?	…いくら ですか?	... i·ku·ra des ka
night	1泊	ip·pa·ku
person	1人	hi·to·ri

air-con	エアコン	air·kon
bathroom	風呂場	fu·ro·ba
window	窓	ma·do

DIRECTIONS

Where's the ...?
…はどこですか? … wa do·ko des ka

Can you show me (on the map)?
(地図で)教えて (chi·zu de) o·shi·e·te
くれませんか? ku·re·ma·sen ka

What's the address?
住所は何ですか? jū·sho wa nan des ka

Could you please write it down?
書いてくれませんか? kai·te ku·re·ma·sen ka

behind ...	…の後ろ	... no u·shi·ro
in front of ...	…の前	... no ma·e
near ...	…の近く	... no chi·ka·ku
next to ...	…のとなり	... no to·na·ri
opposite ...	…の 向かい側	... no mu·kai·ga·wa
straight ahead	この先	ko·no sa·ki

Turn ...	…まがって ください。	... ma·gat·te ku·da·sai
at the corner	その角を	so·no ka·do o
at the traffic lights	その信号を	so·no shin·gō o
left	左へ	hi·da·ri e
right	右へ	mi·gi e

To get by in Japanese, mix and match these simple patterns with words of your choice:

When's (the next bus)?
(次のバスは) (tsu·gi no bas wa)
何時ですか? nan·ji des ka

Where's (the station)?
(駅は)どこですか? (e·ki wa) do·ko des ka

Do you have (a map)?
(地図) (chi·zu)
がありますか? ga a·ri·mas ka

Is there (a toilet)?
(トイレ) (toy·re)
がありますか? ga a·ri·mas ka

I'd like (the menu).
(メニュー) (me·nyū)
をお願いします。 o o·ne·gai shi·mas

Can I (sit here)?
(ここに座って) (ko·ko ni su·wat·te)
もいいですか? mo ī des ka

I need (a can opener).
(缶切り) (kan·ki·ri)
が必要です。 ga hi·tsu·yō des

Do I need (a visa)?
(ビザ) (bi·za)
が必要ですか? ga hi·tsu·yō des ka

I have (a reservation).
(予約)があります。 (yo·ya·ku) ga a·ri·mas

I'm (a teacher).
私は(教師) wa·ta·shi wa (kyō·shi)
です。 des

EATING & DRINKING

I'd like to reserve a table for (two people).
(2人)の予約を (fu·ta·ri) no yo·ya·ku o
お願いします。 o·ne·gai shi·mas

What would you recommend?
なにが na·ni ga
おすすめですか? o·su·su·me des ka

What's in that dish?
あの料理に何 a·no ryō·ri ni na·ni
が入っていますか? ga hait·te i·mas ka

Do you have any vegetarian dishes?
ベジタリアン料理 be·ji·ta·ri·an ryō·ri
がありますか? ga a·ri·mas ka

I'm a vegetarian.
私は wa·ta·shi wa
ベジタリアンです。 be·ji·ta·ri·an des

I'm a vegan.
私は厳格な wa·ta·shi wa gen·ka·ku na
菜食主義者 sai·sho·ku·shu·gi·sha
です。 des

I don't eat ...	…は	... wa
	食べません。	ta·be·ma·sen
dairy products	乳製品	nyū·sē·hin
(red) meat	(赤身の)肉	(a·ka·mi no) ni·ku
meat or dairy products	肉や乳製品は	ni·ku ya nyū·sē·hin
pork	豚肉	bu·ta·ni·ku
seafood	シーフード/海産物	shī·fū·do/kai·sam·bu·tsu

Is it cooked with pork lard or chicken stock?

| これはラードか鶏のだしを使っていますか? | ko·re wa rā·do ka to·ri no da·shi o tsu·kat·te i·mas ka |

I'm allergic to (peanuts).

| 私は(ピーナッツ)にアレルギーがあります。 | wa·ta·shi wa (pī·nat·tsu) ni a·re·ru·gī ga a·ri·mas |

That was delicious!

| おいしかった。 | oy·shi·kat·ta |

Cheers!

| 乾杯! | kam·pai |

Please bring the bill.

| お勘定をください。 | o·kan·jō o ku·da·sai |

Key Words

appetisers	前菜	zen·sai
bottle	ビン	bin
bowl	ボール	bō·ru
breakfast	朝食	chō·sho·ku
cold	冷たい	tsu·me·ta·i
dinner	夕食	yū·sho·ku
fork	フォーク	fō·ku
glass	グラス	gu·ra·su
grocery	食料品	sho·ku·ryō·hin
hot (warm)	熱い	a·tsu·i
knife	ナイフ	nai·fu
lunch	昼食	chū·sho·ku
market	市場	i·chi·ba
menu	メニュー	me·nyū
plate	皿	sa·ra
spicy	スパイシー	spai·shī
spoon	スプーン	spūn
vegetarian	ベジタリアン	be·ji·ta·ri·an
with	いっしょに	is·sho ni
without	なしで	na·shi de

Meat & Fish

beef	牛肉	gyū·ni·ku
chicken	鶏肉	to·ri·ni·ku
duck	アヒル	a·hi·ru
eel	うなぎ	u·na·gi
fish	魚	sa·ka·na
lamb	子羊	ko·hi·tsu·ji
lobster	ロブスター	ro·bus·tā
meat	肉	ni·ku
pork	豚肉	bu·ta·ni·ku
prawn	エビ	e·bi
salmon	サケ	sa·ke
seafood	シーフード/海産物	shī·fū·do/kai·sam·bu·tsu
shrimp	小エビ	ko·e·bi
tuna	マグロ	ma·gu·ro
turkey	七面鳥	shi·chi·men·chō
veal	子牛	ko·u·shi

Fruit & Vegetables

apple	りんご	rin·go
banana	バナナ	ba·na·na
beans	豆	ma·me
capsicum	ピーマン	pī·man
carrot	ニンジン	nin·jin
cherry	さくらんぼ	sa·ku·ram·bo
cucumber	キュウリ	kyū·ri
fruit	果物	ku·da·mo·no
grapes	ブドウ	bu·dō
lettuce	レタス	re·tas
nut	ナッツ	nat·tsu
orange	オレンジ	o·ren·ji
peach	桃	mo·mo
peas	豆	ma·me

Signs	
入口	**Entrance**
出口	**Exit**
営業中/開館	**Open**
閉店/閉館	**Closed**
インフォメーション	**Information**
危険	**Danger**
トイレ	**Toilets**
男	**Men**
女	**Women**

sake	酒	sa·ke
tea	紅茶	kō·cha
water	水	mi·zu
white wine	白ワイン	shi·ro wain
yogurt	ヨーグルト	yō·gu·ru·to

Question Words

How?	どのように?	do·no yō ni
What?	なに?	na·ni
When?	いつ?	i·tsu
Where?	どこ?	do·ko
Which?	どちら?	do·chi·ra
Who?	だれ?	da·re
Why?	なぜ?	na·ze

pineapple	パイナップル	pai·nap·pu·ru
potato	ジャガイモ	ja·ga·i·mo
pumpkin	カボチャ	ka·bo·cha
spinach	ホウレンソウ	hō·ren·sō
strawberry	イチゴ	i·chi·go
tomato	トマト	to·ma·to
vegetables	野菜	ya·sai
watermelon	スイカ	su·i·ka

Other

bread	パン	pan
butter	バター	ba·tā
cheese	チーズ	chī·zu
chilli	唐辛子	tō·ga·ra·shi
egg	卵	ta·ma·go
honey	蜂蜜	ha·chi·mi·tsu
horseradish	わさび	wa·sa·bi
jam	ジャム	ja·mu
noodles	麺	men
pepper	コショウ	ko·shō
rice (cooked)	ごはん	go·han
salt	塩	shi·o
seaweed	のり	no·ri
soy sauce	しょう油	shō·yu
sugar	砂糖	sa·tō

Drinks

beer	ビール	bī·ru
coffee	コーヒー	kō·hī
(orange) juice	(オレンジ) ジュース	(o·ren·ji·) jū·su
lemonade	レモネード	re·mo·nē·do
milk	ミルク	mi·ru·ku
mineral water	ミネラル ウォーター	mi·ne·ra·ru· wō·tā
red wine	赤ワイン	a·ka wain

EMERGENCIES

Help!
たすけて! — tas·ke·te

Go away!
離れろ! — ha·na·re·ro

I'm lost.
迷いました。 — ma·yoy·mash·ta

Call the police.
警察を呼んで。 — kē·sa·tsu o yon·de

Call a doctor.
医者を呼んで。 — i·sha o yon·de

Where are the toilets?
トイレはどこですか? — toy·re wa do·ko des ka

I'm ill.
私は病気です。 — wa·ta·shi wa byō·ki des

It hurts here.
ここが痛いです。 — ko·ko ga i·tai des

I'm allergic to ...
私は… アレルギーです。 — wa·ta·shi wa ... a·re·ru·gī des

SHOPPING & SERVICES

I'd like to buy ...
…をください。 — ... o ku·da·sai

I'm just looking.
見ているだけです。 — mi·te i·ru da·ke des

Can I look at it?
それを見ても いいですか? — so·re o mi·te mo ī des ka

How much is it?
いくらですか? — i·ku·ra des ka

That's too expensive.
高すぎます。 — ta·ka·su·gi·mas

Can you give me a discount?
ディスカウント できますか? — dis·kown·to de·ki·mas ka

There's a mistake in the bill.
請求書に間違いが あります。 — sē·kyū·sho ni ma·chi·gai ga a·ri·mas

ATM	ATM	ē·tī·e·mu
credit card	クレジット カード	ku·re·jit·to· kā·do
post office	郵便局	yū·bin·kyo·ku
public phone	公衆電話	kō·shū·den·wa
tourist office	観光案内所	kan·kō·an·nai·jo

TIME & DATES

What time is it?
何時ですか？ nan·ji des ka

It's (10) o'clock.
(10)時です。 (jū)·ji des

Half past (10).
(10)時半です。 (jū)·ji han des

am	午前	go·zen
pm	午後	go·go

Monday	月曜日	ge·tsu·yō·bi
Tuesday	火曜日	ka·yō·bi
Wednesday	水曜日	su·i·yō·bi
Thursday	木曜日	mo·ku·yō·bi
Friday	金曜日	kin·yō·bi
Saturday	土曜日	do·yō·bi
Sunday	日曜日	ni·chi·yō·bi

January	1月	i·chi·ga·tsu
February	2月	ni·ga·tsu
March	3月	san·ga·tsu
April	4月	shi·ga·tsu
May	5月	go·ga·tsu
June	6月	ro·ku·ga·tsu
July	7月	shi·chi·ga·tsu
August	8月	ha·chi·ga·tsu
September	9月	ku·ga·tsu
October	10月	jū·ga·tsu
November	11月	jū·i·chi·ga·tsu
December	12月	jū·ni·ga·tsu

TRANSPORT

boat	船	fu·ne
bus	バス	bas
metro	地下鉄	chi·ka·te·tsu
plane	飛行機	hi·kō·ki
train	電車	den·sha
tram	市電	shi·den

What time does it leave?
これは何時に ko·re wa nan·ji ni
出ますか？ de·mas ka

Does it stop at (...)?
(…)に (...) ni
停まりますか？ to·ma·ri·mas ka

Please tell me when we get to (...).
(…)に着いたら (...) ni tsu·i·ta·ra
教えてください。 o·shi·e·te ku·da·sai

Numbers

1	一	i·chi
2	二	ni
3	三	san
4	四	shi/yon
5	五	go
6	六	ro·ku
7	七	shi·chi/na·na
8	八	ha·chi
9	九	ku/kyū
10	十	jū
20	二十	ni·jū
30	三十	san·jū
40	四十	yon·jū
50	五十	go·jū
60	六十	ro·ku·jū
70	七十	na·na·jū
80	八十	ha·chi·jū
90	九十	kyū·jū
100	百	hya·ku
1000	千	sen

A one-way/return ticket (to ...).
(…行きの) (...·yu·ki no)
片道/往復 ka·ta·mi·chi/ō·fu·ku
切符。 kip·pu

bus stop	バス停	bas·tē
first	始発の	shi·ha·tsu no
last	最終の	sai·shū no
ticket window	窓口	ma·do·gu·chi
timetable	時刻表	ji·ko·ku·hyō
train station	駅	e·ki

I'd like to …を借りたい … o ka·ri·tai
hire a ... のですが。 no des ga

4WD	四駆	yon·ku
bicycle	自転車	ji·ten·sha
car	自動車	ji·dō·sha
motorbike	オートバイ	ō·to·bai

Is this the road to ...?
この道は … ko·no mi·chi wa ...
まで行きますか？ ma·de i·ki·mas ka

(How long) Can I park here?
(どのくらい)ここに (do·no·ku·rai) ko·ko ni
駐車できますか？ chū·sha de·ki·mas ka

GLOSSARY

For lists of culinary terms, see p787; for useful words when visiting an onsen, see the box, p817; and for train terminology, see p847.

Ainu – indigenous people of Hokkaidō and parts of Northern Honshū

Amaterasu – sun goddess and link to the imperial throne

ANA – All Nippon Airways

annai-sho – information office

asa-ichi – morning market

bama – beach; see also *hama*

bashō – *sumō* tournament

bonsai – the art of growing miniature trees by careful pruning of branches and roots

bugaku – dance piece played by court orchestra in ancient Japan

buke yashiki – *samurai* residence

bunraku – classical puppet theatre which uses huge puppets to portray dramas similar to *kabuki*

Burakumin – traditionally outcasts associated with lowly occupations such as leatherwork; literally 'village people'

bushidō – a set of values followed by the *samurai*; literally 'the way of the warrior'

butsudan – Buddhist altar in Japanese homes

chō – city area (in large cities) between a *ku* and a *chōme* in size; also a street

chōchin – paper lantern

chōme – city area of a few blocks

Daibutsu – Great Buddha

daimyō – regional lord under the *shōgun*

daira – plain; see also *taira*

dake – peak; see also *take*

dani – valley; see also *tani*

danjiri – festival float

dera – temple; see also *tera*

dō – temple or hall of a temple

eki – train station

fu – prefecture; see also *ken*

fusuma – sliding screen door

futsū – local train; literally 'ordinary'

gaijin – foreigner; literally 'outside people'

gasoreen sutando – petrol station

gasshō-zukuri – an architectural style (usually thatch-roofed); literally 'hands in prayer'

gawa – river; see also *kawa*

geiko – the Kyoto word for *geisha*

geisha – woman versed in arts and drama who entertains guests; *not* a prostitute

gekijō – theatre

genkan – foyer area where shoes are removed or replaced when entering or leaving a building

geta – traditional wooden sandals

gū – shrine

gun – county

habu – a venomous snake found in Okinawa

haiku – 17-syllable poem

hama – beach; see also *bama*

hanami – blossom viewing (usually cherry blossoms)

haniwa – earthenware figure found in tombs of the Kōfun period

hantō – peninsula

hara – uncultivated field or plain

hari – dragon-boat race

hatsu-mōde – first shrine visit of the new year

henro – pilgrim on the Shikoku 88 Temple Circuit

Hikari – the second-fastest type of *shinkansen*

hiragana – phonetic syllabary used to write Japanese words

hondō – main route or main hall

honsen – main rail line

ichi-nichi-jōsha-ken – day pass for unlimited travel on bus, tram or subway systems

ikebana – art of flower arrangement

irezumi – a tattoo or the art of tattooing

irori – hearth or fireplace

izakaya – pub-style eatery

JAF – Japan Automobile Federation

JAL – Japan Airlines

ji – temple

jigoku – boiling mineral hot spring, which is definitely not for bathing in; literally 'hells'

jikokuhyō – timetable or book of timetables

jima – island; see also *shima*

jingū – shrine

jinja – shrine

jizō – small stone statue of the Buddhist protector of travellers and children

JNTO – Japan National Tourism Organization

jō – castle

JR – Japan Railways

JTB – Japan Travel Bureau

juku – after-school 'cram' school

JYHA – Japan Youth Hostel Association

kabuki – a form of Japanese theatre based on popular legends, characterised by elaborate costumes, stylised acting and the use of male actors for all roles

kaikan – hall or building

kaikyō – channel/strait

kaisoku – rapid train

kaisū-ken – a book of transport tickets

kami – Shintō gods; spirits of natural phenomena

kamikaze – typhoon that sunk Kublai Khan's 13th-century invasion fleet and the name adopted by suicide pilots in the waning days of WWII; literally 'divine wind'

kana – the two phonetic syllabaries, *hiragana* and *katakana*

kanji – Chinese ideographic script used for writing Japanese; literally 'Chinese script'

Kannon – Bodhisattva of Compassion (commonly referred to as the Buddhist Goddess of Mercy)

karaoke – bar where you sing along with taped music; literally 'empty orchestra'

katakana – phonetic syllabary used to write foreign words

katamichi – one-way transport ticket

katana – Japanese sword

kawa – river; see also *gawa*

ken – prefecture; see also *fu*

kendo – oldest martial art; literally 'the way of the sword'

ki – life force, will

kimono – brightly coloured, robe-like traditional outer garment

kin'en-sha – nonsmoking train carriage

kippu – ticket

kissaten – coffee shop

ko – lake

kō – port

kōban – police box

kōen – park

kōgen – high plain (in the mountains); plateau

kokumin-shukusha – people's lodge; an inexpensive form of accommodation

kokuritsu kōen – national park

kotatsu – heated table with a quilt or cover over it to keep the legs and lower body warm

koto – 13-stringed instrument derived from a Chinese zither that is played flat on the floor

ku – ward

kūkō – airport

kura – earth-walled storehouse

kyō – gorge

kyūkō – ordinary express train (faster than a *futsū*, only stopping at certain stations)

machi – city area (in large cities) between a *ku* and *chōme* in size; also street

machiya – traditional Japanese townhouse or merchant house

maiko – apprentice *geisha*

mama-san – woman who manages a bar or club

maneki-neko – beckoning or welcoming cat figure frequently seen in restaurants and bars; it's supposed to attract customers and trade

manga – Japanese comics

matsuri – festival

meishi – business card

midori-no-madoguchi – ticket counter in large Japan Rail stations, where you can make more complicated bookings (look for the green band across the glass)

mikoshi – portable shrine carried during festivals

minato – harbour

minshuku – the Japanese equivalent of a B&B; family-run budget accommodation

misaki – cape; see also *saki*

mon – gate

mura – village

N'EX – Narita Express

NHK – Nihon Hōsō Kyōkai (Japan Broadcasting Corporation)

Nihon – Japanese word for 'Japan'; literally 'source of the sun'; also *Nippon*

ningyō – Japanese doll

Nippon – see *Nihon*

nō – classical Japanese drama performed on a bare stage

noren – cloth hung as a sunshade, typically carrying the name of the shop or premises; indicates that a restaurant is open for business

norikae-ken – transfer ticket (trams and buses)

NTT – Nippon Telegraph & Telephone Corporation

o- – prefix used to show respect to anything it is applied to

ōfuku – return ticket

o-furo – traditional Japanese bath

OL – 'office lady'; female clerical worker; pronounced 'ō-eru'

onnagata – male actor playing a woman's role (usually in *kabuki*)

onsen – hot spring; mineral-spa area, usually with accommodation

oshibori – hot towel provided in restaurants

pachinko – popular vertical pinball game, played in *pachinko* parlours

rakugo – Japanese raconteur, stand-up comic

rettō – island group; see also *shotō*

Rinzai – school of Zen Buddhism which places an emphasis on *kōan* (riddles)

romaji – Japanese roman script

rōnin – student who must resit university entrance exam; literally 'masterless *samurai*', sometimes referred to as 'wanderer'

ropeway – Japanese word for a cable car, tramway or funicular railway

rotemburo – open-air or outdoor bath

ryokan – traditional Japanese inn

saki – cape; see also *misaki*

sakoku – Japan's period of national seclusion prior to the Meiji Restoration

sakura – cherry blossom

salaryman – male white-collar worker, usually in a large firm

sama – even more respectful suffix than *san;* used in instances such as *o-kyaku-sama* – the 'honoured guest'

samurai – warrior class

san – mountain; also suffix which shows respect to the person it is applied to

san-sō – mountain hut or cottage

sentō – public bath

seppuku – ritual suicide by disembowelment

shamisen – a three-stringed traditional Japanese instrument that resembles a banjo or lute

shi – city (used to distinguish cities from prefectures of the same name, eg Kyoto-shi)

shikki – lacquerware

shima – island; see also *jima*

shinkaisoku – express train or special rapid train (usually on JR lines)

shinkansen – super-express train, known in the West as 'bullet train'

Shintō – the indigenous religion of Japan; literally 'the way of the gods'

shirabyōshi – traditional dancer

shitamachi – traditionally the low-lying, less affluent parts of Tokyo

shodō – Japanese calligraphy; literally the 'way of writing'

shōgekijō – small theatre

shōgi – a version of chess in which each player has 20 pieces and the object is to capture the opponent's king

shōgun – former military ruler of Japan

shōgunate – military government

shōji – sliding rice-paper screen

shōjin ryōri – Buddhist vegetarian meal (served at temple lodgings etc)

shokudō – all-round restaurant

shotō – archipelago or island group; see also *rettō*

Shugendō – offbeat Buddhist school, which incorporates ancient shamanistic rites, *Shintō* beliefs and ascetic Buddhist traditions

shūji – a lesser form of *shodō*; literally 'the practice of letters'

shukubō – temple lodging

soapland – Japanese euphemism for a bathhouse offering sexual services, eg massage parlour

Sōtō – a school of Zen Buddhism which places emphasis on *zazen*

sumi-e – black-ink brush painting

sumō – Japanese wrestling

tabi – split-toed Japanese socks used when wearing *geta*

taiko – drum

taira – plain; see also *daira*

taisha – great shrine

take – peak; see also *dake*

taki – waterfall

tani – valley; see also *dani*

tanuki – racoon or dog-like folklore character frequently represented in ceramic figures

tatami – tightly woven floor matting on which shoes are never worn; traditionally, room size is defined by the number of tatami mats

teien – garden

tera – temple; see also *dera*

to – metropolis, eg Tokyo-to

tō – island

tokkyū – limited express train; faster than a *kyūkō*

tokonoma – sacred alcove in a house in which flowers may be displayed or a scroll hung

torii – entrance gate to a Shinto shrine

tōsu – lavatory

uchiwa – paper fan

ukiyo-e – woodblock print; literally 'pictures of the floating world'

wa – harmony, team spirit; also the old *kanji* used to denote Japan, and still used in Chinese and Japanese as a prefix to indicate things of Japanese origin, eg *wafuku* (Japanese-style clothing)

wabi – enjoyment of peace and tranquillity

wan – bay

washi – Japanese handmade paper

yabusame – samurai-style horseback archery

yakimono – pottery or ceramic ware

yakuza – Japanese mafia

yama – mountain; see also *zan*

yamabushi – mountain priest (Shugendō Buddhism practitioner)

yama-goya – mountain hut

yamato – a term of much debated origins that refers to the Japanese world

yamato-e – traditional Japanese painting

yatai – festival float; hawker stall

yukata – light cotton summer *kimono*, worn for lounging or casual use; standard issue when staying at a *ryokan*

zaibatsu – industrial conglomerate; the term arose pre-WWII but the Japanese economy is still dominated by huge firms such as Mitsui, Marubeni and Mitsubishi, which are involved in many different industries

zaki – cape

zan – mountain; see also *yama*

zazen – seated meditation emphasised in the Sōtō school of Zen Buddhism

Zen – an offshoot of Buddhism, introduced to Japan in the 12th century from China, that emphasises a direct, intuitive approach to enlightenment rather than rational analysis

Behind the Scenes

SEND US YOUR FEEDBACK

We love to hear from travellers – your comments keep us on our toes and help make our books better. Our well-travelled team reads every word on what you loved or loathed about this book. Although we cannot reply individually to postal submissions, we always guarantee that your feedback goes straight to the appropriate authors, in time for the next edition. Each person who sends us information is thanked in the next edition – the most useful submissions are rewarded with a selection of digital PDF chapters.

Visit **lonelyplanet.com/contact** to submit your updates and suggestions or to ask for help. Our award-winning website also features inspirational travel stories, news and discussions.

Note: We may edit, reproduce and incorporate your comments in Lonely Planet products such as guidebooks, websites and digital products, so let us know if you don't want your comments reproduced or your name acknowledged. For a copy of our privacy policy visit lonelyplanet.com/privacy.

OUR READERS

Many thanks to the travellers who used the last edition and wrote to us with helpful hints, useful advice and interesting anecdotes:

Luca Baiotti, Jon Bird, Helen Bonser, Oliver Bracko, Rosemary Candelario, Margaret Cantrell, Agustina Capalbo, Marion Colledge, Hannah Craggs, Rich Crossingham, Justin Dabner, Paul Das, Lois-ellin Datta, Giuseppe Di Nuzzo, Yochay Doutsh, Mónica Durán, Andrew Dye, Sue Ellcome, George Fang, Heather Ferguson, Senan Fox, Jefferson Geck, Simone Gribble, Mark Heylbut, Ikeda Hironobu, John Hoffmann, Torbjörn Janson, Noh Woo Jin, Shin Eun Ju, Karolina Keydel, Kari Kostiainen, Katja Årosin Laursen, Mark Leggate, Jordan Lincez, Paul Malloy, Dorit Maoz, Vivien Mast, Kieran Matheson, Thomas Mayes, Laura Mazza, Anne Mclean, David E Michalik, Maya Morikawa, Melody Ng, Sebastian Orre, Brent Osachuk, Jane Parry, Manuel J Porras, Michael Priest, Moin Qazi, Esther Racoosin, Julie Robert, Jared Rosenthal, Rick Ross, Randy Schain, Johannes Schmid, Stephen Smith, Rudy Snel, Jonathan Streit, Sara Stroman, Hiroshi Sugiura, Kyoji Takahashi, Caitlin Teremchuk, Mathilde Teuben, Robert Uramoto, Cees Vellekoop, Adrianne Vos, Zhang Wei and Frans Wildenborg.

AUTHOR THANKS

Chris Rowthorn

Special thanks to the fantastic author team on this edition of Japan. I'd also like to thank the brilliant inhouse team: Emily Wolman, Barbara Delissen, Diana Von Holdt and all the others who worked on this book. I'd also like to thank Jeffrey Friedl for his excellent photographs of Tōdai-ji, Kana Hattori for her Kōbe picks, Mie Ito for more Kōbe picks, Michael Lambe for Kyoto bar recommendations, and Paul Carty for his input into the environment chapter. I'd also like to thank my wife Hiroe for her incredible support during this whole process. Plus thanks to all the readers who were kind enough to send in your advice for the book. Finally, I'd like to thank all the kind people of Japan who made my research trip such a joy.

Andrew Bender

Yohko Scott, Nick Szasz, Baba Ryoko, Marc Musteric, Rudy Nakaya, Taniguchi Yukiko, Sueyasu Natsu, Odawara Kenji, Kuga Daisuke, Hario Naomi, Satomura Ryo, Nakamura Ryota, Inoue Chika, Sakamoto Hisatoshi, Kawabata Akira, Leo Bromberg, Remy Millot, Nagata Moyoru, Morita Mikiko, Miyahara Ichido, Sean Casey, Kawano Saya, Steve Beimel, Nancy Craft and, in house, Emily Wolman, Chris Rowthorn, David Carroll, Lucy Birchley and Barbara Delissen.

Laura Crawford

Much appreciation goes to fellow travellers, locals and tourist office staff who shared recommendations, with special arigatō to Nicola Jones, Teresa Sadkowsky and Ujita-san in the Oki Islands. In Osaka, thanks to Kate Morgan and Wes Lang for tips, Jools Collis for fine company and foodie insights, and my great friend Naoko Akamatsu. Thank you Emily K Wolman and Chris Rowthorn, and big props to the in-house Japan team. Lastly, thanks to Amrit for always cheering me on.

Trent Holden & Kate Morgan

Firstly, thanks to Emily for giving us a shot at one of our dream books. Thanks to the many helpful staff at tourist offices across the region; particularly Reiko Iwasaki at O-shima, Hanako Kageyama and Yoshihiko Obinata at Ogasawara, and the team at Nikkō. Thanks to Nick and all the staff at K's House, Ito and Fuji, and to all the travellers we met along the way who helped with info. Finally, thanks to the in-house team who worked hard on this book.

Craig McLachlan

A hearty thanks to all those who helped me out on the road, but most of all, to my exceptionally beautiful wife and living kanji dictionary, Yuriko, who let me know when I'd had my daily quota of local Hokkaidō brews!

Rebecca Milner

A big thank you to Julian for trekking all over Tōhoku with me – your company was invaluable! To my parents for first taking me to Tōhoku and to Chikara for his superhuman patience and willingness to check out 'just one more bar'. Also these wonderful, helpful people: Shinji, Kudo-san, Nishimura-san, Takayoshi-san, Maeda-san, Abe-san, Suzuki-san, Tanaka-san, Ando-san, Kuniyoshi-san, Ishiba-san, Sosha, Peter, Honda-san, Kobayashi-san, Jamie, Nakamura-san, Amy and Shiro Shimizu, Hiroko-san, Eri, Tom, Allan and everyone on the *Japan 13* team.

Benedict Walker

I dedicate my small contribution to this guide to my teachers, now passed: Dad (Tony Walker), Nanna (Catherine Cook), my guru, Denise Crundall, and my friend Nanayo Kato-Wilder. Each recognised my connection with Japan and encouraged me to explore it. Thanks also to my families: the Walkers, Cooks, Cheryl and the Cowies, the Delrues and Fauberts, and to Kaori and the Shimizus, in Japan. Finally, much love and gratitude to my mum, Trish, who always believes in me, and to Brintin, who took a risk and helped me to chase my dreams.

Wendy Yanagihara

Special thanks go to Mitsu and Tae, Asada-san, Bartek and Chikae, Toru, Matthew and Nori, Ezaki-san, Kiku-san, Nima, Hiro, Gon-san and lovely wife, Toshi-chan and Ayu. Thanks also to Emily, Chris and all my fellow authors for pulling together this wonderful book. Mad loves to my *otōtō* Jason for hanging with me in Ishigaki, Victoria for surrogate dog-mom duty, Rod for emergency medical advice, Roy for genealogy and translation wisdom, and Laura and Whitney for preserving my fragile sense of sanity.

ACKNOWLEDGMENTS

Climate map data adapted from Peel MC, Finlayson BL & McMahon TA (2007) 'Updated World Map of the Köppen-Geiger Climate Classification', *Hydrology and Earth System Sciences*, 11, 163344.

Illustrations pp94-5 and pp382-3 by Michael Weldon

Cover photograph: Arashiyama Bamboo Grove, Kyoto. Travel Pix Collection, AWL.

BEHIND THE SCENES

THIS BOOK

This guidebook was commissioned in Lonely Planet's Oakland office, and produced by the following:

Commissioning Editor Emily K Wolman

Coordinating Editors Kate Mathews, Sophie Splatt

Senior Cartographers Corey Hutchison, Diana Von Holdt

Coordinating Layout Designer Frank Deim

Managing Editors Barbara Delissen, Bruce Evans, Martine Power, Angela Tinson

Managing Layout Designer Chris Girdler

Assisting Editors Susie Ashworth, Jessica Crouch, Kate Evans, Justin Flynn, Gabrielle Innes, Carly Hall, Robyn Loughnane, Catherine Naghten, Rosemary Neilson, Kristin Odijk, Amanda Williamson

Assisting Cartographers Fatima Bašić, Jeff Cameron, Mick Garrett

Cover Research Naomi Parker

Internal Image Research Kylie McLaughlin

Language Content Branislava Vladisavljevic

Thanks to Shahara Ahmed, Naoko Akamatsu, Anita Banh, David Carroll, Rebecca Chau, Penny Cordner, Ryan Evans, Larissa Frost, Jane Hart, Genesys India, Jouve India, Chris Lee Ack, Annelies Mertens, Korina Miller, Trent Paton, Wibowo Rusli, Dianne Schallmeiner, Kerrianne Southway, Gerard Walker, Juan Winata

Index

Map Pages **000**
Photo Pages **000**

Map Legend

- Beach
- Bird Sanctuary
- Buddhist
- Castle/Palace
- Christian
- Confucian
- Hindu
- Islamic
- Jain
- Jewish
- Monument
- Museum/Gallery/Historic Building
- Ruin
- Sento Hot Baths/Onsen
- Shinto
- Sikh
- Taoist
- Winery/Vineyard
- Zoo/Wildlife Sanctuary
- Other Sight

Activities, Courses & Tours
- Bodysurfing
- Diving/Snorkelling
- Canoeing/Kayaking
- Course/Tour
- Skiing
- Snorkelling
- Surfing
- Swimming/Pool
- Walking
- Windsurfing
- Other Activity

- Bank
- Embassy/Consulate
- Hospital/Medical
- Internet
- Police
- Post Office
- Telephone
- Toilet
- Tourist Information
- Other Information

Geographic
- Beach
- Hut/Shelter
- Lighthouse
- Lookout
- Mountain/Volcano
- Oasis
- Park
- Pass
- Picnic Area
- Waterfall

Population
- Capital (National)
- Capital (State/Province)
- City/Large Town
- Town/Village

Transport
- Airport
- Border crossing
- Bus
- Cable car/Funicular

- Tollway
- Freeway
- Primary
- Secondary
- Tertiary
- Lane
- Unsealed road
- Road under construction
- Plaza/Mall
- Steps
- Tunnel
- Pedestrian overpass
- Walking Tour
- Walking Tour detour
- Path/Walking Trail

Boundaries
- International
- State/Province
- Disputed
- Regional/Suburb
- Marine Park
- Cliff
- Wall

Hydrography
- River, Creek
- Intermittent River
- Canal
- Water
- Dry/Salt/Intermittent Lake
- Reef

Craig McLachlan

Sapporo & Hokkaidō Craig has walked the length of Japan (3200km in 99 days!), climbed Japan's 100 Famous Mountains, hiked the 88 Temples of Shikoku, cycled the 33 Temples of Saigoku, and walked from the Sea of Japan to the Pacific scaling all of Japan's 3000m peaks! Books on these adventures have been published in English and Japanese. A 'freelance anything', Craig has an MBA from the University of Hawaii and is also a pilot, hiking guide, karate instructor and Japanese interpreter. See www.craigmclachlan.com. Craig also wrote the Skiing in Japan chapter of this guide.

Rebecca Milner

Tokyo; Northern Honshū (Tōhoku) Rebecca moved to Tokyo from California in 2002 for 'one year' that turned into 10. She's since lived west of Shinjuku, east of the Sumida-gawa and now calls Meguro home. Even when not on assignment, you can find her cycling around the city in search of new cafes or tracking down obscure onsen in the countryside. She also writes a dining column for the *Japan Times* and has written about travel in Japan for the *Guardian* and *CNN Travel*.

Kate Morgan

Mt Fuji & Around Tokyo Kate's first encounter with Japan was back in 2005 when she moved to Osaka to teach English to kindergarten kids. Since returning to Australia, she manages to find her way back to her 'second home' every couple of years to eat *tako-yaki*, soak in onsen and watch punk bands in basement live houses. Kate lives in Melbourne, Australia, as a freelance writer and editor and has worked on other Lonely Planet books such as Phuket and Southern Africa.

Benedict Walker

The Japan Alps & Central Honshū Inspired by a primary school teacher, or the memory of a past life, Ben's love of Japan blossomed early. At 17 he was runner-up in the Australian finals of the Japan Foundation Japanese Speech Contest, and had made two solo trips to Japan. In 1998, with a degree in communications under his belt, Ben hit the road in earnest. After long stints in Canada and Europe, he found himself teaching English in Osaka until his tattered Lonely Planet guide led him to the mountains of Matsumoto, where he found work as a translator and lived like a local. Dividing his time between Canada, Australia and Japan, Ben has also been known to manage the travel for rockstars and dabble in the arts. For the latest, check out: www.wordsandjourneys.com.

Wendy Yanagihara

Shikoku; Okinawa & the Southwestern Islands As the daughter of an *Issei* (first-generation Japanese-American) in California, Wendy grew up summering in Japan with her mother. It wasn't until this book, however, that she had the pleasure of exploring the 88-temple pilgrimage, the diversity of Ryukyuan dialects and an affinity for *jiimami-dōfu*. Previously, she has worked on several editions of the Japan, Tokyo and Tokyo Encounter guidebooks for Lonely Planet.

OUR STORY

A beat-up old car, a few dollars in the pocket and a sense of adventure. In 1972 that's all Tony and Maureen Wheeler needed for the trip of a lifetime – across Europe and Asia overland to Australia. It took several months, and at the end – broke but inspired – they sat at their kitchen table writing and stapling together their first travel guide, *Across Asia on the Cheap*. Within a week they'd sold 1500 copies. Lonely Planet was born.

Today, Lonely Planet has offices in Melbourne, London and Oakland, with more than 600 staff and writers. We share Tony's belief that 'a great guidebook should do three things: inform, educate and amuse'.

OUR WRITERS

Chris Rowthorn

Coordinating Author; Kyoto; Kansai Born in England and raised in the USA, Chris has lived in Kyoto since 1992. Soon after his arrival in Kyoto, Chris started studying the Japanese language and culture. In 1995 he became a regional correspondent for the *Japan Times*. He joined Lonely Planet in 1996 and has worked on guides to Kyoto, Tokyo, Japan and hiking in Japan. When not on the road, he spends his time seeking out Kyoto's best restaurants, temples, hiking trails and gardens. Chris wrote a book in Japanese with professional guide Koko Ijuin, called *Pro ga Oshieru: Genba no Eigo Tsuyaku Gaido Skiru* (Pro English Guide Skills), for Japanese guides who want to explain the country to Western tourists. Chris also conducts walking tours of Kyoto, Nara and Tokyo. For more on Chris, check out his website at www.chrisrowthorn.com.

Andrew Bender

Kyūshū France was closed, so after college Andy left his native New England for Japan. It was a life-changing journey, as visits to Japan often are. He's since mastered chopsticks, the language, karaoke and shoe etiquette. Now based in Los Angeles, Andy writes about Japan for the *Los Angeles Times*, in-flight magazines and about a dozen Lonely Planet titles, as well as the *Seat 1A* travel blog for Forbes. He also does cross-cultural consulting for Japanese businesses and escorts visitors around Japan. Check out his website: www.wheres-andy-now.com.

Laura Crawford

Osaka; Hiroshima & Western Honshū English born and Australian raised, Laura first arrived in Japan as an undergraduate studying Japanese at a university in Kansai. She later travelled up and down the country, set up home in Osaka for two years, returned to Oz to write a thesis on Japanese English, and eventually landed a job as an editor in Lonely Planet's Melbourne office. Her favourite on-the-road task: touring the Kuniga coast and seeing incredibly old trees on the Oki Islands.

Trent Holden

Mt Fuji & Around Tokyo After several trips to Japan, Trent jumped at the opportunity to head back to discover its coastal beaches and conquer Fuji. A champion of budget travel, he's a connoisseur of combini store *bentō* and vending-machine booze, and a lover of Japanese punk and *okonomiyaki*. Trent has co-authored more than a dozen books for Lonely Planet including guides to India, Nepal and the Philippines.

OVER PAGE MORE WRITERS

Published by Lonely Planet Publications Pty Ltd
ABN 36 005 607 983
13th edition – Sep 2013
ISBN 978 1 74220 414 7
© Lonely Planet 2013   Photographs © as indicated 2013
10 9 8 7 6 5 4 3 2
Printed in China